WRITING ABOUT LITERATURE

This five-chapter guide to writing about literature offers guidance about each stage of the writing process, including information about the latest (2009) MLA guidelines for quotation and citation.

Chapter 15: Paraphrase, Summary, Description (p. 124
    15.1 : Paraphrase
    15.2 : Summary
    15.3 : Description

Chapter 16 : The Elements of the Essay (p. 1248)
    16.1 : Tone (and Audience)
    16.2 : Thesis
    16.3 : Structure
    16.4 : Evidence
    16.5 : Conventions that Can Cause Problems

Chapter 17 : The Writing Process (p. 1258)
    17.1 : Getting Started
    17.2 : Planning
    17.3 : Drafting
    17.4 : Revising
    17.5 : Crafting a Title

Chapter 18 : The Research Essay (p. 1273)
    18.1 : Types and Functions of Secondary Sources
    18.2 : Research and the Writing Process
    18.3 : The Research Process
        18.3.1 : Creating a Working Bibliography
        18.3.2 : Identifying and Locating Sources
        18.3.3 : Evaluating Sources
        18.3.4 : Taking Notes
    18.4 : Integrating Source Material into the Essay

Chapter 19 : Quotation, Citation, and Documentation (p. 1291)
    19.1 : Effective Quotation
    19.2 : Citation and Documentation
        19.2.1 : Parenthetical Citation
        19.2.2 : The List of Works Cited

Chapter 20: Sample Research Paper (p. 1306)

CRITICAL APPROACHES

This short guide to important critical approaches briefly explains the tools that professional critics and theorists employ when they write about literature.

Emphasis on the Text (p. 1319)
  New Criticism
  Structuralism
  Poststructuralism
  Deconstruction
  Narrative Theory

Emphasis on the Source (p. 1327)
  Biographical Criticism
  Psychoanalytic Criticism

Emphasis on the Receiver (p. 1334)
  Reader-Response Criticism

Historical and Ideological Criticism (p. 1336)
  Marxist Criticism
  Feminist Criticism
  Gender Studies and Queer Theory
  African American and Ethnic Literary Studies
  New Historicism
  Cultural Studies
  Postcolonial Criticism and Studies of
    World Literature

The Norton
Introduction to Literature

PORTABLE TENTH EDITION

THE NORTON
INTRODUCTION
TO *Literature*

PORTABLE TENTH EDITION

ALISON BOOTH
University of Virginia

KELLY J. MAYS
University of Nevada, Las Vegas

W. W. NORTON & COMPANY
New York, London

W. W. Norton & Company has been independent since its founding in 1923, when William Warder and Mary D. Herter Norton first published lectures delivered at the People's Institute, the adult education division of New York City's Cooper Union. The firm soon expanded its program beyond the Institute, publishing books by celebrated academics from America and abroad. By mid-century, the two major pillars of Norton's publishing program–trade books and college texts–were firmly established. In the 1950s, the Norton family transferred control of the company to its employees, and today–with a staff of four hundred and a comparable number of trade, college, and professional titles published each year–W.W. Norton & Company stands as the largest and oldest publishing house owned wholly by its employees.

Editor: Peter Simon
Managing editor, College: Marian Johnson
Developmental editor: Beth Ammerman
Manuscript editor: Mike Fleming
Project editor: Melissa Atkin
Assistant editor: Conor Sullivan
Production managers: Christine D'Antonio and Chris Granville
Photo research: Stephanie Romeo
Permissions clearance: Margaret Gorenstein and Nancy Rodwin
Interior design: Charlotte Staub
Interior art direction: Hope Miller Goodell

Composition: Westchester Book Group
Manufacturing: R. R. Donnelley & Sons

Copyright © 2011, 2006
by W. W. Norton & Company, Inc.

Since this page cannot legibly accommodate all the copyright notices, the Permissions Acknowledgments constitute an extension of the copyright page.

Library of Congress Cataloging-in-Publication Data

The Norton introduction to literature / [edited by] Alison Booth,
Kelly J. Mays.—Portable 10th ed.
    p. cm.
  Includes bibliographical references and index.
  ISBN: 978-0-393-91164-0 (pbk.)
  1. Literature—Collections. I. Booth, Alison. II. Mays, Kelly J.
  PN6014.N67 2011
  808—dc22

                                                      2010027159

W. W. Norton & Company, Inc., 500 Fifth Avenue, New York, N.Y. 10110
www.wwnorton.com

W. W. Norton & Company Ltd., Castle House, 75/76 Wells Street, London
W1T 3QT

2 3 4 5 6 7 8 9 0

Brief Contents

Fiction

Fiction: Reading, Responding, Writing   14

Understanding the Text   59

1. PLOT   59
2. NARRATION AND POINT OF VIEW   102
3. CHARACTER   121
4. SETTING   158
5. SYMBOL AND FIGURATIVE LANGUAGE   212
6. THEME   246

Reading More Fiction   294

Biographical Sketches: Fiction Writers   425

Poetry

Poetry: Reading, Responding, Writing   438

ROMANTIC LOVE: An Album   468

Understanding the Text   475

7. THEME AND TONE   475
   FAMILY: An Album   489
8. SPEAKER: WHOSE VOICE DO WE HEAR?   496
9. SITUATION AND SETTING: WHAT HAPPENS? WHERE?
   WHEN?   512
   CULTURAL HOMELANDS: An Album   538
10. LANGUAGE   545
11. THE SOUNDS OF POETRY   587
    WORDS AND MUSIC: An Album   607

12. INTERNAL STRUCTURE 614
13. EXTERNAL FORM 632

Reading More Poetry 655

Biographical Sketches: Poets 729

Drama

Drama: Reading, Responding, Writing 744

Understanding the Text 809

14. ELEMENTS OF DRAMA 809

Reading More Drama 950

Biographical Sketches: Playwrights 1239

Writing about Literature 1243

15. PARAPHRASE, SUMMARY, DESCRIPTION 1244
16. THE ELEMENTS OF THE ESSAY 1248
17. THE WRITING PROCESS 1258
18. THE RESEARCH ESSAY 1273
19. QUOTATION, CITATION, AND DOCUMENTATION 1291
20. SAMPLE RESEARCH PAPER 1306

Critical Approaches 1317

Glossary A1

Permissions Acknowledgments A17

Index of Authors A25

Index of Titles and First Lines A29

Index of Literary Terms A36

Contents

PREFACE FOR INSTRUCTORS   xix

INTRODUCTION   1

   What Is Literature?   1

   What Are the Genres of Literature?   6

   Why Read Literature?   8

   Why Study Literature?   10

Fiction

Fiction: Reading, Responding, Writing   14

   Anonymous, *The Elephant in the Village of the Blind*   16

   READING AND RESPONDING TO FICTION   18

   Linda Brewer, *20/20*   19

      SAMPLE WRITING: *Annotation and Notes on "20/20"*   20

   Marjane Satrapi, *The Shabbat* (from *Persepolis*)   24

   WRITING ABOUT FICTION   32

   Raymond Carver, *Cathedral*   32

      SAMPLE WRITING: Wesley Rupton, *Notes on Raymond Carver's
      "Cathedral"*   45

      SAMPLE WRITING: Wesley Rupton, *Response Paper on Raymond
      Carver's "Cathedral"*   48

      SAMPLE WRITING: Bethany Qualls, *A Narrator's Blindness
      in Raymond Carver's "Cathedral"*   51

Understanding the Text   59

1 **PLOT**   59

   G. B. Trudeau, From *Doonesbury*   62

   Jacob and Wilhelm Grimm, *The Shroud*   63

   Guy de Maupassant, *The Jewelry*   69

   James Baldwin, *Sonny's Blues*   75

2 **NARRATION AND POINT OF VIEW** 102
   EDGAR ALLAN POE, *The Cask of Amontillado* 107
   ERNEST HEMINGWAY, *Hills Like White Elephants* 113
   JAMAICA KINCAID, *Girl* 118

3 **CHARACTER** 121
   CHARLOTTE BRONTË, From *Jane Eyre* 126
   TONI MORRISON, *Recitatif* 130
   HA JIN, *In Broad Daylight* 146

4 **SETTING** 158
   ITALO CALVINO, From *Invisible Cities* 160
   MARGARET MITCHELL, From *Gone with the Wind* 161
   ANTON CHEKHOV, *The Lady with the Dog* 165
   KATHERINE ANNE PORTER, *Flowering Judas* 179
   AMY TAN, *A Pair of Tickets* 189
     SAMPLE WRITING: STEVEN MATVIEW, *How Setting Reflects Emotions in Anton Chekhov's "The Lady with the Dog"* 206

5 **SYMBOL AND FIGURATIVE LANGUAGE** 212
   NATHANIEL HAWTHORNE, *The Birth-Mark* 218
   EDWIDGE DANTICAT, *A Wall of Fire Rising* 232

6 **THEME** 246
   AESOP, *The Two Crabs* 246
   STEPHEN CRANE, *The Open Boat* 250
   GABRIEL GARCÍA MÁRQUEZ, *A Very Old Man with Enormous Wings* 269
   LOUISE ERDRICH, *Love Medicine* 275

Reading More Fiction 294

   TONI CADE BAMBARA, *Gorilla, My Love* 294
   AMBROSE BIERCE, *An Occurrence at Owl Creek Bridge* 299
   KATE CHOPIN, *The Story of an Hour* 306
   WILLIAM FAULKNER, *A Rose for Emily* 308
   CHARLOTTE PERKINS GILMAN, *The Yellow Wallpaper* 315
   JAMES JOYCE, *Araby* 328
   FRANZ KAFKA, *A Hunger Artist* 333

YASUNARI KAWABATA, *The Grasshopper and the Bell Cricket* 341

D. H. LAWRENCE, *The Rocking-Horse Winner* 343

BOBBIE ANN MASON, *Shiloh* 355

HERMAN MELVILLE, *Bartleby, The Scrivener* 367

FLANNERY O'CONNOR, *A Good Man Is Hard to Find* 396

JOHN UPDIKE, *A & P* 409

EUDORA WELTY, *Why I Live at the P.O.* 414

Biographical Sketches: Fiction Writers 425

Poetry

Poetry: Reading, Responding, Writing 438

READING POETRY 439

READING POEMS: FOUR EXAMPLES 439

ELIZABETH BARRETT BROWNING, *How Do I Love Thee?* 439

JAROLD RAMSEY, *The Tally Stick* 440

LINDA PASTAN, *love poem* 441

LIZ ROSENBERG, *Married Love* 443

RESPONDING TO POETRY 444

RESPONDING TO POEMS: TWO EXAMPLES 445

BEN JONSON, *On My First Son* 445

HOWARD NEMEROV, *The Vacuum* 445

RESPONDING TO POEMS: AN EXERCISE 447

RITA DOVE, *Fifth Grade Autobiography* 447

ANNE SEXTON, *The Fury of Overshoes* 448

SEAMUS HEANEY, *Mid-Term Break* 450

RESPONDING TO POETRY: EIGHT CONCRETE STEPS AND AN EXAMPLE 451

APHRA BEHN, *On Her Loving Two Equally* 452

WRITING ABOUT POETRY 458

SAMPLE WRITING: STEPHEN BORDLAND, *Response Paper on W. H. Auden's "[Stop all the clocks, cut off the telephone]"* 460

SAMPLE WRITING: *Multiplying by Dividing in Aphra Behn's "On Her Loving Two Equally"*   464

ROMANTIC LOVE: **An Album**   468

EZRA POUND, *The River-Merchant's Wife: A Letter*   469
W. H. AUDEN, [*Stop all the clocks, cut off the telephone*]   470
ANNE BRADSTREET, *To My Dear and Loving Husband*   471
WILLIAM SHAKESPEARE, [*Let me not to the marriage of true minds*]   472
JOHN DONNE, *The Sun Rising*   472
EDNA ST. VINCENT MILLAY, [*Women have loved before as I love now*]   473

Understanding the Text   475

7   THEME AND TONE   475

LISTENING TO TONE   476
MARGE PIERCY, *Barbie Doll*   476
W. D. SNODGRASS, *Leaving the Motel*   477
THOM GUNN, *In Time of Plague*   478
ETHERIDGE KNIGHT, *Hard Rock Returns to Prison from the Hospital for the Criminal Insane*   479

SETTING AS THEME   482
WILLIAM BLAKE, *London*   483

COMPARING TWO OR MORE POEMS ON SIMILAR TOPICS   484
MAXINE KUMIN, *Woodchucks*   484
ADRIENNE RICH, *Aunt Jennifer's Tigers*   485

FAMILY: **An Album**   489

GALWAY KINNELL, *After Making Love We Hear Footsteps*   490
ROBERT HAYDEN, *Those Winter Sundays*   491
JIMMY SANTIAGO BACA, *Green Chile*   492
KELLY CHERRY, *Alzheimer's*   493
ANDREW HUDGINS, *Begotten*   494

8   SPEAKER: WHOSE VOICE DO WE HEAR?   496
THOMAS HARDY, *The Ruined Maid*   496
X. J. KENNEDY, *In a Prominent Bar in Secaucus One Day*   498

MARGARET ATWOOD, *Death of a Young Son by Drowning*   500
ROBERT BROWNING, *Soliloquy of the Spanish Cloister*   501
DOROTHY PARKER, *A Certain Lady*   504

AUTHOR VERSUS SPEAKER   505
WILLIAM WORDSWORTH, *She Dwelt among
   the Untrodden Ways*   506
ROBERT BURNS, *To a Louse*   507
GWENDOLYN BROOKS, *We Real Cool*   509
WALT WHITMAN, [*I celebrate myself, and sing myself*]   510

9 **SITUATION AND SETTING: WHAT HAPPENS? WHERE?
WHEN?**   512

   SITUATIONS: CARING FOR CHILDREN   514
   RITA DOVE, *Daystar*   514
   LINDA PASTAN, *To a Daughter Leaving Home*   515

   SETTINGS: HISTORICAL CONTEXTS   516
   JOHN MILTON, *On the Late Massacre in Piedmont*   516
   MATTHEW ARNOLD, *Dover Beach*   517
   JOHN BETJEMAN, *In Westminster Abbey*   518

   SITUATION AND SETTING: PREPARING A RESPONSE PAPER   521
   JAMES DICKEY, *Cherrylog Road*   521

   TWO CARPE DIEM POEMS   525
   JOHN DONNE, *The Flea*   526
   ANDREW MARVELL, *To His Coy Mistress*   527

   POEMS OF VARIED SITUATIONS AND SETTINGS   528
   EMILY BRONTË, *The Night-Wind*   529
   SYLVIA PLATH, *Point Shirley*   530
   JOSHUA CLOVER, *The Nevada Glassworks*   531
   DEREK WALCOTT, *Midsummer*   533
   WILLIAM SHAKESPEARE, [*Full many a glorious morning
      have I seen*]   534
   JOHN DONNE, *The Good-Morrow*   535
   SYLVIA PLATH, *Morning Star*   536
   BILLY COLLINS, *Morning*   536

CULTURAL HOMELANDS: An Album 538

PHILLIS WHEATLEY, *On Being Brought from Africa to America* 539

MAYA ANGELOU, *Africa* 540

DEREK WALCOTT, *A Far Cry from Africa* 541

AGHA SHAHID ALI, *Postcard from Kashmir* 543

10 LANGUAGE 545

PRECISION AND AMBIGUITY, DENOTATION AND CONNOTATION 545

SARA CLEGHORN, *[The golf links lie so near the mill]* 545

ANNE FINCH, COUNTESS OF WINCHELSEA, *There's No
    To-morrow* 546

CHARLES BERNSTEIN, *Of Time and the Line* 547

WALTER DE LA MARE, *Slim Cunning Hands* 548

THEODORE ROETHKE, *My Papa's Waltz* 550

WORD ORDER AND WORD PLACEMENT 551

SHARON OLDS, *Sex without Love* 552

EMILY DICKINSON, *[I dwell in Possibility–]* 554

WILLIAM CARLOS WILLIAMS, *The Red Wheelbarrow* 554
    This Is Just to Say 555

GERARD MANLEY HOPKINS, *Pied Beauty* 557

LI-YOUNG LEE, *Persimmons* 557

PICTURING: THE LANGUAGES OF DESCRIPTION 560

OSCAR WILDE, *Symphony in Yellow* 561

RICHARD WILBUR, *The Beautiful Changes* 562

ANDREW MARVELL, *On a Drop of Dew* 563

METAPHOR AND PERSONIFICATION 564

WILLIAM SHAKESPEARE, *[That time of year thou
    mayest in me behold]* 565

LINDA PASTAN, *Marks* 567

SIMILE AND ANALOGY 568

ROBERT BURNS, *A Red, Red Rose* 568

WILLIAM SHAKESPEARE, *[Shall I compare thee to a summer's day?]* 569

ANONYMOUS, *The Twenty-third Psalm* 570

JOHN DONNE, [Batter my heart, three-personed God] 571

    The Canonization 571

DAVID FERRY, At the Hospital 573

RANDALL JARRELL, The Death of the Ball Turret Gunner 573

WILFRED OWEN, Dulce et Decorum Est 574

SYMBOL 575

JAMES DICKEY, The Leap 575

EDMUND WALLER, Song 579

D. H. LAWRENCE, I Am Like a Rose 580

DOROTHY PARKER, One Perfect Rose 580

WILLIAM BLAKE, The Sick Rose 581

ROBERT FROST, Fireflies in the Garden 583

ADRIENNE RICH, Diving into the Wreck 583

ROO BORSON, After a Death 586

11 THE SOUNDS OF POETRY 587

SOUND POEMS: SOME EXAMPLES 587

HELEN CHASIN, The Word Plum 587

KENNETH FEARING, Dirge 588

ALEXANDER POPE, Sound and Sense 589

POETIC METER 592

SAMUEL TAYLOR COLERÍDGE, Metrical Feet 596

PRACTICING SCANSION (READING METER) 597

ANONYMOUS, [There was a young girl from St. Paul] 598

ALFRED, LORD TENNYSON, From The Charge of the Light Brigade 598

SIR JOHN SUCKLING, Song 599

JOHN DRYDEN, To the Memory of Mr. Oldham 599

SCANNING METER: A SELECTION OF POEMS 600

EDGAR ALLAN POE, The Raven 600

WILLIAM SHAKESPEARE, [Like as the waves make towards the pebbled shore] 604

GERARD MANLEY HOPKINS, Spring and Fall 604

EMILY DICKINSON, [A narrow Fellow in the Grass] 605

WORDS AND MUSIC: **An Album**   607

THOMAS CAMPION, *When to Her Lute Corinna Sings*   608
WILLIAM SHAKESPEARE, *Spring*   609
ROBERT HAYDEN, *Homage to the Empress of the Blues*   610
MICHAEL HARPER, *Dear John, Dear Coltrane*   610
BOB DYLAN, *Mr. Tambourine Man*   611

12   **INTERNAL STRUCTURE**   614

NARRATIVE POEMS   614
EDWIN ARLINGTON ROBINSON, *Mr. Flood's Party*   615

DRAMATIC POEMS   617
HOWARD NEMEROV, *The Goose Fish*   618

OTHER TYPES OF POETIC STRUCTURE   620
PAT MORA, *Sonrisas*   620

SHIFTS OF TONE AND SUBJECT   622
SHARON OLDS, *The Victims*   622
ANONYMOUS, *Sir Patrick Spens*   624
WILLIAM CARLOS WILLIAMS, *The Dance*   626
EMILY DICKINSON, *[The Wind begun to knead the Grass–]*   627
WILLIAM SHAKESPEARE, *[Th'expense of spirit in a waste of shame]*   627
PERCY BYSSHE SHELLEY, *Ode to the West Wind*   628

13   **EXTERNAL FORM**   632

RHYME   632
STANZAS   633
STANZAS AND RHYME SCHEMES: SOME EXAMPLES   634
DYLAN THOMAS, *Do Not Go Gentle into That Good Night*   636
MARIANNE MOORE, *Poetry*   637
ELIZABETH BISHOP, *Sestina*   638
ARCHIBALD MACLEISH, *Ars Poetica*   639
DUDLEY RANDALL, *Ballad of Birmingham*   640

THE SONNET   641
HENRY CONSTABLE, *[My lady's presence makes the roses red]*   643
WILLIAM WORDSWORTH, *Nuns Fret Not*   643

DANTE GABRIEL ROSSETTI, *A Sonnet Is a Moment's Monument*   645
JOHN KEATS, *On the Sonnet*   645
   On the Grasshopper and the Cricket   646
   On Seeing the Elgin Marbles   647
GWENDOLYN BROOKS, *First Fight. Then Fiddle.*   647
ROBERT FROST, *Range-Finding*   648
   Design   648
WILLIAM WORDSWORTH, *London, 1802*   649
JOHN MILTON, *[When I consider how my light is spent]*   650
ELIZABETH BARRETT BROWNING, *[When our two souls stand up]*   650
CHRISTINA ROSSETTI, *In an Artist's Studio*   651
EDNA ST. VINCENT MILLAY, *[What lips my lips have kissed,
   and where, and why]*   651
GWEN HARWOOD, *In the Park*   652
WILLIAM SHAKESPEARE, *[My mistress' eyes are nothing like
   the sun]*   653
BILLY COLLINS, *Sonnet*   653

Reading More Poetry   655

W. H. AUDEN, *Musée des Beaux Arts*   655
   In Memory of W. B. Yeats   656
WILLIAM BLAKE, *The Lamb*   658
   The Tyger   658
   The Chimney Sweeper (from *Songs of Innocence*)   659
   The Chimney Sweeper (from *Songs of Experience*)   660
ROBERT BROWNING, *My Last Duchess*   660
SAMUEL TAYLOR COLERIDGE, *Kubla Khan*   662
COUNTEE CULLEN, *Yet Do I Marvel*   663
EMILY DICKINSON, *[Because I could not stop for Death–]*   664
   [I stepped from Plank to Plank]   665
   [We do not play on Graves—]   665
   [The Brain—is wider than the Sky—]   666
   [She dealt her pretty words like Blades—]   666
   [Wild Nights—Wild Nights!]   667
   [My Life had stood—a Loaded Gun—]   667
   [After great pain, a formal feeling comes—]   668

JOHN DONNE, [*Death, be not proud*]   669

    Song   669

    A Valediction: Forbidding Mourning   670

PAUL LAURENCE DUNBAR, *Sympathy*   671

    We Wear the Mask   672

T. S. ELIOT, *The Love Song of J. Alfred Prufrock*   672

ROBERT FROST, *The Road Not Taken*   677

    Stopping by Woods on a Snowy Evening   677

    Home Burial   678

THOMAS GRAY, *Elegy Written in a Country Churchyard*   681

ANGELINA GRIMKÉ, *Tenebris*   685

ROBERT HAYDEN, *The Whipping*   685

    Frederick Douglass   686

SEAMUS HEANEY, *Digging*   687

    Punishment   688

GERARD MANLEY HOPKINS, *God's Grandeur*   689

    The Windhover   690

LANGSTON HUGHES, *Harlem*   690

    The Negro Speaks of Rivers   691

BEN JONSON, [*Come, my Celia, let us prove*]   691

JOHN KEATS, *Ode to a Nightingale*   692

    Ode on a Grecian Urn   694

GALWAY KINNELL, *Blackberry Eating*   696

ROBERT LOWELL, *Skunk Hour*   697

CHRISTOPHER MARLOWE, *The Passionate Shepherd to His Love*   698

ANDREW MARVELL, *The Garden*   699

CLAUDE MCKAY, *The Harlem Dancer*   701

    The White House   702

PAT MORA, *Elena*   702

    Gentle Communion   703

SYLVIA PLATH, *Daddy*   704

    Lady Lazarus   706

EZRA POUND, *In a Station of the Metro*   709

    A Virginal   709

SIR WALTER RALEIGH, *The Nymph's Reply to the Shepherd*   709

JOHN CROWE RANSOM, *Bells for John Whiteside's Daughter*   710

ADRIENNE RICH, *Storm Warnings*   711
   History   712
WILLIAM SHAKESPEARE, [*Not marble, nor the gilded
   monuments*]   713
WALLACE STEVENS, *The Emperor of Ice-Cream*   713
   Anecdote of the Jar   714
ALFRED, LORD TENNYSON, *Tears, Idle Tears*   714
   Ulysses   715
DYLAN THOMAS, *Fern Hill*   717
WALT WHITMAN, *Facing West from California's Shores*   719
   I Hear America Singing   719
   A Noiseless Patient Spider   720
RICHARD WILBUR, *Love Calls Us to the Things of This World*   720
WILLIAM WORDSWORTH, *Lines Written a Few Miles above Tintern
   Abbey, On Revisiting the Banks of the Wye during a Tour,
   July 13, 1798*   721
W. B. YEATS, *The Lake Isle of Innisfree*   725
   The Second Coming   726
   Leda and the Swan   726
   Sailing to Byzantium   727

Biographical Sketches: Poets   729

Drama

Drama: Reading, Responding, Writing   744

READING DRAMA   744
QUESTIONS TO ASK WHEN READING A PLAY   745
SUSAN GLASPELL, *Trifles*   748
TOM STOPPARD, *The Real Inspector Hound*   759

RESPONDING TO DRAMA   794
   SAMPLE WRITING: *Annotating a play*   794
   SAMPLE WRITING: *Reading notes on* Trifles   796

WRITING ABOUT DRAMA   801
   SAMPLE WRITING: LINDA DURAI, *Reading a "Whodunnit?": Stage
   Directions and Repetition in* The Real Inspector Hound   804

Understanding the Text 809

14   ELEMENTS OF DRAMA   809
     CHARACTER   809
     PLOT AND STRUCTURE   812
     STAGES, SETS, AND SETTING   814
     TONE, LANGUAGE, AND SYMBOL   818
     THEME   820
     HENRIK IBSEN, *A Doll House*   821
     AUGUST WILSON, *The Piano Lesson*   879

Reading More Drama 950

LORRAINE HANSBERRY, *A Raisin in the Sun*   950
WILLIAM SHAKESPEARE, *Hamlet*   1024
SOPHOCLES, *Antigone*   1129
TENNESSEE WILLIAMS, *A Streetcar Named Desire*   1165

Biographical Sketches: Playwrights 1239

Writing about Literature 1243

15   PARAPHRASE, SUMMARY, DESCRIPTION   1244

16   THE ELEMENTS OF THE ESSAY   1248

17   THE WRITING PROCESS   1258

18   THE RESEARCH ESSAY   1273

19   QUOTATION, CITATION, AND DOCUMENTATION   1291

20   SAMPLE RESEARCH PAPER: RICHARD GIBSON, *Keeping the Sabbath
     Separately: Emily Dickinson's Rebellious Faith*   1306

Critical Approaches 1317

Glossary A1

Permissions Acknowledgments A17

Index of Authors A25

Index of Titles and First Lines A29

Index of Literary Terms A36

Preface for Instructors

This Portable Tenth Edition of *The Norton Introduction to Literature* offers in a single, compact volume a complete course in reading literature and writing about it. A teaching anthology focused on the actual tasks, challenges, and questions typically faced by college students and instructors, *The Norton Introduction to Literature* offers practical advice to help students transform their first impressions of literary works into fruitful discussions and meaningful critical essays, and it helps students and instructors together tackle the complex questions at the heart of literary study.

We have revised *The Norton Introduction to Literature* with an eye to providing a book that is as flexible and useful as possible—adaptable to many different teaching styles and individual preferences—and that also conveys the excitement at the heart of literature itself.

FEATURES OF *THE NORTON INTRODUCTION TO LITERATURE*

Although this Portable Tenth Edition contains much that is new or refashioned, the essential features of the text have remained consistent over many editions:

Diverse selections with broad appeal

Because readings are the central component of any literature class, our most important task has been to select a rich array of appealing and challenging literary works. Among the 35 stories, 206 poems, and 8 plays in *The Norton Introduction to Literature*'s Portable Edition, readers will find selections by well-established and emerging voices alike, representing a broad range of times, places, cultural perspectives, and styles. The readings are excitingly diverse in terms of subject and style as well as authorship and national origin. In selecting and presenting literary texts, our top priorities continue to be quality as well as pedagogical relevance and usefulness. We have integrated the new with the old and the experimental with the canonical, in the conviction that contrast and variety help students recognize and respond to the unique features of any literary work. In this way, we aim to help students and teachers alike approach the unfamiliar by way of the familiar (and vice versa).

Helpful and unobtrusive editorial matter

As always, the instructional material before and after each selection avoids dictating any particular interpretation or response, instead highlighting essential terms and concepts in order to make the literature that follows more accessible to student readers. Questions and writing suggestions help readers apply general concepts to specific readings in order to develop, articulate, refine, and defend their own responses. As in all Norton anthologies, we have annotated the works with a light hand, seeking to be informative but not interpretive.

An introduction to the study of literature

To introduce students to fiction, poetry, and drama is to open up a complex field of study with a long history. The revised Introduction addresses many of the questions that students may have about the nature of literature as well as the practice of literary criticism. By exploring some of the most compelling reasons for reading and studying literature, we clear away much of the mystery about matters of method and approach, and we provide motivated students with a sense of the issues and opportunities that lie ahead as they continue their study of literature.

Helpful guidance for writing about literature

The Portable Tenth Edition integrates opportunities for student writing at each step of the introduction to literature course, highlighting the mastery of skills for students at every level. Freshly reconceived "Reading, Responding, Writing" chapters at the beginning of every genre section offer students concrete advice about how to transform careful reading into productive and insightful writing. We present sample questions to ask of each work or about each element (e.g., "Questions about Character"), provide exercises for answering these questions or for applying new concepts to particular works, and demonstrate how a student's notes on a story or poem may be developed into a response paper or an organized critical argument. New essays bring the total number of examples of student writing to seven.

The constructive, step-by-step approach to the writing process is thoroughly demonstrated as well in a special section, "Writing about Literature," which was completely rewritten for the previous edition. As in the chapters introducing concepts and literary selections, the first steps presented in the writing section are simple and straightforward, outlining an essay's basic formal elements—thesis, structure, and so on. Following these steps encourages students to approach the essay both as a distinctive genre with its own elements and as an accessible form of writing with a clear purpose. From here, we walk students through the writing process: how to choose a topic, gather evidence, and develop an argument; the methods of writing a research essay; and the mechanics of effective quotation and responsible citation and documentation. We also include a sample research paper—annotated by the editors to call attention to important features of good student writing. The "Critical Approaches" section provides an overview of contemporary critical theory and its terminology and is useful as an introduction, a refresher, or a preparation for further exploration.

A sensible and teachable organization

We have preserved the accessible format of *The Norton Introduction to Literature*, which has worked well for teachers and students for many editions. Each genre is approached in three logical steps. Fiction, for example, is introduced by "Fiction: Reading, Responding, Writing," which treats the purpose and nature of fiction, the reading experience, and the steps one takes to begin writing about fiction. This is followed by the six-chapter section called "Understanding the Text," which concentrates on the genre's key elements. "Reading More Fiction," the final component in the Fiction section, is a reservoir of additional readings for independent study or a different approach. The Poetry and Drama sections, in turn, follow exactly the same organizational format as Fiction.

NEW TO THE PORTABLE TENTH EDITION

Forty-four new selections

There are 12 new stories, 30 new poems, and 2 new plays in this Portable Edition of *The Norton Introduction to Literature*. You will find new selections from canonical writers such as John Updike, Charlotte Brontë, Italo Calvino, Nathaniel Hawthorne, D. H. Lawrence, Sylvia Plath, Emily Dickinson, T. S. Eliot, William Blake, Robert Frost, and Alfred, Lord Tennyson, as well as from contemporary voices such as Marjane Satrapi, Ha Jin, Edwidge Danticat, Toni Morrison, Pat Mora, Rita Dove, Joshvua Clover, Sharon Olds, Li-Young Lee, and Tom Stoppard, among others.

Significantly improved writing pedagogy

In the previous Portable Edition, *The Norton Introduction to Literature* featured a completely reconceived and rewritten "Writing about Literature" section. We are pleased that this revision has proved to be popular with instructors and students. With this edition, we have turned our attention to the "Reading, Responding, Writing" chapters that open each genre section, revising these chapters to reflect and complement the changes made to "Writing about Literature" in the previous edition. Now more concrete than ever, these chapters focus squarely on the tasks involved in transforming close reading into effective critical writing, from time-tested approaches to literary analysis to close reading and note-taking. In addition, five new samples of student writing for different kinds of assignments have been added to the book, bringing the total number of such samples to seven. More generally, throughout the book we have thoroughly revised the writing prompts and suggestions.

STUDENT RESOURCES

LitWeb (wwnorton.com/litweb)

This free online companion to *The Norton Introduction to Literature* builds on the reading and writing pedagogy in the text. In addition to quizzes and other review materials, the site offers many tools that help students read and write about literature with skill and understanding. LitWeb's features include:

- In-depth workshops that now complement the "Reading, Responding, Writing" chapters and include two helpful new sections: a "Before You Read" section that prepares the student for the "Reading" and "Re-reading" process, and a "Writing" section that concludes each workshop with practical exercises and writing prompts to reinforce the text's "Writing about Literature" pedagogy.
- Self-grading multiple-choice quizzes on the most widely taught works offer instant feedback that is designed to hone students' close-reading skills.
- The substantial "Writing about Literature" section from *The Norton Introduction to Literature* is included online in its entirety.
- Tutorials on writing research papers and avoiding plagiarism.
- 2009 MLA documentation guidelines.
- Self-grading multiple-choice quizzes on the elements of literature.
- Access to Norton Poets Online (*nortonpoets.com*), which features interviews with more than 60 contemporary poets, dozens of audio recordings of poets reading their work, essays, online poetry workshops, and an e-mail newsletter.

INSTRUCTOR'S RESOURCES

Instructor's Manual

This thorough guide offers in-depth discussions of nearly all the works in the anthology as well as teaching suggestions and tips for the writing-intensive literature course.

Instructor's Resource Disc and Audio CDs

These easy-to-use media resources will enliven lectures and make class preparation easier. The Instructor's Resource Disc includes a selection of images from the text, PowerPoint slides for shaping lectures, and short multimedia slide shows on select themes, as well as PDF files of the instructor's manual. A two-CD instructor's audio companion includes select poems and stories read by their authors or other readers. All three discs are included in one handy Instructor's Resources folder.

Teaching Poetry: A Handbook of Exercises for Large and Small Classes (Allan J. Gedalof, University of Western Ontario)

This practical handbook offers a wide variety of innovative in-class exercises to enliven classroom discussion of poetry. Each of these flexible teaching exercises includes straightforward, step-by-step guidelines and suggestions for variation.

Blackboard / WebCT coursepack

This free and customizable resource includes lecture PowerPoints; multiple-choice quizzes on the elements of fiction, poetry, and drama; multiple-choice quizzes on selected widely taught individual works of fiction and drama included in the anthology; short-answer questions on selected widely taught poems (with suggested answers in the instructor view); multiple-choice quizzes on the "Writing about Literature" chapters; tutorials on research writing and on avoiding plagiarism; and select short-answer questions from the Instructor's Manual.

Play DVDs

DVDs of most of the plays in the anthology are available to qualified adopters.

To obtain any of these instructional resources, please contact your local Norton representative.

*   *   *

ACKNOWLEDGMENTS

In all our work on this edition, we have been guided by teachers in other English departments and in our own, by students who have used the textbook and written to us with comments and suggestions, and by students in our own classes. We hope that with such capable help we have been able to offer you a solid and stimulating introduction to the experience of literature.

Our collaboration on this book continually reminds us of why we follow the vocation of teaching literature, which after all is a communal rather than a solitary calling. Our own teachers and students as well as our colleagues have shown us how to join private responses to literature with shared learning and interpretation, both in discussion and in writing.

That spirit of collaboration, high standards, and engagement with varieties of literary experience was instilled in *The Norton Introduction to Literature* by its first editors, and we are grateful to carry on the work begun by the late Carl Bain and Jerome Beaty. Paul Hunter and Jerry Beaty welcomed us as part of the editorial team and shaped its success, and Paul has continued to be an inspiring collaborator and colleague. We thank him for his continuing presence, not least in the countless effects of his own editing in the present edition and beyond. Among colleagues and teaching assistants who have enhanced the experience of teaching introduction to literature courses, we would like especially to thank Ellen Malenas Ledoux, Jill Rappoport, Chloe Wigston Smith, and Herbert Tucker. The assistance of Jessica Swope, Nick Lolordo, and Anne Stevens made all the difference at key stages in the preparation of this edition.

The Norton Introduction to Literature continues to thrive because teachers and students who use it take the time to provide us with valuable feedback and suggestions for improvement. We thank everyone who does so. This book is as much your making as ours.

Introduction

In the opening chapters of Charles Dickens's novel *Hard Times* (1854), the aptly named Thomas Gradgrind warns the teachers and pupils at his "model" school to avoid using their imaginations. "Teach these boys and girls nothing but Facts. Facts alone are wanted in life," exclaims Mr. Gradgrind. To press his point, Mr. Gradgrind asks "girl number twenty," Sissy Jupe, the daughter of a circus performer, to define a horse. When she cannot, Gradgrind turns to Bitzer, a pale, spiritless boy who "looked as though, if he were cut, he would bleed white." A "model" student of this "model" school, Bitzer gives exactly the kind of definition to satisfy Mr. Gradgrind:

Literature is not things but a way to comprehend things.
—NORMAN N. HOLLAND

> Quadruped. Graminivorous. Forty teeth, namely, twenty-four grinders, four eyeteeth, and twelve incisive. Sheds coat in spring; in marshy countries, sheds hoofs.

Anyone who has any sense of what a horse is rebels against Bitzer's lifeless picture of that animal and against the "Gradgrind" view of reality. As these first scenes of *Hard Times* lead us to expect, in the course of the novel the fact-grinding Mr. Gradgrind learns that human beings cannot live on facts alone; that it is dangerous to stunt the faculties of imagination and feeling; that, in the words of one of the novel's more lovable characters, "People must be amused." Through the downfall of an exaggerated enemy of the imagination, Dickens reminds us why we like and even *need* to read literature.

What Is Literature?

But what is literature? Before you opened this book, you probably could guess that it would contain the sorts of stories, poems, and plays you have encountered in English classes or in the literature section of a library or bookstore. But why are some written works called *literature* whereas others are not? And who gets to decide? *The American Heritage Dictionary of the English Language* offers a number of definitions for the word *literature*, one of which is "imaginative or creative writing, especially of recognized artistic

Writing is not literature unless it gives to the reader a pleasure which arises not only from the things said, but from the way in which they are said.
—STOPFORD BROOKE

1

value." In this book, we adopt a version of that definition by focusing on fictional stories, poems, and plays—the three major kinds (or *genres*) of "imaginative or creative writing" that form the heart of literature as it has been taught in schools and universities for over a century. Many of the works we have chosen to include are already ones "of recognized artistic value" and thus belong to what scholars call the **canon**, a select, if much-debated and ever-evolving, list of the most highly and widely esteemed works. Though quite a few of the literary texts we include are simply too new to have earned that status, they, too, have already drawn praise, and some have even generated controversy.

Certainly it helps to bear in mind what others have thought of a literary work. Yet one of this book's primary goals is to get you to think for yourself, as well as communicate with others, about what "imaginative writing" and "artistic value" are or might be and thus about what counts as literature. What makes a story or poem different from an essay, a newspaper editorial, or a technical manual? For that matter, what makes a published, canonical story like Herman Melville's "Bartleby, the Scrivener" ("Reading More Fiction") both like and unlike the sorts of stories we tell each other every day? What about so-called *oral literature*, such as the fables and folktales that circulated by word of mouth for hundreds of years before they were ever written down? Or published works such as comic strips and graphic novels that rely little, if at all, on the written word? Or Harlequin romances, television shows, and the stories you collaborate in making when you play a video game like *Grand Theft Auto*? Likewise, how is Shakespeare's poem "[My mistress's eyes are nothing like the sun]" (chapter 13) both like and unlike a verse you might find in a Hallmark card or even a jingle in a mouthwash commercial?

Today, literature departments offer courses in many of these forms of expression, expanding the realm of literature far beyond the limits of the dictionary definition. An essay, a song lyric, a screenplay, a supermarket romance, a novel by Toni Morrison or William Faulkner, and a poem by Walt Whitman or Emily Dickinson—each may be read and interpreted in *literary ways* that yield insight and pleasure. What makes the literary way of reading different from pragmatic reading is, as scholar Louise Rosenblatt explains, that it does not focus "on what will remain . . . *after* the reading—the information to be acquired, the logical solution to a problem, the actions to be carried out," but rather on "what happens *during* . . . reading." The difference between pragmatic and literary reading, in other words, resembles the difference between a journey that is only about reaching a destination and one that is just as much about fully experiencing the ride.

In the pages of this book, you will find cartoons, an excerpt from a graphic novel, song lyrics, folktales, and stories and plays that have spawned movies. Through this inclusiveness, we do not intend to suggest that there are no distinctions among these various forms of expression or between a

good story, poem, or play and a bad one; rather, we want to get you thinking, talking, and writing both about what the key differences and similarities among these forms are and what makes one work a better example of its
genre than another. Sharpening your skills at these peculiarly intensive
and responsive sorts of reading and interpretation is a primary purpose of
this book and of most literature courses.

Another goal of inclusiveness is simply to remind you that literature
doesn't just belong in a textbook or a classroom, even if textbooks and
classrooms are essential means for expanding your knowledge of the literary terrain and of the concepts and techniques essential to thoroughly
enjoying and understanding a broad range of literary forms. You may or
may not be the kind of person who always takes a novel when you go to the
beach or secretly writes a poem about your experience when you get back

home. You may or may not have taken a literature course (or courses) before. Yet you already have a good deal of literary experience and even expertise, as well as much more to discover about literature. A major aim of this book is to make you more conscious of how and to what end you might use the tools you already possess and to add many new ones to your tool belt.

What Does Literature Do?

One quality that may well differentiate stories, poems, and plays from other kinds of writing is that they help us move beyond and probe beneath abstractions by giving us concrete, vivid particulars. Rather than talking *about* things, they bring them to life for us by *representing* experience, and so they *become* an experience for us—one that engages our emotions, our imagination, and all of our senses, as well as our intellects. As the British poet and critic Matthew Arnold put it more than a century ago, "The interpretations of science do not give us this intimate sense of objects as the interpretations of poetry give it; they appeal to a limited faculty, and not to the whole man. It is not Linnaeus . . . who gives us the true sense of animals, or water, or plants, who seizes their secret for us, who makes us participate in their life; it is Shakespeare . . . Wordsworth . . . Keats."

To test Arnold's theory, compare the *American Heritage Dictionary*'s rather dry definition of *literature* with the following poem, in which John Keats describes his first encounter with a specific literary work—George Chapman's translation of *The Iliad* and *The Odyssey*, two epic poems by the ancient Greek poet Homer.

JOHN KEATS
On First Looking into Chapman's Homer[1]

Much have I traveled in the realms of gold,
And many goodly states and kingdoms seen;
Round many western islands have I been
Which bards in fealty to Apollo[2] hold.
5 Oft of one wide expanse had I been told
That deep-browed Homer ruled as his demesne;
Yet did I never breathe its pure serene[3]
Till I heard Chapman speak out loud and bold:

(Continued on next page)

(Continued)

Then felt I like some watcher of the skies
10 When a new planet swims into his ken;[4]
Or like stout Cortez[5] when with eagle eyes
He stared at the Pacific—and all his men
Looked at each other with a wild surmise—
Silent, upon a peak in Darien.

1816

Keats makes us *see* literature as a "wide expanse" by greatly developing this **metaphor** and complementing it with **similes** likening reading to the sighting of a "new planet" and the first glimpse of an undiscovered ocean. More important, he shows us what literature means and why it matters by allowing us to share with him the subjective experience of reading and the complex sensations it inspires—the dizzying exhilaration of discovery; the sense of power, accomplishment, and pride that comes of achieving something difficult; the wonder we feel in those rare moments when a much-anticipated experience turns out to be even greater than we had imagined it would be.

It isn't the definitions of words alone that bring this experience to life for us as we read Keats's poem, but also their sensual qualities—the way the words look, sound, and even feel in our mouths because of the particular way they are put together on the page. The sensation of excitement—of a racing heart and mind—is reproduced *in* us as we read the poem. For example, notice how the lines in the middle run into each other, but then Keats forces us to slow down at the poem's end—stopped short by that dash and comma in the poem's final lines, just as Cortez and his men are when they reach the edge of the known world and peer into what lies beyond.

1. George Chapman's were among the most famous Renaissance translations of Homer; he completed his *Iliad* in 1611, his *Odyssey* in 1616. Keats wrote the sonnet after being led to Chapman by a former teacher and reading the *Iliad* all night long.
2. Greek god of poetry and music. *Fealty*: literally, the loyalty owed by a vassal to his feudal lord.
3. Atmosphere.
4. Range of vision; awareness.
5. Actually, Balboa; he first viewed the Pacific from Darien, in Panama.

What Are the Genres of Literature?

The framework of genre . . . is, when used well, like a comfortable old coat, into which you slip with an anticipatory sigh of comfort.
—NATALIE BENNETT

The conversation that is literature, as well as the conversation about literature, invites all comers, requiring neither a visa nor a special license of any kind. Yet literary studies, like all disciplines, has developed its own terminology and its own systems of classification. Helping you understand and effectively use both is a major focus of this book; especially important terms appear in bold throughout and are defined in a glossary at the back.

Some essential literary terms are common, everyday words used in a special way in the conversation about literature. A case in point, perhaps, is the term *literary criticism*, as well as the closely related term *literary critic*. Despite the usual connotations of the word *criticism*, literary criticism is called *criticism* not because it is negative or corrective but rather because those who write criticism ask searching, analytical, "critical" questions about the works they read. Literary criticism is both the process of interpreting and commenting on literature and the result of that process. If you write an essay on the play *Hamlet*, the poetry of John Keats, or the development of the short story in the 1990s, you engage in literary criticism, and by writing the essay, you've become a literary critic.

Similarly, when we classify works of literature, we use terms that may be familiar to you but have specific meanings in a literary context. All academic disciplines have systems of classification, or taxonomies, as well as jargon. Biologists, for example, classify all organisms into a series of ever-smaller, more specific categories: *kingdom, phylum* or *division, class, order, family, genus*, and *species*. Classification and comparison are just as essential in the study of literature. We expect a poem to work in a certain way, for example, when we know from the outset that it *is* a poem and not, say, a factual news report or a short story. And—whether consciously or not—we compare it, as we read, to other poems we've read in the past. If we know, further, that the poem was first published in eighteenth-century Japan, we expect it to work differently from one that appeared in the latest *New Yorker*. Indeed, we often choose what to read, just as we choose what movie to see, based on the "class" or "order" of book or movie we like or what we are in the mood for that day—horror or comedy, action or science fiction.

As these examples suggest, we generally tend to categorize literary works in two ways: (1) on the basis of contextual factors, especially historical and cultural context—that is, when, by whom, and where it was produced (as in *nineteenth-century* or *Victorian literature, the literature of the Harlem Renaissance, American literature*, or *African American literature*)—and (2) on the basis of formal textual features. For the latter type of classification, the one we focus on in this book, the key term is **genre**, which simply means, as the

Oxford English Dictionary tells us, "A particular style or category of works of art; esp. a type of literary work characterized by a particular form, style, or purpose."

Applied rigorously, *genre* refers to the largest categories around which this book is organized—**fiction**, **poetry**, and **drama** (as well as **nonfiction prose**). The word *subgenre* applies to smaller divisions within a genre, and the word *kind* to divisions within a subgenre. *Subgenres* of fiction include the **novel**, the **novella**, and the **short story**. Kinds of novels, in turn, include things like the **bildungsroman** or the epistolary novel. Similarly, important subgenres of nonfiction include the essay, as well as **biography** and autobiography; a memoir is a particular kind of autobiography, and so on.

However, the terms of literary criticism are not so fixed or so consistently, rigorously used as biologists' are. You will often see the word *genre* applied both much more narrowly—referring to the novel, for example, or even to a kind of novel such as the epistolary novel or the historical novel.

The way we classify a work depends on which aspects of its form or style we concentrate on, and categories may overlap. When we divide fiction, for example, into the subgenres novel, novella, and short story, we take the length of the works as the salient aspect. (Novels are much longer than short stories.) But other fictional subgenres—detective fiction, **gothic fiction**, **historical fiction**, science fiction, and even **romance**—are based on the types of **plots**, **characters**, **settings**, and so on that are customarily featured in these works. These latter categories may include works from all the other, length-based categories. There are, after all, gothic novels (think Anne Rice), as well as gothic short stories (think Edgar Allan Poe).

A few genres even cut across the boundaries dividing poetry, fiction, drama, and nonfiction. A prime example is **satire**—any literary work (whether poem, play, fiction, or nonfiction) "in which prevailing vices and follies are held up to ridicule" (*Oxford English Dictionary*). Examples of satire include poems such as Alexander Pope's *Dunciad*; plays, movies, and television shows, from Moliere's *Tartuffe* to Stanley Kubrick's *Dr. Strangelove* to *South Park* and *The Colbert Report*; works of fiction like Jonathan Swift's *Gulliver's Travels* and Voltaire's *Candide*; and works of nonfiction such as Swift's "A Modest Proposal" and Ambrose Bierce's *The Devil's Dictionary*. Three other major genres that cross the borders between fiction, poetry, drama, and nonfiction are **parody**, **pastoral**, and **romance**.

Individual works can thus belong simultaneously to multiple generic categories or observe some **conventions** of a genre without being an example of that genre in any simple or straightforward way. The Old English poem *Beowulf* is an **epic** and, because it's written in verse, a poem. Yet because (like all epics) it narrates a story, it is also a work of fiction in the more general sense of that term. The novels in the Twilight series contain elements of romance, fantasy, and even the gothic.

Given this complexity, the system of literary genres can be puzzling, especially to the uninitiated. Used well, however, classification schemes are among the most essential and effective tools we use to understand and enjoy just about everything, including literature.

Why Read Literature?

Literature is the human activity that takes the fullest and most precise account of variousness, possibility, complexity, and difficulty.
—LIONEL TRILLING

Because there has never been and never will be absolute, lasting agreement about where exactly the boundaries between one literary genre and another should be drawn or even about what counts as literature at all, it might be more useful from the outset to focus on *why* we look at particular forms of expression.

Over the ages, people have sometimes dismissed *all* literature or at least certain genres as a luxury, a frivolous pastime, even a sinful indulgence. Plato famously banned poetry from his ideal republic on the grounds that it tells beautiful lies that "feed and water our passions" rather than our reason. Thousands of years later, the influential eighteenth-century philosopher Jeremy Bentham decried the "magic art" of literature as doing a good deal of "mischief" by "stimulating our passions, . . . exciting our prejudices." One of Bentham's contemporaries—a minister—blamed the rise of immorality, irreligion, and especially prostitution on the increasing popularity of that particular brand of literature called the novel.

Today, many Americans express their sense of literature's insignificance by simply not reading it: A 2004 government report entitled *Reading at Risk* indicates that less than half of U.S. adults read imaginative literature, with the sharpest declines occurring among the youngest age groups. Even if they very much enjoy reading on their own, many contemporary U.S. college students nonetheless hesitate to study or major in literature for fear that their degree won't provide them with "marketable" credentials, knowledge, or skills.

Yet the enormous success of Oprah's Book Club is only one of many signs that millions of people continue to find both reading literature and discussing it with others to be enjoyable, meaningful, even essential activities. English thrives as a major at most colleges and universities, almost all of which require undergraduates majoring in other areas to take at least one course in literature. (Perhaps that's why you are reading this book!) Schools of medicine, law, and business are today *more* likely to require their students to take literature courses than they were in past decades, and they continue to welcome literature majors as applicants, as do many corporations. So why do so many people read and study literature, and why do schools encourage and even require students to do so? Even if we know what literature is, what does it *do* for us? What is its value?

There are, of course, as many answers to such questions as there are readers. For centuries, a standard answer has been simply that imaginative literature provides a unique brand of "instruction and delight." John Keats's "On Looking into Chapman's Homer" illustrates some of the many forms such delight can take. Some kinds of imaginative writing offer us the delight of immediate escape, but imaginative writing that is more difficult to read and understand than a Harry Potter or Twilight novel offers escape of a different and potentially more instructive sort, liberating us from the confines of our own time, place, and social milieu, as well as our habitual ways of thinking, feeling, and looking at the world. In this way, a story, poem, or play can satisfy our desire for broader experience—including the sorts of experience we might be unable or unwilling to endure in real life. We can learn what it might be like to grow up on a Canadian fox farm or to clean ashtrays in the Singapore airport. We can travel back into the past, experiencing war from the perspective of a soldier watching his comrade drown in air poisoned by mustard gas or of prisoners suffering in a Nazi labor camp. We can journey into the future or into universes governed by entirely different rules than our own. Perhaps we yearn for such knowledge because we can best come to understand our own identities and outlooks by leaping over the boundaries that separate us from other selves and worlds.

Keats's friend and fellow poet Percy Bysshe Shelley argued that literature increases a person's ability to make such leaps, to "imagine intensely and comprehensively" and "put himself in the place of another and of many othe[r]" people in order "to be greatly good." Shelley meant "good" in a moral sense, reasoning that the ability both to accurately imagine and to truly *feel* the human consequences of our actions is the key to ethical behavior. But universities and professional schools today also define this "good" in distinctly pragmatic ways. In virtually any career you choose, you will need to interact positively and productively with both coworkers and clients, and in today's increasingly globalized world, you will need to learn to deal effectively and empathetically with people vastly different from yourself. At the very least, literature written by people from various backgrounds and depicting various places, times, experiences, and feelings will give you some understanding of how others' lives and worldviews may differ from your own—or how they may be very much the same.

Similarly, our rapidly changing world and economy require intellectual flexibility, adaptability, and ingenuity, making ever more essential the human knowledge, general skills, and habits of mind developed through the study of literature. Literature explores issues and questions relevant in any walk of life. Yet rather than offering us neat or comforting solutions and answers, literature enables us to experience difficult situations and human conundrums in all their complexity and to look at them from various points of view. In so doing, it invites us sometimes to question conventional ways of thinking and sometimes to see its wisdom, even as it helps us imagine altogether new possibilities.

Finally, literature awakens us to the richness and complexity of language—our primary tool for engaging with, understanding, and shaping the world around us. As we read more and more, seeing how different writers use language to help us feel their joy, pain, love, rage, or laughter, we begin to recognize the vast range of possibilities for self-expression. Writing and discussion in turn give us invaluable practice in discovering, expressing, and defending our own nuanced, often contradictory thoughts about both literature and life. The study of literature enhances our command of language and our sensitivity to its effects and meanings in every form or medium, providing interpretion and communication skills especially crucial in our "information age." By learning to appreciate and articulate what the language of a story, poem, a play, or an essay does to us and by considering how it affects others, we also learn much about what we can do with language.

Why Study Literature?

Literature is language charged with meaning. . . . Literature is news that stays news.
—EZRA POUND

You may already feel the power and pleasure to be gained from a sustained encounter with challenging reading. Then why not simply enjoy it in solitude, on your own free time? Why take a course in literature? Literary study, like all disciplines, has developed its own terminology and its own techniques. Some knowledge and understanding of both can greatly enhance our personal appreciation of literature and our conversations with others about it. Literature also has a context and a history, and learning something about them can make all the difference in the amount and kind of pleasure and insight you derive from literature. By reading and discussing different genres of literature, as well as works from dramatically different times and places, you may well come to appreciate and even love works that you might never have discovered or chosen to read on your own or that you might have disliked or misunderstood if you did.

Most important, writing about works of literature and discussing them with your teachers and other students will give you practice in analyzing literature in greater depth and in considering alternative views of both the works themselves and the situations and problems the works explore. A clear understanding of the aims and designs of a story, poem, or play never falls like a bolt from the blue. Instead, it emerges from a process that involves trying to put into words *how* and *why* this work had such an effect on you and, just as important, responding to what others say or write about it. Literature itself is essentially a vast, ongoing, ever-evolving conversation in which we most fully participate when we enter into actual conversation with others.

As you engage in this conversation, you will notice that interpretation is always variable, always open to discussion. A great diversity of interpretations might suggest that the discussion is pointless. On the contrary, that's when the discussion gets most interesting. Because there is no single, straight, paved road to an understanding of a literary text, you can explore a variety of blazed trails and less-traveled paths. In sharing your own interpretations, tested against your peers' responses and guided by your instructor's or other critics' expertise, you will hone your skills at both interpretation and communication. After the intricate and interactive process of interpretation, you will find that the work has changed when you read it again. What we do with literature alters what it does to us.

READING, RESPONDING, WRITING

Fiction

Fiction: Reading, Responding, Writing

Stories are a part of daily life in every culture. Stories are what we tell when we return from vacation or survive an accident or illness. They help us make sense of growing up or growing old, of a hurricane or a war, of the country and world we live in. In conversations, a story may be invited by the listener ("What did you do last night?") or initiated by the teller ("Guess what I saw when I was driving home!"). We assume such stories are true, or at least that they are meant to describe an experience honestly. Of course, many of the stories we encounter daily, from jokes to online games to television sitcoms to novels and films, are intended to be **fiction**—that is, stories or narratives about imaginary persons and events. Every story, however, whether a news story, sworn testimony, idle gossip, or a fairy tale, is always a version of events told from a particular (or several) perspectives, and it may be incomplete, biased, misinformed, or just plain made up. As we listen to others' stories, we keep alert to the details, which make the stories rich and entertaining. But we also need to spend considerable time and energy making sure that we accurately interpret what we hear: We ask ourselves who is telling the story, why the story is being told, and whether we have all the information we need to understand it fully.

Even newspaper articles, which are supposed to tell true stories—the facts of what actually happened—may be open to such interpretation. Take as an example the article on the next page, which appeared in the *New York Times* on January 1, 1920.

The report's appearance in a reliable newspaper; its identification of date, location, and other information; and the legalistic adjectives "accused" and "alleged" suggest that it strives to be accurate and objective. But given the distance between us and the events described here, it's also easy to imagine this chain of events being recounted as a play, murder mystery, Hollywood film, or televised trial. In other words, this news story is still fundamentally a *story*. Note that certain points of view are better represented than others and certain details are highlighted, as might be the case in a novel or short story. The news item is based almost entirely on what Kate Uhl asserts, and even the subtitle, "Woman Becomes Desperate," plays up the "dramatic sequel to the woman's dilemma." We don't know what Mervin Uhl said when he allegedly accused his wife and turned her out of the house, and Bryan Pownall, the murdered man, never had a chance to

ACCUSED WIFE KILLS HER ALLEGED LOVER

Cumberland (Md.) Woman Becomes Desperate When Her Husband Orders Her from Home.

Special to The New York Times.

CUMBERLAND, Md., Dec. 31.— Accused by her husband of unfaithfulness, Mrs. Kate Uhl, aged 25, this morning stabbed to death Bryan Pownall, who she alleged was the cause of the estrangement with her husband, Mervin Uhl.

Mrs. Uhl, who is the mother of three children, denies her husband's charge of misconduct with Pownall, asserting that the latter forced his attentions on her by main physical strength against her will.

The stabbing this morning came as a dramatic sequel to the woman's dilemma after she had been ordered to leave her home. Mrs. Uhl summoned Pownall after her husband had gone to work this morning, and according to her story begged him to tell her husband that she, Mrs. Uhl, was not to blame. This Pownall refused to do, but again tried to make love to her, Mrs. Uhl said. When Pownall sought to kiss her Mrs. Uhl seized a thin-bladed butcher knife and stabbed the man to the heart, she admitted.

defend himself. Presumably, the article reports accurately the husband's accusation of adultery and the wife's accusation of rape, but we have no way of knowing whose accusations are true. Further reading in court records about this incident and in newspapers from that time might reveal more of what happened, as far as anyone was able to find out.

Our everyday interpretation of the stories we hear from various sources— including other people, television, newspapers, advertisements, and countless others—has much in common with the interpretation of stories such as those in this anthology. In fact, you'll probably discover that the processes of reading, responding to, and writing about stories are already familiar to you on some level. Most readers already know, for instance, that they should pay close attention to seemingly trivial details; they should ask questions and find out more about any matters of fact that seem mysterious, odd, or unclear. Most readers are well aware that words can have several meanings and that there are alternative ways to tell a story. How would someone else have told the story? What are the storyteller's perspective and motives? What is the context of the tale—for instance, when is it supposed to have taken place and what was the occasion of telling it? These and other questions from our experience of everyday storytelling are equally relevant in reading fiction. Similarly, we can usually tell in reading a story or hearing it whether it is supposed to make us laugh, shock us, or provoke some other response.

TELLING STORIES: INTERPRETATION

Everyone has a unique story to tell. In fact, many stories are about this difference or divergence among people's interpretations of reality. A number of the stories in this chapter explore issues of storytelling and interpretation.

Consider a well-known tale, "The Blind Men and the Elephant," a Buddhist story over two thousand years old. Like other stories that have been transmitted orally, this one exists in many versions. Here's one way of telling it:

The Elephant in the Village of the Blind

Once there was a village high in the mountains in which everyone was born blind. One day a traveler arrived from far away with many fine things to sell and many tales to tell. The villagers asked, "How did you travel so far and so high carrying so much?" The traveler said, "On my elephant." "What is an elephant?" the villagers asked, having never even heard of such an animal in their remote mountain village. "See for yourself," the traveler replied.

The elders of the village were a little afraid of the strange-smelling creature that took up so much space in the middle of the village square. They could hear it breathing and munching on hay, and feel its slow, swaying movements disturbing the air around them. First one elder reached out and felt its flapping ear. "An elephant is soft but tough, and flexible, like a leather fan." Another grasped its back leg. "An elephant is a rough, hairy pillar." An old woman took hold of a tusk and gasped, "An elephant is a cool, smooth staff." A young girl seized the tail and declared, "An elephant is a fringed rope." A boy took hold of the trunk and announced, "An elephant is a water pipe." Soon others were stroking its sides, which were furrowed like a dry plowed field, and others determined that its head was an overturned washing tub attached to the water pipe.

At first each villager argued with the others on the definition of the elephant, as the traveler watched in silence. Two elders were about to come to blows about a fan that could not possibly be a pillar. Meanwhile the elephant patiently enjoyed the investigations as the cries of curiosity and angry debate mixed in the afternoon sun. Soon someone suggested that a list could be made of all the parts: the elephant had four pillars, one tub, two fans, a water pipe, and two staffs, and was covered in tough, hairy leather or dried mud. Four young mothers, sitting on a bench and comparing impressions, realized that the elephant was in fact an enormous, gentle ox with a stretched nose. The traveler agreed, adding only that it was also a powerful draft horse and that if they bought some of his wares for a good price he would be sure to come that way again in the new year.

. . .

The different versions of such a tale, like the different descriptions of the elephant, alter the meaning that is understood. Changing any aspect of the story will inevitably change how it works and what it means to the listener or reader. For example, most versions of this story feature not an entire village of blind people (as this version does), but a small group of blind men who claim to be wiser than their sighted neighbors. These blind men quarrel endlessly because none of them can see; none can put together all the evidence of all their senses or all the elephant's various parts to create a whole. Such traditional versions of the story criticize people who are too proud of what they think they know; these versions imply that sighted people would know better what an elephant is. However, other versions of the tale, like the one above, are set in an imaginary "country" of the blind. This setting changes the emphasis of the story from the errors of a few blind wise men to the value and the insufficiency of *any* one person's perspective. For though it's clear that the various members of the community in this version will never agree entirely on one interpretation of (or story about) the elephant, they do not let themselves get bogged down in endless dispute. Instead they compare and combine their various stories and "readings" in order to form a more satisfying, holistic understanding of the wonder in their midst. Similarly, listening to others' different interpretations of stories, based on their different perspectives, can enhance your experience of a work of literature and your skill in responding to new works.

Just as stories vary depending on who is telling them, their meaning varies depending on who is responding to them. In the elephant story, the villagers pay attention to what the tail or the ear feels like, and then they draw on comparisons to what they already know. But ultimately, the individual interpretations of the elephant depend on what previous experiences each villager brings to bear (of pillars, water pipes, oxen, and dried mud, for example), and also on where (quite literally) he or she stands in relation to the elephant. In the same way, readers participate in re-creating a story as they interpret it. When you read a story for the first time, your response will be informed by other stories you have heard and read as well as your expectations for this kind of story. To grapple with what is new in any story, start by observing one part at a time and gradually trying to understand how those parts work together to form a whole. As you make sense of each new piece of the picture, you adjust your expectations about what is yet to come. When you have read and grasped it as fully as possible, you may share your interpretation with other readers, discussing different ways of seeing the story. Finally, you might express your reflective understanding in writing— in a sense, telling *your* story about the work.

Questions about the Elements of Fiction

- Expectations: What do you expect?
  - from the title? from the first sentence or paragraph?
  - after the first events or interactions of characters?
  - as the conflict is resolved?
- What happens in the story? (See chapter 1.)
  - Do the characters or situation change from the beginning to end?
  - Can you summarize the **plot**? Is it a recognizable kind or **genre** of story?
- How is the story narrated? (See chapter 2.)
  - Is the narrator identified as a character?
  - Is it narrated in the past or present tense?
  - Is it narrated in the first, second, or third person?
  - Do you know what every character is thinking, or only some characters, or none?
- Who are the **characters**? (See chapter 3.)
  - Who is the **protagonist**(s) (hero, heroine)?
  - Who is the **antagonist**(s) (villain, opponent, obstacle)?
  - Who are the other characters? What is their role in the story?
  - Do your expectations change with those of the characters, or do you know more or less than each of the characters?
- What is the **setting** of the story? (See chapter 4.)
  - What is the time of the story? Is it contemporary or set in the past?
  - Where does it take place? Is it in the United States or another country, or in a specific town or region?
  - Does the story move from one setting to another? Does it move in one direction only or back and forth in time and place?
- What do you notice about how the story is written?
  - What is the **style** of the prose? Are the sentences and the vocabulary simple or complex?
  - Are there any **images** or **figures of speech**? (See chapter 5.)
  - What is the **tone** or mood? Does the reader feel sad, amused, worried, curious?
- What does the story mean? Can you express its **theme** or themes? (See chapter 6.)
  - Answers to these big questions may be found in many instances in your answers to the previous questions. The story's meaning or theme depends on all its features.

READING AND RESPONDING TO FICTION

When imaginary events are acted out onstage or onscreen, our experience of those events is that of being a witness to them. In contrast, prose narrative fiction, whether oral or written, is relayed to us by someone. Reading it is more like hearing what happened after the fact than witnessing it before our very eyes. The teller, or **narrator**, of fiction addresses a listener or reader, often referred to as the audience. How much or how little we know about the characters and what they say or do depends on what a narrator tells us.

You should read a story attentively, just as you would listen attentively to someone telling a story out loud. This means limiting distractions and interruptions; you should take a break from social networking and obtrusive music. Literary prose, as well as poetry, works with the sounds as well as meanings of words, just as film works with music and sound as well as images and dramatic action. Be prepared to mark up the text and to make notes.

The following short short story is a contemporary work. As in "The Elephant in the Village of the Blind," this narrator gives us a minimal amount of information, merely observing the characters' different perceptions and interpretations of things they see during a cross-country car trip. As you read the story, pay attention to your expectations, drawing on your personal experience as well as such clues as the title; the characters' opinions, behavior, and speech; specifics of setting (time and place); and any repetitions or changes. When and how does the story begin to challenge and change your initial expectations? You can use the questions given below to guide your reading of any story and help you focus on some of the important features.

LINDA BREWER

20/20

By the time they reached Indiana, Bill realized that Ruthie, his driving companion, was incapable of theoretical debate. She drove okay, she went halves on gas, etc., but she refused to argue. She didn't seem to know how. Bill was used to East Coast women who disputed everything he said, every step of the way. Ruthie stuck to simple observation, like "Look, cows." He chalked it up to the fact that she was from rural Ohio and thrilled to death to be anywhere else.

She didn't mind driving into the setting sun. The third evening out, Bill rested his eyes while she cruised along making the occasional announcement.

"Indian paintbrush. A golden eagle."

Miles later he frowned. There was no Indian paintbrush, that he knew of, near Chicago.

The next evening, driving, Ruthie said, "I never thought I'd see a Bigfoot 5 in real life." Bill turned and looked at the side of the road streaming innocently out behind them. Two red spots winked back—reflectors nailed to a tree stump.

"Ruthie, I'll drive," he said. She stopped the car and they changed places in the light of the evening star.

"I'm so glad I got to come with you," Ruthie said. Her eyes were big, blue, and capable of seeing wonderful sights. A white buffalo near Fargo. A UFO above Twin Falls. A handsome genius in the person of Bill himself. This last vision came to her in Spokane and Bill decided to let it ride.

• • •

SAMPLE WRITING: ANNOTATION AND NOTES

Now re-read the story, along with the brief annotations one reader made in the margins, based on the questions in the box on page 18. The reader then expanded these annotations into longer, more detailed notes.

20/20

Like "20/20 hind-sight" or perfect vision? Also like the way Bill and Ruthie go 50/50 on the trip, and see things in two different ways.

Bill's doubts about Ruthie. Is he reliable? Does she "refuse" or not "know how" to argue? What's her view of him?

Bill's keeping score; maybe Ruthie's nicer, or has better eye-sight. She notices things.

Repetition, like a folk tale: 2nd sun-set drive, 3rd time she speaks. Not much dialogue in story.

By the time they reached Indiana, Bill realized that Ruthie, his driving companion, was incapable of theoretical debate. She drove okay, she went halves on gas, etc., but she refused to argue. She didn't seem to know how. Bill was used to East Coast women who disputed everything he said, every step of the way. Ruthie stuck to simple observation, like "Look, cows." He chalked it up to the fact that she was from rural Ohio and thrilled to death to be anywhere else.

She didn't mind driving into the setting sun. The third evening out, Bill rested his eyes while she cruised along making the occasional announcement.

"Indian paintbrush. A golden eagle."

Miles later he frowned. There was no Indian paintbrush, that he knew of, near Chicago.

The next evening, driving, Ruthie said, "I never thought I'd see a Bigfoot in real life." Bill turned and looked at the side of the road streaming innocently out behind them. Two red spots winked back—reflectors nailed to a tree stump.

Bill's only speech.
Turning point: Bill
sees something
he doesn't already
know.

Repetition, like a
joke, in 3 things
Ruthie sees.

Story begins and
ends in the middle
of things: "By the
time," "let it ride."

"Ruthie, I'll drive," he said. She stopped the car and they changed places in the light of the evening star.

"I'm so glad I got to come with you," Ruthie said. Her eyes were big, blue, and capable of seeing wonderful sights. A white buffalo near Fargo. A UFO above Twin Falls. A handsome genius in the person of Bill himself. This last vision came to her in Spokane and Bill decided to let it ride.

Initial Impressions
Plot: begins in the middle of action, on a journey. *Narration*: past tense, third person. *Character*: Bill is the focal character, and he and Ruthie have been driving for a while. *Setting*: Indiana is a middling, unromantic place.

Paragraph 1
Narration and Character: Bill's judgments of Ruthie show that he prides himself on arguing about abstract ideas; that he thinks Ruthie must be stupid; that they didn't know each other well and aren't suited for a long trip together. Bill is from the unfriendly East Coast; Ruthie, from easy-going, dull "rural Ohio." *Style*: The casual language—"okay" and "etc."—sounds like Bill's voice, but he's not the narrator. The vague "etc." hints that Bill isn't really curious about her. The observation of cows sounds funny, childlike, even stupid. But why does he have to "chalk it up" or keep score?

Paragraph 2
Plot and Character: This is the first specific time given in the story, the "third evening": Ruthie surprises the reader and Bill with more than dull "observation."

Paragraph 4
Style, Character, Setting, and Tone: Dozing in the speeding car, Bill is too late to check out what she says. He frowns (he doesn't argue) because the plant and the bird can't be seen in the Midwest. Brewer uses a series of place names to indicate the route of the car. There's humor in Ruthie's habit of pointing out bizarre sights.

Paragraph 5

Character and Setting: Bigfoot is a legendary monster living in Western forests. Is Ruthie's imagination getting the better of Bill's logic? "Innocently" personifies the road, and the reflectors on the stump wink like the monster; Bill is finally looking (though in hindsight). The scenery seems to be playing a joke on him.

Paragraph 6

Plot and Character: Here the characters change places. He wants to drive (is she hallucinating?), but it's as if she has won. The narration (which has been relying on Bill's voice and perspective) for the first time notices a romantic detail of scenery that Ruthie doesn't point out (the evening star).

Paragraph 7

Character and Theme: Bill begins to see Ruthie and what she is capable of. What they see *is* the journey these characters take toward falling in love, in the West where things become unreal. *Style*: The long "o" sounds and images in "A white buffalo near Fargo. A UFO above Twin Falls" (along with the words Ohio, Chicago, and Spokane) give a feeling for the wildness (notice the Indian place names). The outcome of the story is that they *go far* to Fargo, see double and fall in love at Twin Falls—see and imagine wonderful things in each other. They end up with perfectly matched vision.

These notes could be organized and expanded into a response paper on the story. Some of your insights might even form the basis for a longer essay on one of the elements of the story.

You may approach any kind of narrative with the same kinds of questions that have been applied to "20/20." Try it on the following chapter of Marjane Satrapi's *Persepolis*. This bestselling graphic novel, or graphic memoir, originally written in French and now a successful film, relates Satrapi's own experience as a girl in Iran through her artwork and words. *Persepolis* begins with a portrait of ten-year-old Satrapi, wearing a black veil, in 1980. The Islamic leaders of Iran had recently imposed religious law, including mandatory head coverings for schoolgirls. On September 22, 1980, Iraq invaded Iran, beginning a conflict that lasted until 1988, greatly affecting Satrapi's childhood in Tehran (once known as Persepolis). The Iran-Iraq War was a precursor of the Persian Gulf War of 1990–91 and the ongoing Iraq War or Second Gulf War that began in 2003.

This excerpt resembles an illustrated short story, though it is understood to be closely based on actual events. How do the images and designs of the panels on each page contribute to expectations, narration (here, telling and showing), characterization, plot, setting, style, and themes? Read (and view) with these questions in mind and a pencil in hand. Annotating or taking notes will guide you to a more reflective response.

♦♦♦♦♦ THE SHABBAT

TO KEEP US FROM FORGETTING THAT WE WERE AT WAR, IRAQ OPTED FOR A NEW STRATEGY...

I HEARD THEY'RE GOING TO USE BALLISTIC MISSILES AGAINST US.

WHAT ARE YOU SAYING? WE'RE NOT AT WAR WITH THE SOVIET UNION. I DON'T BELIEVE THE IRAQIS HAVE WEAPONS LIKE THAT.

FROM THE IRAQI BORDER TO TEHRAN IT'S THOUSANDS OF MILES. MISSILES THAT CAN GO THAT FAR COST A FORTUNE!

WELL, THAT'S WHAT THE RUMORS SAY!

WE IRANIANS ARE OLYMPIC CHAMPIONS WHEN IT COMES TO GOSSIP.

SHE'S RIGHT. WE LOVE TO EXAGGERATE.

YOU SEEM TO HAVE THE OPPOSITE SYMPTOM.

WHY DO YOU SAY THAT?

EVEN WHEN YOU SEE SOMETHING WITH YOUR OWN EYES, YOU NEED CONFIRMATION FROM THE BBC.

MY NATURAL OPTIMISM JUST LEADS ME TO BE SKEPTICAL.

Shabbat: Sabbath (Hebrew).

MOM'S PESSIMISM SOON WON OUT OVER DAD'S OPTIMISM. IT TURNED OUT THAT THE IRAQIS DID HAVE MISSILES. THEY WERE CALLED "SCUDS" AND TEHRAN BECAME THEIR TARGET.

WHEN THE SIRENS WENT ON, IT MEANT WE HAD THREE MINUTES TO KNOW IF THE END HAD COME.

WE'RE NOT GOING TO THE BASEMENT?

IT WOULDN'T MAKE ANY DIFFERENCE!!

CONSIDERING THE DAMAGE THEY DO, WHETHER WE'RE IN THE BASEMENT OR ON THE ROOF, IT'S THE SAME THING.

THE THREE MINUTES SEEMED LIKE THREE DAYS. FOR THE FIRST TIME, I REALIZED JUST HOW MUCH DANGER WE WERE IN.

BOOM!!

I DON'T WANT TO DIE!

YOU WON'T DEAR. I PROMISE YOU!

NOW THAT TEHRAN WAS UNDER ATTACK, MANY FLED. THE CITY WAS DESERTED. AS FOR US, WE STAYED. NOT JUST OUT OF FATALISM. IF THERE WAS TO BE A FUTURE, IN MY PARENTS' EYES, THAT FUTURE WAS LINKED TO FRENCH EDUCATION. AND TEHRAN WAS THE ONLY PLACE I COULD GET IT.

SOME PEOPLE, MORE CIRCUMSPECT, TOOK SHELTER IN THE BASEMENTS OF BIG HOTELS, WELL-KNOWN FOR THEIR SAFETY. APPARENTLY, THEIR REINFORCED CONCRETE STRUCTURES WERE BOMBPROOF.

ONE EXAMPLE WAS OUR NEIGHBORS, THE BABA-LEVYS. THEY WERE AMONG THE FEW JEWISH FAMILIES THAT HAD STAYED AFTER THE REVOLUTION. MR. BABA-LEVY SAID THEIR ANCESTORS HAD COME THREE THOUSAND YEARS AGO, AND IRAN WAS THEIR HOME.

...THEIR DAUGHTER NEDA WAS A QUIET GIRL WHO DIDN'T PLAY MUCH, BUT WE WOULD TALK ABOUT ROMANCE FROM TIME TO TIME.

...ONE DAY A BLOND PRINCE WITH BLUE EYES WILL COME AND TAKE ME TO HIS CASTLE...

OH YEAH! ME TOO!

SO LIFE WENT ON...

The Shah: The shah, or king, of Iran was deposed in 1979, the beginning of what was soon known as the Islamic Revolution under the leadership of Ayatollah Ruholla Khomeini (1900–89). An Ayatollah is a high-ranking cleric in the Shia branch of Islam, of which most Iranians are adherents.

FASTER! PLEASE HURRY...

A CROWD HAD GATHERED IN FRONT OF MY STREET! THE BOMB HAD HIT MY STREET!

MA'AM, WHICH BUILDING WAS HIT?

APPARENTLY, IT EXPLODED AT THE END OF THE STREET.

MY BUILDING AND THE BABA-LEVY'S WERE AT THE END OF THE STREET.

LET ME THROUGH.

ONE CHANCE IN TWO THAT IT WAS OUR BUILDING.

PLEASE, LET ME THROUGH.

YOU CAN'T GO BEYOND THIS POINT!

...I LIVE HERE...

AND HE LET ME THROUGH.

I DIDN'T WANT TO LOOK UP. I LOOKED AT MY TREMBLING LEGS. I COULDN'T GO FORWARD, LIKE IN A NIGHTMARE.

LET THEM BE ALIVE. LET THEM BE ALIVE. LET THEM...

MARJI

MARJI!

MOM!

YOU'RE ALL RIGHT? DAD'S ALL RIGHT? GRANDMA'S ALL RIGHT?

EVERYONE'S OK. I WAS THE ONLY ONE HOME.

OH, MOM.

...

WHEN WE WALKED PAST THE BABA-LEVY'S HOUSE, WHICH WAS COMPLETELY DESTROYED, I COULD FEEL THAT SHE WAS DISCREETLY PULLING ME AWAY. SOMETHING TOLD ME THAT THE BABA-LEVYS HAD BEEN AT HOME. SOMETHING CAUGHT MY ATTENTION.

I SAW A TURQUOISE BRACELET. IT WAS NEDA'S. HER AUNT HAD GIVEN IT TO HER FOR HER FOURTEENTH BIRTHDAY...

THE BRACELET WAS STILL ATTACHED TO... I DON'T KNOW WHAT...

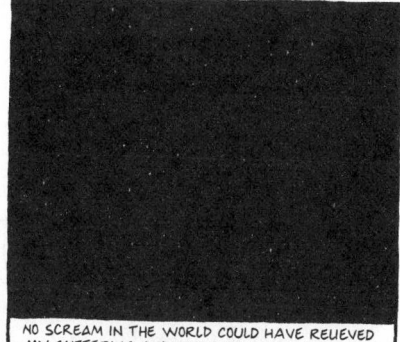

NO SCREAM IN THE WORLD COULD HAVE RELIEVED MY SUFFERING AND MY ANGER.

WRITING ABOUT FICTION

During your first reading of any story, you may want to read without stopping to address each of the questions on page 18. After you have read the whole piece once, re-read it carefully, using the questions as a guide. It's always interesting to compare your initial reactions with your later ones. In fact, a paper may focus on comparing the expectations of readers (and characters) at the beginning of a story and at the end. Responses to fiction may come in unpredictable order, so feel free to address the questions as they arise. Looking at how the story is told and what happens to which characters may lead to observations on expectations or setting. Consideration of setting and style can help explain the personalities, actions, mood, and effect of the story, which can lead to well-informed ideas about the meaning of the whole. But any one of the questions, pursued further, can serve as the focus of more formal writing.

Below are some examples of written responses to Raymond Carver's short story "Cathedral." First, read the story and make notes on any features that you find interesting, important, or confusing. Then look at the notes and response paper by Wesley Rupton and the essay by Bethany Qualls, which show two different ways of writing about "Cathedral."

RAYMOND CARVER
Cathedral

This blind man, an old friend of my wife's, he was on his way to spend the night. His wife had died. So he was visiting the dead wife's relatives in Connecticut. He called my wife from his in-laws'. Arrangements were made. He would come by train, a five-hour trip, and my wife would meet him at the station. She hadn't seen him since she worked for him one summer in Seattle ten years ago. But she and the blind man had kept in touch. They made tapes and mailed them back and forth. I wasn't enthusiastic about his visit. He was no one I knew. And his being blind bothered me. My idea of blindness came from the movies. In the movies, the blind moved slowly and never laughed. Sometimes they were led by seeing-eye dogs. A blind man in my house was not something I looked forward to.

That summer in Seattle she had needed a job. She didn't have any money. The man she was going to marry at the end of the summer was in officers' training school. He didn't have any money, either. But she was in love with the guy, and he was in love with her, etc. She'd seen something in the paper: HELP WANTED—Reading to Blind Man, and a telephone number. She phoned and went over, was hired on the spot. She'd worked with this blind man all summer. She read stuff to him, case studies, reports, that sort of thing. She helped him organize his little office in the county social-service department. They'd become good friends, my wife and the blind man. How do I know these things? She told me. And she told me something else. On her last day in the office, the blind man asked if he could touch her face. She agreed to this. She told me he touched his fingers to every part of her face, her nose—even her neck! She never forgot it. She even tried to write a poem about it. She was always trying to write a poem. She wrote a poem or two every year, usually after something really important had happened to her.

When we first started going out together, she showed me the poem. In the poem, she recalled his fingers and the way they had moved around over her face. In the poem, she talked about what she had felt at the time, about what went through her mind when the blind man touched her nose and lips. I can remember I didn't think much of the poem. Of course, I didn't tell her that. Maybe I just don't understand poetry. I admit it's not the first thing I reach for when I pick up something to read.

Anyway, this man who'd first enjoyed her favors, the officer-to-be, he'd been her childhood sweetheart. So okay. I'm saying that at the end of the summer she let the blind man run his hands over her face, said goodbye to him, married her childhood etc., who was now a commissioned officer, and she moved away from Seattle. But they'd kept in touch, she and the blind man. She made the first contact after a year or so. She called him up one night from an Air Force base in Alabama. She wanted to talk. They talked. He asked her to send him a tape and tell him about her life. She did this. She sent the tape. On the tape, she told the blind man about her husband and about their life together in the military. She told the blind man she loved her husband but she didn't like it where they lived and she didn't like it that he was a part of the military-industrial thing. She told the blind man she'd written a poem and he was in it. She told him that she was writing a poem about what it was like to be an Air Force officer's wife. The poem wasn't finished yet. She was still writing it. The blind man made a tape. He sent her the tape. She made a tape. This went on for years. My wife's officer was posted to one base and then another. She sent tapes from Moody AFB, McGuire, McConnell, and finally Travis, near Sacramento, where one night she got to feeling lonely and cut off from people she kept losing in that moving-around life. She got to feeling she couldn't go it another step. She went in and swallowed all the pills and capsules in the medicine chest and washed them down with a bottle of gin. Then she got into a hot bath and passed out.

But instead of dying, she got sick. She threw up. Her officer—why should 5 he have a name? he was the childhood sweetheart, and what more does he want?—came home from somewhere, found her, and called the ambulance. In time, she put it all on a tape and sent the tape to the blind man. Over the years, she put all kinds of stuff on tapes and sent the tapes off lickety-split. Next to writing a poem every year, I think it was her chief means of recreation. On one tape, she told the blind man she'd decided to live away from her officer for a time. On another tape, she told him about her divorce. She and I began going out, and of course she told her blind man about it. She told him everything, or so it seemed to me. Once she asked me if I'd like to hear the latest tape from the blind man. This was a year ago. I was on the tape, she said. So I said okay, I'd listen to it. I got us drinks and we settled down in the living room. We made ready to listen. First she inserted the tape into the player and adjusted a couple of dials. Then she pushed a lever. The tape squeaked and someone began to talk in this loud voice. She lowered the volume. After a few minutes of harmless chitchat, I heard my own name in the mouth of this stranger, this blind man I didn't even know! And then this: "From all you've said about him, I can only con-clude—" But we were interrupted, a knock at the door, something, and we didn't ever get back to the tape. Maybe it was just as well. I'd heard all I wanted to.

Now this same blind man was coming to sleep in my house.

"Maybe I could take him bowling," I said to my wife. She was at the draining board doing scalloped potatoes. She put down the knife she was using and turned around.

"If you love me," she said, "you can do this for me. If you don't love me, okay. But if you had a friend, any friend, and the friend came to visit, I'd make him feel comfortable." She wiped her hands with the dish towel.

"I don't have any blind friends," I said.

10   "You don't have *any* friends," she said. "Period. Besides," she said, "god-damn it, his wife's just died! Don't you understand that? The man's lost his wife!"

I didn't answer. She'd told me a little about the blind man's wife. Her name was Beulah. Beulah! That's a name for a colored woman.

"Was his wife a Negro?" I asked.

"Are you crazy?" my wife said. "Have you just flipped or something?" She picked up a potato. I saw it hit the floor, then roll under the stove. "What's wrong with you?" she said. "Are you drunk?"

"I'm just asking," I said.

15   Right then my wife filled me in with more detail than I cared to know. I made a drink and sat at the kitchen table to listen. Pieces of the story began to fall into place.

Beulah had gone to work for the blind man the summer after my wife had stopped working for him. Pretty soon Beulah and the blind man had themselves a church wedding. It was a little wedding—who'd want to go to such a wedding in the first place?—just the two of them, plus the minister and the minister's wife. But it was a church wedding just the same. It was what Beulah had wanted, he'd said. But even then Beulah must have been carrying the cancer in her glands. After they had been inseparable for eight years—my wife's word, *inseparable*—Beulah's health went into a rapid decline. She died in a Seattle hospital room, the blind man sitting beside the bed and holding on to her hand. They'd married, lived and worked together, slept together—had sex, sure—and then the blind man had to bury her. All this without his having ever seen what the goddamned woman looked like. It was beyond my understanding. Hearing this, I felt sorry for the blind man for a little bit. And then I found myself thinking what a pitiful life this woman must have led. Imagine a woman who could never see herself as she was seen in the eyes of her loved one. A woman who could go on day after day and never receive the smallest compliment from her beloved. A woman whose husband could never read the expression on her face, be it misery or something better. Someone who could wear makeup or not—what difference to him? She could, if she wanted, wear green eye-shadow around one eye, a straight pin in her nostril, yellow slacks and purple shoes, no matter. And then to slip off into death, the blind man's hand on her hand, his blind eyes streaming tears—I'm imagining now—her last thought maybe this: that he never even knew what she looked like, and she on an express to the grave. Robert was left with a small insurance policy and half of a twenty-peso Mexican coin. The other half of the coin went into the box with her. Pathetic.

So when the time rolled around, my wife went to the depot to pick him up. With nothing to do but wait—sure, I blamed him for that—I was having a drink and watching the TV when I heard the car pull into the drive. I got up from the sofa with my drink and went to the window to have a look.

I saw my wife laughing as she parked the car. I saw her get out of the car and shut the door. She was still wearing a smile. Just amazing. She went around to the other side of the car to where the blind man was already starting to get out. This blind man, feature this, he was wearing a full beard! A beard on a blind man! Too much, I say. The blind man reached into the back seat and dragged out a suitcase. My wife took his arm, shut the car door, and, talking all the way, moved him down the drive and then up the steps to the front porch. I turned off the TV. I finished my drink, rinsed the glass, dried my hands. Then I went to the door.

My wife said, "I want you to meet Robert. Robert, this is my husband. I've told you all about him." She was beaming. She had this blind man by his coat sleeve.

The blind man let go of his suitcase and up came his hand. 20

I took it. He squeezed hard, held my hand, and then he let it go.

"I feel like we've already met," he boomed.

"Likewise," I said. I didn't know what else to say. Then I said, "Welcome. I've heard a lot about you." We began to move then, a little group, from the porch into the living room, my wife guiding him by the arm. The blind man was carrying his suitcase in his other hand. My wife said things like,

"To your left here, Robert. That's right. Now watch it, there's a chair. That's it. Sit down right here. This is the sofa. We just bought this sofa two weeks ago."

I started to say something about the old sofa. I'd liked that old sofa. But I didn't say anything. Then I wanted to say something else, small-talk, about the scenic ride along the Hudson. How going *to* New York, you should sit on the right-hand side of the train, and coming *from* New York, the left-hand side.

25   "Did you have a good train ride?" I said. "Which side of the train did you sit on, by the way?"

"What a question, which side!" my wife said. "What's it matter which side?" she said.

"I just asked," I said.

"Right side," the blind man said. "I hadn't been on a train in nearly forty years. Not since I was a kid. With my folks. That's been a long time. I'd nearly forgotten the sensation. I have winter in my beard now," he said. "So I've been told, anyway. Do I look distinguished, my dear?" the blind man said to my wife.

"You look distinguished, Robert," she said. "Robert," she said. "Robert, it's just so good to see you."

30   My wife finally took her eyes off the blind man and looked at me. I had the feeling she didn't like what she saw. I shrugged.

I've never met, or personally known, anyone who was blind. This blind man was late forties, a heavy-set, balding man with stooped shoulders, as if he carried a great weight there. He wore brown slacks, brown shoes, a light-brown shirt, a tie, a sports coat. Spiffy. He also had this full beard. But he didn't use a cane and he didn't wear dark glasses. I'd always thought dark glasses were a must for the blind. Fact was, I wished he had a pair. At first glance, his eyes looked like anyone else's eyes. But if you looked close, there was something different about them. Too much white in the iris, for one thing, and the pupils seemed to move around in the sockets without his knowing it or being able to stop it. Creepy. As I stared at his face, I saw the left pupil turn in toward his nose while the other made an effort to keep in one place. But it was only an effort, for that eye was on the roam without his knowing it or wanting it to be.

I said, "Let me get you a drink. What's your pleasure? We have a little of everything. It's one of our pastimes."

"Bub, I'm a Scotch man myself," he said fast enough in this big voice.

"Right," I said. Bub! "Sure you are. I knew it."

35   He let his fingers touch his suitcase, which was sitting alongside the sofa. He was taking his bearings. I didn't blame him for that.

"I'll move that up to your room," my wife said.

"No, that's fine," the blind man said loudly. "It can go up when I go up."

"A little water with the Scotch?" I said.

"Very little," he said.

"I knew it," I said.

He said, "Just a tad. The Irish actor, Barry Fitzgerald? I'm like that fellow. When I drink water, Fitzgerald said, I drink water. When I drink whiskey, I drink whiskey." My wife laughed. The blind man brought his hand up under his beard. He lifted his beard slowly and let it drop.

I did the drinks, three big glasses of Scotch with a splash of water in each. Then we made ourselves comfortable and talked about Robert's travels. First the long flight from the West Coast to Connecticut, we covered that. Then from Connecticut up here by train. We had another drink concerning that leg of the trip.

I remembered having read somewhere that the blind didn't smoke because, as speculation had it, they couldn't see the smoke they exhaled. I thought I knew that much and that much only about blind people. But this blind man smoked his cigarette down to the nubbin and then lit another one. This blind man filled his ashtray and my wife emptied it.

When we sat down at the table for dinner, we had another drink. My wife heaped Robert's plate with cube steak, scalloped potatoes, green beans. I buttered him up two slices of bread. I said, "Here's bread and butter for you." I swallowed some of my drink. "Now let us pray," I said, and the blind man lowered his head. My wife looked at me, her mouth agape. "Pray the phone won't ring and the food doesn't get cold," I said.

We dug in. We ate everything there was to eat on the table. We ate like there was no tomorrow. We didn't talk. We ate. We scarfed. We grazed that table. We were into serious eating. The blind man had right away located his foods, he knew just where everything was on his plate. I watched with admiration as he used his knife and fork on the meat. He'd cut two pieces of meat, fork the meat into his mouth, and then go all out for the scalloped potatoes, the beans next, and then he'd tear off a hunk of buttered bread and eat that. He'd follow this up with a big drink of milk. It didn't seem to bother him to use his fingers once in a while, either.

We finished everything, including half a strawberry pie. For a few moments, we sat as if stunned. Sweat beaded on our faces. Finally, we got up from the table and left the dirty plates. We didn't look back. We took ourselves into the living room and sank into our places again. Robert and my wife sat on the sofa. I took the big chair. We had us two or three more drinks while they talked about the major things that had come to pass for them in the past ten years. For the most part, I just listened. Now and then I joined in. I didn't want him to think I'd left the room, and I didn't want her to think I was feeling left out. They talked of things that had happened to them—to them!—these past ten years. I waited in vain to hear my name on my wife's sweet lips: "And then my dear husband came into my life"—something like that. But I heard nothing of the sort. More talk of

Robert. Robert had done a little of everything, it seemed, a regular blind jack-of-all-trades. But most recently he and his wife had had an Amway distributorship, from which, I gathered, they'd earned their living, such as it was. The blind man was also a ham radio operator. He talked in his loud voice about conversations he'd had with fellow operators in Guam, in the Philippines, in Alaska, and even in Tahiti. He said he'd have a lot of friends there if he ever wanted to go visit those places. From time to time, he'd turn his blind face toward me, put his hand under his beard, ask me something. How long had I been in my present position? (Three years.) Did I like my work? (I didn't.) Was I going to stay with it? (What were the options?) Finally, when I thought he was beginning to run down, I got up and turned on the TV.

My wife looked at me with irritation. She was heading toward a boil. Then she looked at the blind man and said, "Robert, do you have a TV?"

The blind man said, "My dear, I have two TVs. I have a color set and a black-and-white thing, an old relic. It's funny, but if I turn the TV on, and I'm always turning it on, I turn on the color set. It's funny, don't you think?"

I didn't know what to say to that. I had absolutely nothing to say to that. No opinion. So I watched the news program and tried to listen to what the announcer was saying.

50 "This is a color TV," the blind man said. "Don't ask me how, but I can tell."

"We traded up a while ago," I said.

The blind man had another taste of his drink. He lifted his beard, sniffed it, and let it fall. He leaned forward on the sofa. He positioned his ashtray on the coffee table, then put the lighter to his cigarette. He leaned back on the sofa and crossed his legs at the ankles.

My wife covered her mouth, and then she yawned. She stretched. She said, "I think I'll go upstairs and put on my robe. I think I'll change into something else. Robert, you make yourself comfortable," she said.

"I'm comfortable," the blind man said.

55 "I want you to feel comfortable in this house," she said.

"I am comfortable," the blind man said.

After she'd left the room, he and I listened to the weather report and then to the sports roundup. By that time, she'd been gone so long I didn't know if she was going to come back. I thought she might have gone to bed. I wished she'd come back downstairs. I didn't want to be left alone with a blind man. I asked him if he wanted another drink, and he said sure. Then I asked if he wanted to smoke some dope with me. I said I'd just rolled a number. I hadn't, but I planned to do so in about two shakes.

"I'll try some with you," he said.

"Damn right," I said. "That's the stuff."

I got our drinks and sat down on the sofa with him. Then I rolled us 60
two fat numbers. I lit one and passed it. I brought it to his fingers. He took
it and inhaled.

"Hold it as long as you can," I said. I could tell he didn't know the first
thing.

My wife came back downstairs wearing her pink robe and her pink
slippers.

"What do I smell?" she said.

"We thought we'd have us some cannabis," I said.

My wife gave me a savage look. Then she looked at the blind man and 65
said, "Robert, I didn't know you smoked."

He said, "I do now, my dear. There's a first time for everything. But I
don't feel anything yet."

"This stuff is pretty mellow," I said. "This stuff is mild. It's dope you
can reason with," I said. "It doesn't mess you up."

"Not much it doesn't, bub," he said, and laughed.

My wife sat on the sofa between the blind man and me. I passed her the
number. She took it and toked and then passed it back to me. "Which way
is this going?" she said. Then she said, "I shouldn't be smoking this. I can
hardly keep my eyes open as it is. That dinner did me in. I shouldn't have
eaten so much."

"It was the strawberry pie," the blind man said. "That's what did it," he 70
said, and he laughed his big laugh. Then he shook his head.

"There's more strawberry pie," I said.

"Do you want some more, Robert?" my wife said.

"Maybe in a little while," he said.

We gave our attention to the TV. My wife yawned again. She said, "Your
bed is made up when you feel like going to bed, Robert. I know you must
have had a long day. When you're ready to go to bed, say so." She pulled his
arm. "Robert?"

He came to and said, "I've had a real nice time. This beats tapes, doesn't 75
it?"

I said, "Coming at you," and I put the number between his fingers. He
inhaled, held the smoke, and then let it go. It was like he'd been doing it
since he was nine years old.

"Thanks, bub," he said. "But I think this is all for me. I think I'm beginning to feel it," he said. He held the burning roach out for my wife.

"Same here," she said. "Ditto. Me, too." She took the roach and passed it
to me. "I may just sit here for a while between you two guys with my eyes
closed. But don't let me bother you, okay? Either one of you. If it bothers
you, say so. Otherwise, I may just sit here with my eyes closed until you're
ready to go to bed," she said. "Your bed's made up, Robert, when you're
ready. It's right next to our room at the top of the stairs. We'll show you up

when you're ready. You wake me up now, you guys, if I fall asleep." She said
that and then she closed her eyes and went to sleep.

The news program ended. I got up and changed the channel. I sat back
down on the sofa. I wished my wife hadn't pooped out. Her head lay across
the back of the sofa, her mouth open. She'd turned so that her robe had
slipped away from her legs, exposing a juicy thigh. I reached to draw her
robe back over her, and it was then that I glanced at the blind man. What
the hell! I flipped the robe open again.

80   "You say when you want some strawberry pie," I said.

"I will," he said.

I said, "Are you tired? Do you want me to take you up to your bed? Are
you ready to hit the hay?"

"Not yet," he said. "No, I'll stay up with you, bub. If that's all right. I'll
stay up until you're ready to turn in. We haven't had a chance to talk.
Know what I mean? I feel like me and her monopolized the evening." He
lifted his beard and he let it fall. He picked up his cigarettes and his
lighter.

"That's all right," I said. Then I said, "I'm glad for the company."

85   And I guess I was. Every night I smoked dope and stayed up as long as I
could before I fell asleep. My wife and I hardly ever went to bed at the same
time. When I did go to sleep, I had these dreams. Sometimes I'd wake up
from one of them, my heart going crazy.

Something about the church and the Middle Ages was on the TV. Not
your run-of-the-mill TV fare. I wanted to watch something else. I turned
to the other channels. But there was nothing on them, either. So I turned
back to the first channel and apologized.

"Bub, it's all right," the blind man said. "It's fine with me. Whatever you
want to watch is okay. I'm always learning something. Learning never
ends. It won't hurt me to learn something tonight. I got ears," he said.

We didn't say anything for a time. He was leaning forward with his head
turned at me, his right ear aimed in the direction of the set. Very disconcerting. Now and then his eyelids drooped and then they snapped open
again. Now and then he put his fingers into his beard and tugged, like he
was thinking about something he was hearing on the television.

On the screen, a group of men wearing cowls was being set upon and
tormented by men dressed in skeleton costumes and men dressed as devils. The men dressed as devils wore devil masks, horns, and long tails. This
pageant was part of a procession. The Englishman who was narrating the
thing said it took place in Spain once a year. I tried to explain to the blind
man what was happening.

90   "Skeletons," he said. "I know about skeletons," he said, and he nodded.

The TV showed this one cathedral. Then there was a long, slow look at
another one. Finally, the picture switched to the famous one in Paris, with

its flying buttresses and its spires reaching up to the clouds. The camera pulled away to show the whole of the cathedral rising above the skyline.

There were times when the Englishman who was telling the thing would shut up, would simply let the camera move around over the cathedrals. Or else the camera would tour the countryside, men in fields walking behind oxen. I waited as long as I could. Then I felt I had to say something. I said, "They're showing the outside of this cathedral now. Gargoyles. Little statues carved to look like monsters. Now I guess they're in Italy. Yeah, they're in Italy. There's paintings on the walls of this one church."

"Are those fresco paintings, bub?" he asked, and he sipped from his drink.

I reached for my glass. But it was empty. I tried to remember what I could remember. "You're asking me are those frescoes?" I said. "That's a good question. I don't know."

The camera moved to a cathedral outside Lisbon. The differences in the Portuguese cathedral compared with the French and Italian were not that great. But they were there. Mostly the interior stuff. Then something occurred to me, and I said, "Something has occurred to me. Do you have any idea what a cathedral is? What they look like, that is? Do you follow me? If somebody says cathedral to you, do you have any notion what they're talking about? Do you know the difference between that and a Baptist church, say?"

He let the smoke dribble from his mouth. "I know they took hundreds of workers fifty or a hundred years to build," he said. "I just heard the man say that, of course. I know generations of the same families worked on a cathedral. I heard him say that, too. The men who began their life's work on them, they never lived to see the completion of their work. In that wise, bub, they're no different from the rest of us, right?" He laughed. Then his eyelids drooped again. His head nodded. He seemed to be snoozing. Maybe he was imagining himself in Portugal. The TV was showing another cathedral now. This one was in Germany. The Englishman's voice droned on. "Cathedrals," the blind man said. He sat up and rolled his head back and forth. "If you want the truth, bub, that's about all I know. What I just said. What I heard him say. But maybe you could describe one to me? I wish you'd do it. I'd like that. If you want to know, I really don't have a good idea."

I stared hard at the shot of the cathedral on the TV. How could I even begin to describe it? But say my life depended on it. Say my life was being threatened by an insane guy who said I had to do it or else.

I stared some more at the cathedral before the picture flipped off into the countryside. There was no use. I turned to the blind man and said, "To begin with, they're very tall." I was looking around the room for clues. "They reach way up. Up and up. Toward the sky. They're so big, some of them, they have to have these supports. To help hold them up, so to speak.

These supports are called buttresses. They remind me of viaducts, for some reason. But maybe you don't know viaducts, either? Sometimes the cathedrals have devils and such carved into the front. Sometimes lords and ladies. Don't ask me why this is," I said.

He was nodding. The whole upper part of his body seemed to be moving back and forth.

100 "I'm not doing so good, am I?" I said.

He stopped nodding and leaned forward on the edge of the sofa. As he listened to me, he was running his fingers through his beard. I wasn't getting through to him, I could see that. But he waited for me to go on just the same. He nodded, like he was trying to encourage me. I tried to think what else to say. "They're really big," I said. "They're massive. They're built of stone. Marble, too, sometimes. In those olden days, when they built cathedrals, men wanted to be close to God. In those olden days, God was an important part of everyone's life. You could tell this from their cathedral-building. I'm sorry," I said, "but it looks like that's the best I can do for you. I'm just no good at it."

"That's all right, bub," the blind man said. "Hey, listen. I hope you don't mind my asking you. Can I ask you something? Let me ask you a simple question, yes or no. I'm just curious and there's no offense. You're my host. But let me ask if you are in any way religious? You don't mind my asking?"

I shook my head. He couldn't see that, though. A wink is the same as a nod to a blind man. "I guess I don't believe in it. In anything. Sometimes it's hard. You know what I'm saying?"

"Sure, I do," he said.

105 "Right," I said.

The Englishman was still holding forth. My wife sighed in her sleep. She drew a long breath and went on with her sleeping.

"You'll have to forgive me," I said. "But I can't tell you what a cathedral looks like. It just isn't in me to do it. I can't do any more than I've done."

The blind man sat very still, his head down, as he listened to me.

I said, "The truth is, cathedrals don't mean anything special to me. Nothing. Cathedrals. They're something to look at on late-night TV. That's all they are."

110 It was then that the blind man cleared his throat. He brought something up. He took a handkerchief from his back pocket. Then he said, "I get it, bub. It's okay. It happens. Don't worry about it," he said. "Hey, listen to me. Will you do me a favor? I got an idea. Why don't you find us some heavy paper? And a pen. We'll do something. We'll draw one together. Get us a pen and some heavy paper. Go on, bub, get the stuff," he said.

So I went upstairs. My legs felt like they didn't have any strength in them. They felt like they did after I'd done some running. In my wife's room, I looked around. I found some ballpoints in a little basket on her table. And then I tried to think where to look for the kind of paper he was talking about.

Downstairs, in the kitchen, I found a shopping bag with onion skins in the bottom of the bag. I emptied the bag and shook it. I brought it into the living room and sat down with it near his legs. I moved some things, smoothed the wrinkles from the bag, spread it out on the coffee table.

The blind man got down from the sofa and sat next to me on the carpet.

He ran his fingers over the paper. He went up and down the sides of the paper. The edges, even the edges. He fingered the corners.

"All right," he said. "All right, let's do her." 115

He found my hand, the hand with the pen. He closed his hand over my hand. "Go ahead, bub, draw," he said. "Draw. You'll see. I'll follow along with you. It'll be okay. Just begin now like I'm telling you. You'll see. Draw," the blind man said.

So I began. First I drew a box that looked like a house. It could have been the house I lived in. Then I put a roof on it. At either end of the roof, I drew spires. Crazy.

"Swell," he said. "Terrific. You're doing fine," he said. "Never thought anything like this could happen in your lifetime, did you, bub? Well, it's a strange life, we all know that. Go on now. Keep it up."

I put in windows with arches. I drew flying buttresses. I hung great doors. I couldn't stop. The TV station went off the air. I put down the pen and closed and opened my fingers. The blind man felt around over the paper. He moved the tips of his fingers over the paper, all over what I had drawn, and he nodded.

"Doing fine," the blind man said. 120

I took up the pen again, and he found my hand. I kept at it. I'm no artist. But I kept drawing just the same.

My wife opened up her eyes and gazed at us. She sat up on the sofa, her robe hanging open. She said, "What are you doing? Tell me, I want to know."

I didn't answer her.

The blind man said, "We're drawing a cathedral. Me and him are working on it. Press hard," he said to me. "That's right. That's good," he said. "Sure. You got it, bub. I can tell. You didn't think you could. But you can, can't you? You're cooking with gas now. You know what I'm saying? We're going to really have us something here in a minute. How's the old arm?" he said. "Put some people in there now. What's a cathedral without people?"

My wife said, "What's going on? Robert, what are you doing? What's 125 going on?"

"It's all right," he said to her. "Close your eyes now," the blind man said to me.

I did it. I closed them just like he said.

"Are they closed?" he said. "Don't fudge."

"They're closed," I said.

130   "Keep them that way," he said. He said, "Don't stop now. Draw."

So we kept on with it. His fingers rode my fingers as my hand went over the paper. It was like nothing else in my life up to now.

Then he said, "I think that's it. I think you got it," he said. "Take a look. What do you think?"

But I had my eyes closed. I thought I'd keep them that way for a little longer. I thought it was something I ought to do.

"Well?" he said. "Are you looking?"

135   My eyes were still closed. I was in my house. I knew that. But I didn't feel like I was inside anything.

"It's really something," I said.

1983

SAMPLE WRITING: NOTES AND RESPONSE PAPER

Wesley Rupton wrote the notes below in response to the questions on page 18. As you read these notes, compare them to the notes you took as you read "Cathedral." Do Rupton's notes reveal anything to you that you didn't notice while reading the story? Did you notice anything he did not, or do you disagree with any of his interpretations?

Notes on Raymond Carver's "Cathedral"

What do you expect?
- Title: The first words are "this blind man," and those words keep being repeated. Why not call it "The Blind Man" or "The Blind Man's Visit"?
- The threatening things the husband says made me expect that he would attack the blind man. I thought the wife might leave her husband for the blind man, who has been nicer to her.
- When they talk about going up to bed, and the wife goes to "get comfortable" and then falls asleep, I thought there was a hint about sex.

What happens in the story?
- Not that much. It is a story about one evening in which a husband and wife and their guest drink, have dinner, talk, and then watch TV.
- These people have probably drunk two bottles of hard liquor (how many drinks?) before, during, and after a meal. And then they smoke marijuana.
- In the final scene, the two men try to describe and draw cathedrals that are on the TV show. Why cathedrals? Though they connect with the title.

- The husband seems to have a different attitude at the end: He likes Robert and seems excited about the experience "like nothing else in my life up to now."

How is the story narrated?

- It's told in first person and past tense. The husband is the narrator. We never get inside another character's thoughts. He seems to be telling someone about the incident, first saying the blind man was coming, and then filling in the background about his wife and the blind man, and then telling what happens after the guest arrives.
- The narrator describes people and scenes and summarizes the past; there is dialogue.
- It doesn't have episodes or chapters, but there are two gaps on the page, before paragraph 57 and before paragraph 88. Maybe time passes here.

Who are the characters?

- Three main characters: husband, wife, and blind man (the blind man's own wife has just died, and the wife divorced her first husband). I don't think we ever know the husband's or wife's names. The blind man, Robert, calls him "Bub," like "buddy." They seem to be white, middle-class Americans. The wife is lonely and looking for meaning. The blind man seems sensitive, and he cares about the poetry and tapes.
- The husband is sort of acting out, though mostly in his own mind. Asking "Was his wife a Negro?" sounds like he wants to make fun of black or blind people. His wife asks, "Are you drunk?" and says that he has no friends; I thought he's an unhappy man who gets drunk and acts "crazy" a lot and that she doesn't really expect him to be that nice.
- It sounds like these people have plenty of food and things, but aren't very happy. They all sound smart, but the narrator is ignorant and he has no religion. All three characters have some bad or nervous habits (alcohol, cigarettes, drugs; insomnia; suicide attempt; divorce).

What is the setting and time of the story?

- Mostly in the house the evening the blind man arrives. But after the intro there's a kind of flashback to the summer in Seattle ten years ago (par. 2). The story about the visit starts again in paragraph 6, and then the wife tells the husband more about the blind man's marriage—another flashback in paragraph 16. In paragraph 17, "the time rolled around" to the story's main event. After that, it's chronological.

- We don't know the name of the town, but it seems to be on the U.S. East Coast (five hours by train from Connecticut [par. 1]). It can't be too long ago or too recent either: They mention trains, audio tapes, color TV, no Internet. No one seems worried about food or health the way they might be today.
- I noticed that travel came up in the story. Part of what drives the wife crazy about her first husband is moving around to different military bases (par. 4). In paragraph 46, Robert tells us about his contact with ham radio operators in places he would like to visit (Guam, Alaska). The TV show takes Robert and the narrator on a tour of France, Italy, and Portugal.

What do you notice about how the story is written?

- The narrator is irritating. He repeats words a lot. He uses stereotypes. He seems to be informally talking to someone, as if he can't get over it. But then he sometimes uses exaggerated or bored-sounding phrases, "this man who'd first enjoyed her favors," "So okay. I'm saying . . . married her childhood etc." (par. 4). His style is almost funny.
- Things he repeats: Paragraphs 2 and 3: "She told me" (3 times), "he could touch her face . . . he touched his fingers to every part of her face . . ." (and later "touched her nose" and "they'd kept in touch"). "She even tried to write a poem . . . always trying to write a poem" (and 4 more times "poem"). The words "talk," "tape," "told" are also repeated.

What does the story mean? Can you express its theme or themes?

- The way the narrator learns to get along with the blind man must be important. The narrator is disgusted by blind people at first, and at the end he closes his eyes on purpose.
- I think it makes a difference that the two men imagine and try to draw a cathedral, not a flower or an airplane. It's something made by human beings, and it's religious. As they mention, the builders of cathedrals don't live to see them finished, but the buildings last for centuries. It's not like the narrator is saved or becomes a great guy, but he gets past whatever he's afraid of at night and he seems inspired for a little while. I don't know why the wife has to be left out of this, but probably the husband couldn't open up if he was worrying about how close she is to Robert.

Now read the following brief paper responding to Raymond Carver's "Cathedral." A response paper may use a less formal organization and style than a longer, more analytical essay, but it should not just be a summary or complete description of the work. Indeed, a response paper could be a step on the way to a longer essay. You need not form a single thesis or argument, but you should try to develop your ideas and feelings about the story through your writing. The point is to get your thoughts in writing without worrying too much about form and style.

Almost everything in the following response paper comes directly from the notes, but notice how the writer has combined observations, adding a few direct quotations or details from the text to support claims about the effects and meaning of the story. Also notice that the writer cites the details from the text by referring to paragraph numbers. Some teachers may ask students to cite the text with page numbers.

Wesley Rupton
Professor Suarez
English 170

Response Paper on Raymond Carver's "Cathedral"

Not much happens in Raymond Carver's short story "Cathedral," and at first I wondered what it was about and why it was called "Cathedral." The narrator, the unnamed husband, seems to be telling someone about the evening that Robert, a blind friend of his wife, came to stay at their house, not long after Robert's own wife has died. After the narrator fills us in about his wife's first marriage and her relationship with the blind man, he describes what the three characters do that evening: they drink a lot of alcohol, eat a huge dinner that leaves them "stunned" (par. 46), smoke marijuana, and after the wife falls asleep the two men watch TV. A show about cathedrals leads the husband to try to describe what a cathedral looks like, and then the men try to draw one together. The husband seems to have a different attitude at the end: he likes Robert and seems excited about an experience "like nothing else in my life up to now" (par. 131).

The husband's way of telling the story is definitely important. He is sort of funny, but also irritating. As he makes jokes about stereotypes, you start to dislike or distrust him. When he hears about Robert's wife, Beulah, he asks, "Was his wife a Negro?" (par. 12) just because her name sounds like a black woman's name to him. In three paragraphs, he flashes back to the time ten years ago when his wife was the blind man's assistant and the blind man asked if he could touch her face. . . . She told me he touched his fingers to every part of her face. . . . She even tried to write a poem about it. . . . In the poem, she recalled his fingers . . . over her face. In the poem, she talked about what she had felt . . . when the blind man touched her nose and lips. (pars. 2, 3)

The narrator seems to be going over and over the same creepy idea of a man feeling his wife's face. It seems to disgust him that his wife and the blind man communicated or expressed themselves, perhaps because he seems incapable of doing so. When his wife asks, "Are you drunk?" and says that he has no friends, I got a feeling that the husband is an unhappy man who gets drunk and acts "crazy" a lot and that his wife doesn't really expect him to be very nice (pars. 8-13). He's going to make fun of their guest (asking a blind man to go bowling). The husband is sort of acting out, though he's mostly rude in his own mind.

There's nothing heroic or dramatic or even unusual about these people (except that one is blind). The events take place in a house somewhere in an American suburb and not too long ago. Other than the quantity of alcohol and drugs they consume, these people don't do anything unusual, though the blind man seems strange to the narrator. The ordinary setting and plot make the idea of something as grand and old as a European cathedral come as a surprise at the end of the story. I wondered if part of the point is that they desperately want to get out of a trap they're in. I noticed that travel came up in the story. Part of what drove the wife crazy with her first husband was moving around to different military bases (par. 4). In paragraph 46, Robert tells us about his contact with ham radio operators in places he would like to visit (Guam, Alaska). The TV show takes Robert and the narrator on a tour of France, Italy, and Portugal.

The way the narrator changes from disliking the blind man to getting along with him must be important to the meaning of the story. After the wife goes up to "get comfortable," suggesting that they might go to bed, the story focuses on the two men. Later she falls asleep on the sofa between them, and the narrator decides not to cover up her leg where her robe has fallen open, as if he has stopped being jealous. At this point the narrator decides he is "glad for the company" of his guest (par. 84). The cooperation between the two men is the turning point. The narrator is disgusted by blind people at first, and at the end he closes his eyes on purpose. The two men try to imagine something and build something together, and Robert is coaching the narrator. Robert says, "let's do her," and then says, "*you're* doing fine" (pars. 115, 118, emphasis added). I think it makes a difference that they imagine and draw a cathedral, not a flower or a cow or an airplane. It's something made by human beings, and it's religious. I don't think the men are converted to believing in God at the end, but this narrow-minded guy gets past whatever he's afraid of at night and finds some sort of inspiring feeling. I don't know why the wife has to be left out, but probably the husband couldn't open up if he was worrying about how close she is to Robert.

The ideas of communicating or being in touch and travel seem connected to me. I think that the husband tries to tell this story about the cathedral the way his wife tried to write a poem. The narrator has had an exciting experience that gets him in touch with something beyond his small house. After drawing the cathedral, the narrator says that he "didn't feel like I was inside anything" (par. 135). Though I still didn't like the narrator, I felt more sympathy, and I thought the story showed that even this hostile person could open up.

SAMPLE WRITING: FIRST-DRAFT ANALYSIS

Bethany Qualls wrote the following first draft of a paper analyzing character and narration in Carver's "Cathedral." Read this paper as you would one of your peers' papers, looking for opportunities for the writer to improve her presentation. Is the language consistently appropriate for academic writing? Does the essay maintain its focus? Does it demonstrate a steady progression of well-supported arguments toward a strong, well-earned conclusion? Is there any redundant or otherwise unnecessary material? Are there ideas that need to be developed further?

Bethany Qualls
Professor Netherton
English 301

A Narrator's Blindness in Raymond Carver's "Cathedral"

A reader in search of an exciting plot will be pretty disappointed by Raymond Carver's "Cathedral" because the truth is nothing much happens. A suburban husband and wife receive a visit from her former boss, who is blind. After the wife falls asleep, the two men watch a TV program about cathedrals and eventually try to draw one. Along the way the three characters down a few cocktails and smoke a little pot. But that's about as far as the action goes. Instead of focusing on plot, then, the story really asks us to focus on the characters, especially the husband who narrates the story. Through his words even more than his actions the narrator unwittingly shows us why nothing much happens to him by continually demonstrating his utter inability to connect with others or to understand himself.

The narrator's isolation is most evident in the distanced way he introduces his own story and the people in it. He does not name the other characters or himself, referring to them only by using labels such as "this blind man," "his wife," "my wife" (par. 1; all page references are to the class

Qualls 2

text, *The Norton Introduction to Literature*, 10th ed.) and "the man [my wife] was going to marry" (par. 2). Even after the narrator's wife starts referring to their visitor as "Robert," the narrator keeps calling him "the blind man." These labels distance him from the other characters and also leave readers with very little connection to them.

At least three times the narrator himself notices that this habit of not naming or really acknowledging people is significant. Referring to his wife's "officer," he asks, "why should he have a name? he was the childhood sweetheart, and what more does he want?" (par. 5). Moments later he describes how freaked out he was when he listened to a tape the blind man had sent his wife and "heard [his] own name in the mouth of this . . . blind man . . . [he] didn't even know!" (par. 5). Yet once the blind man arrives and begins to talk with the wife, the narrator finds himself "wait[ing] in vain to hear [his] name on [his] wife's sweet lips" and disappointed to hear "nothing of the sort" (par. 46). Simply using someone's name suggests a kind of intimacy that the narrator avoids and yet secretly yearns for.

Also reinforcing the narrator's isolation and dissatisfaction with it are the awkward euphemisms and clichés he uses, which emphasize how disconnected he is from his own feelings and how uncomfortable he is with other people's. Referring to his wife's first husband, the narrator says it was he "who'd first enjoyed her favors" (par. 4), an antiquated expression even in 1983, the year the story was published. Such language reinforces our sense that the narrator is unable to speak in language that is meaningful or heartfelt, especially when he actually tries to talk about emotions. He describes his wife's feelings for her first husband, for example, by using generic language and then just trailing off entirely: "she was in love with the guy, and he was in love with her, etc." (par. 2). When he refers to the blind man and his wife as "inseparable," he points out that this is, in fact, his "wife's word," not one that he's come up with (par. 16). And even when he admits that he would like to hear his wife talk about him (par. 46), he speaks in language that seems to come from books or movies rather than the heart.

Once the visit actually begins, the narrator's interactions and conversations with the other characters are even more awkward. His discomfort with the very idea of the visit is obvious to his wife and to the reader. As he says in his usual deadpan manner, "I wasn't enthusiastic about his visit" (par. 1). During the visit he sits silent when his wife and Robert are talking and then answers Robert's questions about his life and feelings with the shortest possible phrases: "How long had I been in my present position? (Three years.) Did I like my work? (I didn't.)" (par. 46). Finally, he tries to escape even that much involvement by simply turning on the TV and tuning Robert out.

Despite Robert's best attempt to make a connection with the narrator, the narrator resorts to a label again, saying that he "didn't want to be left alone with a blind man" (par. 57). Robert, merely "a blind man," remains a category, not a person, and the narrator can initially relate to Robert only by invoking the stereotypes about that category that he has learned "from the movies" (par. 1). He confides to the reader that he believes that blind people always wear dark glasses, that they never smoke (par. 43), and that a beard on a blind man is "too much" (par. 18). It follows that the narrator is amazed about the connection his wife and Robert have because he is unable to see Robert as a person like any other. "Who'd want to go to such a wedding in the first place?" (par. 16) he asks rhetorically about Robert's wedding to his wife, Beulah.

Misconceptions continue as the narrator assumes Beulah would "never receive the smallest compliment from her beloved" since the compliments he is thinking about are physical ones (par. 16). Interestingly, when faced with a name that is specific (Beulah), the narrator immediately assumes that he knows what the person with that name must be like ("a colored woman," par. 11), even though she is not in the room or known to him. Words fail or mislead the narrator in both directions, as he's using them and as he hears them.

There is hope for the narrator at the end as he gains some empathy and forges a bond with Robert over the drawing of a cathedral. That process seems to begin when the narrator admits to himself, the reader, and Robert that he is "glad for the [Robert's] company" (par. 84) and, for the first time, comes close to disclosing the literally nightmarish loneliness of his life. It culminates in a moment of physical and emotional intimacy that the narrator admits is "like nothing else in my life up to now" (par. 131)—a moment in which discomfort with the very idea of blindness gives way to an attempt to actually experience blindness from the inside. Because the narrator has used words to distance himself from the world, it seems fitting that all this happens only when the narrator *stops* using words. They have a tendency to blind him.

However, even at the very end it isn't clear just whether or how the narrator has really changed. He does not completely interact with Robert

Qualls 4

but has to be prodded into action by him. By choosing to keep his eyes closed, he not only temporarily experiences blindness but also shuts out the rest of the world, since he "didn't feel like [he] was inside anything" (par. 135). Perhaps most important, he remains unable to describe his experience meaningfully, making it difficult for readers to decide whether or not he has really changed. For example, he says, "It was like nothing else in my life up to now" (par. 131), but he doesn't explain why this is true. Is it because he is doing something for someone else? Because he is thinking about the world from another's perspective? Because he feels connected to Robert? Because he is drawing a picture while probably drunk and high? There is no way of knowing.

It's possible that not feeling "inside anything" (par. 135) could be a feeling of freedom from his own habits of guardedness and insensitivity, his emotional "blindness." But even with this final hope for connection, for the majority of the story the narrator is a closed, judgmental man who isolates himself and cannot connect with others. The narrator's view of the world is one filled with misconceptions that the visit from Robert starts to slowly change, yet it is not clear what those changes are, how far they will go, or whether they will last.

KEY CONCEPTS: FICTION

As you read, respond to, and write about fiction, some key terms and concepts may be useful in comparing or distinguishing different kinds of stories you read. Stories may be oral rather than written down, and they may be of different lengths. They may be based on true stories or completely invented. They may be written in verse rather than prose, or they may be created in media other than the printed page. While reading and writing, you should always have a good college-level dictionary on hand so that you can look up any unfamiliar terms. In the era of the Internet it's especially easy to learn more about any word or concept—and it can help you enrich the ideas in your papers. Another excellent resource is the *Oxford English Dictionary*, available in the reference section of most academic libraries, which reveals the wide range of meanings words have had over time. Words in English always have a long story to tell because over the centuries so many languages have contributed to our current vocabulary. It's not uncommon for meanings to overlap or even reverse themselves.

Generally speaking, a *story* is a short account of an incident or series of incidents, whether actual or invented. The word is often used to refer to an entertaining tale of imaginary people and events, but it is also used in phrases like "the *story* of my life"—suggesting a true account. The term **narrative** is especially useful as a general concept for the substance rather than the form of what is told about persons and their actions. A story or a tale is usually short, whereas a narrative may be of any length from a sentence to a series of novels and beyond.

Narratives in Daily Life

Narrative plays an important role in our lives beyond the telling of fictional stories. Consider the following:

- Today, sociologists and historians may collect *personal narratives* to present an account of society and everyday life in a certain time or place.
- Since the 1990s, the practice of *narrative medicine* has spread as an improved technique of diagnosis and treatment from the patient's point of view.
- There is a movement to encourage *mediation* rather than litigation in divorce cases. A mediator may collaborate with the couple in arriving at a shared perspective on the divorce; in a sense, they try to agree on the story of their marriage and how it ended.
- Some countries have attempted to recover from the trauma of genocidal ethnic conflict through *official hearings of testimony* by victims as well as defendants. South Africa's Truth and Reconciliation Commission is an example of this use of stories.

We tend to think of stories in their written form, but many of the stories that we now regard as among the world's greatest, such as Homer's *Iliad* and the Old English epic *Beowulf*, were sung or recited by generations of storytellers before being written down. Just as rumors change shape as they circulate, oral stories tend to be more fluid than printed stories. Traditionally oral **tales** such as fairy tales or folktales may endure for a very long time yet take different forms in various countries and eras. And it's often difficult or impossible to trace such a story back to a single "author" or creator. In a sense, then, an oral story is the creation of a whole community or communities, just as oral storytelling tends to be a more communal event than reading.

Certain recognizable signals set a story or tale apart from common speech and encourage us to pay a different kind of attention. Children know that a story is beginning when they hear or read "Once upon a time . . . ," and traditional oral storytellers have formal ways to set up a tale, such as *Su-num-twee* ("listen to me"), as Spokane storytellers say. "And they lived happily ever after," or simply "The End," may similarly indicate when the story is over. Such conventions have been adapted since the invention of printing and the spread of literacy.

FICTION AND NONFICTION

The word *fiction* comes from the Latin root *fingere*, to fashion or form. The earliest definitions concern the act of making something artificial to imi-

Notice to Little Children

Final page of *More English Fairy Tales*, ed. Joseph Jacobs.
Jacobs published volumes of popular tales that had been
collected over several centuries from oral storytellers in the
British countryside.

tate something else. In the past two centuries, *fiction* has become more narrowly defined as "prose narrative about imaginary people and events," the main meaning of the word as we use it in this anthology.

Genres of Prose Fiction by Length

A **novel** is a work of prose fiction of about 40,000 words or more. The form arose in the seventeenth and early eighteenth centuries as prose romances and adventure tales began to adopt techniques of history and travel narrative as well as memoir, letters, and biography.

A **novella** is a work of prose fiction of about 17,000 to 40,000 words. The novella form was especially favored between about 1850 and 1950, largely because it can be more tightly controlled and concentrated than a long novel while focusing on the inner workings of a character.

A **short story** is broadly defined as anywhere between 1,000 and 20,000 words. One expectation of a short story is that it may be read in a single sitting. The modern short story developed in the mid-nineteenth century, in part because of the growing popularity of magazines.

A **short short story**, sometimes called "flash fiction" or "micro-fiction," is generally not much longer than 1,000 words and sometimes much shorter. There have always been very short fictions, including parables and fables, but this genre as we follow it today is an invention cultivated in recent decades.

In contrast with fiction, **nonfiction** usually refers to *factual* prose narrative. Some major nonfiction genres are history, biography, and autobiography. In film, documentaries and "biopics," or biographical feature films, similarly attempt to represent real people, places, and events. The boundary between fiction and nonfiction is often blurred today, as it was centuries ago. So-called true crime novels such as Truman Capote's *In Cold Blood* and novelized biographies such as Colm Tóibín's *The Master*, about the life of the novelist Henry James, use the techniques of fiction writing to narrate actual events. Graphic novels, with a format derived from comic books, have become an increasingly popular medium for memoirs. (Two examples are Art Spiegelman's *Maus* and Marjane Satrapi's *Persepolis*.) Some Hollywood movies and TV shows dramatize real people in everyday situations or contexts, or real events such as the assassination of President John F. Kennedy.

In contrast, **historical fiction**, developed by Sir Walter Scott around 1815, refers to prose narratives that present history in imaginative ways. Such works of prose narrative fiction adhere closely to the facts of history and actual lives, just as many "true" life stories are more or less fictionalized.

. . .

The fiction chapters in this volume present a collection of prose works—mostly short stories—almost all of which were printed within the author's lifetime. Even as you read the short prose fiction in this book, bear in mind the many ways we encounter stories or narrative in everyday life, and consider the almost limitless variety of forms that fiction may take.

Understanding the Text

1 PLOT

At its most basic, every story is an attempt to answer the question, *What happened?* In some cases, this question is easy to answer. J. R. R. Tolkien's *The Lord of the Rings* trilogy (1954–55) is full of battles, chases, and other heart-stopping dramatic action; Mark Twain's *Adventures of Huckleberry Finn* (1884) relates Huck and Jim's adventures as they travel down the Mississippi River. Yet if we ask what happens in other works of fiction, our initial answer might well be, "Not much." In one of the most memorable and pivotal scenes in Henry James's masterly novel *The Portrait of a Lady* (1881), for example, a woman enters a room, sees a man sitting down and a woman standing up, and beats a hasty retreat. Not terribly exciting stuff, it would seem. Yet this event ends up radically transforming the lives of just about everyone in the novel. "On very tiny pivots do human lives turn" would thus seem to be one common message—or **theme**—of fiction.

All fiction, regardless of its subject matter, should make us ask, *What will happen next?* and *How will all this turn out?* And responsive readers of fiction will often pause to answer those questions, trying to articulate just what their expectations are and how the story has shaped them. But great fiction and responsive readers are often just as interested in questions about *why* things happen and about *how* the characters' lives are affected as a result. These *how* and *why* questions are likely to be answered very differently by different readers of the very same fictional work; as a result, such questions will often generate powerful essays, whereas mainly factual questions about what happens in the work usually won't.

PLOT VERSUS ACTION, SEQUENCE, AND SUBPLOT

The term **plot** is sometimes used to refer to the events recounted in a fictional work. But in this book we instead use the term **action** in this way, reserving the term *plot* for the way the author sequences and paces the events so as to shape our response and interpretation.

The difference between action and plot resembles the difference between ancient chronicles that merely list the events of a king's reign in chronological order and more modern histories that make a meaningful sequence out of those events. As the British novelist and critic E. M. Forster put it, "The king died and then the queen died" is not a plot, for it has not been "tampered with." "The queen died after the king died" describes the same events, but the order in which they are reported has been changed. The reader of the first sentence focuses on the king first, the reader of the second on the queen. The second sentence, moreover, subtly encourages us to speculate about *why* things happened, not just *what* happened and *when*: Did the queen die *because* her husband did? If so, was her death the result of her grief? Or was she murdered by a rival who saw the king's death as the perfect opportunity to get rid of her, too? Though our two sentences describe the same action, each has quite a different focus, emphasis, effect, and meaning thanks to its *sequencing*—the precise order in which events are related.

Like chronicles, many fictional works do relate events in chronological order, starting with the earliest and ending with the latest. Folktales, for example, have this sort of plot. But fiction writers have other choices; events need not be recounted in the particular order in which they happened. Quite often, then, a writer will choose to mix things up, perhaps opening a story with the most recent event and then moving backward to show us all that led up to it. Still other stories begin somewhere in the middle of the action or, to use the Latin term, *in medias res* (literally, "in the middle of things"). In such plots, events that occurred before the story's opening are sometimes presented in **flashbacks**. Conversely, a story might jump forward in time to recount a later **episode** or event in a **flashforward. Foreshadowing** occurs when an author merely gives subtle clues or hints about what will happen later in the story.

Though we often talk about the plot of a fictional work, however, keep in mind that some works, especially longer ones, have two or more. A plot that receives significantly less time and attention than another is called a **subplot**.

PACE

In life, we sometimes have little choice about how long a particular event lasts. If you want a driver's license, you may have to spend a boring hour or two at the motor vehicle office. And much as you might prefer to relax and enjoy your lunch, occasionally you have to scarf it down in the ten minutes it takes you to drive to campus.

One of the pleasures of turning experiences into a story, however, is that doing so gives a writer more power over them. In addition to choosing the order in which to recount events, the writer can also decide how much time and attention to devote to each. *Pacing*, or the duration of particular episodes—especially relative to each other and to the time they would have taken in real life—is a vital tool of storytellers and another important factor to consider in analyzing plots. In all fiction, pace as much as sequence determines focus and emphasis, effect and meaning. And though it can be very helpful to differentiate between "fast-paced" and "slow-paced" fiction, all effective stories contain both faster and slower bits. When an author slows down to home in on a particular moment and scene, often introduced by a phrase such as "Later that evening . . ." or "the day before Maggie fell down . . . ," we call this a **discriminated occasion**. For example, the first paragraph of Linda Brewer's "20/20" (in "Fiction: Reading, Responding, Writing") quickly and generally refers to events that occur over three days. Then Brewer suddenly slows down, pinpointing an incident that takes place on "The third evening out. . . ." That episode consumes four paragraphs of the story, even though the action described in those paragraphs accounts for only a few minutes of Bill and Ruthie's time. Next the story devotes two more paragraphs to an incident that occurs "The next evening. . . ." In the last paragraph, Brewer speeds up again, telling us about the series of "wonderful sights" Ruthie sees between Indiana and Spokane, Washington.

CONFLICTS

Whatever their sequence and pace, all plots hinge on at least one **conflict**— some sort of struggle—and its resolution. Conflicts may be *external* or *internal*. External conflicts arise between a character and something or someone outside themselves. Adventure stories and films often present this sort of conflict in its purest form, keeping us poised on the edge of our seats as James Bond struggles to outwit and outfight an arch-villain intent on world domination or destruction. Yet external conflicts can also be much subtler, pitting an individual against nature or fate, against a social force such as racism or poverty, or against another person or group of people with a different way of looking at things (as in "20/20"). The cartoon below presents an external conflict of the latter type and one you may well see quite differently than the cartoonist does.

Internal conflicts occur when a character struggles to reconcile two competing desires, needs, or duties, or two parts or aspects of himself: His head, for instance, might tell him to do one thing, his heart another. Often, a conflict is simultaneously external and internal, as in the following brief folktale, in which a woman seems to struggle simultaneously with nature, with mortality, with God, and with her desire to hold onto someone she loves versus her need to let go.

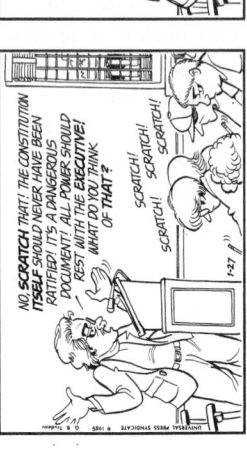

JACOB AND WILHELM GRIMM

The Shroud

There was once a mother who had a little boy of seven years old, who was so handsome and lovable that no one could look at him without liking him, and she herself worshipped him above everything in the world. Now it so happened that he suddenly became ill, and God took him to himself; and for this the mother could not be comforted, and wept both day and night. But soon afterwards, when the child had been buried, it appeared by night in the places where it had sat and played during its life, and if the mother wept, it wept also, and, when morning came, it disappeared. As, however, the mother would not stop crying, it came one night, in the little white shroud in which it had been laid in its coffin, and with its wreath of flowers round its head, and stood on the bed at her feet, and said, "Oh, mother, do stop crying, or I shall never fall asleep in my coffin, for my shroud will not dry because of all thy tears which fall upon it." The mother was afraid when she heard that, and wept no more. The next night the child came again, and held a little light in its hand, and said, "Look, mother, my shroud is nearly dry, and I can rest in my grave." Then the mother gave her sorrow into God's keeping, and bore it quietly and patiently, and the child came no more, but slept in its little bed beneath the earth.

• • •

THE FIVE PARTS OF PLOT

Even compact and simple plots, like that of "The Shroud," have the same five parts or phases as lengthy and complex plots: (1) exposition, (2) rising action,

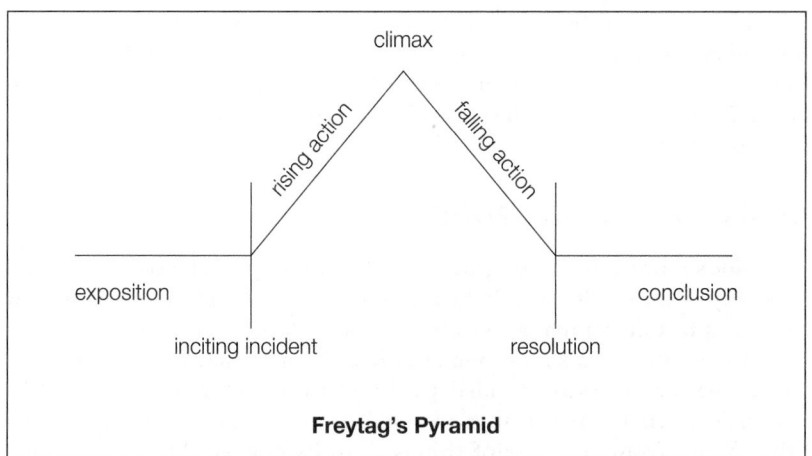

Freytag's Pyramid

(3) climax or turning point, (4) falling action, and (5) conclusion or resolution. The following diagram, known as Freytag's pyramid after the nineteenth-century German scholar Gustav Freytag, maps out a typical plot structure:

EXPOSITION

The first part of the plot, called the **exposition**, introduces the characters, their situations, and, usually, a time and place, giving us all the basic information we need to understand what is to come. In longer works of fiction, exposition may go on for paragraphs or even pages, and some exposition may well be deferred until later phases of the plot. But in our examples, the exposition is all up-front and brief: Trudeau's first panel shows us a teacher (or at least his words), a group of students, and a classroom; the Grimms' first sentence introduces a mother, her young son, and the powerful love she feels for him.

Exposition usually reveals some source or seed of potential conflict in the initial situation, of which the characters may be as yet unaware. In Trudeau's cartoon, the contrast between the talkative teacher, who expects "independent thought" from those in his class, and the silent, scribbling students suggests a conflict in the making. So, too, does the Grimms' statement that the mother "worshipped" her boy "above everything" else in a world in which nothing and no one lasts forever.

RISING ACTION

By suggesting a conflict, exposition may blend into the second phase of the plot, the **rising action**, which begins with an **inciting incident** or *destabilizing event*—that is, some action that destabilizes the initial situation and incites open conflict, as does the death of the little boy in the second sentence of the folktale. Typically, what keeps the action rising is a **complication**, an event that introduces a new conflict or intensifies an existing one. This happens in the third sentence of "The Shroud," when the mother begins to see her little boy every night, although he is dead and buried.

CLIMAX OR TURNING POINT

The plot's **climax** or **turning point** is the moment of greatest emotional intensity. (Notice the way boldface lettering appears and exclamation points replace question marks in the second-to-last panel of the *Doonesbury* strip.) The climax is also the moment when the outcome of the plot and the fate of the characters are decided. (A climax thus tends to be a literally *pivotal* incident that "turns things around," or involves, in Aristotle's words, "the change from one state of things . . . to its opposite.") "The Shroud" reaches its climax when the mother stops crying after her little boy tells her that her grief is what keeps him from sleeping and that peaceful sleep is what he craves.

Here, as in many plots, the turning point involves a discovery or new insight or even an **epiphany,** a sudden revelation of truth inspired by a seemingly trivial event. As a result, turning points often involve internal or psychological events, even if they are prompted by, and lead to, external action. In "The Shroud," for instance, the mother's new insight results in different behavior: She "wept no more."

Sometimes, though, critics differentiate between the story's climax and the **crisis** that precedes and precipitates it. In "The Shroud," for example, these critics would describe the crisis as the moment when the son confronts the mother with information that implicitly requires her to make a choice, the climax as the moment when she makes it. This distinction might be especially helpful when you grapple with longer works of fiction in which much more time and action intervenes between the crisis and the climax.

FALLING ACTION

The **falling action** brings a release of emotional tension and moves us toward the resolution of the conflict or conflicts. This release occurs in "The Shroud" when the boy speaks for the second and last time, assuring his mother that her more peaceful demeanor is giving him peace as well.

In some works of fiction, resolution is achieved through an utterly unexpected twist, as in "Meanwhile, unknown to our hero, the Marines were just on the other side of the hill," or "Susan rolled over in bed and realized the whole thing had been just a dream." Such a device is sometimes called a **deus ex machina.** (This Latin term literally means "god out of a machine" and derives from the ancient theatrical practice of using a machine to lower onto the stage a god who solves the problems of the human characters.)

CONCLUSION

Finally, just as a plot begins with a situation that is later destabilized, so its **conclusion** presents us with a new and at least somewhat stable situation—one that gives a sense of closure because the conflict or conflicts have been resolved, if only temporarily and not necessarily in the way we or the characters had hoped. In "The Shroud," that resolution comes in the last sentence, in which the mother bears her grief "quietly and patiently" and the child quietly sleeps his last sleep. The final *Doonesbury* panel presents us with a situation that is essentially the reverse of the one with which the strip begins—with the teacher silently slumped over his podium, his students suddenly talking to each other instead of scribbling down his words. Many plots instead end with a situation that outwardly looks almost identical to the one with which they began. But thanks to all that has happened between the story's beginning and its end, the final "steady state" at which the characters arrive can never be exactly the same as the one in which they started. A key question to ask at the end of a work of fiction is precisely why, as well as how, things are different.

Some fictional works may also include a final section called an **epilogue**, which ties up loose ends left dangling in the conclusion proper, updates us on what has happened to the characters since their conflicts were resolved, and/or provides some sort of commentary on the story's larger significance. (An epilogue is thus a little like this paragraph, which comes after we have concluded our discussion of the five phases of plot but still feel that there are one or two more terms to deal with.)

A NOTE ON *DÉNOUEMENT*

In discussions of plot, you will very often encounter the French word **dénouement** (literally, "untying," as of a knot). In this anthology, however, we generally try to avoid using *dénouement* because it can be, and often is, used in three different, potentially contradictory ways—as a synonym for *falling action*; as a synonym for *conclusion* or *resolution*; and even as a label for a certain kind of epilogue.

Plot Summary: An Example and an Exercise

Although any good **plot summary** should be a relatively brief recounting (or *synopsis*) of what happens in a work of fiction, it need not necessarily tell what happens in the same order that the work itself does. As a result, many a plot summary is in fact more like an action summary in the sense that we define the terms *action* and *plot* in this book. But unless you have a good reason for reordering events, it is generally a good idea to follow the plot. The following plot summary of Raymond Carver's "Cathedral" does just that:

> The narrator is annoyed to learn that his wife's old friend Robert, a blind man who once employed her as a reader, is coming to visit the couple. The wife has corresponded with her friend for years via cassette tapes, describing the details of her early marriage, divorce, and remarriage to her husband, the narrator. Uncomfortable with

(Continued on next page)

(Continued)

the prospect of having a blind person in his home, the narrator is surprised by Robert's appearance and behavior: his booming voice and full beard are not what he expected, and he eats, drinks, and smokes marijuana with relish. After dinner the three watch television. After the narrator's wife has fallen asleep, a program about cathedrals begins. The narrator asks Robert if he knows what cathedrals look like or represent, and Robert, admitting that he does not, asks the narrator to draw one. With Robert's hand lying on top of his own, the narrator traces roofs, spires, arches, and even people. Eventually Robert instructs the narrator to close his eyes and continue drawing. The narrator reports that this experience was like nothing else in my life up to now. (From "Raymond Carver: 'Cathedral,'" *Characters in Twentieth Century Literature*, Book Two [Gale Research, 1995])

Now try this yourself: Choose any of the stories in this anthology and write a one-paragraph plot summary. Then, in a paragraph or two, reflect on your choices about which details to include, which to omit, and how to order them (especially if you've deviated from the plot). What does your summary imply about the story's focus, meaning, and significance? Now repeat the exercise, summarizing the story in a different way and then reflecting on the significance and effect of the changes you've made.

Alternatively, try the same exercise with a friend who has also read the story: Each of you should write your own summary; then exchange them and (separately or together) write a few paragraphs comparing your summaries and reflecting on the significance of the similarities and differences.

COMMON PLOT TYPES

If most plots are essentially variations on the same five-part pattern, some plots have even more features in common. As you think back over the fiction you have read and the movies you have seen (not to mention the video games you have played), you might be surprised to discover just how many of their plots involve a quest—a character or characters' journey to find something or someone that seems, at least at first, of tremendous material or spiritual value. Traditionally, that requires a literal journey, the challenge being not only to find and acquire the object but also to return home with

As you read the two stories in this chapter, or any other work of fiction, think about what sets each one apart when it comes to plot; how each uses variations on common plot conventions; how each generates, fulfills, and often frustrates our expectations about the action to come; and how each uses sequence, pace, and other techniques to endow action with both emotional charge and meaning. When it comes to action and plot, every good story holds its own surprises and offers a unique answer to the nagging question *What happened?*

GUY DE MAUPASSANT

The Jewelry [1]

Having met the girl one evening, at the house of the office-superintendent, M. Lantin became enveloped in love as in a net.

She was the daughter of a country-tutor, who had been dead for several years. Afterward she had come to Paris with her mother, who made regular visits to several bourgeois families of the neighborhood, in hopes of being able to get her daughter married. They were poor and respectable, quiet and gentle. The young girl seemed to be the very ideal of that pure good woman to whom every young man dreams of entrusting his future. Her modest beauty had a charm of angelic shyness; and the slight smile that always dwelt about her lips seemed a reflection of her heart.

Everybody sang her praises; all who knew her kept saying: "The man who gets her will be lucky. No one could find a nicer girl than that."

M. Lantin, who was then chief clerk in the office of the Minister of the Interior, with a salary of 3,500 francs a year,[2] demanded her hand, and married her.

He was unutterably happy with her. She ruled his home with an economy so adroit that they really seemed to live in luxury. It would be impossible to conceive of any attentions, tendernesses, playful caresses which she did not lavish upon her husband; and such was the charm of her person that, six years after he married her, he loved her even more than he did the first day.

There were only two points upon which he ever found fault with her—her love of the theater, and her passion for false jewelry.

1. Translated by Lafcadio Hearn.
2. Midlevel bureaucratic wage, perhaps about $30,000 to $40,000 today.

Her lady-friends (she was acquainted with the wives of several small office holders) were always bringing her tickets for the theaters; whenever there was a performance that made a sensation, she always had her *loge* secured, even for first performances; and she would drag her husband with her to all these entertainments, which used to tire him horribly after his day's work. So at last he begged her to go to the theater with some lady-acquaintances who would consent to see her home afterward. She refused for quite a while—thinking it would not look very well to go out thus unaccompanied by her husband. But finally she yielded, just to please him; and he felt infinitely grateful to her therefore.

Now this passion for the theater at last evoked in her the desire of dress. It was true that her toilette remained simple, always in good taste, but modest; and her sweet grace, her irresistible grace, ever smiling and shy, seemed to take fresh charm from the simplicity of her robes. But she got into the habit of suspending in her pretty ears two big cut pebbles, fashioned in imitation of diamonds; and she wore necklaces of false pearls, bracelets of false gold, and haircombs studded with paste-imitations of precious stones.

Her husband, who felt shocked by this love of tinsel and show, would often say—"My dear, when one has not the means to afford real jewelry, one should appear adorned with one's natural beauty and grace only—and these gifts are the rarest of jewels."

10   But she would smile sweetly and answer: "What does it matter? I like those things—that is my little whim. I know you are right; but one can't make oneself over again. I've always loved jewelry so much!"

And then she would roll the pearls of the necklaces between her fingers, and make the facets of the cut crystals flash in the light, repeating: "Now look at them—see how well the work is done. You would swear it was real jewelry."

He would then smile in his turn, and declare to her: "You have the tastes of a regular Gypsy."

Sometimes, in the evening, when they were having a chat by the fire, she would rise and fetch the morocco box in which she kept her "stock" (as M. Lantin called it)—would put it on the tea-table, and begin to examine the false jewelry with passionate delight, as if she experienced some secret and mysterious sensations of pleasure in their contemplation; and she would insist on putting one of the necklaces round her husband's neck, and laugh till she couldn't laugh any more, crying out: "Oh! how funny you look!" Then she would rush into his arms, and kiss him furiously.

One winter's night, after she had been to the Opera, she came home chilled through, and trembling. Next day she had a bad cough. Eight days after that, she died of pneumonia.

15   Lantin was very nearly following her into the tomb. His despair was so frightful that in one single month his hair turned white. He wept from

morning till night, feeling his heart torn by inexpressible suffering—ever haunted by the memory of her, by the smile, by the voice, by all the charm of the dead woman.

Time did not assuage his grief. Often during office hours his fellow-clerks went off to a corner to chat about this or that topic of the day—his cheeks might have been seen to swell up all of a sudden, his nose wrinkle, his eyes fill with water—he would pull a frightful face, and begin to sob.

He had kept his dead companion's room just in the order she had left it, and he used to lock himself up in it every evening to think about her—all the furniture, and even all her dresses, remained in the same place they had been on the last day of her life.

But life became hard for him. His salary, which, in his wife's hands, had amply sufficed for all household needs, now proved scarcely sufficient to supply his own few wants. And he asked himself in astonishment how she had managed always to furnish him with excellent wines and with delicate eating which he could not now afford at all with his scanty means.

He got a little into debt, like men obliged to live by their wits. At last one morning that he happened to find himself without a cent in his pocket, and a whole week to wait before he could draw his monthly salary, he thought of selling something; and almost immediately it occurred to him to sell his wife's "stock"—for he had always borne a secret grudge against the flash-jewelry that used to annoy him so much in former days. The mere sight of it, day after day, somewhat spoiled the sad pleasure of thinking of his darling.

He tried a long time to make a choice among the heap of trinkets she 20 had left behind her—for up to the very last day of her life she had kept obstinately buying them, bringing home some new thing almost every night—and finally he resolved to take the big pearl necklace which she used to like the best of all, and which he thought ought certainly to be worth six or eight francs, as it was really very nicely mounted for an imitation necklace.

He put it in his pocket, and walked toward the office, following the boulevards, and looking for some jewelry-store on the way, where he could enter with confidence.

Finally he saw a place and went in; feeling a little ashamed of thus exposing his misery, and of trying to sell such a trifling object.

"Sir," he said to the jeweler, "please tell me what this is worth."

The jeweler took the necklace, examined it, weighed it, took up a magnifying glass, called his clerk, talked to him in whispers, put down the necklace on the counter, and drew back a little bit to judge of its effect at a distance.

M. Lantin, feeling very much embarrassed by all these ceremonies, 25 opened his mouth and began to declare—"Oh! I know it can't be worth much" . . . when the jeweler interrupted him saying:

"Well, sir, that is worth between twelve and fifteen thousand francs; but I cannot buy it unless you can let me know exactly how you came by it."

The widower's eyes opened enormously, and he stood gaping—unable to understand. Then after a while he stammered out: "You said? . . . Are you sure?" The jeweler, misconstruing the cause of this astonishment, replied in a dry tone—"Go elsewhere if you like, and see if you can get any more for it. The very most I would give for it is fifteen thousand. Come back and see me again, if you can't do better."

M. Lantin, feeling perfectly idiotic, took his necklace and departed; obeying a confused desire to find himself alone and to get a chance to think.

But the moment he found himself in the street again, he began to laugh, and he muttered to himself: "The fool!—oh! what a fool; If I had only taken him at his word. Well, well!—a jeweler who can't tell paste from real jewelry!"

30   And he entered another jewelry-store, at the corner of the Rue de la Paix. The moment the jeweler set eyes on the necklace, he examined— "Hello! I know that necklace well—it was sold here!"

M. Lantin, very nervous, asked:

"What's it worth?"

"Sir, I sold it for twenty-five thousand francs. I am willing to buy it back again for eighteen thousand—if you can prove to me satisfactorily, according to legal presciptions, how you came into possession of it."—This time, M. Lantin was simply paralyzed with astonishment. He said: "Well . . . but please look at it again, sir. I always thought until now that it was . . . was false."

The jeweler said:

35   "Will you give me your name, sir?"

"Certainly. My name is Lantin; I am employed at the office of the Minister of the Interior. I live at No. 16, Rue des Martyrs."

The merchant opened the register, looked, and said: "Yes; this necklace was sent to the address of Madame Lantin, 16 Rue des Martyrs, on July 20th, 1876."

And the two men looked into each other's eyes—the clerk wild with surprise; the jeweler suspecting he had a thief before him.

The jeweler resumed:

40   "Will you be kind enough to leave this article here for twenty-four hours only—I'll give you a receipt."

M. Lantin stuttered: "Yes—ah! certainly." And he went out folding up the receipt, which he put in his pocket.

Then he crossed the street, went the wrong way, found out his mistake, returned by way of the Tuileries, crossed the Seine, found out he had taken the wrong road again, and went back to the Champs-Élysées without being able to get one clear idea into his head. He tried to reason, to understand.

His wife could never have bought so valuable an object as that. Certainly not. But then, it must have been a present! . . . A present from whom? What for?

He stopped and stood stock-still in the middle of the avenue.

A horrible suspicion swept across his mind. . . . She? . . . But then all those other pieces of jewelry must have been presents also! . . . Then it seemed to him that the ground was heaving under his feet; that a tree, right in front of him, was falling toward him; he thrust out his arms instinctively, and fell senseless.

He recovered his consciousness again in a drug-store to which some 45 bystanders had carried him. He had them lead him home, and he locked himself into his room.

Until nightfall he cried without stopping, biting his handkerchief to keep himself from screaming out. Then, completely worn out with grief and fatigue, he went to bed, and slept a leaden sleep.

A ray of sunshine awakened him, and he rose and dressed himself slowly to go to the office. It was hard to have to work after such a shock. Then he reflected that he might be able to excuse himself to the superintendent, and he wrote to him. Then he remembered he would have to go back to the jeweler's; and shame made his face purple. He remained thinking a long time. Still he could not leave the necklace there; he put on his coat and went out.

It was a fine day; the sky extended all blue over the city, and seemed to make it smile. Strollers were walking aimlessly about, with their hands in their pockets.

Lantin thought as he watched them passing: "How lucky the men are who have fortunes! With money a man can even shake off grief—you can go where you please—travel—amuse yourself! Oh! if I were only rich!"

He suddenly discovered he was hungry—not having eaten anything 50 since the evening before. But his pockets were empty; and he remembered the necklace. Eighteen thousand francs! Eighteen thousand francs!—that was a sum—that was!

He made his way to the Rue de la Paix and began to walk backward and forward on the sidewalk in front of the store. Eighteen thousand francs! Twenty times he started to go in; but shame always kept him back.

Still he was hungry—very hungry—and had not a cent. He made one brusque resolve, and crossed the street almost at a run, so as not to let himself have time to think over the matter; and he rushed into the jeweler's.

As soon as he saw him, the merchant hurried forward, and offered him a chair with smiling politeness. Even the clerks came forward to stare at Lantin, with gaiety in their eyes and smiles about their lips.

The jeweler said: "Sir, I made inquiries; and if you are still so disposed, I am ready to pay you down the price I offered you."

55   The clerk stammered: "Why, yes—sir, certainly."

The jeweler took from a drawer eighteen big bills,[3] counted them, and held them out to Lantin, who signed a little receipt, and thrust the money feverishly into his pocket.

Then, as he was on the point of leaving, he turned to the ever-smiling merchant, and said, lowering his eyes: "I have some—I have some other jewelry, which came to me in the same—from the same inheritance. Would you purchase them also from me?"

The merchant bowed, and answered: "Why, certainly, sir—certainly...."

One of the clerks rushed out to laugh at his ease; another kept blowing his nose as hard as he could.

Lantin, impassive, flushed and serious, said: "I will bring them to you."

60   And he hired a cab to get the jewelry.

When he returned to the store, an hour later, he had not yet breakfasted. They examined the jewelry—piece by piece—putting a value on each. Nearly all had been purchased from that very house.

Lantin, now, disputed estimates made, got angry, insisted on seeing the books, and talked louder and louder the higher the estimates grew.

The big diamond earrings were worth 20,000 francs; the bracelets, 35,000; the brooches, rings and medallions, 16,000; a set of emeralds and sapphires, 14,000; solitaire, suspended to a gold neckchain, 40,000; the total value being estimated at 196,000 francs.

The merchant observed with mischievous good nature: "The person who owned these must have put all her savings into jewelry."

65   Lantin answered with gravity: "Perhaps that is as good a way of saving money as any other." And he went off, after having agreed with the merchant that an expert should make a counter-estimate for him the next day.

When he found himself in the street again, he looked at the Column Vendôme[4] with the desire to climb it, as if it were a May pole. He felt jolly enough to play leapfrog over the Emperor's head—up there in the blue sky.

He breakfasted at Voisin's[5] restaurant, and ordered wine at 20 francs a bottle.

Then he hired a cab and drove out to the Bois.[6] He looked at the carriages passing with a sort of contempt, and a wild desire to yell out to the passers-by: "I am rich, too—I am! I have 200,000 francs!"

The recollection of the office suddenly came back to him. He drove there, walked right into the superintendent's private room, and said: "Sir, I come to give you my resignation. I have just come into a fortune of *three*

---

3. French paper money varies in size; the larger the bill, the larger the denomination.
4. Famous column with a statue of the emperor Napoleon at the top.
5. Like the Café Anglais below, a well-known and high-priced restaurant.
6. Large Parisian park where the rich took their outings.

hundred thousand francs." Then he shook hands all round with his fellow-clerks; and told them all about his plans for a new career. Then he went to dinner at the Café Anglais.

Finding himself seated at the same table with a man who seemed to him quite genteel, he could not resist the itching desire to tell him, with a certain air of coquetry, that he had just inherited a fortune of *four* hundred thousand francs. 70

For the first time in his life he went to the theater without feeling bored by the performance; and he passed the night in revelry and debauch.

Six months after he married again. His second wife was the most upright of spouses, but had a terrible temper. She made his life very miserable.

1883

QUESTIONS

1. What parts of "The Jewelry" correspond to the five traditional phases of plot: exposition, rising action, turning point or climax, falling action, and conclusion?
2. Once the secret of Madame Lantin's jewelry is revealed, what details from earlier in the story take on a different significance?
3. How and why might the story's end—especially its last paragraph—defy expectations? How does it once again change your interpretation of earlier events and of Lantin's first marriage?

JAMES BALDWIN

Sonny's Blues

I read about it in the paper, in the subway, on my way to work. I read it, and I couldn't believe it, and I read it again. Then perhaps I just stared at it, at the newsprint spelling out his name, spelling out the story. I stared at it in the swinging lights of the subway car, and in the faces and bodies of the people, and in my own face, trapped in the darkness which roared outside.

It was not to be believed and I kept telling myself that, as I walked from the subway station to the high school. And at the same time I couldn't doubt it. I was scared, scared for Sonny. He became real to me again. A great block of ice got settled in my belly and kept melting there slowly all day long, while I taught my classes algebra. It was a special kind of ice. It kept melting, sending trickles of ice water all up and down my veins, but it never got less. Sometimes it hardened and seemed to expand until I felt my guts were going to come spilling out or that I was going to choke or scream. This would always be at a moment when I was remembering some specific thing Sonny had once said or done.

When he was about as old as the boys in my classes his face had been bright and open, there was a lot of copper in it; and he'd had wonderfully direct brown eyes, and great gentleness and privacy. I wondered what he looked like now. He had been picked up, the evening before, in a raid on an apartment downtown, for peddling and using heroin.

I couldn't believe it: but what I mean by that is that I couldn't find any room for it anywhere inside me. I had kept it outside me for a long time. I hadn't wanted to know. I had had suspicions, but I didn't name them, I kept putting them away. I told myself that Sonny was wild, but he wasn't crazy. And he'd always been a good boy, he hadn't ever turned hard or evil or disrespectful, the way kids can, so quick, so quick, especially in Harlem. I didn't want to believe that I'd ever see my brother going down, coming to nothing, all that light in his face gone out, in the condition I'd already seen so many others. Yet it had happened and here I was, talking about algebra to a lot of boys who might, every one of them for all I knew, be popping off needles every time they went to the head.[1] Maybe it did more for them than algebra could.

5   I was sure that the first time Sonny had ever had horse,[2] he couldn't have been much older than these boys were now. These boys, now, were living as we'd been living then, they were growing up with a rush and their heads bumped abruptly against the low ceiling of their actual possibilities. They were filled with rage. All they really knew were two darknesses, the darkness of their lives, which was now closing in on them, and the darkness of the movies, which had blinded them to that other darkness, and in which they now, vindictively, dreamed, at once more together than they were at any other time, and more alone.

When the last bell rang, the last class ended, I let out my breath. It seemed I'd been holding it for all that time. My clothes were wet—I may have looked as though I'd been sitting in a steam bath, all dressed up, all afternoon. I sat alone in the classroom a long time. I listened to the boys outside, downstairs, shouting and cursing and laughing. Their laughter struck me for perhaps the first time. It was not the joyous laughter which—God knows why—one associates with children. It was mocking and insular, its intent was to denigrate. It was disenchanted, and in this, also, lay the authority of their curses. Perhaps I was listening to them because I was thinking about my brother and in them I heard my brother. And myself.

One boy was whistling a tune, at once very complicated and very simple, it seemed to be pouring out of him as though he were a bird, and it sounded very cool and moving through all that harsh, bright air, only just holding its own through all those other sounds.

1. Lavatory.   2. Heroin.

I stood up and walked over to the window and looked down into the courtyard. It was the beginning of the spring and the sap was rising in the boys. A teacher passed through them every now and again, quickly, as though he or she couldn't wait to get out of that courtyard, to get those boys out of their sight and off their minds. I started collecting my stuff. I thought I'd better get home and talk to Isabel.

The courtyard was almost deserted by the time I got downstairs. I saw this boy standing in the shadow of a doorway, looking just like Sonny. I almost called his name. Then I saw that it wasn't Sonny, but somebody we used to know, a boy from around our block. He'd been Sonny's friend. He'd never been mine, having been too young for me, and, anyway, I'd never liked him. And now, even though he was a grown-up man, he still hung around that block, still spent hours on the street corners, was always high and raggy. I used to run into him from time to time and he'd often work around to asking me for a quarter or fifty cents. He always had some real good excuse, too, and I always gave it to him. I don't know why.

But now, abruptly, I hated him. I couldn't stand the way he looked at 10 me, partly like a dog, partly like a cunning child. I wanted to ask him what the hell he was doing in the school courtyard.

He sort of shuffled over to me, and he said, "I see you got the papers. So you already know about it."

"You mean about Sonny? Yes, I already know about it. How come they didn't get you?"

He grinned. It made him repulsive and it also brought to mind what he'd looked like as a kid. "I wasn't there. I stay away from them people."

"Good for you." I offered him a cigarette and I watched him through the smoke. "You come all the way down here just to tell me about Sonny?"

"That's right." He was sort of shaking his head and his eyes looked 15 strange, as though they were about to cross. The bright sun deadened his damp dark brown skin and it made his eyes look yellow and showed up the dirt in his kinked hair. He smelled funky. I moved a little away from him and I said, "Well, thanks. But I already know about it and I got to get home."

"I'll walk you a little ways," he said. We started walking. There were a couple of kids still loitering in the courtyard and one of them said good-night to me and looked strangely at the boy beside me.

"What're you going to do?" he asked me. "I mean, about Sonny?"

"Look. I haven't seen Sonny for over a year, I'm not sure I'm going to do anything. Anyway, what the hell *can* I do?"

"That's right," he said quickly, "ain't nothing you can do. Can't much help old Sonny no more, I guess."

It was what I was thinking and so it seemed to me he had no right to 20 say it.

"I'm surprised at Sonny, though," he went on—he had a funny way of talking, he looked straight ahead as though he were talking to himself—"I thought Sonny was a smart boy, I thought he was too smart to get hung."

"I guess he thought so too," I said sharply, "and that's how he got hung. And how about you? You're pretty goddamn smart, I bet."

Then he looked directly at me, just for a minute. "I ain't smart," he said. "If I was smart, I'd have reached for a pistol a long time ago."

"Look. Don't tell *me* your sad story, if it was up to me, I'd give you one." Then I felt guilty—guilty, probably, for never having supposed that the poor bastard *had* a story of his own, much less a sad one, and I asked, quickly, "What's going to happen to him now?"

25   He didn't answer this. He was off by himself some place.

"Funny thing," he said, and from his tone we might have been discussing the quickest way to get to Brooklyn, "when I saw the papers this morning, the first thing I asked myself was if I had anything to do with it. I felt sort of responsible."

I began to listen more carefully. The subway station was on the corner, just before us, and I stopped. He stopped, too. We were in front of a bar and he ducked slightly, peering in, but whoever he was looking for didn't seem to be there. The juke box was blasting away with something black and bouncy and I half watched the barmaid as she danced her way from the juke box to her place behind the bar. And I watched her face as she laughingly responded to something someone said to her, still keeping time to the music. When she smiled one saw the little girl, one sensed the doomed, still-struggling woman beneath the battered face of the semi-whore.

"I never *give* Sonny nothing," the boy said finally, "but a long time ago I come to school high and Sonny asked me how it felt." He paused, I couldn't bear to watch him, I watched the barmaid, and I listened to the music which seemed to be causing the pavement to shake. "I told him it felt great." The music stopped, the barmaid paused and watched the juke box until the music began again. "It did."

All this was carrying me some place I didn't want to go. I certainly didn't want to know how it felt. It filled everything, the people, the houses, the music, the dark, quicksilver barmaid, with menace; and this menace was their reality.

30   "What's going to happen to him now?" I asked again.

"They'll send him away some place and they'll try to cure him." He shook his head. "Maybe he'll even think he's kicked the habit. Then they'll let him loose"—he gestured, throwing his cigarette into the gutter. "That's all."

"What do you mean, that's *all*?"

But I knew what he meant.

"I *mean*, that's *all*." He turned his head and looked at me, pulling down the corners of his mouth. "Don't you know what I mean?" he asked, softly.

"How the hell *would* I know what you mean?" I almost whispered it, I 35
don't know why.

"That's right," he said to the air, "how would *he* know what I mean?" He
turned toward me again, patient and calm, and yet I somehow felt him
shaking, shaking as though he were going to fall apart. I felt that ice in my
guts again, the dread I'd felt all afternoon; and again I watched the barmaid, moving about the bar, washing glasses, and singing. "Listen. They'll
let him out and then it'll just start all over again. That's what I mean."

"You mean—they'll let him out. And then he'll just start working his
way back in again. You mean he'll never kick the habit. Is that what you
mean?"

"That's right," he said, cheerfully. "*You* see what I mean."

"Tell me," I said at last, "why does he want to die? He must want to die,
he's killing himself, why does he want to die?"

He looked at me in surprise. He licked his lips. "He don't want to die. He 40
wants to live. Don't nobody want to die, ever."

Then I wanted to ask him—too many things. He could not have
answered, or if he had, I could not have borne the answers. I started walking. "Well, I guess it's none of my business."

"It's going to be rough on old Sonny," he said. We reached the subway
station. "This is your station?" he asked. I nodded. I took one step down.
"Damn!" he said, suddenly. I looked up at him. He grinned again. "Damn
it if I didn't leave all my money home. You ain't got a dollar on you, have
you? Just for a couple of days, is all."

All at once something inside gave and threatened to come pouring out
of me. I didn't hate him any more. I felt that in another moment I'd start
crying like a child.

"Sure," I said. "Don't sweat." I looked in my wallet and didn't have a dollar, I only had a five. "Here," I said. "That hold you?"

He didn't look at it—he didn't want to look at it. A terrible, closed look 45
came over his face, as though he were keeping the number on the bill a
secret from him and me. "Thanks," he said, and now he was dying to see
me go. "Don't worry about Sonny. Maybe I'll write him or something."

"Sure," I said. "You do that. So long."

"Be seeing you," he said. I went on down the steps.

And I didn't write Sonny or send him anything for a long time. When I
finally did, it was just after my little girl died, and he wrote me back a letter
which made me feel like a bastard.

Here's what he said:

Dear brother, 50
   You don't know how much I needed to hear from you. I wanted to
write you many a time but I dug how much I must have hurt you and so

I didn't write. But now I feel like a man who's been trying to climb up out of some deep, real deep and funky hole and just saw the sun up there, outside. I got to get outside.

I can't tell you much about how I got here. I mean I don't know how to tell you. I guess I was afraid of something or I was trying to escape from something and you know I have never been very strong in the head (smile). I'm glad Mama and Daddy are dead and can't see what's happened to their son and I swear if I'd known what I was doing I would never have hurt you so, you and a lot of other fine people who were nice to me and who believed in me.

I don't want you to think it had anything to do with me being a musician. It's more than that. Or maybe less than that. I can't get anything straight in my head down here and I try not to think about what's going to happen to me when I get outside again. Sometime I think I'm going to flip and *never* get outside and sometime I think I'll come straight back. I tell you one thing, though, I'd rather blow my brains out than go through this again. But that's what they all say, so they tell me. If I tell you when I'm coming to New York and if you could meet me, I sure would appreciate it. Give my love to Isabel and the kids and I was sure sorry to hear about little Gracie. I wish I could be like Mama and say the Lord's will be done, but I don't know it seems to me that trouble is the one thing that never does get stopped and I don't know what good it does to blame it on the Lord. But maybe it does some good if you believe it.

Your brother,
Sonny

Then I kept in constant touch with him and I sent him whatever I could and I went to meet him when he came back to New York. When I saw him many things I thought I had forgotten came flooding back to me. This was because I had begun, finally, to wonder about Sonny, about the life that Sonny lived inside. This life, whatever it was, had made him older and thinner and it had deepened the distant stillness in which he had always moved. He looked very unlike my baby brother. Yet, when he smiled, when we shook hands, the baby brother I'd never known looked out from the depths of his private life, like an animal waiting to be coaxed into the light.

"How you been keeping?" he asked me.

55　"All right. And you?"

"Just fine." He was smiling all over his face. "It's good to see you again."

"It's good to see you."

The seven years' difference in our ages lay between us like a chasm: I wondered if these years would ever operate between us as a bridge. I was remembering, and it made it hard to catch my breath, that I had been there when he was born; and I had heard the first words he had ever spoken. When he started to walk, he walked from our mother straight to me. I caught him just before he fell when he took the first steps he ever took in this world.

"How's Isabel?"

"Just fine. She's dying to see you." 60

"And the boys?"

"They're fine, too. They're anxious to see their uncle."

"Oh, come on. You know they don't remember me."

"Are you kidding? Of course they remember you."

He grinned again. We got into a taxi. We had a lot to say to each other, 65 far too much to know how to begin.

As the taxi began to move, I asked, "You still want to go to India?"

He laughed. "You still remember that. Hell, no. This place is Indian enough for me."

"It used to belong to them," I said.

And he laughed again. "They damn sure knew what they were doing when they got rid of it."

Years ago, when he was around fourteen, he'd been all hipped on the 70 idea of going to India. He read books about people sitting on rocks, naked, in all kinds of weather, but mostly bad, naturally, and walking barefoot through hot coals and arriving at wisdom. I used to say that it sounded to me as though they were getting away from wisdom as fast as they could. I think he sort of looked down on me for that.

"Do you mind," he asked, "if we have the driver drive alongside the park? On the west side—I haven't seen the city in so long."

"Of course not," I said. I was afraid that I might sound as though I were humoring him, but I hoped he wouldn't take it that way.

So we drove along, between the green of the park and the stony, lifeless elegance of hotels and apartment buildings, toward the vivid, killing streets of our childhood. These streets hadn't changed, though housing projects jutted up out of them now like rocks in the middle of a boiling sea. Most of the houses in which we had grown up had vanished, as had the stores from which we had stolen, the basements in which we had first tried sex, the rooftops from which we had hurled tin cans and bricks. But houses exactly like the houses of our past yet dominated the landscape, boys exactly like the boys we once had been found themselves smothering in these houses, came down into the streets for light and air and found themselves encircled by disaster. Some escaped the trap, most didn't. Those who got out always left something of themselves behind, as some animals amputate a leg and leave it in the trap. It might be said, perhaps, that I had escaped, after all, I was a school teacher; or that Sonny had, he hadn't lived in Harlem for years. Yet, as the cab moved uptown through streets which seemed, with a rush, to darken with dark people, and as I covertly studied Sonny's face, it came to me that what we both were seeking through our separate cab windows was that part of ourselves which had been left behind. It's always at the hour of trouble and confrontation that the missing member aches.

We hit 110th Street and started rolling up Lenox Avenue. And I'd known this avenue all my life, but it seemed to me again, as it had seemed on the day I'd first heard about Sonny's trouble, filled with a hidden menace which was its very breath of life.

75   "We almost there," said Sonny.

"Almost." We were both too nervous to say anything more.

We live in a housing project. It hasn't been up long. A few days after it was up it seemed uninhabitably new, now, of course, it's already rundown. It looks like a parody of the good, clean, faceless life—God knows the people who live in it do their best to make it a parody. The beat-looking grass lying around isn't enough to make their lives green, the hedges will never hold out the streets, and they know it. The big windows fool no one, they aren't big enough to make space out of no space. They don't bother with the windows, they watch the TV screen instead. The playground is most popular with the children who don't play at jacks, or skip rope, or roller skate, or swing, and they can be found in it after dark. We moved in partly because it's not too far from where I teach, and partly for the kids; but it's really just like the houses in which Sonny and I grew up. The same things happen, they'll have the same things to remember. The moment Sonny and I started into the house I had the feeling that I was simply bringing him back into the danger he had almost died trying to escape.

Sonny has never been talkative. So I don't know why I was sure he'd be dying to talk to me when supper was over the first night. Everything went fine, the oldest boy remembered him, and the youngest boy liked him, and Sonny had remembered to bring something for each of them; and Isabel, who is really much nicer than I am, more open and giving, had gone to a lot of trouble about dinner and was genuinely glad to see him. And she's always been able to tease Sonny in a way that I haven't. It was nice to see her face so vivid again and to hear her laugh and watch her make Sonny laugh. She wasn't, or, anyway, she didn't seem to be, at all uneasy or embarrassed. She chatted as though there were no subject which had to be avoided and she got Sonny past his first, faint stiffness. And thank God she was there, for I was filled with that icy dread again. Everything I did seemed awkward to me, and everything I said sounded freighted with hidden meaning. I was trying to remember everything I'd heard about dope addiction and I couldn't help watching Sonny for signs. I wasn't doing it out of malice. I was trying to find out something about my brother. I was dying to hear him tell me he was safe.

"Safe!" my father grunted, whenever Mama suggested trying to move to a neighborhood which might be safer for children. "Safe, hell! Ain't no place safe for kids, nor nobody."

He always went on like this, but he wasn't, ever, really as bad as he 80
sounded, not even on weekends, when he got drunk. As a matter of fact, he
was always on the lookout for "something a little better," but he died
before he found it. He died suddenly, during a drunken weekend in the
middle of the war, when Sonny was fifteen. He and Sonny hadn't ever got
on too well. And this was partly because Sonny was the apple of his father's
eye. It was because he loved Sonny so much and was frightened for him,
that he was always fighting with him. It doesn't do any good to fight with
Sonny. Sonny just moves back, inside himself, where he can't be reached.
But the principal reason that they never hit it off is that they were so much
alike. Daddy was big and rough and loud-talking, just the opposite of
Sonny, but they both had—that same privacy.

Mama tried to tell me something about this, just after Daddy died. I
was home on leave from the army.

This was the last time I ever saw my mother alive. Just the same, this
picture gets all mixed up in my mind with pictures I had of her when she
was younger. The way I always see her is the way she used to be on a Sunday
afternoon, say, when the old folks were talking after the big Sunday dinner. I always see her wearing pale blue. She'd be sitting on the sofa. And my
father would be sitting in the easy chair, not far from her. And the living
room would be full of church folks and relatives. There they sit, in chairs
all around the living room, and the night is creeping up outside, but
nobody knows it yet. You can see the darkness growing against the win-
dowpanes and you hear the street noises every now and again, or maybe
the jangling beat of a tambourine from one of the churches close by, but
it's real quiet in the room. For a moment nobody's talking, but every face
looks darkening, like the sky outside. And my mother rocks a little from the
waist, and my father's eyes are closed. Everyone is looking at something a
child can't see. For a minute they've forgotten the children. Maybe a kid is
lying on the rug, half asleep. Maybe somebody's got a kid in his lap and is
absent-mindedly stroking the kid's head. Maybe there's a kid, quiet and
big-eyed, curled up in a big chair in the corner. The silence, the darkness
coming, and the darkness in the faces frighten the child obscurely. He
hopes that the hand which strokes his forehead will never stop—will never
die. He hopes that there will never come a time when the old folks won't be
sitting around the living room, talking about where they've come from,
and what they've seen, and what's happened to them and their kinfolk.

But something deep and watchful in the child knows that this is bound
to end, is already ending. In a moment someone will get up and turn on
the light. Then the old folks will remember the children and they won't
talk any more that day. And when light fills the room, the child is filled
with darkness. He knows that every time this happens he's moved just a
little closer to that darkness outside. The darkness outside is what the old
folks have been talking about. It's what they've come from. It's what they

endure. The child knows that they won't talk any more because if he knows too much about what's happened to *them,* he'll know too much too soon, about what's going to happen to *him.*

The last time I talked to my mother, I remember I was restless. I wanted to get out and see Isabel. We weren't married then and we had a lot to straighten out between us.

85   There Mama sat, in black, by the window. She was humming an old church song, *Lord, you brought me from a long ways off.* Sonny was out somewhere. Mama kept watching the streets.

"I don't know," she said, "if I'll ever see you again, after you go off from here. But I hope you'll remember the things I tried to teach you."

"Don't talk like that," I said, and smiled. "You'll be here a long time yet."

She smiled, too, but she said nothing. She was quiet for a long time. And I said, "Mama, don't you worry about nothing. I'll be writing all the time, and you be getting the checks. . . ."

"I want to talk to you about your brother," she said, suddenly. "If anything happens to me he ain't going to have nobody to look out for him."

90   "Mama," I said, "ain't nothing going to happen to you *or* Sonny. Sonny's all right. He's a good boy and he's got good sense."

"It ain't a question of his being a good boy," Mama said, "nor of his having good sense. It ain't only the bad ones, nor yet the dumb ones that gets sucked under." She stopped, looking at me. "Your Daddy once had a brother," she said, and she smiled in a way that made me feel she was in pain. "You didn't never know that, did you?"

"No," I said, "I never knew that," and I watched her face.

"Oh, yes," she said, "your Daddy had a brother." She looked out of the window again. "I know you never saw your Daddy cry. But *I* did—many a time, through all these years."

I asked her, "What happened to his brother? How come nobody's ever talked about him?"

95   This was the first time I ever saw my mother look old.

"His brother got killed," she said, "when he was just a little younger than you are now. I knew him. He was a fine boy. He was maybe a little full of the devil, but he didn't mean nobody no harm."

Then she stopped and the room was silent, exactly as it had sometimes been on those Sunday afternoons. Mama kept looking out into the streets.

"He used to have a job in the mill," she said, "and, like all young folks, he just liked to perform on Saturday nights. Saturday nights, him and your father would drift around to different places, go to dances and things like that, or just sit around with people they knew, and your father's brother would sing, he had a fine voice, and play along with himself on his guitar. Well, this particular Saturday night, him and your father was coming home from some place, and they were both a little drunk and there was a moon that night, it was bright like day. Your father's brother was feeling kind of good, and he was whistling to himself, and he had his guitar slung over his shoulder. They was coming down a hill and beneath them was a road that turned off from the highway. Well, your father's brother, being always kind of frisky, decided to run down this hill, and he did, with that guitar banging and clanging behind him, and he ran across the road, and he was making water behind a tree. And your father was sort of amused at him and he was still coming down the hill, kind of slow. Then he heard a car motor and that same minute his brother stepped from behind the tree, into the road, in the moonlight. And he started to cross the road. And your father started to run down the hill, he says he don't know why. This car was full of white men. They was all drunk, and when they seen your father's brother they let out a great whoop and holler and they aimed the car straight at him. They was having fun, they just wanted to scare him, the way they do sometimes, you know. But they was drunk. And I guess the boy, being drunk, too, and scared, kind of lost his head. By the time he jumped it was too late. Your father says he heard his brother scream when the car rolled over him, and he heard the wood of that guitar when it give, and he heard them strings go flying, and he heard them white men shouting, and the car kept on a-going and it ain't stopped till this day. And, time your father got down the hill, his brother weren't nothing but blood and pulp."

Tears were gleaming on my mother's face. There wasn't anything I could say.

"He never mentioned it," she said, "because I never let him mention it 100 before you children. Your Daddy was like a crazy man that night and for many a night thereafter. He says he never in his life seen anything as dark as that road after the lights of that car had gone away. Weren't nothing, weren't nobody on that road, just your Daddy and his brother and that busted guitar. Oh, yes. Your Daddy never did really get right again. Till the day he died he weren't sure but that every white man he saw was the man that killed his brother."

She stopped and took out her handkerchief and dried her eyes and looked at me.

"I ain't telling you all this," she said, "to make you scared or bitter or to make you hate nobody. I'm telling you this because you got a brother. And the world ain't changed."

I guess I didn't want to believe this. I guess she saw this in my face. She turned away from me, toward the window again, searching those streets.

"But I praise my Redeemer," she said at last, "that He called your Daddy home before me. I ain't saying it to throw no flowers at myself, but, I declare, it keeps me from feeling too cast down to know I helped your father get safely through this world. Your father always acted like he was

the roughest, strongest man on earth. And everybody took him to be like
that. But if he hadn't had me there—to see his tears!"

105   She was crying again. Still, I couldn't move. I said, "Lord, Lord, Mama,
I didn't know it was like that."

"Oh, honey," she said, "there's a lot that you don't know. But you are
going to find out." She stood up from the window and came over to me.
"You got to hold on to your brother," she said, "and don't let him fall, no
matter what it looks like is happening to him and no matter how evil you
gets with him. You going to be evil with him many a time. But don't you
forget what I told you, you hear?"

"I won't forget," I said. "Don't you worry, I won't forget. I won't let nothing happen to Sonny."

My mother smiled as though she was amused at something she saw in
my face. Then, "You may not be able to stop nothing from happening. But
you got to let him know you's *there*."

Two days later I was married, and then I was gone. And I had a lot of
things on my mind and I pretty well forgot my promise to Mama until I
got shipped home on a special furlough for her funeral.

110   And, after the funeral, with just Sonny and me alone in the empty
kitchen, I tried to find out something about him.

"What do you want to do?" I asked him.

"I'm going to be a musician," he said.

For he had graduated, in the time I had been away, from dancing to the
juke box to finding out who was playing what, and what they were doing
with it, and he had bought himself a set of drums.

"You mean, you want to be a drummer?" I somehow had the feeling
that being a drummer might be all right for other people but not for my
brother Sonny.

115   "I don't think," he said, looking at me very gravely, "that I'll ever be a
good drummer. But I think I can play a piano."

I frowned. I'd never played the role of the oldest brother quite so seriously before, had scarcely ever, in fact, *asked* Sonny a damn thing. I sensed
myself in the presence of something I didn't really know how to handle,
didn't understand. So I made my frown a little deeper as I asked: "What
kind of musician do you want to be?"

He grinned. "How many kinds do you think there are?"

"Be *serious*," I said.

He laughed, throwing his head back, and then looked at me. "I *am*
serious."

120   "Well, then, for Christ's sake, stop kidding around and answer a serious
question. I mean, do you want to be a concert pianist, you want to play
classical music and all that, or—or what?" Long before I finished he was
laughing again. "For Christ's *sake*, Sonny!"

He sobered, but with difficulty. "I'm sorry. But you sound so—*scared!*"
and he was off again.

"Well, you may think it's funny now, baby, but it's not going to be so funny when you have to make your living at it, let me tell you *that.*" I was furious because I knew he was laughing at me and I didn't know why.

"No," he said, very sober now, and afraid, perhaps, that he'd hurt me, "I don't want to be a classical pianist. That isn't what interests me. I mean"— he paused, looking hard at me, as though his eyes would help me to understand, and then gestured helplessly, as though perhaps his hand would help—"I mean, I'll have a lot of studying to do, and I'll have to study *everything,* but, I mean, I want to play *with*—jazz musicians." He stopped. "I want to play jazz," he said.

Well, the word had never before sounded as heavy, as real, as it sounded that afternoon in Sonny's mouth. I just looked at him and I was probably frowning a real frown by this time. I simply couldn't see why on earth he'd want to spend his time hanging around nightclubs, clowning around on bandstands, while people pushed each other around a dance floor. It seemed—beneath him, somehow. I had never thought about it before, had never been forced to, but I suppose I had always put jazz musicians in a class with what Daddy called "good-time people."

"Are you *serious?*" 125

"Hell, *yes,* I'm serious."

He looked more helpless than ever, and annoyed, and deeply hurt.

I suggested, helpfully: "You mean—like Louis Armstrong?"[3]

His face closed as though I'd struck him. "No. I'm not talking about none of that old-time, down-home crap."

"Well, look, Sonny, I'm sorry, don't get mad. I just don't altogether get it, 130 that's all. Name somebody—you know, a jazz musician you admire."

"Bird."

"Who?"

"Bird! Charlie Parker![4] Don't they teach you nothing in the goddamn army?"

I lit a cigarette. I was surprised and then a little amused to discover that I was trembling. "I've been out of touch," I said. "You'll have to be patient with me. Now. Who's this Parker character?"

"He's just one of the greatest jazz musicians alive," said Sonny, sullenly, 135 his hands in his pockets, his back to me. "Maybe *the* greatest," he added, bitterly, "that's probably why *you* never heard of him."

"All right," I said, "I'm ignorant. I'm sorry. I'll go out and buy all the cat's records right away, all right?"

---

3. New Orleans-born trumpeter and singer (1901–71); by the 1950s, his music would have seemed old-fashioned to a jazz afficionado.

4. Charlie ("Bird") Parker (1920–55), brilliant saxophonist and jazz innovator; working in New York in the mid-1940s, he developed, with Dizzy Gillespie and others, the style of jazz called "bebop." He was a narcotics addict.

"It don't," said Sonny, with dignity, "make any difference to me. I don't care what you listen to. Don't do me no favors."

I was beginning to realize that I'd never seen him so upset before. With another part of my mind I was thinking that this would probably turn out to be one of those things kids go through and that I shouldn't make it seem important by pushing it too hard. Still, I didn't think it would do any harm to ask: "Doesn't all this take a lot of time? Can you make a living at it?"

He turned back to me and half leaned, half sat, on the kitchen table. "Everything takes time," he said, "and—well, yes, sure, I can make a living at it. But what I don't seem to be able to make you understand is that it's the only thing I want to do."

140 "Well, Sonny," I said gently, "you know people can't always do exactly what they *want* to do—"

"*No,* I don't know that," said Sonny, surprising me. "I think people *ought* to do what they want to do, what else are they alive for?"

"You getting to be a big boy," I said desperately, "it's time you started thinking about your future."

"I'm thinking about my future," said Sonny, grimly. "I think about it all the time."

I gave up. I decided, if he didn't change his mind, that we could always talk about it later. "In the meantime," I said, "you got to finish school." We had already decided that he'd have to move in with Isabel and her folks. I knew this wasn't the ideal arrangement because Isabel's folks are inclined to be dicty[5] and they hadn't especially wanted Isabel to marry me. But I didn't know what else to do. "And we have to get you fixed up at Isabel's."

145 There was a long silence. He moved from the kitchen table to the window. "That's a terrible idea. You know it yourself."

"Do you have a *better* idea?"

He just walked up and down the kitchen for a minute. He was as tall as I was. He had started to shave. I suddenly had the feeling that I didn't know him at all.

He stopped at the kitchen table and picked up my cigarettes. Looking at me with a kind of mocking, amused defiance, he put one between his lips. "You mind?"

"You smoking already?"

150 He lit the cigarette and nodded, watching me through the smoke. "I just wanted to see if I'd have the courage to smoke in front of you." He grinned and blew a great cloud of smoke to the ceiling. "It was easy." He looked at my face. "Come on, now. I bet you was smoking at my age, tell the truth."

5. Snobbish, bossy.

I didn't say anything but the truth was on my face, and he laughed. But now there was something very strained in his laugh. "Sure. And I bet that ain't all you was doing."

He was frightening me a little. "Cut the crap," I said. "We already decided that you was going to go and live at Isabel's. Now what's got into you all of a sudden?"

"*You* decided it," he pointed out. "*I* didn't decide nothing." He stopped in front of me, leaning against the stove, arms loosely folded. "Look, brother. I don't want to stay in Harlem no more, I really don't." He was very earnest. He looked at me, then over toward the kitchen window. There was something in his eyes I'd never seen before, some thoughtfulness, some worry all his own. He rubbed the muscle of one arm. "It's time I was getting out of here."

"Where do you want to *go*, Sonny?"

"I want to join the army. Or the navy, I don't care. If I say I'm old enough,   155 they'll believe me."

Then I got mad. It was because I was so scared. "You must be crazy. You goddamn fool, what the hell do you want to go and join the *army* for?"

"I just told you. To get out of Harlem."

"Sonny, you haven't even finished *school*. And if you really want to be a musician, how do you expect to study if you're in the *army?*"

He looked at me, trapped, and in anguish. "There's ways. I might be able to work out some kind of deal. Anyway, I'll have the G.I. Bill when I come out."

"*If* you come out." We stared at each other. "Sonny, please. Be reasonable.   160 I know the setup is far from perfect. But we got to do the best we can."

"I ain't learning nothing in school," he said. "Even when I go." He turned away from me and opened the window and threw his cigarette out into the narrow alley. I watched his back. "At least, I ain't learning nothing you'd want me to learn." He slammed the window so hard I thought the glass would fly out, and turned back to me. "And I'm sick of the stink of these garbage cans!"

"Sonny," I said, "I know how you feel. But if you don't finish school now, you're going to be sorry later that you didn't." I grabbed him by the shoulders. "And you only got another year. It ain't so bad. And I'll come back and I swear I'll help you do *whatever* you want to do. Just try to put up with it till I come back. Will you please do that? For me?"

He didn't answer and he wouldn't look at me.

"Sonny. You hear me?"

He pulled away. "I hear you. But you never hear anything *I* say."   165

I didn't know what to say to that. He looked out of the window and then back at me. "OK," he said, and sighed. "I'll try."

Then I said, trying to cheer him up a little, "They got a piano at Isabel's. You can practice on it."

And as a matter of fact, it did cheer him up for a minute. "That's right," he said to himself. "I forgot that." His face relaxed a little. But the worry, the thoughtfulness, played on it still, the way shadows play on a face which is staring into the fire.

But I thought I'd never hear the end of that piano. At first, Isabel would write me, saying how nice it was that Sonny was so serious about his music and how, as soon as he came in from school, or wherever he had been when he was supposed to be at school, he went straight to that piano and stayed there until suppertime. And, after supper, he went back to that piano and stayed there until everybody went to bed. He was at the piano all day Saturday and all day Sunday. Then he bought a record player and started playing records. He'd play one record over and over again, all day long sometimes, and he'd improvise along with it on the piano. Or he'd play one section of the record, one chord, one change, one progression, then he'd do it on the piano. Then back to the record. Then back to the piano.

170   Well, I really don't know how they stood it. Isabel finally confessed that it wasn't like living with a person at all, it was like living with sound. And the sound didn't make any sense to her, didn't make any sense to any of them—naturally. They began, in a way, to be afflicted by this presence that was living in their home. It was as though Sonny were some sort of god, or monster. He moved in an atmosphere which wasn't like theirs at all. They fed him and he ate, he washed himself, he walked in and out of their door; he certainly wasn't nasty or unpleasant or rude, Sonny isn't any of those things; but it was as though he were all wrapped up in some cloud, some fire, some vision all his own; and there wasn't any way to reach him.

At the same time, he wasn't really a man yet, he was still a child, and they had to watch out for him in all kinds of ways. They certainly couldn't throw him out. Neither did they dare to make a great scene about that piano because even they dimly sensed, as I sensed, from so many thousands of miles away, that Sonny was at that piano playing for his life.

But he hadn't been going to school. One day a letter came from the school board and Isabel's mother got it—there had, apparently, been other letters but Sonny had torn them up. This day, when Sonny came in, Isabel's mother showed him the letter and asked where he'd been spending his time. And she finally got it out of him that he'd been down in Greenwich Village, with musicians and other characters, in a white girl's apartment. And this scared her and she started to scream at him and what came up, once she began—though she denies it to this day—was what sacrifices they were making to give Sonny a decent home and how little he appreciated it.

Sonny didn't play the piano that day. By evening, Isabel's mother had calmed down but then there was the old man to deal with, and Isabel herself. Isabel says she did her best to be calm but she broke down and started crying. She says she just watched Sonny's face. She could tell, by watching him, what was happening with him. And what was happening was that they penetrated his cloud, they had reached him. Even if their fingers had been a thousand times more gentle than human fingers ever are, he could hardly help feeling that they had stripped him naked and were spitting on that nakedness. For he also had to see that his presence, that music, which was life or death to him, had been torture for them and that they had endured it, not at all for his sake, but only for mine. And Sonny couldn't take that. He can take it a little better today than he could then but he's still not very good at it and, frankly, I don't know anybody who is.

The silence of the next few days must have been louder than the sound of all the music ever played since time began. One morning, before she went to work, Isabel was in his room for something and she suddenly realized that all of his records were gone. And she knew for certain that he was gone. And he was. He went as far as the navy would carry him. He finally sent me a postcard from some place in Greece and that was the first I knew that Sonny was still alive. I didn't see him any more until we were both back in New York and the war had long been over.

He was a man by then, of course, but I wasn't willing to see it. He came 175 by the house from time to time, but we fought almost every time we met. I didn't like the way he carried himself, loose and dreamlike all the time, and I didn't like his friends, and his music seemed to be merely an excuse for the life he led. It sounded just that weird and disordered.

Then we had a fight, a pretty awful fight, and I didn't see him for months. By and by I looked him up, where he was living, in a furnished room in the Village, and I tried to make it up. But there were lots of other people in the room and Sonny just lay on his bed, and he wouldn't come downstairs with me, and he treated these other people as though they were his family and I weren't. So I got mad and then he got mad, and then I told him that he might just as well be dead as live the way he was living. Then he stood up and he told me not to worry about him any more in life, that he *was* dead as far as I was concerned. Then he pushed me to the door and the other people looked on as though nothing were happening, and he slammed the door behind me. I stood in the hallway, staring at the door. I heard somebody laugh in the room and then the tears came to my eyes. I started down the steps, whistling to keep from crying, I kept whistling to myself, *You going to need me, baby, one of these cold, rainy days.*

I read about Sonny's trouble in the spring. Little Grace died in the fall. She was a beautiful little girl. But she only lived a little over two years. She died of polio and she suffered. She had a slight fever for a couple of days, but it didn't seem like anything and we just kept her in bed. And we would certainly have called the doctor, but the fever dropped, she seemed to be all right. So we thought it had just been a cold. Then, one day, she was up, playing, Isabel was in the kitchen fixing lunch for the two boys when they'd come in from school, and she heard Grace fall down in the living room. When you have a lot of children you don't always start running when one of them falls, unless they start screaming or something. And, this time, Gracie was quiet. Yet, Isabel says that when she heard that *thump* and then that silence, something happened to her to make her afraid. And she ran to the living room and there was little Grace on the floor, all twisted up, and the reason she hadn't screamed was that she couldn't get her breath. And when she did scream, it was the worst sound, Isabel says, that she'd ever heard in all her life, and she still hears it sometimes in her dreams. Isabel will sometimes wake me up with a low, moaning, strangling sound and I have to be quick to awaken her and hold her to me and where Isabel is weeping against me seems a mortal wound.

I think I may have written Sonny the very day that little Grace was buried. I was sitting in the living room in the dark, by myself, and I suddenly thought of Sonny. My trouble made his real.

One Saturday afternoon, when Sonny had been living with us, or anyway, been in our house, for nearly two weeks, I found myself wandering aimlessly about the living room, drinking from a can of beer, and trying to work up courage to search Sonny's room. He was out, he was usually out whenever I was home, and Isabel had taken the children to see their grandparents. Suddenly I was standing still in front of the living room window, watching Seventh Avenue. The idea of searching Sonny's room made me still. I scarcely dared to admit to myself what I'd be searching for. I didn't know what I'd do if I found it. Or if I didn't.

180   On the sidewalk across from me, near the entrance to a barbecue joint, some people were holding an old-fashioned revival meeting. The barbecue cook, wearing a dirty white apron, his conked[6] hair reddish and metallic in the pale sun, and a cigarette between his lips, stood in the doorway, watching them. Kids and older people paused in their errands and stood there, along with some older men and a couple of very tough-looking women who watched everything that happened on the avenue, as though they owned it, or were maybe owned by it. Well, they were watching this, too. The revival was being carried on by three sisters in black, and a brother. All they had were their voices and their Bibles and a tambourine. The brother was testifying[7] and while he testified two of the sisters stood together, seeming to say, amen, and the third sister walked around with the tambourine outstretched and a couple of people dropped coins into it. Then the brother's testimony ended and the sister who had been taking up the collection dumped the coins into her palm and transferred them to the pocket of her long black robe. Then she raised both hands, striking the tambourine against the air, and then against one hand, and she started to sing. And the two other sisters and the brother joined in.

---

6. Processed: straightened and greased.   7. Publicly professing belief.

JAMES BALDWIN *Sonny's Blues* **93**

It was strange, suddenly, to watch, though I had been seeing these meetings all my life. So, of course, had everybody else down there. Yet, they paused and watched and listened and I stood still at the window. " *'Tis the old ship of Zion,*" they sang, and the sister with the tambourine kept a steady, jangling beat, *"it has rescued many a thousand!"* Not a soul under the sound of their voices was hearing this song for the first time, not one of them had been rescued. Nor had they seen much in the way of rescue work being done around them. Neither did they especially believe in the holiness of the three sisters and the brother, they knew too much about them, knew where they lived, and how. The woman with the tambourine, whose voice dominated the air, whose face was bright with joy, was divided by very little from the woman who stood watching her, a cigarette between her heavy, chapped lips, her hair a cuckoo's nest, her face scarred and swollen from many beatings, and her black eyes glittering like coal. Perhaps they both knew this, which was why, when, as rarely, they addressed each other, they addressed each other as Sister. As the singing filled the air the watching, listening faces underwent a change, the eyes focusing on something within; the music seemed to soothe a poison out of them; and time seemed, nearly, to fall away from the sullen, belligerent, battered faces, as though they were fleeing back to their first condition, while dreaming of their last. The barbecue cook half shook his head and smiled, and dropped his cigarette and disappeared into his joint. A man fumbled in his pockets for change and stood holding it in his hand impatiently, as though he had just remembered a pressing appointment further up the avenue. He looked furious. Then I saw Sonny, standing on the edge of the crowd. He was carrying a wide, flat notebook with a green cover, and it made him look, from where I was standing, almost like a schoolboy. The coppery sun brought out the copper in his skin, he was very faintly smiling, standing very still. Then the singing stopped, the tambourine turned into a collection plate again. The furious man dropped in his coins and vanished, so did a couple of the women, and Sonny dropped some change in the plate, looking directly at the woman with a little smile. He started across the avenue, toward the house. He has a slow, loping walk, something like the way Harlem hipsters walk, only he's imposed on this his own half-beat. I had never really noticed it before.

I stayed at the window, both relieved and apprehensive. As Sonny disappeared from my sight, they began singing again. And they were still singing when his key turned in the lock.

"Hey," he said.

"Hey, yourself. You want some beer?"

"No. Well, maybe." But he came up to the window and stood beside me, 185
looking out. "What a warm voice," he said.

They were singing *If I could only hear my mother pray again!*

"Yes," I said, "and she can sure beat that tambourine."

"But what a terrible song," he said, and laughed. He dropped his notebook on the sofa and disappeared into the kitchen. "Where's Isabel and the kids?"

"I think they went to see their grandparents. You hungry?"

190   "No." He came back into the living room with his can of beer. "You want to come some place with me tonight?"

I sensed, I don't know how, that I couldn't possibly say no. "Sure. Where?"

He sat down on the sofa and picked up his notebook and started leafing through it. "I'm going to sit in with some fellows in a joint in the Village."

"You mean, you're going to play, tonight?"

"That's right." He took a swallow of his beer and moved back to the window. He gave me a sidelong look. "If you can stand it."

195   "I'll try," I said.

He smiled to himself and we both watched as the meeting across the way broke up. The three sisters and the brother, heads bowed, were singing *God be with you till we meet again.* The faces around them were very quiet. Then the song ended. The small crowd dispersed. We watched the three women and the lone man walk slowly up the avenue.

"When she was singing before," said Sonny, abruptly, "her voice reminded me for a minute of what heroin feels like sometimes—when it's in your veins. It makes you feel sort of warm and cool at the same time. And distant. And—and sure." He sipped his beer, very deliberately not looking at me. I watched his face. "It makes you feel—in control. Sometimes you've got to have that feeling."

"Do you?" I sat down slowly in the easy chair.

"Sometimes." He went to the sofa and picked up his notebook again. "Some people do."

200   "In order," I asked, "to play?" And my voice was very ugly, full of contempt and anger.

"Well"—he looked at me with great, troubled eyes, as though, in fact, he hoped his eyes would tell me things he could never otherwise say—"they *think* so. And *if* they think so—!"

"And what do *you* think?" I asked.

He sat on the sofa and put his can of beer on the floor. "I don't know," he said, and I couldn't be sure if he were answering my question or pursuing his thoughts. His face didn't tell me. "It's not so much to *play.* It's to *stand* it, to be able to make it at all. On any level." He frowned and smiled: "In order to keep from shaking to pieces."

"But these friends of yours," I said, "they seem to shake themselves to pieces pretty goddamn fast."

205   "Maybe." He played with the notebook. And something told me that I should curb my tongue, that Sonny was doing his best to talk, that I should listen. "But of course you only know the ones that've gone to pieces.

Some don't—or at least they haven't *yet* and that's just about all *any* of us can say." He paused. "And then there are some who just live, really, in hell, and they know it and they see what's happening and they go right on. I don't know." He sighed, dropped the notebook, folded his arms. "Some guys, you can tell from the way they play, they on something *all* the time. And you can see that, well, it makes something real for them. But of course," he picked up his beer from the floor and sipped it and put the can down again, "they *want* to, too, you've got to see that. Even some of them that say they don't—*some,* not all."

"And what about you?" I asked—I couldn't help it. "What about you? Do *you* want to?"

He stood up and walked to the window and I remained silent for a long time. Then he sighed. "Me," he said. Then: "While I was downstairs before, on my way here, listening to that woman sing, it struck me all of a sudden how much suffering she must have had to go through—to sing like that. It's *repulsive* to think you have to suffer that much."

I said: "But there's no way not to suffer—is there, Sonny?"

"I believe not," he said and smiled, "but that's never stopped anyone from trying." He looked at me. "Has it?" I realized, with this mocking look, that there stood between us, forever, beyond the power of time or forgiveness, the fact that I had held silence—so long!—when he had needed human speech to help him. He turned back to the window. "No, there's no way not to suffer. But you try all kinds of ways to keep from drowning in it, to keep on top of it, and to make it seem—well, like *you.* Like you did something, all right, and now you're suffering for it. You know?" I said nothing. "Well you know," he said, impatiently, "why *do* people suffer? Maybe it's better to do something to give it a reason, *any* reason."

"But we just agreed," I said, "that there's no way not to suffer. Isn't it   210
better, then, just to—take it?"

"But nobody just takes it," Sonny cried, "that's what I'm telling you! *Everybody* tries not to. You're just hung up on the *way* some people try—it's not *your* way!"

The hair on my face began to itch, my face felt wet. "That's not true," I said, "that's not true. I don't give a damn what other people do, I don't even care how they suffer. I just care how *you* suffer." And he looked at me. "Please believe me," I said, "I don't want to see you—die—trying not to suffer."

"I won't," he said flatly, "die trying not to suffer. At least, not any faster than anybody else."

"But there's no need," I said, trying to laugh, "is there? in killing yourself."

I wanted to say more, but I couldn't. I wanted to talk about will power   215
and how life could be—well, beautiful. I wanted to say that it was all within; but was it? or, rather, wasn't that exactly the trouble? And I wanted

to promise that I would never fail him again. But it would all have sounded—empty words and lies.

So I made the promise to myself and prayed that I would keep it.

"It's terrible sometimes, inside," he said, "that's what's the trouble. You walk these streets, black and funky and cold, and there's not really a living ass to talk to, and there's nothing shaking, and there's no way of getting it out—that storm inside. You can't talk it and you can't make love with it, and when you finally try to get with it and play it, you realize *nobody's* listening. So *you've* got to listen. You got to find a way to listen."

And then he walked away from the window and sat on the sofa again, as though all the wind had suddenly been knocked out of him. "Sometimes you'll do *anything* to play, even cut your mother's throat." He laughed and looked at me. "Or your brother's." Then he sobered. "Or your own." Then: "Don't worry. I'm all right now and I think I'll *be* all right. But I can't forget—where I've been. I don't mean just the physical place I've been, I mean where I've *been*. And *what* I've been."

"What have you been, Sonny?" I asked.

220   He smiled—but sat sideways on the sofa, his elbow resting on the back, his fingers playing with his mouth and chin, not looking at me. "I've been something I didn't recognize, didn't know I could be. Didn't know anybody could be." He stopped, looking inward, looking helplessly young, looking old. "I'm not talking about it now because I feel *guilty* or anything like that—maybe it would be better if I did, I don't know. Anyway, I can't really talk about it. Not to you, not to anybody," and now he turned and faced me. "Sometimes, you know, and it was actually when I was most *out* of the world, I felt that I was in it, that I was *with* it, really, and I could play or I didn't really have to *play*, it just came out of me, it was there. And I don't know how I played, thinking about it now, but I know I did awful things, those times, sometimes, to people. Or it wasn't that I *did* anything to them—it was that they weren't real." He picked up the beer can; it was empty; he rolled it between his palms: "And other times—well, I needed a fix, I needed to find a place to lean, I needed to clear a space to *listen*—and I couldn't find it, and I—went crazy, I did terrible things to *me*, I was terrible *for* me." He began pressing the beer can between his hands, I watched the metal begin to give. It glittered, as he played with it like a knife, and I was afraid he would cut himself, but I said nothing. "Oh well. I can never tell you. I was all by myself at the bottom of something, stinking and sweating and crying and shaking, and I smelled it, you know? *my* stink, and I thought I'd die if I couldn't get away from it and yet, all the same, I knew that everything I was doing was just locking me in with it. And I didn't know," he paused, still flattening the beer can, "I didn't know, I still *don't* know, something kept telling me that maybe it was good to smell your own stink, but I didn't think that *that* was what I'd been trying to do— and—who can stand it?" and he abruptly dropped the ruined beer can,

looking at me with a small, still smile, and then rose, walking to the window as though it were the lodestone rock. I watched his face, he watched the avenue. "I couldn't tell you when Mama died—but the reason I wanted to leave Harlem so bad was to get away from drugs. And then, when I ran away, that's what I was running from—really. When I came back, nothing had changed, *I* hadn't changed, I was just—older." And he stopped, drumming with his fingers on the windowpane. The sun had vanished, soon darkness would fall. I watched his face. "It can come again," he said, almost as though speaking to himself. Then he turned to me. "It can come again," he repeated. "I just want you to know that."

"All right," I said, at last. "So it can come again. All right."

He smiled, but the smile was sorrowful. "I had to try to tell you," he said.

"Yes," I said. "I understand that."

"You're my brother," he said, looking straight at me, and not smiling at all.

"Yes," I repeated, "yes. I understand that."   225

He turned back to the window, looking out. "All that hatred down there," he said, "all that hatred and misery and love. It's a wonder it doesn't blow the avenue apart."

We went to the only nightclub on a short, dark street, downtown. We squeezed through the narrow, chattering, jampacked bar to the entrance of the big room, where the bandstand was. And we stood there for a moment, for the lights were very dim in this room and we couldn't see. Then, "Hello, boy," said the voice and an enormous black man, much older than Sonny or myself, erupted out of all that atmospheric lighting and put an arm around Sonny's shoulder. "I been sitting right here," he said, "waiting for you."

He had a big voice, too, and heads in the darkness turned toward us.

Sonny grinned and pulled a little away, and said, "Creole, this is my brother. I told you about him."

Creole shook my hand. "I'm glad to meet you, son," he said, and it was   230
clear that he was glad to meet me *there*, for Sonny's sake. And he smiled, "You got a real musician in *your* family," and he took his arm from Sonny's shoulder and slapped him, lightly, affectionately, with the back of his hand.

"Well. Now I've heard it all," said a voice behind us. This was another musician, and a friend of Sonny's, a coal-black, cheerful-looking man, built close to the ground. He immediately began confiding to me, at the top of his lungs, the most terrible things about Sonny, his teeth gleaming like a lighthouse and his laugh coming up out of him like the beginning of an earthquake. And it turned out that everyone at the bar knew Sonny, or almost everyone; some were musicians, working there, or nearby, or not working, some were simply hangers-on, and some were there to hear Sonny play. I was introduced to all of them and they were all very polite to me. Yet, it was clear that, for them, I was only Sonny's brother. Here, I was in Sonny's world. Or, rather: his kingdom. Here, it was not even a question that his veins bore royal blood.

They were going to play soon and Creole installed me, by myself, at a table in a dark corner. Then I watched them, Creole, and the little black man, and Sonny, and the others, while they horsed around, standing just below the bandstand. The light from the bandstand spilled just a little short of them and, watching them laughing and gesturing and moving about, I had the feeling that they, nevertheless, were being most careful not to step into that circle of light too suddenly; that if they moved into the light too suddenly, without thinking, they would perish in flame. Then, while I watched, one of them, the small black man, moved into the light and crossed the bandstand and started fooling around with his drums. Then—being funny and being, also, extremely ceremonious—Creole took Sonny by the arm and led him to the piano. A woman's voice called Sonny's name and a few hands started clapping. And Sonny, also being funny and being ceremonious, and so touched, I think, that he could have cried, but neither hiding it nor showing it, riding it like a man, grinned, and put both hands to his heart and bowed from the waist.

Creole then went to the bass fiddle and a lean, very bright-skinned brown man jumped up on the bandstand and picked up his horn. So there they were, and the atmosphere on the bandstand and in the room began to change and tighten. Someone stepped up to the microphone and announced them. Then there were all kinds of murmurs. Some people at the bar shushed others. The waitress ran around, frantically getting in the last orders, guys and chicks got closer to each other, and the lights on the bandstand, on the quartet, turned to a kind of indigo. Then they all looked different there. Creole looked about him for the last time, as though he were making certain that all his chickens were in the coop, and then he—jumped and struck the fiddle. And there they were.

All I know about music is that not many people ever really hear it. And even then, on the rare occasions when something opens within, and the music enters, what we mainly hear, or hear corroborated, are personal, private, vanishing evocations. But the man who creates the music is hearing something else, is dealing with the roar rising from the void and imposing order on it as it hits the air. What is evoked in him, then, is of another order, more terrible because it has no words, and triumphant, too, for that same reason. And his triumph, when he triumphs, is ours. I just watched Sonny's face. His face was troubled, he was working hard, but he wasn't with it. And I had the feeling that, in a way, everyone on the bandstand was waiting for him, both waiting for him and pushing him along. But as I began to watch Creole, I realized that it was Creole who held them all back.

He had them on a short rein. Up there, keeping the beat with his whole body, wailing on the fiddle, with his eyes half closed, he was listening to everything, but he was listening to Sonny. He was having a dialogue with Sonny. He wanted Sonny to leave the shoreline and strike out for the deep water. He was Sonny's witness that deep water and drowning were not the same thing—he had been there, and he knew. And he wanted Sonny to know. He was waiting for Sonny to do the things on the keys which would let Creole know that Sonny was in the water.

And, while Creole listened, Sonny moved, deep within, exactly like   235
someone in torment. I had never before thought of how awful the relationship must be between the musician and his instrument. He has to fill it, this instrument, with the breath of life, his own. He has to make it do what he wants it to do. And a piano is just a piano. It's made out of so much wood and wires and little hammers and big ones, and ivory. While there's only so much you can do with it, the only way to find this out is to try; to try and make it do everything.

And Sonny hadn't been near a piano for over a year. And he wasn't on much better terms with his life, not the life that stretched before him now. He and the piano stammered, started one way, got scared, stopped; started another way, panicked, marked time, started again; then seemed to have found a direction, panicked again, got stuck. And the face I saw on Sonny I'd never seen before. Everything had been burned out of it, and, at the same time, things usually hidden were being burned in, by the fire and fury of the battle which was occurring in him up there.

Yet, watching Creole's face as they neared the end of the first set, I had the feeling that something had happened, something I hadn't heard. Then they finished, there was scattered applause, and then, without an instant's warning, Creole started into something else, it was almost sardonic, it was *Am I Blue*.[8] And, as though he commanded, Sonny began to play. Something began to happen. And Creole let out the reins. The dry, low, black man said something awful on the drums, Creole answered, and the drums talked back. Then the horn insisted, sweet and high, slightly detached perhaps, and Creole listened, commenting now and then, dry, and driving, beautiful and calm and old. Then they all came together again, and Sonny was part of the family again. I could tell this from his face. He seemed to have found, right there beneath his fingers, a damn brand-new piano. It seemed that he couldn't get over it. Then, for a while, just being happy with Sonny, they seemed to be agreeing with him that brand-new pianos certainly were a gas.

Then Creole stepped forward to remind them that what they were playing was the blues. He hit something in all of them, he hit something in me, myself, and the music tightened and deepened, apprehension began to

---

8. A favorite jazz standard, brilliantly recorded by Billie Holiday.

beat the air. Creole began to tell us what the blues were all about. They were not about anything very new. He and his boys up there were keeping it new, at the risk of ruin, destruction, madness, and death, in order to find new ways to make us listen. For, while the tale of how we suffer, and how we are delighted, and how we may triumph is never new, it always must be heard. There isn't any other tale to tell, it's the only light we've got in all this darkness.

And this tale, according to that face, that body, those strong hands on those strings, has another aspect in every country, and a new depth in every generation. Listen, Creole seemed to be saying, listen. Now these are Sonny's blues. He made the little black man on the drums know it, and the bright, brown man on the horn. Creole wasn't trying any longer to get Sonny in the water. He was wishing him Godspeed. Then he stepped back, very slowly, filling the air with the immense suggestion that Sonny speak for himself.

240   Then they all gathered around Sonny and Sonny played. Every now and again one of them seemed to say, amen. Sonny's fingers filled the air with life, his life. But that life contained so many others. And Sonny went all the way back, he really began with the spare, flat statement of the opening phrase of the song. Then he began to make it his. It was very beautiful because it wasn't hurried and it was no longer a lament. I seemed to hear with what burning he had made it his, and what burning we had yet to make it ours, how we could cease lamenting. Freedom lurked around us and I understood, at last, that he could help us to be free if we would listen, that he would never be free until we did. Yet, there was no battle in his face now, I heard what he had gone through, and would continue to go through until he came to rest in earth. He had made it his: that long line, of which we knew only Mama and Daddy. And he was giving it back, as everything must be given back, so that, passing through death, it can live forever. I saw my mother's face again, and felt, for the first time, how the stones of the road she had walked on must have bruised her feet. I saw the moonlit road where my father's brother died. And it brought something else back to me, and carried me past it, I saw my little girl again and felt Isabel's tears again, and I felt my own tears begin to rise. And I was yet aware that this was only a moment, that the world waited outside, as hungry as a tiger, and that trouble stretched above us, longer than the sky.

Then it was over. Creole and Sonny let out their breath, both soaking wet, and grinning. There was a lot of applause and some of it was real. In the dark, the girl came by and I asked her to take drinks to the bandstand. There was a long pause, while they talked up there in the indigo light and after awhile I saw the girl put a Scotch and milk on top of the piano for Sonny. He didn't seem to notice it, but just before they started playing again, he sipped from it and looked toward me, and nodded. Then he put it back on top of the piano. For me, then, as they began to play again, it glowed and shook above my brother's head like the very cup of trembling.[9]

1957

QUESTIONS

1. "Sonny's Blues" begins *in medias res*. What does Baldwin achieve by beginning the story as he does? How does the order in which events are related later in the story affect your experience of reading it and interpreting its meaning?
2. What external conflict(s) is (or are) depicted in the story? What internal conflict(s)? How are they resolved?
3. James Baldwin famously avowed that "It is only in his music . . . that the Negro in America has been able to tell his story," and music of various kinds features prominently in "Sonny's Blues." Note all the times when music is mentioned, as well as all the varieties of music. What story seems to be told both *through* and *about* music in "Sonny's Blues"?

SUGGESTIONS FOR WRITING

1. Write an essay comparing the way any two of the stories in this anthology handle the traditional elements of plot: exposition, rising action, climax, falling action, conclusion. Consider especially how plot elements contribute to the overall artistic effect.
2. Many stories depict events out of chronological order. For example, "Sonny's Blues" makes liberal use of flashbacks. Select any story from this anthology, and write an essay discussing the significance of sequence.
3. Write an essay that explores the central conflict in one of the stories in this chapter. What is the nature of the conflict? When, where, and how does it develop or become more complicated as the story unfolds? How is it resolved at the end of the story? Why and how is that resolution satisfying?

---

9. See Isaiah 51.17, 22–23: "Awake, awake, stand up, O Jerusalem, which hast drunk at the hand of the Lord the cup of his fury; thou hast drunken the dregs of the cup of trembling, and wrung them out. . . . Behold, I have taken out of thine hand the cup of trembling, even the dregs of the cup of my fury; thou shalt no more drink it again: But I will put it into the hand of them that afflict thee. . . ."

2 NARRATION AND POINT OF VIEW

When we read fiction, our sense of who is telling us the story is as important as discovering what happens to the characters. Unlike drama, in which
events are acted out in front of an audience, fiction is always mediated or
represented to us by someone else, a **narrator**. Often a reader is very aware
of the **voice** of a narrator telling the story, as if the words are being spoken
aloud. Commonly, stories also reveal a distinct angle of vision or perspective from which the characters, events, and other aspects are viewed. Just as
the verbal quality of narration is called the voice, the visual angle is called
the **focus**. Focus acts much as a camera does, choosing the direction of our
gaze, the proportions and framework in which we see things. Both voice
and focus are generally considered together in the term **point of view**. To
understand how a story is narrated, you need to recognize both voice and
focus. These in turn shape what we know and care about as the plot unfolds,
and they make us feel close to or distant from certain characters.

A story is said to be from a character's point of view, or a character is said
to be a focal or focalizing character, if for the most part the action centers on
that character, as if we see with that character's eyes or we watch that character closely. But the effects of narration certainly involve more than attaching a video camera to a character's head or tracking wherever the character
moves. What about the spoken and unspoken words? In some stories, the
narrator is a character, and we may feel as if we are overhearing his or her
thoughts, whereas in other stories the narrator takes a very distant or critical view of the characters. At times a narrator seems more like a disembod-
ied, unidentified voice. Prose fiction has many ways to convey speech and
thought, so it is important to consider voice as well as focus when we try to
understand the narration of a story.

Besides focus and voice, point of view encompasses more general matters
of value. A story's narrator may explicitly endorse or subtly support whatever
a certain character values, knows, or seeks, even when the character is absent
or silent or unaware. Other narrators may treat characters and their interests
with far more detachment. At the same time, the **style** and **tone** of the narrator's voice—from echoing the characters' feelings to mocking their preten-
tious speech or thoughts to stating their actions in formal diction—may
convey clues that a character or a narrator's perspective is limited. Such dis-

crepancies or gaps between vision and voice, intentions and understandings, or expectations and outcomes generate **irony**. For instance, Sister, the narrator of Eudora Welty's "Why I Live at the P.O.," is unaware that her resentful tone and spiteful behavior undermine both her dignity and her story, which she thinks is a justified complaint and self-defense. Sometimes, too, the point of view shifts, challenging the reader's bias toward any one character. Or the style of narration may even change dramatically from one section to another. Bram Stoker's novel *Dracula* (1897), for example, is variously narrated through characters' journals, letters, reports, and newspaper articles.

Questions about Narration and Point of View

1. Does the narrator speak in the first, second, or third person?
2. Is the story narrated in the past or present tense? Does the verb tense affect your reading of it in any way?
3. Does the narrator use a distinctive vocabulary, style, and tone, or is the language more standard and neutral?
4. Is the narrator identified as a character, and if so, how much does he or she participate in the action?
5. Does the narrator ever seem to speak to the reader directly (addressing "you") or explicitly state opinions or values?
6. Do you know what every character is thinking, or only some characters, or none?
7. Does the narrative voice or focus shift during the story or remain consistent?
8. Do the narrator, the characters, and the reader all perceive matters in the same way, or are there differences in levels of understanding?

The point of view varies according to the narrator's position in the story and the grammatical person (for example, first or third) the narrative voice assumes. These elements determine who is telling the story, whom it is about, and what information the reader has access to.

A *third-person narrator* tells an unidentified listener or reader what happened, referring to all characters using the pronouns *he*, *she*, or *they*. Third-person narration is virtually always external, meaning that the narrator is not a character in and does not participate in the action of the story. Even so, different types of third-person narration—omniscient, limited, and objective—provide the reader with various amounts of information about the characters.

An *omniscient* or *unlimited narrator* has access to the thoughts, perceptions, or experiences of more than one character (often of several), though such narrators usually focus selectively on a few important characters. A *limited narrator* is an external, third-person narrator who tells the story from a distinct point of view, usually that of a single character, revealing that character's thoughts and relating the action from his or her perspective. This focal character is also known as a **central consciousness**. Sometimes, a limited narrator will reveal the thoughts and feelings of a small number of the characters in order to enhance the story told about the central consciousness. Jane Austen's novel *Emma* includes a few episodes from Mr. Knightley's point of view to show what he thinks about Emma Woodhouse, the focal character, and her relationships. Finally, an *objective narrator* does not explicitly report the characters' thoughts and feelings but may obliquely suggest them through the characters' speech and actions. For example, Ernest Hemingway's "Hills Like White Elephants" consists mostly of dialogue interspersed with minimal action and description.

Instead of using third-person narration, an author might choose to tell a story from the point of view of a *first-person narrator*. Most common is first-person singular narration, where the narrator uses the pronoun *I*. The narrator may be a major or minor character within the story and therefore is an *internal narrator*. Notice that the first-person narrator may be telling a story mainly about someone else or about his or her own experience. Sometimes the first-person narrator addresses an **auditor**, a listener within the fiction whose possible reaction is part of the story. Edgar Allan Poe's "The Cask of Amontillado" begins, "The thousand injuries of Fortunato I had borne as best I could. . . . I vowed revenge. You, who so well know the nature of my soul. . . ." Poe's story is controlled by Montresor's point of view: both what he perceived during his act of revenge and what he says about it years later. We never know what the victim, Fortunato, is thinking, nor do we know how the auditor (an unidentified friend) feels about Montresor's character and deeds. We have only Montresor's perspective and voice, but that doesn't stop us from taking a very different view of what happens than Montresor intends for us to have. Such incompatibility between what someone intends to communicate and what auditors understand is one form of irony, as we have noted.

One kind of narrator that is especially effective at producing irony is the *unreliable narrator*. First-person narrators may unintentionally reveal their flaws as they try to impress. Or narrators may make claims that other characters or the audience know to be false or distorted. Some fictions are narrated by villains (Montresor surely counts), insane people, fools, liars, or hypocrites. When we resist a narrator's point of view and judge his or her flaws or misperceptions, we call that narrator unreliable. This does not mean you should dismiss everything such a narrator says, but that you should be on the alert for ironies.

Less common is the first-person plural, where the narrator uses the pronoun *we*. The plural may be used effectively to express a shared perspective of a community. William Faulkner's "A Rose for Emily" is narrated by an unidentified resident of the town. The vision, voice, and tone of the narration suggest that the townspeople all act and speak together. Novels that are about a close-knit community may be narrated primarily in first-person plural. Elizabeth Gaskell's classic short novel *Cranford* (1853) is a good example. The narrator is a young woman who visits a community of genteel widows and spinsters in the English village of Cranford and describes their customs. At one point, a visitor arrives, Lady Glenmire, and all of Cranford society is in awe of her aristocratic rank and title. At an evening party, "We were all very silent at first. We were thinking what we could talk about, that should be high enough to interest My Lady. There had been a rise in the price of sugar, which, as preserving-time was near, was a piece of intelligence to all our housekeeping hearts, and would have been the natural topic if Lady Glenmire had not been by. But we were not sure if the Peerage ate preserves," that is, whether aristocrats like Lord Glenmire ate fruit jam. The high price of sugar doesn't seem "high enough" in another sense for a high-ranked guest to talk about.

The narrator of Cranford does refer to herself as "I" and sometimes addresses the reader as "you." The narrative perspective and voice is rather similar in Kazuo Ishiguro's *Never Let Me Go* (2005), a novel that also portrays an isolated group that follows regulated customs. At a boarding school, a student, Polly, suddenly questions one of the rules: "*We* all went silent. Miss Lucy [the teacher] didn't often get cross, but when she did, *you* certainly knew about it, and we thought for a second Polly was for it [would be punished]. But then we saw Miss Lucy wasn't angry, just deep in thought. *I* remember feeling furious at Polly for so stupidly breaking the unwritten rule, but at the same time, being terribly excited about what answer Miss Lucy might give" (emphasis added). Ishiguro's narrator, like Gaskell's, resorts to different narrative perspectives and voices to represent the experience of a community.

Like narrators who refer to themselves as "we" throughout a work of fiction, *second-person narrators* who consistently speak to *you* are unusual. This technique has the effect of turning the reader into a character in the story. Jay McInerney, for example, in his novel *Bright Lights, Big City* (1984) employed the second-person voice, creating an effect similar to conversational anecdotes. Jamaica Kincaid's "Girl" experiments with second-person narration, addressing the central consciousness, or protagonist, as "you" and using imperative verbs: "Wash the white clothes on Monday" (in "Girl"). Kincaid alternates these direct commands with indirect instructions ("This is how you sew on a button").

Along with the grammatical "person," the verb tense used has an effect on the narration of a story. Since narrative is so wrapped up in memory, most stories rely on the past tense. In contemporary fiction, however, the present tense is also frequently used. The present tense can lend an impression of immediacy, of frequent repetition, or of a dreamlike or magical state that isn't subject to the passage of time. An author might also use the present tense to create a conversational tone. Rarely, for a strange prophetic outlook, a narrator may even use the future tense, predicting what *will* happen.

NARRATOR VERSUS IMPLIED AUTHOR

As you discover how a story is being narrated, by whom, and from what point of view, how should you respond to the shifting points of view, tones of voice, and hints of critical distance or irony toward characters? Who is really shaping the story, and how do you know what is intended? Readers may answer the question "Who is telling this story?" with the name of the author. It is more accurate and practical, however, to distinguish between the narrator who presents the story and the flesh-and-blood author who wrote it, even when the two are hard to tell apart. If you are writing an essay about a short story, you do not need to research the biography of the author or find letters or interviews in which the author comments on the writing process or the intended themes of the work. This sort of biographical information may enrich your study of the story (it can be a good critical approach), but it is not *necessary* to an understanding of the text. And yet if you only consider the narrator when you interpret a story, you may find it difficult to account for the effects of distance and irony that come from a narrator's or a character's limitations. Many critics rely on the concept of the *implied author*, not to be confused with either the flesh-and-blood person who wrote the work or the narrator who relates the words to us. Most of the time, when we ask questions about the "author" of a work, we are asking about its implied author, the perspective and intended values that govern the whole work, including the narrator.

Why not ignore the idea of the narrator or the implied author? What's wrong with writing an essay about *Great Expectations* (1860–61) in which you refer only to the author, Charles Dickens? After all, his name is on the title page, and we know that Pip's coming-of-age story has some autobiographical aspects. Yet from the first sentence of the novel it is clear that someone besides Charles Dickens is telling his life story: Pip, the first-person narrator. "My father's family name being Pirrip, and my Christian name Philip, my infant tongue could make of both names nothing longer or more explicit than Pip. So, I called myself Pip, and came to be called Pip." The reader sympathizes with Pip, the focal character-narrator, as an abused child, but he is also flawed and makes mistakes, as Pip himself realizes when he has grown up and tells the story of his own life. The reader understands Pip's errors through the subtle guidance of the implied author who created the narrator and shaped the plot and other characters. How useful or accurate would it be to attribute Pip's character and experience to the real Charles Dickens? The facts of the flesh-and-blood author's life and his actual personality differ widely from the novel's character, which in turn may differ from what Charles Dickens himself consciously intended. Hence the value of referring to a narrator and an implied author of a work of fiction. In critical essays, these concepts help us make an effort to discover what even the most detailed biography might never pin down: Who in fact was Charles Dickens and what did he actually intend in *Great Expectations*?

Reading a story, we know that it consists of words on a page, but we imagine the narrator speaking to us, giving shape, focus, and voice to a particular history. At the same time, we recognize that the reader should not take the narrator's words as absolute truth, but rather as effects shaped by an implied author. The concept of the implied author helps keep the particulars of the real author's (naturally imperfect) personality and life out of the picture. But it also reminds us to distinguish between the act of writing the work and the imaginary utterance of "telling" the story: The narrator is *neither* the real nor the implied author.

· · ·

Because our responses to a work of fiction are largely guided by the designs and values implied in a certain way of telling the story, questions about narration and point of view can often lead to good essay topics. You might start by considering any other choices the implied author might have made and how these would change your reading of the story. As you read the stories in this chapter, imagine different voices and visions, different narrative techniques, in order to assess the effectiveness of the particular types of narration and point of view. How would the impact of "The Cask of Amontillado" change if an omniscient third-person narrator took turns to show us what Fortunato as well as Montresor was thinking and feeling? Which character in "Hills Like White Elephants" might make the best first-person narrator of the incident, and how would that affect the reader's response? Could you imagine "Girl" rewritten as a single scene or plot with a third-person external narrator? What would be lost in removing the repetitions of actions that "you" might or must perform? Can you show the reader of your essay how the specific narration and point of view of a story contribute to its significant effects?

EDGAR ALLAN POE

The Cask of Amontillado

The thousand injuries of Fortunato I had borne as I best could, but when he ventured upon insult I vowed revenge. You, who so well know the nature of my soul, will not suppose, however, that I gave utterance to a threat. *At length* I would be avenged; this was a point definitively settled—but the very definitiveness with which it was resolved precluded the idea of risk. I must not only punish but punish with impunity. A wrong is unredressed when retribution overtakes its redresser. It is equally unredressed when the avenger fails to make himself felt as such to him who has done the wrong. It must be understood that neither by word nor deed had I given Fortunato cause to doubt my good will. I continued, as was my wont, to smile in his face, and he did not perceive that my smile *now* was at the thought of his immolation.

He had a weak point—this Fortunato—although in other regards he was a man to be respected and even feared. He prided himself upon his connoisseurship in wine. Few Italians have the true virtuoso spirit. For the most part their enthusiasm is adopted to suit the time and opportunity, to practice imposture upon the British and Austrian *millionaires*. In painting and gemmary, Fortunato, like his countrymen, was a quack, but in the matter of old wines he was sincere. In this respect I did not differ from him materially;—I was skilful in the Italian vintages myself, and bought largely whenever I could.

It was about dusk, one evening during the supreme madness of the carnival season, that I encountered my friend. He accosted me with excessive warmth, for he had been drinking much. The man wore motley. He had on a tight-fitting parti-striped dress,[1] and his head was surmounted by the conical cap and bells. I was so pleased to see him that I should never have done wringing his hand.

5   I said to him—"My dear Fortunato, you are luckily met. How remarkably well you are looking to-day. But I have received a pipe[2] of what passes for Amontillado, and I have my doubts."

"How?" said he. "Amontillado? A pipe? Impossible! And in the middle of the carnival!"

"I have my doubts," I replied; "and I was silly enough to pay the full Amontillado price without consulting you in the matter. You were not to be found, and I was fearful of losing a bargain."

"Amontillado!"

"I have my doubts."

10   "Amontillado!"

"And I must satisfy them."

"Amontillado!"

"As you are engaged, I am on my way to Luchresi. If any one has a critical turn it is he. He will tell me——"

"Luchresi cannot tell Amontillado from Sherry."

15   "And yet some fools will have it that his taste is a match for your own."

"Come, let us go."

"Whither?"

---

1. Fortunato wears a jester's costume (i.e., motley), not a woman's dress.   2. Large cask.

"To your vaults."

"My friend, no; I will not impose upon your good nature. I perceive you have an engagement. Luchresi——"

"I have no engagement;—come." 20

"My friend, no. It is not the engagement, but the severe cold with which I perceive you are afflicted. The vaults are insufferably damp. They are encrusted with nitre."

"Let us go, nevertheless. The cold is merely nothing. Amontillado! You have been imposed upon. And as for Luchresi, he cannot distinguish Sherry from Amontillado."

Thus speaking, Fortunato possessed himself of my arm; and putting on a mask of black silk and drawing a *roquelaire*[3] closely about my person, I suffered him to hurry me to my palazzo.

There were no attendants at home; they had absconded to make merry in honour of the time. I had told them that I should not return until the morning, and had given them explicit orders not to stir from the house. These orders were sufficient, I well knew, to insure their immediate disappearance, one and all, as soon as my back was turned.

I took from their sconces two flambeaux,[4] and giving one to Fortu- 25 nato, bowed him through several suites of rooms to the archway that led into the vaults. I passed down a long and winding staircase, requesting him to be cautious as he followed. We came at length to the foot of the descent, and stood together upon the damp ground of the catacombs of the Montresors.

The gait of my friend was unsteady, and the bells upon his cap jingled as he strode.

"The pipe," said he.

"It is farther on," said I; "but observe the white web-work which gleams from these cavern walls."

He turned towards me, and looked into my eyes with two filmy orbs that distilled the rheum of intoxication.

"Nitre[5]?" he asked, at length. 30

"Nitre," I replied. "How long have you had that cough?"

"Ugh! ugh! ugh!—ugh! ugh! ugh!—ugh! ugh! ugh!—ugh! ugh! ugh!— ugh! ugh! ugh!"

My poor friend found it impossible to reply for many minutes.

"It is nothing," he said, at last.

"Come," I said, with decision, "we will go back; your health is precious. 35 You are rich, respected, admired, beloved; you are happy, as once I was. You

---

3. Man's heavy, knee-length cloak.   4. That is, two torches from their wall brackets.
5. Potassium nitrate (saltpeter), a white mineral often found on the walls of damp caves and used in gunpowder.

are a man to be missed. For me it is no matter. We will go back; you will be ill, and I cannot be responsible. Besides, there is Luchresi——"

"Enough," he said; "the cough is a mere nothing; it will not kill me. I shall not die of a cough."

"True—true," I replied; "and, indeed, I had no intention of alarming you unneccessarily—but you should use all proper caution. A draught of this Medoc[6] will defend us from the damps."

Here I knocked off the neck of a bottle which I drew from a long row of its fellows that lay upon the mould.

"Drink," I said, presenting him the wine.

40   He raised it to his lips with a leer. He paused and nodded to me familiarly, while his bells jingled.

"I drink," he said, "to the buried that repose around us."

"And I to your long life."

He again took my arm, and we proceeded.

"These vaults," he said, "are extensive."

45   "The Montresors," I replied, "were a great and numerous family."

"I forget your arms."

"A huge human foot d'or,[7] in a field azure; the foot crushes a serpent rampant whose fangs are imbedded in the heel."

"And the motto?"

"Nemo me impune lacessit."[8]

50   "Good!" he said.

The wine sparkled in his eyes and the bells jingled. My own fancy grew warm with the Medoc. We had passed through long walls of piled skeletons, with casks and puncheons[9] intermingling, into the inmost recesses of the catacombs. I paused again, and this time I made bold to seize Fortunato by an arm above the elbow.

"The nitre!" I said; "see, it increases. It hangs like moss upon the vaults. We are below the river's bed. The drops of moisture trickle among the bones. Come, we will go back ere it is too late. Your cough——"

"It is nothing," he said; "let us go on. But first, another draught of the Medoc."

I broke and reached him a flaçon of De Grâve. He emptied it at a breath. His eyes flashed with a fierce light. He laughed and threw the bottle upwards with a gesticulation I did not understand.

55   I looked at him in surprise. He repeated the movement—a grotesque one.

"You do not comprehend?" he said.

"Not I," I replied.

"Then you are not of the brotherhood."

6. Like De Grâve (below), a French wine.   7. Of gold.   8. No one provokes me with impunity.
9. Large casks.

"How?"

"You are not of the masons."[1]

"Yes, yes," I said; "yes, yes."

"You? Impossible! A mason?"

"A mason," I replied.

"A sign," he said, "a sign."

"It is this," I answered producing from beneath the folds of my *roquelaire* a trowel.

"You jest," he exclaimed, recoiling a few paces. "But let us proceed to the Amontillado."

"Be it so," I said, replacing the tool beneath the cloak and again offering him my arm. He leaned upon it heavily. We continued our route in search of the Amontillado. We passed through a range of low arches, descended, passed on, and descending again, arrived at a deep crypt, in which the foulness of the air caused our flambeaux rather to glow than flame.

At the most remote end of the crypt there appeared another less spacious. Its walls had been lined with human remains, piled to the vault overhead, in the fashion of the great catacombs of Paris. Three sides of this interior crypt were still ornamented in this manner. From the fourth side the bones had been thrown down, and lay promiscuously upon the earth, forming at one point a mound of some size. Within the wall thus exposed by the displacing of the bones, we perceived a still interior crypt or recess, in depth about four feet, in width three, in height six or seven. It seemed to have been constructed for no especial use within itself, but formed merely the interval between two of the colossal supports of the roof of the catacombs, and was backed by one of their circumscribing walls of solid granite.

It was in vain that Fortunato, uplifting his dull torch, endeavoured to pry into the depth of the recess. Its termination the feeble light did not enable us to see.

"Proceed," I said; "herein is the Amontillado. As for Luchresi——"

"He is an ignoramus," interrupted my friend, as he stepped unsteadily forward, while I followed immediately at his heels. In an instant he had reached the extremity of the niche, and finding his progress arrested by the rock, stood stupidly bewildered. A moment more and I had fettered him to the granite. In its surface were two iron staples, distant from each other about two feet, horizontally. From one of these depended a short chain, from the other a padlock. Throwing the links about his waist, it was but the work of a few seconds to secure it. He was too much astounded to resist. Withdrawing the key I stepped back from the recess.

"Pass your hand," I said, "over the wall; you cannot help feeling the nitre. Indeed, it is *very* damp. Once more let me *implore* you to return. No?

1. Masons or Freemasons, an international secret society condemned by the Catholic Church. Montresor means by mason one who builds with stone, brick, etc.

when you expect one outcome and another happens
irony — Thumb

Then I must positively leave you. But I will first render you all the little attentions in my power."

"The Amontillado!" ejaculated my friend, not yet recovered from his astonishment.

"True," I replied; "the Amontillado."

75 As I said these words I busied myself among the pile of bones of which I have before spoken. Throwing them aside, I soon uncovered a quantity of building stone and mortar. With these materials and with the aid of my trowel, I began vigorously to wall up the entrance of the niche.

I had scarcely laid the first tier of the masonry when I discovered that the intoxication of Fortunato had in great measure worn off. The earliest indication I had of this was a low moaning cry from the depth of the recess. It was *not* the cry of a drunken man. There was then a long and obstinate silence. I laid the second tier, and the third, and the fourth; and then I heard the furious vibration of the chain. The noise lasted for several minutes, during which, that I might hearken to it with the more satisfaction, I ceased my labours and sat down upon the bones. When at last the clanking subsided, I resumed the trowel, and finished without interruption the fifth, the sixth, and the seventh tier. The wall was now nearly upon a level with my breast. I again paused, and holding the flambeaux over the mason-work, threw a few feeble rays upon the figure within.

A succession of loud and shrill screams, bursting suddenly from the throat of the chained form, seemed to thrust me violently back. For a brief moment I hesitated, I trembled. Unsheathing my rapier, I began to grope with it about the recess; but the thought of an instant reassured me. I placed my hand upon the solid fabric of the catacombs and felt satisfied. I reapproached the wall. I replied to the yells of him who clamoured. I re-echoed, I aided, I surpassed them in volume and in strength. I did this, and the clamourer grew still.

It was now midnight, and my task was drawing to a close. I had completed the eighth, the ninth and the tenth tier. I had finished a portion of the last and the eleventh; there remained but a single stone to be fitted and plastered in. I struggled with its weight; I placed it partially in its destined position. But now there came from out the niche a low laugh that erected the hairs upon my head. It was succeeded by a sad voice, which I had difficulty in recognizing as that of the noble Fortunato. The voice said—

"Ha! ha! ha!—he! he! he!—a very good joke, indeed—an excellent jest. We will have many a rich laugh about it at the palazzo—he! he! he!—over our wine—he! he! he!"

80 "The Amontillado!" I said.

"He! he! he!—he! he! he!—yes, the Amontillado. But is it not getting late? Will not they be awaiting us at the palazzo—the Lady Fortunato and the rest? Let us be gone."

"Yes," I said, "let us be gone."

"For the love of God, Montresor!"

"Yes," I said, "for the love of God!"

But to these words I hearkened in vain for a reply. I grew impatient. I called aloud— 85

"Fortunato!"

No answer. I called again—

"Fortunato!"

No answer still. I thrust a torch through the remaining aperture and let it fall within. There came forth in return only a jingling of the bells. My heart grew sick; it was the dampness of the catacombs that made it so. I hastened to make an end of my labour. I forced the last stone into its position; I plastered it up. Against the new masonry I re-erected the old rampart of bones. For the half of a century no mortal has disturbed them. *In pace requiescat!*[2]

The end, he 1846

needed to force
what he said

QUESTIONS

1. What can the reader infer about Montresor's social position and character from hints in the text? What evidence does the text provide that Montresor is an unreliable narrator?

2. Who is the auditor, the "You," addressed in the first paragraph of "The Cask of Amontillado"? When is the story being told? Why is it being told? How does your knowledge of the auditor and the occasion influence the effect the story has on you?

3. What devices does Poe use to create and heighten the suspense in the story? Is the outcome ever in doubt?

ERNEST HEMINGWAY

Hills Like White Elephants

The hills across the valley of the Ebro[1] were long and white. On this side there was no shade and no trees and the station was between two lines of rails in the sun. Close against the side of the station there was the warm shadow of the building and a curtain, made of strings of bamboo beads, hung across the open door into the bar, to keep out flies. The American and the girl with him sat at a table in the shade, outside the building. It was very hot and the express from Barcelona would come in forty minutes. It stopped at this junction for two minutes and went on to Madrid.

2. May he rest in peace! 1. River in northern Spain.

"What should we drink?" the girl asked. She had taken off her hat and put it on the table.

"It's pretty hot," the man said.

"Let's drink beer."

5   "Dos cervezas," the man said into the curtain.

"Big ones?" a woman asked from the doorway.

"Yes. Two big ones."

The woman brought two glasses of beer and two felt pads. She put the felt pads and the beer glasses on the table and looked at the man and the girl. The girl was looking off at the line of hills. They were white in the sun and the country was brown and dry.

"They look like white elephants," she said.

10   "I've never seen one," the man drank his beer.

"No, you wouldn't have."

"I might have," the man said. "Just because you say I wouldn't have doesn't prove anything."

The girl looked at the bead curtain. "They've painted something on it," she said. "What does it say?"

"Anis del Toro. It's a drink."

15   "Could we try it?"

The man called "Listen" through the curtain. The woman came out from the bar.

"Four reales."[2]

"We want two Anis del Toro."

"With water?"

20   "Do you want it with water?"

"I don't know," the girl said. "Is it good with water?"

"It's all right."

"You want them with water?" asked the woman.

"Yes, with water."

25   "It tastes like licorice," the girl said and put the glass down.

"That's the way with everything."

"Yes," said the girl. "Everything tastes of licorice. Especially all the things you've waited so long for, like absinthe."

"Oh, cut it out."

"You started it," the girl said. "I was being amused. I was having a fine time."

30   "Well, let's try and have a fine time."

"All right. I was trying. I said the mountains looked like white elephants. Wasn't that bright?"

"That was bright."

2. Spanish coins.

"I wanted to try this new drink. That's all we do, isn't it—look at things and try new drinks?"

"I guess so."

The girl looked across at the hills.   35

"They're lovely hills," she said. "They don't really look like white elephants. I just meant the coloring of their skin through the trees."

"Should we have another drink?"

"All right."

The warm wind blew the bead curtain against the table.

"The beer's nice and cool," the man said.   40

"It's lovely," the girl said.

"It's really an awfully simple operation, Jig," the man said. "It's not really an operation at all."

The girl looked at the ground the table legs rested on.

"I know you wouldn't mind it, Jig. It's really not anything. It's just to let the air in."

The girl did not say anything.   45

"I'll go with you and I'll stay with you all the time. They just let the air in and then it's all perfectly natural."

"Then what will we do afterward?"

"We'll be fine afterward. Just like we were before."

"What makes you think so?"

"That's the only thing that bothers us. It's the only thing that's made us   50
unhappy."

The girl looked at the bead curtain, put her hand out and took hold of two of the strings of beads.

"And you think then we'll be all right and be happy."

"I know we will. You don't have to be afraid. I've known lots of people that have done it."

"So have I," said the girl. "And afterward they were all so happy."

"Well," the man said, "if you don't want to you don't have to. I wouldn't   55
have you do it if you didn't want to. But I know it's perfectly simple."

"And you really want to?"

"I think it's the best thing to do. But I don't want you to do it if you don't really want to."

"And if I do it you'll be happy and things will be like they were and you'll love me?"

"I love you now. You know I love you."

"I know. But if I do it, then it will be nice again if I say things are like   60
white elephants, and you'll like it?"

"I'll love it. I love it now but I just can't think about it. You know how I get when I worry."

"If I do it you won't ever worry?"

"I won't worry about that because it's perfectly simple."

"Then I'll do it. Because I don't care about me."
65   "What do you mean?"
"I don't care about me."
"Well, I care about you."
"Oh, yes. But I don't care about me. And I'll do it and then everything will be fine."
"I don't want you to do it if you feel that way."
70   The girl stood up and walked to the end of the station. Across, on the other side, were fields of grain and trees along the banks of the Ebro. Far away, beyond the river, were mountains. The shadow of a cloud moved across the field of grain and she saw the river through the trees.
"And we could have all this," she said. "And we could have everything and every day we make it more impossible."
"What did you say?"
"I said we could have everything."
"We can have everything."
75   "No, we can't."
"We can have the whole world."
"No, we can't."
"We can go everywhere."
"No, we can't. It isn't ours anymore."
80   "It's ours."
"No, it isn't. And once they take it away, you never get it back."
"But they haven't taken it away."
"We'll wait and see."
"Come on back in the shade," he said. "You mustn't feel that way."
85   "I don't feel any way," the girl said. "I just know things."
"I don't want you to do anything that you don't want to do—"
"Nor that isn't good for me," she said. "I know. Could we have another beer?"
"All right. But you've got to realize—"
"I realize," the girl said. "Can't we maybe stop talking?"
90   They sat down at the table and the girl looked across at the hills on the dry side of the valley and the man looked at her and at the table.
"You've got to realize," he said, "that I don't want you to do it if you don't want to. I'm perfectly willing to go through with it if it means anything to you."
"Doesn't it mean anything to you? We could get along."
"Of course it does. But I don't want anybody but you. I don't want any one else. And I know it's perfectly simple."
"Yes, you know it's perfectly simple."
95   "It's all right for you to say that, but I do know it."
"Would you do something for me now?"
"I'd do anything for you."

"Would you please please please please please please please stop talking?"

He did not say anything but looked at the bags against the wall of the station. There were labels on them from all the hotels where they had spent nights.

"But I don't want you to," he said, "I don't care anything about it." 100

"I'll scream," the girl said.

The woman came out through the curtains with two glasses of beer and put them down on the damp felt pads. "The train comes in five minutes," she said.

"What did she say?" asked the girl.

"That the train is coming in five minutes."

The girl smiled brightly at the woman, to thank her. 105

"I'd better take the bags over to the other side of the station," the man said. She smiled at him.

"All right. Then come back and we'll finish the beer."

He picked up the two heavy bags and carried them around the station to the other tracks. He looked up the tracks but could not see the train. Coming back, he walked through the barroom, where people waiting for the train were drinking. He drank an Anis at the bar and looked at the people. They were all waiting reasonably for the train. He went out through the bead curtain. She was sitting at the table and smiled at him.

"Do you feel better?" he asked.

"I feel fine," she said. "There's nothing wrong with me. I feel fine." 110

1927

QUESTIONS

1. Find the first indication in "Hills Like White Elephants" that the two main characters are not getting along. What is the first clue about the exact nature of their conflict? Why are they going to Madrid? Why do the characters (and the author) refrain from speaking about it explicitly?

2. Point of view includes what characters see. Notice each use of the word "look." What does each person in the story look at, and what does each person seem to understand or feel? Is there anything in the story that none of these people would be able to see or know? How do the different kinds of observation add to the effect of the story?

3. Research the phrase "white elephant." What is the significance of this phrase in the story's title?

JAMAICA KINCAID

Girl

Wash the white clothes on Monday and put them on the stone heap; wash the color clothes on Tuesday and put them on the clothesline to dry; don't walk barehead in the hot sun; cook pumpkin fritters in very hot sweet oil; soak your little cloths right after you take them off; when buying cotton to make yourself a nice blouse, be sure that it doesn't have gum on it, because that way it won't hold up well after a wash; soak salt fish overnight before you cook it; is it true that you sing benna[1] in Sunday school?; always eat your food in such a way that it won't turn someone else's stomach; on Sundays try to walk like a lady and not like the slut you are so bent on becoming; don't sing benna in Sunday school; you mustn't speak to wharf-rat boys, not even to give directions; don't eat fruits on the street—flies will follow you; but I don't sing benna on Sundays at all and never in Sunday school; this is how to sew on a button; this is how to make a buttonhole for the button you have just sewed on; this is how to hem a dress when you see the hem coming down and so to prevent yourself from looking like the slut I know you are so bent on becoming; this is how you iron your father's khaki shirt so that it doesn't have a crease; this is how you iron your father's khaki pants so that they don't have a crease; this is how you grow okra—far from the house, because okra tree harbors red ants; when you are growing dasheen, make sure it gets plenty of water or else it makes your throat itch when you are eating it; this is how you sweep a corner; this is how you sweep a whole house; this is how you sweep a yard; this is how you smile to someone you don't like too much; this is how you smile to someone you don't like at all; this is how you smile to someone you like completely; this is how you set a table for tea; this is how you set a table for dinner; this is how you set a table for dinner with an important guest; this is how you set a table for lunch; this is how you set a table for breakfast; this is how to behave in the presence of men who don't know you very well, and this way they won't recognize immediately the slut I have warned you against becoming; be sure to wash every day, even if it is with your own spit; don't squat down to play marbles—you are not a boy, you know; don't pick people's flowers—you might catch something; don't throw stones at blackbirds, because it might not be a blackbird at all; this is how to make a bread pudding; this is how to make doukona[2] this is how to make pepper pot; this is how to make a good medicine for a cold; this is how to make a

---

1. Caribbean folk-music style.
2. Spicy pudding, often made from plantain and wrapped in a plantain or banana leaf.

good medicine to throw away a child before it even becomes a child; this is how to catch a fish; this is how to throw back a fish you don't like, and that way something bad won't fall on you; this is how to bully a man; this is how a man bullies you; this is how to love a man, and if this doesn't work there are other ways, and if they don't work don't feel too bad about giving up; this is how to spit up in the air if you feel like it, and this is how to move quick so that it doesn't fall on you; this is how to make ends meet; always squeeze bread to make sure it's fresh; *but what if the baker won't let me feel the bread?* you mean to say that after all you are really going to be the kind of woman who the baker won't let near the bread?

All the non-ending sentences.

1983

QUESTIONS

1. Describe the focus or focalization in "Girl." Do we see what one person sees, or observe one person in particular? Describe the voice of the narrator in "Girl." Who is the "you"? How do the focus and voice contribute to the reader's response to the story?
2. Look closely at the indications of time in the story. What actions take place at certain times? Does any event or action happen only once? Is there a plot in "Girl"? If so, how would you summarize it?
3. The instructions in "Girl" have different qualities, as if they come from different people or have different purposes. Why are two phrases in italics? Can you pick out the phrases that are more positive from the girl's point of view? Are there some that seem humorous or ironic?

SUGGESTIONS FOR WRITING

1. Write a parody of "The Cask of Amontillado" set in modern times, perhaps on a college campus ("A Barrel of Bud"?).
2. Hemingway's "Hills Like White Elephants" offers a detached perspective on relationships between men and women at the time the story was published. The story is narrated in a specific style and tone, relying on repetition of some ordinary phrases (e.g., "you've got to realize"). Write an essay on the story, in which you show how the voice (style and tone) of the narration and the point of view help convey the text's perspective on contemporary sexual relationships.
3. Write your own short story, "Boy," modeled on Jamaica Kincaid's "Girl," or write your own version of "Girl." Use either your own point of view or that of an unwelcome advisor.
4. Carry a notebook or tape recorder for a day or two, and note any stories you tell or hear, such as in daydreams, in conversation, on the phone, through e-mail or instant messaging. Consider what makes stories. Your transcripts

condensed like; all the girl reads is that she is being told what to do may be short and may consist of memories, observations about your own character or those of people around you, plans, or predictions about the future. Choose two of your notes and modify them into plot summaries (no more than a paragraph each), using the first or the third person, the present or the past tense. Add a note about whether a full version of each story should give the inner thoughts of one or more characters, and why.

3 CHARACTER

Robert Buss, *Dickens' Dream* (1870)

In the unfinished watercolor *Dickens' Dream*, the nineteenth-century writer peacefully dozes while above and around him float ghostly images of the hundreds of characters that people his novels and, apparently, his dreams. This image captures the undeniable fact that characters loom large in the experience of fiction, for both its writers and its readers. Speaking for the former, Elie Wiesel describes a novelist like himself as practically possessed by characters who "force the writer to tell their stories" because "they want to get out." As readers of fiction, we care about *what* happens and *how* mainly because it happens *to* someone. Indeed, without a "someone," it is unlikely that anything would happen at all.

It is also often a "someone," or the *who* of a story, that sticks with us long after we have forgotten the details of what, where, and how. In this way, characters sometimes seem to take on a life of their own, to float free of the texts where we first encounter them, and even to haunt us. You may know almost nothing about Charles Dickens, but you probably have a vivid sense of his characters Ebenezer Scrooge and Tiny Tim from *A Christmas Carol*.

A **character** is any personage in a literary work who acts, appears, or is referred to as playing a part. Though *personage* usually means a human being, it doesn't have to. Whole genres or subgenres of fiction are distinguished, in part, by the specific kinds of nonhuman characters they conventionally feature, whether alien species and intelligent machines (as in science fiction), animals (as in fables), or elves and monsters (as in traditional fairy tales and modern fantasy). All characters must have at least some human qualities, however, such as the ability to think, to feel pain, or to fall in love.

Evidence to Consider in Analyzing a Character: A Checklist

- the character's name
- the character's physical appearance
- objects and places associated with the character
- the character's actions
- the character's thoughts and speech, including
  - content (what he or she thinks or says)
  - timing (when he or she thinks or says it)
  - phrasing (how he or she thinks or says it)
- other characters' thoughts about the character
- other characters' comments to and about the character
- the narrator's comments about the character

HEROES AND VILLAINS VERSUS PROTAGONISTS AND ANTAGONISTS

A common term for the character with the leading male role is **hero,** the "good guy," who opposes the **villain,** or "bad guy." The leading female character is the **heroine.** Heroes and heroines are usually larger than life, stronger or better than most human beings, sometimes almost godlike. They are characters that a text encourages us to admire and even to emulate, so that the words *hero* and *heroine* can also be applied to especially admirable characters who do not play leading roles.

In most modern fiction, however, the leading character is much more ordinary, not so clearly or simply a "good guy." For that reason, it is usually more appropriate to use the older and more neutral terms *protagonist* and *antagonist* for the leading character and his or her opponent. These terms do not imply either the presence or the absence of outstanding virtue or vice. The claim that a particular character either is or is not heroic might well make a good thesis for an essay, whereas the claim that he is or is not the protagonist generally won't. You might argue, for instance, that Montresor (in Poe's "The Cask of Amontillado," chapter 2) or Ebenezer Scrooge (in Dickens's *A Christmas Carol*) is a hero, but most readers would agree that each is his story's protagonist. Like most rules, however, this one admits of exceptions. Some stories do leave open to debate the question of which character most deserves to be called the *protagonist*. In "Sonny's Blues," for example, Sonny and his brother are equally central. Controversial in a different way is a particular type of protagonist known as an **antihero**. Found mainly in fiction written since around 1850, an antihero, as the name implies, possesses traits that make him or her the opposite of a traditional hero. An antihero may be difficult to like or admire. One early and influential example of an antihero is the narrator-protagonist of Fyodor Dostoevsky's 1864 Russian-language novella *Notes from the Underground*—a man utterly paralyzed by his own hypersensitivity. More familiar and recent examples are Homer and Bart Simpson. Yet it would be a mistake to see the quality of a work of fiction as dependent on whether we find its characters likable or admirable, just as it would be wrong to assume that an author's outlook or values are the same as those of the protagonist. Often, the characters we initially find least likable or admirable may ultimately move and teach us the most.

MAJOR VERSUS MINOR CHARACTERS

The *major* or *main characters* are those we see more of over time; we learn more about them, and we think of them as more complex and, frequently, as more "realistic" than the *minor characters*, the figures who fill out the story. These major characters can grow and change too, sometimes defying our expectations.

Yet even though minor characters are less prominent and may seem less complex, they are ultimately just as indispensable to a story as major characters. Minor characters often play a key role in shaping our interpretations of, and attitudes toward, the major characters, and also in precipitating the changes that major characters undergo. For example, a minor character might function as a **foil**—a character that helps by way of contrast to reveal the unique qualities of another (especially main) character.

Questions about minor characters can lead to good essay topics precisely because such characters' significance to a story is not immediately apparent. Rather, we often have to probe the details of the story to formulate a persuasive interpretation of their roles.

FLAT VERSUS ROUND AND STATIC VERSUS DYNAMIC CHARACTERS

Characters that act from varied, often conflicting motives, impulses, and desires, and who seem to have psychological complexity are said to be *round characters*; they can "surprise convincingly," as one critic puts it. Simple, one-dimensional characters that behave and speak in predictable or repetitive (if sometimes odd) ways are called *flat*. Sometimes, characters seem round to us because our impression of them evolves as a story unfolds. Other times, the characters themselves—not just our impression of them—change as a result of events that occur in the story. A character that changes is *dynamic*; one that doesn't is *static*. Roundness and dynamism tend to go together. But the two qualities are distinct, and one does not require the other: Not all round characters are dynamic, not all dynamic characters are round. Terms like *flat* and *round* or *dynamic* and *static* are useful so long as we do not let them harden into value judgments.

Because flat characters are less complex than round ones, it is easy to assume they are artistically inferior; however, we need only to think of the characters of Charles Dickens, almost all of whom are flat, to realize that this is not always the case. A truly original flat character with only one or two very distinctive traits or behavioral or verbal tics will often prove more memorable than a round one. Unrealistic as such characters might seem, in real life you probably know at least one or two people who can always be counted on to say or do pretty much the same thing every time you see them. Exaggeration can provide insight, as well as humor. Dickens's large gallery of lovable flat characters includes a middle-aged man who constantly pulls himself up by his own hair and an old one who must continually be "fluffed up" by others because he tends to slide right out of his chair. *South Park*'s Kenny is little more than a hooded orange snowsuit and a habit of dying in ever more outrageous ways only to come back to life over and over again.

Flat characters who represent a familiar, frequently recurring type—the dumb blonde, the mad scientist, the inept sidekick, the plain yet ever-sympathetic best friend—are called *stock characters* because they seem to be pulled out of a stockroom of familiar, prefabricated figures. Characters that recur in the myths and literature of many different ages and cultures are instead called **archetypes**, though this term also applies to recurring elements other than characters (such as actions or symbols). One archetypal character is the trickster figure that appears in the guise of Brer Rabbit in the Uncle Remus stories, the spider Anansi in certain African and Afro-

Caribbean folktales, the coyote in Native American folklore, and, perhaps, Bugs Bunny.

READING CHARACTER IN FICTION AND LIFE

On the one hand, we get to know characters in a work of fiction and try to understand them, much as we do people in real life. We observe what they own and wear, what they look like and where they live, how they carry themselves and what expressions flit across their faces, how they behave in various situations, what they say and how they say it, what they do or don't say, what others say about them, and how others act in their presence. Drawing on all that evidence and on our own past experience of both literature and life, we try to deduce characters' motives and desires, their values and beliefs, their strengths and weaknesses—in short, to figure out what makes them tick and how they might react if circumstances changed. In our daily lives, being able to "read" other people in this way is a vital set of skills, one that we may well hone by reading fiction. The skills of observation and interpretation, the enlarged experience and capacity for empathy, that we develop in reading fiction can help us better navigate our real world.

On the other hand, however, fictional characters are not real people; they are imaginary personages crafted by authors. Fiction offers us a more orderly and expansive world than the one we inhabit every day—one in which every person and every gesture and even every word is a meaningful part of a coherent, purposeful design—one in which our responses to people are guided by a narrator and, ultimately, an author; one in which we can sometimes crawl inside other people's heads and know their thoughts; one in which we can get to know murderers and ministers, monsters and miracle workers—the sorts of people (or personages) we might be afraid, unwilling, or simply unable to meet or spend time with in real life.

In other words, fictional characters are the products not of nature, chance, or God, but of careful, deliberate **characterization**—the art and technique of representing fictional personages. In analyzing character, we thus need to consider not only who a character is and what precisely are his or her most important traits, motivations, and values, but also precisely how the text shapes our interpretation of, and degree of sympathy or admiration for, the character; what function the character serves in the story; and what the character might represent.

This last issue is important because all characters, no matter how individualized and idiosyncratic, ultimately become meaningful to us only if they represent something beyond the story, something bigger than themselves— a type of person, a particular set of values or way of looking at the world, a human tendency, a demographic group. When you set out to write about a character, consider how the story would be different without the character and what the author says or shows us through the character.

Direct and Indirect Characterization: An Example and an Exercise

The following conversation appears in the pages of a well-known nineteenth-century novel. Even without being familiar with this novel, you should be able to discern a great deal about the two characters that converse in this scene simply by carefully attending to what each says and how each says it. As you will see, one of the things that differentiates the two speakers is that they hold conflicting views of "character" itself:

"In what order you keep these rooms, Mrs Fairfax!" said I. "No dust, no canvas coverings: except that the air feels chilly, one would think they were inhabited daily."

"Why, Miss Eyre, though Mr Rochester's visits here are rare, they are always sudden and unexpected; and as I observed that it put him out to find everything swathed up, and to have a bustle of arrangement on his arrival, I thought it best to keep the rooms in readiness."

"Is Mr Rochester an exacting, fastidious sort of man?"

"Not particularly so; but he has a gentleman's tastes and habits, and he expects to have things managed in conformity to them."

"Do you like him? Is he generally liked?"

"O yes; the family have always been respected here. Almost all the land in this neighbourhood, as far as you can see, has belonged to the Rochesters time out of mind."

"Well, but leaving his land out of question, do you like him? Is he liked for himself?"

"I have no cause to do otherwise than like him; and I believe he is considered a just and liberal landlord by his tenants: but he has never lived much amongst them."

"But has he no peculiarities? What, in short, is his character?"

"Oh! his character is unimpeachable, I suppose. He is rather peculiar, perhaps: he has travelled a great deal, and seen a great deal of the world, I should think. I daresay he is clever: but I never had much conversation with him."

"In what way is he peculiar?"

"I don't know—it is not easy to describe—nothing striking, but you feel it when he speaks to you: you cannot be always sure whether he is in jest or earnest, whether he is pleased or the

(Continued on next page)

(Continued)

contrary; you don't thoroughly understand him, in short—at least, I don't: but it is of no consequence, he is a very good master."

- What facts about the two speakers can you glean from this conversation? What do you infer about their individual outlooks, personalities, and values?
- What different definitions of the word *character* emerge here? How would you describe each speaker's view of what matters most in the assessment of character?

This scene—from Charlotte Brontë's *Jane Eyre* (1847)—demonstrates the first of the two major methods of presenting character—*indirect characterization* or showing (as opposed to *direct characterization* or telling). In this passage Brontë simply *shows* us what Jane (the narrator) and Mrs. Fairfax say and invites the reader to infer from their words who each character is (including the absent Mr. Rochester), how each looks at the world, and what each cares about.

Sometimes, however, authors present characters more directly, having narrators *tell* us what makes a character tick and what we are to think of him or her. Charlotte Brontë engages in both direct and indirect characterization in the paragraph of *Jane Eyre* that immediately follows the passage above. Here, Jane tells the reader precisely what she thinks this conversation reveals about Mrs. Fairfax, even as she reveals more about herself in the process:

This was all the account I got from Mrs Fairfax of her employer and mine. There are people who seem to have no notion of sketching a character, or observing and describing salient points, either in persons or things: the good lady evidently belonged to this class; my queries puzzled, but did not draw her out. Mr Rochester was Mr Rochester in her eyes; a gentleman, a landed proprietor—nothing more: she inquired and searched no further, and evidently wondered at my wish to gain a more definite notion of his identity.

- How does Jane's interpretation of Mrs. Fairfax compare to yours?
- How and why might this paragraph corroborate or complicate your view of Jane?

CHARACTERS, CONVENTIONS, AND BELIEFS

Just as fiction and the characters that inhabit it operate by somewhat different rules than do the real world and real people, so the rules that govern particular fictional worlds and their characters differ from one another. As the critic James Wood argues,

> our hunger for the particular depth or reality level of a character is tutored by each writer, and adapts to the internal conventions of each book. This is how we can read W. G. Sebald one day and Virginia Woolf or Philip Roth the next, and not demand that each resemble the other. . . . [Works of fiction] tend to fail not when the characters are not vivid or "deep" enough, but when the [work] in question has failed to teach us how to adapt to its conventions, has failed to manage a specific hunger for its own characters, its own reality level.

Works of fiction in various subgenres differ widely in how they handle characterization. Were a folktale, for example, to depict more than a few, mainly flat, archetypal characters, to make us privy to its characters' thoughts, or to offer up detailed descriptions of their physiques and wardrobes, it would cease to be a folktale and cease to yield up the particular sorts of pleasures and insights that only a folktale can. By the same token, readers of a folktale miss out on its pleasures and insights if they expect the wrong things of its characters and modes of characterization.

But even within the same fictional subgenre, the treatment of character varies over time and across cultures. Such variations sometimes reflect profound differences in the way people understand human nature. Individuals and cultures hold conflicting views of what produces personality, whether innate factors such as genes, environmental factors such as upbringing, supernatural forces, unconscious impulses or drives, or a combination of some or all of these. Views differ as well as to whether character is simply an unchanging given or something that can change through experience, conversion, or an act of will. Some works of fiction tackle such issues head on. But many others—especially from cultures or eras different from our own—may raise these questions for us simply because their modes of characterization imply an understanding of the self different from the one we take for granted.

We can thus learn a lot about our own values, prejudices, and beliefs by reading a wide array of fiction. Similarly, we learn from encountering a wide array of fictional characters, including those whose values, beliefs, and ways of life are vastly different from our own.

· · ·

The two stories in this chapter—Toni Morrison's "Recitatif" and Ha Jin's "In Broad Daylight"—differ widely in terms of the number and types of characters they depict and the techniques they use to depict them. In their pages, you will meet a range of diverse individuals—some complex and compelling, some utterly ordinary—struggling to make sense of the people around them just as you work to make sense of them and, through them, yourself.

Questions about Character

1. Who is the protagonist, or might there be more than one? Why and how so? Which other characters, if any, are main or major characters? Which are minor characters?
2. What are the protagonist's most distinctive traits, and what is most distinctive about his or her outlook and values? What motivates the character? What is it about the character that creates internal and/or external conflict?
3. Which textual details and moments reveal most about this character? Which are most surprising or might complicate your interpretation of this character? How is your view of the character affected by what you *don't* know about him or her?
4. What are the roles of other characters? Which, if any, functions as an antagonist? Which, if any, serves as a foil? Why and how so? How would the story as a whole (not just its action or plot) be different if any of these characters disappeared? What points might the author be raising or illustrating through each character?
5. Which of the characters, or which aspects of the characters, does the text encourage us to sympathize with or to admire? to view negatively? Why and how so?
6. Does your view of any character change over the course of the story, or do any of the characters themselves change because of the events in the story? If so, when, how, and why?
7. Does characterization tend to be indirect or direct in the story? What kinds of information do and don't we get about the characters, and how does the story tend to give us that information?

TONI MORRISON

Recitatif[1]

My mother danced all night and Roberta's was sick. That's why we were taken to St. Bonny's. People want to put their arms around you when you tell them you were in a shelter, but it really wasn't bad. No big long room with one hundred beds like Bellevue.[2] There were four to a room, and when Roberta and me came, there was a shortage of state kids, so we were the only ones assigned to 406 and could go from bed to bed if we wanted to. And we wanted to, too. We changed beds every night and for the whole four months we were there we never picked one out as our own permanent bed.

It didn't start out that way. The minute I walked in and the Big Bozo introduced us, I got sick to my stomach. It was one thing to be taken out of your own bed early in the morning—it was something else to be stuck in a strange place with a girl from a whole other race. And Mary, that's my mother, she was right. Every now and then she would stop dancing long enough to tell me something important and one of the things she said was that they never washed their hair and they smelled funny. Roberta sure did. Smell funny, I mean. So when the Big Bozo (nobody ever called her Mrs. Itkin, just like nobody ever said St. Bonaventure)—when she said, "Twyla, this is Roberta. Roberta, this is Twyla. Make each other welcome." I said, "My mother won't like you putting me in here."

"Good," said Bozo. "Maybe then she'll come and take you home."

How's that for mean? If Roberta had laughed I would have killed her, but she didn't. She just walked over to the window and stood with her back to us.

5   "Turn around," said the Bozo. "Don't be rude. Now Twyla. Roberta. When you hear a loud buzzer, that's the call for dinner. Come down to the first floor. Any fights and no movie." And then, just to make sure we knew what we would be missing, "*The Wizard of Oz.*"

Roberta must have thought I meant that my mother would be mad about my being put in the shelter. Not about rooming with her, because as soon as Bozo left she came over to me and said, "Is your mother sick too?"

"No," I said. "She just likes to dance all night."

"Oh," she nodded her head and I liked the way she understood things so fast. So for the moment it didn't matter that we looked like salt and pepper standing there and that's what the other kids called us sometimes. We were eight years old and got F's all the time. Me because I couldn't remember what I read or what the teacher said. And Roberta because she couldn't

---

1. In classical music such as opera, a vocal passage that is sung in a speechlike manner.
2. Large New York City hospital best known for its psychiatric wards.

read at all and didn't even listen to the teacher. She wasn't good at anything except jacks, at which she was a killer: pow scoop pow scoop pow
scoop.

We didn't like each other all that much at first, but nobody else wanted
to play with us because we weren't real orphans with beautiful dead parents in the sky. We were dumped. Even the New York City Puerto Ricans
and the upstate Indians ignored us. All kinds of kids were in there, black
ones, white ones, even two Koreans. The food was good, though. At least I
thought so. Roberta hated it and left whole pieces of things on her plate:
Spam, Salisbury steak—even jello with fruit cocktail in it, and she didn't
care if I ate what she wouldn't. Mary's idea of supper was popcorn and a
can of Yoo-Hoo. Hot mashed potatoes and two weenies was like Thanksgiving for me.

It really wasn't bad, St. Bonny's. The big girls on the second floor pushed 10
us around now and then. But that was all. They wore lipstick and eyebrow
pencil and wobbled their knees while they watched TV. Fifteen, sixteen,
even, some of them were. They were put-out girls, scared runaways most of
them. Poor little girls who fought their uncles off but looked tough to us,
and mean. God did they look mean. The staff tried to keep them separate
from the younger children, but sometimes they caught us watching them
in the orchard where they played radios and danced with each other. They'd
light out after us and pull our hair or twist our arms. We were scared of
them, Roberta and me, but neither of us wanted the other one to know it.
So we got a good list of dirty names we could shout back when we ran from
them through the orchard. I used to dream a lot and almost always the
orchard was there. Two acres, four maybe, of these little apple trees. Hundreds of them. Empty and crooked like beggar women when I first came to
St. Bonny's but fat with flowers when I left. I don't know why I dreamt
about that orchard so much. Nothing really happened there. Nothing all
that important, I mean. Just the big girls dancing and playing the radio.
Roberta and me watching. Maggie fell down there once. The kitchen
woman with legs like parentheses. And the big girls laughed at her. We
should have helped her up, I know, but we were scared of those girls with
lipstick and eyebrow pencil. Maggie couldn't talk. The kids said she had
her tongue cut out, but I think she was just born that way: mute. She was
old and sandy-colored and she worked in the kitchen. I don't know if she
was nice or not. I just remember her legs like parentheses and how she
rocked when she walked. She worked from early in the morning till two
o'clock, and if she was late, if she had too much cleaning and didn't get out
till two-fifteen or so, she'd cut through the orchard so she wouldn't miss
her bus and have to wait another hour. She wore this really stupid little
hat—a kid's hat with ear flaps—and she wasn't much taller than we were. A
really awful little hat. Even for a mute, it was dumb—dressing like a kid
and never saying anything at all.

"But what about if somebody tries to kill her?" I used to wonder about that. "Or what if she wants to cry? Can she cry?"

"Sure," Roberta said. "But just tears. No sounds come out."

"She can't scream?"

"Nope. Nothing."

15　"Can she hear?"

"I guess."

"Let's call her," I said. And we did.

"Dummy! Dummy!" She never turned her head.

"Bow legs! Bow legs!" Nothing. She just rocked on, the chin straps of her baby-boy hat swaying from side to side. I think we were wrong. I think she could hear and didn't let on. And it shames me even now to think there was somebody in there after all who heard us call her those names and couldn't tell on us.

20　We got along all right, Roberta and me. Changed beds every night, got F's in civics and communication skills and gym. The Bozo was disappointed in us, she said. Out of 130 of us state cases, 90 were under twelve. Almost all were real orphans with beautiful dead parents in the sky. We were the only ones dumped and the only ones with F's in three classes including gym. So we got along—what with her leaving whole pieces of things on her plate and being nice about not asking questions.

I think it was the day before Maggie fell down that we found out our mothers were coming to visit us on the same Sunday. We had been at the shelter twenty-eight days (Roberta twenty-eight and a half) and this was their first visit with us. Our mothers would come at ten o'clock in time for chapel, then lunch with us in the teachers' lounge. I thought if my dancing mother met her sick mother it might be good for her. And Roberta thought her sick mother would get a big bang out of a dancing one. We got excited about it and curled each other's hair. After breakfast we sat on the bed watching the road from the window. Roberta's socks were still wet. She washed them the night before and put them on the radiator to dry. They hadn't, but she put them on anyway because their tops were so pretty—scalloped in pink. Each of us had a purple construction-paper basket that we had made in craft class. Mine had a yellow crayon rabbit on it. Roberta's had eggs with wiggly lines of color. Inside were cellophane grass and just the jelly beans because I'd eaten the two marshmallow eggs they gave us. The Big Bozo came herself to get us. Smiling she told us we looked very nice and to come downstairs. We were so surprised by the smile we'd never seen before, neither of us moved.

"Don't you want to see your mommies?"

I stood up first and spilled the jelly beans all over the floor. Bozo's smile disappeared while we scrambled to get the candy up off the floor and put it back in the grass.

She escorted us downstairs to the first floor, where the other girls were lining up to file into the chapel. A bunch of grown-ups stood to one side.

Viewers mostly. The old biddies who wanted servants and the fags who wanted company looking for children they might want to adopt. Once in a while a grandmother. Almost never anybody young or anybody whose face wouldn't scare you in the night. Because if any of the real orphans had young relatives they wouldn't be real orphans. I saw Mary right away. She had on those green slacks I hated and hated even more now because didn't she know we were going to chapel? And that fur jacket with the pocket linings so ripped she had to pull to get her hands out of them. But her face was pretty—like always, and she smiled and waved like she was the little girl looking for her mother—not me.

I walked slowly, trying not to drop the jelly beans and hoping the paper 25 handle would hold. I had to use my last Chiclet because by the time I finished cutting everything out, all the Elmer's was gone. I am left-handed and the scissors never worked for me. It didn't matter, though; I might just as well have chewed the gum. Mary dropped to her knees and grabbed me, mashing the basket, the jelly beans, and the grass into her ratty fur jacket.

"Twyla, baby. Twyla, baby!"

I could have killed her. Already I heard the big girls in the orchard the next time saying, "Twyyyyyla, baby!" But I couldn't stay mad at Mary while she was smiling and hugging me and smelling of Lady Esther dusting powder. I wanted to stay buried in her fur all day.

To tell the truth I forgot about Roberta. Mary and I got in line for the traipse into chapel and I was feeling proud because she looked so beautiful even in those ugly green slacks that made her behind stick out. A pretty mother on earth is better than a beautiful dead one in the sky even if she did leave you all alone to go dancing.

I felt a tap on my shoulder, turned, and saw Roberta smiling. I smiled back, but not too much lest somebody think this visit was the biggest thing that ever happened in my life. Then Roberta said, "Mother, I want you to meet my roommate, Twyla. And that's Twyla's mother."

I looked up it seemed for miles. She was big. Bigger than any man and on 30 her chest was the biggest cross I'd ever seen. I swear it was six inches long each way. And in the crook of her arm was the biggest Bible ever made.

Mary, simple-minded as ever, grinned and tried to yank her hand out of the pocket with the raggedy lining—to shake hands, I guess. Roberta's mother looked down at me and then looked down at Mary too. She didn't say anything, just grabbed Roberta with her Bible-free hand and stepped out of line, walking quickly to the rear of it. Mary was still grinning because she's not too swift when it comes to what's really going on. Then this light bulb goes off in her head and she says "That bitch!" really loud and us almost in the chapel now. Organ music whining; the Bonny Angels singing sweetly. Everybody in the world turned around to look. And Mary would have kept it up—kept calling names if I hadn't squeezed her hand as hard as I could. That helped a little, but she still twitched and crossed and uncrossed her legs all through service. Even groaned a couple of times. Why did I think she would come there and act right? Slacks. No hat like the grandmothers and viewers, and groaning all the while. When we stood for hymns she kept her mouth shut. Wouldn't even look at the words on the page. She actually reached in her purse for a mirror to check her lipstick. All I could think of was that she really needed to be killed. The sermon lasted a year, and I knew the real orphans were looking smug again.

We were supposed to have lunch in the teachers' lounge, but Mary didn't bring anything, so we picked fur and cellophane grass off the mashed jelly beans and ate them. I could have killed her. I sneaked a look at Roberta. Her mother had brought chicken legs and ham sandwiches and oranges and a whole box of chocolate-covered grahams. Roberta drank milk from a thermos while her mother read the Bible to her.

Things are not right. The wrong food is always with the wrong people. Maybe that's why I got into waitress work later—to match up the right people with the right food. Roberta just let those chicken legs sit there, but she did bring a stack of grahams up to me later when the visit was over. I think she was sorry that her mother would not shake my mother's hand. And I liked that and I liked the fact that she didn't say a word about Mary groaning all the way through the service and not bringing any lunch.

Roberta left in May when the apple trees were heavy and white. On her last day we went to the orchard to watch the big girls smoke and dance by the radio. It didn't matter that they said, "Twyyyyyla, baby." We sat on the ground and breathed. Lady Esther. Apple blossoms. I still go soft when I smell one or the other. Roberta was going home. The big cross and the big Bible was coming to get her and she seemed sort of glad and sort of not. I thought I would die in that room of four beds without her and I knew Bozo had plans to move some other dumped kid in there with me. Roberta promised to write every day, which was really sweet of her because she couldn't read a lick so how could she write anybody. I would have drawn pictures and sent them to her but she never gave me her address. Little by little she faded. Her wet socks with the pink scalloped tops and her big serious-looking eyes—that's all I could catch when I tried to bring her to mind.

35   I was working behind the counter at the Howard Johnson's on the Thruway just before the Kingston exit. Not a bad job. Kind of a long ride from Newburgh,[3] but okay once I got there. Mine was the second night shift—eleven to seven. Very light until a Greyhound checked in for breakfast around six-thirty. At that hour the sun was all the way clear of the hills behind the restaurant. The place looked better at night—more like shelter—but I loved it when the sun broke in, even if it did show all the cracks in the vinyl and the speckled floor looked dirty no matter what the mop boy did.

---

3. City on the Hudson River north of New York City.

It was August and a bus crowd was just unloading. They would stand around a long while: going to the john, and looking at gifts and junk-for-sale machines, reluctant to sit down so soon. Even to eat. I was trying to fill the coffee pots and get them all situated on the electric burners when I saw her. She was sitting in a booth smoking a cigarette with two guys smothered in head and facial hair. Her own hair was so big and wild I could hardly see her face. But the eyes. I would know them anywhere. She had on a powder-blue halter and shorts outfit and earrings the size of bracelets. Talk about lipstick and eyebrow pencil. She made the big girls look like nuns. I couldn't get off the counter until seven o'clock, but I kept watching the booth in case they got up to leave before that. My replacement was on time for a change, so I counted and stacked my receipts as fast as I could and signed off. I walked over to the booth, smiling and wondering if she would remember me. Or even if she wanted to remember me. Maybe she didn't want to be reminded of St. Bonny's or to have anybody know she was ever there. I know I never talked about it to anybody.

I put my hands in my apron pockets and leaned against the back of the booth facing them.

"Roberta? Roberta Fisk?"

She looked up. "Yeah?"

"Twyla."   40

She squinted for a second and then said, "Wow."

"Remember me?"

"Sure. Hey. Wow."

"It's been a while," I said, and gave a smile to the two hairy guys.

"Yeah. Wow. You work here?"   45

"Yeah," I said. "I live in Newburgh."

"Newburgh? No kidding?" She laughed then a private laugh that included the guys but only the guys, and they laughed with her. What could I do but laugh too and wonder why I was standing there with my knees showing out from under that uniform. Without looking I could see the blue and white triangle on my head, my hair shapeless in a net, my ankles thick in white oxfords. Nothing could have been less sheer than my stockings. There was this silence that came down right after I laughed. A silence it was her turn to fill up. With introductions, maybe, to her boyfriends or an invitation to sit down and have a Coke. Instead she lit a cigarette off the one she'd just finished and said, "We're on our way to the Coast. He's got an appointment with Hendrix." She gestured casually toward the boy next to her.

"Hendrix? Fantastic," I said. "Really fantastic. What's she doing now?"

Roberta coughed on her cigarette and the two guys rolled their eyes up at the ceiling.

"Hendrix. Jimi Hendrix, asshole. He's only the biggest—Oh, wow. Forget 50 it."

I was dismissed without anyone saying goodbye, so I thought I would do it for her.

"How's your mother?" I asked. Her grin cracked her whole face. She swallowed. "Fine," she said. "How's yours?"

"Pretty as a picture," I said and turned away. The backs of my knees were damp. Howard Johnson's really was a dump in the sunlight.

James is as comfortable as a house slipper. He liked my cooking and I liked his big loud family. They have lived in Newburgh all of their lives and talk about it the way people do who have always known a home. His grandmother is a porch swing older than his father and when they talk about streets and avenues and buildings they call them names they no longer have. They still call the A & P[4] Rico's because it stands on property once a mom and pop store owned by Mr. Rico. And they call the new community college Town Hall because it once was. My mother-in-law puts up jelly and cucumbers and buys butter wrapped in cloth from a dairy. James and his father talk about fishing and baseball and I can see them all together on the Hudson in a raggedy skiff. Half the population of Newburgh is on welfare now, but to my husband's family it was still some upstate paradise of a time long past. A time of ice houses and vegetable wagons, coal furnaces and children weeding gardens. When our son was born my mother-in-law gave me the crib blanket that had been hers.

55 But the town they remembered had changed. Something quick was in the air. Magnificent old houses, so ruined they had become shelter for squatters and rent risks, were bought and renovated. Smart IBM[5] people moved out of their suburbs back into the city and put shutters up and herb gardens in their backyards. A brochure came in the mail announcing the opening of a Food Emporium. Gourmet food it said—and listed items the rich IBM crowd would want. It was located in a new mall at the edge of town and I drove out to shop there one day—just to see. It was late in June. After the tulips were gone and the Queen Elizabeth roses were open everywhere. I trailed my cart along the aisle tossing in smoked oysters and Robert's sauce and things I knew would sit in my cupboard for years. Only when I found some Klondike ice cream bars did I feel less guilty about spending James's fireman's salary so foolishly. My father-in-law ate them with the same gusto little Joseph did.

Waiting in the check-out line I heard a voice say, "Twyla!"

The classical music piped over the aisles had affected me and the woman leaning toward me was dressed to kill. Diamonds on her hand, a smart white summer dress. "I'm Mrs. Benson," I said.

---

4. Supermarket, part of a chain originally known as The Great Atlantic and Pacific Tea Company.
5. The International Business Machine Corporation, which had its executive headquarters in Poughkeepsie, New York.

"Ho. Ho. The Big Bozo," she sang.

For a split second I didn't know what she was talking about. She had a bunch of asparagus and two cartons of fancy water.

"Roberta!" 60

"Right."

"For heaven's sake. Roberta."

"You look great," she said.

"So do you. Where are you? Here? In Newburgh?"

"Yes. Over in Annandale." 65

I was opening my mouth to say more when the cashier called my attention to her empty counter.

"Meet you outside." Roberta pointed her finger and went into the express line.

I placed the groceries and kept myself from glancing around to check Roberta's progress. I remembered Howard Johnson's and looking for a chance to speak only to be greeted with a stingy "wow." But she was waiting for me and her huge hair was sleek now, smooth around a small, nicely shaped head. Shoes, dress, everything lovely and summery and rich. I was dying to know what happened to her, how she got from Jimi Hendrix to Annandale, a neighborhood full of doctors and IBM executives. Easy, I thought. Everything is so easy for them. They think they own the world.

"How long," I asked her. "How long have you been here?"

"A year. I got married to a man who lives here. And you, you're married 70 too, right? Benson, you said."

"Yeah. James Benson."

"And is he nice?"

"Oh, is he nice?"

"Well, is he?" Roberta's eyes were steady as though she really meant the question and wanted an answer.

"He's wonderful, Roberta. Wonderful." 75

"So you're happy."

"Very."

"That's good," she said and nodded her head. "I always hoped you'd be happy. Any kids? I know you have kids."

"One. A boy. How about you?"

"Four." 80

"Four?"

She laughed. "Step kids. He's a widower."

"Oh."

"Got a minute? Let's have a coffee."

I thought about the Klondikes melting and the inconvenience of going 85 all the way to my car and putting the bags in the trunk. Served me right for buying all that stuff I didn't need. Roberta was ahead of me.

"Put them in my car. It's right here."

And then I saw the dark blue limousine.

"You married a Chinaman?"

"No," she laughed. "He's the driver."

90 "Oh, my. If the Big Bozo could see you now."

We both giggled. Really giggled. Suddenly, in just a pulse beat, twenty years disappeared and all of it came rushing back. The big girls (whom we called gar girls—Roberta's misheard word for the evil stone faces described in a civics class) there dancing in the orchard, the ploppy mashed potatoes, the double weenies, the Spam with pineapple. We went into the coffee shop holding on to one another and I tried to think why we were glad to see each other this time and not before. Once, twelve years ago, we passed like strangers. A black girl and a white girl meeting in a Howard Johnson's on the road and having nothing to say. One in a blue and white triangle waitress hat— the other on her way to see Hendrix. Now we were behaving like sisters separated for much too long. Those four short months were nothing in time. Maybe it was the thing itself. Just being there, together. Two little girls who knew what nobody else in the world knew—how not to ask questions. How to believe what had to be believed. There was politeness in that reluctance and generosity as well. Is your mother sick too? No, she dances all night. Oh—and an understanding nod.

We sat in a booth by the window and fell into recollection like veterans.

"Did you ever learn to read?"

"Watch." She picked up the menu. "Special of the day. Cream of corn soup. Entrées. Two dots and a wriggly line. Quiche. Chef salad, scallops . . ."

95 I was laughing and applauding when the waitress came up.

"Remember the Easter baskets?"

"And how we tried to *introduce* them?"

"Your mother with that cross like two telephone poles."

"And yours with those tight slacks."

100 We laughed so loudly heads turned and made the laughter harder to suppress.

"What happened to the Jimi Hendrix date?"

Roberta made a blow-out sound with her lips.

"When he died I thought about you."

"Oh, you heard about him finally?"

105 "Finally. Come on, I was a small-town country waitress."

"And I was a small-town country dropout. God, were we wild. I still don't know how I got out of there alive."

"But you did."

"I did. I really did. Now I'm Mrs. Kenneth Norton."

"Sounds like a mouthful."

110 "It is."

"Servants and all?"

Roberta held up two fingers.

"Ow! What does he do?"

"Computers and stuff. What do I know?"

"I don't remember a hell of a lot from those days, but Lord, St. Bonny's 115 is as clear as daylight. Remember Maggie? The day she fell down and those gar girls laughed at her?"

Roberta looked up from her salad and stared at me. "Maggie didn't fall," she said.

"Yes, she did. You remember."

"No, Twyla. They knocked her down. Those girls pushed her down and tore her clothes. In the orchard."

"I don't—that's not what happened."

"Sure it is. In the orchard. Remember how scared we were?"   120

"Wait a minute. I don't remember any of that."

"And Bozo was fired."

"You're crazy. She was there when I left. You left before me."

"I went back. You weren't there when they fired Bozo."

"What?"   125

"Twice. Once for a year when I was about ten, another for two months when I was fourteen. That's when I ran away."

"You ran away from St. Bonny's?"

"I had to. What do you want? Me dancing in that orchard?"

"Are you sure about Maggie?"

"Of course I'm sure. You've blocked it, Twyla. It happened. Those girls 130 had behavior problems, you know."

"Didn't they, though. But why can't I remember the Maggie thing?"

"Believe me. It happened. And we were there."

"Who did you room with when you went back?" I asked her as if I would know her. The Maggie thing was troubling me.

"Creeps. They tickled themselves in the night."

My ears were itching and I wanted to go home suddenly. This was all 135 very well but she couldn't just comb her hair, wash her face and pretend everything was hunky-dory. After the Howard Johnson's snub. And no apology. Nothing.

"Were you on dope or what that time at Howard Johnson's?" I tried to make my voice sound friendlier than I felt.

"Maybe, a little. I never did drugs much. Why?"

"I don't know; you acted sort of like you didn't want to know me then."

"Oh, Twyla, you know how it was in those days: black—white. You know how everything was."

But I didn't know. I thought it was just the opposite. Busloads of blacks 140 and whites came into Howard Johnson's together. They roamed together then: students, musicians, lovers, protesters. You got to see everything at Howard Johnson's and blacks were very friendly with whites in those days. But sitting there with nothing on my plate but two hard tomato wedges wondering about the melting Klondikes it seemed childish remembering the slight. We went to her car, and with the help of the driver, got my stuff into my station wagon.

"We'll keep in touch this time," she said.

"Sure," I said. "Sure. Give me a call."

"I will," she said, and then just as I was sliding behind the wheel, she leaned into the window. "By the way. Your mother. Did she ever stop dancing?"

I shook my head. "No. Never."

145 Roberta nodded.

"And yours? Did she ever get well?"

She smiled a tiny sad smile. "No. She never did. Look, call me, okay?"

"Okay," I said, but I knew I wouldn't. Roberta had messed up my past somehow with that business about Maggie. I wouldn't forget a thing like that. Would I?

Strife came to us that fall. At least that's what the paper called it. Strife. Racial strife. The word made me think of a bird—a big shrieking bird out of 1,000,000,000 B.C. Flapping its wings and cawing. Its eye with no lid always bearing down on you. All day it screeched and at night it slept on the rooftops. It woke you in the morning and from the *Today* show to the eleven o'clock news it kept you an awful company. I couldn't figure it out from one day to the next. I knew I was supposed to feel something strong, but I didn't know what, and James wasn't any help. Joseph was on the list of kids to be transferred from the junior high school to another one at some far-out-of-the-way place and I thought it was a good thing until I heard it was a bad thing. I mean I didn't know. All the schools seemed dumps to me, and the fact that one was nicer looking didn't hold much weight. But the papers were full of it and then the kids began to get jumpy. In August, mind you. Schools weren't even open yet. I thought Joseph might be frightened to go over there, but he didn't seem scared so I forgot about it, until I found myself driving along Hudson Street out there by the school they were trying to integrate and saw a line of women marching. And who do you suppose was in line, big as life, holding a sign in front of her bigger than her mother's cross? MOTHERS HAVE RIGHTS TOO! it said.

150 I drove on, and then changed my mind. I circled the block, slowed down, and honked my horn.

Roberta looked over and when she saw me she waved. I didn't wave back, but I didn't move either. She handed her sign to another woman and came over to where I was parked.

"Hi."

"What are you doing?"

"Picketing. What's it look like?"

155 "What for?"

"What do you mean. 'What for?' They want to take my kids and send them out of the neighborhood. They don't want to go."
"So what if they go to another school? My boy's being bussed too, and I don't mind. Why should you?"
"It's not about us, Twyla. Me and you. It's about our kids."
"What's more *us* than that?"
"Well, it is a free country."   160
"Not yet, but it will be."
"What the hell does that mean? I'm not doing anything to you."
"You really think that?"
"I know it."
"I wonder what made me think you were different."   165
"I wonder what made me think you were different."
"Look at them," I said. "Just look. Who do they think they are? Swarming all over the place like they own it. And now they think they can decide where my child goes to school. Look at them, Roberta. They're Bozos."
Roberta turned around and looked at the women. Almost all of them were standing still now, waiting. Some were even edging toward us. Roberta looked at me out of some refrigerator behind her eyes. "No, they're not. They're just mothers."
"And what am I? Swiss cheese?"
"I used to curl your hair."   170
"I hated your hands in my hair."
The women were moving. Our faces looked mean to them of course and they looked as though they could not wait to throw themselves in front of a police car, or better yet, into my car and drag me away by my ankles. Now they surrounded my car and gently, gently began to rock it. I swayed back and forth like a sideways yo-yo. Automatically I reached for Roberta, like the old days in the orchard when they saw us watching them and we had to get out of there, and if one of us fell the other pulled her up and if one of us was caught the other stayed to kick and scratch, and neither would leave the other behind. My arm shot out of the car window but no receiving hand was there. Roberta was looking at me sway from side to side in the car and her face was still. My purse slid from the car seat down under the dashboard. The four policemen who had been drinking Tab in their car finally got the message and strolled over, forcing their way through the women. Quietly, firmly they spoke. "Okay, ladies. Back in line or off the streets."
Some of them went away willingly; others had to be urged away from the car doors and the hood. Roberta didn't move. She was looking steadily at me. I was fumbling to turn on the ignition, which wouldn't catch because the gearshift was still in drive. The seats of the car were a mess because the swaying had thrown my grocery coupons all over it and my purse was sprawled on the floor.

"Maybe I am different now, Twyla. But you're not. You're the same little state kid who kicked a poor old black lady when she was down on the ground. You kicked a black lady and you have the nerve to call me a bigot."

175   The coupons were everywhere and the guts of my purse were bunched under the dashboard. What was she saying? Black? Maggie wasn't black.

"She wasn't black," I said.

"Like hell she wasn't, and you kicked her. We both did. You kicked a black lady who couldn't even scream."

"Liar!"

"You're the liar! Why don't you just go on home and leave us alone, huh?"

180   She turned away and I skidded away from the curb.

The next morning I went into the garage and cut the side out of the carton our portable TV had come in. It wasn't nearly big enough, but after a while I had a decent sign: red spray-painted letters on a white background—AND SO DO CHILDREN ****. I meant just to go down to the school and tack it up somewhere so those cows on the picket line across the street could see it, but when I got there, some ten or so others had already assembled—protesting the cows across the street. Police permits and everything. I got in line and we strutted in time on our side while Roberta's group strutted on theirs. That first day we were all dignified, pretending the other side didn't exist. The second day there was name calling and finger gestures. But that was about all. People changed signs from time to time, but Roberta never did and neither did I. Actually my sign didn't make sense without Roberta's. "And so do children what?" one of the women on my side asked me. Have rights, I said, as though it was obvious.

Roberta didn't acknowledge my presence in any way and I got to thinking maybe she didn't know I was there. I began to pace myself in the line, jostling people one minute and lagging behind the next, so Roberta and I could reach the end of our respective lines at the same time and there would be a moment in our turn when we would face each other. Still, I couldn't tell whether she saw me and knew my sign was for her. The next day I went early before we were scheduled to assemble. I waited until she got there before I exposed my new creation. As soon as she hoisted her MOTHERS HAVE RIGHTS TOO I began to wave my new one, which said, HOW WOULD YOU KNOW? I know she saw that one, but I had gotten addicted now. My signs got crazier each day, and the women on my side decided that I was a kook. They couldn't make heads or tails out of my brilliant screaming posters.

I brought a painted sign in queenly red with huge black letters that said, IS YOUR MOTHER WELL? Roberta took her lunch break and didn't come back for the rest of the day or any day after. Two days later I stopped going too and couldn't have been missed because nobody understood my signs anyway.

It was a nasty six weeks. Classes were suspended and Joseph didn't go to anybody's school until October. The children—everybody's children—soon got bored with that extended vacation they thought was going to be so great. They looked at TV until their eyes flattened. I spent a couple of mornings tutoring my son, as the other mothers said we should. Twice I opened a text from last year that he had never turned in. Twice he yawned in my face. Other mothers organized living room sessions so the kids would keep up. None of the kids could concentrate so they drifted back to *The Price Is Right*[6] and *The Brady Bunch*. When the school finally opened there were fights once or twice and some sirens roared through the streets every once in a while. There were a lot of photographers from Albany. And just when ABC was about to send up a news crew, the kids settled down like nothing in the world had happened. Joseph hung my HOW WOULD YOU KNOW? sign in his bedroom. I don't know what became of AND SO DO CHILDREN ****. I think my father-in-law cleaned some fish on it. He was always puttering around in our garage. Each of his five children lived in Newburgh and he acted as though he had five extra homes.

I couldn't help looking for Roberta when Joseph graduated from high school, but I didn't see her. It didn't trouble me much what she had said to me in the car. I mean the kicking part. I know I didn't do that, I couldn't do that. But I was puzzled by her telling me Maggie was black. When I thought about it I actually couldn't be certain. She wasn't pitch-black, I knew, or I would have remembered that. What I remember was the kiddie hat, and the semicircle legs. I tried to reassure myself about the race thing for a long time until it dawned on me that the truth was already there, and Roberta knew it. I didn't kick her; I didn't join in with the gar girls and kick that lady, but I sure did want to. We watched and never tried to help her and never called for help. Maggie was my dancing mother. Deaf, I thought, and dumb. Nobody inside. Nobody who would hear you if you cried in the night. Nobody who could tell you anything important that you could use. Rocking, dancing, swaying as she walked. And when the gar girls pushed her down, and started roughhousing, I knew she wouldn't scream, couldn't—just like me—and I was glad about that.

We decided not to have a tree, because Christmas would be at my mother-in-law's house, so why have a tree at both places? Joseph was at SUNY New Paltz and we had to economize, we said. But at the last minute, I changed my mind. Nothing could be that bad. So I rushed around town looking for a tree, something small but wide. By the time I found a place, it was snowing and very late. I dawdled like it was the most important purchase in the world and the tree man was fed up with me. Finally I chose

185

---

6. Television game show popular in the 1970s. *The Brady Bunch:* television sitcom popular in the 1970s.

one and had it tied onto the trunk of the car. I drove away slowly because the sand trucks were not out yet and the streets could be murder at the beginning of a snowfall. Downtown the streets were wide and rather empty except for a cluster of people coming out of the Newburgh Hotel. The one hotel in town that wasn't built out of cardboard and Plexiglas. A party, probably. The men huddled in the snow were dressed in tails and the women had on furs. Shiny things glittered from underneath their coats. It made me tired to look at them. Tired, tired, tired. On the next corner was a small diner with loops and loops of paper bells in the window. I stopped the car and went in. Just for a cup of coffee and twenty minutes of peace before I went home and tried to finish everything before Christmas Eve.

"Twyla?"

There she was. In a silvery evening gown and dark fur coat. A man and another woman were with her, the man fumbling for change to put in the cigarette machine. The woman was humming and tapping on the counter with her fingernails. They all looked a little bit drunk.

"Well. It's you."

190 "How are you?"

I shrugged. "Pretty good. Frazzled. Christmas and all."

"Regular?" called the woman from the counter.

"Fine," Roberta called back and then, "Wait for me in the car."

She slipped into the booth beside me. "I have to tell you something, Twyla. I made up my mind if I ever saw you again, I'd tell you."

195 "I'd just as soon not hear anything, Roberta. It doesn't matter now, anyway."

"No," she said. "Not about that."

"Don't be long," said the woman. She carried two regulars to go and the man peeled his cigarette pack as they left.

"It's about St. Bonny's and Maggie."

"Oh, please."

200 "Listen to me. I really did think she was black. I didn't make that up. I really thought so. But now I can't be sure. I just remember her as old, so old. And because she couldn't talk—well, you know, I thought she was crazy. She'd been brought up in an institution like my mother was and like I thought I would be too. And you were right. We didn't kick her. It was the gar girls. Only them. But, well, I wanted to. I really wanted them to hurt her. I said we did it, too. You and me, but that's not true. And I don't want you to carry that around. It was just that I wanted to do it so bad that day—wanting to is doing it."

Her eyes were watery from the drinks she'd had, I guess. I know it's that way with me. One glass of wine and I start bawling over the littlest thing.

"We were kids, Roberta."

"Yeah. Yeah. I know, just kids."

"Eight."

"Eight." 205
"And lonely."
"Scared, too."
She wiped her cheeks with the heel of her hand and smiled. "Well, that's all I wanted to say."
I nodded and couldn't think of any way to fill the silence that went from the diner past the paper bells on out into the snow. It was heavy now. I thought I'd better wait for the sand trucks before starting home.
"Thanks, Roberta." 210
"Sure."
"Did I tell you? My mother, she never did stop dancing."
"Yes. You told me. And mine, she never got well." Roberta lifted her hands from the tabletop and covered her face with her palms. When she took them away she really was crying. "Oh shit, Twyla. Shit, shit, shit. What the hell happened to Maggie?"

1983

QUESTIONS

1. At the end of "Recitatif," how does Twyla's and Roberta's exploration of the "truth" of what they had seen at St. Bonny's many years earlier affect your sense of the "truth" of later episodes in the story? Is either Twyla or Roberta more reliable than the other?
2. At what point in the story do you first begin to make assumptions about the race and class of the two main characters, Twyla and Roberta? Why? Do you change your mind later in the story? When and why so—or not? What is the significance of Morrison's choice both to withhold information about the characters' race and class and to have Twyla narrate the story?
3. How does the relationship between Twyla and Roberta evolve over the course of the story?

Authors on Their Work: TONI MORRISON

From "Toni Morrison: The Art of Fiction CXXXIV" (1993)*

MORRISON: [William] Faulkner in *Absalom, Absalom!* spends the entire book tracing race, and you can't find it. No one can see it, even the character who *is* black can't see it. . . . Do you know how hard it is to withhold that kind of information but hinting, pointing

(Continued on next page)

(Continued)

all of the time? And then to reveal it in order to say that it is *not* the point anyway? It is technically just astonishing. As a reader you have been forced to hunt for a drop of black blood that means everything and nothing. The insanity of racism.

• • •

MORRISON: . . . I wrote a story entitled "Recitatif," in which there are two little girls in an orphanage, one white and one black. But the reader doesn't know which is white and which is black. I use class codes, but no racial codes.

INTERVIEWER: Is this meant to confuse the reader?

MORRISON: Well, yes. But to provoke and enlighten. I did that as a lark. What was exciting was to be forced as a writer not to be lazy and rely on obvious codes. Soon as I say, "Black woman . . ." I can rest on or provoke predictable responses, but if I leave it out then I have to talk about her in a complicated way—as a person.

*Elisa Shappell, with Claudia Brodsky Lacour, "Toni Morrison: The Art of Fiction CXXXIV," *Paris Review* 128 (Fall 1993): 82–125.

HA JIN

In Broad Daylight

While I was eating corn cake and jellyfish at lunch, our gate was thrown open and Bare Hips hopped in. His large wooden pistol was stuck partly inside the waist of his blue shorts. "White Cat," he called me by my nickname, "hurry, let's go. They caught Old Whore at her home. They're going to take her through the streets this afternoon."

"Really?" I put down my bowl, which was almost empty, and rushed to the inner room for my undershirt and sandals. "I'll be back in a second."

"Bare Hips, did you say they'll parade Mu Ying today?" I heard Grandma ask in her husky voice.

"Yes, all the kids on our street have left for her house. I came to tell White Cat." He paused. "Hey, White Cat, hurry up!"

5   "Coming," I cried out, still looking for my sandals.

"Good, good!" Grandma said to Bare Hips, while flapping at flies with her large palm-leaf fan. "They should burn the bitch on Heaven Lamp like they did in the old days."

"Come, let's go," Bare Hips said to me the moment I was back. He turned to the door; I picked up my wooden scimitar and followed him.

"Put on your shoes, dear." Grandma stretched out her fan to stop me.

"No time for that, Grandma. I've got to be quick, or I'll miss something and won't be able to tell you the whole story when I get back."

We dashed into the street while Grandma was shouting behind us. 10 "Come back. Take the rubber shoes with you."

We charged toward Mu Ying's home on Eternal Way, waving our weapons above our heads. Grandma was crippled and never came out of our small yard. That was why I had to tell her about what was going on outside. But she knew Mu Ying well, just as all the old women in our town knew Mu well and hated her. Whenever they heard that she had a man in her home again, these women would say, "This time they ought to burn Old Whore on Heaven Lamp."

What they referred to was the old way of punishing an adulteress. Though they had lived in New China for almost two decades, some ancient notions still stuck in their heads. Grandma told me about many of the executions in the old days that she had seen with her own eyes. Officials used to have the criminals of adultery executed in two different ways. They beheaded the man. He was tied to a stake on the platform at the marketplace. At the first blare of horns, a masked headsman ascended the platform holding a broad ax before his chest; at the second blare of horns, the headsman approached the criminal and raised the ax over his head; at the third blare of horns, the head was lopped off and fell to the ground. If the man's family members were waiting beneath the platform, his head would be picked up to be buried together with his body; if no family member was nearby, dogs would carry the head away and chase each other around until they ate up the flesh and returned for the body.

Unlike the man, the woman involved was executed on Heaven Lamp. She was hung naked upside down above a wood fire whose flames could barely touch her scalp. And two men flogged her away with whips made of bulls' penises. Meanwhile she screamed for help and the whole town could hear her. Since the fire merely scorched her head, it took at least half a day for her to stop shrieking and a day and a night to die completely. People used to believe that the way of punishment was justified by Heaven, so the fire was called Heaven Lamp. But that was an old custom; nobody believed they would burn Mu Ying in that way.

Mu's home, a small granite house with cement tiles built a year before, was next to East Wind Inn on the northern side of Eternal Way. When we entered that street, Bare Hips and I couldn't help looking around tremulously, because that area was the territory of the children living there. Two of the fiercest boys, who would kill without having second thoughts, ruled that part of our town. Whenever a boy from another street wandered into Eternal Way, they'd capture him and beat him up. Of course we did the same thing; if we caught one of them in our territory, we'd at least confiscate whatever he had with him: grasshopper cages, slingshots, bottle caps, marbles, cartridge cases, and so on. We would also make him call every one of us "Father" or "Grandfather." But today hundreds of children and grown-ups were pouring into Eternal Way; two dozen urchins on that street surely couldn't hold their ground. Besides, they had already adopted a truce, since they were more eager to see the Red Guards[1] drag Mu Ying out of her den.

15   When we arrived, Mu was being brought out through a large crowd at the front gate. Inside her yard there were three rows of colorful washing hung on iron wires, and there was also a grape trellis. Seven or eight children were in there, plucking off grapes and eating them. Two Red Guards held Mu Ying by the arms, and the other Red Guards, about twenty of them, followed behind. They were all from Dalian City and wore homemade army uniforms. God knew how they came to know that there was a bad woman in our town. Though people hated Mu and called her names, no one would rough her up. Those Red Guards were strangers, so they wouldn't mind doing it.

Surprisingly, Mu looked rather calm; she neither protested nor said a word. The two Red Guards let go of her arms, and she followed them quietly into West Street. We all moved with them. Some children ran several paces ahead to look back at her.

Mu wore a sky-blue dress, which made her different from the other women who always wore jackets and pants suitable for honest work. In fact, even we small boys could tell that she was really handsome, perhaps the best looking woman of her age in our town. Though in her fifties, she didn't have a single gray hair; she was a little plump, but because of her long legs and arms she appeared rather queenly. While most of the women had sallow faces, hers looked white and healthy like fresh milk.

Skipping in front of the crowd, Bare Hips turned around and cried out at her, "Shameless Old Whore!"

She glanced at him, her round eyes flashing; the purple wart beside her left nostril grew darker. Grandma had assured me that Mu's wart was not a beauty-wart but a tear-wart. This meant that her life would be soaked in tears.

20   We knew where we were going, to White Mansion, which was our classroom building, the only two-storied house in the town. As we came to the end of West Street, a short man ran out from a street corner, panting for breath and holding a sickle. He was Meng Su, Mu Ying's husband, who sold bean jelly in summer and sugar-coated haws in winter at the marketplace. He paused in front of the large crowd, as though having forgotten

---

1. National student organization sponsored by Mao Zedong as an instrument to start and develop the Great Proletarian Cultural Revolution (1966–76).

why he had rushed over. He turned his head around to look back; there was nobody behind him. After a short moment he moved close, rather carefully.

"Please let her go," he begged the Red Guards. "Comrade Red Guards, it's all my fault. Please let her go." He put the sickle under his arm and held his hands together before his chest.

"Get out of the way!" commanded a tall young man, who must have been the leader.

"Please don't take her away. It's my fault. I haven't disciplined her well. Please give her a chance to be a new person. I promise, she won't do it again."

The crowd stopped to circle about. "What's your class status?" a square-faced young woman asked in a sharp voice.

"Poor peasant," Meng replied, his small eyes tearful and his cupped ears twitching a little. "Please let her go, sister. Have mercy on us! I'm kneeling down to you if you let her go." Before he was able to fall on his knees, two young men held him back. Tears were rolling down his dark fleshy cheeks, and his gray head began waving about. The sickle was taken away from him.

"Shut up," the tall leader yelled and slapped him across the face. "She's a snake. We traveled a hundred and fifty *li*[2] to come here to wipe out poisonous snakes and worms. If you don't stop interfering, we'll parade you with her together. Do you want to join her?"

Silence. Meng covered his face with his large hands as though feeling dizzy.

A man in the crowd said aloud, "If you can share the bed with her, why can't you share the street?"

Many of the grown-ups laughed. "Take him, take him too!" someone told the Red Guards. Meng looked scared, sobbing quietly.

His wife stared at him without saying a word. Her teeth were clenched; a faint smile passed the corners of her mouth. Meng seemed to wince under her stare. The two Red Guards let his arms go, and he stepped aside, watching his wife and the crowd move toward the school.

Of Meng Su people in our town had different opinions. Some said he was a born cuckold who didn't mind his wife's sleeping with any man as long as she could bring money home. Some believed he was a good-tempered man who had stayed with his wife mainly for their children's sake; they forgot that the three children had grown up long before and were working in big cities far away. Some thought he didn't leave his wife because he had no choice—no woman would marry such a dwarf. Grandma, for some reason, seemed to respect Meng. She told me that Mu Ying had once been raped by a group of Russian soldiers under Northern Bridge and

25

30

2. Approximately 50 miles.

was left on the river bank afterwards. That night her husband sneaked there and carried her back. He looked after her for a whole winter till she recovered. "Old Whore doesn't deserve that good-hearted man," Grandma would say. "She's heartless and knows only how to sell her thighs."

We entered the school's playground where about two hundred people had already gathered. "Hey, White Cat and Bare Hips," Big Shrimp called us, waving his claws. Many boys from our street were there too. We went to join them.

The Red Guards took Mu to the front entrance of the building. Two tables had been placed between the stone lions that crouched on each side of the entrance. On one of the tables stood a tall paper hat with the big black characters on its side: "Down with Old Bitch!"

A young man in glasses raised his bony hand and started to address us, "Folks, we've gathered here today to denounce Mu Ying, who is a demon in this town."

35   "Down with Bourgeois Demons!" a slim woman Red Guard shouted. We raised our fists and repeated the slogan.

"Down with Old Bitch Mu Ying," a middle-aged man cried out with both hands in the air. He was an active revolutionary in our commune. Again we shouted, in louder voices.

The nearsighted man went on, "First, Mu Ying must confess her crime. We must see her attitude toward her own crime. Then we'll make the punishment fit both her crime and her attitude. All right, folks?"

"Right," some voices replied from the crowd.

"Mu Ying," he turned to the criminal, "you must confess everything. It's up to you now."

40   She was forced to stand on a bench. Staying below the steps, we had to raise our heads to see her face.

The questioning began. "Why do you seduce men and paralyze their revolutionary will with your bourgeois poison?" the tall leader asked in a solemn voice.

"I've never invited any man to my home, have I?" she said rather calmly. Her husband was standing at the front of the crowd, listening to her without showing any emotion, as though having lost his mind.

"Then why did they go to your house and not to others' houses?"

"They wanted to sleep with me," she replied.

45   "Shameless!" Several women hissed in the crowd.

"A true whore!"

"Scratch her!"

"Rip apart her filthy mouth!"

"Sisters," she spoke aloud. "All right, it was wrong to sleep with them. But you all know what it feels like when you want a man, don't you? Don't you once in a while have that feeling in your bones?" Contemptuously, she looked at the few withered middle-aged women standing in the front row, then closed her eyes. "Oh, you want that real man to have you in his arms and let him touch every part of your body. For that man alone you want to blossom into a woman, a real woman—"

"Take this, you Fox Spirit!" A stout young fellow struck her on the side 50 with a fist like a sledgehammer. The heavy blow silenced her at once. She held her sides with both hands, gasping for breath.

"You're wrong, Mu Ying," Bare Hips's mother spoke from the front of the crowd, her forefinger pointing upward at Mu. "You have your own man, who doesn't lack an arm or a leg. It's wrong to have others' men and more wrong to pocket their money."

"I have my own man?" Mu glanced at her husband and smirked. She straightened up and said, "My man is nothing. He is no good, I mean in bed. He always comes before I feel anything."

All the adults burst out laughing. "What's that? What's so funny?" Big Shrimp asked Bare Hips.

"You didn't get it?" Bare Hips said impatiently. "You don't know anything about what happens between a man and a woman. It means that whenever she doesn't want him to come close to her he comes. Bad timing."

"It doesn't sound like that," I said. 55

Before we could argue, a large bottle of ink smashed on Mu's head and knocked her off the bench. Prone on the cement terrace, she broke into swearing and blubbering. "Oh, damn your ancestors! Whoever hit me will be childless!" Her left hand was rubbing her head. "Oh Lord of Heaven, they treat their grandma like this!"

"Serves you right!"

"A cheap weasel."

"Even a knife on her throat can't stop her."

"A pig is born to eat slop!" 60

When they put her back up on the bench, she became another person— her shoulders covered with black stains, and a red line trickling down her left temple. The scorching sun was blazing down on her as though all the black parts on her body were about to burn up. Still moaning, she turned her eyes to the spot where her husband had been standing a few minutes before. But he was no longer there.

"Down with Old Whore!" a farmer shouted in the crowd. We all followed him in one voice. She began trembling slightly.

The tall leader said to us, "In order to get rid of her counterrevolutionary airs, first, we're going to cut her hair." With a wave of his hand, he summoned the Red Guards behind him. Four men moved forward and held her down. The square-faced woman raised a large pair of scissors and thrust them into the mass of the dark hair.

"Don't, don't, please. Help, help! I'll do whatever you want me to—"

"Cut!" someone yelled. 65

"Shave her head bald!"

The woman Red Guard applied the scissors skillfully. After four or five strokes, Mu's head looked like the tail of a molting hen. She started blubbering again, her nose running and her teeth chattering.

A breeze came and swept away the fluffy curls from the terrace and scattered them on the sandy ground. It was so hot that some people took out fans, waving them continuously. The crowd stank of sweat.

Wooooo, wooooo, woo, woo. That was the train coming from Sand County at 3:30. It was a freight train, whose young drivers would toot the steam horn whenever they saw a young woman in a field beneath the track.

70   The questioning continued. "How many men have you slept with these years?" the nearsighted man asked.

"Three."

"She's lying," a woman in the crowd cried out.

"I told the truth, sister." She wiped off the tears from her cheeks with the back of her hand.

"Who are they?" the young man asked again. "Tell us more about them."

75   "An officer from the Little Dragon Mountain, and—"

"How many times did he come to your house?"

"I can't remember. Probably twenty."

"What's his name?"

"I don't know. He told me he was a big officer."

80   "Did you take money from him?"

"Yes."

"How much for each time?"

"Twenty *yuan.*"[3]

"How much altogether?"

85   "Probably five hundred."

"Comrades and Revolutionary Masses," the young man turned to us, "how shall we handle this parasite that sucked blood out of a revolutionary officer?"

"Quarter her with four horses!" an old woman yelled.

"Burn her on Heaven Lamp!"

"Poop on her face!" a small fat girl shouted, her hand raised like a tiny pistol with the thumb cocked up and the forefinger aimed at Mu. Some grown-ups snickered.

90   Then a pair of old cloth-shoes, a symbol for a promiscuous woman, were passed to the front. The slim young woman took the shoes and tied them together with the laces. She climbed on a table and was about to hang the shoes around Mu's neck. Mu elbowed the woman aside and knocked the shoes to the ground. The stout young fellow picked up the shoes, and

3. Chinese currency; today, a yuan is worth about 15 cents U.S.

jumped twice to slap her on the cheeks with the soles. "You're so stubborn. Do you want to change yourself or not?" he asked.

"Yes, I do," she replied meekly and dared not stir a bit. Meanwhile the shoes were being hung around her neck.

"Now she looks like a real whore," a woman commented.

"Sing us a tune, Sis," a farmer demanded.

"Comrades," the man in glasses resumed, "let us continue the denunciation." He turned to Mu and asked, "Who are the other men?"

"A farmer from Apple Village." 95

"How many times with him?"

"Once."

"Liar!"

"She's lying!"

"Give her one on the mouth!" 100

The young man raised his hands to calm the crowd down and questioned her again, "How much did you take from him?"

"Eighty *yuan*."

"One night?"

"Yes."

"Tell us more about it. How can you make us believe you?" 105

"That old fellow came to town to sell piglets. He sold a whole litter for eighty, and I got the money."

"Why did you charge him more than the officer?"

"No, I didn't. He did it four times in one night."

Some people were smiling and whispering to each other. A woman said that old man must have been a widower or never married.

"What's his name?" the young man went on. 110

"No idea."

"Was he rich or poor?"

"Poor."

"Comrades," the young man addressed us, "here we have a poor peasant who worked with his sow for a whole year and got only a litter of piglets. That money is the salt and oil money for his family, but this snake swallowed the money with one gulp. What shall we do with her?"

"Kill her!" 115

"Break her skull!"

"Beat the piss out of her!"

A few farmers began to move forward to the steps, waving their fists or rubbing their hands.

"Hold," a woman Red Guard with a huge Chairman Mao badge on her chest spoke in a commanding voice. "The Great Leader has instructed us: 'For our struggle we need words but not force.' Comrades, we can easily wipe her out with words. Force doesn't solve ideological problems." What she said restrained those enraged farmers, who remained in the crowd.

120   *Wooo, woo, wooo, wooooooooooo,* an engine screamed in the south. It was strange, because the drivers of the four o'clock train were a bunch of old men who seldom blew the horn.

"Who is the third man?" the nearsighted man continued to question Mu.

"A Red Guard."

The crowd broke into laughter. Some women asked the Red Guards to give her another bottle of ink. "Mu Ying, you're responsible for your own words," the young man said in a serious voice.

"I told you the truth."

125   "What's his name?"

"I don't know. He led the propaganda team that passed here last month."

"How many times did you sleep with him?"

"Once."

"How much did you make out of him?"

130   "None. That stingy dog wouldn't pay a cent. He said he was the worker who should be paid."

"So you were outsmarted by him?"

Some men in the crowd guffawed. Mu wiped her nose with her thumb, and at once she wore a thick mustache. "I taught him a lesson, though," she said.

"How?"

"I tweaked his ears, gave him a bleeding nose, and kicked him out. I told him never come back."

135   People began talking to each other. Some said that she was a strong woman who knew what was hers. Some said the Red Guard was no good; if you got something you had to pay for it. A few women declared that the rascal deserved such a treatment.

"Dear Revolutionary Masses," the tall leader started to speak. "We all have heard the crime Mu Ying committed. She lured one of our officers and one of our poor peasants into the evil water, and she beat a Red Guard black and blue. Shall we let her go home without punishment or shall we teach her an unforgettable lesson so that she won't do it again?"

"Teach her a lesson!" some voices cried out in unison.

"Then we're going to parade her through the streets."

Two Red Guards pulled Mu off the bench, and another picked up the tall hat. "Brothers and sisters," she begged, "please let me off just for once. Don't, don't! I promise I'll correct my fault. I'll be a new person. Help! Oh, help!"

140   It was no use resisting; within seconds the huge hat was firmly planted on her head. They also hung a big placard between the cloth-shoes lying against her chest. The words on the placard read:

I am a Broken Shoe
My Crime Deserves Death

They put a gong in her hands and ordered her to strike it when she announced the words written on the inner side of the gong.

My pals and I followed the crowd, feeling rather tired. Boys from East Street were wilder; they threw stones at Mu's back. One stone struck the back of her head and blood dropped on her neck. But they were stopped immediately by the Red Guards, because a stone missed Mu and hit a man on the shoulder. Old people, who couldn't follow us, were standing on chairs and windowsills with pipes and towels in their hands. We were going to parade her through every street. It would take several hours to finish the whole thing, as the procession would stop for a short while at every street corner.

Bong, Mu struck the gong and declared, "I am an evil monster."

"Louder!"

Dong, bong—"I have stolen men. I stink for a thousand years."

When we were coming out of the marketplace, Cross Eyes emerged from a narrow lane. He grasped my wrist and Bare Hips's arm and said, "Someone is dead at the train station. Come, let's go there and have a look." The word "dead" at once roused us. We, half a dozen boys, set out running to the train station. 145

The dead man was Meng Su. A crowd had gathered at the railroad a hundred meters east of the station house. A few men were examining the rail that was stained with blood and studded with bits of flesh. One man paced along the darker part of the rail and announced that the train had dragged Meng at least twenty meters.

Beneath the track, Meng's headless body lay in a ditch. One of his feet was missing, and the whitish shinbone stuck out several inches long. There were so many openings on his body that he looked like a large piece of fresh meat on the counter in the butcher's. Beyond him, ten paces away, a big straw hat remained on the ground. We were told that his head was under the hat.

Bare Hips and I went down the slope to have a glimpse at the head. Other boys dared not take a peep. We two looked at each other, asking with our eyes who should raise the straw hat. I held out my wooden scimitar and lifted the rim of the hat a little with the sword. A swarm of bluebottles charged out, droning like provoked wasps. We bent over to peek at the head. Two long teeth pierced through the upper lip. An eyeball was missing. The gray hair was no longer perceivable, as it was covered with mud and dirt. The open mouth filled with purplish mucus. A tiny lizard skipped, sliding away into the grass.

"Oh!" Bare Hips began vomiting. Sorghum gruel mixed with bits of string beans splashed on a yellowish boulder. "Leave it alone, White Cat."

We lingered at the station, listening to different versions of the accident. Some people said that Meng had gotten drunk and dropped asleep on the track. Some said he hadn't slept at all but laughed hysterically 150 walking in the middle of the track toward the coming train. Some said he had not drunk a drop, as he had spoken with tears in his eyes to a few persons he had run into on his way to the station. In any case, he was dead, torn to pieces.

That evening when I was coming home, I heard Mu Ying groaning in the smoky twilight. "Take me home. Oh, help me. Who can help me? Where are you? Why don't you come and carry me home?"

She was lying at the bus stop, alone.

1993

QUESTIONS

1. Which, if any, character seems to be the protagonist of "In Broad Daylight"? Or might its protagonist be the townspeople collectively or even New China as a whole?
2. At one point in the story, the narrator tells us about the "different opinions" of Meng Su held by the townspeople (par. 31). What different opinions about both Meng Su and his wife, Mu Ying, are expressed and enacted by the other characters in the story? Why do the townspeople and the Red Guard seem to behave as they do toward the couple?
3. What do you think happened to Meng Su, and why? What is the effect of Ha Jin's choice not to tell us? What is the significance of Ha Jin's choice to end the story with two very brief paragraphs about Mu Ying?

SUGGESTIONS FOR WRITING

1. Choose any story in this anthology in which a character changes because of the events that occur in the story. Write an essay exploring exactly how, when, and why the character changes.
2. Choose one of the stories in this chapter and write an essay analyzing its handling of character and methods of characterization. Do the story's characters tend to be more flat or round, static or dynamic, highly individualized or nearly indistinguishable? Is indirect or direct characterization more important? How important is each type of evidence listed on the checklist that appears on page 122 in this chapter? Why and how is this treatment of character appropriate to the story?
3. Write an essay comparing how the adult lives and personalities of the two central characters in "Recitatif" are shaped by their experience in the orphanage. Why and how is this experience so traumatic? How does each character understand and cope with this experience over time? In these terms, how are Twyla and Roberta both similar and different, and what role does Maggie play in their efforts to come to terms with their past?
4. Both Maggie in "Recitatif" and Mu Ying in "In Broad Daylight" might be described as *scapegoat* figures (an archetype)—a person or group of people

whom a community harshly punishes, casts out, or even kills in the hope of coming together as a stronger, more united, and purer community. Write an essay exploring the validity of this claim. Why are Maggie and Mu Ying singled out? What do the other characters in each story consciously or unconsciously hope to gain by treating Maggie and Mu Ying as they do? What might these stories suggest about those whom we tend to treat as scapegoats, and why?

4   SETTING

If plot and action are the way fictional works answer the question *What happened?* and characters are the *who*, **setting** is the *where* and *when.* All action in fiction, as in the real world, takes place in a context or setting—a time and place and a social environment or milieu.

TEMPORAL AND PHYSICAL, GENERAL AND PARTICULAR SETTING

The **time**—a work's *temporal setting* or *plot time*—can be roughly the same as that in which the work was written (its *author time*); or it can be much later, as in most science fiction; or much earlier, as in most **historical fiction**. Especially in short stories, which tend not to cover as much time or space as novels do, time may be very restricted, involving only a few hours or even minutes. Yet even in short stories, the action may span years or even decades.

Similarly, the place—a work's *geographical* or *physical setting*—might be limited to a single locale, or it might encompass several disparate ones. Those places might be common and ordinary, unique and extraordinary, or fantastic and even impossible according to the laws of our world (as in modern **fantasy** or **magic realism**).

Even when a story's action takes place in different times and places, we still sometimes refer to its *setting* (singular). By this, we indicate what we might call the entire story's *general setting*—the year(s) and the region, country, or even world in which the story unfolds and which often provides a historical and cultural context for the action. The general setting of Margaret Mitchell's historical novel *Gone with the Wind* (1936), for instance, is the Civil War–era South. But this work, like many, has many *particular settings*; it opens, for instance, on an April morning on the porch of a north Georgia mansion called Tara, where Scarlett O'Hara flirts with two beaus and ignores their talk of a possible war to come. To fully appreciate the nature and role of setting, we thus need to consider the specific time of day and year as well as the specific locales in which the action unfolds.

Sometimes stories merely offer hints about setting; others describe setting in great sensory detail. Especially in the latter case, we might be tempted to skim through what seems like mere "scenery" or "background information" to find out what happens next or how things turn out. But in good fiction, setting always functions as an integral part of the whole.

FUNCTIONS OF SETTING

Fiction often relies on setting to establish mood, situation, and character. The first sentence of Edgar Allan Poe's short story "The Fall of the House of Usher," for example, quickly sets the tone:

> During the whole of a dull, dark, and soundless day in the autumn of the year, when the clouds hung oppressively low in the heavens, I had been passing alone, on horseback, through a singularly dreary tract of country; and at length found myself, as the shades of the evening drew on, within view of the melancholy House of Usher.

This sentence aims to instill in the reader the same fear, "melancholy," and "sense of insufferable gloom" the narrator feels. With it, Poe prepares the reader emotionally, as well as mentally, for the sad and eerie tale that is about to unfold. He also generates suspense and certain expectations about just what might happen, as well as empathy with the narrator-protagonist.

Here, as in other fiction, specific details prove crucial to setting's emotional effect and meaning precisely because, as Poe's narrator himself observes,

> there *are* combinations of very simple natural objects which have the power of thus affecting us. . . . A mere different arrangement of the particulars of the scene, of the details of the picture, would be sufficient to modify, or perhaps to annihilate its capacity for sorrowful impression.

In addition to creating such emotional impressions, setting can reveal or even shape a character's personality, outlook, and values; it can occasionally be an actor in the plot; and it often prompts characters' actions. (Who might you become and what might you do if you lived in the isolated, gloomy House of Usher?) To gloss over descriptions of setting would thus mean not only missing much of the pleasure fiction affords, but also potentially misreading its meanings. Setting is one of the many ways we learn about characters and the chief means by which characters and plots take on a larger historical, social, or even universal significance.

VAGUE AND VIVID SETTINGS

Not all stories, of course, rely so heavily on setting as Poe's does. In some individual works and in some subgenres, the general time, place, or both may be so vague as to seem, at first glance, unimportant. Many folktales and fairy tales take place in **archetypal** settings: "A long time ago," in "the forest" or "a village" or "a cottage," "in a land far, far away." By offering little, if any, specific information about their settings—neither locating the "forest" or "village" or faraway land in a place we can find on a map or a time we can locate on a calendar or clock, nor describing it in any detail—these works implicitly urge us to see the conflicts and aspects of human experience they depict (death, grief, a mother's relationship to her child, the danger and incomprehensibility of the unknown) as timeless and universal. Here, the very lack of attention to setting paradoxically turns out to be all-important.

At the opposite extreme are works and genres of fiction in which setting generates the conflicts, defines the characters, and gives the story purpose and meaning—so much so that there would be little, if any, story left if all the details about setting were removed or the characters and plot somehow transported to a different time, place, and social milieu. Without their settings, what would remain of historical novels like *Gone with the Wind* or Nathaniel Hawthorne's *The Scarlet Letter* (1850)? A more extreme example is Italo Calvino's fantasy novel *Invisible Cities* (1972), which consists almost entirely of a series of descriptions of impossible, yet often hauntingly beautiful places like the following one.

ITALO CALVINO

From *Invisible Cities*

What makes Argia different from other cities is that it has earth instead of air. The streets are completely filled with dirt, clay packs the rooms to the ceiling, on every stair another stairway is set in negative, over the roofs of the houses hang layers of rocky terrain like skies with clouds. We do not know if the inhabitants can move about the city, widening the worm tunnels and the crevices where roots twist: the dampness destroys people's bodies and they have scant strength; everyone is better off remaining still, prone; anyway, it is dark.

From up here, nothing of Argia can be seen; some say, "It's down below there," and we can only believe them. The place is deserted. At night, putting your ear to the ground, you can sometimes hear a door slam.

· · ·

Most fiction, of course, occupies a middle ground between the extremes of Calvino's novel or historical fiction (with their highly particularized settings) versus folklore (with its generic, archetypal setting). Though all fiction may ultimately deal with some types of people, aspects of human experience, and conflicts that can crop up in some form or fashion anywhere or at any time, much fiction also draws our attention to the way people, their experience, and their conflicts are twisted into a particular "form and fashion" by specific contexts.

Analyzing Descriptions of Setting: An Example and an Exercise

The novel *Gone with the Wind*, like the movie, opens on the front porch of Tara, where a carefree Scarlett O'Hara flirts with the Tarleton twins and studiously ignores the first rumors of war. Then, the narrator pulls back to show us, with great detail, both the time of year and the landscape in which that particular place is situated. After you read the following description, write a paragraph or two that draws on details from the passage to explain the feelings and impressions it conjures up, the functions it might serve at the beginning of the novel, and the way it achieves its effects. How, for example, might this description **foreshadow** and even help explain subsequent events? Why else might the novel need all this detail?

Spring had come early that year, with warm quick rains and sudden frothing of pink peach blossoms and dogwood dappling with white stars the dark river swamp and far-off hills. Already the plowing was nearly finished, and the bloody glory of the sunset colored the fresh-cut furrows of red Georgia clay to even redder hues. The moist hungry earth, waiting upturned for the cotton seeds, showed pinkish on the sandy tops of furrows, vermilion and scarlet and maroon where shadows lay along the sides of the trenches. The whitewashed brick plantation house seemed an island set in a wild red sea, a sea of spiraling, curving, crescent billows petrified suddenly at the moment when the pink-tipped waves were breaking into surf. For here were no long, straight furrows, such as could be seen in the yellow clay fields of the flat middle Georgia country or in the lush black earth of the coastal plantations. The rolling foothill country of north Georgia was plowed in a million curves to keep the rich earth from washing down into the river bottoms.

It was a savagely red land, blood-colored after rains, brick dust in droughts, the best cotton land in the world. It was a pleasant land of white houses, peaceful plowed fields and sluggish yellow rivers, but a land of contrasts, of bright sun glare and densest shade. The plantation clearings and miles of cotton fields smiled up to a warm sun, placid, complacent. At their edges rose the virgin forests, dark and cool even in the hottest noons, mysterious, a little sinister, the soughing pines seem to wait with an age-old patience, to threaten with soft sighs: "Be careful! Be careful! We had you once. We can take you back again."

This early scene from the novel *Gone with the Wind* (1939) takes place on the
porch of a mansion in Georgia, just before the start of the Civil War.

TRADITIONAL EXPECTATIONS OF TIME AND PLACE

The effects and meanings evoked by setting depend on our traditional
associations with, and often unconscious assumptions about, particular
times, places, and even such factors as weather conditions—autumn, evening, a deserted country road, a house grand enough to have a name, a sky
full of low and lowering clouds (to refer back to the Poe example).

Traditional associations derive, in part, from literature and myth, and
some are culturally specific. (To someone unfamiliar with the Old Testament, an apple orchard would simply be an apple orchard, without any
suggestion of evil or sin. Likewise, to someone who knows little about the
Civil War, a big white house in the middle of a cotton field might seem
like nothing more than a very beautiful place full of lucky, wealthy, happy
people.) These associations also come from our learning, our experience,

Connecting Setting, Point of View, and Character:
An Example and an Exercise

For the purpose of analysis, we distinguish setting from other elements such as character, plot, point of view, and language. Perhaps paradoxically, we need to do so precisely in order to understand how these elements work together. The following passage from Alice Randall's controversial novel *The Wind Done Gone* (2002), for example, paints a dramatically different picture of the antebellum South than do earlier novels and films like *Gone with the Wind*, in part because it looks at that time and place from a different point of view.

After you read the passage, write a paragraph or two about how its effect and meaning are shaped by point of view and **figurative language** or **imagery**. What might the passage tell us about Randall's narrator? How does the passage encourage us to rethink traditional views of the antebellum South?

Alternatively, compare this passage to the one from Mitchell's *Gone with the Wind* in this chapter's first "Example and Exercise," focusing on how each passage differently depicts the same time and place and how each passage's effect and meaning derive from its point of view and from its distinctive use of somewhat similar language and images.

Mammy worked from can't-see in the morning to can't-see at night, in that great whitewashed wide-columned house surrounded by curvy furrowed fields. The mud, the dirt, was so red, when you looked at the cotton blooming in a field it brought to mind a sleeping gown after childbirth—all soft white cotton and blood.

If it was mine to be able to paint pictures, if I possessed the gift of painting, I would paint a cotton gown balled up and thrown into a corner waiting to be washed, and I would call it "Georgia."

our own specific social and historical context, and even our primal instincts and physical condition as human beings. Almost all of us are more vulnerable in the dark and in inclement weather. And people do behave differently and expect different things to happen in different times and places—on a Saturday versus a Sunday versus a Monday, during spring break versus mid-semester or mid-week, at a posh beach resort we are just visiting versus the grocery store in our own neighborhood, and so on.

Often, however, authors draw on such associations precisely in order to reverse and question them. John Updike has said that he was initially inspired to write "A & P" ("Reading More Fiction") because a suburban grocery store seemed just the sort of mundane place no reader would expect either heroism or a story to take place. ("Why don't you ever read a story set in an A & P?" he reportedly asked his wife.) By reversing expectations in this way, stories not only deepen their emotional effect but also encourage us to rethink our assumptions about particular times and places and the people who inhabit them.

. . .

Setting is key to each of the three stories gathered in this chapter—Anton Chekhov's "The Lady with the Dog," Katherine Anne Porter's "Flowering Judas," and Amy Tan's "A Pair of Tickets." The settings in these stories range from the U.S. and Mexico to Soviet Russia and China; from the late-nineteenth century to the late-twentieth; from coastal resorts to crowded, cosmopolitan cities. The stories take place in just about every season and all kinds of weather, but regardless of the specific setting each paints a revealing portrait of a time and place. Just as our own memories of important experiences include complex impressions of when and where they occurred—the weather, the shape of the room, the music that was playing, even the fashions or the events in the news back then—so stories rely on setting to evoke emotion and generate meaning.

Questions about Setting

General Setting

1. What is the general temporal and geographical setting of this work of fiction? How do you know?
2. How important does the general setting seem to be? In what ways is it important? What about the plot and characters would remain the same if they were magically transported to a different setting? What wouldn't? For example, how does the setting
   • create or shape conflict?
   • affect characters' personalities, outlooks, and actions?

(Continued on next page)

(Continued)

- shape our impressions of who the characters are and what they represent?
- establish mood?

Particular Settings

3. Does all the action occur in one time and place, or in more than one? If the latter, what are those times and places?
4. What patterns do you notice regarding where and when things happen? Which characters are associated with each setting? How do different characters relate to the same setting? When, how, and why do characters move from one setting to another? Are there significant deviations from these patterns?
5. Are particular settings described in detail, or merely sketched? If the former, what seems significant about the details? How might they establish mood, reveal character, and affect individual characters and the characters' interactions with one another?

ANTON CHEKHOV

The Lady with the Dog [1]

I

It was said that a new person had appeared on the sea-front: a lady with a little dog. Dmitri Dmitritch Gurov, who had by then been a fortnight at Yalta,[2] and so was fairly at home there, had begun to take an interest in new arrivals. Sitting in Verney's pavilion, he saw, walking on the sea-front, a fair-haired young lady of medium height, wearing a *béret*; a white Pomeranian dog was running behind her.

And afterwards he met her in the public gardens and in the square several times a day. She was walking alone, always wearing the same *béret*, and always with the same white dog; no one knew who she was, and every one called her simply "the lady with the dog."

"If she is here alone without a husband or friends, it wouldn't be amiss to make her acquaintance," Gurov reflected.

He was under forty, but he had a daughter already twelve years old, and two sons at school. He had been married young, when he was a student in his second year, and by now his wife seemed half as old again as he. She

1. Translated by Constance Garnett.   2. Russian city on the Black Sea; a resort.

was a tall, erect woman with dark eyebrows, staid and dignified, and, as she said of herself, intellectual. She read a great deal, used phonetic spelling, called her husband, not Dmitri, but Dimitri, and he secretly considered her unintelligent, narrow, inelegant, was afraid of her, and did not like to be at home. He had begun being unfaithful to her long ago—had been unfaithful to her often, and, probably on that account, almost always spoke ill of women, and when they were talked about in his presence, used to call them "the lower race."

5   It seemed to him that he had been so schooled by bitter experience that he might call them what he liked, and yet he could not get on for two days together without "the lower race." In the society of men he was bored and not himself, with them he was cold and uncommunicative; but when he was in the company of women he felt free, and knew what to say to them and how to behave; and he was at ease with them even when he was silent. In his appearance, in his character, in his whole nature, there was something attractive and elusive which allured women and disposed them in his favour; he knew that, and some force seemed to draw him, too, to them.

Experience often repeated, truly bitter experience, had taught him long ago that with decent people, especially Moscow people—always slow to move and irresolute—every intimacy, which at first so agreeably diversifies life and appears a light and charming adventure, inevitably grows into a regular problem of extreme intricacy, and in the long run the situation becomes unbearable. But at every fresh meeting with an interesting woman this experience seemed to slip out of his memory, and he was eager for life, and everything seemed simple and amusing.

One evening he was dining in the gardens, and the lady in the *béret* came up slowly to take the next table. Her expression, her gait, her dress, and the way she did her hair told him that she was a lady, that she was married, that she was in Yalta for the first time and alone, and that she was dull there. . . . The stories told of the immorality in such places as Yalta are to a great extent untrue; he despised them, and knew that such stories were for the most part made up by persons who would themselves have been glad to sin if they had been able; but when the lady sat down at the next table three paces from him, he remembered these tales of easy conquests, of trips to the mountains, and the tempting thought of a swift, fleeting love affair, a romance with an unknown woman, whose name he did not know, suddenly took possession of him.

He beckoned coaxingly to the Pomeranian, and when the dog came up to him he shook his finger at it. The Pomeranian growled: Gurov shook his finger at it again.

The lady looked at him and at once dropped her eyes.

10   "He doesn't bite," she said, and blushed.

"May I give him a bone?" he asked; and when she nodded he asked courteously, "Have you been long in Yalta?"

"Five days."

"And I have already dragged out a fortnight here."

There was a brief silence.

"Time goes fast, and yet it is so dull here!" she said, not looking at him. 15
"That's only the fashion to say it is dull here. A provincial will live in Belyov or Zhidra and not be dull, and when he comes here it's 'Oh, the dulness! Oh, the dust!' One would think he came from Grenada."[3]

She laughed. Then both continued eating in silence, like strangers, but after dinner they walked side by side; and there sprang up between them the light jesting conversation of people who are free and satisfied, to whom it does not matter where they go or what they talk about. They walked and talked of the strange light on the sea: the water was of a soft warm lilac hue, and there was a golden streak from the moon upon it. They talked of how sultry it was after a hot day. Gurov told her that he came from Moscow, that he had taken his degree in Arts, but had a post in a bank; that he had trained as an opera-singer, but had given it up, that he owned two houses in Moscow. . . . And from her he learnt that she had grown up in Petersburg, but had lived in S—since her marriage two years before, that she was staying another month in Yalta, and that her husband, who needed a holiday too, might perhaps come and fetch her. She was not sure whether her husband had a post in a Crown Department or under the Provincial Council[4]—and was amused by her own ignorance. And Gurov learnt, too, that she was called Anna Sergeyevna.

Afterwards he thought about her in his room at the hotel—thought she would certainly meet him next day; it would be sure to happen. As he got into bed he thought how lately she had been a girl at school, doing lessons like his own daughter; he recalled the diffidence, the angularity, that was still manifest in her laugh and her manner of talking with a stranger. This must have been the first time in her life she had been alone in surroundings in which she was followed, looked at, and spoken to merely from a secret motive which she could hardly fail to guess. He recalled her slender, delicate neck, her lovely grey eyes.

"There's something pathetic about her, anyway," he thought, and fell asleep.

II

A week had passed since they had made acquaintance. It was a holiday. It 20 was sultry indoors, while in the street the wind whirled the dust round and round, and blew people's hats off. It was a thirsty day, and Gurov often

---

3. Romantic city in southern Spain.
4. That is, a post in a national department, appointed by the czar, or a post in an elective local council.

went into the pavilion, and pressed Anna Sergeyevna to have syrup and water or an ice. One did not know what to do with oneself.

In the evening when the wind had dropped a little, they went out on the groyne to see the steamer come in. There were a great many people walking about the harbour; they had gathered to welcome some one, bringing bouquets. And two peculiarities of a well-dressed Yalta crowd were very conspicuous: the elderly ladies were dressed like young ones, and there were great numbers of generals.

Owing to the roughness of the sea, the steamer arrived late, after the sun had set, and it was a long time turning about before it reached the groyne. Anna Sergeyevna looked through her lorgnette at the steamer and the passengers as though looking for acquaintances, and when she turned to Gurov her eyes were shining. She talked a great deal and asked disconnected questions, forgetting next moment what she had asked; then she dropped her lorgnette in the crush.

The festive crowd began to disperse; it was too dark to see people's faces. The wind had completely dropped, but Gurov and Anna Sergeyevna still stood as though waiting to see some one else come from the steamer. Anna Sergeyevna was silent now, and sniffed the flowers without looking at Gurov.

"The weather is better this evening," he said. "Where shall we go now? Shall we drive somewhere?"

25   She made no answer.

Then he looked at her intently, and all at once put his arm round her and kissed her on the lips, and breathed in the moisture and the fragrance of the flowers; and he immediately looked round him, anxiously wondering whether any one had seen them.

"Let us go to your hotel," he said softly. And both walked quickly.

The room was close and smelt of the scent she had bought at the Japanese shop. Gurov looked at her and thought: "What different people one meets in the world!" From the past he preserved memories of careless, good-natured women, who loved cheerfully and were grateful to him for the happiness he gave them, however brief it might be; and of women like his wife who loved without any genuine feeling, with superfluous phrases, affectedly, hysterically, with an expression that suggested that it was not love nor passion, but something more significant; and of two or three others, very beautiful, cold women, on whose faces he had caught a glimpse of a rapacious expression—an obstinate desire to snatch from life more than it could give, and these were capricious, unreflecting, domineering, unintelligent women not in their first youth, and when Gurov grew cold to them their beauty excited his hatred, and the lace on their linen seemed to him like scales.

But in this case there was still the diffidence, the angularity of inexperienced youth, an awkward feeling; and there was a sense of consternation as though some one had suddenly knocked at the door. The attitude of Anna Sergeyevna—"the lady with the dog"—to what had happened was somehow peculiar, very grave, as though it were her fall—so it seemed, and it was strange and inappropriate. Her face dropped and faded, and on both sides of it her long hair hung down mournfully; she mused in a dejected attitude like "the woman who was a sinner" in an old-fashioned picture.

"It's wrong," she said. "You will be the first to despise me now."   30

There was a water-melon on the table. Gurov cut himself a slice and began eating it without haste. There followed at least half an hour of silence.

Anna Sergeyevna was touching; there was about her the purity of a good, simple woman who had seen little of life. The solitary candle burning on the table threw a faint light on her face, yet it was clear that she was very unhappy.

"How could I despise you?" asked Gurov. "You don't know what you are saying."

"God forgive me," she said, and her eyes filled with tears. "It's awful."

"You seem to feel you need to be forgiven."   35

"Forgiven? No. I am a bad, low woman; I despise myself and don't attempt to justify myself. It's not my husband but myself I have deceived. And not only just now; I have been deceiving myself for a long time. My husband may be a good, honest man, but he is a flunkey! I don't know what he does there, what his work is, but I know he is a flunkey! I was twenty when I was married to him. I have been tormented by curiosity; I wanted something better. 'There must be a different sort of life,' I said to myself. I wanted to live! To live, to live! . . . I was fired by curiosity . . . you don't understand it, but, I swear to God, I could not control myself; something happened to me: I could not be restrained. I told my husband I was ill, and came here. . . . And here I have been walking about as though I were dazed, like a mad creature; . . . and now I have become a vulgar, contemptible woman whom any one may despise."

Gurov felt bored already, listening to her. He was irritated by the naïve tone, by this remorse, so unexpected and inopportune; but for the tears in her eyes, he might have thought she was jesting or playing a part.

"I don't understand," he said softly. "What is it you want?"

She hid her face on his breast and pressed close to him.

"Believe me, believe me, I beseech you . . ." she said. "I love a pure, honest   40 life, and sin is loathsome to me. I don't know what I am doing. Simple people say: 'The Evil One has beguiled me.' And I may say of myself now that the Evil One has beguiled me."

"Hush, hush! . . ." he muttered.

He looked at her fixed, scared eyes, kissed her, talked softly and affectionately, and by degrees she was comforted, and her gaiety returned; they both began laughing.

Afterwards when they went out there was not a soul on the sea-front. The town with its cypresses had quite a deathlike air, but the sea still broke noisily on the shore; a single barge was rocking on the waves, and a lantern was blinking sleepily on it.

They found a cab and drove to Oreanda.

45 "I found out your surname in the hall just now: it was written on the board—Von Diderits," said Gurov. "Is your husband a German?"

"No; I believe his grandfather was a German, but he is an Orthodox Russian himself."

At Oreanda they sat on a seat not far from the church, looked down at the sea, and were silent. Yalta was hardly visible through the morning mist; white clouds stood motionless on the mountain-tops. The leaves did not stir on the trees, grasshoppers chirruped, and the monotonous hollow sound of the sea rising up from below, spoke of the peace, of the eternal sleep awaiting us. So it must have sounded when there was no Yalta, no Oreanda here; so it sounds now, and it will sound as indifferently and monotonously when we are all no more. And in this constancy, in this complete indifference to the life and death of each of us, there lies hid, perhaps, a pledge of our eternal salvation, of the unceasing movement of life upon earth, of unceasing progress towards perfection. Sitting beside a young woman who in the dawn seemed so lovely, soothed and spellbound in these magical surroundings—the sea, mountains, clouds, the open sky— Gurov thought how in reality everything is beautiful in this world when one reflects: everything except what we think or do ourselves when we forget our human dignity and the higher aims of our existence.

A man walked up to them—probably a keeper—looked at them and walked away. And this detail seemed mysterious and beautiful, too. They saw a steamer come from Theodosia, with its lights out in the glow of dawn.

"There is dew on the grass," said Anna Sergeyevna, after a silence.

50 "Yes. It's time to go home."

They went back to the town.

Then they met every day at twelve o'clock on the sea-front, lunched and dined together, went for walks, admired the sea. She complained that she slept badly, that her heart throbbed violently; asked the same questions, troubled now by jealousy and now by the fear that he did not respect her sufficiently. And often in the square or gardens, when there was no one near them, he suddenly drew her to him and kissed her passionately. Complete idleness, these kisses in broad daylight while he looked round in dread of some one's seeing them, the heat, the smell of the sea, and the continual passing to and fro before him of idle, well-dressed, well-fed people, made a new man of him; he told Anna Sergeyevna how beautiful she was, how fascinating. He was impatiently passionate, he would not move a step away from her, while she was often pensive and continually urged him to confess that he did not respect her, did not love her in the least, and thought of her as nothing but a common woman. Rather late almost every evening they drove somewhere out of town, to Oreanda or to the waterfall; and the expedition was always a success, the scenery invariably impressed them as grand and beautiful.

They were expecting her husband to come, but a letter came from him, saying that there was something wrong with his eyes, and he entreated his wife to come home as quickly as possible. Anna Sergeyevna made haste to go.

"It's a good thing I am going away," she said to Gurov. "It's the finger of destiny!"

She went by coach and he went with her. They were driving the whole day. When she had got into a compartment of the express, and when the second bell had rung, she said:

"Let me look at you once more . . . look at you once again. That's right."

She did not shed tears, but was so sad that she seemed ill, and her face was quivering.

"I shall remember you . . . think of you," she said. "God be with you; be happy. Don't remember evil against me. We are parting forever—it must be so, for we ought never to have met. Well, God be with you."

The train moved off rapidly, its lights soon vanished from sight, and a minute later there was no sound of it, as though everything had conspired together to end as quickly as possible that sweet delirium, that madness. Left alone on the platform, and gazing into the dark distance, Gurov listened to the chirrup of the grasshoppers and the hum of the telegraph wires, feeling as though he had only just waked up. And he thought, musing, that there had been another episode or adventure in his life, and it, too, was at an end, and nothing was left of it but a memory. . . . He was moved, sad, and conscious of a slight remorse. This young woman whom he would never meet again had not been happy with him; he was genuinely warm and affectionate with her, but yet in his manner, his tone, and his caresses there had been a shade of light irony, the coarse condescension of a happy man who was, besides, almost twice her age. All the time she had called him kind, exceptional, lofty; obviously he had seemed to her different from what he really was, so he had unintentionally deceived her. . . .

Here at the station was already a scent of autumn; it was a cold evening. 60

"It's time for me to go north," thought Gurov as he left the platform. "High time!"

III

At home in Moscow everything was in its winter routine; the stoves were heated, and in the morning it was still dark when the children were having breakfast and getting ready for school, and the nurse would light the lamp for a short time. The frosts had begun already. When the first snow has fallen, on the first day of sledge-driving it is pleasant to see the white earth, the white roofs, to draw soft, delicious breath, and the season brings back the days of one's youth. The old limes and birches, white with hoar-frost, have a good-natured expression; they are nearer to one's heart than cypresses and palms, and near them one doesn't want to be thinking of the sea and the mountains.

Gurov was Moscow born; he arrived in Moscow on a fine frosty day, and when he put on his fur coat and warm gloves, and walked along Petrovka, and when on Saturday evening he heard the ringing of the bells, his recent trip and the places he had seen lost all charm for him. Little by little he became absorbed in Moscow life, greedily read three newspapers a day, and declared he did not read the Moscow papers on principle! He already felt a longing to go to restaurants, clubs, dinner-parties, anniversary celebrations, and he felt flattered at entertaining distinguished lawyers and artists, and at playing cards with a professor at the doctors' club. He could already eat a whole plateful of salt fish and cabbage. . . .

In another month, he fancied, the image of Anna Sergeyevna would be shrouded in a mist in his memory, and only from time to time would visit him in his dreams with a touching smile as others did. But more than a month passed, real winter had come, and everything was still clear in his memory as though he had parted with Anna Sergeyevna only the day before. And his memories glowed more and more vividly. When in the evening stillness he heard from his study the voices of his children, preparing their lessons, or when he listened to a song or the organ at the restaurant, or the storm howled in the chimney, suddenly everything would rise up in his memory: what had happened on the groyne, and the early morning with the mist on the mountains, and the steamer coming from Theodosia, and the kisses. He would pace a long time about his room, remembering it all and smiling; then his memories passed into dreams, and in his fancy the past was mingled with what was to come. Anna Sergeyevna did not visit him in dreams, but followed him about everywhere like a shadow and haunted him. When he shut his eyes he saw her as though she were living before him, and she seemed to him lovelier, younger, tenderer than she was; and he imagined himself finer than he had been in Yalta. In the evenings she peeped out at him from the bookcase, from the fireplace, from the corner—he heard her breathing, the caressing rustle of her dress. In the street he watched the women, looking for some one like her.

65   He was tormented by an intense desire to confide his memories to some one. But in his home it was impossible to talk of his love, and he had no one outside; he could not talk to his tenants nor to any one at the bank. And what had he to talk of? Had he been in love, then? Had there been anything beautiful, poetical, or edifying or simply interesting in his relations with Anna Sergeyevna? And there was nothing for him but to talk vaguely of love, of woman, and no one guessed what it meant; only his wife

twitched her black eyebrows, and said: "The part of a lady-killer does not suit you at all, Dimitri."

One evening, coming out of the doctors' club with an official with whom he had been playing cards, he could not resist saying:

"If only you knew what a fascinating woman I made the acquaintance of in Yalta!"

The official got into his sledge and was driving away, but turned suddenly and shouted:

"Dmitri Dmitritch!"

"What?"

70

"You were right this evening: the sturgeon was a bit too strong!"

These words, so ordinary, for some reason moved Gurov to indignation, and struck him as degrading and unclean. What savage manners, what people! What senseless nights, what uninteresting, uneventful days! The rage for card-playing, the gluttony, the drunkenness, the continual talk always about the same thing. Useless pursuits and conversations always about the same things absorb the better part of one's time, the better part of one's strength, and in the end there is left a life grovelling and curtailed, worthless and trivial, and there is no escaping or getting away from it—just as though one were in a madhouse or a prison.

Gurov did not sleep all night, and was filled with indignation. And he had a headache all next day. And the next night he slept badly; he sat up in bed, thinking, or paced up and down his room. He was sick of his children, sick of the bank; he had no desire to go anywhere or to talk of anything.

In the holidays in December he prepared for a journey, and told his wife he was going to Petersburg to do something in the interests of a young friend—and he set off for S—. What for? He did not very well know himself. He wanted to see Anna Sergeyevna and to talk with her—to arrange a meeting, if possible.

He reached S—in the morning, and took the best room at the hotel, in 75 which the floor was covered with grey army cloth, and on the table was an inkstand, grey with dust and adorned with a figure on horseback, with its hat in its hand and its head broken off. The hotel porter gave him the necessary information; Von Diderits lived in a house of his own in Old Gontcharny Street—it was not far from the hotel: he was rich and lived in good style, and had his own horses; every one in the town knew him. The porter pronounced the name "Dridirits."

Gurov went without haste to Old Gontcharny Street and found the house. Just opposite the house stretched a long grey fence adorned with nails.

"One would run away from a fence like that," thought Gurov, looking from the fence to the windows of the house and back again.

He considered: to-day was a holiday, and the husband would probably be at home. And in any case it would be tactless to go into the house and upset her. If he were to send her a note it might fall into her husband's hands, and then it might ruin everything. The best thing was to trust to chance. And he kept walking up and down the street by the fence, waiting for the chance. He saw a beggar go in at the gate and dogs fly at him; then an hour later he heard a piano, and the sounds were faint and indistinct. Probably it was Anna Sergeyevna playing. The front door suddenly opened, and an old woman came out, followed by the familiar white Pomeranian. Gurov was on the point of calling to the dog, but his heart began beating violently, and in his excitement he could not remember the dog's name.

He walked up and down, and loathed the grey fence more and more, and by now he thought irritably that Anna Sergeyevna had forgotten him, and was perhaps already amusing herself with some one else, and that that was very natural in a young woman who had nothing to look at from morning till night but that confounded fence. He went back to his hotel room and sat for a long while on the sofa, not knowing what to do, then he had dinner and a long nap.

80   "How stupid and worrying it is!" he thought when he woke and looked at the dark windows: it was already evening. "Here I've had a good sleep for some reason. What shall I do in the night?"

He sat on the bed, which was covered by a cheap grey blanket, such as one sees in hospitals, and he taunted himself in his vexation:

"So much for the lady with the dog . . . so much for the adventure. . . . You're in a nice fix. . . ."

That morning at the station a poster in large letters had caught his eye. "The Geisha"[5] was to be performed for the first time. He thought of this and went to the theatre.

"It's quite possible she may go to the first performance," he thought.

85   The theatre was full. As in all provincial theatres, there was a fog above the chandelier, the gallery was noisy and restless; in the front row the local dandies were standing up before the beginning of the performance, with their hands behind them; in the Governor's box the Governor's daughter, wearing a boa, was sitting in the front seat, while the Governor himself lurked modestly behind the curtain with only his hands visible; the orchestra was a long time tuning up; the stage curtain swayed. All the time the audience were coming in and taking their seats Gurov looked at them eagerly.

Anna Sergeyevna, too, came in. She sat down in the third row, and when Gurov looked at her his heart contracted, and he understood clearly that for him there was in the whole world no creature so near, so precious, and so important to him; she, this little woman, in no way remarkable, lost in a provincial crowd, with a vulgar lorgnette in her hand, filled his whole

5. Operetta by Sidney Jones (1861–1946) that toured eastern Europe in 1898–99.

life now, was his sorrow and his joy, the one happiness that he now desired for himself, and to the sounds of the inferior orchestra, of the wretched provincial violins, he thought how lovely she was. He thought and dreamed.

A young man with small side-whiskers, tall and stooping, came in with Anna Sergeyevna and sat down beside her; he bent his head at every step and seemed to be continually bowing. Most likely this was the husband whom at Yalta, in a rush of bitter feeling, she had called a flunkey. And there really was in his long figure, his side-whiskers, and the small bald patch on his head, something of the flunkey's obsequiousness; his smile was sugary, and in his buttonhole there was some badge of distinction like the number on a waiter.

During the first interval the husband went away to smoke; she remained alone in her stall. Gurov, who was sitting in the stalls, too, went up to her and said in a trembling voice, with a forced smile:

"Good-evening."

She glanced at him and turned pale, then glanced again with horror, 90 unable to believe her eyes, and tightly gripped the fan and the lorgnette in her hands, evidently struggling with herself not to faint. Both were silent. She was sitting, he was standing, frightened by her confusion and not venturing to sit down beside her. The violins and the flute began tuning up. He felt suddenly frightened; it seemed as though all the people in the boxes were looking at them. She got up and went quickly to the door; he followed her, and both walked senselessly along passages, and up and down stairs, and figures in legal, scholastic, and civil service uniforms, all wearing badges, flitted before their eyes. They caught glimpses of ladies, of fur coats hanging on pegs; the draughts blew on them, bringing a smell of stale tobacco. And Gurov, whose heart was beating violently, thought:

"Oh, heavens! Why are these people here and this orchestra! . . ."

And at that instant he recalled how when he had seen Anna Sergeyevna off at the station he had thought that everything was over and they would never meet again. But how far they were still from the end!

On the narrow, gloomy staircase over which was written "To the Amphitheatre," she stopped.

"How you have frightened me!" she said, breathing hard, still pale and overwhelmed. "Oh, how you have frightened me! I am half dead. Why have you come? Why?"

"But do understand, Anna, do understand . . ." he said hastily in a low 95 voice. "I entreat you to understand. . . ."

She looked at him with dread, with entreaty, with love; she looked at him intently, to keep his features more distinctly in her memory.

"I am so unhappy," she went on, not heeding him. "I have thought of nothing but you all the time; I live only in the thought of you. And I wanted to forget, to forget you; but why, oh, why, have you come?"

On the landing above them two schoolboys were smoking and looking down, but that was nothing to Gurov; he drew Anna Sergeyevna to him, and began kissing her face, her cheeks, and her hands.

"What are you doing, what are you doing!" she cried in horror, pushing him away. "We are mad. Go away to-day; go away at once. . . . I beseech you by all that is sacred, I implore you. . . . There are people coming this way!" Some one was coming up the stairs.

"You must go away," Anna Sergeyevna went on in a whisper. "Do you hear, Dmitri Dmitritch? I will come and see you in Moscow. I have never been happy; I am miserable now, and I never, never shall be happy, never! Don't make me suffer still more! I swear I'll come to Moscow. But now let us part. My precious, good, dear one, we must part!"

She pressed his hand and began rapidly going downstairs, looking round at him, and from her eyes he could see that she really was unhappy. Gurov stood for a little while, listened, then, when all sound had died away, he found his coat and left the theatre.

IV

And Anna Sergeyevna began coming to see him in Moscow. Once in two or three months she left S—, telling her husband that she was going to consult a doctor about an internal complaint—and her husband believed her, and did not believe her. In Moscow she stayed at the Slaviansky Bazaar hotel, and at once sent a man in a red cap to Gurov. Gurov went to see her, and no one in Moscow knew of it.

Once he was going to see her in this way on a winter morning (the messenger had come the evening before when he was out). With him walked his daughter, whom he wanted to take to school: it was on the way. Snow was falling in big wet flakes.

"It's three degrees above freezing-point, and yet it is snowing," said Gurov to his daughter. "The thaw is only on the surface of the earth; there is quite a different temperature at a greater height in the atmosphere."

"And why are there no thunderstorms in the winter, father?"

He explained that, too. He talked, thinking all the while that he was going to see *her,* and no living soul knew of it, and probably never would know. He had two lives: one, open, seen and known by all who cared to know, full of relative truth and of relative falsehood, exactly like the lives of his friends and acquaintances; and another life running its course in secret. And through some strange, perhaps accidental, conjunction of circumstances, everything that was essential, of interest and of value to him, everything in which he was sincere and did not deceive himself, everything that made the kernel of his life, was hidden from other people; and all that was false in him, the sheath in which he hid himself to conceal the truth— such, for instance, as his work in the bank, his discussions at the club, his "lower race," his presence with his wife at anniversary festivities—all that was open. And he judged of others by himself, not believing in what he saw, and always believing that every man had his real, most interesting life under the cover of secrecy and under the cover of night. All personal life rested on secrecy, and possibly it was partly on that account that civilised man was so nervously anxious that personal privacy should be respected.

After leaving his daughter at school, Gurov went on to the Slaviansky Bazaar. He took off his fur coat below, went upstairs, and softly knocked at the door. Anna Sergeyevna, wearing his favourite grey dress, exhausted by the journey and the suspense, had been expecting him since the evening before. She was pale; she looked at him, and did not smile, and he had hardly come in when she fell on his breast. Their kiss was slow and prolonged, as though they had not met for two years.

"Well, how are you getting on there?" he asked. "What news?"

"Wait; I'll tell you directly. . . . I can't talk." 110

She could not speak; she was crying. She turned away from him, and pressed her handkerchief to her eyes.

"Let her have her cry out. I'll sit down and wait," he thought, and he sat down in an arm-chair.

Then he rang and asked for tea to be brought him, and while he drank his tea she remained standing at the window with her back to him. She was crying from emotion, from the miserable consciousness that their life was so hard for them; they could only meet in secret, hiding themselves from people, like thieves! Was not their life shattered?

"Come, do stop!" he said.

It was evident to him that this love of theirs would not soon be over, 115 that he could not see the end of it. Anna Sergeyevna grew more and more attached to him. She adored him, and it was unthinkable to say to her that it was bound to have an end some day; besides, she would not have believed it!

He went up to her and took her by the shoulders to say something affectionate and cheering, and at that moment he saw himself in the looking-glass.

His hair was already beginning to turn grey. And it seemed strange to him that he had grown so much older, so much plainer during the last few years. The shoulders on which his hands rested were warm and quivering. He felt compassion for this life, still so warm and lovely, but probably already not far from beginning to fade and wither like his own. Why did she love him so much? He always seemed to women different from what he was, and they loved in him not himself, but the man created by their imagination, whom they had been eagerly seeking all their lives; and afterwards, when they noticed their mistake, they loved him all the same. And not one of them had been happy with him. Time passed, he had made their acquaintance, got on with them, parted, but he had never once loved; it was anything you like, but not love.

And only now when his head was grey he had fallen properly, really in love—for the first time in his life.

Anna Sergeyevna and he loved each other like people very close and akin, like husband and wife, like tender friends; it seemed to them that fate itself had meant them for one another, and they could not understand why he had a wife and she a husband; and it was as though they were a pair of birds of passage, caught and forced to live in different cages. They forgave each other for what they were ashamed of in their past, they forgave everything in the present, and felt that this love of theirs had changed them both.

120 In moments of depression in the past he had comforted himself with any arguments that came into his mind, but now he no longer cared for arguments; he felt profound compassion, he wanted to be sincere and tender. . . .

"Don't cry, my darling," he said. "You've had your cry; that's enough. . . . Let us talk now, let us think of some plan."

Then they spent a long while taking counsel together, talked of how to avoid the necessity for secrecy, for deception, for living in different towns and not seeing each other for long at a time. How could they be free from this intolerable bondage?

"How? How?" he asked, clutching his head. "How?"

And it seemed as though in a little while the solution would be found, and then a new and splendid life would begin; and it was clear to both of them that they had still a long, long road before them, and that the most complicated and difficult part of it was only just beginning.

1899

QUESTIONS

1. When Gurov and Anna take their first walk together, they discuss "the strange light of the sea: the water was of a soft warm lilac hue, and there was a golden streak from the moon upon it." Why do you think Chekhov waits until this moment to provide descriptive details of the story's setting in Yalta?

2. How do the weather and season described in each section relate to the action in that section?

3. What is Gurov's attitude toward his affair with Anna at the outset? What is Anna's attitude? What are some indications that both Gurov and Anna are unprepared for the relationship that develops between them?

KATHERINE ANNE PORTER

Flowering Judas

Braggioni sits heaped upon the edge of a straight-backed chair much too small for him, and sings to Laura in a furry, mournful voice. Laura has begun to find reasons for avoiding her own house until the latest possible moment, for Braggioni is there almost every night. No matter how late she is, he will be sitting there with a surly, waiting expression, pulling at his kinky yellow hair, thumbing the strings of his guitar, snarling a tune under his breath. Lupe the Indian maid meets Laura at the door, and says with a flicker of a glance towards the upper room, "He waits."

Laura wishes to lie down, she is tired of her hairpins and the feel of her long tight sleeves, but she says to him, "Have you a new song for me this evening?" If he says yes, she asks him to sing it. If he says no, she remembers his favorite one, and asks him to sing it again. Lupe brings her a cup of chocolate and a plate of rice, and Laura eats at the small table under the lamp, first inviting Braggioni, whose answer is always the same: "I have eaten, and besides, chocolate thickens the voice."

Laura says, "Sing, then," and Braggioni heaves himself into song. He scratches the guitar familiarly as though it were a pet animal, and sings passionately off key, taking the high notes in a prolonged painful squeal. Laura, who haunts the markets listening to the ballad singers, and stops every day to hear the blind boy playing his reed-flute in Sixteenth of September Street,[1] listens to Braggioni with pitiless courtesy, because she dares not smile at his miserable performance. Nobody dares to smile at him. Braggioni is cruel to everyone, with a kind of specialized insolence, but he is so vain of his talents, and so sensitive to slights, it would require a cruelty and vanity greater than his own to lay a finger on the vast cureless wound of his self-esteem. It would require courage, too, for it is dangerous to offend him, and nobody has this courage.

Braggioni loves himself with such tenderness and amplitude and eternal charity that his followers—for he is a leader of men, a skilled revolutionist, and his skin had been punctured in honorable warfare—warm themselves in the reflected glow, and say to each other: "He has a real nobility, a love of humanity raised above mere personal affections." The excess of this self-love has flowed out, inconveniently for her, over Laura, who, with so many others, owes her comfortable situation and her salary to him. When he is in a very good humor, he tells her, "I am tempted to forgive you for being a *gringa. Gringita!*"[2] and Laura, burning, imagines herself leaning forward suddenly, and with a sound back-handed slap wiping

---

1. Street in Morelia, a city in central Mexico.
2. Diminutive of *gringa:* non-Mexican woman, used pejoratively.

the suety smile from his face. If he notices her eyes at these moments he gives no sign.

5   She knows what Braggioni would offer her, and she must resist tenaciously without appearing to resist, and if she could avoid it she would not admit even to herself the slow drift of his intention. During these long evenings which have spoiled a long month for her, she sits in her deep chair with an open book on her knees, resting her eyes on the consoling rigidity of the printed page when the sight and sound of Braggioni singing threaten to identify themselves with all her remembered afflictions and to add their weight to her uneasy premonitions of the future. The gluttonous bulk of Braggioni has become a symbol of her many disillusions, for a revolutionist should be lean, animated by heroic faith, a vessel of abstract virtues. This is nonsense, she knows it now and is ashamed of it. Revolution must have leaders, and leadership is a career for energetic men. She is, her comrades tell her, full of romantic error, for what she defines as cynicism in them is merely "a developed sense of reality." She is almost too willing to say, "I am wrong, I suppose I don't really understand the principles," and afterward she makes a secret truce with herself, determined not to surrender her will to such expedient logic. But she cannot help feeling that she has been betrayed irreparably by the disunion between her way of living and her feeling of what life should be, and at times she is almost contented to rest in this sense of grievance as a private store of consolation. Sometimes she wishes to run away, but she stays. Now she longs to fly out of this room, down the narrow stairs, and into the street where the houses lean together like conspirators under a single mottled lamp, and leave Braggioni singing to himself.

Instead she looks at Braggioni, frankly and clearly, like a good child who understands the rules of behavior. Her knees cling together under sound blue serge, and her round white collar is not purposely nun-like. She wears the uniform of an idea, and has renounced vanities. She was born Roman Catholic, and in spite of her fear of being seen by someone who might make a scandal of it, she slips now and again into some crumbling little church, kneels on the chilly stone, and says a Hail Mary on the gold rosary she bought in Tehuantepec. It is no good and she ends by examining the altar with its tinsel flowers and ragged brocades, and feels tender about the battered doll-shape of some male saint whose white, lace-trimmed drawers hang limply around his ankles below the hieratic dignity of his velvet robe. She has encased herself in a set of principles derived from her early training, leaving no detail of gesture or of personal taste untouched, and for this reason she will not wear lace made on machines. This is her private heresy, for in her special group the machine is sacred, and will be the salvation of the workers. She loves fine lace, and there is a tiny edge of fluted cobweb on this collar, which is one of twenty precisely alike, folded in blue tissue paper in the upper drawer of her clothes chest.

Braggioni catches her glance solidly as if he had been waiting for it, leans forward, balancing his paunch between his spread knees, and sings with tremendous emphasis, weighing his words. He has, the song relates, no father and no mother, nor even a friend to console him; lonely as a wave of the sea he comes and goes, lonely as a wave. His mouth opens round and yearns sideways, his balloon cheeks grow oily with the labor of song. He bulges marvelously in his expensive garments. Over his lavender collar, crushed upon a purple necktie, held by a diamond hoop: over his ammunition belt of tooled leather worked in silver, buckled cruelly around his gasping middle: over the tops of his glossy yellow shoes Braggioni swells with ominous ripeness, his mauve silk hose stretched taut, his ankles bound with the stout leather thongs of his shoes.

When he stretches his eyelids at Laura she notes again that his eyes are the true tawny yellow cat's eyes. He is rich, not in money, he tells her, but in power, and this power brings with it the blameless ownership of things, and the right to indulge his love of small luxuries. "I have a taste for the elegant refinements," he said once, flourishing a yellow silk handkerchief before her nose. "Smell that? It is Jockey Club, imported from New York." Nonetheless he is wounded by life. He will say so presently. "It is true everything turns to dust in the hand, to gall on the tongue." He sighs and his leather belt creaks like a saddle girth. "I am disappointed in everything as it comes. Everything." He shakes his head. "You, poor thing, you will be disappointed too. You are born for it. We are more alike than you realize in some things. Wait and see. Some day you will remember what I have told you, you will know that Braggioni was your friend."

Laura feels a slow chill, a purely physical sense of danger, a warning in her blood that violence, mutilation, a shocking death, wait for her with lessening patience. She has translated this fear into something homely, immediate, and sometimes hesitates before crossing the street. "My personal fate is nothing, except as the testimony of a mental attitude," she reminds herself, quoting from some forgotten philosophic primer, and is sensible enough to add, "Anyhow, I shall not be killed by an automobile if I can help it."

"It may be true I am as corrupt, in another way, as Braggioni," she ⟨10⟩ thinks in spite of herself, "as callous, as incomplete," and if this is so, any kind of death seems preferable. Still she sits quietly, she does not run. Where could she go? Uninvited she has promised herself to this place; she can no longer imagine herself as living in another country, and there is no pleasure in remembering her life before she came here.

Precisely what is the nature of this devotion, its true motives, and what are its obligations? Laura cannot say. She spends part of her days in Xochimilco, near by, teaching Indian children to say in English, "The cat is on the mat." When she appears in the classroom they crowd about her with smiles on their wise, innocent, clay-colored faces, crying "Good morning,

my titcher!" in immaculate voices, and they make of her desk a fresh garden of flowers every day.

During her leisure she goes to union meetings and listens to busy
important voices quarreling over tactics, methods, internal politics. She
visits the prisoners of her own political faith in their cells, where they
entertain themselves with counting cockroaches, repenting of their indis-
cretions, composing their memoirs, writing out manifestoes and plans
for their comrades who are still walking about free, hands in pockets,
sniffing fresh air. Laura brings them food and cigarettes and a little money,
and she brings messages disguised in equivocal phrases from the men
outside who dare not set foot in the prison for fear of disappearing into
the cells kept empty for them. If the prisoners confuse night and day, and
complain, "Dear little Laura, time doesn't pass in this infernal hole, and
I won't know when it is time to sleep unless I have a reminder," she brings
them their favorite narcotics, and says in a tone that does not wound
them with pity, "Tonight will really be night for you," and though her
Spanish amuses them, they find her comforting, useful. If they lose
patience and all faith, and curse the slowness of their friends in coming to
their rescue with money and influence, they trust her not to repeat everything, and if she inquires, "Where do you think we can find money, or influence?" they are certain to answer, "Well, there is Braggioni, why doesn't he
do something?"

She smuggles letters from headquarters to men hiding from firing
squads in back streets in mildewed houses, where they sit in tumbled beds
and talk bitterly as if all Mexico were at their heels, when Laura knows
positively they might appear at the band concert in the Alameda on Sunday morning, and no one would notice them. But Braggioni says, "Let
them sweat a little. The next time they may be careful. It is very restful to
have them out of the way for a while." She is not afraid to knock on any
door in any street after midnight, and enter in the darkness, and say to
one of these men who is really in danger: "They will be looking for you—
seriously—tomorrow morning after six. Here is some money from Vicente.
Go to Vera Cruz and wait."

She borrows money from the Roumanian agitator to give to his bitter
enemy the Polish agitator. The favor of Braggioni is their disputed territory, and Braggioni holds the balance nicely, for he can use them both. The
Polish agitator talks love to her over café tables, hoping to exploit what he
believes is her secret sentimental preference for him, and he gives her misinformation which he begs her to repeat as the solemn truth to certain
persons. The Roumanian is more adroit. He is generous with his money in
all good causes, and lies to her with an air of ingenuous candor, as if he
were her good friend and confidant. She never repeats anything they may
say. Braggioni never asks questions. He has other ways to discover all that
he wishes to know about them.

Nobody touches her, but all praise her gray eyes, and the soft, round 15
under lip which promises gayety, yet is always grave, nearly always firmly
closed: and they cannot understand why she is in Mexico. She walks back
and forth on her errands, with puzzled eyebrows, carrying her little folder
of drawings and music and school papers. No dancer dances more beautifully than Laura walks, and she inspires some amusing, unexpected ardors,
which cause little gossip, because nothing comes of them. A young captain
who had been a soldier in Zapata's[3] army attempted, during a horseback
ride near Cuernavaca, to express his desire for her with the noble simplicity befitting a rude folk-hero: but gently, because he was gentle. This gentleness was his defeat, for when he alighted, and removed her foot from the
stirrup, and essayed to draw her down into his arms, her horse, ordinarily
a tame one, shied fiercely, reared and plunged away. The young hero's horse
careered blindly after his stable-mate, and the hero did not return to the
hotel until rather late that evening. At breakfast he came to her table in
full charro[4] dress, gray buckskin jacket and trousers with strings of silver
buttons down the leg, and he was in a humorous, careless mood. "May I sit
with you?" and "You are a wonderful rider. I was terrified that you might
be thrown and dragged. I should never have forgiven myself. But I cannot
admire you enough for your riding!"

"I learned to ride in Arizona," said Laura.

"If you will ride with me again this morning, I promise you a horse that
will not shy with you," he said. But Laura remembered that she must
return to Mexico City at noon.

Next morning the children made a celebration and spent their playtime
writing on the blackboard, "We lov ar ticher," and with tinted chalks they
drew wreaths of flowers around the words. The young hero wrote her a letter: "I am a very foolish, wasteful, impulsive man. I should have first said
I love you, and then you would not have run away. But you shall see me
again." Laura thought, "I must send him a box of colored crayons," but she
was trying to forgive herself for having spurred her horse at the wrong
moment.

A brown, shock-haired youth came and stood in her patio one night and
sang like a lost soul for two hours, but Laura could think of nothing to do
about it. The moonlight spread a wash of gauzy silver over the clear spaces
of the garden, and the shadows were cobalt blue. The scarlet blossoms of
the Judas tree were dull purple, and the names of the colors repeated themselves automatically in her mind, while she watched not the boy, but his
shadow, fallen like a dark garment across the fountain rim, trailing in the
water. Lupe came silently and whispered expert counsel in her ear: "If you
will throw him one little flower, he will sing another song or two and go

3. Emiliano Zapata (1879–1919), Mexican peasant-revolutionary general.
4. Costume worn by peasant horsemen of special status.

away." Laura threw the flower, and he sang a last song and went away with the flower tucked in the band of his hat. Lupe said, "He is one of the organizers of the Typographers Union, and before that he sold corridos[5] in the Merced market, and before that, he came from Guanajuato, where I was born. I would not trust any man, but I trust least those from Guanajuato."

20   She did not tell Laura that he would be back again the next night, and the next, nor that he would follow her at a certain fixed distance around the Merced market, through the Zócalo, up Francisco I. Madero Avenue, and so along the Paseo de la Reforma to that Chapultepec Park, and into the Philosopher's Footpath, still with that flower withering in his hat, and an indivisible attention in his eyes.

Now Laura is accustomed to him, it means nothing except that he is nineteen years old and is observing a convention with all propriety, as though it were founded on a law of nature, which in the end it might well prove to be. He is beginning to write poems which he prints on a wooden press, and he leaves them stuck like handbills in her door. She is pleasantly disturbed by the abstract, unhurried watchfulness of his black eyes which will in time turn easily towards another object. She tells herself that throwing the flower was a mistake, for she is twenty-two years old and knows better; but she refuses to regret it, and persuades herself that her negation of all external events as they occur is a sign that she is gradually perfecting herself in the stoicism she strives to cultivate against that disaster she fears, though she cannot name it.

She is not at home in the world. Every day she teaches children who remain strangers to her, though she loves their tender round hands and their charming opportunist savagery. She knocks at unfamiliar doors not knowing whether a friend or a stranger shall answer, and even if a known face emerges from the sour gloom of that unknown interior, still it is the face of a stranger. No matter what this stranger says to her, nor what her message to him, the very cells of her flesh reject knowledge and kinship in one monotonous word. No. No. No. She draws her strength from this one holy talismanic word which does not suffer her to be led into evil. Denying everything, she may walk anywhere in safety, she looks at everything without amazement.

No, repeats this firm unchanging voice of her blood; and she looks at Braggioni without amazement. He is a great man, he wishes to impress this simple girl who covers her great round breasts with thick dark cloth, and who hides long, invaluably beautiful legs under a heavy skirt. She is almost thin except for the incomprehensible fullness of her breasts, like a nursing mother's, and Braggioni, who considers himself a judge of women, speculates again on the puzzle of her notorious virginity, and takes the

5. Popular ballads.

liberty of speech which she permits without a sign of modesty, indeed, without any sort of sign, which is disconcerting.

"You think you are so cold, *gringita!* Wait and see. You will surprise yourself some day! May I be there to advise you!" He stretches his eyelids at her, and his ill-humored cat's eyes waver in a separate glance for the two points of light marking the opposite ends of a smoothly drawn path between the swollen curve of her breasts. He is not put off by that blue serge, nor by her resolutely fixed gaze. There is all the time in the world. His cheeks are bellying with the wind of song. "O girl with the dark eyes," he sings, and reconsiders. "But yours are not dark. I can change all that. O girl with the green eyes, you have stolen my heart away!" then his mind wanders to the song, and Laura feels the weight of his attention being shifted elsewhere. Singing thus, he seems harmless, he is quite harmless, there is nothing to do but sit patiently and say "No," when the moment comes. She draws a full breath, and her mind wanders also, but not far. She dares not wander too far.

Not for nothing has Braggioni taken pains to be a good revolutionist 25 and a professional lover of humanity. He will never die of it. He has the malice, the cleverness, the wickedness, the sharpness of wit, the hardness of heart, stipulated for loving the world profitably. *He will never die of it.* He will live to see himself kicked out from his feeding trough by other hungry world-saviors. Traditionally he must sing in spite of his life which drives him to bloodshed, he tells Laura, for his father was a Tuscany[6] peasant who drifted to Yucatan and married a Maya woman: a woman of race, an aristocrat. They gave him the love and knowledge of music, thus: and under the rip of his thumbnail, the strings of the instrument complain like exposed nerves.

Once he was called Delgadito by all the girls and married women who ran after him; he was so scrawny all his bones showed under his thin cotton clothing, and he could squeeze his emptiness to the very backbone with his two hands. He was a poet and the revolution was only a dream then; too many women loved him and sapped away his youth, and he could never find enough to eat anywhere, anywhere! Now he is a leader of men, crafty men who whisper in his ear, hungry men who wait for hours outside his office for a word with him, emaciated men with wild faces who waylay him at the street gate with a timid, "Comrade, let me tell you . . ." and they blow the foul breath from their empty stomachs in his face.

He is always sympathetic. He gives them handfuls of small coins from his own pocket, he promises them work, there will be demonstrations, they must join the unions and attend the meetings, above all they must be on the watch for spies. They are closer to him than his own brothers, without them he can do nothing—until tomorrow, comrade!

6. Region in northern Italy.

Until tomorrow. "They are stupid, they are lazy, they are treacherous, they would cut my throat for nothing," he says to Laura. He has good food and abundant drink, he hires an automobile and drives in the Paseo on Sunday morning, and enjoys plenty of sleep in a soft bed beside a wife who dares not disturb him; and he sits pampering his bones in easy billows of fat, singing to Laura, who knows and thinks these things about him. When he was fifteen, he tried to drown himself because he loved a girl, his first love, and she laughed at him. "A thousand women have paid for that," and his tight little mouth turns down at the corners. Now he perfumes his hair with Jockey Club, and confides to Laura: "One woman is really as good as another for me, in the dark. I prefer them all."

His wife organizes unions among the girls in the cigarette factories, and walks in picket lines, and even speaks at meetings in the evening. But she cannot be brought to acknowledge the benefits of true liberty. "I tell her I must have my freedom, net. She does not understand my point of view." Laura has heard this many times. Braggioni scratches the guitar and meditates. "She is an instinctively virtuous woman, pure gold, no doubt of that. If she were not, I should lock her up, and she knows it."

30   His wife, who works so hard for the good of the factory girls, employs part of her leisure lying on the floor weeping because there are so many women in the world, and only one husband for her, and she never knows where nor when to look for him. He told her: "Unless you can learn to cry when I am not here, I must go away for good." That day he went away and took a room at the Hotel Madrid.

It is this month of separation for the sake of higher principles that has been spoiled not only for Mrs. Braggioni, whose sense of reality is beyond criticism, but for Laura, who feels herself bogged in a nightmare. Tonight Laura envies Mrs. Braggioni, who is alone, and free to weep as much as she pleases about a concrete wrong. Laura has just come from a visit to the prison, and she is waiting for tomorrow with a bitter anxiety as if tomorrow may not come, but time may be caught immovably in this hour, with herself transfixed, Braggioni singing on forever, and Eugenio's body not yet discovered by the guard.

Braggioni says: "Are you going to sleep?" Almost before she can shake her head, he begins telling her about the May-day disturbances coming on in Morelia, for the Catholics hold a festival in honor of the Blessed Virgin, and the Socialists celebrate their martyrs on that day. "There will be two independent processions, starting from either end of town, and they will march until they meet, and the rest depends . . ." He asks her to oil and load his pistols. Standing up, he unbuckles his ammunition belt, and spreads it laden across her knees. Laura sits with the shells slipping through the cleaning cloth dipped in oil, and he says again he cannot understand why she works so hard for the revolutionary idea unless she loves some man who is in it. "Are you not in love with someone?" "No," says Laura. "And no one is in love with you?" "No." "Then it is your own fault. No woman need go begging. Why, what is the matter with you? The legless beggar woman in the Alameda has a perfectly faithful lover. Did you know that?"

Laura peers down the pistol barrel and says nothing, but a long, slow faintness rises and subsides in her; Braggioni curves his swollen fingers around the throat of the guitar and softly smothers the music out of it, and when she hears him again he seems to have forgotten her, and is speaking in the hypnotic voice he uses when talking in small rooms to a listening, close-gathered crowd. Some day this world, now seemingly so composed and eternal, to the edges of every sea shall be merely a tangle of gaping trenches, of crashing walls and broken bodies. Everything must be torn from its accustomed place where it has rotted for centuries, hurled skyward and distributed, cast down again clean as rain, without separate identity. Nothing shall survive that the stiffened hands of poverty have created for the rich and no one shall be left alive except the elect spirits destined to procreate a new world cleansed of cruelty and injustice, ruled by benevolent anarchy: "Pistols are good, I love them, cannon are even better, but in the end I pin my faith to good dynamite," he concludes, and strokes the pistol lying in her hands. "Once I dreamed of destroying this city, in case it offered resistance to General Ortíz, but it fell into his hands like an overripe pear."

He is made restless by his own words, rises and stands waiting. Laura holds up the belt to him: "Put that on, and go kill somebody in Morelia, and you will be happier," she says softly. The presence of death in the room makes her bold. "Today, I found Eugenio going into a stupor. He refused to allow me to call the prison doctor. He had taken all the tablets I brought him yesterday. He said he took them because he was bored."

"He is a fool, and his death is his own business," says Braggioni, fastening his belt carefully.   35

"I told him if he had waited only a little while longer, you would have got him set free," says Laura. "He said he did not want to wait."

"He is a fool and we are well rid of him," says Braggioni, reaching for his hat.

He goes away. Laura knows his mood has changed, she will not see him any more for a while. He will send word when he needs her to go on errands into strange streets, to speak to the strange faces that will appear, like clay masks with the power of human speech, to mutter their thanks to Braggioni for his help. Now she is free, and she thinks, I must run while there is time. But she does not go.

Braggioni enters his own house where for a month his wife has spent many hours every night weeping and tangling her hair upon her pillow. She is weeping now, and she weeps more at the sight of him, the cause of all her sorrows. He looks about the room. Nothing is changed, the smells are good and familiar, he is well acquainted with the woman who comes toward him with no reproach except grief on her face. He says to her tenderly: "You are so good, please don't cry any more, you dear good creature." She says, "Are you tired, my angel? Sit here and I will wash your feet." She brings a bowl of water, and kneeling, unlaces his shoes, and when from her knees she raises her sad eyes under her blackened lids, he is sorry for everything, and bursts into tears. "Ah, yes, I am hungry, I am tired, let us eat something together," he says, between sobs. His wife leans her head on his arm and says, "Forgive me!" and this time he is refreshed by the solemn, endless rain of her tears.

40   Laura takes off her serge dress and puts on a white linen nightgown and goes to bed. She turns her head a little to one side, and lying still, reminds herself that it is time to sleep. Numbers tick in her brain like little clocks, soundless doors close of themselves around her. If you would sleep, you must not remember anything, the children will say tomorrow, good morning, my teacher, the poor prisoners who come every day bringing flowers to their jailor. 1-2-3-4-5—it is monstrous to confuse love with revolution, night with day, life with death—ah, Eugenio!

The tolling of the midnight bell is a signal, but what does it mean? Get up, Laura, and follow me: come out of your sleep, out of your bed, out of this strange house. What are you doing in this house? Without a word, without fear she rose and reached for Eugenio's hand, but he eluded her with a sharp, sly smile and drifted away. This is not all, you shall see— Murderer, he said, follow me, I will show you a new country, but it is far away and we must hurry. No, said Laura, not unless you take my hand, no; and she clung first to the stair rail, and then to the topmost branch of the Judas tree that bent down slowly and set her upon the earth, and then to the rocky ledge of a cliff, and then to the jagged wave of a sea that was not water but a desert of crumbling stone. Where are you taking me, she asked in wonder but without fear. To death, and it is a long way off, and we must hurry, said Eugenio. No, said Laura, not unless you take my hand. Then eat these flowers, poor prisoner, said Eugenio in a voice of pity, take and eat: and from the Judas tree he stripped the warm bleeding flowers, and held them to her lips. She saw that his hand was fleshless, a cluster of small white petrified branches, and his eye sockets were without light, but she ate the flowers greedily for they satisfied both hunger and thirst. Murderer! said Eugenio, and Cannibal! This is my body and my blood. Laura cried No! and at the sound of her own voice, she awoke trembling, and was afraid to sleep again.

1929, 1930

QUESTIONS

1. The main events in "Flowering Judas" take place on a single evening and mostly in a single room. What is the effect and significance of that temporal

and spatial restriction? How, for example, does the setting affect Laura? How does it reflect or reveal her character? Why does she simply "sit quietly" (par. 10)? What does Porter gain when she deviates from this pattern by taking us inside Braggioni's house near the end of the story?

2. The general setting of "Flowering Judas" is Mexico just after the Mexican revolution of 1910–20. What attracts Laura to Mexico? to the Leftist movement? What keeps her both in Mexico and involved in the movement? What is her relationship to each? To what extent is all this a result and reflection of her personality, outlook, and values? of the place or other people?

3. When and how are the Judas tree and its flowers mentioned and described in the story? What is their significance to the story?

AMY TAN

A Pair of Tickets

The minute our train leaves the Hong Kong border and enters Shenzhen, China, I feel different. I can feel the skin on my forehead tingling, my blood rushing through a new course, my bones aching with a familiar old pain. And I think, My mother was right. I am becoming Chinese.

"Cannot be helped," my mother said when I was fifteen and had vigorously denied that I had any Chinese whatsoever below my skin. I was a sophomore at Galileo High in San Francisco, and all my Caucasian friends agreed: I was about as Chinese as they were. But my mother had studied at a famous nursing school in Shanghai, and she said she knew all about genetics. So there was no doubt in her mind, whether I agreed or not: Once you are born Chinese, you cannot help but feel and think Chinese.

"Someday you will see," said my mother. "It's in your blood, waiting to be let go."

And when she said this, I saw myself transforming like a werewolf, a mutant tag of DNA suddenly triggered, replicating itself insidiously into a *syndrome,* a cluster of telltale Chinese behaviors, all those things my mother did to embarrass me—haggling with store owners, pecking her mouth with a toothpick in public, being color-blind to the fact that lemon yellow and pale pink are not good combinations for winter clothes.

But today I realize I've never really known what it means to be Chinese. 5 I am thirty-six years old. My mother is dead and I am on a train, carrying with me her dreams of coming home. I am going to China.

We are going to Guangzhou, my seventy-two-year-old father, Canning Woo, and I, where we will visit his aunt, whom he has not seen since he was ten years old. And I don't know whether it's the prospect of seeing his aunt or if it's because he's back in China, but now he looks like he's a young boy, so innocent and happy I want to button his sweater and pat his head. We are sitting across from each other, separated by a little table with two cold cups of tea. For the first time I can ever remember, my father has tears in his eyes, and all he is seeing out the train window is a sectioned field of yellow, green, and brown, a narrow canal flanking the tracks, low rising hills, and three people in blue jackets riding an ox-driven cart on this early October morning. And I can't help myself. I also have misty eyes, as if I had seen this a long, long time ago, and had almost forgotten.

In less than three hours, we will be in Guangzhou, which my guidebook tells me is how one properly refers to Canton these days. It seems all the cities I have heard of, except Shanghai, have changed their spellings. I think they are saying China has changed in other ways as well. Chungking is Chongqing. And Kweilin is Guilin. I have looked these names up, because after we see my father's aunt in Guangzhou, we will catch a plane to Shanghai, where I will meet my two half-sisters for the first time.

They are my mother's twin daughters from her first marriage, little babies she was forced to abandon on a road as she was fleeing Kweilin for Chungking in 1944. That was all my mother had told me about these daughters, so they had remained babies in my mind, all these years, sitting on the side of a road, listening to bombs whistling in the distance while sucking their patient red thumbs.

And it was only this year that someone found them and wrote with this joyful news. A letter came from Shanghai, addressed to my mother. When I first heard about this, that they were alive, I imagined my identical sisters transforming from little babies into six-year-old girls. In my mind, they were seated next to each other at a table, taking turns with the fountain pen. One would write a neat row of characters: *Dearest Mama. We are alive.* She would brush back her wispy bangs and hand the other sister the pen, and she would write: *Come get us. Please hurry.*

10   Of course they could not know that my mother had died three months before, suddenly, when a blood vessel in her brain burst. One minute she was talking to my father, complaining about the tenants upstairs, scheming how to evict them under the pretense that relatives from China were moving in. The next minute she was holding her head, her eyes squeezed shut, groping for the sofa, and then crumpling softly to the floor with fluttering hands.

So my father had been the first one to open the letter, a long letter it turned out. And they did call her Mama. They said they always revered her as their true mother. They kept a framed picture of her. They told her about their life, from the time my mother last saw them on the road leaving Kweilin to when they were finally found.

And the letter had broken my father's heart so much—these daughters calling my mother from another life he never knew—that he gave the letter to my mother's old friend Auntie Lindo and asked her to write back and tell my sisters, in the gentlest way possible, that my mother was dead.

But instead Auntie Lindo took the letter to the Joy Luck Club and discussed with Auntie Ying and Auntie An-mei what should be done, because they had known for many years about my mother's search for her twin daughters, her endless hope. Auntie Lindo and the others cried over this double tragedy, of losing my mother three months before, and now again. And so they couldn't help but think of some miracle, some possible way of reviving her from the dead, so my mother could fulfill her dream.

So this is what they wrote to my sisters in Shanghai: "Dearest Daughters, I too have never forgotten you in my memory or in my heart. I never gave up hope that we would see each other again in a joyous reunion. I am only sorry it has been too long. I want to tell you everything about my life since I last saw you. I want to tell you this when our family comes to see you in China...." They signed it with my mother's name.

It wasn't until all this had been done that they first told me about my sisters, the letter they received, the one they wrote back.

"They'll think she's coming, then," I murmured. And I had imagined my sisters now being ten or eleven, jumping up and down, holding hands, their pigtails bouncing, excited that their mother—*their* mother—was coming, whereas my mother was dead.

"How can you say she is not coming in a letter?" said Auntie Lindo. "She is their mother. She is your mother. You must be the one to tell them. All these years, they have been dreaming of her." And I thought she was right.

But then I started dreaming, too, of my mother and my sisters and how it would be if I arrived in Shanghai. All these years, while they waited to be found, I had lived with my mother and then had lost her. I imagined seeing my sisters at the airport. They would be standing on their tiptoes, looking anxiously, scanning from one dark head to another as we got off the plane. And I would recognize them instantly, their faces with the identical worried look.

"*Jyejye, Jyejye.* Sister, Sister. We are here," I saw myself saying in my poor version of Chinese.

"Where is Mama?" they would say, and look around, still smiling, two flushed and eager faces. "Is she hiding?" And this would have been like my mother, to stand behind just a bit, to tease a little and make people's patience pull a little on their hearts. I would shake my head and tell my sisters she was not hiding.

"Oh, that must be Mama, no?" one of my sisters would whisper excitedly, pointing to another small woman completely engulfed in a tower of presents. And that, too, would have been like my mother, to bring mountains of gifts, food, and toys for children—all bought on sale—shunning thanks, saying the gifts were nothing, and later turning the labels over to show my sisters, "Calvin Klein, 100% wool."

I imagined myself starting to say, "Sisters, I am sorry, I have come alone..." and before I could tell them—they could see it in my face—they were wailing, pulling their hair, their lips twisted in pain, as they ran away from me. And then I saw myself getting back on the plane and coming home.

After I had dreamed this scene many times—watching their despair turn from horror into anger—I begged Auntie Lindo to write another letter. And at first she refused.

"How can I say she is dead? I cannot write this," said Auntie Lindo with a stubborn look.

25 "But it's cruel to have them believe she's coming on the plane," I said. "When they see it's just me, they'll hate me."

"Hate you? Cannot be." She was scowling. "You are their own sister, their only family."

"You don't understand," I protested.

"What I don't understand?" she said.

And I whispered, "They'll think I'm responsible, that she died because I didn't appreciate her."

30 And Auntie Lindo looked satisfied and sad at the same time, as if this were true and I had finally realized it. She sat down for an hour, and when she stood up she handed me a two-page letter. She had tears in her eyes. I realized that the very thing I had feared, she had done. So even if she had written the news of my mother's death in English, I wouldn't have had the heart to read it.

"Thank you," I whispered.

The landscape has become gray, filled with low flat cement buildings, old factories, and then tracks and more tracks filled with trains like ours passing by in the opposite direction. I see platforms crowded with people wearing drab Western clothes, with spots of bright colors: little children wearing pink and yellow, red and peach. And there are soldiers in olive green and red, and old ladies in gray tops and pants that stop mid-calf. We are in Guangzhou.

Before the train even comes to a stop, people are bringing down their belongings from above their seats. For a moment there is a dangerous shower of heavy suitcases laden with gifts to relatives, half-broken boxes wrapped in miles of string to keep the contents from spilling out, plastic bags filled with yarn and vegetables and packages of dried mushrooms, and camera cases. And then we are caught in a stream of people rushing, shoving, pushing us along, until we find ourselves in one of a dozen lines waiting to go through customs. I feel as if I were getting on a number 30 Stockton bus in San Francisco. I am in China, I remind myself. And somehow the crowds don't bother me. It feels right. I start pushing too.

I take out the declaration forms and my passport. "Woo," it says at the top, and below that, "June May," who was born in "California, U.S.A.," in 1951. I wonder if the customs people will question whether I'm the same person as in the passport photo. In this picture, my chin-length hair is swept back and artfully styled. I am wearing false eyelashes, eye shadow, and lip liner. My cheeks are hollowed out by bronze blusher. But I had not expected the heat in October. And now my hair hangs limp with the humidity. I wear no makeup; in Hong Kong my mascara had melted into dark circles and everything else had felt like layers of grease. So today my face is plain, unadorned except for a thin mist of shiny sweat on my forehead and nose.

Even without makeup, I could never pass for true Chinese. I stand five- 35 foot-six, and my head pokes above the crowd so that I am eye level only with other tourists. My mother once told me my height came from my grandfather, who was a northerner, and may have even had some Mongol blood. "This is what your grandmother once told me," explained my mother. "But now it is too late to ask her. They are all dead, your grandparents, your uncles, and their wives and children, all killed in the war, when a bomb fell on our house. So many generations in one instant."

She had said this so matter-of-factly that I thought she had long since gotten over any grief she had. And then I wondered how she knew they were all dead.

"Maybe they left the house before the bomb fell," I suggested.

"No," said my mother. "Our whole family is gone. It is just you and I."

"But how do you know? Some of them could have escaped."

"Cannot be," said my mother, this time almost angrily. And then her 40 frown was washed over by a puzzled blank look, and she began to talk as if she were trying to remember where she had misplaced something. "I went back to that house. I kept looking up to where the house used to be. And it wasn't a house, just the sky. And below, underneath my feet, were four stories of burnt bricks and wood, all the life of our house. Then off to the side I saw things blown into the yard, nothing valuable. There was a bed someone used to sleep in, really just a metal frame twisted up at one corner. And a book, I don't know what kind, because every page had turned black. And I saw a teacup which was unbroken but filled with ashes. And then I found my doll, with her hands and legs broken, her hair burned off.... When I was a little girl, I had cried for that doll, seeing it all alone in the store window, and my mother had bought it for me. It was an American doll with yellow hair. It could turn its legs and arms. The eyes moved up and down. And when I married and left my family home, I gave the doll to my youngest niece, because she was like me. She cried if that doll was not with her always. Do you see? If she was in the house with that doll, her parents were there, and so everybody was there, waiting together, because that's how our family was."

The woman in the customs booth stares at my documents, then glances at me briefly, and with two quick movements stamps everything and sternly nods me along. And soon my father and I find ourselves in a large area filled with thousands of people and suitcases. I feel lost and my father looks helpless.

"Excuse me," I say to a man who looks like an American. "Can you tell me where I can get a taxi?" He mumbles something that sounds Swedish or Dutch.

"Syau Yen! Syau Yen!" I hear a piercing voice shout from behind me. An old woman in a yellow knit beret is holding up a pink plastic bag filled with wrapped trinkets. I guess she is trying to sell us something. But my father is staring down at this tiny sparrow of a woman, squinting into her eyes. And then his eyes widen, his face opens up and he smiles like a pleased little boy.

"*Aiyi! Aiyi!*"—Auntie Auntie!—he says softly.

45   "Syau Yen!" coos my great-aunt. I think it's funny she has just called my father "Little Wild Goose." It must be his baby milk name, the name used to discourage ghosts from stealing children.

They clasp each other's hands—they do not hug—and hold on like this, taking turns saying, "Look at you! You are so old. Look how old you've become!" They are both crying openly, laughing at the same time, and I bite my lip, trying not to cry. I'm afraid to feel their joy. Because I am thinking how different our arrival in Shanghai will be tomorrow, how awkward it will feel.

Now Aiyi beams and points to a Polaroid picture of my father. My father had wisely sent pictures when he wrote and said we were coming. See how smart she was, she seems to intone as she compares the picture to my father. In the letter, my father had said we would call her from the hotel once we arrived, so this is a surprise, that they've come to meet us. I wonder if my sisters will be at the airport.

It is only then that I remember the camera. I had meant to take a picture of my father and his aunt the moment they met. It's not too late.

"Here, stand together over here," I say, holding up the Polaroid. The camera flashes and I hand them the snapshot. Aiyi and my father still stand close together, each of them holding a corner of the picture, watching as their images begin to form. They are almost reverentially quiet. Aiyi is only five years older than my father, which makes her around seventy-seven. But she looks ancient, shrunken, a mummified relic. Her thin hair is pure white, her teeth are brown with decay. So much for stories of Chinese women looking young forever, I think to myself.

50   Now Aiyi is crooning to me: "*Jandale.*" So big already. She looks up at me, at my full height, and then peers into her pink plastic bag—her gifts to us, I have figured out—as if she is wondering what she will give to me, now that I am so old and big. And then she grabs my elbow with her sharp pincerlike grasp and turns me around. A man and a woman in their fifties are shaking hands with my father, everybody smiling and saying, "Ah! Ah!" They are Aiyi's oldest son and his wife, and standing next to them are four

other people, around my age, and a little girl who's around ten. The introductions go by so fast, all I know is that one of them is Aiyi's grandson, with his wife, and the other is her granddaughter, with her husband. And the little girl is Lili, Aiyi's great-granddaughter.

Aiyi and my father speak the Mandarin dialect from their childhood, but the rest of the family speaks only the Cantonese of their village. I understand only Mandarin but can't speak it that well. So Aiyi and my father gossip unrestrained in Mandarin, exchanging news about people from their old village. And they stop only occasionally to talk to the rest of us, sometimes in Cantonese, sometimes in English.

"Oh, it is as I suspected," says my father, turning to me. "He died last summer." And I already understood this. I just don't know who this person, Li Gong, is. I feel as if I were in the United Nations and the translators had run amok.

"Hello," I say to the little girl. "My name is Jing-mei." But the little girl squirms to look away, causing her parents to laugh with embarrassment. I try to think of Cantonese words I can say to her, stuff I learned from friends in Chinatown, but all I can think of are swear words, terms for bodily functions, and short phrases like "tastes good," "tastes like garbage," and "she's really ugly." And then I have another plan: I hold up the Polaroid camera, beckoning Lili with my finger. She immediately jumps forward, places one hand on her hip in the manner of a fashion model, juts out her chest, and flashes me a toothy smile. As soon as I take the picture she is standing next to me, jumping and giggling every few seconds as she watches herself appear on the greenish film.

By the time we hail taxis for the ride to the hotel, Lili is holding tight onto my hand, pulling me along.

In the taxi, Aiyi talks nonstop, so I have no chance to ask her about the different sights we are passing by. 55

"You wrote and said you would come only for one day," says Aiyi to my father in an agitated tone. "One day! How can you see your family in one day! Toishan is many hours' drive from Guangzhou. And this idea to call us when you arrive. This is nonsense. We have no telephone."

My heart races a little. I wonder if Auntie Lindo told my sisters we would call from the hotel in Shanghai?

Aiyi continues to scold my father. "I was so beside myself, ask my son, almost turned heaven and earth upside down trying to think of a way! So we decided the best was for us to take the bus from Toishan and come into Guangzhou—meet you right from the start."

And now I am holding my breath as the taxi driver dodges between trucks and buses, honking his horn constantly. We seem to be on some sort of long freeway overpass, like a bridge above the city. I can see row after row of apartments, each floor cluttered with laundry hanging out to dry on the balcony. We pass a public bus, with people jammed in so tight their faces are nearly wedged against the window. Then I see the skyline of what must be downtown Guangzhou. From a distance, it looks like a major American city, with highrises and construction going on everywhere. As we slow down in the more congested part of the city, I see scores of little shops, dark inside, lined with counters and shelves. And then there is a building, its front laced with scaffolding made of bamboo poles held together with plastic strips. Men and women are standing on narrow platforms, scraping the sides, working without safety straps or helmets. Oh, would OSHA[1] have a field day here, I think.

60   Aiyi's shrill voice rises up again: "So it is a shame you can't see our village, our house. My sons have been quite successful, selling our vegetables in the free market. We had enough these last few years to build a big house, three stories, all of new brick, big enough for our whole family and then some. And every year, the money is even better. You Americans aren't the only ones who know how to get rich!"

The taxi stops and I assume we've arrived, but then I peer out at what looks like a grander version of the Hyatt Regency. "This is communist China?" I wonder out loud. And then I shake my head toward my father. "This must be the wrong hotel." I quickly pull out our itinerary, travel tickets, and reservations. I had explicitly instructed my travel agent to choose something inexpensive, in the thirty-to-forty-dollar range. I'm sure of this. And there it says on our itinerary: Garden Hotel, Huanshi Dong Lu. Well, our travel agent had better be prepared to eat the extra, that's all I have to say.

The hotel is magnificent. A bellboy complete with uniform and sharp-creased cap jumps forward and begins to carry our bags into the lobby. Inside, the hotel looks like an orgy of shopping arcades and restaurants all encased in granite and glass. And rather than be impressed, I am worried about the expense, as well as the appearance it must give Aiyi, that we rich Americans cannot be without our luxuries even for one night.

But when I step up to the reservation desk, ready to haggle over this booking mistake, it is confirmed. Our rooms are prepaid, thirty-four dollars each. I feel sheepish, and Aiyi and the others seem delighted by our temporary surroundings. Lili is looking wide-eyed at an arcade filled with video games.

Our whole family crowds into one elevator, and the bellboy waves, saying he will meet us on the eighteenth floor. As soon as the elevator door shuts, everybody becomes very quiet, and when the door finally opens again, everybody talks at once in what sounds like relieved voices. I have the feeling Aiyi and the others have never been on such a long elevator ride.

65   Our rooms are next to each other and are identical. The rugs, drapes, bedspreads are all in shades of taupe. There's a color television with remote-control panels built into the lamp table between the two twin beds. The

---

1. The Occupational Safety and Health Administration, a division of the U.S. Department of Labor.

bathroom has marble walls and floors. I find a built-in wet bar with a small refrigerator stocked with Heineken beer, Coke Classic, and Seven-Up, mini-bottles of Johnnie Walker Red, Bacardi rum, and Smirnoff vodka, and packets of M & M's, honey-roasted cashews, and Cadbury chocolate bars. And again I say out loud, "This is communist China?"

My father comes into my room. "They decided we should just stay here and visit," he says, shrugging his shoulders. "They say, Less trouble that way. More time to talk."

"What about dinner?" I ask. I have been envisioning my first real Chinese feast for many days already, a big banquet with one of those soups steaming out of a carved winter melon, chicken wrapped in clay, Peking duck, the works.

My father walks over and picks up a room service book next to a *Travel & Leisure* magazine. He flips through the pages quickly and then points to the menu. "This is what they want," says my father.

So it's decided. We are going to dine tonight in our rooms, with our family, sharing hamburgers, french fries, and apple pie à la mode.

Aiyi and her family are browsing the shops while we clean up. After a hot 70 ride on the train, I'm eager for a shower and cooler clothes.

The hotel has provided little packets of shampoo which, upon opening, I discover is the consistency and color of hoisin sauce.[2] This is more like it, I think. This is China. And I rub some in my damp hair.

Standing in the shower, I realize this is the first time I've been by myself in what seems like days. But instead of feeling relieved, I feel forlorn. I think about what my mother said, about activating my genes and becoming Chinese. And I wonder what she meant.

Right after my mother died, I asked myself a lot of things, things that couldn't be answered, to force myself to grieve more. It seemed as if I wanted to sustain my grief, to assure myself that I had cared deeply enough.

But now I ask the questions mostly because I want to know the answers. What was that pork stuff she used to make that had the texture of sawdust? What were the names of the uncles who died in Shanghai? What had she dreamt all these years about her other daughters? All the times when she got mad at me, was she really thinking about them? Did she wish I were they? Did she regret that I wasn't?

At one o'clock in the morning, I awake to tapping sounds on the window. I 75 must have dozed off and now I feel my body uncramping itself. I'm sitting on the floor, leaning against one of the twin beds. Lili is lying next to me. The others are asleep, too, sprawled out on the beds and floor. Aiyi is

---

2. Sweet brownish-red sauce made from soybeans, sugar, water, spices, garlic, and chili.

seated at a little table, looking very sleepy. And my father is staring out the window, tapping his fingers on the glass. The last time I listened my father was telling Aiyi about his life since he last saw her. How he had gone to Yenching University, later got a post with a newspaper in Chungking, met my mother there, a young widow. How they later fled together to Shanghai to try to find my mother's family house, but there was nothing there. And then they traveled eventually to Canton and then to Hong Kong, then Haiphong and finally to San Francisco. . . .

"Suyuan didn't tell me she was trying all these years to find her daughters," he is now saying in a quiet voice. "Naturally, I did not discuss her daughters with her. I thought she was ashamed she had left them behind."

"Where did she leave them?" asks Aiyi. "How were they found?"

I am wide awake now. Although I have heard parts of this story from my mother's friends.

"It happened when the Japanese took over Kweilin," says my father.

80 "Japanese in Kweilin?" says Aiyi. "That was never the case. Couldn't be. The Japanese never came to Kweilin."

"Yes, that is what the newspapers reported. I know this because I was working for the news bureau at the time. The Kuomintang[3] often told us what we could say and could not say. But we knew the Japanese had come into Kwangsi Province. We had sources who told us how they had captured the Wuchang-Canton railway. How they were coming overland, making very fast progress, marching toward the provincial capital."

Aiyi looks astonished. "If people did not know this, how could Suyuan know the Japanese were coming?"

"An officer of the Kuomintang secretly warned her," explains my father. "Suyuan's husband also was an officer and everybody knew that officers and their families would be the first to be killed. So she gathered a few possessions and, in the middle of the night, she picked up her daughters and fled on foot. The babies were not even one year old."

"How could she give up those babies!" sighs Aiyi. "Twin girls. We have never had such luck in our family." And then she yawns again.

85 "What were they named?" she asks. I listen carefully. I had been planning on using just the familiar "Sister" to address them both. But now I want to know how to pronounce their names.

"They have their father's surname, Wang," says my father. "And their given names are Chwun Yu and Chwun Hwa."

"What do the names mean?" I ask.

"Ah." My father draws imaginary characters on the window. "One means 'Spring Rain,' the other 'Spring Flower,'" he explains in English, "because

---

3. National People's Party, led by Generalissimo Chiang Kai-shek (1887–1975), which fought successfully against the Japanese occupation before being defeated militarily in 1949 by the Chinese Communist Party, led by Mao Zedong (1893–1976).

they born in the spring, and of course rain come before flower, same order these girls are born. Your mother like a poet, don't you think?"

I nod my head. I see Aiyi nod her head forward, too. But it falls forward and stays there. She is breathing deeply, noisily. She is asleep.

"And what does Ma's name mean?" I whisper. 90

"'Suyuan,'" he says, writing more invisible characters on the glass. "The way she write it in Chinese, it mean 'Long-Cherished Wish.' Quite a fancy name, not so ordinary like flower name. See this first character, it mean something like 'Forever Never Forgotten.' But there is another way to write 'Suyuan.' Sound exactly the same, but the meaning is opposite." His finger creates the brushstrokes of another character. "The first part look the same: 'Never Forgotten.' But the last part add to first part make the whole word mean 'Long-Held Grudge.' Your mother get angry with me, I tell her her name should be Grudge."

My father is looking at me, moist-eyed. "See, I pretty clever, too, hah?"

I nod, wishing I could find some way to comfort him. "And what about my name," I ask, "what does 'Jing-mei' mean?"

"Your name also special," he says. I wonder if any name in Chinese is not something special. "'Jing' like excellent *jing*. Not just good, it's something pure, essential, the best quality. *Jing* is good leftover stuff when you take impurities out of something like gold, or rice, or salt. So what is left—just pure essence. And 'Mei,' this is common *mei*, as in *meimei*, 'younger sister.'"

I think about this. My mother's long-cherished wish. Me, the younger 95 sister who was supposed to be the essence of the others. I feed myself with the old grief, wondering how disappointed my mother must have been. Tiny Aiyi stirs suddenly, her head rolls and then falls back, her mouth opens as if to answer my question. She grunts in her sleep, tucking her body more closely into the chair.

"So why did she abandon those babies on the road?" I need to know, because now I feel abandoned too.

"Long time I wondered this myself," says my father. "But then I read that letter from her daughters in Shanghai now, and I talk to Auntie Lindo, all the others. And then I knew. No shame in what she done. None."

"What happened?"

"Your mother running away—" begins my father.

"No, tell me in Chinese," I interrupt. "Really, I can understand." 100

He begins to talk, still standing at the window, looking into the night.

After fleeing Kweilin, your mother walked for several days trying to find a main road. Her thought was to catch a ride on a truck or wagon, to catch enough rides until she reached Chungking, where her husband was stationed.

She had sewn money and jewelry into the lining of her dress, enough, she thought, to barter rides all the way. If I am lucky, she thought, I will not have to trade the heavy gold bracelet and jade ring. These were things from her mother, your grandmother.

By the third day, she had traded nothing. The roads were filled with people, everybody running and begging for rides from passing trucks. The trucks rushed by, afraid to stop. So your mother found no rides, only the start of dysentery pains in her stomach.

105　　Her shoulders ached from the two babies swinging from scarf slings. Blisters grew on the palms from holding two leather suitcases. And then the blisters burst and began to bleed. After a while, she left the suitcases behind, keeping only the food and a few clothes. And later she also dropped the bags of wheat flour and rice and kept walking like this for many miles, singing songs to her little girls, until she was delirious with pain and fever.

Finally, there was not one more step left in her body. She didn't have the strength to carry those babies any farther. She slumped to the ground. She knew she would die of her sickness, or perhaps from thirst, from starvation, or from the Japanese, who she was sure were marching right behind her.

She took the babies out of the slings and sat them on the side of the road, then lay down next to them. You babies are so good, she said, so quiet. They smiled back, reaching their chubby hands for her, wanting to be picked up again. And then she knew she could not bear to watch her babies die with her.

She saw a family with three young children in a cart going by. "Take my babies, I beg you," she cried to them. But they stared back with empty eyes and never stopped.

She saw another person pass and called out again. This time a man turned around, and he had such a terrible expression—your mother said it looked like death itself—she shivered and looked away.

110　　When the road grew quiet, she tore open the lining of her dress, and stuffed jewelry under the shirt of one baby and money under the other. She reached into her pocket and drew out the photos of her family, the picture of her father and mother, the picture of herself and her husband on their wedding day. And she wrote on the back of each the names of the babies and this same message: "Please care for these babies with the money and valuables provided. When it is safe to come, if you bring them to Shanghai, 9 Weichang Lu, the Li family will be glad to give you a generous reward. Li Suyuan and Wang Fuchi."

And then she touched each baby's cheek and told her not to cry. She would go down the road to find them some food and would be back. And without looking back, she walked down the road, stumbling and crying, thinking only of this one last hope, that her daughters would be found by a kindhearted person who would care for them. She would not allow herself to imagine anything else.

She did not remember how far she walked, which direction she went, when she fainted, or how she was found. When she awoke, she was in the back of a bouncing truck with several other sick people, all moaning. And she began to scream, thinking she was now on a journey to Buddhist hell. But the face of an American missionary lady bent over her and smiled, talking to her in a soothing language she did not understand. And yet she could somehow understand. She had been saved for no good reason, and it was now too late to go back and save her babies.

When she arrived in Chungking, she learned her husband had died two weeks before. She told me later she laughed when the officers told her this news, she was so delirious with madness and disease. To come so far, to lose so much and to find nothing.

I met her in a hospital. She was lying on a cot, hardly able to move, her dysentery had drained her so thin. I had come in for my foot, my missing toe, which was cut off by a piece of falling rubble. She was talking to herself, mumbling.

"Look at these clothes," she said, and I saw she had on a rather unusual 115 dress for wartime. It was silk satin, quite dirty, but there was no doubt it was a beautiful dress.

"Look at this face," she said, and I saw her dusty face and hollow cheeks, her eyes shining black. "Do you see my foolish hope?"

"I thought I had lost everything, except these two things," she murmured. "And I wondered which I would lose next. Clothes or hope? Hope or clothes?"

"But now, see here, look what is happening," she said, laughing, as if all her prayers had been answered. And she was pulling hair out of her head as easily as one lifts new wheat from wet soil.

It was an old peasant woman who found them. "How could I resist?" the peasant woman later told your sisters when they were older. They were still sitting obediently near where your mother had left them, looking like little fairy queens waiting for their sedan to arrive.

The woman, Mei Ching, and her husband, Mei Han, lived in a stone 120 cave. There were thousands of hidden caves like that in and around Kweilin so secret that the people remained hidden even after the war ended. The Meis would come out of their cave every few days and forage for food supplies left on the road, and sometimes they would see something that they both agreed was a tragedy to leave behind. So one day they took back to their cave a delicately painted set of rice bowls, another day a little footstool with a velvet cushion and two new wedding blankets. And once, it was your sisters.

They were pious people, Muslims, who believed the twin babies were a sign of double luck, and they were sure of this when, later in the evening, they discovered how valuable the babies were. She and her husband had never seen rings and bracelets like those. And while they admired the pictures, knowing the babies came from a good family, neither of them could read or write. It was not until many months later that Mei Ching found someone who could read the writing on the back. By then, she loved these baby girls like her own.

In 1952 Mei Han, the husband, died. The twins were already eight years old, and Mei Ching now decided it was time to find your sisters' true family.

She showed the girls the picture of their mother and told them they had been born into a great family and she would take them back to see their true mother and grandparents. Mei Ching told them about the reward, but she swore she would refuse it. She loved these girls so much, she only wanted them to have what they were entitled to—a better life, a fine house, educated ways. Maybe the family would let her stay on as the girls' amah.[4] Yes, she was certain they would insist.

Of course, when she found the place at 9 Weichang Lu, in the old French Concession, it was something completely different. It was the site of a factory building, recently constructed, and none of the workers knew what had become of the family whose house had burned down on that spot.

125   Mei Ching could not have known, of course, that your mother and I, her new husband, had already returned to that same place in 1945 in hopes of finding both her family and her daughters.

Your mother and I stayed in China until 1947. We went to many different cities—back to Kweilin, to Changsha, as far south as Kunming. She was always looking out of one corner of her eye for twin babies, then little girls. Later we went to Hong Kong, and when we finally left in 1949 for the United States, I think she was even looking for them on the boat. But when we arrived, she no longer talked about them. I thought, At last, they have died in her heart.

When letters could be openly exchanged between China and the United States, she wrote immediately to old friends in Shanghai and Kweilin. I did not know she did this. Auntie Lindo told me. But of course, by then, all the street names had changed. Some people had died, others had moved away. So it took many years to find a contact. And when she did find an old schoolmate's address and wrote asking her to look for her daughters, her friend wrote back and said this was impossible, like looking for a needle on the bottom of the ocean. How did she know her daughters were in Shanghai and not somewhere else in China? The friend, of course, did not ask, How do you know your daughters are still alive?

So her schoolmate did not look. Finding babies lost during the war was a matter of foolish imagination, and she had no time for that.

---

4. Maidservant or nurse.

But every year, your mother wrote to different people. And this last year, I think she got a big idea in her head, to go to China and find them herself. I remember she told me, "Canning, we should go, before it is too late, before we are too old." And I told her we were already too old, it was already too late.

I just thought she wanted to be a tourist! I didn't know she wanted to go and look for her daughters. So when I said it was too late, that must have put a terrible thought in her head that her daughters might be dead. And I think this possibility grew bigger and bigger in her head, until it killed her.

Maybe it was your mother's dead spirit who guided her Shanghai school-mate to find her daughters. Because after your mother died, the school-mate saw your sisters, by chance, while shopping for shoes at the Number One Department Store on Nanjing Dong Road. She said it was like a dream, seeing these two women who looked so much alike, moving down the stairs together. There was something about their facial expressions that reminded the schoolmate of your mother.

She quickly walked over to them and called their names, which of course, they did not recognize at first, because Mei Ching had changed their names. But your mother's friend was so sure, she persisted. "Are you not Wang Chwun Yu and Wang Chwun Hwa?" she asked them. And then these double-image women became very excited, because they remembered the names written on the back of an old photo, a photo of a young man and woman they still honored, as their much-loved first parents, who had died and become spirit ghosts still roaming the earth looking for them.

———

At the airport, I am exhausted. I could not sleep last night. Aiyi had fol-lowed me into my room at three in the morning, and she instantly fell asleep on one of the twin beds, snoring with the might of a lumberjack. I lay awake thinking about my mother's story, realizing how much I have never known about her, grieving that my sisters and I had both lost her.

And now at the airport, after shaking hands with everybody, waving good-bye, I think about all the different ways we leave people in this world. Cheerily waving good-bye to some at airports, knowing we'll never see each other again. Leaving others on the side of the road, hoping that we will. Finding my mother in my father's story and saying good-bye before I have a chance to know her better.

Aiyi smiles at me as we wait for our gate to be called. She is so old. I put one arm around her and one arm around Lili. They are the same size, it seems. And then it's time. As we wave good-bye one more time and enter the waiting area, I get the sense I am going from one funeral to another. In my hand I'm clutching a pair of tickets to Shanghai. In two hours we'll be there.

The plane takes off. I close my eyes. How can I describe to them in my broken Chinese about our mother's life? Where should I begin?

"Wake up, we're here," says my father. And I awake with my heart pounding in my throat. I look out the window and we're already on the runway. It's gray outside.

And now I'm walking down the steps of the plane, onto the tarmac and toward the building. If only, I think, if only my mother had lived long enough to be the one walking toward them. I am so nervous I cannot even feel my feet. I am just moving somehow.

Somebody shouts, "She's arrived!" And then I see her. Her short hair. Her small body. And that same look on her face. She has the back of her hand pressed hard against her mouth. She is crying as though she had gone through a terrible ordeal and were happy it is over.

140 And I know it's not my mother, yet it is the same look she had when I was five and had disappeared all afternoon, for such a long time, that she was convinced I was dead. And when I miraculously appeared, sleepy-eyed, crawling from underneath my bed, she wept and laughed, biting the back of her hand to make sure it was true.

And now I see her again, two of her, waving, and in one hand there is a photo, the Polaroid I sent them. As soon as I get beyond the gate, we run toward each other, all three of us embracing, all hesitations and expectations forgotten.

"Mama, Mama," we all murmur, as if she is among us.

My sisters look at me, proudly. *"Meimei jandale,"* says one sister proudly to the other. "Little Sister has grown up." I look at their faces again and I see no trace of my mother in them. Yet they still look familiar. And now I also see what part of me is Chinese. It is so obvious. It is my family. It is in our blood. After all these years, it can finally be let go.

My sisters and I stand, arms around each other, laughing and wiping the tears from each other's eyes. The flash of the Polaroid goes off and my father hands me the snapshot. My sisters and I watch quietly together, eager to see what develops.

145 The gray-green surface changes to the bright colors of our three images, sharpening and deepening all at once. And although we don't speak, I know we all see it: Together we look like our mother. Her same eyes, her same mouth, open in surprise to see, at last, her long-cherished wish.

1989

QUESTIONS

1. Why is the opening scene of "A Pair of Tickets"—the train journey from Hong Kong to Guangzhou—an appropriate setting for June May's remark that she is "becoming Chinese"?

2. When June May arrives in Guangzhou, what are some details that seem familiar to her, and what are some that seem exotic? Why is she so preoccupied with comparing China to America?
3. June May says that "she could never pass for true Chinese," yet by the end of the story she has discovered "the part of me that is Chinese." How does the meaning of "Chinese" evolve throughout the story?

SUGGESTIONS FOR WRITING

1. Write an essay in which you compare the use of setting in any two stories in this book. You might compare the re-creation of two similar settings, such as landscapes far from home, foreign cities, or stifling suburbs; or you might contrast the treatment of different kinds of settings. Be sure to consider not only the authors' descriptive techniques but also the way the authors use setting to shape plot, point of view, and character.
2. In "A Pair of Tickets," Amy Tan provides detailed descriptions of June May's journeys to Guangzhou and Shanghai. In his account of his wife's escape from Kweilin, June May's father says little about the landscape. Write an essay in which you compare the two very different storytelling techniques used in this story.
3. In at least two of the stories in this chapter, a place encountered for the first time by a traveler is described with great vividness: the city of Guangzhou in "A Pair of Tickets" and the city of Yalta in "The Lady with the Dog." Citing examples from these stories, write an essay in which you discuss the effect of new surroundings on our perceptions, emotions, and memories.
4. Choose any story in this chapter and write an essay that explores how the story both draws on and also encourages us to rethink our ideas about a particular place and time and social milieu, perhaps (but not necessarily) by showing us characters who themselves either come to see a setting differently or refuse to do so.
5. Write a fifth section for "The Lady with the Dog."
6. Write a story in which a newcomer brings a fresh perspective to a familiar setting.

SAMPLE WRITING

In the following essay, student writer Steven Matview explores the role of setting in Anton Chekhov's "The Lady with the Dog." His essay could well have been written in response to the second of the "Suggestions for Writing" in this chapter. Read the essay responsively and critically, taking time to consider the details Steven chooses to highlight and the way he interprets them. Does he manage to build a convincing and thorough argument about the role of setting in "The Lady with the Dog"? What other details from the story might deserve a place in this argument? In particular, notice how Steven concentrates on temporal setting (the seasons) while commenting only briefly on spatial setting and on the interconnections between time and space in the story. If Steven were your classmate, what three things would you suggest he most needs to do in order to improve the essay in revision?

Steven Matview
Professor Anne Stevens
English 298
12 March 2008

The Importance of Good Setting: How Setting Reflects Emotions
in Anton Chekhov's "The Lady with the Dog"

Setting is important to Chekhov's "The Lady with the Dog." But wait, isn't setting important to all stories? Not necessarily. In many stories, like Hemingway's "Hills like White Elephants," the plot could be happening anywhere, and it would not matter. But in "The Lady with the Dog" the setting plays an important role in the story, in particular to Dmitri, who is the main character and who experiences the most growth throughout. He goes from being a man at 40 who is full of youthful energy and thinks he has been loved by many women to an old man who realizes that he is just experiencing love for the first time. During the course of the narrative, the setting Chekhov maps out shows the progression of Dmitri's affair with Anna Sergeyevna,

Dmitri's state of mind, and the changes that Dmitri undergoes. The setting in this story is just as important as any character. In fact, I would argue that the setting is the single most important component of the story.

Dmitri's relationship with the lady with the dog has its ups and downs, which are reflected in the seasons and the descriptions of weather. Anna, the lady with the dog, makes this apparent when she says, "The weather is better this evening" (184). Their lives are better when they are together in the summer. This is the time Dmitri and Anna meet and start their courtship. Both are married, and both have spent so much time forcing themselves to love their partners that they do not recognize real love when they feel it. Dmitri initially only wants a fling and doesn't even learn or use Anna's name, referring to her only as "the lady with the dog." There isn't any stress yet, and the two can be just happy with things the way they are. They go on dates and spend time together in Anna's hotel room. Dmitri starts to think of her as "Anna Sergeyevna—'the lady with the dog'" (par. 29), showing a shift within the relationship. He shows he's started to think of this as more of a relationship by using her full name but doesn't completely switch, as he adds in that epithet "lady with the dog." He is trying to resist because he is still married. Dmitri feels young and alive and thinks back to all the women he has made happy in his life.

Another aspect of the setting are the places described in the story, which relate to things the characters feel or know on a subconscious level. At the start of the story, Dmitri is staying at a seaside resort in Yalta. We know that a resort is an impersonal place, where someone can reinvent themselves or get away from the things they don't like about home. Dmitri reinvents his idea about what love is while getting away from a wife he does not care for. Dmitri meets Anna for the first time "in the public gardens" (par. 2). A garden is a place of growth, reflecting the soon-to-be growth of their relationship, as well as the growth Dmitri will experience as a person. They then go on a date, and we become privy to a metaphor describing Dmitri's marriage and how things will go with Anna: "Owing to the roughness of the sea, the steamer arrived late, after the sun had set, and it was a long time turning about before it reached the groyne" (par. 22). The steamer is Dmitri, the sea is his life, and the groyne, a device designed to disrupt the flow of water, is Anna. It took Dmitri longer to find true love, and he has gone through a rough time in a boring marriage, and now there is someone to break that up. This is when Dmitri starts to feel love for Anna, though he does not realize it is love because it is so different from what he has known in the past.

Things change as soon as the next season approaches. The first challenges that arise in the courtship of Dmitri and Anna come when the season begins to change from summer to autumn. Dmitri mentions here that "it's a cold evening" (par. 60), the first time cold is mentioned in the present (before it was only used to describe the unhappy places Anna and Dmitri were escaping from) and a stark contrast to Anna's comment about the weather earlier in the story. Things are starting to get worse for the relationship. Word gets to Anna that she must travel back to her home to be with her husband, who has fallen ill. Dmitri finds that he does not want to let Anna go, that the fling he wanted has turned into something much more. Dmitri thinks that he was "warm and affectionate with [Anna]" (par. 59), terms associated with summer weather. But, with autumn approaching, Dmitri decides that they were not really in love. This is because the feeling he has does not resemble the forced love he has always experienced with his wife and mistresses, but it is brought up as the object of his "warm feelings" leaves and is replaced with the "cold night."

Change of place goes hand in hand with a change of seasons and weather here. And we are told shortly before Anna leaves that "Yalta was hardly visible through the morning mist; white clouds stood motionless on mountain-tops" (par. 47). The mist covering Yalta is like the uncertainty that lies in their future as the summer is winding down. Neither can see clearly what will come from their summer tryst when the time comes to separate. White is a color that is often associated with purity, and Dmitri is experiencing a pure, true kind of love for the first time, but he also has obstacles to overcome that are represented by the mountains.

Dmtri thinks he will get over Anna quickly now that she's gone, but winter brings him even more hardships. The most difficult time the couple face comes in the season of winter. Winter is a cold season often affiliated with sadness and the absence of hope. We find out that "the frosts had begun already" (par. 62), meaning the bad times have already started, and we join Dmitri after he's already been back in Moscow for a short time. In Moscow Dmitri has not stopped thinking of Anna Sergeyevna, who is only referred to by her full name now. Referring to her as "Anna Sergeyevna" instead of "the lady with the dog" is a subtle way of letting us know that Dmitri is thinking of her as more than a fling that has gone by, as we saw earlier that he only called her "the lady with the dog" when he didn't have feelings for her. They are separated by cities and by circumstance, and it seems the relationship might be over. In winter all the plants die, and Dmitri and Anna, whose relationship first blossomed in a garden, seem to have a dead relationship. We find out that "more than a month has past" and that "real winter has come" (186), real winter representing the increasing feelings of separation anxiety Dmitri is suffering from.

We get more visual descriptions in Moscow and Anna's unnamed city relating to the characters' thoughts. After Anna leaves and Dmitri returns to his home in Moscow, we find out that he wants to escape to "restaurants, clubs, dinner-parties, [and] anniversary celebrations" (par. 63), showing us that Dmitri is feeling repressed at home compared to the freedom he had at the resort. After confiding in a local his problems, Dmitri thinks, "there is no escaping or getting away from it—just as though one were in a madhouse or a prison" (par. 72). A madhouse and a prison are two places that no one wants to be. Both places are where you are kept from loved ones. But they are also places you are put in when you have done something wrong, a hint that Dmitri feels he's made mistakes in the past, done his time, and now wants to be free to be with Anna.

Dmitri then decides to go to Anna's city, which is left unnamed in the story. This reflects that it is really Dmitri's journey. Dmitri has a hard time reaching Anna at first, as she is tucked away in the house she shares with her husband. When Dmitri finally does confront Anna she does not initially seem happy to see him. Dmitri confronts Anna at a performance of the play *The Geisha*. The opera and the opera house it is performed in have many qualities that suggest Dmitri's emotional state. The opera house is described as having "a thick fog above the chandelier," and its "gallery was noisy and restless" (par. 85). Dmitri has lots of noisy thoughts in his head as he approaches Anna with uncertainty. As Dmitri approaches Anna the musicians begin tuning their instruments. They are getting ready for the big performance, as Dmitri is getting ready to renew his relationship with Anna. Anna at first appears to be unhappy and takes Dmitri down a path of winding corridors and then up and down a "narrow, gloomy staircase" (par. 93). The outlook seems gloomy for Dmitri, but she does agree to see him again and proceeds to profess her love for him.

At the end of winter, with spring fast approaching, things between Dmitri and Anna begin to show slight improvement over early winter. The weather is described as being "three degrees above freezing-point, and yet it is snowing" (par. 105). Things are getting better for Dmitri, who knows now that Anna loves him and wants to be with him, but it's not all great yet as both are still married and forced to keep their relationship a secret. The open-air setting of the gardens that their relationship started in is replaced by a hotel room, giving the final scene a claustrophobic feel as Anna wonders how they can be together. At the end of the story the couple is still trying to find a way to make their relationship work when we are told, "it seemed as though in a little while the solution would be found" (par. 124). Winter is ending, and spring, a season of growth, new beginnings, and love, is on the horizon. From this we might deduce that the couple will make it, at least into the spring.

But will they? The fact that the story ends with the couple in a "gray area" is fitting because gray, a color associated with ambiguity (shades of gray compared to a black-and-white situation; a "gray area"), in fact appears often in the story. Dmitri is in a situation that involves a lot of moral ambiguity. During the course of the narrative he ends up in love with a married woman while he himself is also married. They begin existing in this gray area where we as readers begin to wonder if what they are doing is really wrong, since they are committing adultery. Anna's eyes are gray, reminding us that Dmitri is entering into a moral gray area whenever he is engaging in this relationship. When Dmitri goes to find Anna and resume their relationship in her home town, he stays at a hotel room whose "floor was covered with grey army cloth" (par. 75) and where there is gray dust and a gray blanket. He enters another gray area when he wants to do what his heart says is right by reuniting with Anna, but doing so is committing more adultery.

But I feel that the recurring gray colors also imply something besides ambiguity—the sadness and lack of excitement that Dmitri has always had in his life thanks to his unhappy marriage and that he might, paradoxically, have come to expect or even need. We can see this when he refers to his hotel in Anna's city as "the best room at the hotel" (par. 75), but filled with items of gray, or when Anna is "wearing his favourite grey dress" (par. 108). The hotel room and Anna are both things that are great or that he adores, but they have that tinge of sadness, represented by the gray, that he needs.

Looking back over the story, we as readers can come to our own conclusions about whether or not Dmitri and Anna stay together. From looking at the progression of the weather we see that in the summer things are good, in fall bad situations arise, winter is the worst time, and the dawn of spring shows slight hope. Following this progression, I believe that when spring finally hits they will be able to come up with a plan to stay a couple.

Dmitri and Anna would be happy. We would see Dmitri and Anna figuring out a way to make their relationship public and no longer to be confined to enclosed hiding places. The real question then would be whether the gray would fade out of Dmitri's life after he finds a happiness with Anna that will last past the following summer or whether the cycle is just doomed to repeat itself, as summer eventually turns into winter and the brightest of colors and emotions fade into gray.

5 SYMBOL AND FIGURATIVE LANGUAGE

A symbol is something that stands for or represents something else. Sometimes a symbol resembles or closely relates to what it represents, but often the association is arbitrary or subtle. Even so, through common usage, many symbols are instantly understood by almost everyone in a particular group. Although we rarely think of them as such, the letters of the English alphabet are themselves symbols, representing different sounds. We simply learn to recognize them, however, without thinking about whether there is any resemblance between what the symbols look like and what they represent. In other languages, one character may stand for an object or concept, such as the Chinese characters for "fire." Yet some symbols do help us by resembling what they stand for, such as the symbol for a fire alarm.

Similarly, abstractions may be represented by symbols that resemble things that are associated with them:

Although the smiley face can simply mean "Smile!" its meanings as an "emoticon" in e-mails and text messages range from "I like this" to "Just joking." The skull and crossbones symbol is used on warning labels to indicate that the contents are poisonous, but it has also been associated with death, cemeteries, and pirates.

Other symbols are more arbitrary, having no literal connection with what they represent. Octagons and the color red have little to do with stopping a car, but most Americans, even if they are too young to drive, understand what a stop sign means. Such symbols, though not based on resemblances, elicit an unconscious and reflexive response from us. The meaning of a symbol is not always so concrete and practical, however. The U.S. national flag is an arbitrary symbol, having no direct resemblance to what it represents, but most people recognize its primary significance; the "stars and stripes" undoubtedly stands for the United States. Nevertheless, the flag differs from a traffic sign in the sense that people respond on various levels to the many meanings associated with that vast country.

LITERARY SYMBOLISM

A **symbol** in a work of literature compares or puts together two things that are in some ways dissimilar. But literary symbolism rarely comes down to a simple equation of one thing to another. Unlike an arbitrary symbol such as a letter or traffic sign, a symbol in literature usually carries richer and various meanings, as does a flag or a religious image. And because of its significance, a symbol usually appears or is hinted at numerous times throughout the work. In reading literature, it may be challenging to recognize symbols, and readers may have good reasons to disagree about their interpretation, since literary works often incorporate symbolism for which there is no single "correct" interpretation. No one would say that reading a short story should be like a treasure hunt for some shiny symbol that clearly reveals all the hidden meanings; the complexity remains and requires further exploration even when we have recognized a symbol's significance at some level. A literary symbol may be understood as an extended figure of speech that rewards further interpretation.

A symbol usually conveys an abstraction or cluster of abstractions, from the ideal to the imperceptible or the irrational, in a more concrete form. Some symbols have been in use by many people for a long time (in which case it is known as a *traditional symbol*); a white dove, for example, is a traditional symbol of peace and love. A rose can be a symbol of godly love, of romantic desire, of female beauty, of mortality (because the flower wilts), or of hidden cruelty (because it has thorns). The snake has traditionally been a symbol of evil, but in Rudyard Kipling's *The Jungle Book*, the python Ka, while frightening, is on the side of law and order. A few symbolic character types, plots, objects, or settings—for example, the trickster, the quest, the garden—have become so pervasive and have recurred in so many cultures that they are considered **archetypes** (literary elements that recur in cultural and cross-cultural myth). Fire, water, a flower, or a tree can all be considered archetypes because numerous cultures use them symbolically, often within their system of religion or myth. Literary symbolism frequently borrows from the symbols and archetypes associated with religion or myth.

A common literary form, especially in works written by and for religious believers, is the **allegory**, which may be regarded as an "extended" symbol or series of symbols that encompasses a whole work. In an allegory, concrete things and abstract concepts may be associated with each other across a narrative with at least two distinct levels of meaning. Because allegories set up series of correspondences, they usually help the reader translate these correspondences through the use of names that readily function as labels, often with obvious moral implications. In *The Pilgrim's Progress*, probably the most famous prose allegory in English, the central character is named Christian; he was born in the City of Destruction and sets out for the Celestial City, passes through the Slough of Despond and Vanity Fair, meets men named Pliable and Obstinate, and so on. The point of an allegory is not to make us hunt for disguised meanings, so it is no defect if an allegory's intended meaning is clear. Instead, the purpose is to let us enjoy an invented world where everything is especially meaningful and everything corresponds to something else according to a moral or otherwise "correct" plan.

When an entire story is allegorical or symbolic, it is sometimes called a **myth**. *Myth* originally referred to a story of communal origin that provided an explanation or religious interpretation of humanity, nature, the universe, or the relations among them. Sometimes we apply the term *myth* to stories associated with religions we do not believe in, and sometimes to literature that seeks to express experiences or truths that transcend any one location, culture, or time.

FIGURES OF SPEECH

Figures of speech, or **figurative language**, are similar to symbols in that they supplement or replace literal meaning, often by creating imaginative connections between our ideas and our senses. Sometimes referred to as *tropes* (literally, "turnings"), figures of speech could be described as *bending* the usual meaning of language and *shaping* our response to a work. Whether or not they have anything to do with spatial forms or "figures," or whether they rely on vision, such tropes contribute to what are called the **images** or **imagery** of a story. Many figures of speech are known by the Latin or Greek names used in classical Greek and Roman *rhetoric*, the art and science of speech and persuasion.

Just as you can enjoy gymnastics or diving events during the Olympics without knowing the names of the specific twists and turns, you can enjoy the figurative language in a story without identifying each figure of speech. Yet for the purposes of interpreting and writing about literature, it is important to learn some basic terms and distinctions. The box below defines some of the most frequently encountered figures of speech.

Key Figures of Speech

allegory an extended association, often sustained in every element (character, plot, setting, etc.) and throughout an entire work, between two levels of meaning, usually literal and abstract. In *Animal Farm* (1945), for example, George Orwell uses an uprising of barnyard animals as an allegory for the Bolshevik revolution in Russia.

allusion a reference, usually brief, to another text or some person or entity external to the work. Examples may range from a direct quotation of the Bible to the mention of a famous name.

irony a meaning or outcome contrary to what is expected; in *verbal irony*, the text says one thing and means the reverse. When the intended meaning is harshly critical or mocking, it is called *sarcasm*. Sister in "Why I Live at the P.O." ("Reading More Fiction") unintentionally creates verbal irony in recalling how Stella-Rondo stole Mr. Whitaker from her: "Told him I was one-sided. Bigger on one side than the other, which is a deliberate, calculated falsehood: I'm the same." "One-sided" in this quarrel means having breasts of different sizes, but Sister doesn't realize that she truly is biased or one-sided as a personality. She tells her own calculated falsehoods. An example of sarcasm occurs when the girl in "Hills Like White Elephants" (chapter 2) agrees that many people have had the operation, "And afterward they were all so happy." She means the opposite, bitterly mocking her companion's promise that they will be happy.

metaphor a representation of one thing as if it were something else, without a verbal signal such as *like* or *as*. "She was the queen," Sammy tells us in John Updike's story "A & P" ("Reading More Fiction")—not *like* a queen, but simply "the queen." Sammy calls her this to express her high status, beauty, and leadership among the girls.

metonymy using the name of one thing to refer to another thing associated with it. The common phrase *red tape* is a metonymy for

(Continued on next page)

(Continued)

excessive paperwork and procedure that slows down an official trans-action, based on the fact that papers used to be tied up with red tape.

oxymoron   a combination of contradictory or opposite ideas, quali-ties, or entities, as in *wise fool.*

personification   sometimes called *anthropomorphism*, attributing human qualities to objects or animals. In "The Open Boat" (chapter 6), Stephen Crane personifies the birds who "sat comfortably in groups" and looked at the men with "unblinking scrutiny." He pushes personifi-cation to comic extreme in the shipwrecked men's thoughts: "If this old ninny-woman, Fate, cannot do better than this . . . she is an old hen who knows not her intention." Here, "hen" is a metaphor for a silly woman, who in turn personifies the idea of destiny or fate.

simile   a representation of one thing as if it were something else, with an explicit verbal signal such as *like* or *as*. A. S. Byatt's story "The Thing in the Forest" begins by describing the forlorn and slightly gro-tesque child evacuees in World War II England with the help of several similes: They wear gloves "like a scarecrow" and march "like a disor-derly dwarf regiment."

symbol   a person, place, object, or image that represents more than its literal meaning. A symbol is more than a passing comparison (such as a simile); instead, as in allegory, its meaning usually relates to most details and themes of the work. Unlike allegory, a symbol usually associates more than two entities or ideas and may be obscure or ambiguous in its meaning. Short stories (or poems) may refer to their central symbolic figure in the title, as in "Cathedral" ("Fiction: Read-ing, Responding, Writing") or "The Birth-Mark."

synecdoche   a form of metonymy (or name substitution) in which the part represents the whole (a *sail* refers to a ship).

INTERPRETING SYMBOLISM AND FIGURATIVE LANGUAGE

The context of an entire story or poem or play can guide you in deciding how far to push your own "translation" of a figure of speech or whether a metaphor has the deeper significance of a symbol. It is best to read the entire story and note all of the figures of speech or imagery before you examine one as a symbol. Often, a symbol is a focal point in a story, a single object or situation that draws the attention of one or more characters.

In Edwidge Danticat's "A Wall of Fire Rising," for example, the hot-air balloon takes on a central and multilayered significance, though there is no longstanding tradition of symbolic meaning for hot-air balloons. Although the story appears to be a matter-of-fact picture of a poor family in Haiti, the climactic action focuses on the father's desire to fly in the balloon, which in turn relates to the title's allusion to a line in a revolutionary speech. Thus the balloon flight, as an effort to rise in every sense, becomes symbolic—but a symbol of what, exactly? The fact that we cannot say with certainty what the balloon flight "means" does not diminish but rather increases its symbolic power. In Nathaniel Hawthorne's "The Birth-Mark," Aylmer explicitly calls Georgiana's one defect "the symbol of his wife's liability to sin, sorrow, decay, and death." The symbolism, allegory, and moral of Hawthorne's story are traditional and accessible. Yet the story remains ambiguous and complex because of its distinctive combination of literal and figurative elements and meanings.

Effective symbols and figurative language cannot be extracted from the story in which they serve, but they can leave a lasting image of what the story is about. With guidance and practice, identifying and interpreting literary symbolism and other figurative language will begin to feel almost as familiar to you as reading the letter symbols on a page, though the meanings may be subtle, ambiguous, and far-reaching rather than straightforward.

Responding to Symbolism: Some Guidelines

1. Read the story carefully, noting any details that seem to have exceptional significance such as names, repeated actions or statements, recurring references to objects, peculiar places, allusions, or other figures of speech.

2. Using your list of such possibly symbolic details, look back through the story to find the passages that feature these details. Are any of the passages connected to each other in a pattern? Do any of these interconnected details suggest themes of the story?

3. Note any symbols or images that you recognize from mythology, religion, or any other literature, art, or popular culture. Look again at the way the story presents such material. What are the signals that the fire is more than a fire, the tree is more than a tree, the ring is more than a ring? If the story invents its own symbol, find any words in the story that show how the characters see something meaningful in the birthmark, monster, hot-air balloon, or coin.

4. Once you have found a symbol—an aspect of the story that is a figure of speech, trope, image, or connection between literal and nonliteral; is extended beyond a few sentences; is more complicated than an alle-

(Continued on next page)

(Continued)

gory's one-to-one translation; and may be interpreted in multiple ways—review every aspect of the story, on the literal level, that relates to this symbol.

5. As you write about the symbol or symbolism in a story, consider your claims about its meaning. Try not to narrow down the possible meanings of either the symbol or the story, but at the same time don't make too grand claims for their ability to reveal the meaning of life. When in doubt, refer back to the story and its literal level of characterization, plot, and setting.

6. Remember to cite specific passages that will help your reader understand the symbol's significance. Your reader may suspect that you are reading too much into it, so this evidence will help you both explain your interpretation and persuade your reader that it is reasonable.

NATHANIEL HAWTHORNE

The Birth-Mark

In the latter part of the last century[1] there lived a man of science, an eminent proficient in every branch of natural philosophy,[2] who not long before our story opens had made experience of a spiritual affinity more attractive than any chemical one. He had left his laboratory to the care of an assistant, cleared his fine countenance from the furnace-smoke, washed the stain of acids from his fingers, and persuaded a beautiful woman to become his wife. In those days, when the comparatively recent discovery of electricity and other kindred mysteries of Nature seemed to open paths into the region of miracle, it was not unusual for the love of science to rival the love of woman in its depth and absorbing energy. The higher intellect, the imagination, the spirit, and even the heart might all find their congenial aliment in pursuits which, as some of their ardent votaries believed, would ascend from one step of powerful intelligence to another, until the philosopher should lay his hand on the secret of creative force and perhaps make new worlds for himself. We know not whether Aylmer possessed this degree of faith in man's ultimate control over nature. He had devoted him-

---

1. That is, the eighteenth century; this story was first published in 1843.
2. The body of knowledge we now call science.

self, however, too unreservedly to scientific studies ever to be weakened from them by any second passion. His love for his young wife might prove the stronger of the two; but it could only be by intertwining itself with his love of science and uniting the strength of the latter to his own. Such a union accordingly took place, and was attended with truly remarkable consequences and a deeply impressive moral. One day, very soon after their marriage, Aylmer sat gazing at his wife with a trouble in his countenance that grew stronger until he spoke.

"Georgiana," said he, "has it never occurred to you that the mark upon your cheek might be removed?"

"No, indeed," said she, smiling; but, perceiving the seriousness of his manner, she blushed deeply. "To tell you the truth, it has been so often called a charm, that I was simple enough to imagine it might be so."

"Ah, upon another face perhaps it might," replied her husband; "but 5 never on yours. No, dearest Georgiana, you came so nearly perfect from the hand of Nature, that this slightest possible defect, which we hesitate whether to term a defect or a beauty, shocks me, as being the visible mark of earthly imperfection."

"Shocks you, my husband!" cried Georgiana, deeply hurt; at first reddening with momentary anger, but then bursting into tears. "Then why did you take me from my mother's side? You cannot love what shocks you!"

To explain this conversation, it must be mentioned that in the center of Georgiana's left cheek there was a singular mark, deeply interwoven, as it were, with the texture and substance of her face. In the usual state of her complexion—a healthy though delicate bloom—the mark wore a tint of deeper crimson, which imperfectly defined its shape amid the surrounding rosiness. When she blushed it gradually became more indistinct, and finally vanished amid the triumphant rush of blood that bathed the whole cheek with its brilliant glow. But if any shifting motion caused her to turn pale there was the mark again, a crimson stain upon the snow, in what Aylmer sometimes deemed an almost fearful distinctness. Its shape bore not a little similarity to the human hand, though of the smallest pygmy size. Georgiana's lovers were wont to say that some fairy at her birth-hour had laid her tiny hand upon the infant's cheek, and left this impress there in token of the magic endowments that were to give her such sway over all hearts. Many a desperate swain would have risked life for the privilege of pressing his lips to the mysterious hand. It must not be concealed, however, that the impression wrought by this fairy sign-manual varied exceedingly according to the difference of temperament in the beholders. Some fastidious persons—but they were exclusively of her own sex—affirmed that the bloody hand, as they chose to call it, quite destroyed the effect of Georgiana's beauty and rendered her countenance even hideous. But it would be as reasonable to say that one of those small blue stains which sometimes occur in the purest statuary marble would convert the Eve of

Powers[3] to a monster. Masculine observers, if the birthmark did not heighten their admiration, contented themselves with wishing it away, that the world might possess one living specimen of ideal loveliness without the semblance of a flaw. After his marriage—for he thought little or nothing of the matter before—Aylmer discovered that this was the case with himself.

Had she been less beautiful—if Envy's self could have found aught else to sneer at—he might have felt his affection heightened by the prettiness of this mimic hand, now vaguely portrayed, now lost, now stealing forth again and glimmering to and fro with every pulse of emotion that throbbed within her heart; but, seeing her otherwise so perfect, he found this one defect grow more and more intolerable with every moment of their united lives. It was the fatal flaw of humanity which Nature, in one shape or another, stamps ineffaceably on all her productions, either to imply that they are temporary and finite, or that their perfection must be wrought by toil and pain. The crimson hand expressed the ineludible gripe in which mortality clutches the highest and purest of earthly mould, degrading them into kindred with the lowest, and even with the very brutes, like whom their visible frames return to dust. In this manner, selecting it as the symbol of his wife's liability to sin, sorrow, decay, and death, Aylmer's somber imagination was not long in rendering the birthmark a frightful object, causing him more trouble and horror than ever Georgiana's beauty, whether of soul or sense, had given him delight.

10   At all the seasons which should have been their happiest he invariably, and without intending it, nay, in spite of a purpose to the contrary, reverted to this one disastrous topic. Trifling as it at first appeared, it so connected itself with innumerable trains of thought and modes of feeling that it became the central point of all. With the morning twilight Aylmer opened his eyes upon his wife's face and recognized the symbol of imperfection; and when they sat together at the evening hearth his eyes wandered stealthily to her cheek, and beheld, flickering with the blaze of the wood-fire, the spectral hand that wrote mortality where he would fain[4] have worshipped. Georgiana soon learned to shudder at his gaze. It needed but a glance with the peculiar expression that his face often wore to change the roses of her cheek into a death-like paleness, amid which the crimson hand was brought strongly out, like a bas relief of ruby on the whitest marble.

Late one night, when the lights were growing dim so as hardly to betray the stain on the poor wife's cheek, she herself, for the first time, voluntarily took up the subject.

---

3. Hiram Powers (1805–73), American sculptor and friend of Hawthorne, produced noted marble statues, including *Eve Tempted* and *Eve Disconsolate*.   4. Eagerly, preferably.

"Do you remember, my dear Aylmer," said she, with a feeble attempt at a smile, "have you any recollection, of a dream last night about this odious hand?"

"None! none whatever!" replied Aylmer, starting; but then he added, in a dry, cold tone, affected for the sake of concealing the real depth of his emotion, "I might well dream of it; for, before I fell asleep, it had taken a pretty firm hold of my fancy."

"And you did dream of it?" continued Georgiana, hastily; for she dreaded lest a gush of tears should interrupt what she had to say. "A terrible dream! I wonder that you can forget it. Is it possible to forget this one expression?—'It is in her heart now; we must have it out!' Reflect, my husband; for by all means I would have you recall that dream."

The mind is in a sad state when Sleep, the all-involving, cannot confine her specters within the dim region of her sway, but suffers them to break forth, affrighting this actual life with secrets that perchance belong to a deeper one. Aylmer now remembered his dream. He had fancied himself with his servant Aminadab attempting an operation for the removal of the birth-mark; but the deeper went the knife, the deeper sank the hand, until at length its tiny grasp appeared to have caught hold of Georgiana's heart; whence, however, her husband was inexorably resolved to cut or wrench it away.

When the dream had shaped itself perfectly in his memory, Aylmer sat in his wife's presence with a guilty feeling. Truth often finds its way to the mind close muffled in robes of sleep, and then speaks with uncompromising directness of matters in regard to which we practice an unconscious self-deception during our waking moments. Until now he had not been aware of the tyrannizing influence acquired by one idea over his mind, and of the lengths which he might find in his heart to go for the sake of giving himself peace.

"Aylmer," resumed Georgiana, solemnly, "I know not what may be the cost to both of us to rid me of this fatal birth-mark. Perhaps its removal may cause cureless deformity; or it may be the stain goes as deep as life itself. Again: do we know that there is a possibility, on any terms, of unclasping the firm gripe of this little hand which was laid upon me before I came into the world?"

"Dearest Georgiana, I have spent much thought upon the subject," hastily interrupted Aylmer. "I am convinced of the perfect practicability of its removal."

"If there be the remotest possibility of it," continued Georgiana, "let the attempt be made, at whatever risk. Danger is nothing to me; for life, while this hateful mark makes me the object of your horror and disgust—life is a burden which I would fling down with joy. Either remove this dreadful hand, or take my wretched life! You have deep science. All the world bears witness of it. You have achieved great wonders. Cannot you remove this little, little mark, which I cover with the tips of two small fingers? Is this beyond your power, for the sake of your own peace, and to save your poor wife from madness?"

20   "Noblest, dearest, tenderest wife," cried Aylmer, rapturously, "doubt not my power. I have already given this matter the deepest thought—thought which might almost have enlightened me to create a being less perfect than yourself. Georgiana, you have led me deeper than ever into the heart of science. I feel myself fully competent to render this dear cheek as fault-less as its fellow; and then, most beloved, what will be my triumph when I shall have corrected what Nature left imperfect in her fairest work! Even Pygmalion,[5] when his sculptured woman assumed life, felt not greater ecstasy than mine will be."

"It is resolved, then," said Georgiana, faintly smiling. "And, Aylmer, spare me not, though you should find the birth-mark take refuge in my heart at last."

Her husband tenderly kissed her cheek—her right cheek—not that which bore the impress of the crimson hand.

The next day Aylmer apprised his wife of a plan that he had formed whereby he might have opportunity for the intense thought and constant watchfulness which the proposed operation would require; while Georgi-ana, likewise, would enjoy the perfect repose essential to its success. They were to seclude themselves in the extensive apartments occupied by Aylmer as a laboratory, and where, during his toilsome youth, he had made discov-eries in the elemental powers of Nature that had roused the admiration of all the learned societies in Europe. Seated calmly in this laboratory, the pale philosopher had investigated the secrets of the highest cloud-region and of the profoundest mines; he had satisfied himself of the causes that kindled and kept alive the fires of the volcano; and had explained the mys-tery of fountains, and how it is that they gush forth, some so bright and pure, and others with such rich medicinal virtues, from the dark bosom of the earth. Here, too, at an earlier period, he had studied the wonders of the human frame, and attempted to fathom the very process by which Nature assimilates all her precious influences from earth and air, and from the spiritual world, to create and foster man, her masterpiece. The latter pur-suit, however, Aylmer had long laid aside in unwilling recognition of the truth—against which all seekers sooner or later stumble—that our great creative Mother, while she amuses us with apparently working in the broadest sunshine, is yet severely careful to keep her own secrets, and, in spite of her pretended openness, shows us nothing but results. She permits us, indeed, to mar, but seldom to mend, and, like a jealous patentee, on no account to make. Now, however, Aylmer resumed these half-forgotten

---

5. Pygmalion was a legendary artist of Cyprus who fell in love with the statue he made of a beauti-ful woman; in Ovid's *Metamorphoses,* she comes to life.

investigations; not, of course, with such hopes or wishes as first suggested them; but because they involved much physiological truth and lay in the path of his proposed scheme for the treatment of Georgiana.

As he led her over the threshold of the laboratory Georgiana was cold and tremulous. Aylmer looked cheerfully into her face, with intent to reassure her, but was so startled with the intense glow of the birth-mark upon the whiteness of her cheek that he could not restrain a strong convulsive shudder. His wife fainted.

"Aminadab! Aminadab!" shouted Aylmer, stamping violently on the 25 floor.

Forthwith there issued from an inner apartment a man of low stature, but bulky frame, with shaggy hair hanging about his visage, which was grimed with the vapors of the furnace. This personage had been Aylmer's underworker during his whole scientific career, and was admirably fitted for that office by his great mechanical readiness, and the skill with which, while incapable of comprehending a single principle, he executed all the details of his master's experiments. With his vast strength, his shaggy hair, his smoky aspect, and the indescribable earthiness that incrusted him, he seemed to represent man's physical nature; while Aylmer's slender figure, and pale, intellectual face, were no less apt a type of the spiritual element.

"Throw open the door of the boudoir, Aminadab," said Aylmer, "and burn a pastil."[6]

"Yes, master," answered Aminadab, looking intently at the lifeless form of Georgiana; and then he muttered to himself. "If she were my wife, I'd never part with that birth-mark."

When Georgiana recovered consciousness she found herself breathing an atmosphere of penetrating fragrance, the gentle potency of which had recalled her from her death-like faintness. The scene around her looked like enchantment. Aylmer had converted those smoky, dingy, somber rooms, where he had spent his brightest years in recondite pursuits, into a series of beautiful apartments not unfit to be the secluded abode of a lovely woman. The walls were hung with gorgeous curtains, which imparted the combination of grandeur and grace that no other species of adornment can achieve; and, as they fell from the ceiling to the floor, their rich and ponderous folds, concealing all angles and straight lines, appeared to shut in the scene from infinite space. For aught Georgiana knew, it might be a pavilion among the clouds. And Aylmer, excluding the sunshine, which would have interfered with his chemical processes, had supplied its place with perfumed lamps, emitting flames of various hue, but all uniting in a soft, impurpled radiance. He now knelt by his wife's side, watching her earnestly, but without alarm; for he was confident in his science, and felt that he could draw a magic circle round her within which no evil might intrude.

6. Pastille, a lozenge or tablet of medicinal incense.

30   "Where am I? Ah, I remember," said Georgiana, faintly; and she placed
her hand over her cheek to hide the terrible mark from her husband's eyes.
"Fear not, dearest!" exclaimed he. "Do not shrink from me! Believe me,
Georgiana, I even rejoice in this single imperfection, since it will be such a
rapture to remove it."
"O, spare me!" sadly replied his wife. "Pray do not look at it again. I never
can forget that convulsive shudder."
     In order to soothe Georgiana, and, as it were, to release her mind from
the burden of actual things, Aylmer now put in practice some of the light
and playful secrets which science had taught him among its profounder
lore. Airy figures, absolutely bodiless ideas, and forms of unsubstantial
beauty came and danced before her, imprinting their momentary footsteps on beams of light. Though she had some indistinct idea of the method
of these optical phenomena, still the illusion was almost perfect enough
to warrant the belief that her husband possessed say over the spiritual
world. Then again, when she felt a wish to look forth from her seclusion,
immediately, as if her thoughts were answered, the procession of external
existence flitted across a screen. The scenery and the figures of actual life
were perfectly represented but with that bewitching yet indescribable difference which always makes a picture, an image, or a shadow so much
more attractive than the original. When wearied of this, Aylmer bade her
cast her eyes upon a vessel containing a quantity of earth. She did so, with
little interest at first; but was soon startled to perceive the germ of a plant
shooting upward from the soil. Then came the slender stalk; the leaves
gradually unfolded themselves; and amid them was a perfect and lovely
flower.
     "It is magical!" cried Georgiana. "I dare not touch it."
35   "Nay, pluck it," answered Aylmer— "pluck it, and inhale its brief perfume
while you may. The flower will wither in a few moments and leave nothing
save its brown seed vessels; but theence may be perpetuated a race as ephem-
eral as itself."
     But Georgiana had no sooner touched the flower than the whole plant
suffered a blight, its leaves turning coal-black as if by the agency of fire.
     "There was too powerful a stimulus," said Aylmer, thoughtfully.
     To make up for this abortive experiment, he proposed to take her por-
trait by a scientific process of his own invention. It was to be affected by
rays of light striking upon a polished plate of metal. Georgiana assented;
but, on looking at the result, was affrighted to find the features of the portrait blurred and indefinable; while the minute figure of a hand appeared
where the cheek should have been. Aylmer snatched the metallic plate and
threw it into a jar of corrosive acid.
     Soon, however, he forgot these mortifying failures. In the intervals of
study and chemical experiment he came to her flushed and exhausted, but
seemed invigorated by her presence, and spoke in glowing language of the

resources of his art. He gave a history of the long dynasty of the alchemists, who spent so many ages in quest of the universal solvent by which the golden principle might be elicited from all things vile and base.[7] Aylmer appeared to believe that, by the plainest scientific logic, it was altogether within the limits of possibility to discover this long-sought medium. "But," he added, "a philosopher who should go deep enough to acquire the power would attain too lofty a wisdom to stoop to the exercise of it." Not less singular were his opinions in regard to the elixir vitae.[8] He more than intimated that it was at his option to concoct a liquid that should prolong life for years, perhaps interminably; but that it would produce a discord in Nature which all the world, and chiefly the quaffer of the immortal nostrum, would find cause to curse.

"Aylmer, are you in earnest?" asked Georgiana, looking at him with 40 amazement and fear. "It is terrible to possess such power, or even to dream of possessing it."

"O, do not tremble, my love," said her husband. "I would not wrong either you or myself by working such inharmonious effects upon our lives; but I would have you consider how trifling, in comparison, is the skill requisite to remove this little hand."

At the mention of the birth-mark, Georgiana, as usual, shrank as if a red-hot iron had touched her cheek.

Again Aylmer applied himself to his labors. She could hear his voice in the distant furnace-room giving directions to Aminadab, whose harsh, uncouth, misshapen tones were audible in response, more like the grunt or growl of a brute than human speech. After hours of absence, Aylmer reappeared and proposed that she should now examine his cabinet of chemical products and natural treasures of the earth. Among the former he showed her a small vial, in which, he remarked, was contained a gentle yet most powerful fragrance, capable of impregnating all the breezes that blow across a kingdom. They were of inestimable value, the contents of that little vial; and, as he said so, he threw some of the perfume into the air and filled the room with piercing and invigorating delight.

"And what is this?" asked Georgiana, pointing to a small crystal globe containing a gold-colored liquid. "It is so beautiful to the eye that I could imagine it the elixir of life."

"In one sense it is," replied Aylmer; "or rather, the elixir of immortality. 45 It is the most precious poison that ever was concocted in this world. By its aid I could apportion the lifetime of any mortal at whom you might point your finger. The strength of the dose would determine whether he were to linger out years, or drop dead in the midst of a breath. No king on his

---

7. Before the advent of modern chemistry, alchemists studied the properties of matter in a search for spiritual essences and the secret of transforming base metals into gold.
8. Literally, the drink or potion of life (Latin), imagined to give immortality.

guarded throne could keep his life if I, in my private station, should deem that the welfare of millions justified me in depriving him of it."

"Why do you keep such a terrific drug?" inquired Georgiana, in horror.

"Do not mistrust me, dearest," said her husband, smiling; "its virtuous potency is yet greater than its harmful one. But see! here is a powerful cosmetic. With a few drops of this in a vase of water, freckles may be washed away as easily as the hands are cleansed. A stronger infusion would take the blood out of the cheek, and leave the rosiest beauty a pale ghost."

"Is it with this lotion that you intend to bathe my cheek?" asked Georgiana, anxiously.

"O no," hastily replied her husband; "this is merely superficial. Your case demands a remedy that shall go deeper."

50   In his interviews with Georgiana, Aylmer generally made minute inquiries as to her sensations, and whether the confinement of the rooms and the temperature of the atmosphere agreed with her. These questions had such a particular drift that Georgiana began to conjecture that she was already subjected to certain physical influences, either breathed in with the fragrant air or taken with her food. She fancied likewise, but it might be altogether fancy, that there was a stirring up of her system—a strange, indefinite sensation creeping through her veins, and tingling, half painfully, half pleasurably, at her heart. Still, whenever she dared to look into the mirror, there she beheld herself pale as a white rose and with the crimson birth-mark stamped upon her cheek. Not even Aylmer now hated it so much as she.

To dispel the tedium of the hours which her husband found it necessary to devote to the processes of combination and analysis, Georgiana turned over the volumes of his scientific library. In many dark old tomes she met with chapters full of romance and poetry. They were the works of the philosophers of the Middle Ages, such as Albertus Magnus, Cornelius Agrippa, Paracelsus, and the famous friar who created the prophetic Brazen Head.[9] All these antique naturalists stood in advance of their centuries, yet were imbued with some of their credulity, and therefore were believed, and perhaps imagined themselves to have acquired from the investigation of Nature a power above Nature, and from physics a away over the spiritual world. Hardly less curious and imaginative were the early volumes of the Transactions of the Royal Society,[1] in which the members, knowing little of the limits of natural possibility, were continually recording wonders or proposing methods whereby wonders might be wrought.

9. The Brazen Head, a brass bust of a man, was supposed to be able to answer any question; the "famous friar" is Roger Bacon (c. 1214–94), an English natural philosopher, as scientists were then called. Albertus Magnus (1193/1206–80), Agrippa (1496–1535), and Paracelsus (1493–1541) were all European experimenters reputed to have near-magical powers in alchemy or astrology.
1. The Philosophical Transactions of the Royal Society is the oldest scientific journal in English, published since 1665.

But, to Georgiana, the most engrossing volume was a large folio from her husband's own hand, in which he had recorded every experiment of his scientific career, its original aim, the methods adopted for its development, and its final success or failure, with the circumstances to which either event was attributable. The book, in truth was both the history and emblem of his ardent, ambitious, imaginative, yet practical and laborious life. He handled physical details as if there were nothing beyond them; yet spiritualized them all, and redeemed himself from materialism by his strong and eager aspiration towards the infinite. In his grasp the veriest clod of earth assumed a soul. Georgiana, as she read, reverenced Aylmer and loved him more profoundly than ever, but with a less entire dependence on his judgment than heretofore. Much as he had accomplished, she could not but observe that his most splendid successes were almost invariably failures, if compared with the ideal at which he aimed. His brightest diamonds were the merest pebbles, and felt to be so by himself, in comparison with the inestimable gems which lay hidden beyond his reach. The volume, rich with achievements that had won renown for its author, was yet as melancholy a record as ever mortal hand had penned. It was the sad confession and continual exemplification of the shortcomings of the composite man, the spirit burdened with clay and working in matter, and of the despair that assails the higher nature at finding itself so miserably thwarted by the earthly part. Perhaps every man of genius, in whatever sphere, might recognize the image of his own experience in Aylmer's journal.

So deeply did these reflections affect Georgiana that she laid her face upon the open volume and burst into tears. In this situation she was found by her husband.

"It is dangerous to read in a sorcerer's books," said he with a smile, though his countenance was uneasy and displeased. "Georgiana, there are pages in that volume which I can scarcely glance over and keep my senses. Take heed lest it prove as detrimental to you."

"It has made me worship you more than ever," said she.   55

"Ah, wait for this one success," rejoined he, "then worship me if you will. I shall deem myself hardly unworthy of it. But come, I have sought you for the luxury of your voice. Sing to me, dearest."

So she poured out the liquid music of her voice to quench the thirst of his spirit. He then took his leave with a boyish exuberance of gayety, assuring her that her seclusion would endure but a little longer, and that the result was already certain. Scarcely had he departed when Georgiana felt irresistibly impelled to follow him. She had forgotten to inform Aylmer of a symptom which for two or three hours past had begun to excite her attention. It was a sensation in the fatal birth-mark, not painful, but which induced a restlessness throughout her system. Hastening after her husband, she intruded for the first time into the laboratory.

The first thing that struck her eye was the furnace, that hot and feverish worker, with the intense glow of its fire, which by the quantities of soot clustered above it seemed to have been burning for ages. There was a distilling-apparatus in full operation. Around the room were retorts, tubes, cylinders, crucibles, and other apparatus of chemical research. An electrical machine stood ready for immediate use. The atmosphere felt oppressively close, and was tainted with gaseous odors which had been tormented forth by the processes of science. The severe and homely simplicity of the apartment, with its naked walls and brick pavement, looked strange, accustomed as Georgiana had become to the fantastic elegance of her boudoir. But what chiefly, indeed almost solely, drew her attention, was the aspect of Aylmer himself.

He was pale as death, anxious and absorbed, and hung over the furnace as if it depended upon his utmost watchfulness whether the liquid which it was distilling should be the draught of immortal happiness or misery. How different from the sanguine and joyous mien that he had assumed for Georgiana's encouragement!

60   "Carefully now, Aminadab; carefully, thou human machine; carefully, thou man of clay," muttered Aylmer, more to himself than his assistant. "Now, if there be a thought too much or too little, it is all over."

"Ho! ho!" mumbled Aminadab. "Look, master! look!"

Aylmer raised his eyes hastily, and at first reddened, then grew paler than ever, on beholding Georgiana. He rushed towards her and seized her arm with a gripe that left the print of his fingers upon it.

"Why do you come hither? Have you no trust in your husband?" cried he, impetuously. "Would you throw the blight of that fatal birth-mark over my labors? It is not well done. Go, prying woman! go!"

"Nay, Aylmer," said Georgiana with the firmness of which she possessed no stinted endowment, "it is not you that have a right to complain. You mistrust your wife; you have concealed the anxiety with which you watch the development of this experiment. Think not so unworthily of me, my husband. Tell me all the risk we run, and fear not that I shall shrink; for my share in it is far less than your own."

65   "No, no, Georgiana!" said Aylmer, impatiently; "it must not be."

"I submit," replied she, calmly. "And, Aylmer, I shall quaff whatever draught you bring me; but it will be on the same principle that would induce me to take a dose of poison if offered by your hand."

"My noble wife," said Aylmer, deeply moved, "I knew not the height and depth of your nature until now. Nothing shall be concealed. Know, then, that this crimson hand, superficial as it seems, has clutched its grasp into your being with a strength of which I had no previous conception. I have already administered agents powerful enough to do aught except to change your entire physical system. Only one thing remains to be tried. If that fail us we are ruined."

"Why did you hesitate to tell me this?" asked she.

"Because, Georgiana," said Aylmer, in a low voice, "there is danger."

"Danger? There is but one danger—that this horrible stigma shall be 70 left upon my cheek!" cried Georgiana. "Remove it, remove it, whatever be the cost, or we shall both go mad!"

"Heaven knows your words are too true," said Aylmer, sadly. "And now, dearest, return to your boudoir. In a little while all will be tested."

He conducted her back and took leave of her with a solemn tenderness which spoke far more than his words how much was now at stake. After his departure Georgiana became rapt in musings. She considered the character of Aylmer, and did it completer justice than at any previous moment. Her heart exulted, while it trembled, at his honorable love—so pure and lofty that it would accept nothing less than perfection, nor miserably make itself contented with an earthlier nature than he had dreamed of. She felt how much more precious was such a sentiment than that meaner kind which would have borne with the imperfection for her sake, and have been guilty of treason to holy love by degrading its perfect idea to the level of the actual; and with her whole spirit she prayed that, for a single moment, she might satisfy his highest and deepest conception. Longer than one moment she well knew it could not be; for his spirit was ever on the march, ever ascending, and each instant required something that was beyond the scope of the instant before.

The sound of her husband's footsteps aroused her. He bore a crystal goblet containing a liquor colorless as water, but bright enough to be the draught of immortality. Aylmer was pale; but it seemed rather the consequence of a highly wrought state of mind and tension of spirit than of fear or doubt.

"The concoction of the draught has been perfect," said he, in answer to Georgiana's look. "Unless all my science have deceived me, it cannot fail."

"Save on your account, my dearest Aylmer," observed his wife, "I might 75 wish to put off this birth-mark of mortality by relinquishing mortality itself in preference to any other mode. Life is but a sad possession to those who have attained precisely the degree of moral advancement at which I stand. Were I weaker and blinder, it might be happiness. Were I stronger, it might be endured hopefully. But, being what I find myself, methinks I am of all mortals the most fit to die."

"You are fit for heaven without tasting death!" replied her husband. "But why do we speak of dying? The draught cannot fail. Behold its effect upon this plant."

On the window-seat there stood a geranium diseased with yellow blotches, which had overspread all its leaves. Aylmer poured a small quantity of the liquid upon the soil in which it grew. In a little time, when the roots of the plant had taken up the moisture, the unsightly blotches began to be extinguished in a living verdure.

"There needed no proof," said Georgiana, quietly. "Give me the goblet. I joyfully stake all upon your word."

"Drink, then, thou lofty creature!" exclaimed Aylmer, with fervid admiration. "There is no taint of imperfection on thy spirit. Thy sensible frame, too, shall soon be all perfect."

80   She quaffed the liquid and returned the goblet to his hand.

"It is grateful," said she, with a placid smile. "Methinks it is like water from a heavenly fountain; for it contains I know not what of unobtrusive fragrance and deliciousness. It allays a feverish thirst that had parched me for many days. Now, dearest, let me sleep. My earthly senses are closing over my spirit like the leaves around the heart of a rose at sunset."

She spoke the last words with a gentle reluctance, as if it required almost more energy than she could command to pronounce the faint and lingering syllables. Scarcely had they loitered through her lips ere she was lost in slumber. Aylmer sat by her side, watching her aspect with the emotions proper to a man, the whole value of whose existence was involved in the process now to be tested. Mingled with this mood, however, was the philosophic investigation characteristic of the man of science. Not the minutest symptom escaped him. A heightened flush of the cheek, a slight irregularity of breath, a quiver of the eyelid, a hardly perceptible tremor through the frame—such were the details which, as the moments passed, he wrote down in his folio volume. Intense thought had set its stamp upon every previous page of that volume; but the thoughts of years were all concentrated upon the last.

While thus employed, he failed not to gaze often at the fatal hand, and not without a shudder. Yet once, by a strange and unaccountable impulse, he pressed it with his lips. His spirit recoiled, however, in the very act; and Georgiana, out of the midst of her deep sleep, moved uneasily and murmured, as if in remonstrance. Again Aylmer resumed his watch. Nor was it without avail. The crimson hand, which at first had been strongly visible upon the marble paleness of Georgiana's cheek, now grew more faintly outlined. She remained not less pale than ever; but the birth-mark, with every breath that came and went, lost somewhat of its former distinctness. Its presence had been awful; its departure was more awful still. Watch the stain of the rainbow fading out of the sky, and you will know how that mysterious symbol passed away.

"By Heaven! it is wellnigh gone!" said Aylmer to himself, in almost irrepressible ecstasy. "I can scarcely trace it now. Success! success! And now it is like the faintest rose-color. The lightest flush of blood across her cheek would overcome it. But she is so pale!"

85   He drew aside the window-curtain and suffered the light of natural day to fall into the room and rest upon her cheek. At the same time he heard a gross, hoarse chuckle, which he had long known as his servant Aminadab's expression of delight.

"Ah, clod! ah, earthly mass!" cried Aylmer, laughing in a sort of fenzy, "you have served me well! Matter and spirit—earth and heaven—have both done their part in this! Laugh, thing of the senses! You have earned the right to laugh."

These exclamations broke Georgiana's sleep. She slowly unclosed her eyes and gazed into the mirror which her husband had arranged for that purpose. A faint smile fitted over her lips when she recognized how barely perceptible was now that crimson hand which had once blazed forth with such disastrous brilliancy as to scare away all their happiness. But then her eyes sought Aylmer's face with a trouble and anxiety that he could by no means account for.

"My poor Aylmer!" murmured she.

"Poor? Nay, richest, happiest, most favored!" exclaimed he. "My peerless bride, it is successful! You are perfect!"

"My poor Aylmer," she repeated, with a more than human tenderness, "you have aimed loftily; you have done nobly. Do not repent that, with so high and pure a feeling, you have rejected the best the earth could offer. Aylmer, dearest Aylmer, I am dying!" 90

Alas! it was too true! The fatal hand had grappled with the mystery of life, and was the bond by which an angelic spirit kept itself in union with a mortal frame. As the last crimson tint of the birth-mark—that sole token of human imperfection—faded from her cheek, the parting breath of the now perfect woman passed into the atmosphere, and her soul, lingering a moment near her husband, took its heavenward flight. Then a hoarse, chuckling laugh was heard again! Thus ever does the gross fatality of earth exult in its invariable triumph over the immortal essence which, in this dim sphere of half-development, demands the completeness of a higher state. Yet, had Aylmer reached a profounder wisdom, he need not thus have flung away the happiness which would have woven his mortal life of the selfsame texture with the celestial. The momentary circumstance was too strong for him; he failed to look beyond the shadowy scope of time, and, living once for all in eternity, to find the perfect future in the present.

1843

QUESTIONS

1. What difference would it make if the mark on Georgiana's cheek were shaped like a fish, a heart, or an irregular oval? Why (and when) does the mark appear redder or more visible or fainter? If the birthmark is explicitly a "symbol of imperfection" (par. 9), what *kinds* of imperfection does it represent?
2. Aylmer says to his wife, "Even Pygmalion, when his sculptured woman assumed life, felt not greater ecstasy than mine will be" (par. 19). How does this literary allusion to the myth of Pygmalion enhance the meaning of "The Birth-Mark"? Is this allusion ironic, given what happens to Alymer's project to make his wife perfect?

3. Look closely at the setting of the story, from the laboratory to the boudoir. Note the similes, metaphors, and other figures of speech that help characterize these places. How do these different patterns of imagery contribute to the symbolism of the story? to an allegorical reading of the story?

EDWIDGE DANTICAT

A Wall of Fire Rising

"Listen to what happened today," Guy said as he barged through the rattling door of his tiny shack.

His wife, Lili, was squatting in the middle of their one-room home, spreading cornmeal mush on banana leaves for their supper.

"Listen to what happened to *me* today!" Guy's seven-year-old son—Little Guy—dashed from a corner and grabbed his father's hand. The boy dropped his composition notebook as he leaped to his father, nearly stepping into the corn mush and herring that his mother had set out in a trio of half gourds on the clay floor.

"Our boy is in a play." Lili quickly robbed Little Guy of the honor of telling his father the news.

5   "A play?" Guy affectionately stroked the boy's hair.

The boy had such tiny corkscrew curls that no amount of brushing could ever make them all look like a single entity. The other boys at the Lycée Jean-Jacques[1] called him "pepper head" because each separate kinky strand was coiled into a tight tiny ball that looked like small peppercorns.

"When is this play?" Guy asked both the boy and his wife. "Are we going to have to buy new clothes for this?"

Lili got up from the floor and inclined her face towards her husband's in order to receive her nightly peck on the cheek.

"What role do you have in the play?" Guy asked, slowly rubbing the tip of his nails across the boy's scalp. His fingers made a soft grating noise with each invisible circle drawn around the perimeters of the boy's head. Guy's fingers finally landed inside the boy's ears, forcing the boy to giggle until he almost gave himself the hiccups.

10   "Tell me, what is your part in the play?" Guy asked again, pulling his fingers away from his son's ear.

"I am Boukman," the boy huffed out, as though there was some laughter caught in his throat.

---

1. Haiti is French-speaking; Little Guy attends a *lycée* (school) named after Jean-Jacques Dessalines (1758–1806), the founder of independent Haiti. A former slave, Dessalines was declared emperor Jacques I in 1804.

"Show Papy your lines," Lili told the boy as she arranged the three open gourds on a piece of plywood raised like a table on two bricks, in the middle of the room. "My love, Boukman is the hero of the play."

The boy went back to the corner where he had been studying and pulled out a thick book carefully covered in brown paper.

"You're going to spend a lifetime learning those." Guy took the book from the boy's hand and flipped through the pages quickly. He had to strain his eyes to see the words by the light of an old kerosene lamp, which that night—like all others—flickered as though it was burning its very last wick.

"All these words seem so long and heavy," Guy said. "You think you can do this, son?" 15

"He has one very good speech," Lili said. "Page forty, remember, son?"

The boy took back the book from his father. His face was crimped in an of-course-I-remember look as he searched for page forty.

"Bouk-man," Guy struggled with the letters of the slave revolutionary's name as he looked over his son's shoulders. "I see some very hard words here, son."

"He already knows his speech," Lili told her husband.

"Does he now?" asked Guy. 20

"We've been at it all afternoon," Lili said. "Why don't you go on and recite that speech for your father?"

The boy tipped his head towards the rusting tin on the roof as he prepared to recite his lines.

Lili wiped her hands on an old apron tied around her waist and stopped to listen.

"Remember what you are," Lili said, "a great rebel leader. Remember, it is the revolution."

"Do we want him to be all of that?" Guy asked. 25

"He is Boukman," Lili said. "What is the only thing on your mind now, Boukman?"

"Supper," Guy whispered, enviously eyeing the food cooling off in the middle of the room. He and the boy looked at each other and began to snicker.

"Tell us the other thing that is on your mind," Lili said, joining in their laughter.

"Freedom!" shouted the boy, as he quickly slipped into his role.

"Louder!" urged Lili. 30

"Freedom is on my mind!" yelled the boy.

"Why don't you start, son?" said Guy. "If you don't, we'll never get to that other thing that we have on our minds."

The boy closed his eyes and took a deep breath. At first, his lips parted but nothing came out. Lili pushed her head forward as though she were holding her breath. Then like the last burst of lightning out of clearing sky, the boy began.

"A wall of fire is rising and in the ashes, I see the bones of my people. Not only those people whose dark hollow faces I see daily in the fields, but all those souls who have gone ahead to haunt my dreams. At night I relive once more the last caresses from the hand of a loving father, a valiant love, a beloved friend."[2]

35   It was obvious that this was a speech written by a European man, who gave to the slave revolutionary Boukman the kind of European phrasing that might have sent the real Boukman turning in his grave. However, the speech made Lili and Guy stand on the tips of their toes from great pride. As their applause thundered in the small space of their shack that night, they felt as though for a moment they had been given the rare pleasure of hearing the voice of one of the forefathers of Haitian independence in the forced baritone of their only child. The experience left them both with a strange feeling that they could not explain. It left the hair on the back of their necks standing on end. It left them feeling much more love than they ever knew that they could add to their feeling for their son.

"Bravo," Lili cheered, pressing her son into the folds of her apron. "Long live Boukman and long live my boy."

"Long live our supper," Guy said, quickly batting his eyelashes to keep tears from rolling down his face.

The boy kept his eyes on his book as they ate their supper that night. Usually Guy and Lili would not have allowed that, but this was a special occasion. They watched proudly as the boy muttered his lines between swallows of cornmeal.

The boy was still mumbling the same words as the three of them used the last of the rainwater trapped in old gasoline containers and sugarcane pulp from the nearby sugarcane mill to scrub the gourds that they had eaten from.

40   When things were really bad for the family, they boiled clean sugarcane pulp to make what Lili called her special sweet water tea. It was supposed to suppress gas and kill the vermin in the stomach that made poor children hungry. That and a pinch of salt under the tongue could usually quench hunger until Guy found a day's work or Lili could manage to buy spices on credit and then peddle them for a profit at the marketplace.

That night, anyway, things were good. Everyone had eaten enough to put all their hunger vermin to sleep.

The boy was sitting in front of the shack on an old plastic bucket turned upside down, straining his eyes to find the words on the page. Sometimes when there was no kerosene for the lamp, the boy would have to go sit by

---

2. On the night of August 22, 1791, slaves led by a slave foreman named Boukman (who was secretly a voodoo high priest) built a "wall of fire" that destroyed many plantations in the north of the French colony of Saint-Domingue, marking the beginning of a mass slave revolt that would lead, fourteen years later, to the establishment of independent Haiti.

the side of the road and study under the street lamps with the rest of the neighborhood children. Tonight, at least, they had a bit of their own light.

Guy bent down by a small clump of old mushrooms near the boy's feet, trying to get a better look at the plant. He emptied the last drops of rainwater from a gasoline container on the mushroom, wetting the bulging toes sticking out of his sons' sandals, which were already coming apart around his endlessly growing feet.

Guy tried to pluck some of the mushrooms, which were being pushed into the dust as though they wanted to grow beneath the ground as roots. He took one of the mushrooms in his hand, running his smallest finger over the round bulb. He clipped the stem and buried the top in a thick strand of his wife's hair.

The mushroom looked like a dried insect in Lili's hair.   45

"It sure makes you look special," Guy said, teasing her.

"Thank you so much," Lili said, tapping her husband's arm. "It's nice to know that I deserve these much more than roses."

Taking his wife's hand, Guy said, "Let's go to the sugar mill."

"Can I study my lines there?" the boy asked.

"You know them well enough already," Guy said.   50

"I need many repetitions," the boy said.

Their feet sounded as though they were playing a wet wind instrument as they slipped in and out of the puddles between the shacks in the shantytown. Near the sugar mill was a large television screen in an iron grill cage that the government had installed so that the shantytown dwellers could watch the state-sponsored news at eight o'clock every night. After the news, a gendarme[3] would come and turn off the television set, taking home the key. On most nights, the people stayed at the site long after this gendarme had gone and told stories to one another beneath the big blank screen. They made bonfires with dried sticks, corn husks, and paper, cursing the authorities under their breath.

There was a crowd already gathering for the nightly news event. The sugar mill workers sat in the front row in chairs or on old buckets.

Lili and Guy passed the group, clinging to their son so that in his childhood naïveté he wouldn't accidentally glance at the wrong person and be called an insolent child. They didn't like the ambiance of the nightly news watch. They spared themselves trouble by going instead to the sugar mill, where in the past year they had discovered their own wonder.

Everyone knew that the family who owned the sugar mill were eccentric   55 "Arabs," Haitians of Lebanese or Palestinian descent whose family had been in the country for generations. The Assad family had a son who, it seems, was into all manner of odd things, the most recent of which was a

3. Policeman or guard (French).

hot-air balloon, which he had brought to Haiti from America and occasionally flew over the shantytown skies.

As they approached the fence surrounding the field where the large wicker basket and deflated balloon rested on the ground, Guy let go of the hands of both his wife and the boy.

Lili walked on slowly with her son. For the last few weeks, she had been feeling as though Guy was lost to her each time he reached this point, twelve feet away from the balloon. As Guy pushed his hand through the barbed wire, she could tell from the look on his face that he was thinking of sitting inside the square basket while the smooth rainbow surface of the balloon itself floated above his head. During the day, when the field was open, Guy would walk up to the basket, staring at it with the same kind of longing that most men display when they admire very pretty girls.

Lili and the boy stood watching from a distance as Guy tried to push his hand deeper, beyond the chain link fence that separated him from the balloon. He reached into his pants pocket and pulled out a small pocketknife, sharpening the edges on the metal surface of the fence. When his wife and child moved closer, he put the knife back in his pocket, letting his fingers slide across his son's tightly coiled curls.

"I wager you I can make this thing fly," Guy said.

60   "Why do you think you can do that?" Lili asked.

"I know it," Guy replied.

He followed her as she circled the sugar mill, leading to their favorite spot under a watch light. Little Guy lagged faithfully behind them. From this distance, the hot-air balloon looked like an odd spaceship.

Lili stretched her body out in the knee-high grass in the field. Guy reached over and tried to touch her between her legs.

"You're not one to worry, Lili," he said. "You're not afraid of the frogs, lizards, or snakes that could be hiding in this grass?"

65   "I am here with my husband," she said. "You are here to protect me if anything happens."

Guy reached into his shirt pocket and pulled out a lighter and a crumpled piece of paper. He lit the paper until it burned to an ashy film. The burning paper floated in the night breeze for a while, landing in fragments on the grass.

"Did you see that, Lili?" Guy asked with a flame in his eyes brighter than the lighter's. "Did you see how the paper floated when it was burned? This is how that balloon flies."

"What did you mean by saying that you could make it fly?" Lili asked.

"You already know all my secrets," Guy said as the boy came charging towards them.

70   "Papa, could you play *Lago* with me?" the boy asked.

Lili lay peacefully on the grass as her son and husband played hide-and-seek. Guy kept hiding and his son kept finding him as each time Guy made it easier for the boy.

"We rest now." Guy was becoming breathless.

The stars were circling the peaks of the mountains, dipping into the cane fields belonging to the sugar mill. As Guy caught his breath, the boy raced around the fence, running as fast as he could to purposely make himself dizzy.

"Listen to what happened today," Guy whispered softly in Lili's ear.

"I heard you say that when you walked in the house tonight," Lili said. 75 "With the boy's play, I forgot to ask you."

The boy sneaked up behind them, his face lit up, though his brain was spinning. He wrapped his arms around both their necks.

"We will go back home soon," Lili said.

"Can I recite my lines?" asked the boy.

"We have heard them," Guy said. "Don't tire your lips."

The boy mumbled something under his breath. Guy grabbed his ear 80 and twirled it until it was a tiny ball in his hand. The boy's face contorted with agony as Guy made him kneel in the deep grass in punishment.

Lili looked tortured as she watched the boy squirming in the grass, obviously terrified of the crickets, lizards, and small snakes that might be there.

"Perhaps we should take him home to bed," she said.

"He will never learn," Guy said, "if I say one thing and you say another."

Guy got up and angrily started walking home. Lili walked over, took her son's hand, and raised him from his knees.

"You know you must not mumble," she said.   85

"I was saying my lines," the boy said.

"Next time say them loud," Lili said, "so he knows what is coming out of your mouth."

That night Lili could hear her son muttering his lines as he tucked himself in his corner of the room and drifted off to sleep. The boy still had the book with his monologue in it clasped under his arm as he slept.

Guy stayed outside in front of the shack as Lili undressed for bed. She loosened the ribbon that held the old light blue cotton skirt around her waist and let it drop past her knees. She grabbed half a lemon that she kept in the corner by the folded mat that she and Guy unrolled to sleep on every night. Lili let her blouse drop to the floor as she smoothed the lemon over her ashen legs.

Guy came in just at that moment and saw her bare chest by the light of 90 the smaller castor oil lamp that they used for the later hours of the night. Her skin had coarsened a bit over the years, he thought. Her breasts now drooped from having nursed their son for two years after he was born. It was now easier for him to imagine their son's lips around those breasts than to imagine his anywhere near them.

He turned his face away as she fumbled for her nightgown. He helped her open the mat, tucking the blanket edges underneath.

Fully clothed, Guy dropped onto the mat next to her. He laid his head on her chest, rubbing the spiky edges of his hair against her nipples.

"What was it that happened today?" Lili asked, running her fingers along Guy's hairline, an angular hairline, almost like a triangle, in the middle of his forehead. She nearly didn't marry him because it was said that people with angular hairlines often have very troubled lives.

"I got a few hours' work for tomorrow at the sugar mill," Guy said. "That's what happened today."

95   "It was such a long time coming," Lili said.

It was almost six months since the last time Guy had gotten work there. The jobs at the sugar mill were few and far between. The people who had them never left, or when they did they would pass the job on to another family member who was already waiting on line.

Guy did not seem overjoyed about the one day's work.

"I wish I had paid more attention when you came in with the news," Lili said. "I was just so happy about the boy."

"I was born in the shadow of that sugar mill," Guy said. "Probably the first thing my mother gave me to drink as a baby was some sweet water tea from the pulp of the sugarcane. If anyone deserves to work there, I should."

100   "What will you be doing for your day's work?"

"Would you really like to know?"

"There is never any shame in honest work," she said.

"They want me to scrub the latrines."

"It's honest work," Lili said, trying to console him.

105   "I am still number seventy-eight on the permanent hire list," he said. "I was thinking of putting the boy on the list now, so maybe by the time he becomes a man he can be up for a job."

Lili's body jerked forward, rising straight up in the air. Guy's head dropped with a loud thump onto the mat.

"I don't want him on that list," she said. "For a young boy to be on any list like that might influence his destiny. I don't want him on the list."

"Look at me," Guy said. "If my father had worked there, if he had me on the list, don't you think I would be working?"

"If you have any regard for me," she said, "you will not put him on the list."

110   She groped for her husband's chest in the dark and laid her head on it. She could hear his heart beating loudly as though it were pumping double, triple its normal rate.

"You won't put the boy on any lists, will you?" she implored.

"Please, Lili, no more about the boy. He will not go on the list."

"Thank you."

"Tonight I was looking at that balloon in the yard behind the sugar mill," he said. "I have been watching it real close."

"I know." 115

"I have seen the man who owns it," he said. "I've seen him get in it and put it in the sky and go up there like it was some kind of kite and he was the kite master. I see the men who run after it trying to figure out where it will land. Once I was there and I was one of those men who were running and I actually guessed correctly. I picked a spot in the sugarcane fields. I picked the spot from a distance and it actually landed there."

"Let me say something to you, Guy—"

"Pretend that this is the time of miracles and we believed in them. I watched the owner for a long time, and I think I can fly that balloon. The first time I saw him do it, it looked like a miracle, but the more and more I saw it, the more ordinary it became."

"You're probably intelligent enough to do it," she said.

"I am intelligent enough to do it. You're right to say that I can." 120

"Don't you think about hurting yourself?"

"Think like this. Can't you see yourself up there? Up in the clouds somewhere like some kind of bird?"

"If God wanted people to fly, he would have given us wings on our backs."

"You're right, Lili, you're right. But look what he gave us instead. He gave us reasons to want to fly. He gave us the air, the birds, our son."

"I don't understand you," she said. 125

"Our son, your son, you do not want him cleaning latrines."

"He can do other things."

"Me too. I can do other things too."

A loud scream came from the corner where the boy was sleeping. Lili and Guy rushed to him and tried to wake him. The boy was trembling when he opened his eyes.

"What is the matter?" Guy asked. 130

"I cannot remember my lines," the boy said.

Lili tried to string together what she could remember of her son's lines. The words slowly came back to the boy. By the time he fell back to sleep, it was almost dawn.

The light was slowly coming up behind the trees. Lili could hear the whispers of the market women, their hisses and swearing as their sandals dug into the sharp-edged rocks on the road.

She turned her back to her husband as she slipped out of her nightgown, quickly putting on her day clothes.

"Imagine this," Guy said from the mat on the floor. "I have never really 135 seen your entire body in broad daylight."

Lili shut the door behind her, making her way out to the yard. The empty gasoline containers rested easily on her head as she walked a few miles to the public water fountains. It was harder to keep them steady when the containers were full. The water splashed all over her blouse and rippled down her back.

The sky was blue as it was most mornings, a dark indigo-shaded turquoise that would get lighter when the sun was fully risen.

Guy and the boy were standing in the yard waiting for her when she got back.

"You did not get much sleep, my handsome boy," she said, running her wet fingers over the boy's face.

140   "He'll be late for school if we do not go right now," Guy said. "I want to drop him off before I start work."

"Do we remember our lines this morning?" Lili asked, tucking the boy's shirt down deep into his short pants.

"We just recited them," Guy said. "Even I know them now."

Lili watched them walk down the footpath, her eyes following them until they disappeared.

As soon as they were out of sight, she poured the water she had fetched into a large calabash, letting it stand beside the house.

145   She went back into the room and slipped into a dry blouse. It was never too early to start looking around, to scrape together that night's meal.

"Listen to what happened again today," Lili said when Guy walked through the door that afternoon.

Guy blotted his face with a dust rag as he prepared to hear the news. After the day he'd had at the factory, he wanted to sit under a tree and have a leisurely smoke, but he did not want to set a bad example for his son by indulging his very small pleasures.

"You tell him, son," Lili urged the boy, who was quietly sitting in a corner, reading.

"I've got more lines," the boy announced, springing up to his feet. "Papy, do you want to hear them?"

150   "They are giving him more things to say in the play," Lili explained, "because he did such a good job memorizing so fast."

"My compliments, son. Do you have your new lines memorized too?" Guy asked.

"Why don't you recite your new lines for your father?" Lili said.

The boy walked to the middle of the room and prepared to recite. He cleared his throat, raising his eyes towards the ceiling.

"There is so much sadness in the faces of my people. I have called on their gods, now I call on our gods. I call on our young. I call on our old. I call on our mighty and the weak. I call on everyone and anyone so that we shall all let out one piercing cry that we may either live freely or we should die."

155   "I see your new lines have as much drama as the old ones," Guy said. He wiped a tear away, walked over to the chair, and took the boy in his arms. He pressed the boy's body against his chest before lowering him to the ground.

"Your new lines are wonderful, son. They're every bit as affecting as the old." He tapped the boy's shoulder and walked out of the house.

"What's the matter with Papy?" the boy asked as the door slammed shut behind Guy.

"His heart hurts," Lili said.

After supper, Lili took her son to the field where she knew her husband would be. While the boy ran around, she found her husband sitting in his favorite spot behind the sugar mill.

"Nothing, Lili," he said. "Ask me nothing about this day that I have had." 160
She sat down on the grass next to him, for once feeling the sharp edges of the grass blades against her ankles.

"You're really good with that boy," he said, drawing circles with his smallest finger on her elbow. "You will make a performer of him. I know you will. You can see the best in that whole situation. It's because you have those stars in your eyes. That's the first thing I noticed about you when I met you. It was your eyes, Lili, so dark and deep. They drew me like danger draws a fool."

He turned over on the grass so that he was staring directly at the moon up in the sky. She could tell that he was also watching the hot-air balloon behind the sugar mill fence out of the corner of his eye.

"Sometimes I know you want to believe in me," he said. "I know you're wishing things for me. You want me to work at the mill. You want me to get a pretty house for us. I know you want these things too, but mostly you want me to feel like a man. That's why you're not one to worry about, Lili. I know you can take things as they come."

"I don't like it when you talk this way," she said. 165
"Listen to this, Lili. I want to tell you a secret. Sometimes, I just want to take that big balloon and ride it up in the air. I'd like to sail off somewhere and keep floating until I got to a really nice place with a nice plot of land where I could be something new. I'd build my own house, keep my own garden. Just *be* something new."

"I want you to stay away from there."

"I know you don't think I should take it. That can't keep me from wanting."

"You could be injured. Do you ever think about that?"

"Don't you ever want to be something new?" 170
"I don't like it," she said.

"Please don't get angry with me," he said, his voice straining almost like the boy's.

"If you were to take that balloon and fly away, would you take me and the boy?"

"First you don't want me to take it and now you want to go?"

"I just want to know that when you dream, me and the boy, we're always 175 in your dreams."

He leaned his head on her shoulders and drifted off to sleep. Her back ached as she sat there with his face pressed against her collar bone. He drooled and the saliva dripped down to her breasts, soaking her frayed polyester bra. She listened to the crickets while watching her son play, muttering his lines to himself as he went in a circle around the field. The moon was glowing above their heads. Winking at them, as Guy liked to say, on its way to brighter shores.

Opening his eyes, Guy asked her, "How do you think a man is judged after he's gone?"

How did he expect her to answer something like that?

"People don't eat riches," she said. "They eat what it can buy."

180   "What does that mean, Lili? Don't talk to me in parables. Talk to me honestly."

"A man is judged by his deeds," she said. "The boy never goes to bed hungry. For as long as he's been with us, he's always been fed."

Just as if he had heard himself mentioned, the boy came dashing from the other side of the field, crashing in a heap on top of his parents.

"My new lines," he said. "I have forgotten my new lines."

"Is this how you will be the day of this play, son?" Guy asked. "When people give you big responsibilities, you have to try to live up to them."

185   The boy had relearned his new lines by the time they went to bed.

That night, Guy watched his wife very closely as she undressed for bed.

"I would like to be the one to rub that piece of lemon on your knees tonight," he said.

She handed him the half lemon, then raised her skirt above her knees. Her body began to tremble as he rubbed his fingers over her skin.

190   "You know that question I asked you before," he said, "how a man is remembered after he's gone? I know the answer now. I know because I remember my father, who was a very poor struggling man all his life. I remember him as a man that I would never want to be."

Lili got up with the break of dawn the next day. The light came up quickly above the trees. Lili greeted some of the market women as they walked together to the public water fountain.

On her way back, the sun had already melted a few gray clouds. She found the boy standing alone in the yard with a terrified expression on his face, the old withered mushrooms uprooted at his feet. He ran up to meet her, nearly knocking her off balance.

"What happened?" she asked. "Have you forgotten your lines?"

The boy was breathing so heavily that his lips could not form a single word.

195   "What is it?" Lili asked, almost shaking him with anxiety.

"It's Papa," he said finally, raising a stiff finger in the air.

The boy covered his face as his mother looked up at the sky. A rainbow-colored balloon was floating aimlessly above their heads.

"It's Papa," the boy said. "He is in it."

She wanted to look down at her son and tell him that it wasn't his father, but she immediately recognized the spindly arms, in a bright flowered shirt that she had made, gripping the cables.

From the field behind the sugar mill a group of workers were watching the balloon floating in the air. Many were clapping and cheering, calling out Guy's name. A few of the women were waving their head rags at the sky, shouting, "Go! Beautiful, go!"

Lili edged her way to the front of the crowd. Everyone was waiting, watching the balloon drift higher up into the clouds.

"He seems to be right over our heads," said the factory foreman, a short slender mulatto with large buckteeth.

Just then, Lili noticed young Assad, his thick black hair sticking to the beads of sweat on his forehead. His face had the crumpled expression of disrupted sleep.

"He's further away than he seems," said young Assad. "I still don't understand. How did he get up there? You need a whole crew to fly these things."

"I don't know," the foreman said. "One of my workers just came in saying there was a man flying above the factory."

"But how the hell did he start it?" Young Assad was perplexed.

"He just did it," the foreman said.

"Look, he's trying to get out!" someone hollered.

A chorus of screams broke out among the workers.

The boy was looking up, trying to see if his father was really trying to jump out of the balloon. Guy was climbing over the side of the basket. Lili pressed her son's face into her skirt.

Within seconds, Guy was in the air hurtling down towards the crowd. Lili held her breath as she watched him fall. He crashed not far from where Lili and the boy were standing, his blood immediately soaking the landing spot.

The balloon kept floating free, drifting on its way to brighter shores. Young Assad rushed towards the body. He dropped to his knees and checked the wrist for a pulse, then dropped the arm back to the ground.

"It's over!" The foreman ordered the workers back to work.

Lili tried to keep her son's head pressed against her skirt as she moved closer to the body. The boy yanked himself away and raced to the edge of the field where his father's body was lying on the grass. He reached the body as young Assad still knelt examining the corpse. Lili rushed after him.

"He is mine," she said to young Assad. "He is my family. He belongs to me."

Young Assad got up and raised his head to search the sky for his aimless balloon, trying to guess where it would land. He took one last glance at Guy's bloody corpse, then raced to his car and sped away.

The foreman and another worker carried a cot and blanket from the factory.

Little Guy was breathing quickly as he looked at his father's body on the ground. While the foreman draped a sheet over Guy's corpse, his son began to recite the lines from his play.

"A wall of fire is rising and in the ashes, I see the bones of my people. Not only those people whose dark hollow faces I see daily in the fields, but all those souls who have gone ahead to haunt my dreams. At night I relive once more the last caresses from the hand of a loving father, a valiant love, a beloved friend."

220   "Let me look at him one last time," Lili said, pulling back the sheet.

She leaned in very close to get a better look at Guy's face. There was little left of that countenance that she had loved so much. Those lips that curled when he was teasing her. That large flat nose that felt like a feather when rubbed against hers. And those eyes, those night-colored eyes. Though clouded with blood, Guy's eyes were still bulging open. Lili was searching for some kind of sign—a blink, a smile, a wink—something that would remind her of the man that she had married.

"His eyes aren't closed," the foreman said to Lili. "Do you want to close them, or should I?"

The boy continued reciting his lines, his voice rising to a man's grieving roar. He kept his eyes closed, his fists balled at his side as he continued with his newest lines.

"There is so much sadness in the faces of my people. I have called on their gods, now I call on our gods. I call on our young. I call on our old. I call on our mighty and the weak. I call on everyone and anyone so that we shall all let out one piercing cry that we may either live freely or we should die."

225   "Do you want to close the eyes?" the foreman repeated impatiently.

"No, leave them open," Lili said. "My husband, he likes to look at the sky."

1991

QUESTIONS

1. What do you think the hot-air balloon symbolizes to Assad, its owner? to Guy? to Edwidge Danticat?

2. The title of the story alludes to a speech that Little Guy must memorize for a school play about Haiti's history. The lines of the speech are rich in figurative language, including metaphors: "A wall of fire is rising and in the ashes I see the bones of my people" (par. 34). How do the title's allusion and other aspects of the story confirm that the speech's image of "a wall of fire" is symbolic?

3. What do you think happens at the end of "A Wall of Fire Rising"? Is Guy's plunge to the earth a deliberate suicide or an accident? What are some symbolic interpretations of both possibilities?

SUGGESTIONS FOR WRITING

1. Choose one of the stories in this chapter, read it thoroughly, and follow the guidelines for responding to symbolism on pages 217–18. Write an essay in which you explore the various meanings of the story's major symbol and the way these emerge over the course of the story.
2. In "The Birth-Mark," Aylmer the scientist is portrayed as "spiritual" and "intellectual," in contrast with his crudely physical laboratory assistant, Aminadab (par. 25). Write an essay in which you argue that the allegory of Aylmer's terrible experiment on his wife refers not only to a man's desire for immortal beauty but also to his desire for control of everything physical, including the laborer.
3. Write an essay in which you compare and contrast the way symbolism works in "The Birth-Mark" and "A Wall of Fire Rising." For example, what is the effect and significance of both the magical atmosphere of Hawthorne's story and the way its characters explicitly refer to particular objects as symbols? How might symbolism work differently in Danticat's story because of its realistic, contemporary setting and plot and the fact that its characters don't explicitly refer to anything as a symbol?
4. To what extent are characters aware of the symbolism in a story? Do characters accept the symbolism as objective and real, even if what happens seems magical or impossible? Write an essay focused on characters' different ways of responding to or believing in a symbol or symbolism in one or both stories in this chapter. For instance, compare and contrast the characters' awareness and response to the respective symbols in Danticat's and Hawthorne's stories.
5. Write a parody of any of the stories in this chapter. See if you can make the symbolism deliberately heavy-handed and obvious, or perhaps obscure and puzzling.

6 THEME

At some point, a responsive reader of any story or novel will inevitably ask, *Why does it all matter? What does it all mean? What's the point?* When we ask what a text means, we are inquiring, at least in part, about its **theme**—a general idea or insight conveyed by the work in its entirety. Theme is certainly not the only way fiction matters nor the only thing we take away from our experience of reading it. Nor is theme fiction's *point* in the sense of its sole "objective" or "purpose." Yet theme is a fictional work's *point* in the sense of its "essential meaning" (or meanings). And our experience of any work isn't complete unless we grapple with the question of its theme.

On rare occasions, we might not have to grapple hard or look far: A very few texts, such as **fables** and certain fairy tales and folktales, explicitly state their themes. To succeed, however, even these works must ultimately "earn" their themes, bringing a raw statement to life through their characters, plot, setting, symbols, and narration. The following fable, by Aesop, succinctly makes its point through a brief dialogue.

AESOP

The Two Crabs

ONE fine day two crabs came out from their home to take a stroll on the sand. "Child," said the mother, "you are walking very ungracefully. You should accustom yourself to walking straight forward without twisting from side to side."

"Pray, mother," said the young one, "do but set the example yourself, and I will follow you."

"EXAMPLE IS THE BEST PRECEPT."

• • •

In most works, however, all the elements work together to imply an unstated theme that usually requires re-reading to decipher. Even the most careful and responsive readers will likely disagree about just what the theme is or how best to state it. And each statement of a given theme will imply a slightly different view of what matters most and why.

THEME(S): SINGULAR OR PLURAL?

In practice, readers disagree about the precise meaning of the term *theme*. One source of disagreement hinges on the question of whether any single work of fiction can convey more than one theme. On one side of the debate are those who use the word *theme* to refer only to the central or main idea of a work. On the other are those who use the term, as we generally do in this book, to refer to any idea a work conveys. While the former readers tend to talk about *the* theme, the latter instead refer to *a* theme in order to stress that each theme is only one of many. Regardless of whether we call all of the ideas expressed in a work *themes* or instead refer to some of them as *subthemes*, the essential points on which all agree are that a single literary work often expresses multiple ideas, and that at least one of those ideas is likely to be more central or overarching and inclusive than others. "The Two Crabs" demonstrates that even the most simple and straightforward of stories can have more than one theme. This fable's main, stated theme, "Example is the best precept," emerges only because the little crab "back-talks" to its mother, implicitly suggesting another theme: that children are sometimes wiser than their parents or even that we sometimes learn by questioning, rather than blindly following, authority. The fact that crabs naturally "twist from side to side"—that no crab *can* walk straight—certainly adds **irony** to the fable, but might it also imply yet another theme?

BE SPECIFIC: THEME AS IDEA VERSUS TOPIC OR SUBJECT

Often, you will see the term *theme* used very loosely to refer to a topic or subject captured in a noun phrase—"the wisdom of youth," "loss of innocence," "the dangers of perfectionism"—or even a single noun—"loss," "youth," "grief," or "prejudice." Identifying such topics—especially those specific enough to require a noun phrase rather than a simple noun—can be a useful first step on the way to figuring out a particular story's themes and also to grouping stories together for the purpose of comparison.

For now, though, we urge you to consider this merely a first step on the path to interpreting a story. The truth is, we haven't yet said anything very insightful, revealing, or debatable about the meaning of an individual story until we articulate the idea it expresses *about* a topic such as love, prejudice, or grief. To state a theme in this much more restricted and helpful sense you will need at least one complete sentence. Note, however, that a complete sentence is still not necessarily a statement of theme. For example, an online student essay begins with the less than scintillating sentence, "In Nathaniel

Hawthorne's 'The Birthmark' the reader finds several themes—guilt, evil, love and alienation." One reason this sentence is both unexciting and unhelpful is that—despite its specific list of topics—we could in fact substitute for "The Birth-Mark" almost any other story in this book. (Try it yourself.) Notice how much more interesting things get, however, when we instead articulate the story's particular insight about just one of these very general topics: "Nathaniel Hawthorne's 'The Birth-Mark' shows us that we too often destroy the very thing we love by trying to turn the good into the perfect."

DON'T BE TOO SPECIFIC: THEME AS *GENERAL* IDEA

Though a theme is specific in the sense that it is a complete idea or statement rather than a topic, it is nonetheless a *general* idea rather than one that describes the characters, plot, or settings unique to one story. Theme is a general insight illustrated *through* these elements rather than an insight *about* any of them. Look again at the statement above—"Nathaniel Hawthorne's 'The Birth-Mark' shows us that we too often destroy the very thing we love by trying to turn the good into the perfect." Now compare this statement with one such as this: "In Nathaniel Hawthorne's 'The Birth-Mark,' the scientist Aylmer kills his wife because he can't tolerate imperfection." Though both statements are valid, only the first of them is truly a statement of theme—of what the story shows us about love through Aylmer rather than what it suggests about Aylmer himself.

THEME VERSUS MORAL

In some cases, a theme may take the form of a **moral**—a rule of conduct or maxim for living. But most themes are instead general observations and insights about how humans actually *do* behave, or about how life, the world, or some particular corner of it actually *is*, rather than moral imperatives about how people *should* behave or how life *should* ideally be. As one contemporary critic puts it, a responsive reader should thus "ask not *What does this story teach?* but *What does this story reveal?*" By the same token, we're usually on safer and more fertile ground if we phrase a theme as a statement rather than a command. Hawthorne's "The Birth-Mark," for example, certainly demonstrates the dangers of arrogantly seeking a perfection that isn't natural or human. As a result, we might well be tempted to reduce its theme to a moral such as "Accept imperfection," "Avoid arrogance," or "Don't mess with Mother Nature." None of these statements is wholly inappropriate to the story. Yet each of them seems to underestimate the story's complexity and especially its implicit emphasis on all that humanity gains, as well as loses, in the search for perfection. As a result, a better statement of the story's theme might be "Paradoxically, both our drive for perfection and our inevitable imperfection together make us human."

· · ·

As you decipher and discuss the themes of the three powerful stories that follow—Stephen Crane's "The Open Boat," Gabriel García Márquez's "A Very Old Man with Enormous Wings," and Louise Erdrich's "Love Medicine"—keep in mind that to identify a theme is not to "close the case" but rather to begin a more searching investigation of the details that make each story vivid and unique. Theme is an abstraction from the story; the story and its details do not disappear or lose significance once distilled into theme, nor could you reconstruct a story merely from a statement of its theme. Indeed, theme and story are fused, inseparable. Often difficult to put into words, themes are the common ground that helps you recognize and care about a story, and relate it to your own life—even though it seems to be about lives and experiences very different from your own.

Tips for Identifying Themes

Because theme emerges from a work in its entirety and from all the other elements working together, there is no "one-size-fits-all" method for identifying theme. Here, however, are some things to look for and consider as you read and re-read the work.

1. Pay attention to the title. A title will seldom spell out in full a work's main theme, but some titles do suggest a central topic or topics or a clue to theme. Probe the rest of the story to see what, if any, insights about that topic it ultimately seems to offer.

2. List any recurring phrases and words, especially those for abstract concepts (love, honor). Certain concrete terms (especially if noted in the title) may likewise provide clues; objects of value or potency might attract significant attention in the text (an heirloom, a weapon, a tree in a garden). Then probe the story to see how and where else it might implicitly deal with that concept or entity and what, if any, conclusions the story proposes.

3. Identify any statements that the characters or narrator(s) make about a general concept, issue, or topic such as human nature, the natural world, and so on. Look, too, for statements that potentially have a general meaning or application beyond the story, even if they refer to a specific situation. Then consider whether and how the story as a whole corroborates, overturns, or complicates any one such view or statement.

4. If a character changes over the course of the story, articulate the truth or insight that he or she seems to discover. Then consider whether and how the story as a whole corroborates or complicates that insight.

5. Identify a conflict depicted in the work and state it in general terms or turn it into a general question, leaving out any reference to specific characters, situations, and so on. Then think about the insight or theme that might be implied by the way the conflict is resolved.

STEPHEN CRANE

The Open Boat

A Tale Intended to Be after the Fact:[1] Being the Experience
of Four Men from the Sunk Steamer Commodore

I

None of them knew the color of the sky. Their eyes glanced level and were fastened upon the waves that swept toward them. These waves were of the hue of slate, save for the tops, which were of foaming white, and all of the men knew the colors of the sea. The horizon narrowed and widened, and dipped and rose, and at all times its edge was jagged with waves that seemed thrust up in points like rocks.

Many a man ought to have a bathtub larger than the boat which here rode upon the sea. These waves were most wrongfully and barbarously abrupt and tall, and each froth-top was a problem in small-boat navigation.

The cook squatted in the bottom, and looked with both eyes at the six inches of gunwale which separated him from the ocean. His sleeves were rolled over his fat forearms, and the two flaps of his unbuttoned vest dangled as he bent to bail out the boat. Often he said, "Gawd! that was a narrow clip." As he remarked it he invariably gazed eastward over the broken sea.

The oiler, steering with one of the two oars in the boat, sometimes raised himself suddenly to keep clear of water that swirled in over the stern. It was a thin little oar, and it seemed often ready to snap.

5   The correspondent, pulling at the other oar, watched the waves and wondered why he was there.

The injured captain, lying in the bow, was at this time buried in that profound dejection and indifference which comes, temporarily at least, to even the bravest and most enduring when, willy-nilly, the firm fails, the army loses, the ship goes down. The mind of the master of a vessel is rooted deep in the timbers of her, though he command for a day or a decade; and this captain had on him the stern impression of a scene in the grays of dawn of seven turned faces, and later a stump of a topmast with a white ball on it, that slashed to and fro at the waves, went low and lower, and down. Thereafter there was something strange in his voice. Although steady, it was deep with mourning, and of a quality beyond oration or tears.

"Keep 'er a little more south, Billie," said he.

"A little more south, sir," said the oiler in the stern.

---

1. Crane had an experience very like the one here re-created in fiction. His autobiographical account of his adventure at sea was published in the *New York Press* on January 7, 1897.

A seat in his boat was not unlike a seat upon a bucking broncho, and by the same token a broncho is not much smaller. The craft pranced and reared and plunged like an animal. As each wave came, and she rose for it, she seemed like a horse making at a fence outrageously high. The manner of her scramble over these walls of water is a mystic thing, and, moreover, at the top of them were ordinarily these problems in white water, the foam racing down from the summit of each wave requiring a new leap, and a leap from the air. Then, after scornfully bumping a crest, she would slide and race and splash down a long incline, and arrive bobbing and nodding in front of the next menace.

A singular disadvantage of the sea lies in the fact that after successfully 10 surmounting one wave you discover that there is another behind it just as important and just as nervously anxious to do something effective in the way of swamping boats. In a ten-foot dinghy one can get an idea of the resources of the sea in the line of waves that is not probable to the average experience, which is never at sea in a dinghy. As each slaty wall of water approached, it shut all else from the view of the men in the boat, and it was not difficult to imagine that this particular wave was the final outburst of the ocean, the last effort of the grim water. There was a terrible grace in the move of the waves, and they came in silence, save for the snarling of the crests.

In the wan light the faces of the men must have been gray. Their eyes must have glinted in strange ways as they gazed steadily astern. Viewed from a balcony, the whole thing would, doubtless, have been weirdly picturesque. But the men in the boat had no time to see it, and if they had had leisure, there were other things to occupy their minds. The sun swung steadily up the sky, and they knew it was broad day because the color of the sea changed from slate to emerald-green streaked with amber lights, and the foam was like tumbling snow. The process of the breaking day was unknown to them. They were aware only of this effect upon the color of the waves that rolled toward them.

In disjointed sentences the cook and the correspondent argued as to the difference between a life-saving station and a house of refuge. The cook had said: "There's a house of refuge just north of the Mosquito Inlet Light, and as soon as they see us they'll come off in their boat and pick us up."

"As soon as who see us?" said the correspondent.

"The crew," said the cook.

"Houses of refuge don't have crews," said the correspondent. "As I 15 understand them, they are only places where clothes and grub are stored for the benefit of shipwrecked people. They don't carry crews."

"Oh, yes, they do," said the cook.

"No, they don't," said the correspondent.

"Well, we're not there yet, anyhow," said the oiler, in the stern.

"Well," said the cook, "perhaps it's not a house of refuge that I'm thinking of as being near Mosquito Inlet Light; perhaps it's a life-saving station."

20   "We're not there yet," said the oiler in the stern.

II

As the boat bounced from the top of each wave the wind tore through the hair of the hatless men, and as the craft plopped her stern down again the spray slashed past them. The crest of each of these waves was a hill, from the top of which the men surveyed for a moment a broad tumultuous expanse, shining and wind-riven. It was probably splendid, it was probably glorious, this play of the free sea, wild with lights of emerald and white and amber.

"Bully good thing it's an on-shore wind," said the cook. "If not, where would we be? Wouldn't have a show."

"That's right," said the correspondent.

The busy oiler nodded his assent.

25   Then the captain, in the bow, chuckled in a way that expressed humor, contempt, tragedy, all in one. "Do you think we've got much of a show now, boys?" said he.

Whereupon the three were silent, save for a trifle of hemming and hawing. To express any particular optimism at this time they felt to be childish and stupid, but they all doubtless possessed this sense of the situation in their minds. A young man thinks doggedly at such times. On the other hand, the ethics of their condition was decidedly against any open suggestion of hopelessness. So they were silent.

"Oh, well," said the captain, soothing his children, "we'll get ashore all right."

But there was that in his tone which made them think; so the oiler quoth, "Yes! if this wind holds."

The cook was bailing. "Yes! if we don't catch hell in the surf."

30   Canton-flannel[2] gulls flew near and far. Sometimes they sat down on the sea, near patches of brown seaweed that rolled over the waves with a movement like carpets on a line in a gale. The birds sat comfortably in groups, and they were envied by some in the dinghy, for the wrath of the sea was no more to them than it was to a covey of prairie chickens a thousand miles inland. Often they came very close and stared at the men with black bead-like eyes. At these times they were uncanny and sinister in their unblinking scrutiny, and the men hooted angrily at them, telling them to be gone. One came, and evidently decided to alight on the top of the captain's head. The bird flew parallel to the boat and did not circle, but made short sidelong jumps in the air in chicken fashion. His black eyes were wistfully fixed upon the captain's head. "Ugly brute," said the oiler to the

---

2. Plain-weave cotton fabric.

bird. "You look as if you were made with a jackknife." The cook and the correspondent swore darkly at the creature. The captain naturally wished to knock it away with the end of the heavy painter,[3] but he did not dare do it, because anything resembling an emphatic gesture would have capsized this freighted boat; and so, with his open hand, the captain gently and carefully waved the gull away. After it had been discouraged from the pursuit the captain breathed easier on account of his hair, and others breathed easier because the bird struck their minds at this time as being somehow gruesome and ominous.

In the meantime the oiler and the correspondent rowed; and also they rowed. They sat together in the same seat, and each rowed an oar. Then the oiler took both oars; then the correspondent took both oars, then the oiler; then the correspondent. They rowed and they rowed. The very ticklish part of the business was when the time came for the reclining one in the stern to take his turn at the oars. By the very last star of truth, it is easier to steal eggs from under a hen than it was to change seats in the dinghy. First the man in the stern slid his hand along the thwart and moved with care, as if he were of Sèvres.[4] Then the man in the rowing-seat slid his hand along the other thwart. It was all done with the most extraordinary care. As the two sidled past each other, the whole party kept watchful eyes on the coming wave, and the captain cried: "Look out, now! Steady, there!"

The brown mats of seaweed that appeared from time to time were like islands, bits of earth. They were travelling, apparently, neither one way nor the other. They were, to all intents, stationary. They informed the men in the boat that it was making progress slowly toward the land.

The captain, rearing cautiously in the bow after the dinghy soared on a great swell, said that he had seen the lighthouse at Mosquito Inlet. Presently the cook remarked that he had seen it. The correspondent was at the oars then, and for some reason he too wished to look at the lighthouse; but his back was toward the far shore, and the waves were important, and for some time he could not seize an opportunity to turn his head. But at last there came a wave more gentle than the others, and when at the crest of it he swiftly scoured the western horizon.

"See it?" said the captain.

"No," said the correspondent, slowly; "I didn't see anything." 35

"Look again," said the captain. He pointed. "It's exactly in that direction."

At the top of another wave the correspondent did as he was bid, and this time his eyes chanced on a small, still thing on the edge of the swaying horizon. It was precisely like the point of a pin. It took an anxious eye to find a lighthouse so tiny.

"Think we'll make it, Captain?"

---

3. Mooring rope attached to the bow of a boat.   4. Type of fine china.

"If this wind holds and the boat don't swamp, we can't do much else," said the captain.

40   The little boat, lifted by each towering sea and splashed viciously by the crests, made progress that in the absence of seaweed was not apparent to those in her. She seemed just a wee thing wallowing, miraculously top up, at the mercy of five oceans. Occasionally a great spread of water, like white flames, swarmed into her.

"Bail her, cook," said the captain, serenely.

"All right, Captain," said the cheerful cook.

III

It would be difficult to describe the subtle brotherhood of men that was here established on the seas. No one said that it was so. No one mentioned it. But it dwelt in the boat, and each man felt it warm him. They were a captain, an oiler, a cook, and a correspondent, and they were friends—friends in a more curiously iron-bound degree than may be common. The hurt captain, lying against the water jar in the bow, spoke always in a low voice and calmly; but he could never command a more ready and swiftly obedient crew than the motley three of the dinghy. It was more than a mere recognition of what was best for the common safety. There was surely in it a quality that was personal and heart-felt. And after this devotion to the commander of the boat, there was this comradeship, that the correspondent, for instance, who had been taught to be cynical of men, knew even at the time was the best experience of his life. But no one said that it was so. No one mentioned it.

"I wish we had a sail," remarked the captain. "We might try my overcoat on the end of an oar, and give you two boys a chance to rest." So the cook and the correspondent held the mast and spread wide the overcoat; the oiler steered; and the little boat made good way with her new rig. Sometimes the oiler had to scull sharply to keep a sea from breaking into the boat, but otherwise sailing was a success.

45   Meanwhile the lighthouse had been growing slowly larger. It had now almost assumed color, and appeared like a little gray shadow on the sky. The man at the oars could not be prevented from turning his head rather often to try for a glimpse of this little gray shadow.

At last, from the top of each wave, the men in the tossing boat could see land. Even as the lighthouse was an upright shadow on the sky, this land seemed but a long black shadow on the sea. It certainly was thinner than paper. "We must be about opposite New Smyrna,"[5] said the cook, who had coasted this shore often in schooners. "Captain, by the way, I believe they abandoned that life-saving station there about a year ago."

"Did they?" said the captain.

---

5. Town on the Florida coast.

The wind slowly died away. The cook and the correspondent were not now obliged to slave in order to hold high the oar. But the waves continued their old impetuous swooping at the dinghy, and the little craft, no longer underway, struggled woundily over them. The oiler or the correspondent took the oars again.

Shipwrecks are *apropos* of nothing. If men could only train for them and have them occur when the men had reached pink condition, there would be less drowning at sea. Of the four in the dinghy none had slept any time worth mentioning for two days and two nights previous to embarking in the dinghy, and in the excitement of clambering about the deck of a foundering ship they had also forgotten to eat heartily.

For these reasons, and for others, neither the oiler nor the correspon- 50 dent was fond of rowing at this time. The correspondent wondered ingenuously how in the name of all that was sane could there be people who thought it amusing to row a boat. It was not an amusement; it was a diabolical punishment, and even a genius of mental aberrations could never conclude that it was anything but a horror to the muscles and a crime against the back. He mentioned to the boat in general how the amusement of rowing struck him, and the weary-faced oiler smiled in full sympathy. Previously to the foundering, by the way, the oiler had worked a double watch in the engine-room of the ship.

"Take her easy, now, boys," said the captain. "Don't spend yourselves. If we have to run a surf you'll need all your strength, because we'll sure have to swim for it. Take your time."

Slowly the land arose from the sea. From a black line it became a line of black and a line of white—trees and sand. Finally the captain said that he could make out a house on the shore. "That's the house of refuge, sure," said the cook. "They'll see us before long, and come out after us."

The distant lighthouse reared high. "The keeper ought to be able to make us out now, if he's looking through a glass," said the captain. "He'll notify the life-saving people."

"None of those other boats could have got ashore to give word of the wreck," said the oiler, in a low voice, "else the life-boat would be out hunting us."

Slowly and beautifully the land loomed out of the sea. The wind came 55 again. It had veered from the northeast to the southeast. Finally a new sound struck the ears of the men in the boat. It was the low thunder of the surf on the shore. "We'll never be able to make the lighthouse now," said the captain. "Swing her head a little more north, Billie."

"A little more north, sir," said the oiler.

Whereupon the little boat turned her nose once more down the wind, and all but the oarsman watched the shore grow. Under the influence of this expansion doubt and direful apprehension were leaving the minds of the men. The management of the boat was still most absorbing, but it could not prevent a quiet cheerfulness. In an hour, perhaps, they would be ashore.

Their backbones had become thoroughly used to balancing in the boat, and they now rode this wild colt of a dinghy like circus men. The correspondent thought that he had been drenched to the skin, but happening to feel in the top pocket of his coat, he found therein eight cigars. Four of them were soaked with sea-water; four were perfectly scatheless. After a search, somebody produced three dry matches; and thereupon the four waifs rode impudently in their little boat and, with an assurance of an impending rescue shining in their eyes, puffed at the big cigars, and judged well and ill of all men. Everybody took a drink of water.

IV

"Cook," remarked the captain, "there don't seem to be any signs of life about your house of refuge."

60   "No," replied the cook. "Funny they don't see us!"

A broad stretch of lowly coast lay before the eyes of the men. It was of low dunes topped with dark vegetation. The roar of the surf was plain, and sometimes they could see the white lip of a wave as it spun up the beach. A tiny house was blocked out black upon the sky. Southward, the slim lighthouse lifted its little gray length.

Tide, wind, and waves were swinging the dinghy northward. "Funny they don't see us," said the men.

The surf's roar was here dulled, but its tone was nevertheless thunderous and mighty. As the boat swam over the great rollers the men sat listening to this roar. "We'll swamp sure," said everybody.

It is fair to say here that there was not a life-saving station within twenty miles in either direction; but the men did not know this fact, and in consequence they made dark and opprobrious remarks concerning the eyesight of the nation's life-savers. Four scowling men sat in the dinghy and surpassed records in the invention of epithets.

65   "Funny they don't see us."

The light-heartedness of a former time had completely faded. To their sharpened minds it was easy to conjure pictures of all kinds of incompetency and blindness and, indeed, cowardice. There was the shore of the populous land, and it was bitter and bitter to them that from it came no sign.

"Well," said the captain, ultimately, "I suppose we'll have to make a try for ourselves. If we stay out here too long, we'll none of us have strength left to swim after the boat swamps."

And so the oiler, who was at the oars, turned the boat straight for the shore. There was a sudden tightening of muscles. There was some thinking.

"If we don't all get ashore," said the captain—"if we don't all get ashore, I suppose you fellows know where to send news of my finish?"

They then briefly exchanged some addresses and admonitions. As for 70
the reflections of the men, there was a great deal of rage in them. Perchance
they might be formulated thus: "If I am going to be drowned—if I am
going to be drowned—if I am going to be drowned, why, in the name of the
seven mad gods who rule the sea, was I allowed to come thus far and contemplate sand and trees? Was I brought here merely to have my nose
dragged away as I was about to nibble the sacred cheese of life? It is prepos-
terous. If this old ninny-woman, Fate, cannot do better than this, she
should be deprived of the management of men's fortunes. She is an old hen
who knows not her intention. If she has decided to drown me, why did she
not do it in the beginning and save me all this trouble? The whole affair is
absurd. . . . But no; she cannot mean to drown me. She dare not drown me.
She cannot drown me. Not after all this work." Afterward the man might
have had an impulse to shake his fist at the clouds. "Just you drown me,
now, and then hear what I call you!"

The billows that came at this time were more formidable. They seemed
always just about to break and roll over the little boat in a turmoil of foam.
There was a preparatory and long growl in the speech of them. No mind
unused to the sea would have concluded that the dinghy could ascend
these sheer heights in time. The shore was still afar. The oiler was a wily
surfman. "Boys," he said, swiftly, "she won't live three minutes more, and
we're too far out to swim. Shall I take her to sea again, Captain?"

"Yes; go ahead!" said the captain.

This oiler, by a series of quick miracles and fast and steady oarsmanship,
turned the boat in the middle of the surf and took her safely to sea again.

There was a considerable silence as the boat bumped over the furrowed
sea to deeper water. Then somebody in gloom spoke: "Well, anyhow, they
must have seen us from the shore by now."

The gulls went in slanting flight up the wind toward the gray, desolate 75
east. A squall, marked by dingy clouds and clouds brick-red, like smoke
from a burning building, appeared from the southeast.

"What do you think of those life-saving people? Ain't they peaches?"

"Funny they haven't seen us."

"Maybe they think we're out here for sport! Maybe they think we're
fishin'. Maybe they think we're damned fools."

It was a long afternoon. A changed tide tried to force them southward,
but wind and wave said northward. Far ahead, where coast-line, sea, and
sky formed their mighty angle, there were little dots which seemed to indicate a city on the shore.

"St. Augustine." 80

The captain shook his head. "Too near Mosquito Inlet."

And the oiler rowed, and then the correspondent rowed; then the oiler
moved. It was a weary business. The human back can become the seat of
more aches and pains than are registered in books for the composite

anatomy of a regiment. It is a limited area, but it can become the theatre of innumerable muscular conflicts, tangles, wrenches, knots, and other comforts.

"Did you ever like to row, Billie?" asked the correspondent.

"No," said the oiler. "Hang it."

85 When one exchanged the rowing-seat for a place in the bottom of the boat, he suffered a bodily depression that caused him to be careless of everything save an obligation to wiggle one finger. There was cold sea-water swashing to and fro in the boat, and he lay in it. His head, pillowed on a thwart, was within an inch of the swirl of a wave-crest, and sometimes a particularly obstreperous sea came inboard and drenched him once more. But these matters did not annoy him. It is almost certain that if the boat had capsized he would have tumbled comfortably out upon the ocean as if he felt sure that it was a great soft mattress.

"Look! There's a man on the shore!"

"There? See 'im? See 'im?"

"Yes, sure! He's walking along."

"Now he's stopped. Look! He's facing us!"

90 "He's waving at us!"

"So he is! By thunder!"

"Ah, now we're all right! Now we're all right! There'll be a boat out here for us in half an hour."

"He's going on. He's running. He's going up to that house there."

The remote beach seemed lower than the sea, and it required a searching glance to discern the little black figure. The captain saw a floating stick, and they rowed to it. A bath towel was by some weird chance in the boat, and, tying this on the stick, the captain waved it. The oarsman did not dare turn his head, so he was obliged to ask questions.

95 "What's he doing now?"

"He's standing still again. He's looking, I think.... There he goes again—toward the house.... Now he's stopped again."

"Is he waving at us?"

"No, not now; he was, though."

"Look! There comes another man!"

100 "He's running."

"Look at him go, would you!"

"Why, he's on a bicycle. Now he's met the other man. They're both waving at us. Look!"

"There comes something up the beach."

"What the devil is that thing?"

105 "Why, it looks like a boat."

"Why, certainly, it's a boat."

"No; it's on wheels."

"Yes, so it is. Well, that must be the life-boat. They drag them along shore on a wagon."

"That's the life-boat, sure."

"No, by God, it's—it's an omnibus." 110

"I tell you it's a life-boat."

"It is not! It's an omnibus. I can see it plain. See? One of these big hotel omnibuses."

"By thunder, you're right. It's an omnibus, sure as fate. What do you suppose they are doing with an omnibus? Maybe they are going around collecting the life-crew, hey?"

"That's it, likely. Look! There's a fellow waving a little black flag. He's standing on the steps of the omnibus. There comes those other two fellows. Now they're all talking together. Look at the fellow with the flag. Maybe he ain't waving it!"

"That ain't a flag, is it? That's his coat. Why, certainly, that's his coat." 115

"So it is: it's his coat. He's taken it off and is waving it around his head. But would you look at him swing it!"

"Oh, say, there isn't any life-saving station there. That's just a winter-resort."

"What's that idiot with the coat mean? What's he signaling, anyhow?"

"It looks as if he were trying to tell us to go north. There must be a life-saving station up there."

"No; he thinks we're fishing. Just giving us a merry hand. See? Ah, there, 120 Willie!"

"Well, I wish I could make something out of those signals. What do you suppose he means?"

"He don't mean anything; he's just playing."

"Well, if he'd just signal us to try the surf again, or to go to sea and wait, or go north, or go south, or go to hell, there would be some reason in it. But look at him! He just stands there and keeps his coat revolving like a wheel. The ass!"

"There come more people."

"Now there's quite a mob. Look! Isn't that a boat?" 125

"Where? Oh, I see where you mean. No, that's no boat."

"That fellow is still waving his coat."

"He must think we like to see him to do that. Why don't he quit? It don't mean anything."

"I don't know. I think he is trying to make us go north. It must be that there's a life-saving station there somewhere."

"Say, he ain't tired yet. Look at 'im wave!" 130

"Wonder how long he can keep that up. He's been revolving his coat ever since he caught sight of us. He's an idiot. Why aren't they getting men to bring a boat out? A fishing boat—one of those big yawls—could come out here all right. Why don't he do something?"

"Oh, it's all right now."

"They'll have a boat out here for us in less than no time, now that they've seen us."

A faint yellow tone came into the sky over the low land. The shadows on the sea slowly deepened. The wind bore coldness with it, and the men began to shiver.

135 "Holy smoke!" said one, allowing his voice to express his impious mood, "if we keep on monkeying out here! If we've got to flounder out here all night!"

"Oh, we'll never have to stay here all night! Don't you worry. They've seen us now, and it won't be long before they'll come chasing out after us."

The shore grew dusky. The man waving a coat blended gradually into this gloom, and it swallowed in the same manner the omnibus and the group of people. The spray, when it dashed uproariously over the side, made the voyagers shrink and swear like men who were being branded.

"I'd like to catch the chump who waved the coat. I feel like socking him one, just for luck."

"Why? What did he do?"

140 "Oh, nothing, but then he seemed so damned cheerful."

In the meantime the oiler rowed, and then the correspondent rowed, and then the oiler rowed. Gray-faced and bowed forward, they mechanically, turn by turn, plied the leaden oars. The form of the lighthouse had vanished from the southern horizon, but finally a pale star appeared, just lifting from the sea. The streaked saffron in the west passed before the all-merging darkness, and the sea to the east was black. The land had vanished, and was expressed only by the low and drear thunder of the surf.

"If I am going to be drowned—if I am going to be drowned—if I am going to be drowned, why, in the name of the seven mad gods who rule the sea, was I allowed to come thus far and contemplate sand and trees? Was I brought here merely to have my nose dragged away as I was about to nibble the sacred cheese of life?"

The patient captain, drooped over the water-jar, was sometimes obliged to speak to the oarsman.

"Keep her head up! Keep her head up!"

145 "Keep her head up, sir." The voices were weary and low.

This was surely a quiet evening. All save the oarsman lay heavily and listlessly in the boat's bottom. As for him, his eyes were just capable of noting the tall black waves that swept forward in a most sinister silence, save for an occasional subdued growl of a crest.

The cook's head was on a thwart, and he looked without interest at the water under his nose. He was deep in other scenes. Finally he spoke. "Billie," he murmured, dreamfully, "what kind of pie do you like best?"

V

"Pie!" said the oiler and the correspondent, agitatedly. "Don't talk about those things, blast you!"

"Well," said the cook, "I was just thinking about ham sandwiches, and——"

A night on the sea in an open boat is a long night. As darkness settled 150
finally, the shine of the light, lifting from the sea in the south, changed to
full gold. On the northern horizon a new light appeared, a small bluish
gleam on the edge of the waters. These two lights were the furniture of the
world. Otherwise there was nothing but waves.

Two men huddled in the stern, and distances were so magnificent in the
dinghy that the rower was enabled to keep his feet partly warm by thrusting them under his companions. Their legs indeed extended far under the
rowing-seat until they touched the feet of the captain forward. Sometimes,
despite the efforts of the tired oarsman, a wave came piling into the boat,
an icy wave of the night, and the chilling water soaked them anew. They
would twist their bodies for a moment and groan, and sleep the dead sleep
once more, while the water in the boat gurgled about them as the craft
rocked.

The plan of the oiler and the correspondent was for one to row until he
lost the ability, and then arouse the other from his sea-water couch in the
bottom of the boat.

The oiler plied the oars until his head drooped forward and the overpowering sleep blinded him; and he rowed yet afterward. Then he touched
a man in the bottom of the boat, and called his name. "Will you spell me
for a little while?" he said meekly.

"Sure, Billie," said the correspondent, awaking and dragging himself to
a sitting position. They exchanged places carefully, and the oiler, cuddling
down in the sea-water at the cook's side, seemed to go to sleep instantly.

The particular violence of the sea had ceased. The waves came without 155
snarling. The obligation of the man at the oars was to keep the boat headed
so that the tilt of the rollers would not capsize her, and to preserve her from
filling when the crests rushed past. The black waves were silent and hard
to be seen in the darkness. Often one was almost upon the boat before the
oarsman was aware.

In a low voice the correspondent addressed the captain. He was not sure
that the captain was awake, although this iron man seemed to be always
awake. "Captain, shall I keep her making for that light north, sir?"

The same steady voice answered him. "Yes. Keep it about two points off
the port bow."

The cook had tied a life-belt around himself in order to get even the
warmth which this clumsy cork contrivance could donate, and he seemed
almost stove-like when a rower, whose teeth invariably chattered wildly as
soon as he ceased his labor, dropped down to sleep.

The correspondent, as he rowed, looked down at the two men sleeping
underfoot. The cook's arm was around the oiler's shoulders, and, with
their fragmentary clothing and haggard faces, they were the babes of the
sea—a grotesque rendering of the old babes in the wood.

Later he must have grown stupid at his work, for suddenly there was a 160
growling of water, and a crest came with a roar and a swash into the boat,

and it was a wonder that it did not set the cook afloat in his life-belt. The cook continued to sleep, but the oiler sat up, blinking his eyes and shaking with the new cold.

"Oh, I'm awful sorry, Billie," said the correspondent, contritely.

"That's all right, old boy," said the oiler, and lay down again and was asleep.

Presently it seemed that even the captain dozed, and the correspondent thought that he was the one man afloat on all the ocean. The wind had a voice as it came over the waves, and it was sadder than the end.

There was a long, loud swishing astern of the boat, and a gleaming trail of phosphorescence, like blue flame, was furrowed on the black waters. It might have been made by a monstrous knife.

165   Then there came a stillness, while the correspondent breathed with open mouth and looked at the sea.

Suddenly there was another swish and another long flash of bluish light, and this time it was alongside the boat, and might almost have been reached with an oar. The correspondent saw an enormous fin speed like a shadow through the water, hurling the crystalline spray and leaving the long glowing trail.

The correspondent looked over his shoulder at the captain. His face was hidden, and he seemed to be asleep. He looked at the babes of the sea. They certainly were asleep. So, being bereft of sympathy, he leaned a little way to one side and swore softly into the sea.

But the thing did not then leave the vicinity of the boat. Ahead or astern, on one side or the other, at intervals long or short, fled the long sparkling streak, and there was to be heard the *whirroo* of the dark fin. The speed and power of the thing was greatly to be admired. It cut the water like a gigantic and keen projectile.

The presence of this biding thing did not affect the man with the same horror that it would if he had been a picnicker. He simply looked at the sea dully and swore in an undertone.

170   Nevertheless, it is true that he did not wish to be alone with the thing. He wished one of his companions to awake by chance and keep him company with it. But the captain hung motionless over the water-jar and the oiler and the cook in the bottom of the boat were plunged in slumber.

VI

"If I am going to be drowned—if I am going to be drowned—if I am going to be drowned, why, in the name of the seven mad gods who rule the sea, was I allowed to come thus far and contemplate sand and trees?"

During this dismal night, it may be remarked that a man would conclude that it was really the intention of the seven mad gods to drown him, despite the abominable injustice of it. For it was certainly an abominable injustice to drown a man who had worked so hard, so hard. The man felt it would be a crime most unnatural. Other people had drowned at sea since galleys swarmed with painted sails, but still—

When it occurs to a man that nature does not regard him as important, and that she feels she would not maim the universe by disposing of him, he at first wishes to throw bricks at the temple, and he hates deeply the fact that there are no bricks and no temples. Any visible expression of nature would surely be pelleted with his jeers.

Then, if there be no tangible thing to hoot, he feels, perhaps, the desire to confront a personification and indulge in pleas, bowed to one knee, and with hands supplicant, saying, "Yes, but I love myself."

A high cold star on a winter's night is the word he feels that she says to him. Thereafter he knows the pathos of his situation.

The men in the dinghy had not discussed these matters, but each had, no doubt, reflected upon them in silence and according to his mind. There was seldom any expression upon their faces save the general one of complete weariness. Speech was devoted to the business of the boat.

To chime the notes of his emotions, a verse mysteriously entered the correspondent's head. He had even forgotten that he had forgotten this verse, but it suddenly was in his mind.

A soldier of the Legion lay dying in Algiers;
There was lack of woman's nursing, there was dearth of woman's tears;
But a comrade stood beside him, and he took the comrade's hand,
And he said, "I never more shall see my own, my native land."[6]

In his childhood the correspondent had been made acquainted with the fact that a soldier of the Legion lay dying in Algiers, but he had never regarded it as important. Myriads of his schoolfellows had informed him of the soldier's plight, but the dinning had naturally ended by making him perfectly indifferent. He had never considered it his affair that a soldier of the Legion lay dying in Algiers, nor had it appeared to him as a matter for sorrow. It was less to him than the breaking of a pencil's point.

Now, however, it quaintly came to him as a human, living thing. It was no longer merely a picture of a few throes in the breast of a poet, meanwhile drinking tea and warming his feet at the grate; it was an actuality—stern, mournful, and fine.

The correspondent plainly saw the soldier. He lay on the sand with his feet out straight and still. While his pale left hand was upon his chest in an attempt to thwart the going of his life, the blood came between his fingers. In the far Algerian distance, a city of low square forms was set against a sky that was faint with the last sunset hues. The correspondent, plying the oars and dreaming of the slow and slower movements of the lips of the soldier, was moved by a profound and perfectly impersonal

---

6. From "Bingen on the Rhine," by Caroline Norton (1808–77).

comprehension. He was sorry for the soldier of the Legion who lay dying in Algiers.

180 The thing which had followed the boat and waited had evidently grown bored at the delay. There was no longer to be heard the slash of the cutwater, and there was no longer the flame of the long trail. The light in the north still glimmered, but it was apparently no nearer to the boat. Sometimes the boom of the surf rang in the correspondent's ears, and he turned the craft seaward then and rowed harder. Southward, some one had evidently built a watch-fire on the beach. It was too low and too far to be seen, but it made a shimmering, roseate reflection upon the bluff in back of it, and this could be discerned from the boat. The wind came stronger, and sometimes a wave suddenly raged out like a mountain-cat, and there was to be seen the sheen and sparkle of a broken crest.

The captain, in the bow, moved on his water-jar and sat erect. "Pretty long night," he observed to the correspondent. He looked at the shore. "Those life-saving people take their time."

"Did you see that shark playing around?"

"Yes, I saw him. He was a big fellow, all right."

"Wish I had known you were awake."

185 Later the correspondent spoke into the bottom of the boat. "Billie!" There was a slow and gradual disentanglement. "Billie, will you spell me?"

"Sure," said the oiler.

As soon as the correspondent touched the cold, comfortable seawater in the bottom of the boat and had huddled close to the cook's life-belt he was deep in sleep, despite the fact that his teeth played all the popular airs. This sleep was so good to him that it was but a moment before he heard a voice call his name in a tone that demonstrated the last stages of exhaustion. "Will you spell me?"

"Sure, Billie."

The light in the north had mysteriously vanished, but the correspondent took his course from the wide-awake captain.

190 Later in the night they took the boat farther out to sea, and the captain directed the cook to take one oar at the stern and keep the boat facing the seas. He was to call out if he should hear the thunder of the surf. This plan enabled the oiler and the correspondent to get respite together. "We'll give those boys a chance to get into shape again," said the captain. They curled down and, after a few preliminary chatterings and trembles, slept once more the dead sleep. Neither knew they had bequeathed to the cook the company of another shark, or perhaps the same shark.

As the boat caroused on the waves, spray occasionally bumped over the side and gave them a fresh soaking, but this had no power to break their repose. The ominous slash of the wind and the water affected them as it would have affected mummies.

"Boys," said the cook, with the notes of every reluctance in his voice, "she's drifted in pretty close. I guess one of you had better take her to sea again." The correspondent, aroused, heard the crash of the toppled crests.

As he was rowing, the captain gave him some whiskey-and-water, and this steadied the chills out of him. "If I ever get ashore and anybody shows me even a photograph of an oar——"

At last there was a short conversation.

"Billie! . . . Billie, will you spell me?"   195

"Sure," said the oiler.

VII

When the correspondent again opened his eyes, the sea and the sky were each of the gray hue of the dawning. Later, carmine and gold was painted upon the waters. The morning appeared finally, in its splendor, with a sky of pure blue, and the sunlight flamed on the tips of the waves.

On the distant dunes were set many little black cottages, and a tall white windmill reared above them. No man, nor dog, nor bicycle appeared on the beach. The cottages might have formed a deserted village.

The voyagers scanned the shore. A conference was held in the boat. "Well," said the captain, "if no help is coming, we might better try a run through the surf right away. If we stay out here much longer we will be too weak to do anything for ourselves at all." The others silently acquiesced in this reasoning. The boat was headed for the beach. The correspondent wondered if none ever ascended the tall wind-tower,[7] and if then they never looked seaward. This tower was a giant, standing with its back to the plight of the ants. It represented in a degree, to the correspondent, the serenity of nature amid the struggles of the individual—nature in the wind, and nature in the vision of men. She did not seem cruel to him then, nor beneficent, nor treacherous, nor wise. But she was indifferent, flatly indifferent. It is, perhaps, plausible that a man in this situation, impressed with the unconcern of the universe, should see the innumerable flaws of his life, and have them taste wickedly in his mind, and wish for another chance. A distinction between right and wrong seems absurdly clear to him, then, in this new ignorance of the grave-edge, and he understands that if he were given another opportunity he would mend his conduct and his words, and be better and brighter during an introduction or at a tea.

"Now, boys," said the captain, "she is going to swamp sure. All we can   200 do is to work her in as far as possible, and then when she swamps, pile out and scramble for the beach. Keep cool now, and don't jump until she swamps sure."

The oiler took the oars. Over his shoulders he scanned the surf. "Captain," he said, "I think I'd better bring her about and keep her head-on to the seas and back her in."

---

7. Watchtower for observing weather.

"All right, Billie," said the captain. "Back her in." The oiler swung the boat then, and, seated in the stern, the cook and the correspondent were obliged to look over their shoulders to contemplate the lonely and indifferent shore.

The monstrous inshore rollers heaved the boat high until the men were again enabled to see the white sheets of water scudding up the slanted beach. "We won't get in very close," said the captain. Each time a man could wrest his attention from the rollers, he turned his glance toward the shore, and in the expression of the eyes during this contemplation there was a singular quality. The correspondent, observing the others, knew that they were not afraid, but the full meaning of their glances was shrouded.

As for himself, he was too tired to grapple fundamentally with the fact. He tried to coerce his mind into thinking of it, but the mind was dominated at this time by the muscles, and the muscles said they did not care. It merely occurred to him that if he should drown it would be a shame.

205   There were no hurried words, no pallor, no plain agitation. The men simply looked at the shore. "Now, remember to get well clear of the boat when you jump," said the captain.

Seaward the crest of a roller suddenly fell with a thunderous crash, and the long white comber came roaring down upon the boat.

"Steady now," said the captain. The men were silent. They turned their eyes from the shore to the comber and waited. The boat slid up the incline, leaped at the furious top, bounced over it, and swung down the long back of the wave. Some water had been shipped, and the cook bailed it out.

But the next crest crashed also. The tumbling, boiling flood of white water caught the boat and whirled it almost perpendicular. Water swarmed in from all sides. The correspondent had his hands on the gunwale at this time, and when the water entered at that place he swiftly withdrew his fingers, as if he objected to wetting them.

The little boat, drunken with this weight of water, reeled and snuggled deeper into the sea.

210   "Bail her out, cook! Bail her out!" said the captain.

"All right, Captain," said the cook.

"Now, boys, the next one will do for us sure," said the oiler. "Mind to jump clear of the boat."

The third wave moved forward, huge, furious, implacable. It fairly swallowed the dinghy, and almost simultaneously the men tumbled into the sea. A piece of life-belt had lain in the bottom of the boat, and as the correspondent went overboard he held this to his chest with his left hand.

The January water was icy, and reflected immediately that it was colder than he had expected to find it off the coast of Florida. This appeared to his dazed mind as a fact important enough to be noted at the time. The coldness of the water was sad; it was tragic. This fact was somehow mixed and confused with his opinion of his own situation, so that it seemed almost a proper reason for tears. The water was cold.

When he came to the surface he was conscious of little but the noisy 215
water. Afterward he saw his companions in the sea. The oiler was ahead in
the race. He was swimming strongly and rapidly. Off to the correspondent's left, the cook's great white and corked back bulged out of the water,
and in the rear the captain was hanging with his one good hand to the keel
of the overturned dinghy.

There is a certain immovable quality to a shore, and the correspondent
wondered at it amid the confusion of the sea.

It seemed also very attractive; but the correspondent knew that it was a
long journey, and he paddled leisurely. The piece of life-preserver lay under
him, and sometimes he whirled down the incline of a wave as if he were on
a hand-sled.

But finally he arrived at a place in the sea where travel was beset with
difficulty. He did not pause swimming to inquire what manner of current
had caught him, but there his progress ceased. The shore was set before
him like a bit of scenery on a stage, and he looked at it and understood
with his eyes each detail of it.

As the cook passed, much farther to the left, the captain was calling
to him, "Turn over on your back, cook! Turn over on your back and use
the oar."

"All right, sir." The cook turned on his back, and, paddling with an oar, 220
went ahead as if he were a canoe.

Presently the boat also passed to the left of the correspondent, with the
captain clinging with one hand to the keel. He would have appeared like a
man raising himself to look over a board fence if it were not for the extraordinary gymnastics of the boat. The correspondent marvelled that the captain could still hold to it.

They passed on nearer to shore—the oiler, the cook, the captain—and
following them went the water-jar, bouncing gaily over the seas.

The correspondent remained in the grip of this strange new enemy, a
current. The shore, with its white slope of sand and its green bluff topped
with little silent cottages, was spread like a picture before him. It was very
near to him then, but he was impressed as one who, in a gallery, looks at a
scene from Brittany or Algiers.

He thought: "I am going to drown? Can it be possible? Can it be possible?
Can it be possible?" Perhaps an individual must consider his own death to
be the final phenomenon of nature.

But later a wave perhaps whirled him out of this small deadly current, 225
for he found suddenly that he could again make progress toward the shore.
Later still he was aware that the captain, clinging with one hand to the
keel of the dinghy, had his face turned away from the shore and toward
him, and was calling his name. "Come to the boat! Come to the boat!"

In his struggle to reach the captain and the boat, he reflected that
when one gets properly wearied drowning must really be a comfortable

arrangement—a cessation of hostilities accompanied by a large degree of relief; and he was glad of it, for the main thing in his mind for some moments had been horror of the temporary agony; he did not wish to be hurt.

Presently he saw a man running along the shore. He was undressing with most remarkable speed. Coat, trousers, shirt, everything flew magically off him.

"Come to the boat!" called the captain.

"All right, Captain." As the correspondent paddled, he saw the captain let himself down to bottom and leave the boat. Then the correspondent performed his one little marvel of the voyage. A large wave caught him and flung him with ease and supreme speed completely over the boat and far beyond it. It struck him even then as an event in gymnastics and a true miracle of the sea. An overturned boat in the surf is not a plaything to a swimming man.

230   The correspondent arrived in water that reached only to his waist, but his condition did not enable him to stand for more than a moment. Each wave knocked him into a heap, and the undertow pulled at him.

Then he saw the man who had been running and undressing, and undressing and running, come bounding into the water. He dragged ashore the cook, and then waded toward the captain; but the captain waved him away and sent him to the correspondent. He was naked—naked as a tree in winter; but a halo was about his head, and he shone like a saint. He gave a strong pull, and a long drag, and a bully heave at the correspondent's hand. The correspondent, schooled in the minor formulae, said, "Thanks, old man." But suddenly the man cried, "What's that?" He pointed a swift finger. The correspondent said, "Go."

In the shallows, face downward, lay the oiler. His forehead touched sand that was periodically, between each wave, clear of the sea.

The correspondent did not know all that transpired afterward. When he achieved safe ground he fell, striking the sand with each particular part of his body. It was as if he had dropped from a roof, but the thud was grateful to him.

It seems that instantly the beach was populated with men with blankets, clothes, and flasks, and women with coffee-pots and all the remedies sacred to their minds. The welcome of the land to the men from the sea was warm and generous; but a still and dripping shape was carried slowly up the beach, and the land's welcome for it could only be the different and sinister hospitality of the grave.

235   When it came night, the white waves paced to and fro in the moonlight, and the wind brought the sound of the great sea's voice to the men on the shore, and they felt that they could then be interpreters.

1898

QUESTIONS

1. When do you become aware that your view of events in "The Open Boat" is limited to things seen and heard by the four men in the boat? In what specific ways is that important to the story's effect? Where does the story's perspective "expand" to include larger reflections and generalizations? How are they justified by the narrative point of view?
2. Examine paragraphs 3–6; then differentiate the four men as fully as you can. What distinguishing features help you keep them straight as the narrative proceeds? What facts are provided later about each of the men? In which of the men do you become most interested as the story develops?
3. Which, if any, of the following seem like apt statements of the story's theme, and why? Which, if any, seems most central?

    a. All human beings are ultimately the same in that we are all equally powerless against nature.
    b. As the novelist George Eliot once said, "Character is destiny."
    c. In the face of disaster, people tend to become selfless, forgetting their differences and bonding together.
    d. Our individual fates are ultimately determined by forces beyond our control.
    e. We can never know the full truth; all we have is our own limited individual perspective.
    f. Pride is man's downfall.

GABRIEL GARCÍA MÁRQUEZ

A Very Old Man with Enormous Wings [1]

A Tale for Children

On the third day of rain they had killed so many crabs inside the house that Pelayo had to cross his drenched courtyard and throw them into the sea, because the newborn child had a temperature all night and they thought it was due to the stench. The world had been sad since Tuesday. Sea and sky were a single ashgray thing and the sands of the beach, which on March nights glimmered like powdered light, had become a stew of mud and rotten shellfish. The light was so weak at noon that when Pelayo was coming back to the house after throwing away the crabs, it was hard for him see what it was that was moving and groaning in the rear of the courtyard. He had to go very close to see that it was an old man, a very old man, lying face down in the mud, who, in spite of his tremendous efforts, couldn't get up, impeded by his enormous wings.

---

1. Translated by Gregory Rabassa.

Frightened by that nightmare, Pelayo ran to get Elisenda, his wife, who was putting compresses on the sick child, and he took her to the rear of the courtyard. They both looked at the fallen body with mute stupor. He was dressed like a ragpicker.[2] There were only a few faded hairs left on his bald skull and very few teeth in his mouth, and his pitiful condition of a drenched great-grandfather had taken away any sense of grandeur he might have had. His huge buzzard wings, dirty and half-plucked, were forever entangled in the mud. They looked at him so long and so closely that Pelayo and Elisenda very soon overcame their surprise and in the end found him familiar. Then they dared speak to him, and he answered in an incomprehensible dialect with a strong sailor's voice. That was how they skipped over the inconvenience of the wings and quite intelligently concluded that he was a lonely castaway from some foreign ship wrecked by the storm. And yet, they called in a neighbor woman who knew everything about life and death to see him, and all she needed was one look to show them their mistake.

"He's an angel," she told them. "He must have been coming for the child, but the poor fellow is so old that the rain knocked him down."

On the following day everyone knew that a flesh-and-blood angel was held captive in Pelayo's house. Against the judgment of the wise neighbor woman, for whom angels in those times were the fugitive survivors of a celestial conspiracy, they did not have the heart to club him to death. Pelayo watched over him all afternoon from the kitchen, armed with his bailiff's[3] club, and before going to bed he dragged him out of the mud and locked him up with the hens in the wire chicken coop. In the middle of the night, when the rain stopped, Pelayo and Elisenda were still killing crabs. A short time afterward the child woke up without a fever and with a desire to eat. Then they felt magnanimous and decided to put the angel on a raft with fresh water and provisions for three days and leave him to his fate on the high seas. But when they went out into the courtyard with the first light of dawn, they found the whole neighborhood in front of the chicken coop having fun with the angel, without the slightest reverence, tossing him things to eat through the openings in the wire as if he weren't a supernatural creature but a circus animal.

5   Father Gonzaga arrived before seven o'clock, alarmed at the strange news. By that time onlookers less frivolous than those at dawn had already arrived and they were making all kinds of conjectures concerning the captive's future. The simplest among them thought that he should be named mayor of the world. Others of sterner mind felt that he should be promoted to the rank of five-star general in order to win all wars. Some visionaries hoped that he could be put to stud in order to implant on earth a race of winged wise men who could take charge of the universe. But Father

2. Someone who earns a living by collecting rags and other refuse.
3. Local government official, usually one employed to make arrests and serve warrants.

Gonzaga, before becoming a priest, had been a robust woodcutter. Standing by the wire, he reviewed his catechism in an instant and asked them to open the door so that he could take a close look at that pitiful man who looked more like a huge decrepit hen among the fascinated chickens. He was lying in a corner drying his open wings in the sunlight among the fruit peels and breakfast leftovers that the early risers had thrown him. Alien to the impertinences of the world, he only lifted his antiquarian eyes and murmured something in his dialect when Father Gonzaga went into the chicken coop and said good morning to him in Latin. The parish priest had his first suspicion of an imposter when he saw that he did not understand the language of God or know how to greet His ministers. Then he noticed that seen close up he was much too human: he had an unbearable smell of the outdoors, the back side of his wings was strewn with parasites and his main feathers had been mistreated by terrestrial winds, and nothing about him measured up to the proud dignity of angels. Then he came out of the chicken coop and in a brief sermon warned the curious against the risks of being ingenuous. He reminded them that the devil had the bad habit of making use of carnival tricks in order to confuse the unwary. He argued that if wings were not the essential element in determining the difference between a hawk and an airplane, they were even less so in the recognition of angels. Nevertheless, he promised to write a letter to his bishop so that the latter would write to his primate[4] so that the latter would write to the Supreme Pontiff in order to get the final verdict from the highest courts.

His prudence fell on sterile hearts. The news of the captive angel spread with such rapidity that after a few hours the courtyard had the bustle of a marketplace and they had to call in troops with fixed bayonets to disperse the mob that was about to knock the house down. Elisenda, her spine all twisted from sweeping up so much marketplace trash, then got the idea of fencing in the yard and charging five cents admission to see the angel.

The curious came from far away. A traveling carnival arrived with a flying acrobat who buzzed over the crowd several times, but no one paid any attention to him because his wings were not those of an angel but, rather, those of a sidereal[5] bat. The most unfortunate invalids on earth came in search of health: a poor woman who since childhood had been counting her heartbeats and had run out of numbers; a Portuguese man who couldn't sleep because the noise of the stars disturbed him; a sleepwalker who got up at night to undo the things he had done while awake; and many others with less serious ailments. In the midst of that shipwreck disorder that made the earth tremble, Pelayo and Elisenda were happy with fatigue, for in less than a week they had crammed their rooms with money and the line of pilgrims waiting their turn to enter still reached beyond the horizon.

4. Highest bishop of a given state.   5. Of, or relating to, the stars.

The angel was the only one who took no part in his own act. He spent his time trying to get comfortable in his borrowed nest, befuddled by the hellish heat of the oil lamps and sacramental candles that had been placed along the wire. At first they tried to make him eat some mothballs, which, according to the wisdom of the wise neighbor woman, were the food prescribed for angels. But he turned them down, just as he turned down the papal lunches[6] that the penitents brought him, and they never found out whether it was because he was an angel or because he was an old man that in the end he ate nothing but eggplant mush. His only supernatural virtue seemed to be patience. Especially during the first days, when the hens pecked at him, searching for the stellar parasites that proliferated in his wings, and the cripples pulled out feathers to touch their defective parts with, and even the most merciful threw stones at him, trying to get him to rise so they could see him standing. The only time they succeeded in arousing him was when they burned his side with an iron for branding steers, for he had been motionless for so many hours that they thought he was dead. He awoke with a start, ranting in his hermetic language and with tears in his eyes, and he flapped his wings a couple of times, which brought on a whirlwind of chicken dung and lunar dust and a gale of panic that did not seem to be of this world. Although many thought that his reaction had been one not of rage but of pain, from then on they were careful not to annoy him, because the majority understood that his passivity was not that of a hero taking his ease but that of a cataclysm in repose.

Father Gonzaga held back the crowd's frivolity with formulas of maidservant inspiration while awaiting the arrival of a final judgment on the nature of the captive. But the mail from Rome showed no sense of urgency. They spent their time finding out if the prisoner had a navel, if his dialect had any connection with Aramaic, how many times he could fit on the head of a pin, or whether he wasn't just a Norwegian with wings. Those meager letters might have come and gone until the end of time if a providential event had not put an end to the priest's tribulations.

10   It so happened that during those days, among so many other carnival attractions, there arrived in town the traveling show of the woman who had been changed into a spider for having disobeyed her parents. The admission to see her was not only less than the admission to see the angel, but people were permitted to ask her all manner of questions about her absurd state and to examine her up and down so that no one would ever doubt the truth of her horror. She was a frightful tarantula the size of a ram and with the head of a sad maiden. What was most heart-rending, however, was not her outlandish shape but the sincere affliction with which she recounted the details of her misfortune. While still practically a child she had sneaked out of her parents' house to go to a dance, and while she was coming back through the woods after having danced all night without permission, a

6. Expensive, elaborately prepared meals.

fearful thunderclap rent the sky in two and through the crack came the lightning bolt of brimstone that changed her into a spider. Her only nourishment came from the meatballs that charitable souls chose to toss into her mouth. A spectacle like that, full of so much human truth and with such a fearful lesson, was bound to defeat without even trying that of a haughty angel who scarcely deigned to look at mortals. Besides, the few miracles attributed to the angel showed a certain mental disorder, like the blind man who didn't recover his sight but grew three new teeth, or the paralytic who didn't get to walk but almost won the lottery, and the leper whose sores sprouted sunflowers. Those consolation miracles, which were more like mocking fun, had already ruined the angel's reputation when the woman who had been changed into a spider finally crushed him completely. That was how Father Gonzaga was cured forever of his insomnia and Pelayo's courtyard went back to being as empty as during the time it had rained for three days and crabs walked through the bedrooms.

The owners of the house had no reason to lament. With the money they saved they built a two-story mansion with balconies and gardens and high netting so that crabs wouldn't get in during the winter, and with iron bars on the windows so that angels wouldn't get in. Pelayo also set up a rabbit warren close to town and gave up his job as bailiff for good, and Elisenda bought some satin pumps with high heels and many dresses of iridescent silk, the kind worn on Sunday by the most desirable women in those times. The chicken coop was the only thing that didn't receive any attention. If they washed it down with creolin[7] and burned tears of myrrh inside it every so often, it was not in homage to the angel but to drive away the dungheap stench that still hung everywhere like a ghost and was turning the new house into an old one. At first, when the child learned to walk, they were careful that he not get too close to the chicken coop. But then they began to lose their fears and got used to the smell, and before the child got his second teeth he'd gone inside the chicken coop to play, where the wires were falling apart. The angel was no less standoffish with him than with other mortals, but he tolerated the most ingenious infamies with the patience of a dog who had no illusions. They both came down with chicken pox at the same time. The doctor who took care of the child couldn't resist the temptation to listen to the angel's heart, and he found so much whistling in the heart and so many sounds in his kidneys that it seemed impossible for him to be alive. What surprised him most, however, was the logic of his wings. They seemed so natural on that completely human organism that he couldn't understand why other men didn't have them too.

When the child began school it had been some time since the sun and rain had caused the collapse of the chicken coop. The angel went dragging himself about here and there like a stray dying man. They would drive him out of the bedroom with a broom and a moment later find him in the

7. Disinfectant.

kitchen. He seemed to be in so many places at the same time that they grew to think that he'd been duplicated, that he was reproducing himself all through the house, and the exasperated and unhinged Elisenda shouted that it was awful living in that hell full of angels. He could scarcely eat and his antiquarian eyes had also become so foggy that he went about bumping into posts. All he had left were the bare cannulae of his last feathers. Pelayo threw a blanket over him and extended him the charity of letting him sleep in the shed, and only then did they notice that he had a temperature at night, and was delirious with the tongue twisters of an old Norwegian. That was one of the few times they became alarmed, for they thought he was going to die and not even the wise neighbor woman had been able to tell them what to do with dead angels.

And yet he not only survived his worst winter, but seemed improved with the first sunny days. He remained motionless for several days in the farthest corner of the courtyard, where no one would see him, and at the beginning of December some large, stiff feathers began to grow on his wings, the feathers of a scarecrow, which looked more like another misfortune of decrepitude. But he must have known the reason for those changes, for he was quite careful that no one should notice them, that no one should hear the sea chanteys that he sometimes sang under the stars. One morning Elisenda was cutting some bunches of onions for lunch when a wind that seemed to come from the high seas blew into the kitchen. Then she went to the window and caught the angel in his first attempts at flight. They were so clumsy that his fingernails opened a furrow in the vegetable patch and he was on the point of knocking the shed down with the ungainly flapping that slipped on the light and couldn't get a grip on the air. But he did manage to gain altitude. Elisenda let out a sigh of relief, for herself and for him, when she saw him pass over the last houses, holding himself up in some way with the risky flapping of a senile vulture. She kept watching him even when she was through cutting the onions and she kept on watching until it was no longer possible for her to see him, because then he was no longer an annoyance in her life but an imaginary dot on the horizon of the sea.

1968

QUESTIONS

1. The subtitle of this story is "A Tale for Children." Why and how does this seem like an apt description? an inapt or ironic one?

2. How do the various characters interpret the winged man? How do they arrive at their interpretations? What might their interpretations reveal about them? about people and/or the process of interpretation in general?

3. Why do so many people at first come to see the winged man and later stop doing so? Why is Elisenda so relieved when he finally flies away? What insights into human behavior might be revealed here?

LOUISE ERDRICH

Love Medicine

I never really done much with my life, I suppose. I never had a television. Grandma Kashpaw had one inside her apartment at the Senior Citizens, so I used to go there and watch my favorite shows. For a while she used to call me the biggest waste on the reservation and hark back to how she saved me from my own mother, who wanted to tie me in a potato sack and throw me in a slough. Sure, I was grateful to Grandma Kashpaw for saving me like that, for raising me, but gratitude gets old. After a while, stale. I had to stop thanking her. One day I told her I had paid her back in full by staying at her beck and call. I'd do anything for Grandma. She knew that. Besides, I took care of Grandpa like nobody else could, on account of what a handful he'd gotten to be.

But that was nothing. I know the tricks of mind and body inside out without ever having trained for it, because I got the touch. It's a thing you got to be born with. I got secrets in my hands that nobody ever knew to ask. Take Grandma Kashpaw with her tired veins all knotted up in her legs like clumps of blue snails. I take my fingers and I snap them on the knots. The medicine flows out of me. The touch. I run my fingers up the maps of those rivers of veins or I knock very gentle above their hearts or I make a circling motion on their stomachs, and it helps them. They feel much better. Some women pay me five dollars.

I couldn't do the touch for Grandpa, though. He was a hard nut. You know, some people fall right through the hole in their lives. It's invisible, but they come to it after time, never knowing where. There is this woman here, Lulu Lamartine, who always had a thing for Grandpa. She loved him since she was a girl and always said he was a genius. Now she says that his mind got so full it exploded.

How can I doubt that? I know the feeling when your mental power builds up too far. I always used to say that's why the Indians got drunk. Even statistically we're the smartest people on the earth. Anyhow with Grandpa I couldn't hardly believe it, because all my youth he stood out as a hero to me. When he started getting toward second childhood he went through different moods. He would stand in the woods and cry at the top of his shirt. It scared me, scared everyone, Grandma worst of all.

Yet he was so smart—do you believe it?—that he *knew* he was getting foolish.

He said so. He told me that December I failed school and come back on the train to Hoopdance. I didn't have nowhere else to go. He picked me up there and he said it straight out: "I'm getting into my second childhood." And then he said something else I still remember: "I been chosen for it. I couldn't say no." So I figure that a man so smart all his life—tribal chairman and the star of movies and even pictured in the statehouse and on cans of snuff—would know what he's doing by saying yes. I think he was called to second childhood like anybody else gets a call for the priesthood or the army or whatever. So I really did not listen too hard when the doctor said this was some kind of disease old people got eating too much sugar. You just can't tell me that a man who went to Washington and gave them bureaucrats what for could lose his mind from eating too much Milky Way. No, he put second childhood on himself.

Behind those songs he sings out in the middle of Mass, and back of those stories that everybody knows by heart, Grandpa is thinking hard about life. I know the feeling. Sometimes I'll throw up a smokescreen to think behind. I'll hitch up to Winnipeg and play the Space Invaders[1] for six hours, but all the time there and back I will be thinking some fairly deep thoughts that surprise even me, and I'm used to it. As for him, if it was just the thoughts there wouldn't be no problem. Smokescreen is what irritates the social structure, see, and Grandpa has done things that just distract people to the point they want to throw him in the cookie jar where they keep the mentally insane. He's far from that, I know for sure, but even Grandma had trouble keeping her patience once he started sneaking off to Lamartine's place. He's not supposed to have his candy, and Lulu feeds it to him. That's *one* of the reasons why he goes.

Grandma tried to get me to put the touch on Grandpa soon after he began stepping out. I didn't want to, but before Grandma started telling me again what a bad state my bare behind was in when she first took me home, I thought I should at least pretend.

I put my hands on either side of Grandpa's head. You wouldn't look at him and say he was crazy. He's a fine figure of a man, as Lamartine would say, with all his hair and half his teeth, a beak like a hawk, and cheeks like the blades of a hatchet. They put his picture on all the tourist guides to North Dakota and even copied his face for artistic paintings. I guess you could call him a monument all of himself. He started grinning when I put my hands on his templates, and I knew right then he knew how come I touched him. I knew the smokescreen was going to fall.

10   And I was right: just for a moment it fell.

"Let's pitch whoopee," he said across my shoulder to Grandma.

They don't use that expression much around here anymore, but for damn sure it must have meant something. It got her goat right quick.

She threw my hands off his head herself and stood in front of him, overmatching him pound for pound, and taller too, for she had a growth spurt in middle age while he had shrunk, so now the length and breadth of her surpassed him. She glared and spoke her piece into his face about how he was off at all hours tomcatting and chasing Lamartine again and making a damn old fool of himself.

1. Extremely popular and influential 1980s arcade video game.

"And you got no more whoopee to pitch anymore anyhow!" she yelled at last, surprising me so my jaw just dropped, for us kids all had pretended for so long that those rustling sounds we heard from their side of the room at night never happened. She sure had pretended it, up till now, anyway. I saw that tears were in her eyes. And that's when I saw how much grief and love she felt for him. And it gave me a real shock to the system. You see I thought love got easier over the years so it didn't hurt so bad when it hurt, or feel so good when it felt good. I thought it smoothed out and old people hardly noticed it. I thought it curled up and died, I guess. Now I saw it rear up like a whip and lash.

She loved him. She was jealous. She mourned him like the dead. 15
And he just smiled into the air, trapped in the seams of his mind.

So I didn't know what to do. I was in a laundry then. They was like parents to me, the way they had took me home and reared me. I could see her point for wanting to get him back the way he was so at least she could argue with him, sleep with him, not be shamed out by Lamartine. She'd always love him. That hit me like a ton of bricks. For one whole day I felt this odd feeling that cramped my hands. When you have the touch, that's where longing gets you. I never loved like that. It made me feel all inspired to see them fight, and I wanted to go out and find a woman who I would love until one of us died or went crazy. But I'm not like that really. From time to time I heal a person all up good inside, however when it comes to the long shot I doubt that I got staying power.

And you need that, staying power, going out to love somebody. I knew this quality was not going to jump on me with no effort. So I turned my thoughts back to Grandma and Grandpa. I felt her side of it with my hands and my tangled guts, and I felt his side of it within the stretch of my mentality. He had gone out to lunch one day and never came back. He was fishing in the middle of Matchimanito. And there was big thoughts on his line, and he kept throwing them back for even bigger ones that would explain to him, say, the meaning of how we got here and why we have to leave so soon. All in all, I could not see myself treating Grandpa with the touch, bringing him back, when the real part of him had chose to be off thinking somewhere. It was only the rest of him that stayed around causing trouble, after all, and we could handle most of it without any problem.

Besides, it was hard to argue with his reasons for doing some things. Take Holy Mass. I used to go there just every so often, when I got frustrated mostly, because even though I know the Higher Power dwells everyplace, there's something very calming about the cool greenish inside of our mission. Or so I thought, anyway. Grandpa was the one who stripped off my delusions in this matter, for it was he who busted right through what Father calls the sacred serenity of the place.

We filed in that time. Me and Grandpa. We sat down in our pews. Then 20
the rosary got started up pre-Mass and that's when Grandpa filled up his chest and opened his mouth and belted out them words.

HAIL MARIE FULL OF GRACE.

He had a powerful set of lungs.

And he kept on like that. He did not let up. He hollered and he yelled them prayers, and I guess people was used to him by now, because they only muttered theirs and did not quit and gawk like I did. I was getting red-faced, I admit. I give him the elbow once or twice, but that wasn't nothing to him. He kept on. He shrieked to heaven and he pleaded like a movie actor and he pounded his chest like Tarzan in the Lord I Am Not Worthies. I thought he might hurt himself. Then after a while I guess I got used to it, and that's when I wondered: how come?

So afterwards I out and asked him. "How come? How come you yelled?"

25   "God don't hear me otherwise," said Grandpa Kashpaw.

I sweat. I broke right into a little cold sweat at my hairline because I knew this was perfectly right and for years not one damn other person had noticed it. God's been going deaf. Since the Old Testament, God's been deafening up on us. I read, see. Besides the dictionary, which I'm constantly in use of, I had this Bible once. I read it. I found there was discrepancies between then and now. It struck me. Here God used to raineth bread from clouds, smite the Phillipines, sling fire down on red-light districts where people got stabbed. He even appeared in person every once in a while. God used to pay attention, is what I'm saying.

Now there's your God in the Old Testament and there is Chippewa Gods as well. Indian Gods, good and bad, like tricky Nanabozho or the water monster, Missepeshu, who lives over in Matchimanito. That water monster was the last God I ever heard to appear. It had a weakness for young girls and grabbed one of the Pillagers off her rowboat. She got to shore all right, but only after this monster had its way with her. She's an old lady now. Old Lady Pillager. She still doesn't like to see her family fish that lake.

Our Gods aren't perfect, is what I'm saying, but at least they come around. They'll do a favor if you ask them right. You don't have to yell. But you do have to know, like I said, how to ask in the right way. That makes problems, because to ask proper was an art that was lost to the Chippewas once the Catholics gained ground. Even now, I have to wonder if Higher Power turned it back, if we got to yell, or if we just don't speak its language.

I looked around me. How else could I explain what all I had seen in my short life—King smashing his fist in things, Gordie drinking himself down to the Bismarck hospitals, or Aunt June left by a white man to wander off in the snow. How else to explain the times my touch don't work, and farther back, to the oldtime Indians who was swept away in the outright germ warfare and dirty-dog killing of the whites. In those times, us Indians was so much kindlier than now.

30   We took them in.

Oh yes, I'm bitter as an old cutworm just thinking of how they done to us and doing still.

So Grandpa Kashpaw just opened my eyes a little there. Was there any sense relying on a God whose ears was stopped? Just like the government? I says then, right off, maybe we got nothing but ourselves. And that's not much, just personally speaking. I know I don't got the cold hard potatoes it takes to understand everything. Still, there's things I'd like to do. For instance, I'd like to help some people like my Grandpa and Grandma Kashpaw get back some happiness within the tail ends of their lives.

I told you once before I couldn't see my way clear to putting the direct touch on Grandpa's mind, and I kept my moral there, but something soon happened to make me think a little bit of mental adjustment wouldn't do him and the rest of us no harm.

It was after we saw him one afternoon in the sunshine courtyard of the Senior Citizens with Lulu Lamartine. Grandpa used to like to dig there. He had his little dandelion fork out, and he was prying up them dandelions right and left while Lamartine watched him.

"He's scratching up the dirt, all right," said Grandma, watching Lamartine watch Grandpa out the window. 35

Now Lamartine was about half the considerable size of Grandma, but you would never think of sizes anyway. They were different in an even more noticeable way. It was the difference between a house fixed up with paint and picky fence, and a house left to weather away into the soft earth, is what I'm saying. Lamartine was jacked up, latticed, shuttered, and vinyl sided, while Grandma sagged and bulged on her slipped foundations and let her hair go the silver gray of rain-dried lumber. Right now, she eyed the Lamartine's pert flowery dress with such a look it despaired me. I knew what this could lead to with Grandma. Alternating tongue storms and rock-hard silences was hard on a man, even one who didn't notice, like Grandpa. So I went fetching him.

But he was gone when I popped through the little screen door that led out on the courtyard. There was nobody out there either, to point which way they went. Just the dandelion fork quibbling upright in the ground. That gave me an idea. I snookered over to the Lamartine's door and I listened in first, then knocked. But nobody. So I went walking through the lounges and around the card tables. Still nobody. Finally it was my touch that led me to the laundry room. I cracked the door. I went in. There they were. And he was really loving her up good, boy, and she was going hell for leather. Sheets was flapping on the lines above, and washcloths, pillowcases, shirts was also flying through the air, for they was trying to clear out a place for themselves in a high-heaped but shallow laundry cart. The washers and dryers was all on, chock-full of quarters, shaking and moaning. I couldn't hear what Grandpa and the Lamartine was billing and cooing, and they couldn't hear me.

I didn't know what to do, so I went inside and shut the door.

The Lamartine wore a big curly light-brown wig. Looked like one of them squeaky little white-people dogs. Poodles they call them. Anyway, that wig is what saved us from the worse. For I could hardly shout and tell them I was in there, no more could I try and grab him. I was trapped where I was. There was nothing I could really do but hold the door shut. I was scared of somebody else upsetting in and really getting an eyeful. Turned out though, in the heat of the clinch, as I was trying to avert my eyes you see, the Lamartine's curly wig jumped off her head. And if you ever been in the midst of something and had a big change like that occur in the someone, you can't help know how it devastates your basic urges. Not only that, but her wig was almost with a life of its own. Grandpa's eyes were bugging at the change already, and swear to God if the thing didn't rear up and pop him in the face like it was going to start something. He scrambled up, Grandpa did, and the Lamartine jumped up after him all addled looking. They just stared at each other, huffing and puffing, with quizzical expression. The surprise seemed to drive all sense completely out of Grandpa's mind.

40   "The letter was what started the fire," he said. "I never would have done it."

"What letter?" said the Lamartine. She was stiff-necked now, and elegant, even bald, like some alien queen. I gave her back the wig. The Lamartine replaced it on her head, and whenever I saw her after that, I couldn't help thinking of her bald, with special powers, as if from another planet.

"That was a close call," I said to Grandpa after she had left.

But I think he had already forgot the incident. He just stood there all quiet and thoughtful. You really wouldn't think he was crazy. He looked like he was just about to say something important, explaining himself. He said something, all right, but it didn't have nothing to do with anything that made sense.

He wondered where the heck he put his dandelion fork. That's when I decided about the mental adjustment.

45 Now what was mostly our problem was not so much that he was not all there, but that what was there of him often hankered after Lamartine. If we could put a stop to that, I thought, we might be getting someplace. But here, see, my touch was of no use. For what could I snap my fingers at to make him faithful to Grandma? Like the quality of staying power, this faithfulness was invisible. I know it's something that you got to acquire, but I never known where from. Maybe there's no rhyme or reason to it, like my getting the touch, and then again maybe it's a kind of magic.

It was Grandma Kashpaw who thought of it in the end. She knows things. Although she will not admit she has a scrap of Indian blood in her, there's no doubt in my mind she's got some Chippewa. How else would you explain the way she'll be sitting there, in front of her TV story, rocking in her armchair and suddenly she turns on me, her brown eyes hard as lake-bed flint.

"Lipsha Morrissey," she'll say, "you went out last night and got drunk." How did she know that? I'll hardly remember it myself. Then she'll say she just had a feeling or ache in the scar of her hand or a creak in her shoulder. She is constantly being told things by little aggravations in her joints or by her household appliances. One time she told Gordie never to ride with a crazy Lamartine boy. She had seen something in the polished-up tin of her bread toaster. So he didn't. Sure enough, the time came we heard how Lyman and Henry went out of control in their car, ending up in the river. Lyman swam to the top, but Henry never made it.

Thanks to Grandma's toaster, Gordie was probably spared.

Someplace in the blood Grandma Kashpaw knows things. She also 50 remembers things, I found. She keeps things filed away. She's got a memory like them video games that don't forget your score. One reason she remembers so many details about the trouble I gave her in early life is so she can flash back her total when she needs to.

Like now. Take the love medicine. I don't know where she remembered that from. It came tumbling from her mind like an asteroid off the corner of the screen.[2]

Of course she starts out by mentioning the time I had this accident in church and did she leave me there with wet overhalls? No she didn't. And ain't I glad? Yes I am. Now what you want now, Grandma?

But when she mentions them love medicines, I feel my back prickle at the danger. These love medicines is something of an old Chippewa specialty. No other tribe has got them down so well. But love medicines is not for the layman to handle. You don't just go out and get one without paying for it. Before you get one, even, you should go through one hell of a lot of mental condensation. You got to think it over. Choose the right one. You could really mess up your life grinding up the wrong little thing.

So anyhow, I said to Grandma I'd give this love medicine some thought. I knew the best thing was to go ask a specialist like Old Lady Pillager, who lives up in a tangle of bush and never shows herself. But the truth is I was afraid of her, like everyone else. She was known for putting the twisted mouth on people, seizing up their hearts. Old Lady Pillager was serious business, and I have always thought it best to steer clear of that whenever I could. That's why I took the powers in my own hands. That's why I did what I could.

I put my whole mentality to it, nothing held back. After a while I started 55 to remember things I'd heard gossiped over.

I heard of this person once who carried a charm of seeds that looked like baby pearls. They was attracted to a metal knife, which made them

---

2. Allusion to *Asteroids*, another popular 1980s video arcade game.

powerful. But I didn't know where them seeds grew. Another love charm I heard about I couldn't go along with, because how was I suppose to catch frogs in the act, which it required. Them little creatures is slippery and fast. And then the powerfullest of all, the most extreme, involved nail clips and such. I wasn't anywhere near asking Grandma to provide me all the little body bits that this last love recipe called for. I went walking around for days just trying to think up something that would work.

Well I got it. If it hadn't been the early fall of the year, I never would have got it. But I was sitting underneath a tree one day down near the school just watching people's feet go by when something tells me, look up! Look up! So I look up, and I see two honkers, Canada geese, the kind with little masks on their faces, a bird what mates for life. I see them flying right over my head naturally preparing to land in some slough on the reservation, which they certainly won't get off of alive.

It hits me, anyway. Them geese, they mate for life. And I think to myself, just what if I went out and got a pair? And just what if I fed some part—say the goose heart—of the female to Grandma and Grandpa ate the other heart? Wouldn't that work? Maybe it's all invisible, and then maybe again it's magic. Love is a stony road. We know that for sure. If it's true that the higher feelings of devotion get lodged in the heart like people say, then we'd be home free. If not, eating goose heart couldn't harm nobody anyway. I thought it was worth my effort, and Grandma Kashpaw thought so, too. She had always known a good idea when she heard one. She borrowed me Grandpa's gun.

So I went out to this particular slough, maybe the exact same slough I never got thrown in by my mother, thanks to Grandma Kashpaw, and I hunched down in a good comfortable pile of rushes. I got my gun loaded up. I ate a few of these soft baloney sandwiches Grandma made me for lunch. And then I waited. The cattails blown back and forth above my head. Them stringy blue herons was spearing up their prey. The thing I know how to do best in this world, the thing I been training for all my life, is to wait. Sitting there and sitting there was no hardship on me. I got to thinking about some funny things that happened. There was this one time that Lulu Lamartine's little blue tweety bird, a paraclete, I guess you'd call it, flown up inside her dress and got lost within there. I recalled her running out into the hallway trying to yell something, shaking. She was doing a right good jig there, cutting the rug for sure, and the thing is it *never* flown out. To this day people speculate where it went. They fear she might perhaps of crushed it in her corsets. It sure hasn't ever yet been seen alive. I thought of funny things for a while, but then I used them up, and strange things that happened started weaseling their way into my mind.

60   I got to thinking quite naturally of the Lamartine's cousin named Wristwatch. I never knew what his real name was. They called him Wristwatch because he got his father's broken wristwatch as a young boy when

his father passed on. Never in his whole life did Wristwatch take his father's watch off. He didn't care if it worked, although after a while he got sensitive when people asked what time it was, teasing him. He often put it to his ear like he was listening to the tick. But it was broken for good and forever, people said so, at least that's what they thought.

Well I saw Wristwatch smoking in his pickup one afternoon and by nine that evening he was dead.

He died sitting at the Lamartine's table, too. As she told it, Wristwatch had just eaten himself a good-size dinner and she said would he take seconds on the hot dish when he fell over to the floor. They turnt him over. He was gone. But here's the strange thing: when the Senior Citizen's orderly took the pulse he noticed that the wristwatch Wristwatch wore was now working. The moment he died the wristwatch started keeping perfect time. They buried him with the watch still ticking on his arm.

I got to thinking. What if some gravediggers dug up Wristwatch's casket in two hundred years and that watch was still going? I thought what question they would ask and it was this: Whose hand wound it?

I started shaking like a piece of grass at just the thought.

Not to get off the subject or nothing. I was still hunkered in the slough. It was passing late into the afternoon and still no honkers had touched down. Now I don't need to tell you that the waiting did not get to me, it was the chill. The rushes was very soft, but damp. I was getting cold and debating to leave, when they landed. Two geese swimming here and there as big as life, looking deep into each other's little pinhole eyes. Just the ones I was looking for. So I lifted Grandpa's gun to my shoulder and I aimed perfectly, and *blam! Blam!* I delivered two accurate shots. But the thing is, them shots missed. I couldn't hardly believe it. Whether it was that the stock had warped or the barrel got bent someways, I don't quite know, but anyway them geese flown off into the dim sky, and Lipsha Morrissey was left there in the rushes with evening fallen and his two cold hands empty. He had before him just the prospect of another day of bone-cracking chill in them rushes, and the thought of it got him depressed.

Now it isn't my style, in no way, to get depressed.

So I said to myself, Lipsha Morrissey, you're a happy S.O.B. who could be covered up with weeds by now down at the bottom of this slough, but instead you're alive to tell the tale. You might have problems in life, but you still got the touch. You got the power, Lipsha Morrissey. Can't argue that. So put your mind to it and figure out how not to be depressed.

I took my advice. I put my mind to it. But I never saw at the time how my thoughts led me astray toward a tragic outcome none could have known. I ignored all the danger, all the limits, for I was tired of sitting in the slough and my feet were numb. My face was aching. I was chilled, so I played with fire. I told myself love medicine was simple. I told myself the old superstitions was just that—strange beliefs. I told myself to take the ten dollars

Mary MacDonald had paid me for putting the touch on her arthritis joint, and the other five I hadn't spent yet from winning bingo last Thursday. I told myself to go down to the Red Owl store.

And here is what I did that made the medicine backfire. I took an evil shortcut. I looked at birds that was dead and froze.

70 All right. So now I guess you will say, "Slap a malpractice suit on Lipsha Morrissey."

I heard of those suits. I used to think it was a color clothing quack doctors had to wear so you could tell them from the good ones. Now I know better that it's law.

As I walked back from the Red Owl with the rock-hard, heavy turkeys, I argued to myself about malpractice. I thought of faith. I thought to myself that faith could be called belief against the odds and whether or not there's any proof. How does that sound? I thought how we might have to yell to be heard by Higher Power, but that's not saying it's not *there*. And that is faith for you. It's belief even when the goods don't deliver. Higher Power makes promises we all know they can't back up, but anybody ever go and slap an old malpractice suit on God? Or the U.S. government? No they don't. Faith might be stupid, but it gets us through. So what I'm heading at is this. I finally convinced myself that the real actual power to the love medicine was not the goose heart itself but the faith in the cure.

I didn't believe it, I knew it was wrong, but by then I had waded so far into my lie I was stuck there. And then I went one step further.

The next day, I cleaned the hearts away from the paper packages of gizzards inside the turkeys. Then I wrapped them hearts with a clean hankie and brung them both to get blessed up at the mission. I wanted to get official blessings from the priest, but when Father answered the door to the rectory, wiping his hands on a little towel, I could tell he was a busy man.

75 "Booshoo,[3] Father," I said. "I got a slight request to make of you this afternoon."

"What is it?" he said.

"Would you bless this package?" I held out the hankie with the hearts tied inside it.

He looked at the package, questioning it.

"It's turkey hearts," I honestly had to reply.

80 A look of annoyance crossed his face.

"Why don't you bring this matter over to Sister Martin," he said. "I have duties."

And so, although the blessing wouldn't be as powerful, I went over to the Sisters with the package.

---

3. That is, *Bonjour,* French for "good day" or "hello."

I rung the bell, and they brought Sister Martin to the door. I had her as
a music teacher, but I was always so shy then. I never talked out loud. Now,
I had grown taller than Sister Martin. Looking down, I saw that she was
not feeling up to snuff. Brown circles hung under her eyes.

"What's the matter?" she said, not noticing who I was.

"Remember me, Sister?"   85

She squinted up at me.

"Oh yes," she said after a moment. "I'm sorry, you're the youngest of the
Kashpaws. Gordie's brother."

Her face warmed up.

"Lipsha," I said, "that's my name."

"Well, Lipsha," she said, smiling broad at me now, "what can I do for   90
you?"

They always said she was the kindest-hearted of the Sisters up the hill,
and she was. She brought me back into their own kitchen and made me
take a big yellow wedge of cake and a glass of milk.

"Now tell me," she said, nodding at my package. "What have you got
wrapped up so carefully in those handkerchiefs?"

Like before, I answered honestly.

"Ah," said Sister Martin. "Turkey hearts." She waited.

"I hoped you could bless them."   95

She waited some more, smiling with her eyes. Kindhearted though she
was, I began to sweat. A person could not pull the wool down over Sister
Martin. I stumbled through my mind for an explanation, quick, that
wouldn't scare her off.

"They're a present," I said, "for Saint Kateri's[4] statue."

"She's not a saint yet."

"I know," I stuttered on. "In the hopes they will crown her."

"Lipsha," she said, "I never heard of such a thing."   100

So I told her. "Well the truth is," I said, "it's a kind of medicine."

"For what?"

"Love."

"Oh Lipsha," she said after a moment, "you don't need any medicine.
I'm sure any girl would like you exactly the way you are."

I just sat there. I felt miserable, caught in my pack of lies.   105

"Tell you what," she said, seeing how bad I felt, "my blessing won't make
any difference anyway. But there is something you can do."

I looked up at her, hopeless.

---

4. Kateri Kekakwitha (1656–80), "Lily of the Mohawk," was born in what is now upstate New York
to a Mohawk father and an Algonquin mother who was a devout Christian. Following the deaths
of her parents, Kateri moved to a Jesuit mission near Montreal to spend the rest of her short life in
prayer and chastity. Miracles were attributed to her after her death; she was beatified in 1980 and
canonized in 1991.

"Just be yourself."

I looked down at my plate. I knew I wasn't much to brag about right then, and I shortly became even less. For as I walked out the door I stuck my fingers in the cup of holy water that was sacred from their touches. I put my fingers in and blessed the hearts, quick, with my own hand.

110   I went back to Grandma and sat down in her little kitchen at the Senior Citizens. I unwrapped them hearts on the table, and her hard agate eyes went soft. She said she wasn't even going to cook those hearts up but eat them raw so their power would go down strong as possible.

I couldn't hardly watch when she munched hers. Now that's true love. I was worried about how she would get Grandpa to eat his, but she told me she'd think of something and don't worry. So I did not. I was supposed to hide off in her bedroom while she put dinner on a plate for Grandpa and fixed up the heart so he'd eat it. I caught a glint of the plate she was making for him. She put that heart smack on a piece of lettuce like in a restaurant and then attached to it a little heap of boiled peas.

He sat down. I was listening in the next room.

She said, "Why don't you have some mash potato?" So he had some mash potato. Then she gave him a little piece of boiled meat. He ate that. Then she said, "Why you didn't never touch your salad yet. See that heart? I'm feeding you it because the doctor said your blood needs building up."

I couldn't help it, at that point I peeked through a crack in the door.

115   I saw Grandpa picking at that heart on his plate with a certain look. He didn't look appetized at all, is what I'm saying. I doubted our plan was going to work. Grandma was getting worried, too. She told him one more time, loudly, that he had to eat that heart.

"Swallow it down," she said. "You'll hardly notice it."

He just looked at her straight on. The way he looked at her made me think I was going to see the smokescreen drop a second time, and sure enough it happened.

"What you want me to eat this for so bad?" he asked her uncannily.

Now Grandma knew the jig was up. She knew that he knew she was working medicine. He put his fork down. He rolled the heart around his saucer plate.

120   "I don't want to eat this," he said to Grandma. "It don't look good."

"Why it's fresh grade-A," she told him. "One hundred percent."

He didn't ask percent what, but his eyes took on an even more warier look.

"Just go on and try it," she said, taking the salt shaker up in her hand. She was getting annoyed. "Not tasty enough? You want me to salt it for you?" She waved the shaker over his plate.

"All right, skinny white girl!" She had got Grandpa mad. Oopsy-daisy, he popped the heart into his mouth. I was about to yawn loudly and come out of the bedroom. I was about ready for this crash of wills to be over, when I saw he was still up to his old tricks. First he rolled it into one side of his cheek. "Mmmmm," he said. Then he rolled it into the other side of his cheek. "Mmmmmmm," again. Then he stuck his tongue out with the heart on it and put it back, and there was no time to react. He had pulled Grandma's leg once too far. Her goat was got. She was so mad she hopped up quick as a wink and slugged him between the shoulderblades to make him swallow.

Only thing is, he choked. 125

He choked real bad. A person can choke to death. You ever sit down at a restaurant table and up above you there is a list of instructions what to do if something slides down the wrong pipe? It sure makes you chew slow, that's for damn sure. When Grandpa fell off his chair better believe me that little graphic illustrated poster fled into my mind. I jumped out the bedroom. I done everything within my power that I could do to unlodge what was choking him. I squeezed underneath his rib cage. I socked him in the back. I was desperate. But here's the factor of decision: he wasn't choking on the heart alone. There was more to it than that. It was other things that choked him as well. It didn't seem like he wanted to struggle or fight. Death came and tapped his chest, so he went just like that. I'm sorry all through my body at what I done to him with that heart, and there's those who will say Lipsha Morrissey is just excusing himself off the hook by giving song and dance about how Grandpa gave up.

Maybe I can't admit what I did. My touch had gone worthless, that is true. But here is what I seen while he lay in my arms.

You hear a person's life will flash before their eyes when they're in danger. It was him in danger, not me, but it was *his* life come over me. I saw him dying, and it was like someone pulled the shade down in a room. His eyes clouded over and squeezed shut, but just before that I looked in. He was still fishing in the middle of Matchimanito. Big thoughts was on his line and he had half a case of beer in the boat. He waved at me, grinned, and then the bobber went under.

Grandma had gone out of the room crying for help. I bunched my force up in my hands and I held him. I was so wound up I couldn't even breathe. All the moments he had spent with me, all the times he had hoisted me on his shoulders or pointed into the leaves was concentrated in that moment. Time was flashing back and forth like a pinball machine. Lights blinked and balls hopped and rubber bands chirped, until suddenly I realized the last ball had gone down the drain and there was nothing. I felt his force leaving him, flowing out of Grandpa never to return. I felt his mind weakening. The bobber going under in the lake. And I felt the touch retreat back into the darkness inside my body, from where it came.

One time, long ago, both of us were fishing together. We caught a big 130 old snapper what started towing us around like it was a motor. "This here fishline is pretty damn good," Grandpa said. "Let's keep this turtle on and see where he takes us." So we rode along behind that turtle, watching as from time to time it surfaced. The thing was just about the size of a washtub. It took us all around the lake twice, and as it was traveling, Grandpa said something as a joke. "Lipsha," he said, "we are glad your mother didn't want you because we was always looking for a boy like you who would tow us around the lake."

"I ain't no snapper. Snappers is so stupid they stay alive when their head's chopped off," I said.

"That ain't stupidity," said Grandpa. "Their brain's just in their heart, like yours is."

When I looked up, I knew the fuse had blown between my heart and my mind and that a terrible understanding was to be given.

Grandma got back into the room and I saw her stumble. And then she went down too. It was like a house you can't hardly believe has stood so long, through years of record weather, suddenly goes down in the worst yet. It makes sense, is what I'm saying, but you still can't hardly believe it. You think a person you know has got through death and illness and being broke and living on commodity rice will get through anything. Then they fold and you see how fragile were the stones that underpinned them. You see how instantly the ground can shift you thought was solid. You see the stop signs and the yellow dividing markers of roads you traveled and all the instructions you had played according to vanish. You see how all the everyday things you counted on was just a dream you had been having by which you run your whole life. She had been over me, like a sheer overhang of rock dividing Lipsha Morrissey from outer space. And now she went underneath. It was as though the banks gave way on the shores of Matchimanito, and where Grandpa's passing was just the bobber swallowed under by his biggest thought, her fall was the house and the rock under it sliding after, sending half the lake splashing up to the clouds.

135   Where there was nothing.

You play them games never knowing what you see. When I fell into the dream alongside of both of them I saw that the dominions I had defended myself from anciently was but delusions of the screen. Blips of light. And I was scot-free now, whistling through space.

I don't know how I come back. I don't know from where. They was slapping my face when I arrived back at Senior Citizens and they was oxygenating her. I saw her chest move, almost unwilling. She sighed the way she would when somebody bothered her in the middle of a row of beads she was counting. I think it irritated her to no end that they brought her back. I knew from the way she looked after they took the mask off, she was not going to forgive them disturbing her restful peace. Nor was she forgiving Lipsha Morrissey. She had been stepping out onto the road of death, she told the children later at the funeral. I asked was there any stop signs or dividing markers on that road, but she clamped her lips in a vise the way she always done when she was mad.

Which didn't bother me. I knew when things had cleared out she wouldn't have no choice. I was not going to speculate where the blame was put for Grandpa's death. We was in it together. She had slugged him between the shoulders. My touch had failed him, never to return.

All the blood children and the took-ins, like me, came home from Minneapolis and Chicago, where they had relocated years ago. They stayed with friends on the reservation or with Aurelia or slept on Grandma's floor. They were struck down with grief and bereavement to be sure, every one of them. At the funeral I sat down in the back of the church with Albertine. She had gotten all skinny and ragged haired from cramming all her years of study into two or three. She had decided that to be a nurse was not enough for her so she was going to be a doctor. But the way she was straining her mind didn't look too hopeful. Her eyes were bloodshot from driving and crying. She took my hand. From the back we watched all the children and the mourners as they hunched over their prayers, their hands stuffed full of Kleenex. It was someplace in that long sad service that my vision shifted. I began to see things different, more clear. The family kneeling down turned to rocks in a field. It struck me how strong and reliable grief was, and death. Until the end of time, death would be our rock.

So I had perspective on it all, for death gives you that. All the Kashpaw 140 children had done various things to me in their lives—shared their folks with me, loaned me cash, beat me up in secret—and I decided, because of death, then and there I'd call it quits. If I ever saw King again, I'd shake his hand. Forgiving somebody else made the whole thing easier to bear.

Everybody saw Grandpa off into the next world. And then the Kashpaws had to get back to their jobs, which was numerous and impressive. I had a few beers with them and I went back to Grandma, who had sort of got lost in the shuffle of everybody being sad about Grandpa and glad to see one another.

Zelda had sat beside her the whole time and was sitting with her now. I wanted to talk to Grandma, say how sorry I was, that it wasn't her fault, but only mine. I would have, but Zelda gave me one of her looks of strict warning as if to say, "I'll take care of Grandma. Don't horn in on the women."

If only Zelda knew, I thought, the sad realities would change her. But of course I couldn't tell the dark truth.

It was evening, late. Grandma's light was on underneath a crack in the door. About a week had passed since we buried Grandpa. I knocked first but there wasn't no answer, so I went right in. The door was unlocked. She was there but she didn't notice me at first. Her hands were tied up in her rosary, and her gaze was fully absorbed in the easy chair opposite her, the one that had always been Grandpa's favorite. I stood there, staring with her, at the little green nubs in the cloth and plastic armrest covers and the sad little hair-tonic stain he had made on the white doily where he laid his head. For the life of me I couldn't figure what she was staring at. Thin space. Then she turned.

145   "He ain't gone yet," she said.

Remember that chill I luckily didn't get from waiting in the slough? I got it now. I felt it start from the very center of me, where fear hides, waiting to attack. It spiraled outward so that in minutes my fingers and teeth were shaking and clattering. I knew she told the truth. She seen Grandpa. Whether or not he had been there is not the point. She had *seen* him, and that meant anybody else could see him, too. Not only that but, as is usually the case with these here ghosts, he had a certain uneasy reason to come back. And of course Grandma Kashpaw had scanned it out.

I sat down. We sat together on the couch watching his chair out of the corner of our eyes. She had found him sitting in his chair when she walked in the door.

"It's the love medicine, my Lipsha," she said. "It was stronger than we thought. He came back even after death to claim me to his side."

I was afraid. "We shouldn't have tampered with it," I said. She agreed. For a while we sat still. I don't know what she thought, but my head felt screwed on backward. I couldn't accurately consider the situation, so I told Grandma to go to bed. I would sleep on the couch keeping my eye on Grandpa's chair. Maybe he would come back and maybe he wouldn't. I guess I feared the one as much as the other, but I got to thinking, see, as I lay there in darkness, that perhaps even through my terrible mistakes some good might come. If Grandpa did come back, I thought he'd return in his right mind. I could talk with him. I could tell him it was all my fault for playing with power I did not understand. Maybe he'd forgive me and rest in peace. I hoped this. I calmed myself and waited for him all night.

150   He fooled me though. He knew what I was waiting for, and it wasn't what he was looking to hear. Come dawn I heard a blood-splitting cry from the bedroom and I rushed in there. Grandma turnt the lights on. She was sitting on the edge of the bed and her face looked harsh, pinched-up, gray.

"He was here," she said. "He came and laid down next to me in bed. And he touched me."

Her heart broke down. She cried. His touch was so cold. She laid back in bed after a while, as it was morning, and I went to the couch. As I lay there, falling asleep, I suddenly felt Grandpa's presence and the barrier between us like a swollen river. I felt how I had wronged him. How awful was the place where I had sent him. Behind the wall of death, he'd watched the living eat and cry and get drunk. He was lonesome, but I understood he meant no harm.

"Go back," I said to the dark, afraid and yet full of pity. "You got to be with your own kind now," I said. I felt him retreating, like a sigh, growing less. I felt his spirit as it shrunk back through the walls, the blinds, the brick courtyard of Senior Citizens. "Look up Aunt June," I whispered as he left.

I slept late the next morning, a good hard sleep allowing the sun to rise and warm the earth. It was past noon when I awoke. There is nothing, to my mind, like a long sleep to make those hard decisions that you neglect under stress of wakefulness. Soon as I woke up that morning, I saw exactly what I'd say to Grandma. I had gotten humble in the past week, not just losing the touch but getting jolted into the understanding that would prey on me from here on out. Your life feels different on you, once you greet death and understand your heart's position. You wear your life like a garment from the mission bundle sale ever after—lightly because you realize you never paid nothing for it, cherishing because you know you won't ever come by such a bargain again. Also you have the feeling someone wore it before you and someone will after. I can't explain that, not yet, but I'm putting my mind to it.

"Grandma," I said, "I got to be honest about the love medicine." 155
She listened. I knew from then on she would be listening to me the way I had listened to her before. I told her about the turkey hearts and how I had them blessed. I told her what I used as love medicine was purely a fake, and then I said to her what my understanding brought me.

"Love medicine ain't what brings him back to you, Grandma. No, it's something else. He loved you over time and distance, but he went off so quick he never got the chance to tell you how he loves you, how he doesn't blame you, how he understands. It's true feeling, not no magic. No supermarket heart could have brung him back."

She looked at me. She was seeing the years and days I had no way of knowing, and she didn't believe me. I could tell this. Yet a look came on her face. It was like the look of mothers drinking sweetness from their children's eyes. It was tenderness.

"Lipsha," she said, "you was always my favorite."
She took the beads off the bedpost, where she kept them to say at night, 160 and she told me to put out my hand. When I did this, she shut the beads inside of my fist and held them there a long minute, tight, so my hand hurt. I almost cried when she did this. I don't really know why. Tears shot up behind my eyelids, and yet it was nothing. I didn't understand, except her hand was so strong, squeezing mine.

The earth was full of life and there were dandelions growing out the window, thick as thieves, already seeded, fat as big yellow plungers. She let my hand go. I got up. "I'll go out and dig a few dandelions," I told her.

Outside, the sun was hot and heavy as a hand on my back. I felt it flow down my arms, out my fingers, arrowing through the ends of the fork into the earth. With every root I prized up there was return, as if I was kin to its secret lesson. The touch got stronger as I worked through the grassy afternoon. Uncurling from me like a seed out of the blackness where I was lost, the touch spread. The spiked leaves full of bitter mother's milk. A buried root. A nuisance people dig up and throw in the sun to wither. A globe of frail seeds that's indestructible.

1982

QUESTIONS

1. How, if at all, do you think Lipsha changes over the course of the story? What might he learn by the end? What might the story show us through him?
2. What different meanings does the phrase *love medicine* take on over the course of the story? How might you use the phrase to state the story's theme?
3. Lipsha tells the stories of Lulu's "tweety bird" that disappeared up her dress and of Wristwatch, whose broken watch started keeping time after its owner dropped dead. He then says, "Not to get off the subject or nothing" (par. 65). Are these stories off the subject? How do they arouse expectations? How do they function in the plot? What do they tell you of Lipsha's character? of the nature of the people on the reservation? Are they related to the theme? If so, how?

SUGGESTIONS FOR WRITING

1. Choose any story in this chapter and write an essay exploring how character, point of view, setting, symbolism, or any recurring word or phrase contributes to the development of theme. Be sure to state that theme in a sentence.
2. Sometimes the theme in a work of literature can be expressed as a strong, clear statement: "A always follows from B," or "An X can never be a Y." More often, though, especially in modern literature, authors offer subtler, often ambiguous themes that deliberately undermine our faith in simple absolutes: "A doesn't necessarily always follow B," or "There are times when an X can be a Y." Write an essay in which you argue that one of the four stories in this chapter has an "always" or "never" kind of theme, and contrast it to the more indeterminate theme in one of the other three stories.
3. Write an essay exploring how theme is developed through the juxtaposition of realistic detail and fantastic elements in "A Very Old Man with Enormous Wings," especially (but not exclusively) in the description of the winged man himself.
4. Though the main theme of "Love Medicine" may well be a universal one (an insight that applies to all or most people), its major characters are all Native Americans living on a reservation. Write an essay exploring how the story

characterizes contemporary Native American life and how this characterization shapes the story's theme, perhaps giving the story a culturally and historically specific, as well as universal, resonance and relevance.

5. Write an essay comparing the way Stephen Crane's "The Open Boat" and Nathaniel Hawthorne's "The Birth-Mark" portray the relationship between human beings and nature. What is similar and different about the nature-related themes of the two stories?

6. Write two versions of a poem or short story. In the first version, be explicit, even obvious, about your theme. In the second, employ any strategies you wish for veiling the theme as much as possible. Then write a brief essay discussing which version is more successful, and why.

Reading More Fiction

TONI CADE BAMBARA

Gorilla, My Love

That was the year Hunca Bubba changed his name. Not a change up, but a change back, since Jefferson Winston Vale was the name in the first place. Which was news to me cause he'd been my Hunca Bubba my whole life-time, since I couldn't manage Uncle to save my life. So far as I was con-cerned it was a change completely to somethin soundin very geographical weatherlike to me, like somethin you'd find in a almanac. Or somethin you'd run across when you sittin in the navigator seat with a wet thumb on the map crinkly in your lap, watchin the roads and signs so when Grand-daddy Vale say "Which way, Scout," you got sense enough to say take the next exit or take a left or whatever it is. Not that Scout's my name. Just the name Granddaddy call whoever sittin in the navigator seat. Which is usu-ally me cause I don't feature sittin in the back with the pecans. Now, you figure pecans all right to be sittin with. If you thinks so, that's your busi-ness. But they dusty sometime and make you cough. And they got a way of slidin around and dippin down sudden, like maybe a rat in the buckets. So if you scary like me, you sleep with the lights on and blame it on Baby Jason and, so as not to waste good electric, you study the maps. And that's how come I'm in the navigator seat most times and get to be called Scout.

So Hunca Bubba in the back with the pecans and Baby Jason, and he in love. And we got to hear all this stuff about this woman he in love with and all. Which really ain't enough to keep the mind alive, though Baby Jason got no better sense than to give his undivided attention and keep grabbin at the photograph which is just a picture of some skinny woman in a countrified dress with her hand shot up to her face like she shame fore cameras. But there's a movie house in the background which I ax about. Cause I am a movie freak from way back, even though it do get me in trouble sometime.

Like when me and Big Brood and Baby Jason was on our own last Easter and couldn't go to the Dorset cause we'd seen all the Three Stooges they was. And the RKO Hamilton was closed readying up for the Easter Pag-eant that night. And the West End, the Regun and the Sunset was too far, less we had grownups with us which we didn't. So we walk up Amsterdam Avenue to the Washington and *Gorilla, My Love* playin, they say, which suit me just fine, though the "my love" part kinda drag Big Brood some. As for

Baby Jason, shoot, like Granddaddy say, he'd follow me into the fiery furnace if I say come on. So we go in and get three bags of Havmore potato chips which not only are the best potato chips but the best bags for blowin up and bustin real loud so the matron come trottin down the aisle with her chunky self, flashin that flashlight dead in your eye so you can give her some lip, and if she answer back and you already finish seein the show anyway, why then you just turn the place out. Which I love to do, no lie. With Baby Jason kickin at the seat in front, egging me on, and Big Brood mumblin bout what fiercesome things we goin do. Which means me. Like when the big boys come up on us talkin bout Lemme a nickel. It's me that hide the money. Or when the bad boys in the park take Big Brood's Spaudeen[1] way from him. It's me that jump on they back and fight awhile. And it's me that turns out the show if the matron get too salty.

So the movie come on and right away it's this churchy music and clearly not about no gorilla. Bout Jesus. And I am ready to kill, not cause I got anything gainst Jesus. Just that when you fixed to watch a gorilla picture you don't wanna get messed around with Sunday School stuff. So I am mad. Besides, we see this raggedy old brown film *King of Kings*[2] every year and enough's enough. Grownups figure they can treat you just anyhow. Which burns me up. There I am, my feet up and my Havmore potato chips really salty and crispy and two jawbreakers in my lap and the money safe in my shoe from the big boys, and there comes this Jesus stuff. So we all go wild. Yellin, booin, stompin and carryin on. Really to wake the man in the booth up there who musta went to sleep and put on the wrong reels. But no, cause he holler down to shut up and then he turn the sound up so we really gotta holler like crazy to even hear ourselves good. And the matron ropes off the children section and flashes her light all over the place and we yell some more and some kids slip under the rope and run up and down the aisle just to show it take more than some dusty ole velvet rope to tie us down. And I'm flingin the kid in front of me's popcorn. And Baby Jason kickin seats. And it's really somethin. Then here come the big and bad matron, the one they let out in case of emergency. And she totin that flashlight like she gonna use it on somebody. This here the colored matron Brandy and her friends call Thunderbuns. She do not play. She do not smile. So we shut up and watch the simple ass picture.

Which is not so simple as it is stupid. Cause I realized that just about 5 anybody in my family is better than this god they always talkin about. My daddy wouldn't stand for nobody treatin any of us that way. My mama specially. And I can just see it now, Big Brood up there on the cross talkin bout Forgive them Daddy cause they don't know what they doin. And my

---

1. Probably refers to "Spaldeen," the small pink rubber ball made by the Spalding company and used for stickball.
2. Although there is a 1961 version, this probably refers to the silent movie made in the 1920s.

Mama say Get on down from there you big fool, whatcha think this is, playtime? And my Daddy yellin to Granddaddy to get him a ladder cause Big Brood actin the fool, his mother side of the family showin up. And my mama and her sister Daisy jumpin on them Romans beatin them with they pocketbooks. And Hunca Bubba tellin them folks on they knees they better get out the way and go get some help or they goin to get trampled on. And Granddaddy Vale sayin Leave the boy alone, if that's what he wants to do with his life we ain't got nothin to say about it. Then Aunt Daisy givin him a taste of that pocketbook, fussin bout what a damn fool old man Granddaddy is. Then everybody jumpin in his chest like the time Uncle Clayton went in the army and come back with only one leg and Granddaddy say somethin stupid about that's life. And by this time Big Brood off the cross and in the park playin handball or skully[3] or somethin. And the family in the kitchen throwin dishes at each other, screamin bout if you hadn't done this I wouldn't had to do that. And me in the parlor trying to do my arithmetic yellin Shut it off.

Which is what I was yellin all by myself which make me a sittin target for Thunderbuns. But when I yell We want our money back, that gets everybody in chorus. And the movie windin up with this heavenly cloud music and the smartass up there in his hole in the wall turns up the sound again to drown us out. Then there comes Bugs Bunny which we already seen so we know we been had. No gorilla my nuthin. And Big Brood say Awwww sheeet, we goin to see the manager and get our money back. And I know from this we business. So I brush the potato chips out of my hair which is where Baby Jason like to put em, and I march myself up the aisle to deal with the manager who is a crook in the first place for lyin out there sayin *Gorilla, My Love* playin. And I never did like the man cause he oily and pasty at the same time like the bad guy in the serial, the one that got a hideout behind a pushbutton bookcase and play "Moonlight Sonata"[4] with gloves on. I knock on the door and I am furious. And I am alone, too. Cause Big Brood suddenly got to go so bad even though my mama told us bout goin in them nasty bathrooms. And I hear him sigh like he disgusted when he get to the door and see only a little kid there. And now I'm really furious cause I get so tired grownups messin over kids cause they little and can't take em to court. What is it, he say to me like I lost my mittens or wet myself or am somebody's retarded child. When in reality I am the smartest kid P.S. 186 ever had in its whole lifetime and you can ax anybody. Even them teachers that don't like me cause I won't sing them Southern songs or back off when they tell me my questions are out of order. And cause my Mama come up

---

3. Basketball game that tests shooting skill and can be played alone or as a contest between two people.

4. Popular name for Beethoven's *Piano Sonata in C Sharp Minor*, Opus 27, No. 2. The "bad guy" who plays this piece is the Phantom of the Opera.

there in a minute when them teachers start playin the dozens[5] behind colored folks. She stalks in with her hat pulled down bad and that Persian lamb coat draped back over one hip on account of she got her fist planted there so she can talk that talk which gets us all hypnotized, and teacher be comin undone cause she know this could be her job and her behind cause Mama got pull with the Board and bad by her own self anyhow.

So I kick the door open wider and just walk right by him and sit down and tell the man about himself and that I want my money back and that goes for Baby Jason and Big Brood too. And he still trying to shuffle me out the door even though I'm sittin which shows him for the fool he is. Just like them teachers do fore they realize Mama like a stone on that spot and ain't backin up. So he ain't gettin up off the money. So I was forced to leave, takin the matches from under his ashtray, and set a fire under the candy stand, which closed the raggedy ole Washington down for a week. My Daddy had the suspect it was me cause Big Brood got a big mouth. But I explained right quick what the whole thing was about and I figured it was even-steven. Cause if you say Gorilla, My Love, you supposed to mean it. Just like when you say you goin to give me a party on my birthday, you gotta mean it. And if you say me and Baby Jason can go South pecan haulin with Granddaddy Vale, you better not be comin up with no stuff about the weather look uncertain or did you mop the bathroom or any other trickified business. I mean even gangsters in the movies say My word is my bond. So don't nobody get away with nothin far as I'm concerned. So Daddy put his belt back on. Cause that's the way I was raised. Like my Mama say in one of them situations when I won't back down, Okay Badbird, you right. Your point is well-taken. Not that Badbird my name, just what she say when she tired arguin and know I'm right. And Aunt Jo, who is the hardest head in the family and worse even than Aunt Daisy, she say, You absolutely right Miss Muffin, which also ain't my real name but the name she gave me one time when I got some medicine shot in my behind and wouldn't get up off her pillows for nothin. And even Granddaddy Vale—who got no memory to speak of, so sometime you can just plain lie to him, if you want to be like that—he say, Well if that's what I said, then that's it. But this name business was different they said. It wasn't like Hunca Bubba had gone back on his word or anything. Just that he was thinkin bout gettin married and was usin his real name now. Which ain't the way I saw it at all.

So there I am in the navigator seat. And I turned to him and just plain ole ax him. I mean I come right on out with it. No sense goin all around that barn the old folks talk about. And like my mama say, Hazel—which is my real name and what she remembers to call me when she bein serious—when you got somethin on your mind, speak up and let the chips fall where they may. And if anybody don't like it, tell em to come see your mama. And

---

5. Ritualized game or contest in which two participants exchange artfully stylized insults.

Daddy look up from the paper and say, You hear your Mama good, Hazel. And tell em to come see me first. Like that. That's how I was raised.

So I turn clear round in the navigator seat and say, "Look here, Hunca Bubba or Jefferson Windsong Vale or whatever your name is, you gonna marry this girl?"

10   "Sure am," he say, all grins.

And I say, "Member that time you was baby-sittin me when we lived at four-o-nine and there was this big snow and Mama and Daddy got held up in the country so you had to stay for two days?"

And he say, "Sure do."

"Well. You remember how you told me I was the cutest thing that ever walked the earth?"

"Oh, you were real cute when you were little," he say, which is supposed to be funny. I am not laughin.

15   "Well. You remember what you said?"

And Granddaddy Vale squintin over the wheel and axin Which way, Scout. But Scout is busy and don't care if we all get lost for days.

"Watcha mean, Peaches?"

"My name is Hazel. And what I mean is you said you were going to marry *me* when I grew up. You were going to wait. That's what I mean, my dear Uncle Jefferson." And he don't say nuthin. Just look at me real strange like he never saw me before in life. Like he lost in some weird town in the middle of night and lookin for directions and there's no one to ask. Like it was me that messed up the maps and turned the road posts round. "Well, you said it, didn't you?" And Baby Jason lookin back and forth like we playin ping-pong. Only I ain't playin. I'm hurtin and I can hear that I am screamin. And Granddaddy Vale mumblin how we never gonna get to where we goin if I don't turn around and take my navigator job serious.

"Well, for cryin out loud, Hazel, you just a little girl. And I was just teasin."

20   "'And I was just teasin,'" I say back just how he said it so he can hear what a terrible thing it is. Then I don't say nuthin. And he don't say nuthin. And Baby Jason don't say nuthin nohow. Then Granddaddy Vale speak up. "Look here, Precious, it was Hunca Bubba what told you them things. This here, Jefferson Winston Vale." And Hunca Bubba say, "That's right. That was somebody else. I'm a new somebody."

"You a lyin dawg," I say, when I meant to say treacherous dog, but just couldn't get hold of the word. It slipped away from me. And I'm crying and crumplin down in the seat and just don't care. And Granddaddy say to hush and steps on the gas. And I'm losin my bearins and don't even know where to look on the map cause I can't see for cryin. And Baby Jason cryin too. Cause he is my blood brother and understands that we must stick together or be forever lost, what with grown-ups playin change-up and turnin you round every which way so bad. And don't even say they sorry.

1971

AMBROSE BIERCE

An Occurrence at Owl Creek Bridge

I

A man stood upon a railroad bridge in Northern Alabama, looking down into the swift waters twenty feet below. The man's hands were behind his back, the wrists bound with a cord. A rope loosely encircled his neck. It was attached to a stout cross-timber above his head, and the slack fell to the level of his knees. Some loose boards laid upon the sleepers supporting the metals of the railway supplied a footing for him and his executioners—two private soldiers of the Federal army, directed by a sergeant, who in civil life may have been a deputy sheriff. At a short remove upon the same temporary platform was an officer in the uniform of his rank, armed. He was a captain. A sentinel at each end of the bridge stood with his rifle in the position known as "support," that is to say, vertical in front of the left shoulder, the hammer resting on the forearm thrown straight across the chest—a formal and unnatural position, enforcing an erect carriage of the body. It did not appear to be the duty of these two men to know what was occurring at the centre of the bridge; they merely blockaded the two ends of the foot plank which traversed it.

Beyond one of the sentinels nobody was in sight; the railroad ran straight away into a forest for a hundred yards, then, curving, was lost to view. Doubtless there was an outpost further along. The other bank of the stream was open ground—a gentle acclivity crowned with a stockade of vertical tree trunks, loopholed for rifles, with a single embrasure through which protruded the muzzle of a brass cannon commanding the bridge. Midway of the slope between bridge and fort were the spectators—a single company of infantry in line, at "parade rest," the butts of the rifles on the ground, the barrels inclining slightly backward against the right shoulder, the hands crossed upon the stock. A lieutenant stood at the right of the line, the point of his sword upon the ground, his left hand resting upon his right. Excepting the group of four at the centre of the bridge not a man moved. The company faced the bridge, staring stonily, motionless. The sentinels, facing the banks of the stream, might have been statues to adorn the bridge. The captain stood with folded arms, silent, observing the work of his subordinates but making no sign. Death is a dignitary who, when he comes announced, is to be received with formal manifestations of respect, even by those most familiar with him. In the code of military etiquette silence and fixity are forms of deference.

The man who was engaged in being hanged was apparently about thirty-five years of age. He was a civilian, if one might judge from his dress, which was that of a planter. His features were good—a straight nose, firm mouth, broad forehead, from which his long, dark hair was combed straight back, falling behind his ears to the collar of his well-fitting frock coat. He wore a moustache and pointed beard, but no whiskers; his eyes were large and dark grey and had a kindly expression which one would hardly have expected in one whose neck was in the hemp. Evidently this was no vulgar assassin. The liberal military code makes provision for hanging many kinds of people, and gentlemen are not excluded.

The preparations being complete, the two private soldiers stepped aside and each drew away the plank upon which he had been standing. The sergeant turned to the captain, saluted and placed himself immediately behind that officer, who in turn moved apart one pace. These movements left the condemned man and the sergeant standing on the two ends of the same plank, which spanned three of the cross-ties of the bridge. The end upon which the civilian stood almost, but not quite, reached a fourth. This plank had been held in place by the weight of the captain; it was now held by that of the sergeant. At a signal from the former, the latter would step aside, the plank would tilt and the condemned man go down between two ties. The arrangement commended itself to his judgment as simple and effective. His face had not been covered nor his eyes bandaged. He looked a moment at his "unsteadfast footing," then let his gaze wander to the swirling water of the stream racing madly beneath his feet. A piece of dancing driftwood caught his attention and his eyes followed it down the current. How slowly it appeared to move! What a sluggish stream!

5   He closed his eyes in order to fix his last thoughts upon his wife and children. The water, touched to gold by the early sun, the brooding mists under the banks at some distance down the stream, the fort, the soldiers, the piece of drift—all had distracted him. And now he became conscious of a new disturbance. Striking through the thought of his dear ones was a sound which he could neither ignore nor understand, a sharp, distinct, metallic percussion like the stroke of a blacksmith's hammer upon the anvil; it had the same ringing quality. He wondered what it was, and whether immeasurably distant or near by—it seemed both. Its recurrence was regular, but as slow as the tolling of a death knell. He awaited each stroke with impatience and—he knew not why—apprehension. The intervals of silence grew progressively longer, the delays became maddening. With their greater infrequency the sounds increased in strength and sharpness. They hurt his ear like the thrust of a knife; he feared he would shriek. What he heard was the ticking of his watch.

He unclosed his eyes and saw again the water below him. "If I could free my hands," he thought, "I might throw off the noose and spring into the stream. By diving I could evade the bullets, and, swimming vigorously, reach the bank, take to the woods, and get away home. My home, thank God, is as yet outside their lines; my wife and little ones are still beyond the invader's farthest advance."

As these thoughts, which have here to be set down in words, were flashed into the doomed man's brain rather than evolved from it, the captain nodded to the sergeant. The sergeant stepped aside.

II

Peyton Farquhar was a well-to-do planter, of an old and highly-respected Alabama family. Being a slave owner, and, like other slave owners, a politician, he was naturally an original secessionist and ardently devoted to the Southern cause. Circumstances of an imperious nature which it is unnecessary to relate here, had prevented him from taking service with the gallant army which had fought the disastrous campaigns ending with the fall of Corinth,[1] and he chafed under the inglorious restraint, longing for the release of his energies, the larger life of the soldier, the opportunity for distinction. That opportunity, he felt, would come, as it comes to all in war time. Meanwhile he did what he could. No service was too humble for him to perform in aid of the South, no adventure too perilous for him to undertake if consistent with the character of a civilian who was at heart a soldier, and who in good faith and without too much qualification assented to at least a part of the frankly villainous dictum that all is fair in love and war.

One evening while Farquhar and his wife were sitting on a rustic bench near the entrance to his grounds, a grey-clad soldier rode up to the gate and asked for a drink of water. Mrs. Farquhar was only too happy to serve him with her own white hands. While she was gone to fetch the water, her husband approached the dusty horseman and inquired eagerly for news from the front.

"The Yanks are repairing the railroads," said the man, "and are getting 10 ready for another advance. They have reached the Owl Creek bridge, put it in order, and built a stockade on the other bank. The commandant has issued an order, which is posted everywhere, declaring that any civilian caught interfering with the railroad, its bridges, tunnels, or trains, will be summarily hanged. I saw the order."

"How far is it to the Owl Creek bridge?" Farquhar asked.

"About thirty miles."

"Is there no force on this side the creek?"

"Only a picket post half a mile out, on the railroad, and a single sentinel at this end of the bridge."

"Suppose a man—a civilian and student of hanging—should elude the 15 picket post and perhaps get the better of the sentinel," said Farquhar, smiling, "what could he accomplish?"

The soldier reflected. "I was there a month ago," he replied. "I observed that the flood of last winter had lodged a great quantity of driftwood

---

1. Corinth, Mississippi, captured by General Ulysses S. Grant in April 1862.

against the wooden pier at this end of the bridge. It is now dry and would burn like tow."

The lady had now brought the water, which the soldier drank. He thanked her ceremoniously, bowed to her husband, and rode away. An hour later, after nightfall, he repassed the plantation, going northward in the direction from which he had come. He was a Federal scout.

III

As Peyton Farquhar fell straight downward through the bridge, he lost consciousness and was as one already dead. From this state he was awakened—ages later, it seemed to him—by the pain of a sharp pressure upon his throat, followed by a sense of suffocation. Keen, poignant agonies seemed to shoot from his neck downward through every fibre of his body and limbs. These pains appeared to flash along well-defined lines of ramification, and to beat with an inconceivably rapid periodicity. They seemed like streams of pulsating fire heating him to an intolerable temperature. As to his head, he was conscious of nothing but a feeling of fullness—of congestion. These sensations were unaccompanied by thought. The intellectual part of his nature was already effaced; he had power only to feel, and feeling was torment. He was conscious of motion. Encompassed in a luminous cloud, of which he was now merely the fiery heart, without material substance, he swung through unthinkable arcs of oscillation, like a vast pendulum. Then all at once, with terrible suddenness, the light about him shot upward with the noise of a loud plash; a frightful roaring was in his ears, and all was cold and dark. The power of thought was restored; he knew that the rope had broken and he had fallen into the stream. There was no additional strangulation; the noose about his neck was already suffocating him, and kept the water from his lungs. To die of hanging at the bottom of a river!—the idea seemed to him ludicrous. He opened his eyes in the blackness and saw above him a gleam of light, but how distant, how inaccessible! He was still sinking, for the light became fainter and fainter until it was a mere glimmer. Then it began to grow and brighten, and he knew that he was rising toward the surface—knew it with reluctance, for he was now very comfortable. "To be hanged and drowned," he thought, "that is not so bad; but I do not wish to be shot. No; I will not be shot; that is not fair."

He was not conscious of an effort, but a sharp pain in his wrist apprised him that he was trying to free his hands. He gave the struggle his attention, as an idler might observe the feat of a juggler, without interest in the outcome. What splendid effort!—what magnificent, what superhuman strength! Ah, that was a fine endeavour! Bravo! The cord fell away; his arms parted and floated upward, the hands dimly seen on each side in the growing light. He watched them with a new interest as first one and then the other pounced upon the noose at his neck. They tore it away and thrust it fiercely aside, its undulations resembling those of a water-snake. "Put it back, put it back!" He thought he shouted these words to his hands, for the undoing of the noose had been succeeded by the direst pang which he had yet experienced. His neck ached horribly; his brain was on fire; his heart, which had been fluttering faintly, gave a great leap, trying to force itself out at his mouth. His whole body was racked and wrenched with an insupportable anguish! But his disobedient hands gave no heed to the command. They beat the water vigorously with quick, downward strokes, forcing him to the surface. He felt his head emerge; his eyes were blinded by the sunlight; his chest expanded convulsively, and with a supreme and crowning agony his lungs engulfed a great draught of air, which instantly he expelled in a shriek!

He was now in full possession of his physical senses. They were, indeed, 20 preternaturally keen and alert. Something in the awful disturbance of his organic system had so exalted and refined them that they made record of things never before perceived. He felt the ripples upon his face and heard their separate sounds as they struck. He looked at the forest on the bank of the stream, saw the individual trees, the leaves and the veining of each leaf—the very insects upon them, the locusts, the brilliant-bodied flies, the grey spiders stretching their webs from twig to twig. He noted the prismatic colors in all the dewdrops upon a million blades of grass. The humming of the gnats that danced above the eddies of the stream, the beating of the dragon flies' wings, the strokes of the water spiders' legs, like oars which had lifted their boat—all these made audible music. A fish slid along beneath his eyes and he heard the rush of its body parting the water.

He had come to the surface facing down the stream; in a moment the visible world seemed to wheel slowly round, himself the pivotal point, and he saw the bridge, the fort, the soldiers upon the bridge, the captain, the sergeant, the two privates, his executioners. They were in silhouette against the blue sky. They shouted and gesticulated, pointing at him; the captain had drawn his pistol, but did not fire; the others were unarmed. Their movements were grotesque and horrible, their forms gigantic.

Suddenly he heard a sharp report and something struck the water smartly within a few inches of his head, spattering his face with spray. He heard a second report, and saw one of the sentinels with his rifle at his shoulder, a light cloud of blue smoke rising from the muzzle. The man in the water saw the eye of the man on the bridge gazing into his own through the sights of the rifle. He observed that it was a grey eye, and remembered having read that grey eyes were keenest and that all famous marksmen had them. Nevertheless, this one had missed.

A counter swirl had caught Farquhar and turned him half round; he was again looking into the forest on the bank opposite the fort. The sound of a clear, high voice in a monotonous singsong now rang out behind him and came across the water with a distinctness that pierced and subdued all other sounds, even the beating of the ripples in his ears. Although no soldier, he had frequented camps enough to know the dread significance of that deliberate, drawling, aspirated chant; the lieutenant on shore was taking a part in the morning's work. How coldly and pitilessly—with what an even, calm intonation, presaging and enforcing tranquillity in the men—with what accurately-measured intervals fell those cruel words:

"Attention, company.... Shoulder arms.... Ready.... Aim.... Fire."

25   Farquhar dived—dived as deeply as he could. The water roared in his ears like the voice of Niagara, yet he heard the dulled thunder of the volley, and rising again toward the surface, met shining bits of metal, singularly flattened, oscillating slowly downward. Some of them touched him on the face and hands, then fell away, continuing their descent. One lodged between his collar and neck; it was uncomfortably warm, and he snatched it out.

As he rose to the surface, gasping for breath, he saw that he had been a long time under water; he was perceptibly farther down stream—nearer to safety. The soldiers had almost finished reloading; the metal ramrods flashed all at once in the sunshine as they were drawn from the barrels, turned in the air, and thrust into their sockets. The two sentinels fired again, independently and ineffectually.

The hunted man saw all this over his shoulder; he was now swimming vigorously with the current. His brain was as energetic as his arms and legs; he thought with the rapidity of lightning.

"The officer," he reasoned, "will not make that martinet's error a second time. It is as easy to dodge a volley as a single shot. He has probably already given the command to fire at will. God help me, I cannot dodge them all!"

An appalling plash within two yards of him, followed by a loud rushing sound, *diminuendo*, which seemed to travel back through the air to the fort and died in an explosion which stirred the very river to its deeps! A rising sheet of water, which curved over him, fell down upon him, blinded him, strangled him! The cannon had taken a hand in the game. As he shook his head free from the commotion of the smitten water, he heard the deflected shot humming through the air ahead, and in an instant it was cracking and smashing the branches in the forest beyond.

30   "They will not do that again," he thought; "the next time they will use a charge of grape. I must keep my eye upon the gun; the smoke will apprise me—the report arrives too late; it lags behind the missile. It is a good gun."

Suddenly he felt himself whirled round and round—spinning like a top. The water, the banks, the forest, the now distant bridge, fort and men—all were commingled and blurred. Objects were represented by their colors only; circular horizontal streaks of color—that was all he saw. He had been caught in a vortex and was being whirled on with a velocity of advance and gyration which made him giddy and sick. In a few moments he was flung upon the gravel at the foot of the left bank of the stream—the southern bank—and behind a projecting point which concealed him from his enemies. The sudden arrest of his motion, the abrasion of one of his hands on the gravel, restored him and he wept with delight. He dug his fingers into the sand, threw it over himself in handfuls and audibly blessed it. It looked like gold, like diamonds, rubies, emeralds; he could think of nothing beautiful which it did not resemble. The trees upon the bank were giant garden plants; he noted a definite order in their arrangement, inhaled the fragrance of their blooms. A strange, roseate light shone through the spaces among their trunks, and the wind made in their branches the music of æolian harps. He had no wish to perfect his escape, was content to remain in that enchanting spot until retaken.

A whizz and rattle of grapeshot among the branches high above his head roused him from his dream. The baffled cannoneer had fired him a random farewell. He sprang to his feet, rushed up the sloping bank, and plunged into the forest.

All that day he travelled, laying his course by the rounding sun. The forest seemed interminable; nowhere did he discover a break in it, not even a woodman's road. He had not known that he lived in so wild a region. There was something uncanny in the revelation.

By nightfall he was fatigued, footsore, famishing. The thought of his wife and children urged him on. At last he found a road which led him in what he knew to be the right direction. It was as wide and straight as a city street, yet it seemed untravelled. No fields bordered it, no dwelling anywhere. Not so much as the barking of a dog suggested human habitation. The black bodies of the great trees formed a straight wall on both sides, terminating on the horizon in a point, like a diagram in a lesson in perspective. Overhead, as he looked up through this rift in the wood, shone great golden stars looking unfamiliar and grouped in strange constellations. He was sure they were arranged in some order which had a secret and malign significance. The wood on either side was full of singular noises, among which—once, twice, and again—he distinctly heard whispers in an unknown tongue.

His neck was in pain, and, lifting his hand to it, he found it horribly 35 swollen. He knew that it had a circle of black where the rope had bruised it. His eyes felt congested; he could no longer close them. His tongue was swollen with thirst; he relieved its fever by thrusting it forward from between his teeth into the cool air. How softly the turf had carpeted the untravelled avenue! He could no longer feel the roadway beneath his feet!

Doubtless, despite his suffering, he fell asleep while walking, for now he sees another scene—perhaps he has merely recovered from a delirium. He stands at the gate of his own home. All is as he left it, and all bright and beautiful in the morning sunshine. He must have travelled the entire night. As he pushes open the gate and passes up the wide white walk, he sees a flutter of female garments; his wife, looking fresh and cool and sweet, steps down from the verandah to meet him. At the bottom of the steps she stands waiting, with a smile of ineffable joy, an attitude of matchless grace and dignity. Ah, how beautiful she is! He springs forward with extended arms. As he is about to clasp her, he feels a stunning blow upon the back of the neck; a blinding white light blazes all about him, with a sound like the shock of a cannon—then all is darkness and silence!

Peyton Farquhar was dead; his body, with a broken neck, swung gently from side to side beneath the timbers of the Owl Creek bridge.

1891

KATE CHOPIN

The Story of an Hour

Knowing that Mrs. Mallard was afflicted with a heart trouble, great care was taken to break to her as gently as possible the news of her husband's death.

It was her sister Josephine who told her, in broken sentences; veiled hints that revealed in half concealing. Her husband's friend Richards was there, too, near her. It was he who had been in the newspaper office when intelligence of the railroad disaster was received, with Brently Mallard's name leading the list of "killed." He had only taken the time to assure himself of its truth by a second telegram, and had hastened to forestall any less careful, less tender friend in bearing the sad message.

She did not hear the story as many women have heard the same, with a paralyzed inability to accept its significance. She wept at once, with sudden, wild abandonment, in her sister's arms. When the storm of grief had spent itself she went away to her room alone. She would have no one follow her.

There stood, facing the open window, a comfortable, roomy armchair. Into this she sank, pressed down by a physical exhaustion that haunted her body and seemed to reach into her soul.

5   She could see in the open square before her house the tops of trees that were all aquiver with the new spring life. The delicious breath of rain was in the air. In the street below a peddler was crying his wares. The notes of a distant song which some one was singing reached her faintly, and countless sparrows were twittering in the eaves.

There were patches of blue sky showing here and there through the clouds that had met and piled one above the other in the west facing her window.

She sat with her head thrown back upon the cushion of the chair, quite motionless, except when a sob came up into her throat and shook her, as a child who has cried itself to sleep continues to sob in its dreams.

She was young, with a fair, calm face, whose lines bespoke repression and even a certain strength. But now there was a dull stare in her eyes, whose gaze was fixed away off yonder on one of those patches of blue sky.

It was not a glance of reflection, but rather indicated a suspension of intelligent thought.

There was something coming to her and she was waiting for it, fearfully. What was it? She did not know; it was too subtle and elusive to name. But she felt it, creeping out of the sky, reaching toward her through the sounds, the scents, the color that filled the air.

Now her bosom rose and fell tumultuously. She was beginning to recognize this thing that was approaching to possess her, and she was striving to beat it back with her will—as powerless as her two white slender hands would have been.

When she abandoned herself a little whispered word escaped her slightly parted lips. She said it over and over under her breath: "free, free, free!" The vacant stare and the look of terror that had followed it went from her eyes. They stayed keen and bright. Her pulses beat fast, and the coursing blood warmed and relaxed every inch of her body.

She did not stop to ask if it were or were not a monstrous joy that held her. A clear and exalted perception enabled her to dismiss the suggestion as trivial.

She knew that she would weep again when she saw the kind, tender hands folded in death; the face that had never looked save with love upon her, fixed and gray and dead. But she saw beyond that bitter moment a long procession of years to come that would belong to her absolutely. And she opened and spread her arms out to them in welcome.

There would be no one to live for her during those coming years; she would live for herself. There would be no powerful will bending hers in that blind persistence with which men and women believe they have a right to impose a private will upon a fellow-creature. A kind intention or a cruel intention made the act seem no less a crime as she looked upon it in that brief moment of illumination.

And yet she had loved him—sometimes. Often she had not. What did it matter! What could love, the unsolved mystery, count for in face of this possession of self-assertion which she suddenly recognized as the strongest impulse of her being!

"Free! Body and soul free!" she kept whispering.

Josephine was kneeling before the closed door with her lips to the keyhold, imploring for admission. "Louise, open the door! I beg; open the door—you will make yourself ill. What are you doing, Louise? For heaven's sake open the door."

"Go away. I am not making myself ill." No; she was drinking in a very elixir of life through that open window.

Her fancy was running riot along those days ahead of her. Spring days, and summer days, and all sorts of days that would be her own. She breathed a quick prayer that life might be long. It was only yesterday she had thought with a shudder that life might be long.

20   She arose at length and opened the door to her sister's importunities. There was a feverish triumph in her eyes, and she carried herself unwittingly like a goddess of Victory. She clasped her sister's waist, and together they descended the stairs. Richards stood waiting for them at the bottom. Some one was opening the front door with a latchkey. It was Brently Mallard who entered, a little travel-stained, composedly carrying his gripsack and umbrella. He had been far from the scene of accident, and did not even know there had been one. He stood amazed at Josephine's piercing cry; at Richards' quick motion to screen him from the view of his wife.

But Richards was too late.

When the doctors came they said she had died of heart disease—of joy that kills.

1894

WILLIAM FAULKNER

A Rose for Emily

I

When Miss Emily Grierson died, our whole town went to her funeral: the men through a sort of respectful affection for a fallen monument, the women mostly out of curiosity to see the inside of her house, which no one save an old man-servant—a combined gardener and cook—had seen in at least ten years.

It was a big, squarish frame house that had once been white, decorated with cupolas and spires and scrolled balconies in the heavily lightsome style of the seventies,[1] set on what had once been our most select street. But garages and cotton gins had encroached and obliterated even the august names of that neighborhood; only Miss Emily's house was left, lifting its stubborn and coquettish decay above the cotton wagons and the gasoline pumps—an eyesore among eyesores. And now Miss Emily had gone to join the representatives of those august names where they lay in the cedar-bemused cemetery among the ranked and anonymous graves of Union and Confederate soldiers who fell at the battle of Jefferson.

Alive, Miss Emily had been a tradition, a duty, and a care; a sort of hereditary obligation upon the town, dating from that day in 1894 when Colonel Sartoris, the mayor—he who fathered the edict that no Negro woman should appear on the streets without an apron—remitted her taxes, the dispensation dating from the death of her father on into perpetuity. Not that Miss Emily would have accepted charity. Colonel Sartoris invented an

1. The 1870s, the decade following the Civil War between the "Union and Confederate soldiers" mentioned at the end of the paragraph.

involved tale to the effect that Miss Emily's father had loaned money to the town, which the town, as a matter of business, preferred this way of repaying. Only a man of Colonel Sartoris' generation and thought could have invented it, and only a woman could have believed it.

When the next generation, with its more modern ideas, became mayors and aldermen, this arrangement created some little dissatisfaction. On the first of the year they mailed her a tax notice. February came, and there was no reply. They wrote her a formal letter, asking her to call at the sheriff's office at her convenience. A week later the mayor wrote her himself, offering to call or to send his car for her, and received in reply a note on paper of an archaic shape, in a thin, flowing calligraphy in faded ink, to the effect that she no longer went out at all. The tax notice was also enclosed, without comment.

They called a special meeting of the Board of Aldermen. A deputation 5 waited upon her, knocked at the door through which no visitor had passed since she ceased giving china-painting lessons eight or ten years earlier. They were admitted by the old Negro into a dim hall from which a stairway mounted into still more shadow. It smelled of dust and disuse—a close, dank smell. The Negro led them into the parlor. It was furnished in heavy, leather-covered furniture. When the Negro opened the blinds of one window, a faint dust rose sluggishly about their thighs, spinning with slow motes in the single sun-ray. On a tarnished gilt easel before the fireplace stood a crayon portrait of Miss Emily's father.

They rose when she entered—a small, fat woman in black, with a thin gold chain descending to her waist and vanishing into her belt, leaning on an ebony cane with a tarnished gold head. Her skeleton was small and spare; perhaps that was why what would have been merely plumpness in another was obesity in her. She looked bloated, like a body long submerged in motionless water, and of that pallid hue. Her eyes, lost in the fatty ridges of her face, looked like two small pieces of coal pressed into a lump of dough as they moved from one face to another while the visitors stated their errand.

She did not ask them to sit. She just stood in the door and listened quietly until the spokesman came to a stumbling halt. Then they could hear the invisible watch ticking at the end of the gold chain.

Her voice was dry and cold. "I have no taxes in Jefferson. Colonel Sartoris explained it to me. Perhaps one of you can gain access to the city records and satisfy yourselves."

"But we have. We are the city authorities, Miss Emily. Didn't you get a notice from the sheriff, signed by him?"

"I received a paper, yes," Miss Emily said. "Perhaps he considers himself 10 the sheriff. . . . I have no taxes in Jefferson."

"But there is nothing on the books to show that, you see. We must go by the—"

"See Colonel Sartoris. I have no taxes in Jefferson."

"But, Miss Emily—"

"See Colonel Sartoris." (Colonel Sartoris had been dead almost ten years.) "I have no taxes in Jefferson. Tobe!" The Negro appeared. "Show these gentlemen out."

II

15   So she vanquished them, horse and foot, just as she had vanquished their fathers thirty years before about the smell. That was two years after her father's death and a short time after her sweetheart—the one we believed would marry her—had deserted her. After her father's death she went out very little; after her sweetheart went away, people hardly saw her at all. A few of the ladies had the temerity to call, but were not received, and the only sign of life about the place was the Negro man—a young man then—going in and out with a market basket.

"Just as if a man—any man—could keep a kitchen properly," the ladies said; so they were not surprised when the smell developed. It was another link between the gross, teeming world and the high and mighty Griersons.

A neighbor, a woman, complained to the mayor, Judge Stevens, eighty years old.

"But what will you have me do about it, madam?" he said.

"Why, send her word to stop it," the woman said. "Isn't there a law?"

20   "I'm sure that won't be necessary," Judge Stevens said. "It's probably just a snake or a rat that nigger of hers killed in the yard. I'll speak to him about it."

The next day he received two more complaints, one from a man who came in diffident deprecation. "We really must do something about it, Judge. I'd be the last one in the world to bother Miss Emily, but we've got to do something." That night the Board of Aldermen met—three gray-beards and one younger man, a member of the rising generation.

"It's simple enough," he said. "Send her word to have her place cleaned up. Give her a certain time to do it in, and if she don't . . ."

"Dammit, sir," Judge Stevens said, "will you accuse a lady to her face of smelling bad?"

So the next night, after midnight, four men crossed Miss Emily's lawn and slunk about the house like burglars, sniffing along the base of the brickwork and at the cellar openings while one of them performed a regular sowing motion with his hand out of a sack slung from his shoulder. They broke open the cellar door and sprinkled lime there, and in all the outbuildings. As they recrossed the lawn, a window that had been dark was lighted and Miss Emily sat in it, the light behind her, and her upright torso motionless as that of an idol. They crept quietly across the lawn and into the shadow of the locusts that lined the street. After a week or two the smell went away.

25   That was when people had begun to feel really sorry for her. People in our town, remembering how old lady Wyatt, her great-aunt, had gone com-

pletely crazy at last, believed that the Griersons held themselves a little too high for what they really were. None of the young men were quite good enough for Miss Emily and such. We had long thought of them as a tableau; Miss Emily a slender figure in white in the background, her father a spraddled silhouette in the foreground, his back to her and clutching a horsewhip, the two of them framed by the back-flung front door. So when she got to be thirty and was still single, we were not pleased exactly, but vindicated; even with insanity in the family she wouldn't have turned down all of her chances if they had really materialized.

When her father died, it got about that the house was all that was left to her; and in a way, people were glad. At last they could pity Miss Emily. Being left alone, and a pauper, she had become humanized. Now she too would know the old thrill and the old despair of a penny more or less.

The day after his death all the ladies prepared to call at the house and offer condolence and aid, as is our custom. Miss Emily met them at the door, dressed as usual and with no trace of grief on her face. She told them that her father was not dead. She did that for three days, with the ministers calling on her, and the doctors, trying to persuade her to let them dispose of the body. Just as they were about to resort to law and force, she broke down, and they buried her father quickly.

We did not say she was crazy then. We believed she had to do that. We remembered all the young men her father had driven away, and we knew that with nothing left, she would have to cling to that which had robbed her, as people will.

III

She was sick for a long time. When we saw her again, her hair was cut short, making her look like a girl, with a vague resemblance to those angels in colored church windows—sort of tragic and serene.

The town had just let the contracts for paving the sidewalks, and in the summer after her father's death they began to work. The construction company came with niggers and mules and machinery, and a foreman named Homer Barron, a Yankee—a big, dark, ready man, with a big voice and eyes lighter than his face. The little boys would follow in groups to hear him cuss the niggers, and the niggers singing in time to the rise and fall of picks. Pretty soon he knew everybody in town. Whenever you heard a lot of laughing anywhere about the square, Homer Barron would be in the center of the group. Presently we began to see him and Miss Emily on Sunday afternoons driving in the yellow-wheeled buggy and the matched team of bays from the livery stable.

At first we were glad that Miss Emily would have an interest, because the ladies all said, "Of course a Grierson would not think seriously of a Northerner, a day laborer." But there were still others, older people, who said that even grief could not cause a real lady to forget *noblesse oblige*—without calling it *noblesse oblige*.[2] They just said, "Poor Emily. Her kinsfolk should come to her." She had some kin in Alabama; but years ago her father had fallen out with them over the estate of old lady Wyatt, the crazy woman, and there was no communication between the two families. They had not even been represented at the funeral.

And as soon as the old people said, "Poor Emily," the whispering began. "Do you suppose it's really so?" they said to one another. "Of course it is. What else could . . ." This behind their hands; rustling of craned silk and satin behind jalousies[3] closed upon the sun of Sunday afternoon as the thin, swift clop-clop-clop of the matched team passed: "Poor Emily."

She carried her head high enough—even when we believed that she was fallen. It was as if she demanded more than ever the recognition of her dignity as the last Grierson; as if it had wanted that touch of earthiness to reaffirm her imperviousness. Like when she bought the rat poison, the arsenic. That was over a year after they had begun to say "Poor Emily," and while the two female cousins were visiting her.

"I want some poison," she said to the druggist. She was over thirty then, still a slight woman, though thinner than usual, with cold, haughty black eyes in a face the flesh of which was strained across the temples and about the eyesockets as you imagine a lighthouse-keeper's face ought to look. "I want some poison," she said.

35   "Yes, Miss Emily. What kind? For rats and such? I'd recom—"

"I want the best you have. I don't care what kind."

The druggist named several. "They'll kill anything up to an elephant. But what you want is—"

"Arsenic," Miss Emily said. "Is that a good one?"

"Is . . . arsenic? Yes ma'am. But what you want—"

40   "I want arsenic."

The druggist looked down at her. She looked back at him, erect, her face like a strained flag. "Why, of course," the druggist said. "If that's what you want. But the law requires you to tell what you are going to use it for."

Miss Emily just stared at him, her head tilted back in order to look him eye for eye, until he looked away and went and got the arsenic and wrapped it up. The Negro delivery boy brought her the package; the druggist didn't come back. When she opened the package at home there was written on the box, under the skull and bones: "For rats."

IV

So the next day we all said, "She will kill herself"; and we said it would be the best thing. When she had first begun to be seen with Homer Barron, we had said, "She will marry him." Then we said, "She will persuade him yet," because Homer himself had remarked—he liked men, and it was known

2. The obligation, coming with noble or upper-class birth, to behave with honor and generosity toward those less privileged.   3. Window blinds made of adjustable horizontal slats.

that he drank with the younger men in the Elk's Club—that he was not a marrying man. Later we said, "Poor Emily," behind the jalousies as they passed on Sunday afternoon in the glittering buggy, Miss Emily with her head high and Homer Barron with his hat cocked and a cigar in his teeth, reins and whip in a yellow glove.

Then some of the ladies began to say that it was a disgrace to the town and a bad example to the young people. The men did not want to interfere, but at last the ladies forced the Baptist minister—Miss Emily's people were Episcopal—to call upon her. He would never divulge what happened during that interview, but he refused to go back again. The next Sunday they again drove about the streets, and the following day the minister's wife wrote to Miss Emily's relations in Alabama.

So she had blood-kin under her roof again and we sat back to watch developments. At first nothing happened. Then we were sure that they were to be married. We learned that Miss Emily had been to the jeweler's and ordered a man's toilet set in silver, with the letters H. B. on each piece. Two days later we learned that she had bought a complete outfit of men's clothing, including a nightshirt, and we said, "They are married." We were really glad. We were glad because the two female cousins were even more Grierson than Miss Emily had ever been.

So we were not surprised when Homer Barron—the streets had been finished some time since—was gone. We were a little disappointed that there was not a public blowing-off, but we believed that he had gone on to prepare for Miss Emily's coming, or to give her a chance to get rid of the cousins. (By that time it was a cabal, and we were all Miss Emily's allies to help circumvent the cousins.) Sure enough, after another week they departed. And, as we had expected all along, within three days Homer Barron was back in town. A neighbor saw the Negro man admit him at the kitchen door at dusk one evening.

And that was the last we saw of Homer Barron. And of Miss Emily for some time. The Negro man went in and out with the market basket, but the front door remained closed. Now and then we would see her at a window for a moment, as the men did that night when they sprinkled the lime, but for almost six months she did not appear on the streets. Then we knew that this was to be expected too; as if that quality of her father which had thwarted her woman's life so many times had been too virulent and too furious to die.

When we next saw Miss Emily, she had grown fat and her hair was turning gray. During the next few years it grew grayer and grayer until it attained an even pepper-and-salt iron-gray, when it ceased turning. Up to the day of her death at seventy-four it was still that vigorous iron-gray, like the hair of an active man.

From that time on her front door remained closed, save for a period of six or seven years, when she was about forty, during which she gave lessons in china-painting. She fitted up a studio in one of the downstairs rooms, where the daughters and grand-daughters of Colonel Sartoris' contemporaries were sent to her with the same regularity and in the same spirit that they were sent on Sundays with a twenty-five cent piece for the collection plate. Meanwhile her taxes had been remitted.

50   Then the newer generation became the backbone and the spirit of the town, and the painting pupils grew up and fell away and did not send their children to her with boxes of color and tedious brushes and pictures cut from the ladies' magazines. The front door closed upon the last one and remained closed for good. When the town got free postal delivery Miss Emily alone refused to let them fasten the metal numbers above her door and attach a mailbox to it. She would not listen to them.

Daily, monthly, yearly we watched the Negro grow grayer and more stooped, going in and out with the market basket. Each December we sent her a tax notice, which would be returned by the post office a week later, unclaimed. Now and then we would see her in one of the downstairs windows—she had evidently shut up the top floor of the house—like the carven torso of an idol in a niche, looking or not looking at us, we could never tell which. Thus she passed from generation to generation—dear, inescapable, impervious, tranquil, and perverse.

And so she died. Fell ill in the house filled with dust and shadows, with only a doddering Negro man to wait on her. We did not even know she was sick; we had long since given up trying to get any information from the Negro. He talked to no one, probably not even to her, for his voice had grown harsh and rusty, as if from disuse.

She died in one of the downstairs rooms, in a heavy walnut bed with a curtain, her gray head propped on a pillow yellow and moldy with age and lack of sunlight.

V

The Negro met the first of the ladies at the front door and let them in, with their hushed, sibilant voices and their quick, curious glances, and then he disappeared. He walked right through the house and out the back and was not seen again.

55   The two female cousins came at once. They held the funeral on the second day, with the town coming to look at Miss Emily beneath a mass of bought flowers, with the crayon face of her father musing profoundly above the bier and the ladies sibilant and macabre; and the very old men—some in their brushed Confederate uniforms—on the porch and the lawn, talking of Miss Emily as if she had been a contemporary of theirs, believing that they had danced with her and courted her perhaps, confusing time with its mathematical progression, as the old do, to whom all the past is not a diminishing road, but, instead, a huge meadow which no winter ever quite touches, divided from them now by the narrow bottleneck of the most recent decade of years.

Already we knew that there was one room in that region above stairs which no one had seen in forty years, and which would have to be forced. They waited until Miss Emily was decently in the ground before they opened it.

The violence of breaking down the door seemed to fill this room with pervading dust. A thin, acrid pall as of the tomb seemed to lie everywhere upon this room decked and furnished as for a bridal: upon the valance curtains of faded rose color, upon the rose-shaded lights, upon the dressing table, upon the delicate array of crystal and the man's toilet things backed with tarnished silver, silver so tarnished that the monogram was obscured. Among them lay a collar and tie, as if they had just been removed, which, lifted, left upon the surface a pale crescent in the dust. Upon a chair hung the suit, carefully folded; beneath it the two mute shoes and the discarded socks.

The man himself lay in the bed.

For a long while we just stood there, looking down at the profound and fleshless grin. The body had apparently once lain in the attitude of an embrace, but now the long sleep that outlasts love, that conquers even the grimace of love, had cuckolded him. What was left of him, rotted beneath what was left of the nightshirt, had become inextricable from the bed in which he lay; and upon him and upon the pillow beside him lay that even coating of the patient and biding dust.

Then we noticed that in the second pillow was the indentation of a head. 60 One of us lifted something from it, and leaning forward, that faint and invisible dust dry and acrid in the nostrils, we saw a long strand of iron-gray hair.

1931

CHARLOTTE PERKINS GILMAN

The Yellow Wallpaper

It is very seldom that mere ordinary people like John and myself secure ancestral halls for the summer.

A colonial mansion, a hereditary estate, I would say a haunted house, and reach the height of romantic felicity—but that would be asking too much of fate!

Still I will proudly declare that there is something queer about it.

Else, why should it be let so cheaply? And why have stood so long untenanted?

John laughs at me, of course, but one expects that in marriage. 5

John is practical in the extreme. He has no patience with faith, an intense horror of superstition, and he scoffs openly at any talk of things not to be felt and seen and put down in figures.

John is a physician, and *perhaps*—(I would not say it to a living soul, of course, but this is dead paper and a great relief to my mind—) *perhaps* that is one reason I do not get well faster.

You see he does not believe I am sick!

And what can one do?

10   If a physician of high standing, and one's own husband, assures friends and relatives that there is really nothing the matter with one but temporary nervous depression—a slight hysterical tendency—what is one to do?

My brother is also a physician, and also of high standing, and he says the same thing.

So I take phosphates or phosphites—whichever it is, and tonics, and journeys, and air, and exercise, and am absolutely forbidden to "work" until I am well again.

Personally, I disagree with their ideas.

Personally, I believe that congenial work, with excitement and change, would do me good.

15   But what is one to do?

I did write for a while in spite of them; but it *does* exhaust me a good deal—having to be so sly about it, or else meet with heavy opposition.

I sometimes fancy that in my condition if I had less opposition and more society and stimulus—but John says the very worst thing I can do is to think about my condition, and I confess it always makes me feel bad.

So I will let it alone and talk about the house.

The most beautiful place! It is quite alone, standing well back from the road, quite three miles from the village. It makes me think of English places that you read about, for there are hedges and walls and gates that lock, and lots of separate little houses for the gardeners and people.

20   There is a *delicious* garden! I never saw such a garden—large and shady, full of box-bordered paths, and lined with long grape-covered arbors with seats under them.

There were greenhouses, too, but they are all broken now.

There was some legal trouble, I believe, something about the heirs and co-heirs; anyhow, the place has been empty for years.

That spoils my ghostliness, I am afraid, but I don't care—there is something strange about the house—I can feel it.

I even said so to John one moonlight evening, but he said what I felt was a *draught,* and shut the window.

25   I get unreasonably angry with John sometimes. I'm sure I never used to be so sensitive. I think it is due to this nervous condition.

But John says if I feel so, I shall neglect proper self-control; so I take pains to control myself—before him, at least, and that makes me very tired.

I don't like our room a bit. I wanted one downstairs that opened on the piazza and had roses all over the window, and such pretty old-fashioned chintz hangings! but John would not hear of it.

He said there was only one window and not room for two beds, and no near room for him if he took another.

He is very careful and loving, and hardly lets me stir without special direction.

I have a schedule prescription for each hour in the day; he takes all care 30 from me, and so I feel basely ungrateful not to value it more.

He said we came here solely on my account, that I was to have perfect rest and all the air I could get. "Your exercise depends on your strength, my dear," said he, "and your food somewhat on your appetite; but air you can absorb all the time." So we took the nursery at the top of the house.

It is a big, airy room, the whole floor nearly, with windows that look all ways, and air and sunshine galore. It was nursery first and then playroom and gymnasium, I should judge; for the windows are barred for little children, and there are rings and things in the walls.

The paint and paper look as if a boys' school had used it. It is stripped off—the paper—in great patches all around the head of my bed, about as far as I can reach, and in a great place on the other side of the room low down. I never saw a worse paper in my life.

One of those sprawling flamboyant patterns committing every artistic sin.

It is dull enough to confuse the eye in following, pronounced enough to 35 constantly irritate and provoke study, and when you follow the lame uncertain curves for a little distance they suddenly commit suicide—plunge off at outrageous angles, destroy themselves in unheard of contradictions.

The color is repellant, almost revolting; a smouldering unclean yellow, strangely faded by the slow-turning sunlight.

It is a dull yet lurid orange in some places, a sickly sulphur tint in others.

No wonder the children hated it! I should hate it myself if I had to live in this room long.

There comes John, and I must put this away,—he hates to have me write a word.

We have been here two weeks, and I haven't felt like writing before, since 40 that first day.

I am sitting by the window now, up in this atrocious nursery, and there is nothing to hinder my writing as much as I please, save lack of strength.

John is away all day, and even some nights when his cases are serious.

I am glad my case is not serious!

But these nervous troubles are dreadfully depressing.

John does not know how much I really suffer. He knows there is no *rea-* 45 *son* to suffer, and that satisfies him.

Of course it is only nervousness. It does weigh on me so not to do my duty in any way!

I mean to be such a help to John, such a real rest and comfort, and here I am a comparative burden already!

Nobody would believe what an effort it is to do what little I am able,—to dress and entertain, and order things.

It is fortunate Mary is so good with the baby. Such a dear baby!

50   And yet I *cannot* be with him, it makes me so nervous.

I suppose John never was nervous in his life. He laughs at me so about this wallpaper!

At first he meant to repaper the room, but afterwards he said that I was letting it get the better of me, and that nothing was worse for a nervous patient than to give way to such fancies.

He said that after the wallpaper was changed it would be the heavy bedstead, and then the barred windows, and then that gate at the head of the stairs, and so on.

"You know the place is doing you good," he said, "and really, dear, I don't care to renovate the house just for a three months' rental."

55   "Then do let us go downstairs," I said, "there are such pretty rooms there."

Then he took me in his arms and called me a blessed little goose, and said he would go down cellar, if I wished, and have it whitewashed into the bargain.

But he is right enough about the beds and windows and things.

It is an airy and comfortable room as any one need wish, and, of course, I would not be so silly as to make him uncomfortable just for a whim.

I'm really getting quite fond of the big room, all but that horrid paper.

60   Out of one window I can see the garden, those mysterious deep-shaded arbors, the riotous old-fashioned flowers, and bushes and gnarly trees.

Out of another I get a lovely view of the bay and a little private wharf belonging to the estate. There is a beautiful shaded lane that runs down there from the house. I always fancy I see people walking in these numerous paths and arbors, but John has cautioned me not to give way to fancy in the least. He says that with my imaginative power and habit of story-making, a nervous weakness like mine is sure to lead to all manner of excited fancies, and that I ought to use my will and good sense to check the tendency. So I try.

I think sometimes that if I were only well enough to write a little it would relieve the press of ideas and rest me.

But I find I get pretty tired when I try.

It is so discouraging not to have any advice and companionship about my work. When I get really well, John says we will ask Cousin Henry and Julia down for a long visit; but he says he would as soon put fireworks in my pillow-case as to let me have those stimulating people about now.

65   I wish I could get well faster.

But I must not think about that. This paper looks to me as if it *knew* what a vicious influence it had!

There is a recurrent spot where the pattern lolls like a broken neck and two bulbous eyes stare at you upside down.

I get positively angry with the impertinence of it and the everlastingness. Up and down and sideways they crawl, and those absurd, unblinking eyes are everywhere. There is one place where two breadths didn't match, and the eyes go all up and down the line, one a little higher than the other.

I never saw so much expression in an inanimate thing before, and we all know how much expression they have! I used to lie awake as a child and get more entertainment and terror out of blank walls and plain furniture than most children could find in a toy-store.

I remember what a kindly wink the knobs of our big, old bureau used to have, and there was one chair that always seemed like a strong friend. 70

I used to feel that if any of the other things looked too fierce I could always hop into that chair and be safe.

The furniture in this room is no worse than inharmonious, however, for we had to bring it all from downstairs. I suppose when this was used as a playroom they had to take the nursery things out, and no wonder! I never saw such ravages as the children have made here.

The wallpaper, as I said before, is torn off in spots, and it sticketh closer than a brother—they must have had perseverance as well as hatred.

Then the floor is scratched and gouged and splintered, the plaster itself is dug out here and there, and this great heavy bed which is all we found in the room, looks as if it had been through the wars.

But I don't mind it a bit—only the paper. 75

There comes John's sister. Such a dear girl as she is, and so careful of me! I must not let her find me writing.

She is a perfect and enthusiastic housekeeper, and hopes for no better profession. I verily believe she thinks it is the writing which made me sick!

But I can write when she is out, and see her a long way off from these windows.

There is one that commands the road, a lovely shaded winding road, and one that just looks off over the country. A lovely country, too, full of great elms and velvet meadows.

This wallpaper has a kind of sub-pattern in a different shade, a particu- 80 larly irritating one, for you can only see it in certain lights, and not clearly then.

But in the places where it isn't faded and where the sun is just so—I can see a strange, provoking, formless sort of figure, that seems to skulk about behind that silly and conspicuous front design.

There's sister on the stairs!

Well, the Fourth of July is over! The people are all gone and I am tired out. John thought it might do me good to see a little company, so we just had mother and Nellie and the children down for a week.

Of course I didn't do a thing. Jennie sees to everything now.

85   But it tired me all the same.

John says if I don't pick up faster he shall send me to Weir Mitchell[1] in the fall.

But I don't want to go there at all. I had a friend who was in his hands once, and she says he is just like John and my brother, only more so!

Besides, it is such an undertaking to go so far.

I don't feel as if it was worth while to turn my hand over for anything, and I'm getting dreadfully fretful and querulous.

90   I cry at nothing, and cry most of the time.

Of course I don't when John is here, or anybody else, but when I am alone.

And I am alone a good deal just now. John is kept in town very often by serious cases, and Jennie is good and lets me alone when I want her to.

So I walk a little in the garden or down that lovely lane, sit on the porch under the roses, and lie down up here a good deal.

I'm getting really fond of the room in spite of the wallpaper. Perhaps *because* of the wallpaper.

95   It dwells in my mind so!

I lie here on this great immovable bed—it is nailed down, I believe—and follow that pattern about by the hour. It is as good as gymnastics, I assure you. I start, we'll say, at the bottom, down in the corner over there where it has not been touched, and I determine for the thousandth time that I *will* follow that pointless pattern to some sort of conclusion.

I know a little of the principle of design, and I know this thing was not arranged on any laws of radiation, or alternation, or repetition, or symmetry, or anything else that I ever heard of.

It is repeated, of course, by the breadths, but not otherwise.

Looked at in one way each breadth stands alone, the bloated curves and flourishes—a kind of "debased Romanesque" with *delirium tremens*—go waddling up and down in isolated columns of fatuity.

100   But, on the other hand, they connect diagonally, and the sprawling outlines run off in great slanting waves of optic horror, like a lot of wallowing seaweeds in full chase.

The whole thing goes horizontally, too, at least it seems so, and I exhaust myself in trying to distinguish the order of its going in that direction.

They have used a horizontal breadth for a frieze, and that adds wonderfully to the confusion.

There is one end of the room where it is almost intact, and there, when the crosslights fade and the low sun shines directly upon it, I can almost fancy radiation after all,—the interminable grotesque seem to form around a common center and rush off in headlong plunges of equal distraction.

It makes me tired to follow it. I will take a nap I guess.

1. Silas Weir Mitchell (1829-1914), American physician, novelist, and specialist in nerve disorders, popularized the rest cure.

I don't know why I should write this. 105
    I don't want to.
    I don't feel able.
    And I know John would think it absurd. But I *must* say what I feel and think in some way—it is such a relief!
    But the effort is getting to be greater than the relief.
    Half the time now I am awfully lazy, and lie down ever so much. 110
    John says I mustn't lose my strength, and has me take cod liver oil and lots of tonics and things, to say nothing of ale and wine and rare meat.
    Dear John! He loves me very dearly, and hates to have me sick. I tried to have a real earnest reasonable talk with him the other day, and tell him how I wish he would let me go and make a visit to Cousin Henry and Julia.
    But he said I wasn't able to go, nor able to stand it after I got there; and I did not make out a very good case for myself, for I was crying before I had finished.
    It is getting to be a great effort for me to think straight. Just this nervous weakness I suppose.
    And dear John gathered me up in his arms, and just carried me upstairs 115 and laid me on the bed, and sat by me and read to me till it tired my head.
    He said I was his darling and his comfort and all he had, and that I must take care of myself for his sake, and keep well.
    He says no one but myself can help me out of it, that I must use my will and self-control and not let any silly fancies run away with me.
    There's one comfort, the baby is well and happy, and does not have to occupy this nursery with the horrid wallpaper.
    If we had not used it, that blessed child would have! What a fortunate escape! Why, I wouldn't have a child of mine, an impressionable little thing, live in such a room for worlds.
    I never thought of it before, but it is lucky that John kept me here after 120 all, I can stand it so much easier than a baby, you see.
    Of course I never mention it to them any more—I am too wise,—but I keep watch of it all the same.
    There are things in that paper that nobody knows but me, or ever will.
    Behind that outside pattern the dim shapes get clearer every day.
    It is always the same shape, only very numerous.
    And it is like a woman stooping down and creeping about behind that 125 pattern. I don't like it a bit. I wonder—I begin to think—I wish John would take me away from here!

It is so hard to talk with John about my case, because he is so wise, and because he loves me so.
    But I tried it last night.
    It was moonlight. The moon shines in all around just as the sun does.

I hate to see it sometimes, it creeps so slowly, and always comes in by one window or another.

130   John was asleep and I hated to waken him, so I kept still and watched the moonlight on that undulating wallpaper till I felt creepy.

The faint figure behind seemed to shake the pattern, just as if she wanted to get out.

I got up softly and went to feel and see if the paper *did* move, and when I came back John was awake.

"What is it, little girl?" he said. "Don't go walking about like that—you'll get cold."

I thought it was a good time to talk, so I told him that I really was not gaining here, and that I wished he would take me away.

135   "Why, darling!" said he, "our lease will be up in three weeks, and I can't see how to leave before.

"The repairs are not done at home, and I cannot possibly leave town just now. Of course if you were in any danger, I could and would, but you really are better, dear, whether you can see it or not. I am a doctor, dear, and I know. You are gaining flesh and color, your appetite is better, I feel really much easier about you."

"I don't weigh a bit more," said I, "nor as much; and my appetite may be better in the evening when you are here, but it is worse in the morning when you are away!"

"Bless her little heart!" said he with a big hug, "she shall be as sick as she pleases! But now let's improve the shining hours by going to sleep, and talk about it in the morning!"

"And you won't go away?" I asked gloomily.

140   "Why, how can I, dear? It is only three weeks more and then we will take a nice little trip of a few days while Jennie is getting the house ready. Really dear you are better!"

"Better in body perhaps—" I began, and stopped short, for he sat up straight and looked at me with such a stern, reproachful look that I could not say another word.

"My darling," said he, "I beg of you, for my sake and for our child's sake, as well as for your own, that you will never for one instant let that idea enter your mind! There is nothing so dangerous, so fascinating, to a temperament like yours. It is a false and foolish fancy. Can you not trust me as a physician when I tell you so?"

So of course I said no more on that score, and we went to sleep before long. He thought I was asleep first, but I wasn't, and lay there for hours trying to decide whether that front pattern and the back pattern really did move together or separately.

On a pattern like this, by daylight, there is a lack of sequence, a defiance of law, that is a constant irritant to a normal mind.

The color is hideous enough, and unreliable enough, and infuriating 145 enough, but the pattern is torturing.

You think you have mastered it, but just as you get well underway in following, it turns a back-somersault and there you are. It slaps you in the face, knocks you down, and tramples upon you. It is like a bad dream.

The outside pattern is a florid arabesque, reminding one of a fungus. If you can imagine a toadstool in joints, an interminable string of toadstools, budding and sprouting in endless convolutions—why, that is something like it.

That is, sometimes!

There is one marked peculiarity about this paper, a thing nobody seems to notice but myself, and that is that it changes as the light changes.

When the sun shoots in through the east window—I always watch for 150 that first long, straight ray—it changes so quickly that I never can quite believe it.

That is why I watch it always.

By moonlight—the moon shines in all night when there is a moon—I wouldn't know it was the same paper.

At night in any kind of light, in twilight, candlelight, lamplight, and worst of all by moonlight, it becomes bars! The outside pattern I mean, and the woman behind it is as plain as can be.

I didn't realize for a long time what the thing was that showed behind, that dim sub-pattern, but now I am quite sure it is a woman.

By daylight she is subdued, quiet. I fancy it is the pattern that keeps her 155 so still. It is so puzzling. It keeps me quiet by the hour.

I lie down ever so much now. John says it is good for me, and to sleep all I can.

Indeed he started the habit by making me lie down for an hour after each meal.

It is a very bad habit I am convinced, for you see I don't sleep.

And that cultivates deceit, for I don't tell them I'm awake—O no!

The fact is I am getting a little afraid of John. 160

He seems very queer sometimes, and even Jennie has an inexplicable look.

It strikes me occasionally, just as a scientific hypothesis,—that perhaps it is the paper!

I have watched John when he did not know I was looking, and come into the room suddenly on the most innocent excuses, and I've caught him several times *looking at the paper!* And Jennie too. I caught Jennie with her hand on it once.

She didn't know I was in the room, and when I asked her in a quiet, a very quiet voice, with the most restrained manner possible, what she was doing with the paper—she turned around as if she had been caught stealing, and looked quite angry—asked me why I should frighten her so!

165   Then she said that the paper stained everything it touched, that she had found yellow smooches on all my clothes and John's, and she wished we would be more careful!

Did not that sound innocent? But I know she was studying that pattern, and I am determined that nobody shall find it out but myself!

Life is very much more exciting now than it used to be. You see I have something more to expect, to look forward to, to watch. I really do eat better, and am more quiet than I was.

John is so pleased to see me improve! He laughed a little the other day, and said I seemed to be flourishing in spite of my wallpaper.

I turned it off with a laugh. I had no intention of telling him it was *because* of the wallpaper—he would make fun of me. He might even want to take me away.

170   I don't want to leave now until I have found it out. There is a week more, and I think that will be enough.

I'm feeling ever so much better! I don't sleep much at night, for it is so interesting to watch developments; but I sleep a good deal in the daytime.

In the daytime it is tiresome and perplexing.

There are always new shoots on the fungus, and new shades of yellow all over it. I cannot keep count of them, though I have tried conscientiously.

It is the strangest yellow, that wallpaper! It makes me think of all the yellow things I ever saw—not beautiful ones like buttercups, but old foul, bad yellow things.

175   But there is something else about that paper—the smell! I noticed it the moment we came into the room, but with so much air and sun it was not bad. Now we have had a week of fog and rain, and whether the windows are open or not, the smell is here.

It creeps all over the house.

I find it hovering in the dining-room, skulking in the parlor, hiding in the hall, lying in wait for me on the stairs.

It gets into my hair.

Even when I go to ride, if I turn my head suddenly and surprise it—there is that smell!

180   Such a peculiar odor, too! I have spent hours in trying to analyze it, to find what it smelled like.

It is not bad—at first, and very gentle, but quite the subtlest, most enduring odor I ever met.

In this damp weather it is awful, I wake up in the night and find it hanging over me.

It used to disturb me at first. I thought seriously of burning the house— to reach the smell.

But now I am used to it. The only thing I can think of that it is like is the *color* of the paper! A yellow smell.

There is a very funny mark on this wall, low down, near the mopboard. A streak that runs round the room. It goes behind every piece of furniture, except the bed, a long, straight, even *smooch,* as if it had been rubbed over and over.

I wonder how it was done and who did it, and what they did it for. Round and round and round—round and round and round—it makes me dizzy!

I really have discovered something at last.

Through watching so much at night, when it changes so, I have finally found out.

The front pattern *does* move—and no wonder! The woman behind shakes it!

Sometimes I think there are a great many women behind, and sometimes only one, and she crawls around fast, and her crawling shakes it all over.

Then in the very bright spots she keeps still, and in the very shady spots she just takes hold of the bars and shakes them hard.

And she is all the time trying to climb through. But nobody could climb through that pattern—it strangles so; I think that is why it has so many heads.

They get through, and then the pattern strangles them off and turns them upside down, and makes their eyes white!

If those heads were covered or taken off it would not be half so bad.

I think that woman gets out in the daytime!

And I'll tell you why—privately—I've seen her!

I can see her out of every one of my windows!

It is the same woman, I know, for she is always creeping, and most women do not creep by daylight.

I see her in that long shaded lane, creeping up and down. I see her in those dark grape arbors, creeping all around the garden.

I see her on that long road under the trees, creeping along, and when a carriage comes she hides under the blackberry vines.

I don't blame her a bit. It must be very humiliating to be caught creeping by daylight!

I always lock the door when I creep by daylight. I can't do it at night, for I know John would suspect something at once.

And John is so queer now, that I don't want to irritate him. I wish he would take another room! Besides, I don't want anybody to get that woman out at night but myself.

I often wonder if I could see her out of all the windows at once.

But, turn as fast as I can, I can only see out of one at one time.

And though I always see her, she *may* be able to creep faster than I can turn!

I have watched her sometimes away off in the open country, creeping as fast as a cloud shadow in a high wind.

If only that top pattern could be gotten off from the under one! I mean to try it, little by little.

I have found out another funny thing, but I shan't tell it this time! It does not do to trust people too much.

210 There are only two more days to get this paper off, and I believe John is beginning to notice. I don't like the look in his eyes.

And I heard him ask Jennie a lot of professional questions about me. She had a very good report to give.

She said I slept a good deal in the daytime.

John knows I don't sleep very well at night, for all I'm so quiet!

He asked me all sorts of questions, too, and pretended to be very loving and kind.

215 As if I couldn't see through him!

Still, I don't wonder he acts so, sleeping under this paper for three months.

It only interests me, but I feel sure John and Jennie are secretly affected by it.

Hurrah! This is the last day, but it is enough. John is to stay in town over night, and won't be out until this evening.

Jennie wanted to sleep with me—the sly thing! but I told her I should undoubtedly rest better for a night all alone.

220 That was clever, for really I wasn't alone a bit! As soon as it was moonlight and that poor thing began to crawl and shake the pattern, I got up and ran to help her.

I pulled and she shook, I shook and she pulled, and before morning we had peeled off yards of that paper.

A strip about as high as my head and half around the room.

And then when the sun came and that awful pattern began to laugh at me, I declared I would finish it to-day!

We go away to-morrow, and they are moving all my furniture down again to leave things as they were before.

225 Jennie looked at the wall in amazement, but I told her merrily that I did it out of pure spite at the vicious thing.

She laughed and said she wouldn't mind doing it herself, but I must not get tired.

How she betrayed herself that time!

But I am here, and no person touches this paper but me,—not *alive!*

She tried to get me out of the room—it was too patent! But I said it was so quiet and empty and clean now that I believed I would lie down again and sleep all I could; and not to wake me even for dinner—I would call when I woke.

So now she is gone, and the servants are gone, and the things are gone, and there is nothing left but that great bedstead nailed down, with the canvas mattress we found on it.

We shall sleep downstairs to-night, and take the boat home to-morrow.

I quite enjoy the room, now it is bare again.

How those children did tear about here!

This bedstead is fairly gnawed!

But I must get to work.

I have locked the door and thrown the key down into the front path.

I don't want to go out, and I don't want to have anybody come in, till John comes.

I want to astonish him.

I've got a rope up here that even Jennie did not find. If that woman does get out, and tries to get away, I can tie her!

But I forgot I could not reach far without anything to stand on!

This bed will *not* move!

I tried to lift and push it until I was lame, and then I got so angry I bit off a little piece at one corner—but it hurt my teeth.

Then I peeled off all the paper I could reach standing on the floor. It sticks horribly and the pattern just enjoys it! All those strangled heads and bulbous eyes and waddling fungus growths just shriek with derision!

I am getting angry enough to do something desperate. To jump out of the window would be admirable exercise, but the bars are too strong even to try.

Besides I wouldn't do it. Of course not. I know well enough that a step like that is improper and might be misconstrued.

I don't like to *look* out of the windows even—there are so many of those creeping women, and they creep so fast.

I wonder if they all come out of that wallpaper as I did?

But I am securely fastened now by my well-hidden rope—you don't get *me* out in the road there!

I suppose I shall have to get back behind the pattern when it comes night, and that is hard!

It is so pleasant to be out in this great room and creep around as I please!

I don't want to go outside. I won't, even if Jennie asks me to.

For outside you have to creep on the ground, and everything is green instead of yellow.

But here I can creep smoothly on the floor, and my shoulder just fits in that long smooch around the wall, so I cannot lose my way.

Why there's John at the door!

It is no use, young man, you can't open it!

How he does call and pound!

Now he's crying for an axe.

It would be a shame to break down that beautiful door!

"John dear!" said I in the gentlest voice, "the key is down by the front steps, under a plantain leaf!"

260   That silenced him for a few moments.

Then he said—very quietly indeed, "Open the door, my darling!"

"I can't," said I. "The key is down by the front door under a plantain leaf!"

And then I said it again, several times, very gently and slowly, and said it so often that he had to go and see, and he got it of course, and came in. He stopped short by the door.

"What is the matter?" he cried. "For God's sake, what are you doing!"

265   I kept on creeping just the same, but I looked at him over my shoulder.

"I've got out at last," said I, "in spite of you and Jane. And I've pulled off most of the paper, so you can't put me back!"

Now why should that man have fainted? But he did, and right across my path by the wall, so that I had to creep over him every time!

                                                                        1892

JAMES JOYCE

Araby

North Richmond Street, being blind,[1] was a quiet street except at the hour when the Christian Brothers' School set the boys free. An uninhabited house of two storeys stood at the blind end, detached from its neighbours in a square ground. The other houses of the street, conscious of decent lives within them, gazed at one another with brown imperturbable faces.

The former tenant of our house, a priest, had died in the back drawing-room. Air, musty from having been long enclosed, hung in all the rooms, and the waste room behind the kitchen was littered with old useless papers. Among these I found a few paper-covered books, the pages of which were curled and damp: *The Abbot*, by Walter Scott, *The Devout Communicant* and *The Memoirs of Vidocq*.[2] I liked the last best because its leaves were yellow. The wild garden behind the house contained a central apple-tree and a few straggling bushes under one of which I found the late tenant's rusty

1. That is, a dead-end street.
2. The "memoirs" were probably *not* written by François Vidocq (1775-1857), a French criminal who became chief of detectives and who died poor and disgraced for his part in a crime that he solved; the 1820 novel by Sir Walter Scott (1771-1834) is a romance about the Catholic Mary, Queen of Scots (1542-87), who was beheaded; *The Devout Communicant: or Pious Meditations and Aspirations for the Three Days Before and Three Days after Receiving the Holy Eucharist* (1813) is a Catholic religious tract.

bicycle-pump. He had been a very charitable priest; in his will he had left all his money to institutions and the furniture of his house to his sister.

When the short days of winter came dusk fell before we had well eaten our dinners. When we met in the street the houses had grown sombre. The space of sky above us was the colour of ever-changing violet and towards it the lamps of the street lifted their feeble lanterns. The cold air stung us and we played till our bodies glowed. Our shouts echoed in the silent street. The career of our play brought us through the dark muddy lanes behind the houses where we ran the gantlet of the rough tribes from the cottages, to the back doors of the dark dripping gardens where odours arose from the ashpits,[3] to the dark odorous stables where a coachman smoothed and combed the horse or shook music from the buckled harness. When we returned to the street light from the kitchen windows had filled the areas. If my uncle was seen turning the corner we hid in the shadow until we had seen him safely housed. Or if Mangan's sister came out on the doorstep to call her brother in to his tea we watched her from our shadow peer up and down the street. We waited to see whether she would remain or go in and, if she remained, we left our shadow and walked up to Mangan's steps resignedly. She was waiting for us, her figure defined by the light from the half-opened door. Her brother always teased her before he obeyed and I stood by the railings looking at her. Her dress swung as she moved her body and the soft rope of her hair tossed from side to side.

Every morning I lay on the floor in the front parlour watching her door. The blind was pulled down to within an inch of the sash so that I could not be seen. When she came out on the doorstep my heart leaped. I ran to the hall, seized my books and followed her. I kept her brown figure always in my eye and, when we came near the point at which our ways diverged, I quickened my pace and passed her. This happened morning after morning. I had never spoken to her, except for a few casual words, and yet her name was like a summons to all my foolish blood.

Her image accompanied me even in places the most hostile to romance. 5 On Saturday evenings when my aunt went marketing I had to go to carry some of the parcels. We walked through the flaring streets, jostled by drunken men and bargaining women, amid the curses of labourers, the shrill litanies of shop-boys who stood on guard by the barrels of pigs' cheeks, the nasal chanting of street-singers, who sang a *come-all-you* about O'Donovan Rossa,[4] or a ballad about the troubles in our native land. These noises converged in a single sensation of life for me: I imagined that

---

3. Where fireplace ashes and other household refuse were dumped.
4. Jeremiah O'Donovan (1831–1915) was a militant Irish nationalist who fought on despite terms in prison and banishment. *Come-all-you:* a song, of which there were many, that began "Come, all you Irishmen."

I bore my chalice safely through a throng of foes. Her name sprang to my lips at moments in strange prayers and praises which I myself did not understand. My eyes were often full of tears (I could not tell why) and at times a flood from my heart seemed to pour itself out into my bosom. I thought little of the future. I did not know whether I would ever speak to her or not or, if I spoke to her, how I could tell her of my confused adoration. But my body was like a harp and her words and gestures were like fingers running upon the wires.

One evening I went into the back drawing-room in which the priest had died. It was a dark rainy evening and there was no sound in the house. Through one of the broken panes I heard the rain impinge upon the earth, the fine incessant needles of water playing in the sodden beds. Some distant lamp or lighted window gleamed below me. I was thankful that I could see so little. All my senses seemed to desire to veil themselves and, feeling that I was about to slip from them, I pressed the palms of my hands together until they trembled, murmuring: *O love! O love!* many times.

At last she spoke to me. When she addressed the first words to me I was so confused that I did not know what to answer. She asked me was I going to *Araby.*[5] I forget whether I answered yes or no. It would be a splendid bazaar, she said; she would love to go.

—And why can't you? I asked.

While she spoke she turned a silver bracelet round and round her wrist. She could not go, she said, because there would be a retreat[6] that week in her convent. Her brother and two other boys were fighting for their caps

5. A charity bazaar billed as a "Grand Oriental Fete," Dublin, May 1894.
6. A period of withdrawal dedicated to prayer and religious study.

and I was alone at the railings. She held one of the spikes, bowing her head towards me. The light from the lamp opposite our door caught the white curve of her neck, lit up her hair that rested there and, falling, lit up the hand upon the railing. It fell over one side of her dress and caught the white border of a petticoat, just visible as she stood at ease.

—It's well for you, she said.   10

—If I go, I said, I will bring you something.

What innumerable follies laid waste my waking and sleeping thoughts after that evening! I wished to annihilate the tedious intervening days. I chafed against the work of school. At night in my bedroom and by day in the classroom her image came between me and the page I strove to read. The syllables of the word *Araby* were called to me through the silence in which my soul luxuriated and cast an Eastern enchantment over me. I asked for leave to go to the bazaar on Saturday night. My aunt was surprised and hoped it was not some Freemason[7] affair. I answered few questions in class. I watched my master's face pass from amiability to sternness; he hoped I was not beginning to idle. I could not call my wandering thoughts together. I had hardly any patience with the serious work of life which, now that it stood between me and my desire, seemed to me child's play, ugly monotonous child's play.

On Saturday morning I reminded my uncle that I wished to go to the bazaar in the evening. He was fussing at the hall-stand, looking for the hat-brush, and answered me curtly:

—Yes, boy, I know.

As he was in the hall I could not go into the front parlour and lie at the   15
window. I left the house in bad humour and walked slowly towards the school. The air was pitilessly raw and already my heart misgave me.

When I came home to dinner my uncle had not yet been home. Still it was early. I sat staring at the clock for some time and, when its ticking began to irritate me, I left the room. I mounted the staircase and gained the upper part of the house. The high cold empty gloomy rooms liberated me and I went from room to room singing. From the front window I saw my companions playing below in the street. Their cries reached me weakened and indistinct and, leaning my forehead against the cool glass, I looked over at the dark house where she lived. I may have stood there for an hour, seeing nothing but the brown-clad figure cast by my imagination, touched discreetly by the lamplight at the curved neck, at the hand upon the railings and at the border below the dress.

When I came downstairs again I found Mrs Mercer sitting at the fire. She was an old garrulous woman, a pawnbroker's widow, who collected used stamps for some pious purpose. I had to endure the gossip of the tea-table.

---

7. Freemasons—members of an influential, secretive, and highly ritualistic fraternal organization—were considered enemies of the Catholics.

The meal was prolonged beyond an hour and still my uncle did not come. Mrs Mercer stood up to go: she was sorry she couldn't wait any longer, but it was after eight o'clock and she did not like to be out late, as the night air was bad for her. When she had gone I began to walk up and down the room, clenching my fists. My aunt said:

—I'm afraid you may put off your bazaar for this night of Our Lord.

At nine o'clock I heard my uncle's latchkey in the halldoor. I heard him talking to himself and heard the hallstand rocking when it had received the weight of his overcoat. I could interpret these signs. When he was midway through his dinner I asked him to give me the money to go to the bazaar. He had forgotten.

20   —The people are in bed and after their first sleep now, he said.

I did not smile. My aunt said to him energetically:

—Can't you give him the money and let him go? You've kept him late enough as it is.

My uncle said he was very sorry he had forgotten. He said he believed in the old saying: *All work and no play makes Jack a dull boy.* He asked me where I was going and, when I had told him a second time he asked me did I know *The Arab's Farewell to his Steed.*[8] When I left the kitchen he was about to recite the opening lines of the piece to my aunt.

I held a florin[9] tightly in my hand as I strode down Buckingham Street towards the station. The sight of the streets thronged with buyers and glaring with gas recalled to me the purpose of my journey. I took my seat in a third-class carriage of a deserted train. After an intolerable delay the train moved out of the station slowly. It crept onward among ruinous houses and over the twinkling river. At Westland Row Station a crowd of people pressed to the carriage doors; but the porters moved them back, saying that it was a special train for the bazaar. I remained alone in the bare carriage. In a few minutes the train drew up beside an improvised wooden platform. I passed out on to the road and saw by the lighted dial of a clock that it was ten minutes to ten. In front of me was a large building which displayed the magical name.

25   I could not find any sixpenny entrance and, fearing that the bazaar would be closed, I passed in quickly through a turnstile, handing a shilling to a weary-looking man. I found myself in a big hall girdled at half its height by a gallery. Nearly all the stalls were closed and the greater part of the hall was in darkness. I recognized a silence like that which pervades a church after a service. I walked into the centre of the bazaar timidly. A few people were gathered about the stalls which were still open. Before a curtain, over which the words *Café Chantant*[1] were written in coloured lamps,

---

8. Or *The Arab's Farewell to His Horse,* a sentimental nineteenth-century poem by Caroline Norton. The speaker has sold the horse.

9. A two-shilling piece; thus four times the "sixpenny entrance" fee.   1. Café with music (French).

two men were counting money on a salver. I listened to the fall of the coins.

Remembering with difficulty why I had come I went over to one of the stalls and examined porcelain vases and flowered tea-sets. At the door of the stall a young lady was talking and laughing with two young gentlemen. I remarked their English accents and listened vaguely to their conversation.

—O, I never said such a thing!

—O, but you did!

—O, but I didn't!

—Didn't she say that?   30

—Yes. I heard her.

—O, there's a . . . fib!

Observing me the young lady came over and asked me did I wish to buy anything. The tone of her voice was not encouraging; she seemed to have spoken to me out of a sense of duty. I looked humbly at the great jars that stood like eastern guards at either side of the dark entrance to the stall and murmured:

—No, thank you.

The young lady changed the position of one of the vases and went back 35 to the two young men. They began to talk of the same subject. Once or twice the young lady glanced at me over her shoulder.

I lingered before her stall, though I knew my stay was useless, to make my interest in her wares seem the more real. Then I turned away slowly and walked down the middle of the bazaar. I allowed the two pennies to fall against the sixpence in my pocket. I heard a voice call from one end of the gallery that the light was out. The upper part of the hall was now completely dark.

Gazing up into the darkness I saw myself as a creature driven and derided by vanity; and my eyes burned with anguish and anger.

1914

FRANZ KAFKA

A Hunger Artist[1]

During these last decades the interest in professional fasting has markedly diminished. It used to pay very well to stage such great performances under one's own management, but today that is quite impossible. We live in a different world now. At one time the whole town took a lively interest

---

1. Translated by Edwin and Willa Muir.

in the hunger artist; from day to day of his fast the excitement mounted; everybody wanted to see him at least once a day; there were people who bought season tickets for the last few days and sat from morning till night in front of his small barred cage; even in the nighttime there were visiting hours, when the whole effect was heightened by torch flares; on fine days the cage was set out in the open air, and then it was the children's special treat to see the hunger artist; for their elders he was often just a joke that happened to be in fashion, but the children stood open-mouthed, holding each other's hands for greater security, marveling at him as he sat there pallid in black tights, with his ribs sticking out so prominently, not even on a seat but down among straw on the ground, sometimes giving a courteous nod, answering questions with a constrained smile, or perhaps stretching an arm through the bars so that one might feel how thin it was, and then again withdrawing deep into himself, paying no attention to anyone or anything, not even to the all-important striking of the clock that was the only piece of furniture in his cage, but merely staring into vacancy with half shut eyes, now and then taking a sip from a tiny glass of water to moisten his lips.

Besides casual onlookers there were also relays of permanent watchers selected by the public, usually butchers, strangely enough, and it was their task to watch the hunger artist day and night, three of them at a time, in case he should have some secret recourse to nourishment. This was nothing but a formality, instituted to reassure the masses, for the initiates knew well enough that during his fast the artist would never in any circumstances, not even under forcible compulsion, swallow the smallest morsel of food: the honor of his profession forbade it. Not every watcher, of course, was capable of understanding this, there were often groups of night watchers who were very lax in carrying out their duties and deliberately huddled together in a retired corner to play cards with great absorption, obviously intending to give the hunger artist the chance of a little refreshment, which they supposed he could draw from some private hoard. Nothing annoyed the artist more than such watchers; they made him miserable; they made his fast seem unendurable; sometimes he mastered his feebleness sufficiently to sing during their watch for as long as he could keep going, to show them how unjust their suspicions were. But that was of little use; they only wondered at his cleverness in being able to fill his mouth even while singing. Much more to his taste were the watchers who sat close up to the bars, who were not content with the dim night lighting of the hall but focused him in the full glare of the electric pocket torch[2] given them by the impresario. The harsh light did not trouble him at all, in any case he could never sleep properly, and he could always drowse a little, whatever the light, at any hour, even when the hall was thronged with noisy onlookers. He was quite happy at the prospect of spending a sleepless night with such watchers; he was ready

2. Flashlight.

to exchange jokes with them, to tell them stories out of his nomadic life, anything at all to keep them awake and demonstrate to them again that he had no eatables in his cage and that he was fasting as not one of them could fast. But his happiest moment was when the morning came and an enormous breakfast was brought them, at his expense, on which they flung themselves with the keen appetite of healthy men after a weary night of wakefulness. Of course there were people who argued that this breakfast was an unfair attempt to bribe the watchers, but that was going rather too far, and when they were invited to take on a night's vigil without a breakfast, merely for the sake of the cause, they made themselves scarce, although they stuck stubbornly to their suspicions.

Such suspicions, anyhow, were a necessary accompaniment to the profession of fasting. No one could possibly watch the hunger artist continuously, day and night, and so no one could produce first-hand evidence that the fast had really been rigorous and continuous; only the artist himself could know that, he was therefore bound to be the sole completely satisfied spectator of his own fast. Yet for other reasons he was never satisfied; it was not perhaps mere fasting that had brought him to such skeleton thinness that many people had regretfully to keep away from his exhibitions, because the sight of him was too much for them, perhaps it was dissatisfaction with himself that had worn him down. For he alone knew, what no other initiate knew, how easy it was to fast. It was the easiest thing in the world. He made no secret of this, yet people did not believe him, at the best they set him down as modest; most of them, however, thought he was out for publicity or else was some kind of cheat who found it easy to fast because he had discovered a way of making it easy, and then had the impudence to admit the fact, more or less. He had to put up with all that, and in the course of time had got used to it, but his inner dissatisfaction always rankled, and never yet, after any term of fasting—this must be granted to his credit—had he left the cage of his own free will. The longest period of fasting was fixed by his impresario at forty days,[3] beyond that term he was not allowed to go, not even in great cities, and there was good reason for it, too. Experience had proved that for about forty days the interest of the public could be stimulated by a steadily increasing pressure of advertisement, but after that the town began to lose interest, sympathetic support began notably to fall off; there were of course local variations as between one town and another or one country and another, but as a general rule forty days marked the limit. So on the fortieth day the flower-bedecked cage was opened, enthusiastic spectators filled the hall, a military band played, two doctors entered the cage to measure the results of the fast, which were announced through a megaphone, and finally two young ladies appeared, blissful at having been

3. A common biblical length of time; in the New Testament, Jesus fasts for forty days in the desert and has visions of both God and the devil.

selected for the honor, to help the hunger artist down the few steps leading to a small table on which was spread a carefully chosen invalid repast.
And at this very moment the artist always turned stubborn. True, he would
entrust his bony arms to the outstretched helping hands of the ladies bending over him, but stand up he would not. Why stop fasting at this particular
moment, after forty days of it? He had held out for a long time, an illimit-
ably long time; why stop now, when he was in his best fasting form, or rather,
not yet quite in his best fasting form? Why should he be cheated of the
fame he would get for fasting longer, for being not only the record hunger
artist of all time, which presumably he was already, but for beating his own
record by a performance beyond human imagination, since he felt that there
were no limits to his capacity for fasting? His public pretended to admire
him so much, why should it have so little patience with him; if he could
endure fasting longer, why shouldn't the public endure it? Besides, he was
tired, he was comfortable sitting in the straw, and now he was supposed to
lift himself to his full height and go down to a meal the very thought of
which gave him a nausea that only the presence of the ladies kept him from
betraying, and even that with an effort. And he looked up into the eyes of
the ladies who were apparently so friendly and in reality so cruel, and shook
his head, which felt too heavy on its strengthless neck. But then there happened yet again what always happened. The impresario came forward, without a word—for the band made speech impossible—lifted his arms in the air
above the artist, as if inviting Heaven to look down upon its creature here
in the straw, this suffering martyr, which indeed he was, although in quite
another sense; grasped him round the emaciated waist, with exaggerated
caution, so that the frail cndition he was in might be appreciated; and
committed him to the care of the blenching ladies, not without secretly
giving him a shaking so that his legs and body tottered and swayed. The
artist now submitted completely; his head lolled on his breast as if it had
landed there by chance; his body was hollowed out; his legs in a spasm of
self-preservation clung close to each other at the knees, yet scraped on the
ground as if it were not really solid ground, as if they were only trying to
find solid ground; and the whole weight of his body, a feather-weight after
all, relapsed onto one of the ladies, who, looking round for help and panting a little—this post of honor was not at all what she had expected it to
be—first stretched her neck as far as she could to keep her face at least free
from contact with the artist, when finding this impossible, and her more
fortunate companion not coming to her aid but merely holding extended
on her own trembling hand the little bunch of knucklebones that was the
artist's, to the great delight of the spectators burst into tears and had to be
replaced by an attendant who had long been stationed in readiness. Then
came the food, a little of which the impresario managed to get between the
artist's lips, while he sat in a kind of half-fainting trance, to the accompaniment of cheerful patter designed to distract the public's attention from

the artist's condition; after that, a toast was drunk to the public, supposedly prompted by a whisper from the artist in the impresario's ear; the band confirmed it with a mighty flourish, the spectators melted away, and no one had any cause to be dissatisfied with the proceedings, no one except the hunger artist himself, he only, as always.

So he lived for many years, with small regular intervals of recuperation, in visible glory, honored by the world, yet in spite of that troubled in spirit, and all the more troubled because no one would take his trouble seriously. What comfort could he possibly need? What more could he possibly wish for? And if some good-natured person, feeling sorry for him, tried to console him by pointing out that his melancholy was probably caused by fasting, it could happen, especially when he had been fasting for some time, that he reacted with an outburst of fury and to the general alarm began to shake the bars of his cage like a wild animal. Yet the impresario had a way of punishing these outbreaks which he rather enjoyed putting into operation. He would apologize publicly for the artist's behavior, which was only to be excused, he admitted, because of the irritability caused by fasting, a condition hardly to be understood by well-fed people; then by natural transition he went on to mention the artist's equally incomprehensible boast that he could fast for much longer than he was doing; he praised the high ambition, the good will, the great self-denial undoubtedly implicit in such a statement; and then quite simply countered it by bringing out photographs, which were also on sale to the public, showing the artist on the fortieth day of a fast lying in bed almost dead from exhaustion. This perversion of the truth, familiar to the artist though it was, always unnerved him afresh and proved too much for him. What was a consequence of the premature ending of his fast was here presented as the cause of it! To fight against this lack of understanding, against a whole world of non-understanding, was impossible. Time and again in good faith he stood by the bars listening to the impresario, but as soon as the photographs appeared he always let go and sank with a groan back on to his straw, and the reassured public could once more come close and gaze at him.

A few years later when the witnesses of such scenes called them to mind, they often failed to understand themselves at all. For meanwhile the aforementioned change in public interest had set in; it seemed to happen almost overnight; there may have been profound causes for it, but who was going to bother about that; at any rate the pampered hunger artist suddenly found himself deserted one fine day by the amusement seekers, who went streaming past him to other more favored attractions. For the last time the impresario hurried him over half Europe to discover whether the old interest might still survive here and there; all in vain; everywhere, as if by secret agreement, a positive revulsion from professional fasting was in evidence. Of course it could not really have sprung up so suddenly as all that, and many premonitory symptoms which had not been sufficiently remarked or suppressed during the rush and glitter of success now came retrospectively to mind, but it was now too late to take any countermeasures. Fasting would surely come into fashion again at some future date, yet that was no comfort for those living in the present. What, then, was the hunger artist to do? He had been applauded by thousands in his time and could hardly come down to showing himself in a street booth at village fairs, and as for adopting another profession, he was not only too old for that but too fanatically devoted to fasting. So he took leave of the impresario, his partner in an unparalleled career, and hired himself to a large circus; in order to spare his own feelings he avoided reading the conditions of his contract.

A large circus with its enormous traffic in replacing and recruiting men, animals and apparatus can always find a use for people at any time, even for a hunger artist, provided of course that he does not ask too much, and in this particular case anyhow it was not only the artist who was taken on but his famous and long-known name as well, indeed considering the peculiar nature of his performance, which was not impaired by advancing age, it could not be objected that here was an artist past his prime, no longer at the height of his professional skill, seeking a refuge in some quiet corner of a circus; on the contrary, the hunger artist averred that he could fast as well as ever, which was entirely credible, he even alleged that if he were allowed to fast as he liked, and this was at once promised him without more ado, he could astound the world by establishing a record never yet achieved, a statement which certainly provoked a smile among the other professionals, since it left out of account the change in public opinion, which the hunger artist in his zeal conveniently forgot.

He had not, however, actually lost his sense of the real situation and took it as a matter of course that he and his cage should be stationed, not in the middle of the ring as a main attraction, but outside, near the animal cages, on a site that was after all easily accessible. Large and gaily painted placards made a frame for the cage and announced what was to be seen inside it. When the public came thronging out in the intervals to see the animals, they could hardly avoid passing the hunger artist's cage and stopping there for a moment, perhaps they might even have stayed longer had not those pressing behind them in the narrow gangway, who did not understand why they should be held up on their way toward the excitements of the menagerie, made it impossible for anyone to stand gazing quietly for any length of time. And that was the reason why the hunger artist, who had of course been looking forward to these visiting hours as the main achievement of his life, began instead to shrink from them. At first he could hardly wait for the intervals; it was exhilarating to watch the crowds come streaming his way, until only too soon—not even the most obstinate self-deception, clung to almost consciously, could hold out against the fact—the conviction was borne in upon him that these people, most of them, to judge from their actions, again and again, without exception, were all on their way to the menagerie. And the first sight of them from the distance remained the best. For when they reached his cage he was at once deafened by the storm of shouting and abuse that arose from the two contending factions, which renewed themselves continuously, of those who wanted to stop and stare at him—he soon began to dislike them more than the others—not out of real interest but only out of obstinate self-assertiveness, and those who wanted to go straight on to the animals. When the first great rush was past, the stragglers came along, and these, whom nothing could have prevented from stopping to look at him as long as they had breath, raced past with long strides, hardly even glancing at him, in their haste to get to the menagerie in time. And all too rarely did it happen that he had a stroke of luck, when some father of a family fetched up before him with his children, pointed a finger at the hunger artist and explained at length what the phenomenon meant, telling stories of earlier years when he himself had watched similar but much more thrilling performances, and the children, still rather uncomprehending, since neither inside nor outside school had they been sufficiently prepared for this lesson—what did they care about fasting?— yet showed by the brightness of their intent eyes that new and better times might be coming. Perhaps, said the hunger artist to himself many a time, things would be a little better if his cage were set not quite so near the menagerie. That made it too easy for people to make their choice, to say nothing of what he suffered from the stench of the menagerie, the animals' restlessness by night, the carrying past of raw lumps of flesh for the beasts of prey, the roaring at feeding times, which depressed him continually. But he did not dare to lodge a complaint with the management; after all, he had the animals to thank for the troops of people who passed his cage, among whom there might always be one here and there to take an interest in him, and who could tell where they might seclude him if he called attention to his existence and thereby to the fact that, strictly speaking, he was only an impediment on the way to the menagerie.

A small impediment, to be sure, one that grew steadily less. People grew familiar with the strange idea that they could be expected, in times like these, to take an interest in a hunger artist, and with this familiarity the verdict went out against him. He might fast as much as he could, and he did so; but nothing could save him now, people passed him by. Just try to explain to anyone the art of fasting! Anyone who has no feeling for it cannot be made to understand it. The fine placards grew dirty and illegible, they were torn down; the little notice board telling the number of fast days achieved, which at first was changed carefully every day, had long stayed at the same figure, for after the first few weeks even this small task seemed pointless to the staff; and so the artist simply fasted on and on, as he had once dreamed of doing, and it was no trouble to him, just as he had always foretold, but no one counted the days, no one, not even the artist himself, knew what records he was already breaking, and his heart grew heavy. And when once in a time some leisurely passer-by stopped, made merry over the old figure on the board and spoke of swindling, that was in its way the stupidest lie ever invented by indifference and inborn malice, since it was not the hunger artist who was cheating; he was working honestly, but the world was cheating him of his reward.

Many more days went by, however, and that too came to an end. An overseer's eye fell on the cage one day and he asked the attendants why this perfectly good cage should be left standing there unused with dirty straw inside it; nobody knew, until one man, helped out by the notice board, remembered about the hunger artist. They poked into the straw with sticks and found him in it. "Are you still fasting?" asked the overseer. "When on earth do you mean to stop?" "Forgive me, everybody," whispered the hunger artist; only the overseer, who had his ear to the bars, understood him. "Of course," said the overseer, and tapped his forehead with a finger to let the attendants know what state the man was in, "we forgive you." "I always wanted you to admire my fasting," said the hunger artist. "We do admire it," said the overseer, affably. "But you shouldn't admire it," said the hunger artist. "Well, then we don't admire it," said the overseer, "but why shouldn't we admire it?" "Because I have to fast, I can't help it," said the hunger artist. "What a fellow you are," said the overseer, "and why can't you help it?" "Because," said the hunger artist, lifting his head a little and speaking, with his lips pursed, as if for a kiss, right into the overseer's ear, so that no syllable might be lost, "because I couldn't find the food I liked. If I had found it, believe me, I should have made no fuss and stuffed myself like you or anyone else." These were his last words, but in his dimming eyes remained the firm though no longer proud persuasion that he was still continuing to fast.

"Well, clear this out now!" said the overseer, and they buried the hunger artist, straw and all. Into the cage they put a young panther. Even the most insensitive felt it refreshing to see this wild creature leaping around the cage that had so long been dreary. The panther was all right. The food he liked was brought him without hesitation by the attendants; he seemed not even to miss his freedom; his noble body, furnished almost to the bursting point with all that it needed, seemed to carry freedom around with it too; somewhere in his jaws it seemed to lurk; and the joy of life streamed with such ardent passion from his throat that for the onlookers it was not easy to stand the shock of it. But they braced themselves, crowded round the cage, and did not want ever to move away.

1924

YASUNARI KAWABATA

The Grasshopper and the Bell Cricket [1]

Walking along the tile-roofed wall of the university, I turned aside and approached the upper school. Behind the white board fence of the school playground, from a dusky clump of bushes under the black cherry trees, an insect's voice could be heard. Walking more slowly and listening to that voice, and furthermore reluctant to part with it, I turned right so as not to leave the playground behind. When I turned to the left, the fence gave way to an embankment planted with orange trees. At the corner, I exclaimed with surprise. My eyes gleaming at what they saw up ahead, I hurried forward with short steps.

At the base of the embankment was a bobbing cluster of beautiful varicolored lanterns, such as one might see at a festival in a remote country village. Without going any farther, I knew that it was a group of children on an insect chase among the bushes of the embankment. There were about twenty lanterns. Not only were there crimson, pink, indigo, green, purple, and yellow lanterns, but one lantern glowed with five colors at once. There were even some little red store-bought lanterns. But most of the lanterns were beautiful square ones which the children had made themselves with love and care. The bobbing lanterns, the coming together of children on this lonely slope—surely it was a scene from a fairy tale?

One of the neighborhood children had heard an insect sing on this slope one night. Buying a red lantern, he had come back the next night to find the insect. The night after that, there was another child. This new child could not buy a lantern. Cutting out the back and front of a small carton and papering it, he placed a candle on the bottom and fastened a string to the top. The number of children grew to five, and then to seven. They learned how to color the paper that they stretched over the windows of the cutout cartons, and to draw pictures on it. Then these wise child-artists, cutting out round, three-cornered, and lozenge leaf shapes in the cartons, coloring each little window a different color, with circles and diamonds, red and green, made a single and whole decorative pattern. The child with the red lantern discarded it as a tasteless object that could be bought at a store. The child who had made his own lantern threw it away because the design was too simple. The pattern of light that one had had in hand the night before was unsatisfying the morning after. Each day, with cardboard, paper, brush, scissors, penknife, and glue, the children made new lanterns out of their hearts and minds. Look at my lantern! Be the most unusually beautiful! And each night, they had gone out on their insect hunts. These were the twenty children and their beautiful lanterns that I now saw before me.

1. Translated by Lane Dunlop.

Wide-eyed, I loitered near them. Not only did the square lanterns have old-fashioned patterns and flower shapes, but the names of the children who had made them were cut out in squared letters of the syllabary. Different from the painted-over red lanterns, others (made of thick cutout cardboard) had their designs drawn onto the paper windows, so that the candle's light seemed to emanate from the form and color of the design itself. The lanterns brought out the shadows of the bushes like dark light. The children crouched eagerly on the slope wherever they heard an insect's voice.

5   "Does anyone want a grasshopper?" A boy, who had been peering into a bush about thirty feet away from the other children, suddenly straightened up and shouted.

"Yes! Give it to me!" Six or seven children came running up. Crowding behind the boy who had found the grasshopper, they peered into the bush. Brushing away their outstretched hands and spreading out his arms, the boy stood as if guarding the bush where the insect was. Waving the lantern in his right hand, he called again to the other children.

"Does anyone want a grasshopper? A grasshopper!"

"I do! I do!" Four or five more children came running up. It seemed you could not catch a more precious insect than a grasshopper. The boy called out a third time.

"Doesn't anyone want a grasshopper?"

10   Two or three more children came over.

"Yes. I want it."

It was a girl, who just now had come up behind the boy who'd discovered the insect. Lightly turning his body, the boy gracefully bent forward. Shifting the lantern to his left hand, he reached his right hand into the bush.

"It's a grasshopper."

"Yes. I'd like to have it."

15   The boy quickly stood up. As if to say "Here!" he thrust out his fist that held the insect at the girl. She, slipping her left wrist under the string of her lantern, enclosed the boy's fist with both hands. The boy quietly opened his fist. The insect was transferred to between the girl's thumb and index finger.

"Oh! It's not a grasshopper. It's a bell cricket." The girl's eyes shone as she looked at the small brown insect.

"It's a bell cricket! It's a bell cricket!" The children echoed in an envious chorus.

"It's a bell cricket. It's a bell cricket."

Glancing with her bright intelligent eyes at the boy who had given her the cricket, the girl opened the little insect cage hanging at her side and released the cricket in it.

20   "It's a bell cricket."

"Oh, it's a bell cricket," the boy who'd captured it muttered. Holding up the insect cage close to his eyes, he looked inside it. By the light of his beautiful many colored lantern, also held up at eye level, he glanced at the girl's face.

Oh, I thought. I felt slightly jealous of the boy, and sheepish. How silly of me not to have understood his actions until now! Then I caught my breath in surprise. Look! It was something on the girl's breast which neither the boy who had given her the cricket, nor she who had accepted it, nor the children who were looking at them noticed.

In the faint greenish light that fell on the girl's breast, wasn't the name "Fujio" clearly discernible? The boy's lantern, which he held up alongside the girl's insect cage, inscribed his name, cut out in the green papered aperture, onto her white cotton kimono. The girl's lantern, which dangled loosely from her wrist, did not project its pattern so clearly, but still one could make out, in a trembling patch of red on the boy's waist, the name "Kiyoko." This chance interplay of red and green—if it was chance or play—neither Fujio nor Kiyoko knew about.

Even if they remembered forever that Fujio had given her the cricket and that Kiyoko had accepted it, not even in dreams would Fujio ever know that his name had been written in green on Kiyoko's breast or that Kiyoko's name had been inscribed in red on his waist, nor would Kiyoko ever know that Fujio's name had been inscribed in green on her breast or that her own name had been written in red on Fujio's waist.

Fujio! Even when you have become a young man, laugh with pleasure at 25 a girl's delight when, told that it's a grasshopper, she is given a bell cricket; laugh with affection at a girl's chagrin when, told that it's a bell cricket, she is given a grasshopper.

Even if you have the wit to look by yourself in a bush away from the other children, there are not many bell crickets in the world. Probably you will find a girl like a grasshopper whom you think is a bell cricket.

And finally, to your clouded, wounded heart, even a true bell cricket will seem like a grasshopper. Should that day come, when it seems to you that the world is only full of grasshoppers, I will think it a pity that you have no way to remember tonight's play of light, when your name was written in green by your beautiful lantern on a girl's breast.

1988

D. H. LAWRENCE

The Rocking-Horse Winner

There was a woman who was beautiful, who started with all the advantages, yet she had no luck. She married for love, and the love turned to dust. She had bonny children, yet she felt they had been thrust upon her, and she could not love them. They looked at her coldly, as if they were find-ing fault with her. And hurriedly she felt she must cover up some fault in herself. Yet what it was that she must cover up she never knew. Neverthe-less, when her children were present, she always felt the centre of her heart go hard. This troubled her, and in her manner she was all the more gentle and anxious for her children, as if she loved them very much. Only she herself knew that at the centre of her heart was a hard little place that could not feel love, no, not for anybody. Everybody else said of her: "She is such a good mother. She adores her children." Only she herself, and her children themselves, knew it was not so. They read it in each other's eyes.

There were a boy and two little girls. They lived in a pleasant house, with a garden, and they had discreet servants, and felt themselves superior to anyone in the neighbourhood.

Although they lived in style, they felt always an anxiety in the house. There was never enough money. The mother had a small income, and the father had a small income, but not nearly enough for the social position which they had to keep up. The father went in to town to some office. But though he had good prospects, these prospects never materialized. There was always the grinding sense of the shortage of money, though the style was always kept up.

At last the mother said: "I will see if *I* can't make something." But she did not know where to begin. She racked her brains, and tried this thing and the other, but could not find anything successful. The failure made deep lines come into her face. Her children were growing up, they would have to go to school. There must be more money, there must be more money. The father, who was always very handsome and expensive in his tastes, seemed as if he never *would* be able to do anything worth doing. And the mother, who had a great belief in herself, did not succeed any better, and her tastes were just as expensive.

5   And so the house came to be haunted by the unspoken phrase: *There must be more money! There must be more money!* The children could hear it all the time, though nobody said it aloud. They heard it at Christmas, when the expensive and splendid toys filled the nursery. Behind the shining modern rocking-horse, behind the smart doll's-house, a voice would start whispering: "There *must* be more money! There *must* be more money!" And the children would stop playing, to listen for a moment. They would look into each other's eyes, to see if they had all heard. And each one saw in the eyes of the other two that they too had heard. "There *must* be more money! There *must* be more money!"

It came whispering from the springs of the still-swaying rocking-horse, and even the horse, bending his wooden, champing head, heard it. The big doll, sitting so pink and smirking in her new pram,[1] could hear it quite

---

1. Baby carriage.

plainly, and seemed to be smirking all the more self-consciously because of it. The foolish puppy, too, that took the place of the teddy-bear, he was looking so extraordinarily foolish for no other reason but that he heard the secret whisper all over the house: "There *must* be more money!"

Yet nobody ever said it aloud. The whisper was everywhere, and therefore no one spoke it. Just as no one ever says: "We are breathing!" in spite of the fact that breath is coming and going all the time.

"Mother," said the boy Paul one day, "why don't we keep a car of our own? Why do we always use uncle's, or else a taxi?"

"Because we're the poor members of the family," said the mother.

"But why *are* we, mother?" 10

"Well—I suppose," she said slowly and bitterly, "it's because your father has no luck."

The boy was silent for some time.

"Is luck money, mother?" he asked rather timidly.

"No, Paul. Not quite. It's what causes you to have money."

"Oh!" said Paul vaguely. "I thought when Uncle Oscar said *filthy lucker*, it 15 meant money."

"*Filthy lucre* does mean money," said the mother. "But it's lucre, not luck."

"Oh!" said the boy. "Then what *is* luck, mother?"

"It's what causes you to have money. If you're lucky you have money. That's why it's better to be born lucky than rich. If you're rich, you may lose your money. But if you're lucky, you will always get more money."

"Oh! Will you? And is father not lucky?"

"Very unlucky, I should say," she said bitterly. 20

The boy watched her with unsure eyes.

"Why?" he asked.

"I don't know. Nobody ever knows why one person is lucky and another unlucky."

"Don't they? Nobody at all? Does *nobody* know?"

"Perhaps God. But He never tells." 25

"He ought to, then. And aren't you lucky either, mother?"

"I can't be, if I married an unlucky husband."

"But by yourself, aren't you?"

"I used to think I was, before I married. Now I think I am very unlucky indeed."

"Why?" 30

"Well—never mind! Perhaps I'm not really," she said.

The child looked at her, to see if she meant it. But he saw, by the lines of her mouth, that she was only trying to hide something from him.

"Well, anyhow," he said stoutly, "I'm a lucky person."

"Why?" said his mother, with a sudden laugh.

He stared at her. He didn't even know why he had said it. 35

"God told me," he asserted, brazening it out.

"I hope He did, dear!" she said, again with a laugh, but rather bitter.

"He did, mother!"

"Excellent!" said the mother, using one of her husband's exclamations.

40   The boy saw she did not believe him; or, rather, that she paid no attention to his assertion. This angered him somewhat, and made him want to compel her attention.

He went off by himself, vaguely, in a childish way, seeking for the clue to "luck." Absorbed, taking no heed of other people, he went about with a sort of stealth, seeking inwardly for luck. He wanted luck, he wanted it, he wanted it. When the two girls were playing dolls in the nursery, he would sit on his big rocking-horse, charging madly into space, with a frenzy that made the little girls peer at him uneasily. Wildly the horse careered, the waving dark hair of the boy tossed, his eyes had a strange glare in them. The little girls dared not speak to him.

When he had ridden to the end of his mad little journey, he climbed down and stood in front of his rocking-horse, staring fixedly into its lowered face. Its red mouth was slightly open, its big eye was wide and glassy-bright.

"Now!" he would silently command the snorting steed. "Now, take me to where there is luck! Now take me!"

And he would slash the horse on the neck with the little whip he had asked Uncle Oscar for. He *knew* the horse could take him to where there was luck, if only he forced it. So he would mount again, and start on his furious ride, hoping at last to get there. He knew he could get there.

45   "You'll break your horse, Paul!" said the nurse.

"He's always riding like that! I wish he'd leave off!" said his elder sister Joan.

But he only glared down on them in silence. Nurse gave him up. She could make nothing of him. Anyhow he was growing beyond her.

One day his mother and his Uncle Oscar came in when he was on one of his furious rides. He did not speak to them.

"Hallo, you young jockey! Riding a winner?" said his uncle.

50   "Aren't you growing too big for a rocking-horse? You're not a very little boy any longer, you know," said his mother.

But Paul only gave a blue glare from his big, rather close-set eyes. He would speak to nobody when he was in full tilt. His mother watched him with an anxious expression on her face.

At last he suddenly stopped forcing his horse into the mechanical gallop, and slid down.

"Well, I got there!" he announced fiercely, his blue eyes still flaring, and his sturdy long legs straddling apart.

"Where did you get to?" asked his mother.

55   "Where I wanted to go," he flared back at her.

"That's right, son!" said Uncle Oscar. "Don't you stop till you get there. What's the horse's name?"

"He doesn't have a name," said the boy.

"Gets on without all right?" asked the uncle.

"Well, he has different names. He was called Sansovino last week."

"Sansovino, eh? Won the Ascot.[2] How did you know his name?"   60

"He always talks about horse-races with Bassett," said Joan.

The uncle was delighted to find that his small nephew was posted with all the racing news. Bassett, the young gardener, who had been wounded in the left foot in the war[3] and had got his present job through Oscar Cresswell, whose batman[4] he had been, was a perfect blade of the "turf."[5] He lived in the racing events, and the small boy lived with him.

Oscar Cresswell got it all from Bassett.

"Master Paul comes and asks me, so I can't do more than tell him, sir," said Bassett, his face terribly serious, as if he were speaking of religious matters.

"And does he ever put anything on a horse he fancies?"   65

"Well—I don't want to give him away—he's a young sport, a fine sport, sir. Would you mind asking him himself? He sort of takes a pleasure in it, and perhaps he'd feel I was giving him away, sir, if you don't mind."

Bassett was serious as a church.

The uncle went back to his nephew and took him off for a ride in the car.

"Say, Paul, old man, do you ever put anything on a horse?" the uncle asked.

The boy watched the handsome man closely.   70

"Why, do you think I oughtn't to?" he parried.

"Not a bit of it! I thought perhaps you might give me a tip for the Lincoln."

The car sped on into the country, going down to Uncle Oscar's place in Hampshire.

"Honour bright?" said the nephew.

"Honour bright, son!" said the uncle.   75

"Well, then, Daffodil."

"Daffodil! I doubt it, sonny. What about Mirza?"

"I only know the winner," said the boy. "That's Daffodil."

"Daffodil, eh?"

There was a pause. Daffodil was an obscure horse comparatively.   80

"Uncle!"

---

2. A race run at a course of that name in Berkshire. Other races mentioned in the story are Lincolnshire Handicap, then run at Lincoln Downs; the St. Leger Stakes, run at Doncaster; the Grand National Steeplechase, run at Aintree, the most famous steeplechase in the world; the famous Derby, a mile-and-a-half race for three-year-olds run at Epsom Downs.
3. World War I, 1914–18.   4. British officer's orderly.   5. That is, a dashing young horseplayer.

"Yes, son?"

"You won't let it go any further, will you? I promised Bassett."

"Bassett be damned, old man! What's he got to do with it?"

85   "We're partners. We've been partners from the first. Uncle, he lent me my first five shillings, which I lost. I promised him, honour bright, it was only between me and him; only you gave me that ten-shilling note I started winning with, so I thought you were lucky. You won't let it go any further, will you?"

The boy gazed at his uncle from those big, hot, blue eyes, set rather close together. The uncle stirred and laughed uneasily.

"Right you are, son! I'll keep your tip private. Daffodil, eh? How much are you putting on him?"

"All except twenty pounds," said the boy. "I keep that in reserve."

The uncle thought it a good joke.

90   "You keep twenty pounds in reserve, do you, you young romancer? What are you betting, then?"

"I'm betting three hundred," said the boy, gravely. "But it's between you and me, Uncle Oscar! Honour bright?"

The uncle burst into a roar of laughter.

"It's between you and me all right, you young Nat Gould,"[6] he said, laughing. "But where's your three hundred?"

"Bassett keeps it for me. We're partners."

95   "You are, are you! And what is Bassett putting on Daffodil?"

"He won't go quite as high as I do, I expect. Perhaps he'll go a hundred and fifty."

"What, pennies?" laughed the uncle.

"Pounds," said the child, with a surprised look at his uncle. "Bassett keeps a bigger reserve than I do."

Between wonder and amusement Uncle Oscar was silent. He pursued the matter no further, but he determined to take his nephew with him to the Lincoln races.

100   "Now, son," he said, "I'm putting twenty on Mirza, and I'll put five for you on any horse you fancy. What's your pick?"

"Daffodil, uncle."

"No, not the fiver on Daffodil!"

"I should if it was my own fiver," said the child.

"Good! Good! Right you are! A fiver for me and a fiver for you on Daffodil."

105   The child had never been to a race-meeting before, and his eyes were blue fire. He pursed his mouth tight, and watched. A Frenchman just in front had put his money on Lancelot. Wild with excitement, he flayed his arms up and down, yelling *"Lancelot! Lancelot!"* in his French accent.

---

6. Nathaniel Gould (1857–1919), novelist and journalist who wrote about horse racing.

Daffodil came in first, Lancelot second, Mirza third. The child, flushed and with eyes blazing, was curiously serene. His uncle brought him four five-pound notes, four to one.

"What am I to do with these?" he cried, waving them before the boy's eyes.

"I suppose we'll talk to Bassett," said the boy. "I expect I have fifteen hundred now; and twenty in reserve; and this twenty."

His uncle studied him for some moments.

"Look here, son!" he said. "You're not serious about Bassett and that fifteen hundred, are you?"

"Yes, I am. But it's between you and me, uncle. Honour bright!"

"Honour bright all right, son! But I must talk to Bassett."

"If you'd like to be a partner, uncle, with Bassett and me, we could all be partners. Only, you'd have to promise, honour bright, uncle, not to let it go beyond us three. Bassett and I are lucky, and you must be lucky, because it was your ten shillings I started winning with. . . ."

Uncle Oscar took both Bassett and Paul into Richmond Park for an afternoon, and there they talked.

"It's like this, you see, sir," Bassett said. "Master Paul would get me talking about racing events, spinning yarns, you know, sir. And he was always keen on knowing if I'd made or if I'd lost. It's about a year since, now, that I put five shillings on Blush of Dawn for him—and we lost. Then the luck turned, with the ten shillings he had from you, that we put on Singhalese. And since that time, it's been pretty steady, all things considering. What do you say, Master Paul?"

"We're all right when we're sure," said Paul. "It's when we're not quite sure that we go down."

"Oh, but we're careful then," said Bassett.

"But when are you *sure?*" smiled Uncle Oscar.

"It's Master Paul, sir," said Bassett, in a secret, religious voice. "It's as if he had it from heaven. Like Daffodil, now, for the Lincoln. That was as sure as eggs."

"Did you put anything on Daffodil?" asked Oscar Cresswell.

"Yes, sir. I made my bit."

"And my nephew?"

Bassett was obstinately silent, looking at Paul.

"I made twelve hundred, didn't I, Bassett? I told uncle I was putting three hundred on Daffodil."

"That's right," said Bassett, nodding.

"But where's the money?" asked the uncle.

"I keep it safe locked up, sir. Master Paul he can have it any minute he likes to ask for it."

"What, fifteen hundred pounds?"

"And twenty! And *forty,* that is, with the twenty he made on the course."

130 "It's amazing!" said the uncle.

"If Master Paul offers you to be partners, sir, I would, if I were you; if you'll excuse me," said Bassett.

Oscar Cresswell thought about it.

"I'll see the money," he said.

They drove home again, and sure enough, Bassett came round to the garden-house with fifteen hundred pounds in notes. The twenty pounds reserve was left with Joe Glee, in the Turf Commission deposit.

135 "You see, it's all right, uncle, when I'm *sure!* Then we go strong, for all we're worth. Don't we, Bassett?"

"We do that, Master Paul"

"And when are you sure?" said the uncle, laughing.

"Oh, well, sometimes I'm *absolutely* sure, like about Daffodil," said the boy; "and sometimes I have an idea; and sometimes I haven't even an idea, have I, Bassett? Then we're careful, because we mostly go down."

"You do, do you! And when you're sure, like about Daffodil, what makes you sure, sonny?"

140 "Oh, well, I don't know," said the boy uneasily. "I'm sure, you know, uncle; that's all."

"It's as if he had it from heaven, sir," Bassett reiterated.

"I should say so!" said the uncle.

But he became a partner. And when the Leger was coming on, Paul was "sure" about Lively Spark, which was a quite inconsiderable horse. The boy insisted on putting a thousand on the horse, Bassett went for five hundred, and Oscar Cresswell two hundred. Lively Spark came in first, and the betting had been ten to one against him. Paul had made ten thousand.

"You see," he said, "I was absolutely sure of him."

145 Even Oscar Cresswell had cleared two thousand.

"Look here, son," he said, "this sort of thing makes me nervous."

"It needn't, uncle! Perhaps I shan't be sure again for a long time."

"But what are you going to do with your money?" asked the uncle.

"Of course," said the boy, "I started it for mother. She said she had no luck, because father is unlucky, so I thought if *I* was lucky, it might stop whispering."

150 "What might stop whispering?"

"Our house. I *hate* our house for whispering."

"What does it whisper?"

"Why—why"—the boy fidgeted—"why, I don't know. But it's always short of money, you know, uncle."

"I know it, son, I know it."

155 "You know people send mother writs, don't you, uncle?"

"I'm afraid I do," said the uncle.

"And then the house whispers, like people laughing at you behind your back. It's awful, that is! I thought if I was lucky . . ."

"You might stop it," added the uncle.

The boy watched him with big blue eyes, that had an uncanny cold fire in them, and he said never a word.

"Well, then!" said the uncle. "What are we doing?"

"I shouldn't like mother to know I was lucky," said the boy.

"Why not, son?"

"She'd stop me."

"I don't think she would."

"Oh!"—and the boy writhed in an odd way—"I *don't* want her to know, uncle."

"All right, son! We'll manage it without her knowing."

They managed it very easily. Paul, at the other's suggestion, handed over five thousand pounds to his uncle, who deposited it with the family lawyer, who was then to inform Paul's mother that a relative had put five thousand pounds into his hands, which sum was to be paid out a thousand pounds at a time, on the mother's birthday, for the next five years.

"So she'll have a birthday present of a thousand pounds for five successive years," said Uncle Oscar. "I hope it won't make it all the harder for her later."

Paul's mother had her birthday in November. The house had been "whispering" worse than ever lately, and, even in spite of his luck, Paul could not bear up against it. He was very anxious to see the effect of the birthday letter, telling his mother about the thousand pounds.

When there were no visitors, Paul now took his meals with his parents, as he was beyond the nursery control. His mother went into town nearly every day. She had discovered that she had an odd knack of sketching furs and dress materials, so she worked secretly in the studio of a friend who was the chief "artist" for the leading drapers. She drew the figures of ladies in furs and ladies in silk and sequins for the newspaper advertisements. This young woman artist earned several thousand pounds a year, but Paul's mother only made several hundreds, and she was again dissatisfied. She so wanted to be first in something, and she did not succeed, even in making sketches for drapery advertisements.

She was down to breakfast on the morning of her birthday. Paul watched her face as she read her letters. He knew the lawyer's letter. As his mother read it, her face hardened and became more expressionless. Then a cold, determined look came on her mouth. She hid the letter under the pile of others, and said not a word about it.

"Didn't you have anything nice in the post for your birthday, mother?" said Paul.

"Quite moderately nice," she said, her voice cold and absent.

She went away to town without saying more.

But in the afternoon Uncle Oscar appeared. He said Paul's mother had had a long interview with the lawyer, asking if the whole five thousand could not be advanced at once, as she was in debt.

"What do you think, uncle?" said the boy.

"I leave it to you, son."

"Oh, let her have it, then! We can get some more with the other," said the boy.

"A bird in the hand is worth two in the bush, laddie!" said Uncle Oscar.

180   "But I'm sure to *know* for the Grand National; or the Lincolnshire; or else the Derby. I'm sure to know for *one* of them," said Paul.

So Uncle Oscar signed the agreement, and Paul's mother touched the whole five thousand. Then something very curious happened. The voices in the house suddenly went mad, like a chorus of frogs on a spring evening. There were certain new furnishings, and Paul had a tutor. He was *really* going to Eton, his father's school, in the following autumn. There were flowers in the winter, and a blossoming of the luxury Paul's mother had been used to. And yet the voices in the house, behind the sprays of mimosa and almond blossom, and from under the piles of iridescent cushions, simply trilled and screamed in a sort of ecstasy: "There *must* be more money! Oh-h-h; there *must* be more money Oh, now, now-w! Now-w-w— there *must* be more money!—more than ever! More than ever!"

It frightened Paul terribly. He studied away at his Latin and Greek with his tutors. But his intense hours were spent with Bassett. The Grand National had gone by: he had not "known," and had lost a hundred pounds. Summer was at hand. He was in agony for the Lincoln. But even for the Lincoln he didn't "know," and he lost fifty pounds. He became wild-eyed and strange, as if something were going to explode in him.

"Let it alone, son! Don't you bother about it!" urged Uncle Oscar. But it was as if the boy couldn't really hear what his uncle was saying.

"I've got to know for the Derby! I've got to know for the Derby!" the child reiterated, his big blue eyes blazing with a sort of madness.

185   His mother noticed how overwrought he was.

"You'd better go to the seaside. Wouldn't you like to go now to the seaside, instead of waiting? I think you'd better," she said, looking down at him anxiously, her heart curiously heavy because of him.

But the child lifted his uncanny blue eyes.

"I couldn't possibly go before the Derby, mother!" he said. "I couldn't possibly!"

"Why not?" she said, her voice becoming heavy when she was opposed. "Why not? You can still go from the seaside to see the Derby with your Uncle Oscar, if that's what you wish. No need for you to wait here. Besides, I think you care too much about these races. It's a bad sign. My family has been a gambling family, and you won't know till you grow up how much damage it has done. But it has done damage. I shall have to send Bassett away, and ask Uncle Oscar not to talk racing to you, unless you promise to be reasonable about it; go away to the seaside and forget it. You're all nerves!"

190   "I'll do what you like, mother, so long as you don't send me away till after the Derby," the boy said.

"Send you away from where? Just from this house?"

"Yes," he said, gazing at her.

"Why, you curious child, what makes you care about this house so much, suddenly? I never knew you loved it."

He gazed at her without speaking. He had a secret within a secret, something he had not divulged, even to Bassett or to his Uncle Oscar.

But his mother, after standing undecided and a little bit sullen for some moments, said: 195

"Very well, then! Don't go to the seaside till after the Derby, if you don't wish it. But promise me you won't let your nerves go to pieces. Promise you won't think so much about horse-racing and events, as you call them!"

"Oh, no," said the boy casually. "I won't think much about them, mother. You needn't worry. I wouldn't worry, mother, if I were you."

"If you were me and I were you," said his mother, "I wonder what we *should* do!"

"But you know you needn't worry, mother, don't you?" the boy repeated.

"I should be awfully glad to know it," she said wearily. 200

"Oh, well, you *can*, you know. I mean, you *ought* to know you needn't worry," he insisted.

"Ought I? Then I'll see about it," she said.

Paul's secret of secrets was his wooden horse, that which had no name. Since he was emancipated from a nurse and a nursery-governess, he had had his rocking-horse removed to his own bedroom at the top of the house.

"Surely, you're too big for a rocking-horse!" his mother had remonstrated.

"Well, you see, mother, till I can have a *real* horse, I like to have *some* sort 205 of animal about," had been his quaint answer.

"Do you feel he keeps you company?" she laughed.

"Oh, yes! He's very good, he always keeps me company, when I'm there," said Paul.

So the horse, rather shabby, stood in an arrested prance in the boy's bedroom.

The Derby was drawing near, and the boy grew more and more tense. He hardly heard what was spoken to him, he was very frail, and his eyes were really uncanny. His mother had sudden strange seizures of uneasiness about him. Sometimes, for half-an-hour, she would feel a sudden anxiety about him that was almost anguish. She wanted to rush to him at once, and know he was safe.

Two nights before the Derby, she was at a big party in town, when one of 210 her rushes of anxiety about her boy, her first-born, gripped her heart till she could hardly speak. She fought with the feeling, might and main, for she believed in common-sense. But it was too strong. She had to leave the dance and go downstairs to telephone to the country. The children's nursery-governess was terribly surprised and startled at being rung up in the night.

"Are the children all right, Miss Wilmot?"

"Oh, yes, they are quite all right."

"Master Paul? Is he all right?"

"He went to bed as right as a trivet. Shall I run up and look at him?"

215 "No," said Paul's mother reluctantly. "No! Don't trouble. It's all right. Don't sit up. We shall be home fairly soon." She did not want her son's privacy intruded upon.

"Very good," said the governess.

It was about one o'clock when Paul's mother and father drove up to their house. All was still. Paul's mother went to her room and slipped off her white fur cloak. She had told her maid not to wait up for her. She heard her husband downstairs, mixing a whisky-and-soda.

And then, because of the strange anxiety at her heart, she stole upstairs to her son's room. Noiselessly she went along the upper corridor. Was there a faint noise? What was it?

She stood, with arrested muscles, outside his door, listening. There was a strange, heavy, and yet not loud noise. Her heart stood still. It was a soundless noise, yet rushing and powerful. Something huge, in violent, hushed motion. What was it? What in God's name was it? She ought to know. She felt that she knew the noise. She knew what it was.

220 Yet she could not place it. She couldn't say what it was. And on and on it went, like a madness.

Softly, frozen with anxiety and fear, she turned the door-handle.

The room was dark. Yet in the space near the window, she heard and saw something plunging to and fro. She gazed in fear and amazement.

Then suddenly she switched on the light, and saw her son, in his green pyjamas, madly surging on the rocking-horse. The blaze of light suddenly lit him up, as he urged the wooden horse, and lit her up, as she stood, blonde, in her dress of pale green and crystal, in the doorway.

"Paul!" she cried. "Whatever are you doing?"

225 "It's Malabar!" he screamed, in a powerful, strange voice. "It's Malabar!"

His eyes blazed at her for one strange and senseless second, as he ceased urging his wooden horse. Then he fell with a crash to the ground, and she, all her tormented motherhood flooding upon her, rushed to gather him up.

But he was unconscious, and unconscious he remained, with some brain-fever. He talked and tossed, and his mother sat stonily by his side.

"Malabar! It's Malabar! Bassett, Bassett, I *know*! It's Malabar!"

So the child cried, trying to get up and urge the rocking-horse that gave him his inspiration.

230 "What does he mean by Malabar?" asked the heart-frozen mother.

"I don't know," said the father stonily.

"What does he mean by Malabar?" she asked her brother Oscar.

"It's one of the horses running for the Derby," was the answer.

And, in spite of himself, Oscar Cresswell spoke to Bassett, and himself put a thousand on Malabar: at fourteen to one.

The third day of the illness was critical: they were waiting for a change. 235 The boy, with his rather long, curly hair, was tossing ceaselessly on the pillow. He neither slept nor regained consciousness, and his eyes were like blue stones. His mother sat, feeling her heart had gone, turned actually into a stone.

In the evening, Oscar Cresswell did not come, but Bassett sent a message, saying could he come up for one moment, just one moment? Paul's mother was very angry at the intrusion, but on second thought she agreed. The boy was the same. Perhaps Bassett might bring him to consciousness.

The gardener, a shortish fellow with a little brown moustache, and sharp little brown eyes, tip-toed into the room, touched his imaginary cap to Paul's mother, and stole to the bedside, staring with glittering, smallish eyes, at the tossing, dying child.

"Master Paul!" he whispered. "Master Paul! Malabar came in first all right, a clean win. I did as you told me. You've made over seventy thousand pounds, you have; you've got over eighty thousand. Malabar came in all right, Master Paul."

"Malabar! Malabar! Did I say Malabar, mother? Did I say Malabar? Do you think I'm lucky, mother? I knew Malabar, didn't I? Over eighty thousand pounds! I call that lucky, don't you, mother? Over eighty thousand pounds! I knew, didn't I know I knew! Malabar came in all right. If I ride my horse till I'm sure, then I tell you, Bassett, you can go as high as you like. Did you go for all you were worth, Bassett?"

"I went a thousand on it, Master Paul." 240

"I never told you, mother, that if I can ride my horse, and *get there,* then I'm absolutely sure—oh absolutely! Mother, did I ever tell you? I *am* lucky!"

"No, you never did," said the mother.

But the boy died in the night.

And even as he lay dead, his mother heard her brother's voice saying to her: "My God, Hester, you're eighty-odd thousand to the good, and a poor devil of a son to the bad. But, poor devil, poor devil, he's best gone out of a life where he rides his rocking-horse to find a winner."

1932

BOBBIE ANN MASON

Shiloh

Leroy Moffitt's wife, Norma Jean, is working on her pectorals. She lifts three-pound dumbbells to warm up, then progresses to a twenty-pound barbell. Standing with her legs apart, she reminds Leroy of Wonder Woman.

"I'd give anything if I could just get these muscles to where they're real hard," says Norma Jean. "Feel this arm. It's not as hard as the other one."

"That's cause you're right-handed," says Leroy, dodging as she swings the barbell in an arc.

"Do you think so?"

5   "Sure."

Leroy is a truckdriver. He injured his leg in a highway accident four months ago, and his physical therapy, which involves weights and a pulley, prompted Norma Jean to try building herself up. Now she is attending a body-building class. Leroy has been collecting temporary disability since his tractor-trailer jack-knifed in Missouri, badly twisting his left leg in its socket. He has a steel pin in his hip. He will probably not be able to drive his rig again. It sits in the backyard, like a gigantic bird that has flown home to roost. Leroy has been home in Kentucky for three months, and his leg is almost healed, but the accident frightened him and he does not want to drive any more long hauls. He is not sure what to do next. In the meantime, he makes things from craft kits. He started by building a miniature log cabin from notched Popsicle sticks. He varnished it and placed it on the TV set, where it remains. It reminds him of a rustic Nativity scene. Then he tried string art (sailing ships on black velvet), a macramé owl kit, a snap-together B-17 Flying Fortress,[1] and a lamp made out of a model truck, with a light fixture screwed in the top of the cab. At first the kits were diversions, something to kill time, but now he is thinking about building a full-scale log house from a kit. It would be considerably cheaper than building a regular house, and besides, Leroy has grown to appreciate how things are put together. He has begun to realize that in all the years he was on the road he never took time to examine anything. He was always flying past scenery.

"They won't let you build a log cabin in any of the new subdivisions," Norma Jean tells him.

"They will if I tell them it's for you," he says, teasing her. Ever since they were married, he has promised Norma Jean he would build her a new home one day. They have always rented, and the house they live in is small and nondescript. It does not even feel like a home, Leroy realizes now.

Norma Jean works at the Rexall drugstore, and she has acquired an amazing amount of information about cosmetics. When she explains to Leroy the three stages of complexion care, involving creams, toners, and moisturizers, he thinks happily of other petroleum products—axle grease, diesel fuel. This is a connection between him and Norma Jean. Since he has been home, he has felt unusually tender about his wife and guilty over his long absences. But he can't tell what she feels about him. Norma Jean has never complained about his traveling; she has never made hurt remarks, like calling his truck a "widow-maker." He is reasonably certain she has been faithful to him, but he wishes she would celebrate his permanent homecoming more happily. Norma Jean is often startled to find Leroy at home, and he thinks she seems

1. American World War II bomber.

a little disappointed about it. Perhaps he reminds her too much of the early days of their marriage, before he went on the road. They had a child who died as an infant, years ago. They never speak about their memories of Randy, which have almost faded, but now that Leroy is home all the time, they sometimes feel awkward around each other, and Leroy wonders if one of them should mention the child. He has the feeling that they are waking up out of a dream together—that they must create a new marriage, start afresh. They are lucky they are still married. Leroy has read that for most people losing a child destroys the marriage—or else he heard this on *Donahue*. He can't always remember where he learns things anymore.

At Christmas, Leroy bought an electric organ for Norma Jean. She used 10 to play the piano when she was in high school. "It don't leave you," she told him once. "It's like riding a bicycle."

The new instrument had so many keys and buttons that she was bewildered by it at first. She touched the keys tentatively, pushed some buttons, then pecked out "Chopsticks." It came out in an amplified fox-trot rhythm, with marimba sounds.

"It's an orchestra!" she cried.

The organ had a pecan-look finish and eighteen preset chords, with optional flute, violin, trumpet, clarinet, and banjo accompaniments. Norma Jean mastered the organ almost immediately. At first she played Christmas songs. Then she bought *The Sixties Songbook* and learned every tune in it, adding variations to each with the rows of brightly colored buttons.

"I didn't like these old songs back then," she said. "But I have this crazy feeling I missed something."

"You didn't miss a thing," said Leroy. 15

Leroy likes to lie on the couch and smoke a joint and listen to Norma Jean play "Can't Take My Eyes Off You" and "I'll Be Back."[2] He is back again. After fifteen years on the road, he is finally settling down with the woman he loves. She is still pretty. Her skin is flawless. Her frosted curls resemble pencil trimmings.

Now that Leroy has come home to stay, he notices how much the town has changed. Subdivisions are spreading across western Kentucky like an oil slick. The sign at the edge of town says "Pop: 11,500"—only seven hundred more than it said twenty years before. Leroy can't figure out who is living in all the new houses. The farmers who used to gather around the courthouse square on Saturday afternoons to play checkers and spit tobacco juice have gone. It has been years since Leroy has thought about the farmers, and they have disappeared without his noticing.

Leroy meets a kid named Stevie Hamilton in the parking lot at the new shopping center. While they pretend to be strangers meeting over a stalled

2. Hit songs of the 1960s.

car, Stevie tosses an ounce of marijuana under the front seat of Leroy's car. Stevie is wearing orange jogging shoes and a T-shirt that says CHATTA-HOOCHEE SUPER-RAT. His father is a prominent doctor who lives in one of the expensive subdivisions in a new white-columned brick house that looks like a funeral parlor. In the phone book under his name there is a separate number, with the listing "Teenagers."

"Where do you get this stuff?" asks Leroy. "From your pappy!"

20   "That's for me to know and you to find out," Stevie says. He is slit-eyed and skinny.

"What else you got?"

"What you interested in?"

"Nothing special. Just wondered."

Leroy used to take speed on the road. Now he has to go slowly. He needs to be mellow. He leans back against the car and says, "I'm aiming to build me a log house, soon as I get time. My wife, though, I don't think she likes the idea."

25   "Well, let me know when you want me again," Stevie says. He has a cigarette in his cupped palm, as though sheltering it from the wind. He takes a long drag, then stomps it on the asphalt and slouches away.

Stevie's father was two years ahead of Leroy in high school. Leroy is thirty-four. He married Norma Jean when they were both eighteen, and their child Randy was born a few months later, but he died at the age of four months and three days. He would be about Stevie's age now. Norma Jean and Leroy were at the drive-in, watching a double feature (*Dr. Strangelove* and *Lover Come Back*),[3] and the baby was sleeping in the back seat. When the first movie ended, the baby was dead. It was the sudden infant death syndrome. Leroy remembers handing Randy to a nurse at the emergency room, as though he were offering her a large doll as a present. A dead baby feels like a sack of flour. "It just happens sometimes," said the doctor, in what Leroy always recalls as a nonchalant tone. Leroy can hardly remember the child anymore, but he still sees vividly a scene from *Dr. Strangelove* in which the President of the United States was talking in a folksy voice on the hot line to the Soviet premier about the bomber accidentally headed toward Russia. He was in the War Room, and the world map was lit up. Leroy remembers Norma Jean catatonically beside him in the hospital and himself thinking: Who is this strange girl? He had forgotten who she was. Now scientists are saying that crib death is caused by a virus. Nobody knows anything, Leroy thinks. The answers are always changing.

When Leroy gets home from the shopping center, Norma Jean's mother, Mabel Beasley, is there. Until this year, Leroy has not realized how much time she spends with Norma Jean. When she visits, she inspects the closets

---

3. A 1963 satire on nuclear war and a 1961 Rock Hudson-Doris Day romantic comedy satirizing the advertising business, respectively.

and then the plants, informing Norma Jean when a plant is droopy or yellow. Mabel calls the plants "flowers," although there are never any blooms. She always notices if Norma Jean's laundry is piling up. Mabel is a short, overweight woman whose tight, brown-dyed curls look more like a wig than the actual wig she sometimes wears. Today she has brought Norma Jean an off-white dust ruffle she made for the bed; Mabel works in a custom-upholstery shop.

"This is the tenth one I made this year," Mabel says. "I got started and couldn't stop."

"It's real pretty," says Norma Jean.

"Now we can hide things under the bed," says Leroy, who gets along   30
with his mother-in-law primarily by joking with her. Mabel has never really forgiven him for disgracing her by getting Norma Jean pregnant. When the baby died, she said that fate was mocking her.

"What's that thing?" Mabel says to Leroy in a loud voice, pointing to a tangle of yarn on a piece of canvas.

Leroy holds it up for Mabel to see. "It's my needlepoint," he explains. "This is a *Star Trek* pillow cover."

"That's what a woman would do," says Mabel. "Great day in the morning!"

"All the big football players on TV do it," he says.

"Why, Leroy, you're always trying to fool me. I don't believe you for one   35
minute. You don't know what to do with yourself—that's the whole trouble. Sewing!"

"I'm aiming to build us a log house," says Leroy. "Soon as my plans come."

"Like *heck* you are," says Norma Jean. She takes Leroy's needlepoint and shoves it into a drawer. "You have to find a job first. Nobody can afford to build now anyway."

Mabel straightens her girdle and says, "I still think before you get tied down y'all ought to take a little run to Shiloh."

"One of these days, Mama," Norma Jean says impatiently.

Mabel is talking about Shiloh, Tennessee. For the past few years, she   40
has been urging Leroy and Norma Jean to visit the Civil War battle-ground there.[4] Mabel went there on her honeymoon—the only real trip she ever took. Her husband died of a perforated ulcer when Norma Jean was ten, but Mabel, who was accepted into the United Daughters of the Confederacy in 1975, is still preoccupied with going back to Shiloh.

4. Where, in April 1862, more than twenty-three thousand troops of the North and South, one-quarter of those who fought there, died. This was the first real indication of how bitter and bloody the war was to be. When Union reinforcements arrived, General Ulysses S. Grant drove the Confederate forces, which had gained an initial victory by a surprise attack, back to their base in Corinth, Mississippi.

"I've been to kingdom come and back in that truck out yonder," Leroy says to Mabel, "but we never yet set foot in that battleground. Ain't that something? How did I miss it?"

"It's not even that far," Mabel says.

After Mabel leaves, Norma Jean reads to Leroy from a list she has made. "Thing you could do," she announces. "You could get a job as a guard at Union Carbide, where they'd let you set on a stool. You could get on at the lumberyard. You could do a little carpenter work, if you want to build so bad. You could—"

"I can't do something where I'd have to stand up all day."

45   "You ought to try standing up all day behind a cosmetics counter. It's amazing that I have strong feet, coming from two parents that never had strong feet at all." At the moment Norma Jean is holding on to the kitchen counter, raising her knees one at a time as she talks. She is wearing two-pound ankle weights.

"Don't worry," says Leroy. "I'll do something."

"You could truck calves to slaughter for somebody. You wouldn't have to drive any big old truck for that."

"I'm going to build you this house," says Leroy. "I want to make you a real home."

"I don't want to live in any log cabin."

50   "It's not a cabin. It's a house."

"I don't care. It looks like a cabin."

"You and me together could lift those logs. It's just like lifting weights."

Norma Jean doesn't answer. Under her breath, she is counting. Now she is marching through the kitchen. She is doing goose steps.

Before his accident, when Leroy came home he used to stay in the house with Norma Jean, watching TV in bed and playing cards. She would cook fried chicken, picnic ham, chocolate pie—all his favorites. Now he is home alone much of the time. In the mornings, Norma Jean disappears, leaving a cooling place in the bed. She eats a cereal called Body Buddies, and she leaves the bowl on the table, with soggy tan balls floating in a milk puddle. He sees things about Norma Jean that he never realized before. When she chops onions, she stares off into a corner, as if she can't bear to look. She puts on her house slippers almost precisely at nine o'clock every evening and nudges her jogging shoes under the couch. She saves bread heels for the birds. Leroy watches the birds at the feeder. He notices the peculiar way goldfinches fly past the window. They close their wings, then fall, then spread their wings to catch and lift themselves. He wonders if they close their eyes when they fall. Norma Jean closes her eyes when they are in bed. She wants the lights turned out. Even then, he is sure she closes her eyes.

55   He goes for long drives around town. He tends to drive a car rather carelessly. Power steering and an automatic shift make a car feel so small and

inconsequential that his body is hardly involved in the driving process. His injured leg stretches out comfortably. Once or twice he has almost hit something, but even the prospect of an accident seems minor in a car. He cruises the new subdivisions, feeling like a criminal rehearsing for a robbery. Norma Jean is probably right about a log house being inappropriate here in the new subdivisions. All the houses look grand and complicated. They depress him.

One day when Leroy comes home from a drive he finds Norma Jean in tears. She is in the kitchen making a potato and mushroom-soup casserole, with grated-cheese topping. She is crying because her mother caught her smoking.

"I didn't hear her coming. I was standing here puffing away pretty as you please," Norma Jean says, wiping her eyes.

"I knew it would happen sooner or later," says Leroy, putting his arm around her.

"She don't know the meaning of the word 'knock,'" says Norma Jean. "It's a wonder she hadn't caught me years ago."

"Think of it this way," Leroy says. "What if she caught me with a joint?" 60

"You better not let her!" Norma Jean shrieks. "I'm warning you, Leroy Moffitt!"

"I'm just kidding. Here, play me a tune. That'll help you relax."

Norma Jean puts the casserole in the oven and sets the timer. Then she plays a ragtime tune, with horns and banjo, as Leroy lights up a joint and lies on the couch, laughing to himself about Mabel's catching him at it. He thinks of Stevie Hamilton—a doctor's son pushing grass. Everything is funny. The whole town seems crazy and small. He is reminded of Virgil Mathis, a boastful policeman Leroy used to shoot pool with. Virgil recently led a drug bust in a back room at a bowling alley, where he seized ten thousand dollars' worth of marijuana. The newspaper had a picture of him holding up the bags of grass and grinning widely. Right now, Leroy can imagine Virgil breaking down the door and arresting him with a lungful of smoke. Virgil would probably have been alerted to the scene because of all the racket Norma Jean is making. Now she sounds like a hard-rock band. Norma Jean is terrific. When she switches to a Latin-rhythm version of "Sunshine Superman," Leroy hums along. Norma Jean's foot goes up and down, up and down.

"Well, what do you think?" Leroy says, when Norma Jean pauses to search through her music.

"What do I think about what?" 65

His mind has gone blank. Then he says, "I'll sell my rig and build us a house." That wasn't what he wanted to say. He wanted to know what she thought—what she *really* thought—about them.

"Don't start in on that again," says Norma Jean. She begins playing "Who'll Be the Next in Line?"

Leroy used to tell hitchhikers his whole life story—about his travels, his hometown, the baby. He would end with a question: "Well, what do you think?" It was just a rhetorical question. In time, he had the feeling that he'd been telling the same story over and over to the same hitchhikers. He quit talking to hitchhikers when he realized how his voice sounded— whining and self-pitying, like some teenage-tragedy song. Now Leroy has the sudden impulse to tell Norma Jean about himself, as if he had just met her. They have known each other so long they have forgotten a lot about each other. They could become reacquainted. But when the oven timer goes off and she runs to the kitchen, he forgets why he wants to do this.

The next day, Mabel drops by. It is Saturday and Norma Jean is cleaning. Leroy is studying the plans of his log house, which have finally come in the mail. He has them spread out on the table—big sheets of stiff blue paper, with diagrams and numbers printed in white. While Norma Jean runs the vacuum, Mabel drinks coffee. She sets her coffee cup on a blueprint.

70   "I'm just waiting for time to pass," she says to Leroy, drumming her fingers on the table.

As soon as Norma Jean switches off the vacuum, Mabel says in a loud voice, "Did you hear about the datsun dog that killed the baby?"

Norma Jean says, "The word is 'dachshund.'"

"They put the dog on trial. It chewed the baby's legs off. The mother was in the next room all the time." She raises her voice. "They thought it was neglect."

Norma Jean is holding her ears. Leroy manages to open the refrigerator and get some Diet Pepsi to offer Mabel. Mabel still has some coffee and she waves away the Pepsi.

75   "Datsuns are like that," Mabel says. "They're jealous dogs. They'll tear a place to pieces if you don't keep an eye on them."

"You better watch out what you're saying, Mabel," says Leroy.

"Well, facts is facts."

Leroy looks out the window at his rig. It is like a huge piece of furniture gathering dust in the backyard. Pretty soon it will be an antique. He hears the vacuum cleaner. Norma Jean seems to be cleaning the living room rug again.

Later, she says to Leroy, "She just said that about the baby because she caught me smoking. She's trying to pay me back."

80   "What are you talking about?" Leroy says, nervously shuffling blueprints.

"You know good and well," Norma Jean says. She is sitting in a kitchen chair with her feet up and her arms wrapped around her knees. She looks small and helpless. She says, "The very idea, her bringing up a subject like that! Saying it was neglect."

"She didn't mean that," Leroy says.

"She might not have *thought* she meant it. She always says things like that. You don't know how she goes on."

"But she didn't really mean it. She was just talking."

Leroy opens a king-sized bottle of beer and pours it into two glasses, 85 dividing it carefully. He hands a glass to Norma Jean and she takes it from him mechanically. For a long time, they sit by the kitchen window watching the birds at the feeder.

Something is happening. Norma Jean is going to night school. She has graduated from her six-week body-building course and now she is taking an adult-education course in composition at Paducah Community College. She spends her evenings outlining paragraphs.

"First you have a topic sentence," she explains to Leroy. "Then you divide it up. Your secondary topic has to be connected to your primary topic."

To Leroy, this sounds intimidating. "I never was any good in English," he says.

"It makes a lot of sense."

"What are you doing this for, anyhow?" 90

She shrugs. "It's something to do." She stands up and lifts her dumbbells a few times.

"Driving a rig, nobody cared about my English."

"I'm not criticizing your English."

Norma Jean used to say, "If I lose ten minutes' sleep, I just drag all day." Now she stays up late, writing compositions. She got a B on her first paper—a how-to theme on soup-based casseroles. Recently Norma Jean has been cooking unusual foods—tacos, lasagna, Bombay chicken. She doesn't play the organ anymore, though her second paper was called "Why Music Is Important to Me." She sits at the kitchen table, concentrating on her outlines, while Leroy plays with his log house plans, practicing with a set of Lincoln Logs. The thought of getting a truckload of notched, numbered logs scares him, and he wants to be prepared. As he and Norma Jean work together at the kitchen table, Leroy has the hopeful thought that they are sharing something, but he knows he is a fool to think this. Norma Jean is miles away. He knows he is going to lose her. Like Mabel, he is just waiting for time to pass.

One day, Mabel is there before Norma Jean gets home from work, and 95 Leroy finds himself confiding in her. Mabel, he realizes, must know Norma Jean better than he does.

"I don't know what's got into that girl," Mabel says. "She used to go to bed with the chickens. Now you say she's up all hours. Plus her a-smoking. I like to died."

"I want to make her this beautiful home," Leroy says, indicating the Lincoln Logs. "I don't think she even wants it. Maybe she was happier with me gone."

"She don't know what to make of you, coming home like this."

"Is that it?"

100 Mabel takes the roof off his Lincoln Log cabin. "You couldn't get *me* in a log cabin," she says. "I was raised in one. It's no picnic, let me tell you."

"They're different now," says Leroy.

"I tell you what," Mabel says, smiling oddly at Leroy.

"What?"

"Take her on down to Shiloh. Y'all need to get out together, stir a little. Her brain's all balled up over them books."

105 Leroy can see traces of Norma Jean's features in her mother's face. Mabel's face has the texture of crinkled cotton, but suddenly she looks pretty. It occurs to Leroy that Mabel has been hinting all along that she wants them to take her with them to Shiloh.

"Let's all go to Shiloh," he says. "You and me and her. Come Sunday."

Mabel throws up her hands in protest. "Oh, no, not me. Young folks want to be by theirselves."

When Norma Jean comes in with groceries, Leroy says excitedly, "Your mama here's been dying to go to Shiloh for thirty-five years. It's about time we went, don't you think?"

"I'm not going to butt in on anybody's second honeymoon," Mabel says.

110 "Who's going on a honeymoon, for Christ's sake?" Norma Jean says loudly.

"I never raised no daughter of mine to talk that-a-way," Mabel says.

"You ain't seen nothing yet," says Norma Jean. She starts putting away boxes and cans, slamming cabinet doors.

"There's a log cabin at Shiloh." Mabel says, "It was there during the battle. There's bullet holes in it."

"When are you going to *shut up* about Shiloh, Mama?" asks Norma Jean.

115 "I always thought Shiloh was the prettiest place, so full of history," Mabel goes on. "I just hoped y'all could see it once before I die, so you could tell me about it." Later, she whispers to Leroy, "You do what I said. A little change is what she needs."

"Your name means 'the king,'" Norma Jean says to Leroy that evening. He is trying to get her to go to Shiloh, and she is reading a book about another century.

"Well, I reckon I ought to be right proud."

"I guess so."

"Am I still king around here?"

120 Norma Jean flexes her biceps and feels them for hardness. "I'm not fooling around with anybody, if that's what you mean," she says.

"Would you tell me if you were?"

"I don't know."

"What does *your* name mean?"

"It was Marilyn Monroe's real name."

"No kidding!"   125

"Norma comes from the Normans. They were invaders," she says. She closes her book and looks hard at Leroy. "I'll go to Shiloh with you if you'll stop staring at me."

On Sunday, Norma Jean packs a picnic and they go to Shiloh. To Leroy's relief, Mabel says she does not want to come with them. Norma Jean drives, and Leroy, sitting beside her, feels like some boring hitchhiker she has picked up. He tries some conversation, but she answers him in monosyllables. At Shiloh, she drives aimlessly through the park, past bluffs and trails and steep ravines. Shiloh is an immense place, and Leroy cannot see it as a battleground. It is not what he expected. He thought it would look like a golf course. Monuments are everywhere, showing through the thick clusters of trees. Norma Jean passes the log cabin Mabel mentioned. It is surrounded by tourists looking for bullet holes.

"That's not the kind of log house I've got in mind," says Leroy apologetically.

"I know *that*."

"This is a pretty place. Your mama was right."   130

"It's O.K.," says Norma Jean. "Well, we've seen it. I hope she's satisfied."

They burst out laughing together.

At the park museum, a movie on Shiloh is shown every half hour, but they decide that they don't want to see it. They buy a souvenir Confederate flag for Mabel, and then they find a picnic spot near the cemetery. Norma Jean has brought a picnic cooler, with pimiento sandwiches, soft drinks, and Yodels. Leroy eats a sandwich and then smokes a joint, hiding it behind the picnic cooler. Norma Jean has quit smoking altogether. She is picking cake crumbs from the cellophane wrapper, like a fussy bird.

Leroy says, "So the boys in gray ended up in Corinth. The Union soldiers zapped 'em finally. April 7, 1862."

They both know that he doesn't know any history. He is just talking   135 about some of the historical plaques they have read. He feels awkward, like a boy on a date with an older girl. They are still just making conversation.

"Corinth is where Mama eloped to," says Norma Jean.

They sit in silence and stare at the cemetery for the Union dead and, beyond, at a tall cluster of trees. Campers are parked nearby, bumper to bumper, and small children in bright clothing are cavorting and squealing. Norma Jean wads up the cake wrapper and squeezes it tightly in her hand. Without looking at Leroy, she says, "I want to leave you."

Leroy takes a bottle of Coke out of the cooler and flips off the cap. He holds the bottle poised near his mouth but cannot remember to take a drink. Finally he says, "No, you don't."

"Yes, I do."

140   "I won't let you."
        "You can't stop me."
        "Don't do me that way."
        Leroy knows Norma Jean will have her own way. "Didn't I promise to be
        home from now on?" he says.
        "In some ways, a woman prefers a man who wanders," says Norma Jean.
        "That sounds crazy, I know."
145   "You're not crazy."
        Leroy remembers to drink from his Coke. Then he says, "Yes, you *are*
        crazy. You and me could start all over again. Right back at the beginning."
        "We *have* started all over again," says Norma Jean. "And this is how it
        turned out."
        "What did I do wrong?"
        "Nothing."
150   "Is this one of those women's lib things?" Leroy asks.
        "Don't be funny."
        The cemetery, a green slope dotted with white markers, looks like a sub-
        division site. Leroy is trying to comprehend that his marriage is breaking
        up, but for some reason he is wondering about white slabs in a graveyard.
        "Everything was fine till Mama caught me smoking," says Norma Jean,
        standing up. "That set something off."
        "What are you talking about?"
155   "She won't leave me alone—*you* won't leave me alone." Norma Jean seems
        to be crying, but she is looking away from him. "I feel eighteen again. I
        can't face that all over again." She starts walking away. "No, it *wasn't* fine. I
        don't know what I'm saying. Forget it."
        Leroy takes a lungful of smoke and closes his eyes as Norma Jean's words
        sink in. He tries to focus on the fact that thirty-five hundred soldiers died on
        the grounds around him. He can only think of that war as a board game
        with plastic soldiers. Leroy almost smiles, as he compares the Confederates'
        daring attack on the Union camps and Virgil Mathis's raid on the bowling
        alley. General Grant, drunk and furious, shoved the Southerners back to
        Corinth, where Mabel and Jet Beasley were married years later, when Mabel
        was still thin and good-looking. The next day, Mabel and Jet visited the bat-
        tleground, and then Norma Jean was born, and then she married Leroy and
        they had a baby, which they lost, and now Leroy and Norma Jean are here
        at the same battleground. Leroy knows he is leaving out a lot. He is leaving
        out the insides of history. History was always just names and dates to him. It
        occurs to him that building a house out of logs is similarly empty—too sim-
        ple. And the real inner workings of a marriage, like most of history, have
        escaped him. Now he sees that building a log house is the dumbest idea he
        could have had. It was clumsy of him to think Norma Jean would want a log
        house. It was a crazy idea. He'll have to think of something else, quickly. He
        will wad the blueprints into tight balls and fling them into the lake. Then

he'll get moving again. He opens his eyes. Norma Jean has moved away and is walking through the cemetery, following a serpentine brick path.

Leroy gets up to follow his wife, but his good leg is asleep and his bad leg still hurts him. Norma Jean is far away, walking rapidly toward the bluff by the river, and he tries to hobble toward her. Some children run past him, screaming noisily. Norma Jean has reached the bluff, and she is looking out over the Tennessee River. Now she turns toward Leroy and waves her arms. Is she beckoning to him? She seems to be doing an exercise for her chest muscles. The sky is unusually pale—the color of the dust ruffle Mabel made for their bed.

1982

HERMAN MELVILLE

Bartleby, the Scrivener

A Story of Wall Street

I am a rather elderly man. The nature of my avocations for the last thirty years has brought me into more than ordinary contact with what would seem an interesting and somewhat singular set of men, of whom as yet nothing that I know of has ever been written:—I mean the law-copyists or scriveners. I have known very many of them, professionally and privately, and if I pleased, could relate divers histories, at which good-natured gentlemen might smile, and sentimental souls might weep. But I waive the biographies of all other scriveners for a few passages in the life of Bartleby, who was a scrivener the strangest I ever saw or heard of. While of other law-copyists I might write the complete life, of Bartleby nothing of that sort can be done. I believe that no materials exist for a full and satisfactory biography of this man. It is an irreparable loss to literature. Bartleby was one of those beings of whom nothing is ascertainable, except from the original sources, and in his case those are very small. What my own astonished eyes saw of Bartleby, *that* is all I know of him, except, indeed, one vague report which will appear in the sequel.[1]

Ere introducing the scrivener, as he first appeared to me, it is fit I make some mention of myself, my *employées*, my business, my chambers, and general surroundings; because some such description is indispensable to an adequate understanding of the chief character about to be presented.

Imprimis:[2] I am a man who, from his youth upwards, has been filled with a profound conviction that the easiest way of life is the best. Hence,

---

1. That is, in the following story. 2. In the first place.

though I belong to a profession proverbially energetic and nervous, even to turbulence, at times, yet nothing of that sort have I ever suffered to invade my peace. I am one of those unambitious lawyers who never addresses a jury, or in any way draws down public applause; but in the cool tranquillity of a snug retreat, do a snug business among rich men's bonds and mortgages and title-deeds. All who know me, consider me an eminently *safe* man. The late John Jacob Astor,[3] a personage little given to poetic enthusiasm, had no hesitation in pronouncing my first grand point to be prudence; my next, method. I do not speak it in vanity, but simply record the fact, that I was not unemployed in my profession by the late John Jacob Astor; a name which, I admit, I love to repeat, for it hath a rounded and orbicular sound to it, and rings like unto bullion. I will freely add that I was not insensible to the late John Jacob Astor's good opinion.

Some time prior to the period at which this little history begins, my avocations had been largely increased. The good old office, now extinct in the State of New York, of a Master in Chancery[4] had been conferred upon me. It was not a very arduous office, but very pleasantly remunerative. I seldom lose my temper; much more seldom indulge in dangerous indignation at wrongs and outrages; but I must be permitted to be rash here and declare, that I consider the sudden and violent abrogation of the office of Master in Chancery, by the new Constitution, as a—premature act; inasmuch as I had counted upon a life-lease of the profits, whereas I only received those of a few short years. But this is by the way.

5   My chambers were up stairs at No. —— Wall Street. At one end they looked upon the white wall of the interior of a spacious skylight shaft, penetrating the building from top to bottom. This view might have been considered rather tame than otherwise, deficient in what landscape painters call "life." But if so, the view from the other end of my chambers offered, at least, a contrast, if nothing more. In that direction my windows commanded an unobstructed view of a lofty brick wall, black by age and everlasting shade; which wall required no spyglass to bring out its lurking beauties, but for the benefit of all near-sighted spectators, was pushed up to within ten feet of my window panes. Owing to the great height of the surrounding buildings, and my chambers being on the second floor, the interval between this wall and mine not a little resembled a huge square cistern.

At the period just preceding the advent of Bartleby, I had two persons as copyists in my employment, and a promising lad as an office-boy. First, Turkey; second, Nippers, third, Ginger Nut. These may seem names the like of which are not usually found in the Directory.[5] In truth they were nick-

---

3. New York fur merchant and landowner (1763–1848) who died the richest man in the United States.

4. A court of chancery can temper the law, applying "dictates of conscience" or "the principles of natural justice"; the office of Master was abolished in 1847.

5. Post Office Directory.

names, mutually conferred upon each other by my three clerks, and were deemed expressive of their respective persons or characters. Turkey was a short, pursy [6] Englishman of about my own age, that is, somewhere not far from sixty. In the morning, one might say, his face was of a fine florid hue, but after twelve o'clock, meridian—his dinner hour—it blazed like a grate full of Christmas coals; and continued blazing—but, as it were, with a gradual wane—till 6 o'clock, P.M. or thereabouts, after which I saw no more of the proprietor of the face, which gaining its meridian with the sun, seemed to set with it, to rise, culminate, and decline the following day, with the like regularity and undiminished glory. There are many singular coincidences I have known in the course of my life, not the least among which was the fact, that exactly when Turkey displayed his fullest beams from his red and radiant countenance, just then, too, at that critical moment, began the daily period when I considered his business capacities as seriously disturbed for the remainder of the twenty-four hours. Not that he was absolutely idle, or averse to business then; far from it. The difficulty was, he was apt to be altogether too energetic. There was a strange, inflamed, flurried, flighty recklessness of activity about him. He would be incautious in dipping his pen into his inkstand. All his blots upon my documents were dropped there after twelve o'clock, meridian. Indeed, not only would he be reckless and sadly given to making blots in the afternoon, but some days he went further, and was rather noisy. At such times, too, his face flamed with augmented blazonry, as if cannel coal had been heaped on anthracite.[7] He made an unpleasant racket with his chair; spilled his sand-box; in mending his pens, impatiently split them all to pieces, and threw them on the floor in a sudden passion; stood up and leaned over his table, boxing his papers about in a most indecorous manner, very sad to behold in an elderly man like him. Nevertheless, as he was in many ways a most valuable person to me, and all the time before twelve o'clock, meridian, was the quickest, steadiest creature too, accomplishing a great deal of work in a style not easy to be matched—for these reasons, I was willing to overlook his eccentricities, though indeed, occasionally, I remonstrated with him. I did this very gently, however, because, though the civilest, nay, the blandest and most reverential of men in the morning, yet in the afternoon he was disposed, upon provocation, to be slightly rash with his tongue, in fact, insolent. Now, valuing his morning services as I did, and resolved not to lose them; yet, at the same time made uncomfortable by his inflamed ways after twelve o'clock; and being a man of peace, unwilling by my admonitions to call forth unseemly retorts from him; I took upon me, one Saturday noon (he was always worse on Saturdays), to hint to him, very kindly, that perhaps now that he was growing old, it might be well to abridge his labors; in short, he need not come to my chambers after twelve o'clock, but, dinner over, had best go home to his lodgings and rest himself till tea-time. But

---

6. Fat, short-winded.   7. Fast, bright-burning coal heaped on slow-burning, barely glowing coal.

no; he insisted upon his afternoon devotions. His countenance became intolerably fervid, as he oratorically assured me—gesticulating with a long ruler at the other end of the room—that if his services in the morning were useful, how indispensable, then, in the afternoon?

"With submission, sir," said Turkey on this occasion, "I consider myself your right-hand man. In the morning I but marshal and deploy my columns; but in the afternoon I put myself at their head, and gallantly charge the foe, thus!"—and he made a violent thrust with the ruler.

"But the blots, Turkey," intimated I.

"True,—but, with submission, sir, behold these hairs! I am getting old. Surely, sir, a blot or two of a warm afternoon is not to be severely urged against gray hairs. Old age—even if it blot the page—is honorable. With submission, sir, we *both* are getting old."

10   This appeal to my fellow-feeling was hardly to be resisted. At all events, I saw that go he would not. So I made up my mind to let him stay, resolving, nevertheless, to see to it, that during the afternoon he had to do with my less important papers.

Nippers, the second on my list, was a whiskered, sallow, and, upon the whole, rather piratical-looking young man of about five and twenty. I always deemed him the victim of two evil powers—ambition and indigestion. The ambition was evinced by a certain impatience of the duties of a mere copyist, an unwarrantable usurpation of strictly professional affairs, such as the original drawing up of legal documents. The indigestion seemed betokened in an occasional nervous testiness and grinning irritability, causing the teeth to audibly grind together over mistakes committed in copying; unnecessary maledictions, hissed, rather than spoken, in the heat of business; and especially by a continual discontent with the height of the table where he worked. Though of a very ingenious mechanical turn, Nippers could never get this table to suit him. He put chips under it, blocks of various sorts, bits of pasteboard, and at last went so far as to attempt an exquisite adjustment by final pieces of folded blotting-paper. But no invention would answer. If, for the sake of easing his back, he brought the table lid at a sharp angle well up towards his chin, and wrote there like a man using the steep roof of a Dutch house for his desk:—then he declared that it stopped the circulation in his arms. If now he lowered the table to his waistbands, and stooped over it in writing, then there was a sore aching in his back. In short, the truth of the matter was, Nippers knew not what he wanted. Or, if he wanted any thing, it was to be rid of a scrivener's table altogether. Among the manifestations of his diseased ambition was a fondness he had for receiving visits from certain ambiguous-looking fellows in seedy coats, whom he called his clients. Indeed I was aware that not only was he, at times, considerable of a ward-politician, but he occasionally did a little business at the Justices' courts, and was not unknown on the steps of the Tombs.[8]

8. Prison in New York City.

I have good reason to believe, however, that one individual who called upon him at my chambers, and who, with a grand air, he insisted was his client, was no other than a dun,[9] and the alleged title-deed, a bill. But with all his failings, and the annoyances he caused me, Nippers, like his compatriot Turkey, was a very useful man to me; wrote a neat, swift hand; and, when he chose, was not deficient in a gentlemanly sort of deportment. Added to this, he always dressed in a gentlemanly sort of way: and so, incidentally, reflected credit upon my chambers. Whereas with respect to Turkey, I had much ado to keep him from being a reproach to me. His clothes were apt to look oily and smell of eating-houses. He wore his pantaloons very loose and baggy in summer. His coats were execrable; his hat not to be handled. But while the hat was a thing of indifference to me, inasmuch as his natural civility and deference, as a dependent Englishman, always led him to doff it the moment he entered the room, yet his coat was another matter. Concerning his coats, I reasoned with him; but with no effect. The truth was, I suppose, that a man with so small an income, could not afford to sport such a lustrous face and a lustrous coat at one and the same time. As Nippers once observed, Turkey's money went chiefly for red ink. One winter day I presented Turkey with a highly-respectable looking coat of my own, a padded gray coat, of a most comfortable warmth, and which buttoned straight up from the knee to the neck. I thought Turkey would appreciate the favor, and abate his rashness and obstreperousness of afternoons. But no. I verily believe that buttoning himself up in so downy and blanket-like a coat had a pernicious effect upon him; upon the same principle that too much oats are bad for horses. In fact, precisely as a rash, restive horse is said to feel his oats, so Turkey felt his coat. It made him insolent. He was a man whom prosperity harmed.

Though concerning the self-indulgent habits of Turkey I had my own private surmises, yet touching Nippers I was well persuaded that whatever might be his faults in other respects, he was, at least, a temperate young man. But indeed, nature herself seemed to have been his vintner,[1] and at his birth charged him so thoroughly with an irritable, brandy-like disposition, that all subsequent potations were needless. When I consider how, amid the stillness of my chambers, Nippers would sometimes impatiently rise from his seat, and stooping over his table, spread his arms wide apart, seize the whole desk, and move it, and jerk it, with a grim, grinding motion on the floor, as if the table were a perverse voluntary agent, intent on thwarting and vexing him; I plainly perceive that for Nippers, brandy and water were altogether superfluous.

It was fortunate for me that, owing to its peculiar cause—indigestion—the irritability and consequent nervousness of Nippers, were mainly observable in the morning, while in the afternoon he was comparatively mild. So that Turkey's paroxysms only coming on about twelve o'clock, I never had to do with their eccentricities at one time. Their fits relieved each other like

---

9. Bill collector.   1. Wine seller.

guards. When Nippers' was on, Turkey's was off; and *vice versa*. This was a good natural arrangement under the circumstances.

Ginger Nut, the third on my list, was a lad some twelve years old. His father was a carman,[2] ambitious of seeing his son on the bench instead of a cart, before he died. So he sent him to my office as student at law, errand boy, and cleaner and sweeper, at the rate of one dollar a week. He had a little desk to himself, but he did not use it much. Upon inspection, the drawer exhibited a great array of the shells of various sorts of nuts. Indeed, to this quick-witted youth the whole noble science of the law was contained in a nutshell. Not the least among the employments of Ginger Nut, as well as one which he discharged with the most alacrity, was his duty as cake and apple purveyor for Turkey and Nippers. Copying law papers being proverbially a dry, husky sort of business, my two scriveners were fain to moisten their mouths very often with Spitzenbergs[3] to be had at the numerous stalls nigh the Custom House and Post Office. Also, they sent Ginger Nut very frequently for that peculiar cake—small, flat, round, and very spicy—after which he had been named by them. Of a cold morning when business was but dull, Turkey would gobble up scores of these cakes, as if they were mere wafers—indeed they sell them at the rate of six or eight for a penny—the scrape of his pen blending with the crunching of the crisp particles in his mouth. Of all the fiery afternoon blunders and flurried rashnesses of Turkey, was his once moistening a ginger-cake between his lips, and clapping it on to a mortgage for a seal. I came within an ace of dismissing him then. But he mollified me by making an oriental bow, and saying—"With submission, sir, it was generous of me to find you in[4] stationery on my own account."

15   Now my original business—that of a conveyancer and title hunter,[5] and drawer-up of recondite documents of all sorts—was considerably increased by receiving the master's office. There was now great work for scriveners. Not only must I push the clerks already with me, but I must have additional help. In answer to my advertisement, a motionless young man one morning stood upon my office threshold, the door being open, for it was summer. I can see that figure now—pallidly neat, pitiably respectable, incurably forlorn! It was Bartleby. *first meet at main character*

After a few words touching his qualifications, I engaged him, glad to have among my corps of copyists a man of so singularly sedate an aspect, which I thought might operate beneficially upon the flighty temper of Turkey, and the fiery one of Nippers.

I should have stated before that ground glass folding-doors divided my premises into two parts, one of which was occupied by my scriveners, the

2. Driver of wagon or cart that hauls goods.   3. Red-and-yellow American apple.
4. Supply you with.
5. Lawyer who draws up deeds for transferring property, and one who searches out legal control of title deeds.

other by myself. According to my humor I threw open these doors, or closed them. I resolved to assign Bartleby a corner by the folding-doors, but on my side of them, so as to have this quiet man within easy call, in case any trifling thing was to be done. I placed his desk close up to a small side-window in that part of the room, a window which originally had afforded a lateral view of certain grimy backyards and bricks, but which, owing to subsequent erections, commanded at present no view at all, though it gave some light. Within three feet of the panes was a wall, and the light came down from far above, between two lofty buildings, as from a very small opening in a dome. Still further to a satisfactory arrangement, I procured a high green folding screen, which might entirely isolate Bartleby from my sight, though not remove him from my voice. And thus, in a manner, privacy and society were conjoined.

At first Bartleby did an extraordinary quantity of writing. As if long famishing for something to copy, he seemed to gorge himself on my documents. There was no pause for digestion. He ran a day and night line, copying by sunlight and by candlelight. I should have been quite delighted with his application, had he been cheerfully industrious. But he wrote on silently, palely, mechanically.

It is, of course, an indispensable part of a scrivener's business to verify the accuracy of his copy, word by word. Where there are two or more scriveners in an office, they assist each other in this examination, one reading from the copy, the other holding the original. It is a very dull, wearisome, and lethargic affair. I can readily imagine that to some sanguine temperaments it would be altogether intolerable. For example, I cannot credit that the mettlesome poet Byron would have contentedly sat down with Bartleby to examine a law document of, say, five hundred pages, closely written in a crimpy hand.

Now and then, in the haste of business, it had been my habit to assist in comparing some brief document myself, calling Turkey or Nippers for this purpose. One object I had in placing Bartleby so handy to me behind the screen, was to avail myself of his services on such trivial occasions. It was on the third day, I think, of his being with me, and before any necessity had arisen for having his own writing examined, that, being much hurried to complete a small affair I had in hand, I abruptly called to Bartleby. In my haste and natural expectancy of instant compliance, I sat with my head bent over the original on my desk, and my right hand sideways, and somewhat nervously extended with the copy, so that immediately upon emerging from his retreat, Bartleby might snatch it and proceed to business without the least delay.

In this very attitude did I sit when I called to him, rapidly stating what it was I wanted him to do—namely, to examine a small paper with me. Imagine my surprise, nay, my consternation, when without moving from his privacy, Bartleby, in a singularly mild, firm voice, replied, "I would prefer not to."

I sat awhile in perfect silence, rallying my stunned faculties. Immediately it occurred to me that my ears had deceived me, or Bartleby had entirely misunderstood my meaning. I repeated my request in the clearest tone I could assume. But in quite as clear a one came the previous reply, "I would prefer not to."

"Prefer not to," echoed I, rising in high excitement, and crossing the room with a stride. "What do you mean? Are you moon-struck?[6] I want you to help me compare this sheet here—take it," and I thrust it towards him.

"I would prefer not to," said he.

25   I looked at him steadfastly. His face was leanly composed; his gray eye dimly calm. Not a wrinkle of agitation rippled him. Had there been the least uneasiness, anger, impatience or impertinence in his manner; in other words, had there been anything ordinarily human about him, doubtless I should have violently dismissed him from the premises. But as it was, I should have as soon thought of turning my pale plaster-of-paris bust of Cicero[7] out-of-doors. I stood gazing at him awhile, as he went on with his own writing, and then reseated myself at my desk. This is very strange, thought I. What had one best do? But my business hurried me. I concluded to forget the matter for the present, reserving it for my future leisure. So calling Nippers from the other room, the paper was speedily examined.

A few days after this, Bartleby concluded four lengthy documents, being quadruplicates of a week's testimony taken before me in my High Court of Chancery. It became necessary to examine them. It was an important suit, and great accuracy was imperative. Having all things arranged I called Turkey, Nippers and Ginger Nut from the next room, meaning to place the four copies in the hands of my four clerks, while I should read from the original. Accordingly Turkey, Nippers and Ginger Nut had taken their seats in a row, each with his document in hand, when I called to Bartleby to join this interesting group.

"Bartleby! quick, I am waiting."

I heard a slow scrape of his chair legs on the uncarpeted floor, and soon he appeared standing at the entrance of his hermitage.

"What is wanted?" said he mildly.

30   "The copies, the copies," said I hurriedly. "We are going to examine them. There"—and I held towards him the fourth quadruplicate.

"I would prefer not to," he said, and gently disappeared behind the screen.

For a few moments I was turned into a pillar of salt,[8] standing at the head of my seated column of clerks. Recovering myself, I advanced towards the screen, and demanded the reason for such extraordinary conduct.

6. Crazy.
7. Marcus Tullius Cicero (106–43 B.C.E.), pro-republican Roman statesman, barrister, writer, and orator.
8. Struck dumb; in Genesis 19.26, Lot's wife, defying God's command, "looked back from behind him, and she became a pillar of salt."

"*Why* do you refuse?"

"I would prefer not to."

With any other man I should have flown outright into a dreadful pas- 35
sion, scorned all further words, and thrust him ignominiously from my
presence. But there was something about Bartleby that not only strangely
disarmed me, but in a wonderful manner touched and disconcerted me. I
began to reason with him.

"These are your own copies we are about to examine. It is labor saving
to you, because one examination will answer for your four papers. It is
common usage. Every copyist is bound to help examine his copy. Is it not
so? Will you not speak? Answer!"

"I prefer not to," he replied in a flute-like tone. It seemed to me that
while I had been addressing him, he carefully revolved every statement
that I made; fully comprehended the meaning; could not gainsay the irresistible conclusion; but, at the same time, some paramount consideration
prevailed with him to reply as he did.

"You are decided, then, not to comply with my request—a request made
according to common usage and common sense?"

He briefly gave me to understand that on that point my judgment was
sound. Yes: his decision was irreversible.

It is not seldom the case that when a man is browbeaten in some unpre- 40
cedented and violently unreasonable way, he begins to stagger in his own
plainest faith. He begins, as it were, vaguely to surmise that, wonderful as
it may be, all the justice and all the reason is on the other side. Accordingly,
if any disinterested persons are present, he turns to them for some rein-
forcement for his own faltering mind.

"Turkey," said I, "what do you think of this? Am I not right?"

"With submission, sir," said Turkey, with his blandest tone, "I think
that you are." *I like this phrase*

"Nippers," said I, "what do *you* think of it?"

"I think I should kick him out of the office."

(The reader of nice perceptions will here perceive that, it being morn- 45
ing, Turkey's answer is couched in polite and tranquil terms, but Nippers
replies in ill-tempered ones. Or, to repeat a previous sentence, Nippers's
ugly mood was on duty, and Turkey's off.) *only Turk + character*

"Ginger Nut," said I, willing to enlist the smallest suffrage[9] in my
behalf, "what do *you* think of it?"

"I think, sir, he's a little *luny*," replied Ginger Nut, with a grin.

"You hear what they say," said I, turning towards the screen, "come
forth and do your duty."

But he vouchsafed no reply. I pondered a moment in sore perplexity. But
once more business hurried me. I determined again to postpone the consideration of this dilemma to my future leisure. With a little trouble we

9. Favorable vote.

made out to examine the papers without Bartleby, though at every page or two, Turkey deferentially dropped his opinion that this proceeding was quite out of the common; while Nippers, twitching in his chair with a dyspeptic nervousness, ground out between his set teeth occasional hissing maledictions against the stubborn oaf behind the screen. And for his (Nippers's) part, this was the first and the last time he would do another man's business without pay.

50   Meanwhile Bartleby sat in his hermitage, oblivious to everything but his own peculiar business there.

Some days passed, the scrivener being employed upon another lengthy work. His late remarkable conduct led me to regard his ways narrowly. I observed that he never went to dinner; indeed that he never went anywhere. As yet I had never of my personal knowledge known him to be outside of my office. He was a perpetual sentry in the corner. At about eleven o'clock though, in the morning, I noticed that Ginger Nut would advance toward the opening in Bartleby's screen, as if silently beckoned thither by a gesture invisible to me where I sat. The boy would then leave the office jingling a few pence, and reappear with a handful of ginger-nuts which he delivered in the hermitage, receiving two of the cakes for his trouble.

He lives, then, on ginger-nuts, thought I; never eats a dinner, properly speaking; he must be a vegetarian then; but no; he never eats even vegetables, he eats nothing but ginger-nuts. My mind then ran on in reveries concerning the probable effects upon the human constitution of living entirely on ginger-nuts. Ginger-nuts are so called because they contain ginger as one of their peculiar constituents, and the final flavoring one. Now what was ginger? A hot, spicy thing. Was Bartleby hot and spicy? Not at all. Ginger, then, had no effect upon Bartleby. Probably he preferred it should have none.

Nothing so aggravates an earnest person as a passive resistance. If the individual so resisted be of a not inhumane temper, and the resisting one perfectly harmless in his passivity; then, in the better moods of the former, he will endeavor charitably to construe to his imagination what proves impossible to be solved by his judgment. Even so, for the most part, I regarded Bartleby and his ways. Poor fellow! thought I, he means no mischief; it is plain he intends no insolence; his aspect sufficiently evinces that his eccentricities are involuntary. He is useful to me. I can get along with him. If I turn him away, the chances are he will fall in with some less indulgent employer, and then he will be rudely treated, and perhaps driven forth miserably to starve. Yes. Here I can cheaply purchase a delicious self-approval. To befriend Bartleby; to humor him in his strange wilfulness, will cost me little or nothing, while I lay up in my soul what will eventually prove a sweet morsel for my conscience. But this mood was not invariable with me. The passiveness of Bartleby sometimes irritated me. I felt strangely goaded on to encounter him in new opposition, to elicit some angry spark from him answerable to my own. But indeed I might as well have essayed to strike fire with my knuckles against a bit of Windsor soap.[1] But one afternoon the evil impulse in me mastered me, and the following little scene ensued:

"Bartleby," said I, "when those papers are all copied, I will compare them with you."

"I would prefer not to."   55

"How? Surely you do not mean to persist in that mulish vagary?"

No answer.

I threw open the folding-doors near by, and turning upon Turkey and Nippers, exclaimed in an excited manner—

"He says, a second time, he won't examine his papers. What do you think of it, Turkey?"

It was afternoon, be it remembered. Turkey sat glowing like a brass boiler,   60 his bald head steaming, his hands reeling among his blotted papers.

"Think of it?" roared Turkey; "I think I'll just step behind his screen, and black his eyes for him!"

So saying, Turkey rose to his feet and threw his arms into a pugilistic position. He was hurrying away to make good his promise, when I detained him, alarmed at the effect of incautiously rousing Turkey's combativeness after dinner.

"Sit down, Turkey," said I, "and hear what Nippers has to say. What do you think of it, Nippers? Would I not be justified in immediately dismissing Bartleby?"

"Excuse me, that is for you to decide, sir. I think his conduct quite unusual, and indeed unjust, as regards Turkey and myself. But it may only be a passing whim."

"Ah," exclaimed I, "you have strangely changed your mind then—you   65 speak very gently of him now."

"All beer," cried Turkey; "gentleness is effects of beer—Nippers and I dined together today. You see how gentle *I* am, sir. Shall I go and black his eyes?"

"You refer to Bartleby, I suppose. No, not today, Turkey," I replied; "pray, put up your fists."

I closed the doors, and again advanced towards Bartleby. I felt additional incentives tempting me to my fate. I burned to be rebelled against again. I remembered that Bartleby never left the office.

"Bartleby," said I, "Ginger Nut is away; just step round to the Post Office, won't you? (it was but a three minutes' walk,) and see if there is anything for me."

"I would prefer not to."   70

"You *will* not?"

"I *prefer* not."

I staggered to my desk, and sat there in a deep study. My blind inveteracy returned. Was there any other thing in which I could procure myself to

---

1. Scented soap, usually brown.

be ignominiously repulsed by this lean, penniless wight?—my hired clerk? What added thing is there, perfectly reasonable, that he will be sure to refuse to do?

"Bartleby!"

75   No answer.

"Bartleby," in a louder tone.

No answer.

"Bartleby," I roared.

Like a very ghost, agreeably to the laws of magical invocation, at the third summons, he appeared at the entrance of his hermitage.

80   "Go to the next room, and tell Nippers to come to me."

"I prefer not to," he respectfully and slowly said, and mildly disappeared.

"Very good, Bartleby," said I, in a quiet sort of serenely severe self-possessed tone, intimating the unalterable purpose of some terrible retribution very close at hand. At the moment I half intended something of the kind. But upon the whole, as it was drawing towards my dinner-hour, I thought it best to put on my hat and walk home for the day, suffering much from perplexity and distress of mind.

Shall I acknowledge it? The conclusion of this whole business was, that it soon became a fixed fact of my chambers, that a pale young scrivener, by the name of Bartleby, had a desk there; that he copied for me at the usual rate of four cents a folio (one hundred words); but he was permanently exempt from examining the work done by him, that duty being transferred to Turkey and Nippers, one of compliment doubtless to their superior acuteness; moreover, said Bartleby was never on any account to be dispatched on the most trivial errand of any sort; and that even if entreated to take upon him such a matter, it was generally understood that he would prefer not to—in other words, that he would refuse point-blank.

As days passed on, I became considerably reconciled to Bartleby. His steadiness, his freedom from all dissipation, his incessant industry (except when he chose to throw himself into a standing revery behind his screen), his great stillness, his unalterableness of demeanor under all circumstances, made him a valuable acquisition. One prime thing was this,—*he was always there*;—first in the morning, continually through the day, and the last at night. I had a singular confidence in his honesty. I felt my most precious papers perfectly safe in his hands. Sometimes to be sure I could not, for the very soul of me, avoid falling into sudden spasmodic passions with him. For it was exceeding difficult to bear in mind all the time those strange peculiarities, privileges, and unheard of exemptions, forming the tacit stipulations on Bartleby's part under which he remained in my office. Now and then, in the eagerness of dispatching pressing business, I would inadvertently summon Bartleby, in a short, rapid tone, to put his finger, say, on the incipient tie of a bit of red tape with which I was about compressing some papers. Of course, from behind the screen the usual answer, "I prefer not to," was sure to come; and then, how could a human creature with the common infirmities of our nature, refrain from bitterly exclaiming upon such perverseness—such unreasonableness? However, every added repulse of this sort which I received only tended to lessen the probability of my repeating the inadvertence.

Here it must be said, that according to the custom of most legal gentle- 85 men occupying chambers in densely-populated law buildings, there were several keys to my door. One was kept by a woman residing in the attic, which person weekly scrubbed and daily swept and dusted my apartments. Another was kept by Turkey for convenience sake. The third I sometimes carried in my own pocket. The fourth I knew not who had.

Now, one Sunday morning I happened to go to Trinity Church, to hear a celebrated preacher, and finding myself rather early on the ground, I thought I would walk round to my chambers for a while. Luckily I had my key with me; but upon applying it to the lock, I found it resisted by something inserted from the inside. Quite surprised, I called out; when to my consternation a key was turned from within; and thrusting his lean visage at me, and holding the door ajar, the apparition of Bartleby appeared, in his shirt sleeves, and otherwise in a strangely tattered dishabille, saying quietly that he was sorry, but he was deeply engaged just then, and—preferred not admitting me at present. In a brief word or two, he moreover added, that perhaps I had better walk round the block two or three times, and by that time he would probably have concluded his affairs.

Now, the utterly unsurmised appearance of Bartleby, tenanting my law-chambers of a Sunday morning, with his cadaverously gentlemanly *non-chalance*, yet withal firm and self-possessed, had such a strange effect upon me, that incontinently I slunk away from my own door, and did as desired. But not without sundry twinges of impotent rebellion against the mild effrontery of this unaccountable scrivener. Indeed, it was his wonderful mildness, chiefly, which not only disarmed me, but unmanned me, as it were. For I consider that one, for the time, is sort of unmanned when he tranquilly permits his hired clerk to dictate to him, and order him away from his own premises. Furthermore, I was full of uneasiness as to what Bartleby could possibly be doing in my office in his shirt sleeves, and in an otherwise dismantled condition of a Sunday morning. Was anything amiss going on? Nay, that was out of the question. It was not to be thought of for a moment that Bartleby was an immoral person. But what could he be doing there?—copying? Nay again, whatever might be his eccentricities, Bartleby was an eminently decorous person. He would be the last man to sit down to his desk in any state approaching to nudity. Besides, it was Sunday; and there was something about Bartleby that forbade the supposition that he would by any secular occupation violate the proprieties of the day.

Nevertheless, my mind was not pacified; and full of a restless curiosity, at last I returned to the door. Without hindrance I inserted my key, opened it, and entered. Bartleby was not to be seen. I looked round anxiously, peeped behind his screen; but it was very plain that he was gone. Upon more closely examining the place, I surmised that for an indefinite period Bartleby must have ate, dressed, and slept in my office, and that too without plate, mirror, or bed. The cushioned seat of a ricketty old sofa in one corner bore the faint impress of a lean, reclining form. Rolled away under his desk, I found a blanket under the empty grate, a blacking box[2] and brush; on a chair, a tin basin, with soap and a ragged towel; in a newspaper a few crumbs of ginger-nuts and a morsel of cheese. Yes, thought I, it is evident enough that Bartleby has been making his home here, keeping bachelor's hall all by himself. Immediately then the thought came sweeping across me, What miserable friendlessness and loneliness are here revealed! His poverty is great; but his solitude, how horrible! Think of it. Of a Sunday, Wall Street is deserted as Petra;[3] and every night of every day it is an emptiness. This building too, which of weekdays hums with industry and life, at nightfall echoes with sheer vacancy, and all through Sunday is forlorn. And here Bartleby makes his home; sole spectator of a solitude which he has seen all populous—a sort of innocent and transformed Marius brooding among the ruins of Carthage![4]

For the first time in my life a feeling of overpowering stinging melancholy seized me. Before, I had never experienced aught but a not-unpleasing sadness. The bond of a common humanity now drew me irresistibly to gloom. A fraternal melancholy! For both I and Bartleby were sons of Adam. I remembered the bright silks and sparkling faces I had seen that day, in gala trim, swan-like sailing down the Mississippi of Broadway; and I contrasted them with the pallid copyist, and thought to myself, Ah, happiness courts the light, so we deem the world is gay; but misery hides aloof, so we deem that misery there is none. These sad fancyings—chimeras, doubtless, of a sick and silly brain—led on to other and more special thoughts, concerning the eccentricities of Bartleby. Presentiments of strange discoveries hovered round me. The scrivener's pale form appeared to me laid out, among uncaring strangers, in its shivering winding sheet.

90   Suddenly I was attracted by Bartleby's closed desk, the key in open sight left in the lock.

I mean no mischief, seek the gratification of no heartless curiosity, thought I; besides, the desk is mine, and its contents too, so I will make

---

2. Box of black shoe polish.   3. Once a flourishing Middle Eastern trade center, long in ruins.
4. Gaius (or Caius) Marius (157–86 B.C.E.), Roman consul and general, expelled from Rome in 88 B.C.E. by Sulla; when an officer of Sextilius, the governor, forbade him to land in Africa, Marius replied, "Go tell him that you have seen Caius Marius sitting in exile among the ruins of Carthage," applying the example of the fortune of that city to the change of his own condition. The image was so common that a few years after "Bartleby," Dickens apologizes for using it: "like that lumbering Marius among the ruins of Carthage, who has sat heavy on a thousand millions of similes" ("The Calais Night-Mail," in *The Uncommercial Traveler*).

bold to look within. Everything was methodically arranged, the papers smoothly placed. The pigeonholes were deep, and removing the files of documents, I groped into their recesses. Presently I felt something there, and dragged it out. It was an old bandanna handkerchief, heavy and knotted. I opened it, and saw it was a savings' bank.

I now recalled all the quiet mysteries which I had noted in the man. I remembered that he never spoke but to answer; that though at intervals he had considerable time to himself, yet I had never seen him reading—no, not even a newspaper; that for long periods he would stand looking out, at his pale window behind the screen, upon the dead brick wall; I was quite sure he never visited any refectory or eating house; while his pale face clearly indicated that he never drank beer like Turkey, or tea and coffee even, like other men; that he never went anywhere in particular that I could learn; never went out for a walk, unless indeed that was the case at present; that he had declined telling who he was, or whence he came, or whether he had any relatives in the world; that though so thin and pale, he never complained of ill health. And more than all, I remembered a certain unconscious air of pallid—how shall I call it?—of pallid haughtiness, say, or rather an austere reserve about him, which had positively awed me into my tame compliance with his eccentricities, when I had feared to ask him to do the slightest incidental thing for me, even though I might know, from his long-continued motionlessness, that behind his screen he must be standing in one of those dead-wall reveries of his.

Revolving all these things, and coupling them with the recently discovered fact that he made my office his constant abiding place and home, and not forgetful of his morbid moodiness; revolving all these things, a prudential feeling began to steal over me. My first emotions had been those of pure melancholy and sincerest pity; but just in proportion as the forlornness of Bartleby grew and grew to my imagination, did that same melancholy merge into fear, that pity into repulsion. So true it is, and so terrible too, that up to a certain point the thought or sight of misery enlists our best affections; but, in certain special cases, beyond that point it does not. They err who would assert that invariably this is owing to the inherent selfishness of the human heart. It rather proceeds from a certain hopelessness of remedying excessive and organic ill. To a sensitive being, pity is not seldom pain. And when at last it is perceived that such pity cannot lead to effectual succor, common sense bids the soul be rid of it. What I saw that morning persuaded me that the scrivener was the victim of innate and incurable disorder. I might give alms to his body; but his body did not pain him; it was his soul that suffered, and his soul I could not reach.

I did not accomplish the purpose of going to Trinity Church that morning. Somehow, the things I had seen disqualified me for the time from churchgoing. I walked homeward, thinking what I would do with Bartleby. Finally, I resolved upon this;—I would put certain calm questions to him the next morning, touching his history, &c., and if he declined to answer them openly and unreservedly (and I supposed he would prefer not), then to give him a twenty-dollar bill over and above whatever I might owe him, and tell him his services were no longer required; but that if in any other way I could assist him, I would be happy to do so, especially if he desired to return to his native place, wherever that might be, I would willingly help to defray the expenses. Moreover, if, after reaching home, he found himself at any time in want of aid, a letter from him would be sure of a reply.

95   The next morning came.

"Bartleby," said I, gently calling to him behind his screen.

No reply.

"Bartleby," said I, in a still gentler tone, "come here; I am not going to ask you to do anything you would prefer not to do—I simply wish to speak to you."

Upon this he noiselessly slid into view.

100   "Will you tell me, Bartleby, where you were born?"

"I would prefer not to."

"Will you tell me *anything* about yourself?"

"I would prefer not to."

"But what reasonable objection can you have to speak to me? I feel friendly towards you."

105   He did not look at me while I spoke, but kept his glance fixed upon my bust of Cicero, which as I then sat, was directly behind me, some six inches above my head.

"What is your answer, Bartleby?" said I, after waiting a considerable time for a reply, during which his countenance remained immovable, only there was the faintest conceivable tremor of the white attenuated mouth.

"At present I prefer to give no answer," he said, and retired into his hermitage.

It was rather weak in me I confess, but his manner on this occasion nettled me. Not only did there seem to lurk in it a certain calm disdain, but his perverseness seemed ungrateful, considering the undeniable good usage and indulgence he had received from me.

Again I sat ruminating what I should do. Mortified as I was at his behavior, and resolved as I had been to dismiss him when I entered my office, nevertheless I strangely felt something superstitious knocking at my heart, and forbidding me to carry out my purpose, and denouncing me for a villain if I dared to breathe one bitter word against this forlornest of mankind. At last, familiarly drawing my chair behind his screen, I sat down and said: "Bartleby, never mind then about revealing your history; but let me entreat you, as a friend, to comply as far as may be with the usages of this office. Say now you will help to examine papers tomorrow or next day: in short, say now that in a day or two you will begin to be a little reasonable:—say so, Bartleby."

"At present I would prefer not to be a little reasonable," was his mildly 110
cadaverous reply.

Just then the folding-doors opened, and Nippers approached. He seemed
suffering from an unusually bad night's rest, induced by severer indigestion than common. He overheard those final words of Bartleby.

"*Prefer not,* eh?" gritted Nippers—"I'd *prefer* him, if I were you, sir,"
addressing me—"I'd *prefer* him; I'd give him preferences, the stubborn
mule! What is it, sir, pray, that he *prefers* not to do now?"

Bartleby moved not a limb.

"Mr. Nippers," said I, "I'd prefer that you would withdraw for the
present."

Somehow, of late I had got into the way of involuntarily using this word 115
"prefer" upon all sorts of not exactly suitable occasions. And I trembled to
think that my contact with the scrivener had already and seriously affected
me in a mental way. And what further and deeper aberration might it not
yet produce? This apprehension had not been without efficacy in determining me to summary means.

As Nippers, looking very sour and sulky, was departing, Turkey blandly
and deferentially approached.

"With submission, sir," said he, "yesterday I was thinking about Bartleby here, and I think that if he would but prefer to take a quart of good
ale every day, it would do much towards mending him and enabling him
to assist in examining his papers."

"So you have got the word too," said I, slightly excited.

"With submission, what word, sir?" asked Turkey, respectfully crowding himself into the contracted space behind the screen, and by so doing
making me jostle the scrivener. "What word, sir?"

"I would prefer to be left alone here," said Bartleby, as if offended at 120
being mobbed in his privacy.

"*That's* the word, Turkey," said I—"*that's* it."

"Oh, *prefer*? oh yes—queer word. I never use it myself. But, sir, as I was
saying, if he would but prefer—"

"Turkey," interrupted I, "you will please withdraw."

"Oh certainly, sir, if you prefer that I should."

As he opened the folding-door to retire, Nippers at his desk caught a 125
glimpse of me, and asked whether I would prefer to have a certain paper
copied on blue paper or white. He did not in the least roguishly accent the
word *prefer.* It was plain that it involuntarily rolled from his tongue. I
thought to myself, surely I must get rid of a demented man, who already
has in some degree turned the tongues, if not the heads of myself and
clerks. But I thought it prudent not to break the dismission at once.

The next day I noticed that Bartleby did nothing but stand at his window in his dead-wall revery. Upon asking him why he did not write, he said
that he had decided upon doing no more writing.

"Why, how now? what next?" exclaimed I, "do no more writing?"

"No more."

"And what is the reason?"

130   "Do you not see the reason for yourself," he indifferently replied.

I looked steadfastly at him, and perceived that his eyes looked dull and glazed. Instantly it occurred to me, that his unexampled diligence in copying by his dim window for the first few weeks of his stay with me might have temporarily impaired his vision.

I was touched. I said something in condolence with him. I hinted that of course he did wisely in abstaining from writing for a while; and urged him to embrace that opportunity of taking wholesome exercise in the open air. This, however, he did not do. A few days after this, my other clerks being absent, and being in a great hurry to dispatch certain letters by the mail, I thought that, having nothing else earthly to do, Bartleby would surely be less inflexible than usual, and carry these letters to the post office. But he blankly declined. So, much to my inconvenience, I went myself.

Still added days went by. Whether Bartleby's eyes improved or not, I could not say. To all appearance, I thought they did. But when I asked him if they did, he vouchsafed no answer. At all events, he would do no copying. At last, in reply to my urgings, he informed me that he had permanently given up copying.

"What!" exclaimed I; "suppose your eyes should get entirely well—better than ever before—would you not copy then?"

135   "I have given up copying," he answered, and slid aside.

He remained, as ever, a fixture in my chamber. Nay—if that were possible—he became still more of a fixture than before. What was to be done? He would do nothing in the office: why should he stay there? In plain fact, he had now become a millstone[5] to me, not only useless as a necklace, but afflictive to bear. Yet I was sorry for him. I speak less than truth when I say that, on his own account, he occasioned me uneasiness. If he would but have named a single relative or friend, I would instantly have written, and urged their taking the poor fellow away to some convenient retreat. But he seemed alone, absolutely alone in the universe. A bit of wreck in the mid-Atlantic. At length, necessities connected with my business tyrannized over all other considerations. Decently as I could, I told Bartleby that in six days' time he must unconditionally leave the office. I warned him to take measures, in the interval, for procuring some other abode. I offered to assist him in this endeavor, if he himself would but take the first step towards a removal. "And when you finally quit me, Bartleby," added I, "I shall see that you go not away entirely unprovided. Six days from this hour, remember."

---

5. Heavy stone for grinding grain. See Matthew 18.6: "But whoso shall offend one of these little ones which believe in me, it were better for him that a millstone were hanged about his neck, and that he were drowned in the depth of the sea."

At the expiration of that period, I peeped behind the screen, and lo! Bartleby was there.

I buttoned up my coat, balanced myself; advanced slowly towards him, touched his shoulder, and said, "The time has come; you must quit this place; I am sorry for you; here is money; but you must go."

"I would prefer not," he replied, with his back still towards me.

"You *must*." 140

He remained silent.

Now I had an unbounded confidence in this man's common honesty. He had frequently restored to me sixpences and shillings[6] carelessly dropped upon the floor, for I am apt to be very reckless in such shirt-button affairs. The proceeding then which followed will not be deemed extraordinary.

"Bartleby," said I, "I owe you twelve dollars on account; here are thirty-two; the odd twenty are yours.—Will you take it?" and I handed the bills towards him.

But he made no motion.

"I will leave them here then," putting them under a weight on the table. 145 Then taking my hat and cane and going to the door I tranquilly turned and added—"After you have removed your things from these offices, Bartleby, you will of course lock the door—since everyone is now gone for the day but you—and if you please, slip your key underneath the mat, so that I may have it in the morning. I shall not see you again; so good-bye to you. If hereafter in your new place of abode I can be of any service to you, do not fail to advise me by letter. Good-bye, Bartleby, and fare you well."

But he answered not a word; like the last column of some ruined temple, he remained standing mute and solitary in the middle of the otherwise deserted room.

As I walked home in a pensive mood, my vanity got the better of my pity. I could not but highly plume myself on my masterly management in getting rid of Bartleby. Masterly I call it, and such it must appear to any dispassionate thinker. The beauty of my procedure seemed to consist in its perfect quietness. There was no vulgar bullying, no bravado of any sort, no choleric hectoring, and striding to and fro across the apartment, jerking out vehement commands for Bartleby to bundle himself off with his beggarly traps.[7] Nothing of the kind. Without loudly bidding Bartleby depart—as an inferior genius might have done—I *assumed* the ground that depart he must; and upon that assumption built all I had to say. The more I thought over my procedure, the more I was charmed with it. Nevertheless, next morning, upon awakening, I had my doubts,—I had somehow slept off the fumes of vanity. One of the coolest and wisest hours a man has is just after he awakes in the morning. My procedure seemed as sagacious as ever,—but only in theory. How it would prove in practice—there was the rub. It was

6. Coins. 7. Personal belongings, luggage.

truly a beautiful thought to have assumed Bartleby's departure; but, after all, that assumption was simply my own, and none of Bartleby's. The great point was, not whether I had assumed that he would quit me, but whether he would prefer so to do. He was more a man of preferences than assumptions.

After breakfast, I walked downtown, arguing the probabilities *pro* and *con*. One moment I thought it would prove a miserable failure, and Bartleby would be found all alive at my office as usual; the next moment it seemed certain that I should see his chair empty. And so I kept veering about. At the corner of Broadway and Canal Street, I saw quite an excited group of people standing in earnest conversation.

"I'll take odds he doesn't," said a voice as I passed.

150   "Doesn't go?—done!" said I, "put up your money."

I was instinctively putting my hand in my pocket to produce my own, when I remembered that this was an election day. The words I had overheard bore no reference to Bartleby, but to the success or non-success of some candidate for the mayoralty. In my intent frame of mind, I had, as it were, imagined that all Broadway shared in my excitement, and were debating the same question with me. I passed on, very thankful that the uproar of the street screened my momentary absent-mindedness.

As I had intended, I was earlier than usual at my office door. I stood listening for a moment. All was still. He must be gone. I tried the knob. The door was locked. Yes, my procedure had worked to a charm; he indeed must be vanished. Yet a certain melancholy mixed with this: I was almost sorry for my brilliant success. I was fumbling under the door mat for the key, which Bartleby was to have left there for me, when accidentally my knee knocked against a panel, producing a summoning sound, and in response a voice came to me from within—"Not yet; I am occupied."

It was Bartleby.

I was thunderstruck. For an instant I stood like the man who, pipe in mouth, was killed one cloudless afternoon long ago in Virginia, by summer lightning; at his own warm open window he was killed, and remained leaning out there upon the dreamy afternoon, till some one touched him, when he fell.

155   "Not gone!" I murmured at last. But again obeying that wondrous ascendancy which the inscrutable scrivener had over me, and from which ascendancy, for all my chafing, I could not completely escape, I slowly went downstairs and out into the street, and while walking round the block, considered what I should next do in this unheard-of perplexity. Turn the man out by an actual thrusting I could not; to drive him away by calling him hard names would not do; calling in the police was an unpleasant idea; and yet, permit him to enjoy his cadaverous triumph over me,—this too I could not think of. What was to be done? or, if nothing could be done, was there anything further that I could *assume* in the matter? Yes, as

before I had prospectively assumed that Bartleby would depart, so now I might retrospectively assume that departed he was. In the legitimate carrying out of this assumption, I might enter my office in a great hurry, and pretending not to see Bartleby at all, walk straight against him as if he were air. Such a proceeding would in a singular degree have the appearance of a home-thrust.[8] It was hardly possible that Bartleby could withstand such an application of the doctrine of assumptions. But upon second thoughts the success of the plan seemed rather dubious. I resolved to argue the matter over with him again.

"Bartleby," said I, entering the office, with a quietly severe expression, "I am seriously displeased. I am pained, Bartleby. I had thought better of you. I had imagined you of such a gentlemanly organization, that in any delicate dilemma a slight hint would suffice—in short, an assumption. But it appears I am deceived. Why," I added, unaffectedly starting, "you have not even touched that money yet," pointing to it, just where I had left it the evening previous.

He answered nothing.

"Will you, or will you not, quit me?" I now demanded in a sudden passion, advancing close to him.

"I would prefer *not* to quit you," he replied, gently emphasizing the *not*.

"What earthly right have you to stay here? Do you pay any rent? Do you 160 pay my taxes? Or is this property yours?"

He answered nothing.

"Are you ready to go on and write now? Are your eyes recovered? Could you copy a small paper for me this morning? or help examine a few lines? or step round to the post office? In a word, will you do anything at all, to give a coloring to your refusal to depart the premises?"

He silently retired into his hermitage.

I was now in such a state of nervous resentment that I thought it but prudent to check myself at present from further demonstrations. Bartleby and I were alone. I remembered the tragedy of the unfortunate Adams and the still more unfortunate Colt in the solitary office of the latter;[9] and how poor Colt, being dreadfully incensed by Adams, and imprudently permitting himself to get wildly excited, was at unawares hurried into his fatal act—an act which certainly no man could possibly deplore more than the actor himself. Often it had occurred to me in my ponderings upon the subject, that had that altercation taken place in the public street, or at a private residence, it would not have terminated as it did. It was the circumstance of being alone in a solitary office, up stairs, of a building entirely unhallowed by humanizing domestic associations—an uncarpeted office, doubtless, of

8. In fencing, a successful thrust to the opponent's body.
9. In 1841, John C. Colt, brother of the famous gunmaker, unintentionally killed Samuel Adams, a printer, when he hit him on the head during a fight.

a dusty, haggard sort of appearance;—this it must have been, which greatly helped to enhance the irritable desperation of the hapless Colt.

165   But when this old Adam[1] of resentment rose in me and tempted me concerning Bartleby, I grappled him and threw him. How? Why, simply by recalling the divine injunction: "A new commandment[2] give I unto you, that ye love one another." Yes, this it was that saved me. Aside from higher considerations, charity often operates as a vastly wise and prudent principle—a great safeguard to its possessor. Men have committed murder for jealousy's sake, and anger's sake, and hatred's sake, and selfishness' sake, and spiritual pride's sake; but no man that ever I heard of, ever committed a diabolical murder for sweet charity's sake. Mere self-interest, then, if no better motive can be enlisted, should, especially with high-tempered men, prompt all beings to charity and philanthropy. At any rate, upon the occasion in question, I strove to drown my exasperated feelings towards the scrivener by benevolently construing his conduct. Poor fellow, poor fellow! thought I, he don't mean anything; and besides, he has seen hard times, and ought to be indulged.

I endeavored also immediately to occupy myself, and at the same time to comfort my despondency. I tried to fancy that in the course of the morning, at such time as might prove agreeable to him, Bartleby, of his own free accord, would emerge from his hermitage, and take up some decided line of march in the direction of the door. But no. Half-past twelve o'clock came; Turkey began to glow in the face, overturn his inkstand, and become generally obstreperous; Nippers abated down into quietude and courtesy; Ginger Nut munched his noon apple; and Bartleby remained standing at his window in one of his profoundest dead-wall reveries. Will it be credited? Ought I to acknowledge it? That afternoon I left the office without saying one further word to him.

Some days now passed, during which, at leisure intervals I looked a little into "Edwards on the Will," and "Priestley on Necessity."[3] Under the circumstances, those books induced a salutary feeling. Gradually I slid into the persuasion that these troubles of mine touching the scrivener, had been all predestinated from eternity, and Bartleby was billeted upon me for

---

1. Sinful element in human nature; see, e.g., "Invocation of Blessing on the Child" in the *Book of Common Prayer:* "Grant that the old Adam in this child may be so buried, that the new man may be raised up in him." Christ is sometimes called the "new Adam."

2. In John 13.34, where, however, the phrasing is "I give unto . . ."

3. Jonathan Edwards (1703–58), New England Calvinist theologian and revivalist, in *The Freedom of the Will* (1754) argued that human beings are not in fact free, for though they choose according to the way they see things, that way is predetermined (by biography, environment, and character), and they act out of personality rather than by will. Joseph Priestley (1733–1804), dissenting preacher, scientist, grammarian, and philosopher, argued in *The Doctrine of Philosophical Necessity* (1777) that free will is theologically objectionable, metaphysically incomprehensible, and morally undesirable.

some mysterious purpose of an all-wise Providence, which it was not for a mere mortal like me to fathom. Yes, Bartleby, stay there behind your screen, thought I; I shall persecute you no more; you are harmless and noiseless as any of these old chairs; in short, I never feel so private as when I know you are here. At least I see it, I feel it; I penetrate to the predestinated purpose of my life. I am content. Others may have loftier parts to enact; but my mission in this world, Bartleby, is to furnish you with office-room for such period as you may see fit to remain.

I believe that this wise and blessed frame of mind would have continued with me, had it not been for the unsolicited and uncharitable remarks obtruded upon me by my professional friends who visited the rooms. But thus it often is, that the constant friction of illiberal minds wears out at last the best resolves of the more generous. Though to be sure, when I reflected upon it, it was not strange that people entering my office should be struck by the peculiar aspect of the unaccountable Bartleby, and so be tempted to throw out some sinister observations concerning him. Sometimes an attorney having business with me, and calling at my office, and finding no one but the scrivener there, would undertake to obtain some sort of precise information from him touching my whereabouts; but without heeding his idle talk, Bartleby would remain standing immovable in the middle of the room. So after contemplating him in that position for a time, the attorney would depart, no wiser than he came.

Also, when a Reference[4] was going on, and the room full of lawyers and witnesses and business was driving fast; some deeply occupied legal gentleman present, seeing Bartleby wholly unemployed, would request him to run round to his (the legal gentleman's) office and fetch some papers for him. Thereupon, Bartleby would tranquilly decline, and yet remain idle as before. Then the lawyer would give a great stare, and turn to me. And what could I say? At last I was made aware that all through the circle of my professional acquaintance, a whisper of wonder was running round, having reference to the strange creature I kept at my office. This worried me very much. And as the idea came upon me of his possibly turning out a long-lived man, and keep occupying my chambers, and denying my authority; and perplexing my visitors; and scandalizing my professional reputation; and casting a general gloom over the premises; keeping soul and body together to the last upon his savings (for doubtless he spent but half a dime a day), and in the end perhaps outlive me, and claim possession of my office by right of his perpetual occupancy: as all these dark anticipations crowded upon me more and more, and my friends continually intruded their relentless remarks upon the apparition in my room; a great change was wrought in me. I resolved to gather all my faculties together, and forever rid me of this intolerable incubus.[5]

4. Consultation or committee meeting.   5. Evil spirit.

170   Ere revolving any complicated project, however, adapted to this end, I first simply suggested to Bartleby the propriety of his permanent departure. In a calm and serious tone, I commended the idea to his careful and mature consideration. But having taken three days to meditate upon it, he apprised me that his original determination remained the same; in short, that he still preferred to abide with me.

What shall I do? I now said to myself, buttoning up my coat to the last button. What shall I do? what ought I to do? what does conscience say I *should* do with this man, or rather ghost. Rid myself of him, I must; go, he shall. But how? You will not thrust him, the poor, pale, passive mortal,—you will not thrust such a helpless creature out of your door? you will not dishonor yourself by such cruelty? No, I will not, I cannot do that. Rather would I let him live and die here, and then mason up his remains in the wall. What then will you do? For all your coaxing, he will not budge. Bribes he leaves under your own paperweight on your table; in short, it is quite plain that he prefers to cling to you.

Then something severe, something unusual must be done. What! surely you will not have him collared by a constable, and commit his innocent pallor to the common jail? And upon what ground could you procure such a thing to be done?—a vagrant, is he? What! he a vagrant, a wanderer, who refuses to budge? It is because he will *not* be a vagrant, then, that you seek to count him *as* a vagrant. That is too absurd. No visible means of support: there I have him. Wrong again: for indubitably he *does* support himself, and that is the only unanswerable proof that any man can show of his possessing the means so to do. No more then. Since he will not quit me, I must quit him. I will change my offices; I will move elsewhere; and give him fair notice, that if I find him on my new premises I will then proceed against him as a common trespasser.

Acting accordingly, next day I thus addressed him: "I find these chambers too far from the City Hall; the air is unwholesome. In a word, I propose to remove my offices next week, and shall no longer require your services. I tell you this now, in order that you may seek another place."

He made no reply, and nothing more was said.

175   On the appointed day I engaged carts and men, proceeded to my chambers, and having but little furniture, everything was removed in a few hours. Throughout, the scrivener remained standing behind the screen, which I directed to be removed the last thing. It was withdrawn; and being folded up like a huge folio, left him the motionless occupant of a naked room. I stood in the entry watching him a moment, while something from within me upbraided me.

I re-entered, with my hand in my pocket—and—and my heart in my mouth.

"Good-bye, Bartleby; I am going—good-bye, and God some way bless you; and take that," slipping something in his hand. But it dropped upon the floor, and then,—strange to say—I tore myself from him whom I had so longed to be rid of.

Established in my new quarters, for a day or two I kept the door locked, and started at every footfall in the passages. When I returned to my rooms after any little absence, I would pause at the threshold for an instant, and attentively listen, ere applying my key. But these fears were needless. Bartleby never came nigh me.

I thought all was going well, when a perturbed-looking stranger visited me, inquiring whether I was the person who had recently occupied rooms at No.——Wall Street.

Full of forebodings, I replied that I was. 180

"Then sir," said the stranger, who proved a lawyer, "you are responsible for the man you left there. He refuses to do any copying; he refuses to do anything; he says he prefers not to; and he refuses to quit the premises."

"I am very sorry, sir," said I, with assumed tranquillity, but an inward tremor, "but, really, the man you allude to is nothing to me—he is no relation or apprentice of mine, that you should hold me responsible for him."

"In mercy's name, who is he?"

"I certainly cannot inform you. I know nothing about him. Formerly I employed him as a copyist; but he has done nothing for me now for some time past."

"I shall settle him then,—good morning, sir." 185

Several days passed, and I heard nothing more; and though I often felt a charitable prompting to call at the place and see poor Bartleby, yet a certain squeamishness of I know not what withheld me.

All is over with him, by this time, thought I at last, when through another week no further intelligence reached me. But coming to my room the day after, I found several persons waiting at my door in a high state of nervous excitement.

"That's the man—here he comes," cried the foremost one, whom I recognized as the lawyer who had previously called upon me alone.

"You must take him away, sir, at once," cried a portly person among them, advancing upon me, and whom I knew to be the landlord of No. —— Wall Street. "These gentlemen, my tenants, cannot stand it any longer; Mr. B——" pointing to the lawyer, "has turned him out of his room, and he now persists in haunting the building generally, sitting upon the banisters of the stairs by day, and sleeping in the entry by night. Everybody is concerned; clients are leaving the offices; some fears are entertained of a mob; something you must do, and that without delay."

Aghast at this torrent, I fell back before it, and would fain have locked 190 myself in my new quarters. In vain I persisted that Bartleby was nothing to me—no more than to anyone else. In vain:—I was the last person known to have anything to do with him, and they held me to the terrible account.

Fearful then of being exposed in the papers (as one person present obscurely threatened) I considered the matter, and at length said, that if the lawyer would give me a confidential interview with the scrivener, in his (the lawyer's) own room, I would that afternoon strive my best to rid them of the nuisance they complained of.

Going upstairs to my old haunt, there was Bartleby silently sitting upon the banister at the landing.

"What are you doing here, Bartleby?" said I.

"Sitting upon the banister," he mildly replied.

I motioned him into the lawyer's room, who then left us.

195 "Bartleby," said I, "are you aware that you are the cause of great tribulation to me, by persisting in occupying the entry after being dismissed from the office?"

No answer.

"Now one of two things must take place. Either you must do something, or something must be done to you. Now what sort of business would you like to engage in? Would you like to re-engage in copying for someone?"

"No; I would prefer not to make any change."

"Would you like a clerkship in a drygoods store?"

200 "There is too much confinement about that. No, I would not like a clerkship; but I am not particular."

"Too much confinement," I cried, "why you keep yourself confined all the time!"

"I would prefer not to take a clerkship," he rejoined, as if to settle that little item at once.

"How would a bartender's business suit you? There is no trying of the eyesight in that."

"I would not like it at all; though, as I said before, I am not particular."

205 His unwonted wordiness inspirited me. I returned to the charge.

"Well then, would you like to travel through the country collecting bills for the merchants? That would improve your health."

"No, I would prefer to be doing something else."

"How then would going as a companion to Europe, to entertain some young gentleman with your conversation,—how would that suit you?"

"Not at all. It does not strike me that there is anything definite about that. I like to be stationary. But I am not particular."

210 "Stationary you shall be then," I cried, now losing all patience, and for the first time in all my exasperating connection with him fairly flying into a passion. "If you do not go away from these premises before night, I shall feel bound—indeed I *am* bound—to—to—to quit the premises myself!" I rather absurdly concluded, knowing not with what possible threat to try to frighten his immobility into compliance. Despairing of all further efforts, I was precipitately leaving him, when a final thought occurred to me—one which had not been wholly unindulged before.

"Bartleby," said I, in the kindest tone I could assume under such exciting circumstances, "will you go home with me now—not to my office, but my dwelling—and remain there till we can conclude upon some convenient arrangement for you at our leisure? Come, let us start now, right away."

"No: at present I would prefer not to make any change at all."

I answered nothing; but effectually dodging everyone by the suddenness and rapidity of my flight, rushed from the building, ran up Wall Street toward Broadway, and jumping into the first omnibus was soon removed from pursuit. As soon as tranquillity returned I distinctly perceived that I had now done all that I possibly could, both in respect to the demands of the landlord and his tenants, and with regard to my own desire and sense of duty, to benefit Bartleby, and shield him from rude persecution. I now strove to be entirely carefree and quiescent; and my conscience justified me in the attempt; though indeed it was not so successful as I could have wished. So fearful was I of being again hunted out by the incensed landlord and his exasperated tenants, that, surrendering my business to Nippers, for a few days I drove about the upper part of the town and through the suburbs, in my rockaway;[6] crossed over to Jersey City and Hoboken, and paid fugitive visits to Manhattanville and Astoria. In fact I almost lived in my rockaway for the time.

When again I entered my office, lo, a note from the landlord lay upon the desk. I opened it with trembling hands. It informed me that the writer had sent to the police, and had Bartleby removed to the Tombs as a vagrant. Moreover, since I knew more about him than anyone else, he wished me to appear at that place, and make a suitable statement of the facts. These tidings had a conflicting effect upon me. At first I was indignant; but at last almost approved. The landlord's energetic, summary disposition had led him to adopt a procedure which I do not think I would have decided upon myself; and yet as a last resort, under such peculiar circumstances, it seemed the only plan.

As I afterwards learned, the poor scrivener, when told that he must be conducted to the Tombs, offered not the slightest obstacle, but in his pale unmoving way, silently acquiesced. 215

Some of the compassionate and curious bystanders joined the party; and headed by one of the constables arm in arm with Bartleby, the silent procession filed its way through all the noise, and heat, and joy of the roaring thoroughfares at noon.

The same day I received the note I went to the Tombs, or to speak more properly, the Halls of Justice. Seeking the right officer, I stated the purpose of my call, and was informed that the individual I described was indeed within. I then assured the functionary that Bartleby was a perfectly honest man, and greatly to be compassionated, however unaccountably eccentric.

6. Light, four-wheeled carriage.

I narrated all I knew, and closed by suggesting the idea of letting him remain in as indulgent confinement as possible till something less harsh might be done—though indeed I hardly knew what. At all events, if nothing else could be decided upon, the alms-house must receive him. I then begged to have an interview.

Being under no disgraceful charge, and quite serene and harmless in all his ways, they had permitted him freely to wander about the prison, and especially in the inclosed grass-platted yards thereof. And so I found him there, standing all alone in the quietest of the yards, his face towards a high wall, while all around, from the narrow slits of the jail windows, I thought I saw peering out upon him the eyes of murderers and thieves.

"Bartleby!"

220   "I know you," he said, without looking round,—"and I want nothing to say to you."

"It was not I that brought you here, Bartleby," said I, keenly pained at his implied suspicion. "And to you, this should not be so vile a place. Nothing reproachful attaches to you by being here. And see, it is not so sad a place as one might think. Look, there is the sky, and here is the grass."

"I know where I am," he replied, but would say nothing more, and so I left him.

As I entered the corridor again, a broad meat-like man, in an apron, accosted me, and jerking his thumb over his shoulder said—"Is that your friend?"

"Yes."

225   "Does he want to starve? If he does, let him live on the prison fare, that's all."

"Who are you?" asked I, not knowing what to make of such an unofficially-speaking person in such a place.

"I am the grub-man. Such gentlemen as have friends here, hire me to provide them with something good to eat."

"Is this so?" said I, turning to the turnkey.

He said it was.

230   "Well then," said I, slipping some silver into the grub-man's hands (for so they called him). "I want you to give particular attention to my friend there; let him have the best dinner you can get. And you must be as polite to him as possible."

"Introduce me, will you?" said the grub-man, looking at me with an expression which seemed to say he was all impatience for an opportunity to give a specimen of his breeding.

Thinking it would prove of benefit to the scrivener, I acquiesced; and asking the grub-man his name, went up with him to Bartleby.

"Bartleby, this is Mr. Cutlets; you will find him very useful to you."

"Your sarvant, sir, your sarvant," said the grub-man, making a low salutation behind his apron. "Hope you find it pleasant here, sir;—spacious grounds—cool apartments, sir—hope you'll stay with us some time—try to make it agreeable. May Mrs. Cutlets and I have the pleasure of your company to dinner, sir, in Mrs. Cutlets' private room?"

"I prefer not to dine today," said Bartleby, turning away. "It would dis- 235 agree with me; I am unused to dinners." So saying he slowly moved to the other side of the inclosure, and took up a position fronting the dead-wall.

"How's this?" said the grub-man, addressing me with a stare of astonishment. "He's odd, ain't he?"

"I think he is a little deranged," said I, sadly.

"Deranged? deranged is it? Well now, upon my word, I thought that friend of yourn was a gentleman forger; they are always pale and genteel-like, them forgers. I can't help pity 'em—can't help it, sir. Did you know Monroe Edwards?"[7] he added touchingly, and paused. Then laying his hand pityingly on my shoulder, sighed, "he died of consumption at Sing Sing. So you weren't acquainted with Monroe?"

"No, I was never socially acquainted with any forgers. But I cannot stop longer. Look to my friend yonder. You will not lose by it. I will see you again."

Some few days after this, I again obtained admission to the Tombs, and 240 went through the corridors in quest of Bartleby; but without finding him.

"I saw him coming from his cell not long ago," said a turnkey, "may be he's gone to loiter in the yards."

So I went in that direction.

"Are you looking for the silent man?" said another turnkey passing me. "Yonder he lies—sleeping in the yard there. 'Tis not twenty minutes since I saw him lie down."

The yard was entirely quiet. It was not accessible to the common prisoners. The surrounding walls, of amazing thickness, kept off all sounds behind them. The Egyptian character of the masonry weighed upon me with its gloom. But a soft imprisoned turf grew under foot. The heart of the eternal pyramids, it seemed, wherein, by some strange magic, through the clefts, grass seed, dropped by birds, had sprung.

Strangely huddled at the base of the wall, his knees drawn up, and lying 245 on his side, his head touching the cold stones, I saw the wasted Bartleby. But nothing stirred. I paused; then went close up to him; stooped over, and saw that his dim eyes were open; otherwise he seemed profoundly sleeping. Something prompted me to touch him. I felt his hand, when a tingling shiver ran up my arm and down my spine to my feet.

The round face of the grub-man peered upon me now. "His dinner is ready. Won't he dine today, either? Or does he live without dining?"

"Lives without dining," said I, and closed the eyes.

"Eh!—He's asleep, ain't he?"

---

7. Famously flamboyant swindler and forger (1808–47) who died in Sing Sing prison, north of New York City.

"With kings and counsellors,"[8] murmured I.

250   There would seem little need for proceeding further in this history. Imagination will readily supply the meager recital of poor Bartleby's interment. But ere parting with the reader, let me say, that if this little narrative has sufficiently interested him, to awaken curiosity as to who Bartleby was, and what manner of life he led prior to the present narrator's making his acquaintance, I can only reply, that in such curiosity I fully share, but am wholly unable to gratify it. Yet here I hardly know whether I should divulge one little item of rumor, which came to my ear a few months after the scrivener's decease. Upon what basis it rested, I could never ascertain; and hence, how true it is I cannot now tell. But inasmuch as this vague report has not been without a certain strange suggestive interest to me, however sad, it may prove the same with some others; and so I will briefly mention it. The report was this: that Bartleby had been a subordinate clerk in the Dead Letter Office at Washington, from which he had been suddenly removed by a change in the administration. When I think over this rumor, I cannot adequately express the emotions which seize me. Dead letters! does it not sound like dead men? Conceive a man by nature and misfortune prone to a pallid hopelessness, can any business seem more fitted to heighten it than that of continually handling these dead letters, and assorting them for the flames? For by the cartload they are annually burned. Sometimes from out the folded paper the pale clerk takes a ring:—the finger it was meant for, perhaps, molders in the grave; a banknote sent in swiftest charity:—he whom it would relieve, nor eats nor hungers any more; pardon for those who died despairing; hope for those who died unhoping; good tidings for those who died stifled by unrelieved calamities. On errands of life, these letters speed to death.

Ah Bartleby! Ah humanity!

1853

FLANNERY O'CONNOR

A Good Man Is Hard to Find

The grandmother didn't want to go to Florida. She wanted to visit some of her connections in east Tennessee and she was seizing at every chance to change Bailey's mind. Bailey was the son she lived with, her only boy. He was sitting on the edge of his chair at the table, bent over the orange sports section of the *Journal*. "Now look here, Bailey," she said, "see here, read

8. I.e., dead. See Job 3.13-14: "then had I been at rest, With kings and counsellors of the earth, which built desolate places for themselves."

this," and she stood with one hand on her thin hip and the other rattling the newspaper at his bald head. "Here this fellow that calls himself The Misfit is aloose from the Federal Pen and headed toward Florida and you read here what it says he did to these people. Just you read it. I wouldn't take my children in any direction with a criminal like that aloose in it. I couldn't answer to my conscience if I did."

Bailey didn't look up from his reading so she wheeled around then and faced the children's mother, a young woman in slacks, whose face was as broad and innocent as a cabbage and was tied around with a green head-kerchief that had two points on the top like a rabbit's ears. She was sitting on the sofa, feeding the baby his apricots out of a jar. "The children have been to Florida before," the old lady said. "You all ought to take them somewhere else for a change so they would see different parts of the world and be broad. They never have been to east Tennessee."

The children's mother didn't seem to hear her but the eight-year-old boy, John Wesley, a stocky child with glasses, said, "If you don't want to go to Florida, why dontcha stay at home?" He and the little girl, June Star, were reading the funny papers on the floor.

"She wouldn't stay at home to be queen for a day," June Star said without raising her yellow head.

"Yes and what would you do if this fellow, The Misfit, caught you?" the grandmother asked. 5

"I'd smack his face," John Wesley said.

"She wouldn't stay at home for a million bucks," June Star said. "Afraid she'd miss something. She has to go everywhere we go."

"All right, Miss," the grandmother said. "Just remember that the next time you want me to curl your hair."

June Star said her hair was naturally curly.

The next morning the grandmother was the first one in the car, ready to go. She had her big black valise that looked like the head of a hippopotamus in one corner, and underneath it she was hiding a basket with Pitty Sing,[1] the cat, in it. She didn't intend for the cat to be left alone in the house for three days because he would miss her too much and she was afraid he might brush against one of the gas burners and accidentally asphyxiate himself. Her son, Bailey, didn't like to arrive at a motel with a cat. 10

She sat in the middle of the back seat with John Wesley and June Star on either side of her. Bailey and the children's mother and the baby sat in front and they left Atlanta at eight forty-five with the mileage on the car at 55890. The grandmother wrote this down because she thought it would be interesting to say how many miles they had been when they got back. It took them twenty minutes to reach the outskirts of the city.

---

1. Named after Pitti-Sing, one of the "three little maids from school" in Gilbert and Sullivan's operetta *The Mikado* (1885).

The old lady settled herself comfortably, removing her white cotton gloves and putting them up with her purse on the shelf in front of the back window. The children's mother still had on slacks and still had her head tied up in a green kerchief, but the grandmother had on a navy blue straw sailor hat with a bunch of white violets on the brim and a navy blue dress with a small white dot in the print. Her collars and cuffs were white organdy trimmed with lace and at her neckline she had pinned a purple spray of cloth violets containing a sachet. In case of an accident, anyone seeing her dead on the highway would know at once that she was a lady.

She said she thought it was going to be a good day for driving, neither too hot nor too cold, and she cautioned Bailey that the speed limit was fifty-five miles an hour and that the patrolmen hid themselves behind billboards and small clumps of trees and sped out after you before you had a chance to slow down. She pointed out interesting details of the scenery: Stone Mountain; the blue granite that in some places came up to both sides of the highway; the brilliant red clay banks slightly streaked with purple; and the various crops that made rows of green lace-work on the ground. The trees were full of silver-white sunlight and the meanest of them sparkled. The children were reading comic magazines and their mother had gone back to sleep.

"Let's go through Georgia fast so we won't have to look at it much," John Wesley said.

15   "If I were a little boy," said the grandmother, "I wouldn't talk about my native state that way. Tennessee has the mountains and Georgia has the hills."

"Tennessee is just a hillbilly dumping ground," John Wesley said, "and Georgia is a lousy state too."

"You said it," June Star said.

"In my time," said the grandmother, folding her thin veined fingers, "children were more respectful of their native states and their parents and everything else. People did right then. Oh look at the cute little pickaninny!" she said and pointed to a Negro child standing in the door of a shack. "Wouldn't that make a picture, now?" she asked and they all turned and looked at the little Negro out of the back window. He waved.

"He didn't have any britches on," June Star said.

20   "He probably didn't have any," the grandmother explained. "Little niggers in the country don't have things like we do. If I could paint, I'd paint that picture," she said.

The children exchanged comic books.

The grandmother offered to hold the baby and the children's mother passed him over the front seat to her. She set him on her knee and bounced him and told him about the things they were passing. She rolled her eyes and screwed up her mouth and stuck her leathery thin face into his smooth bland one. Occasionally he gave her a faraway smile. They passed a large cotton field with five or six graves fenced in the middle of it, like a small island. "Look at the graveyard!" the grandmother said, pointing it out. "That was the old family burying ground. That belonged to the plantation."

"Where's the plantation?" John Wesley asked.

"Gone with the Wind,"[2] said the grandmother. "Ha. Ha."

When the children finished all the comic books they had brought, they 25 opened the lunch and ate it. The grandmother ate a peanut butter sandwich and an olive and would not let the children throw the box and the paper napkins out the window. When there was nothing else to do they played a game by choosing a cloud and making the other two guess what shape it suggested. John Wesley took one the shape of a cow and June Star guessed a cow and John Wesley said, no, an automobile, and June Star said he didn't play fair, and they began to slap each other over the grandmother.

The grandmother said she would tell them a story if they would keep quiet. When she told a story, she rolled her eyes and waved her head and was very dramatic. She said once when she was a maiden lady she had been courted by a Mr. Edgar Atkins Teagarden from Jasper, Georgia. She said he was a very good-looking man and a gentleman and that he brought her a watermelon every Saturday afternoon with his initials cut in it, E. A. T. Well, one Saturday, she said, Mr. Teagarden brought the watermelon and there was nobody at home and he left it on the front porch and returned in his buggy to Jasper, but she never got the watermelon, she said, because a nigger boy ate it when he saw the initials, E. A. T.! This story tickled John Wesley's funny bone and he giggled and giggled but June Star didn't think it was any good. She said she wouldn't marry a man that just brought her a watermelon on Saturday. The grandmother said she would have done well to marry Mr. Teagarden because he was a gentleman and had bought Coca-Cola stock when it first came out and that he had died only a few years ago, a very wealthy man. *Coca-cola came out 1886*

They stopped at The Tower for barbecued sandwiches. The Tower was a part stucco and part wood filling station and dance hall set in a clearing outside of Timothy. A fat man named Red Sammy Butts ran it and there were signs stuck here and there on the building and for miles up and down the highway saying, TRY RED SAMMY'S FAMOUS BARBECUE. NONE LIKE FAMOUS RED SAMMY'S! RED SAM! THE FAT BOY WITH THE HAPPY LAUGH! A VETERAN! RED SAMMY'S YOUR MAN!

Red Sammy was lying on the bare ground outside The Tower with his head under a truck while a gray monkey about a foot high, chained to a

---

2. Title of an immensely popular novel, published in 1936, by Margaret Mitchell (1900–49); the novel depicts a large, prosperous Southern plantation, Tara, that is destroyed by Northern troops in the American Civil War.

small chinaberry tree, chattered nearby. The monkey sprang back into the tree and got on the highest limb as soon as he saw the children jump out of the car and run toward him.

Inside, The Tower was a long dark room with a counter at one end and tables at the other and dancing space in the middle. They all sat down at a board table next to the nickelodeon[3] and Red Sam's wife, a tall burnt-brown woman with hair and eyes lighter than her skin, came and took their order. The children's mother put a dime in the machine and played "The Tennessee Waltz," and the grandmother said that tune always made her want to dance. She asked Bailey if he would like to dance but he only glared at her. He didn't have a naturally sunny disposition like she did and trips made him nervous. The grandmother's brown eyes were very bright. She swayed her head from side to side and pretended she was dancing in her chair. June Star said play something she could tap to so the children's mother put in another dime and played a fast number and June Star stepped out onto the dance floor and did her tap routine.

"Ain't she cute?" Red Sam's wife said, leaning over the counter. "Would you like to come be my little girl?"

"No I certainly wouldn't," June Star said. "I wouldn't live in a broken-down place like this for a million bucks!" and she ran back to the table.

"Ain't she cute?" the woman repeated, stretching her mouth politely.

"Aren't you ashamed?" hissed the grandmother.

Red Sam came in and told his wife to quit lounging on the counter and hurry up with these people's order. His khaki trousers reached just to his hip bones and his stomach hung over them like a sack of meal swaying under his shirt. He came over and sat down at a table nearby and let out a combination sigh and yodel. "You can't win," he said. "You can't win," and he wiped his sweating red face off with a gray handkerchief. "These days you don't know who to trust," he said. "Ain't that the truth?"

"People are certainly not nice like they used to be," said the grandmother.

"Two fellers come in here last week," Red Sammy said, "driving a Chrysler. It was a old beat-up car but it was a good one and these boys looked all right to me. Said they worked at the mill and you know I let them fellers charge the gas they bought? Now why did I do that?"

"Because you're a good man!" the grandmother said at once.

"Yes'm, I suppose so," Red Sam said as if he were struck with this answer.

His wife brought the orders, carrying the five plates all at once without a tray, two in each hand and one balanced on her arm. "It isn't a soul in this green world of God's that you can trust," she said. "And I don't count nobody out of that, not nobody," she repeated, looking at Red Sammy.

3. Jukebox.

"Did you read about that criminal, The Misfit, that's escaped?" asked 40 the grandmother.

"I wouldn't be a bit surprised if he didn't attact this place right here," said the woman. "If he hears about it being here, I wouldn't be none surprised to see him. If he hears it's two cent in the cash register, I wouldn't be a tall surprised if he . . ."

"That'll do," Red Sam said. "Go bring these people their Co'-Colas," and the woman went off to get the rest of the order.

"A good man is hard to find," Red Sammy said. "Everything is getting terrible. I remember the day you could go off and leave your screen door unlatched. Not no more."

He and the grandmother discussed better times. The old lady said that in her opinion Europe was entirely to blame for the way things were now. She said the way Europe acted you would think we were made of money and Red Sam said it was no use talking about it, she was exactly right. The children ran outside into the white sunlight and looked at the monkey in the lacy chinaberry tree. He was busy catching fleas on himself and biting each one carefully between his teeth as if it were a delicacy.

They drove off again into the hot afternoon. The grandmother took cat 45 naps and woke up every few minutes with her own snoring. Outside of Toombsboro she woke up and recalled an old plantation that she had visited in this neighborhood once when she was a young lady. She said the house had six white columns across the front and that there was an avenue of oaks leading up to it and two little wooden trellis arbors on either side in front where you sat down with your suitor after a stroll in the garden. She recalled exactly which road to turn off to get to it. She knew that Bailey would not be willing to lose any time looking at an old house, but the more she talked about it, the more she wanted to see it once again and find out if the little twin arbors were still standing. "There was a secret panel in this house," she said craftily, not telling the truth but wishing that she were, "and the story went that all the family silver was hidden in it when Sherman came through but it was never found . . ."

"Hey!" John Wesley said. "Let's go see it! We'll find it! We'll poke all the woodwork and find it! Who lives there? Where do you turn off at? Hey Pop, can't we turn off there?"

"We never have seen a house with a secret panel!" June Star shrieked. "Let's go to the house with the secret panel! Hey Pop, can't we go see the house with the secret panel!"

"It's not far from here, I know," the grandmother said. "It wouldn't take over twenty minutes."

Bailey was looking straight ahead. His jaw was as rigid as a horseshoe. "No," he said.

The children began to yell and scream that they wanted to see the house 50 with the secret panel. John Wesley kicked the back of the front seat and

June Star hung over her mother's shoulder and whined desperately into her ear that they never had any fun even on their vacation, that they could never do what THEY wanted to do. The baby began to scream and John Wesley kicked the back of the seat so hard that his father could feel the blows in his kidney.

"All right!" he shouted and drew the car to a stop at the side of the road. "Will you all shut up? Will you all just shut up for one second? If you don't shut up, we won't go anywhere."

"It would be very educational for them," the grandmother murmured.

"All right," Bailey said, "but get this: this is the only time we're going to stop for anything like this. This is the one and only time."

"The dirt road that you have to turn down is about a mile back," the grandmother directed. "I marked it when we passed."

55   "A dirt road," Bailey groaned.

After they had turned around and were headed toward the dirt road, the grandmother recalled other points about the house, the beautiful glass over the front doorway and the candle-lamp in the hall. John Wesley said that the secret panel was probably in the fireplace.

"You can't go inside this house," Bailey said. "You don't know who lives there."

"While you all talk to the people in front, I'll run around behind and get in a window," John Wesley suggested.

"We'll all stay in the car," his mother said.

60   They turned onto the dirt road and the car raced roughly along in a swirl of pink dust. The grandmother recalled the times when there were no paved roads and thirty miles was a day's journey. The dirt road was hilly and there were sudden washes in it and sharp curves on dangerous embankments. All at once they would be on a hill, looking down over the blue tops of trees for miles around, then the next minute, they would be in a red depression with the dust-coated trees looking down on them.

"This place had better turn up in a minute," Bailey said, "or I'm going to turn around."

The road looked as if no one had traveled on it in months.

"It's not much farther," the grandmother said and just as she said it, a horrible thought came to her. The thought was so embarrassing that she turned red in the face and her eyes dilated and her feet jumped up, upsetting her valise in the corner. The instant the valise moved, the newspaper top she had over the basket under it rose with a snarl and Pitty Sing, the cat, sprang onto Bailey's shoulder.

The children were thrown to the floor and their mother, clutching the baby, out the door onto the ground; the old lady was thrown into the front seat. The car turned over once and landed right-side-up in a gulch off the side of the road. Bailey remained in the driver's seat with the cat—gray-striped with a broad white face and an orange nose—clinging to his neck like a caterpillar.

As soon as the children saw they could move their arms and legs, they 65
scrambled out of the car, shouting, "We've had an ACCIDENT!" The
grandmother was curled up under the dashboard, hoping she was injured
so that Bailey's wrath would not come down on her all at once. The horrible thought she had had before the accident was that the house she had
remembered so vividly was not in Georgia but in Tennessee.

Bailey removed the cat from his neck with both hands and flung it out
the window against the side of a pine tree. Then he got out of the car and
started looking for the children's mother. She was sitting against the side
of the red gutted ditch, holding the screaming baby, but she only had a cut
down her face and a broken shoulder. "We've had an ACCIDENT!" the
children screamed in a frenzy of delight.

"But nobody's killed," June Star said with disappointment as the grandmother limped out of the car, her hat still pinned to her head but the broken front brim standing up at a jaunty angle and the violet spray hanging
off the side. They all sat down in the ditch, except the children, to recover
from the shock. They were all shaking.

"Maybe a car will come along," said the children's mother hoarsely.

"I believe I have injured an organ," said the grandmother, pressing her
side, but no one answered her. Bailey's teeth were clattering. He had on a
yellow sport shirt with bright blue parrots designed in it and his face was
as yellow as the shirt. The grandmother decided that she would not mention that the house was in Tennessee.

The road was about ten feet above and they could see only the tops of 70
the trees on the other side of it. Behind the ditch they were sitting in there
were more woods, tall and dark and deep. In a few minutes they saw a car
some distance away on top of a hill, coming slowly as if the occupants were
watching them. The grandmother stood up and waved both arms dramatically to attract their attention. The car continued to come on slowly,
disappeared around a bend and appeared again, moving even slower, on
top of the hill they had gone over. It was a big black battered hearselike
automobile. There were three men in it.

It came to a stop just over them and for some minutes, the driver looked
down with a steady expressionless gaze to where they were sitting, and didn't
speak. Then he turned his head and muttered something to the other two
and they got out. One was a fat boy in black trousers and a red sweat shirt
with a silver stallion embossed on the front of it. He moved around on the
right side of them and stood staring, his mouth partly open in a kind of
loose grin. The other had on khaki pants and a blue striped coat and a gray
hat pulled down very low, hiding most of his face. He came around slowly
on the left side. Neither spoke.

The driver got out of the car and stood by the side of it, looking down at
them. He was an older man than the other two. His hair was just beginning
to gray and he wore silver-rimmed spectacles that gave him a scholarly look.
He had a long creased face and didn't have on any shirt or undershirt. He

had on blue jeans that were too tight for him and was holding a black hat and a gun. The two boys also had guns.

"We've had an ACCIDENT!" the children screamed.

The grandmother had the peculiar feeling that the bespectacled man was someone she knew. His face was as familiar to her as if she had known him all her life but she could not recall who he was. He moved away from the car and began to come down the embankment, placing his feet carefully so that he wouldn't slip. He had on tan and white shoes and no socks, and his ankles were red and thin. "Good afternoon," he said. "I see you all had you a little spill."

75   "We turned over twice!" said the grandmother.

"Oncet," he corrected. "We seen it happen. Try their car and see will it run, Hiram," he said quietly to the boy with the gray hat.

"What you got that gun for?" John Wesley asked. "Whatcha gonna do with that gun?"

"Lady," the man said to the children's mother, "would you mind calling them children to sit down by you? Children make me nervous. I want all you all to sit down right together there where you're at."

"What are you telling US what to do for?" June Star asked.

80   Behind them the line of woods gaped like a dark open mouth. "Come here," said their mother.

"Look here now," Bailey began suddenly, "we're in a predicament! We're in . . ."

The grandmother shrieked. She scrambled to her feet and stood staring. "You're The Misfit!" she said. "I recognized you at once!"

"Yes'm," the man said, smiling slightly as if he were pleased in spite of himself to be known, "but it would have been better for all of you, lady, if you hadn't of reckernized me."

Bailey turned his head sharply and said something to his mother that shocked even the children. The old lady began to cry and The Misfit reddened.

85   "Lady," he said, "don't you get upset. Sometimes a man says things he don't mean. I don't reckon he meant to talk to you thataway."

"You wouldn't shoot a lady, would you?" the grandmother said and removed a clean handkerchief from her cuff and began to slap at her eyes with it.

The Misfit pointed the toe of his shoe into the ground and made a little hole and then covered it up again. "I would hate to have to," he said.

"Listen," the grandmother almost screamed, "I know you're a good man. You don't look a bit like you have common blood. I know you must come from nice people!"

"Yes mam," he said, "finest people in the world." When he smiled he showed a row of strong white teeth. "God never made a finer woman than my mother and my daddy's heart was pure gold," he said. The boy with the red sweat shirt had come around behind them and was standing with his gun at his hip. The Misfit squatted down on the ground. "Watch them children, Bobby Lee," he said. "You know they make me nervous." He looked at the six of them huddled together in front of him and he seemed to be embarrassed as if he couldn't think of anything to say. "Ain't a cloud in the sky," he remarked, looking up at it. "Don't see no sun but don't see no cloud neither."

"Yes, it's a beautiful day," said the grandmother. "Listen," she said, "you 90 shouldn't call yourself The Misfit because I know you're a good man at heart. I can just look at you and tell."

"Hush!" Bailey yelled. "Hush! Everybody shut up and let me handle this!" He was squatting in the position of a runner about to sprint forward but he didn't move.

"I pre-chate that, lady," The Misfit said and drew a little circle in the ground with the butt of his gun.

"It'll take a half a hour to fix this here car," Hiram called, looking over the raised hood of it.

"Well, first you and Bobby Lee get him and that little boy to step over yonder with you," The Misfit said, pointing to Bailey and John Wesley. "The boys want to ast you something," he said to Bailey. "Would you mind stepping back in them woods there with them?"

"Listen," Bailey began, "we're in a terrible predicament! Nobody real- 95 izes what this is," and his voice cracked. His eyes were as blue and intense as the parrots in his shirt and he remained perfectly still.

The grandmother reached up to adjust her hat brim as if she were going to the woods with him but it came off in her hand. She stood staring at it and after a second she let it fall on the ground. Hiram pulled Bailey up by the arm as if he were assisting an old man. John Wesley caught hold of his father's hand and Bobby Lee followed. They went off toward the woods and just as they reached the dark edge, Bailey turned and supporting himself against a gray naked pine trunk, he shouted, "I'll be back in a minute, Mamma, wait on me!"

"Come back this instant!" his mother shrilled but they all disappeared into the woods.

"Bailey Boy!" the grandmother called in a tragic voice but she found she was looking at The Misfit squatting on the ground in front of her. "I just know you're a good man," she said desperately. "You're not a bit common!"

"Nome, I ain't a good man," The Misfit said after a second as if he had considered her statement carefully, "but I ain't the worst in the world neither. My daddy said I was a different breed of dog from my brothers and sisters. 'You know,' Daddy said, 'it's some that can live their whole life out without asking about it and it's others has to know why it is, and this boy is one of the latters. He's going to be into everything!'" He put on his black hat and looked up suddenly and then away deep into the woods as if he were embarrassed again. "I'm sorry I don't have on a shirt before you ladies," he said, hunching his shoulders slightly. "We buried our clothes that we had on when we escaped and we're just making do until we can get better. We borrowed these from some folks we met," he explained.

100   "That's perfectly all right," the grandmother said. "Maybe Bailey has an extra shirt in his suitcase."

"I'll look and see terrectly," The Misfit said.

"Where are they taking him?" the children's mother screamed.

"Daddy was a card himself," The Misfit said. "You couldn't put anything over on him. He never got in trouble with the Authorities though. Just had the knack of handling them."

"You could be honest too if you'd only try," said the grandmother. "Think how wonderful it would be to settle down and live a comfortable life and not have to think about somebody chasing you all the time."

105   The Misfit kept scratching in the ground with the butt of his gun as if he were thinking about it. "Yes'm, somebody is always after you," he murmured.

The grandmother noticed how thin his shoulder blades were just behind his hat because she was standing up looking down on him. "Do you ever pray?" she asked.

He shook his head. All she saw was the black hat wiggle between his shoulder blades. "Nome," he said.

There was a pistol shot from the woods, followed closely by another. Then silence. The old lady's head jerked around. She could hear the wind move through the tree tops like a long satisfied insuck of breath. "Bailey Boy!" she called.

"I was a gospel singer for a while," The Misfit said. "I been most everything. Been in the arm service, both land and sea, at home and abroad, been twict married, been an undertaker, been with the railroads, plowed Mother Earth, been in a tornado, seen a man burnt alive oncet," and looked up at the children's mother and the little girl who were sitting close together, their faces white and their eyes glassy; "I even seen a woman flogged," he said.

110   "Pray, pray," the grandmother began, "pray, pray. . . ."

"I never was a bad boy that I remember of," The Misfit said in an almost dreamy voice, "but somewheres along the line I done something wrong and got sent to the penitentiary. I was buried alive," and he looked up and held her attention to him by a steady stare.

"That's when you should have started to pray," she said. "What did you do to get sent to the penitentiary that first time?"

"Turn to the right, it was a wall," The Misfit said, looking up again at the cloudless sky. "Turn to the left, it was a wall. Look up it was a ceiling, look down it was a floor. I forgot what I done, lady. I set there and set there, trying to remember what it was I done and I ain't recalled it to this day. Oncet in a while, I would think it was coming to me, but it never come."

"Maybe they put you in by mistake," the old lady said vaguely.

"Nome," he said. "It wasn't no mistake. They had the papers on me." 115

"You must have stolen something," she said.

The Misfit sneered slightly. "Nobody had nothing I wanted," he said. "It was a head-doctor at the penitentiary said what I had done was kill my daddy but I known that for a lie. My daddy died in nineteen ought nineteen of the epidemic flu and I never had a thing to do with it. He was buried in the Mount Hopewell Baptist churchyard and you can go there and see for yourself."

"If you would pray," the old lady said, "Jesus would help you."

"That's right," The Misfit said.

"Well then, why don't you pray?" she asked trembling with delight 120 suddenly.

"I don't want no hep," he said. "I'm doing all right by myself."

Bobby Lee and Hiram came ambling back from the woods. Bobby Lee was dragging a yellow shirt with bright blue parrots in it.

"Thow me that shirt, Bobby Lee," The Misfit said. The shirt came flying at him and landed on his shoulder and he put it on. The grandmother couldn't name what the shirt reminded her of. "No, lady," The Misfit said while he was buttoning it up, "I found out the crime don't matter. You can do one thing or you can do another, kill a man or take a tire off his car, because sooner or later you're going to forget what it was you done and just be punished for it."

The children's mother had begun to make heaving noises as if she couldn't get her breath. "Lady," he asked, "would you and that little girl like to step off yonder with Bobby Lee and Hiram and join your husband?"

"Yes, thank you," the mother said faintly. Her left arm dangled help- 125 lessly and she was holding the baby, who had gone to sleep, in the other. "Hep that lady up, Hiram," The Misfit said as she struggled to climb out of the ditch, "and Bobby Lee, you hold onto that little girl's hand."

"I don't want to hold hands with him," June Star said. "He reminds me of a pig."

The fat boy blushed and laughed and caught her by the arm and pulled her off into the woods after Hiram and her mother.

Alone with The Misfit, the grandmother found that she had lost her voice. There was not a cloud in the sky nor any sun. There was nothing around her but woods. She wanted to tell him that he must pray. She opened and closed her mouth several times before anything came out. Finally she found herself saying, "Jesus, Jesus," meaning, Jesus will help you, but the way she was saying it, it sounded as if she might be cursing.

"Yes'm," The Misfit said as if he agreed. "Jesus thown everything off balance. It was the same case with Him as with me except He hadn't committed any crime and they could prove I had committed one because they had the papers on me. Of course," he said, "they never shown me my papers.

That's why I sign myself now. I said long ago, you get you a signature and sign everything you do and keep a copy of it. Then you'll know what you done and you can hold up the crime to the punishment and see do they match and in the end you'll have something to prove you ain't been treated right. I call myself The Misfit," he said, "because I can't make what all I done wrong fit what all I gone through in punishment."

130   There was a piercing scream from the woods, followed closely by a pistol report. "Does it seem right to you, lady, that one is punished a heap and another ain't punished at all?"

"Jesus!" the old lady cried. "You've got good blood! I know you wouldn't shoot a lady! I know you come from nice people! Pray! Jesus, you ought not to shoot a lady. I'll give you all the money I've got!"

"Lady," The Misfit said, looking beyond her far into the woods, "there never was a body that give the undertaker a tip."

There were two more pistol reports and the grandmother raised her head like a parched old turkey hen crying for water and called, "Bailey Boy, Bailey Boy!" as if her heart would break.

"Jesus was the only One that ever raised the dead." The Misfit continued, "and He shouldn't have done it. He thown everything off balance. If He did what He said, then it's nothing for you to do but thow away everything and follow Him, and if He didn't, then it's nothing for you to do but enjoy the few minutes you got left the best way you can—by killing somebody or burning down his house or doing some other meanness to him. No pleasure but meanness," he said and his voice had become almost a snarl.

135   "Maybe He didn't raise the dead," the old lady mumbled, not knowing what she was saying and feeling so dizzy that she sank down in the ditch with her legs twisted under her.

"I wasn't there so I can't say He didn't," The Misfit said. "I wisht I had of been there," he said, hitting the ground with his fist. "It ain't right I wasn't there because if I had of been there I would of known. Listen lady," he said in a high voice, "if I had of been there I would of known and I wouldn't be like I am now." His voice seemed about to crack and the grandmother's head cleared for an instant. She saw the man's face twisted close to her own as if he were going to cry and she murmured, "Why you're one of my babies. You're one of my own children!" She reached out and touched him on the shoulder. The Misfit sprang back as if a snake had bitten him and shot her three times through the chest. Then he put his gun down on the ground and took off his glasses and began to clean them.

Hiram and Bobby Lee returned from the woods and stood over the ditch, looking down at the grandmother who half sat and half lay in a puddle of blood with her legs crossed under her like a child's and her face smiling up at the cloudless sky.

Without his glasses, The Misfit's eyes were red-rimmed and pale and defenseless-looking. "Take her off and thow her where you thown the others," he said, picking up the cat that was rubbing itself against his leg.

"She was a talker, wasn't she?" Bobby Lee said, sliding down the ditch with a yodel.

"She would of been a good woman," The Misfit said, "if it had been 140 somebody there to shoot her every minute of her life."

"Some fun!" Bobby Lee said.

"Shut up, Bobby Lee," The Misfit said. <u>"It's no real pleasure in life."</u>

~~misfit~~   1953

JOHN UPDIKE

A & P[1]

In walks these three girls in nothing but bathing suits. I'm in the third checkout slot, with my back to the door, so I don't see them until they're over by the bread. The one that caught my eye first was the one in the plaid green two-piece. She was a chunky kid, with a good tan and a sweet broad soft-looking can with those two crescents of white just under it, where the sun never seems to hit, at the top of the backs of her legs. I stood there with my hand on a box of HiHo crackers trying to remember if I rang it up or not. I ring it up again and the customer starts giving me hell. She's one of these cash-register-watchers, a witch about fifty with rouge on her cheekbones and no eyebrows, and I know it made her day to trip me up. She'd been watching cash registers for fifty years and probably never seen a mistake before.

By the time I got her feathers smoothed and her goodies into a bag—she gives me a little snort in passing, if she'd been born at the right time they would have burned her over in Salem[2]—by the time I get her on her way the girls had circled around the bread and were coming back, without a pushcart, back my way along the counters, in the aisle between the checkouts and the Special bins. They didn't even have shoes on. There was this chunky one, with the two-piece—it was bright green and the seams on the bra were still sharp and her belly was still pretty pale so I guessed she just got it (the suit)—there was this one, with one of those chubby berry-faces, the lips all bunched together under her nose, this one, and a tall one, with black hair that hadn't quite frizzed right, and one of these sunburns right across under the eyes, and a chin that was too long—you know, the kind of girl other girls think is very "striking" and "attractive" but never quite makes it, as they very well know, which is why they like her so much—and then the

---

1. The Great Atlantic and Pacific Tea Company, so named in 1869, became by the 1930s the leading national chain of supermarkets. The A&P Corporation today has more than 400 stores under various names.

2. The store is located not far from Salem, Massachusetts, where in 1692 nineteen women and men were hanged after being convicted of witchcraft.

third one, that wasn't quite so tall. She was the queen. She kind of led them, the other two peeking around and making their shoulders round. She didn't look around, not this queen, she just walked straight on slowly, on these long white prima-donna legs. She came down a little hard on her heels, as if she didn't walk in her bare feet that much, putting down her heels and then letting the weight move along to her toes as if she was testing the floor with every step, putting a little deliberate extra action into it. You never know for sure how girls' minds work (do you really think it's a mind in there or just a little buzz like a bee in a glass jar?) but you got the idea she had talked the other two into coming in here with her, and now she was showing them how to do it, walk slow and hold yourself straight.

She had on a kind of dirty-pink—beige maybe, I don't know—bathing suit with a little nubble all over it and, what got me, the straps were down. They were off her shoulders looped loose around the cool tops of her arms, and I guess as a result the suit had slipped a little on her, so all around the top of the cloth there was this shining rim. If it hadn't been there you wouldn't have known there could have been anything whiter than those shoulders. With the straps pushed off, there was nothing between the top of the suit and the top of her head except just *her*, this clean bare plane of the top of her chest down from the shoulder bones like a dented sheet of metal tilted in the light. I mean, it was more than pretty.

She had sort of oaky hair that the sun and salt had bleached, done up in a bun that was unravelling, and a kind of prim face. Walking into the A & P with your straps down, I suppose it's the only kind of face you *can* have. She held her head so high her neck, coming up out of those white shoulders, looked kind of stretched, but I didn't mind. The longer her neck was, the more of her there was.

5   She must have felt in the corner of her eye me and over my shoulder Stokesie in the second slot watching, but she didn't tip. Not this queen. She kept her eyes moving across the racks, and stopped, and turned so slow it made my stomach rub the inside of my apron, and buzzed to the other two, who kind of huddled against her for relief, and then they all three of them went up the cat-and-dog-food-breakfast-cereal-macaroni-rice-raisins-seasonings-spreads-spaghetti-soft-drinks-crackers-and-cookies aisle. From the third slot I look straight up this aisle to the meat counter, and I watched them all the way. The fat one with the tan sort of fumbled with the cookies, but on second thought she put the package back. The sheep pushing their carts down the aisle—the girls were walking against the usual traffic (not that we have one-way signs or anything)—were pretty hilarious. You could see them, when Queenie's white shoulders dawned on them, kind of jerk, or hop, or hiccup, but their eyes snapped back to their own baskets and on they pushed. I bet you could set off dynamite in an A & P and the people would by and large keep reaching and checking oatmeal off their lists and muttering "Let me see, there was a third thing, began with A, asparagus, no, ah, yes, applesauce!" or whatever it is they do mutter. But there was no doubt,

this jiggled them. A few houseslaves in pin curlers even looked around after pushing their carts past to make sure what they had seen was correct.

You know, it's one thing to have a girl in a bathing suit down on the beach, where what with the glare nobody can look at each other much anyway, and another thing in the cool of the A & P, under the fluorescent lights, against all those stacked packages, with her feet paddling along naked over our checkerboard green-and-cream rubber-tile floor.

"Oh Daddy," Stokesie said beside me. "I feel so faint."

"Darling," I said. "Hold me tight." Stokesie's married, with two babies chalked up on his fuselage already, but as far as I can tell that's the only difference. He's twenty-two, and I was nineteen this April.

"Is it done?" he asks, the responsible married man finding his voice. I forgot to say he thinks he's going to be manager some sunny day, maybe in 1990 when it's called the Great Alexandrov and Petrooshki Tea Company or something.

What he meant was, our town is five miles from a beach, with a big summer colony out on the Point, but we're right in the middle of town, and the women generally put on a shirt or shorts or something before they get out of the car into the street. And anyway these are usually women with six children and varicose veins mapping their legs and nobody, including them, could care less. As I say, we're right in the middle of town, and if you stand at our front doors you can see two banks and the Congregational church and the newspaper store and three real-estate offices and about twenty-seven old freeloaders tearing up Central Street because the sewer broke again. It's not as if we're on the Cape; we're north of Boston and there's people in this town haven't seen the ocean for twenty years. 10

The girls had reached the meat counter and were asking McMahon something. He pointed, they pointed, and they shuffled out of sight behind a pyramid of Diet Delight peaches. All that was left for us to see was old McMahon patting his mouth and looking after them sizing up their joints. Poor kids, I began to feel sorry for them, they couldn't help it.

• • •

Now here comes the sad part of the story, at least my family says it's sad, but I don't think it's so sad myself. The store's pretty empty, it being Thursday afternoon, so there was nothing much to do except lean on the register and wait for the girls to show up again. The whole store was like a pinball machine and I didn't know which tunnel they'd come out of. After a while they come around out of the far aisle, around the light bulbs, records at discount of the Caribbean Six or Tony Martin Sings[3] or some such gunk you wonder they waste the wax on, sixpacks of candy bars, and plastic toys done up in cellophane that fall apart when a kid looks at them anyway. Around they come, Queenie still leading the way, and holding a little gray

---

3. Typical titles of record albums at the time of the story (1962). Tony Martin (b. 1913), a popular singer and actor, was featured on radio and television in the 1940s and 1950s.

jar in her hand. Slots Three through Seven are unmanned and I could see her wondering between Stokes and me, but Stokesie with his usual luck draws an old party in baggy gray pants who stumbles up with four giant cans of pineapple juice (what do these bums *do* with all that pineapple juice? I've often asked myself) so the girls come to me. Queenie puts down the jar and I take it into my fingers icy cold. Kingfish Fancy Herring Snacks in Pure Sour Cream: 49¢. Now her hands are empty, not a ring or a bracelet, bare as God made them, and I wonder where the money's coming from. Still with that prim look she lifts a folded dollar bill out of the hollow at the center of her nubbled pink top. The jar went heavy in my hand. Really, I thought that was so cute.

Then everybody's luck begins to run out. Lengel comes in from haggling with a truck full of cabbages on the lot and is about to scuttle into that door marked MANAGER behind which he hides all day when the girls touch his eye. Lengel's pretty dreary, teaches Sunday school and the rest, but he doesn't miss that much. He comes over and says, "Girls, this isn't the beach."

Queenie blushes, though maybe it's just a brush of sunburn I was noticing for the first time, now that she was so close. "My mother asked me to pick up a jar of herring snacks." Her voice kind of startled me, the way voices do when you see the people first, coming out so flat and dumb yet kind of tony, too, the way it ticked over "pick up" and "snacks." All of a sudden I slid right down her voice into her living room. Her father and the other men were standing around in ice-cream coats and bow ties and the women were in sandals picking up herring snacks on toothpicks off a big glass plate and they were all holding drinks the color of water with olives and sprigs of mint in them. When my parents have somebody over they get lemonade and if it's a real racy affair Schlitz in tall glasses with "They'll Do It Every Time" cartoons stencilled on.[4]

15   "That's all right," Lengel said. "But this isn't the beach." His repeating this struck me as funny, as if it had just occurred to him, and he had been thinking all these years the A & P was a great big dune and he was the head lifeguard. He didn't like my smiling—as I say he doesn't miss much—but he concentrates on giving the girls that sad Sunday-school-superintendent stare.

Queenie's blush is no sunburn now, and the plump one in plaid, that I liked better from the back—a really sweet can—pipes up, "We weren't doing any shopping. We just came in for the one thing."

"That makes no difference," Lengel tells her, and I could see from the way his eyes went that he hadn't noticed she was wearing a two-piece before. "We want you decently dressed when you come in here."

4. Schlitz is an inexpensive brand of beer. The cheap glasses are decorated with a popular saying derived from a syndicated series of single-panel cartoons printed between 1929–2008.

"We *are* decent," Queenie says suddenly, her lower lip pushing, getting sore now that she remembers her place, a place from which the crowd that runs the A & P must look pretty crummy. Fancy Herring Snacks flashed in her very blue eyes.

"Girls, I don't want to argue with you. After this come in here with your shoulders covered. It's our policy." He turns his back. That's policy for you. Policy is what the kingpins want. What the others want is juvenile delinquency.

All this while, the customers had been showing up with their carts but, you know, sheep, seeing a scene, they had all bunched up on Stokesie, who shook open a paper bag as gently as peeling a peach, not wanting to miss a word. I could feel in the silence everybody getting nervous, most of all Lengel, who asks me, "Sammy, have you rung up their purchase?"

I thought and said "No" but it wasn't about that I was thinking. I go through the punches, 4, 9, GROC, TOT—it's more complicated than you think, and after you do it often enough, it begins to make a little song, that you hear words to, in my case "Hello (*bing*) there, you (*gung*) hap-py pee-pul (*splat*)!"—the *splat* being the drawer flying out. I uncrease the bill, tenderly as you may imagine, it just having come from between the two smoothest scoops of vanilla I had ever known were there, and pass a half and a penny into her narrow pink palm, and nestle the herrings in a bag and twist its neck and hand it over, all the time thinking.

The girls, and who'd blame them, are in a hurry to get out, so I say "I quit" to Lengel quick enough for them to hear, hoping they'll stop and watch me, their unsuspected hero. They keep right on going, into the electric eye; the door flies open and they flicker across the lot to their car, Queenie and Plaid and Big Tall Goony-Goony (not that as raw material she was so bad), leaving me with Lengel and a kink in his eyebrow.

"Did you say something, Sammy?"

"I said I quit."

"I thought you did."

"You didn't have to embarrass them."

"It was they who were embarrassing us."

I started to say something that came out "Fiddle-de-doo." It's a saying of my grandmother's, and I know she would have been pleased.

"I don't think you know what you're saying," Lengel said.

"I know you don't," I said. "But I do." I pull the bow at the back of my apron and start shrugging it off my shoulders. A couple customers that had been heading for my slot begin to knock against each other, like scared pigs in a chute.

Lengel sighs and begins to look very patient and old and gray. He's been a friend of my parents for years. "Sammy, you don't want to do this to your Mom and Dad," he tells me. It's true, I don't. But it seems to me that once you begin a gesture it's fatal not to go through with it. I fold the apron,

"Sammy" stitched in red on the pocket, and put it on the counter, and drop the bow tie on top of it. The bow tie is theirs, if you've ever wondered. "You'll feel this for the rest of your life," Lengel says, and I know that's true, too, but remembering how he made that pretty girl blush makes me so scrunchy inside I punch the No Sale tab and the machine whirs "pee-pul" and the drawer splats out. One advantage to this scene taking place in summer, I can follow this up with a clean exit, there's no fumbling around getting your coat and galoshes, I just saunter into the electric eye in my white shirt that my mother ironed the night before, and the door heaves itself open, and outside the sunshine is skating around on the asphalt.

I look around for my girls, but they're gone, of course. There wasn't anybody but some young married screaming with her children about some candy they didn't get by the door of a powder-blue Falcon station wagon. Looking back in the big windows, over the bags of peat moss and aluminum lawn furniture stacked on the pavement, I could see Lengel in my place in the slot, checking the sheep through. His face was dark gray and his back stiff, as if he'd just had an injection of iron, and my stomach kind of fell as I felt how hard the world was going to be to me hereafter.

1962

EUDORA WELTY

Why I Live at the P.O.

I was getting along fine with Mama, Papa-Daddy, and Uncle Rondo until my sister Stella-Rondo just separated from her husband and came back home again. Mr. Whitaker! Of course I went with Mr. Whitaker first, when he first appeared here in China Grove, taking "Pose Yourself" photos, and Stella-Rondo broke us up. Told him I was one-sided. Bigger on one side than the other, which is a deliberate, calculated falsehood: I'm the same. Stella-Rondo is exactly twelve months to the day younger than I am and for that reason she's spoiled.

She's always had anything in the world she wanted and then she'd throw it away. Papa-Daddy give her this gorgeous Add-a-Pearl necklace when she was eight years old and she threw it away playing baseball when she was nine, with only two pearls.

So as soon as she got married and moved away from home the first thing she did was separate! From Mr. Whitaker! This photographer with the popeyes she said she trusted. Came home from one of those towns up in Illinois and to our complete surprise brought this child of two.

Mama said she like to make her drop dead for a second. "Here you had this marvelous blonde child and never so much as wrote your mother a word about it," says Mama. "I'm thoroughly ashamed of you." But of course she wasn't.

Stella-Rondo just calmly takes off this *hat*, I wish you could see it. She says, "Why, Mama, Shirley-T.'s adopted, I can prove it." 5

"How?" says Mama, but all I says was, "H'm!" There I was over the hot stove, trying to stretch two chickens over five people and a completely unexpected child into the bargain without one moment's notice.

"What do you mean—'H'm'?" says Stella-Rondo, and Mama says, "I heard that, Sister."

I said that oh, I didn't mean a thing, only that whoever Shirley-T. was, she was the spit-image of Papa-Daddy if he'd cut off his beard, which of course he'd never do in the world. Papa-Daddy's Mama's papa and sulks.

Stella-Rondo got furious! She said, "Sister, I don't need to tell you you got a lot of nerve and always did have and I'll thank you to make no future reference to my adopted child whatsoever."

"Very well," I said. "Very well, very well. Of course I noticed at once she 10 looks like Mr. Whitaker's side too. That frown. She looks like a cross between Mr. Whitaker and Papa-Daddy."

"Well, all I can say is she isn't."

"She looks exactly like Shirley Temple to me," says Mama, but Shirley-T. just ran away from her.

So the first thing Stella-Rondo did at the table was turn Papa-Daddy against me.

"Papa-Daddy," she says. He was trying to cut up his meat. "Papa-Daddy!" I was taken completely by surprise. Papa-Daddy is about a million years old and's got this long-long beard. "Papa-Daddy, Sister says she fails to understand why you don't cut off your beard."

So Papa-Daddy l-a-y-s down his knife and fork! He's real rich. Mama 15 says he is, he says he isn't. So he says, "Have I heard correctly? You don't understand why I don't cut off my beard?"

"Why," I says, "Papa-Daddy, of course I understand, I did not say any such a thing, the idea!"

He says, "Hussy!"

I says, "Papa-Daddy, you know I wouldn't any more want you to cut off your beard than the man in the moon. It was the farthest thing from my mind! Stella-Rondo sat there and made that up while she was eating breast of chicken."

But he says, "So the postmistress fails to understand why I don't cut off my beard. Which job I got you through my influence with the government. 'Bird's nest'—is that what you call it?"

Not that it isn't the next to smallest P.O. in the entire state of Missis- 20 sippi.

I says, "Oh, Papa-Daddy," I says, "I didn't say any such a thing, I never dreamed it was a bird's nest, I have always been grateful though this is the next to smallest P.O. in the state of Mississippi, and I do not enjoy being referred to as a hussy by my own grandfather."

But Stella-Rondo says, "Yes, you did say it too. Anybody in the world could of heard you, that had ears."

"Stop right there," says Mama, looking at *me*.

So I pulled my napkin straight back through the napkin ring and left the table.

25 As soon as I was out of the room Mama says, "Call her back, or she'll starve to death," but Papa-Daddy says, "This is the beard I started growing on the Coast when I was fifteen years old." He would of gone on till nightfall if Shirley-T. hadn't lost the Milky Way she ate in Cairo.

So Papa-Daddy says, "I am going out and lie in the hammock, and you can all sit here and remember my words: I'll never cut off my beard as long as I live, even one inch, and I don't appreciate it in you at all." Passed right by me in the hall and went straight out and got in the hammock.

It would be a holiday. It wasn't five minutes before Uncle Rondo suddenly appeared in the hall in one of Stella-Rondo's flesh-colored kimonos, all cut on the bias, like something Mr. Whitaker probably thought was gorgeous.

"Uncle Rondo!" I says. "I didn't know who that was! Where are you going?"

"Sister," he says, "get out of my way, I'm poisoned."

30 "If you're poisoned stay away from Papa-Daddy," I says. "Keep out of the hammock. Papa-Daddy will certainly beat you on the head if you come within forty miles of him. He thinks I deliberately said he ought to cut off his beard after he got me the P.O., and I've told him and told him and told him, and he acts like he just don't hear me. Papa-Daddy must of gone stone deaf."

"He picked a fine day to do it then," says Uncle Rondo, and before you could say "Jack Robinson" flew out in the yard.

What he'd really done, he'd drunk another bottle of that prescription. He does it every single Fourth of July as sure as shooting, and it's horribly expensive. Then he falls over in the hammock and snores. So he insisted on zigzagging right on out to the hammock, looking like a half-wit.

Papa-Daddy woke with this horrible yell and right there without moving an inch he tried to turn Uncle Rondo against me. I heard every word he said. Oh, he told Uncle Rondo I didn't learn to read till I was eight years old and he didn't see how in the world I ever got the mail put up at the P.O., much less read it all, and he said if Uncle Rondo could only fathom the lengths he had gone to get me that job! And he said on the other hand he thought Stella-Rondo had a brilliant mind and deserved credit for getting out of town. All the time he was just lying there swinging as pretty as you please and looping out his beard, and poor Uncle Rondo was *pleading* with him to slow down the hammock, it was making him as dizzy as a witch to watch it. But that's what Papa-Daddy likes about a hammock. So Uncle Rondo was too dizzy to get turned against me for the time being. He's Mama's only brother and is a good case of a one-track mind. Ask anybody. A certified pharmacist.

Just then I heard Stella-Rondo raising the upstairs window. While she was married she got this peculiar idea that it's cooler with the windows shut and locked. So she has to raise the window before she can make a soul hear her outdoors.

So she raises the window and says, "*Oh!*" You would have thought she was mortally wounded. 35

Uncle Rondo and Papa-Daddy didn't even look up, but kept right on with what they were doing. I had to laugh.

I flew up the stairs and threw the door open! I says, "What in the wide world's the matter, Stella-Rondo? You mortally wounded?"

"No," she says, "I am not mortally wounded but I wish you would do me the favor of looking out that window there and telling me what you see."

So I shade my eyes and look out the window.

"I see the front yard," I says. 40

"Don't you see any human beings?"

"I see Uncle Rondo trying to run Papa-Daddy out of the hammock," I says. "Nothing more. Naturally, it's so suffocating-hot in the house, with all the windows shut and locked, everybody who cares to stay in their right mind will have to go out and get in the hammock before the Fourth of July is over."

"Don't you notice anything different about Uncle Rondo?" asks Stella-Rondo.

"Why, no, except he's got on some terrible-looking flesh-colored contraption I wouldn't be found dead in, is all I can see," I says.

"Never mind, you won't be found dead in it, because it happens to be part of my trousseau, and Mr. Whitaker took several dozen photographs of me in it," says Stella-Rondo. "What on earth could Uncle Rondo *mean* by wearing part of my trousseau out in the broad open daylight without saying so much as 'Kiss my foot,' *knowing* I only got home this morning after my separation and hung my negligee up on the bathroom door, just as nervous as I could be?" 45

"I'm sure I don't know, and what do you expect me to do about it?" I says. "Jump out the window?"

"No, I expect nothing of the kind. I simply declare that Uncle Rondo looks like a fool in it, that's all," she says. "It makes me sick to my stomach."

"Well, he looks as good as he can," I says. "As good as anybody in reason could." I stood up for Uncle Rondo, please remember. And I said to Stella-Rondo, "I think I would do well not to criticize so freely if I were you and came home with a two-year-old child I had never said a word about, and no explanation whatever about my separation."

"I asked you the instant I entered this house not to refer one more time to my adopted child, and you gave me your word of honor you would not," was all Stella-Rondo would say, and started pulling out every one of her eyebrows with some cheap Kress tweezers.

50 So I merely slammed the door behind me and went down and made some green-tomato pickle. Somebody had to do it. Of course Mama had turned both the Negroes loose; she always said no earthly power could hold one anyway on the Fourth of July, so she wouldn't even try. It turned out that Jaypan fell in the lake and came within a very narrow limit of drowning.

So Mama trots in. Lifts up the lid and says, "H'm! Not very good for your Uncle Rondo in his precarious condition, I must say. Or poor little adopted Shirley-T. Shame on you!"

That made me tired. I says, "Well, Stella-Rondo had better thank her lucky stars it was her instead of me came trotting in with that very peculiar-looking child. Now if it had been me that trotted in from Illinois and brought a peculiar-looking child or two, I shudder to think of the reception I'd of got, much less controlled the diet of an entire family."

"But you must remember, Sister, that you were never married to Mr. Whitaker in the first place and didn't go up to Illinois to live," says Mama, shaking a spoon in my face. "If you had I would of been just as overjoyed to see you and your little adopted girl as I was to see Stella-Rondo, when you wound up with your separation and came on back home."

"You would not," I says.

55 "Don't contradict me, I would," says Mama.

But I said she couldn't convince me though she talked till she was blue in the face. Then I said, "Besides, you know as well as I do that that child is not adopted."

"She most certainly is adopted," says Mama, stiff as a poker.

I says, "Why, Mama, Stella-Rondo had her just as sure as anything in this world, and just too stuck up to admit it."

"Why, Sister," said Mama. "Here I thought we were going to have a pleasant Fourth of July, and you start right out not believing a word your own baby sister tells you!"

60 "Just like Cousin Annie Flo. Went to her grave denying the facts of life," I reminded Mama.

"I told you if you ever mentioned Annie Flo's name I'd slap your face," says Mama, and slaps my face.

"All right, you wait and see," I says.

"I," says Mama, "I prefer to take my children's word for anything when it's humanly possible." You ought to see Mama, she weighs two hundred pounds and has real tiny feet.

Just then something perfectly horrible occurred to me.

65 "Mama," I says, "can that child talk?" I simply had to whisper! "Mama, I wonder if that child can be—you know—in any way? Do you realize?" I

says, "that she hasn't spoke one single, solitary word to a human being up to this minute? This is the way she looks," I says, and I looked like this.

Well, Mama and I just stood there and stared at each other. It was horrible!

"I remember well that Joe Whitaker frequently drank like a fish," says Mama. "I believed to my soul he drank *chemicals*." And without another word she marches to the foot of the stairs and calls Stella-Rondo.

"Stella-Rondo? O-o-o-o-o! Stella-Rondo!"

"What?" says Stella-Rondo from upstairs. Not even the grace to get up off the bed.

"Can that child of yours talk?" asks Mama.   70

Stella-Rondo says, "Can she what?"

"Talk! Talk!" says Mama. "Burdyburdyburdyburdy!"

So Stella-Rondo yells back, "Who says she can't talk?"

"Sister says so," says Mama.

"You didn't have to tell me, I know whose word of honor don't mean a   75
thing in this house," says Stella-Rondo.

And in a minute the loudest Yankee voice I ever heard in my life yells out, "OE'm Pop-OE the Sailor-r-r-r Ma-a-an!" and then somebody jumps up and down in the upstairs hall. In another second the house would of fallen down.

"Not only talks, she can tap-dance!" calls Stella-Rondo. "Which is more than some people I won't name can do."

"Why, the little precious darling thing!" Mama says, so surprised. "Just as smart as she can be!" Starts talking baby talk right there. Then she turns on me. "Sister, you ought to be thoroughly ashamed! Run upstairs this instant and apologize to Stella-Rondo and Shirley-T."

"Apologize for what?" I says. "I merely wondered if the child was normal, that's all. Now that she's proved she is, why, I have nothing further to say."

But Mama just turned on her heel and flew out, furious. She ran right   80
upstairs and hugged the baby. She believed it was adopted. Stella-Rondo hadn't done a thing but turn her against me from upstairs while I stood there helpless over the hot stove. So that made Mama, Papa-Daddy, and the baby all on Stella-Rondo's side.

Next, Uncle Rondo.

I must say that Uncle Rondo has been marvelous to me at various times in the past and I was completely unprepared to be made to jump out of my skin, the way it turned out. Once Stella-Rondo did something perfectly horrible to him—broke a chain letter from Flanders Field—and he took the radio back he had given her and gave it to me. Stella-Rondo was furious! For six months we all had to call her Stella instead of Stella-Rondo, or she wouldn't answer. I always thought Uncle Rondo had all the brains of the entire family. Another time he sent me to Mammoth Cave with all expenses paid.

But this would be the day he was drinking that prescription, the Fourth of July.

So at supper Stella-Rondo speaks up and says she thinks Uncle Rondo ought to try to eat a little something. So finally Uncle Rondo said he would try a little cold biscuits and ketchup, but that was all. So *she* brought it to him.

85 "Do you think it wise to disport with ketchup in Stella-Rondo's flesh-colored kimono?" I says. Trying to be considerate! If Stella-Rondo couldn't watch out for her trousseau, somebody had to.

"Any objections?" asks Uncle Rondo, just about to pour out all of the ketchup.

"Don't mind what she says, Uncle Rondo," says Stella-Rondo. "Sister has been devoting this solid afternoon to sneering out my bedroom window at the way you look."

"What's that?" says Uncle Rondo. Uncle Rondo has got the most terrible temper in the world. Anything is liable to make him tear the house down if it comes at the wrong time.

So Stella-Rondo says, "Sister says, 'Uncle Rondo certainly does look like a fool in that pink kimono!'"

90 Do you remember who it was really said that?

Uncle Rondo spills out all the ketchup and jumps out of his chair and tears off the kimono and throws it down on the dirty floor and puts his foot on it. It had to be sent all the way to Jackson to the cleaners and re-pleated.

"So that's your opinion of your Uncle Rondo, is it?" he says. "I look like a fool, do I? Well, that's the last straw. A whole day in this house with nothing to do, and then to hear you come out with a remark like that behind my back!"

"I didn't say any such of a thing, Uncle Rondo," I says, "and I'm not saying who did, either. Why, I think you look all right. Just try to take care of yourself and not talk and eat at the same time," I says. "I think you better go lie down."

"Lie down my foot," says Uncle Rondo. I ought to of known by that he was fixing to do something perfectly horrible.

95 So he didn't do anything that night in the precarious state he was in— just played Casino with Mama and Stella-Rondo and Shirley-T. and gave Shirley-T. a nickel with a head on both sides. It tickled her nearly to death, and she called him "Papa." But at 6:30 A.M. the next morning, he threw a whole five-cent package of some unsold one-inch firecrackers from the store as hard as he could into my bedroom and they every one went off. Not one bad one in the string. Anybody else, there'd be one that wouldn't go off.

Well, I'm just terribly susceptible to noise of any kind, the doctor has always told me I was the most sensitive person he had ever seen in his whole life, and I was simply prostrated. I couldn't eat! People tell me they heard it as far as the cemetery, and old Aunt Jep Patterson, that had been holding her own so good, thought it was Judgment Day and she was going to meet her whole family. It's usually so quiet here.

And I'll tell you it didn't take me any longer than a minute to make up my mind what to do. There I was with the whole entire house on Stella-Rondo's side and turned against me. If I have anything at all I have pride.

So I just decided I'd go straight down to the P.O. There's plenty of room there in the back, I says to myself.

Well! I made no bones about letting the family catch on to what I was up to. I didn't try to conceal it.

The first thing they knew, I marched in where they were all playing Old 100
Maid and pulled the electric oscillating fan out by the plug, and everything got real hot. Next I snatched the pillow I'd done the needlepoint on right off the davenport from behind Papa-Daddy. He went "Ugh!" I beat Stella-Rondo up the stairs and finally found my charm bracelet in her bureau drawer under a picture of Nelson Eddy.[1]

"So that's the way the land lies," says Uncle Rondo. There he was, piecing on the ham. "Well, Sister, I'll be glad to donate my army cot if you got any place to set it up, providing you'll leave right this minute and let me get some peace." Uncle Rondo was in France.

"Thank you kindly for the cot and 'peace' is hardly the word I would select if I had to resort to firecrackers at 6:30 A.M. in a young girl's bedroom," I says to him. "And as to where I intend to go, you seem to forget my position as postmistress of China Grove, Mississippi," I says. "I've always got the P.O."

Well, that made them all sit up and take notice.

I went out front and started digging up some four-o'clocks to plant around the P.O.

"Ah-ah-ah!" says Mama, raising the window. "Those happen to be my 105
four-o'clocks. Everything planted in that star is mine. I've never known you to make anything grow in your life."

"Very well," I says. "But I take the fern. Even you, Mama, can't stand there and deny that I'm the one watered that fern. And I happen to know where I can send in a box top and get a packet of one thousand mixed seeds, no two the same kind, free."

"Oh, where?" Mama wants to know.

But I says, "Too late. You 'tend to your house, and I'll 'tend to mine. You hear things like that all the time if you know how to listen to the radio. Perfectly marvelous offers. Get anything you want free."

---

1. Opera singer (1901–67) who enjoyed phenomenal popularity in the 1930s and 1940s when he costarred in numerous film musicals with Jeanette MacDonald. The two were known as "America's Singing Sweethearts."

So I hope to tell you I marched in and got that radio, and they could of all bit a nail in two, especially Stella-Rondo, that it used to belong to, and she well knew she couldn't get it back, I'd sue for it like a shot. And I very politely took the sewing-machine motor I helped pay the most on to give Mama for Christmas back in 1929, and a good big calendar, with the first-aid remedies on it. The thermometer and the Hawaiian ukulele certainly were rightfully mine, and I stood on the step-ladder and got all my watermelon-rind preserves and every fruit and vegetable I'd put up, every jar. Then I began to pull the tacks out of the bluebird wall vases on the archway to the dining room.

110   "Who told you you could have those, Miss Priss?" says Mama, fanning as hard as she could.

"I bought 'em and I'll keep track of 'em," I says. "I'll tack 'em up one on each side of the post-office window, and you can see 'em when you come to ask me for your mail, if you're so dead to see 'em."

"Not I! I'll never darken the door to that post office again if I live to be a hundred," Mama says. "Ungrateful child! After all the money we spent on you at the Normal."[2]

"Me either," says Stella-Rondo. "You can just let my mail lie there and *rot*, for all I care. I'll never come and relieve you of a single, solitary piece."

"I should worry," I says. "And who you think's going to sit down and write you all those big fat letters and postcards, by the way? Mr. Whitaker? Just because he was the only man ever dropped down in China Grove and you got him—unfairly—is he going to sit down and write you a lengthy correspondence after you come home giving no rhyme nor reason whatsoever for your separation and no explanation for the presence of that child? I may not have your brilliant mind, but I fail to see it."

115   So Mama says, "Sister, I've told you a thousand times that Stella-Rondo simply got homesick, and this child is far too big to be hers," and she says, "Now, why don't you just sit down and play Casino?"

Then Shirley-T. sticks out her tongue at me in this perfectly horrible way. She has no more manners than the man in the moon. I told her she was going to cross her eyes like that some day and they'd stick.

"It's too late to stop me now," I says. "You should have tried that yesterday. I'm going to the P.O. and the only way you can possibly see me is to visit me there."

So Papa-Daddy says, "You'll never catch me setting foot in that post office, even if I should take a notion into my head to write a letter some place." He says, "I won't have you reachin' out of that little old window with a pair of shears and cuttin' off any beard of mine. I'm too smart for you!"

"We all are," says Stella-Rondo.

---

2. That is, normal school (teachers' college).

But I said, "If you're so smart, where's Mr. Whitaker?"   120

So then Uncle Rondo says, "I'll thank you from now on to stop reading all the orders I get on postcards and telling everybody in China Grove what you think is the matter with them," but I says, "I draw my own conclusions and will continue in the future to draw them." I says, "If people want to write their innermost secrets on penny postcards, there's nothing in the wide world you can do about it, Uncle Rondo."

"And if you think we'll ever *write* another postcard you're sadly mistaken," says Mama.

"Cutting off your nose to spite your face then," I says. "But if you're all determined to have no more to do with the U.S. mail, think of this: What will Stella-Rondo do now, if she wants to tell Mr. Whitaker to come after her?"

"Wah!" says Stella-Rondo. I knew she'd cry. She had a conniption fit right there in the kitchen.

"It will be interesting to see how long she holds out," I says. "And now—I   125
am leaving."

"Good-bye," says Uncle Rondo.

"Oh, I declare," says Mama, "to think that a family of mine should quarrel on the Fourth of July, or the day after, over Stella-Rondo leaving old Mr. Whitaker and having the sweetest little adopted child! It looks like we'd all be glad!"

"Wah!" says Stella-Rondo, and has a fresh conniption fit.

"He left *her*—you mark my words," I says. "That's Mr. Whitaker. I know Mr. Whitaker. After all, I knew him first. I said from the beginning he'd up and leave her. I foretold every single thing that's happened."

"Where did he go?" asks Mama.   130

"Probably to the North Pole, if he knows what's good for him," I says.

But Stella-Rondo just bawled and wouldn't say another word. She flew to her room and slammed the door.

"Now look what you've gone and done, Sister," says Mama. "You go apologize."

"I haven't the time, I'm leaving," I says.

"Well, what are you waiting around for?" asks Uncle Rondo.   135

So I just picked up the kitchen clock and marched off, without saying, "Kiss my foot," or anything, and never did tell Stella-Rondo good-bye.

There was a girl going along on a little wagon right in front.

"Girl," I says, "come help me haul these things down the hill, I'm going to live in the post office."

Took her nine trips in her express wagon. Uncle Rondo came out on the porch and threw her a nickel.

And that's the last I've laid eyes on any of my family or my family laid   140
eyes on me for five solid days and nights. Stella-Rondo may be telling the

most horrible tales in the world about Mr. Whitaker, but I haven't heard them. As I tell everybody, I draw my own conclusions.

But oh, I like it here. It's ideal, as I've been saying. You see, I've got everything cater-cornered, the way I like it. Hear the radio? All the war news. Radio, sewing machine, book ends, ironing board and that great big piano lamp—peace, that's what I like. Butter-bean vines planted all along the front where the strings are.

Of course, there's not much mail. My family are naturally the main people in China Grove, and if they prefer to vanish from the face of the earth, for all the mail they get or the mail they write, why, I'm not going to open my mouth. Some of the folks here in town are taking up for me and some turned against me. I know which is which. There are always people who will quit buying stamps just to get on the right side of Papa-Daddy.

But here I am, and here I'll stay. I want the world to know I'm happy.

And if Stella-Rondo should come to me this minute, on bended knees, and *attempt* to explain the incidents of her life with Mr. Whitaker, I'd simply put my fingers in both my ears and refuse to listen.

1941

Biographical Sketches Fiction Writers

AESOP
(c. 620 B.C.E.–c. 560 B.C.E.)

Little is known for certain about the ancient Greek fabulist Aesop. Because the name *Aesop* is itself a Greek reference to Ethiopia and because many of the fables today attributed to Aesop feature characters very like the trickster figures in African tales, scholars today speculate that Aesop himself may well have been of African birth or descent. The first recorded mention of Aesop came some one hundred years after his supposed death, in the work of the Greek historian Herodotus, who indicated only that the storyteller had lived around 550 B.C., had once been a slave, and ultimately died at Delphi. Over the centuries, this and a few other sketchy ancient references grew into a full-fledged legend: Aesop was a slave who earned his freedom through his talent as a storyteller, served King Croesus as an ambassador, and yet was ultimately framed for the theft of a gold cup from Apollo's temple at Delphi and was thrown off the cliffs to his death. Whatever the truth of this story, it is almost certainly true that Aesop was an oral storyteller who never wrote down the tales first attributed to him in 320 B.C. when a Greek writer compiled the first known anthology of the fables, which eventually made their way to medieval Europe through a fifth-century Latin verse translation.

JAMES BALDWIN
(1924–1987)

For much of his life, James Baldwin was a leading literary spokesman for civil rights and racial equality in America. Born in New York City but long a resident of France, he first attracted critical attention with two extraordinary novels, *Go Tell It on the Mountain* (1953), drawing upon his past as a teenage preacher in the Fireside Pentecostal Church, and *Giovanni's Room* (1956), which dealt with the anguish of being black and homosexual in a largely white and heterosexual society. Other works include the novels *Another Country* (1962) and *If Beale Street Could Talk* (1974), the play *Blues for Mr. Charlie* (1964), and a story collection, *Going to Meet the Man* (1965). Baldwin is perhaps best remembered as a perceptive and eloquent essayist, the author of *Notes of a Native Son* (1955), *Nobody Knows My Name* (1961), *The Fire Next Time* (1963), *No Name in the Street* (1972), and *The Price of a Ticket* (1985).

TONI CADE BAMBARA
(1939–1995)

Born in New York City, Toni Cade Bambara grew up in Harlem and Bedford-Stuyvesant, two of New York's poorest neighborhoods. She began writing as a child and took her last name from a signature on a sketchbook she found in a trunk belonging to her great-grandmother. (The Bambara are a people of northwest Africa.) After graduating from "Queens College, she wrote fiction in "the pre-dawn in-betweens" while studying for her MA at the City College of New York and working at a great variety of jobs: dancer, social worker, recreation director, psychiatric counselor, college English teacher, literary critic, and film producer. Bambara began to publish her stories in 1962. Her fiction includes two collections of stories, *Gorilla, My Love* (1972) and *The Sea Birds Are Still Alive* (1977), as well as two novels, *The Salt Eaters* (1980) and *If Blessing Comes* (1987). Bambara also edited two anthologies, *The Black Woman* (1970) and *Stories for Black Folks* (1971).

AMBROSE BIERCE
(1842–1914?)

The tenth child of a poor Ohio family, Ambrose Bierce served with distinction in the Union Army during the Civil War, rising to the rank of major. After the war he worked as a journalist in California and London, where his boisterous western mannerisms and savage wit made him a celebrity and earned him the name "Bitter Bierce." He is probably best known as the author of *The Cynic's Word Book* (1906; later called *The Devil's Dictionary*), but his finest achievement may be his two volumes of short stories—*Tales of Soldiers and Civilians* (1891; later called *In the Midst of Life*) and *Can Such Things Be?* (1893)—and *The Monk and the Hangman's Daughter* (1892), an adaptation of a German story. Disillusioned and depressed after his divorce and the deaths of his two sons, Bierce went to Mexico in 1913, where he reportedly rode with Pancho Villa's revolutionaries. He disappeared and is presumed to have died there.

LINDA BREWER
(b. 1946)

Western writer Linda Brewer grew up in Oregon's Siuslaw and now lives in the Sonora Desert of southern Arizona, where she works in a medical lab and writes features and food articles for a Tucson publication, *The Desert Leaf.* A finalist in the World's Best Short Story Contest, she won the 2002 Raymond Carver Short Story Contest. Her story "20/20" was featured in *Micro Fiction: An Anthology of Really Short Stories* (1996).

RAYMOND CARVER
(1938–1988)

Born in the logging town of Clatskanie, Oregon, to a working-class family, Raymond Carver married at nineteen and had two children by the time he was twenty-one. Despite these early responsibilities and a struggle with alcoholism that was to continue for the rest of his life, Carver published his first story in 1961 and graduated from Humboldt State College in 1963. He published his first book, *Near Klamath*, a collection of poems, in 1968 and thereafter supported himself with visiting lectureships at the University of California at Berkeley, Syracuse University, and the Iowa Writer's Workshop, among other institutions. His short-story collections include *What We Talk About When We Talk About Love* (1981), *Will You Please Be Quiet, Please?* (1976), *Cathedral* (1983), *My Father's Life* (1986), and *Where I'm Calling From* (1989). His poetry is collected in *All of Us* (2000).

ANTON CHEKHOV
(1860–1904)

The grandson of an emancipated serf, Anton Chekhov was born in the Russian town of Taganrog. In 1875, his father, a grocer facing bankruptcy and imprisonment, fled to Moscow, and soon the rest of the family lost their house to a former friend and lodger, a situation that Chekhov would revisit in his play *The Cherry Orchard.* In 1884, Chekhov received his M.D. from the University of Moscow. He purchased an estate near Moscow in the early 1890s and became both an industrious landowner and doctor to the local peasants. After contributing stories to magazines and journals throughout the 1880s, he began writing for the stage in 1887. His plays, now regarded as classics, were generally ill-received in his lifetime. *The Wood Demon* (later rewritten as *Uncle Vanya*) was performed only a few times in 1889 before closing, while the 1896 premiere of *The Seagull* sparked a riot when an audience expecting comedy was confronted with an experimental tragedy.

KATE CHOPIN

(1850–1904)
Katherine O'Flaherty was born in St. Louis, Missouri, to a Creole-Irish family that enjoyed a high place in society. Her father died when she was four, and Kate was raised by her mother, grandmother, and great-grandmother. Very well read at a young age, she received her formal education at the St. Louis Academy of the Sacred Heart. In 1870, she married Oscar Chopin, a Louisiana businessman, and lived with him in Natchitoches parish and New Orleans, where she became a close observer of Creole and Cajun life. Following her husband's sudden death in 1884, she returned to St. Louis, where she raised her six children and began her literary career. In slightly more than a decade she produced a substantial body of work, including the story collections *Bayou Folk* (1894) and *A Night in Acadie* (1897) and the classic novella *The Awakening* (1899), which was greeted with a storm of criticism for its frank treatment of female sexuality.

STEPHEN CRANE

(1871–1900)
One of fourteen children, Stephen Crane and his family moved frequently before settling, after his father's death in 1880, in Asbury Park, New Jersey. Crane sporadically attended various preparatory schools and colleges without excelling at much besides baseball. Determined to be a journalist, he left school for the last time in 1891 and began contributing pieces to New York newspapers. His city experiences led him to write *Maggie: A Girl of the Streets,* a realist social-reform novel published in 1893 at his own expense. His next novel, *The Red Badge of Courage* (1895), presented a stark picture of the Civil War and brought him widespread fame; many of his stories were published in the collections *The Open Boat and Other Tales of Adventure* (1898) and *The Monster and Other Stories* (1899). Crane served as a foreign correspondent, reporting on conflicts in Cuba and Greece, and lived his last years abroad, dying of tuberculosis at the age of 28.

EDWIDGE DANTICAT

(b. 1969)
When she was twelve, Edwidge Danticat moved from Port-au-Prince, Haiti, to Brooklyn, New York, where her parents had relocated eight years before. Danticat published her first writing in English two years later, a newspaper article about her immigration to the United States that developed into her first novel, *Breath, Eyes, Memory* (1994). Danticat received a degree in French literature from Barnard College and an MFA from Brown University. *Krik? Krak!* (1991), a collection of short stories, was nominated for the National Book Award. Her second novel, *The Farming of Bones* (1998), is based on the 1937 massacre of Haitians at the border of the

Dominican Republic. In 2002 Danticat published *After the Dance: A Walk through Carnival in Jacmel, Haiti,* an account of her travels. More recent publications include *The Dew Breaker* (2004), a collection of stories that examine the life of a Haitian torturer, and *Brother, I'm Dying* (2007), winner of the National Book Critics Circle Award for Autobiography.

LOUISE ERDRICH
(b. 1954)

Born in Minnesota of German-American and French-Chippewa descent, Louise Erdrich grew up in Wahpeton, North Dakota, as a member of the Turtle Mountain Band of Chippewa. She attended Dartmouth College and received an MFA in creative writing from Johns Hopkins University. Her first novel, *Love Medicine* (1984), a collection of linked stories, won the National Book Critics Circle Award. In her subsequent publications—*The Beet Queen* (1986), *Tracks* (1988), *The Bingo Palace* (1993), and *Tales of Burning Love* (1996)—she pursued her focus on the lives of Native Americans in contemporary North Dakota. In 1991, she jointly authored the best-selling novel *The Crown of Columbus* with her husband, Michael Dorris. Her recent works include the novels *The Last Report on the Miracles at Little No Horse* (2001), *Four Souls* (2004), *The Plague of Doves* (2008), and a series of novels for young readers. She lives in Minnesota with her family and dogs.

WILLIAM FAULKNER
(1897–1962)

A native of Oxford, Mississippi, William Faulkner left high school without graduating, joined the Royal Canadian Air Force in 1918, and in the mid-1920s lived briefly in New Orleans, where he was encouraged as a writer by Sherwood Anderson. He then spent a few miserable months as a clerk in a New York bookstore, published a collection of poems, *The Marble Faun,* in 1924, and took a long walking tour of Europe in 1925 before returning to Mississippi. With the publication of *Sartoris* in 1929, Faulkner began a cycle of works, featuring recurrent characters and set in fictional Yoknapatawpha County, including *The Sound and the Fury* (1929), *As I Lay Dying* (1930), *Light in August* (1932), *Absalom, Absalom!* (1936), *The Hamlet* (1940), and *Go Down, Moses* (1942). He spent time in Hollywood, writing screenplays for *The Big Sleep* and other films, and lived his last years in Charlottesville, Virginia. Faulkner received the Nobel Prize for Literature in 1950.

GABRIEL GARCÍA MÁRQUEZ
(b. 1928)

Born in Aracataca, Colombia, a remote town near the Caribbean coast, Gabriel García Márquez studied law at the University of Bogotá and then worked as a journalist in Latin America, Europe, and the United States. In 1967, he took up permanent residence in Barcelona, Spain. His first published book, *Leaf Storm* (1955), set in the fictional small town of Macondo, is based on the myths and legends of his childhood home. His most famous novel, *One Hundred Years of Solitude* (1967), fuses magic, reality, fable, and fantasy to present six generations of one Macondo family, a microcosm of many of the social, political, and economic problems of Latin America. Among his many works are *The Autumn of the Patriarch* (1975), *Chronicle of a Death Foretold* (1981), *Love in the Time of Cholera* (1987), *Of Love and Other Demons* (1994), and *Living to Tell the Tale* (2003), a three-volume set of memoirs. Márquez won the Nobel Prize for Literature in 1982.

CHARLOTTE PERKINS GILMAN
(1860–1935)

Charlotte Anna Perkins was born in Hartford, Connecticut. After a painful, lonely childhood and several years of supporting herself as a governess, art teacher, and designer of greeting cards, Perkins married the artist Charles Stetson. Following Gilman's several extended periods of depression, her husband put her in the care of a doctor who "sent me home with the solemn advice to 'live as domestic a life as . . . possible,' to 'have but two hours' intellectual life a day,' and 'never to touch pen, brush, or pencil again' as long as I lived." Three months of this regimen brought her "near the borderline of utter mortal ruin" and inspired her masterpiece, "The Yellow Wallpaper." In 1900, she married George Houghton Gilman, having divorced Stetson in 1892. Her nonfiction works, springing from the early women's movement, include *Women and Economics* (1898) and *Man-Made World* (1911). She also wrote several utopian novels, including *Moving the Mountain* (1911) and *Herland* (1915).

JACOB AND WILHELM GRIMM (1785–1863, 1786–1859)

Among the world's first, as well as most famous, folklorists, the German "Brothers Grimm" were only two of nine children born into the family of a lawyer and judge. After what they described as an idyllic childhood was cut short by the death of their father in 1796, both brothers studied law only to become fascinated with medieval German literature and history. With the death of their mother in 1808, the brothers became the sole support of their four surviving siblings. For the next 23 years, both would work as private librarians even as they began to collect the traditional legends and tales they published in the famed two-volume *Nursery and Household Tales* (1812, 1816). Appointed university librarians and lecturers, the brothers, along with Wilhelm's wife and growing brood of children, moved first to Göttingen (1830) and then to Berlin (1840). Here, they not only revised their *Tales* but also undertook important research into the history of German law, customs, and mythology, as well as grammar and historical linguistics. Modern scholars estimate that their tales have been translated into some 160 languages, rivaling the Bible in overall sales.

HA JIN (b. 1956)

Born Xuefei Jin, Ha Jin grew up in mainland China. During his teenage years, he served in the People's Army. He then worked for a railroad company while teaching himself English, before receiving degrees from Heilongjiang and Shandong universities in China. While earning his Ph.D. from Brandeis, Jin watched television coverage of the Tiananmen Square massacre and decided to remain, with his wife and son, in the United States, where he now teaches English and creative writing at Emory University. He has published the poetry collections *Between Silences* (1990), *Facing Shadows* (1996), and *Wreckage* (2001); the short-story collections *Ocean of Words: Army Stories* (1996), *Under the Red Flag* (1997), and *The Bridegroom* (2000); and the novels *In the Pond* (1998) and *Waiting* (1999), which won both the National Book Award and the 2000 PEN/Faulkner Award for Fiction. Ha Jin's most recent novels are *The Crazed* (2002), *War Trash* (2004), which also won the PEN/Faulkner Award, and *A Free Life* (2007). Jin's opera *The First Emperor*, co-authored with composer Tan Dun, opened at New York's Metropolitan Opera in 2006.

NATHANIEL HAWTHORNE
(1804–1864)

Nathaniel Hawthorne was born in Salem, Massachusetts, a descendant of Puritan immigrants. Educated at Bowdoin College, he was agonizingly slow in winning recognition for his work and supported himself from time to time in government service—working in the customhouses of Boston and Salem and serving as the United States consul in Liverpool. His early collections of stories, *Twice-Told Tales* (1837) and *Mosses from an Old Manse* (1846), did not sell well, and it was not until the publication of his most famous novel, *The Scarlet Letter* (1850), that his fame spread beyond a discerning few. His other novels include *The House of the Seven Gables* (1851) and *The Blithedale Romance* (1852). Burdened by a deep sense of guilt for his family's role in the notorious Salem witchcraft trials over a century before he was born (one ancestor had been a judge), Hawthorne used fiction as a means of exploring the moral dimensions of sin and the human soul.

ERNEST HEMINGWAY
(1899–1961)

Born in Oak Park, Illinois, Ernest Hemingway became a reporter after graduating from high school. During World War I, he served as an ambulance-service volunteer in France and an infantryman in Italy, where he was wounded and decorated for valor. After the war, he lived for a time in Paris, part of the "Lost Generation" of American expatriates that also included Gertrude Stein and F. Scott Fitzgerald. Two volumes of stories, *In Our Time* (1925) and *Death in the Afternoon* (1932), and two major novels, *The Sun Also Rises* (1926) and *A Farewell to Arms* (1929), established his international reputation. Hemingway supported the Loyalists in the Spanish Civil War—the subject of *For Whom the Bell Tolls* (1940)—served as a war correspondent during World War II, and from 1950 until his death lived in Cuba. His novel *The Old Man and the Sea* (1952) won a Pulitzer Prize, and Hemingway was awarded the Nobel Prize for Literature in 1954.

JAMES JOYCE
(1882–1941)

In 1902, after graduating from University College, Dublin, James Joyce left Ireland for Paris, returning a year later. In October 1904, he eloped with Nora Barnacle and settled in Trieste, where he taught English for the Berlitz school. Though he lived as an expatriate for the rest of his life, all of his fiction is set in his native Dublin. Joyce had more than his share of difficulties with publication and censorship. His volume of short stories, *Dubliners*, completed in 1905, was not published until 1914. His novel *Portrait of the Artist as a Young Man*, dated "Dublin 1904, Trieste 1914," appeared first in America, in 1916. His great novel *Ulysses* (1921) was banned for a dozen years in the United States and as long or longer elsewhere. In addition, Joyce published a play, *Exiles* (1918); two collections of poetry, *Chamber Music* (1907) and *Pomes Penyeach* (1927); and the monumental, experimental, and puzzling novel *Finnegans Wake* (1939).

FRANZ KAFKA
(1883–1924)

Born into a middle-class Jewish family in Prague, Franz Kafka earned a doctorate in law from the German University in that city and held an inconspicuous position in the civil service for many years. Emotionally and physically ill for the last seven or eight years of his short life, he died of tuberculosis in Vienna, never having married (though he was twice engaged to the same woman and lived with an actress in Berlin for some time before he died) and not having published his three major novels, *The Trial* (1925), *The Castle* (1926), and *Amerika* (1927). Indeed, he ordered his friend Max Brod to destroy them and other works he had left in manuscript. Fortunately, Brod did not; and not long after Kafka's death, his sometimes-dreamlike, sometimes-nightmarish work was known and admired all over the world. His stories in English translation are collected in *The Great Wall of China* (1933), *The Penal Colony* (1948), and *The Complete Stories* (1976).

YASUNARI KAWABATA
(1899–1972)

Born in Osaka, Japan, to a prosperous family, Yasunari Kawabata graduated from Tokyo Imperial University in 1924 and had his first literary success with the semiautobiographical novella *The Izu Dancer* (1926). He cofounded the journal *Contemporary Literature* in support of the Neosensualist movement, which had much in common with the European literary movements of Dadaism, Expressionism, and Cubism. His best-known works include *Snow Country* (1937), *Thousand Cranes* (1952), *The Sound of the Mountain* (1954), *The Lake* (1955), *The Sleeping Beauty* (1960), *The Old Capital* (1962), and the collection *Palm-of-the-Hand Stories* (translated in 1988). Kawabata was awarded the Nobel Prize for Literature in 1968. After long suffering from poor health, he committed suicide in 1972.

JAMAICA KINCAID
(b. 1949)

Born in St. John's, Antigua, Elaine Potter Richardson left her native island and her family at seventeen. Changing her name to Jamaica Kincaid, she worked in New York City as an au pair and a receptionist before studying photography at the New School for Social Research, then briefly continuing her studies at Franconia College in New Hampshire. After returning to New York, she became a regular contributor to *The New Yorker*, for which she wrote from 1976 until 1995. Her publications include a collection of short stories, *At the Bottom of the River* (1983); a book-length essay about Antigua, *A Small Place* (1988); a book for children, *Annie, Gwen, Lilly, Pam, and Tulip* (1986); the novels *Annie John* (1985), *Lucy* (1990), and *The Autobiography of My Mother* (1996); the memoir *My Brother* (1997); and a collection of her *New Yorker* pieces, *Talk Stories* (2001). Her most recent novel, *Mr. Potter* (2002), takes place on the island of Antigua.

D. H. LAWRENCE
(1885–1930)

The son of a coal miner and a schoolteacher, David Herbert Lawrence was able to attend high school only briefly. He worked for a surgical-appliance manufacturer, attended Nottingham University College, and taught school in Croydon, near London. After publishing his first novel, *The White Peacock* (1911), he devoted his time exclusively to writing; *Sons and Lovers* (1913) established him as a major literary figure. In 1912, he eloped with Frieda von Richthofen, and in 1914, after her divorce, they were married. During World War I, both his novels and his wife's German nationality gave him trouble: *The Rainbow* was published in September 1915 and suppressed in November. In 1919, the Lawrences left England and began years of wandering: first to Italy, then Ceylon, Australia, Mexico, and New Mexico, then back to England and Italy. Lawrence published *Women in Love* in 1920 and *Lady Chatterley's Lover,* his most sexually explicit novel, in 1928. Through it all he suffered from tuberculosis, eventually dying from the disease.

BOBBIE ANN MASON
(b. 1940)

Bobbie Ann Mason was born and raised in Mayfield, Kentucky, where her parents were dairy farmers. She received a B.A. from the University of Kentucky, an M.A. from the State University of New York at Binghamton, and a Ph.D. in English from the University of Connecticut. After her stories appeared in such magazines as *The New Yorker* and *Redbook*, Mason published her first collection, *Shiloh and Other Stories* (1982), which won the Ernest Hemingway Foundation Award and established her literary reputation. Her works include the novels *In Country* (1985), *Feather Crowns* (1993), and *Atomic Romance* (2005); a short novel, *Spence and Lila* (1988); three collections of stories—*Love Life* (1989), *Midnight Magic* (1998), and *Zigzagging Down a Wild Trail* (2001); and a memoir, *Clear Springs* (1999), which was a finalist for the Pulitzer Prize.

GUY DE MAUPASSANT
(1850–1893)

Born Henri René Albert in Normandy, France, Maupassant was expelled at sixteen from a Rouen seminary and finished his education at a public high school. After serving in the Franco-Prussian War, he worked as a government clerk in Paris for ten years. A protégé of Flaubert, he published during the 1880s some three hundred stories, half a dozen novels, and plays. The short stories, which appeared regularly in popular periodicals, sampled military and peasant life, the decadent world of politics and journalism, prostitution, the supernatural, and the hypocrisies of solid citizens; with Chekhov, he may be said to have created the modern short story. His life ended somewhat like one of his own stories: he died of syphilis in an asylum. His novels include *Une Vie* (*A Life*, 1883), *Bel Ami* (*Handsome Friend*, 1885), and *Pierre et Jean* (1888).

HERMAN MELVILLE
(1819–1891)

When his father died in debt, twelve-year-old Herman Melville's life of privilege became one of struggle. At eighteen, he left his native New York to teach in a backwoods Massachusetts school, then trained as a surveyor; finding no work, he became a sailor in 1839. After five years in the South Seas, he wrote *Typee* (1846) and *Omoo* (1847), sensationalized and wildly popular accounts of his voyages. They proved the pinnacle of Melville's career in his lifetime, however; *Mardi* (1849) was judged too abstruse, the travel narratives *Redburn* (1849) and *White-Jacket* (1850) too listless. Melville's magnum opus, *Moby-Dick* (1851), was alternately shunned and condemned. His later novels—*Pierre* (1852), *Israel Potter* (1853), and *The Confidence-Man* (1856)—as well as his poetry collection *Battle-Pieces* (1866) were all but ignored. Melville's reputation as one of the giants of American literature was established only after his death; the novella *Billy Budd, Sailor* (not published until 1924), like *Moby-Dick*, is judged a masterpiece.

TONI MORRISON
(b. 1931)

Born in Lorain, Ohio, a steel town on the shores of Lake Erie, Chloe Anthony Wofford was the first member of her family to go to college, graduating from Howard University in 1953 and earning an M.A. from Cornell. She taught at both Texas Southern University and at Howard before becoming an editor at Random House, where she worked for nearly twenty years. In such novels as *The Bluest Eye* (1969), *Sula* (1973), *Song of Solomon*

(1977), *Beloved* (1987), and *Paradise* (1998), Morrison traces the problems and possibilities faced by black Americans struggling with slavery and its aftermath in the United States. More recent work includes her eighth novel, *Love* (2003); two picture books for children co-authored with her son, Slade—*The Bog Box* (1999) and *Book of Mean People* (2002); a book for young adults, *Remember: The Journey to School Integration* (2004); and *What Moves at the Margin: Selected Nonfiction* (2008). In 1993 she became the first African American author to win the Nobel Prize for literature.

FLANNERY O'CONNOR
(1925–1964)

Mary Flannery O'Connor was born in Savannah, Georgia, studied at the Georgia State College for Women, and won a fellowship to the Writer's Workshop of the University of Iowa, from which she received her MFA. In 1950, she was first diagnosed with lupus, a painful autoimmune disorder that had killed her father and would trouble her for the rest of her brief life. Her first novel, *Wise Blood,* was published in 1952, and her first collection of stories, *A Good Man Is Hard to Find,* in 1955. She was able to complete only one more novel, *The Violent Bear It Away* (1960), and a second collection of stories, *Everything That Rises Must Converge* (1965), before dying of lupus in Milledgeville, Georgia. Her posthumously published *Complete Stories* won the National Book Award in 1972. A collection of letters, edited by Sally Fitzgerald under the title *The Habit of Being,* appeared in 1979.

EDGAR ALLAN POE
(1809–1849)

Orphaned before he was three, Edgar Poe was adopted by John Allan, a wealthy Richmond businessman. Poe received his early schooling in Richmond and in England before a brief, unsuccessful stint at the University of Virginia. After serving for two years in the army, he was appointed to West Point in 1830 but expelled within the year for cutting classes. Living in Baltimore with his grandmother, aunt, and cousin Virginia (whom he married in 1835, when she was thirteen), Poe eked out a precarious living as an editor; his keen-edged reviews earned him numerous literary enemies. His two-volume *Tales of the Grotesque and Arabesque* received little critical attention when published in 1839, but his poem "The Raven" (1845) made him a literary celebrity. After his wife's death of tuberculosis in 1847, Poe, already an alcoholic, became increasingly erratic; two years later he died mysteriously in Baltimore.

KATHERINE ANNE PORTER
(1890–1980)

A native of Indian Creek, Texas, and a descendant of Daniel Boone, Katherine Anne Porter was raised by her grandmother and educated in convent schools. Forced by tuberculosis to abandon an acting career, she worked as a journalist in Denver, Chicago, and Mexico. She published her first short story in 1922; her first collection, *Flowering Judas* (1930), won critical acclaim. Porter's only full-length novel, *Ship of Fools* (1962), established her as a major American writer and made her rich. She won numerous awards for her work, including both a Pulitzer Prize and a National Book Award for her *Collected Short Stories* (1965) and a Gold Medal from the National Institute of Arts and Letters. Among her works are the story collections *Pale Horse, Pale Rider* (1939) and *The Leaning Tower and Other Stories* (1944); a volume of essays, *The Days Before* (1952); and an account of the controversial Sacco and Vanzetti murder trial, *The Never-Ending Wrong* (1977).

MARJANE SATRAPI
(b. 1969)

As the granddaughter of Nasreddine Shah, the last Quadjar emperor of Iran, Iranian-born Marjane Satrapi is a princess by birth and a self-declared pacifist by inclination. Only 10 years old at the time of the 1979 Islamist revolution, she was reportedly expelled at age 14 from her French-language school after hitting a principal who demanded she stop wearing jewelry. Fearing for her safety, Satrapi's secularist parents sent her to Vienna, Austria, where she would remain until age 18, when she returned to Iran to attend college. After a brief marriage ended in divorce, Satrapi moved to France in 1994, where her graphic memoir, *Persepolis*, was published to great acclaim in 2000. Subsequently translated into numerous languages, it appeared in the United States as *Persepolis: The Story of a Childhood* (2003) and *Persepolis 2: The Story of a Return* (2004). A 2007 animated movie version garnered the Jury Prize at the Cannes Film Festival and was nominated for an Academy Award in 2008. Satrapi's other works are *Embroideries* (2005), which explores Iranian women's views of sex and love through a conversation among Satrapi's female relatives; *Chicken with Plums* (2006), which tells the story of both the 1953 CIA-backed Iranian coup d'etat and the last days of Satrapi's great-uncle, a musician who committed suicide; and several children's books.

AMY TAN (b. 1952)

Amy Tan was born in Oakland, California, just two and a half years after her parents immigrated from China. She received her M.A. in linguistics from San Jose State University and has worked on programs for disabled children and as a freelance writer. In 1987, she visited China for the first time—"As soon as my feet touched China, I became Chinese"—and returned to write her first book, *The Joy Luck Club* (1989). Tan has since published four more novels—*The Kitchen God's Wife* (1991), *The Hundred Secret Senses* (1995), *The Bonesetter's Daughter* (2000) and *Saving Fish from Drowning* (2006)—and has co-authored two children's books. Her first book of nonfiction, *The Opposite of Fate: A Book of Musings* (2003), explores lucky accidents, choice, and memory. Tan is also the lead singer for the Rock Bottom Remainders, a rock band made up of fellow writers, including Stephen King and Dave Barry; they make appearances at benefits that support literacy programs for children.

GARRY TRUDEAU
(b. 1948)

A New York native of Canadian descent, Garry Trudeau began his career as a cartoonist while still a student at Yale University. His popular comic strip *Doonesbury* debuted nationally in 1970. In the almost forty years since, the controversial, often-political strip has earned Trudeau a Pulitzer Prize (1975) and spawned an Academy Award–nominated animated film (1977), a Broadway musical (1983), and numerous books—all written by Trudeau. (His most recent books are *The Revolt of the English Majors* [2001] and The *Long Road Home* [2005], a collection of strips inspired by the war in Iraq.) The cartoonist—who calls drama his "earliest passion"—is also the author of *Rap Master Ronnie* (1984), a Broadway musical about President Ronald Reagan; and, with famed film director Robert Altman, the HBO series *Tanner 88* (1988), which portrayed the ongoing presidential campaign through the eyes of a fictional Democratic candidate, as well as a 2004 sequel for the Sundance Channel. Known as something of a recluse, the father of three has been married to journalist and television personality Jane Pauley since 1980.

JOHN UPDIKE
(1932–2009)

The man *The Oxford Encyclopedia of American Literature* dubs "perhaps America's most versatile, prolific, and distinguished man of letters of the second half of the twentieth century" spent the early years of his life in Reading and rural Shillington, Pennsylvania. John Updike went on to study English literature at Harvard, where he also contributed cartoons and articles to the famous *Lampoon.* Marrying a Radcliffe fine-arts student in 1953, Updike the next year graduated summa cum laude and sold both his first poem and his first story to *The New Yorker,* whose staff he joined in 1955. Though he would continue to contribute essays, poems, and fiction to *The New Yorker* for the rest of his life, in 1957 Updike moved with his young family from Manhattan to rural Massachusetts. In the two years following the move, he published both his first book, a collection of poems (1958), and his first novel (1959). Updike went on to publish some 21 novels, 13 short-story collections, seven volumes of poetry (including *Collected Poems, 1953–1993* [1993]), as well as seven collections of essays, a play, and a memoir. He is best known for the tetralogy tracing the life of high-school basketball star turned car salesman Harry C. Rabbit Angstrom. Begun with *Rabbit, Run* in 1960, the series of novels includes *Rabbit Is Rich* (1981) and *Rabbit at Rest* (1990), both of which were awarded Pulitzer Prizes.

EUDORA WELTY
(1909–2001)

Known as the "First Lady of Southern Literature," Eudora Welty was born and raised in Jackson, Mississippi, attended Mississippi State College for Women, and earned a B.A. from the University of Wisconsin. Among the countless awards she received were two Guggenheim Fellowships, six O. Henry Awards, a Pulitzer Prize, the French Legion of Honor, the National Medal for Literature, and the Presidential Medal of Freedom. Although she wrote five novels, including *The Robber Bridegroom* (1942), *Ponder Heart* (1954), and *The Optimist's Daughter* (1972), she is best known for her short stories, many of which appear in *The Collected Stories of Eudora Welty* (1980). Among her nonfiction works are *One Writer's Beginnings* (1984), *A Writer's Eye: Collected Book Reviews* (1994), and five collections of her photographs, including *One Place, One Time* (1978) and *Photographs* (1989). In 1998 the Library of America published a two-volume edition of her selected works, making her the first living author they had published.

READING, RESPONDING, WRITING

Poetry

Poetry: Reading, Responding, Writing

If you're a reader of poetry, you already know that poetry reading is not just an intellectual and bookish activity; it is about feeling. Reading poetry well means responding to it. If you respond emotionally, you are likely to read more accurately, with deeper understanding, and with greater pleasure. Conversely, if you read poetry accurately and with attention to detail, you will almost certainly respond to it—or learn how to respond—on an emotional level. Reading and responding come to be, for experienced readers of poetry, very nearly one. But those who teach poetry have discovered something else: Writing about poetry helps both the reading and the responding processes.

Responding involves remembering and reflecting. As you recall your own past and make associations between things in the text and things you already know and feel, you will not only respond more fully to a particular poem but also improve your general reading skills. Your knowledge and life experience inform your reading of what is before you and allow you to connect elements within the text—events, images, words, sounds—so that meanings and feelings develop and accumulate. Prior learning creates expectations: of pattern, repetition, association, or causality. Reflecting on the text—and on expectations produced by the text—re-creates old feelings but directs them in new, often unusual ways. Poems, even when they are about things we have no experience of, connect to things we do know and order our memories, thoughts, and feelings in new and newly challenging ways.

A course in reading poetry can enrich your life by helping you become more articulate and more sensitive to both ideas and feelings; that's the larger goal. But the more immediate goal—and the route to the larger one—is to become a better reader of texts and a more precise and careful writer. Close attention to one text makes you appreciate and understand textuality and its possibilities more generally. Texts may be complex and even unstable in some ways; they do not affect all readers the same way, and they work through language that has its own volatilities and complexities. But paying attention to how you read—developing specific questions to ask and working on your reading skills systematically—can take a lot of the guesswork out of reading texts and make your interpretations more satisfying.

READING POETRY

Poems, perhaps even more than other texts, can sharpen your reading skills because they tend to be so compact, so fully dependent on concise expression of feeling. In poems, ideas and feelings may be packed tightly into just a few lines. The experiences of life are very concentrated here, and meanings emerge quickly, word by word.

Poems often show us the very process of putting feelings into a language that can be shared with others. Poetry can be intellectual, too, explaining and exploring ideas, but its focus is more often on how people feel than on how they think. Poems work out a shareable language for feeling, and one of poetry's most insistent virtues arises from its attempt to express the inexpressible. How can anyone, for example, put into words what it means to be in love or how it feels to lose someone one cares about? Poetry tries, and it often captures a shade of emotion that feels just right to a reader. No single poem can be said to represent all the things that love or death feels like or means, but one of the joys of poetry comes when we read a poem and want to say, "Yes, that is just what it is like; I know exactly what that line means, but I've never been able to express it so well." Poetry can be the voice of our feelings even when our minds are speechless with grief or joy. Reading is no substitute for living, but it can make living more abundant and more available. At the same time, poetry does not always celebrate or make us feel better. Sometimes, it questions easy expectations about how we are supposed to feel. Even the most appealing subjects may be handled very differently than we expect, challenging our assumptions and understanding.

READING POEMS: FOUR EXAMPLES

The following four poems talk about the love between two people—a familiar poetic subject and something we all have our own ideas and expectations about. Each poem is written as if it were spoken by one person to his or her lover, and each powerfully conveys the intensity, sincerity, and depth of the love. But the poems work in different ways. As you read these poems, make mental (or actual) notes about what you think makes them alike and different, both in terms of what they suggest about love and how they suggest it.

ELIZABETH BARRETT BROWNING

How Do I Love Thee?

How do I love thee? Let me count the ways.
I love thee to the depth and breadth and height

My soul can reach, when feeling out of sight
For the ends of Being and ideal Grace.
5 I love thee to the level of every day's
Most quiet need, by sun and candlelight.
I love thee freely, as men strive for Right;
I love thee purely, as they turn from Praise;
I love thee with the passion put to use
10 In my old griefs, and with my childhood's faith.
I love thee with a love I seemed to lose
With my lost saints—I love thee with the breath,
Smiles, tears of all my life!—and, if God choose,
I shall but love thee better after death.

                                        1850

JAROLD RAMSEY

The Tally Stick

Here from the start, from our first of days, look:
I have carved our lives in secret on this stick
of mountain mahogany the length of your arms
outstretched, the wood clear red, so hard and rare.
5 It is time to touch and handle what we know we share.

Near the butt, this intricate notch where the grains
converge and join: it is our wedding.
I can read it through with a thumb and tell you now
who danced, who made up the songs, who meant us joy.
10 These little arrowheads along the grain,
they are the births of our children. See,
they make a kind of design with these heavy crosses,
the deaths of our parents, the loss of friends.

Over it all as it goes, of course, I
15 have chiseled Events, History—random
hashmarks cut against the swirling grain.
See, here is the Year the World Went Wrong,
we thought, and here the days the Great Men fell.
The lengthening runes of our lives run through it all.

20 See, our tally stick is whittled nearly end to end;
delicate as scrimshaw, it would not bear you up.
Regrets have polished it, hand over hand.

Yet let us take it up, and as our fingers
like children leading on a trail cry back
25 our unforgotten wonders, sign after sign,
we will talk softly as of ordinary matters,
and in one another's blameless eyes go blind.

1977

LINDA PASTAN

love poem

I want to write you
a love poem as headlong
as our creek
after thaw
5 when we stand
on its dangerous
banks and watch it carry
with it every twig
every dry leaf and branch
10 in its path
every scruple
when we see it
so swollen
with runoff
15 that even as we watch
we must grab
each other
and step back
we must grab each
20 other or
get our shoes
soaked we must
grab each other

1988

"How Do I Love Thee?" is direct but fairly abstract. It lists several ways the poet feels love and connects them to some noble ideas of higher obligations—to justice (line 7), for example, and to spiritual aspiration (lines 2–4). It suggests a wide range of things that love can mean and evokes a variety of emotions. It does not say much about the everyday relationship between the two lovers, the experiences they have had together, or the ways in which their relationship is unlike those of other devoted or ideal lovers. Its appeal is to our general sense of what love is like and of how intense feelings can be; it does not offer details.

"The Tally Stick" is much more concrete. The whole poem concentrates on a single object that "counts" or "tallies" the ways in which this couple love one another, as does "How Do I Love Thee?" This stick stands for their love and becomes a kind of physical totem for it: The stick's natural features (lines 4, 6-7, 10, and 16) and the marks carved on it (lines 6, 10, 12 15-16, 20-21) indicate events in the story of the relationship—their wedding and the births of their children, for example. We could say that the stick *symbolizes* their love, but for now it is enough to notice that the stick serves the lovers as a marker and a reminder of some specific details of their love. It is a special kind of reminder because its language is "secret" (line 2), something they can share privately. The stick itself becomes a very personal object, and in the last stanza of the poem it is as if we watch the lovers touching the stick together and reminiscing over it, gradually dissolving into their emotions and each other as they recall the "unforgotten wonders" (line 25) of their lives together.

Linda Pastan's direct and seemingly simple "love poem" suggests as much about the art and craft of poetry as it does about love. The poem expresses the desire to write a love poem even as the love poem itself materializes before our eyes; the desire and the resultant poem exist side by side, and in reading the poem we seem to watch and hear the poet's creative process at work in developing appropriate metaphors and means of expression. The poem must be "headlong" (line 2) to match the power of a love comparable to the irresistible forces of nature. The poem should, like the love it expresses and the swollen creek it describes, sweep everything along, and it should represent (and reproduce) the sense of watching that the lovers have when they observe natural processes at work. The poem, like the action it represents, suggests to readers the kind of desire that propels the lovers.

The poem suggests that love straddles a border between safety and danger. Instead of bringing passivity and peace, it requires activity and boldness and deep passion. Everything—twigs, leaves, branches, scruples—is carried along by the powerful currents of love and the creek, and the poem replicates the repeated action of the lovers as if to power along observant readers, too, just as the lovers are powered along by what they see. Love here is no quiet or simple matter even if the expression of it in poems can be direct and can stem from a simple observation of experience. The "love poem" itself—linked as it is with the headlong currents of the creek from which the lovers are protecting themselves even as they step close—seems to represent that which is beyond love and that which, therefore, both threatens love and at the same time is love's source. The poem thus affirms the power of poetry, but it also suggests that the subject of poetry—love and life—is what matters most.

Of course, love does not always go smoothly, and poems are not always about emotional fulfillment. Many poems are about disappointment, suggesting the contradictions and uncertainties in relationships. The following poem is a kind of **monologue**, recording the complex longings of a married woman whose attitudes toward marriage are quite different from those of Barrett Browning or Ramsay. How are they different? What emotions are expressed in the poem? How might this poem challenge your assumptions about what married love might feel like?

LIZ ROSENBERG

Married Love

The trees are uncurling their first
green messages: Spring, and some man
lets his arm brush my arm in a darkened
theatre. Faint-headed, I fight the throb.
5 Later I dream
the gas attendant puts a cool hand
on my breast, asking a question.
Slowly I rise through the surface of the dream,
brushing his hand and my own heat away.

10 Young, I burned to marry. Married,
the smolder goes on underground;
clutching at weeds, writhing everywhere.
I'm trying to talk to a friend on burning
issues, flaming from the feet up,
15 drinking in his breath, touching his wrist.
I want to grab the pretty woman
on the street, seize the falcon
by its neck, beat my way into whistling steam.

I turn to you in the dark, oh husband,
20 watching your lit breath circle the pillow.
Then you turn to me, throwing first one limb
and then another over me, in the easy brotherly
lust of marriage. I cling to you
as if I were a burning ship and you
25 could save me, as if I won't go sliding down
beneath you soon; as if our lives are made of rise
and fall, and we could ride this out forever,
with longing's thunder rolling heavy in our arms.

1986

The initial expectations of springtime and newness here quickly turn into signs, both conscious and unconscious, of desire ("throb") for anonymous sex ("some man"). Reality and fantasy are nearly one here, as the woman tries to repress arousal she does not wish to feel. The poem is full of fire and burning, in fact, which the speaker cannot ignore, subdue, or quench; there is hurt here and bewilderment and fear, and the easy habitual comforts of married love are not exactly reassuring ("brotherly lust"), nor do they seem to satisfy desire. The woman feels herself to be a burning (and sinking) ship, and her marital clinging seems an act of desperation; she hopes for salvation (or at least a "rid[ing] out"), but "longing's thunder" remains far more powerful than any sense of satisfaction or solution.

RESPONDING TO POETRY

Various readers will respond differently to the same poem; some will prefer one poem and some another. Personal preference does not mean that objective standards for poetry cannot be found—some poems *are* better than others, and in later chapters we will look in detail at features that help us evaluate and interpret poems—but there are no unquestionable standards as to what poetry must be or how it must work. Some good poems are quite abstract, others quite specific. Some deal with familiar, comfortable feelings, others with more difficult ones. Any poem that helps us articulate and clarify human feelings and ideas has a legitimate claim on us as readers. Watching how poems discover a language for feeling can help us discover a language for our own feelings, but the process is also reciprocal: Being conscious of feelings we already have can lead us into poems more surely and with more satisfaction. Readers with a strong romantic bent—and with strong yearnings or positive memories of desire—will be likely to find a poem like "The Tally Stick" easy to respond to and admire, while those more skeptical of human institutions and male behavior may find the wifely despair of "Married Love" more compelling.

You may also come across poems about events or feelings you have never experienced—or even ones you can hardly imagine. But sharing unfamiliar experiences through language often enables us to uncover feelings—of love or anger, fear or confidence—we did not know we had, or could have, thus increasing what some people call our *emotional literacy*. We don't have to be a person who has been married for years or a parent who has lost a child to respond emotionally to a poem that describes such an experience: Our own experiences give us some idea of what such a love or loss would feel like. And the words and strategies of the poem may arouse expectations created by our previous experiences.

Indeed, poets often write about experiences and feelings that they have not themselves had. Like a dramatist or writer of fiction, the poet may simply *imagine* an event in order to analyze and articulate how it might feel. A work of literature can be *true* without being *actual*.

RESPONDING TO POEMS: TWO EXAMPLES

In the following poems, a father and a husband struggle to deal with the death of a loved one, though each poem handles the subject quite differently.

BEN JONSON

On My First Son

Farewell, thou child of my right hand,[1] and joy;
My sin was too much hope of thee, loved boy:
Seven years thou wert lent to me, and I thee pay,
Exacted by thy fate, on the just[2] day.
5 O could I lose all father now! for why
Will man lament the state he should envý,
To have so soon 'scaped world's and flesh's rage,
And, if no other misery, yet age?
Rest in soft peace, and asked, say, "Here doth lie
10 Ben Jonson his[3] best piece of poetry."
For whose sake henceforth all his vows be such
As what he loves may never like too much.

                                                                1616

HOWARD NEMEROV

The Vacuum

The house is so quiet now
The vacuum cleaner sulks in the corner closet,
Its bag limp as a stopped lung, its mouth
Grinning into the floor, maybe at my
5 Slovenly life, my dog-dead youth.

I've lived this way long enough,
But when my old woman died her soul

1. A literal translation of the son's name, Benjamin.
2. Exact; the son died on his seventh birthday, in 1603.
3. That is, Ben Jonson's (this was a common Renaissance form of the possessive).

Went into that vacuum cleaner, and I can't bear
To see the bag swell like a belly, eating the dust
10 And the woolen mice, and begin to howl

Because there is old filth everywhere
She used to crawl, in the corner and under the stair.
I know now how life is cheap as dirt,
And still the hungry, angry heart
15 Hangs on and howls, biting at air.

1955

The first poem's attempts to rationalize the boy's death are quite conventional. Although the father tries to be comforted by pious thoughts, his feelings keep showing through. The poem's beginning—with its formal "farewell" and the rather distant-sounding address to his dead son ("child of my right hand")—cannot be sustained for long: Both of the first two lines end with bursts of emotion. It is as if the father is trying to explain the death to himself and to keep his emotions under control, but he cannot quite manage it. Even the punctuation suggests the way his feelings compete with conventional attempts to put the death into some sort of perspective that will soften the grief, and the comma near the end of each of the first two lines marks a pause that cannot quite hold back the overflowing emotion. But finally the only "idea" that the poem supports is that the father wishes he did not feel so intensely; in the fifth line he fairly blurts that he wishes he could lose his fatherly emotions, and in the final lines he resolves never again to "like" so much that he can be this deeply hurt. Philosophy and religion offer their useful counsels in this poem, but they prove far less powerful than feeling. Rather than drawing some kind of moral about what death means, the poem presents the actuality of feeling as inevitable and nearly all-consuming.

The husband in the second poem also tries to suppress the rawness of his feelings, but this survivor is haunted by memories of his loved one when he sees a physical object—a vacuum cleaner—that he associates with her. The poem's title refers most obviously to the vacuum cleaner that, like the tally stick in Ramsey's poem, seems to stand for many of the things that were once important in the life he had together with his wife. Yet the poem is ultimately more about the vacuum in the husband's life created by his wife's death. The machine is a reminder of the dead wife ("my old woman," line 7) because of her devotion to cleanliness. But to the surviving husband buried in the filth of his life it seems as if the machine has become almost human, a kind of ghost of her: it "sulks" (line 2), it has lungs and a mouth (line 3), and it seems to grin, making fun of what has become of him. He "can't bear" (line 8) to see it in action because it then seems too much alive, too much a reminder of her life.

The poem records his paralysis, his inability to do more than discover that life is "cheap as dirt" without her ordering and cleansing presence for him. At the end it is *his* angry heart that acts like the haunting machine, howling and biting at air as if he has merged with her spirit and the physical object that memorializes her. This poem puts a strong emphasis on the stillness of death and the way it makes things seem to stop; it captures in words the hurt, the anger, the inability to understand, the vacuum that remains when a loved one dies and leaves a vacant space. But here we do not see the body or hear a direct good-bye to the dead person; rather we encounter the feeling that lingers and won't go away, recalled through memory by an especially significant object, a mere thing but one that has been personalized to the point of becoming nearly human itself. (The event described here is, by the way, fictional; the poet's wife did not actually die.)

Responding to Poems: An Exercise

Though you may never have been in love or lost a loved one, you were once a child, and adult memories of childhood are the subject of the following poems. In the first, written as if the person speaking the poem were in the fifth grade, a child's sense of death is portrayed through the speaker's exploration of a photograph that makes her grandfather's presence vivid to her memory—a memory that lingers primarily through smell and touch. In the second poem, another childhood memory—this time of overshoes—takes an adult almost physically back into childhood. In the third poem, a man remembers an even more traumatic event—the aftermath of his brother's death. As you read the three poems, jot down your responses. How much are your responses shaped by your past experiences? In what specific places did these experiences occur? What family photographs do you remember most vividly? What feelings do they evoke that make them so memorable? Which feelings expressed in each poem are similar to your own? Where do your feelings differ most strongly? How would you articulate your responses to such memories differently? In what ways does an awareness of your similar—and different—experiences and feelings make you a better reader?

RITA DOVE

Fifth Grade Autobiography

I was four in this photograph fishing
with my grandparents at a lake in Michigan.

(Continued on next page)

(Continued)

My brother squats in poison ivy.
His Davy Crockett cap
5 sits squared on his head so the raccoon tail
flounces down the back of his sailor suit.

My grandfather sits to the far right
in a folding chair,
and I know his left hand is on
10 the tobacco in his pants pocket
because I used to wrap it for him
every Christmas. Grandmother's hips
bulge from the brush, she's leaning
into the ice chest, sun through the trees
15 printing her dress with soft
luminous paws.

I am staring jealously at my brother;
the day before he rode his first horse, alone.
I was strapped in a basket
20 behind my grandfather.
He smelled of lemons. He's died—

but I remember his hands.

1989

ANNE SEXTON

The Fury of Overshoes

They sit in a row
outside the kindergarten,
black, red, brown, all
with those brass buckles.
5 Remember when you couldn't
buckle your own
overshoe
or tie your own
shoe
10 or cut your own meat

(Continued on next page)

(Continued)

and the tears
running down like mud
because you fell off your
tricycle?
15 Remember, big fish,
when you couldn't swim
and simply slipped under
like a stone frog?
The world wasn't
20 yours.
It belonged to
the big people.
Under your bed
sat the wolf
25 and he made a shadow
when cars passed by
at night.
They made you give up
your nightlight
30 and your teddy
and your thumb.
Oh overshoes,
don't you
remember me,
35 pushing you up and down
in the winter snow?
Oh thumb,
I want a drink,
it is dark,
40 where are the big people,
when will I get there,
taking giant steps
all day,
each day
45 and thinking
nothing of it?

1974

(Continued on next page)

(Continued)

SEAMUS HEANEY

Mid-Term Break

I sat all morning in the college sick bay
Counting bells knelling classes to a close.
At two o'clock our neighbors drove me home.

In the porch I met my father crying—
5 He had always taken funerals in his stride—
And Big Jim Evans saying it was a hard blow.

The baby cooed and laughed and rocked the pram
When I came in, and I was embarrassed
By old men standing up to shake my hand

10 And tell me they were "sorry for my trouble,"
Whispers informed strangers I was the eldest,
Away at school, as my mother held my hand

In hers and coughed out angry tearless sighs.
At ten o'clock the ambulance arrived
15 With the corpse, stanched and bandaged by the nurses.

Next morning I went up into the room. Snowdrops
And candles soothed the bedside; I saw him
For the first time in six weeks. Paler now,

Wearing a poppy bruise on his left temple,
20 He lay in the four foot box as in his cot.
No gaudy scars, the bumper knocked him clear.

A four foot box, a foot for every year.

1966

Not all poems are as accessible as those in this chapter, and even the accessible ones yield themselves to us more readily and more fully if we approach them systematically by developing specific reading habits and skills—just as someone learning to play tennis or to make pottery systematically learns the rules, the techniques, the things to watch out for that are distinctive to that activity. It helps if you develop a sense of what to expect, and the chapters that follow will show you the things that poets can do—and thus what you can do with poetry.

But knowing what to expect isn't everything. As a reader of poetry, you should always be open—to new experiences, new feelings, new ideas. Every poem is a potential new experience, and no matter how sophisticated you become, you can still be surprised (and delighted) by new poems—and by re-reading old ones. Good poems bear many re-readings, and you may often discover something new with every reading: There is no such thing as "mastering" a poem. Let poems surprise you when you come to them, let them come on their own terms, let them be themselves. If you are open to poetry, you are also open to much more that the world can offer you.

Reading and Responding: Three General Tips

1. *Take a poem on its own terms.* Adjust to the poem; don't make the poem adjust to you. Be prepared to hear things you do not want to hear. Not all poems are about your ideas, nor will they always present emotions you want to feel. But be tolerant and listen to the poem's ideas first; later you can explore the ways you do or don't agree with the poem.
2. *Assume there is a reason for everything.* Poets do make mistakes, but when a poem shows some degree of verbal control it is usually safest to assume that the poet chose each word carefully; if the choice seems peculiar, you may be missing something. Try to account for everything in a poem, see what kind of sense you can make of it, and figure out a coherent pattern that explains the text as it stands.
3. *Remember that poems exist in time, and times change.* Not only the meanings of words, but whole ways of looking at the universe vary in different ages. Consciousness of time works two ways: Your knowledge of history provides a context for reading the poem, and the poem's use of a word or idea may modify your notion of a particular age.

RESPONDING TO POETRY: EIGHT CONCRETE STEPS AND AN EXAMPLE

No one can give you a method that will offer you total experience of all poems. But because individual poems often share characteristics with other poems, taking certain steps can prompt you to ask the right questions. If you are relatively new to poetry or are faced with a poem that seems especially difficult, you may need to tackle these steps one at a time, pausing to write even as you read and respond. With more accessible poems and with further experience, though, you will find that you can skip steps or run through them quickly and almost automatically.

The following list and description of the steps shows you how this process might work in practice. First, though, we need a poem to work on.

APHRA BEHN

On Her Loving Two Equally

I

How strongly does my passion flow,
Divided equally twixt[4] two?
Damon had ne'er subdued my heart
Had not Alexis took his part;
5 Nor could Alexis powerful prove,
Without my Damon's aid, to gain my love.

II

When my Alexis present is,
Then I for Damon sigh and mourn;
But when Alexis I do miss,
10 Damon gains nothing but my scorn.
But if it chance they both are by,
For both alike I languish, sigh, and die.

III

Cure then, thou mighty wingèd god,[5]
This restless fever in my blood;
15 One golden-pointed dart take back:
But which, O Cupid, wilt thou take?
If Damon's, all my hopes are crossed;
Or that of my Alexis, I am lost.

1684

Now that you've read Behn's poem, read through the steps below and see how one reader used them as a guide for responding. Later, you may want to return to these steps as you read and respond to other poems.

---

4. Between.
5. Cupid, who, according to myth, shot darts of lead and of gold at the hearts of lovers, corresponding to false love and true love, respectively.

1. **Articulate your expectations, starting with the title.** Poets often use false leads and try to surprise readers, but defining your expectations makes you more conscious of where you are when you begin. As you read the poem, pay attention to what you expect and where, when, and how the poem fulfills, or perhaps frustrates, your expectations.

> The title of Aphra Behn's "On Her Loving Two Equally" both creates certain expectations and defies other expectations about love, as well as love poems. Can someone really "love two equally"? Perhaps this will be the question the poem seeks to answer.

2. **Read the syntax literally.** What the sentences literally say is only a starting point, but it is vital. Not all poems use normal prose syntax, but most of them do, and you can save yourself from going astray by first "translating" the poem accurately and not simply free-associating from an isolated word or phrase. To do this, especially with poems written before the twentieth century, you may need to break this step down into the following smaller steps:

   a. *Identify sentences.* For now, ignore the line breaks and look for sentences or independent clauses (word groups that can function as complete sentences). These will typically be preceded and followed by a period (.), a semicolon (;), a colon (:), or a dash (—).

   > The 18 lines of Aphra Behn's "On Her Loving Two Equally" can be broken down into nine sentences.

   > 1. How strongly does my passion flow, Divided equally twixt two?
   > 2. Damon had ne'er subdued my heart Had not Alexis took his part;
   > 3. Nor could Alexis powerful prove, Without my Damon's aid, to gain my love.
   > 4. When my Alexis present is, Then I for Damon sigh and mourn;
   > 5. But when Alexis I do miss, Damon gains nothing but my scorn.
   > 6. But if it chance they both are by, For both alike I languish, sigh, and die.
   > 7. Cure then, thou mighty wingèd god, This restless fever in my blood;
   > 8. One golden-pointed dart take back: But which, O Cupid, wilt thou take?
   > 9. If Damon's, all my hopes are crossed; Or that of my Alexis, I am lost.

   b. *Reorder sentences.* Identify the main elements—subject(s), verb(s), object(s)—of each sentence or independent clause, and if necessary rearrange them in normative word order. (By "normative word order," we mean the normal way words are ordered. In English, that is usually *subject,* then *verb,* then *object,* with dependent clauses at the beginning or end of the main clause and next to whatever main element they modify.) Have you clarified which subjects and verbs belong together, what pronouns refer to what nouns, and so on?

In the following sentences, the reordered words appear in italics:

1. How strong does my passion flow, Divided equally twixt two?
2. Damon had ne'er subdued my heart Had not Alexis took his part;
3. Nor *Without my Damon's aid* could Alexis *prove* powerful *to gain my love.*
4. When my Alexis *is* present, Then I *sigh and mourn* for Damon;
5. But when *I do miss* Alexis, Damon gains nothing but my scorn.
6. But if it chance they both are by, *I languish, sigh, and die* For both alike.
7. *thou mighty wingèd god,* Cure then This restless fever in my blood;
8. *take back* One golden-pointed dart: But which wilt thou take, *O Cupid?*
9. If Damon's, all my hopes are crossed; Or that of my Alexis, I am lost.

c. *Translate sentences into modern prose, defining unfamiliar or ambiguous words.* Be sure to link the parts of the sentence logically and to link one sentence logically to the sentence that comes before it by adding any implied words necessary to make the connection. At this stage, don't move to outright paraphrase; instead, stick closely to the original.

Below, added words appear in brackets, definitions of words in parentheses:

1. How strongly does my passion flow [when it is] divided equally between two [people]?
2. Damon would never have (*conquered* or *tamed*) my heart if Alexis had not taken his [own] (portion) [of my heart].
3. Nor without my Damon's aid could Alexis have proven powerful [enough] to gain my love.
4. When my Alexis is present, then I sigh and mourn for Damon;
5. But when I miss Alexis, Damon doesn't gain anything (except) my scorn.
6. But if it (so happens) that [Damon and Alexis] are both (near) [me], I languish, sigh, and die for both [Damon and Alexis] alike.
7. [Cupid,] (you) mighty wingèd god, cure then this restless fever in my blood;
8. Take back one [of your two] darts [with] pointed gold [tips]: But which [of these arrows] will you take, O Cupid?
9. If [on the one hand, you take away] Damon's [arrow], all my hopes are (*opposed, invalidated, spoiled*); Or [if, on the other hand, you take away] Alexis's arrow, I am lost.

d. *Note any ambiguities in the original language that might be ignored in your translation.* Look for modifiers that might modify more than one thing, verbs that might have multiple subjects and objects, words that have multiple, relevant meanings:

The translation of lines 3 and 4—"Damon would never have (*conquered* or *tamed*) my heart if Alexis had not taken his [own] (portion) [of my heart]"— ignores the ambiguity of the phrase "Alexis took his part." *His* could refer to

Alexis or Damon because both are mentioned in the first part of the sentence, so this phrase could be translated as "Alexis took Damon's part" or "Alexis took his own part." But what about the word *part?* At least three different meanings of this word make equal sense in this context:

- "one of the . . . subdivisions into which something is . . . divided," the most obvious "something" here being the "heart" mentioned in the last line and in exactly the same place in the line that *part* comes in this line.
- "the role of a character in a play" or "one's . . . allotted task (as in an action)."
- "one of the opposing sides in a conflict or dispute," which in this case could be the "conflict" over the speaker's love.

On the one hand, then, this phrase could mean something like "Alexis took his own portion of my heart"; "Alexis played his own role in my life or in this three-way courtship drama"; "Alexis defended his own side in the battle for my love." On the other hand, it could mean "Alexis took *Damon's* part of my heart"; "Alexis played *Damon's* role"; or even "Alexis defended *Damon's* side in the battle for my love."

3. **Use your dictionary, other reference books, and reliable Web sites.** Look up anything that you either don't understand or that you suspect might be ambiguous: an unfamiliar word, a word used in an unfamiliar way, a word that seems to have multiple meanings, a place, a person, a myth, an idea—anything the poem uses. When you can't find what you need or don't know where to look, ask the reference librarian to help.

This step has been addressed above to get at the precise meanings of *part* and other words, but you could also consult a source to find out more about Cupid, for example.

4. **Figure out who, where, when, and what happens.** Once you have gotten a sense of the literal meaning of each sentence, ask the following very general factual questions about the whole poem. Remember that not all of the questions will suit every poem. At this point, stick to the facts. What do you know for sure?

Who?
- Who is, or who are, the poem's **speaker(s)**?
- Who is the **auditor**? That is, whom does the speaker address in the poem?
- Which other **characters**, if any, appear within the poem?

The title "On *Her* Loving Two Equally" suggests that the speaker is a woman who equally loves two people. In the body of the poem, she identifies these as two men—Damon and Alexis. At the beginning of the poem, the woman doesn't seem to be addressing anyone in particular (certainly not the two men she talks *about*). But in the third stanza, she addresses Cupid—first through the epithet "mighty wingèd god" (line 13) and then by name (line 16). (Because Cupid isn't present, this is an apostrophe.)

Where? When?

Where is the speaker and when are the events he or she describes? That is, what is the poem's temporal and physical **setting**?

No place or time is specified in Behn's poem. The antiquated diction ("twixt," line 2; "wilt," line 16) implies that the poem wasn't written recently, and the publication date is 1684. But there is nothing in the poem to limit the situation or feelings it describes to any specific time or place.

What?

- What is the **situation** described in the poem?
- What, if anything, literally happens over the course of it, or what **action**, if any, does it describe?
- Or, if the poem doesn't tell a story, then how is it structured internally? Does the speaker's subject or focus shift over the course of the poem? When and how?

The basic situation is that the speaker loves two men equally. Beyond that, the poem doesn't say much about what has happened. Instead, the speaker alludes in the second stanza to general situations—when she is with one of the men and not the other or when she is with both of them at once—and the feelings that result. Then, in the third stanza, she imagines what would happen if she stopped loving one of them. The topic or subject essentially remains the same throughout, though there are two subtle shifts. First is the shift from addressing anyone in stanzas one and two to addressing Cupid in stanza three. Second, there are shifts in verb tense and time: The first stanza floats among various tenses ("does," line 1; "took," line 4), the second sticks to the present tense ("is," "sigh," "mourn," etc.), and the third shifts to future ("wilt," line 16).

5. **Formulate tentative answers to the questions, Why does it matter? What does it all mean?**

- Why should the poem matter to anyone other than the poet, or what might the poem show and say to readers?
- What problems, issues, questions, or conflicts does the poem explore that might be relevant to people other than the speaker(s) or the poet—to humanity in general, to the poet's contemporaries, to people of a certain type or in a certain situation, and so forth?
- How is each problem or conflict developed and resolved over the course of the poem, or how is each question answered? What con-

clusions does the poem seem to reach about these, or what are its
themes?

The title and first two lines pose a question: How strong is our love if we love
two people instead of one? We tend to assume that anything that is "divided" is
less strong than something that unified. The use of the word *flow* in the first line reinforces that assumption because it implicitly compares love to something that
flows: A river, for example, "flows," and when a river divides into two streams,
each is smaller and its flow less strong than the river's. So the way the speaker
articulates the question implies an answer: Love, like a river, isn't strong and
sure when divided.

But the rest of the poem undermines that answer. In the first stanza, the
speaker points out that each lover and his love has "aided" and added to the
"power" of the other: Neither man would have "gain[ed her] love" if the other
hadn't. The second stanza gives a more concrete sense of why this might happen: Since we tend to yearn for what we don't have at the moment, being with
one of these men makes her miss the other one. But if both men are present, she
feels the same about both and perhaps even feels *more* complete and satisfied.

As if realizing she can't solve the problem herself, she turns in the third
stanza to Cupid and asks him to solve it by taking away her love for either Damon
or Alexis. As soon as she asks for this, though, she indicates that the result
would be unhappiness. In the end, the poem seems to say (or its theme is) that
love *doesn't* flow or work like a river because love can actually be stronger when
we love more than one person, as if it's multiplied instead of lessened by division.

6. **Consider how the poem's form contributes to its effect and
meaning.**

   • **How is the poem put together? What are its formal features?**
   • **How do the poem's overall form and its various specific formal
   features contribute to its meaning?**
   • **In other words, what gets lost when you translate the poem into
   modern prose?**

Formal features to consider include **diction** (or word choice) and
syntax (or word order), **figures of speech** (**metaphor, simile**, etc.),
symbolism, sound patterns (**rhyme, alliteration, assonance,
meter**), and the organization of lines and stanzas—the length,
shape, and arrangement of lines (as opposed to sentences). Here,
you might note where you see a **caesura, end-stopped lines,
enjambment**, and so on.

The stanza organization underscores shifts in the speaker's approach to her situation. But organization reinforces meaning in other ways as well. On the one
hand, the division into three stanzas and the choice to number them, plus the
fact that each stanza has three sentences, mirror the three-way struggle or "love
triangle" described in the poem. On the other hand—as the fact that the poem

has 18 *lines* and 9 *sentences* suggests—every sentence is "divided equally twixt two" *lines*. Sound and especially rhyme reinforce this pattern since the two lines that make up one sentence usually rhyme with each other (to form a couplet). The only lines that aren't couplets are those that begin the second stanza, where we instead have alternating rhyme—*is* (line 7) rhymes with *miss* (line 9), *mourn* (line 8) rhymes with *scorn* (line 10). Notice, though, the content of these lines: They describe how the speaker "miss[es]" one man when the other is "by," a sensation she arguably reproduces in readers by ensuring that they twice "miss" the rhyme that the rest of the poem leads us to expect.

7. **Investigate and consider the ways the poem draws on and departs from poetic tradition, especially (but not exclusively) in terms of its formal features.** Find out whether the poem conforms to any traditional poetic formal patterns or what particular subgenre or kind of poem it might be—a **sonnet**, an **ode**, a **ballad**, and so forth—and ask why and how that affects the meaning of the poem. Certain patterns of rhythm and rhyme, particular verse forms, and poetic genres and kinds have traditionally been used in certain ways and to certain ends. As a result, they generate particular expectations for readers familiar with such traditions, and poems gain additional meaning by both fulfilling and defying those expectations, following and departing from tradition. For example, **anapestic** meter (two unstressed syllables followed by a stressed one, as in *Tennessee*) is usually used for comic poems, so when poets use it in a serious poem they are probably making a point.

8. **Argue.** Discussion with others—both out loud and in writing—usually results in clarification and keeps you from being too dependent on personal biases and preoccupations that sometimes mislead even the best readers. Discussing a poem with someone else (especially someone who thinks very differently) or sharing what you've written about the poem can expand your perspective and enrich your experience.

WRITING ABOUT POETRY

If you have followed the steps outlined above and kept notes on your personal responses to the poems you've read, you have already taken an important step toward more formal writing about them. Two examples of such writing appear in this chapter: an informal student response paper on W. H. Auden's "[Stop all the clocks]," a poem included in "Romantic Love: An Album," and a more formal essay on Aphra Behn's "On Her Loving Two Equally," based on the notes on the poem presented in the previous section.

There are many different ways to write about poems, just as there are many different things to say. (The section of the anthology called "Writing about Literature" suggests some ways to come up with and develop a good topic.) But all writing begins with a clear sense of the poem itself and your responses to it, so the first steps (long before formally sitting down to write) are to read the poem several times and take notes on the things that strike you and the questions that remain.

* * *

What *is* poetry? Let your definition be cumulative as you read more and more poems. No dictionary definition will cover all that you find, and it is better to discover for yourself poetry's many ingredients, its many effects, its many ways of acting. What can it do for you? Wait and see. Add up its effects after you have read carefully—after you have re-read and studied—a hundred or so poems; then continue to read new poems or re-read old ones.

SAMPLE WRITING

In the response paper that follows, Stephen Bordland works through Auden's poem "[Stop all the clocks, cut off the telephone]" more or less line-by-line, writing down whatever ideas come to him. The form of this paper is less important than the process of thinking carefully about the poem's music, emotions, and meanings. As you can see, by the time Stephen reaches the end of his response, he has decided on a topic for the more formal paper that he will write later.

Stephen Bordland
Professor O'Connor
English 157
2 February 2005

Response Paper on
W. H. Auden's "[Stop all the clocks, cut off the telephone]"

I first heard this poem read aloud when I saw the movie *Four Weddings and a Funeral* on cable. The character who read the poem was reading it at the funeral of his lover. It was perfectly suited to the story and was very moving. I was struck by the actor's reading because the poem seemed to have a steady rhythm for several lines and then suddenly hit what sounded like a dead end—"I thought that love would last forever: I was wrong." Hearing the actor's reading of this poem made me want to read it myself, to see if the poem would still affect me if I read/heard it outside of the context of an emotional scene in a movie. It did, and I think that the "I was wrong" line is the key—a turning point, I guess.

In the anthology, the poem seems to have no actual title (at least that's how I interpret the fact that the first line is in brackets where the title usually goes), but I did some searching on the Internet and found that this poem was once called "Funeral Blues." If I were reading the poem for the first time under that title, I would at least know that the poem has something to do with death right from the start. But this title makes the poem sound

Bordland 2

irreverent rather than sincerely painful. I wonder if that would have been true in the 1930s, when Auden wrote the poem. There were lots of blues and jazz songs of that era whose titles ended in "Blues" (like Robert Johnson's "Kindhearted Woman Blues"), so maybe the title wasn't meant to be read the way that I'm reading it. Anyway, I don't know if Auden himself changed the title, or if there's another story there, but I think it's a better poem without the title.

The poem starts with a request to an unknown person (everyone?) to make some common aspects of daily life go away: "Stop all the clocks," presumably because time seems to be standing still; "cut off the telephone," presumably because the speaker wants to be alone and undisturbed, cut off from human contact. I'm not sure what's implied by "Prevent the dog from barking with a juicy bone," mainly because I'm confused about the literal meaning: Are we supposed to prevent the dog from barking by giving him a juicy bone (one way to interpret "with a juicy bone"), or are we supposed to prevent the dog with a juicy bone in his mouth (another way of interpreting "with a juicy bone") from barking at all? I don't think I really have a handle on what this line means in relation to the other ones, but I'll leave it for now. In the next line, "Silence the pianos" clearly means that the speaker wants no music now that his lover is dead, except for the "muffled drum" that will accompany the coffin and mourners in the fourth line. It's interesting that all of these things so far are sounds—the tick-tock of the clock, the ring of the telephone, a barking dog, music. They all seem to stand in for something, too—for the passing of time, contact with other people (and with pets?), joy as expressed by music.

The image of "aeroplanes" circling overhead (and "moaning"—that's a really good choice of words) writing "He is Dead" is very strong and would have been a very modern reference at the time of this poem (1936). A *Christian Science Monitor* article about a "skywriting" pilot says that "Skywriting's heyday was from the 1930s to the early 1950s when Pepsi Cola used skywriting as its main way of advertising," so the reference here is to a commercial medium being used to make as many people as possible aware of the speaker's loss. If a poet tried to make a reference to something equivalent today, it would have to be a television advertisement or a blog, maybe. I wonder if a modern poet could really pull off a reference to a TV ad and still make it sound sincerely sad.

I'm not sure what the "crepe bows round the white necks of the public doves" means. Would the bows even be visible? Does "crepe" imply a color, or is it just a type of fabric? And what is a public dove? I'm not sure I like the repetition in this line of three adjective/noun pairs: "crepe bows," "white necks," "public doves." It seems too precious or "poetic." The "traffic policemen" that I've seen all wear white gloves so that their hand movements can be seen clearly. The speaker wants them all to wear "black cotton gloves," the appropriate color for mourning, but that would probably create real problems for the drivers trying to see what the policemen are directing them to do. So, I wonder if the bows on doves and black gloves on cops are both there to show us that the speaker is feeling not just the sort of grief that moves him to write poetry, but also the sort of intense pain that makes him want to throw the rest of the world into the same confusion and chaos he's experiencing. Or at least, he's not only asking to be alone, but also wanting the rest of the world to share his grief.

In the next four lines, the speaker turns to himself and his lover: "He was my North, my South, my East and West / My working week and my Sunday rest." These lines flow so smoothly, with a soothing, regular rhythm; they're almost sing-songy. But they don't seem sappy or wrong in this poem; they seem painfully sincere. The author uses place (as described by the compass) and time (the whole week, the reference to noon and midnight) to make very clear, in case we hadn't figured it out from the preceding lines, that his lover was everything to him. In the fourth line of this section, this regular rhythm is interrupted, or even stopped dead: "I thought that love would last for ever: I was wrong." This is a very true and moving conclusion to reach, but it also seems ironic, once we read to the end of the poem. If the speaker was wrong to believe (before the death of his lover) that love would last forever, isn't it possible that he's wrong about the conclusion "nothing now can ever come to any good"—that grief will last forever.

I think that Auden probably intended us to be aware of this irony. It seems to me that the poem is broken into three major parts. First, we sympathize with the speaker's grief and sense of loss. Then we're supposed to stop at the point where the speaker makes a judgment about his understanding of the world prior to that loss ("I thought that love would last for ever: I was wrong") and to spend a moment absorbing the meaning of that judgment. Finally, as we read the most extreme expression of the speaker's loss ("Pack up the moon and dismantle the sun"), we can see that although we sympathize and understand, we also know something that the speaker doesn't know at the moment. Just as his love apparently blinded the speaker to love's inevitable end, his profound grief is probably blinding him to grief's inevitable end.

Bordland 4

Also, it may just be me, but it seems that this last part is almost too dramatic or theatrical, as if maybe the speaker has made some sort of transition from being unself-consciously mournful to being self-consciously aware that the way he's expressing himself is poetic.

Back to the idea about the irony: The poem itself seems to be arguing against the notion that love cannot last forever (or, okay, a very long time). After all, people are still reading this poem, and I bet people will continue to read it for as long as people read poetry. That's about as close to forever as we get on this earth, so even though the lovers of this poem are long dead, their love lives on, in a way. Auden must have been aware of this when he was writing the poem. I wonder if he ever said anything in letters, essays, or speeches about art and immortality? If so, I think I'll write a paper on that topic as addressed in this poem.

SAMPLE WRITING

The following sample essay develops the observations about Aphra Behn's "On Her Loving Two Equally" in this chapter, demonstrating how you can turn notes about a poem into a coherent, well-structured essay. As this essay also shows, however, you will often discover new ways of looking at a poem (or any literary text) in the very process of writing about it. (For guidelines on correctly quoting and citing poetry, see "Writing about Literature.")

The writer begins by considering why she is drawn to the poem, even though it does not express her ideal of love. She then uses her personal response to the poem as a starting point for analyzing it in greater depth.

Multiplying by Dividing in Aphra Behn's "On Her Loving Two Equally"

My favorite poem in "Reading, Responding, Writing" is Aphra Behn's "On Her Loving Two Equally"—not because it expresses my ideal of love, but because it challenges conventional ideals. The main ideal or assumption explored in the poem is that true love is exclusive and monogamous, as the very titles of two other poems in the chapter and the "Romantic Love" album insist: "How Do *I* [singular] Love *Thee* [singular]?" or "To *My* Dear and Loving [and One and Only] Husband." The mere title of Behn's poem upsets that idea by insisting that at least one woman is capable of "Loving Two Equally." In fact, one thing that is immediately interesting about Behn's poem is that, though it poses and explores a question, its question is not "Can a woman love two equally?" The title and the poem take it for granted that she can. Instead, the poem asks whether equally loving two people lessens the power or quality of love—or, as the speaker puts it in the first two lines, "How strongly does my passion flow, / Divided equally twixt two?" Every aspect of this poem suggests that when it comes to love, as opposed to math, "division" leads to multiplication.

This answer grabs attention because it is so counterintuitive and unconventional. Forget love for just a minute: It's common sense that

---

anything that is "divided" is smaller and weaker than something unified. In math, for example, division is the opposite of multiplication; if we divide one number by another, we get a number smaller than the first number, if not the second. Although Behn's use of the word *flow* to frame her question compares love to a river instead of a number, the implication is the same: When a river divides into two streams, each of them is smaller than the river, and its flow less strong; as a result, each stream is more easily dammed up or diverted than the undivided river. So the way the speaker initially poses her question seems to support the conventional view: Love is stronger when it "flows" toward one person, weaker when divided between two.

However conventional and comforting that implied answer, however, it's one the poem immediately rejects. In the remaining lines of the first stanza, the speaker insists that each of her two lovers and the love she feels for him has *not* lessened the strength of her feelings for the other, but the reverse. Each lover and each love has "aid[ed]" (line 6) the other, making him and it more "powerful" (line 5). Indeed, she says, neither man would have "subdued [her] heart" (line 3) or "gain[ed her] love" (line 6) at all if the other hadn't done so as well.

In the second stanza, the speaker gives us a somewhat more concrete sense of why and how this might be the case. On the one hand, being with either one of these men ("When Alexis present is," line 7) actually makes her both "scorn" him (line 10) and "miss" (line 9) the man who's not there ("I for Damon sigh and mourn," line 8). This isn't really a paradox; we often yearn more for the person or thing we don't have (the grass is always greener on the *other* side of the fence), and we often lose our appreciation for nearby, familiar things and people. What is far away and inaccessible is often dearer to us because its absence either makes us aware of what it means to us or allows us to forget its flaws and idealize it.

Perhaps because all of this makes the speaker feel that she can't possibly solve the problem by herself, the speaker turns in the third stanza to Cupid—the deity who is supposed to control these things by shooting a "golden-pointed dart" (line 15) into the heart of each lover. She asks him to solve her dilemma for her by "tak[ing] back" her love for either Damon or Alexis (line 15). As with her question in the first stanza, however, this plea is taken back as soon as it's formulated, for if she loses Damon, "all [her] hopes are crossed"; if she loses Alexis, she is "lost" (lines 17–18).

Here and throughout the poem, the speaker's main preoccupation seems to be what *she* feels and what this situation is like for *her*—"*my* passion" (line 1), "*my* heart" (line 3), "*my* Damon's aid, . . . *my* love" (line 6), "*my* Alexis" (line 7), "*I* . . . sigh and mourn" (line 8), "*I* do miss" (line 9), "*my* scorn" (line 10), "*I* languish, sigh, and die" (line 12), "This restless fever in *my* blood" (line 14), "*my* hopes" (line 17), "*my* Alexis" and "*I* am lost" (line 18). Yet the poem implies that the payoff here is not hers alone and that her feelings are not purely selfish. Both times the word *gain* appears in the poem, for example, her lovers' gains and feelings are the focus—the fact that Alexis is able "to gain [her] love" thanks to "Damon's aid" (line 6) and that "Damon gains nothing but my scorn" when she is missing Alexis (line 10). Moreover, ambiguous wording in the first stanza suggests that the men here may be actively, intentionally helping to create this situation and even themselves acting in contradictory, selfish and unselfish, ways. For when the speaker says that "Damon had ne'er subdued my heart / Had not Alexis took his part" (lines 3–4), *his* could refer to Alexis or Damon and *part* could mean "a portion" (of her "heart," presumably), "a role" (in her life or in this courtship drama), or a "side in a dispute or conflict" (over and for her love). Thus, she could be saying that Alexis (unselfishly) defended Damon's suit; (selfishly) fought against Damon or took a share or role that properly belonged to Damon; and/or (neutrally) took his (Alexis's) own share or role or defended his (Alexis's) own cause. Perhaps all of this *has* been the case at various times; people do behave in contradictory ways when they are in love, especially when they perceive that they have a rival. It's also true that men and women alike often more highly prize something or someone that someone else prizes, too. So perhaps each lover's "passion" for her also "flow[s]" more strongly than it would otherwise precisely because he has a rival.

In the end, the poem thus seems to say that love *doesn't* flow or work like a river because love isn't a tangible or quantifiable thing. As a result, love is also different from the sort of battle conjured up by the martial language of the first stanza in which someone wins only if someone else loses. The poem attributes this to the perversity of the human heart—especially our tendency to yearn for what we can't have and what we think other people want, too.

Through its form, the poem demonstrates that division can increase instead of lessen meaning, as well as love. On the one hand, just as the poem's content stresses the power of the love among *three people,* so the poem's form also stresses "threeness" as well as "twoness." It is after all divided into *three* distinctly numbered stanzas, and each stanza consists of *three* sentences. On the other hand, every *sentence* is "divided equally twixt two" *lines,* just as the speaker's "passion" is divided equally between two men. Formally, then, the poem mirrors the kinds of division it describes. Sound and especially rhyme reinforce this pattern since the two lines that make up one sentence usually rhyme with each other to form a couplet. The only lines that don't conform to this pattern come at the beginning of the second stanza where we instead have alternating rhyme—*is* (line 7) rhymes with *miss* (line 9), *mourn* (line 8) rhymes with *scorn* (line 10). But here, again, form reinforces content. For these lines describe how the speaker "miss[es]" one man when the other is "by," a sensation that she arguably reproduces in us as we read by ensuring we twice "miss" the rhyme that the rest of the poem leads us to expect.

Because of the way it challenges our expectations and our conventional ideas about romantic love, the poem might well make us uncomfortable, perhaps all the more so because the speaker and poet here are female. For though we tend to think all true lovers should be loyal and monogamous, this has been expected even more of women than of men. What the poem says about love might make more sense and seem less strange and even objectionable, however, if we think of other, nonromantic kinds of love: After all, do we really think that our mother and father love us less if their love is "divided equally twixt" ourselves and our siblings, or do we love each of our parents less because there are two of *them*? If we think of these familial kinds of love, it becomes much easier to accept Behn's suggestion that love multiplies when we spread it around.

WORK CITED

Behn, Aphra. "On Her Loving Two Equally." *The Norton Introduction to Literature*. Eds. Alison Booth and Kelly J. Mays. 10th ed. New York: Norton, 2010. Print.

Romantic Love: An Album

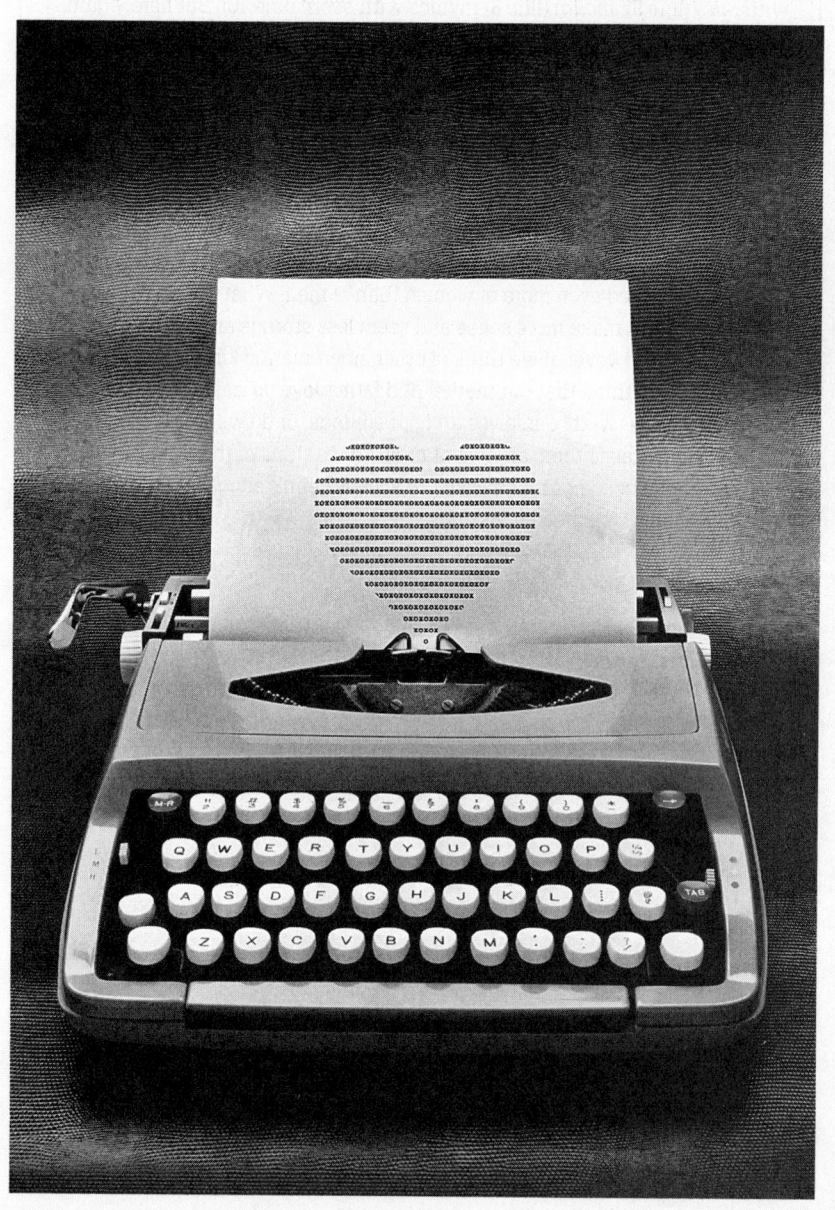

Said Elizabeth . . . , "I wonder who first discovered the efficacy of poetry in driving away love!"
"I have been used to consider poetry as the food of love," said Darcy.
"Of a fine, stout, healthy love it may. Everything nourishes what is strong already. But if it be only a slight, thin sort of inclination, I am convinced that one good sonnet will starve it entirely away."

–JANE AUSTEN, *Pride and Prejudice*

If poetry is a way to probe, understand, and express our emotions, then the emotion most readily associated with poetry is love. Whether or not you "consider poetry as the food of love" (as does Jane Austen's Mr. Darcy) or the quickest way to starve it right out of existence (as Austen's Elizabeth Bennet would have it), there is no doubt that poetry has, over the ages, fed, even feasted, on the feeling we call *love*. What some of the greatest poetry reminds us, however, is that romantic love is not one emotion but innumerable different, even contradictory ones—desire, lust, excitement, and affection; astonishment, admiration, desperation, and delight; jealousy, joy, anger, annoyance, and regret. The list goes on and on.

What is "true love"? What defines it? What destroys it? What on earth do we do when it is threatened or lost? The poems gathered in this album offer a range of answers to such questions, even as they raise a host of others. As you read them, look closely at the way love grows or dies, finds expression or fails to be shared. Which one or two poems best capture your own feelings and ideas about love? Which ones challenge your vision of love? Which describe feelings you have either felt or would like to feel about a lover, a partner, a spouse? Which reveal to you something utterly new about what love is and what it might be? Above all, how and why—after all these years and all these words—can a poem on this oldest, most traditional of all poetic subjects still manage to surprise?

EZRA POUND

The River-Merchant's Wife: A Letter

(after Rihaku)[1]

While my hair was still cut straight across my forehead
I played about the front gate, pulling flowers.
You came by on bamboo stilts, playing horse,

---

1. The Japanese name for Li Po, an eighth-century Chinese poet. Pound's poem is a loose paraphrase of one by Li Po.

You walked about my seat, playing with blue plums.
5 And we went on living in the village of Chokan:
Two small people, without dislike or suspicion.

At fourteen I married My Lord you.
I never laughed, being bashful.
Lowering my head, I looked at the wall.
10 Called to, a thousand times, I never looked back.

At fifteen I stopped scowling,
I desired my dust to be mingled with yours
For ever and for ever and for ever.
Why should I climb the look out?

15 At sixteen you departed,
You went into far Ku-to-yen, by the river of swirling eddies,
And you have been gone five months.
The monkeys make sorrowful noise overhead.

You dragged your feet when you went out.
20 By the gate now, the moss is grown, the different mosses,
Too deep to clear them away!

The leaves fall early this autumn, in wind.
The paired butterflies are already yellow with August
Over the grass in the West garden;
25 They hurt me. I grow older.
If you are coming down through the narrows of the river
    Kiang,
Please let me know beforehand,
And I will come out to meet you
    As far as Cho-fu-Sa.

                          1915

- How have the speaker's feelings about her husband changed
  over time? How do you know?

W. H. AUDEN

[Stop all the clocks, cut off the telephone]

Stop all the clocks, cut off the telephone,
Prevent the dog from barking with a juicy bone,
Silence the pianos and with muffled drum
Bring out the coffin, let the mourners come.

5 Let aeroplanes circle moaning overhead
   Scribbling on the sky the message He Is Dead,
   Put crêpe bows round the white necks of the public doves,
   Let the traffic policemen wear black cotton gloves.

   He was my North, my South, my East and West,
10 My working week and my Sunday rest,
   My noon, my midnight, my talk, my song;
   I thought that love would last for ever: I was wrong.

   The stars are not wanted now: put out every one;
   Pack up the moon and dismantle the sun;
15 Pour away the ocean and sweep up the wood;
   For nothing now can ever come to any good.

                                                   ca. 1936

• Whom does the speaker of this poem seem to be addressing?
  Why might the poet have proclaimed his grief with such a
  public declaration as this poem?

ANNE BRADSTREET

To My Dear and Loving Husband

   If ever two were one, then surely we.
   If ever man were loved by wife, then thee;
   If ever wife was happy in a man,
   Compare with me ye women if you can.
5 I prize thy love more than whole mines of gold,
   Or all the riches that the East doth hold.
   My love is such that rivers cannot quench,
   Nor aught but love from thee give recompense.
   Thy love is such I can no way repay;
10 The heavens reward thee manifold, I pray.
   Then while we live, in love let's so persever,
   That when we live no more we may live ever.
                                                   1678

• How does Bradstreet's strategy of characterizing her love
  through a series of comparisons compare with Barrett
  Browning's strategy in "How Do I Love Thee?"

WILLIAM SHAKESPEARE

[Let me not to the marriage of true minds]

Let me not to the marriage of true minds
Admit impediments.[2] Love is not love
Which alters when it alteration finds,
Or bends with the remover to remove:
5 Oh, no! it is an ever-fixèd mark,
That looks on tempests and is never shaken;
It is the star to every wandering bark,
Whose worth's unknown, although his height be taken.[3]
Love's not Time's fool, though rosy lips and cheeks
10 Within his bending sickle's compass come;
Love alters not with his brief hours and weeks,
But bears it out even to the edge of doom.
If this be error and upon me proved,
I never writ, nor no man ever loved.

1609

- What might the speaker mean when he says that love doesn't "ben[d] with the remover to remove" (line 4)? How might the rest of the poem explain and develop this statement?

JOHN DONNE

The Sun Rising

Busy old fool, unruly sun,
Why dost thou thus,
Through windows, and through curtains, call on us?
Must to thy motions lovers' seasons run?
5 Saucy pedantic wretch, go chide
Late schoolboys, and sour prentices,[4]
Go tell court-huntsmen that the king will ride,
Call country ants[5] to harvest offices;
Love, all alike, no season knows, nor clime,

---

2. The Church of England's Marriage Service contains this address to the witnesses: "If any of you know cause or just impediments why these persons should not be joined together. . . ."
3. That is, measuring the altitude of stars (for purposes of navigation) is not a way to measure value.
4. Apprentices.   5. Farmworkers.

10 Nor hours, days, months, which are the rags of time.
     Thy beams, so reverend and strong
     why shouldst thou think?
  I could eclipse and cloud them with a wink,
  But that I would not lose her sight so long:
15   If her eyes have not blinded thine,
     Look, and tomorrow late, tell me
     Whether both the Indias[6] of spice and mine
     Be where thou left'st them, or lie here with me.
  Ask for those kings whom thou saw'st yesterday,
20 And thou shalt hear, all here in one bed lay.

     She is all states, and all princes I,
     Nothing else is.
  Princes do but play us; compared to this,
  All honor's mimic,[7] all wealth alchemy.
25   Thou, sun, art half as happy as we,
     In that the world's contracted thus;
     Thine age asks[8] ease, and since thy duties be
     To warm the world, that's done in warming us.
  Shine here to us, and thou art every where;
30 This bed thy center[9] is, these walls thy sphere.

                           1633

- What does the poem as a whole suggest about how and why the world has "contracted" for the speaker (line 26)?

EDNA ST. VINCENT MILLAY

[*Women have loved before as I love now*]

Women have loved before as I love now;
At least, in lively chronicles of the past—
Of Irish waters by a Cornish prow
Or Trojan waters by a Spartan mast
5 Much to their cost invaded—here and there,
Hunting the amorous line, skimming the rest,
I find some woman bearing as I bear
Love like a burning city in the breast.
I think however that of all alive

6. The East and West Indies, commercial sources of spices and gold.   7. Hypocritical.
8. Requires.   9. Of orbit.

10   I only in such utter, ancient way
     Do suffer love; in me alone survive
     The unregenerate passions of a day
     When treacherous queens, with death upon the tread,
     Heedless and wilful, took their knights to bed.

                                                         1931

- What does this poem imply about the difference between ancient and modern ways of loving?

SUGGESTIONS FOR WRITING

1. Of all the love poems in this album, which one would you most like to have addressed to you? which least? Write an essay in which you answer the author of either poem you have chosen, explaining what seemed to you most (or least) complimentary in what the poem said about you.
2. Which of the poems in this album or in the preceding chapter ("Poetry: Reading, Responding, Writing") do you find most moving, and why? Write a short response paper or essay in which you explore your response and explain when, how, and why the poem evoked it. What about the situation, relationship, or feelings described in the poem do you find especially moving? What aspects of the poem itself do you find most moving, and why?
3. Consider your responses to all the poems in this album. Which one most accurately expresses your ideal of love? Why do you think so? What does your choice say about you? Write an essay in which you reflect on how these poems reinforce, refine, or perhaps challenge your views of love.

Understanding the Text

7 THEME AND TONE

Poetry is full of surprises. Poems express anger or outrage just as effectively as love or sadness, and good poems can be written about going to a rock concert or having lunch or mowing the lawn, as well as about making love or smelling flowers or listening to Beethoven. Even poems on "predictable" subjects can surprise us with unpredicted attitudes, unusual events, or sudden twists. Knowing that a poem is about some particular subject or topic—love, for example, or death—may give us a general idea of what to expect, but it never tells us altogether what we will find in a particular poem. Labeling a poem a "love poem" or a "death poem" is a convenient way to speak of its topic. But poems that may be loosely called "love poems" or "death poems" may have little else in common, may express utterly different attitudes or ideas, and may concentrate on very different aspects of the subject. Letting a poem speak to us means more than merely figuring out its topic; it means listening to *how* the poem says what it says. *What* a poem says involves its **theme**. *How* a poem makes that statement involves its **tone**—the poem's attitude or feelings toward the theme. No two poems on the same subject affect us in exactly the same way; their themes and tones vary, and even similar themes may be expressed in various ways, creating different tones and effects.

Tone, a term borrowed from acoustics and music, refers to the qualities of the language a speaker uses in social situations or in a poem, and it also refers to a speaker's intended effect. Tone is closely related to style and diction; it is an effect of the speaker's expressions, *as if* showing a real person's feelings, manner, and attitude or relationship to a listener and to the particular subject or situation. (Note that the speaker of a poem does not necessarily represent the voice of the author, as we discuss in chapter 8.) Thus, the speaker may use angry or mocking words, may address the listener intimately or distantly, may sincerely confess or coolly observe, may paint a grand picture or narrate a legend. Our response to the tone of the poem, however it surprises or jars or stirs us, becomes a starting point for a clearer restatement of the poem's subject and theme(s).

The tone of a poem thus guides us to understand its theme (or themes): what the poem expresses about its topic. A theme is not simply a work's subject or its topic; it is a statement *about* that topic. Although we can usually agree on what a poem is about without much difficulty, it is harder to determine how to state a poem's theme. Not only may a theme be expressed in several different ways, but also many poems arguably have more than one theme. Sometimes the poet explicitly states a poem's theme, and such a statement may clarify why the author chose a particular mode of presentation and how the poem fits into the author's own patterns of thinking and growing. However, the author's words may give a misleading view of how most people read the poem, just as a person's self-assessment may not be all we need in order to understand his or her character. Further study of the poem is necessary to understand how it fulfills—or fails to fulfill—the author's intentions. Despite the difficulty of identifying and expressing themes, doing so is an important step in understanding and writing about poetry.

LISTENING TO TONE

Reading two or more poems with similar topics side by side may suggest how each is distinctive in what it has to say and how it does so—its theme and tone. The following poems differ widely from those in the previous chapter and from each other. Each focuses on a striking topic that pushes the limits of what was commonly considered polite for conversation—or poetry—at the time it was written. The tones of these poems vary according to the situation and the implied attitude of the speaker and the reader. Arguably, some have similar topics, and some could be said to include themes such as *Love is dangerous* or *Desire can be deadly*. But each unique poem makes its own statements about specific topics that have broad significance.

MARGE PIERCY

Barbie Doll

This girlchild was born as usual
and presented dolls that did pee-pee
and miniature GE stoves and irons
and wee lipsticks the color of cherry candy.
5 Then in the magic of puberty, a classmate said:
You have a great big nose and fat legs.

She was healthy, tested intelligent,
possessed strong arms and back,
abundant sexual drive and manual dexterity.
10 She went to and fro apologizing.
Everyone saw a fat nose on thick legs.

She was advised to play coy,
exhorted to come on hearty,
exercise, diet, smile and wheedle.
15 Her good nature wore out
like a fan belt.
So she cut off her nose and her legs
and offered them up.

In the casket displayed on satin she lay
20 with the undertaker's cosmetics painted on,
a turned-up putty nose,
dressed in a pink and white nightie.
Doesn't she look pretty? everyone said.
Consummation at last.
25 To every woman a happy ending.

                                          1973

W. D. SNODGRASS

Leaving the Motel

Outside, the last kids holler
Near the pool: they'll stay the night.
Pick up the towels; fold your collar
Out of sight.

5 Check: is the second bed
Unrumpled, as agreed?
Landlords have to think ahead
In case of need,

Too. Keep things straight: don't take
10 The matches, the wrong keyrings—
We've nowhere we could keep a keepsake—
Ashtrays, combs, things

That sooner or later others
Would accidentally find.
15 Check: take nothing of one another's
And leave behind

Your license number only,
Which they won't care to trace;
We've paid. Still, should such things get lonely,
20 Leave in their vase

An aspirin to preserve
Our lilacs, the wayside flowers
We've gathered and must leave to serve
A few more hours;

25 That's all. We can't tell when
We'll come back, can't press claims,
We would no doubt have other rooms then,
Or other names.

1968

THOM GUNN

In Time of Plague

My thoughts are crowded with death
and it draws so oddly on the sexual
that I am confused
confused to be attracted
5 by, in effect, my own annihilation.
Who are these two, these fiercely attractive men
who want me to stick their needle in my arm?
They tell me they are called Brad and John,
one from here, one from Denver, sitting the same
10 on the bench as they talk to me,
their legs spread apart, their eyes attentive.
I love their daring, their looks, their jargon,
and what they have in mind.
Their mind is the mind of death.

15 They know it, and do not know it,
and they are like me in that
(I know it, and do not know it)
and like the flow of people through this bar.
Brad and John thirst heroically together
20 for euphoria—for a state of ardent life
in which we could all stretch ourselves
and lose our differences. I seek
to enter their minds: am I a fool,
and they direct and right, properly
25 testing themselves against risk,
as a human must, and does,
or are they the fools, their alert faces
mere death's heads lighted glamorously?

I weigh possibilities
30 till I am afraid of the strength
of my own health
and of their evident health.

They get restless at last with my indecisiveness
and so, first one, and then the other,
35 move off into the moving concourse of people
who are boisterous and bright
carrying in their faces and throughout their bodies
the news of life and death.

1992

ETHERIDGE KNIGHT

Hard Rock Returns to Prison from the Hospital for the Criminal Insane

Hard Rock was "known not to take no shit
From nobody," and he had the scars to prove it:
Split purple lips, lumped ears, welts above
His yellow eyes, and one long scar that cut
5 Across his temple and plowed through a thick
Canopy of kinky hair.

The WORD was that Hard Rock wasn't a mean nigger
Anymore, that the doctors had bored a hole in his head,
Cut out part of his brain, and shot electricity
10 Through the rest. When they brought Hard Rock back,
Handcuffed and chained, he was turned loose,
Like a freshly gelded stallion, to try his new status.
And we all waited and watched, like indians at a corral,
To see if the WORD was true.

15 As we waited we wrapped ourselves in the cloak
Of his exploits: "Man, the last time, it took eight
Screws to put him in the Hole."[1] "Yeah, remember when he
Smacked the captain with his dinner tray?" "He set
The record for time in the Hole—67 straight days!"
20 "Ol Hard Rock! man, that's one crazy nigger."
And then the jewel of a myth that Hard Rock had once bit
A screw on the thumb and poisoned him with syphilitic spit.

---

1. Solitary confinement. *Screws:* guards

The testing came, to see if Hard Rock was really tame.
A hillbilly called him a black son of a bitch
25 And didn't lose his teeth, a screw who knew Hard Rock
From before shook him down and barked in his face.
And Hard Rock did *nothing.* Just grinned and looked silly,
His eyes empty like knot holes in a fence.

And even after we discovered that it took Hard Rock
30 Exactly 3 minutes to tell you his first name,
We told ourselves that he had just wised up,
Was being cool; but we could not fool ourselves for long,
And we turned away, our eyes on the ground. Crushed.
He had been our Destroyer, the doer of things
35 We dreamed of doing but could not bring ourselves to do,
The fears of years, like a biting whip,
Had cut grooves too deeply across our backs.

1968

These poems approach a range of topics from unusual angles (and situations) and using different tones. "Barbie Doll" has an objective or distant speaker who retells a kind of legend (albeit with familiar twentieth-century toys) about the grotesque life and early death of a "girlchild" who is expected to embody the perfect beauty of a Barbie doll. The title and details of "Leaving the Motel" indicate that two secret lovers are at the end of an afternoon sexual encounter in a motel room (perhaps one is speaking for both of them), reminding themselves not to leave or take with them any clues for "others"—their spouses?—to find. The speaker of "In the Time of Plague" is a participant in the action of the poem; he describes his attraction to two gay men who entice him to share both sex and drugs during the AIDS epidemic in American gay culture—a new manifestation of the plagues that ravaged medieval Europe, as the title suggests. "Hard Rock Returns to Prison from the Hospital for the Criminal Insane" tells a story of defeat not unlike "Barbie Doll," but this time the speaker of the poem appears to be the spokesman for a group of fellow African American prisoners who looked up to one unconquerable prisoner as a hero for doing the things they "dreamed of doing," until a lobotomy left him brain damaged.

The set of topics these poems offer us—from illicit and deadly sexuality to the potentially destructive forces of gender, race, and class—is hardly cheerful. But the tone of these poems varies significantly, in keeping with their themes, the ideas or feelings that they express on their subjects.

"Barbie Doll," as the title suggests, satirizes romance plots with happy endings and the commercialized standards of femininity represented by Barbie. However we choose to state the theme—*Girls are willing to kill themselves to live up to the unrealistic body images society pushes on them*, perhaps—that theme is expressed with humor, particularly in the comparisons between a doll and a baby ("did pee-pee," [line 2]) and between the girl and an object of a scientific study ("tested intelligent, / possessed strong arms and back, / abundant sexual drive and manual dexterity," [lines 7–9]). The outcome is also ironically neat: In her pretty coffin (like Sleeping Beauty), she gets the nose and the "consummation" of her dreams, if not with the missing Prince Charming. The playful tone parodying these sinister stereotypes is probably more effective in conveying the theme than a sincere and overt statement of political protest would be. A reader knows the final "happy ending" is ironic, just as the made-up corpse sugar-coats the sad life.

Whereas many poems on the topic of love confirm an enduring attachment or express desire or suggest erotic experience, "Leaving the Motel" focuses on the effort to erase a stolen encounter. Like the "she" of "Barbie Doll," the two lovers in this poem have no names; indeed, they have registered under false names. They have already paid for this temporary shelter, can't stay the night like other guests or build a home with children of their own, and are running through a checklist of their agreements and duties ("Check." "Keep things straight." "Check" [lines 5, 9, 15]). Other than the "wayside" lilacs, the objects are daily trivia (with some hints of association with weddings and marriage), from matches and keyrings to license numbers. The matter-of-fact but hurried tone suggests that they wish to hide any deep feelings (hinted at in the last two stanzas in the wish to make "claims" or preserve flowers). The failure to express love—or guilt—enhances the effect when the tone shifts, at the word "still" (line 19), to the second thoughts about leaving something behind. The poem's short rhyming lines, sounding brisk and somewhat impersonal, contrast with the situation and add to the tone of subdued regret that nothing lasts.

The speaker in Gunn's "In the Time of the Plague" seems to address himself in the present tense—"My thoughts are crowded with death" (line 1)—as if writing a diary while simultaneously experiencing an encounter in a gay bar that ends without incident. The tone of doubt and contradiction, set up by the first lines with the repetition of "confused / confused" (lines 3 and 4), requires that the debate go on silently in his own mind and that words be frequently repeated and balanced with their opposites. "Who are these two," a fearful or even hostile rhetorical question (line 6), receives a hesitant response, weighing "possibilities" (line 29). Both the pair of similar men and the speaker "know" and "do not know" (lines 15 and 17) that their proposition is a deadly idea, an invitation to death. Imagery such as the "death's heads" or skulls suggests a medieval worldview in which the flesh is sinful, corrupt, and transitory. The mixture of grand thoughts about mortality with an informal manner of speech ("one from here, one from Denver, sitting the same") complements the speaker's mixed feelings. He is tempted by the two men and "what they have in mind" (line 13), but the poem is about a mental state rather than a physical action. The tone is carefully poised between excitement and fear—so much so that the two emotions are nearly one; here, lust for life and attraction to death are closely related. The speaker realizes that he is "attracted by . . . my own annihilation" (lines 4–5), and he vacillates in an internal debate between desire and self-protection.

Etheridge Knight's "Hard Rock Returns to Prison from the Hospital for the Criminal Insane" identifies with those who wait; they are hopeful that Hard Rock's spirit has not been broken by lobotomy or shock treatments, and the lines crawl almost to a stop with disappointment in stanza 4. The "*nothing*" (line 27) of Hard Rock's response to taunting and the emptiness of his eyes ("like knot holes in a fence," line 28) reduce the speaker's hopes to despair. The final stanza recounts the observers' attempts to reinterpret, to hang onto hope for their symbol of heroism. But the spirit has gone out of the hero-worshipers, too. The tone of street slang and gossip about an undefeated fighter, which makes the first stanzas so rapid-fire, becomes tame within the single word "Crushed" (line 33). The poem records despair and vain resistance in the grip of a system that can quash even a defiant figure such as Hard Rock.

SETTING AS THEME

The **setting** of a work of literature often makes a powerful statement, serving as the subject of a poem (or story or play) and shaping its theme as well as its tone. Setting is abstract in "Barbie Doll," but in "Leaving the Motel" it determines the title and situation as well as the theme. Certain kinds of setting, such as *the country* or *the city*, have a broad significance in literary tradition. The great metropolises such as Rome, Paris, London, and New York have inspired a large body of poetry as well as visual art, while certain landscapes or natural scenes (the Lake District in England, the West in North America, for example) and certain familiar types of places like the country estate or the family farm have similarly inspired literary themes. Some poems devote many lines to evocative descriptions of setting. In other poems, we can quickly recognize the setting and fill in the details, so the poem may not need to devote much space to description.

In the following poem, the speaker responds to setting as a record of social and political changes—that is, setting develops the poem's theme of protest against injustice and suffering; the tone of the poem conveys outrage and grief, while the author's historical context informs the poem's depiction of the London streets. How does Blake use place to develop the speaker's protest against violence? Does the speaker address a companion, or does he walk alone through the places he wishes the reader to imagine?

WILLIAM BLAKE

London

I wander through each chartered street,
Near where the chartered Thames does flow,
And mark in every face I meet
Marks of weakness, marks of woe.

5 In every cry of every man,
In every Infant's cry of fear,
In every voice, in every ban,
The mind-forged manacles I hear.

How the Chimney-sweeper's cry
10 Every black'ning Church appalls;
And the hapless Soldier's sigh
Runs in blood down Palace walls.

But most through midnight streets I hear
How the youthful Harlot's curse
15 Blasts the new-born Infant's tear,
And blights with plagues the Marriage hearse.

                                    1794

Whereas Etheridge Knight's poem about Hard Rock is set in an actual
prison, Blake's "London" envisions an entire metropolis as a kind of mental prison. Blake's speaker appears to be taking a walk through that city ("I
wander," line 1), though it might be a repeated action over many occasions.
The time (around midnight?) as well as the specific locations (river, church,
palace) are unspecific, but everything observed implies multitudes of individuals (*every* infant, lines 5–7; the typical chimney-sweep or prostitute,
lines 9 and 14).

The word "chartered," used twice (lines 1 and 2), implies strong feelings,
too. The streets, instead of seeming alive with people or bustling with
movement, are rigidly, coldly determined, controlled, cramped. Likewise
the river seems as if it were planned, programmed, and laid out by an
oppressor. In fact, the course of the Thames through the city had been
altered (slightly) by the government before Blake's time, but most important is the word's emotional force, the sense it projects of constriction and
artificiality: The speaker experiences London as if human artifice had
usurped nature. Moreover, according to the poem, people are victimized,
"marked" (lines 3 and 4) by their confrontations with the city and its faceless institutions. The "Soldier's sigh" that "runs in blood down Palace

walls" (lines 11–12) vividly suggests, through metaphor, both the power-lessness of the individual and the headless violence of power. This descrip-tion of the city is clearly a subjective, highly emotional, and vivid expression of how the speaker feels about London and what it represents to him. The unidentified, formal speaker at first looks at the miserable people and then listens to a worsening series of voices expressing the social wrongs, from economic to gender oppression. The time of a lifespan is compressed into single lines. The infant is cursed by the "Harlot" (line 14), whose disease infects even those who legitimately marry, making weddings into funerals ("Marriage hearse," line 16).

COMPARING TWO OR MORE POEMS ON SIMILAR TOPICS

The following two poems are about animals, although both of them place their final emphasis on human beings: The animal in each case is only the means to the end of exploring human nature. The poems share the assump-tion that animal behavior may appear to reflect human habits and conduct, and that it may reveal much about ourselves; in each case the character cen-tral to the poem is revealed to be surprisingly unlike the way she thinks of herself. But the poems differ in their tones, in the specific relationship between the woman and the animals, and in their themes.

MAXINE KUMIN

Woodchucks

Gassing the woodchucks didn't turn out right.
The knockout bomb from the Feed and Grain Exchange
was featured as merciful, quick at the bone
and the case we had against them was airtight,
5 both exits shoehorned shut with puddingstone,[2]
but they had a sub-sub-basement out of range.

Next morning they turned up again, no worse
for the cyanide than we for our cigarettes
and state-store Scotch, all of us up to scratch.
10 They brought down the marigolds as a matter of course
and then took over the vegetable patch
nipping the broccoli shoots, beheading the carrots.

---

2. A mixture of cement, pebbles, and gravel.

The food from our mouths, I said, righteously thrilling
to the feel of the .22, the bullets' neat noses.
15 I, a lapsed pacifist fallen from grace
puffed with Darwinian pieties for killing,
now drew a bead on the littlest woodchuck's face.
He died down in the everbearing roses.

Ten minutes later I dropped the mother. She
20 flipflopped in the air and fell, her needle teeth
still hooked in a leaf of early Swiss chard.
Another baby next. O one-two-three
the murderer inside me rose up hard,
the hawkeye killer came on stage forthwith.

25 There's one chuck left. Old wily fellow, he keeps
me cocked and ready day after day after day.
All night I hunt his humped-up form. I dream
I sight along the barrel in my sleep.
If only they'd all consented to die unseen
30 gassed underground the quiet Nazi way.

                                            1972

ADRIENNE RICH

Aunt Jennifer's Tigers

Aunt Jennifer's tigers prance across a screen,
Bright topaz denizens of a world of green.
They do not fear the men beneath the tree;
They pace in sleek chivalric certainty.

5 Aunt Jennifer's fingers fluttering through her wool
Find even the ivory needle hard to pull.
The massive weight of Uncle's wedding band
Sits heavily upon Aunt Jennifer's hand.

When Aunt is dead, her terrified hands will lie
10 Still ringed with ordeals she was mastered by.
The tigers in the panel that she made
Will go on prancing, proud and unafraid.

                                            1951

Authors on their Work: ADRIENNE RICH

From "When We Dead Awaken" (1971)*

Twenty years after writing "Aunt Jennifer's Tigers," Adrienne Rich said this about the poem:

> In writing this poem, composed and apparently cool as it is, I thought I was creating a portrait of an imaginary woman. But this woman suffers from the opposition of her imagination, worked out in tapestry, and her lifestyle, "ringed with ordeals she was mastered by." It was important to me that Aunt Jennifer was a person as distinct from myself as possible—distanced by the formalism of the poem, by its objective, observant tone—even by putting the woman in a different generation. In those years formalism was part of the strategy—like asbestos gloves, it allowed me to handle materials I couldn't pick up bare-handed.

*From "When We Dead Awaken: Writing As Re-Vision," a talk given in December 1971 at the Women's Forum of the Modern Language Association.

As you read "Woodchucks" aloud, how does your tone of voice change from beginning to end? What tone do you use to read the ending? How does the hunter feel about her increasing attraction to violence? Why does the poem begin by calling the gassing of the woodchucks "merciful" and end by describing it as "the quiet Nazi way"? What names does the hunter call herself? How does the name-calling affect your feelings about her? Exactly when does the hunter begin to *enjoy* the feel of the gun and the idea of killing? How does the poet make that clear?

Questions for Comparing Two Poems

Here are some questions and steps for identifying, interpreting, and comparing the topics, themes, and tones of more than one poem. Some of these steps will be familiar to you already, and you may discover other ways to illuminate poetic topics, themes, and tones in addition to the guidelines offered here. As you respond to these questions, note line numbers to cite your evidence, according to this format: "puddingstone" (line 5) or "her terrified hands will lie / Still ringed with ordeals" (lines 9–10).

(Continued on next page)

(Continued)

1. Read each poem through slowly and carefully.
2. Compare the titles. How do the titles point to the topics and possible themes, and are these similar or different? Take "Woodchucks" and "Aunt Jennifer's Tigers," for example. What different qualities do we associate with woodchucks or tigers, animals rarely kept as pets?
3. What is the situation and setting in each poem? Make a list of the words in each poem that name objects or state physical actions. Which things or scenes are most significant, and how would you visualize or imagine them? Compare and contrast your notes on situation, setting, objects, and actions in both poems.
4. Who are the speakers? Is there an "I" present in the action of either poem, or are the speakers external and unidentified? Are there other people in the poems? Is anyone identified as a listener or auditor? Are any things or beings (such as animals) personified or given human traits? Compare and contrast the speakers and other personalities in the poems.
5. What happens in each poem? Look closely at each stanza. Could the stanzas or lines be rearranged without making a difference? Does one poem tell of a single event or short passage of time, whereas another describes repeated actions or longer periods? Is one poem more eventful than the other?
6. Write down four or five words that describe the tone of first one poem and then the other. Do these words also describe the language or style of each poem? Can you use all or some of the same words for both poems? What is different about the two styles and forms, including length? Notice the rhythms and sounds, any regular or irregular patterns of meter or rhyme, and the shape of the stanzas.
7. Reread the poems and try to express their themes in sentences or phrases. Then try to combine the two themes in a statement that notes similarities and differences between them. Does your statement comparing the themes resemble your comparison of the tone and style of the two poems? Do the themes relate to similar or different historical, political, and social issues or contexts featured in the poems? Do the poems develop their themes with comparable allusions to myth, religion, literature, art, or other familiar or traditional ideas or associations?
8. Combining your notes and responses to the other questions, outline and write an essay comparing the two poems. Your argument on how and why the two poems are different and similar may be chosen from responses to the questions above and include evidence that you may have noted.

In the second poem, why are tigers a particularly appropriate contrast to the woman embroidering or cross-stitching a hunting scene? What words describing the tigers seem particularly significant? Why are Aunt Jennifer's hands described as "terrified"? What clues does the poem give about why Aunt Jennifer is so afraid? How does the poem make you feel about Aunt Jennifer's life and death? How would you describe the tone of the poem? Why does the poem begin and end with the tigers?

SUGGESTIONS FOR WRITING

1. Choose any two poems in this chapter that associate positive and negative feelings on their topics—for example, the death of a loved one. How do the tones of the poems combine or contrast the feelings about these topics? Is there a shift in tone in each poem? If so, where? How is the shift revealed through language? Write an essay in which you compare and contrast the way each poet accomplishes this shifting of tone.

2. Write an essay in which you consider the use of language to create tone in any two or more poems on the same subject. How do the tones suit the themes of these poems?

3. Write an essay on Maxine Kumin's "Woodchucks" in which you show that the speaker's conflict between sympathy and murderous instinct is reflected in the mixed tone and varied vocabulary. Focus on formal and informal tone, noting phrases from law or religion—"the case we had against them"; "fallen from grace"—or from everyday speech—"up to scratch," "food from our mouths." How does the diction, or word choice, of the poem affect its tone?

4. Imagine W. D. Snodgrass's "Leaving the Motel" as a poem in which the speaker and lover are happy and delighted with each other and certain that the relationship will last forever. What details and phrases would need to be changed for the poem to express a positive feeling about the relationship? Write an essay in which you relate the tone of the poem to the subject of secret and short-lived sexual relationships.

Family: An Album

F amilies are the groundwork of society, and most people's earliest memories involve family members. Families may be nuclear or extended, biological or adoptive, emotionally demonstrative or distant. Families may pass down traditions, or younger generations may choose to abandon them. Adults who have left home may dwell on memories, good or bad, of their mothers, fathers, brothers, or sisters. Each renewed contact with family can spark conflicted thoughts and feelings. Hope, disappointment, or grief for one's child can find expression as a concentrated moment in a poem. A spouse or a child can remind the speaker of the passage of time and mortality.

Because the family is such a basic unit of social interaction, many poems explore family relations. The following poems are all, in different ways, about families. What do these poems have in common? How do they differ? Which have the most unusual situations or relationships compared with the rest? Can you find two poems that address the same theme—in other words, can you accurately state their themes in the same way? How do any two poems differ in tone, whether or not they have similar themes? Which poems have surprising shifts in tone? Do any poems express surprising or disturbing attitudes toward loved ones? Are some relatives not beloved?

GALWAY KINNELL

After Making Love We Hear Footsteps

    For I can snore like a bullhorn
    or play loud music
    or sit up talking with any reasonably sober Irishman
    and Fergus will only sink deeper
5   into his dreamless sleep, which goes by all in one flash,
    but let there be that heavy breathing
    or a stifled come-cry anywhere in the house
    and he will wrench himself awake
    and make for it on the run—as now, we lie together,
10   after making love, quiet, touching along the length of our
       bodies,
    familiar touch of the long-married,
    and he appears—in his baseball pajamas, it happens,
    the neck opening so small
    he has to screw them on, which one day may make him wonder
15   about the mental capacity of baseball players—
    and says, "Are you loving and snuggling? May I join?"

He flops down between us and hugs us and snuggles himself to
   sleep,
his face gleaming with satisfaction at being this very child.

In the half darkness we look at each other
20 and smile
and touch arms across his little, startlingly muscled body—
this one whom habit of memory propels to the ground of his
   making,
sleeper only the mortal sounds can sing awake,
this blessing love gives again into our arms.

                                 1980

- How does the language in lines 1–5 establish the poem's tone?
Do the last lines (starting with line 22) alter the tone in any
way?

ROBERT HAYDEN

Those Winter Sundays

Sundays too my father got up early
and put his clothes on in the blueblack cold,
then with cracked hands that ached
from labor in the weekday weather made
5 banked fires blaze. No one ever thanked him.

I'd wake and hear the cold splintering, breaking.
When the rooms were warm, he'd call,
and slowly I would rise and dress,
fearing the chronic angers of that house,

10 Speaking indifferently to him,
who had driven out the cold
and polished my good shoes as well.
What did I know, what did I know
of love's austere and lonely offices?

                                 1966

- Why does the poem begin with the words "Sundays too"
(rather than, say, "On Sundays")? What are the "austere and
lonely offices" of love in the poem's final line?

JIMMY SANTIAGO BACA

Green Chile

I prefer red chile over my eggs
and potatoes for breakfast.
Red chile *ristras*[1] decorate my door,
dry on my roof, and hang from eaves.
5 They lend open-air vegetable stands
historical grandeur, and gently swing
with an air of festive welcome.
I can hear them talking in the wind,
haggard, yellowing, crisp, rasping
10 tongues of old men, licking the breeze.

But grandmother loves green chile.
When I visit her,
she holds the green chile pepper
in her wrinkled hands.
15 Ah, voluptuous, masculine,
an air of authority and youth simmers
from its swan-neck stem, tapering to a flowery
collar, fermenting resinous spice.
A well-dressed gentleman at the door
20 my grandmother takes sensuously in her hand,
rubbing its firm glossed sides,
caressing the oily rubbery serpent,
with mouth-watering fulfillment,
fondling its curves with gentle fingers.
25 Its bearing magnificent and taut
as flanks of a tiger in mid-leap,
she thrusts her blade into
and cuts it open, with lust
on her hot mouth, sweating over the stove,
30 bandanna round her forehead,
mysterious passion on her face
and she serves me green chile con carne
between soft warm leaves of corn tortillas,
with beans and rice—her sacrifice
35 to her little prince.
I slurp from my plate
with last bit of tortilla, my mouth burns
and I hiss and drink a tall glass of cold water.

1. Braided strings of peppers.

All over New Mexico, sunburned men and women
40 drive rickety trucks stuffed with gunny-sacks
of green chile, from Belen, Veguita, Willard, Estancia,
San Antonio y Socorro, from fields
to roadside stands, you see them roasting green chile
in screen-sided homemade barrels, and for a dollar a bag,
45 we relive this old, beautiful ritual again and again.

1989

- What different qualities do the red and green chiles have?
  Which words in the poem help personify the chiles? How fully
  do these words reflect the differences between the speaker
  and the grandmother?

KELLY CHERRY

Alzheimer's

He stands at the door, a crazy old man
Back from the hospital, his mind rattling
Like the suitcase, swinging from his hand,
That contains shaving cream, a piggy bank,
5 A book he sometimes pretends to read,
His clothes. On the brick wall beside him
Roses and columbine slug it out for space, claw the mortar.
The sun is shining, as it does late in the afternoon
In England, after rain.
10 Sun hardens the house, reifies it,
Strikes the iron grillwork like a smithy
And sparks fly off, burning in the bushes—
The rosebushes—
While the white wood trim defines solidity in space.
15 This is his house. He remembers it as his,
Remembers the walkway he built between the front room
And the garage, the rhododendron he planted in back,
The car he used to drive. He remembers himself,
A younger man, in a tweed hat, a man who loved
20 Music. There is no time for that now. No time for music,
The peculiar screeching of strings, the luxurious
Fiddling with emotion.
Other things have become more urgent.
Other matters are now of greater import, have more
25 Consequence, must be attended to. The first

Thing he must do, now that he is home, is decide who
This woman is, this old, white-haired woman
Standing here in the doorway,
Welcoming him in.

1997

- How do phrases like "a crazy old man" and "a book he sometimes pretends to read" indicate the speaker's feelings toward
her father? Does her attitude shift at some point? Where?

ANDREW HUDGINS

Begotten

I've never, as some children do,
looked at my folks and thought, I *must*
have come from someone else—
rich parents who'd misplaced me, but
5 who would, as in a myth or novel,
return and claim me. Hell, no. I saw
my face in cousins' faces, heard
my voice in their high drawls. And Sundays,
after the dinner plates were cleared,
10 I lingered, elbow propped on red
oilcloth, and studied great-uncles, aunts,
and cousins new to me. They squirmed.
I stared till I discerned the features
they'd gotten from the family larder:
15 eyes, nose, lips, hair? I stared until,
uncomfortable, they'd snap, "Hey, boy—
what are you looking at? At me?"
"No, sir," I'd lie. "No, ma'am." I'd count ten
and then continue staring at them.
20 I never had to ask, What am I?
I stared at my blood-kin, and thought,
So *this*, dear God, is what I am.

1994

- What can you infer from the language in this poem about
the speaker's attitude toward his life? What does the poem's
title evoke?

SUGGESTIONS FOR WRITING

1. Choose any two poems in this album that associate positive and negative feelings of one family member toward another. How do the tones shift from one tone to another? Where, in each poem, is this shift of tone? How is the shift revealed through language? Write an essay in which you compare and contrast the way each poet accomplishes this shifting tone.

2. What words in Robert Hayden's "Those Winter Sundays" suggest the son's feelings toward his father and his home? What words indicate that the poet's attitudes have changed since the time depicted in the poem? Write an essay in which you compare the speaker's feelings, as a youth and then later as a man, about his father and his home.

3. Kelly Cherry's "Alzheimer's" uses contrasts—especially before and after—to characterize the ravages of Alzheimer's disease. What evidence does the poem provide about what the man used to be like? What specific changes have come about? How does the setting of the poem suggest some of those changes? In what ways do the stabilities of house, landscape, and other people clarify what has happened? Write an essay about the function of the poem's setting.

4. Write an essay in which you consider the use of language to create tone in two or more poems on the same subject. How do the tones suit the themes of these poems?

8 SPEAKER: WHOSE VOICE DO WE HEAR?

Poems are personal. The thoughts and feelings they express belong to a specific person, and however general or universal their sentiments seem to be, poems come to us as the expression of an individual human voice. That voice is often the voice of the poet, but not always. Poets sometimes create "characters" just as writers of fiction or drama do—people who speak for them only indirectly. A character may, in fact, be very different from the poet, just as a character in a play or story is not necessarily the author, and that person, the **speaker** of the poem, may express ideas or feelings very different from the poet's own. In the following poem, rather than speaking directly to us himself, the poet has created two speakers, both female, each of whom has a distinctive voice, personality, and character. A third speaker here acts as a **narrator**, telling us who said what. (We can thus describe this poem as a **narrative poem** rather than a **lyric**.)

THOMAS HARDY

The Ruined Maid

"O 'Melia,[1] my dear, this does everything crown!
Who could have supposed I should meet you in Town?
And whence such fair garments, such prosperi-ty?"—
"O didn't you know I'd been ruined?" said she.

5 —"You left us in tatters, without shoes or socks,
Tired of digging potatoes, and spudding up docks;[2]
And now you've gay bracelets and bright feathers three!"—
"Yes: that's how we dress when we're ruined," said she.

—"At home in the barton[3] you said 'thee' and 'thou,'
10 And 'thik oon,' and 'theäs oon,' and 't'other'; but now
Your talking quite fits 'ee for high compa-ny!"—

1. Short for Amelia. 2. Spading up weeds. 3. Farmyard.

496

"Some polish is gained with one's ruin," said she.

—"Your hands were like paws then, your face blue and bleak
But now I'm bewitched by your delicate cheek,
15   And your little gloves fit as on any la-dy!"—
"We never do work when we're ruined," said she.

—"You used to call home-life a hag-ridden dream,
And you'd sigh, and you'd sock;[4] but at present you seem
To know not of megrims[5] or melancho-ly!"—
20   "True. One's pretty lively when ruined," said she.

—"I wish I had feathers, a fine sweeping gown,
And a delicate face, and could strut about Town!"—
"My dear—a raw country girl, such as you be,
Cannot quite expect that. You ain't ruined," said she.

1866

The first voice, that of a young woman who has remained back on the farm, is designated typographically (that is, by the way the poem is printed): There are dashes at the beginning and end of all but the first of her speeches. She speaks the first part of each **stanza** (a stanza is a section of a poem designated by spacing), usually the first three lines. The second young woman, a companion and coworker on the farm in years gone by, regularly gets the last line in each stanza (and in the last stanza, two lines), so it is clear who is talking at every point.

The two women are just as clearly distinguished by what they say, how they say it, and what sort of person each proves to be. The nameless stay-at-home shows little knowledge of the world, and everything surprises her: seeing her former companion at all, but especially seeing her well clothed, cheerful, and polished. And as the poem develops she shows increasing envy of her more worldly friend. She is the "raw country girl" (line 23) that the other speaker says she is, and she still speaks the country dialect ("fits 'ee," line 11, for example) that she notices her friend has lost (lines 9–11). The "ruined" young woman ('Melia), on the other hand, says little except the refrain about having been ruined, but even the slight variations she plays on that theme suggest her sophistication and amusement at her rural friend, although she still uses a country "ain't" at the end.

We are not told the full story of their lives (Was the "ruined" young woman thrown out? Did she run away from home or work?), but we know enough (that they've been separated for some time, that the stay-at-home did not know where the other had gone) to allow the dialogue to articulate the contrast between them: One is still rural, inexperienced, and innocent;

---

4. Deliver angry blows.   5. Migraine headaches.

the other is sophisticated, citified—and "ruined." Each speaker's style of
speech then does the rest.

It is equally obvious that there are two speakers (or, in this case, a speaker
and a singer) in the following poem: The first functions as a narrator, the
second speaks in stanzas 2 through 9.

X. J. KENNEDY

In a Prominent Bar in Secaucus One Day

To the tune of "The Old Orange Flute" or the tune of
"Sweet Betsy from Pike"

In a prominent bar in Secaucus[6] one day
Rose a lady in skunk with a topheavy sway,
Raised a knobby red finger—all turned from their beer—
While with eyes bright as snowcrust she sang high and clear:

5 "Now who of you'd think from an eyeload of me
That I once was a lady as proud as could be?
Oh I'd never sit down by a tumbledown drunk
If it wasn't, my dears, for the high cost of junk.

"All the gents used to swear that the white of my calf
10 Beat the down of a swan by a length and a half.
In the kerchief of linen I caught to my nose
Ah, there never fell snot, but a little gold rose.

"I had seven gold teeth and a toothpick of gold.
My Virginia cheroot was a leaf of it rolled
15 And I'd light it each time with a thousand in cash—
Why the bums used to fight if I flicked them an ash.

"Once the toast of the Biltmore,[7] the belle of the Taft,
I would drink bottle beer at the Drake, never draft,
And dine at the Astor on Salisbury steak
20 With a clean tablecloth for each bite I did take.

"In a car like the Roxy[8] I'd roll to the track,
A steel-guitar trio, a bar in the back,

6. Small town on the Hackensack River in New Jersey, a few miles west of Manhattan.
7. Like the Taft, Drake, and Astor, a once-fashionable New York hotel.
8. Luxurious old New York theater and movie house, the site of many "world premieres" in the
heyday of Hollywood.

And the wheels made no noise, they turned over so fast,
Still it took you ten minutes to see me go past.

25 "When the horses bowed down to me that I might choose,
I bet on them all, for I hated to lose.
Now I'm saddled each night for my butter and eggs
And the broken threads race down the backs of my legs.

"Let you hold in mind, girls, that your beauty must pass
30 Like a lovely white clover that rusts with its grass.
Keep your bottoms off barstools and marry you young
Or be left—an old barrel with many a bung.

"For when time takes you out for a spin in his car
You'll be hard-pressed to stop him from going too far
35 And be left by the roadside, for all your good deeds,
Two toadstools for tits and a face full of weeds."

All the house raised a cheer, but the man at the bar
Made a phonecall and up pulled a red patrol car
And she blew us a kiss as they copped her away
40 From that prominent bar in Secaucus, N.J.

1961

Again, we learn about the singer primarily through her own words, although we may not believe everything she tells us about her past. From her introduction in the first stanza we get some general notion of her appearance and condition, but it is she who tells us that she is a junkie (line 8) and a prostitute (lines 27, 32) and that her face and figure have seen better days (lines 32, 36). That information could make her a sad case, and the poem might lament her state or encourage us to lament it, but instead she presents herself in a light, friendly, and theatrical way. The comedy is bittersweet, perhaps, but she is allowed to present herself, through her own words and attitudes, as a likable character—someone who has survived life's disappointments and retained her dignity. The self-portrait accumulates almost completely through how she talks about herself, and the poet develops our attitude toward her by allowing her to recount her story herself, in her own words—or rather in words he has chosen for her.

Sometimes poets "borrow" a character from history and ask readers to factor in historical facts and contexts. In the following poem, for example, the Canadian poet Margaret Atwood draws heavily on facts and traditions about a nineteenth-century émigré from Scotland to Canada. The poem is a lyric spoken in the first person, but its speaker is a fictional character based on a real woman.

MARGARET ATWOOD

Death of a Young Son by Drowning

He, who navigated with success
the dangerous river of his own birth
once more set forth

on a voyage of discovery
5   into the land I floated on
but could not touch to claim.

His feet slid on the bank,
the currents took him;
he swirled with ice and trees in the swollen water

10   and plunged into distant regions,
his head a bathysphere;
through his eyes' thin glass bubbles

he looked out, reckless adventurer
on a landscape stranger than Uranus
15   we have all been to and some remember.

There was an accident; the air locked,
he was hung in the river like a heart.
They retrieved the swamped body,

cairn of my plans and future charts,
20   with poles and hooks
from among the nudging logs.

It was spring, the sun kept shining, the new grass
leapt to solidity;
my hands glistened with details.

25   After the long trip I was tired of waves.
My foot hit rock. The dreamed sails
collapsed, ragged.

        I planted him in this country
        like a flag.

                  1970

The poem comes from a volume called *The Journals of Susanna Moodie: Poems by Margaret Atwood* (1970). A frontier pioneer, Moodie herself wrote two books about Canada, *Roughing It in the Bush* and *Life in the Clearings*, and Atwood found their observations rather stark and disorganized. She wrote her Susanna Moodie poems to refocus the "character" and to reconstruct Moodie's actual geographical exploration and self-discovery. To fully understand these thoughts and meditations, then, we need to know something of the history behind them. Yet even without such knowledge, we can appreciate the poem's powerful evocation of the speaker's situation and feelings.

Some speakers in poems are not nearly so heroic or attractive, and some poems create a speaker we are made to dislike, as the following poem does. A **dramatic monologue**, it consists entirely of the words of a single, fictional speaker in a specific time, place, and dramatic situation, very like a character in a play.

ROBERT BROWNING

Soliloquy of the Spanish Cloister

Gr-r-r—there go, my heart's abhorrence!
    Water your damned flower-pots, do!
If hate killed men, Brother Lawrence,
    God's blood, would not mine kill you!
5 What? your myrtle-bush wants trimming?
    Oh, that rose has prior claims—
Needs its leaden vase filled brimming?
    Hell dry you up with its flames!

At the meal we sit together:
10   *Salve tibi!*[9] I must hear
Wish talk of the kind of weather,
    Sort of season, time of year:
Not a plenteous cork-crop: scarcely
    Dare we hope oak-galls,[1] *I doubt:*
15 *What's the Latin name for "parsley"?*
    What's the Greek name for Swine's Snout?

Whew! We'll have our platter burnished,
    Laid with care on our own shelf!
With a fire-new spoon we're furnished,
20   And a goblet for ourself,
Rinsed like something sacrificial

---

9. Hail to thee (Latin). Italics usually indicate the words of Brother Lawrence.
1. Abnormal growth on oak trees, used for tanning.

Ere 'tis fit to touch our chaps²—
Marked with L. for our initial!
(He-he! There his lily snaps!)

25 *Saint*, forsooth! While brown Dolores
    —Squats outside the Convent bank
With Sanchicha, telling stories,
    Steeping tresses in the tank,
Blue-black, lustrous, thick like horsehairs,
30   —Can't I see his dead eye glow,
Bright as 'twere a Barbary corsair's?³
    (That is, if he'd let it show!)

When he finishes refection,
    Knife and fork he never lays
35 Cross-wise, to my recollection,
    As do I, in Jesu's praise.
I the Trinity illustrate,
    Drinking watered orange-pulp—
In three sips the Arian⁴ frustrate;
40   —While he drains his at one gulp.

Oh, those melons? If he's able
    We're to have a feast! so nice!
One goes to the Abbot's table,
    All of us get each a slice.
45 How go on your flowers? None double?
    Not one fruit-sort can you spy?
Strange!—And I, too, at such trouble,
    —Keep them close-nipped on the sly!

There's a great text in Galatians,
50   Once you trip on it, entails
Twenty-nine distinct damnations,⁵
    One sure, if another fails:
If I trip him just a-dying,
    Sure of heaven as sure can be,
55 Spin him round and send him flying
    Off to hell, a Manichee?⁶

---

2. Jaws.   3. African pirate's.   4. Heretical sect that denied the Trinity.
5. Galatians 5.15–23 provides a long list of possible offenses, though they do not add up to twenty-nine.
6. Heretic. According to the Manichean heresy, the world was divided into the forces of good and evil, each equally powerful.

Or, my scrofulous French novel
 On gray paper with blunt type!
Simply glance at it, you grovel
60 Hand and foot in Belial's gripe:[7]
If I double down its pages
 At the woeful sixteenth print,
When he gathers his greengages,
 Ope a sieve and slip it in't?

65 Or, there's Satan!—one might venture
 Pledge one's soul to him, yet leave
Such a flaw in the indenture
 —As he'd miss till, past retrieve,
Blasted lay that rose-acacia
70 We're so proud of! *Hy, Zy, Hine* . . .[8]
'St, there's Vespers! *Plena gratiâ*
 Ave, Virgo.[9] Gr-r-r—you swine!

       1842

Not many poems begin with a growl, and this harsh sound turns out to be fair warning that we are about to meet a real beast, even though he is in the clothing of a religious man. In line 1 he shows himself to hold a most uncharitable attitude toward his fellow monk, Brother Lawrence, and by line 4 he has uttered two profanities and admitted his intense feelings of hatred and vengefulness. His ranting and roaring is full of exclamation points (four in the first stanza!), and he reveals his own personality and character when he imagines curses and unflattering nicknames for Brother Lawrence or plots malicious jokes on him. By the end, we have accumulated no knowledge of Brother Lawrence that makes him seem a fit target for such rage (except that he is pious, dutiful, and pleasant—perhaps enough to make this sort of speaker despise him), but we should have discovered much about the speaker's character and habits.

 The speaker characterizes himself; the details accumulate into a fairly full portrait, and here we do not have even an opening and closing "objective" narrator's description (as in Kennedy's "In a Prominent Bar") or another speaker (as in Hardy's "The Ruined Maid") to give us perspective. Except for the moments when the speaker mimics or parodies Brother Lawrence (usually in italic type), we have only the speaker's own words and thoughts. But that is enough; the poet has controlled them so carefully that we know what he thinks of the speaker. The whole poem has been about the

---

7. That is, in the devil's clutches. 8. Possibly the beginning of an incantation or curse.
9. Opening words of the *Ave Maria,* here reversed: "Full of grace, Hail, Virgin" (Latin).

speaker and his attitudes; the point has been to characterize the speaker and develop in us a dislike of him and what he stands for.

In reading a poem like this aloud, we would want our voice to suggest all the speaker's unlikable features. We would also need to suggest, through tone of voice, the author's contemptuous mocking of them, and we would want, like an actor, to create strong disapproval in the hearer. The poem's words (the ones the author has given to the speaker) clearly imply those attitudes, and we would want our voice to express them.

Usually there is much more to a poem than the characterization of the speaker, but often it is necessary first to identify the speaker and determine his or her character before we can appreciate what else goes on in the poem. And sometimes, as here, in looking for the speaker of the poem, we discover the gist of the entire poem.

Analyzing Speakers: An Exercise

In the following poem, we do not get a full sense of the speaker until well into the poem. As you read, try to imagine the tone of voice you think this person would use. Exactly when do you begin to know what she sounds like?

DOROTHY PARKER

A Certain Lady

Oh, I can smile for you, and tilt my head,
    And drink your rushing words with eager lips,
And paint my mouth for you a fragrant red,
    And trace your brows with tutored finger-tips.
5 When you rehearse your list of loves to me,
    Oh, I can laugh and marvel, rapturous-eyed.
And you laugh back, nor can you ever see
    The thousand little deaths my heart has died.
And you believe, so well I know my part,
10   That I am gay as morning, light as snow,
And all the straining things within my heart
    You'll never know.

(Continued on next page)

(Continued)

      Oh, I can laugh and listen, when we meet,
        And you bring tales of fresh adventurings—
15 Of ladies delicately indiscreet,
        Of lingering hands, and gently whispered things.
      And you are pleased with me, and strive anew
        To sing me sagas of your late delights.
      Thus do you want me—marveling, gay, and true—
20   Nor do you see my staring eyes of nights.
      And when, in search of novelty, you stray,
        Oh, I can kiss you blithely as you go . . .
      And what goes on, my love, while you're away,
        You'll never know.

                                   1937

    To whom does the speaker seem to be talking? What sort of person is he? How do you feel about him? Which habits and attitudes of his do you like least? How soon can you tell that the speaker is not altogether happy about his conversation and conduct? In what tone of voice would you read the first twenty-two lines aloud? What attitude would you try to express toward the person spoken to? What tone would you use for the last two lines? How would you describe the speaker's personality? What aspects of her behavior are most crucial to the poem's effect?

AUTHOR VERSUS SPEAKER

It is easy to assume that the speaker in a poem is an extension of the poet, especially when the voice is as distinctively self-assured as in "A Certain Lady." So, is the speaker in the poem above Dorothy Parker? Maybe. A lot of Parker's poems present a similar world-weary posture and a wry cynicism about romantic love. But the poem is hardly a case of self-revelation, a giving away of personal secrets. If it were, it would be silly, not to say risky, to address her lover in a way that gives damaging facts about a pose she has been so careful to set up.

    In poems such as "The Ruined Maid," "In a Prominent Bar," and "Soliloquy of the Spanish Cloister," we are in no danger of mistaking the speaker for the poet, once we recognize that poets may create speakers who participate in specific situations, much as in fiction or drama. When there is a pointed discrepancy between the speaker and what we know of the poet—when the speaker is a woman, for example, and the poet is a man—we know we have a created speaker to contend with and that the point (or at least *one* point) in the poem is to observe the characterization carefully. In "A Certain Lady" we may be less sure, and in other poems the discrepancy between speaker and poet may be even more uncertain. What are we to make, for example, of the speaker in "Woodchucks" in the previous chapter? Is that speaker the real Maxine Kumin? At best (without knowing something quite specific about the author) we can only say "maybe" to that question. What we can be sure of is the sort of person the speaker is portrayed to be—someone (a man? a woman?) surprised to discover feelings and attitudes that contradict values apparently held with confidence. And that is exactly what we need to know for the poem to have its effect.

Even when poets present themselves as if they were speaking directly to us in their own voices, their poems present only a partial portrait, something considerably less than the full personality and character of the poet. Even when there is not an obviously created character—someone with distinct characteristics that are different from those of the poet—strategies of characterization are used to present the person speaking in one way and not another. Even when reading a poem like the following one, which contains identifiable autobiographical details, you should still think of the speaker instead of the poet, although here the poet is probably writing about a personal, actual experience, and he is certainly making a character of himself—that is, characterizing himself in a certain way, emphasizing some parts of himself and not others.

WILLIAM WORDSWORTH

She Dwelt among the Untrodden Ways

She dwelt among the untrodden ways
    Beside the springs of Dove,[1]
A Maid whom there were none to praise
    And very few to love:

5 A violet by a mossy stone
    Half hidden from the eye!
—Fair as a star, when only one
    Is shining in the sky.

She lived unknown, and few could know
10   When Lucy ceased to be;

---

1. Small stream in the Lake District in northern England, near where Wordsworth lived.

But she is in her grave, and, oh,
The difference to me!

1800

Is this poem more about Lucy or about the speaker's feelings concerning her death? Her simple life, far removed from fame and known only to a few, is said to have been beautiful, but we know little about her beyond her name and where she lived, in a beautiful but then-isolated section of northern England. We don't know if she was young or old, only that the speaker thinks of her as "fair" and compares her to a "violet by a mossy stone." We do know that the speaker is deeply pained by her death, so deeply that he is almost inarticulate with grief, lapsing into simple exclamation ("oh," line 11) and hardly able to articulate the "difference" that her death makes.

Did Lucy actually live? Was she a friend of the poet? We don't know; the poem doesn't tell us, and even biographers of Wordsworth are unsure. What we do know is that Wordsworth was able to represent grief very powerfully. Whether the speaker is the historical Wordsworth or not, that speaker is a major focus of the poem, and it is his feelings that the poem isolates and expresses. We need to recognize some characteristics of the speaker and be sensitive to his feelings for the poem to work.

The poems we have looked at in this chapter—and the group that follows—all suggest the value of beginning the reading of any poem with three simple questions: Who is speaking? What do we know about him or her? What kind of person is she or he? Putting together the evidence that the poem presents in answer to such questions can often take us a long way into the poem. For some poems, such questions won't help a great deal because the speaking voice is too indistinct or the character behind the poem too scantily presented. But starting with such questions will often lead you toward the central experience the poem offers. At the very least, the question of speaker helps clarify the tone of voice, and it often provides guidance to the larger situation the poem explores.

. . .

ROBERT BURNS

To a Louse

On Seeing One on a Lady's Bonnet at Church

Ha! whare ya gaun, ye crowlan ferlie!²
Your impudence protects you sairly:³

---

2. Crawling miracle! (The speaker uses Scots dialect.) 3. Sorely.

I canna say but ye strunt[4] rarely,
    Owre gauze and lace;
5 Tho' faith, I fear ye dine but sparely,
    On sic a place.

Ye ugly, creepan, blastit wonner,[5]
Detested, shunn'd, by saunt an' sinner,
How daur ye set your fit[6] upon her,
10   Sae fine a Lady!
Gae somewhere else and seek your dinner,
    On some poor body.

Swith, in some beggar's haffet squattle;[7]
There ye may creep, and sprawl, and sprattle,[8]
15 Wi'ither kindred, jumping cattle,
    In shoals and, nations;
Whare horn nor bane[9] ne'er daur unsettle,
    Your thick plantations.

Now haud you there ye're out o'sight,
20 Below the fatt'rels,[1] snug and tight,
Na faith ye yet![2] ye'll no be right,
    Till ye've got on it,
The vera tapmost, towrin height
    O' Miss's bonnet.

25 My sooth! right bauld ye set your nose out,
As plump an' gray as onie grozet:[3]
O for some rank, mercurial rozet,[4]
    Or fell, red smeddum,[5]
I'd gie you sic a hearty dose o't,
30   Wad dress your droddum![6]

I wad na been surpriz'd to spy
You on an auld wife's flainen toy,[7]
Or aiblins some bit duddie boy,[8]
    On 's wylecoat;[9]
35 But Miss's fine Lunardi,[1] fye!
    How daur ye do't?

O Jenny dinna toss your head,
An' set your beauties a' abread![2]

4. Strut.   5. Wonder.   6. Foot.   7. Swift, in some beggar's hair sprawl.   8. Struggle.
9. Bone.   1. Ribbon ends.   2. No matter!   3. Gooseberry.   4. Rosin.
5. Or sharp, red powder.   6. Buttocks.   7. Flannel cap.
8. Or perhaps some small ragged boy.   9. Undershirt.   1. Bonnet.   2. Abroad.

Ye little ken what cursed speed
40   The blastie's³ makin!
Thae⁴ winks and finger-ends, I dread,
      Are notice takin!

O wad some Pow'r the giftie gie us
To see oursels as others see us!
45 It wad frae monie a blunder free us
      An foolish notion:
What airs in dress an' gait wad lea'e us,
      And ev'n Devotion!⁵

                                        1785

• What is the speaker's attitude toward the louse? toward
  Jenny? How do the speaker's attitude and focus change in the
  last two stanzas? What lines best summarize the speaker's
  main point?

GWENDOLYN BROOKS

We Real Cool

      THE POOL PLAYERS,
      SEVEN AT THE GOLDEN SHOVEL.

We real cool. We
Left school. We

Lurk late. We
Strike straight. We

5 Sing sin. We
Thin gin. We

Jazz June. We
Die soon.
                    1950

• Who are "we" in this poem? Do you think that the speaker
  and the poet share the same idea of what is "cool"?

3. Creature's.   4. Those.   5. Piety.

Authors on Their Work: GWENDOLYN BROOKS (1917–2000)*

From "An Interview with Gwendolyn Brooks"
(1970)*

Q. Are your characters literally true to your experience or do you set out to change experience?

A. Some of them are, are invented, some of them are very real people.

. . .

Q. How about the seven pool players in the poem "We Real Cool"?

A. They have no pretensions to any glamor. They are supposedly dropouts, or at least they're in the poolroom when they should possibly be in school, since they're probably young enough, or at least those I saw were when I looked in a poolroom. . . . First of all, let me tell you how that's supposed to be said, because there's a reason why I set it out as I did. These are people who are essentially saying, "Kilroy is here. We are." But they're a little uncertain of the strength of their identity. . . .

The "We"—you're supposed to stop after the "We" and think about their validity, and of course there's no way for you to tell whether it should be said softly or not, I suppose, but I say it rather softly because I want to represent their basic uncertainty, which they don't bother to question every day, of course.

Q. Are you saying that the form of this poem, then, was determined by the colloquial rhythm you were trying to catch?

A. No, determined by my feeling about these boys, these young men.

*Gwendolyn Brooks and George Stavros, "An Interview with Gwendolyn Brooks." *Contemporary Literature* 11.1 (Winter 1970), 7, 9–10.

WALT WHITMAN

[*I celebrate myself, and sing myself*]

I celebrate myself, and sing myself,
And what I assume you shall assume,
For every atom belonging to me as good belongs to you.

I loafe and invite my soul,
5 I lean and loafe at my ease observing a spear of summer grass.

My tongue, every atom of my blood, form'd from this soil, this air,
Born here of parents born here from parents the same, and their
  parents the same,
I, now thirty-seven years old in perfect health begin,
Hoping to cease not till death.
10 Creeds and schools in abeyance,
Retiring back a while sufficed at what they are, but never
  forgotten,
I harbor for good or bad, I permit to speak at every hazard,
Nature without check with original energy.

                                                              1855, 1881

- What is characteristically American about the speaker of this
  poem?

SUGGESTIONS FOR WRITING

1. Several of the poems in this chapter create characters and imply situations, as in drama. Write an essay in which you describe and analyze the main speaker of "The Ruined Maid" by Thomas Hardy, "In a Prominent Bar in Secaucus One Day" by X. J. Kennedy, "Soliloquy of the Spanish Cloister" by Robert Browning, or "A Certain Lady" by Dorothy Parker.

2. Choose any of the poems in this or the previous chapter and write an essay about the way a poet can create irony and humor through the use of a speaker who is clearly distinct from the poet himself or herself.

3. Write a poem, short story, or personal essay in which the speaker or narrator is a character mentioned by a speaker in any of the poems in this chapter—for example, Amelia in Hardy's "The Ruined Maid," someone who hears the song sung in X. J. Kennedy's "In a Prominent Bar in Secaucus One Day," the lover in Dorothy Parker's "A Certain Lady," or Jenny in Robert Burns's "To a Louse." How might the same situation, as well as the main speaker of these poems, look and sound different when viewed from another speaker's point of view and described in another speaker's voice?

9 SITUATION AND SETTING: WHAT HAPPENS? WHERE? WHEN?

Questions about the speaker (*Who* questions) in a poem lead to questions about *What?* and *Why?* as well as *Where?* and *When?* First you identify the imagined **situation** in the poem: Who is speaking? To whom is the speaker speaking? Is there an auditor in the poem, or simply an audience outside of it? Is anyone else present or referred to in the poem? What is happening? Why is this event or communication occurring, and why is it significant? As soon as you zoom in on answers to such questions about persons and actions, you also encounter questions about place (Where does the action or communication take place?) and time (When is the poem set?). In other words, situation entails **setting**.

The place involved in a poem is its *spatial setting*, and the time is its *temporal setting*. The temporal setting may be a specific date or an era, a season of the year or a time of day. We tend, for example, to think of spring as a time of discovery and growth, and poems set in spring are likely to make use of that association. Similarly, morning usually suggests discovery—beginnings, vitality, the world fresh and new—even to those of us who in reality take our waking slow. Temporal or spatial setting often influences our expectations of theme and tone, although a poet may surprise us by making something very different from what we had thought was familiar.

Not all poems have an identifiable situation or setting, just as not all poems have a speaker who is entirely distinct from the author. Poems that simply present a series of thoughts and feelings directly, in a reflective way, may not present anything resembling a scene with action and dialogue. But many poems depend crucially on a sense of place, a sense of time, and an understanding of human interaction in scenes that resemble those in plays or films. And questions about these matters will often lead you to define not only the "facts" but also the feelings central to the design a poem has on its readers.

To understand the dialogue in Hardy's "The Ruined Maid" (chapter 8), for example, we need to recognize that the two women are meeting after an extended period of separation, and that they meet in a town setting rather than the rural area in which they grew up together. We infer (from the opening lines) that the meeting is accidental and that no other friends are present for the conversation. The poem's whole "story" depends on their situation: After leading separate lives for a while, they have some catching up to do. We don't know what specific town they are in or what year, season, or time of day it is—and those details are not important to the poem's effect.

More specific settings matter in other poems. X. J. Kennedy's "lady in skunk" sings her life story "in a prominent bar in Secaucus," a working-class town in New Jersey, but on no particular occasion ("one day"). In Browning's "Soliloquy of the Spanish Cloister," the setting, a monastery, adds to the irony because of the gross inappropriateness of the speaker's sentiments and attitudes in a supposedly holy place.

Situation and setting may be treated in various ways in a text, ranging from silence to the barest hints of description to full photographic detail. Often it is relatively easy to identify the situation at the beginning of a poem, but the implications of setting, and what happens as the poem unfolds, may be subtler. Poets often rely on readers to fill in the gaps in what is mentioned, drawing on their knowledge of circumstances and familiar experiences in the present or in the past. The poem may specify only a few aspects of a *kind* of setting, such as a motel room in the afternoon.

Frequently a poem's setting draws on common notions of a particular time or place. Setting a poem in a garden, for example, or writing about apples almost inevitably reminds many readers of the Garden of Eden because it is an important and widely recognized part of the Western heritage of belief and knowledge. Even people who don't read at all or who lack Judeo-Christian religious commitments are likely to know about Eden, and poets writing in Western cultures can count on that knowledge. A reference to something outside the poem that carries a history of meaning and strong emotional associations is called an **allusion**. For example, gardens may carry suggestions of innocence and order, or temptation and the Fall, or both, depending on how the poem handles the allusion.

Specific, well-known places from history or myth may similarly be associated with particular ideas or values or ways of life. The titles of many poems refer directly to specific places or times. Or the poem itself may indicate a well-known place such as Paris, or a historic event or period such as D-Day or the Great Depression. Indeed, while much of the poetry in this anthology expresses personal feelings, and while some of it is tied to the poet's autobiographical circumstances, a great deal of poetry written over the centuries has focused not on individuals but on political or historical topics and themes. The "setting" of epic poetry may be as broad as a nation or even the cosmos. Poems have been written to instruct readers about religion, science, philosophy, and the art of poetry, among many other themes, with an appropriate range of settings and situations. The poet may wish to influence readers' sympathies or loyalties toward different sides in a conflict, or to record and honor a specific event such as an inauguration. A poem written about or for a specific occasion is called an *occasional poem*, and such a poem is *referential*; that is, it *refers* to a certain historical time or event.

Sometimes it is hard to place ourselves fully in another time or place in order to imagine sympathetically what a particular historical moment would have been like, and even the best poetic efforts, by themselves, do not necessarily transport us there. For such poems we need, at the least, specific historical information—plus a willingness to be transported by a name, a date, or a dramatic situation.

SITUATIONS: CARING FOR CHILDREN

RITA DOVE

Daystar

She wanted a little room for thinking:
but she saw diapers steaming on the line,
a doll slumped behind the door.
So she lugged a chair behind the garage
5 to sit out the children's naps.

Sometimes there were things to watch—
the pinched armor of a vanished cricket,
a floating maple leaf. Other days
she stared until she was assured
10 when she closed her eyes
she'd see only her own vivid blood.

She had an hour, at best, before Liza appeared
pouting from the top of the stairs.
And just *what* was mother doing
15 out back with the field mice? Why,
building a palace. Later
that night when Thomas rolled over and
lurched into her, she would open her eyes
and think of the place that was hers
20 for an hour—where
she was nothing,
pure nothing, in the middle of the day.

1986

LINDA PASTAN

To a Daughter Leaving Home

When I taught you
at eight to ride
a bicycle, loping along
beside you
5 as you wobbled away
on two round wheels,
my own mouth rounding
in surprise when you pulled
ahead down the curved
10 path of the park,
I kept waiting
for the thud
of your crash as I
sprinted to catch up,
15 while you grew
smaller, more breakable
with distance,
pumping, pumping
for your life, screaming
20 with laughter,
the hair flapping
behind you like a
handkerchief waving
goodbye.

1988

Both of these poems involve motherhood, but they take entirely different stances about it and have very different tones. The mother in Dove's
"Daystar," overwhelmed by the demands of young children, needs a room
of her own. All she can manage, however, is a brief hour of respite. The situation is virtually the whole story here. Nothing really happens except that
daily events (washing diapers, picking up toys, looking at crickets and
leaves, explaining the world to children, having sex) surround her brief private hour and make it precious. Being "nothing" (lines 21 and 22) takes on
great value in these circumstances, and the poem makes much of the setting: an isolated chair behind the garage. Setting in poems often means
something much more specific about a particular culture or social history,
but here time and place get their value from the circumstances of the situation for one frazzled mother.

The particulars of time and place in Pastan's "To a Daughter Leaving Home" are even less specific; the incident the poem describes happened a long time ago, and its vividness is a function of memory. The speaker here thinks back nostalgically to a moment when her daughter made an earlier (but briefer) departure. Though we learn very little about the speaker, at least directly, we may infer quite a bit about her—her affection for her daughter, the kind of mother she has been, her anxiety at the new departure that seems to reflect the earlier wobbly ride into the distance. The daughter is now, the poem implies, old enough to "leave" home in a full sense, but we do not know the specific reason or what the present circumstances are. Only the title tells us the situation, and (like "Daystar") the poem is all situation.

SETTINGS: HISTORICAL CONTEXTS

JOHN MILTON

On the Late Massacre in Piedmont

Avenge, O Lord, thy slaughtered saints, whose bones
  Lie scattered on the Alpine mountains cold;
  Even them who kept thy truth so pure of old
  When all our fathers worshiped stocks and stones,[1]
5 Forget not: in thy book record their groans
  Who were thy sheep and in their ancient fold
  Slain by the bloody Piemontese that rolled
  Mother with infant down the rocks. Their moans
  The vales redoubled to the hills, and they
10 To heaven. Their martyred blood and ashes sow
  O'er all th' Italian fields, where still doth sway
  The triple tyrant:[2] that from these may grow
  A hundredfold, who having learnt thy way
  Early may fly the Babylonian woe.[3]

1655

---

1. Idols of wood and stone.   2. The pope's tiara featured three crowns.
3. In Milton's day, Protestants often likened the Roman Church to Babylonian decadence, calling the church "the whore of Babylon," and they read Revelation 17 and 18 as an allegory of its coming destruction.

MATTHEW ARNOLD

Dover Beach[4]

The sea is calm tonight.
The tide is full, the moon lies fair
Upon the straits; on the French coast the light
Gleams and is gone; the cliffs of England stand,
5 Glimmering and vast, out in the tranquil bay.
Come to the window, sweet is the night-air!
Only, from the long line of spray
Where the sea meets the moon-blanched land,
Listen! you hear the grating roar
10 Of pebbles which the waves draw back, and fling,
At their return, up the high strand,
Begin, and cease, and then again begin,
With tremulous cadence slow, and bring
The eternal note of sadness in.

15 Sophocles long ago
Heard it on the Aegean, and it brought
Into his mind the turbid ebb and flow
Of human misery;[5] we
Find also in the sound a thought,
20 Hearing it by this distant northern sea.

The Sea of Faith
Was once, too, at the full, and round earth's shore
Lay like the folds of a bright girdle furled.
But now I only hear
25 Its melancholy, long, withdrawing roar,
Retreating, to the breath
Of the night-wind, down the vast edges drear
And naked shingles[6] of the world.

Ah, love, let us be true
30 To one another! for the world, which seems
To lie before us like a land of dreams,
So various, so beautiful, so new,
Hath really neither joy, nor love, nor light,

---

4. At the narrowest point on the English Channel. The light on the French coast (lines 3–4) would be about twenty miles away.
5. In Sophocles' *Antigone*, lines 637–46, the chorus compares the fate of the house of Oedipus to the waves of the sea. 6. Pebble-strewn beaches.

Nor certitude, nor peace, nor help for pain;
35 And we are here as on a darkling plain
Swept with confused alarms of struggle and flight,
Where ignorant armies clash by night.

ca. 1851

JOHN BETJEMAN

In Westminster Abbey[7]

Let me take this other glove off
  As the *vox humana*[8] swells,
And the beauteous fields of Eden
  Bask beneath the Abbey bells.
5 Here, where England's statesmen lie,
Listen to a lady's cry.

Gracious Lord, oh bomb the Germans.
  Spare their women for Thy Sake,
And if that is not too easy
10   We will pardon Thy Mistake.
But, gracious Lord, whate'er shall be,
Don't let anyone bomb me.

Keep our Empire undismembered
  Guide our Forces by Thy Hand,
15 Gallant blacks from far Jamaica,
    Honduras and Togoland;
Protect them Lord in all their fights,
And, even more, protect the whites.

Think of what our Nation stands for,
20   Books from Boots[9] and country lanes,
Free speech, free passes, class distinction,
    Democracy and proper drains.
Lord, put beneath Thy special care
One-eighty-nine Cadogan Square.[1]

25 Although dear Lord I am a sinner,
    I have done no major crime;

7. Gothic church in London in which English monarchs are crowned and many famous
Englishmen are buried (see lines 5, 39–40).   8. Organ tones that resemble the human voice.
9. A chain of British pharmacies.
1. Presumably where the speaker lives, in a fashionable section of central London.

Now I'll come to Evening Service
Whensoever I have the time.
So, Lord, reserve for me a crown,[2]
30 And do not let my shares go down.

I will labor for Thy Kingdom,
Help our lads to win the war,
Send white feathers to the cowards[3]
Join the Women's Army Corps,[4]
35 Then wash the Steps around Thy Throne
In the Eternal Safety Zone.

Now I feel a little better,
What a treat to hear Thy Word
Where the bones of leading statesmen,
40 Have so often been interred.
And now, dear Lord, I cannot wait
Because I have a luncheon date.

1940

These three poems, with their distinctive meter and rhyme and varied tones, would be difficult to interpret without reference to specific English perspectives on European traditions, to specific events such as war, and to specific places such as Dover (where many British travelers embarked for tours of the European continent) and Westminster Abbey (the church near the Houses of Parliament in London where many famous Englishmen, including writers as well as leaders, are buried). The poems were written at different times—1655, 1851, and 1940—but each reflects the latest news and outlook at the time of writing. Milton's speaker is scarcely identified, and the sonnet resembles a public prayer addressed to God on current religious and political conflicts. Arnold's speaker closely resembles the poet himself, and eventually addresses a companion in a room overlooking the sea at Dover, contemplating the history of the West since Sophocles. Betjeman, in contrast, creates an ironic or unreliable speaker who is, unlike the poet, an upper-class woman praying for special favors in the abbey during World War II.

What does the reader need to know in order to understand the situations and settings in these poems? Milton's occasional poem requires the

2. Coin worth five shillings (but also an afterlife reward).
3. White feathers were sometimes given or sent to men not in uniform to suggest that they were cowards and should join the armed forces.
4. The speaker uses the old World War I name (Women's Army Auxiliary Corps) of the Auxiliary Territorial Service, an organization that performed domestic (and some foreign) defense duties.

most explanation, largely because it is the most historically removed from what is familiar to readers today. (Imagine a poem written about the Hurricane Katrina disaster when the evacuation of New Orleans was still in the news; few details would need to be explained for contemporary readers.) Milton wrote the poem when the news reached England that many of the Waldensians, a heretical sect living in southern France and northern Italy (the Piedmont), had been massacred. Until 1655, they had been allowed freedom of worship, but when their legal protection was withdrawn, local Catholics attacked them. Milton's readers would have perceived parallels between events in the Piedmont and current English politics. "Saints" was the term then regularly used by English Protestants of the Puritan stamp to describe all individual Christian believers, in contrast with the few saints worshipped by Catholics. Milton was warning his fellow Puritans that, if the Stuart monarchy were reestablished, what had just happened to the Waldensians could happen to them as well. The heir to the English throne, who would be crowned as Charles II in 1660, was suspected of being a Catholic—anathema to the Protestant English. Indeed, following the Restoration in 1660, tight restrictions were placed on the Puritan "sects" under the new British monarchy. In lines 12 and 14, the poem alludes to dangers of religious rule by dominant groups by invoking standard images of Catholic power and persecution.

The situation and setting of "Dover Beach" are more concrete and specific. It is night by the seashore, and the speaker is gazing at the view from a room with someone he invites to "come to the window" (line 6) and "listen" (line 9); later he says to this person, "Ah, love, let us be true / To one another!" (lines 29–30). Most readers have assumed that the speaker and his companion are about to travel from Dover across the sea to France and that the situation is a honeymoon, or at least that the couple is young and married; after all the "world . . . seems to lie before us . . . so new" (lines 30–32). Although this poem is not a prayer, it is a kind of plea for hope despite the modern loss of faith. The tide is now full, but the poet hears a destructive repetition of rising and falling waves (the pebbles will be worn down eventually), and he dwells on the "withdrawing" side of this pattern. For centuries, Christian belief ("the Sea of Faith") was at high tide, beholding the world as a glorious whole, but both the ancient Greeks and the Victorians took a longer view of the recurring calamities of history. England had been at war with France throughout most of the eighteenth century and until 1815; a wave of European revolutions (as recently as 1848 in France), as well as colonial conflicts, made the shore of England feel vulnerable enough. In 1854, England was to embroil itself in the disastrous Crimean War. As an island, England had some protection; as an imperial power, it depended on its navy and was coming close to ruling the majority of the world's territories. Yet the sea and its rocky shore suggest both time that extends beyond empires and the exposed fossil evidence of deep time before human history.

The speaker, at this threshold, is moved to cling to love as the only refuge from a nightmarish vision of the history of the world.

Instead of a melancholy ode, "In Westminster Abbey" is a mocking satire of British imperialism during World War II (with allusions to World War I), spoken in the voice of a patriotic, snobbish, self-centered woman; of these three historical poems, its time and place are the most specific. The supposed prayer is uttered during a morning service amid the tombs of great statesmen, before the speaker hurries off to lunch. Her wishes are racist and chauvinistic, imagining a deity that takes her side in the war against the Germans and will prevent the speaker's own house (she gives the exact address) from being bombed, as many buildings in London were during the Blitz. The repeated references to the setting emphasize the political target of the satire: the nationalism and narrow materialism of the official state religion of Britain, in which statesmen are worshiped like saints and the worshipers ask for a good return on their investments.

SITUATION AND SETTING: PREPARING A RESPONSE PAPER

The title of the following poem suggests that place may be important, and it is, although you may be surprised to discover exactly what exists at this address and what uses the speaker makes of it. What happens in "Cherrylog Road" is fairly easy to sort out, but its effect is more complex than the simple story suggests, largely because of the wealth of details the poem provides about setting. First, read the poem through once, pausing only when you come to a period and allowing your immediate personal impressions to form on their own. Then, reread the poem, following the steps provided for analyzing and taking notes on specific elements, which will help you understand—and write about—the centrality of its setting.

JAMES DICKEY

Cherrylog Road

Off Highway 106
At Cherrylog Road I entered
The '34 Ford without wheels,
Smothered in kudzu,
5   With a seat pulled out to run
Corn whiskey down from the hills,

And then from the other side
Crept into an Essex
With a rumble seat of red leather

10 And then out again, aboard
   A blue Chevrolet, releasing
   The rust from its other color,

   Reared up on three building blocks.
   None had the same body heat;
15 I changed with them inward, toward
   The weedy heart of the junkyard,
   For I knew that Doris Holbrook
   Would escape from her father at noon

   And would come from the farm
20 To seek parts owned by the sun
   Among the abandoned chassis,
   Sitting in each in turn
   As I did, leaning forward
   As in a wild stock-car race

25 In the parking lot of the dead.
   Time after time, I climbed in
   And out the other side, like
   An envoy or movie star
   Met at the station by crickets.
30 A radiator cap raised its head,

   Become a real toad or a kingsnake
   As I neared the hub of the yard,
   Passing through many states,
   Many lives, to reach
35 Some grandmother's long Pierce-Arrow
   Sending platters of blindness forth

   From its nickel hubcaps
   And spilling its tender upholstery
   On sleepy roaches,
40 The glass panel in between
   Lady and colored driver
   Not all the way broken out,

   The back-seat phone
   Still on its hook.
45 I got in as though to exclaim,
   "Let us go to the orphan asylum,
   John; I have some old toys
   For children who say their prayers."

   I popped with sweat as I thought
50 I heard Doris Holbrook scrape
   Like a mouse in the southern-state sun

That was eating the paint in blisters
From a hundred car tops and hoods.
She was tapping like code,

55　Loosening the screws,
Carrying off headlights,
Sparkplugs, bumpers,
Cracked mirrors and gear-knobs,
Getting ready, already,
60　To go back with something to show

Other than her lips' new trembling
I would hold to me soon, soon,
Where I sat in the ripped back seat
Talking over the interphone,
65　Praying for Doris Holbrook
To come from her father's farm

And to get back there
With no trace of me on her face
To be seen by her red-haired father
70　Who would change, in the squalling barn,
Her back's pale skin with a strop,
Then lay for me

In a bootlegger's roasting car
With a string-triggered 12-gauge shotgun
75　To blast the breath from the air.
Not cut by the jagged windshields,
Through the acres of wrecks she came
With a wrench in her hand,

Through dust where the blacksnake dies
80　Of boredom, and the beetle knows
The compost has no more life.
Someone outside would have seen
The oldest car's door inexplicably
Close from within:

85　I held her and held her and held her,
Convoyed at terrific speed
By the stalled, dreaming traffic around us,
So the blacksnake, stiff
With inaction, curved back
90　Into life, and hunted the mouse

With deadly overexcitement,
The beetles reclaimed their field
As we clung, glued together,

With the hooks of the seat springs
95 Working through to catch us red-handed
Amidst the gray breathless batting

That burst from the seat at our backs.
We left by separate doors
Into the changed, other bodies
100 Of cars, she down Cherrylog Road
And I to my motorcycle
Parked like the soul of the junkyard

Restored, a bicycle fleshed
With power, and tore off
105 Up Highway 106, continually
Drunk on the wind in my mouth,
Wringing the handlebar for speed,
Wild to be wreckage forever.

                                          1964

Now consider your response to Dickey's poem.

1. First, answer the basic questions at the beginning of this chapter:
   Who is speaking? To whom is the speaker speaking? Is there an
   auditor in the poem, or simply an audience outside of it? Is anyone
   else present or referred to in the poem?

2. Underline or list the words or lines in which setting is first indicated.

3. Underline (perhaps in a different color) or list the words or lines
   that gave you your first impression of the situation. What do you
   notice about the connection between setting and situation? Could
   the action occur in a different place or kind of place?

4. Similarly, list the proper or improper nouns that fill in your sense of
   the setting. Sort these into different kinds of entities: plants, animals, machines, real or imaginary people. Consider and compare
   the items you list under each category. How do they contribute to
   the specific spatial setting and temporal setting of the poem? How
   do they contribute to the situation of the poem?

5. Make a similar inventory of the verbs in the poem in order to understand the action step by step. Which actions are real? Which are
   remembered? Which are repeated? Which are imagined?

6. As your inventories show, the poem relies on personification (attributing human qualities to natural or inanimate things). Find lines
   in which insects, reptiles, or mammals interact with the parts of
   cars, either helping destroy them or making them come back to life.
   Find lines in which creatures and humans are compared.

7. Now that you have comprehended the details of the poem, try to summarize each stanza in a phrase and to place it in time and place, whether within the scene or within the twentieth century in the United States. What is the significance of "Time after time" (line 26)? Of "Passing through many states, / Many lives" (lines 33–34)? Of "the southern-state sun" (line 51)? What is implied about the region and the time period in two references to illegal alcohol: "run / Corn whiskey down from the hills" (lines 5–6) and "a bootlegger's roasting car" (line 73)? What is implied about local social rules in the scenario of the "Lady and colored driver" with her plans to donate toys to orphans (lines 40–48)? Or in the idea of the menacing father who would whip his daughter in the barn and gun down her seducer (lines 65–75)?

8. Review the action of the poem and your answers in number 1 above. Why does the speaker arrive at the junkyard first and explore the cars before Doris Holbrook arrives? Why does the poem begin with the names of two roads in the first two lines and end with Doris departing "down Cherrylog Road" in the next-to-last stanza, followed by the speaker speeding on his motorcycle "up Highway 106" in the final stanza (lines 100, 105)? What does the last line suggest not only about the speaker's desire but also about the temporal and spatial setting?

9. Did the sexual experience happen once, a few times, or many times? Is the memory of the encounter recent? Is the speaker still a young boy? Find specific evidence in the poem for your answers to these questions.

10. What is the significance of the title "Cherrylog Road"? (There is a real Cherrylog Road in North Georgia, but no Highway 106 near it.)

Based on your answers and discoveries, write a short response paper on "Cherrylog Road" in which you argue that the poem's specific, richly detailed setting is essential to its situation, theme, and tone, finding your own way to express the theme and tone. Support your claim by showing that James Dickey uses personification to bring to life a particular setting, a car junkyard in the heat of a southern summer, as a metaphor for the situation—the reckless, instinctive, and fleeting lovemaking of teenagers.

TWO CARPE DIEM POEMS

The following two poems from the 1600s could be said to represent a similar situation to that in "Cherrylog Road": The male speaker desires a woman who also appears in the scene represented in the poem. As in Dickey's poem, their possible sexual acts and the delay or foreplay are described figuratively in relation to natural or other objects—in Donne's poem through the symbol of the flea that has bitten both lovers, and in Marvell's poem through the series of metaphors of the history of the world and cosmos, birds of prey, and a ball bombarding iron gates. The poems belong to the tradition of **carpe diem** (Latin for *seize the day*) because the speaker is urging his auditor, his lover, to enjoy pleasures now, before they die. The woman is resisting because of her concern for chastity ("That long preserved virginity" in Marvell's poem, line 28) or social rules ("parents grudge" in Donne's poem, line 14). The most significant differences from "Cherrylog Road" emerge from the situation (the speaker is directly appealing to the woman, who has not yet agreed to have sex) and from the setting (we learn little about the place, time of day, weather, or other details of the scene in either poem). The action of these poems is implied in the shifts in what the speaker is saying. What does the woman do in "The Flea"? Can you imagine the woman's response in "To His Coy Mistress"? How do the images in the poems create a sense of time and space?

JOHN DONNE

The Flea

Mark but this flea, and mark in this[5]
How little that which thou deny'st me is;
It sucked me first, and now sucks thee,
And in this flea our two bloods mingled be;
5   Thou know'st that this cannot be said
A sin, nor shame, nor loss of maidenhead.
    Yet this enjoys before it woo,
        And pampered[6] swells with one blood made of two,
    And this, alas, is more than we would do.[7]

10 Oh stay,[8] three lives in one flea spare,
Where we almost, yea more than, married are.
This flea is you and I, and this
Our marriage bed, and marriage temple is;
Though parents grudge, and you, we're met
15 And cloistered in these living walls of jet.
    Though use[9] make you apt to kill me,
        Let not to that, self-murder added be,
        And sacrilege, three sins in killing three.

Cruel and sudden, hast thou since
20 Purpled thy nail in blood of innocence?

---

5. Medieval preachers and rhetoricians asked their hearers to "mark" (look at) an object that illustrated a moral or philosophical lesson they wished to emphasize.   6. Fed luxuriously.
7. According to the medical theory of Donne's era, conception involved the literal mingling of the lovers' blood.   8. Desist.   9. Habit.

Wherein could this flea guilty be,
Except in that drop which it sucked from thee?
Yet thou triumph'st, and say'st that thou
Find'st not thyself, nor me, the weaker now;
25   'Tis true; then learn how false, fears be;
Just so much honor, when thou yield'st to me,
Will waste, as this flea's death took life from thee.

                                                    1633

- Is the setting of the encounter between the speaker and the
  woman described or hinted at? What lines help you imagine
  where they are and what the woman does or says?

ANDREW MARVELL

To His Coy Mistress

Had we but world enough, and time,
This coyness,[1] lady, were no crime.
We would sit down, and think which way
To walk, and pass our long love's day.
5 Thou by the Indian Ganges' side
Shouldst rubies[2] find: I by the tide
Of Humber would complain.[3] I would
Love you ten years before the Flood,
And you should if you please refuse
10 Till the conversion of the Jews.[4]
My vegetable love[5] should grow
Vaster than empires, and more slow;
An hundred years should go to praise
Thine eyes, and on thy forehead gaze;
15 Two hundred to adore each breast,
But thirty thousand to the rest.
An age at least to every part,
And the last age should show your heart.
For, lady, you deserve this state;[6]

---

1. Hesitancy, modesty (not necessarily suggesting calculation).
2. Talismans that are supposed to preserve virginity.
3. Write love complaints, conventional songs lamenting the cruelty of love. *Humber*: a river and estuary in Marvell's hometown of Hull.
4. Which, according to popular Christian belief, will occur just before the end of the world.
5. Which is capable only of passive growth, not of consciousness. The "vegetable soul" is lower than the other two divisions of the soul, "animal" and "rational."   6. Dignity.

20 Nor would I love at lower rate.
      But at my back I always hear
  Time's wingèd chariot hurrying near;
  And yonder all before us lie
  Deserts of vast eternity.
25 Thy beauty shall no more be found,
  Nor, in thy marble vault, shall sound
  My echoing song; then worms shall try
  That long preserved virginity,
  And your quaint honor turn to dust,
30 And into ashes all my lust:
  The grave's a fine and private place,
  But none, I think, do there embrace.
      Now therefore, while the youthful hue
  Sits on thy skin like morning dew,[7]
35 And while thy willing soul transpires[8]
  At every pore with instant fires,
  Now let us sport us while we may,
  And now, like am'rous birds of prey,
  Rather at once our time devour
40 Than languish in his slow-chapped[9] pow'r.
  Let us roll all our strength and all
  Our sweetness up into one ball,
  And tear our pleasures with rough strife
  Thorough[1] the iron gates of life.
45 Thus, though we cannot make our sun
  Stand still,[2] yet we will make him run.[3]

                                        1681

- Whom is the speaker trying to persuade in this poem? Is his
  argument persuasive?

POEMS OF VARIED SITUATIONS AND SETTINGS

Consider the *Who? What? Why? Where?* and *When?* questions as you read the
following poems.

---

7. The text reads "glew." "Lew" (warmth) has also been suggested as an emendation.
8. Breathes forth.
9. Slow-jawed. Chronos (Time), ruler of the world in early Greek myth, devoured all of his children
except Zeus, who was hidden. Later, Zeus seized power (see line 46 and note).   1. Through.
2. To lengthen his night of love with Alcmene, Zeus made the sun stand still.
3. Each sex act was believed to shorten life by one day.

EMILY BRONTË

The Night-Wind

In summer's mellow midnight,
A cloudless moon shone through
Our open parlor window
And rosetrees wet with dew.

5 I sat in silent musing,
The soft wind waved my hair:
It told me Heaven was glorious,
And sleeping Earth was fair.

I needed not its breathing
10 To bring such thoughts to me,
But still it whispered lowly,
"How dark the woods will be!

"The thick leaves in my murmur
Are rustling like a dream,
15 And all their myriad voices
Instinct[4] with spirit seem."

I said, "Go, gentle singer,
Thy wooing voice is kind,
But do not think its music
20 Has power to reach my mind.

"Play with the scented flower,
The young tree's supple bough,
And leave my human feelings
In their own course to flow."

25 The wanderer would not leave me;
Its kiss grew warmer still—
"O come," it sighed so sweetly,
"I'll win thee 'gainst thy will.

"Have we not been from childhood friends?
30 Have I not loved thee long?
As long as thou hast loved the night
Whose silence wakes my song.

"And when thy heart is laid at rest
Beneath the church-yard stone

---

4. Infused.

35 I shall have time enough to mourn
And thou to be alone."

September 11, 1840

- What might it mean that the speaker feels tempted by the
  wind to go wandering in the darkness? What might she find
  there?

SYLVIA PLATH

Point Shirley

From Water-Tower Hill to the brick prison
The shingle booms, bickering under
The sea's collapse.
Snowcakes break and welter. This year
5 The gritted wave leaps
The seawall and drops onto a bier
Of quahog chips,[5]
Leaving a salty mash of ice to whiten

In my grandmother's sand yard. She is dead,
10 Whose laundry snapped and froze here, who
Kept house against
What the sluttish, rutted sea could do.
Squall waves once danced
Ship timbers in through the cellar window;
15 A thresh-tailed, lanced
Shark littered in the geranium bed—

Such collusion of mulish elements
She wore her broom straws to the nub.
Twenty years out
20 Of her hand; the house still hugs in each drab
Stucco socket
The purple egg-stones: from Great Head's knob
To the filled-in Gut
The sea in its cold gizzard ground those rounds.

25 Nobody wintering now behind
The planked-up windows where she set
Her wheat loaves

---

5. Chips from quahog clamshells, common on the New England coast.

And apple cakes to cool. What is it
Survives, grieves
30 So, over this battered, obstinate spit
Of gravel? The waves'
Spewed relics clicker masses in the wind,

Gray waves the stub-necked eiders ride.
A labor of love, and that labor lost.
35 Steadily the sea
Eats at Point Shirley. She died blessed,
And I come by
Bones, bones only, pawed and tossed,
A dog-faced sea.
40 The sun sinks under Boston, bloody red.

I would get from these dry-papped stones
The milk your love instilled in them.
The black ducks dive.
And though your graciousness might stream,
45 And I contrive,
Grandmother, stones are nothing of home
To that spumiest dove.
Against both bar and tower the black sea runs.

1960

- How important is the specific setting of Point Shirley near
  Boston? How are memories mixed with the specific "now" of
  the poem?

JOSHUA CLOVER

The Nevada Glassworks

Ka-Boom! They're making glass in Nevada![6]
Figure August, 1953,
mom's 13, it's hot as a simile.
Ker-Pow! Transmutation in Nevada!
5 Imagine mom: pre-PostModern new teen,
innocent for Elvis, ditto "Korean
conflict," John Paul George Ringo[7] Viet Nam.
Mom's 1 state west of the glassworks, she's

6. Sand fused into glass in the intense heat of the atomic bombs tested in Nevada in the 1950s.
7. The four Beatles, whose musical career would help define the 1960s.

in a tree / K*I*S*S*I*N*G,
10 lurid cartoon-colored kisses. Ka-Blam!
They're blowing peacock-tinted New World glass
in southern Nevada, the alchemists
& architects of mom's duck-&-cover[8]
adolescence, they're making Las Vegas
15 turn to gold—real neon gold—in the blast
furnace heat that reaches clear to Clover
Ranch in dry Central Valley: O the dust—
It is the Golden State! O the landscape—
dreaming of James Dean! O mom in a tree
20 close-range kissing as in Nevada just
now they're making crazy ground-zero shapes
of radiant see-through geography.
What timing! What kisses! What a fever
this day's become, humming hundred degree
25 California afternoon that she's
sure she could never duplicate, never,
she feels transparent, gone—isn't this heat
suffocating?—no, she forgot to breathe
for a flash while in the Nevada flats
30 factory glassblowers exhale . . . exhale . . .
a philosopher's stone,[9] a crystal ball,
a spectacular machine. Hooray! Hats
off—they're making a window in the sand!
Mom's in the tree—picture this—all alone!
35 Unforgettable kisses, comic book
mnemonic kisses, O something's coming
out of the ranch road heat mirage. That drone—
an engine? Mom quits practice & looks
east, cups an ear to the beloved humming,
40 the hazy gold dust kicked wildly west
ahead of something almost . . . in . . . sight. Vroom!
It's the Future, hot like nothing else, dressed
as a sonic-boom Cadillac. O mom!
This land is your land / This land Amnesia—
45 they're dropping some new science out there,
a picture-perfect hole blown clear to Asia:
everything in the desert—Shazam!—turns

---

8. During the Cold War era, American school children were trained to "duck and cover" in case of nuclear attack.

9. Legendary substance long sought by alchemists, who believed it would transmute base metals to gold and confer immortal life.

to glass, gold glass, a picture-window where
the bomb-dead kids are burned & burn & burn
1997

- In what line do you discover that the speaker is not himself a
  boy in 1953, but is writing from his mother's teenage perspective? What words especially convey the place and time
  period?

DEREK WALCOTT

Midsummer

Certain things here [1] are quietly American—
that chain-link fence dividing the absent roars
of the beach from the empty ball park, its holes
muttering the word umpire instead of empire;
5   the gray, metal light where an early pelican
coasts, with its engine off, over the pink fire
of a sea whose surface is as cold as Maine's.
The light warms up the sides of white, eager Cessnas [2]
parked at the airstrip under the freckling hills
10 of St. Thomas. The sheds, the brown, functional hangar,
are like those of the Occupation in the last war.
The night left a rank smell under the casuarinas,
the villas have fenced-off beaches where the natives walk,
illegal immigrants from unlucky islands
15 who envy the smallest polyp its right to work.
Here the wetback crab and the mollusc are citizens,
and the leaves have green cards. Bulldozers jerk
and gouge out a hill, but we all know that the dust
is industrial and must be suffered. Soon—
20 the sea's corrugations are sheets of zinc
soldered by the sun's steady acetylene. This
drizzle that falls now is American rain,
stitching stars in the sand. My own corpuscles
are changing as fast. I fear what the migrant envies:
25 the starry pattern they make—the flag on the post office—
the quality of the dirt, the fealty changing under my foot.
1984

---

1. Trinidad.   2. Small airplanes.

- What is "American" (line 22) about the images described in this poem? Why does the speaker say he fears "the starry pattern" made by the raindrops in the sand (line 25)?

SETTINGS: IN THE MORNING

The setting of the following poems is clearly temporal as well as spatial. All four of these poems identify the early time of day in their titles. August Kleinzahler's "Aubade on East 12th Street" may at first appear not to state its topic, "morning," in the title, but an **aubade** is a morning song or poem (from the French term for dawn). Although morning suggests fresh beginnings and hope, an aubade often expresses sadness because the new day means that two lovers must part—time has moved on. Do you detect a sad or a hopeful tone in each of these poems? Some of the poems refer to times of day metaphorically or more abstractly. Do the poems help you visualize a particular day? How do some of these poems use space, such as the idea of the earth and the sun? How does the specific place in some of these poems, such as a city or the writer's home, affect the speaker's response to the time of day? What references to darkness or light, to sleep or waking, or to other times of day do you notice in these poems?

WILLIAM SHAKESPEARE

[*Full many a glorious morning have I seen*]

Full many a glorious morning have I seen
Flatter the mountain-tops with sovereign eye,
Kissing with golden face the meadows green,
Gilding pale streams with heavenly alchymy;
5 Anon permit the basest clouds to ride
With ugly rack[3] on his celestial face,
And from the forlorn world his visage hide,
Stealing unseen to west with this disgrace:
Even so my sun one early morn did shine,
10 With all-triumphant splendor on my brow;
But, out! alack! he was but one hour mine,
The region cloud hath mask'd him from me now.
　　Yet him for this my love no whit disdaineth;
　　Suns of the world may stain when heaven's sun staineth.

1609

3. Moss.

• What words and phrases mark the shifts of the clouds back and forth across the face of the sun in "Full many a glorious morning"? What distinction is Shakespeare making between "suns of the world" and "heaven's sun"?

JOHN DONNE

The Good-Morrow

I wonder, by my troth, what thou and I
    Did, till we loved? were we not weaned till then?
But sucked on country pleasures, childishly?
    Or snorted we in the Seven Sleepers' den?[4]
5 'Twas so; but[5] this, all pleasures fancies be.
    If ever any beauty I did see,
Which I desired, and got,[6] twas but a dream of thee.

And now good-morrow to our waking souls,
    Which watch not one another out of fear;
10 For love, all love of other sights controls,
    And makes one little room an everywhere.
Let sea-discoverers to new worlds have gone,
Let maps to other,[7] worlds on worlds have shown,
Let us possess one world, each hath one, and is one.

15 My face in thine eye, thine in mine appears,[8]
    And true plain hearts do in the faces rest;
Where can we find two better hemispheres,
    Without sharp north, without declining west?
Whatever dies was not mixed equally,[9]
20 If our two loves be one, or, thou and I
Love so alike that none do slacken, none can die.

1633

• Like so many of Donne's poems, this one attempts to persuade. What is the situation of this poem? What does the speaker wish to demonstrate?

---

4. According to legend, seven Christian youths escaped Roman persecution by sleeping in a cave for 187 years. *Snorted*: snored.   5. Except for.   6. Sexually possessed.   7. Other people.
8. That is, each is reflected in the other's eyes.
9. Perfectly mixed elements, according to scholastic philosophy, were stable and immortal.

SYLVIA PLATH

Morning Song

Love set you going like a fat gold watch.
The midwife slapped your footsoles, and your bald cry
Took its place among the elements.

Our voices echo, magnifying your arrival. New statue.
5   In a drafty museum, your nakedness
Shadows our safety. We stand round blankly as walls.

I'm no more your mother
Than the cloud that distils a mirror to reflect its own slow
Effacement at the wind's hand.

10   All night your moth-breath
Flickers among the flat pink roses. I wake to listen:
A far sea moves in my ear.

One cry, and I stumble from bed, cow-heavy and floral
In my Victorian nightgown.
15   Your mouth opens clean as a cat's. The window square

Whitens and swallows its dull stars. And now you try
Your handful of notes;
The clear vowels rise like balloons.

                                                                        1961

• How does this poem's language emphasize the distinctions
  between the speaker and her baby? How does the poem's setting in time—morning—affect its meaning?

BILLY COLLINS

Morning

Why do we bother with the rest of the day,
the swale of the afternoon,
the sudden dip into evening,

then night with his notorious perfumes,
5   his many-pointed stars?

This is the best—
throwing off the light covers,

feet on the cold floor,
and buzzing around the house on espresso—

10 maybe a splash of water on the face,
a palmful of vitamins—
but mostly buzzing around the house on espresso,

dictionary and atlas open on the rug,
the typewriter waiting for the key of the head,
15 a cello on the radio,

and, if necessary, the windows—
trees fifty, a hundred years old
out there,
heavy clouds on the way
20 and the lawn steaming like a horse
in the early morning.

1998

- What words and phrases help color the reader's perceptions of the various times of day mentioned in this poem? Why is morning "the best" (line 6)?

SUGGESTIONS FOR WRITING

1. Matthew Arnold's "Dover Beach" is a meditation on history and human destiny derived from the poet's close observation of the ebb and flow of the sea. Write an essay in which you examine the poem's descriptive language and the way it creates a suitable setting for Arnold's philosophical musings.

2. Certain seventeenth-century poets, such as John Donne and Andrew Marvell, have been called "metaphysical poets" for their ingenuity in using apparently far-fetched analogies to create apt and insightful comparisons, usually intended to persuade. What is the line of reasoning in Donne's "The Flea" or Marvell's "To His Coy Mistress?" Who is the intended audience for each poem? Write an essay in which you discuss the way that either or both of these poems uses situation as the basis for comparison and persuasion.

3. This chapter contains a number of poems that, in both obvious and subtle ways, associate love with the morning—Shakespeare's "[Full many a glorious morning have I seen]," Donne's "The Good-Morrow," Sylvia Plath's "Morning Song," and Billy Collins's "Morning." Write an essay in which you compare and contrast the poetic use of the morning setting in any two of these poems.

4. Choose any of the poems in this or the previous chapters and write an essay about the way a poet can use situation and setting to evoke a rich intermingling of language, subject, and feeling.

Cultural Homelands: An Album

Rosemary Woods, *Africa Collage*

One of the most ancient topics of literature is the quest or journey away from home. Sacred literature, including the Bible, tells of exile and a long period of suffering before returning to or reaching a homeland. Epic poems and romances may concern the hero's wanderings or adventures to reach or to defend a realm that is deeply associated with his birth, inheritance, or fate. Since the 1500s, global exploration, colonialism, slavery, mass migration, and economic transformation have meant that many of the world's populations have experienced dislocation and loss of roots. Those who find themselves displaced try to remember where they came from; they may seek to honor their heritage or yearn for a sense of belonging. The poems in this album were written at different times in different cultural contexts. Each speaker suggests some kind of double vision on the past and present, on a more modern or recent location and the former place. What is the role of dislocation or altered identity in these poems? How do these poems represent the speaker's divided loyalties or distance from home? How do they indicate the passage of time, whether in history, over generations, or within one person's life?

PHILLIS WHEATLEY

On Being Brought from Africa to America

'Twas mercy brought me from my Pagan land,
Taught my benighted soul to understand
That there's a God, that there's a Saviour too:
Once I redemption neither sought nor knew.
5 Some view our sable race with scornful eye,
"Their colour is a diabolic die."
Remember, Christians, Negroes, black as Cain,[1]
May be refin'd, and join th' angelic train.

                                                    1773

- How does this compressed poem appeal to "Christians" (line 7)? If Africa was "Pagan" and "benighted" (lines 1, 2), why are "some" people wrong to see Africans as "diabolic" or dark because of devilish sin (lines 5, 6)?

---

1. One of Adam's sons, who killed his brother Abel. See Genesis 4.

MAYA ANGELOU

Africa

Thus she had lain
sugar cane sweet
deserts her hair
golden her feet
5 mountains her breasts
two Niles her tears
Thus she has lain
Black through the years.

Over the white seas
10 rime white and cold
brigands ungentled
icicle bold
took her young daughters
sold her strong sons
15 churched her with Jesus
bled her with guns.
Thus she has lain.

Now she is rising
remember her pain
20 remember the losses
her screams loud and vain
remember her riches
her history slain
now she is striding
25 although she had lain.

1975

- Why do the phrases describing Africa's action—"had lain," "is rising," and so forth—repeat with variations throughout the poem?

DEREK WALCOTT

A Far Cry from Africa

A wind is ruffling the tawny pelt
Of Africa. Kikuyu,[2] quick as flies,
Batten upon the bloodstreams of the veldt.[3]
Corpses are scattered through a paradise.
5   Only the worm, colonel of carrion, cries:
"Waste no compassion on these separate dead!"
Statistics justify and scholars seize
The salients of colonial policy.
What is that to the white child hacked in bed?
10 To savages, expendable as Jews?

Threshed out by beaters,[4] the long rushes break
In a white dust of ibises whose cries
Have wheeled since civilization's dawn
From the parched river or beast-teeming plain.
15 The violence of beast on beast is read
As natural law, but upright man
Seeks his divinity by inflicting pain.
Delirious as these worried beasts, his wars
Dance to the tightened carcass of a drum,
20 While he calls courage still that native dread
Of the white peace contracted by the dead.

Again brutish necessity wipes its hands
Upon the napkin of a dirty cause, again
A waste of our compassion, as with Spain,[5]
25 The gorilla wrestles with the superman.
I who am poisoned with the blood of both,
Where shall I turn, divided to the vein?
I who have cursed
The drunken officer of British rule, how choose
30 Between this Africa and the English tongue I love?
Betray them both, or give back what they give?

2. An East African tribe whose members, as Mau Mau fighters, conducted an eight-year insurrection against British colonial settlers in Kenya.
3. Open plains, neither cultivated nor thickly forested (Afrikaans).
4. In big-game hunting, natives are hired to beat the brush, driving birds—such as ibises—and other animals into the open.
5. The Spanish Civil War (1936-39), in which the Republican loyalists were supported politically by liberals in the West and militarily by Soviet Communists, and the Nationalist rebels by Nazi Germany and Fascist Italy.

How can I face such slaughter and be cool?
How can I turn from Africa and live?

1962

- How does the speaker express his divided loyalties in the
  questions that conclude the poem? Can be choose a homeland to return to?

Authors on Their Work: DEREK WALCOTT

From "An Interview with Derek Walcott" (1979)*

Q. . . . "A Far Cry from Africa" . . . closes with "How
can I turn from Africa and live?" And yet at another
juncture you speak of the African revival as a kind
of simplification, although a glamorous one, for the
Caribbean writer. Do you want to talk about the
Caribbean writer's special relationship to Africa?

A. . . . I have been British; I have been a citizen of the Caribbean federa-
tion; now I'm supposed to be either a Trinidadian or a St. Lucian but
with a British passport. I find that I am able to make a living in
America (and I owe America a great deal for its recognition and the
fact that I can work here); and there is the same danger, the same
seduction in saying I really am African and should be in Africa, or
that my whole experience is African. This can be simply another
longing, even a slave longing, for another master. There is no West
Indian who is black, or even one who is not black, who is not aware of
the existence of Africa in all of us. I was writing against the African
influence during a period when the political nostalgia seemed to be a
deceit because it meant that if one was lifting up a spade or fork, all
one had to do was to throw it down and turn and look toward Africa
and say, well, I shouldn't be digging up the ground in St. Lucia, or I
shouldn't be doing whatever job I am doing in any one of the islands.
I should really be in some sort of pastoral idealized place where I
won't have to work, or where I may be working for Mother Africa. The
fact is that every West Indian has been severed from a continent, whether
he be Indian, Chinese, Portuguese, or black. To have the population
induced into a mass nostalgia to be somewhere else seemed to me
about as ennobling as wishing that the whole population was in
Brooklyn. . . . What I think was especially irritating to me was the
fact that this idea was continually being dramatized in poems
being offered to the masses—mainly the urban masses—as an

(Continued on next page)

escape. It would be equally abhorrent to me to say "I wish we were English again" as to say "I wish we were African again." The reality is that one has to build in the West Indies. But that is not to say one doesn't know who one is: our music, our speech—all the things that are organic in the way we live—are African.

. . .

I . . . felt that it was a privilege to grow up as an English colonial child [in the West Indies] because politically and culturally the British heritage was supposed to be mine. It was no problem for me to feel that since I was writing in English, I was in tune with the growth of the language. I was the contemporary of anyone writing in English anywhere in the world. What is more important, however—and I'm still working on this—was to find a voice that was not inflected by influences. One didn't develop an English accent in speech; one kept as close as possible to an inflection that was West Indian. The aim was that a West Indian or an Englishman could read a single poem, each with his own accent, without either one feeling that it was written in dialect.

*Edward Hirsch and Derek Walcott, "An Interview with Derek Walcott," *Contemporary Literature* 20.3 (Summer 1979): 279–292.

AGHA SHAHID ALI

Postcard from Kashmir

(for Pavan Sahgal)

Kashmir shrinks into my mailbox,
my home a neat four by six inches.

I always loved neatness. Now I hold
the half-inch Himalayas in my hand.
5 This is home. And this the closest
I'll ever be to home. When I return,
the colors won't be so brilliant,
the Jhelum's waters[6] so clean,
so ultramarine. My love
10 so overexposed.

6. The river Jhelum runs through Kashmir and Pakistan.

> And my memory will be a little
> out of focus, in it
> a giant negative, black
> and white, still undeveloped.

1987

- What words characterize the speaker's dreams of home in this poem? What words reveal a more realistic attitude?

SUGGESTIONS FOR WRITING

1. Look closely at the three stanzas of "A Far Cry from Africa" by Derek Walcott. Be sure to note any changes—rhyme patterns or meter, subject matter or tone—across the three stanzas. Where does the speaker clarify who he is and where his loyalties lie? Why is the last part of the poem a series of questions? Write an essay in which you interpret the form and theme of the poem as itself a kind of "far cry from Africa," in every sense: far from that homeland, part of non-African tradition, "crying" for connection.

2. Imagine receiving in your mailbox a postcard from the place where you or your parents were born. (You may imagine receiving digital pictures or messages in other formats.) Write a poem or a short prose description in which you express a response similar to the speaker's in Agha Shahid Ali's "Postcard from Kashmir": How would the place be changed if you could visit, and how would it differ from the way you or your family think about it now?

10 LANGUAGE

Fiction and drama depend on language just as poetry does, but in a poem almost everything comes down to the particular meanings and implications, as well as sound and shape, of individual words. When we read stories and plays, we generally focus our attention on character and plot, and although words determine how we imagine those characters and how we respond to what happens to them, we are not as likely to pause over any one word as we may need to when reading a poem. Because poems are often short, much depends on every word in them. Sometimes, as though they were distilled prose, poems contain only the essential words. They say just barely enough to communicate in the most basic way, using elemental signs—each of which is chosen for exactly the right shade of meaning or feeling or both. But elemental does not necessarily mean simple, and these signs may be very rich in their meanings and complex in their effects. The poet's word choice—the **diction** of a poem—determines not only meaning but just about every effect the poem produces.

PRECISION AND AMBIGUITY, DENOTATION AND CONNOTATION

Let's look first at poems that create some of their effects by examining—or playing with—a single word. Often multiple meanings or shiftiness and uncertainty of a word are at issue. The following short poem, for example, depends almost entirely on the ways we use the word *play*.

SARAH CLEGHORN

[*The golf links lie so near the mill*]

The golf links lie so near the mill
That almost every day
The laboring children can look out
And see the men at play.

1915

While traveling in the American South, Cleghorn had seen, right next to a golf course, a textile mill that employed quite young children. Her poem doesn't *say* that we expect men to work and children to play; it just assumes our expectation and builds an effect of *dramatic* **irony**—an incongruity between what we expect and what actually occurs—out of the observation. The poem saves almost all of its devastating effect for the final word, after the situation has been carefully described and the irony set up.

In the following two poems, a word used over and over acquires multiple meanings and refuses to be limited to a single one.

ANNE FINCH, COUNTESS OF WINCHELSEA

There's No To-morrow

A Fable imitated from Sir Roger L'Estrange

Two long had Lov'd, and now the Nymph desir'd,
The Cloak of Wedlock, as the Case requir'd;
Urg'd that, the Day he wrought her to this Sorrow,
He Vow'd, that he wou'd marry her To-Morrow.
5   Agen he Swears, to shun the present Storm,
That he, To-Morrow, will that Vow perform.
The Morrows in their due Successions came;
Impatient still on Each, the pregnant Dame
Urg'd him to keep his Word, and still he swore the same.
10   When tir'd at length, and meaning no Redress,
But yet the Lye not caring to confess,
He for his Oath this Salvo chose to borrow,
That he was Free, since there was no To-Morrow;
For when it comes in Place to be employ'd,
15   'Tis then To-Day; To-Morrow's ne'er enjoy'd.
The Tale's a Jest, the Moral is a Truth;
To-Morrow and To-Morrow, cheat our Youth:
In riper Age, To-Morrow still we cry,
Not thinking, that the present Day we Dye;
20   Unpractis'd all the Good we had Design'd;
There's No To-Morrow to a Willing Mind.

1713

CHARLES BERNSTEIN

Of Time and the Line

George Burns[1] likes to insist that he always
takes the straight lines; the cigar in his mouth
is a way of leaving space between the
lines for a laugh. He weaves lines together
5 by means of a picaresque narrative;
not so Hennie Youngman,[2] whose lines are strictly paratactic. My father pushed a
line of ladies' dresses—not down the street
in a pushcart but upstairs in a fact'ry
10 office. My mother has been more concerned
with her hemline. Chairman Mao[3] put forward
Maoist lines, but that's been abandoned (mostly) for the East-West line of malarkey
so popular in these parts. The prestige
15 of the iambic line has recently
suffered decline, since it's no longer so
clear who "I" am, much less who *you* are. When
making a line, better be double sure
what you're lining in & what you're lining
20 out & which side of the line you're on; the
world is made up so (Adam didn't so much
name as delineate). Every poem's got
a prosodic lining, some of which will
unzip for summer wear. The lines of an
25 imaginary are inscribed on the
social flesh by the knifepoint of history.
Nowadays, you can often spot a work
of poetry by whether it's in lines
or no; if it's in prose, there's a good chance
30 it's a poem. While there is no lesson in
the line more useful than that of the picket line, the line that has caused the most ad-
versity is the bloodline. In Russia
everyone is worried about long lines;
35 back in the USA, it's strictly soup-
lines. "Take a chisel to write," but for an

---

1. American comedian (1896–1996) who played straight man to his wife, Gracie Allen.
2. American stand-up comedian (1906–98), king of the one-liner.
3. Mao Zedong (1893–1976), leader of the revolution that established China as a communist nation.

actor a line's got to be cued. Or, as
they say in math, it takes two lines to make
an angle but only one lime to make
40   a Margarita.

1991

In these poems, the importance of a word involves its ambiguity (that is, its having more than one possible meaning) rather than its precision or exactness. The Finch poem repeatedly explores the shifting sands of the word *tomorrow*, first noting how different people may think of its meanings differently, and then showing how these shifts are anchored in time and the whole process of meaning. The Bernstein poem finds a great variety of completely different meanings of the word *line*. How many different meanings can you distinguish in the poem? What does "Time" (in the title) have to do with the poem?

Although the unambiguous or "dictionary" meaning of words—that is, what words denote, their **denotation**—is certainly important, words are more than hard blocks of meaning on whose sense everyone agrees. They also have a more personal side, and they carry emotional force and shades of suggestion. The words we use indicate not only what we mean but how we feel about it, and we choose words that we hope will engage others emotionally and persuasively, in conversation and daily usage as well as in poems. A person who holds office is, quite literally (and unemotionally), an *officeholder*—the word denotes what he or she does. But if we want to convey that a particular officeholder is wise, trustworthy, and deserving of political support we may call that person a *civil servant*, a *political leader*, or an *elected official*, whereas if we want to promote distrust or contempt of that same officeholder we might say *politician* or *bureaucrat* or *political hack*. These terms have clear **connotations**—suggestions of emotional coloration that imply our attitude and invite a similar one from our hearers. What words connote can be just as important to a poem as what they denote; some poems work primarily through denotation and some more through connotation.

The following **epitaph**, for example, which describes one person's mixed feelings about another, depends heavily on the connotations of fairly common words.

WALTER DE LA MARE

Slim Cunning Hands

Slim cunning hands at rest, and cozening eyes—
Under this stone one loved too wildly lies;

How false she was, no granite could declare;
Nor all earth's flowers, how fair.

1950

What the speaker in "Slim Cunning Hands" remembers about the dead woman—her hands, her eyes—tells part of the story; her physical presence was clearly important to him. The poem's other nouns—stone, granite, flowers—all remind us of her death and its finality. All these words denote objects having to do with the rituals that memorialize a departed life. Granite and stone connote finality as well, and flowers connote fragility and suggest the shortness of life (which is why they have become the symbolic language of funerals). The way the speaker talks about the woman expresses, in just a few words, the complexity of his love for her. She was loved, he says, too "wildly"— by him perhaps, and apparently by others. The excitement she offered is suggested by the word, and also the lack of control. The words *cunning* and *cozening* help us interpret both her wildness and her falsity; they suggest her calculation, cleverness, and untrustworthiness as well as her skill, persuasiveness, and ability to please. Moreover, coming at the end of the second line, the word *lies* has more than one meaning. The body "lies" under the stone, but the woman's falsity has by now become too prominent to ignore as a second meaning. And the word *fair*, a simple yet very inclusive word, suggests how totally attractive the speaker finds her: Her beauty can no more be expressed by flowers than her fickleness can be expressed by something as permanent as words in stone. But the word *fair*, in the emphatic position as the final word, also implies two other meanings that seem to resonate, ironically, with what we have already learned about her from the speaker: "impartial" and "just." "Impartial" she may be in her preferences (as the word *false* suggests), but to the speaker she is hardly "just," and the final defining word speaks both to her appearance and (ironically) to her character. Simple words here tell us perhaps all we need to know of a long story—or at least the speaker's version of it.

Words like *fair* and *cozening* are clearly loaded. They imply more emotionally than they mean literally. They have strong, clear connotations; they tell us what to think, what evaluation to make; and they suggest the basis for the evaluation.

Sometimes word choice in poems is less dramatic and less obviously significant but equally important. Often, in fact, simple appropriateness makes the words in a poem work, and words that do not call special attention to themselves can be the most effective. Precision of denotation may be just as impressive and productive of specific effects as the resonance or ambiguous suggestiveness of connotation. Often poems achieve their power by a combination of verbal effects, setting off elaborate figures of speech or other complicated strategies with simple words chosen to mark exact actions, moments, or states of mind.

Words are the starting point for all poetry, of course, and almost every word is likely to be significant, either denotatively or connotatively or both. Poets who know their craft pick each word with care to express exactly what needs to be expressed and to suggest every emotional shade that the poem is calculated to evoke in us.

Word Choice: An Example and an Exercise

Before you read the following poem, notice the three words in the title. What do they lead you to expect? What questions do they raise? Jot down your thoughts on a piece of paper. Then, as you read the poem, take note of key words and try to be conscious of the emotional effects and impressions they create.

THEODORE ROETHKE

My Papa's Waltz

The whiskey on your breath
Could make a small boy dizzy;
But I hung on like death:
Such waltzing was not easy.

5 We romped until the pans
Slid from the kitchen shelf;
My mother's countenance
Could not unfrown itself.

The hand that held my wrist
10 Was battered on one knuckle;
At every step you missed
My right ear scraped a buckle.

You beat time on my head
With a palm caked hard by dirt,
15 Then waltzed me off to bed
Still clinging to your shirt.

1948

(Continued on next page)

(Continued)

Exactly how does the situation in "My Papa's Waltz" and the poem itself fulfill or deny your expectations? How does it answer your questions? How does it characterize the waltz and the speaker's feelings about it? Which words are most suggestive in these terms? What clues are there in the word choice that an adult is remembering a childhood experience? How scared was the boy at the time? How does the grown adult now evaluate his emotions when he was a boy?

WORD ORDER AND WORD PLACEMENT

Often individual words qualify and amplify one another—suggestions clarify other suggestions, and meanings grow upon meanings—and thus how words are put together and where individual words are located can be important, too. Notice, for example, that in "Slim Cunning Hands" the final emphasis is on how *fair* in appearance the woman was; the speaker's last word describes the quality he can't forget despite her lack of a different kind of fairness and his distrust of her. Even though it doesn't justify everything else, her beauty mitigates all the disappointment and hurt. Putting the word *fair* at the end of the line and of the poem gives it special emphasis and meaning.

That one word, *fair*, does not stand all by itself, however, any more than any other word in a poem can be considered all alone. Every word exists within larger units of meaning—sentences, patterns of comparisons and contrasts, the whole poem—and where the word is and how it is used are often important. The final word or words may be especially emphatic (as in "Slim Cunning Hands"), and words that are repeated take on a special intensity, as *line* does in "Of Time and the Line," or as *chartered* and *cry* do in "London" (chapter 7), or *what did I know?* in "Those Winter Sundays" (Family: An Album). Certain words may stand out because they are used in an unusual way (like *chartered* in "London") or because they are given an artificial prominence—through unusual sentence structure, for example, or because the title calls special attention to them. In a poem, as opposed to a prose work, moreover, the number and placement of words in a line and the spacing of the words and lines stays the same in every printed version. Where words come—in a line, in a stanza—and how they are spatially and visually related to other words also helps determine their force and meaning.

The subtlety and force of word choice are sometimes strongly affected by **syntax**—the way the sentences are put together. When you find unusual syntax or spacing, you can be pretty sure that something there merits special attention. Notice the odd sentence constructions in the second and third stanzas of "My Papa's Waltz"—the way the speaker talks about the abrasion of buckle on ear in line 12, for example. He does not say that the buckle scraped his ear, but rather "My right ear scraped a buckle." Reversing the more common expression makes a big difference in the effect created; the speaker avoids placing blame and refuses to specify any unpleasant effect. Had he said that the buckle scraped his ear, we would have to worry about the fragile ear. The syntax of the poem channels our feeling and helps control what we think of the "waltz."

In the most curious part of the poem, the second stanza, the silent mother appears, and the syntax on both sides of the semicolon is peculiar. In lines 5-6, the connection between the romping and the pans falling is stated oddly: "We romped *until* the pans / Slid from the kitchen shelf" (emphasis added). The speaker does not say that they knocked down the pans or imply awkwardness, but he does suggest energetic activity and duration. He implies intensity, almost intention—as though the romping would not be complete until the pans fell. And the clause about the mother—odd but effective— makes her position clear. A silent bystander in this male ritual, she doesn't seem frightened or angry. She seems to be holding a frown, or to have it molded on her face, as though it were part of her own ritual, and perhaps a facet of her stern character as well. The syntax implies that she *has to* maintain the frown, and the falling of the pans almost seems to be for her benefit. She disapproves, but she remains their audience.

Sometimes poems create, as well, a powerful sense of the way minds and emotions work by varying normal syntactical order in special ways. Listen and watch, for example, what happens a few lines into the following poem. What does it suggest about what is happening inside the speaker?

SHARON OLDS

Sex without Love

How do they do it, the ones who make love
without love? Beautiful as dancers,
gliding over each other like ice-skaters
over the ice, fingers hooked
5 inside each other's bodies, faces
red as steak, wine, wet as the
children at birth whose mothers are going to
give them away. How do they come to the
come to the   come to the   God   come to the

10 still waters, and not love
    the one who came there with them, light
    rising slowly as steam off their joined
    skin? These are the true religious,
    the purists, the pros, the ones who will not
15 accept a false Messiah, love the
    priest instead of the God. They do not
    mistake the lover for their own pleasure,
    they are like great runners: they know they are alone
    with the road surface, the cold, the wind,
20 the fit of their shoes, their over-all cardio-
    vascular health—just factors, like the partner
    in the bed, and not the truth, which is the
    single body alone in the universe
    against its own best time.

                                1984

The poem starts calmly enough, with a simple rhetorical question implying that the speaker just cannot understand sex without love. Lines 2–4
carefully compare such sexual activity with two other artful activities, and
the speaker—although plainly disapproving—seems coolly in control of the
analysis and evaluation. But by the end of the fourth line, something begins
to seem odd: "Hooked" seems too ugly and extreme a way to characterize the
lovers' fingers, however much the speaker may disapprove, and by line 6 the
syntax seems to break down. How does "wine" fit the syntax of the line? Is it
parallel with "steak," another example of redness? Or is it somehow related
to the last part of the sentence, parallel with "faces"? Neither of these possibilities quite works. At best, the punctuation is inadequate; at worst, the
speaker's mind is working too fast for the language it generates, scrambling its images. We can't yet be sure what is going on, but by the ninth line
the lack of control is manifest with the compulsive repeating (three times)
of "come to the" and the interjected "God."

Such verbal behavior—here concretized by the way the poem orders its
words and spaces them on the page—invites us to reevaluate the speaker's
moralizing relative to her emotional involvement with the issues and with
her representation of sexuality itself. The speaker's own values, as well as
those who have sex without love, become a subject for evaluation.

Words, the basic materials of poetry, come in many kinds and can be
used in many different ways and in different—sometimes surprising—
combinations. They are seldom simple or transparent, even when we know
their meanings and recognize their syntactical combinations as ordinary
and conventional. Carefully examining them, individually and collectively,
is a crucial part of reading poems, and being able to ask good questions

about the words that poems use and the way they use them is one of the most basic—and rewarding—skills a reader of poetry can develop.

EMILY DICKINSON

[*I dwell in Possibility—*]

I dwell in Possibility—
A fairer House than Prose—
More numerous of Windows—
Superior—for Doors—

5 Of Chambers as the Cedars—
Impregnable of Eye—
And for an Everlasting Roof
The Gambrels[4] of the Sky—

Of Visitors—the fairest—
10 For Occupation—This—
The spreading wide my narrow Hands
To gather Paradise—

ca. 1862

• What does Dickinson seem to mean by "Possibility"? How does the poem's ending broaden this meaning?

WILLIAM CARLOS WILLIAMS

The Red Wheelbarrow

so much depends
upon

a red wheel
barrow

5 glazed with rain
water

beside the white
chickens.

1923

---

4. Roofs with double slopes.

- How does setting the words *barrow, water,* and *chickens* on lines of their own help to substantiate the poem's first line?

This Is Just to Say

I have eaten
the plums
that were in
the icebox

5 and which
you were probably
saving
for breakfast

Forgive me
10 they were delicious
so sweet
and so cold

                    1934

- What is meant by "This" in the poem's title? What is the apparent occasion for this poem?

Authors on Their Work: WILLIAM CARLOS WILLIAMS

From reading and commentary at Princeton University (1952)*

I've . . . gotten some fame, but I should probably say notoriety, from a very brief little poem called "The Red Wheelbarrow." . . . I had a letter from a lady in Boston after that appearance that said, "I love it. It's perfectly wonderful. But what does it *mean?*" [audience laughs] In the first place, I say modestly it's a perfect poem. [laughs] . . . It means just the same as the opening lines of [John Keats's] *Endymion,* "A thing of beauty is a joy forever." And so much depends upon it. But instead of saying "A thing of beauty," I say, "a red wheel / barrow // glazed with rain / water // beside the white / chickens." Isn't that beautiful?

(Continued on next page)

(Continued)

* * *

From interview with John W. Gerber (1950)**

WILLIAMS: It actually took place just as it . . . says here [in "This Is Just to Say"]. And my wife being out, I left a note for her just that way, and she replied very beautifully. Unfortunately, I lost it. . . . I think what she wrote was quite as good as this, a little more complex, but quite as good. Perhaps the virtue of this is its simplicity.

INTERVIEWER: Now, what I want to ask you about that [is], What makes that a poem?

WILLIAMS: In the first place, it's metrically absolutely regular. . . . [reads poem] So, dogmatically speaking, it has to be a poem because it goes that way, don't you see?

INTERVIEWER: Well, this goes against so many preconceived ideas of the poem, though, because it's the kind of thing that almost anybody might say.

WILLIAMS: Yes, because no one believes that poetry can exist in its own light. That's one of our immediate fallacies. . . . Imagine reading a poem in the American dialects, how impossible! That's the first hazard, that's the first hurdle. We have to get over that. . . . It can't be that we poor colonials, as we have been ever since the Revolution, we poor people who are not living in the centers of Europe can have anything happen in our lives important enough to be put down in words and given a form. But everything in our lives, if it's sufficiently authentic to our lives and touches us deeply enough, with a certain amount of feeling, is capable of being organized into a form which can be a poem. . . . Your wife, . . . the woman who's there with whom you are supposed to be in love and sometimes are . . . had these things saved for supper, and here you come along and raid it. Why, it's practically rape of the icebox, and there you are. So I think that's material for a poem. [laughs] That's a definite poem—without even writing it. But then if you can give it conventional metrical form, why . . . you're just simply superb, that's all. [laughs] You've done a great deed.

* Reading and commentary at Princeton University, March 19, 1952. *Penn Sound.* Web. 17 June 2009.
** Interview with John W. Gerber, Rutherford, New Jersey, June 1950. *Penn Sound.* Web. 17 June 2009.

GERARD MANLEY HOPKINS

Pied Beauty[5]

Glory be to God for dappled things—
  For skies of couple-color as a brinded[6] cow;
    For rose-moles all in stipple[7] upon trout that swim;
Fresh-firecoal chestnut-falls;[8] finches' wings;
5   Landscape plotted and pieced—fold, fallow, and plow;
  And all trades, their gear and tackle and trim.
All things counter, original, spare, strange;
  Whatever is fickle, freckled (who knows how?)
    With swift, slow; sweet, sour; adazzle, dim;
10 He fathers-forth whose beauty is past change;
      Praise him.

                                            1887

• How many ways of expressing mixed color can you find in
  this poem? How does Hopkins expand the meaning of "pied
  beauty"?

LI-YOUNG LEE

Persimmons

In sixth grade Mrs. Walker
slapped the back of my head
and made me stand in the corner
for not knowing the difference
5 between *persimmon* and *precision*.
How to choose
persimmons. This is precision.
Ripe ones are soft and brown-spotted.
Sniff the bottoms. The sweet one
10 will be fragrant. How to eat:
put the knife away, lay down newspaper.
Peel the skin tenderly, not to tear the meat.
Chew the skin, suck it,

5. Particolored beauty: having patches or sections of more than one color.
6. Streaked or spotted.   7. Rose-colored dots or flecks.
8. Fallen chestnuts as red as burning coals.

and swallow. Now, eat
15 the meat of the fruit,
so sweet,
all of it, to the heart.

Donna undresses, her stomach is white.
In the yard, dewy and shivering
20 with crickets, we lie naked,
face-up, face-down.
I teach her Chinese.
Crickets: *chiu chiu.* Dew: I've forgotten.
Naked: I've forgotten.
25 *Ni, wo:*   you and me.
I part her legs,
remember to tell her
she is beautiful as the moon.

Other words
30 that got me into trouble were
fight and *fright, wren* and *yarn.*
Fight was what I did when I was frightened,
fright was what I felt when I was fighting.
Wrens are small, plain birds,
35 yarn is what one knits with.
Wrens are soft as yarn.
My mother made birds out of yarn.
I loved to watch her tie the stuff;
a bird, a rabbit, a wee man.

40 Mrs. Walker brought a persimmon to class
and cut it up
so everyone could taste
a *Chinese apple.* Knowing
it wasn't ripe or sweet, I didn't eat
45 but watched the other faces.

My mother said every persimmon has a sun
inside, something golden, glowing,
warm as my face.

Once, in the cellar, I found two wrapped in newspaper,
50 forgotten and not yet ripe.
I took them and set both on my bedroom windowsill,
where each morning a cardinal
sang, *The sun, the sun.*
Finally understanding

55 he was going blind,
  my father sat up all one night
  waiting for a song, a ghost.
  I gave him the persimmons,
  swelled, heavy as sadness,
60 and sweet as love.

  This year, in the muddy lighting
  of my parents' cellar, I rummage, looking
  for something I lost.
  My father sits on the tired, wooden stairs,
65 black cane between his knees,
  hand over hand, gripping the handle.

  He's so happy that I've come home.
  I ask how his eyes are, a stupid question.
  All gone, he answers.

70 Under some blankets, I find a box.
  Inside the box I find three scrolls.
  I sit beside him and untie
  three paintings by my father:
  Hibiscus leaf and a white flower.
75 Two cats preening.
  Two persimmons, so full they want to drop from the cloth.

  He raises both hands to touch the cloth,
  asks, *Which is this?*

  This is persimmons, Father.

80 *Oh, the feel of the wolftail on the silk,*
  the strength, the tense
  precision in the wrist.
  I painted them hundreds of times
  eyes closed. These I painted blind.
85 *Some things never leave a person:*
  scent of the hair of one you love,
  the texture of persimmons,
  in your palm, the ripe weight.

                              1986

* How does the poem play on the words *precision* and *persimmons*? What different kinds of precision are discussed and demonstrated in the poem?

PICTURING: THE LANGUAGES OF DESCRIPTION

The language of poetry is often visual and pictorial. Rather than depending primarily on abstract ideas and elaborate reasoning, poems depend more on concrete and specific words that create images in our minds. Poems thus help us see things afresh or feel them suggestively through our other physical senses, such as hearing or touch. Sound is, as we will see, a vital aspect of poetry. But most poems use the sense of sight to help us form, in our minds, visual impressions, images that communicate more directly than concepts. We "see" yellow leaves on a branch, a father and son waltzing precariously, or two lovers sitting together on the bank of a stream, so that our response begins from a vivid visual impression of exactly what is happening. Some people think that those media and arts that challenge the imagination of a hearer or reader—radio drama, for example, or poetry—allow us to respond more fully than those (such as television or theater) that actually show things more fully to our physical senses. Certainly these media leave more to our imagination, to our mind's eye.

Poems are sometimes quite abstract—they can even be *about* abstractions. But usually they are quite concrete in what they ask us to see. One reason is that they often begin in a poet's mind with a picture or an image: of a person, a place, an event, or an object of observation. That image may be based on something the poet has seen—that is, it may be a picture of something remembered by the poet—but it may also be totally imaginary and only based on the "real world" in the sense that it draws on the poet's physical sense of what the world is like, including the people and things in it. Even when a poet begins with an idea that draws on visual experience, however, the reader still has to *imagine* (through the poem's words) an image, some person or thing or action that the poem describes. The poet must rely on words to help the reader to flesh out that mental image. In a sense, then, the reader becomes a visual artist, but the poet directs the visualization by evoking specific responses through words. *How* that happens can involve quite complicated verbal strategies—or even *visual* ones that draw on the possibilities of print.

The languages of description are quite varied. The visual qualities of poetry result partly from the two aspects of poetic language described in the previous section: on the one hand, the precision of individual words, and, on the other hand, precision's opposite—the reach, richness, and ambiguity of suggestion that words sometimes accrue. Visualization can also derive from sophisticated rhetorical and literary devices (**figures of speech** and **symbols,** for example, as we will see later in this chapter). But often description begins simply with naming—providing the word (noun, verb, adjective, or adverb) that will trigger images familiar from a reader's own experience. A reader can readily imagine a *dog* or *cat* or *house* or *flower* when each word is named, but not all readers will envision the same kind of dog or flower (because of our individual experiences) until the word is qualified in some way. So the poet may specify that the dog is a greyhound or poodle, or that the flower is a daffodil or a lilac or Queen Anne's lace; or the poet may provide colors, sizes, specific movements, or particular identifying features. Such description can involve either narrowing by category or expanding through detail, and often comparisons are either explicitly or implicitly involved. In Richard Wilbur's "The Beautiful Changes" (later in this chapter), for example, the similarity between wading through flowers in a meadow and wading among waves in the sea both suggests how the first experience feels and etches it visually in our minds. More than just a matter of naming, using precise words, and providing basic information, description involves qualification and comparison; sometimes the poet needs to tell us what not to picture, dissociating what the poem describes from other possible images we may have in mind. Different features in the language of description add up to something that describes a whole—a picture or scene—as well as a series of individualized objects.

Seeing in the mind's eye—the re-creation of visual experience—requires different skills from poets and readers. Poets use all the languistic strategies they can think of to re-create for us something they have already "seen." Poets depend on our having had a rich variety of visual experiences and try to draw on those experiences by using common, evocative words and then refining the process through more elaborate verbal devices. We as readers inhabit the process the other way around, trying to draw on our previous knowledge so that we can "see" by following verbal clues. In the poems that follow, notice the ways that description inspires specific images, and pay attention to how shape, color, relationship, and perspective become clear, not only through individual words but also through combinations of words and phrases that suggest appearance and motion.

. . .

OSCAR WILDE

Symphony in Yellow

An omnibus across the bridge
   Crawls like a yellow butterfly,
   And, here and there, a passer-by
Shows like a little restless midge.[9]

5 Big barges full of yellow hay
   Are moored against the shadowy wharf,

9. Tiny mosquito-like insect.

And, like a yellow silken scarf,
The thick fog hangs along the quay.

The yellow leaves begin to fade
10   And flutter from the Temple[1] elms,
And at my feet the pale green Thames
Lies like a rod of rippled jade.

1909

• What can you infer about London, its climate, and the season from each of the yellow images in this poem?

RICHARD WILBUR

The Beautiful Changes

One wading a Fall meadow finds on all sides
The Queen Anne's Lace[2] lying like lilies
On water; it glides
So from the walker, it turns
5 Dry grass to a lake, as the slightest shade of you
Valleys my mind in fabulous blue Lucernes.[3]

The beautiful changes as a forest is changed
By a chameleon's tuning his skin to it;
As a mantis, arranged
10 On a green leaf, grows
Into it, makes the leaf leafier, and proves
Any greenness is deeper than anyone knows.

Your hands hold roses always in a way that says
They are not only yours; the beautiful changes
15 In such kind ways,
Wishing ever to sunder
Things and things' selves for a second finding, to lose
For a moment all that it touches back to wonder.

1947

1. The law-courts area of London.
2. Plant sometimes called "wild carrot," with delicate, finger-like leaves and flat clusters of small
white flowers.
3. Alfalfa, a plant resembling clover, with small purple flowers. Lake Lucerne is famed for its deep
blue color and picturesque Swiss setting amid limestone mountains.

- What part of speech is "Beautiful" in the poem's title and lines 7 and 14? What part of speech is "Changes"? What is meant by "the beautiful changes / In such kind ways" (lines 14–15)?

ANDREW MARVELL

On a Drop of Dew

See how the orient[4] dew
Shed from the bosom of the morn
   Into the blowing roses,
Yet careless of its mansion new
5 For[5] the clear region where 'twas born
   Round in itself incloses,
   And in its little globe's extent
Frames as it can its native element;
   How it the purple flow'r does slight,
10   Scarce touching where it lies,
But gazing back upon the skies,
   Shines with a mournful light
   Like its own tear,
Because so long divided from the sphere.[6]
15 Restless it rolls and unsecure,
   Trembling lest it grow impure,

   Till the warm sun pity its pain,
And to the skies exhale it back again.
   So the soul, that drop, that ray
20 Of the clear fountain of eternal day,
   Could it within the human flower be seen,
   Rememb'ring still its former height,
   Shuns the sweet leaves and blossoms green;
   And, recollecting its own light,
25 Does, in its pure and circling thoughts, express
The greater Heaven in an Heaven less.
   In how coy[7] a figure wound,
   Every way it turns away;
   So the world excluding round,
30   Yet receiving in the day:

4. Shining. 5. By reason of. 6. Of heaven. 7. Reserved, withdrawn, modest.

Dark beneath, but bright above,
Here disdaining, there in love.

How loose and easy hence to go,
How girt and ready to ascend;
35   Moving but on a point below,
It all about does upwards bend.
Such did the manna's sacred dew distill,
White and entire, though congealed and chill;[8]
Congealed on earth, but does, dissolving, run
Into the glories of th' almighty sun.

1681

- How does the sun "exhale" (line 17) the drop of dew? "Back
  again" to where? Explain the comparison between the dew-
  drop and the human soul.

METAPHOR AND PERSONIFICATION

Being visual does not just mean describing; telling us facts; indicating
shapes, colors, and specific details; and giving us precise discriminations
through exacting verbs, nouns, adverbs, and adjectives. Often the vividness
of the picture in our minds depends on comparisons made through figures
of speech. What we are trying to imagine is pictured in terms of something
else familiar to us, and we are asked to think of one thing as if it were something else. Many such comparisons, in which something is pictured or figured forth in terms of something already familiar to us, are taken for
granted in daily life. Things we can't see or that aren't familiar to us are
imaged as things we already know; for example, God is said to be like a
father; Italy is said to be shaped like a boot; life is compared to a forest, a
journey, or a sea. When the comparison is implicit, describing something as
if it were something else, it is called a **metaphor.**

Poems use **figurative language** much of the time. A poem may insist
that death is like a sunset or sex like an earthquake or that the way to imagine how it feels to be spiritually secure is to think of the way a sheep is taken
care of by a shepherd. The pictorialness of our imagination may *clarify*
things for us—scenes, states of mind, ideas—but at the same time it stimu-
lates us to think of how those pictures make us *feel.* Pictures, even when
they are mental pictures or imagined visions, may be both denotative and

---

8. In the wilderness, the Israelites fed upon manna from heaven (distilled from the dew; see Exodus 16.10–21); manna became a traditional symbol for divine grace.

connotative, just as individual words are: They may clarify and make precise, and they may evoke a range of feelings.

In the poem that follows, the poet helps us visualize old age and approaching death by making comparisons with familiar things—the coming of winter, the approach of sunset, and the dying embers of a fire.

WILLIAM SHAKESPEARE

[*That time of year thou mayst in me behold*]

That time of year thou mayst in me behold
When yellow leaves, or none, or few, do hang
Upon those boughs which shake against the cold,
Bare ruined choirs, where late the sweet birds sang.
5 In me thou see'st the twilight of such day
As after sunset fadeth in the west;
Which by and by[9] black night doth take away,
Death's second self,[1] that seals up all in rest.
In me thou see'st the glowing of such fire,
10 That on the ashes of his youth doth lie,
As the deathbed whereon it must expire,
Consumed with that which it was nourished by.
This thou perceiv'st, which makes thy love more strong,
To love that well which thou must leave ere long.

1609

The first four lines of "That time of year" evoke images of the late autumn, but notice that the poet does not have the speaker say directly that his physical condition and age make him resemble autumn. He draws the comparison without stating it as a comparison: You can see my own state, he says, in the coming of winter, when almost all the leaves have fallen from the trees. The speaker portrays himself *indirectly* by talking about the passing of the year. The poem uses metaphor; that is, one thing is pictured *as if* it were something else. "That time of year" goes on to another metaphor in lines 5–8 and still another in lines 9–12, and each metaphor contributes to our understanding of the speaker's sense of his old age and approaching death. More important, however, is the way the metaphors give us feelings, an emotional sense of the speaker's age and of his own attitude toward aging. Through the metaphors we come to understand, appreciate, and to

9. Shortly.   1. Sleep.

some extent share the increasing sense of urgency that the poem expresses. Our emotional sense of the poem depends largely on the way each metaphor is developed and by the way each metaphor leads, with its own kind of internal logic, to another.

The images of late autumn in the first four lines all suggest loneliness, loss, and nostalgia for earlier times. As in the rest of the poem, the speaker presents our eyes as the main vehicle for noticing his age and condition; in the phrase "thou mayst in me behold" (line 1), he introduces what he is asking us to see, and in both lines 5 and 9 he tells us similarly, "In me thou see'st. . . ." The picture of the trees shedding their leaves suggests that autumn is nearly over, and we can imagine trees either with yellow leaves, or without leaves, or with just a trace of foliage remaining—the latter perhaps most feelingly suggesting the bleakness and loneliness that characterize the change of seasons, the ending of the life cycle. But other senses are invoked, too. The boughs shaking against the cold represent an appeal to our tactile sense, and the next line appeals to our sense of hearing, although only by the silence of birds no longer singing. (Notice how exact the visual representation is of the bare, or nearly bare, limbs, even as the speaker notes the cold and the lack of birds; birds lined up like a choir on risers would have made a striking visual image on the barren limbs one above the other, but now there is only the *reminder* of what used to be. The present is quiet, bleak, and lonely; it is the absence of color, song, and life that underscores the visual impression, a reminder of what formerly was.)

The next four lines have a slightly different tone, and the color changes. From a black-and-white landscape with a few yellow leaves, we come upon a rich and almost warm reminder of a faded sunset. But a somber note enters the poem in these lines through another figure of speech, **personification,** which involves treating an abstraction, such as death or justice or beauty, as if it were a person. As the poem talks about the coming of night and of sleep, Sleep is personified as the "second self" of Death (that is, as a kind of "double" for death). The main emphasis is on how night and sleep close in on the twilight, and only secondarily does a reminder of death enter the poem. But it does enter.

The third metaphor—that of the dying embers of a fire—begins in line 9 and continues to color and warm the bleak cold that the poem began with, but it also sharpens the reminder of death. The three main metaphors in the poem work to make our sense of old age and approaching death not only more familiar but also more immediate: Moving from barren trees, to fading twilight, to dying embers suggests a sensuous increase of color and warmth—and an increasing urgency. The first metaphor involves a whole season, or at least a segment of one, a matter of days or possibly weeks; the second involves the passing of a single day, reducing the time scale to a matter of minutes, and the third draws our attention to that split second when a glowing ember dies into a gray ash. The final part of the fire metaphor introduces the most explicit sense of death so far, as the metaphor of embers shifts into a direct reminder of death. Embers, which had been a metaphor of the speaker's aging body, now themselves become, metaphorically, a deathbed; the vitality that nourishes youth is used up just as a log in a fire is. The urgency of the reminder of coming death has now peaked. It is friendlier but now seems immediate and inevitable, a natural part of the life process, and the final two lines offer an explicit plea to make good and intense use of the remaining moments of human relationship.

"That time of year" represents an unusually intricate use of images to organize a poem and focus its emotional impact. Not all poems are so skillfully made, and not all depend on such a full and varied use of metaphor. But most poems use metaphors for at least part of their effect. Sometimes a single metaphor extends over a section of a poem (in which it is called an *extended metaphor*) or even over the whole poem (in which case it is called a *controlling metaphor*). The following poem depends from the beginning— even from its title—on a single controlling metaphor.

LINDA PASTAN

Marks

My husband gives me an A
for last night's supper,
an incomplete for my ironing,
a B plus in bed.
5 My son says I am average,
an average mother, but if
I put my mind to it
I could improve.
My daughter believes
10 in Pass/Fail and tells me
I pass. Wait 'til they learn
I'm dropping out.

1978

The speaker in "Marks" is obviously less than pleased with the idea of continually being judged, and the metaphor of marks (or grades) as a way of talking about her performance of family duties suggests her irritation. The list of the roles implies the many things expected of her, and the three different systems of marking (letter grades, categories to be checked off on a chart, and pass/fail) detail the difficulties of multiple standards. The poem retains the language of schooldays all the way to the end ("learn," line 11; "dropping out," line 12), and the major effect of the poem depends on the irony of the speaker's surrendering to the metaphor the family has thrust upon her; if she is to be judged as if she were a student, she retains the right to leave the system. Ironically, she joins the system (adopts the metaphor for herself) in order to defeat it.

SIMILE AND ANALOGY

Sometimes, in poetry as in prose, comparisons are made explicitly, as in the following poem:

ROBERT BURNS

A Red, Red Rose

O, my luve's like a red, red rose
That's newly sprung in June.
O, my luve is like the melodie
That's sweetly played in tune.

5 As fair art thou, my bonnie lass,
So deep in luve am I;
And I will luve thee still, my dear,
Till a' the seas gang² dry.

Till a' the seas gang dry, my dear,
10 And the rocks melt wi' the sun;
And I will luve thee still, my dear,
While the sands o' life shall run.

And fare thee weel, my only luve,
And fare thee weel a while!
15 And I will come again, my luve,
Though it were ten thousand mile.

1796

2. Go.

The first four lines make two explicit comparisons: The speaker says that his love is "like a . . . rose" and "like [a] melodie." Such *explicit* comparisons are called **similes**, and usually (as here) the comparison involves the word *like* or the word *as*. Similes work much as do metaphors, except that usually they are used more passingly, more incidentally; they make a quick comparison and usually do not elaborate.

The two similes in "A Red, Red Rose" assume that we already have a favorable opinion of roses and of melodies. Here the poet does not develop the comparison or even remind us of attractive details about roses or tunes. He pays the quick compliment and moves on. Similes sometimes develop more elaborate comparisons than this and occasionally, as in Marvell's "On a Drop of Dew," even govern long sections of a poem (in which case they are called *analogies*). Usually, though, a simile is briefer and relies more fully on something we already know. The speaker in "My Papa's Waltz" says that he hung on "like death." He doesn't have to explain or elaborate on the comparison: We know the anxiety he refers to.

Like metaphors, similes may imply both meaning and feeling; they may both explain something and invoke feelings about it. All figurative language involves an attempt to clarify something *and* to prompt readers to feel a certain way about it. Saying that one's love is like a rose implies a delicate and fragile beauty and invites our senses into play so that we can share sensuously a response to appealing fragrance and soft touch, just as the shivering boughs and dying embers in "That time of year" suggest separation and loss at the same time that they invite us to share both the cold sense of loneliness and the warmth of old friendship.

Once you start looking for them, you will find figures of speech in poem after poem; they are among the most common devices through which poets share their visions with us.

. . .

WILLIAM SHAKESPEARE

[Shall I compare thee to a summer's day?]

Shall I compare thee to a summer's day?
Thou art more lovely and more temperate.
Rough winds do shake the darling buds of May,
And summer's lease hath all too short a date.
5 Sometime too hot the eye of heaven shines,
And often is his gold complexion dimmed;
And every fair from fair sometime declines,

By chance or nature's changing course untrimmed.
But thy eternal summer shall not fade,
10 Nor lose possession of that fair thou ow'st,
Nor shall Death brag thou wand'rest in his shade,
When in eternal lines to time thou grow'st.
    So long as men can breathe or eyes can see,
    So long lives this,[3] and this gives life to thee.

1609

- What sort of promise does the speaker make with this poem? Why can he boast that "thy eternal summer shall not fade" (line 9)?

ANONYMOUS[4]

The Twenty-third Psalm

The Lord is my shepherd; I shall not want.
He maketh me to lie down in green pastures: he leadeth me
    beside the still waters.
He restoreth my soul: he leadeth me in the paths of righteousness
    for his name's sake.
Yea, though I walk through the valley of the shadow of death,
    I will fear no evil: for thou art with me;
    thy rod and thy staff they comfort me.
5 Thou preparest a table before me in the presence of mine
    enemies: thou anointest my head with oil; my cup runneth
    over.
Surely goodness and mercy shall follow me all the days of my life:
    and I will dwell in the house of the Lord for ever.

- What is the controlling metaphor in this poem? At what point in the psalm does the controlling metaphor shift?

3. This poem.   4. Traditionally attributed to King David. This English translation is from the King James Version of the Bible (1611)

JOHN DONNE

[*Batter my heart, three-personed God*]⁵

Batter my heart, three-personed God; for You *A*
As yet but knock, breathe, shine, and seek to mend; *B*
That I may rise and stand, o'erthrow me, and bend *B*
Your force, to break, blow, burn, and make me new. *A*
5 I, like an usurped town, to another due, *A*
Labor to admit You, but Oh, to no end! *B*
Reason, Your viceroy⁶ in me, me should defend, *B*
But is captived, and proves weak or untrue. *A*
Yet dearly I love You, and would be loved fain,⁷ *C*
10 But am betrothed unto Your enemy: *D*
Divorce me, untie or break that knot again, *C*
Take me to You, imprison me, for I, *D*
Except You enthrall me, never shall be free, *E*
Nor ever chaste, except You ravish me. *E*

1633

- In the poem's controlling metaphor, who is the speaker?
  Who, or what, is God? To whom is the speaker "betrothed"
  (line 10)?

haven't we Elizabeth forgive to answer this for 1000's of years

The Canonization

For God's sake hold your tongue and let me love!
    Or⁸ chide my palsy or my gout,
My five gray hairs or ruined fortune flout;
With wealth your state, your mind with arts improve,
5   Take you a course, get you a place,
        Observe his Honor or his Grace,
Or the king's real or his stampèd face⁹
        Contemplate; what you will, approve,
            So you will let me love.

10 Alas, alas, who's injured by my love?
        What merchant's ships have my sighs drowned?
    Who says my tears have overflowed his ground?

---

5. From the sequence *Holy Sonnets,* 14.   6. One who rules as the representative of a higher power.
7. Gladly.   8. Either.   9. On coins.

When did my colds a forward spring remove?
When did the heats which my veins fill
15 Add one man to the plaguy bill?[1]
Soldiers find wars, and lawyers find out still
Litigious men which quarrels move,
Though she and I do love.

Call us what you will, we are made such by love.
20 Call her one, me another fly,
We're tapers too, and at our own cost die;[2]
And we in us find th' eagle and the dove.[3]
The phoenix riddle hath more wit[4]
By us; we two, being one, are it.
25 So to one neutral thing both sexes fit,
We die and rise the same, and prove
Mysterious by this love.

We can die by it, if not live by love;
And if unfit for tombs and hearse
30 Our legend be, it will be fit for verse;[5]
And if no piece of chronicle we prove,
We'll build in sonnets pretty rooms[6]
(As well a well-wrought urn becomes[7]
The greatest ashes, as half-acre tombs),
35 And by these hymns all shall approve
Us canonized for love.

And thus invoke us: "You whom reverent love
Made one another's hermitage,
You to whom love was peace, that now is rage,
40 Who did the whole world's soul extract, and drove[8]
Into the glasses of your eyes
(So made such mirrors and such spies
That they did all to you epitomize)

1. List of plague victims.
2. Tapers (candles) consume themselves. To "die" is Renaissance slang for consummating the
sexual act, which was popularly believed to shorten life by one day. *Fly*: a traditional symbol of
transitory life. 3. Traditional symbols of strength and purity.
4. Meaning. According to tradition, only one phoenix existed at a time, dying in a funeral pyre of
its own making and being reborn from its own ashes. The bird's existence was thus a riddle akin
to a religious mystery (line 27), and a symbol sometimes fused with Christian representations of
immortality.
5. That is, if we don't turn out to be an authenticated piece of historical narrative.
6. In Italian, *stanza* means "room."   7. Befits.   8. Compressed.

Countries, towns, courts; beg from above
45   A pattern of your love!"

                                1633

* Whom does the speaker address in the first line, "hold your tongue"? Why does the speaker concede that he and his lover may not "prove" a "piece of chronicle" (line 31)?

DAVID FERRY

At the Hospital

She was the sentence the cancer spoke at last,
Its blurred grammar finally clarified.

                                1983

* What, exactly, has "clarified" the cancer's "blurred grammar"?

RANDALL JARRELL

The Death of the Ball Turret Gunner[9]

From my mother's sleep I fell into the State,
And I hunched in its belly till my wet fur froze.
Six miles from earth, loosed from its dream of life,
5 I woke to black flak and the nightmare fighters.
When I died they washed me out of the turret with a hose.

                                1945

* What is meant by "I fell into the State"? What do the words "sleep," "dream," and "nightmare" suggest about the poem's basic situation?

---

9. A ball turret was a plexiglass sphere set into the belly of a B-17 or B-24 and inhabited by two .50 caliber machine-guns and one short, small man. When this gunner tracked with his machine-guns a fighter attacking his bomber from below, he revolved with the turret; hunched upside-down in his little sphere, he looked like the foetus in the womb. The fighters which attacked him were armed with cannon firing explosive shells. The hose was a steam hose. [Jarrell's note was erased.]

WILFRED OWEN

Dulce et Decorum Est [1]

Bent double, like old beggars under sacks,
Knock-kneed, coughing like hags, we cursed through sludge,
Till on the haunting flares we turned our backs
And towards our distant rest began to trudge.
5 Men marched asleep. Many had lost their boots
But limped on, blood-shod. All went lame; all blind;
Drunk with fatigue; deaf even to the hoots
Of disappointed shells that dropped behind.

Gas! Gas! Quick, boys!—An ecstasy of fumbling,
10 Fitting the clumsy helmets just in time;
But someone still was yelling out and stumbling
And floundering like a man in fire or lime.—
Dim, through the misty panes and thick green light
As under a green sea, I saw him drowning.

15 In all my dreams, before my helpless sight,
He plunges at me, guttering, choking, drowning.

If in some smothering dreams you too could pace
Behind the wagon that we flung him in,
And watch the white eyes writhing in his face,
20 His hanging face, like a devil's sick of sin;
If you could hear, at every jolt, the blood
Come gargling from the froth-corrupted lungs,
Obscene as cancer, bitter as the cud
Of vile, incurable sores on innocent tongues,—
25 My friend, you would not tell with such high zest
To children ardent for some desperate glory,
The old Lie: Dulce et decorum est
Pro patria mori.

1917

- Note all the similes in this poem. What patterns do you see
  here? What do the similes individually and collectively contribute to the poem, especially in terms of undermining the
  — "lie" to which Owen alludes?

---

1. Part of a phrase from Horace (Roman poet and satirist, 65–8 B.C.E.), quoted in full in the last
lines: "It is sweet and proper to die for one's country."

SYMBOL

Properly used, the term *symbol* suggests one of the most basic things about poems—their ability to get beyond what words signify and to make larger claims about meanings in the verbal world. All words go beyond themselves. They are not simply a collection of sounds: They signify something beyond their sounds, often things or actions or ideas. Words describe not only a verbal universe but also a world in which actions occur, acts have implications, and events have meaning. Sometimes words signify something beyond themselves, say, *rock* or *tree* or *cloud*, and symbolize something as well, such as solidity or life or dreams. Words can—when their implications are agreed on by tradition, convention, or habit—stand for things beyond their most immediate meanings or significations and become symbols, and even simple words that have accumulated no special power from previous use may be given special significance in special circumstances—in poetry as in life itself.

A **symbol** is, put simply, something that stands for something else. The everyday world is full of common examples; a flag, a logo, a trademark, or a skull and crossbones all suggest things beyond themselves, and everyone likely understands what their display indicates, whether or not each viewer shares a commitment to what is thus represented. In common usage a prison symbolizes confinement, constriction, and loss of freedom, and in specialized traditional usage a cross may symbolize oppression, cruelty, suffering, death, resurrection, triumph, or an intersection of some kind (as in *crossroads* and *crosscurrents*). The specific symbolic significance depends on the context; for example, a reader might determine significance by looking at contiguous details in a poem and by examining the poem's attitude toward a particular tradition or body of beliefs. A star means one thing to a Jewish poet and something else to a Christian poet, still something else to a sailor or an actor. In a very literal sense, words themselves are all symbols (they stand for objects, actions, or qualities, not just for letters or sounds), but symbols in poetry are those words and phrases that have a range of reference beyond their literal signification or denotation.

Poems sometimes create a symbol out of a thing, action, or event that has no previously agreed-upon symbolic significance. The following poem, for example, gives an action symbolic significance.

JAMES DICKEY

The Leap

The only thing I have of Jane MacNaughton
Is one instant of a dancing-class dance.

She was the fastest runner in the seventh grade,
My scrapbook says, even when boys were beginning
5   To be as big as the girls,
But I do not have her running in my mind,
Though Frances Lane is there, Agnes Fraser,
Fat Betty Lou Black in the boys-against-girls
Relays we ran at recess: she must have run

10 Like the other girls, with her skirts tucked up
So they would be like bloomers,
But I cannot tell; that part of her is gone.
What I do have is when she came,
With the hem of her skirt where it should be
15 For a young lady, into the annual dance
Of the dancing class we all hated, and with a light
Grave leap, jumped up and touched the end
Of one of the paper-ring decorations

To see if she could reach it. She could,
20 And reached me now as well, hanging in my mind
From a brown chain of brittle paper, thin
And muscular, wide-mouthed, eager to prove
Whatever it proves when you leap
In a new dress, a new womanhood, among the boys
25 Whom you easily left in the dust
Of the passionless playground. If I said I saw
In the paper where Jane MacNaughton Hill,

Mother of four, leapt to her death from a window
Of a downtown hotel, and that her body crushed-in
30 The top of a parked taxi, and that I held
Without trembling a picture of her lying cradled
In that papery steel as though lying in the grass,
One shoe idly off, arms folded across her breast,
I would not believe myself. I would say
35 The convenient thing, that it was a bad dream
Of maturity, to see that eternal process

Most obsessively wrong with the world
Come out of her light, earth-spurning feet
Grown heavy: would say that in the dusty heels
40 Of the playground some boy who did not depend
On speed of foot, caught and betrayed her.
Jane, stay where you are in my first mind:
It was odd in that school, at that dance.

I and the other slow-footed yokels sat in corners
45 Cutting rings out of drawing paper

Before you leapt in your new dress
And touched the end of something I began,
Above the couples struggling on the floor,
New men and women clutching at each other
50 And prancing foolishly as bears: hold on
To that ring I made for you, Jane—
My feet are nailed to the ground
By dust I swallowed thirty years ago—
While I examine my hands.

                     1967

Memory is crucial to "The Leap." The fact that Jane MacNaughton's graceful leap in dancing class has stuck in the speaker's mind all these years means that this leap was important to him, meant something to him, stood for something in his mind. For the speaker, the leap is an "instant" and the "only thing" he has of Jane. He remembers its grace and ease, and he struggles at several points to articulate its meaning (lines 16–26, 44–50), but even without articulation or explanation it remains in his head as a visual memory, a symbol of something beyond himself, something he cannot do, something he wanted to be. What that leap stood for, or symbolized, was boldness, confidence, accomplishment, maturity, Jane's ability to go beyond her fellow students in dancing class—the transcending of childhood by someone entering adulthood. Her feet now seem "earth-spurning" (line 38) in that original leap, and they separate her from everyone else. Jane MacNaughton was beyond the speaker's abilities and any attempt he could make to articulate his hopes, but she was not beyond his dreams. And even before he could say so, she symbolized a dream.

The leap to her death seems cruelly wrong and ironic after the grace of her earlier leap. In memory she is suspended in air, as if there were no gravity, no coming back to earth, as if life could exist as dream. And so the photograph, re-created in precise detail, is a cruel dashing of the speaker's dream—a detailed record of the ending of a leap, a denial of the suspension in which his memory had held her. His dream is grounded; her mortality is insistent. But the speaker still wants to hang on to that symbolic moment (line 42), which he confronts in a more mature context but will never altogether replace or surrender.

The leap is ultimately symbolic in the *poem*, too, not just in the speaker's mind. In the poem (and for us as readers) its symbolism is double: The first leap symbolizes aspiration, and the second symbolizes the frustration and grounding of high hopes; the two are complementary, one impossible to imagine without the other. The poem is horrifying in some ways, a dramatic reminder that human beings don't ultimately transcend their mortality, their limits, no matter how heroic or unencumbered by gravity they may once have seemed. But the poem is not altogether sad and despairing, partly because it still affirms the validity of the original leap and partly because it creates and elaborates another symbol: the paper chain.

The chain connects Jane to the speaker both literally and figuratively. It is, in part, *his* paper chain that she had leaped to touch in dancing class (lines 18–19), and he thinks of her first leap as "touch[ing] the end of something I began" (line 47). He and the other earthbound, "slow-footed yokels" (line 44) made the chain, and it connects them to her original leap, just as a photograph glimpsed in the newspaper connects the speaker to her second leap. The paper in the chain is "brittle" (line 21), and its creators seem dull artisans compared to the artistic performer that Jane was. They are heavy and "left in the dust" (lines 25, 52–53), but she is "light" (line 16) and able to transcend them, even in transcendence touching their lives. And so the paper chain becomes the poem's symbol of linkage, connecting lower accomplishment to higher possibility, the artisan to the artist, material substance to the act of imagination. And at the end the speaker examines the hands that made the chain because those hands certify his connection to her and the imaginative leap she had made for him. The chain thus symbolizes not only the lower capabilities of those who cannot leap like the budding Jane could, but (later) the connection with her leap as both transcendence and mortality. Like the leap, the chain is elevated to special meaning, given symbolic significance, by the poet's treatment of it. A leap and a chain have no necessary significance in themselves to most of us—at least no significance that we have all agreed upon—but they may take on significance in specific circumstances or a specific text.

Other objects and acts have a built-in significance because of past usage in literature, or tradition, or the stories a culture develops to explain itself and its beliefs. Over the years some things have acquired an agreed-upon significance, an accepted value in our minds. They already stand for something before the poet cites them; they are *traditional symbols*. Poets assume that their readers will recognize the traditional meanings of these symbols, and the poem does not have to propose or argue a particular symbolic value. Birds, for example, traditionally symbolize flight, freedom from confinement, detachment from earthbound limits, the ability to soar beyond rationality and transcend mortal limits. Traditionally, birds have also been linked with imagination, especially poetic imagination, and poets often identify with them as pure and ideal singers of songs, as in Keats's "Ode to a Nightingale" (see "Reading More Poetry").

One traditional symbol, the rose, may be a simple and fairly plentiful flower in its season, but it has so long stood for particular qualities that merely to name it raises predictable expectations. Its beauty, delicacy, fragrance, shortness of life, and depth of color have made it a symbol of the transitoriness of beauty, and countless poets have counted on its accepted symbolism—sometimes to compliment a friend (as Burns does in "A Red, Red Rose") or sometimes to make a point about the nature of symbolism. The following poem draws, in quite a traditional way, on the traditional meanings.

EDMUND WALLER

Song

    Go, lovely rose!
Tell her that wastes her time and me
    That now she knows,
When I resemble[2] her to thee,
5 How sweet and fair she seems to be.

    Tell her that's young,
And shuns to have her graces spied,
    That hadst thou sprung
In deserts, where no men abide,
10 Thou must have uncommended died.

    Small is the worth
Of beauty from the light retired;
    Bid her come forth,
Suffer herself to be desired,
15 And not blush so to be admired.

    Then die! that she
The common fate of all things rare
    May read in thee;
How small a part of time they share
That are so wondrous sweet and fair!
              1645

The speaker in "Song" sends the rose to his love in order to have it speak its traditional meanings of beauty and transitoriness. He counts on accepted symbolism to make his point and hurry her into accepting his advances. Likewise, the poet does not elaborate or argue these things because he does not need to; he counts on the familiarity of the tradition (though, of course,

2. Compare.

readers unfamiliar with the tradition will not respond in the same way—that is one reason it is difficult to fully appreciate texts from another linguistic or cultural tradition).

Poets may use traditional symbols to invoke predictable responses—in effect using shortcuts to meaning by repeating acts of signification sanctioned by time and cultural habit. But often poets examine the tradition even as they employ it, and sometimes they revise or reverse meanings built into the tradition. Symbols do not necessarily stay the same over time, and poets often turn even the most traditional symbols to their own original uses. Knowing the traditions of poetry—reading a lot of poems and observing how they tend to use certain words, metaphors, and symbols—can be very useful in reading new poems, but traditions evolve and individual poems do highly individual things. Knowing the past never means being able to interpret new texts with certainty. Symbolism makes things happen, but individual poets and texts determine what will happen and how. The following two poems work important variations on the traditional associations of roses.

D. H. LAWRENCE

I Am Like a Rose

I am myself at last; now I achieve
My very self. I, with the wonder mellow,
Full of fine warmth, I issue forth in clear
And single me, perfected from my fellow.

5 Here I am all myself. No rose-bush heaving
Its limpid sap to culmination has brought
Itself more sheer and naked out of the green
In stark-clear roses, than I to myself am brought.

1917

DOROTHY PARKER

One Perfect Rose

A single flow'r he sent me, since we met.
    All tenderly his messenger he chose;
Deep-hearted, pure, with scented dew still wet—
    One perfect rose.

5 I knew the language of the floweret;
     "My fragile leaves," it said, "his heart enclose."
   Love long has taken for his amulet
     One perfect rose.

   Why is it no one ever sent me yet
10   One perfect limousine, do you suppose?
   Ah no, it's always just my luck to get
     One perfect rose.

                                                    1937

Sometimes symbols—traditional or not—become so insistent in the world of a poem that the larger referential world is left almost totally behind. In such cases the symbol is everything, and the poem does not just *use* symbols but becomes a **symbolic poem**, usually a highly individualized one dependent on an internal system introduced by the individual poet.

Here is an example of such a poem:

WILLIAM BLAKE
The Sick Rose[3]

O rose, thou art sick.
The invisible worm
That flies in the night
In the howling storm

5 Has found out thy bed
Of crimson joy,
And his dark secret love
Does thy life destroy.
                        1794

The poem does not seem to be about a rose, but about what the rose represents—not in this case something altogether understandable through the traditional meanings of *rose*.

We usually associate the rose with beauty and love, often with sex; and here several key terms have sexual connotations: "worm," "bed," and

---

3. In Renaissance emblem books, the scarab beetle, worm, and rose are closely associated: The beetle feeds on dung, and the smell of the rose is fatal to it.

"crimson joy." The violation of the rose by the worm is the poem's main concern; the violation seems to have involved secrecy, deceit, and "dark" motives, and the result is sickness rather than the joy of love. The poem is sad; it involves a sense of hurt and tragedy, nearly of despair. The poem cries out against the misuse of the rose, against its desecration, implying that instead of a healthy joy in sensuality and sexuality, there has been in this case destruction and hurt, perhaps because of misunderstanding and repression and lack of sensitivity.

But to say so much about this poem we have to extrapolate from other poems by Blake, and we have to introduce information from outside the poem. Fully symbolic poems often require that we thus go beyond the formal procedures of reading that we have discussed so far. As presented in this poem, the rose is not part of the normal world that we ordinarily see, and it is symbolic in a special sense. The poet does not simply take an object from our everyday world and give it special significance, making it a symbol in the same sense that the leap becomes a symbol for James Dickey. Here the rose seems to belong to its own world, a world made entirely inside the poem or the poet's head. The rose is not referential, or not primarily so. The whole poem is symbolic; it is not paraphrasable; it lives in its own world. But what is the rose here a symbol of? In general terms, we can say from what the poem tells us; but we may not be as confident as we can be in the more nearly recognizable world of "The Leap" or "I Am Like a Rose." In "The Sick Rose," it seems inappropriate to ask the standard questions: What rose? Where? Which worm? What are the particulars here? In the world of this poem worms can fly and may be invisible. We are altogether in a world of meanings that have been formulated according to a special system of knowledge and code of belief. We will feel comfortable and confident in that world only if we read many poems written by the poet (in this case, William Blake) within the same symbolic system.

Negotiation of meanings in symbolic poems can be very difficult indeed. Reading symbolic poems is an advanced skill that depends on knowledge of context, especially the lives and work of authors and their special literary and cultural traditions. But usually the symbols you will find in poems *are* referential of meanings we all share, and you can readily discover these meanings by carefully studying the poems themselves.

· · ·

ROBERT FROST

Fireflies in the Garden

Here come real stars to fill the upper skies,
And here on earth come emulating flies,
That though they never equal stars in size,
(And they were never really stars at heart)
5   Achieve at times a very star-like start.
Only, of course, they can't sustain the part.

                    1928

- What is the tone of this poem? What does the poem say about the limits of symbolism?

ADRIENNE RICH

Diving into the Wreck

First having read the book of myths,
and loaded the camera,
and checked the edge of the knife-blade,
I put on
5   the body-armor of black rubber
the absurd flippers
the grave and awkward mask.
I am having to do this
not like Cousteau[4] with his
10 assiduous team
aboard the sun-flooded schooner
but here alone.

There is a ladder.
The ladder is always there
15 hanging innocently
close to the side of the schooner.
We know what it is for,
we who have used it.
Otherwise
20 it's a piece of maritime floss
some sundry equipment.

4. Jacques-Yves Cousteau (1910–97), French underwater explorer and writer.

I go down.
Rung after rung and still
the oxygen immerses me
25   the blue light
the clear atoms
of our human air.
I go down.
My flippers cripple me,
30   I crawl like an insect down the ladder
and there is no one
to tell me when the ocean
will begin.

First the air is blue and then
35   it is bluer and then green and then
black I am blacking out and yet
my mask is powerful
it pumps my blood with power
the sea is another story
40   the sea is not a question of power
I have to learn alone
to turn my body without force
in the deep element.

And now: it is easy to forget
45   what I came for
among so many who have always
lived here
swaying their crenellated fans
between the reefs
50   and besides
you breathe differently down here.

I came to explore the wreck.
The words are purposes.
The words are maps.
55   I came to see the damage that was done
and the treasures that prevail.
I stroke the beam of my lamp
slowly along the flank
of something more permanent
60   than fish or weed

the thing I came for:
the wreck and not the story of the wreck

the thing itself and not the myth
the drowned face always staring
65 toward the sun
the evidence of damage
worn by salt and sway into this threadbare beauty
the ribs of the disaster
curving their assertion
70 among the tentative haunters.

This is the place.
And I am here, the mermaid whose dark hair
streams black, the merman in his armored body
We circle silently
75 about the wreck
we dive into the hold.
I am she: I am he

whose drowned face sleeps with open eyes
whose breasts still bear the stress
80 whose silver, copper, vermeil cargo lies
obscurely inside barrels
half-wedged and left to rot
we are the half-destroyed instruments
that once held to a course
85 the water-eaten log
the fouled compass

We are, I am, you are
by cowardice or courage
the one who find our way
90 back to this scene
carrying a knife, a camera
a book of myths
in which
our names do not appear.
1972   1973

- What word or phrase first signals that "Diving into the
  Wreck" is to be understood symbolically, not literally? What
  are some possible symbolic interpretations of the wreck and
  the dive?

ROO BORSON

After a Death

Seeing that there's no other way,
I turn his absence into a chair.
I can sit in it,
gaze out through the window.
5   I can do what I do best
and then go out into the world.
And I can return then with my useless love,
to rest,
because the chair is there.

1989

• Why do you think the speaker chooses to symbolize her
  absent loved one with a chair?

SUGGESTIONS FOR WRITING

1. Choose one poem you have read in this book in which a single word seems
   crucial to that poem's total effect. Write an essay in which you work out carefully how the poem's meaning and tone depend on that one word.
2. Choose any poem in this chapter and explore the meaning and effect of its
   metaphor(s). Does the poem make use of an extended or controlling metaphor or of multiple metaphors? If the latter, how do the metaphors relate to
   and build on each other?
3. Consider the poems about roses in this chapter and write a paragraph about
   each poem showing how it establishes specific symbolism for the rose. What
   generalizations can you draw about the rose's traditional meanings in poetry?
   If you can, find other poems about roses outside of this book to determine if
   your generalizations still apply.
4. Is there a "correct" interpretation of Adrienne Rich's "Diving into the
   Wreck"? If one interpretation seems to fit all the particulars of the poem,
   does that mean it's better than other possible interpretations? Write an essay
   in which you explore the poem's symbolism and argue for or against the idea
   that there is a single best way to understand this poem. Can ambiguity serve
   a poet's purpose, or does it ultimately undercut a poem's meaning and
   significance?
5. Research the design of World War II bombers like the B-17 and the B-24. Try
   to find a picture of the gunner in the ball turret of such an airplane, and note
   carefully his body position. Write an essay in which you explain how Randall
   Jarrell's "The Death of the Ball Turret Gunner" uses visual details to create
   its fetal and birth metaphors.

11 THE SOUNDS OF POETRY

Much of what happens in a poem happens in your mind's eye, but some of it happens in your "mind's ear" and in your voice. Poems are full of meaningful sounds and silences as well as words and sentences. Besides choosing words for their meanings, poets choose words because they have certain sounds, and poems use sound effects to create a mood or establish a tone, just as films do.

Historically, poetry began as an oral phenomenon. Early bards in many cultures chanted or recited their verses, often accompanied by a musical instrument of some kind—and poetry remains a vocal art, dependent on the human voice. Often poems that seem very difficult when looked at silently come alive when turned into sound. The music and rhythms become clearer, and saying the words aloud or hearing them spoken is very good practice for learning to hear in your mind's ear when you read silently.

Sometimes the sounds in poems just provide special effects, rather like a musical score behind a film, setting the mood and getting us into an appropriate frame of mind. But often sound and meaning go hand in hand, and the poet finds words whose sounds echo the action. A word that captures or approximates the sound of what it describes, such as "splash" or "squish" or "murmur," is an *onomatopoeic* word, and the device itself is **onomatopoeia**. Poets can do similar things with pacing and rhythm, sounds and pauses. The punctuation, the length of vowels, and the combination of consonant sounds help control the way we read so that our voices imitate what is being described.

SOUND POEMS: SOME EXAMPLES

HELEN CHASIN

The Word Plum

The word *plum* is delicious

pout and push, luxury of
self-love, and savoring murmur

full in the mouth and falling
5   like fruit

taut skin
pierced, bitten, provoked into
juice, and tart flesh

question
10   and reply, lip and tongue
of pleasure.

1968

KENNETH FEARING

Dirge

1-2-3 was the number he played but today the number came 3-2-1;
Bought his Carbide at 30, and it went to 29; had the favorite at
Bowie[1] but the track was slow—

O executive type, would you like to drive a floating-power, knee-
action, silk-upholstered six? Wed a Hollywood star? Shoot the
course in 58? Draw to the ace, king, jack?
O fellow with a will who won't take no, watch out for three cigarettes on the same, single match; O democratic voter born in
August under Mars, beware of liquidated rails—

5   Denouement to denouement, he took a personal pride in the
certain, certain way he lived his own, private life,
But nevertheless, they shut off his gas; nevertheless, the bank
foreclosed; nevertheless, the landlord called; nevertheless, the
radio broke,

And twelve o'clock arrived just once too often,
Just the same he wore one gray tweed suit, bought one straw hat,
drank one straight Scotch, walked one short step, took one
long look, drew one deep breath,
Just one too many,

10   And wow he died as wow he lived,
Going whop to the office and blooie home to sleep and biff got
married and bam had children and oof got fired,
Zowie did he live and zowie did he die,

---

1. A racetrack in Maryland. *Carbide:* stock in the Union Carbide Corporation.

With who the hell are you at the corner of his casket, and where
the hell're we going on the right-hand silver knob, and who the
hell cares walking second from the end with an American
Beauty[2] wreath from why the hell not,

Very much missed by the circulation staff of the New York Evening Post; deeply, deeply mourned by the B.M.T.[3]

15 Wham, Mr. Roosevelt; pow, Sears Roebuck; awk, big dipper; bop,
summer rain;

Bong, Mr., bong, Mr., bong, Mr., bong.

1935

ALEXANDER POPE

Sound and Sense[4]

337 But most by numbers[5] judge a poet's song,
And smooth or rough, with them, is right or wrong;
In the bright muse though thousand charms conspire,[6]
340 Her voice is all these tuneful fools admire,
Who haunt Parnassus[7] but to please their ear,
Not mend their minds; as some to church repair,
Not for the doctrine, but the music there.
These, equal syllables[8] alone require,
345 Though oft the ear the open vowels tire,
While expletives[9] their feeble aid do join,
And ten low words oft creep in one dull line,
While they ring round the same unvaried chimes,
With sure returns of still expected rhymes.
350 Where'er you find "the cooling western breeze,"
In the next line, it "whispers through the trees";
If crystal streams "with pleasing murmurs creep,"
The reader's threatened (not in vain) with "sleep."
Then, at the last and only couplet fraught

2. A variety of rose.   3. A New York City subway line.
4. From *An Essay on Criticism*, Pope's poem on the art of poetry and the problems of literary criticism. The passage excerpted here follows a discussion of several common weaknesses of critics—
failure to regard an author's intention, for example, or overemphasis on clever metaphors and
ornate style.   5. Meter, rhythm, sound.   6. Unite.
7. A mountain in Greece, traditionally associated with the Muses and considered the seat of
poetry and music.   8. Regular accents.   9. Filler words, such as "do."

355 With some unmeaning thing they call a thought,
A needless Alexandrine¹ ends the song,
That, like a wounded snake, drags its slow length along.
Leave such to tune their own dull rhymes, and know
What's roundly smooth, or languishingly slow;
360 And praise the easy vigor of a line,
Where Denham's strength and Waller's² sweetness join.
True ease in writing comes from art, not chance,
As those move easiest who have learned to dance.
'Tis not enough no harshness gives offense,
365 The sound must seem an echo to the sense:
Soft is the strain when Zephyr³ gently blows,
And the smooth stream in smoother numbers flows;
But when loud surges lash the sounding shore,
The hoarse, rough verse should like the torrent roar.
370 When Ajax⁴ strives, some rock's vast weight to throw,
The line too labors, and the words move slow;
Not so, when swift Camilla⁵ scours the plain,
Flies o'er th' unbending corn, and skims along the main.
Hear how Timotheus'⁶ varied lays surprise,
375 And bid alternate passions fall and rise!
While, at each change, the son of Libyan Jove⁷
Now burns with glory, and then melts with love;
Now his fierce eyes with sparkling fury glow,
Now sighs steal out, and tears begin to flow:
380 Persians and Greeks like turns of nature⁸ found,
And the world's victor stood subdued by sound!
The pow'r of music all our hearts allow,
And what Timotheus was, is DRYDEN now.

1711

---

1. A line of six metrical feet, sometimes used in pentameter poems to vary the pace mechanically. Line 357 is an alexandrine.
2. Sir John Denham and Edmund Waller, seventeenth-century poets credited with perfecting the heroic couplet.   3. The west wind.   4. A Greek hero of the Trojan War, noted for his strength.
5. A woman warrior in Virgil's *Aeneid*.
6. The court musician of Alexander the Great, celebrated in a famous poem by John Dryden (see line 383) for the power of his music over Alexander's emotions.
7. In Greek tradition, the chief god of any people was often given the name Zeus (Jove), and the chief god of Libya (the Greek name for all of Africa) was called Zeus Ammon. Alexander visited his oracle and was proclaimed son of the god.   8. Similar alternations of emotion.

Helen Chasin's poem "The Word *Plum*" savors the sounds of the word as well as the taste and feel of the fruit itself. It is almost as if the poem is tasting the sounds and rolling them slowly on the tongue. The second and third lines even replicate the *p, l, uh,* and *m* sounds of the word while imitating the squishy sounds of eating the fruit. Words like "delicious" and "luxury" sound juicy, and other words, such as "murmur," imitate sounds of satisfaction and pleasure. Even the process of eating is in part re-created aurally. The tight, clipped sounds of "taut skin / pierced" suggest the way teeth sharply break the skin and slice quickly into the soft flesh of a plum, and the words describing the tartness ("provoked," "question") force the lips to pucker and the tongue and palate to meet and hold, as if the mouth were savoring a tart fruit. The poet is having fun here refashioning the sensual appeal of a plum, teasing the sounds and meanings out of available words. The words must mean something appropriate and describe something accurately first of all, of course, but when they also imitate the sounds and feel of the process, they do double duty.

As the title implies, Kenneth Fearing's "Dirge" is a musical lament, in this case for a businessman who took many chances and saw his investments and life go down the drain in the Great Depression of the early 1930s. The expressive cartoon words here, like "oof" and "blooie," echo the action. Reading aloud, you will notice that the poem employs rhythms much as a song would and that it frequently shifts its pace and mood. Notice how carefully the first two lines are balanced, and then how quickly the rhythm shifts as the "executive type" is addressed directly in line 3. (Especially long lines, like line 2, and irregular line lengths here create some of the poem's special sound effects.) In the direct address, the poem first picks up the rapid lingo of advertising. In stanza 3, the rhythm shifts again, but the poem gives us helpful clues about how to read. Line 5 sounds like prose and is long, drawn out, and rather dull (rather like its subject), but line 6 sets up a regular (and monotonous) rhythm with its repeated "nevertheless," which punctuates the rhythm like a drumbeat: "But nevertheless, *tuh-tuh-tuh-tuh-tuh*; nevertheless, *tuh-tuh-tuh-tuh*; nevertheless, *tuh-tuh-tuh-tuh*; nevertheless, *tuh-tuh-tuh-tuh-tuh*." In the next stanza comes more repetitive phrasing, this time guided by the word "one" in conjunction with other one-syllable words: "wore *one* gray tweed suit, bought *one* straw hat, *tuh* one *tuh-tuh, tuh* one *tuh-tuh, tuh* one *tuh-tuh, tuh* one *tuh-tuh*." And then a new rhythm and a new technique begin in stanza 5, which again imitates the language of comic books. You have to say words like "whop" and "zowie" aloud and in the rhythm of the whole sentence to get the full effect of how boring his life is, no matter how he tries to jazz it up. And so it goes—the repeating rhythms of routine—until the final bell ("Bong . . . bong . . . bong . . . bong") tolls rhythmically for the dead man in the final clanging line.

Written in a very different era and style, Pope's "Sound and Sense" uses a number of echoic or onomatopoeic words. In some lines pleasant and unpleasant consonant sounds underline a particular point or emphasize a mood. When the poet talks about a particular weakness in poetry, he illustrates it at the same time—by using open vowels (line 345), expletives (line 346), monosyllabic words (line 347), predictable rhymes (lines 350–53), or long, slow lines (line 357). He similarly illustrates the good qualities of poetry as well (line 360, for example). But the main effects of the passage come from an interaction of several ingenious strategies at once. In lines 339 and 340, for example, Pope produces complex sound effects in addition to the harmony of a rhyming couplet ("conspire," "admire"). Assonance echoes in the *oo* vowel sounds in "muse," "tuneful," and "fools"; alliteration repeats consonants in "*r*ight or *wr*ong" and "tune*f*ul *f*ools." Ironically, the *muse*-ical voice here is a bit out of tune to those who have good poetic taste: Pope intends the *r* and *f* sounds to feel both cute and awkward, as a comment on people who only want easy listening and miss poetry's other "charms," including its meaning (compared to the "doctrine" that is the real purpose of a church service, in line 343).

With a similar technique of demonstrating principles of poetic style and taste, the pace of lines 347, 357, and 359 is controlled by clashing consonant sounds as well as long vowels. Line 347 seems much longer than it is because almost every one-syllable word ends in a consonant that refuses to blend with the beginning of the next word, making the words hard to say without distinct, awkward pauses between them. In lines 357 and 359, long vowels such as those in "wounded," "snake," "slow," "along," "roundly," and "smooth" slow down the pace, and awkward, hard-to-pronounce consonants are again juxtaposed. The commas also provide nearly full stops in the middle of these lines to slow us down still more. Similarly, the harsh lashing of the shore in lines 368–69 is accomplished partly by onomatopoeia, partly by a shift in the pattern of stress, which creates irregular waves in line 368, and partly by the dominance of rough consonants in line 369. (In Pope's time, the English *r* was still trilled gruffly so that it could be made to sound extremely *rrr*ough and ha*rrr*sh.) Almost every line in this passage demonstrates how to make sound echo sense.

POETIC METER

In the Western world, we can thank the ancient Greeks for systematizing an understanding of meter and providing a vocabulary (including the words **rhythm** and **meter**) that enables us to discuss the art of poetry. *Meter* comes from a Greek word meaning "measure": What we measure in the English language are the patterns of stressed (or accented) syllables that occur naturally when we speak, and, just as when we measure length, the unit we use in measuring poetry is the **foot**. Most traditional poetry in English uses the accentual-syllabic form of meter—meaning that its rhythmic pattern is based on both a set number of syllables per line and a regular pattern of accents in each line. Not all poems have a regular metrical pattern, and not all metered poems follow only one pattern throughout. But like everyday speech, the language of poetry always has *some* accents (as in this italic emphasis on "some"), and poets arrange that rhythm for effect. Thus in non-metrical as well as metrical poetry, a reader should "listen" for patterns of stress.

The Basic Metrical Feet of Poetry in English

iamb: an unstressed or unaccented syllable followed by a stressed or accented one ("she wént," "belíeve"). This meter is called *iambic.*

trochee: a stressed syllable followed by an unstressed one ("méter," "Hómer"). This meter is called *trochaic.*

anapest: two unstressed syllables followed by a stressed one ("comprehénd," "after yóu"). This meter is called *anapestic.*

dactyl: a stressed syllable followed by two unstressed ones ("róundabout," "dínnertime"). This meter is called *dactylic.*

long or **short, strong** or **weak**: various terms that have been used for the syllables that we call stressed and unstressed.

rising or **falling**: the above feet either begin or end with the stressed syllable, as if they lose or gain momentum or "height." Hence iambic and anapestic are called rising meters, and trochaic and dactylic are called falling meters.

Other Kinds of Feet

spondee: two stressed syllables. Spondaic feet vary or interrupt the prevailing rhythm, emphasizing a syllable that we would expect to be unstressed ("Lást cáll," "Dón't gó").

pyrrhic: two unstressed syllables. Pyrrhic feet similarly interrupt the expected rising or falling beats, placing an unstressed syllable where we expect an emphasis ("ŭntŏ," "ĭs ă").

Spondees and pyrrhic feet depend on prevailing meter and usually appear singly or only a few times in a row. It is difficult to imagine (or to write or speak) a line or sentence either that has no unstressed syllables—a constant strong beat (spondaic)—or one that lacks stressed syllables—a rippling monotone (pyrrhic).

Because the concept of meter derives from poetic traditions in Greek and Latin that counted syllables rather than accents, other

(Continued on next page)

(Continued)

possible combinations of syllables acquired names, for instance, *amphibrach* (unstressed, stressed, unstressed—noted by Coleridge in his demonstration of meter, "Metrical Feet," below). But since most meter in poetry in English depends on accents rather than the number of syllables, the terms above cover most of the variations that you will encounter.

Counting Feet, or Meter

A line of poetry is subdivided into feet in order to "measure" its meter. The terms are easy enough to understand if you recall geometry or other numeric terminology. Remember that this is a count *not* of the number of syllables but of stresses; thus, for example, monometer could have two or three syllables per line.

monometer:	one foot
dimeter:	two feet
trimeter:	three feet
tetrameter:	four feet
pentameter:	five feet
hexameter:	six feet
heptameter:	seven feet
octameter:	eight feet

Counting the number of feet, that is, the number of accents, stresses, or strong beats per line, helps you identify the *kind* of feet in the line. Thus the terms are combined: *Iambic pentameter* has five iambs per line; *trochaic tetrameter* has four trochees per line, and so on.

Although scanning lines of poetry by reading them aloud, marking syllables as "short" or "long" (unstressed or stressed), and adding up feet may seem like a counting game that has little to do with the meaning of poetry, it is an important way to understand the sound effects of a poem. Like different styles of music, different meters tend to express different moods or to be appropriate to different themes. When you know the basic meter of a poem, you are more alert to subtle variations in the pattern. Poets avoid the predictable or the lulling by using certain "change-ups" in the dominant meter or line length, such as substitution of a different foot (e.g., a trochee or spondee instead of an iamb); **caesura**, a short pause within a line often signaled by punctuation; or **enjambment**, extending the end of the grammatical sentence beyond the end of the poetic line.

Here are the first two lines of Alexander Pope's "Sound and Sense," marked to show the stressed syllables:

(Continued on next page)

(Continued)

> But móst | by núm- | bers júdge | a pó- | et's sóng,
> And smóoth | or róugh, | with thém, | is ríght | or wróng.

These lines, like so many in English literature, provide an example of *iambic pentameter*—that is, the lines are written in a meter consisting of five iambic feet. Notice that there is nothing forced or artificial in the sound of these lines; the words flow easily. In fact, linguists contend that English is naturally iambic, and even the most ordinary, "unpoetic" utterances often fall into this pattern: "Please tell me if you've heard this one before." "They said she had a certain way with words." "The baseball game was televised at nine."

> **iambic pentameter**: "In sé- | quent tóil | all fór- | wards dó | con- | ténd…" (William Shakespeare)
> **trochaic octameter**: "Ónce u- | pón a | mídnight | dréary, | whíle I | póndered, | wéak and | wéary…" (Edgar Allan Poe)
> **anapestic tetrameter**: "There are mán- | y who sáy | that a dóg | has his dáy…" (Dylan Thomas)
> **dactylic hexameter**: "Thís is the | fórest pri- | méval. The | múrmuring | pínes and the | hémlocks…" (Henry Wadsworth Longfellow)

Notice that this final example is perfectly regular until the final foot, a trochee. Also notice that Poe and Longfellow have placed a caesura within a long line. Substitution of one metrical foot for another—to accommodate idioms and conversational habits or to create a special effect or emphasis—is quite common, especially in the first foot of a line. Shakespeare often begins an iambic line with a trochee:

> Líke as | the wáves | make towárds | the péb- | bled shóre…

Or consider this line from John Milton's *Paradise Lost*, a poem written mainly in iambic pentameter:

> Rócks, cáves, | lákes, féns, | bógs, déns, | and Shádes | of Déath…

Here Milton substitutes three spondees for the first three iambs in a pentameter line. John Dryden's "To the Memory of Mr. Oldham" arguably begins with two spondees, a pyrrhic, and an iamb before settling into a regular iambic pentameter (here the slashes mark the feet):

(Continued on next page)

(Continued)

> Fárewéll, | tóo lít | tle, and | tóo láte | ly knówn,

As Dryden's poem shows, meter does leave room for discussion; some readers might read the line above as iambic throughout, and others might read the last three feet as iambic: The natural emphasis on the first word after the caesura, "and," could make the predictable word "too" unstressed.

In the following poem, Samuel Taylor Coleridge playfully names and illustrates many types of meter.

SAMUEL TAYLOR COLERIDGE

Metrical Feet

Lesson for a Boy

Trōchĕe trīps frŏm lōng tŏ shōrt;[9]
From long to long in solemn sort
Slōw Spōndēe stālks; strŏng fŏŏt! yet ill able
Ēvĕr tŏ cōme ŭp wĭth Dāctȳl trĭsȳllāblĕ.
5 Īāmbĭcs mārch frŏm shōrt tŏ lōng—
   Wĭth ă lēap ănd ă bōund thĕ swĭft Ānăpĕsts thrōng;
   One syllable long, with one short at each side,
   Ămphībrăchȳs hāstes wĭth ă stātelȳ stride—
   Fīrst ănd lāst bēĭng lōng, mīddlĕ shōrt, Ămphīmācer
10 Strīkes hĭs thūndērĭng hŏŏfs līke ă prōud hīgh-brĕd Rācer.
   If Derwent[1] be innocent, steady, and wise,
   And delight in the things of earth, water, and skies;
   Tender warmth at his heart, with these meters to show it,
   With sound sense in his brains, may make Derwent a poet—
15 May crown him with fame, and must win him the love
   Of his father on earth and his Father above.
              My dear, dear child!

---

9. The long and short marks over syllables are Coleridge's.
1. Written originally for Coleridge's son Hartley, the poem was later adapted for his younger son, Derwent.

Could you stand upon Skiddaw,[2] you would not from its whole
  ridge
See a man who so loves you as your fond S. T. COLERIDGE.

1806

PRACTICING SCANSION (READING METER)

Scansion is the technique of listening to and marking stressed and unstressed syllables, counting the syllables and feet, and checking the rhyme patterns. Often, you will need to scan several lines before you can be sure of the "controlling" metrical pattern of a poem. Though there is no easy substitute for this work, it will help you appreciate the subtleties of a poet's craft.

Hearing a poem properly involves practice—listening to others read poetry and especially to yourself as you read poems aloud. Your dictionary will show you the stresses for every word of more than one syllable, and the governing stress of individual words will largely control the patterns in a line: If you read a line for its sense (almost as if it were prose), you will usually see the line's basic pattern. But single-syllable words can be a challenge because they may or may not be stressed, depending on their syntactic function and the full meaning of the sentence. Normally, important functional words, such as one-syllable nouns and verbs, are stressed (as in normal conversation or in prose), but conjunctions (such as *and* or *but*), prepositions (such as *on* or *with*), and articles (such as *an* or *the*) are not.

The way you actually read a line, once you have "heard" the basic rhythm, is influenced by two factors: normal pronunciation and prose sense (on the one hand) and the predominant pattern of the poem (on the other). Since these two forces are constantly in tension and are sometimes contradictory, you can almost never fully predict the actual reading of a line, and good reading aloud (like every other art) depends less on formula than on subtlety and flexibility. Sometimes very good readers plausibly disagree about whether or not to stress certain syllables. We have noted the use of substitution, and many poems since around 1900 have taken liberties with meter and rhyme. Some poets (such as Marianne Moore) have favored counting syllables rather than accents. Even more widespread is **free verse**, which does without any governing pattern of stresses or line lengths.

Each of the following poems is written in a different meter. Using the terms defined in "Poetic Meter" (on pp. 592–596) as well as in Coleridge's poem "Metrical Feet," pair the following poems with their corresponding meter. (The answers are on p. 599.)

---

2. A mountain in the lake country of northern England (where Coleridge lived in his early years), near the town of Derwent.

1. ANONYMOUS

[*There was a young girl from St. Paul*]

There was a young girl from St. Paul,
Wore a newspaper-dress to a ball.
    The dress caught on fire
    And burned her entire
Front page, sporting section and all.

2. ALFRED, LORD TENNYSON

From *The Charge of the Light Brigade*

1.

Half a league, half a league,
    Half a league onward,
All in the valley of Death
    Rode the six hundred.
5 "Forward, the Light Brigade!
"Charge for the guns!" he said:
Into the valley of Death
    Rode the six hundred.

2.

"Forward, the Light Brigade!"
10 Was there a man dismay'd?
Not tho' the soldier knew
    Someone had blunder'd:
Theirs not to make reply,
Theirs not to reason why,
15 Theirs but to do and die:
Into the valley of Death
    Rode the six hundred.

1854

3. SIR JOHN SUCKLING

Song

Why so pale and wan, fond Lover?
  Prithee why so pale?
Will, when looking well can't move her,
  Looking ill prevail?
5 Prithee why so pale?

Why so dull and mute, young Sinner?
  Prithee why so mute?
Will, when speaking well can't win her,
  Saying nothing do 't?
10 Prithee why so mute?

Quit, quit, for shame, this will not move,
  This cannot take her;
If of her self she will not love,
  Nothing can make her,
15 The Devil take her.

        1646

4. JOHN DRYDEN

To the Memory of Mr. Oldham[3]

Farewell, too little, and too lately known,
Whom I began to think and call my own;
For sure our souls were near allied, and thine
Cast in the same poetic mold with mine.
5 One common note on either lyre did strike,
And knaves and fools we both abhorred alike.
To the same goal did both our studies drive;
The last set out the soonest did arrive.
Thus Nisus fell upon the slippery place,
10 While his young friend performed and won the race.[4]
O early ripe! to thy abundant store

---

*ANSWERS: 1. anapestic, 2. dactylic, 3. trochaic, 4. iambic.
3. John Oldham (1653–83), like Dryden (see lines 3–6), wrote satiric poetry.
4. In Virgil's *Aeneid* (Book 5), Nisus (who is leading the race) falls and then trips the second runner so that his friend Euryalus can win.

What could advancing age have added more?
It might (what nature never gives the young)
Have taught the numbers[5] of thy native tongue.
15 But satire needs not those, and wit will shine
Through the harsh cadence of a rugged line.[6]
A noble error, and but seldom made,
When poets are by too much force betrayed.
Thy generous fruits, though gathered ere their prime,
20 Still showed a quickness; and maturing time
But mellows what we write to the dull sweets of rhyme.
Once more, hail and farewell; farewell, thou young,
But ah too short, Marcellus[7] of our tongue;
Thy brows with ivy, and with laurels bound;
25 But fate and gloomy night encompass thee around.

                                                    1684

· · ·

SCANNING METER: A SELECTION OF POEMS

EDGAR ALLAN POE

The Raven

Once upon a midnight dreary, while I pondered, weak and weary,
Over many a quaint and curious volume of forgotten lore,
While I nodded, nearly napping, suddenly there came a tapping,
As of some one gently rapping, rapping at my chamber door.
5 "'Tis some visitor," I muttered, "tapping at my chamber door—
            Only this, and nothing more."

Ah, distinctly I remember it was in the bleak December,
And each separate dying ember wrought its ghost upon the floor.
Eagerly I wished the morrow;—vainly I had sought to borrow
10 From my books surcease of sorrow—sorrow for the lost Lenore—
For the rare and radiant maiden whom the angels name Lenore—
            Nameless here for evermore.

And the silken sad uncertain rustling of each purple curtain
Thrilled me—filled me with fantastic terrors never felt before;

---

5. Rhythms.   6. In Dryden's time, the English *r* was pronounced with a harsh, trilling sound.
7. Nephew of the Roman emperor Augustus who died at twenty, celebrated by Virgil in the *Aeneid*,
Book 6.

15 So that now, to still the beating of my heart, I stood repeating
   " 'Tis some visitor entreating entrance at my chamber door;—
   Some late visitor entreating entrance at my chamber door;
                    This it is, and nothing more."

   Presently my soul grew stronger; hesitating then no longer,
20 "Sir," said I, "or Madam, truly your forgiveness I implore;
   But the fact is I was napping, and so gently you came rapping,
   And so faintly you came tapping, tapping at my chamber door,
   That I scarce was sure I heard you"—here I opened wide the door;—
                    Darkness there, and nothing more.

25 Deep into that darkness peering, long I stood there wondering,
      fearing,
   Doubting, dreaming dreams no mortal ever dared to dream
      before;
   But the silence was unbroken, and the darkness gave no token,
   And the only word there spoken was the whispered word,
      "Lenore!"
   This I whispered, and an echo murmured back the word, "Lenore!"—
30   Merely this, and nothing more.

   Back into the chamber turning, all my soul within me burning,
   Soon I heard again a tapping somewhat louder than before.
   "Surely," said I, "surely that is something at my window lattice;
   Let me see, then, what thereat is, and this mystery explore—
35 Let my heart be still a moment and this mystery explore;—
                    'Tis the wind and nothing more!"

   Open here I flung the shutter, when, with many a flirt and flutter,
   In there stepped a stately raven of the saintly days of yore;
   Not the least obeisance made he; not an instant stopped or
      stayed he;
40 But, with mien of lord or lady, perched above my chamber door—
   Perched upon a bust of Pallas[8] just above my chamber door—
                    Perched, and sat, and nothing more.

   Then this ebony bird beguiling my sad fancy into smiling,
   By the grave and stern decorum of the countenance it wore,
45 "Though thy crest be shorn and shaven, thou," I said, "art sure no
      craven,
   Ghastly grim and ancient raven wandering from the Nightly shore—
   Tell me what thy lordly name is on the Night's Plutonian[9] shore!"
                    Quoth the raven, "Nevermore."

---

8. Athena, the Greek goddess of wisdom.   9. Dark; Pluto was god of the underworld.

Much I marvelled this ungainly fowl to hear discourse so plainly,
50 Though its answer little meaning—little relevancy bore,
For we cannot help agreeing that no living human being
Ever yet was blessed with seeing bird above his chamber door—
Bird or beast upon the sculptured bust above his chamber door,
With such name as "Nevermore."

55 But the raven, sitting lonely on the placid bust, spoke only
That one word, as if his soul in that one word he did outpour.
Nothing farther then he uttered—not a feather then he fluttered—
Till I scarcely more than muttered "Other friends have flown before—
On the morrow *he* will leave me, as my hopes have flown before."
60 Then the bird said "Nevermore."

Startled at the stillness broken by reply so aptly spoken,
"Doubtless," said I, "what it utters is its only stock and store
Caught from some unhappy master whom unmerciful Disaster
Followed fast and followed faster till his songs one burden bore—
65 Till the dirges of his Hope that melancholy burden bore
Of 'Never—nevermore.' "

But the raven still beguiling all my sad soul into smiling,
Straight I wheeled a cushioned seat in front of bird and bust and
door;
Then, upon the velvet sinking, I betook myself to linking
70 Fancy unto fancy, thinking what this ominous bird of yore—
What this grim, ungainly, ghastly, gaunt, and ominous bird of
yore
Meant in croaking "Nevermore."

This I sat engaged in guessing, but no syllable expressing
To the fowl whose fiery eyes now burned into my bosom's core;
75 This and more I sat divining, with my head at ease reclining
On the cushion's velvet lining that the lamplight gloated o'er,
But whose velvet violet lining with the lamplight gloating o'er,
She shall press, ah, nevermore!

Then, methought, the air grew denser, perfumed from an unseen
censer
80 Swung by angels whose faint foot-falls tinkled on the tufted
floor.
"Wretch," I cried, "thy God hath lent thee—by these angels he
hath sent thee
Respite—respite and nepenthe[1] from thy memories of Lenore!

1. A drug reputed by the Greeks to cause forgetfulness or sorrow (pronounced "ne-PEN-thee").

Quaff, oh quaff this kind nepenthe and forget this lost Lenore!"
                    Quoth the raven, "Nevermore."

85 "Prophet!" said I, "thing of evil!—prophet still, if bird or devil!—
    Whether Tempter sent, or whether tempest tossed thee here
        ashore,
    Desolate, yet all undaunted, on this desert land enchanted—
    On this home by Horror haunted—tell me truly, I implore—
    Is there—*is* there balm in Gilead?² —tell me—tell me, I implore!"
90   Quoth the raven, "Nevermore."

    "Prophet!" said I, "thing of evil—prophet still, if bird or devil!
    By that Heaven that bends above us—by that God we both adore—
    Tell this soul with sorrow laden if, within the distant Aidenn,³
    It shall clasp a sainted maiden whom the angels name Lenore—
95 Clasp a rare and radiant maiden whom the angels name Lenore."
                    Quoth the raven, "Nevermore."

    "Be that word our sign of parting, bird or fiend!" I shrieked
        upstarting—
    "Get thee back into the tempest and the Night's Plutonian shore!
    Leave no black plume as a token of that lie thy soul hath spoken!
100 Leave my loneliness unbroken!—quit the bust above my door!
    Take thy beak from out my heart, and take thy form from off my
        door!"
                    Quoth the raven, "Nevermore."

    And the raven, never flitting, still is sitting, still is sitting
    On the pallid bust of Pallas just above my chamber door;
105 And his eyes have all the seeming of a demon's that is dreaming,
    And the lamp-light o'er him streaming throws his shadow on the
        floor;
    And my soul from out that shadow that lies floating on the floor
                    Shall be lifted—nevermore!

                                                    1844

- Describing the composition of "The Raven," Poe wrote of the
  need to use sounds "in the fullest possible keeping with that
  melancholy which I had predetermined as the tone of the
  poem." List at least five of the sound effects (e.g., rhyme, alliteration, etc.) that Poe uses in "The Raven." How does each of
  these contribute to the poem's tone of "melancholy"?

2. See Jeremiah 8.22. 3. Eden.

WILLIAM SHAKESPEARE

[Like as the waves make towards the pebbled shore]

Like as the waves make towards the pebbled shore,
So do our minutes hasten to their end,
Each changing place with that which goes before,
In sequent toil all forwards do contend.[4]
5 Nativity, once in the main[5] of light,
Crawls to maturity, wherewith being crowned,
Crooked[6] eclipses 'gainst his glory fight,
And Time that gave doth now his gift confound.[7]
Time doth transfix[8] the flourish set on youth
10 And delves the parallels[9] in beauty's brow,
Feeds on the rarities of nature's truth,
And nothing stands but for his scythe to mow.
And yet to times in hope[1] my verse shall stand,
Praising thy worth, despite his cruel hand.

1609

• Which lines in this poem vary the basic iambic metric
scheme? What is the effect of these variations?

GERARD MANLEY HOPKINS

Spring and Fall

to a young child

Márgarét áre you gríeving[2]
Over Goldengrove unleaving?
Leáves, like the things of man, you
With your fresh thoughts care for, can you?
5 Áh! ás the heart grows older
It will come to such sights colder
By and by, nor spare a sigh

---

4. Struggle. *Sequent:* successive.   5. High seas. *Nativity:* newborn life.   6. Perverse.
7. Bring to nothing.   8. Pierce.   9. Lines, wrinkles.   1. In the future.
2. Hopkins's own accent markings.

Though worlds of wanwood leafmeal³ lie;
And yet you wíll weep and know why.
10 Now no matter, child, the name:
Sórrow's spríngs áre the same.
Nor mouth had, no nor mind, expressed
What heart heard of, ghost⁴ guessed:
It ís the blight man was born for,
15 It is Margaret you mourn for.

1880

• How does this poem's heavy use of alliteration serve its
themes of youth and age, life and death?

EMILY DICKINSON

[*A narrow Fellow in the Grass*]

A narrow Fellow in the Grass
Occasionally rides—
You may have met Him—did you not
His notice sudden is—

5 The Grass divides as with a Comb—
A spotted shaft is seen—
And then it closes at your feet
And opens further on—

He likes a Boggy Acre
10 A Floor too cool for Corn—
Yet when a Boy, and Barefoot—
I more than once at Noon

Have passed, I thought, a Whip lash
Unbraiding in the Sun
15 When stooping to secure it
It wrinkled, and was gone—

Several of Nature's People
I know, and they know me—
I feel for them a transport
20 Of cordiality—

3. Broken up, leaf by leaf (analogous to "piecemeal"). *Wanwood:* pale, gloomy woods.   4. Soul.

> But never met this Fellow
> Attended, or alone
> Without a tighter breathing
> And Zero at the Bone—

1866

• How does Dickinson use sound devices such as alliteration
  to underscore the images and themes of the poem?

SUGGESTIONS FOR WRITING

1. Read Pope's "Sound and Sense" carefully twice—once silently and once
   aloud—and then mark the stressed and unstressed syllables. Single out all
   the lines that have major variations from the basic iambic pentameter pattern. Pick out six lines with variations that seem to you worthy of comment,
   and write a paragraph on each in which you show how the varied metrical
   pattern contributes to the specific effects achieved in that line and the corresponding point Pope conveys about poetic style.

2. Try your hand at writing limericks in imitation of "There was a young girl
   from St. Paul"; study the rhythmic patterns and line lengths carefully, and
   imitate them exactly in your poem. Begin your limerick with "There once
   was a _____ from _____" (using a place for which you think you can find a
   comic rhyme).

3. Read Poe's "The Raven" aloud, paying particular attention to pacing. Do you
   find yourself speeding up as you continue through the poem? Does a quick-
   ening pace suit the speaker's growing exasperation and madness? Write an
   essay in which you examine the way that Poe underlines the poem's story and
   emotional flow with a range of poetic devices: line length, punctuation,
   rhyme, meter, and the sounds of words.

4. Pope's "Sound and Sense" contains this advice for poets: "But when loud
   surges lash the sounding shore, / The hoarse, rough verse should like the torrent roar" (lines 368–69). In other words, he counsels that the sound of the
   poet's description should match the sense of what the poem is describing.
   Write an essay in which you examine the sound and sense in Shakespeare's
   "[Like as the waves make towards the pebbled shore]." How does the poem
   achieve a harmony of meaning and sound?

5. Write an essay in which you discuss any of the poems you have read in this
   book in which sound seems a more important element than anything else,
   even the meaning of words. What is the point of writing and reading this
   kind of poetry? Can it achieve its effects through silent reading, or must it be
   experienced aloud?

Words and Music: An Album

People often associate poetry with music, for good reason. The word lyric—the standard term for a short, harmonious, pleasant, and often romantic poem—derives from the ancient Greeks' practice of reciting certain poems to the accompaniment of a harplike instrument, the lyre. Throughout history, poems have been set to music and many "lyrics" have been created specifically to fit musical compositions. Many poems, especially during the Renaissance, were simply called "Song" (or "Chanson" or "Lied" or similar terms in other languages), and some were constructed in hybrid musical-poetic forms such as the madrigal, the dirge, and the hymn.

The most fundamental link between poetry and music involves their almost equal dependence on the principles of rhythm. Both art forms have a basis in mathematics: A regular beat or syncopated sound pattern shapes their phrasing and formal movement. Performers of both arts must keep count and consider quantities as well as qualities of sounds. Just as good musicians learn to listen and count so easily that it seems "natural," poets often develop an ear for rhythm that makes their sound choices seem effortless. Readers, too, can develop such an ear.

Both poetry and music use representational or imitative strategies to create the illusion of sounds—bells, waves, motorcycles, for example—but words operate referentially in a way that sounds normally do not, and their syntax is of a different kind from that in musical composition. The referential fact of language almost always alters the "pure" effects of sound (though in nonsense lyrics, sounds or tonal expressions may be merely recorded in letters).

Poems composed to or for music obviously rely on rhythmic or harmonic effects even more than those created solely by words. Reading the lyrics of a song you know well is quite different from reading words that have for you no musical association or history. But the "music" created by a poem itself can work in a similar way when there is no musical "source" or co-creation.

The poems that follow were all written for, in conjunction with, or to imitate music. Can you add your own song lyrics from your favorite contemporary singers and groups? Are the words as effective without the music? Do they make good poems? Can you, in the lyrics you know well, separate the actual musical implications from those of the words alone?

THOMAS CAMPION

When to Her Lute Corinna Sings

When to her lute Corinna sings,
Her voice revives the leaden[1] strings,

---

1. Heavy.

And doth in highest notes appear
As any challenged[2] echo clear;
5 But when she doth of mourning speak,
Ev'n with her sighs the strings do break.
And as her lute doth live or die,
Led by her passion, so must I:
For when of pleasure she doth sing,
10 My thoughts enjoy a sudden spring;
But if she doth of sorrow speak,
Ev'n from my heart the strings do break.

1601

- How does Campion mimic an "echo" in this poem? What is
the effect of this echoing?

WILLIAM SHAKESPEARE

Spring[3]

When daisies pied[4] and violets blue
And ladysmocks all silver-white
And cuckoobuds of yellow hue
Do paint the meadows with delight,
5 The cuckoo then, on every tree,
Mocks married men;[5] for thus sings he,
Cuckoo;
Cuckoo, cuckoo: Oh word of fear,
Unpleasing to a married ear!

10 When shepherds pipe on oaten straws,
And merry larks are plowmen's clocks,
When turtles tread,[6] and rooks, and daws,
And maidens bleach their summer smocks,
The cuckoo then, on every tree,
15 Mocks married men; for thus sings he,
Cuckoo;
Cuckoo, cuckoo: Oh word of fear,
Unpleasing to a married ear!

ca. 1595

---

2. Aroused.   3. Song from *Love's Labour's Lost*.   4. Of varied colors.
5. That is, by the resemblance of its call to the word *cuckold*.   6. Turtledoves copulate.

• What words or phrases might a singer emphasize in order to enhance this poem's comic effect?

ROBERT HAYDEN

Homage to the Empress of the Blues[7]

Because there was a man somewhere in a candystripe silk shirt,
gracile and dangerous as a jaguar and because a woman moaned
for him in sixty-watt gloom and mourned him Faithless Love
Twotiming Love Oh Love Oh Careless Aggravating Love,

5   She came out on the stage in yards of pearls, emerging like
a favorite scenic view, flashed her golden smile and sang.

Because grey laths began somewhere to show from underneath
torn hurdygurdy[8] lithographs of dollfaced heaven;
and because there were those who feared alarming fists of snow
10 on the door and those who feared the riot-squad of statistics,

She came out on the stage in ostrich feathers, beaded satin,
and shone that smile on us and sang.

1962

• How do the two short stanzas beginning with "She came out" complete the thoughts of the longer stanzas that start with "Because"?

MICHAEL HARPER

Dear John, Dear Coltrane

a love supreme, a love supreme
a love supreme, a love supreme[9]

Sex fingers toes
in the marketplace

7. Bessie Smith (1894 [or 1898?]–1937); legendary blues singer whose theatrical style grew out of the black American vaudeville tradition.   8. A disreputable kind of dance hall.
9. Coltrane wrote "A Love Supreme" in response to a spiritual experience in 1957 that also led to his quitting heroin and alcohol. Mainly an instrumental improvisation featuring Coltrane's saxophone, the piece begins with the repeated chant of "a love supreme." The record was released in 1965.

near your father's church
in Hamlet, North Carolina—[1]
5 witness to this love
in this calm fallow
of these minds,
there is no substitute for pain:
genitals gone or going,
10 seed burned out,
you tuck the roots in the earth,

BOB DYLAN

Mr. Tambourine Man

Hey! Mr. Tambourine Man, play a song for me,
I'm not sleepy and there is no place I'm going to.
Hey! Mr. Tambourine Man, play a song for me,
In the jingle jangle morning I'll come followin' you.

5 Though I know that evenin's empire has returned into sand,
Vanished from my hand,
Left me blindly here to stand but still not sleeping.
My weariness amazes me, I'm branded on my feet,
I have no one to meet
10 And the ancient empty street's too dead for dreaming.

Hey! Mr. Tambourine Man, play a song for me,
I'm not sleepy and there is no place I'm going to.
Hey! Mr. Tambourine Man, play a song for me,
In the jingle jangle morning I'll come followin' you.

15 Take me on a trip upon your magic swirlin' ship,
My senses have been stripped, my hands can't feel to grip,
My toes too numb to step, wait only for my boot heels
To be wanderin'.
I'm ready to go anywhere, I'm ready for to fade
20 Into my own parade, cast your dancing spell my way,
I promise to go under it.

Hey! Mr. Tambourine Man, play a song for me,
I'm not sleepy and there is no place I'm going to.

---

1. Coltrane's birthplace. His family shared a house with Coltrane's grandfather, who was the minister of St. Stephen's AME Zion Church.

Hey! Mr. Tambourine Man, play a song for me,
25 In the jingle jangle morning I'll come followin' you.

Though you might hear laughin', spinnin', swingin' madly across
    the sun,
It's not aimed at anyone, it's just escapin' on the run
And but for the sky there are no fences facin'.
And if you hear vague traces of skippin' reels of rhyme
30 To your tambourine in time, it's just a ragged clown behind,
I wouldn't pay it any mind, it's just a shadow you're
Seein' that he's chasing.

Hey! Mr. Tambourine Man, play a song for me,
I'm not sleepy and there is no place I'm going to.
35 Hey! Mr. Tambourine Man, play a song for me,
In the jingle jangle morning I'll come followin' you.

Then take me disappearin' through the smoke rings of my mind,
Down the foggy ruins of time, far past the frozen leaves,
The haunted, frightened trees, out to the windy beach,
40 Far from the twisted reach of crazy sorrow.
Yes, to dance beneath the diamond sky with one hand waving
    free,
Silhouetted by the sea, circled by the circus sands,
With all memory and fate driven deep beneath the waves,
Let me forget about today until tomorrow.

45 Hey! Mr. Tambourine Man, play a song for me,
I'm not sleepy and there is no place I'm going to.
Hey! Mr. Tambourine Man, play a song for me,
In the jingle jangle morning I'll come followin' you.

1964

- How does familiarity with "Mr. Tambourine Man" as a song
  affect our sense of it as a poem? Do successful song lyrics
  necessarily work as poetry?

SUGGESTIONS FOR WRITING

1. Is there a meaningful difference between poetry and song lyrics? between
   poetry and rap? Is hip-hop a form of literature? Write an essay in which you
   explore the definitions of "poetry" and "lyrics." Be sure to cite enough examples to illustrate your ideas.
2. Find on the Internet the lyrics of a song (of any genre) that in your opinion uses
   words well, and download or print out one or more versions. First, notice any
   variations between the text(s) you find and the words you hear when listening

to the song. Using a correct version of the lyrics (as you determine it), scan the lines for meter and rhyme. Are any words or syllables used to keep the beat without adding to the meaning (like the word "do," in Pope's "Sound and Sense")? Are any rhymes dependent on vowel sounds rather than consonants (that is, do they not quite rhyme in print)? How does the refrain (if any) vary from the rest of the lyrics, and how does it relate to the title or theme of the song? Which lines or verses are most important in the "story" or the feeling relayed by the song? How would you describe the diction and tone of the "speaker" of the words, and how does it compare with the vocal style of the singer? Write a descriptive response paper on these words as a poem without music, and as lyrics within the song. Are they equally successful in print as they are when performed with music?

12 INTERNAL STRUCTURE

"Proper words in proper places": That is how one great writer of English prose, Jonathan Swift, described good writing. A good poet finds appropriate words, and already we have looked at some implications for readers of the verbal choices a poet makes. But the poet must also decide where to put those words—how to arrange them for maximum effect—because individual words, metaphors, and symbols exist not only within phrases and sentences and rhythmic patterns, but also within the larger whole of the poem. How should the words be arranged and the poem organized? What comes first and what last? Will the poem have a "plot"? What principle or idea of organization will inform it? How can words, sentences, images, ideas, and feelings be combined into a structure that holds together, seems complete, and affects readers?

Considering these questions from the poet's point of view (What is my plan? Where shall I begin?) can help us notice the effects of structural choices. Every poem works in its own unique way, and therefore every poet must make independent decisions about how to organize an individual poem. But poems do fall into patterns of organization, sometimes because of subject matter, sometimes because of effects intended, sometimes for other reasons. A poet may consciously decide on a particular strategy, may reach instinctively for one, or may happen into one that suits the needs of the moment—a framework onto which words and sentences will hang, one by one and group by group.

NARRATIVE POEMS

A **narrative poem** tells a story, and its organization may be fairly straightforward. The following poem, for example, tells a simple story largely in chronological order:

EDWIN ARLINGTON ROBINSON

Mr. Flood's Party

Old Eben Flood, climbing alone one night
Over the hill between the town below
And the forsaken upland hermitage
That held as much as he should ever know
5   On earth again of home, paused warily.
The road was his and not a native near;
And Eben, having leisure, said aloud,
For no man else in Tilbury Town to hear:

"Well, Mr. Flood, we have the harvest moon
10   Again, and we may not have many more;
The bird is on the wing, the poet says,[1]
And you and I have said it here before.
Drink to the bird." He raised up to the light
The jug that he had gone so far to fill,
15   And answered huskily: "Well, Mr. Flood,
Since you propose it, I believe I will."

Alone, as if enduring to the end
A valiant armor of scarred hopes outworn
He stood there in the middle of the road
20   Like Roland's ghost winding a silent horn.[2]
Below him, in the town among the trees,
Where friends of other days had honored him,
A phantom salutation of the dead
Rang thinly till old Eben's eyes were dim.

25   Then, as a mother lays her sleeping child
Down tenderly, fearing it may awake
He set the jug down slowly at his feet
With trembling care, knowing that most things break;
And only when assured that on firm earth
30   It stood, as the uncertain lives of men
Assuredly did not, he paced away,
And with his hand extended paused again:

---

1. Edward FitzGerald, in "The Rubáiyát of Omar Khayyám" (more or less a translation of an Arab original), so describes the "Bird of Time."
2. According to French legend, the hero Roland used his powerful ivory horn to warn his allies of impending attack.

> "Well, Mr. Flood, we have not met like this
> In a long time; and many a change has come
> 35 To both of us, I fear, since last it was
> We had a drop together. Welcome home!"
> Convivially returning with himself,
> Again he raised the jug up to the light;
> And with an acquiescent quaver said:
> 40 "Well, Mr. Flood, if you insist, I might.
>
> "Only a very little, Mr. Flood—
> For auld lang syne. No more, sir; that will do."
> So, for the time, apparently it did,
> And Eben evidently thought so too;
> 45 For soon amid the silver loneliness
> Of night he lifted up his voice and sang,
> Secure, with only two moons listening,
> Until the whole harmonious landscape rang—
>
> "For auld lang syne." The weary throat gave out,
> 50 The last word wavered, and the song was done.
> He raised again the jug regretfully
> And shook his head, and was again alone.
> There was not much that was ahead of him,
> And there was nothing in the town below—
> 55 Where strangers would have shut the many doors
> That many friends had opened long ago.

1921

The fairly simple narrative structure here is based on the gradual unfolding of the story. After old Eben is introduced and situated in relation to the town and his home, the "plot" unfolds: He sits down in the road, reviews his life, reflects on the present, and has a drink—several drinks, in fact, as he thinks about passing time and growing old; then he sings and considers going "home." Not much happens, really; we get a vignette of Mr. Flood between two places and two times. But there *is* **action**, and the poem's movement—its organization and structure—depends on it: Mr. Flood in motion, in stasis, and then, again, contemplating motion. This counts as action, and a certain, limited chronological movement. We could say that a spare sort of story takes place, like that in Dickey's "Cherrylog Road" (chapter 9). The poem's organization—its structural principle—involves the passing of time, action moving forward, a larger story being revealed by the few moments depicted here.

"Mr. Flood's Party" presents about as much story as a short poem ever does, but like many poems it doesn't really emphasize the developing action—

which all seems fairly predictable once we "get" who Eben is, how old he is, and what place he occupies in the communal memory of Tilbury Town and vice versa. Rather, the movement forward in time dictates the shape of the poem, determines the way it presents its images, ideas, themes. Nearly everything occurs within an easy-to-follow chronology.

But even here, in this most simple narrative structure, we note complications. One complication is in the use of time itself, for "old" time and "present" time seem posed against each other as a structural principle, too, one in tension with the chronological movement: Eben's past, as contrasted with his present and limited future, focuses the poem's attention, and in some ways the contrast between what was and what is seems even more important than the brief movement through present time that gets the most obvious attention in the poem. Then, too, "character"—Eben's character and that of the townspeople of later generations—gets a lot of attention, even as the chronology moves forward. More than one structural principle is at work here. We may identify the main movement of the poem as chronological and its principal structure as narrative, but to be fair and full in our discussion we have to note several other competing organizational forces at work—principles of comparison and contrast, for example, and of descriptive elaboration.

Most poems work with this kind of complexity, and identifying a single structure behind any poem involves a sense of the organizational principle that makes it work; at the same time, other principles repeatedly, perhaps continually, compete for our attention. A poem's structure involves its conceptual framework—what principle best explains its organization and movement—and it is often useful to identify one dominating kind of structure, such as narrative structure, that gives the poem its shape. But we need to recognize from the start that most poems follow structural models loosely. Finding an appropriate label to describe the structure of a particular poem can help us analyze the poem's other aspects, but the label itself has no magic.

Purely narrative poems are often very long and often include many features that are not, strictly speaking, closely connected to the narrative or linked to a strict chronology. Very often a poem moves from a narrative of an event to some sort of commentary or reflection on it. Such reflection can be included along the way or may be implicit in the way the story is narrated, as in Maxine Kumin's "Woodchucks" (chapter 7), where we focus more on the narrator and her responses than on the events in the story.

DRAMATIC POEMS

Just as poems sometimes take on a structure like that of a story, they sometimes borrow the structure of plays. Indeed, some plays *are* written in verse and are thus examples of **verse drama**. What we here call **dramatic poems** are instead merely modeled on drama. The following poem has a dramatic structure; although it, too, is technically a narrative poem insofar as its speaker narrates what happens to the characters in it, the poem consists wholly of a series of scenes, each of which is presented vividly and in detail, as if on stage.

HOWARD NEMEROV

The Goose Fish

On the long shore, lit by the moon
To show them properly alone,
Two lovers suddenly embraced
So that their shadows were as one.
5   The ordinary night was graced
For them by the swift tide of blood
That silently they took at flood.
And for a little time they prized
    Themselves emparadised.

10   Then, as if shaken by stage-fright
Beneath the hard moon's bony light,
They stood together on the sand
Embarrassed in each other's sight
But still conspiring hand in hand,
15   Until they saw, there underfoot,
As though the world had found them out,
The goose fish turning up, though dead,
    His hugely grinning head.

There in the china light he lay,
20   Most ancient and corrupt and gray.
They hesitated at his smile,
Wondering what it seemed to say
To lovers who a little while
Before had thought to understand,
25   By violence upon the sand,
The only way that could be known
    To make a world their own.

It was a wide and moony grin
Together peaceful and obscene;
30   They knew not what he would express,
So finished a comedian
He might mean failure or success,

But took it for an emblem of
Their sudden, new and guilty love
35 To be observed by, when they kissed,
   That rigid optimist.

So he became their patriarch,
Dreadfully mild in the half-dark.
His throat that the sand seemed to choke,
40 His picket teeth, these left their mark
   But never did explain the joke
   That so amused him, lying there
   While the moon went down to disappear
   Along the still and tilted track
45 That bears the zodiac.

                              1955

The first stanza sets the scene—a sandy shore in moonlight—and presents, in fact, the major action of the poem. The rest of the poem dramatizes the lovers' reactions: their initial embarrassment and feelings of guilt (stanza 2); their attempt to interpret the goose fish's smile (stanza 3); their decision to make him, whatever his meaning, the "emblem" of their love (stanza 4); and their acceptance of the fish's ambiguity and of their own relationship (stanza 5). The five stanzas do not exactly present five different scenes or angles on the action, but they do present separate dramatic moments, even if little time has elapsed between them. Almost like a play of five very short acts, the poem traces the drama of the lovers' discovery of themselves and their coming to terms with the meaning of their action. As in many plays, the central event (their lovemaking) is not the focus of the drama, although the drama is based on that event and could not take place without it. The poem depicts the event swiftly but very vividly through figurative language: "they took at flood" the "swift tide of blood" (lines 7, 6). The lovers then briefly feel "emparadised" (line 9), but the poem concentrates on their later reactions.

Their sudden discovery of the fish, a rude shock, injects a grotesque, almost macabre, note into the poem. From a vision of paradise, the poem seems for a moment to turn toward gothic horror when the lovers discover that they have, after all, been seen—and by such a ghoulish spectator. The last three stanzas gradually re-create the intruder in their minds, as they admit that their act of love exists not in isolation, but rather as part of a continuum, as part of their relationship to the larger world, even (at the end) within the context of the earth itself, and the moon, and the stars. In retrospect, we can see that even at the moment of passion the lovers were in touch with larger processes controlled by the presiding moon ("the swift *tide* of blood"), but neither they nor we had understood their act as such then, and the poem is about this gradual recognition of their "place" in time and space.

Stages of feeling and knowing rather than specific visual scenes determine the poem's progress, and its dramatic structure depends on internal perceptions and internal states of mind rather than dialogue and events. Visualization and images help organize the poem, too. Notice in particular how the two most striking visual features—the fish and the moon—are presented stanza by stanza. In stanza 1, the fish does not appear; the moon is only mentioned, not described, and its light provides a stage spotlight to assure not center-stage attention, but rather total privacy: The moon serves as a lookout for the lovers. The stage imagery, barely suggested by the light in stanza 1, is articulated in stanza 2, and there the moon is "hard" and its light "bony"; its characteristics seem more appropriate to the fish, which has now become visible. In stanza 3, the moon's light comes to seem fragile ("china") as it exposes the fish directly; the moon's role as lookout and protector seems abandoned, or at least endangered. No moon appears in stanza 4, but the fish's grin is "wide and moony," almost as if the two onlookers, one earthly and dead, the other heavenly and eternal, have merged, as they nearly were by the imagery in stanza 2. And in stanza 5, the fish becomes a friend, a comedian, an optimist, an emblem, and a patriarch of their love— and his new position in collaboration with the lovers is presided over by the moon going about its eternal business. The moon—providing the stage light for the poem and the means by which not only the fish but also the meaning of the lovers' act is discovered—has also helped to organize the poem, partly as a dramatic accessory, partly as imagery.

OTHER TYPES OF POETIC STRUCTURE

Some poems are also (or instead) organized by contrasts, and they conveniently set one thing up against another that is quite different. Notice, for example, how the following poem carefully contrasts two worlds:

PAT MORA

Sonrisas

    I live in a doorway
    between two rooms, I hear
    quiet clicks, cups of black
    coffee, *click, click* like facts
  5   budgets, tenure, curriculum,

from careful women in crisp beige
suits, quick beige smiles
that seldom sneak into their eyes.

I peek
10 in the other room señoras
in faded dresses stir sweet
milk coffee, laughter whirls
with steam from fresh *tamales*
sh, sh, mucho ruido,[3]
15 they scold one another,
press their lips, trap smiles
in their dark, Mexican eyes.

1986

Here different words, habits, sights, sounds, and values characterize the worlds of the two sets of characters, and the poem is organized largely by the contrasts between them. The meaning of the poem (the difference between the two worlds) is very nearly the same as the structure.

Poems can have **discursive structures**; that is, they may be organized like a treatise, an argument, or an essay. "First," they say, "and second . . . and third . . ." This sort of 1-2-3 structure takes a variety of forms depending on what is being enumerated or argued. Discursive structures help organize poems such as Shelley's "Ode to the West Wind" (later in this chapter), where the wind drives a leaf in part I, a cloud in part II, a wave in part III, and then, after a summary and statement of the speaker's ambitious hope in part IV, is asked to make the speaker a lyre in part V.

Poems may borrow their organizational strategies from many places, imitating chronological, visual, or discursive shapes in reality or in other works of art. Sometimes poems strive to be almost purely descriptive of someone or something (using **descriptive structures**), in which case poets have to make organizational decisions much as painters or photographers would, deciding first how a whole scene should look, then putting the parts into proper place for the whole. Of course, poems must present their details sequentially, not all at once as actual pictures more or less can, so poets must decide where to start a description (at the left? center? top?) and what sort of movement to use (linear across the scene? clockwise?). But if using words instead of paint or film has some drawbacks, it also has particular advantages: **Figurative language** can be a part of description, or an adjunct to it. Poets can insert comparisons at any point without necessarily disturbing the unity of their descriptions.

3. A lot of noise.

Some poems use **imitative structures,** mirroring as exactly as possible the structure of something that already exists as an object and can be seen— often, another poem. Other poems use **reflective** (or *meditative*) **structures,** pondering a subject, theme, or event, and letting the mind play with it, skipping (logically or not) from one sound to another, or to related thoughts or objects as the mind encounters them.

SHIFTS OF TONE AND SUBJECT

Most poems, regardless of which structure or mix of structures they use, depend on shifts of focus, attitude, tone, or subject that are sometimes subtle but always important. Such shifts divide the poem into parts, even when those parts aren't marked by line or stanza breaks or changes in sound or rhythm. Being attuned to such shifts is key to fully responsive reading, and explaining them is often equally key to effective interpretation.

Although the following poem employs several organizational principles, it ultimately takes its structure from an important shift in the speaker's attitude as she reviews, ponders, and rethinks events of long ago.

SHARON OLDS

The Victims

When Mother divorced you, we were glad. She took it and
took it, in silence, all those years and then
kicked you out, suddenly, and her
kids loved it. Then you were fired, and we
5 grinned inside, the way people grinned when
Nixon's helicopter lifted off the South
Lawn for the last time.[4] We were tickled
to think of your office taken away,
your secretaries taken away,
10 your lunches with three double bourbons,
your pencils, your reams of paper. Would they take your
suits back, too, those dark
carcasses hung in your closet, and the black
noses of your shoes with their large pores?
15 She had taught us to take it, to hate you and take it
until we pricked with her for your

---

4. When Richard Nixon resigned the U.S. presidency on August 8, 1974, his exit from the White House (by helicopter from the lawn) was televised live.

annihilation, Father. Now I
pass the bums in doorways, the white
slugs of their bodies gleaming through slits in their
20 suits of compressed silt, the stained
flippers of their hands, the underwater
fire of their eyes, ships gone down with the
lanterns lit, and I wonder who took it and
took it from them in silence until they had
25 given it all away and had nothing
left but this.

1984

"The Victims" divides basically into two parts. In the first two-thirds of the poem (from line 1 to the middle of line 17), the speaker evokes her father (the "you" of lines 1, 3, and so forth), who had been guilty of terrible behavior during the speaker's youth and was kicked out suddenly and divorced by the speaker's mother (lines 1–3). The father seems to have led a luxurious and insensitive life, with lots of support in his office (lines 8–11), fancy clothes (lines 12–14), and decadent lunches (line 10); his artificial identity seemed haunting and frightening (lines 11–14) to the speaker as child. He was then fired from his job (line 4) and lost his whole way of life (lines 8–12), and the speaker (taught by the mother, lines 15–17) recalls celebrating every defeat and every loss ("we pricked with her for your annihilation," lines 16–17). The mother is regarded as a victim ("She took it and took it, in silence, all those years" [lines 1–2]), and the speaker forms an indivisible unit with her and the other children ("her kids," lines 3–4). They are the "we" of the first part of the poem. They were "glad" (line 1) at the divorce; they "loved it" (line 4) when the mother kicked out the father; they "grinned" (line 5) when the father was fired; they were "tickled" (line 7) when he lost his job, his secretaries, and his daily life. Only at the end of the first section does the speaker (now older but remembering what it was like to be a child) recognize that the mother was responsible for the easy, childish vision of the father's guilt ("She had taught us to take it, to hate you and take it" [line 15]); nevertheless, all sympathy in this part of the poem is with the mother and her children, while all of the imagery is entirely unfavorable to the father. The family reacted to the father's misfortunes the way observers responded to the retreat in disgrace of Richard Nixon from the U.S. presidency.

But in line 17, the poem shifts its focus and tone. The "you" in the poem is now, suddenly, "Father." A bit of sympathy begins to surface for "bums in doorways" (line 18), who begin to seem like victims, too; their bodies are "slugs" (line 19), their suits are made of residual waste (lines 19–20), and their hands are reduced to nearly useless "flippers" (line 21). Their eyes contain fire (line 22), but it is as if they retain only a spark of life in their submerged and dying state. The speaker has not forgotten the cruelty and insensitivity recalled in the first part of the poem, but the blame seems to have shifted somewhat, and the father is not the only villain, nor are the mother and children the only victims. Look carefully at how the existence of street people recalls earlier details about the father, how sympathy for his plight is elicited from us, and how the definition of *victim* shifts.

Imagery, words, attitudes, and narrative are different in the two parts of the poem, and the second half carefully qualifies the first, as if to illustrate the more mature and considered attitudes of the speaker in her older years—a qualification of the easy imitation of the earlier years, when the mother's views dominated and set the tone. Change has governed the poem's structure here; differences in age and attitude are supported by an entirely different point of view and frame of reference.

• • •

The paradigms (or models) for organizing poems are, finally, not all that different from those of prose. It may be easier to organize something short (like many a poem) rather than something long (like a short story or biography), but the question of intensity becomes comparatively more important in shorter works. Basically, the problem of how to organize one's material is, for the writer, first of all a matter of deciding what kind of thing one wants to create, of having its purposes and effects clearly in mind. That means that every poem will differ somewhat from every other, but it also means that purposeful patterns—narrative, dramatic, descriptive, imitative, or reflective—may help writers organize and develop their ideas. A consciousness of purpose and effect can help the reader see *how* a poem proceeds toward its goal. And seeing how a poem is organized is, in turn, often a good way of seeing where it is going and what its real concerns, purposes, and **themes** may be. Often a poem's organization helps clarify the particular effects that the poet wishes to generate. In a good poem, means and ends are closely related, and a reader who is a good observer of one will be rewarded with the other.

• • •

ANONYMOUS

Sir Patrick Spens

The king sits in Dumferling toune,[5]
Drinking the blude-reid[6] wine:

---

5. Town.   6. Blood-red.

"O whar will I get guid sailor,
  To sail this ship of mine?"

5 Up and spake an eldern knicht,
      Sat at the king's richt knee:
    "Sir Patrick Spens is the best sailor
      That sails upon the sea."

The king has written a braid[7] letter
10   And signed it wi' his hand,
    And sent it to Sir Patrick Spens,
      Was walking on the sand.

The first line that Sir Patrick read,
      A loud lauch[8] lauched he;
15 The next line that Sir Patrick read,
      The tear blinded his ee.[9]

"O wha is this has done this deed,
      This il deed done to me,
    To send me out this time o' the year,
20   To sail upon the sea?

"Make haste, make haste, my merry men all,
      Our guid ship sails the morn."
    "O say na sae,[1] my master dear,
      For I fear a deadly storm.

25 "Late, late yestre'en I saw the new moon
      Wi' the auld moon in her arm,
    And I fear, I fear, my dear mastér,
      That we will come to harm."

O our Scots nobles were richt laith[2]
30   To weet their cork-heeled shoon,[3]
    But lang owre a'[4] the play were played
      Their hats they swam aboon.[5]

O lang, lang, may their ladies sit,
      Wi' their fans into their hand,
35 Or ere they see Sir Patrick Spens
      Come sailing to the land.

---

7. Broad: explicit. 8. Laugh. 9. Eye. 1. Not so. 2. Right loath: very reluctant.
3. To wet their cork-heeled shoes. Cork was expensive, and therefore such shoes were a mark of
wealth and status. 4. Before all. 5. Their hats swam above them.

O lang, lang, may the ladies stand
    Wi' their gold kems[6] in their hair,
Waiting for their ain[7] dear lords,
40   For they'll see them na mair.

Half o'er, half o'er to Aberdour
    It's fifty fadom deep,
And there lies guid Sir Patrick Spens
    Wi' the Scots lords at his feet.

ca. 13th century

- What event is hinted at in line 32 ("Their hats they swam aboon") and in the poem's final stanza? What is the effect of depicting the poem's principal action indirectly?

WILLIAM CARLOS WILLIAMS

The Dance

In Brueghel's great picture, The Kermess,[8]
the dancers go round, they go round and
around, the squeal and the blare and the
tweedle of bagpipes, a bugle and fiddles
5 tipping their bellies (round as the thick-
sided glasses whose wash they impound)
their hips and their bellies off balance
to turn them. Kicking and rolling about
the Fair Grounds, swinging their butts, those
10 shanks must be sound to bear up under such
rollicking measures, prance as they dance
in Brueghel's great picture, The Kermess.

1944

- Why is it appropriate to the subject, a painting, to begin and end the poem with the same line? In what ways is the poem like the dance it depicts?

6. Combs.   7. Own.   8. A painting by Pieter Brueghel the Elder (1525?-69).

EMILY DICKINSON

[*The Wind begun to knead the Grass—*]

The Wind begun to knead the Grass—
As Women do a Dough—
He flung a Hand full at the Plain—
A Hand full at the Sky—
5 The Leaves unhooked themselves from Trees—
And started all abroad—
The Dust did scoop itself like Hands—
And throw away the Road—
The Wagons quickened on the Street—
10 The Thunders gossiped low—
The Lightning showed a Yellow Head—
And then a livid Toe—
The Birds put up the Bars to Nests—
The Cattle flung to Barns—
15 Then came one drop of Giant Rain—
And then, as if the Hands
That held the Dams—had parted hold—
The Waters Wrecked the Sky—
20 But overlooked my Father's House—
Just Quartering a Tree—

                                             1864

• How would you describe this poem's structure? What happens in this poem's final line? How is this the work of "the Hands" (line 16)?

WILLIAM SHAKESPEARE

[*Th'expense of spirit in a waste of shame*]

Th'expense of spirit in a waste[9] of shame
Is lust in action; and, till action, lust
Is perjured, murderous, bloody, full of blame,
Savage, extreme, rude, cruel, not to trust;
5 Enjoyed no sooner but despisèd straight:
Past reason hunted; and no sooner had,

---

9. Using up; also, desert. *Expense:* expending

Past reason hated, as a swallowed bait,
On purpose laid to make the taker mad:
Mad in pursuit, and in possession so;
10 Had, having, and in quest to have, extreme;
A bliss in proof;[1] and proved, a very woe;
Before, a joy proposed; behind, a dream.
All this the world well knows; yet none knows well
To shun the heaven that leads men to this hell.

1609

• Paraphrase this poem. What emotional stages accompany
the carrying out of a violent or lustful act? What is the poem's
major insight about how lust works? How does the poem's
structure contribute to its effect and meaning?

PERCY BYSSHE SHELLEY

Ode to the West Wind

I

O wild West Wind, thou breath of Autumn's being,
Thou, from whose unseen presence the leaves dead
Are driven, like ghosts from an enchanter fleeing,

Yellow, and black, and pale, and hectic red,
5 Pestilence-stricken multitudes: O thou,
Who chariotest to their dark wintry bed

The wingèd seeds, where they lie cold and low,
Each like a corpse within its grave, until
Thine azure sister of the Spring shall blow

10 Her clarion[2] o'er the dreaming earth, and fill
(Driving sweet buds like flocks to feed in air)
With living hues and odors plain and hill:

Wild Spirit, which art moving everywhere;
Destroyer and preserver; hear, oh, hear!

II

15 Thou on whose stream, mid the steep sky's commotion,
Loose clouds like earth's decaying leaves are shed,
Shook from the tangled boughs of Heaven and Ocean,

1. In the act.   2. Trumpet call.

Angels[3] of rain and lightning: there are spread
On the blue surface of thine aëry surge,
20 Like the bright hair uplifted from the head

Of some fierce Maenad,[4] even from the dim verge
Of the horizon to the zenith's height,
The locks of the approaching storm. Thou dirge

Of the dying year, to which this closing night
25 Will be the dome of a vast sepulcher,
Vaulted with all thy congregated might

Of vapors, from whose solid atmosphere
Black rain, and fire, and hail will burst: oh, hear!

III
Thou who didst waken from his summer dreams
30 The blue Mediterranean, where he lay,
Lulled by the coil of his crystàlline streams,

Beside a pumice isle in Baiae's bay,[5]
And saw in sleep old palaces and towers
Quivering within the wave's intenser day,

35 All overgrown with azure moss and flowers
So sweet, the sense faints picturing them! Thou
For whose path the Atlantic's level powers

Cleave themselves into chasms, while far below
The sea-blooms and the oozy woods which wear
40 The sapless foliage of the ocean, know

Thy voice, and suddenly grow gray with fear,
And tremble and despoil themselves:[6] oh, hear!

IV
If I were a dead leaf thou mightest bear;
If I were a swift cloud to fly with thee;
45 A wave to pant beneath thy power, and share

The impulse of thy strength, only less free
Than thou, O uncontrollable! If even
I were as in my boyhood, and could be

---

3. Messengers.
4. Frenzied female votary of Dionysus, the Greek god of vegetation and fertility who was supposed to die in the fall and rise again each spring.
5. Where Roman emperors had erected villas, west of Naples.
6. The vegetation at the bottom of the sea . . . sympathizes with that of the land in the change of seasons. [Shelley's note]

The comrade of thy wanderings over Heaven,
50 As then, when to outstrip thy skyey speed
Scarce seemed a vision; I would ne'er have striven

As thus with thee in prayer in my sore need.
Oh, lift me as a wave, a leaf, a cloud!
I fall upon the thorns of life! I bleed!

55 A heavy weight of hours has chained and bowed
One too like thee: tameless, and swift, and proud.

V

Make me thy lyre, even as the forest is:
What if my leaves are falling like its own!
The tumult of thy mighty harmonies

60 Will take from both a deep, autumnal tone,
Sweet though in sadness. Be thou, Spirit fierce,
My spirit! Be thou me, impetuous one!

Drive my dead thoughts over the universe
Like withered leaves to quicken a new birth!
65 And, by the incantation of this verse,

Scatter, as from an unextinguished hearth
Ashes and sparks, my words among mankind!
Be through my lips to unawakened earth

The trumpet of a prophecy! O Wind,
70 If Winter comes, can Spring be far behind?

                                                    1820

- What attributes of the West Wind does the speaker want his
  poetry to embody? In what ways is this poem like the wind it
  describes? What is the effect of its structure?

SUGGESTIONS FOR WRITING

1. How many different "scenes" can you identify in "Sir Patrick Spens"? Write
   an essay in which you first summarize the story recounted by the poem, and
   then discuss the methods of storytelling employed by the poem. Consider
   the transitions from one scene to another and the almost cinematic "fading"
   effect between scenes.
2. What words and patterns are repeated in the different stanzas of Shelley's
   "Ode to the West Wind"? What differences are there from stanza to stanza?
   What "progress" does the poem make? Write an essay in which you discuss
   the ways that meaning and structure are intertwined in Shelley's poem.

3. Write an essay that explores the use of contrast in Pat Mora's "Sonrisas." How is each of the two rooms in the poem characterized by way of contrast with the other? What do they individually and jointly symbolize? What does the poem show through this contrast?

4. Pick out any poem you have read in this book that seems particularly effective in the way it is put together. Write an essay in which you consider how the poem is organized—that is, what structural principles it employs. What do the choices of speaker, situation, and setting have to do with the poem's structure? What other artistic decisions contribute to its structure?

13 EXTERNAL FORM

The previous chapters have discussed many of the *internal* features of a poem that make it unique: the tone and characteristics of its speaker; its situation and setting and its themes; its diction, imagery, and sounds. This chapter ventures into what is called the *external* form of a poem. These formal aspects are external in being recognizable; like the fashion and fabric of clothing that expresses the personality of an individual, the external form is an appropriate garb or guise for the unique internal action and meaning of the poem. When reading a poem, you might immediately notice its stanza breaks and even its rhyme scheme before you comprehend the words and meaning. Or you might quickly recognize that the poem takes a traditional form such as the sonnet. These forms guide readers as well as the poet. They help readers feel and appreciate repetitions and connections, changes and gaps, in the language as well as the meaning of the poem.

RHYME

Early English poetry used **alliteration**, instead of rhyming words at the end of the poetic lines, to balance the first and second half of each line. From the later Middle Ages until the twentieth century, the music of **rhyme** was central to both the sound and the formal conception of most poems in the Western world. Because poetry was originally an oral art (many poems were only later written down, if at all), various kinds of memory devices (sometimes called mnemonic devices) were built into poems to help reciters remember them. Rhyme was one such device, and most people still find it easier to memorize poetry that rhymes. The simple pleasure of hearing familiar sounds repeated at regular intervals may help account for the traditional popularity of rhyme. Rhyme also gives poetry a special aural quality that distinguishes it from prose. According to the established taste in eras before our own, there was a decorum or proper behavior in poetry as in other things: A poem should not in any way be mistaken for prose (though it might serve prosaic functions). Hence, the literary critics in those ages made extraordinary efforts to distinguish poetry, which was thought to be artistically superior, from prose, which was thought to be primarily utilitarian.

Some English poets (especially in the Renaissance) did experiment—often very successfully—with **blank verse** (that is, verse that does not rhyme but that nevertheless conforms to strict metrical requirements), but the cultural pressure for rhyme was almost constant. Why? Custom combined with the sense of proper decorum accounted in part for the assumption that rhyme was necessary to poetry, but there was probably more to it than that. Rather, the poets' sense that poetry was an imitation of larger relationships in the universe made it seem natural to use rhyme to represent or re-create a sense of pattern, harmony, correspondence, symmetry, and order. The sounds of poetry were thus, they reasoned, reminders of the harmonious cosmos, of the music of the spheres that animated all creation. In a modern world increasingly perceived as fragmented and chaotic, there may be less of a tendency to assert a sense of harmony and symmetry. It would be too simple to say that rhyme in a poem specifically means that the poet has a firm sense of cosmic order, or that an unrhymed poem testifies to chaos. Unrhymed medieval alliterative poetry certainly presupposed a divinely ordered universe, for instance. In different ways, the norms of poetry and the cultural assumptions of the time interact to influence the expectations of both poets and readers.

Rhyme also provides a kind of discipline for the poet, a way of harnessing poetic talents and keeping a rein on the imagination, so that the results have a recognizable form. Robert Frost said that writing **free verse**—that is, poems without rhyme or regular meter—was pointless, like playing tennis without a net. Frost speaks for many (perhaps most) traditional poets in suggesting that writing good poetry requires discipline and great care with formal elements such as rhyme or rhythm. More recent poets have often chosen to play by new rules or to invent their own as they go along, preferring the sparer tones that unrhymed poetry provides. Contemporary poets of course still care about the sounds of their poetry, but they may replace rhyme and meter with other aural and metrical devices and other strategies for organizing stanzas. Nevertheless, some contemporary poets mix regular rhyme and meter with more flexible lines to suggest a tribute to tradition as well as the unexpectedness of experience; even the search for rhyming words may lead to surprising discoveries.

STANZAS

Most poems of more than a few lines are divided into **stanzas**—groups of lines divided from other groups by white space on the page. Putting some space between groupings of lines has the effect of sectioning a poem, giving its physical appearance a series of divisions that often mark turns of thought, changes of scene or image, or other shifts in structure or direction. In Donne's "The Flea" (chapter 9), for example, the stanza divisions mark distinct stages in the action: Between the first and second stanzas, the speaker stops his companion from killing the flea; between the second and third stanzas, the companion follows through on her intention and kills the flea. In Nemerov's "The Goose Fish" (chapter 12), the stanzas mark stages in the self-perception of the lovers: Each stanza is a more or less distinct scene, and the scenes unfold almost like a series of slides. Any formal division of a poem into stanzas is important to consider; what appear to be gaps or silences may be structural markers.

Historically, stanzas have most often been organized by patterns of rhyme, and thus stanza divisions have traditionally been a visual indicator of patterns in sound. Highly elaborate verse forms have been developed that set up stanzas as part of a scheme for the whole poem. The poets of medieval Provence were especially inventive, subtle, and elaborate in their construction of complex verse forms, such as the sestina; some of these forms have been adapted by poets ever since. Different cultures develop their own patterns and measures, and they vary from age to age as well as from region to region. In most traditional stanza forms, the pattern of rhyme is repeated in stanza after stanza throughout the poem, until voice and ear become familiar with the pattern and come to expect it. The repetition of pattern allows us to hear deviations from the pattern as well, just as we do in music.

STANZAS AND RHYME SCHEMES: SOME EXAMPLES

In Shelley's "Ode to the West Wind," the first and third lines in each stanza rhyme, and the middle line then rhymes with the first and third lines of the next stanza. (In indicating rhyme, we conventionally use a different letter of the alphabet to represent each rhyme sound. Remember to reuse a letter if the same sound repeats in later lines or stanzas; for instance, a poem may return to *a* and *b* rhymes for the last lines after *g* and *h*, to bring a feeling of closure and coherence. In the following example, if we begin with "being" as *a* and "dead" as *b*, then "fleeing" is also *a*, "red" and "bed" are *b*, and so forth.)

O wild West Wind, thou breath of Autumn's being,	*a*
Thou, from whose unseen presence the leaves dead	*b*
Are driven, like ghosts from an enchanter fleeing,	*a*
Yellow, and black, and pale, and hectic red,	*b*
Pestilence-stricken multitudes: O thou,	*c*
Who chariotest to their dark wintry bed	*b*
The wingèd seeds, where they lie cold and low,	*c*
Each like a corpse within its grave, until	*d*
Thine azure sister of the Spring shall blow	*c*

In this stanza form, known as **terza rima**, the stanzas are linked to each other by a common sound: One rhyme sound from each stanza is picked up in the next stanza, and so on to the end of the poem (though sometimes poems in this form have sections that use varied rhyme schemes). This stanza form was used by Dante in *The Divine Comedy*, written in Italian in the early 1300s.

Terza rima requires many rhymes, and thus many different rhyme words, and therefore it is not very common in English, a relatively rhyme-poor language (not as rich in rhyme possibilities as Italian or French). English is derived from so many different language families that it has fewer similar word endings than languages that mainly derive from a single language family.

The **Spenserian stanza** is even more rhyme-rich than terza rima, using only three rhyme sounds in nine rhymed lines, as in Keats's *The Eve of St. Agnes*:

Her falt'ring hand upon the balustrade,	*a*
Old Angela was feeling for the stair,	*b*
When Madeline, St. Agnes' charmèd maid,	*a*
Rose, like a missioned spirit, unaware:	*b*
With silver taper's light, and pious care,	*b*
She turned, and down the agèd gossip led	*c*
To a safe level matting. Now prepare,	*b*
Young Porphyro, for gazing on that bed;	*c*
She comes, she comes again, like ring dove frayed and fled	*c*

On the other hand, the **ballad stanza** (as in "Sir Patrick Spens") has only one set of rhymes in four lines; lines 1 and 3 in each stanza do not rhyme at all:

The king sits in Dumferling toune,	*a*
Drinking the blude-reid wine:	*b*
"O whar will I get guid sailor,	*c*
To sail this ship of mine?"	*b*

Most stanza forms use a metrical pattern as well as a rhyme scheme. Terza rima, like most English stanza and verse forms, involves **iambic** meter (unstressed and stressed syllables alternating regularly), and each line has five beats (**pentameter**). The first eight lines of a Spenserian stanza are also in iambic pentameter, but the ninth line in each stanza has one extra foot (iambic **hexameter**). The ballad stanza, also iambic, alternates three-beat and four-beat lines; lines 1 and 3 are unrhymed iambic **tetrameter** (four beats), and lines 2 and 4 are rhymed iambic **trimeter** (three beats).

You can probably deduce the principles involved in each of the following stanza or verse forms by looking carefully at a poem that uses it; if you have trouble, look at the definitions in the glossary. Some examples of these and other forms follow.

heroic couplet	"Sound and Sense"
tetrameter couplet	"To His Coy Mistress"
limerick	"[There was a young girl from St. Paul]"
free verse	"Dirge"
blank verse	"Lines Written a Few Miles above Tintern Abbey"
sestina	"Sestina"
villanelle	"Do Not Go Gentle into That Good Night"

• • •

DYLAN THOMAS

Do Not Go Gentle into That Good Night [1]

Do not go gentle into that good night,
Old age should burn and rave at close of day;
Rage, rage against the dying of the light.

Though wise men at their end know dark is right,
5 Because their words had forked no lightning they
Do not go gentle into that good night.

Good men, the last wave by, crying how bright
Their frail deeds might have danced in a green bay,
Rage, rage against the dying of the light.

10 Wild men who caught and sang the sun in flight,
And learn, too late, they grieved it on its way,
Do not go gentle into that good night.

Grave men, near death, who see with blinding sight
Blind eyes could blaze like meteors and be gay,
15 Rage, rage against the dying of the light.

And you, my father, there on the sad height,
Curse, bless, me now with your fierce tears, I pray.
Do not go gentle into that good night.
Rage, rage against the dying of the light.

1952

---

1. Written during the final illness of the poet's father.

- What do the wise, good, wild, and grave men have in common with the speaker's father? Why do you think Thomas chose such a strict form, the villanelle, for such an emotionally charged subject?

MARIANNE MOORE

Poetry

I, too, dislike it: there are things that are important beyond all
    this fiddle.
Reading it, however, with a perfect contempt for it, one discov-
    ers in
it after all, a place for the genuine.
    Hands that can grasp, eyes
5   that can dilate, hair that can rise
       if it must, these things are important not because a

high-sounding interpretation can be put upon them but because
    they are
useful. When they become so derivative as to become
    unintelligible,
the same thing may be said for all of us, that we
10   do not admire what
    we cannot understand: the bat
       holding on upside down or in quest of something to

eat, elephants pushing, a wild horse taking a roll, a tireless wolf
    under
a tree, the immovable critic twitching his skin like a horse that
    feels a flea, the base-
15   ball fan, the statistician—
    nor is it valid
       to discriminate against "business documents and

school-books";[2] all these phenomena are important. One must
    make a distinction
however: when dragged into prominence by half poets, the
    result is not poetry,

---

2. *Diary of Tolstoy* (Dutton), p. 84. "Where the boundary between prose and poetry lies, I shall never be able to understand. The question is raised in manuals of style, yet the answer to it lies beyond me. Poetry is verse: Prose is not verse. Or else poetry is everything with the exception of business documents and school books" [Moore's note].

20   nor till the poets among us can be
      "literalists of
      the imagination"[3]—above
          insolence and triviality and can present

      for inspection, "imaginary gardens with real toads in them,"
          shall we have
25   it. In the meantime, if you demand on the one hand,
      the raw material of poetry in
          all its rawness and
      that which is on the other hand
          genuine, you are interested in poetry.

                                                           1921

- In what ways does this poem resemble prose? Does it follow
  any rules of line endings or stanza forms? Is there a regular
  meter? (Hint: The first line of each stanza has nineteen
  syllables.)

ELIZABETH BISHOP

Sestina

September rain falls on the house.
In the failing light, the old grandmother
sits in the kitchen with the child
beside the Little Marvel Stove,
5 reading the jokes from the almanac,
laughing and talking to hide her tears.

She thinks that her equinoctial tears
and the rain that beats on the roof of the house
were both foretold by the almanac,
10 but only known to a grandmother.
The iron kettle sings on the stove.
She cuts some bread and says to the child,

---

3. Yeats, *Ideas of Good and Evil* (A. H. Bullen, 1903), p. 182. "The limitation of [William Blake's] view
was from the very intensity of his vision; he was a too literal realist of imagination, as others are of
nature; and because he believed that the figures seen by the mind's eye, when exalted by inspiration, were 'eternal existences,' symbols of divine essences, he hated every grace of style that might
obscure their lineaments" [Moore's note]. The phrase "imaginary . . . in them," in the next stanza,
has no known source.

It's time for tea now; but the child
is watching the teakettle's small hard tears
15 dance like mad on the hot black stove,
the way the rain must dance on the house.
Tidying up, the old grandmother
hangs up the clever almanac

on its string. Birdlike, the almanac
20 hovers half open above the child,
hovers above the old grandmother
and her teacup full of dark brown tears.
She shivers and says she thinks the house
feels chilly, and puts more wood in the stove.

25 *It was to be,* says the Marvel Stove.
I know what I know, says the almanac.
With crayons the child draws a rigid house
and a winding pathway. Then the child
puts in a man with buttons like tears
30 and shows it proudly to the grandmother.

But secretly, while the grandmother
busies herself about the stove,
the little moons fall down like tears
from between the pages of the almanac
35 into the flower bed the child
has carefully placed in the front of the house.

Time to plant tears, says the almanac.
The grandmother sings to the marvellous stove
and the child draws another inscrutable house.

1965

- Try to derive from "Sestina" the "rules" that govern the sestina form. Why do you think Bishop chose this form for her poem?

ARCHIBALD MacLEISH

Ars Poetica [4]

A poem should be palpable and mute
As a globed fruit,

4. "The Art of Poetry," title of a poetical treatise by the Roman poet Horace (65–8 B.C.E.).

Dumb
As old medallions to the thumb,

5 Silent as the sleeve-worn stone
Of casement ledges where the moss has grown—

A poem should be wordless
As the flight of birds.

A poem should be motionless in time
10 As the moon climbs.

Leaving, as the moon releases
Twig by twig the night-entangled trees,

Leaving, as the moon behind the winter leaves,
Memory by memory the mind—

15 A poem should be motionless in time
As the moon climbs.

A poem should be equal to:
Not true.

For all the history of grief
20 An empty doorway and a maple leaf.

For love
The leaning grasses and two lights above the sea—

A poem should not mean
But be.

                                                    1926

- Can you summarize this poem's ideas about what poetry
  should be? How does the poem itself illustrate these principles?

DUDLEY RANDALL

Ballad of Birmingham

(On the bombing of a church in Birmingham, Alabama, 1963)

"Mother dear, may I go downtown
Instead of out to play,
And march the streets of Birmingham
In a Freedom March today?"

5 "No, baby, no, you may not go,
For the dogs are fierce and wild,
And clubs and hoses, guns and jails
Aren't good for a little child."

"But, mother, I won't be alone.
10 Other children will go with me,
And march the streets of Birmingham
To make our country free."

"No, baby, no, you may not go,
For I fear those guns will fire.
15 But you may go to church instead
And sing in the children's choir."

She has combed and brushed her night-dark hair,
And bathed rose petal sweet,
And drawn white gloves on her small brown hands,
20 And white shoes on her feet.

The mother smiled to know her child
Was in the sacred place,
But that smile was the last smile
To come upon her face.

25 For when she heard the explosion,
Her eyes grew wet and wild.
She raced through the streets of Birmingham
Calling for her child.

She clawed through bits of glass and brick,
30 Then lifted out a shoe.
"Oh, here's the shoe my baby wore,
But, baby, where are you?"

                                              1969

• Compare this poem to other ballads in this volume and elsewhere. Why is the form appropriate for commemorating this
  violent event?

THE SONNET

The **sonnet**, one of the most persistent verse forms, originated in the Middle Ages in Italian and French poetry. It dominated English poetry in the
late sixteenth and early seventeenth centuries and then was revived several
times from the early nineteenth century onward. Except for some early
experiments with length, the sonnet has always been fourteen lines long,

and it usually is written in iambic pentameter. It is most often printed as if it were a single stanza, although it actually has formal divisions defined by its various rhyme schemes and structures. (In discussions of poetry, the word *formal* simply means "relating to form.") For more than four centuries, the sonnet has been surprisingly resilient, and it continues to attract a variety of poets. As a verse form, the sonnet is contained, compact, demanding; whatever it does, it must do concisely. It is best suited to intensity of feeling and concentration of figurative language and expression.

Most sonnets are structured according to one of two principles of division. The *English*, or *Shakespearean, sonnet* is divided into three units of four lines each and a final unit of two lines, and sometimes the line spacing reflects this division. Ordinarily its rhyme scheme reflects the structure: The scheme of *abab cdcd efef gg* is the classic one, but many variations from that pattern still reflect the basic 4-4-4-2 division. In the *Italian*, or *Petrarchan, sonnet* (the Italian poet Petrarch was an early master of this structure), the fundamental break is between the first eight lines (called an **octave**) and the last six (called a **sestet**). Its "typical" rhyme scheme is *abbaabba cdecde*, although it too produces many variations that still reflect the basic division into two parts, an octave and a sestet.

The two kinds of sonnet structures are useful for different sorts of argument. The 4-4-4-2 structure works very well for constructing a poem that makes a three-step argument (with a quick summary at the end) or for setting up brief, cumulative images. Shakespeare's "[That time of year thou mayst in me behold]" (chapter 10), for example, uses the 4-4-4-2 structure to mark the progressive steps toward death and the parting of lovers by using three distinct images and then summarizing. In the two-part structure of the Italian sonnet, the octave states a proposition or generalization and the sestet provides a particular example, consequence, or application of it; alternatively, the second part may turn away from the first to present a new position or response. The final lines may, for example, reverse the first eight and achieve a paradox or irony in the poem, or the poem may nearly balance two comparable arguments. Basically, the 8-6 structure lends itself to poems with two points to make, or to those that make one point and then illustrate it.

During the Renaissance, poets regularly employed the sonnet for love poems; many modern sonnets continue to be about love or private life, and many poets continue to use a personal, apparently open and sincere tone in their sonnets. But poets often find the sonnet's compact form and rigid demands equally useful for a variety of subjects and tones. Sonnets may be about subjects other than love: politics, philosophy, discovery. And their tones vary widely, too, from the anger and remorse of "[Th' expense of spirit in a waste of shame]" (chapter 12) and righteous outrage of "On the Late Massacre in Piedmont" (chapter 9) to the tender awe of "How Do I Love Thee?" ("Poetry: Reading, Responding, Writing"). Many poets seem to take the kind of comfort in the careful limits of the form that William Wordsworth describes in "Nuns Fret Not" (below), finding in its two basic variations, the English sonnet and the Italian sonnet, a wealth of ways to organize their materials into coherent structures.

TWO SONNETS: PRACTICING

Can you identify the rhyme scheme in each of these poems and the type of sonnet each poem is?

HENRY CONSTABLE

[My lady's presence makes the roses red]

My lady's presence makes the roses red,
Because to see her lips they blush for shame.
The lily's leaves, for envy, pale became,
And her white hands in them this envy bred.
5 The marigold the leaves abroad doth spread,
Because the sun's and her power is the same.
The violet of purple colour came,
Dyed in the blood she made my heart to shed.
In brief: all flowers from her their virtue take;
10 From her sweet breath their sweet smells do proceed;
The living heat which her eyebeams doth make
Warmeth the ground and quickeneth the seed.
The rain, wherewith she watereth the flowers,
Falls from mine eyes, which she dissolves in showers.
                                                      1594

WILLIAM WORDSWORTH

Nuns Fret Not

Nuns fret not at their convent's narrow room;
And hermits are contented with their cells;
And students with their pensive citadels;
Maids at the wheel, the weaver at his loom,
5 Sit blithe and happy; bees that soar for bloom,
High as the highest Peak of Furness-fells,[5]

___
5. Mountains in England's Lake District, where Wordsworth lived.

Will murmur by the hour in foxglove bells:
In truth the prison, unto which we doom
Ourselves, no prison is: and hence for me,
10 In sundry moods, 'twas pastime to be bound
Within the sonnet's scanty plot of ground;
Pleased if some souls (for such there needs must be)
Who have felt the weight of too much liberty,
Should find brief solace there, as I have found.

1807

Mark with letters of the alphabet the rhyme sounds at the end of all fourteen lines of both sonnets. Then decide whether each poem is an Italian or an English sonnet. Do you notice any variations from the descriptions above of these two sonnet forms?

Do the last two lines of Wordsworth's sonnet rhyme? In which line do you first see or hear a third end-rhyme sound? What feelings might be expressed by the sound as well as sense of the last words in each line? For instance, "room," "loom," and "bloom" rhyme with "gloom" and "tomb"; not all these words have dark or haunting meanings, but readers may vaguely sense such associations, especially when they anticipate and then hear the sound again, in "doom" (line 8). Where do you first notice the speaker referring to himself and his views ("me")? Can you summarize two or more basic points this sonnet makes?

What is the rhyme scheme of Constable's sonnet? How many of the end-rhymes (last words of the lines) end with the letter *d*? How many of the end-rhymes have a long *a* vowel sound, as in "shame"? Which end rhymes have a single syllable? Which have two syllables? Are these word patterns meaningful, or do they simply enhance the pleasing sounds of this poem about love? Why do the new rhyme sounds begin in line 9? What do the first eight lines argue? How do the next four lines add to or follow from the argument? What happens to rhyme and meaning in the final couplet?

Sometimes a neat and precise structure is altered—either slightly, as in Wordsworth's "Nuns Fret Not," or more radically as particular needs or effects may demand. And the two basic structures, Shakespearean and Petrarchan, certainly do not define all the structural possibilities within a fourteen-line poem, even if they are the most traditional ways of taking advantage of the sonnet's compact and contained form.

THE SONNET: EXAMPLES

DANTE GABRIEL ROSSETTI
A Sonnet Is a Moment's Monument

A Sonnet is a moment's monument—
Memorial from the Soul's eternity
To one dead deathless hour. Look that it be,
Whether for lustral[6] rite or dire portent,
5   Of its own arduous fullness reverent.
   Carve it in ivory or in ebony,
   As Day or Night may rule; and let Time see
Its flowering crest impearled and orient.[7]

A Sonnet is a coin: its face reveals
10   The soul—its converse, to what Power 'tis due—
Whether for tribute to the august appeals
   Of Life or dower in Love's high retinue,

It serve; or 'mid the dark wharf's cavernous breath,
In Charon's palm it pay the toll to Death.[8]

                                        1881

• In Rossetti's metaphor comparing the sonnet to a coin (lines
  9–14), what are the two "sides" of a sonnet?

JOHN KEATS
On the Sonnet

If by dull rhymes our English must be chained,
And like Andromeda,[9] the sonnet sweet
Fettered, in spite of painèd loveliness,
Let us find, if we must be constrained,

---

6. Purificatory.   7. Sparkling.
8. In classical myth, Charon was the boatman who rowed the souls of the dead across the river
Styx. Ancient Greeks put a small coin in the hand of the dead to pay his fee.
9. According to Greek myth, Andromeda was chained to a rock so that she would be devoured by
a sea monster. She was rescued by Perseus, who married her. When she died she was placed among
the stars.

5 Sandals more interwoven and complete
To fit the naked foot of Poesy:[1]
Let us inspect the lyre, and weigh the stress
Of every chord,[2] and see what may be gained
By ear industrious, and attention meet;
10 Misers of sound and syllable, no less
Than Midas[3] of his coinage, let us be
Jealous of dead leaves in the bay-wreath crown;[4]
So, if we may not let the Muse be free,
She will be bound with garlands of her own.

1819

- What is the rhyme scheme of this poem? How well does this
  unusual structure meet the challenge implied by the poem?

On the Grasshopper and the Cricket

The poetry of earth is never dead:
When all the birds are faint with the hot sun,
And hide in cooling trees, a voice will run
From hedge to hedge about the new-mown mead;
5 That is the grasshopper's—he takes the lead
In summer luxury—he has never done
With his delights; for when tired out with fun
He rests at ease beneath some pleasant weed.
The poetry of earth is ceasing never:
10 On a lone winter evening, when the frost
Has wrought a silence, from the stove there shrills
The cricket's song, in warmth increasing ever,
And seems to one in drowsiness half lost,
The grasshopper's among some grassy hills.

December 30, 1816

- How does this sonnet connect and compare two scenes and
  two "singers" in its two-part "Italian" form?

1. In a letter that contained this sonnet, Keats expressed impatience with the traditional Petrarchan and Shakespearean sonnet forms: "I have been endeavoring to discover a better sonnet stanza than we have." 2. Lyre string. *Meet:* proper.
3. The legendary king of Phrygia who asked, and got, the power to turn all he touched to gold.
4. The bay tree was sacred to Apollo, god of poetry, and bay wreaths came to symbolize true poetic achievement. The withering of the bay tree is sometimes considered an omen of death. *Jealous:* suspiciously watchful.

On Seeing the Elgin Marbles[5]

My spirit is too weak—mortality
Weighs heavily on me like unwilling sleep,
And each imagined pinnacle and steep
Of godlike hardship tells me I must die
5 Like a sick eagle looking at the sky.
Yet 'tis a gentle luxury to weep
That I have not the cloudy winds to keep
Fresh for the opening of the morning's eye.
Such dim-conceivèd glories of the brain
10 Bring round the heart an indescribable feud;
So do these wonders a most dizzy pain,
That mingles Grecian grandeur with the rude
Wasting of old Time—with a billowy main—
A sun—a shadow of a magnitude.

1817

• Most of the octet and the beginning of the sestet describe the
speaker's desire for imagined "pinnacles" of vision. Why are
the carved stone ruins referred to so late and so obliquely in
the poem?

GWENDOLYN BROOKS

First Fight. Then Fiddle.

First fight. Then fiddle. Ply the slipping string
With feathery sorcery; muzzle the note
With hurting love; the music that they wrote
Bewitch, bewilder. Qualify to sing
5 Threadwise. Devise no salt, no hempen thing
For the dear instrument to bear. Devote
The bow to silks and honey. Be remote
A while from malice and from murdering.
But first to arms, to armor. Carry hate
10 In front of you and harmony behind.
Be deaf to music and to beauty blind.

---

5. Figures and friezes from the Athenian Parthenon, they were taken from the site by Lord Elgin,
brought to England in 1806, and then sold to the British Museum, where Keats saw them.

Win war. Rise bloody, maybe not too late
For having first to civilize a space
Wherein to play your violin with grace.

1949

- After advising "First fight. Then fiddle," the speaker discusses first music, then conflict. Why do you think the poet has arranged her argument this way?

ROBERT FROST

Range-Finding

The battle rent a cobweb diamond-strung
And cut a flower beside a groundbird's nest
Before it stained a single human breast.
The stricken flower bent double and so hung.
5 And still the bird revisited her young.
A butterfly its fall had dispossessed,
A moment sought in air his flower of rest,
Then slightly stooped to it and fluttering clung.
On the bare upland pasture there had spread
10 O'ernight 'twixt mullein stalks a wheel of thread
And straining cables wet with silver dew.
A sudden passing bullet shook it dry.
The indwelling spider ran to greet the fly,
But finding nothing, sullenly withdrew.

1916

- What is the "battle" of line 1? What is the poem's actual subject?

Design

I found a dimpled spider, fat and white,
On a white heal-all,[6] holding up a moth
Like a white piece of rigid satin cloth—
Assorted characters of death and blight
5 Mixed ready to begin the morning right,

---

6. A plant, also called the "all-heal" and "self-heal," with tightly clustered violet-blue flowers.

Like the ingredients of a witches' broth—
A snow-drop spider, a flower like a froth,
And dead wings carried like a paper kite.

What had that flower to do with being white,
10 The wayside blue and innocent heal-all?
What brought the kindred spider to that height,
Then steered the white moth thither in the night?
What but design of darkness to appall?—
If design govern in a thing so small.

1936

- How does this poem confound our usual preconceptions
  about "light" and "darkness"? How does its elaborate form
  complement its theme?

WILLIAM WORDSWORTH

London, 1802

Milton! thou should'st be living at this hour:
England hath need of thee: she is a fen
Of stagnant waters: altar, sword, and pen,
Fireside, the heroic wealth of hall and bower,
5 Have forfeited their ancient English dower
Of inward happiness. We are selfish men;
Oh! raise us up, return to us again;
And give us manners, virtue, freedom, power.
Thy soul was like a star, and dwelt apart:
10 Thou hadst a voice whose sound was like the sea:
Pure as the naked heavens, majestic, free,
So didst thou travel on life's common way,
In cheerful godliness; and yet thy heart
The lowliest duties on herself did lay.

1802

- What is Wordsworth asserting about the power of poetry in
  this sonnet? Why do you think he chose the sonnet form for
  this poem?

JOHN MILTON

[*When I consider how my light is spent*]

When I consider how my light is spent,
  Ere half my days, in this dark world and wide,
  And that one talent which is death to hide[7]
  Lodged with me useless, though my soul more bent
5 To serve therewith my Maker, and present
  My true account, lest he returning chide;
  "Doth God exact day-labor, light denied?"
  I fondly ask; but Patience to prevent[8]
That murmur, soon replies, "God doth not need
10   Either man's work or his own gifts; who best
  Bear his mild yoke, they serve him best. His state
Is kingly. Thousands at his bidding speed
  And post o'er land and ocean without rest:
  They also serve who only stand and wait."

                      ca. 1652

- Paraphrase the speaker's question and Patience's reply. Does knowing that Milton was blind alter your interpretation of this poem?

ELIZABETH BARRETT BROWNING

[*When our two souls stand up*]

When our two souls stand up erect and strong,
Face to face, silent, drawing nigh and nigher,
Until the lengthening wings break into fire
At either curvèd point,—what bitter wrong
5 Can the earth do to us, that we should not long
Be here contented? Think. In mounting higher,
The angels would press on us and aspire
To drop some golden orb of perfect song
Into our deep, dear silence. Let us stay
10 Rather on earth, Belovèd,—where the unfit
Contrarious moods of men recoil away

---

7. In the parable of the talents (Matthew 25), the servants who earned interest on their master's money (his talents) while he was away were called "good and faithful"; the one who simply hid the money and then returned it was condemned and sent away.   8. Forestall. *Fondly:* foolishly.

And isolate pure spirits, and permit
A place to stand and love in for a day,
With darkness and the death-hour rounding it.

                                    1897

* Explain the metaphor of this poem's first four lines. What
  will cause "the lengthening wings" to "break into fire"?

CHRISTINA ROSSETTI

In an Artist's Studio

One face looks out from all his canvases,
    One selfsame figure sits or walks or leans;
    We found her hidden just behind those screens,
That mirror gave back all her loveliness.
5 A queen in opal or in ruby dress,
    A nameless girl in freshest summer-greens,
    A saint, an angel—every canvas means
The same one meaning, neither more nor less.
He feeds upon her face by day and night,
10   And she with true kind eyes looks back on him
Fair as the moon and joyful as the light:
    Not wan with waiting, not with sorrow dim;
Not as she is, but was when hope shone bright;
    Not as she is, but as she fills his dream.

                                    1856

* Does this sonnet show a single view of "the same one meaning" the speaker sees in every portrait in the studio, or is
  there a shift or turn at line 9 or line 13?

EDNA ST. VINCENT MILLAY

[What lips my lips have kissed, and where, and why]

What lips my lips have kissed, and where, and why,
I have forgotten, and what arms have lain
Under my head till morning; but the rain

Is full of ghosts tonight, that tap and sigh
5 Upon the glass and listen for reply,
And in my heart there stirs a quiet pain
For unremembered lads that not again
Will turn to me at midnight with a cry.
Thus in the winter stands the lonely tree,
10 Nor knows what birds have vanished one by one,
Yet knows its boughs more silent than before:
I cannot say what loves have come and gone;
I only know that summer sang in me
A little while, that in me sings no more.

1923

- What are the poem's principal parts? Why does the
  Petrarchan model suit this sonnet?

GWEN HARWOOD

In the Park

She sits in the park. Her clothes are out of date.
Two children whine and bicker, tug her skirt.
A third draws aimless patterns in the dirt.
Someone she loved once passes by—too late

5 to feign indifference to that casual nod.
"How nice," et cetera. "Time holds great surprises."
From his neat head unquestionably rises
a small balloon . . . "but for the grace of God . . ."

They stand a while in flickering light, rehearsing
10 the children's names and birthdays. "It's so sweet
to hear their chatter, watch them grow and thrive,"
she says to his departing smile. Then, nursing
the youngest child, sits staring at her feet.
To the wind she says, "They have eaten me alive."

1963

- What is the implication of the "small balloon" that rises
  from the head of the man who passes by?

WILLIAM SHAKESPEARE

[*My mistress' eyes are nothing like the sun*]

My mistress' eyes are nothing like the sun;
Coral is far more red than her lips' red;
If snow be white, why then her breasts are dun;[9]
If hairs be wires, black wires grow on her head.
5 I have seen roses damasked[1] red and white,
But no such roses see I in her cheeks;
And in some perfumes is there more delight
Than in the breath that from my mistress reeks.
I love to hear her speak, yet well I know
10 That music hath a far more pleasing sound;
I grant I never saw a goddess go;[2]
My mistress, when she walks, treads on the ground.
And yet, by heaven, I think my love as rare
As any she belied with false compare.

1609

• In addition to the speaker's mistress, what might be another
subject of this poem?

BILLY COLLINS

Sonnet

All we need is fourteen lines, well, thirteen now,
and after this one just a dozen
to launch a little ship on love's storm-tossed seas,
then only ten more left like rows of beans.
5 How easily it goes unless you get Elizabethan
and insist the iambic bongos must be played
and rhymes positioned at the ends of lines,
one for every station of the cross.
But hang on here while we make the turn
10 into the final six where all will be resolved,
where longing and heartache will find an end,
where Laura will tell Petrarch[3] to put down his pen,

---

9. Mouse-colored.   1. Variegated.   2. Walk
3. Italian poet Francesco Petrarca (1304–74), regarded as a father of the sonnet form. Many of his
love poems were inspired by Laura, who may have been the wife of a local nobleman.

take off those crazy medieval tights,
blow out the lights, and come at last to bed.

1999

- In what respects is Collins's poem a traditional sonnet? In what respects is it not?

SUGGESTIONS FOR WRITING

1. Trace the variations on imagery of light and darkness in Thomas's "Do Not Go Gentle into That Good Night." How do we know that light represents life and darkness death (rather than, say, sight and blindness)? How does the poet use the strict formal requirements of the villanelle to emphasize this interplay of light and darkness? Write an essay in which you discuss the interaction of form and content in "Do Not Go Gentle into That Good Night."

2. Chart the rhyme scheme of Keats's "On the Sonnet"; then, after reading the poem aloud, mark the major structural divisions of the poem. At what points do these structural divisions and the breaks in rhyme coincide? At what points do they conflict? Write an essay in which you discuss how these patterns and variations relate to the poem's meaning.

3. Consider carefully the structure of and sequencing in Brooks's "First Fight. Then Fiddle." How do various uses of sound in the poem (rhyme, onomatopoeia, and alliteration, for example) reinforce its themes and tones? Write an essay in which you explore the relationship between "sound and sense" in the poem.

4. Some of the sonnets in this book, such as those by Shakespeare, adhere closely to the classic English model; others, such as Milton's "[When I consider how my light is spent]," follow the Italian model; and some bear only slight resemblance to either of the traditional sonnet models. Take any four sonnets in this book as the basis for an essay in which you compare and contrast the various ways poets have used the sonnet form to achieve their unique artistic purposes.

5. Every poem has a structure, whether or not it adheres to a traditional form or to conventional ideas about line, rhythm, or spacing. Examine closely the structure of any poem or group of poems in this book. How does the poet use form to shape sound, emotion, and meaning? Write an essay in which you examine the structural choices that determine both the form and the content of these poems.

Reading More Poetry

W. H. AUDEN

Musée des Beaux Arts[1]

About suffering they were never wrong,
The Old Masters: how well they understood
Its human position; how it takes place
While someone else is eating or opening a window or just
    walking dully along;
5 How, when the aged are reverently, passionately waiting
For the miraculous birth, there always must be
— Children who did not specially want it to happen, skating
On a pond at the edge of the wood:
They never forgot
10 That even the dreadful martyrdom must run its course
Anyhow in a corner, some untidy spot
Where the dogs go on with their doggy life and the torturer's horse
Scratches its innocent behind on a tree.

In Brueghel's *Icarus*,[2] for instance: how everything turns away
15 Quite leisurely from the disaster; the plowman may
Have heard the splash, the forsaken cry,
But for him it was not an important failure; the sun shone
As it had to on the white legs disappearing into the green
Water; and the expensive delicate ship that must have seen
20 Something amazing, a boy falling out of the sky,
Had somewhere to get to and sailed calmly on.

                    1938

---

1. The Museum of the Fine Arts, in Brussels.
2. *Landscape with the Fall of Icarus*, by Pieter Bruegel the Elder (1525?–69), located in the Brussels museum. According to Greek myth, Daedalus and his son, Icarus, escaped from imprisonment by using homemade wings of feathers and wax; but Icarus flew too near the sun, the wax melted, and he fell into the sea and drowned. In the Bruegel painting the central figure is a peasant plowing, and several other figures are more immediately noticeable than Icarus, who, disappearing into the sea, is easy to miss in the lower right-hand corner.

W. H. AUDEN

In Memory of W. B. Yeats

(d. January, 1939)

I

He disappeared in the dead of winter:
The brooks were frozen, the airports almost deserted,
And snow disfigured the public statues;
The mercury sank in the mouth of the dying day.
5 What instruments we have agree
The day of his death was a dark cold day.

Far from his illness
The wolves ran on through the evergreen forests,
The peasant river was untempted by the fashionable quays;
10 By mourning tongues
The death of the poet was kept from his poems.

But for him it was his last afternoon as himself,
An afternoon of nurses and rumors;
The provinces of his body revolted,
15 The squares of his mind were empty,
Silence invaded the suburbs,
The current of his feeling failed; he became his admirers.

Now he is scattered among a hundred cities
And wholly given over to unfamiliar affections,
20 To find his happiness in another kind of wood
And be punished under a foreign code of conscience.
The words of a dead man
Are modified in the guts of the living.

But in the importance and noise of tomorrow
25 When the brokers are roaring like beasts on the floor of the
     Bourse,[3]
And the poor have the sufferings to which they are fairly
     accustomed,
And each in the cell of himself is almost convinced of his freedom,
A few thousand will think of this day
As one thinks of a day when one did something slightly unusual.
30 What instruments we have agree
The day of his death was a dark cold day.

3. The Paris stock exchange.

II

You were silly like us; your gift survived it all:
The parish of rich women, physical decay,
Yourself. Mad Ireland hurt you into poetry.
35 Now Ireland has her madness and her weather still,
For poetry makes nothing happen: it survives
In the valley of its making where executives
Would never want to tamper, flows on south
From ranches of isolation and the busy griefs,
40 Raw towns that we believe and die in; it survives,
A way of happening, a mouth.

III

Earth, receive an honored guest:
William Yeats is laid to rest.
Let the Irish vessel lie
45 Emptied of its poetry.

In the nightmare of the dark
All the dogs of Europe bark,
And the living nations wait,
Each sequestered in its hate;

50 Intellectual disgrace
Stares from every human face,
And the seas of pity lie
Locked and frozen in each eye.

Follow, poet, follow right
55 To the bottom of the night,
With your unconstraining voice
Still persuade us to rejoice;

With the farming of a verse
Make a vineyard of the curse,
60 Sing of human unsuccess
In a rapture of distress;

In the deserts of the heart
Let the healing fountain start,
In the prison of his days
65 Teach the free man how to praise.

1939

WILLIAM BLAKE

The Lamb

Little Lamb, who made thee?
Dost thou know who made thee?
Gave thee life, and bid thee feed
By the stream and o'er the mead;
5   Gave thee clothing of delight,
Softest clothing woolly bright;
Gave thee such a tender voice,
Making all the vales rejoice?
Little Lamb, who made thee?
10   Dost thou know who made thee?

Little Lamb, I'll tell thee!
Little Lamb, I'll tell thee:
He is callèd by thy name,
For he calls himself a Lamb,
15   He is meek and he is mild;
He became a little child.
I a child and thou a lamb,
We are callèd by his name.
Little Lamb, God bless thee!
20   Little Lamb, God bless thee!

                                        1789

The Tyger

Tyger! Tyger! burning bright
In the forests of the night,
What immortal hand or eye
Could frame thy fearful symmetry?

5   In what distant deeps or skies
Burnt the fire of thine eyes?
On what wings dare he aspire?
What the hand dare seize the fire?

And what shoulder, & what art,
10   Could twist the sinews of thy heart?
And when thy heart began to beat,
What dread hand? & what dread feet?

What the hammer? what the chain?
In what furnace was thy brain?
15 What the anvil? what dread grasp
Dare its deadly terrors clasp?

When the stars threw down their spears
And water'd heaven with their tears,
Did he smile his work to see?
20 Did he who made the Lamb make thee?

Tyger! Tyger! burning bright
In the forests of the night,
What immortal hand or eye
Dare frame thy fearful symmetry?

1794

The Chimney Sweeper

(from *Songs of Innocence*)

When my mother died I was very young,
And my father sold me while yet my tongue,
Could scarcely cry weep weep weep weep.
So your chimneys I sweep & in soot I sleep.

5 Theres little Tom Dacre, who cried when his head
That curl'd like a lambs back, was shav'd, so I said.
Hush Tom never mind it, for when your head's bare,
You know that the soot cannot spoil your white hair.

And so he was quiet, & that very night,
10 As Tom was a sleeping he had such a sight,
That thousands of sweepers Dick, Joe Ned & Jack
Were all of them lock'd up in coffins of black

And by came an Angel who had a bright key,
And he open'd the coffins & set them all free.
15 Then down a green plain leaping laughing they run
And wash in a river and shine in the Sun.

Then naked & white, all their bags left behind,
They rise upon clouds, and sport in the wind.
And the Angel told Tom if he'd be a good boy,
20 He'd have God for his father & never want[4] joy.

4. Lack.

And so Tom awoke and we rose in the dark
And got with our bags & our brushes to work.
Tho' the morning was cold, Tom was happy & warm,
So if all do their duty, they need not fear harm.

1789

The Chimney Sweeper

(from *Songs of Experience*)

A little black thing among the snow:
Crying weep, weep, in notes of woe!
Where are thy father & mother? say?
They are both gone up to the church to pray.

5 Because I was happy upon the heath,
And smil'd among the winters snow:
They clothed me in the clothes of death,
And taught me to sing the notes of woe.

And because I am happy, & dance & sing,
10 They think they have done me no injury:
And are gone to praise God & his Priest & King
Who make up a heaven of our misery.

1794

ROBERT BROWNING

My Last Duchess

Ferrara[5]

That's my last Duchess painted on the wall,
Looking as if she were alive. I call
That piece a wonder, now: Frà Pandolf's hands[6]
Worked busily a day, and there she stands.
5 Will't please you sit and look at her? I said

---

5. Alfonso II, duke of Ferrara in Italy in the mid-sixteenth century, is the presumed speaker of the poem, which is loosely based on historical events. The duke's first wife—whom he had married when she was fourteen—died under suspicious circumstances at seventeen, and he then negotiated through an agent (to whom the poem is spoken) for the hand of the niece of the count of Tyrol in Austria.   6. Frà Pandolf is, like Claus (line 56), fictitious.

"Frà Pandolf" by design, for never read
Strangers like you that pictured countenance,
The depth and passion of its earnest glance,
But to myself they turned (since none puts by
10 The curtain I have drawn for you, but I)
And seemed as they would ask me, if they durst,
How such a glance came there; so, not the first
Are you to turn and ask thus. Sir, 'twas not
Her husband's presence only, called that spot
15 Of joy into the Duchess' cheek: perhaps
Frà Pandolf chanced to say "Her mantle laps
Over my lady's wrist too much," or "Paint
Must never hope to reproduce the faint
Half-flush that dies along her throat": such stuff
20 Was courtesy, she thought, and cause enough
For calling up that spot of joy. She had
A heart—how shall I say?—too soon made glad,
Too easily impressed; she liked whate'er
She looked on, and her looks went everywhere.
25 Sir, 'twas all one! My favor at her breast,
The dropping of the daylight in the West,
The bough of cherries some officious fool
Broke in the orchard for her, the white mule
She rode with round the terrace—all and each
30 Would draw from her alike the approving speech,
Or blush, at least. She thanked men,—good! but thanked
Somehow—I know not how—as if she ranked
My gift of a nine-hundred-years-old name
With anybody's gift. Who'd stoop to blame
35 This sort of trifling? Even had you skill
In speech—which I have not—to make your will
Quite clear to such an one, and say, "Just this
Or that in you disgusts me; here you miss,
Or there exceed the mark"—and if she let
40 Herself be lessoned so, nor plainly set
Her wits to yours, forsooth, and made excuse,
—E'en then would be some stooping; and I choose
Never to stoop. Oh sir, she smiled, no doubt,
Whene'er I passed her; but who passed without
45 Much the same smile? This grew; I gave commands;
Then all smiles stopped together. There she stands
As if alive. Will't please you rise? We'll meet
The company below, then. I repeat,
The Count your master's known munificence
50 Is ample warrant that no just pretense

Of mine for dowry will be disallowed;
Though his fair daughter's self, as I avowed
At starting, is my object. Nay, we'll go
Together down, sir. Notice Neptune, though,
55 Taming a sea-horse, thought a rarity,
Which Claus of Innsbruck cast in bronze for me!

1842

SAMUEL TAYLOR COLERIDGE

Kubla Khan

Or, a Vision in a Dream[7]

In Xanadu did Kubla Khan
A stately pleasure-dome decree:
Where Alph, the sacred river, ran
Through caverns measureless to man
5   Down to a sunless sea.
So twice five miles of fertile ground
With walls and towers were girdled round:
And here were gardens bright with sinuous rills
Where blossomed many an incense-bearing tree;
10 And here were forests ancient as the hills,
Enfolding sunny spots of greenery.

But oh! that deep romantic chasm which slanted
Down the green hill athwart a cedarn cover![8]
A savage place! as holy and enchanted
15 As e'er beneath a waning moon was haunted
By woman wailing for her demon-lover![9]
And from this chasm, with ceaseless turmoil seething,
As if this earth in fast thick pants were breathing,
A mighty fountain momently[1] was forced,
20 Amid whose swift half-intermitted burst
Huge fragments vaulted like rebounding hail,
Or chaffy grain beneath the thresher's flail:
And 'mid these dancing rocks at once and ever

---

7. Coleridge said that he wrote this fragment immediately after waking from an opium dream and that after he was interrupted by a caller he was unable to finish the poem.
8. That is, from side to side beneath a cover of cedar trees.
9. In a famous and often-imitated German ballad, the lady Lenore is carried off on horseback by the specter of her lover and married to him at his grave.   1. Suddenly.

It flung up momently the sacred river.
25 Five miles meandering with a mazy motion
Through wood and dale the sacred river ran,
Then reached the caverns measureless to man,
And sank in tumult to a lifeless ocean:
And 'mid this tumult Kubla heard from far
30 Ancestral voices prophesying war!

The shadow of the dome of pleasure
Floated midway on the waves;
Where was heard the mingled measure
From the fountain and the caves.
35 It was a miracle of rare device,
A sunny pleasure-dome with caves of ice!

A damsel with a dulcimer
In a vision once I saw:
It was an Abyssinian maid,
40 And on her dulcimer she played,
Singing of Mount Abora.
Could I revive within me
Her symphony and song,
To such a deep delight 'twould win me,
45 That with music loud and long,
I would build that dome in air,
That sunny dome! those caves of ice!
And all who heard should see them there,
And all should cry, Beware! Beware!
50 His flashing eyes, his floating hair!
Weave a circle round him thrice,
And close your eyes with holy dread,
For he on honey-dew hath fed,
And drunk the milk of Paradise.

1798

COUNTEE CULLEN

Yet Do I Marvel

I doubt not God is good, well-meaning, kind,
And did He stoop to quibble could tell why
The little buried mole continues blind,
Why flesh that mirrors Him must some day die,

5   Make plain the reason tortured Tantalus[2]
Is baited by the fickle fruit, declare
If merely brute caprice dooms Sisyphus[3]
To struggle up a never-ending stair.
Inscrutable His ways are, and immune
10   To catechism by a mind too strewn
With petty cares to slightly understand
What awful brain compels His awful hand.
Yet do I marvel at this curious thing:
To make a poet black, and bid him sing!

                                                              1925

EMILY DICKINSON

[Because I could not stop for Death—]

Because I could not stop for Death—
He kindly stopped for me—
The Carriage held but just Ourselves—
And Immortality.

5   We slowly drove—He knew no haste
And I had put away
My labor and my leisure too,
For His Civility—

We passed the School, where Children strove
10   At Recess—in the Ring—
We passed the Fields of Gazing Grain—
We passed the Setting Sun—

Or rather—He passed Us—
The Dews drew quivering and chill—
15   For only Gossamer,[4] my Gown—
My Tippet—only Tulle[5]—

We paused before a House that seemed
A Swelling of the Ground—
The Roof was scarcely visible—
20   The Cornice—in the Ground—

---

2. In Greek myth he was condemned, for ambiguous reasons, to stand up to his neck in water he couldn't drink and to be within sight of fruit he couldn't reach to eat.
3. The king of Corinth who, in Greek myth, was condemned eternally to roll a huge stone uphill.
4. Soft, sheer fabric.   5. Fine net fabric. *Tippet*: shawl.

Since then—'tis Centuries—and yet
Feels shorter than the Day
I first surmised the Horses' Heads
Were toward Eternity—

ca. 1863

- What vision of death and the afterlife is implied by the way
  death is personified and characterized in the poem? by the
  details the speaker offers about the carriage ride she takes
  with him?

[*I stepped from Plank to Plank*]

I stepped from Plank to Plank
A slow and cautious way
The Stars about my Head I felt
About my Feet the Sea.

5 I knew not but the next
Would be my final inch—
This gave me that precarious Gait
Some call Experience.

ca. 1864

- For what does "stepp[ing] from Plank to Plank" become a
  metaphor in the poem (line 1)? Is this experience a positive or
  a negative one?

[*We do not play on Graves—*]

We do not play on Graves—
Because there isn't Room—
Besides—it isn't even—it slants
And People come—

5 And put a Flower on it—
And hang their faces so—
We're fearing that their Hearts will drop—
And crush our pretty play—

And so we move as far
10 As Enemies—away—

Just looking round to see how far
It is—Occasionally—

ca. 1862

- What can we infer about the speaker's age and experience? Who are "We"? Why do the speaker and her companions "loo[k] round . . . / Occasionally" (lines 11–12)?

[The Brain—is wider than the Sky—]

The Brain—is wider than the Sky—
For—put them side by side—
The one the other will contain
With ease—and You—beside—

5 The Brain is deeper than the sea—
For—hold them—Blue to Blue—
The one the other will absorb—
As Sponges—Buckets—do—

The Brain is just the weight of God—
10 For—Heft them—Pound for Pound—
And they will differ—if they do—
As Syllable from Sound—

ca. 1862

- What does this poem imply about the human brain by focusing on its width, depth, and weight? by comparing it to the sky, the sea, and God?

[She dealt her pretty words like Blades—]

She dealt her pretty words like Blades—
How glittering they shone—
And every One unbared a Nerve
Or wantoned with a Bone—

5 She never deemed—she hurt—
That—is not Steel's Affair—
A vulgar grimace in the Flesh—
How ill the Creatures bear—

To Ache is human—not polite—
10 The Film upon the eye
Mortality's old Custom—
Just locking up—to Die.

1862

- What kind of person and situation might the poem describe?
  What does the end of the poem imply about how someone
  should respond to such a situation and person?

[*Wild Nights—Wild Nights!*]

Wild Nights—Wild Nights!
Were I with thee
Wild Nights should be
Our luxury!

5 Futile—the Winds—
To a Heart in port—
Done with the Compass—
Done with the Chart!

Rowing in Eden—
10 Ah, the Sea!
Might I but moor—Tonight—
In Thee!

ca. 1861

- Whom might the speaker be addressing? What might it mean
  to be "Done with the Chart" (line 8)?

[*My Life had stood—a Loaded Gun—*]

My Life had stood—a Loaded Gun—
In Corners—till a Day
The Owner passed—identified—
And carried Me away—

5 And now We roam in Sovereign Woods—
And now We hunt the Doe—
And every time I speak for Him—
The Mountains straight reply—

And do I smile, such cordial light
10 Upon the Valley glow—
It is as a Vesuvian face
Had let its pleasure through—

And when at Night—Our good Day done—
I guard My Master's Head—
15 'Tis better than the Eider-Duck's
Deep Pillow—to have shared—

To foe of His—I'm deadly foe—
None stir the second time—
On whom I lay a Yellow Eye—
20 Or an emphatic Thumb—

Though I than He—may longer live
He longer must—than I—
For I have but the power to kill,
Without—the power to die—

ca. 1863

- How does Dickinson set up and then defy the reader's expectations through the poem's controlling metaphor—the speaker's life as a loaded gun? How do the poem's quirks (e.g., the jerky rhythm, the strange syntax, the slant rhymes) contribute to its overall effect?

[*After great pain, a formal feeling comes*—]

After great pain, a formal feeling comes—
The Nerves sit ceremonious, like Tombs—
The stiff Heart questions was it He, that bore,
And Yesterday, or Centuries before?

5 The Feet, mechanical, go round—
Of Ground, or Air, or Ought—
A Wooden way
Regardless grown,
A Quartz contentment, like a stone—

10 This is the Hour of Lead—
Remembered, if outlived,
As Freezing Persons recollect the Snow—
First—Chill—then Stupor—then the letting go—

ca. 1862

- What different metaphors and similes are used here, and what does each contribute to the poem's portrayal of how we feel "After great pain"?

JOHN DONNE

[*Death, be not proud*]

Death be not proud, though some have callèd thee
Mighty and dreadful, for thou art not so;
For those whom thou think'st thou dost overthrow
Die not, poor Death, nor yet canst thou kill me.
5 From rest and sleep, which but thy pictures[6] be,
Much pleasure; then from thee much more must flow,
And soonest[7] our best men with thee do go,
Rest of their bones, and soul's delivery.[8]
Thou art slave to Fate, Chance, kings, and desperate men,
10 And dost with Poison, War, and Sickness dwell;
And poppy or charms can make us sleep as well,
And better than thy stroke; why swell'st[9] thou then?
One short sleep past, we wake eternally
And death shall be no more; Death, thou shalt die.

1633

Song

Go, and catch a falling star,
  Get with child a mandrake root,[1]
Tell me, where all past years are,
  Or who cleft the devil's foot,
5 Teach me to hear mermaids singing
Or to keep off envy's stinging,
    And find
    What wind
Serves to advance an honest mind.

10 If thou beest born to strange sights,[2]
    Things invisible to see,

6. Likenesses. 7. Most willingly. 8. Deliverance. 9. Puff with pride.
1. The forked mandrake root looks vaguely like a pair of human legs.
2. That is, if you have supernatural powers.

Ride ten thousand days and nights,
  Till age snow white hairs on thee;
Thou, when thou return'st, wilt tell me
15 All strange wonders that befell thee,
     And swear
     No where
Lives a woman true, and fair.

If thou find'st one, let me know:
20   Such a pilgrimage were sweet.
Yet do not, I would not go,
  Though at next door we might meet:
Though she were true when you met her,
And last till you write your letter,
25   Yet she
    Will be
False, ere I come, to two, or three.

1633

A Valediction: Forbidding Mourning

As virtuous men pass mildly away,
  And whisper to their souls to go,
Whilst some of their sad friends do say,
  "The breath goes now," and some say, "No,"

5 So let us melt, and make no noise,
    No tear-floods, nor sigh-tempests move;
'Twere profanation of our joys
    To tell the laity our love.

Moving of the earth[3] brings harms and fears,
10   Men reckon what it did and meant;
But trepidation of the spheres,[4]
    Though greater far, is innocent.

Dull sublunary[5] lovers' love
    (Whose soul is sense) cannot admit

---

3. Earthquakes.
4. Renaissance theory that the celestial spheres trembled and thus caused unexpected variations in their orbits. Such movements are "innocent" because earthlings do not observe or fret about them.
5. Below the moon—that is, changeable. According to the traditional cosmology that Donne invokes here, the moon is the dividing line between the immutable celestial world and the mutable earthly one.

15 Absence, because it doth remove
    Those things which elemented[6] it.

But we, by a love so much refined
    That our selves know not what it is,
Inter-assured of the mind,
20   Care less, eyes, lips, and hands to miss.

Our two souls therefore, which are one,
    Though I must go, endure not yet
A breach, but an expansion,
    Like gold to airy thinness beat.

25 If they be two, they are two so
    As stiff twin compasses are two:
Thy soul, the fixed foot, makes no show
    To move, but doth, if the other do;

And though it in the center sit,
30   Yet when the other far doth roam,
It leans, and hearkens after it,
    And grows erect, as that comes home.

Such wilt thou be to me, who must,
    Like the other foot, obliquely run;
35 Thy firmness makes my circle[7] just,
    And makes me end where I begun.

                               1611?

PAUL LAURENCE DUNBAR

Sympathy

I know what the caged bird feels, alas!
    When the sun is bright on the upland slopes;
When the wind stirs soft through the springing grass,
    And the river flows like a stream of glass;
5   When the first bird sings and the first bud opens,
And the faint perfume from its chalice steals—
I know what the caged bird feels!

I know why the caged bird beats his wing
    Till its blood is red on the cruel bars;
10 For he must fly back to his perch and cling

---

6. Comprised.   7. Traditional symbol of perfection.

When he fain[8] would be on the bough a-swing;
   And a pain still throbs in the old, old scars
And they pulse again with a keener sting—
I know why he beats his wing!

15 I know why the caged bird sings, ah me,
   When his wing is bruised and his bosom sore,—
When he beats his bars and he would be free;
It is not a carol of joy or glee,
   But a prayer that he sends from his heart's deep core,
20 But a plea, that upward to Heaven he flings—
I know why the caged bird sings!

1893

We Wear the Mask

We wear the mask that grins and lies,
It hides our cheeks and shades our eyes,—
This debt we pay to human guile;
With torn and bleeding hearts we smile,
5 And mouth with myriad subtleties.

Why should the world be over-wise,
In counting all our tears and sighs?
Nay, let them only see us, while
   We wear the mask.

10 We smile, but, O great Christ, our cries
To thee from tortured souls arise.
We sing, but oh the clay is vile
Beneath our feet, and long the mile;
But let the world dream otherwise,
15   We wear the mask!

1895

T. S. ELIOT

The Love Song of J. Alfred Prufrock

*S'io credessi che mia risposta fosse
a persona che mai tornasse al mondo,
questa fiamma staria senza più scosse.*

8. Gladly.

Ma per ciò che giammai di questo fondo
non tornò vivo alcun, s'i'odo il vero,
senza tema d'infamia ti rispondo.[9]

Let us go then, you and I,
When the evening is spread out against the sky
Like a patient etherised upon a table;
Let us go, through certain half-deserted streets,
5 The muttering retreats
Of restless nights in one-night cheap hotels
And sawdust restaurants with oyster-shells:
Streets that follow like a tedious argument
Of insidious intent
10 To lead you to an overwhelming question . . .
Oh, do not ask, 'What is it?'
Let us go and make our visit.

In the room the women come and go
Talking of Michelangelo.[1]

15 The yellow fog that rubs its back upon the window-panes,
The yellow smoke that rubs its muzzle on the window-panes,
Licked its tongue into the corners of the evening,
Lingered upon the pools that stand in drains,
Let fall upon its back the soot that falls from chimneys,
20 Slipped by the terrace, made a sudden leap,
And seeing that it was a soft October night,
Curled once about the house, and fell asleep.

And indeed there will be time[2]
For the yellow smoke that slides along the street
25 Rubbing its back upon the window-panes;
There will be time, there will be time
To prepare a face to meet the faces that you meet;
There will be time to murder and create,

9. From Dante, *Inferno* (27.61-66): "If I thought that my reply would be / to one who would ever
return to the world, / this flame would stay without further movement; / but since none has ever
returned alive from this depth, / if what I hear is true, / I answer you without fear of infamy." The
words are spoken by the character Guido da Montefeltro—imprisoned in flame in the depths
of hell as a punishment for giving false counsel—to Dante, whom da Montefeltro believes will
never return from his journey into the inferno.
1. Italian artist Michelangelo Buonarroti (1475-1564).
2. Echo of Andrew Marvell's "To His Coy Mistress" (1681), which famously begins, "Had we but
world enough, and time / This coyness, lady, were no crime."

And time for all the works and days[3] of hands
30 That lift and drop a question on your plate;
Time for you and time for me,
And time yet for a hundred indecisions,
And for a hundred visions and revisions,
Before the taking of a toast and tea.

35 In the room the women come and go
Talking of Michelangelo.

And indeed there will be time
To wonder, 'Do I dare?' and, 'Do I dare?'
Time to turn back and descend the stair,
40 With a bald spot in the middle of my hair—
(They will say: 'How his hair is growing thin!')
My morning coat, my collar mounting firmly to the chin,
My necktie rich and modest, but asserted by a simple pin—
(They will say: 'But how his arms and legs are thin!')
45 Do I dare
Disturb the universe?
In a minute there is time
For decisions and revisions which a minute will reverse.

For I have known them all already, known them all—
50 Have known the evenings, mornings, afternoons,
I have measured out my life with coffee spoons;
I know the voices dying with a dying fall
Beneath the music from a farther room.
       So how should I presume?

55 And I have known the eyes already, known them all—
The eyes that fix you in a formulated phrase,
And when I am formulated, sprawling on a pin,
When I am pinned and wriggling on the wall,
Then how should I begin
60 To spit out all the butt-ends of my days and ways?
       And how should I presume?

And I have known the arms already, known them all—
Arms that are braceleted and white and bare
(But in the lamplight, downed with light brown hair!)

3. *Works and Days* is a poem composed about 700 B.C.E. by the Greek writer Hesiod; lamenting the moral decay of the present, it celebrates simple life and hard work, especially agricultural labor.

65 Is it perfume from a dress
That makes me so digress?
Arms that lie along a table, or wrap about a shawl.
And should I then presume?
And how should I begin?

· · · · ·

70 Shall I say, I have gone at dusk through narrow streets
And watched the smoke that rises from the pipes
Of lonely men in shirt-sleeves, leaning out of windows? . . .

I should have been a pair of ragged claws
Scuttling across the floors of silent seas.

· · · · ·

75 And the afternoon, the evening, sleeps so peacefully!
Smoothed by long fingers,
Asleep . . . tired . . . or it malingers,
Stretched on the floor, here beside you and me.
Should I, after tea and cakes and ices,
80 Have the strength to force the moment to its crisis?
But though I have wept and fasted, wept and prayed,
Though I have seen my head (grown slightly bald) brought in
       upon a platter,[4]
I am no prophet—and here's no great matter;
I have seen the moment of my greatness flicker,
85 And I have seen the eternal Footman hold my coat, and snicker,
And in short, I was afraid.

And would it have been worth it, after all,
After the cups, the marmalade, the tea,
Among the porcelain, among some talk of you and me,
90 Would it have been worth while,
To have bitten off the matter with a smile,
To have squeezed the universe into a ball[5]
To roll it towards some overwhelming question,
To say: 'I am Lazarus, come from the dead,[6]
95 Come back to tell you all, I shall tell you all'—
If one, settling a pillow by her head,

4. Like John the Baptist; at a banquet, King Herod has the prophet's head delivered on a plate to Salome, the woman who requested his execution (Mark 6.17-28; Matthew 14.3-11).
5. Another echo of "To His Coy Mistress": "Let us roll all our strength and all / Our sweetness up into one ball, / And tear our pleasures with rough strife / Through the iron gates of life" (lines 41-44).
6. The New Testament relates the story of Jesus raising Lazarus from the dead in John 11.1-44.

Should say: 'That is not what I meant at all.
That is not it, at all.'

And would it have been worth it, after all,
100 Would it have been worth while,
After the sunsets and the dooryards and the sprinkled streets,
After the novels, after the teacups, after the skirts that trail along
    the floor—
And this, and so much more?—
It is impossible to say just what I mean!
105 But as if a magic lantern threw the nerves in patterns on a screen:
Would it have been worth while
If one, settling a pillow or throwing off a shawl,
And turning toward the window, should say:
    'That is not it at all,
110   That is not what I meant, at all.'

· · · · ·

No! I am not Prince Hamlet,[7] nor was meant to be;
Am an attendant lord, one that will do
To swell a progress,[8] start a scene or two,
Advise the prince; no doubt, an easy tool,
115 Deferential, glad to be of use,
Politic, cautious, and meticulous;
Full of high sentence,[9] but a bit obtuse;
At times, indeed, almost ridiculous—
Almost, at times, the Fool.

120 I grow old . . . I grow old . . .
I shall wear the bottoms of my trousers rolled.

Shall I part my hair behind? Do I dare to eat a peach?
I shall wear white flannel trousers, and walk upon the beach.
125 I have heard the mermaids singing, each to each.

I do not think that they will sing to me.

I have seen them riding seaward on the waves
Combing the white hair of the waves blown back
When the wind blows the water white and black.

7. Protagonist of Shakespeare's tragedy *Hamlet*, who is indecisive for much of the play.
8. Journey of a royal or noble person, or the representation of such a journey onstage as part of a play (as was common in the age of Shakespeare).
9. In either of its two archaic senses: official opinion, as of a judge; maxim, general truth, or proverbial saying.

130 We have lingered in the chambers of the sea
    By sea-girls wreathed with seaweed red and brown
    Till human voices wake us, and we drown.

                                                        1915

ROBERT FROST

The Road Not Taken

Two roads diverged in a yellow wood,
And sorry I could not travel both
And be one traveler, long I stood
And looked down one as far as I could
5 To where it bent in the undergrowth;

Then took the other, as just as fair,
And having perhaps the better claim,
Because it was grassy and wanted wear;
Though as for that the passing there
10 Had worn them really about the same,

And both that morning equally lay
In leaves no step had trodden black.
Oh, I kept the first for another day!
Yet knowing how way leads on to way,
15 I doubted if I should ever come back.

I shall be telling this with a sigh
Somewhere ages and ages hence:
Two roads diverged in a wood, and I—
I took the one less traveled by,
20 And that has made all the difference.

                                                        1916

Stopping by Woods on a Snowy Evening

Whose woods these are I think I know.
His house is in the village, though;
He will not see me stopping here
To watch his woods fill up with snow.

5 My little horse must think it queer
To stop without a farmhouse near

Between the woods and frozen lake
The darkest evening of the year.

He gives his harness bells a shake
10   To ask if there is some mistake.
The only other sound's the sweep
Of easy wind and downy flake.

The woods are lovely, dark, and deep,
But I have promises to keep,
15   And miles to go before I sleep,
And miles to go before I sleep.

                                        1923

Home Burial

He saw her from the bottom of the stairs
Before she saw him. She was starting down,
Looking back over her shoulder at some fear.
She took a doubtful step and then undid it
5   To raise herself and look again. He spoke
Advancing toward her: "What is it you see
From up there always?—for I want to know."
She turned and sank upon her skirts at that,
And her face changed from terrified to dull.
10   He said to gain time: "What is it you see?"
Mounting until she cowered under him.
"I will find out now—you must tell me, dear."
She, in her place, refused him any help,
With the least stiffening of her neck and silence.
15   She let him look, sure that he wouldn't see,
Blind creature; and awhile he didn't see.
But at last he murmured, "Oh," and again, "Oh."

"What is it—what?" she said.

                              "Just that I see."

"You don't," she challenged. "Tell me what it is."

20   "The wonder is I didn't see at once.
I never noticed it from here before.
I must be wonted to it—that's the reason.
The little graveyard where my people are!
So small the window frames the whole of it.
25   Not so much larger than a bedroom, is it?

There are three stones of slate and one of marble,
Broad-shouldered little slabs there in the sunlight
On the sidehill. We haven't to mind *those*.
But I understand: it is not the stones,
But the child's mound——"

                  "Don't, don't, don't,

30   don't," she cried.

She withdrew, shrinking from beneath his arm
That rested on the banister, and slid downstairs;
And turned on him with such a daunting look,
He said twice over before he knew himself:
35 "Can't a man speak of his own child he's lost?"

"Not you!—Oh, where's my hat? Oh, I don't need it!
I must get out of here. I must get air.—
I don't know rightly whether any man can."

"Amy! Don't go to someone else this time.
40 Listen to me. I won't come down the stairs."
He sat and fixed his chin between his fists.
"There's something I should like to ask you, dear."

"You don't know how to ask it."

                  "Help me, then."

45 Her fingers moved the latch for all reply.

"My words are nearly always an offense.
I don't know how to speak of anything
So as to please you. But I might be taught,
I should suppose. I can't say I see how.
50 A man must partly give up being a man
With womenfolk. We could have some arrangement
By which I'd bind myself to keep hands off
Anything special you're a-mind to name.
Though I don't like such things 'twixt those that love.
Two that don't love can't live together without them.
55 But two that do can't live together with them."
She moved the latch a little. "Don't—don't go.
Don't carry it to someone else this time.
Tell me about it if it's something human.
Let me into your grief. I'm not so much
60 Unlike other folks as your standing there
Apart would make me out. Give me my chance.
I do think, though, you overdo it a little.

What was it brought you up to think it the thing
To take your mother-loss of a first child
65 So inconsolably—in the face of love.
You'd think his memory might be satisfied—"

"There you go sneering now!"

                              "I'm not, I'm not!
You make me angry. I'll come down to you.
God, what a woman! And it's come to this,
70 A man can't speak of his own child that's dead."

"You can't because you don't know how to speak.
If you had any feelings, you that dug
With your own hand—how could you?—his little grave;
I saw you from that very window there,
75 Making the gravel leap and leap in air,
Leap up, like that, like that, and land so lightly
And roll back down the mound beside the hole.
I thought, Who is that man? I didn't know you.
And I crept down the stairs and up the stairs
80 To look again, and still your spade kept lifting.
Then you came in. I heard your rumbling voice
Out in the kitchen, and I don't know why,
But I went near to see with my own eyes.
You could sit there with the stains on your shoes
85 Of the fresh earth from your own baby's grave
And talk about your everyday concerns.
You had stood the spade up against the wall
Outside there in the entry, for I saw it."

"I shall laugh the worst laugh I ever laughed.
90 I'm cursed. God, if I don't believe I'm cursed."

"I can repeat the very words you were saying:
'Three foggy mornings and one rainy day
Will rot the best birch fence a man can build.'
Think of it, talk like that at such a time!
95 What had how long it takes a birch to rot
To do with what was in the darkened parlor?
You *couldn't* care! The nearest friends can go
With anyone to death, comes so far short
They might as well not try to go at all.
100 No, from the time when one is sick to death,
One is alone, and he dies more alone.
Friends make pretense of following to the grave,

But before one is in it, their minds are turned
And making the best of their way back to life
105 And living people, and things they understand.
But the world's evil. I won't have grief so
If I can change it. Oh, I won't, I won't!"

"There, you have said it all and you feel better.
You won't go now. You're crying. Close the door.
110 The heart's gone out of it: why keep it up?
Amy! There's someone coming down the road!"
"*You*—oh, you think the talk is all. I must go—
Somewhere out of this house. How can I make you—"

"If—you—do!" She was opening the door wider.
115 "Where do you mean to go? First tell me that.
I'll follow and bring you back by force. I *will!*—"

1915

THOMAS GRAY

Elegy Written in a Country Churchyard

The curfew tolls the knell of parting day,
   The lowing herd wind slowly o'er the lea,
The plowman homeward plods his weary way,
   And leaves the world to darkness and to me.

5 Now fades the glimmering landscape on the sight,
   And all the air a solemn stillness holds,
Save where the beetle wheels his droning flight,
   And drowsy tinklings lull the distant folds;

Save that from yonder ivy-mantled tower
10   The moping owl does to the moon complain
Of such, as wandering near her secret bower,
   Molest her ancient solitary reign.

Beneath those rugged elms, that yew tree's shade,
   Where heaves the turf in many a moldering heap,
15 Each in his narrow cell forever laid,
   The rude[1] forefathers of the hamlet sleep.

---

1. Unlearned.

The breezy call of incense-breathing Morn,
   The swallow twittering from the straw-built shed,
The cock's shrill clarion, or the echoing horn.[2]
20 No more shall rouse them from their lowly bed.

For them no more the blazing hearth shall burn,
   Or busy housewife ply her evening care;
No children run to lisp their sire's return,
   Or climb his knees the envied kiss to share.

25 Oft did the harvest to their sickle yield,
   Their furrow oft the stubborn glebe[3] has broke;
How jocund did they drive their team afield!
   How bowed the woods beneath their sturdy stroke!

Let not Ambition mock their useful toil,
30   Their homely joys, and destiny obscure;
Nor Grandeur hear with a disdainful smile
   The short and simple annals of the poor.

The boast of heraldry,[4] the pomp of power,
   And all that beauty, all that wealth e'er gave,
35 Awaits alike the inevitable hour.
   The paths of glory lead but to the grave.

Nor you, ye proud, impute to these the fault,
   If Memory o'er their tomb no trophies[5] raise,
Where through the long-drawn aisle and fretted[6] vault
40   The pealing anthem swells the note of praise

Can storied urn or animated[7] bust
   Back to its mansion call the fleeting breath?
Can Honor's voice provoke the silent dust,
   Or Flattery soothe the dull cold ear of Death?

45 Perhaps in this neglected spot is laid
   Some heart once pregnant with celestial fire;
Hands that the rod of empire might have swayed,
   Or waked to ecstasy the living lyre.

But Knowledge to their eyes her ample page
50   Rich with the spoils of time did ne'er unroll;
Chill Penury repressed their noble rage,
   And froze the genial current of the soul.

---

2. Hunter's horn.   3. Soil.   4. That is, noble birth.
5. Ornamental or symbolic groups of figures depicting the achievements of the deceased.
6. Decorated with intersecting lines in relief.
7. Lifelike. *Storied urn*: a funeral urn with an epitaph or pictured story inscribed on it.

Full many a gem of purest ray serene,
    The dark unfathomed caves of ocean bear:
55 Full many a flower is born to blush unseen,
    And waste its sweetness on the desert air.

Some village Hampden,[8] that with dauntless breast
    The little tyrant of his fields withstood;
Some mute inglorious Milton[9] here may rest,
60 Some Cromwell[1] guiltless of his country's blood.

The applause of listening senates to command,
    The threats of pain and ruin to despise,
To scatter plenty o'er a smiling land,
    And read their history in a nation's eyes,

65 Their lot forbade: nor circumscribed alone
    Their growing virtues, but their crimes confined;
Forbade to wade through slaughter to a throne,
    And shut the gates of mercy on mankind,

The struggling pangs of conscious truth to hide,
70 To quench the blushes of ingenuous shame,
Or heap the shrine of Luxury and Pride
    With incense kindled at the Muse's flame.

Far from the madding crowd's ignoble strife,
    Their sober wishes never learned to stray;
75 Along the cool sequestered vale of life
    They kept the noiseless tenor of their way.

Yet even these bones from insult to protect
    Some frail memorial still erected nigh,
With uncouth rhymes and shapeless sculpture decked,[2]
80 Implores the passing tribute of a sigh.

Their name, their years, spelt by the unlettered Muse,
    The place of fame and elegy supply:
And many a holy text around she strews,
    That teach the rustic moralist to die.

85 For who to dumb Forgetfulness a prey,
    This pleasing anxious being e'er resigned,

---

8. John Hampden (1594-1643), both as a private citizen and as a member of Parliament, zealously defended the rights of the people against the autocratic policies of King Charles I.
9. John Milton (1608-74), great English poet.
1. Oliver Cromwell (1599-1658), Lord Protector of England during the Commonwealth, or Interregnum, noted for military genius but also cruelty and intolerance.
2. Cf. the "storied urn or animated bust" (line 41) dedicated inside the church to the "proud" (line 37).

Left the warm precincts of the cheerful day,
Nor cast one longing lingering look behind?

On some fond breast the parting soul relies,
90   Some pious drops the closing eye requires;
Even from the tomb the voice of Nature cries,
Even in our ashes live their wonted fires.

For thee, who mindful of the unhonored dead
Dost in these lines their artless tale relate;
95 If chance, by lonely contemplation led,
Some kindred spirit shall inquire thy fate,

Haply[3] some hoary-headed swain may say,
"Oft have we seen him at the peep of dawn
Brushing with hasty steps the dews away
100   To meet the sun upon the upland lawn.

"There at the foot of yonder nodding beech
That wreathes its old fantastic roots so high,
His listless length at noontide would he stretch,
And pore upon the brook that babbles by.

105 "Hard by yon wood, now smiling as in scorn,
Muttering his wayward fancies he would rove,
Now drooping, woeful wan, like one forlorn,
Or crazed with care, or crossed in hopeless love.

"One morn I missed him on the customed hill,
110   Along the heath and near his favorite tree;
Another came; nor[4] yet beside the rill,
Nor up the lawn, nor at the wood was he;

"The next with dirges due in sad array
Slow through the churchway path we saw him borne.
115 Approach and read (for thou canst read) the lay,
Graved on the stone beneath yon aged thorn."

The Epitaph

Here rests his head upon the lap of Earth
A youth to Fortune and to Fame unknown.
Fair Science[5] frowned not on his humble birth,
120   *And Melancholy marked him for her own.*

Large was his bounty, and his soul sincere,
Heaven did a recompense as largely send:

3. Perhaps.   4. Neither.   5. Learning.

He gave to Misery all he had, a tear,
    He gained from Heaven ('twas all he wished) a friend.

125 No farther seek his merits to disclose,
    Or draw his frailties from their dread abode
    (There they alike in trembling hope repose),
    The bosom of his Father and his God.

                                                        1751

ANGELINA GRIMKÉ

Tenebris[6]

There is a tree, by day,
That, at night,
Has a shadow,
A hand huge and black,
5 With fingers long and black.
    All through the dark,
Against the white man's house,
    In the little wind,
The black hand plucks and plucks
10   At the bricks.
The bricks are the color of blood and very small.
    Is it a black hand,
    Or is it a shadow?

                                                        1927

ROBERT HAYDEN

The Whipping

The old woman across the way
    is whipping the boy again
and shouting to the neighborhood
    her goodness and his wrongs.

5 Wildly he crashes through elephant ears,
    pleads in dusty zinnias,

---

6. In darkness (Latin).

while she in spite of crippling fat
pursues and corners him.

She strikes and strikes the shrilly circling
10   boy till the stick breaks
in her hand. His tears are rainy weather
to woundlike memories:

My head gripped in bony vise
of knees, the writing struggle
15 to wrench free, the blows, the fear
worse than blows that hateful

Words could bring, the face that I
no longer knew or loved. . . .
Well, it is over now, it is over,
20   and the boy sobs in his room,

And the woman leans muttering against
a tree, exhausted, purged—
avenged in part for lifelong hidings
she has had to bear.

1962, 1966

Frederick Douglass

When it is finally ours, this freedom,[7] this liberty, this beautiful
and terrible thing, needful to man as air,
usable as earth; when it belongs at last to all,
when it is truly instinct, brain matter, diastole, systole,
5 reflex action; when it is finally won; when it is more
than the gaudy mumbo jumbo of politicians:
this man, this Douglass, this former slave, this Negro
beaten to his knees, exiled, visioning a world
where none is lonely, none hunted, alien,
10 this man, superb in love and logic, this man
shall be remembered. Oh, not with statues' rhetoric,
not with legends and poems and wreaths of bronze alone,
but with the lives grown out of his life, the lives
fleshing his dream of the beautiful, needful thing.

1966

7. Frederick Douglass (1817–95), an escaped slave, was involved in the Underground Railroad and
became publisher of the famous abolitionist newspaper the *North Star*, in Rochester, New York.

SEAMUS HEANEY

Digging

Between my finger and my thumb
The squat pen rests; snug as a gun.

Under my window, a clean rasping sound
When the spade sinks into gravelly ground:
5 My father, digging. I look down

Till his straining rump among the flowerbeds
Bends low, comes up twenty years away
Stooping in rhythm through potato drills[8]
Where he was digging.

10 The coarse boot nestled on the lug, the shaft
Against the inside knee was levered firmly.
He rooted out tall tops, buried the bright edge deep
To scatter new potatoes that we picked
Loving their cool hardness in our hands.

15 By God, the old man could handle a spade.
Just like his old man.

My grandfather cut more turf[9] in a day
Than any other man on Toner's bog.
Once I carried him milk in a bottle
20 Corked sloppily with paper. He straightened up
To drink it, then fell to right away.
Nicking and slicing neatly, heaving sods
Over his shoulder, going down and down
For the good turf. Digging.

25 The cold smell of potato mould, the squelch and slap
Of soggy peat, the curt cuts of an edge
Through living roots awaken in my head.
But I've no spade to follow men like them.

Between my finger and my thumb
30 The squat pen rests.
I'll dig with it.

1966

8. Small furrows in which seeds are sown.
9. Peat cut into slabs and dried to be used as fuel in stoves and furnaces.

Punishment[1]

I can feel the tug
of the halter at the nape
of her neck, the wind
on her naked front.

5   It blows her nipples
to amber beads,
it shakes the frail rigging
of her ribs.

I can see her drowned
10   body in the bog,
the weighing stone,
the floating rods and boughs.

Under which at first
she was a barked sapling
15   that is dug up
oak-bone, brain-firkin:

her shaved head
like a stubble of black corn,
her blindfold a soiled bandage,
20   her noose a ring

to store
the memories of love.
Little adulteress,
before they punished you

25   you were flaxen-haired,
undernourished, and your
tar-black face was beautiful.
My poor scapegoat,

I almost love you
30   but would have cast, I know,
the stones of silence.
I am the artful voyeur

1. According to the Roman historian Tacitus (ca. 56–ca. 120 C.E.), Germanic peoples punished
adulterous women by first shaving their heads and then banishing or killing them. In 1951, in
Windeby, Germany, the naked body of a young girl from the first century C.E. was pulled from the
bog where she had been murdered. In contemporary Ireland, "betraying sisters" (38) have sometimes been punished by the Irish Republican Army (IRA) for associating with British soldiers.

of your brain's exposed
and darkened combs,
35 your muscles' webbing
and all your numbered bones:

I who have stood dumb
when your betraying sisters,
cauled[2] in tar,
40 wept by the railings,

who would connive
in civilized outrage
yet understand the exact
and tribal, intimate revenge.

1975

GERARD MANLEY HOPKINS

God's Grandeur

The world is charged with the grandeur of God.
  It will flame out, like shining from shook foil;[3]
  It gathers to a greatness, like the ooze of oil
Crushed. Why do men then now not reck his rod?[4]
5 Generations have trod, have trod, have trod;
  And all is seared with trade; bleared, smeared with toil;
  And wears man's smudge and shares man's smell: the soil
Is bare now, nor can foot feel, being shod.

And for all this, nature is never spent;
10   There lives the dearest freshness deep down things;
And though the last lights off the black West went
  Oh, morning, at the brown brink eastward, springs—
Because the Holy Ghost over the bent
  World broods with warm breast and with ah! bright wings.

ca. 1877

---

2. Wrapped or enclosed as if in a caul (the inner fetal membrane of higher vertebrates that sometimes covers the head at birth).
3. "I mean foil in its sense of leaf or tinsel. . . . Shaken goldfoil gives off broad glares like sheet lightning and also, and this is true of nothing else, owing to its zig-zag dints and creasings and network of small many cornered facets, a sort of fork lightning too" (*Letters of Gerard Manley Hopkins to Robert Bridges*, ed. C. C. Abbott [1955], p. 169).   4. Heed his authority.

The Windhover[5]

To Christ our Lord

I caught this morning morning's minion,[6] king-
    dom of daylight's dauphin,[7] dapple-dawn-drawn Falcon, in his
      riding
Of the rolling level underneath him steady air, and striding
High there, how he rung upon the rein of a wimpling[8] wing
5 In his ecstasy! then off, off forth on swing,
    As a skate's heel sweeps smooth on a bow-bend: the hurl and
      gliding
Rebuffed the big wind. My heart in hiding
Stirred for a bird,—the achieve of, the mastery of the thing!

Brute beauty and valor and act, oh, air, pride, plume, here
10   Buckle![9] AND the fire that breaks from thee then, a billion
Times told lovelier, more dangerous, O my chevalier![1]

No wonder of it: shéer plód makes plow down sillion[2]
Shine, and blue-bleak embers, ah my dear,
    Fall, gall themselves, and gash gold-vermilion.

1877

LANGSTON HUGHES

Harlem

What happens to a dream deferred?

    Does it dry up
    Like a raisin in the sun? *A*
    Or fester like a sore—
5   And then run? *A*
    Does it stink like rotten meat? *B*
    Or crust and sugar over—
    Like a syrupy sweet? *B*

5. Small hawk, the kestrel, which habitually hovers in the air, headed into the wind.
6. Favorite, beloved.   7. Heir to regal splendor.   8. Rippling.
9. Several meanings may apply: to join closely, to prepare for battle, to grapple with, to collapse.
1. Horseman, knight.
2. Narrow strip of land between furrows in an open field divided for separate cultivation.

Maybe it just sags
10 Like a heavy load. (

Or does it explode? (

1951

The Negro Speaks of Rivers

I've known rivers:
I've known rivers ancient as the world and older than the flow of
   human blood in human veins.

My soul has grown deep like the rivers.

I bathed in the Euphrates when dawns were young.
5 I built my hut near the Congo and it lulled me to sleep.
I looked upon the Nile and raised the pyramids above it.
I heard the singing of the Mississippi when Abe Lincoln went
      down to New Orleans, and I've seen its muddy bosom turn
      all golden in the sunset.

I've known rivers:
Ancient, dusky rivers.

10 My soul has grown deep like the rivers.

1926

BEN JONSON

[*Come, my Celia, let us prove*]³

Come, my Celia, let us prove,⁴
While we can, the sports of love;
Time will not be ours forever:
He at length our good will sever.
5 Spend not, then, his gifts in vain;
Suns that set may rise again,
But if once we lose this light,
'Tis with us perpetual night.

---

3. A song from *Volpone*, sung by the play's villain and would-be seducer. Part of the poem paraphrases Catullus, poem 5. The speaker's invitation echoes Satan's temptation of Eve in Genesis.
4. Experience.

Why should we defer our joys?
10 Fame and rumor are but toys.
Cannot we delude the eyes
Of a few poor household spies?
Or his easier ears beguile,
Thus removèd by our wile?
15 'Tis no sin love's fruits to steal,
But the sweet thefts to reveal;
To be taken, to be seen,
These have crimes accounted been.

                                    1606

JOHN KEATS

Ode to a Nightingale

I

My heart aches, and a drowsy numbness pains
    My sense, as though of hemlock I had drunk,
Or emptied some dull opiate to the drains
    One minute past, and Lethe-wards[5] had sunk:
5 'Tis not through envy of thy happy lot,
    But being too happy in thine happiness,
        That thou, light-wingèd Dryad[6] of the trees,
            In some melodious plot
Of beechen green, and shadows numberless,
10   Singest of summer in full-throated ease.

II

O, for a draught of vintage! that hath been
    Cooled a long age in the deep-delvèd earth,
Tasting of Flora[7] and the country green,
    Dance, and Provençal song,[8] and sunburnt mirth!
15 O for a beaker full of the warm South,
    Full of the true, the blushful Hippocrene,[9]
        With beaded bubbles winking at the brim,
            And purple-stainèd mouth;

5. Toward the river of forgetfulness (Lethe) in Hades.   6. Wood nymph.
7. Roman goddess of flowers.
8. The medieval troubadours of Provence were famous for their love songs.
9. The fountain of the Muses on Mt. Helicon, whose waters bring poetic inspiration

That I might drink, and leave the world unseen,
20   And with thee fade away into the forest dim:

III

Fade far away, dissolve, and quite forget
    What thou among the leaves hast never known,
The weariness, the fever, and the fret
    Here, where men sit and hear each other groan;
25 Where palsy shakes a few, sad, last gray hairs,
    Where youth grows pale, and specter-thin, and dies;
        Where but to think is to be full of sorrow
            And leaden-eyed despairs,
        Where Beauty cannot keep her lustrous eyes,
30   Or new Love pine at them beyond tomorrow.

IV

Away! away! for I will fly to thee,
    Not charioted by Bacchus and his pards,[1]
But on the viewless[2] wings of Poesy,
    Though the dull brain perplexes and retards:
35 Already with thee! tender is the night,
    And haply the Queen-Moon is on her throne,
        Clustered around by all her starry Fays;[3]
            But here there is no light,
        Save what from heaven is with the breezes blown
40   Through verdurous glooms and winding mossy ways.

V

I cannot see what flowers are at my feet,
    Nor what soft incense hangs upon the boughs,
But, in embalmèd[4] darkness, guess each sweet
    Wherewith the seasonable month endows
45 The grass, the thicket, and the fruit-tree wild;
    White hawthorn, and the pastoral eglantine;[5]
        Fast fading violets covered up in leaves;
            And mid-May's eldest child,
        The coming musk-rose, full of dewy wine,
50   The murmurous haunt of flies on summer eves.

VI

Darkling[6] I listen; and, for many a time
    I have been half in love with easeful Death,

---

1. The Roman god of wine was sometimes portrayed in a chariot drawn by leopards.
2. Invisible.   3. Fairies.   4. Fragrant, aromatic.   5. Sweetbriar or honeysuckle.   6. In the dark.

Called him soft names in many a musèd rhyme,
　　To take into the air my quiet breath;
55 Now more than ever seems it rich to die,
　　To cease upon the midnight with no pain,
　　　While thou art pouring forth thy soul abroad
　　　　In such an ecstasy!
　　Still wouldst thou sing, and I have ears in vain—
60 　　To thy high requiem become a sod.

VII

Thou wast not born for death, immortal Bird!
　　No hungry generations tread thee down;
The voice I hear this passing night was heard
　　In ancient days by emperor and clown:
65 Perhaps the selfsame song that found a path
　　Through the sad heart of Ruth,[7] when, sick for home,
　　　She stood in tears amid the alien corn;
　　　　The same that ofttimes hath
　　Charmed magic casements, opening on the foam
70 　　Of perilous seas, in faery lands forlorn.

VIII

Forlorn! the very word is like a bell
　　To toll me back from thee to my sole self!
Adieu! the fancy cannot cheat so well
　　As she is famed to do, deceiving elf.
75 Adieu! adieu! thy plaintive anthem fades
　　Past the near meadows, over the still stream,
　　　Up the hillside; and now 'tis buried deep
　　　　In the next valley-glades:
　　Was it a vision, or a waking dream?
80 　　Fled is that music:—Do I wake or sleep?

　　　　　　　　　　　　　　　　　　May 1819

Ode on a Grecian Urn

I

Thou still unravished bride of quietness,
　　Thou foster-child of silence and slow time,

---

7. A virtuous Moabite widow who, according to the Old Testament Book of Ruth, left her own country to accompany her mother-in-law, Naomi, back to Naomi's native land. She supported herself
as a gleaner.

Sylvan historian, who canst thus express
A flowery tale more sweetly than our rhyme:
5 What leaf-fringed legend haunts about thy shape
Of deities or mortals, or of both,
In Tempe or the dales of Arcady?[8]
What men or gods are these? What maidens loath?
What mad pursuit? What struggle to escape?
10   What pipes and timbrels? What wild ecstasy?

II

Heard melodies are sweet, but those unheard
Are sweeter; therefore, ye soft pipes, play on;
Not to the sensual[9] ear, but, more endeared,
Pipe to the spirit ditties of no tone:
15 Fair youth, beneath the trees, thou canst not leave
Thy song, nor ever can those trees be bare;
Bold Lover, never, never canst thou kiss,
Though winning near the goal—yet, do not grieve;
She cannot fade, though thou hast not thy bliss,
20   For ever wilt thou love, and she be fair!

III

Ah, happy, happy boughs! that cannot shed
Your leaves, nor ever bid the Spring adieu;
And, happy melodist, unwearièd,
For ever piping songs for ever new;
25 More happy love! more happy, happy love!
For ever warm and still to be enjoyed,
For ever panting, and for ever young;
All breathing human passion far above,
That leaves a heart high-sorrowful and cloyed,
30   A burning forehead, and a parching tongue.

IV

Who are these coming to the sacrifice?
To what green altar, O mysterious priest,
Lead'st thou that heifer lowing at the skies,
And all her silken flanks with garlands dressed?
35 What little town by river or sea shore,
Or mountain-built with peaceful citadel,
Is emptied of this folk, this pious morn?
And, little town, thy streets for evermore

8. Arcadia. Tempe is a beautiful valley near Mt. Olympus in Greece, and the valleys ("dales") of
Arcadia are a picturesque section of the Peloponnesus; both came to be associated with the pastoral ideal.   9. Of the senses, as distinguished from the "ear" of the spirit or imagination.

Will silent be; and not a soul to tell
40   Why thou art desolate, can e'er return.

V

O Attic shape! Fair attitude! with brede[1]
Of marble men and maidens overwrought,[2]
With forest branches and the trodden weed;
Thou, silent form, dost tease us out of thought
45 As doth eternity: Cold Pastoral!
When old age shall this generation waste,
Thou shalt remain, in midst of other woe
Than ours, a friend to man, to whom thou say'st,
Beauty is truth, truth beauty[3]—that is all
50   Ye know on earth, and all ye need to know.
                                                    May 1819

GALWAY KINNELL

Blackberry Eating

I love to go out in late September
among the fat, overripe, icy, black blackberries
to eat blackberries for breakfast,
the stalks very prickly, a penalty
5 they earn for knowing the black art
of blackberry-making; and as I stand among them
lifting the stalks to my mouth, the ripest berries
fall almost unbidden to my tongue,
as words sometimes do, certain peculiar words
10 like *strengths* or *squinched*,
many-lettered, one-syllabled lumps,
which I squeeze, squinch open, and splurge well
in the silent, startled, icy, black language
of blackberry-eating in late September.
                                                    1980

---

1. Woven pattern. *Attic*: Attica was the district of ancient Greece surrounding Athens.
2. Ornamented all over.
3. In some texts of the poem, "Beauty is truth, truth beauty" is in quotation marks, and in some texts it is not, leading to critical disagreements about whether the last line and a half are also inscribed on the urn or spoken by the poet.

ROBERT LOWELL

Skunk Hour

for Elizabeth Bishop

Nautilus Island's hermit
heiress still lives through winter in her Spartan cottage;
her sheep still graze above the sea.
Her son's a bishop. Her farmer
5   is first selectman[4] in our village,
she's in her dotage.

Thirsting for
the hierarchic privacy
of Queen Victoria's century,
10 she buys up all
the eyesores facing her shore,
and lets them fall.

The season's ill—
we've lost our summer millionaire,
15 who seemed to leap from an L. L. Bean[5]
catalogue. His nine-knot yawl
was auctioned off to lobstermen.
A red fox stain covers Blue Hill.

And now our fairy
20 decorator brightens his shop for fall,
his fishnet's filled with orange cork,
orange, his cobbler's bench and awl,
there is no money in his work,
he'd rather marry.

25 One dark night,
my Tudor Ford climbed the hill's skull,
I watched for love-cars. Lights turned down,
they lay together, hull to hull,
where the graveyard shelves on the town. . . .
30 My mind's not right.

A car radio bleats,
"Love, O careless Love. . . ."[6] I hear
my ill-spirit sob in each blood cell,

---

4. Elected New England town official.   5. Famous old Maine sporting goods firm.
6. Popular folk song recorded many times, as by Frankie Laine (1959).

as if my hand were at its throat. . . .
35 I myself am hell;
nobody's here—

only skunks, that search
in the moonlight for a bite to eat.
They march on their soles up Main Street:
40 white stripes, moonstruck eyes' red fire
under the chalk-dry and spar spire
of the Trinitarian Church.

I stand on top
of our back steps and breathe the rich air—
45 a mother skunk with her column of kittens swills the garbage pail.
She jabs her wedge head in a cup
of sour cream, drops her ostrich tail,
and will not scare.

1959

CHRISTOPHER MARLOWE

The Passionate Shepherd to His Love

Come live with me and be my love,
And we will all the pleasures prove[7]
That valleys, groves, hills, and fields,
Woods, or steepy mountain yields.

5 And we will sit upon the rocks,
Seeing the shepherds feed their flocks,
By shallow rivers to whose falls
Melodious birds sing madrigals.

And I will make thee beds of roses
10 And a thousand fragrant posies,
A cap of flowers, and a kirtle[8]
Embroidered all with leaves of myrtle;

A gown made of the finest wool
Which from our pretty lambs we pull;
15 Fair linèd slippers for the cold,
With buckles of the purest gold;

7. Experience 8. Gown.

A belt of straw and ivy buds,
With coral clasps and amber studs:
And if these pleasures may thee move,
20 Come live with me, and be my love.

The shepherd swains[9] shall dance and sing
For thy delight each May morning:
If these delights thy mind may move,
Then live with me and be my love.

1600

ANDREW MARVELL

The Garden

How vainly men themselves amaze[1]
To win the palm, the oak, or bays,[2]
And their incessant labors see
Crowned from some single herb, or tree,
5 Whose short and narrow-vergèd[3] shade
Does prudently their toils upbraid;
While all flowers and all trees do close[4]
To weave the garlands of repose!

Fair Quiet, have I found thee here,
10 And Innocence, thy sister dear?
Mistaken long, I sought you then
In busy companies of men.
Your sacred plants,[5] if here below,
Only among the plants will grow;
15 Society is all but rude[6]
To[7] this delicious solitude.

No white nor red was ever seen
So am'rous as this lovely green.
Fond lovers, cruel as their flame,
20 Cut in these trees their mistress' name:
Little, alas, they know, or heed
How far these beauties hers exceed!

9. Youths.   1. Become frenzied.
2. Awards for athletic, civic, and literary achievements, respectively.   3. Narrowly cropped.
4. Unite.   5. Cuttings.   6. Barbarous.   7. Compared to.

Fair trees, wheresoe'er your barks I wound,
No name shall but your own be found.

25 When we have run our passion's heat,
Love hither makes his best retreat.
The gods, that mortal beauty chase,
Still in a tree did end their race:
Apollo hunted Daphne so,
30 Only that she might laurel grow;
And Pan did after Syrinx speed,
Not as a nymph, but for a reed.[8]

What wondrous life is this I lead!
Ripe apples drop about my head;
35 The luscious clusters of the vine
Upon my mouth do crush their wine;
The nectarine and curious[9] peach
Into my hands themselves do reach;
Stumbling on melons, as I pass,
40 Insnared with flowers, I fall on grass.

Meanwhile the mind, from pleasure less,
Withdraws into its happiness;[1]
The mind, that ocean where each kind
Does straight its own resemblance find;[2]
45 Yet it creates, transcending these,
Far other worlds and other seas,
Annihilating[3] all that's made
To a green thought in a green shade.

Here at the fountain's sliding foot,
50 Or at some fruit tree's mossy root,
Casting the body's vest[4] aside,
My soul into the boughs does glide:
There, like a bird, it sits and sings,
Then whets[5] and combs its silver wings,
55 And, till prepared for longer flight,
Waves in its plumes the various[6] light.

---

8. In Ovid's *Metamorphoses*, Daphne, pursued by Apollo, is turned into a laurel, and Syrinx, pursued by Pan, into a reed that Pan makes into a flute.   9. Exquisite.
1. That is, the mind withdraws from lesser-sense pleasure into contemplation.
2. All land creatures supposedly had corresponding sea creatures.
3. Reducing to nothing by comparison.
4. Vestment, clothing; the flesh is being considered as simply clothing for the soul.   5. Preens.
6. Many-colored.

Such was that happy garden-state,
While man there walked without a mate:
After a place so pure, and sweet,
60 What other help could yet be meet![7]
But 'twas beyond a mortal's share
To wander solitary there:
Two paradises 'twere in one
To live in paradise alone.

65 How well the skillful gardener drew
Of flowers and herbs this dial[8] new,
Where, from above, the milder sun
Does through a fragrant zodiac run;
And as it works, th' industrious bee
70 Computes its time as well as we!
How could such sweet and wholesome hours
Be reckoned but with herbs and flowers?

1681

CLAUDE McKAY

The Harlem Dancer

Applauding youths laughed with young prostitutes
And watched her perfect, half-clothed body sway;
Her voice was like the sound of blended flutes
Blown by black players upon a picnic day.
5 She sang and danced on gracefully and calm,
The light gauze hanging loose about her form;
To me she seemed a proudly-swaying palm
Grown lovelier for passing through a storm.
Upon her swarthy neck black shiny curls
10 Luxuriant fell; and tossing coins in praise,
The wine-flushed, bold-eyed boys, and even the girls,
Devoured her shape with eager, passionate gaze;
But looking at her falsely-smiling face,
I knew her self was not in that strange place.

1922

---

7. Appropriate.   8. Garden planted in the shape of a sundial, complete with zodiac.

The White House

Your door is shut against my tightened face,
And I am sharp as steel with discontent;
But I possess the courage and the grace
To bear my anger proudly and unbent.
5 The pavement slabs burn loose beneath my feet,
And passion rends my vitals as I pass,
A chafing savage, down the decent street,
Where boldly shines your shuttered door of glass.
Oh, I must search for wisdom every hour,
10 Deep in my wrathful bosom sore and raw,
And find in it the superhuman power
To hold me to the letter of your law!
Oh, I must keep my heart inviolate
Against the poison of your deadly hate.

1937

PAT MORA

Elena

My Spanish isn't enough.
I remember how I'd smile
listening to my little ones,
understanding every word they'd say,
5 their jokes, their songs, their plots.
    Vamos a pedirle dulces a mamá. Vamos.[9]
But that was in Mexico.
Now my children go to American high schools.
They speak English. At night they sit around
10 the kitchen table, laugh with one another.
I stand by the stove and feel dumb, alone.
I bought a book to learn English.
My husband frowned, drank more beer.
My oldest said, "*Mamá,* he doesn't want you
15 to be smarter than he is." I'm forty,
embarrassed at mispronouncing words,
embarrassed at the laughter of my children,

9. "Let's go ask mama for sweets. Let's go" (Spanish).

the grocer, the mailman. Sometimes I take
my English book and lock myself in the bathroom,
20 say the thick words softly,
for if I stop trying, I will be deaf
when my children need my help.

1985

(annof generation)

Gentle Communion

Even the long-dead are willing to move.
Without a word, she came with me from the desert.
Mornings she wanders through my rooms
making beds, folding socks.

5 Since she can't hear me anymore,
Mamande[1] ignores the questions I never knew
to ask, about her younger days, her red
hair, the time she fell and broke her nose
in the snow. I will never know.

10 When I try to make her laugh,
to disprove her sad album face, she leaves
the room, resists me as she resisted
grinning for cameras, make-up, English.

While I write, she sits and prays,
15 feet apart, legs never crossed,
the blue housecoat buttoned high
as her hair dries white, girlish
around her head and shoulders.

She closes her eyes, bows her head,
20 and like a child presses her hands together,
her patient flesh steeple, the skin
worn, like the pages of her prayer book.

Sometimes I sit in her wide-armed
chair as I once sat in her lap.
25 Alone, we played a quiet I Spy.
She peeled grapes I still taste.

She removes the thin skin, places
the luminous coolness on my tongue.

---

1. Child's conflation of *mama grande* (Spanish for "grandmother").

I know not to bite or chew. I wait
30 for the thick melt,
our private green honey.

1991

- How does this poem draw on the various meanings of the
  word *communion*? Why might it be significant that the grandmother comes "Without a word" (line 2)?

SYLVIA PLATH

Daddy[2]

You do not do, you do not do
Any more, black shoe
In which I have lived like a foot
For thirty years, poor and white,
5 Barely daring to breathe or Achoo.

Daddy, I have had to kill you.
You died before I had time—
Marble-heavy, a bag full of God,
Ghastly statue with one gray toe[3]
10 Big as a Frisco seal

And a head in the freakish Atlantic
Where it pours bean green over blue
In the waters off beautiful Nauset.[4]
I used to pray to recover you.
15 Ach, du.[5]

In the German tongue, in the Polish town[6]
Scraped flat by the roller
Of wars, wars, wars.
But the name of the town is common.
20 My Polack friend

Says there are a dozen or two.
So I never could tell where you

2. First published in *Ariel*, a volume of poems that appeared two years after Plath's suicide.
3. Otto Plath, Sylvia's father, lost a toe to gangrene that resulted from diabetes.
4. Inlet on Cape Cod.
5. Oh, you (German). Plath often portrays herself as Jewish and her oppressors as German.
6. Otto Plath, an ethnic German, was born in Grabow, Poland.

Put your foot, your root,
I never could talk to you.
25 The tongue stuck in my jaw.

It stuck in a barb wire snare.
Ich,[7] ich, ich, ich,
I could hardly speak.
I thought every German was you.
30 And the language obscene

An engine, an engine
Chuffing me off like a Jew.
A Jew to Dachau, Auschwitz, Belsen.[8]
I began to talk like a Jew.
35 I think I may well be a Jew.

The snows of the Tyrol, the clear beer of Vienna[9]
Are not very pure or true.
With my gypsy-ancestress and my weird luck
And my Taroc[1] pack and my Taroc pack
40 I may be a bit of a Jew.

I have always been scared of *you*,
With your Luftwaffe,[2] your gobbledygoo.
And your neat moustache
And your Aryan[3] eye, bright blue.
45 Panzer[4]-man, panzer-man, O You—

Not God but a swastika
So black no sky could squeak through.
Every woman adores a Fascist,
The boot in the face, the brute
50 Brute heart of a brute like you.

You stand at the blackboard, daddy,
In the picture I have of you,
A cleft in your chin instead of your foot
But no less a devil for that, no not
55 Any less the black man who

Bit my pretty red heart in two.
I was ten when they buried you.

7. German for "I."   8. Sites of World War II Nazi death camps.
9. The snow in the Tyrol (an Alpine region in Austria and northern Italy) is, legendarily, as pure as the beer is clear in Vienna.   1. Tarot, playing cards used mainly for fortune-telling.
2. German air force.   3. People of Germanic lineage, often blond-haired and blue-eyed.
4. Literally "panther," the Nazi tank corps' term for an armored vehicle.

At twenty I tried to die
And get back, back, back to you.
60 I thought even the bones would do

But they pulled me out of the sack,
And they stuck me together with glue.[5]
And then I knew what to do.
I made a model of you,
65 A man in black with a Meinkampf[6] look

And a love of the rack and the screw.
And I said I do, I do.
So daddy, I'm finally through.
The black telephone's off at the root,
70 The voices just can't worm through.

If I've killed one man, I've killed two—
The vampire who said he was you
And drank my blood for a year,
Seven years, if you want to know.
75 Daddy, you can lie back now.

There's a stake in your fat black heart
And the villagers never liked you.
They are dancing and stamping on you.
They always *knew* it was you.
80 Daddy, daddy, you bastard, I'm through.

1966

Lady Lazarus

I have done it again.
One year in every ten
I manage it—

A sort of walking miracle, my skin
5 Bright as a Nazi lampshade,
My right foot

A paperweight,
My face a featureless, fine
Jew linen.[7]

5. Allusion to Plath's recovery from her first suicide attempt.
6. The title of Adolf Hitler's autobiography and manifesto (1925-27); German for "my struggle."
7. During World War II, prisoners in some Nazi camps were gassed to death and their body parts then turned into objects such as lampshades and paperweights.

10 Peel off the napkin
    O my enemy.
    Do I terrify?—

    The nose, the eye pits, the full set of teeth?
    The sour breath
15 Will vanish in a day.

    Soon, soon the flesh
    The grave cave ate will be
    At home on me

    And I a smiling woman.
20 I am only thirty.
    And like the cat I have nine times to die.

    This is Number Three.
    What a trash
    To annihilate each decade.

25 What a million filaments.
    The peanut-crunching crowd
    Shoves in to see

    Them unwrap me hand and foot—
    The big strip tease.
30 Gentlemen, ladies

    These are my hands
    My knees.
    I may be skin and bone,

    Nevertheless, I am the same, identical woman.
35 The first time it happened I was ten.
    It was an accident.

    The second time I meant
    To last it out and not come back at all.
    I rocked shut

40 As a seashell.
    They had to call and call
    And pick the worms off me like sticky pearls.

    Dying
    Is an art, like everything else.
45 I do it exceptionally well.

    I do it so it feels like hell.
    I do it so it feels real.
    I guess you could say I've a call.

It's easy enough to do it in a cell.
50 It's easy enough to do it and stay put.
It's the theatrical

Comeback in broad day
To the same place, the same face, the same brute
Amused shout:

55 "A miracle!"
That knocks me out.
There is a charge

For the eyeing of my scars, there is a charge
For the hearing of my heart—
60 It really goes.

And there is a charge, a very large charge
For a word or a touch
Or a bit of blood

Or a piece of my hair or my clothes.
65 So, so Herr Doktor.
So, Herr Enemy.

I am your opus,
I am your valuable,
The pure gold baby

70 That melts to a shriek.
I turn and burn.
Do not think I underestimate your great concern

Ash, ash—
You poke and stir.
75 Flesh, bone, there is nothing there—

A cake of soap,
A wedding ring,
A gold filling.

Herr God, Herr Lucifer
80 Beware
Beware.

Out of the ash
I rise with my red hair
And I eat men like air.

1965

EZRA POUND

In a Station of the Metro[8]

The apparition of these faces in the crowd;
Petals on a wet, black bough.

1913

A Virginal

No, no! Go from me. I have left her lately.
I will not spoil my sheath with lesser brightness,
For my surrounding air hath a new lightness;
Slight are her arms, yet they have bound me straitly
5 And left me cloaked as with a gauze of aether;
As with sweet leaves; as with a subtle clearness.
Oh, I have picked up magic in her nearness
To sheathe me half in half the things that sheathe her.
No, no! Go from me, I have still the flavor,
10 Soft as spring wind that's come from birchen bowers.
Green come the shoots, aye April in the branches,
As winter's wound with her sleight hand she staunches,
Hath of the trees a likeness of the savor:
As white their bark, so white this lady's hours.

1912

SIR WALTER RALEIGH

The Nymph's Reply to the Shepherd

If all the world and love were young,
And truth in every shepherd's tongue,
These pretty pleasures might me move
To live with thee and be thy love.

5 Time drives the flocks from field to fold,
When rivers rage, and rocks grow cold,
And Philomel[9] becometh dumb;
The rest complain of cares to come.

8. Paris subway.   9. The nightingale.

The flowers do fade, and wanton fields
10 To wayward winter reckoning yields:
A honey tongue, a heart of gall,
Is fancy's spring, but sorrow's fall.

Thy gowns, thy shoes, thy beds of roses,
Thy cap, thy kirtle, and thy posies
15 Soon break, soon wither, soon forgotten;
In folly ripe, in reason rotten.

Thy belt of straw and ivy buds,
Thy coral clasps and amber studs,
All these in me no means can move
20 To come to thee and be thy love.

But could youth last, and love still breed,
Had joys no date,[1] nor age no need,
Then these delights my mind might move
To live with thee and be thy love.

                                        1600

JOHN CROWE RANSOM

Bells for John Whiteside's Daughter

There was such speed in her little body,
And such lightness in her footfall,
It is no wonder her brown study[2]
Astonishes us all.

5 Her wars were bruited in our high window.
We looked among orchard trees and beyond
Where she took arms against her shadow,
Or harried unto the pond

The lazy geese, like a snow cloud
10 Dripping their snow on the green grass,
Tricking and stopping, sleepy and proud,
Who cried in goose, Alas,

For the tireless heart within the little
Lady with rod that made them rise
15 From their noon apple-dreams and scuttle
Goose-fashion under the skies!

1. End.   2. Stillness, as if in meditation or deep thought.

But now go the bells, and we are ready,
In one house we are sternly stopped
To say we are vexed at her brown study,
20 Lying so primly propped.

1924

ADRIENNE RICH

Storm Warnings

The glass has been falling all the afternoon,
And knowing better than the instrument
What winds are walking overhead, what zone
Of gray unrest is moving across the land,
5 I leave the book upon a pillowed chair
And walk from window to closed window, watching
Boughs strain against the sky

And think again, as often when the air
Moves inward toward a silent core of waiting,
10 How with a single purpose time has traveled
By secret currents of the undiscerned
Into this polar realm. Weather abroad
And weather in the heart alike come on
Regardless of prediction.

15 Between foreseeing and averting change
Lies all the mastery of elements
Which clocks and weatherglasses cannot alter.
Time in the hand is not control of time,
Nor shattered fragments of an instrument
20 A proof against the wind; the wind will rise,
We can only close the shutters.

I draw the curtains as the sky goes black
And set a match to candles sheathed in glass
Against the keyhole draught, the insistent whine
25 Of weather through the unsealed aperture.
This is our sole defense against the season;
These are the things that we have learned to do
Who live in troubled regions.

1951

History[3]

Should I simplify my life for you?
Don't ask how I began to love men.
Don't ask how I began to love women.
Remember the forties songs, the slowdance numbers
5 the small sex-filled gas-rationed Chevrolet?
Remember walking in the snow and who was gay?
Cigarette smoke of the movies, silver-and-gray
profiles, dreaming the dreams of he-and-she
breathing the dissolution of the wisping silver plume?
10 Dreaming that dream we leaned applying lipstick
by the gravestone's mirror when we found ourselves
playing in the cemetery. In Current Events she said
the war in Europe is over, the Allies
and she wore no lipstick have won the war
15 and we raced screaming out of Sixth Period.

Dreaming that dream
we had to maze our ways through a wood
where lips were knives breasts razors and I hid
in the cage of my mind scribbling
20 *this map stops where it all begins*
into a red-and-black notebook.
Remember after the war when peace came down
as plenty for some and they said we were saved
in an eternal present and we knew the world could end?
25 —Remember after the war when peace rained down
on the winds from Hiroshima Nagasaki Utah Nevada?[4]
and the socialist queer Christian teacher jumps from the hotel
    window?[5]
and L.G. saying *I want to sleep with you but not for sex*
and the red-and-black enamelled coffee-pot dripped slow
    through the
dark grounds
30 —appetite terror power tenderness
the long kiss in the stairwell the switch thrown
on two Jewish Communists[6] married to each other

---

3. This is poem 4 in Rich's sequence "Inscriptions."
4. Sites of atomic bomb explosions, the first two in Japan near the end of World War II, the last two at test sites in the American desert.
5. This line alludes to the critic Francis Otto Matthiessen (1902–50), who taught at Harvard while Rich was an undergraduate there.
6. Julius and Ethel Rosenberg, executed as spies by the U.S. in 1953.

the definitive crunch of glass at the end of the wedding?[7]
(When shall we learn, what should be clear as day,
35 *We cannot choose what we are free to love?)*[8]

1995

WILLIAM SHAKESPEARE

[Not marble, nor the gilded monuments]

Not marble, nor the gilded monuments
Of princes, shall outlive this powerful rhyme;
But you shall shine more bright in these contènts
Than unswept stone, besmeared with sluttish time.
5 When wasteful war shall statues overturn,
And broils[9] root out the work of masonry,
Nor[1] Mars his sword nor war's quick fire shall burn
The living record of your memory.
'Gainst death and all-oblivious enmity
10 Shall you pace forth; your praise shall still find room
Even in the eyes of all posterity
That wear this world out to the ending doom.[2]
So, till the judgment that yourself arise,
You live in this, and dwell in lovers' eyes.

1609

WALLACE STEVENS

The Emperor of Ice-Cream

Call the roller of big cigars,
The muscular one, and bid him whip
In kitchen cups concupiscent curds.[3]
Let the wenches dawdle in such dress
5 As they are used to wear, and let the boys

---

7. Reference to the custom at Jewish weddings in which the groom breaks a glass to commemorate the loss of Jerusalem and the Temple.
8. The italicized last two lines are the opening lines of W. H. Auden's poem "Canzone."
9. Riots. 1. Neither. *Mars his:* Mars's. 2. Judgment Day.
3. "The words 'concupiscent curds' have no genealogy; they are merely expressive: at least, I hope they are expressive. They express the concupiscence of life, but, by contrast with the things in relation in the poem, they express or accentuate life's destitution, and it is this that gives them something more than a cheap lustre" (*Letters,* p. 500).

Bring flowers in last month's newspapers.
Let be be finale of seem.[4]
The only emperor is the emperor of ice-cream.

Take from the dresser of deal,
10 Lacking the three glass knobs, that sheet
On which she embroidered fantails[5] once
And spread it so as to cover her face.
If her horny feet protrude, they come
To show how cold she is, and dumb.
15 Let the lamp affix its beam.
The only emperor is the emperor of ice-cream.

                                                        1923

Anecdote of the Jar

I placed a jar in Tennessee,
And round it was, upon a hill.
It made the slovenly wilderness
Surround that hill.

5 The wilderness rose up to it,
And sprawled around, no longer wild.
The jar was round upon the ground
And tall and of a port in air.

It took dominion everywhere.
10 The jar was gray and bare.
It did not give of bird or bush,
Like nothing else in Tennessee.

                                                        1923

ALFRED, LORD TENNYSON

Tears, Idle Tears [6]

Tears, idle tears, I know not what they mean,
Tears from the depth of some divine despair

---

4. "The true sense of Let be be the finale of seem is let being become the conclusion or denouement of appearing to be: in short, ice cream is an absolute good. The poem is obviously not about ice cream, but about being as distinguished from seeming to be" (*Letters*, p. 341).   5. Fantail pigeons.
6. One of the songs from Tennyson's book-length narrative poem *The Princess*.

Rise in the heart, and gather to the eyes,
In looking on the happy autumn-fields,
5 And thinking of the days that are no more.

    Fresh as the first beam glittering on a sail,
That brings our friends up from the underworld,
Sad as the last which reddens over one
That sinks with all we love below the verge;
10 So sad, so fresh, the days that are no more.

    Ah, sad and strange as in dark summer dawns
The earliest pipe of half-awakened birds
To dying ears, when unto dying eyes
The casement slowly grows a glimmering square;
15 So sad, so strange, the days that are no more.

    Dear as remembered kisses after death,
And sweet as those by hopeless fancy feigned
On lips that are for others; deep as love,
Deep as first love, and wild with all regret;
20 O Death in Life, the days that are no more!

                               1847

ALFRED, LORD TENNYSON

Ulysses[7]

    It little profits that an idle king,
By this still hearth, among these barren crags,
Matched with an agèd wife,[8] I mete and dole
Unequal laws unto a savage race,
5 That hoard, and sleep, and feed, and know not me.

    I cannot rest from travel; I will drink
Life to the lees.[9] All times I have enjoyed
Greatly, have suffered greatly, both with those
That loved me, and alone; on shore, and when
10 Through scudding drifts the rainy Hyades[1]
Vexed the dim sea. I am become a name;
For always roaming with a hungry heart

---

7. After the end of the Trojan War, Ulysses (or Odysseus), king of Ithaca and one of the war's Greek heroes, returned to his island home (line 34). Homer's account of the situation is in book 11 of *The Odyssey*, but Dante's account of Ulysses in canto 26 of the *Inferno* is the more immediate background of the poem. 8. Penelope. 9. That is, all the way down to the bottom of the cup.
1. Group of stars that were supposed to predict the rain when they rose at the same time as the sun.

Much have I seen and known—cities of men
And manners, climates, councils, governments,
15 Myself not least, but honored of them all—
And drunk delight of battle with my peers,
Far on the ringing plains of windy Troy.
I am a part of all that I have met;
Yet all experience is an arch wherethrough
20 Gleams that untraveled world, whose margin fades
For ever and for ever when I move.
How dull it is to pause, to make an end,
To rust unburnished, not to shine in use!
As though to breathe were life. Life piled on life
25 Were all too little, and of one to me
Little remains; but every hour is saved
From that eternal silence, something more,
A bringer of new things; and vile it were
For some three suns to store and hoard myself,
30 And this gray spirit yearning in desire
To follow knowledge like a sinking star,
Beyond the utmost bound of human thought.

   This is my son, mine own Telemachus,
To whom I leave the scepter and the isle—
35 Well-loved of me, discerning to fulfill
This labor by slow prudence to make mild
A rugged people, and through soft degrees
Subdue them to the useful and the good.
Most blameless is he, centered in the sphere
40 Of common duties, decent not to fail
In offices of tenderness, and pay
Meet adoration to my household gods,
When I am gone. He works his work, I mine.

   There lies the port; the vessel puffs her sail:
45 There gloom the dark, broad seas. My mariners,
Souls that have toiled, and wrought, and thought with me—
That ever with a frolic welcome took
The thunder and the sunshine, and opposed
Free hearts, free foreheads—you and I are old;
50 Old age hath yet his honor and his toil.
Death closes all; but something ere the end,
Some work of noble note, may yet be done,
Not unbecoming men that strove with Gods.
The lights begin to twinkle from the rocks;
55 The long day wanes; the slow moon climbs; the deep

Moans round with many voices. Come, my friends.
'Tis not too late to seek a newer world.
Push off, and sitting well in order smite
The sounding furrows; for my purpose holds
60   To sail beyond the sunset, and the baths
Of all the western stars, until I die.
It may be that the gulfs will wash us down;[2]
It may be we shall touch the Happy Isles,[3]
And see the great Achilles, whom we knew.
65   Though much is taken, much abides; and though
We are not now that strength which in old days
Moved earth and heaven, that which we are, we are:
One equal temper of heroic hearts,
Made weak by time and fate, but strong in will
70   To strive, to seek, to find, and not to yield.

                                                            1833

DYLAN THOMAS

Fern Hill

Now as I was young and easy under the apple boughs
About the lilting house and happy as the grass was green,
      The night above the dingle starry,
         Time let me hail and climb
5   Golden in the heydays of his eyes,
And honored among wagons I was prince of the apple towns
And once below a time I lordly had the trees and leaves
         Trail with daisies and barley
      Down the rivers of the windfall light.

10 And as I was green and carefree, famous among the barns
About the happy yard and singing as the farm was home,
      In the sun that is young once only,
         Time let me play and be
      Golden in the mercy of his means,
15 And green and golden I was huntsman and herdsman, the calves
Sang to my horn, the foxes on the hills barked clear and cold,
         And the sabbath rang slowly
      In the pebbles of the holy streams.

2. Beyond the Gulf of Gibraltar was supposed to lie a chasm that led to Hades.
3. Elysium, the Islands of the Blessed, where heroes like Achilles (line 64) go after death.

All the sun long it was running, it was lovely, the hay
20 Fields high as the house, the tunes from the chimneys, it was air
    And playing, lovely and watery
        And fire green as grass.
    And nightly under the simple stars
As I rode to sleep the owls were bearing the farm away,
25 All the moon long I heard, blessed among stables, the nightjars[4]
Flying with the ricks,[5] and the horses
        Flashing into the dark.

And then to awake, and the farm, like a wanderer white
With the dew, come back, the cock on his shoulder: it was all
30   Shining, it was Adam and maiden,
        The sky gathered again
    And the sun grew round that very day.
So it must have been after the birth of the simple light
In the first, spinning place, the spellbound horses walking warm
35   Out of the whinnying green stable
        On to the fields of praise.

And honored among foxes and pheasants by the gay house
Under the new made clouds and happy as the heart was long,
    In the sun born over and over,
40   I ran my heedless ways,
      My wishes raced through the house-high hay
And nothing I cared, at my sky-blue trades, that time allows
In all his tuneful turning so few and such morning songs
    Before the children green and golden
45   Follow him out of grace,

Nothing I cared, in the lamb white days, that time would take me
Up to the swallow-thronged loft by the shadow of my hand,
    In the moon that is always rising,
        Nor that riding to sleep
50   I should hear him fly with the high fields
And wake to the farm forever fled from the childless land.
Oh as I was young and easy in the mercy of his means,
        Time held me green and dying
    Though I sang in my chains like the sea.

                        1946

---

4. Birds also known as goatsuckers.   5. Haystacks.

WALT WHITMAN

Facing West from California's Shores

Facing west, from California's shores,
Inquiring, tireless, seeking what is yet unfound,
I, a child, very old, over waves, towards the house of maternity,[6]
    the land of migrations, look afar,
Look off the shores of my Western sea, the circle almost circled:
5 For starting westward from Hindustan, from the vales of
    Kashmere,
From Asia, from the north, from the God, the sage, and the hero,
From the south, from the flowery peninsulas and the spice
    islands,
Long having wandered since, round the earth having wandered,
Now I face home again, very pleased and joyous;
10 (But where is what I started for, so long ago?
And why is it yet unfound?)

        1860

I Hear America Singing

I hear America singing, the varied carols I hear,
Those of mechanics, each one singing his as it should be blithe
    and strong,
The carpenter singing his as he measures his plank or beam,
The mason singing his as he makes ready for work, or leaves off
    work,
5 The boatman singing what belongs to him in his boat, the
    deckhand singing on the steamboat deck,
The shoemaker singing as he sits on his bench, the hatter singing
    as he stands,
The wood-cutter's song, the ploughboy's on his way in the
    morning, or at noon intermission or at sundown,
The delicious singing of the mother, or of the young wife at work,
    or of the girl sewing or washing,
Each singing what belongs to him or her and to none else,
10 The day what belongs to the day—at night the party of young
    fellows, robust, friendly,
Singing with open mouths their strong melodious songs.

        1860

6. Asia, as the supposed birthplace of the human race.

A Noiseless Patient Spider

A noiseless patient spider,
I marked where on a little promontory it stood isolated,
Marked how to explore the vacant vast surrounding,
It launched forth filament, filament, filament, out of itself,
5 Ever unreeling them, ever tirelessly speeding them.

And you O my soul where you stand,
Surrounded, detached, in measureless oceans of space,
Ceaselessly musing, venturing, throwing, seeking the spheres to
    connect them,
Till the bridge you will need be formed, till the ductile anchor hold,
10 Till the gossamer thread you fling catch somewhere, O my soul.

                                                              1881

RICHARD WILBUR

Love Calls Us to the Things of This World

The eyes open to a cry of pulleys,
And spirited from sleep, the astounded soul
Hangs for a moment bodiless and simple
As false dawn.
5   Outside the open window
The morning air is all awash with angels.

    Some are in bed-sheets, some are in blouses,
Some are in smocks: but truly there they are.
Now they are rising together in calm swells
10 Of halcyon[7] feeling, filling whatever they wear
With the deep joy of their impersonal breathing;
    Now they are flying in place, conveying
The terrible speed of their omnipresence, moving
And staying like white water; and now of a sudden
15 They swoon down into so rapt a quiet
That nobody seems to be there.
                        The soul shrinks

    From all that it is about to remember,
From the punctual rape of every blessed day,

7. Serene.

20 And cries,
          "Oh, let there be nothing on earth but laundry,
     Nothing but rosy hands in the rising steam
     And clear dances done in the sight of heaven."

     Yet, as the sun acknowledges
25 With a warm look the world's hunks and colors,
     The soul descends once more in bitter love
     To accept the waking body, saying now
     In a changed voice as the man yawns and rises,

          "Bring them down from their ruddy gallows;
30 Let there be clean linen for the backs of thieves;
     Let lovers go fresh and sweet to be undone,
     And the heaviest nuns walk in a pure floating
     Of dark habits,
               keeping their difficult balance."

                                                            1956

WILLIAM WORDSWORTH

Lines Written a Few Miles above Tintern Abbey, On Revisiting the Banks of the Wye during a Tour, July 13, 1798[8]

     Five years have passed; five summers, with the length
     Of five long winters! and again I hear
     These waters, rolling from their mountain-springs
     With a soft inland murmur. Once again
5 Do I behold these steep and lofty cliffs,
     That on a wild secluded scene impress
     Thoughts of more deep seclusion; and connect
     The landscape with the quiet of the sky.
     The day is come when I again repose
10 Here, under this dark sycamore, and view
     These plots of cottage-ground, these orchard tufts,
     Which at this season, with their unripe fruits,
     Are clad in one green hue, and lose themselves

---

8. Wordsworth had first visited the Wye valley in Wales and the ruins of the medieval abbey there in 1793, while on a solitary walking tour. He was twenty-three then, twenty-eight when he wrote this poem.   9. Thickets.

'Mid groves and copses.[1] Once again I see
15 These hedge-rows, hardly hedge-rows, little lines
Of sportive wood run wild: these pastoral farms,
Green to the very door; and wreaths of smoke
Sent up, in silence, from among the trees!
With some uncertain notice, as might seem
20 Of vagrant dwellers in the houseless woods,
Or of some hermit's cave, where by his fire
The hermit sits alone.

                    These beauteous forms,
Through a long absence, have not been to me
As is a landscape to a blind man's eye;
25 But oft, in lonely rooms, and 'mid the din
Of towns and cities, I have owed to them,
In hours of weariness, sensations sweet,
Felt in the blood, and felt along the heart;
And passing even into my purer mind,
30 With tranquil restoration—feelings too
Of unremembered pleasure: such, perhaps,
As have no slight or trivial influence
On that best portion of a good man's life,
His little, nameless, unremembered acts
35 Of kindness and of love. Nor less, I trust,
To them I may have owed another gift,
Of aspect more sublime; that blessèd mood,
In which the burthen[2] of the mystery,
In which the heavy and the weary weight
40 Of all this unintelligible world,
Is lightened—that serene and blessèd mood,
In which the affections gently lead us on—
Until, the breath of this corporeal frame
And even the motion of our human blood
45 Almost suspended, we are laid asleep
In body, and become a living soul;
While with an eye made quiet by the power
Of harmony, and the deep power of joy,
We see into the life of things.

                    If this
50 Be but a vain belief, yet, oh! how oft—
In darkness and amid the many shapes
Of joyless daylight; when the fretful stir

1. Burden.

Unprofitable, and the fever of the world,
Have hung upon the beatings of my heart—
55 How oft, in spirit, have I turned to thee,
O sylvan Wye! thou wanderer through the woods,
How often has my spirit turned to thee!

And now, with gleams of half-extinguished thought,
With many recognitions dim and faint,
60 And somewhat of a sad perplexity,
The picture of the mind revives again;
While here I stand, not only with the sense
Of present pleasure, but with pleasing thoughts
That in this moment there is life and food
65 For future years. And so I dare to hope,
Though changed, no doubt, from what I was when first
I came among these hills; when like a roe
I bounded o'er the mountains, by the sides
Of the deep rivers, and the lonely streams,
70 Wherever nature led: more like a man
Flying from something that he dreads than one
Who sought the thing he loved. For nature then
(The coarser[3] pleasures of my boyish days,
And their glad animal movements all gone by)
75 To me was all in all—I cannot paint
What then I was. The sounding cataract
Haunted me like a passion; the tall rock,
The mountain, and the deep and gloomy wood,
Their colors and their forms, were then to me
80 An appetite; a feeling and a love,
That had no need of a remoter charm,
By thought supplied, nor any interest
Unborrowed from the eye. That time is past,
And all its aching joys are now no more,
85 And all its dizzy raptures. Not for this
Faint I,[4] nor mourn nor murmur; other gifts
Have followed; for such loss, I would believe,
Abundant recompense. For I have learned
To look on nature, not as in the hour
90 Of thoughtless youth; but hearing oftentimes
The still, sad music of humanity,
Nor[5] harsh nor grating, though of ample power
To chasten and subdue. And I have felt
A presence that disturbs me with the joy

2. Physical. 3. Am I discouraged. 4. Neither.

95 Of elevated thoughts, a sense sublime
    Of something far more deeply interfused,
    Whose dwelling is the light of setting suns,
    And the round ocean and the living air,
    And the blue sky, and in the mind of man:
100 A motion and a spirit, that impels
    All thinking things, all objects of all thought,
    And rolls through all things. Therefore am I still
    A lover of the meadows and the woods
    And mountains; and of all that we behold
105 From this green earth; of all the mighty world
    Of eye, and ear—both what they half create,
    And what perceive; well pleased to recognize
    In nature and the language of the sense
    The anchor of my purest thoughts, the nurse,
110 The guide, the guardian of my heart, and soul
    Of all my moral being.

                        Nor perchance,
    If I were not thus taught, should I the more
    Suffer my genial spirits[6] to decay:
    For thou art with me here upon the banks
115 Of this fair river; thou my dearest Friend,[7]
    My dear, dear Friend; and in thy voice I catch
    The language of my former heart, and read
    My former pleasures in the shooting lights
    Of thy wild eyes. Oh! yet a little while
120 May I behold in thee what I was once,
    My dear, dear Sister! and this prayer I make,
    Knowing that Nature never did betray
    The heart that loved her; 'tis her privilege,
    Through all the years of this our life, to lead
125 From joy to joy: for she can so inform
    The mind that is within us, so impress
    With quietness and beauty, and so feed
    With lofty thoughts, that neither evil tongues,
    Rash judgments, nor the sneers of selfish men,
130 Nor greetings where no kindness is, nor all
    The dreary intercourse of daily life,
    Shall e'er prevail against us, or disturb
    Our cheerful faith that all which we behold
    Is full of blessings. Therefore let the moon
135 Shine on thee in thy solitary walk;
    And let the misty mountain-winds be free

5. Natural disposition; that is, the spirits are part of his individual genius.   6. His sister Dorothy.

To blow against thee: and, in after years,
When these wild ecstasies shall be matured
Into a sober pleasure; when thy mind
140 Shall be a mansion for all lovely forms,
Thy memory be as a dwelling-place
For all sweet sounds and harmonies; oh! then,
If solitude, or fear, or pain, or grief,
Should be thy portion, with what healing thoughts
145 Of tender joy wilt thou remember me,
And these my exhortations! No, perchance—
If I should be where I no more can hear
Thy voice, nor catch from thy wild eyes these gleams
Of past existence—wilt thou then forget
150 That on the banks of this delightful stream
We stood together; and that I, so long
A worshiper of Nature, hither came
Unwearied in that service; rather say
With warmer love—oh! with far deeper zeal
155 Of holier love. Nor wilt thou then forget,
That after many wanderings, many years
Of absence, these steep woods and lofty cliffs,
And this green pastoral landscape, were to me
More dear, both for themselves and for thy sake!

                                                              1798

W. B. YEATS

The Lake Isle of Innisfree[7]

I will arise and go now, and go to Innisfree,
And a small cabin build there, of clay and wattles made,
Nine bean-rows will I have there, a hive for the honey-bee,
And live alone in the bee-loud glade.

5 And I shall have some peace there, for peace comes dropping slow,
Dropping from the veils of the morning to where the cricket sings;
There midnight's all a glimmer, and noon a purple glow,
And evening full of the linnet's wings.

I will arise and go now, for always night and day
10 I hear lake water lapping with low sounds by the shore;
While I stand on the roadway, or on the pavements grey,
I hear it in the deep heart's core.

                                                              1890

7. Island in Lough Gill, County Sligo, Ireland.

The Second Coming[8]

Turning and turning in the widening gyre[9]
The falcon cannot hear the falconer;
Things fall apart; the center cannot hold;
Mere anarchy is loosed upon the world,
5 The blood-dimmed tide is loosed, and everywhere
The ceremony of innocence is drowned;
The best lack all conviction, while the worst
Are full of passionate intensity.
Surely some revelation is at hand;
10 Surely the Second Coming is at hand.
The Second Coming! Hardly are those words out
When a vast image out of *Spiritus Mundi*[1]
Troubles my sight: somewhere in sands of the desert
A shape with lion body and the head of a man,
15 A gaze blank and pitiless as the sun,
Is moving its slow thighs, while all about it
Reel shadows of the indignant desert birds.[2]
The darkness drops again; but now I know
That twenty centuries of stony sleep
20 Were vexed to nightmare by a rocking cradle,
And what rough beast, its hour come round at last,
Slouches towards Bethlehem to be born?

                                        January 1919

Leda and the Swan[3]

A sudden blow: the great wings beating still
Above the staggering girl, her thighs caressed

8. The Second Coming of Christ, according to Matthew 24.29–44, will follow a time of "tribulation." Disillusioned by Ireland's continued civil strife, Yeats saw his time as the end of another historical cycle. In *A Vision* (1937), Yeats describes his view of history as dependent on cycles of about two thousand years: the birth of Christ had ended the cycle of Greco-Roman civilization, and now the Christian cycle seemed near an end, to be followed by an antithetical cycle, ominous in its portents.
9. Literally, the widening spiral of a falcon's flight. "Gyre" is Yeats's term for a cycle of history, which he diagrammed as a series of interpenetrating cones.
1. Or *Anima Mundi* (Latin), the spirit or soul of the world. Yeats considered this universal consciousness or memory a fund from which poets drew their images and symbols.
2. Yeats later wrote of the "brazen winged beast . . . described in my poem *The Second Coming*" as "associated with laughing, ecstatic destruction."
3. According to Greek myth, Zeus took the form of a swan to rape Leda, who became the mother of Helen of Troy; of Castor; and also of Clytemnestra, Agamemnon's wife and murderer. Helen's

By the dark webs, her nape caught in his bill,
He holds her helpless breast upon his breast.

5 How can those terrified vague fingers push
The feathered glory from her loosening thighs?
And how can body, laid in that white rush,
But feel the strange heart beating where it lies?

A shudder in the loins engenders there
10 The broken wall, the burning roof and tower
And Agamemnon dead.
                                    Being so caught up,
So mastered by the brute blood of the air,
Did she put on his knowledge with his power
Before the indifferent beak could let her drop?

                                    1923

Sailing to Byzantium[4]

I

That[5] is no country for old men. The young
In one another's arms, birds in the trees
—Those dying generations—at their song,
The salmon-falls, the mackerel-crowded seas,
5 Fish, flesh, or fowl, commend all summer long
Whatever is begotten, born, and dies.
Caught in that sensual music all neglect
Monuments of unaging intellect.

II

An aged man is but a paltry thing,
10 A tattered coat upon a stick, unless
Soul clap its hands and sing, and louder sing
For every tatter in its mortal dress,
Nor is there singing school but studying
Monuments of its own magnificence;

---

abduction from her husband, Menelaus, brother of Agamemnon, began the Trojan War (line 10).
Yeats described the visit of Zeus to Leda as an annunciation like that to Mary (see Luke 1.26–38);
"I imagine the annunciation that founded Greece as made to Leda" (*A Vision*).
4. Ancient name of Istanbul, the capital and holy city of Eastern Christendom from the late
fourth century until 1453. It was famous for its stylized and formal mosaics; its symbolic, non-
naturalistic art; and its highly developed intellectual life. Yeats repeatedly uses it to symbolize a
world of artifice and timelessness, free from the decay and death of the natural and sensual world.
5. Ireland, as an instance of the natural, temporal world.

15   And therefore I have sailed the seas and come
     To the holy city of Byzantium.

                 III

     O sages standing in God's holy fire
     As in the gold mosaic of a wall,
     Come from the holy fire, perne in a gyre,[6]
20   And be the singing-masters of my soul.
     Consume my heart away; sick with desire
     And fastened to a dying animal
     It knows not what it is; and gather me
     Into the artifice of eternity.

                 IV

25   Once out of nature I shall never take
     My bodily form from any natural thing,
     But such a form as Grecian goldsmiths make
     Of hammered gold and gold enameling
     To keep a drowsy Emperor awake;[7]
30   Or set upon a golden bough[8] to sing
     To lords and ladies of Byzantium
     Of what is past, or passing, or to come.

                                              1927

6. That is, whirl in a coiling motion, so that his soul may merge with its motion as the timeless world invades the cycles of history and nature. "Perne" is Yeats's coinage (from the noun *pirn*): to spin around in the kind of spiral pattern that thread makes as it comes off a bobbin or spool.
7. "I have read somewhere that in the Emperor's palace at Byzantium was a tree made of gold and silver, and artificial birds that sang" [Yeats's note].
8. In Book 6 of the *Aeneid,* the sibyl tells Aeneas that he must pluck a golden bough from a nearby tree in order to descend to Hades. Each time Aeneas plucks the one such branch there, an identical one takes its place.

Biographical Sketches
Poets

Sketches are included for all poets represented by two or more poems.

W. H. AUDEN
(1907–1973)

Wystan Hugh Auden was born in York, England, to a medical officer and a nurse. Intending at first to become a scientist, Auden studied at Oxford, where he became the center of the "Oxford Group" of poets and leftist intellectuals. His travels during the 1930s led him to Germany, Iceland, China, Spain (where he was an ambulance driver in the civil war), and the United States (where he taught at various universities and, in 1946, became a naturalized citizen). A prolific writer of poems, plays, essays, and criticism, Auden won the Pulitzer Prize in 1948 for his collection of poems *The Age of Anxiety*, set in a New York City bar. Late in life he returned to Christ Church College, Oxford, where he was writer in residence. He is regarded as a masterly poet of political and intellectual conscience as well as one of the twentieth century's greatest lyric craftsmen.

WILLIAM BLAKE
(1757–1828)

The son of a London haberdasher and his wife, William Blake studied drawing at ten and at fourteen was apprenticed to an engraver for seven years. After a first book of poems, *Poetical Sketches* (1783), he began experimenting with what he called "illuminated printing"—the words and pictures of each page were engraved in relief on copper, which was used to print sheets that were then partly colored by hand—a laborious and time-consuming process that resulted in books of singular beauty, no two of which are exactly alike. His great *Songs of Innocence and of Experience* (1794) were produced in this manner, as were his increasingly mythic and prophetic books, including *The Marriage of Heaven and Hell* (1793), *The Four Zoas* (1803), *Milton* (1804), and *Jerusalem* (1809). Blake devoted his later life to pictorial art, illustrating *The Canterbury Tales*, the Book of Job, and *The Divine Comedy*, on which he was hard at work when he died.

GWENDOLYN BROOKS
(1917–2000)

Gwendolyn Brooks was born in Topeka, Kansas, and raised in Chicago, where she began writing poetry at the age of seven, and where she graduated from Wilson Junior College in 1936. Shortly after beginning her formal study of modern poetry at Chicago's Southside Community Art Center, Brooks produced her first book of poems, *A Street in Bronzeville* (1945). With her second volume, *Annie Allen* (1949), she became the first African American to win the Pulitzer Prize. Though her early work focused on what Langston Hughes called the "ordinary aspects of black life," during the mid-1960s she devoted her poetry to raising African American consciousness and to social activism. In 1968, she was named the Poet Laureate of Illinois; from 1985 to 1986, she served as poetry consultant to the Library of Congress. Her *Selected Poems* appeared in 1999.

ELIZABETH BARRETT BROWNING
(1806–1861)

Elizabeth Barrett was born into a wealthy family in Durham, England, and raised in Herefordshire. She received no formal schooling, but was very well educated at home in the classics and in English literature, and published her first volume of poetry at the age of thirteen. Despite her status as a prominent woman of letters, deteriorating health forced Barrett to live in semi-seclusion. Her collection *Poems* (1844) inspired the poet Robert Browning to write to her in May 1845, and thus began a courtship that resulted in their eloping to Italy in 1846. Following the publication of *Sonnets from the Portuguese* (1850), Barrett Browning received serious consideration to succeed Wordsworth as Poet Laureate (although the laureateship went instead to Tennyson); one critic hailed her as "the greatest female poet that England has produced." Her most admired work is *Aurora Leigh* (1857), a nine-book verse novel.

ROBERT BROWNING
(1812–1889)

Born in London, Robert Browning attended London University but was largely self-educated, learning Latin, Greek, French, and Italian by the time he was fourteen. He was an accomplished but little-known poet and playwright when he began courting the already famous poet Elizabeth Barrett. After they eloped to Italy in 1846, the Brownings enjoyed a period of happiness during which they produced most of their best-known work. Following Elizabeth's death in 1861, Robert returned to England with their son and for the rest of his life enjoyed great literary and social success. His major collections are *Men and Women* (1855), dedicated to his wife, and *Dramatis Personae* (1864), which contains some of his finest dramatic monologues.

Lionized as one of England's greatest poets by the time of his death, Browning is buried in Poets' Corner at Westminster Abbey.

ROBERT BURNS
(1759–1796)

Robert Burns was born and raised in Ayrshire, Scotland. The son of impoverished tenant farmers, he attended school sporadically but was largely self-taught. He collected subscriptions to publish his first collection, *Poems, Chiefly in the Scottish Dialect* (1786), which made his reputation in both Edinburgh and London. These poems were new in their rebellious individualism and in their pre-Romantic sensitivity to nature, yet they seemed to speak in an authentic "auld Scots" voice. A perennial failure as a farmer, Burns became a tax inspector and settled in the country town of Dumfries. Despite financial difficulties and failing health, he continued to write poems and songs (including "Auld Lang Syne") and devoted his last years to collecting Scottish folk songs for a cultural-preservation project. His work, frequently bawdy, politically zealous, and critical of organized religion, remains deeply loved throughout the world.

SAMUEL TAYLOR COLERIDGE
(1772–1834)

Born in the small town of Ottery St. Mary in rural Devonshire, England, Samuel Taylor Coleridge is among the greatest and most original of the nineteenth-century Romantic poets. He wrote three of the most haunting and powerful poems in English—*The Rime of the Ancient Mariner* (1798), *Christabel* (1816), and "Kubla Khan" (1816)—as well as immensely influential literary criticism and a treatise on biology. In 1795, in the midst of a failed experiment to establish a "Pantisocracy" (his form of ideal community), he met William Wordsworth, and in 1798 they jointly published their enormously influential *Lyrical Ballads.* Coleridge's physical ailments, addiction to opium, and profound sense of despair made his life difficult and tumultuous and certainly affected his work. Still, he remains a central figure in English literature.

BILLY COLLINS
(b. 1941)

Born in New York, Billy Collins received a B.A. from the College of the Holy Cross in Massachusetts and a Ph.D. from the University of California at Riverside before becoming a professor of English at Lehman College, City University of New York. His publications, several of which have broken sales records for poetry, include *Pokerface* (1977), *Video Poems* (1980), *The Apple That Astonished Paris* (1988), *Questions about Angels* (1991), *The Art of Drowning* (1995), *Picnic, Lightning* (1998), *Sailing Alone around the Room: New and Selected Poems* (2000), *Taking off Emily Dickinson's Clothes* (2000), *The Trouble with Poetry* (2005), and *Ballistics* (2008). He reads regularly on National Public Radio, performs live, and has recorded two spoken-word CDs, *The Best Cigarette* (1997) and *Billy Collins Live* (2005). He served two terms as Poet Laureate of the United States (2001-2003).

JAMES DICKEY
(1923–1997)

James Dickey did not become seriously interested in poetry until he joined the Air Force in 1942. When he returned from World War II, he earned a B.A. and an M.A. at Vanderbilt University, publishing his first poem in *Sewanee Review* in his senior year. Following the publication of his first volume of poems, *Into the Stone* (1960), Dickey, while primarily a poet, worked in advertising, wrote novels, and taught at various universities. His 1965 collection, *Buckdancer's Choice*, received the National Book Award, and from 1967 to 1969 Dickey was Consultant in Poetry to the Library of Congress. He is widely known for his best-selling novel *Deliverance* (1970), which he later adapted for Hollywood. Other publications include *The Whole Motion: Collected Poems 1949–1992* (1992) and another novel, *To the White Sea* (1993).

EMILY DICKINSON
(1830–1886)

From childhood on, Emily Dickinson led a sequestered and obscure life. Yet her verse has traveled far beyond the cultured yet relatively circumscribed environment in which she lived: her room, her father's house, her family, a few close friends, and the small town of Amherst, Massachusetts. Indeed, along with Walt Whitman, her far more public contemporary, she all but invented American poetry. Born in Amherst, the daughter of a respected lawyer whom she revered ("His heart was pure and terrible," she once wrote), Dickinson studied for less than a year at the Mount Holyoke Female Seminary, returning permanently to her family home. She became more and more reclusive, dressing only in white, seeing no visitors, yet working ceaselessly at her poems—nearly eighteen hundred in all, only a few of which were published during her lifetime. After her death, her sister Lavinia discovered the rest in a trunk, neatly bound into packets with blue ribbons—among the most important bodies of work in all of American literature.

JOHN DONNE
(1572–1631)

The first and greatest of the English writers who came to be known as the Metaphysical poets, John Donne wrote in a revolutionary style that combined highly intellectual conceits with complex, compressed phrasing. Born into an old Roman Catholic family at a time when Catholics were subject to constant harassment, Donne quietly abandoned his religion and had a promising legal career until a politically disastrous marriage ruined his worldly hopes. He struggled for years to support a large family; impoverished and despairing, he even wrote a treatise (*Biathanatos*) on the lawfulness of suicide. King James (who had ambitions for him as a preacher) eventually pressured Donne to take Anglican orders in 1615, and Donne became one of the great sermonizers of his day, rising to the position of dean of St. Paul's Cathedral in 1621. Donne's private devotions ("Meditations") were published in 1624, and he continued to write poetry until a few years before his death.

RITA DOVE (b. 1952)

A native of Akron, Ohio, Rita Dove attended Miami University in Ohio, studied for a year in West Germany as a Fulbright scholar, and received an M.F.A. in creative writing from the University of Iowa. She is now a professor of English at the University of Virginia as well as associate editor of *Callaloo*, a journal of African American arts and letters. In 1987, Dove became the second African American poet (after Gwendolyn Brooks, in 1950) to win the Pulitzer Prize (for *Thomas and Beulah*). In 1993, she was appointed Poet Laureate of the United States, ultimately serving two terms. Her books include *The Yellow House on the Corner* (1980), *Museum* (1983), *Grace Notes* (1989), *Mother Love* (1995), *On the Bus with Rosa Parks* (1999), and, most recently, *American Smooth* (2004). A tireless advocate for poetry, Dove edited *The Best American Poetry 2000* and, from 2000 to 2002, authored the weekly column "Poet's Choice" in the *Washington Post Book World*.

PAUL LAURENCE DUNBAR
(1872–1906)

The son of former slaves, Paul Laurence Dunbar was born in Dayton, Ohio. He attended a white high school, where he showed an early talent for writing and was elected class president. Unable to afford further education, he then worked as an elevator operator, writing poems and newspaper articles in his spare time. Dunbar took out a loan to subsidize the printing of his first book, *Oak and Ivy* (1893), but with the publication of *Majors and Minors* (1895) and *Lyrics of Lowly Life* (1896), his growing reputation enabled him to support himself by writing and lecturing. Though acclaimed during his lifetime for his lyrical use of rural black dialect in volumes such as *Candle-Lightin' Time* (1902), Dunbar was later criticized for adopting "white" literary conventions and accused of pandering to racist images of slaves and ex-slaves. He wrote novels and short stories in addition to poetry and dealt frankly with racial injustice in works such as *The Sport of the Gods* (1903) and *The Fourth of July and Race Outrages* (1903).

ROBERT FROST
(1874–1963)

Though his poetry identifies Frost with rural New England, he was born and lived to the age of eleven in San Francisco. Moving to New England after his father's death, Frost studied classics in high school, entered and dropped out of both Dartmouth and Harvard, and spent difficult years as an unrecognized poet before his first book, *A Boy's Will* (1913), was accepted and published in England. Frost's character was full of contradiction—he held "that we get forward as much by hating as by loving"—yet by the end of his long life he was one of the most honored poets of his time, and the most widely read. In 1961, two years before his death, he was invited to read a poem at John F. Kennedy's presidential inauguration ceremony. Frost's poems—masterfully crafted, sometimes deceptively simple—are collected in *The Poetry of Robert Frost* (1969).

ROBERT HAYDEN
(1913–1980)

Robert Hayden was born Asa Bundy Sheffey, in Detroit, Michigan, and raised by foster parents. He studied at Detroit City College (later Wayne State University), but left in 1936 to work for the Federal Writers' Project, where he researched black history and folk culture. He received an M.A. from the University of Michigan, taught at Fisk University from 1949 until 1969, and then taught at Michigan until his retirement. Although he published ten volumes of poetry, he did not receive acclaim until late in life. His collections include *Heart-Shape in the Dust* (1940), *The Lion and the Archer, Figures of Time* (1955), *A Ballad of Remembrance* (1962), *Selected Poems* (1966), *Words in the Mourning Time* (1970), *Night-Blooming Cereus* (1972), *Angle of Ascent* (1975), *American Journal* (1978 and 1982), and *Collected Poems* (1985).

SEAMUS HEANEY
(b. 1939)

Seamus Heaney, whose poems explore themes of rural life, memory, and history, was born on a farm in Mossbawn, County Derry (Castledawson, Londonderry), Northern Ireland. Educated at Queen's University in Belfast, he has taught at the University of California at Berkeley, Carysfort College in Dublin, Oxford University and Harvard. Once called by Robert Lowell "the most important Irish poet since Yeats," Heaney received the 1995 Nobel Prize for Literature. His poetry collections include *Eleven Poems* (1965), *Death of a Naturalist* (1966), *Wintering Out* (1972), *The*

Haw Lantern (1987), *Seeing Things* (1991), *The Spirit Level* (1996), *Electric Light* (2001), and *District and Circle* (2006). Heaney's translation of *Beowulf* (2000) from Anglo-Saxon into modern English gave new life to the oldest of English poems; it not only won Britain's prestigious Whitbread Award but also become a best-seller.

GERARD MANLEY HOPKINS
(1844–1889)

Born the eldest of eight children of a marine-insurance adjuster and his wife, Gerard Manley Hopkins attended Oxford, where his ambition was to become a painter—until, at the age of 22, he converted to Roman Catholicism and burned all his early poetry as too worldly. Not until after his seminary training and ordination as a Jesuit priest, in 1877, did he resume writing poetry, though he made few attempts to publish his verse, which many of his contemporaries found nearly incomprehensible. Near the end of his life, Hopkins was appointed professor of Greek at University College, Dublin, where—out of place, deeply depressed, and all but unknown—he died of typhoid. His poetry, collected and published by his friends, has been championed by modern poets, who admire its controlled tension, strong rhythm, and sheer exuberance.

LANGSTON HUGHES
(1902–1967)

Born in Joplin, Missouri, Langston Hughes was raised mainly by his maternal grandmother, though he lived intermittently with each of his parents. He studied at Columbia University, but left to travel and work at a variety of jobs. Having already published poems in periodicals, anthologies, and his own first collection, *The Weary Blues* (1926), he graduated from Lincoln University; published a successful novel,

Not without Laughter (1930); and became a major writer in the intellectual and literary movement called the Harlem Renaissance. During the 1930s, he became involved in radical politics and traveled the world as a correspondent and columnist; during the 1950s, though, the FBI classified him as a security risk and limited his ability to travel. In addition to poems and novels, he wrote essays, plays, screenplays, and an autobiography; he also edited anthologies of literature and folklore. His *Collected Poems* appeared in 1994.

BEN JONSON
(1572?–1637)

Poet, playwright, actor, scholar, critic, and translator, Ben Jonson was the posthumous son of a clergyman and the stepson of a master bricklayer of Westminster. Jonson had an eventful early life, going to war against the Spanish, working as an actor, killing an associate in a duel, and converting to Roman Catholicism. Meanwhile, Jonson wrote a number of plays that have remained popular to this day, including *Every Man in His Humour* (in which Shakespeare acted a leading role; 1598), *Volpone* (1606), and *The Alchemist* (1610). He was named Poet Laureate in 1616 and spent the latter part of his life at the center of a large circle of friends and admirers known as the "Tribe of Ben." Often considered the first English author to deem writing his primary career, he published *The Works of Benjamin Jonson* in 1616.

JOHN KEATS
(1795–1821)

Because John Keats was the son of a London livery stable owner and his wife, reviewers would later disparage him as a working-class "Cockney poet." At fifteen he was apprenticed to a surgeon, and at twenty-one he became a licensed pharmacist—in the same year that his first two published poems, including the sonnet "On First Looking into Chapman's Homer," appeared in *The Examiner*, a journal edited by the critic and poet Leigh Hunt. Hunt introduced Keats to such literary figures as the poet Percy Bysshe Shelley and helped him publish his *Poems by John Keats* (1817). When his second book, the long poem *Endymion* (1818), was fiercely attacked by critics, Keats, suffering from a steadily worsening case of tuberculosis, knew that he would not live to realize his poetic promise. In July 1820, he published *Lamia, Isabella, The Eve of St. Agnes, and Other Poems*, which contained the poignant "To Autumn" and three other great odes: "Ode on a Grecian Urn," "Ode on Melancholy," and "Ode to a Nightingale"; early the next year, he died in Rome. In the years after Keats's death, his letters became almost as famous as his poetry.

GALWAY KINNELL
(b. 1927)

Born in Providence, Rhode Island, Galway Kinnell earned a B.A. from Princeton and an M.A. from the University of Rochester. He served in the navy and has been a journalist, a civil-rights field-worker, and a teacher at numerous colleges and universities. His early poetry, collected in *What a Kingdom It Was* (1960) and *First Poems 1946–1954* (1970), is highly formal; his subsequent work employs a more colloquial style. "Poetry," he has said, "is the attempt to find a language that can speak the unspeakable." He received both a Pulitzer Prize and the American Book Award for *Selected Poems* (1982), and in 2000 he culled *A New Selected Poems* from eight collections spanning twenty-four years. He lives in New York and Vermont.

ANDREW MARVELL
(1621–1678)

The son of a clergyman and his wife, Andrew Marvell was born in Yorkshire, England, and educated at Trinity College, Cambridge. There is no evidence that he fought in the English Civil War, which broke out in 1642, but his poem "An Horatian Ode upon Cromwell's Return from Ireland" appeared in 1650, shortly after the beheading of King Charles I in 1649, and may represent straightforward praise of England's new Puritan leader. Some regard it as strong satire, however—Marvell was known in his day for his satirical prose and verse. Today he is better known for lyric poems such as the *carpe diem* manifesto "To His Coy Mistress," which he probably wrote while serving as tutor to a Yorkshire nobleman's daughter. In 1657, on the recommendation of John Milton, Marvell accepted a position in Cromwell's government that he held until his election to Parliament in 1659. After helping restore the monarchy in 1660, he continued to write and to serve as a member of Parliament until the end of his life.

CLAUDE MCKAY
(1889–1948)

Festus Claudius McKay was born and raised in Sunny Ville, Clarendon Parish, Jamaica, the youngest of eleven children. He worked as a wheelwright and cabinetmaker, then briefly as a police constable, before writing and publishing two books of poetry in Jamaican dialect. In 1912, he emigrated to the United States, where he attended Booker T. Washington's Tuskegee Institute in Alabama, studied agricultural science at Kansas State College, and then moved to New York City. McKay supported himself through various jobs while becoming a prominent literary and political figure. The oldest Harlem Renaissance writer, McKay was also the first to publish, with the poetry collection *Harlem Shadows* (1922). His other works include the novels *Home to Harlem* (1928) and *Banana Bottom* (1933), and his autobiography, *A Long Way from Home* (1937).

EDNA ST. VINCENT MILLAY
(1892–1950)

Born in Rockland, Maine, Edna St. Vincent Millay published her first poem at twenty, her first poetry collection at twenty-five. After graduating from Vassar College, she moved to New York City's Greenwich Village, where she both gained a reputation as a brilliant poet and became notorious for her bohemian life and her association with prominent artists, writers, and radicals. In 1923, she won the Pulitzer Prize for her collection *The Ballad of the Harp-Weaver*; in 1925, growing weary of fame, she and her husband moved to Austerlitz, New York, where she lived for the rest of her life. Although her work fell out of favor with mid-twentieth century modernists, who rejected her formalism as old-fashioned, her poetry—witty, acerbic, and superbly crafted—has found many new admirers today.

JOHN MILTON
(1608–1674)

Born in London, the elder son of a self-made businessman and his wife, John Milton exhibited unusual literary and scholarly gifts at an early age; before entering Cambridge University, he was adept at Latin and Greek and was well on his way to mastering Hebrew and a number of European languages. After graduation, he spent six more years of intense study and composed, among other works, his great pastoral elegy, "Lycidas" (1637). After a year of travel in Europe, Milton return to England and found his country embroiled in religious strife and civil war. Milton took up the

Puritan cause and, in 1641, began writing pamphlets defending everything from free speech to Cromwell's execution of Charles I; Milton also served as Cromwell's Latin secretary until, in 1651, he lost his sight. After the monarchy was restored in 1660, Milton was briefly imprisoned, and his property confiscated. Blind, impoverished, and isolated, he devoted himself to the great spiritual epics of his later years: *Paradise Lost* (1667), *Paradise Regained* (1671), and *Samson Agonistes* (1671).

PAT MORA (b. 1942)

Born to Mexican American parents in El Paso, Texas, Pat Mora earned a B.A. and an M.A. from the University of Texas at El Paso. She has been a consultant on U.S.-Mexico youth exchanges; a museum director and administrator at her alma mater; and a teacher of English at all levels. Her poetry—collected in *Chants* (1985), *Borders* (1986), *Communion* (1991), *Agua Santa* (1995), and *Aunt Carmen's Book of Practical Saints* (1997)—reflects and addresses her Chicana and southwestern background. Mora's other publications include *Nepantla: Essays from the Land in the Middle* (1993); a family memoir, *House of Houses* (1997); and many works for children and young adults.

HOWARD NEMEROV
(1920–1991)

Born and raised in New York City, Howard Nemerov graduated from Harvard University, served in the U.S. Army Air Corps during World War II, and returned to New York to complete his first book, *The Image and the Law* (1948). He taught at a number of colleges and universities and published books of poetry, plays, short stories, novels, and essays. His *Collected Poems* won the Pulitzer Prize and the National Book Award in 1978. He served as Consultant in Poetry to the Library of Congress from 1963 to 1964, and Poet Laureate of the United States from 1988 to 1990. *Trying Conclusions: New and Selected Poems 1961–1991* was published in 1991.

SHARON OLDS
(b. 1942)

Born in San Francisco, Sharon Olds earned a B.A. from Stanford University and a Ph.D. from Columbia University. She was founding chair of the Writing Program at Goldwater Hospital (a public facility for the severely physically disabled), and she currently teaches in New York University's Creative Writing Program. She has received a National Endowment for the Arts Grant and a Guggenheim Fellowship, and served as New York State Poet Laureate from 1998 to 2000. Her books include *Satan Says* (1980); the National Book Critics Circle Award-winning *The Dead and the Living* (1983); *The Gold Cell* (1987); *The Father* (1992); *The Wellspring* (1997); *Blood, Tin, Straw* (1999); and *The Unswept Room*, a National Book Award nominee in 2002. Her *Strike Sparks: Selected Poems: 1980–2002* appeared in 2004.

DOROTHY PARKER
(1893–1967)

Born in West End, New Jersey, Dorothy Rothschild worked for both *Vogue* and *Vanity Fair* magazines before becoming a freelance writer. In 1917, she married Edwin Pond Parker II, whom she divorced in 1928. Her first book of verse, *Enough Rope* (1926), was a best-seller and was followed by *Sunset Gun* (1928), *Death and Taxes* (1931), and *Collected Poems: Not So Deep as a Well* (1936). In 1927, Parker became a book reviewer for *The New Yorker*, to which she contributed for most of her career. In 1933, Parker and her second husband, Alan Campbell, moved to Hollywood, where they collaborated as film writers. In addition, Parker wrote criticism, two plays, short stories, and news reports from the Spanish Civil War. She is probably best remembered, though, as the reigning wit at the "Round Table" at Manhattan's Algonquin Hotel, where, in the 1920s and '30s, she traded barbs with other prominent writers and humorists.

LINDA PASTAN
(b. 1932)

Linda Pastan was born in New York City and raised in nearby Westchester County. After graduating from Radcliffe College, she received an M.A. in literature from Brandeis University. Although her first published poems appeared in *Mademoiselle* in 1955, Pastan spent many years concentrating on her husband and children—indeed, much of her poetry deals with her own family life. Her many collections include *A Perfect Circle of Sun* (1971), *The Five Stages of Grief* (1978), American Book Award nominee *PM/AM: New and Selected Poems* (1982), *Carnival Evening: New and Selected Poems 1968–1998* (1998), and *Queen of a Rainy Country* (2006). She lives in Potomac, Maryland, and was named Poet Laureate of Maryland in 1991.

SYLVIA PLATH
(1932–1963)

Sylvia Plath was born in Boston; her father, a Polish immigrant, died when she was eight. After graduating from Smith College, Plath attended Cambridge University on a Fulbright scholarship, and there she met and married the poet Ted Hughes, with whom she had two children. As she documented in her novel *The Bell Jar* (1963), in 1953—between her junior and senior years of college—Plath became seriously depressed, attempted suicide, and was hospitalized. In 1963, the break-up of her marriage led to another suicide attempt, this time successful. Plath has attained cult status as much for her poems as for her "martyr-

dom" to art and life. In addition to her first volume of poetry, *The Colossus* (1960), Plath's work has been collected in *Ariel* (1966), *Crossing the Water* (1971), and *Winter Trees* (1972). Her selected letters were published in 1975; her expurgated journals in 1983; and her unabridged journals in 2000.

EZRA POUND
(1885–1972)

Born in Hailey, Idaho, Ezra Pound studied at the University of Pennsylvania and Hamilton College before traveling to Europe in 1908. He remained there, living in Ireland, England, France, and Italy, for much of his life. Pound's tremendous ambition—to succeed in his own work and to influence the development of poetry and Western culture in general—led him to found the Imagist school of poetry, to advise and assist many great writers (Eliot, Joyce, Williams, Frost, and Hemingway, to name a few), and to write a number of highly influential critical works. His increasingly fiery and erratic behavior led to a charge of treason (he served as a propagandist for Mussolini during World War II), a diagnosis of insanity, and twelve years at St. Elizabeth's, an institution for the criminally insane. His verse is collected in *Personae: The Collected Poems* (1949) and *The Cantos* (1976).

ADRIENNE RICH
(b. 1929)

Adrienne Rich was born in Baltimore. Since the selection of her first volume by W. H. Auden for the Yale Series of Younger Poets (1951), her work has continually evolved, from the tightly controlled early poems to the politically and personally charged verse for which she is known today. Rich's books of poetry include *Collected Early Poems 1950–1970* (1993), *The Dream of a Common Language* (1978), *Your*

Native Land, Your Life (1986), *Time's Power* (1988), *An Atlas of the Difficult World* (1991), *Dark Fields of the Republic* (1995), *Midnight Salvage* (1999), *Fox* (2001), and *The School among the Ruins* (2004). Her prose works include *Of Woman Born: Motherhood as Experience and Institution* (1976), *On Lies, Secrets, and Silence* (1979), and *Blood, Bread, and Poetry* (1986), all influential feminist texts; *What Is Found There: Notebooks on Poetry and Politics* (1993); and *Arts of the Possible: Essays and Conversations* (2001). Her many awards include a MacArthur Fellowship and a Lanning Foundation Lifetime Achievement Award.

CHRISTINA ROSSETTI

(1830–1894)

The daughter of Italian political refugees, Christina Rossetti was born in London and educated at home. Though associated with the Pre-Raphaelite group of artists and writers through her brother, Dante Gabriel Rossetti, Christina withdrew into the more personal world of her quiet but intense devotion to poetry and Anglican spirituality. Published under the pseudonym "Ellen Alleyn," her first poems appeared when she was only eighteen; her first adult collection, *Goblin Market and Other Poems* (1862), was a popular and critical success. Never marrying, Rossetti instead devoted herself to her writing and to a variety of moral and educational causes. Her collected *Poetical Works* (1904) was published a decade after her death.

WILLIAM SHAKESPEARE

(1554–1616)

Considering the great fame of his work, surprisingly little is known of William Shakespeare's life. Between 1585 and 1592, he left his birthplace of Stratford-upon-Avon for London to begin a career as playwright and actor. No dates of his professional career are recorded, however, nor can the order in which he composed his plays and poetry be determined with any certainty. By 1594, he had established himself as a poet with two long works—*Venus and Adonis* and *The Rape of Lucrece*—and his more than 150 sonnets are supreme expressions of the form. His reputation, though, rests on the works he wrote for the theater. Shakespeare produced perhaps thirty-five plays in twenty-five years, proving himself a master of every dramatic genre: tragedy (in works such as *Macbeth, Hamlet, King Lear,* and *Othello*); historical drama (for example, *Richard III* and *Henry IV*); comedy (*Twelfth Night, As You Like It,* and many more); and romance (in plays such as *The Tempest* and *Cymbaline*). Without question, Shakespeare is the most quoted, discussed, and beloved English writer.

WALLACE STEVENS

(1879–1955)

Born and raised in Reading, Pennsylvania, Wallace Stevens attended Harvard University and New York Law School. In New York City, he worked for a number of law firms, published poems in magazines, and befriended such literary figures as William Carlos Williams and Marianne Moore. In 1916, Stevens moved to Connecticut and began working for the Hartford Accident and Indemnity Company, where he became a vice-president in 1934 and where he worked for the rest of his life, writing poetry at night and during vacations. He published his first collection, *Harmonium*, in 1923, and followed it with a series of volumes from 1935 until 1950, establishing himself as one of the twentieth century's most important poets. His lectures were collected in *The Necessary Angel: Essays on Reality and Imagination* (1951); his *Collected Poems* appeared in 1954.

ALFRED, LORD TENNYSON
(1809–1892)

Certainly the most popular and perhaps the most important of the Victorian poets, Alfred, Lord Tennyson demonstrated his talents at an early age; he published his first volume in 1827. Encouraged to devote his life to poetry by a group of undergraduates at Cambridge University known as the "Apostles," Tennyson was particularly close to Arthur Hallam, whose sudden death in 1833 inspired the long elegy *In Memoriam* (1850). With that poem he achieved lasting fame and recognition; he was appointed Poet Laureate the year of its publication, succeeding Wordsworth. Despite the great popularity of his "journalistic" poems— "The Charge of the Light Brigade" (1854) is perhaps the best known—Tennyson's great theme was the past, both personal (*In the Valley of Cauteretz*, 1864) and national (*Idylls of the King*, 1869). Tennyson was made a baron in 1884; when he died, eight years later, he was buried in Poets' Corner in Westminster Abbey.

DYLAN THOMAS
(1914–1953)

Born in Swansea, Wales, into what he called "the smug darkness of a provincial town," Dylan Thomas published his first book, *Eighteen Poems* (1934), at twenty, in the same year that he moved to London. Thereafter he had a successful, though turbulent, career publishing poetry, short stories, and plays, including the highly successful *Under Milk Wood* (1954). In his last years he supported himself with lecture tours and poetry readings in the United States, but his excessive drinking caught up with him, and he died in New York City of chronic alcoholism. His *Collected Poems, 1934–1952* (1952) was the last book he published during his short life-

time; his comic novel, *Adventures in the Skin Trade*, was never completed.

DEREK WALCOTT
(b. 1930)

Born of mixed heritage on the West Indian island of St. Lucia, Derek Walcott grew up speaking French and patois but was educated in English. In 1953, he earned his B.A. in English, French, and Latin from the University College of the West Indies in Jamaica. In 1950, with his twin brother, Roderick, he founded the St. Lucia Arts Guild, a dramatic society; nine years later, he founded the Little Carib Theatre Workshop in Trinidad, which he ran until 1976, writing many plays for production there. Walcott has published many volumes of poetry, including *In a Green Night* (1962), *The Castaway* (1965), *Another Life* (1973), *Sea Grapes* (1976), *The Fortunate Traveller* (1981), *Omeros* (1990), *The Bounty* (1997), *Tiepolo's Hound* (2000), and *The Prodigal: A Poem* (2004). His work draws on diverse influences, from West Indian folk tales to Homer to Yeats. The first Caribbean poet to win the Nobel Prize (in 1992), Walcott now lives and teaches in the United States.

WALT WHITMAN
(1819–1892)

Walt Whitman was born on a farm in West Hills, Long Island, to a British father and a Dutch mother. After working as a journalist throughout New York for many years, he taught for a time and founded his own newspaper, *The Long Islander*, in 1838; he then left journalism to work on *Leaves of Grass*, originally intended as a poetic treatise on American democratic idealism. Published privately in multiple editions from 1855 to 1874, the book at first failed to reach a mass audience. In 1881, Boston's Osgood and Company published another edition of *Leaves of Grass*, which sold well until the district attorney called it "obscene literature" and stipulated that Whitman remove certain poems and phrases. He refused, and it was many years before his works were again published, this time in Philadelphia. By the time Whitman died, his work was revered, as it still is today, for its greatness of spirit and its exuberant American voice.

RICHARD WILBUR
(b. 1921)

Born in New York City and raised in New Jersey, Richard Wilbur received his B.A. from Amherst College and his M.A. from Harvard. He started to write while serving as an army cryptographer during World War II, and his collections *The Beautiful Changes* (1947) and *Ceremony* (1950) established his reputation as a serious poet. In addition to subsequent volumes such as the Pulitzer Prize–winning *Things of This World* (1956), *Walking to Sleep* (1969), *The Mind Reader* (1976), the Pulitzer Prize–winning *New and Collected Poems* (1988), and *Mayflies: New Poems and Translations* (2000), he has published children's books, critical essays, and numerous translations of classic French works by Racine and Molière. He has taught at various colleges and universities, including Harvard, Wellesley, Wesleyan, and Smith. In 1987, he was named Poet Laureate of the United States.

WILLIAM CARLOS WILLIAMS
(1883–1963)

Born in Rutherford, New Jersey, William Carlos Williams attended school in Switzerland and New York and studied medicine at the University of Pennsylvania and the University of Leipzig in Germany. He spent most of his life in Rutherford, practicing medicine and gradually establishing himself as one of the great figures in American poetry. Early in his writing career he left the European-inspired Imagist movement in favor of a more uniquely American poetic style comprised of vital, local language, and "no ideas but in things." His shorter poems have been published in numerous collected editions and other volumes, including the Pulitzer Prize–winning *Brueghel, and Other Poems* (1963); his five-volume philosophical poem, *Paterson*, was published in 1963. Among his other works are plays such as *A Dream of Love* (1948) and *Many Loves* (1950); a trilogy of novels—*White Mules* (1937), *In the Money* (1940), and *The Build-Up* (1952); his *Autobiography* (1951); his *Selected Essays* (1954); and his *Selected Letters* (1957).

WILLIAM WORDS-WORTH
(1770–1850)

Regarded by many as the greatest of the Romantic poets, William Wordsworth was born in Cockermouth in the English Lake District, a beautiful, mountainous region that his poetry helped make a popular tourist destination even in his own lifetime. He studied at Cambridge and then spent a year in France, hoping to witness the French Revolution firsthand; as the Revolution's "glorious renovation" dissolved into anarchy and then tyranny, Wordsworth was forced to return to England. Remarkably, he managed to establish "a saving intercourse with my true self" and to write some of his finest poetry, including the early version of his masterpiece, *The Prelude*, which first appeared in 1805 and then again, much altered, in 1850. In 1798, Wordsworth and his friend Samuel Taylor Coleridge published *Lyrical Ballads*, which contains many of their greatest poems as well as a preface that can be considered the founding document of English Romanticism. Wordsworth was revered by the reading public and in 1843 was named Poet Laureate.

WILLIAM BUTLER YEATS (1865–1939)

William Butler Yeats was born in Dublin and, though he spent most of his youth in London, became the pre-eminent Irish poet of the twentieth century. Immersed in Irish history, folklore, and politics, as well as spiritualism and the occult, he attended art school for a time but left to devote himself to poetry that was, early in his career, self-consciously dreamy and ethereal. Yeats's poems became tighter and more passionate with his reading of philosophers such as Nietzsche, his involvement (mainly through theater) with the Irish nationalist cause, and his desperate love for the actress and nationalist Maud Gonne. He was briefly a senator in the newly independent Irish government before withdrawing from active public life to Thoor Ballylee, a crumbling Norman tower that Yeats and his wife fashioned into a home. There he developed an elaborate mythology (published as *A Vision* in 1925) and wrote poems that explored fundamental questions of history and identity. He was awarded the Nobel Prize for Literature in 1923. His works, in many genres, have been selected and collected in various editions.

Drama

Drama: Reading, Responding, Writing

As noted in the introduction, many cultures have had oral literatures: histories, romances, poems to be recited or sung. Our own era has its share of oral art forms, of course, but "literary" fiction and poetry are now most often read privately, silently, from the printed page. Most contemporary fiction writers and poets write with an understanding that their work will be experienced and enjoyed this way.

In contrast, **drama** is written primarily to be performed—by actors, on a stage, for an audience. Playwrights work with an understanding that the words on the page are just the first step—a map of sorts—toward the ultimate goal: a collaborative, publicly performed work of art. They create plays fully aware of the possibilities that go beyond printed words and extend to physical actions, stage devices, and other theatrical techniques for creating special effects and modifying audience responses. Although the script of a play may be the most essential piece in the puzzle that makes up the final work of art, the play text is not the final, complete work.

To attend a play—that is, to be part of an audience—represents a very different kind of experience from the usually solitary act of reading. On the stage, real human beings, standing for imaginary characters, deliver lines and perform actions for you to see and hear. In turn, the actors adapt in subtle ways to the reactions of the people who attend the performance and whose responses are no longer wholly private but have become, in part, communal.

When you attend the performance of a play, then, you become a collaborator in the creation of a unique work of art: not the play *text* but instead a specific *interpretation* of that text. No two performances of a play can ever be identical, just as no two interpretations of a play can be exactly the same.

READING DRAMA

In many respects, of course, reading drama is similar to reading fiction. In both cases we anticipate what will happen next; we imagine the characters, settings, and actions; we respond to the symbolic suggestiveness of images; and we notice thematic patterns that are likely to matter in the end. But

because most plays are written to be performed, reading plays is also somewhat different from reading fiction or poetry on the printed page. In narrative fiction, for example, there is a mediator or narrator, someone standing
between us and the events to help us relate to the characters, actions, and
meanings. In contrast, drama rarely has such an interpreter or mediator to
tell us what is happening or to shape our responses. Play texts instead rely
on **stage directions** (the italicized descriptions of the set, characters, and
actions), while **exposition** (the explanation of the past and current situation) emerges only here and there in the dialogue.

For this reason, reading drama may place a greater demand on the imagination than reading fiction does: The reader must be his or her own narrator and interpreter. Such an exercise for the imagination can prove rewarding,
however, for it has much in common with the imaginative work that a director, actors, and other artists involved in a staged production bring to their
performance of a play. In re-creating a play as we read it, we are essentially
imagining the play as if it were being performed by live actors in real time.
We "cast" the characters, we design the set with its furniture and props,
and we choreograph or "block" the physical action, according to the cues in
the text.

In reading drama even more than in reading fiction, we construct our
ideas of character and personality from what a character says. In some
plays, especially those with a modernist or experimental bent, certain lines
of dialogue can be mystifying; other characters, as well as the audience or
readers, can be left wondering what a speech meant. On the one hand, such
puzzling lines can become clearer in performance, in which actors physically express the intentions and interactions of the characters. On the other
hand, plays that call for several characters to speak at once or to talk at
cross purposes can be much easier to understand from the printed script
than in performance. In interpreting dialogue, you will naturally draw on
your own experiences of comparable situations or similar personalities, as
well as your familiarity with other plays or stories.

QUESTIONS TO ASK WHEN READING A PLAY

As mentioned above, reading drama has much in common with reading fiction. You can begin to understand a play by asking some basic questions
about the elements of drama, similar to those in fiction. Most critics would
agree that plays, as well as most films and television shows, generally have
no narrator. At times there may be a voiceover or an actor onstage or offstage telling us something, but usually this device will be dropped as the
action gets under way and the actors perform what happens. Again, your
questions will be somewhat different when you attend a performance of a
play from your questions when you read a printed play.

- **Expectations:** What do you expect:
  - from the title? from the first sentence, paragraph, or speech?
  - after the first events or interactions of characters? as the conflict is resolved?
- **Characterization:** Who are the characters? Is there a list of characters printed after the title of the play? What do you notice about their names or any identification of their roles, character types, or relationships?
  - Who is/are the **protagonist**(s) (hero, heroine)?
  - Who is/are the **antagonist**(s) (villain, opponent, obstacle)?
  - Who are the other characters?
  - What does each character know at any moment in the action? What does each character expect at any point? What does the audience know or expect that is different from what the characters know or expect?
- **Plot:** What happens in the play?
  - Do the characters or situations change during the play?
  - What are the differences between the beginning, middle, and end of the play? Is it divided into acts? Would there be an intermission in a performance?
  - Can you summarize the plot? Is it a recognizable kind or genre such as tragedy, comedy, farce, or mystery?
- **Setting:** What is the setting of the play?
  - What is the *time* of the play? Is it contemporary or set in the past? Do the stage directions specify a day of the week, a season, a time of day?
  - Are there any time changes during the play? Are the scenes in chronological order, or are there any scenes that are supposed to take place earlier or simultaneously? Does the passage of time in the lives of the characters correspond with the passage of time onstage during the performance? Or do we understand that time has passed and events have occurred offstage and between scenes?
  - *Where* does it take place? Is it in the United States or another country, or in a specific town or region? Do the stage directions describe the scene that an audience would see on stage, and does this remain the same or does it change during the play? How many scene changes are there?
- **Style:** What do you notice about how the play is written?
  - What is the **style** of the dialogue? Are the sentences and speeches short or long? Is the vocabulary simple or complex? Do characters ever speak at the same time, or do they always take turns? Does the play instruct actors to be silent for periods of time? Which characters speak most often?

◦ Are there any **images** or figures of speech?

◦ What is the **tone** or mood? Does the play make the reader or audience feel sad, amused, worried, curious?

• **Theme:** What does the play mean? Can you express its theme or themes?

◦ Answers to these big questions may be found in many instances by returning to your answers to the questions above. The play's meaning or theme depends on all its features.

Later in this chapter you will find an example of responses to these questions in the form of reading notes on Susan Glaspell's play *Trifles*.

As you read a play, you should not only make mental or written notes but also raise some of the questions an actor might ask in preparing a role, or that a director might ask before choosing a cast: How should this line be spoken? What kind of person is this character, and what are his or her motives in each scene? What does the play imply or state about what made the character this way—family, environment, experience? Which characters are present or absent (onstage or off) in which scenes, and how do the characters onstage or off influence one another?

Besides trying to understand the characters, you should consider ways that the play could be produced, designed, staged, and acted. How might a set designer create a kitchen, drawing room, garden, woods, or other space for the actors to move in, and how many set changes are there in the play? What would the audience see through any windows or doors in an imaginary building? How would lighting give an impression of the time of day or season? Would sound effects or music be necessary (such as a gunshot, radio, or telephone)? What sort of costumes are specified in the stage directions, and how would costumes help express character types and their relationships, as well as the historical time period? What essential props must be provided for the actors to use, and what other props are optional? Would you, as "director" of an imaginary performance, tell the actors to move in certain directions, together or apart; to express certain emotions and intentions; to speak in quiet, angry, sarcastic, or agonized tones?

As you read Susan Glaspell's *Trifles* and Tom Stoppard's *The Real Inspector Hound*, below, keep these kinds of questions in mind. Try to create a mental image of the settings and of each character, and think about different ways the lines might be delivered that would affect an audience's response.

SUSAN GLASPELL

Trifles

CHARACTERS

SHERIFF   MRS. PETERS, *Sheriff's wife*
COUNTY ATTORNEY   MRS. HALE
HALE

SCENE: *The kitchen in the now abandoned farmhouse of* JOHN WRIGHT, *a gloomy kitchen, and left without having been put in order—unwashed pans under the sink, a loaf of bread outside the bread-box, a dish-towel on the table—other signs of incompleted work. At the rear the outer door opens and the* SHERIFF *comes in followed by the* COUNTY ATTORNEY *and* HALE. *The* SHERIFF *and* HALE *are men in middle life, the* COUNTY ATTORNEY *is a young man; all are much bundled up and go at once to the stove. They are followed by the two women—the* SHERIFF'S *wife first; she is a slight wiry woman, a thin nervous face.* MRS. HALE *is larger and would ordinarily be called more comfortable looking, but she is disturbed now and looks fearfully about as she enters. The women have come in slowly, and stand close together near the door.*

COUNTY ATTORNEY: [*Rubbing his hands.*] This feels good. Come up to the fire, ladies.

MRS. PETERS: [*After taking a step forward.*] I'm not—cold.

SHERIFF: [*Unbuttoning his overcoat and stepping away from the stove as if to mark the beginning of official business.*] Now, Mr. Hale, before we move things about, you explain to Mr. Henderson just what you saw when you came here yesterday morning.

COUNTY ATTORNEY: By the way, has anything been moved? Are things just as you left them yesterday?

SHERIFF: [*Looking about.*] It's just the same. When it dropped below zero last night I thought I'd better send Frank out this morning to make a fire for us—no use getting pneumonia with a big case on, but I told him not to touch anything except the stove—and you know Frank.

COUNTY ATTORNEY: Somebody should have been left here yesterday.

SHERIFF: Oh—yesterday. When I had to send Frank to Morris Center for that man who went crazy—I want you to know I had my hands full yesterday. I knew you could get back from Omaha by today and as long as I went over everything here myself—

COUNTY ATTORNEY: Well, Mr. Hale, tell just what happened when you came here yesterday morning.

HALE: Harry and I had started to town with a load of potatoes. We came along the road from my place and as I got here I said, "I'm going to see if I can't get John Wright to go in with me on a party telephone."[1] I spoke

1. That is, a party line in which a number of households each have extensions of a single line, a common arrangement in the early twentieth century, especially in rural areas.

to Wright about it once before and he put me off, saying folks talked too much anyway, and all he asked was peace and quiet—I guess you know about how much he talked himself; but I thought maybe if I went to the house and talked about it before his wife, though I said to Harry that I didn't know as what his wife wanted made much difference to John—

COUNTY ATTORNEY: Let's talk about that later, Mr. Hale. I do want to talk about that, but tell now just what happened when you got to the house.

HALE: I didn't hear or see anything; I knocked at the door, and still it was all quiet inside. I knew they must be up, it was past eight o'clock. So I knocked again, and I thought I heard somebody say, "Come in." I wasn't sure, I'm not sure yet, but I opened the door—this door [*Indicating the door by which the two women are still standing.*] and there in that rocker— [*Pointing to it.*] sat Mrs. Wright.

[*They all look at the rocker.*]

COUNTY ATTORNEY: What—was she doing?

HALE: She was rockin' back and forth. She had her apron in her hand and was kind of—pleating it.

COUNTY ATTORNEY: And how did she—look?

HALE: Well, she looked queer.

COUNTY ATTORNEY: How do you mean—queer?

HALE: Well, as if she didn't know what she was going to do next. And kind of done up.

COUNTY ATTORNEY: How did she seem to feel about your coming?

HALE: Why, I don't think she minded—one way or other. She didn't pay much attention. I said, "How do, Mrs. Wright, it's cold, ain't it?" And she said, "Is it?"—and went on kind of pleating at her apron. Well, I was surprised; she didn't ask me to come up to the stove, or to set down, but just sat there, not even looking at me, so I said, "I want to see John." And then she—laughed. I guess you would call it a laugh. I thought of Harry and the team outside, so I said a little sharp: "Can't I see John?" "No," she says, kind o' dull like. "Ain't he home?" says I. "Yes," says she, "he's home." "Then why can't I see him?" I asked her, out of patience. "'Cause he's dead," says she. "*Dead?*" says I. She just nodded her head, not getting a bit excited, but rockin' back and forth. "Why—where is he?" says I, not knowing what to say. She just pointed upstairs—like that. [*Himself pointing to the room above.*] I got up, with the idea of going up there. I walked from there to here—then I says, "Why, what did he die of?" "He died of a rope round his neck," says she, and just went on pleatin' at her apron. Well, I went out and called Harry. I thought I might—need help. We went upstairs and there he was lyin'—

COUNTY ATTORNEY: I think I'd rather have you go into that upstairs, where you can point it all out. Just go on now with the rest of the story.

HALE: Well, my first thought was to get that rope off. It looked . . . [*Stops, his face twitches.*] . . . but Harry, he went up to him, and he said, "No, he's dead all right, and we'd better not touch anything." So we went back downstairs. She was still sitting that same way. "Has anybody been notified?" I asked. "No," says she unconcerned. "Who did this, Mrs. Wright?" said Harry. He said it business-like—and she stopped pleatin' of her apron. "I don't know," she says. "You don't *know*?" says Harry. "No," says she. "Weren't you sleepin' in the bed with him?" says Harry. "Yes," says she, "but I was on the inside." "Somebody slipped a rope round his neck and strangled him and you didn't wake up?" says Harry. "I didn't wake up," she said after him. We must 'a looked as if we didn't see how that could be, for after a minute she said, "I sleep sound." Harry was going to ask her more questions but I said maybe we ought to let her tell her story first to the coroner, or the sheriff, so Harry went fast as he could to Rivers' place, where there's a telephone.

COUNTY ATTORNEY: And what did Mrs. Wright do when she knew that you had gone for the coroner?

HALE: She moved from that chair to this one over here [*Pointing to a small chair in the corner.*] and just sat there with her hands held together and looking down. I got a feeling that I ought to make some conversation, so I said I had come in to see if John wanted to put in a telephone, and at that she started to laugh, and then she stopped and looked at me— scared. [*The* COUNTY ATTORNEY, *who has had his notebook out, makes a note.*] I dunno, maybe it wasn't scared. I wouldn't like to say it was. Soon Harry got back, and then Dr. Lloyd came, and you, Mr. Peters, and so I guess that's all I know that you don't.

COUNTY ATTORNEY: [*Looking around.*] I guess we'll go upstairs first—and then out to the barn and around there. [*To the* SHERIFF.] You're convinced that there was nothing important here—nothing that would point to any motive?

SHERIFF: Nothing here but kitchen things.

[*The* COUNTY ATTORNEY, *after again looking around the kitchen, opens the door of a cupboard closet. He gets up on a chair and looks on a shelf. Pulls his hand away, sticky.*]

COUNTY ATTORNEY: Here's a nice mess.

[*The women draw nearer.*]

MRS. PETERS: [*To the other woman.*] Oh, her fruit; it did freeze. [*To the* LAWYER.] She worried about that when it turned so cold. She said the fire'd go out and her jars would break.

SHERIFF: Well, can you beat the women! Held for murder and worryin' about her preserves.

COUNTY ATTORNEY: I guess before we're through she may have something more serious than preserves to worry about.

HALE: Well, women are used to worrying over trifles.

[*The two women move a little closer together.*]

COUNTY ATTORNEY: [*With the gallantry of a young politician.*] And yet, for all their worries, what would we do without the ladies? [*The women do not unbend. He goes to the sink, takes a dipperful of water from the pail and pouring it into a basin, washes his hands. Starts to wipe them on the roller towel, turns it for a cleaner place.*] Dirty towels! [*Kicks his foot against the pans under the sink.*] Not much of a housekeeper, would you say, ladies?

MRS. HALE: [*Stiffly.*] There's a great deal of work to be done on a farm.

COUNTY ATTORNEY: To be sure. And yet [*With a little bow to her.*] I know there are some Dickson county farmhouses which do not have such roller towels. [*He gives it a pull to expose its length again.*]

MRS. HALE: Those towels get dirty awful quick. Men's hands aren't always as clean as they might be.

COUNTY ATTORNEY: Ah, loyal to your sex, I see. But you and Mrs. Wright were neighbors. I suppose you were friends, too.

MRS. HALE: [*Shaking her head.*] I've not seen much of her of late years. I've not been in this house—it's more than a year.

COUNTY ATTORNEY: And why was that? You didn't like her?

MRS. HALE: I liked her all well enough. Farmers' wives have their hands full, Mr. Henderson. And then—

COUNTY ATTORNEY: Yes—?

MRS. HALE: [*Looking about.*] It never seemed a very cheerful place.

COUNTY ATTORNEY: No—it's not cheerful. I shouldn't say she had the home-making instinct.

MRS. HALE: Well, I don't know as Wright had, either.

COUNTY ATTORNEY: You mean that they didn't get on very well?

MRS. HALE: No, I don't mean anything. But I don't think a place'd be any cheerfuller for John Wright's being in it.

COUNTY ATTORNEY: I'd like to talk more of that a little later. I want to get the lay of things upstairs now. [*He goes to the left, where three steps lead to a stair door.*]

SHERIFF: I suppose anything Mrs. Peters does'll be all right. She was to take in some clothes for her, you know, and a few little things. We left in such a hurry yesterday.

COUNTY ATTORNEY: Yes, but I would like to see what you take, Mrs. Peters, and keep an eye out for anything that might be of use to us.

MRS. PETERS: Yes, Mr. Henderson. [*The women listen to the men's steps on the stairs, then look about the kitchen.*]

MRS. HALE: I'd hate to have men coming into my kitchen, snooping around and criticizing. [*She arranges the pans under sink which the LAWYER had shoved out of place.*]

MRS. PETERS: Of course it's no more than their duty.

MRS. HALE: Duty's all right, but I guess that deputy sheriff that came out to make the fire might have got a little of this on. [*Gives the roller towel a pull.*] Wish I'd thought of that sooner. Seems mean to talk about her for not having things slicked up when she had to come away in such a hurry.

MRS. PETERS: [*Who has gone to a small table in the left rear corner of the room, and lifted one end of a towel that covers a pan.*] She had bread set. [*Stands still.*]

MRS. HALE: [*Eyes fixed on a loaf of bread beside the bread box, which is on a low shelf at the other side of the room. Moves slowly toward it.*] She was going to put this in there. [*Picks up loaf, then abruptly drops it. In a manner of returning to familiar things.*] It's a shame about her fruit. I wonder if it's all gone. [*Gets up on the chair and looks.*] I think there's some here that's all right, Mrs. Peters. Yes—here; [*Holding it toward the window.*] this is cherries, too. [*Looking again.*] I declare I believe that's the only one. [*Gets down, bottle in her hand. Goes to the sink and wipes it off on the outside.*] She'll feel awful bad after all her hard work in the hot weather. I remember the afternoon I put up my cherries last summer. [*She puts the bottle on the big kitchen table, center of the room. With a sigh, is about to sit down in the rocking-chair. Before she is seated realizes what chair it is; with a slow look at it, steps back. The chair, which she has touched, rocks back and forth.*]

MRS. PETERS: Well, I must get those things from the front room closet. [*She goes to the door at the right, but after looking into the other room, steps back.*] You coming with me, Mrs. Hale? You could help me carry them. [*They go in the other room; reappear,* MRS. PETERS *carrying a dress and skirt,* MRS. HALE *following with a pair of shoes.*] My, it's cold in there. [*She puts the clothes on the big table, and hurries to the stove.*]

MRS. HALE: [*Examining the skirt.*] Wright was close. I think maybe that's why she kept so much to herself. She didn't even belong to the Ladies Aid. I suppose she felt she couldn't do her part, and then you don't enjoy things when you feel shabby. She used to wear pretty clothes and be lively, when she was Minnie Foster, one of the town girls singing in the choir. But that—oh, that was thirty years ago. This all you was to take in?

MRS. PETERS: She said she wanted an apron. Funny thing to want, for there isn't much to get you dirty in jail, goodness knows. But I suppose just to make her feel more natural. She said they was in the top drawer in this cupboard. Yes, here. And then her little shawl that always hung behind the door. [*Opens stair door and looks.*] Yes, here it is. [*Quickly shuts door leading upstairs.*]

MRS. HALE: [*Abruptly moving toward her.*] Mrs. Peters?

MRS. PETERS: Yes, Mrs. Hale?

MRS. HALE: Do you think she did it?

MRS. PETERS: [*In a frightened voice.*] Oh, I don't know.

MRS. HALE: Well, I don't think she did. Asking for an apron and her little shawl. Worrying about her fruit.

MRS. PETERS: [*Starts to speak, glances up, where footsteps are heard in the room above. In a low voice.*] Mr. Peters says it looks bad for her. Mr. Henderson is awful sarcastic in a speech and he'll make fun of her sayin' she didn't wake up.

MRS. HALE: Well, I guess John Wright didn't wake when they was slipping that rope under his neck.

MRS. PETERS: No, it's strange. It must have been done awful crafty and still. They say it was such a—funny way to kill a man, rigging it all up like that.

MRS. HALE: That's just what Mr. Hale said. There was a gun in the house. He says that's what he can't understand.

MRS. PETERS: Mr. Henderson said coming out that what was needed for the case was a motive; something to show anger, or—sudden feeling.

MRS. HALE: [*Who is standing by the table.*] Well, I don't see any signs of anger around here. [*She puts her hand on the dish towel which lies on the table, stands looking down at table, one half of which is clean, the other half messy.*] It's wiped to here. [*Makes a move as if to finish work, then turns and looks at loaf of bread outside the bread box. Drops towel. In that voice of coming back to familiar things.*] Wonder how they are finding things upstairs. I hope she had it a little more red-up[2] up there. You know, it seems kind of *sneaking*. Locking her up in town and then coming out here and trying to get her own house to turn against her!

MRS. PETERS: But Mrs. Hale, the law is the law.

MRS. HALE: I s'pose 'tis. [*Unbuttoning her coat.*] Better loosen up your things, Mrs. Peters. You won't feel them when you go out.

[MRS. PETERS *takes off her fur tippet, goes to hang it on hook at back of room, stands looking at the under part of the small corner table.*]

MRS. PETERS: She was piecing a quilt. [*She brings the large sewing basket and they look at the bright pieces.*]

MRS. HALE: It's log cabin pattern. Pretty, isn't it? I wonder if she was goin' to quilt it or just knot it?

[*Footsteps have been heard coming down the stairs. The* SHERIFF *enters followed by* HALE *and the* COUNTY ATTORNEY.]

SHERIFF: They wonder if she was going to quilt it or just knot it!

[*The men laugh, the women look abashed.*]

COUNTY ATTORNEY: [*Rubbing his hands over the stove.*] Frank's fire didn't do much up there, did it? Well, let's go out to the barn and get that cleared up.

[*The men go outside.*]

---

2. Tidied up.

MRS. HALE: [*Resentfully.*] I don't know as there's anything so strange, our takin' up our time with little things while we're waiting for them to get the evidence. [*She sits down at the big table smoothing out a block with decision.*] I don't see as it's anything to laugh about.

MRS. PETERS: [*Apologetically.*] Of course they've got awful important things on their minds. [*Pulls up a chair and joins* MRS. HALE *at the table.*]

MRS. HALE: [*Examining another block.*] Mrs. Peters, look at this one. Here, this is the one she was working on, and look at the sewing! All the rest of it has been so nice and even. And look at this! It's all over the place! Why, it looks as if she didn't know what she was about! [*After she has said this they look at each other, then start to glance back at the door. After an instant* MRS. HALE *has pulled at a knot and ripped the sewing.*]

MRS. PETERS: Oh, what are you doing, Mrs. Hale?

MRS. HALE: [*Mildly.*] Just pulling out a stitch or two that's not sewed very good. [*Threading the needle.*] Bad sewing always made me fidgety.

MRS. PETERS: [*Nervously.*] I don't think we ought to touch things.

MRS. HALE: I'll just finish up this end. [*Suddenly stopping and leaning forward.*] Mrs. Peters?

MRS. PETERS: Yes, Mrs. Hale?

MRS. HALE: What do you suppose she was so nervous about?

MRS. PETERS: Oh—I don't know. I don't know as she was nervous. I sometimes sew awful queer when I'm just tired. [MRS. HALE *starts to say something, looks at* MRS. PETERS, *then goes on sewing.*] Well, I must get these things wrapped up. They may be through sooner than we think. [*Putting apron and other things together.*] I wonder where I can find a piece of paper, and string.

MRS. HALE: In that cupboard, maybe.

MRS. PETERS: [*Looking in cupboard.*] Why, here's a bird-cage. [*Holds it up.*] Did she have a bird, Mrs. Hale?

MRS. HALE: Why, I don't know whether she did or not—I've not been here for so long. There was a man around last year selling canaries cheap, but I don't know as she took one; maybe she did. She used to sing real pretty herself.

MRS. PETERS: [*Glancing around.*] Seems funny to think of a bird here. But she must have had one, or why would she have a cage? I wonder what happened to it.

MRS. HALE: I s'pose maybe the cat got it.

MRS. PETERS: No, she didn't have a cat. She's got that feeling some people have about cats—being afraid of them. My cat got in her room and she was real upset and asked me to take it out.

MRS. HALE: My sister Bessie was like that. Queer, ain't it?

MRS. PETERS: [*Examining the cage.*] Why, look at this door. It's broke. One hinge is pulled apart.

MRS. HALE: [*Looking too.*] Looks as if someone must have been rough with it.

MRS. PETERS: Why, yes. [*She brings the cage forward and puts it on the table.*]

MRS. HALE: I wish if they're going to find any evidence they'd be about it. I don't like this place.

MRS. PETERS: But I'm awful glad you came with me, Mrs. Hale. It would be lonesome for me sitting here alone.

MRS. HALE: It would, wouldn't it? [*Dropping her sewing.*] But I tell you what I do wish, Mrs. Peters. I wish I had come over sometimes when *she* was here. I—[*Looking around the room.*]—wish I had.

MRS. PETERS: But of course you were awful busy, Mrs. Hale—your house and your children.

MRS. HALE: I could've come. I stayed away because it weren't cheerful—and that's why I ought to have come. I—I've never liked this place. Maybe because it's down in a hollow and you don't see the road. I dunno what it is, but it's a lonesome place and always was. I wish I had come over to see Minnie Foster sometimes. I can see now—[*Shakes her head.*]

MRS. PETERS: Well, you mustn't reproach yourself, Mrs. Hale. Somehow we just don't see how it is with other folks until—something comes up.

MRS. HALE: Not having children makes less work—but it makes a quiet house, and Wright out to work all day, and no company when he did come in. Did you know John Wright, Mrs. Peters?

MRS. PETERS: Not to know him; I've seen him in town. They say he was a good man.

MRS. HALE: Yes—good; he didn't drink, and kept his word as well as most, I guess, and paid his debts. But he was a hard man, Mrs. Peters. Just to pass the time of day with him—[*Shivers.*] Like a raw wind that gets to the bone. [*Pauses, her eye falling on the cage.*] I should think she would 'a wanted a bird. But what do you suppose went with it?

MRS. PETERS: I don't know, unless it got sick and died. [*She reaches over and swings the broken door, swings it again, both women watch it.*]

MRS. HALE: You weren't raised round here, were you? [MRS. PETERS *shakes her head.*] You didn't know—her?

MRS. PETERS: Not till they brought her yesterday.

MRS. HALE: She—come to think of it, she was kind of like a bird herself—real sweet and pretty, but kind of timid and—fluttery. How—she—did—change. [*Silence; then as if struck by a happy thought and relieved to get back to everyday things.*] Tell you what, Mrs. Peters, why don't you take the quilt in with you? It might take up her mind.

MRS. PETERS: Why, I think that's a real nice idea, Mrs. Hale. There couldn't possibly be any objection to it, could there? Now, just what would I take? I wonder if her patches are in here—and her things. [*They look in the sewing basket.*]

MRS. HALE: Here's some red. I expect this has got sewing things in it. [*Brings out a fancy box.*] What a pretty box. Looks like something somebody would give you. Maybe her scissors are in here. [*Opens box. Suddenly puts* her hand to her nose.] Why—[MRS. PETERS *bends nearer, then turns her face away.*] There's something wrapped up in this piece of silk.

MRS. PETERS: Why, this isn't her scissors.

MRS. HALE: [*Lifting the silk.*] Oh, Mrs. Peters—it's—

[MRS. PETERS *bends closer.*]

MRS. PETERS: It's the bird.

MRS. HALE: [*Jumping up.*] But, Mrs. Peters—look at it! Its neck! Look at its neck! It's all—other side *to.*

MRS. PETERS: Somebody—wrung—its—neck.

[*Their eyes meet. A look of growing comprehension, of horror. Steps are heard outside.* MRS. HALE *slips box under quilt pieces, and sinks into her chair. Enter* SHERIFF *and* COUNTY ATTORNEY. MRS. PETERS *rises.*]

COUNTY ATTORNEY: [*As one turning from serious things to little pleasantries.*] Well ladies, have you decided whether she was going to quilt it or knot it?

MRS. PETERS: We think she was going to—knot it.

COUNTY ATTORNEY: Well, that's interesting, I'm sure. [*Seeing the bird-cage.*] Has the bird flown?

MRS. HALE: [*Putting more quilt pieces over the box.*] We think the—cat got it.

COUNTY ATTORNEY: [*Preoccupied.*] Is there a cat?

[MRS. HALE *glances in a quick covert way at* MRS. PETERS.]

MRS. PETERS: Well, not *now.* They're superstitious, you know. They leave.

COUNTY ATTORNEY: [*To* SHERIFF PETERS, *continuing an interrupted conversation.*] No sign at all of anyone having come from the outside. Their own rope. Now let's go up again and go over it piece by piece. [*They start upstairs.*] It would have to have been someone who knew just the—

[MRS. PETERS *sits down. The two women sit there not looking at one another, but as if peering into something and at the same time holding back. When they talk now it is in the manner of feeling their way over strange ground, as if afraid of what they are saying, but as if they cannot help saying it.*]

MRS. HALE: She liked the bird. She was going to bury it in that pretty box.

MRS. PETERS: [*In a whisper.*] When I was a girl—my kitten—there was a boy took a hatchet, and before my eyes—and before I could get there—[*Covers her face an instant.*] If they hadn't held me back I would have—[*Catches herself, looks upstairs where steps are heard, falters weakly.*]—hurt him.

MRS. HALE: [*With a slow look around her.*] I wonder how it would seem never to have had any children around. [*Pause.*] No, Wright wouldn't like the bird—a thing that sang. She used to sing. He killed that, too.

MRS. PETERS: [*Moving uneasily.*] We don't know who killed the bird.

MRS. HALE: I knew John Wright.

MRS. PETERS: It was an awful thing was done in this house that night, Mrs. Hale. Killing a man while he slept, slipping a rope around his neck that choked the life out of him.

MRS. HALE: His neck. Choked the life out of him. [*Her hand goes out and rests on the bird-cage.*]

MRS. PETERS: [*With rising voice.*] We don't know who killed him. We don't know.

MRS. HALE: [*Her own feeling not interrupted.*] If there's been years and years of nothing, then a bird to sing to you, it would be awful—still, after the bird was still.

MRS. PETERS: [*Something within her speaking.*] I know what stillness is. When we homesteaded in Dakota, and my first baby died—after he was two years old, and me with no other then—

MRS. HALE: [*Moving.*] How soon do you suppose they'll be through, looking for the evidence?

MRS. PETERS: I know what stillness is. [*Pulling herself back.*] The law has got to punish crime, Mrs. Hale.

MRS. HALE: [*Not as if answering that.*] I wish you'd seen Minnie Foster when she wore a white dress with blue ribbons and stood up there in the choir and sang. [*A look around the room.*] Oh, I *wish* I'd come over here once in a while! That was a crime! That was a crime! Who's going to punish that?

MRS. PETERS: [*Looking upstairs.*] We mustn't—take on.

MRS. HALE: I might have known she needed help! I know how things can be—for women. I tell you, it's queer, Mrs. Peters. We live close together and we live far apart. We all go through the same things—it's all just a different kind of the same thing. [*Brushes her eyes, noticing the bottle of fruit, reaches out for it.*] If I was you, I wouldn't tell her her fruit was gone. Tell her it *ain't*. Tell her it's all right. Take this in to prove it to her. She—she may never know whether it was broke or not.

MRS. PETERS: [*Takes the bottle, looks about for something to wrap it in; takes petticoat from the clothes brought from the other room, very nervously begins winding this around the bottle. In a false voice.*] My, it's a good thing the men couldn't hear us. Wouldn't they just laugh! Getting all stirred up over a little thing like a—dead canary. As if that could have anything to do with—with—wouldn't they *laugh*!

[*The men are heard coming down stairs.*]

MRS. HALE: [*Under her breath.*] Maybe they would—maybe they wouldn't.

COUNTY ATTORNEY: No, Peters, it's all perfectly clear except a reason for doing it. But you know juries when it comes to women. If there was some definite thing. Something to show—something to make a story about—a thing that would connect up with this strange way of doing it—

[*The women's eyes meet for an instant. Enter HALE from outer door.*]

HALE: Well, I've got the team around. Pretty cold out there.

COUNTY ATTORNEY: I'm going to stay here a while by myself. [*To the* SHERIFF.] You can send Frank out for me, can't you? I want to go over everything. I'm not satisfied that we can't do better.

SHERIFF: Do you want to see what Mrs. Peters is going to take in?

[*The* LAWYER *goes to the table, picks up the apron, laughs.*]

COUNTY ATTORNEY: Oh, I guess they're not very dangerous things the ladies have picked out. [*Moves a few things about, disturbing the quilt pieces which cover the box. Steps back.*] No, Mrs. Peters doesn't need supervising. For that matter, a sheriff's wife is married to the law. Ever think of it that way, Mrs. Peters?

MRS. PETERS: Not—just that way.

SHERIFF: [*Chuckling.*] Married to the law. [*Moves toward the other room.*] I just want you to come in here a minute, George. We ought to take a look at these windows.

COUNTY ATTORNEY: [*Scoffingly.*] Oh, windows!

SHERIFF: We'll be right out, Mr. Hale.

[HALE *goes outside. The* SHERIFF *follows the* COUNTY ATTORNEY *into the other room. Then* MRS. HALE *rises, hands tight together, looking intensely at* MRS. PETERS, *whose eyes make a slow turn, finally meeting* MRS. HALE*'s. A moment* MRS. HALE *holds her, then her own eyes point the way to where the box is concealed. Suddenly* MRS. PETERS *throws back quilt pieces and tries to put the box in the bag she is wearing. It is too big. She opens box, starts to take bird out, cannot touch it, goes to pieces, stands there helpless. Sound of a knob turning in the other room.* MRS. HALE *snatches the box and puts it in the pocket of her big coat. Enter* COUNTY ATTORNEY *and* SHERIFF.]

COUNTY ATTORNEY: [*Facetiously.*] Well, Henry, at least we found out that she was not going to quilt it. She was going to—what is it you call it, ladies?

MRS. HALE: [*Her hand against her pocket.*] We call it—knot it, Mr. Henderson.

CURTAIN

1916

QUESTIONS

1. If we were watching a production of *Trifles* and had no cast list, how would we gradually piece together the fact that Mrs. Peters is the sheriff's wife? What are the earliest lines of dialogue that allow an audience to infer this fact?

2. What lines in the play characterize Mrs. Hale's reaction to the men's behavior and attitudes? What lines characterize Mrs. Peters's reaction to the men early in the play, and what lines show her feelings changing later in the play?

What might account for both their initial differences and then their evolving solidarity with Mrs. Wright?

3. What are the "trifles" that the men ignore and the two women notice? Why do the men dismiss them, and why do the women see these things as significant clues? What is the thematic importance of these "trifles"?

4. How would you stage the key moment of the play, Mrs. Hale's discovery of the bird in the sewing basket? What facial expression would she have, what body language? Where would you place Mrs. Peters, and what would she be doing? How would you use lighting to heighten the effectiveness of the scene?

5. To what degree is each of the characters in the play "round," or well developed? To what degree are any of them stereotypes?

6. If a twenty-first-century playwright were to write an updated version of *Trifles*, what details of plot, character, and setting would be different from those in Glaspell's play? What would be the same? What are some possible "trifles" that might serve the same dramatic functions as those in Glaspell's play?

forget forget to read

TOM STOPPARD

The Real Inspector Hound

CHARACTERS

MOON	SIMON	MAGNUS
BIRDBOOT	FELICITY	INSPECTOR HOUND
MRS. DRUDGE	CYNTHIA	

The first thing is that the audience appear to be confronted by their own reflection in a huge mirror. Impossible. However, back there in the gloom—not at the footlights—a bank of plush seats and pale smudges of faces. The total effect having been established, it can be progressively faded out as the play goes on, until the front row remains to remind us of the rest and then, finally, merely two seats in that row—one of which is now occupied by MOON. *Between* MOON *and the auditorium is an acting area which represents, in as realistic an idiom as possible, the drawing-room of Muldoon Manor. French windows at one side. A telephone fairly well upstage (i.e. towards* MOON). *The body of a man lies sprawled face down on the floor in front of a large settee. This settee must be of a size and design to allow it to be wheeled over the body, hiding it completely. Silence. The room. The body.* MOON.

MOON *stares blankly ahead. He turns his head to one side then the other, then up, then down—waiting. He picks up his programme and reads the front cover. He turns over the page and reads.*

He turns over the page and reads.
He turns over the page and reads.
He turns over the page and reads.
He looks at the back cover and reads.

He puts it down and crosses his legs and looks about. He stares front. Behind him and to one side, barely visible, a man enters and sits down: BIRDBOOT.

Pause. MOON *picks up his programme, glances at the front cover and puts it down impatiently. Pause . . . Behind him there is the crackle of a chocolate-box, absurdly loud.* MOON *looks round. He and* BIRDBOOT *see each other. They are clearly known to each other. They acknowledge each other with constrained waves.* MOON *looks straight ahead.* BIRDBOOT *comes down to join him.*

Note: *Almost always,* MOON *and* BIRDBOOT *converse in tones suitable for an auditorium, sometimes a whisper. However good the acoustics might be, they will have to have microphones where they are sitting. The effect must be* not *of sound picked up, amplified and flung out at the audience, but of sound picked up, carried and gently dispersed around the auditorium.*

Anyway, BIRDBOOT, *with a box of Black Magic,*[1] *makes his way down to join* MOON *and plumps himself down next to him, plumpish middle-aged* BIRDBOOT *and younger, taller, less-relaxed* MOON.

BIRDBOOT: [*sitting down; conspiratorially*] Me and the lads have had a meeting in the bar and decided it's first-class family entertainment but if it goes on beyond half-past ten it's self-indulgent—pass it on . . . [*and laughs jovially*] I'm on my own tonight, don't mind if I join you?

MOON: Hello, Birdboot.

BIRDBOOT: Where's Higgs?

MOON: I'm standing in.

MOON AND BIRDBOOT: Where's Higgs?

MOON: Every time.

BIRDBOOT: What?

MOON: It is as if we only existed one at a time, combining to achieve continuity. I keep space warm for Higgs. My presence defines his absence, his absence confirms my presence, his presence precludes mine. . . . When Higgs and I walk down this aisle together to claim our common seat, the oceans will fall into the sky and the trees will hang with fishes.

BIRDBOOT: [*he has not been paying attention, looking around vaguely, now catches up*] Where's Higgs?

MOON: The very sight of me with a complimentary ticket is enough. The streets are impassable tonight, the country is rising and the cry goes up from hill to hill—Where—is—Higgs? [*Small pause.*] Perhaps he's dead at last, or trapped in a lift[2] somewhere, or succumbed to amnesia, wandering the land with his turn-ups stuffed with ticket-stubs.

[BIRDBOOT *regards him doubtfully for a moment.*]

---

1. Popular brand of chocolates sold in London theaters.
2. Elevator. *Turn-ups*: trouser cuffs.

BIRDBOOT: Yes.... Yes, well I didn't bring Myrtle tonight—not exactly her cup of tea, I thought, tonight.

MOON: Over her head, you mean?

BIRDBOOT: Well, no—I mean it's a sort of a *thriller*, isn't it?

MOON: Is it?

BIRDBOOT: That's what I heard. Who killed thing?—no one will leave the house.

MOON: I suppose so. Underneath.

BIRDBOOT: *Underneath*?!? It's a whodunnit, man!—Look at it!

[*They look at it. The room. The body. Silence.*]

Has it started yet?

MOON: Yes.

[*Pause. They look at it.*]

BIRDBOOT: Are you sure?

MOON: It's a pause.

BIRDBOOT: You can't start with a *pause*! If you want my opinion there's total panic back there. [*Laughs and subsides.*] Where's Higgs tonight, then?

MOON: It will follow me to the grave and become my epitaph—Here lies Moon the second string: where's Higgs? ... Sometimes I dream of revolution, a bloody *coup d'etat* by the second rank—troupes of actors slaughtered by their understudies, magicians sawn in half by indefatigably smiling glamour girls, cricket teams wiped out by marauding bands of twelfth men[3]—I dream of champions chopped down by rabbit-punching sparring partners while eternal bridesmaids turn and rape the bridegrooms over the sausage rolls and parliamentary private secretaries plant bombs in the Minister's Humber[4]—comedians die on provincial stages, robbed of their feeds by mutely triumphant stooges—and—march—an army of assistants and deputies, the seconds-in-command, the runners-up, the right-hand men—storming the palace gates wherein the second son has already mounted the throne having committed regicide with a croquet-mallet—stand-ins of the world stand up!—

[*Beat.*][5] Sometimes I dream of Higgs.

[*Pause.* BIRDBOOT *regards him doubtfully. He is at a loss, and grasps reality in the form of his box of chocolates.*]

BIRDBOOT: [*Chewing into mike.*] Have a chocolate!

MOON: What kind?

BIRDBOOT: [*Chewing into mike.*] Black Magic.

---

3. Substitutes. A cricket team ("side") fields eleven players at a time.

4. A car once manufactured in Britain. *Feeds:* cues provided to comedians by straight men, "stooges." 5. In drama, a "beat" is a pause.

MOON: No thanks.

> [*Chewing stops dead.*]
> [*Of such tiny victories and defeats. . . .*]

BIRDBOOT: I'll give you a tip, then. Watch the girl.

MOON: You think she did it?

BIRDBOOT: No, no—the *girl*, watch her.

MOON: What girl?

BIRDBOOT: You won't know her, I'll give you a nudge.

MOON: *You* know her, do you?

BIRDBOOT: [*suspiciously, bridling*] What's *that* supposed to mean?

MOON: I beg your pardon?

BIRDBOOT: I'm trying to tip you a wink—give you a nudge as good as a tip—
for God's sake, Moon, what's the matter with you?—you could do yourself some good, spotting her first time out—she's new, from the provinces,
going straight to the top. I don't want to put words into your mouth but
a word from us and we could make her.

MOON: I suppose you've made dozens of them, like that.

BIRDBOOT: [*Instantly outraged.*] I'll have you know I'm a family man devoted
to my homely but good-natured wife, and if you're suggesting—

MOON: No, no—

BIRDBOOT: —A man of my scrupulous morality—

MOON: I'm sorry—

BIRDBOOT: —falsely besmirched.

MOON: Is that her?

> [*For* MRS. DRUDGE *has entered.*]

BIRDBOOT: —don't be absurd, wouldn't be seen dead with the old—ah.

> [MRS. DRUDGE *is the char,*[6] *middle-aged, turbanned. She heads straight for the
> radio, dusting on the trot.*]

MOON: [*reading his programme*] Mrs. Drudge the Help.

RADIO: [*without preamble, having been switched on by* MRS. DRUDGE] We interrupt our programme for a special police message.

> [MRS. DRUDGE *stops to listen.*]

The search still goes on for the escaped madman who is on the run in
Essex.

MRS. DRUDGE: [*fear and dismay*] Essex!

RADIO: County police led by Inspector Hound have received a report that
the man has been seen in the desolate marshes around Muldoon
Manor.

---

6. British term for cleaning lady or maid who does not live in the house.

[*Fearful gasp from* MRS. DRUDGE.]

The man is wearing a darkish suit with a lightish shirt. He is of medium height and build and youngish. Anyone seeing a man answering to this description and acting suspiciously, is advised to phone the nearest police station.

[*A man answering this description has appeared behind* MRS. DRUDGE. *He is acting suspiciously. He creeps in. He creeps out.* MRS. DRUDGE *does not see him. He does not see the body.*]

That is the end of the police message.

[MRS. DRUDGE *turns off the radio and resumes her cleaning. She does not see the body. Quite fortuitously, her view of the body is always blocked, and when it isn't she has her back to it. However, she is dusting and polishing her way towards it.*]

BIRDBOOT: So that's what they say about me, is it?

MOON: What?

BIRDBOOT: Oh, I know what goes on behind my back—sniggers—slanders—hole-in-corner innuendo—What have you heard?

MOON: Nothing.

BIRDBOOT: [*urbanely*] Tittle tattle. Tittle, my dear fellow, tattle. I take no notice of it—the sly envy of scandal mongers—I can afford to ignore them, I'm a respectable married man—

MOON: Incidentally—

BIRDBOOT: Water off a duck's back, I assure you.

MOON: Who was that lady I saw you with last night?

BIRDBOOT: [*unexpectedly stung into fury*] How dare you! [*More quietly*] How dare you. Don't you come here with your slimy insinuations! My wife Myrtle understands perfectly well that a man of my critical standing is obliged occasionally to mingle with the world of the footlights, simply by way of keeping *au fait*[7] with the latest—

MOON: I'm sorry—

BIRDBOOT: That a critic of my scrupulous integrity should be vilified and pilloried in the stocks of common gossip—

MOON: Ssssh—

BIRDBOOT: I have nothing to hide!—why, if this should reach the ears of my beloved Myrtle—

MOON: Can I have a chocolate?

BIRDBOOT: What? Oh—[*Mollified.*] Oh yes—my dear fellow—yes, let's have a chocolate—No point in—yes, good show. [*Pops chocolate into his mouth*

---

7. In touch; knowledgeable (French).

and chews.] Which one do you fancy?—Cherry? Strawberry? Coffee cream? Turkish delight?

MOON: I'll have montelimar.

[*Chewing stops.*]

BIRDBOOT: Ah. Sorry. [*Just missed that one.*]

MOON: Gooseberry fondue?

BIRDBOOT: No.

MOON: Pistacchio fudge? Nectarine cluster? Hickory nut praline? Chateau Neuf du Pape '55 cracknell?[8]

BIRDBOOT: I'm afraid not . . . Caramel?

MOON: Yes, all right.

BIRDBOOT: Thanks very much. [*He gives* MOON *a chocolate. Pause.*] Incidentally, old chap, I'd be grateful if you didn't mention—I mean, you know how these misunderstandings get about. . . .

MOON: What?

BIRDBOOT: The fact is, Myrtle simply doesn't *like* the theatre. . . .

[*He tails off hopelessly.* MRS. DRUDGE, *whose discovery of the body has been imminent, now—by way of tidying the room—slides the couch over the corpse, hiding it completely. She resumes dusting and humming.*]

MOON: By the way, congratulations, Birdboot.

BIRDBOOT: What?

MOON: At the Theatre Royal. Your entire review reproduced in neon!

BIRDBOOT: [*pleased.*] Oh . . . that old thing.

MOON: You've seen it, of course.

BIRDBOOT: [*vaguely.*] Well, I was passing. . . .

MOON: I definitely intend to take a second look when it has settled down.

BIRDBOOT: As a matter of fact I have a few colour transparencies—I don't know whether you'd care to . . . ?

MOON: Please, please—love to, love to. . . .

[BIRDBOOT *hands over a few colour slides and a battery-powered viewer which* MOON *holds up to his eyes as he speaks.*]

Yes . . . yes . . . lovely . . . awfully sound. It has scale, it has colour, it is, in the best sense of the word, electric. Large as it is, it is a small masterpiece—I would go so far as to say—kinetic without being pop, and having said that, I think it must be said that here we have a review that adds a new dimension to the critical scene. I urge you to make haste to the Theatre Royal, for this is the stuff of life itself. [*Handing*

---

8. A hard, sweet biscuit. *Chateau Neuf du Pape '55*: a fine wine in an excellent vintage year. The flavors that Moon requests, after "montelimar," are all fanciful—not found in any Black Magic box.

back the slides, *morosely*]: All I ever got was "Unforgettable" on the posters for . . . What was it?

BIRDBOOT: Oh—yes—I know. . . . Was that you? I thought it was Higgs.

[*The phone rings.* MRS. DRUDGE *seems to have been waiting for it to do so and for the last few seconds has been dusting it with an intense concentration. She snatches it up.*]

MRS. DRUDGE: [*into phone*] Hello, the drawing-room of Lady Muldoon's country residence one morning in early spring? . . . Hello!—the draw— Who? Who did you wish to speak to? I'm afraid there is no one of that name here, this is all very mysterious and I'm sure it's leading up to something. I hope nothing is amiss for we, that is Lady Muldoon and her houseguests, are here cut off from the world, including Magnus, the wheelchair-ridden half-brother of her ladyship's husband Lord Albert Muldoon who ten years ago went out for a walk on the cliffs and was never seen again—and all alone, for they had no children.

MOON: Derivative, of course.

BIRDBOOT: But quite sound.

MRS. DRUDGE: Should a stranger enter our midst, which I very much doubt, I will tell him you called. Good-bye.

[*She puts down the phone and catches sight of the previously seen suspicious character who has now entered again, more suspiciously than ever, through the french windows. He senses her stare, freezes, and straightens up.*]

SIMON: Ah!—hello there! I'm Simon Gascoyne, I hope you don't mind, the door was open so I wandered in. I'm a friend of Lady Muldoon, the lady of the house, having made her acquaintance through a mutual friend, Felicity Cunningham, shortly after moving into this neighbourhood just the other day.

MRS. DRUDGE: I'm Mrs. Drudge. I don't live in but I pop in on my bicycle when the weather allows to help in the running of charming though somewhat isolated Muldoon Manor. Judging by the time [*she glances at the clock*] you did well to get here before high water cut us off for all practical purposes from the outside world.

SIMON: I took the short cut over the cliffs and followed one of the old smugglers' paths through the treacherous swamps that surround this strangely inaccessible house.

MRS. DRUDGE: Yes, many visitors have remarked on the topographical quirk in the local strata whereby there are no roads leading from the Manor, though there *are* ways of getting *to* it, weather allowing.

SIMON: Yes, well I must say it's a lovely day so far.

MRS. DRUDGE: Ah, but now that the cuckoo-beard is in bud there'll be fog before the sun hits Foster's Ridge.

SIMON: I say, it's wonderful how you country people really know weather.

MRS. DRUDGE: [*suspiciously*] Know whether what?

SIMON: [*glancing out of the window.*] Yes, it does seem to be coming on a bit foggy.

MRS. DRUDGE: The fog is very treacherous around here—it rolls off the sea without warning, shrouding the cliffs in a deadly mantle of blind man's buff.

SIMON: Yes, I've heard it said.

MRS. DRUDGE: I've known whole week-ends when Muldoon Manor, as this lovely old Queen Anne House is called, might as well have been floating on the pack ice for all the good it would have done phoning the police. It was on such a week-end as this that Lord Muldoon who had lately brought his beautiful bride back to the home of his ancestors, walked out of this house ten years ago, and his body was never found.

SIMON: Yes, indeed, poor Cynthia.

MRS. DRUDGE: His name was Albert.

SIMON: Yes indeed, poor Albert. But tell me, is Lady Muldoon about?

MRS. DRUDGE: I believe she is playing tennis on the lawn with Felicity Cunningham.

SIMON: [*startled*] Felicity Cunningham?

MRS. DRUDGE: A mutual friend, I believe you said. A happy chance. I will tell them you are here.

SIMON: Well, I can't really stay as a matter of fact—please don't disturb them—I really should be off.

MRS. DRUDGE: They would be very disappointed. It is some time since we have had a four for pontoon bridge at the Manor, and I don't play cards myself.

SIMON: There is another guest, then?

MRS. DRUDGE: Major Magnus, the crippled half-brother of Lord Muldoon who turned up out of the blue from Canada just the other day, completes the house-party.

[MRS. DRUDGE *leaves on this,* SIMON *is undecided.*]

MOON: [*ruminating quietly*] I think I must be waiting for Higgs to die.

BIRDBOOT: What?

MOON: Half afraid that I will vanish when he does.

[*The phone rings.* SIMON *picks it up.*]

SIMON: Hello?

MOON: I wonder if it's the same for Puckeridge?

BIRDBOOT AND SIMON: [*together*] Who?

MOON: Third string.

BIRDBOOT: Your stand-in?

MOON: Does he wait for Higgs and I to write each other's obituary—does he dream——?

SIMON: To whom did you wish to speak?

BIRDBOOT: What's he like?

MOON: Bitter.

SIMON: There is no one of that name here.

BIRDBOOT: No—as a critic, what's Puckeridge like as a critic?

MOON: [*laughs poisonously*] Nobody knows——

SIMON: You must have got the wrong number!

MOON: —there's always been me and Higgs.

[SIMON *replaces the phone and paces nervously. Pause.* BIRDBOOT *consults his programme.*]

BIRDBOOT: Simon Gascoyne. It's not him, of course.

MOON: What?

BIRDBOOT: I said it's not him.

MOON: Who is it, then?

BIRDBOOT: My guess is Magnus.

MOON: In disguise, you mean?

BIRDBOOT: What?

MOON: You think he's Magnus in disguise?

BIRDBOOT: I don't think you're concentrating, Moon.

MOON: I thought you said——

BIRDBOOT: You keep chattering on about Higgs and Puckeridge—what's the matter with you?

MOON: [*thoughtfully*] I wonder if they talk about me . . . ?

[*A strange impulse makes* SIMON *turn on the radio.*]

RADIO: Here is another police message. Essex county police are still searching in vain for the madman who is at large in the deadly marshes of the coastal region. Inspector Hound who is masterminding the operation, is not available for comment but it is widely believed that he has a secret plan. . . . Meanwhile police and volunteers are combing the swamps with loud-hailers, shouting, "Don't be a madman, give yourself up." That is the end of the police message. [SIMON *turns off the radio. He is clearly nervous.* MOON *and* BIRDBOOT *are on separate tracks.*]

BIRDBOOT: [*knowingly*] Oh yes . . .

MOON: Yes, I should think my name is seldom off Puckeridge's lips . . . sad, really. I mean, it's no life at all, a stand-in's stand-in.

BIRDBOOT: Yes . . . yes . . .

MOON: Higgs never gives me a second thought. I can tell by the way he nods.

BIRDBOOT: Revenge, of course.

MOON: What?

BIRDBOOT: Jealousy.

MOON: Nonsense—there's nothing *personal* in it——

BIRDBOOT: The paranoid grudge—
MOON: [*sharply first, then starting to career . . .*] It is merely that it is not enough to wax at another's wane, to be held in reserve, to be on hand, on call, to step in or not at all, the substitute—the near offer—the temporary-acting—for I am Moon, continuous Moon, in my own shoes, Moon in June, April, September and no member of the human race keeps warm my bit of space—yes, I can tell by the way he nods.
BIRDBOOT: Quite mad, of course.
MOON: What?
BIRDBOOT: The answer lies out there in the swamps.
MOON: Oh.
BIRDBOOT: The skeleton in the cupboard is coming home to roost.
MOON: Oh yes. [*He clears his throat . . . for both he and* BIRDBOOT *have a "public" voice, a critic voice which they turn on for sustained pronouncements of opinion.*] Already in the opening stages we note the classic impact of the catalystic figure—the outsider—plunging through to the centre of an ordered world and setting up the disruptions—the shock waves—which unless I am much mistaken, will strip these comfortable people—these crustaceans in the rock pool of society—strip them of their shells and leave them exposed as the trembling raw meat which, at heart, is all of us. But there is more to it than that—
BIRDBOOT: I agree—keep your eye on Magnus.

[*A tennis ball bounces through the french windows, closely followed by* FELICITY, *who is in her 20's. She wears a pretty tennis outfit, and carries a racket.*]

FELICITY: [*calling behind her*] Out!

[*It takes her a moment to notice* SIMON *who is standing shiftily to one side.* MOON *is stirred by a memory.*]

MOON: I say, Birdboot . . .
BIRDBOOT: That's the one.
FELICITY: [*catching sight of* SIMON] You!

[FELICITY's *manner at the moment is one of great surprise but some pleasure.*]

SIMON: [*nervously*] Er, yes—hello again.
FELICITY: What are you doing here?
SIMON: Well, I . . .
MOON: She's—
BIRDBOOT: Sssh . . .
SIMON: No doubt you're surprised to see me.
FELICITY: Honestly, darling, you really are extraordinary.
SIMON: Yes, well, here I am.

FELICITY: You must have been desperate to see me—I mean, I'm *flattered*, but couldn't it wait till I got back?

SIMON: [*bravely*] There is something you don't know.

FELICITY: What is it?

SIMON: Look, about the things I said—it may be that I got carried away a little—we both did—

FELICITY: [*stiffly*] What are you trying to say?

SIMON: I love another!

FELICITY: I see.

SIMON: I didn't make any promises—I merely—

FELICITY: You don't have to say any more—

SIMON: Oh, I didn't want to hurt you—

FELICITY: Of all the nerve!

SIMON: Well, I—

FELICITY: You philandering coward—

SIMON: Let me explain—

FELICITY: This is hardly the time and place—you think you can barge in anywhere, whatever I happen to be doing—

SIMON: But I want you to know that my admiration for you is sincere—I don't want you to think that I didn't mean those things I said—

FELICITY: I'll kill you for this, Simon Gascoyne!

[*She leaves in tears, passing* MRS. DRUDGE *who has entered in time to overhear her last remark.*]

MOON: It was her.

BIRDBOOT: I told you—straight to the top—

MOON: No, no—

BIRDBOOT: Sssh . . .

SIMON: [*to* MRS. DRUDGE] Yes, what is it?

MRS. DRUDGE: I have come to set up the card table, sir.

SIMON: I don't think I can stay.

MRS. DRUDGE: Oh, Lady Muldoon *will* be disappointed.

SIMON: Does she know I'm here?

MRS. DRUDGE: Oh yes, sir, I just told her and it put her in quite a tizzy.

SIMON: Really? . . . Well, I suppose now that I've cleared the air. . . . Quite a tizzy, you say . . . really . . . really . . .

[*He and* MRS. DRUDGE *start setting up for card game.* MRS. DRUDGE *leaves when this is done.*]

MOON: Felicity!—she's the one.

BIRDBOOT: Nonsense—red herring.

MOON: I mean, it was *her*!

BIRDBOOT: [*exasperated*] *What* was?

MOON: That lady I saw you with last night!

BIRDBOOT: [*inhales with fury*] Are you suggesting that a man of my scrupulous integrity would trade his pen for a mess of potage?!⁹ Simply because in the course of my profession I happen to have struck up an acquaintance—to have, that is, a warm regard, if you like, for a fellow toiler in the vineyard of greasepaint—I find it simply intolerable to be pillified and villoried—

MOON: I never implied—

BIRDBOOT: —to find myself the object of uninformed malice, the petty slanders of little men—

MOON: I'm sorry—

BIRDBOOT: —to suggest that my good opinion in a journal of unimpeachable integrity is at the disposal of the first coquette who gives me what I want—

MOON: Ssssh—

BIRDBOOT: A ladies' man! . . . Why, Myrtle and I have been together now for—Christ!—who's *that*?

[*Enter* LADY CYNTHIA MULDOON *through french windows. A beautiful woman in her thirties. She wears a cocktail dress, is formally coiffured, and carries a tennis racket.*]
[*Her effect on* BIRDBOOT *is also impressive. He half rises and sinks back agape.*]

CYNTHIA: [*entering*] Simon!

[*A dramatic freeze between her and* SIMON].

MOON: Lady Muldoon.
BIRDBOOT: No, I mean—who *is* she?
SIMON: [*coming forward*] Cynthia!
CYNTHIA: Don't say anything for a moment—just hold me.

[*He seizes her and glues his lips to hers, as they say. While their lips are glued*—]

BIRDBOOT: She's *beautiful*—a vision of eternal grace, a poem . . .
MOON: I think she's got her mouth open.

[CYNTHIA *breaks away dramatically.*]

CYNTHIA: We can't go on meeting like this!
SIMON: We have nothing to be ashamed of!
CYNTHIA: But darling, this is madness!
SIMON: Yes!—I am mad with love for you!

9. In the Bible, Jacob persuades his elder brother Esau to give up his right of inheritance in exchange for a "mess of potage" or dish of stew—that is, for a very cheap price. *Toiler in the vineyard of greasepaint*: theater professional. *Pillified and villoried*: vilified and pilloried.

CYNTHIA: Please—remember where we are!

SIMON: Cynthia, I love you!

CYNTHIA: Don't—I love Albert!

SIMON: He's dead! [*Shaking her.*] Do you understand me—Albert's dead!

CYNTHIA: No—I'll never give up hope! Let me go! We are not free!

SIMON: I don't care, we were meant for each other—had we but met in time.

CYNTHIA: You're a cad, Simon! You will use me and cast me aside as you have cast aside so many others.

SIMON: No, Cynthia!—you can make me a better person!

CYNTHIA: You're ruthless—so strong, so cruel—

[*Ruthlessly he kisses her.*]

MOON: The son she never had, now projected in this handsome stranger and transformed into lover—youth, vigour, the animal, the athlete as aesthete—breaking down the barriers at the deepest level of desire.

BIRDBOOT: By jove, I think you're right. Her mouth *is* open.

[CYNTHIA *breaks away.* MRS. DRUDGE *has entered.*]

CYNTHIA: Stop—can't you see you're making a fool of yourself!

SIMON: I'll kill anyone who comes between us!

CYNTHIA: Yes, what is it, Mrs. Drudge?

MRS. DRUDGE: Should I close the windows, my lady? The fog is beginning to roll off the sea like a deadly—

CYNTHIA: Yes, you'd better. It looks as if we're in for one of those days. Are the cards ready?

MRS. DRUDGE: Yes, my lady.

CYNTHIA: Would you tell Miss Cunningham we are waiting.

MRS. DRUDGE: Yes, my lady.

CYNTHIA: And fetch the Major down.

MRS. DRUDGE: I think I hear him coming downstairs now [*as she leaves*].

[*She does: the sound of a wheelchair approaching down several flights of stairs with landings in between. It arrives bearing* MAGNUS *at about 15 m.p.h., knocking* SIMON *over violently.*]

CYNTHIA: Simon!

MAGNUS: [*roaring*] Never had a chance! Ran under the wheels!

CYNTHIA: Darling, are you all right?

MAGNUS: I have witnesses!

CYNTHIA: Oh, Simon—say something!

SIMON: [*sitting up suddenly*] I'm most frightfully sorry.

MAGNUS: [*shouting yet*] How long have you been a pedestrian?

SIMON: Ever since I could walk.

CYNTHIA: Can you walk now . . . ?

[SIMON *rises and walks.*]

Thank God! Magnus, this is Simon Gascoyne.

MAGNUS: What's he doing here?

CYNTHIA: He just turned up.

MAGNUS: Really? How do you like it here?

SIMON: [*to* CYNTHIA] I could stay forever.

[FELICITY *enters.*]

FELICITY: So—you're still here.

CYNTHIA: Of course he's still here. We're going to play cards. There's no need to introduce you two, is there, for I recall now that you, Simon, met me through Felicity, our mutual friend.

FELICITY: Yes, Simon is an old friend, though not as old as you, Cynthia dear.

SIMON: Yes, I haven't seen Felicity since—

FELICITY: Last night.

CYNTHIA: Indeed? Well, you deal, Felicity. Simon, you help me with the sofa. Will you partner Felicity, Magnus, against Simon and me?

MAGNUS: [*aside*] Will Simon and you always be partnered against me, Cynthia?

CYNTHIA: What do you mean, Magnus?

MAGNUS: You are a damned attractive woman, Cynthia.

CYNTHIA: Please! Please! Remember Albert!

MAGNUS: Albert's dead, Cynthia—and you are still young. I'm sure he would have wished that you and I—

CYNTHIA: No, Magnus, this is not to be!

MAGNUS: It's Gascoyne, isn't it? I'll kill him if he comes between us!

CYNTHIA: [*calling*] Simon!

[*The sofa is shoved towards the card table, once more revealing the corpse, though not to the players.*]

BIRDBOOT: Simon's for the chop[1] all right.

CYNTHIA: Right! Who starts?

MAGNUS: I do. No bid.

CYNTHIA: Did I hear you say you saw Felicity last night, Simon?

SIMON: Did I?—Ah yes, yes, quite—your turn, Felicity.

FELICITY: I've had my turn, haven't I, Simon?—now, it seems, it's Cynthia's turn.

CYNTHIA: That's my trick, Felicity dear.

FELICITY: Hell hath no fury like a woman scorned,[2] Simon.

---

1. In danger; slated for execution.
2. A saying adapted from a line in William Congreve's play *The Mourning Bride* (1697), warning that rejected or jealous women are roused to overwhelming, violent revenge.

SIMON: Yes, I've heard it said.

FELICITY: So I hope you have not been cheating, Simon.

SIMON: [*standing up and throwing down his cards*] No, Felicity, it's just that I hold the cards!

CYNTHIA: Well done, Simon!

[MAGNUS *pays* SIMON, *while* CYNTHIA *deals.*]

FELICITY: Strange how Simon appeared in the neighborhood from nowhere. We know so little about him.

SIMON: It doesn't always pay to show your hand!

CYNTHIA: Right! Simon, it's your opening on the minor bid.

[SIMON *plays.*]

CYNTHIA: Hm, let's see . . . [*Plays.*]

FELICITY: I hear there's a dangerous madman on the loose.

CYNTHIA: Simon?

SIMON: Yes—yes—sorry. [*Plays.*]

CYNTHIA: I meld.

FELICITY: Yes—personally, I think he's been hiding out in the deserted cottage [*plays*] on the cliffs.

SIMON: Flush!

CYNTHIA: No! Simon—your luck's in tonight!

FELICITY: We shall see—the night is not over yet, Simon Gascoyne! [*She exits.*]

[MAGNUS *pays* SIMON *again.*]

SIMON: [*to* MAGNUS] So you're the crippled half-brother of Lord Muldoon who turned up out of the blue from Canada just the other day, are you? It's taken you a long time to get here. What did you do—walk? Oh, I say, I'm most frightfully sorry!

MAGNUS: Care for a spin round the rose garden, Cynthia?

CYNTHIA: No, Magnus, I must talk to Simon.

SIMON: My round, I think, Major.

MAGNUS: You think so?

SIMON: Yes, Major—I do.

MAGNUS: There's an old Canadian proverb handed down from the Bladfoot Indians, which says: He who laughs last laughs longest.[3]

SIMON: Yes, I've heard it said.

[SIMON *turns away to* CYNTHIA.]

MAGNUS: Well, I think I'll go and oil my gun. [*He exits.*]

---

3. The usual proverb, possibly of Italian origin, is "He who laughs last laughs best." The Bladfoot Indians, like Magnus's association with Canada, are fictitious.

CYNTHIA: I think Magnus suspects something. And Felicity . . . Simon, was there anything between you and Felicity?

SIMON: No, no—it's over between her and me, Cynthia—it was a mere passing fleeting thing we had—but now that I have found you——

CYNTHIA: If I find that you have been untrue to me—if I find that you have falsely seduced me from my dear husband Albert—I will kill you, Simon Gascoyne!

> [MRS. DRUDGE *has entered silently to witness this. On this tableau, pregnant with significance, the act ends, the body still undiscovered. Perfunctory applause.*]
> [MOON *and* BIRDBOOT *seem to be completely preoccupied, becoming audible, as it were.*]

MOON: Camps it around the Old Vic in his opera cloak and passes me the tat.[4]

BIRDBOOT: Do you believe in love at first sight?

MOON: It's not that I think I'm a better critic——

BIRDBOOT: I feel my whole life changing——

MOON: I am but it's not that.

BIRDBOOT: Oh, the world will laugh at me, I know. . . .

MOON: It is not that they are much in the way of shoes to step into. . . .

BIRDBOOT: . . . call me an infatuated old fool . . .

MOON: . . . They are not.

BIRDBOOT: . . . condemn me . . .

MOON: He is standing in my light, that is all.

BIRDBOOT: . . . betrayer of my class . . .

MOON: . . . an almost continuous eclipse, interrupted by the phenomenon of moonlight.

BIRDBOOT: I don't care, I'm a goner.

MOON: And I dream . . .

BIRDBOOT: The Blue Angel[5] all over again.

MOON: . . . of the day his temperature climbs through the top of his head . . .

BIRDBOOT: Ah, the sweet madness of love . . .

MOON: . . . of the spasm on the stairs . . .

BIRDBOOT: Myrtle, farewell . . .

MOON: . . . dreaming of the stair he'll never reach——

BIRDBOOT: . . . for I only live but once. . . .

MOON: Sometimes I dream that I've killed him.

BIRDBOOT: What?

---

4. That is, puts on a grand act when he goes to the Old Vic (a prestigious London theater) and treats Moon as an underling.

5. A 1931 film directed by Josef von Sternberg and starring Marlene Dietrich and Emil Jennings; it tells the story of a middle-aged professor falling for a nightclub performer.

MOON: What?

[*They pull themselves together.*]

BIRDBOOT: Yes . . . yes. . . . A beautiful performance, a collector's piece. I shall say so.

MOON: A very promising debut. I'll put in a good word.

BIRDBOOT: It would be as hypocritical of me to withhold praise on grounds of personal feelings, as to withhold censure.

MOON: You're right. Courageous.

BIRDBOOT: Oh, I know what people will say— There goes Birdboot buttering up his latest—

MOON: Ignore them—

BIRDBOOT: But I rise above that— The fact is I genuinely believe her performance to be one of the summits in the range of contemporary theatre.

MOON: Trim-buttocked, that's the word for her.

BIRDBOOT: —the radiance, the inner sadness—

MOON: Does she actually come across with it?

BIRDBOOT: The part as written is a mere cypher but she manages to make Cynthia a real person—

MOON: *Cynthia?*

BIRDBOOT: And should she, as a result, care to meet me over a drink, simply by way of er—thanking me, as it were—

MOON: Well, you fickle old bastard!

BIRDBOOT: [*aggressively*] Are you suggesting . . . ?

[BIRDBOOT *shudders to a halt and clears his throat.*]

BIRDBOOT: Well now—shaping up quite nicely, wouldn't you say?

MOON: Oh yes, yes. A nice trichotomy of forces. One must reserve judgement of course, until the confrontation, but I think it's pretty clear where we're heading.

BIRDBOOT: I agree. It's Magnus a mile off.

[*Small pause.*]

MOON: What's Magnus a mile off?

BIRDBOOT: If we knew that we wouldn't be here.

MOON: [*clears throat*] Let me at once say that it has *élan*[6] while at the same time avoiding *éclat.* Having said that, and I think it must be said, I am bound to ask—does this play know where it is going?

BIRDBOOT: Well, it seems open and shut to me, Moon—Magnus is not what he pretends to be and he's got his next victim marked down—

---

6. Flair; grace (French). *Éclat*: a public sensation; a splashy production (French).

MOON: Does it, I repeat, declare its affiliations? There are moments, and I
would not begrudge it this, when the play, if we can call it that, and I
think on balance we can, aligns itself uncompromisingly on the side of
life. *Je suis,* it seems to be saying, *ergo sum.*[7] But is that enough? I think we
are entitled to ask. For what in fact is this play concerned with? It is my
belief that here we are concerned with what I have referred to elsewhere
as the nature of identity. I think we are entitled to ask—and here one is
irresistibly reminded of Voltaire's cry, *"Violà!"*—I think we are entitled to
ask—*Where is God?*
BIRDBOOT: [*stunned*] Who?
MOON: Go-od.
BIRDBOOT: [*peeping furtively into his programme*] God?
MOON: I think we are entitled to ask.

> [*The phone rings.*]
> [*The set re-illumines to reveal* CYNTHIA, FELICITY *and* MAGNUS *about to take
> coffee, which is being taken round by* MRS. DRUDGE. SIMON *is missing. The
> body lies in position.*]

MRS. DRUDGE: [*into phone*] The same, half an hour later? . . . No, I'm sorry—
there's no one of that name here. [*She replaces phone and goes round with
coffee. To* CYNTHIA]: Black or white, my lady?
CYNTHIA: White please.

> [MRS. DRUDGE *pours.*]

MRS. DRUDGE: [*to* FELICITY] Black or white, miss?
FELICITY: White please.

> [MRS. DRUDGE *pours.*]

MRS. DRUDGE: [*to* MAGNUS] Black or white, Major?
MAGNUS: White please.

> [*Ditto.*]

MRS. DRUDGE: [*to* CYNTHIA] Sugar, my lady?
CYNTHIA: Yes please.

> [*Puts sugar in.*]

MRS. DRUDGE: [*to* FELICITY] Sugar, miss?
FELICITY: Yes please.

> [*Ditto.*]

---

7. Moon misquotes and misapplies the French philosopher Descartes's principle *Cogito, ergo sum,*
Latin for "I think, therefore I am." *"Je suis"* means "I am" in French; that is, Moon says, "I am . . .
therefore I am." *Voilà:* French expression meaning "Look!" or "You see!" There is no common reference to the French philosopher Voltaire (1694–1778) ever saying this.

MRS. DRUDGE: [*to* MAGNUS] Sugar, Major?

MAGNUS: Yes please.

[*Ditto.*]

MRS. DRUDGE: [*to* CYNTHIA] Biscuit, my lady?

CYNTHIA: No thank you.

BIRDBOOT: [*writing elaborately in his notebook*] The second act, however, fails to fulfil the promise. . . .

FELICITY: If you ask me, there's something funny going on.

[MRS. DRUDGE's *approach to* FELICITY *makes* FELICITY *jump to her feet in impatience. She goes to the radio while* MAGNUS *declines his biscuit, and* MRS. DRUDGE *leaves.*]

RADIO: We interrupt our programme for a special police message. The search for the dangerous madman who is on the loose in Essex has now narrowed to the immediate vicinity of Muldoon Manor. Police are hampered by the deadly swamps and the fog, but believe that the madman spent last night in a deserted cottage on the cliffs. The public is advised to stick together and make sure none of their number is missing. That is the end of the police message.

[FELICITY *turns off the radio nervously. Pause.*]

CYNTHIA: Where's Simon?

FELICITY: Who?

CYNTHIA: Simon. Have you seen him?

FELICITY: No.

CYNTHIA: Have you, Magnus?

MAGNUS: No.

CYNTHIA: Oh.

FELICITY: Yes, there's something foreboding in the air, it is as if one of *us*—

CYNTHIA: Oh, Felicity, the house is locked up tight—no one can get in—and the police are practically on the doorstep.

FELICITY: I don't know—it's just a feeling.

CYNTHIA: It's only the fog.

MAGNUS: Hound will never get through on a day like this.

CYNTHIA: [*shouting at him*] Fog!

FELICITY: He means the Inspector.

CYNTHIA: Is he bringing a dog?

FELICITY: Not that I know of.

MAGNUS: —never get through the swamps. Yes, I'm afraid the madman can show his hand in safety now.

[*A mournful baying hooting is heard in the distance, scary.*]

CYNTHIA: What's that?!

FELICITY: [*tensely*] It sounded like the cry of a gigantic hound!

MAGNUS: Poor devil!

CYNTHIA: Ssssh!

[*They listen. The sound is repeated, nearer.*]

FELICITY: There it is again!

CYNTHIA: It's coming this way—it's right outside the house!

[MRS. DRUDGE *enters.*]

MRS. DRUDGE: Inspector Hound!

CYNTHIA: A *police* dog?

[*Enter* INSPECTOR HOUND. *On his feet are his swamp boots. These are two inflatable—and inflated—pontoons with flat bottoms about two feet across. He carries a foghorn.*]

HOUND: Lady Muldoon?

CYNTHIA: Yes.

HOUND: I came as soon as I could. Where shall I put my foghorn and my swamp boots?

CYNTHIA: Mrs. Drudge will take them out. Be prepared, as the Force's motto has it, eh, Inspector? How very resourceful!

HOUND: [*divesting himself of boots and foghorn*] It takes more than a bit of weather to keep a policeman from his duty.

[MRS. DRUDGE *leaves with chattels. A pause.*]

CYNTHIA: Oh—er, Inspector Hound—Felicity Cunningham, Major Magnus Muldoon.

HOUND: Good evening.

[*He and* CYNTHIA *continue to look expectantly at each other.*]

CYNTHIA AND HOUND: [*together*] Well?—Sorry——

CYNTHIA: No, do go on.

HOUND: Thank you. Well, tell me about it in your own words—take your time, begin at the beginning and don't leave anything out.

CYNTHIA: I beg your pardon?

HOUND: Fear nothing. You are in safe hands now. I hope you haven't touched anything.

CYNTHIA: I'm afraid I don't understand.

HOUND: I'm Inspector Hound.

CYNTHIA: Yes.

HOUND: Well, what's it all about?

CYNTHIA: I really have no idea.

HOUND: How did it begin?

CYNTHIA: What?

HOUND: The . . . thing.

CYNTHIA: What thing?

HOUND: [*rapidly losing confidence but exasperated*] The trouble!

CYNTHIA: There hasn't *been* any trouble!

HOUND: Didn't you phone the police?

CYNTHIA: No.

FELICITY: I didn't.

MAGNUS: What for?

HOUND: I see. [*Pause.*] This puts me in a very difficult position. [*A steady pause.*] Well, I'll be getting along, then. [*He moves towards the door.*]

CYNTHIA: I'm terribly sorry.

HOUND: [*stiffly*] That's perfectly all right.

CYNTHIA: Thank you so much for coming.

HOUND: Not at all. You never know, there might have been a serious matter.

CYNTHIA: Drink?

HOUND: More serious than that, even.

CYNTHIA: [*correcting*] Drink before you go?

HOUND: No thank you. [*Leaves.*]

CYNTHIA: [*through the door*] I do hope you find him.

HOUND: [*reappearing at once*] Find who, Madam?—out with it!

CYNTHIA: I thought you were looking for the lunatic.

HOUND: And what do you know about that?

CYNTHIA: It was on the radio.

HOUND: Was it, indeed? Well, that's what I'm here about, really. I didn't want to mention it because I didn't know how much you knew. No point in causing unnecessary panic, even with a murderer in our midst.

FELICITY: Murderer, did you say?

HOUND: Ah—so that was not on the radio?

CYNTHIA: Whom has he murdered, Inspector?

HOUND: Perhaps no one—yet. Let us hope we are in time.

MAGNUS: You believe he is in our midst, Inspector?

HOUND: I do. If anyone of you have recently encountered a youngish good-looking fellow in a smart suit, white shirt, hatless, well-spoken—someone possibly claiming to have just moved into the neighbourhood, someone who on the surface seems as sane as you or I, then now is the time to speak!

FELICITY: I——

HOUND: Don't interrupt!

FELICITY: Inspector——

HOUND: Very well.

CYNTHIA: No. Felicity!

HOUND: Please, Lady Cynthia, we are all in this together. I must ask you to put yourself completely in my hands.

CYNTHIA: Don't, Inspector. I love Albert.

HOUND: I don't think you quite grasp my meaning.

MAGNUS: Is one of us in danger, Inspector?

HOUND: Didn't it strike you as odd that on his escape the madman made a beeline for Muldoon Manor? It is my guess that he bears a deep-seated grudge against someone in this very house! Lady Muldoon—where is your husband?

CYNTHIA: My husband?—you don't mean——?

HOUND: I don't know—but I have a reason to believe that one of you is the real McCoy![8]

FELICITY: The real what?

HOUND: William Herbert McCoy who as a young man, meeting the madman in the street and being solicited for sixpence for a cup of tea, replied, "Why don't you do a decent day's work, you shifty old bag of horse manure," in Canada all those many years ago and went on to make his fortune. [*He starts to pace intensely.*] The madman was a mere boy at the time but he never forgot that moment, and thenceforth carried in his heart the promise of revenge! [*At which point he finds himself standing on top of the corpse. He looks down carefully.*]

HOUND: Is there anything you have forgotten to tell me?

[*They all see the corpse for the first time.*]

FELICITY: So the madman has struck!

CYNTHIA: Oh—it's horrible—horrible—

HOUND: Yes, just as I feared. Now you see the sort of man you are protecting.

CYNTHIA: I can't believe it!

FELICITY: I'll have to tell him, Cynthia—Inspector, a stranger of that description has indeed appeared in our midst—Simon Gascoyne. Oh, he had charm, I'll give you that, and he took me in completely. I'm afraid I made a fool of myself over him, and so did Cynthia.

HOUND: Where is he now?

MAGNUS: He must be around the house—he couldn't get away in these conditions.

HOUND: You're right. Fear naught, Lady Muldoon—I shall apprehend the man who killed your husband.

CYNTHIA: My husband? I don't understand.

HOUND: Everything points to Gascoyne.

CYNTHIA: But who's that? [*The corpse.*]

HOUND: Your husband.

8. This expression, meaning the genuine original, the real article among fakes, has many possible origins, none of which has anything to do with the fanciful explanation in Inspector Hound's next speech.

CYNTHIA: No, it's not.

HOUND: Yes, it is.

CYNTHIA: I tell you it's not.

HOUND: *I'm* in charge of this case!

CYNTHIA: But that's not my husband.

HOUND: Are you sure?

CYNTHIA: For goodness sake!

HOUND: Then who is it?

CYNTHIA: I don't know.

HOUND: Anybody?

FELICITY: I've never seen him before.

MAGNUS: Quite unlike anybody I've ever met.

HOUND: This case is becoming an utter shambles.

CYNTHIA: But what are we going to do?

HOUND: [*snatching the phone*] I'll phone the police!

CYNTHIA: But you are the police!

HOUND: Thank God I'm here—the lines have been cut!

CYNTHIA: You mean——?

HOUND: Yes!—we're on our own, cut off from the world and in grave danger!

FELICITY: You mean——?

HOUND: Yes!—I think the killer will strike again!

MAGNUS: You mean——?

HOUND: Yes! One of us ordinary mortals thrown together by fate and cut off by the elements, is the murderer! He must be found—search the house!

[*All depart speedily in different directions leaving a momentarily empty stage.* SIMON *strolls on.*]

SIMON: [*entering, calling*] Anyone about?—funny . . .

[*He notices the corpse and is surprised. He approaches it and turns it over. He stands up and looks about in alarm.*]

BIRDBOOT: This is where Simon gets the chop.

[*There is a shot.* SIMON *falls dead.*]

[INSPECTOR HOUND *runs on and crouches down by* SIMON*'s body.* CYNTHIA *appears at the french windows. She stops there and stares.*]

CYNTHIA: What happened, Inspector?!

[HOUND *turns to face her.*]

HOUND: He's dead . . . Simon Gascoyne, I presume. Rough justice even for a killer—unless—unless—We assumed that the body could not have been lying there before Simon Gascoyne entered the house . . . but . . . [*he slides*

the sofa over the body] there's your answer. And now—who killed Simon
Gascoyne? And why?

[*"Curtain", freeze, applause, exeunt.*[9]]

MOON: Why not?

BIRDBOOT: Exactly. Good riddance.

MOON: Yes, getting away with murder must be quite easy provided that
one's motive is sufficiently inscrutable.

BIRDBOOT: Fickle young pup! He was deceiving her right, left and centre.

MOON: [*thoughtfully*] Of course. I'd still have Puckeridge behind *me*—

BIRDBOOT: She needs someone steadier, more mature—

MOON: —And if I could, so could he—

BIRDBOOT: Yes, I know of this rather nice hotel, very discreet, run by a man
of the world—

MOON: Uneasy lies the head that wears the crown.[1]

BIRDBOOT: Breakfast served in one's room and no questions asked.

MOON: Does Puckeridge dream of me?

BIRDBOOT: [*pause*] Hello—what's happened?

MOON: What? Oh yes—what do you make of it, so far?

BIRDBOOT: [*clears throat*] It is at this point that the play for me comes alive.
The groundwork has been well and truly laid, and the author has taken
the trouble to learn from the masters of the genre. He has created a real
situation, and few will doubt his ability to resolve it with a startling
denouement. Certainly that is what it so far lacks, but it has a beginning, a middle and I have no doubt it will prove to have an end. For this
let us give thanks, and double thanks for a good clean show without a
trace of smut. But perhaps even all this would be for nothing were it not
for a performance which I consider to be one of the summits in the
range of contemporary theatre. In what is possibly the finest Cynthia
since the war—

MOON: If we examine this more closely, and I think close examination is
the least tribute that this play deserves, I think we will find that within
the austere framework of what is seen to be on one level a country-
house week-end, and what a useful symbol that is, the author has given
us—yes, I will go so far—he has given us the human condition—

BIRDBOOT: More talent in her little finger—

MOON: An uncanny ear that might have belonged to a Van Gogh[2]—

9. Literally, "They go out" (Latin).
1. Shakespeare, *2 Henry IV* 3.1.31. The king is lamenting his insomnia, in contrast with a poor
sailor boy's ability to sleep soundly during a storm at sea.
2. Dutch artist (1853–90); Van Gogh cut off his ear, possibly because of suffering from Meniere's
disease, which causes ringing in the inner ear and loss of balance.

BIRDBOOT: —a public scandal that the Birthday Honours[3] to date have neglected—

MOON: Faced as we are with such ubiquitous obliquity, it is hard, it is hard indeed, and therefore I will not attempt, to refrain from invoking the names of Kafka, Sartre, Shakespeare, St. Paul, Beckett, Birkett, Pinero, Pirandello, Dante and Dorothy L. Sayers.[4]

BIRDBOOT: A rattling good evening out. I was held.

[*The phone starts to ring on the empty stage.* MOON *tries to ignore it.*]

MOON: Harder still—— Harder still if possible—— Harder still if it is possible to be—— Neither do I find it easy—— Dante and Dorothy L. Sayers. Harder still—

BIRDBOOT: Others taking part included—*Moon!*

[*For* MOON *has lost patience and is bearing down on the ringing phone. He is frankly irritated.*]

MOON: [*picking up phone, barks*] Hel-lo! [*Pause, turns to* BIRDBOOT, *quietly.*] It's for you. [*Pause.*]

[BIRDBOOT *gets up. He approaches cautiously.* MOON *gives him the phone and moves back to his seat.* BIRDBOOT *watches him go. He looks round and smiles weakly, expiating himself.*]

BIRDBOOT: [*into phone*] Hello . . . [*Explosion.*] Oh, for God's sake, Myrtle!—I've told you never to phone me at work! [*He is naturally embarrassed, looking about with surreptitious fury.*] What? Last night? Good God, woman, this is hardly the time to—I assure you, Myrtle, there is absolutely nothing going on between me and—I took her to dinner simply by way of keeping *au fait* with the world of the paint and the motley[5]—— Yes, I promise—— Yes, I do—— Yes, I *said* yes—I *do*—and you are mine too, Myrtle—darling—I can't—[*whispers*] *I'm not alone*—[*up*]. No, she's not!—[*he looks around furtively, licks his lips and mumbles*]. All *right*! I love your little pink ears and you are my own fluffy bunny-boo—— Now for God's sake—— Good-bye, Myrtle— [*puts down phone*].

[BIRDBOOT *mops his brow with his handkerchief. As he turns, a tennis ball bounces in through the french windows, followed by* FELICITY, *as before, in tennis outfit. The lighting is as it was. Everything is as it was. It is, let us say, the same moment of time.*]

FELICITY: [*calling*] Out! [*She catches sight of* BIRDBOOT *and is amazed.*] You!

3. A list of honorees for public service in various fields; the list is issued yearly in Britain to mark Queen Elizabeth's birthday.
4. A range of writers' names, biblical, classic, and modern, ending with one of the most famous detective novelists. "Birkett" apparently is an invention to chime with "Beckett."
5. That is, the world of the theater. ("Motley" refers to a jester's patchwork costume.)

BIRDBOOT: Er, yes—hello again.

FELICITY: What are you doing here?!

BIRDBOOT: Well, I . . .

FELICITY: Honestly, darling, you really are extraordinary—

BIRDBOOT: Yes, well, here I am. [*He looks round sheepishly.*]

FELICITY: You must have been desperate to see me—I mean, I'm flattered, but couldn't it wait till I got back?

BIRDBOOT: No, no, you've got it all wrong—

FELICITY: What is it?

BIRDBOOT: And about last night—perhaps I gave you the wrong impression— got carried away a bit, perhaps—

FELICITY: [*stiffly*] What are you trying to say?

BIRDBOOT: I want to call it off.

FELICITY: I see.

BIRDBOOT: I didn't promise anything—and the fact is, I have my reputation— people do talk—

FELICITY: You don't have to say any more—

BIRDBOOT: And my wife, too—I don't know how she got to hear of it, but—

FELICITY: Of all the nerve! To march in here and—

BIRDBOOT: I'm sorry you had to find out like this—the fact is I didn't mean it this way—

FELICITY: You philandering coward!

BIRDBOOT: I'm sorry—but I want you to know that I meant those things I said—oh yes—shows brilliant promise—I shall say so—

FELICITY: I'll kill you for this, Simon Gascoyne!

[*She leaves in tears, passing* MRS. DRUDGE *who has entered in time to overhear her last remark.*]

BIRDBOOT: [*wide-eyed*] Good God. . . .

MRS. DRUDGE: I have come to set up the card table, sir.

BIRDBOOT: [*wildly*] I can't stay for a game of *cards*!

MRS. DRUDGE: Oh, Lady Muldoon *will* be disappointed.

BIRDBOOT: You mean . . . you mean, she wants to meet me . . . ?

MRS. DRUDGE: Oh yes, sir, I just told her and it put her in quite a tizzy.

BIRDBOOT: Really? Yes, well, a man of my influence is not to be sneezed at—I think I have some small name for the making of reputations—mmm, yes, quite a tizzy, you say?

[MRS. DRUDGE *is busied with the card table.* BIRDBOOT *stands marooned and bemused for a moment.*]

MOON: [*from his seat*] Birdboot!—[*a tense whisper*]. Birdboot!

[BIRDBOOT *looks round vaguely.*]

What the hell are you doing?

BIRDBOOT: Nothing.

MOON: Stop making an ass of yourself. Come back.

BIRDBOOT: Oh, I know what you're thinking—but the fact is I genuinely consider her performance to be one of the summits—

[CYNTHIA *enters as before.* MRS. DRUDGE *has gone.*]

CYNTHIA: Darling!

BIRDBOOT: Ah, good evening—may I say that I genuinely consider—

CYNTHIA: Don't say anything for a moment—just hold me.

[*She falls into his arms.*]

BIRDBOOT: All right! [*They kiss.*] My God!—she *does* have her mouth open!
Dear lady, from the first moment I saw you, I felt my whole life changing—

CYNTHIA: [*breaking free*] We can't go on meeting like this!

BIRDBOOT: I am not ashamed to proclaim nightly my love for you!—but fortunately that will not be necessary— I know of a very good hotel, discreet—run by a man of the world—

CYNTHIA: But darling, this is madness!

BIRDBOOT: Yes! I am mad with love.

CYNTHIA: Please!—remember where we are!

BIRDBOOT: I don't care! Let them think what they like, I love you!

CYNTHIA: Don't—I love Albert!

BIRDBOOT: He's dead. [*Shaking her.*] Do you understand me—Albert's dead!

CYNTHIA: No—I'll never give up hope! Let me go! We are not free!

BIRDBOOT: You mean Myrtle? She means nothing to me—nothing!—she's all cocoa and blue nylon fur slippers—not a spark of creative genius in her whole slumping knee-length-knickered body—

CYNTHIA: You're a cad, Simon! You will use me and cast me aside as you have cast aside so many others!

BIRDBOOT: No, Cynthia—now that I have found you—

CYNTHIA: You're ruthless—so strong—so cruel—

[BIRDBOOT *seizes her in an embrace, during which* MRS. DRUDGE *enters, and* MOON's *fevered voice is heard.*]

MOON: Have you taken leave of your tiny mind?

[CYNTHIA *breaks free.*]

CYNTHIA: Stop—can't you see you're making a fool of yourself!

MOON: She's right.

BIRDBOOT: [*to* MOON] You keep out of this.

CYNTHIA: Yes, what is it, Mrs. Drudge?

MRS. DRUDGE: Should I close the windows, my lady? The fog—

CYNTHIA: Yes, you'd better.

MOON: Look, they've got your number—

BIRDBOOT: I'll leave in my own time, thank you very much.

MOON: It's the finish of you, I suppose you know that—

BIRDBOOT: I don't need your twopenny Grubb Street prognostications[6]—I have found something bigger and finer—

MOON: [*bemused, to himself*] If only it were Higgs. . . .

CYNTHIA: . . . And fetch the Major down.

MRS. DRUDGE: I think I hear him coming downstairs now.

> [*She leaves. The sound of a wheelchair's approach as before.* BIRDBOOT *prudently keeps out of the chair's former path but it enters from the next wing down and knocks him flying. A babble of anguish and protestation.*]

CYNTHIA: Simon—say something!

BIRDBOOT: That reckless bastard [*as he sits up*].

CYNTHIA: Thank God!—

MAGNUS: What's *he* doing here?

CYNTHIA: He just turned up.

MAGNUS: Really? How do you like it here?

BIRDBOOT: I couldn't take it night after night.

> [FELICITY *enters.*]

FELICITY: So—you're still here.

CYNTHIA: Of course he's still here. We're going to play cards. There is no need to introduce you two, is there, for I recall now that you, Simon, met me through Felicity, our mutual friend.

FELICITY: Yes, Simon is an old friend—

BIRDBOOT: Ah—yes—well, I like to give young up and comers the benefit of my—er—Of course, she lacks technique as yet—

FELICITY: Last night.

BIRDBOOT: I'm not talking about last night!

CYNTHIA: Indeed? Well, you deal, Felicity. Simon, you help me with the sofa.

BIRDBOOT: [*to* MOON] Did you see that? Tried to kill me. I told you it was Magnus—not that it *is* Magnus.

MOON: Who did it, you mean?

BIRDBOOT: What?

MOON: You think it's not Magnus who did it?

BIRDBOOT: Get a grip on yourself, Moon—the facts are staring you in the face. He's after Cynthia for one thing.

MAGNUS: It's Gascoyne, isn't it?

BIRDBOOT: Over my dead body!

MAGNUS: If he comes between us . . .

---

6. Cheap predictions from hack journalists. Grubb Street, in London, was once home to low-market writers and publishers.

MOON: [*angrily*] For God's sake sit down!
CYNTHIA: Simon!
BIRDBOOT: She needs me, Moon. I've got to make up a four.

[CYNTHIA *and* BIRDBOOT *move the sofa as before, and they all sit at the table.*]

CYNTHIA: Right! Who starts?
MAGNUS: I do. I'll dummy for a no-bid ruff and double my holding on South's queen.[7] [*While he moves cards.*]
CYNTHIA: Did I hear you say you saw Felicity last night, Simon?
BIRDBOOT: Er—er—
FELICITY: Pay twenty-ones or trump my contract. [*Discards.*] Cynthia's turn.
CYNTHIA: I'll trump your contract with five dummy no-trumps there [*discards*], and I'll move West's rook for the re-bid with a banker ruff on his second trick there. [*Discards.*] Simon?
BIRDBOOT: Would you mind doing that again?
CYNTHIA: And I'll ruff your dummy with five no-bid trumps there, [*discards*] and I support your re-bid with a banker for the solo ruff in the dummy trick there. [*Discards.*]
BIRDBOOT: [*standing up and throwing down his cards*] And I call your bluff!
CYNTHIA: Well done, Simon!

[MAGNUS *pays* BIRDBOOT *while* CYNTHIA *deals.*]

FELICITY: Strange how Simon appeared in the neighbourhood from nowhere, we know so little about him.
CYNTHIA: Right, Simon, it's your opening on the minor bid. Hmm. Let's see. I think I'll overbid the spade convention with two no-trumps and King's gambit offered there—[*discards*] and West's dummy split double to Queen's Bishop four there!
MAGNUS: [*as he plays cards*] Faites vos jeux.[8] Rien ne va plus. Rouge et noir. Zero.
CYNTHIA: Simon?
BIRDBOOT: [*triumphant, leaping to his feet*] And I call your bluff!
CYNTHIA: [*imperturbably*] I meld.
FELICITY: I huff.
MAGNUS: I ruff.
BIRDBOOT: I bluff.
CYNTHIA: Twist.

---

7. Like much of the dialogue that follows, a fanciful mishmash of card-game and chess terminology.
8. Place your bets. *Rien ne va plus:* The betting is closed. (Literally: "No more.") *Rouge et noir:* Red and black. These are all French phrases that would be used at a roulette table (though not a card table) by a croupier—a casino employee in charge of table games like blackjack and roulette.

FELICITY: Bust.
MAGNUS: Check.
BIRDBOOT: Snap.
CYNTHIA: How's that?
FELICITY: Not out.
MAGNUS: Double top.
BIRDBOOT: Bingo!
CYNTHIA: No! Simon—your luck's in tonight.
FELICITY: We shall see—the night is not over yet, Simon Gascoyne! [*She quickly exits.*]
BIRDBOOT: [*looking after* FELICITY] Red herring[9]—smell it a mile off. [*To* MAGNUS.] Oh, yes, she's as clean as a whistle, I've seen it a thousand times. And I've seen you before too, haven't I? Strange—there's something about you——
MAGNUS: Care for a spin round the rose garden, Cynthia?
CYNTHIA: No, Magnus, I must talk to Simon.
BIRDBOOT: There's nothing for you there, you know.
MAGNUS: You think so?
BIRDBOOT: Oh, yes, she knows which side her bread is buttered. I am a man not without a certain influence among those who would reap the limelight—she's not going to throw me over for a heavily disguised cripple.
MAGNUS: There's an old Canadian proverb——
BIRDBOOT: Don't give me that—I tumbled to you[1] right from the start—oh, yes, you chaps are not as clever as you think. . . . Sooner or later you makeyourmistake. . . . Incidentally,wherewasitIsawyou? . . . I'vedefinitely——
MAGNUS: [*leaving*] Well, I think I'll go and oil my gun. [*Exit.*]
BIRDBOOT: [*after* MAGNUS] Double bluff!—[*to* CYNTHIA] I've seen it a thousand times.
CYNTHIA: I think Magnus suspects something. And Felicity? Simon, was there anything between you and Felicity?
BIRDBOOT: No, no—that's all over now. I merely flattered her a little over a drink, told her she'd go far, that sort of thing. Dear me, the fuss that's been made over a simple flirtation——
CYNTHIA: [*as* MRS. DRUDGE *enters behind*] If I find you have falsely seduced me from my dear husband Albert, I will kill you, Simon Gascoyne!

[*The "*CURTAIN*" as before.* MRS. DRUDGE *and* CYNTHIA *leave.* BIRDBOOT *starts to follow them.*]

MOON: *Birdboot!*

[BIRDBOOT *stops.*]

9. False lead; distraction.   1. That is, I was on to you; I suspected you.

MOON: For God's sake pull yourself together.

BIRDBOOT: I can't help it.

MOON: What do you think you're doing? You're turning it into a complete farce!

BIRDBOOT: I know, I know—but I can't live without her. [*He is making erratic neurotic journeys about the stage.*] I shall resign my position, of course. I don't care I'm a goner, I tell you—— [*He has arrived at the body. He looks at it in surprise, hesitates, bends and turns it over.*]

MOON: Birdboot, think of your family, your friends—your high standing in the world of letters—I say, what are you doing?

[BIRDBOOT *is staring at the body's face.*]

Birdboot . . . leave it alone. Come and sit down—what's the matter with you?

BIRDBOOT: [*dead-voiced*] It's Higgs.

MOON: What?

BIRDBOOT: It's Higgs.

[*Pause.*]

MOON: Don't be silly.

BIRDBOOT: I tell you it's Higgs!

[MOON *half rises. Bewildered.*]

I don't understand. . . . He's dead.

MOON: Dead?

BIRDBOOT: Who would want to . . . ?

MOON: He must have been lying there all the time . . .

BIRDBOOT: . . . kill Higgs?

MOON: But what's he doing here? I was standing in tonight. . . .

BIRDBOOT: [*turning*] Moon? . . .

MOON: [*in wonder, quietly*] So it's me and Puckeridge now.

BIRDBOOT: *Moon* . . . ?

MOON: [*faltering*] But I swear I. . . .

BIRDBOOT: I've got it——

MOON: But I didn't——

BIRDBOOT: [*quietly*] My God . . . so that was it . . . [*Up.*] Moon—now I see——

MOON: —I swear I didn't——

BIRDBOOT: Now—finally—I see it all——

[*There is a shot and* BIRDBOOT *falls dead.*]

MOON: Birdboot! [*He runs on, to* BIRDBOOT's *body.*]

[CYNTHIA *appears at the french windows. She stops and stares. All as before.*]

CYNTHIA: Oh my God—what happened, Inspector?

MOON: [*almost to himself*] He's dead.... [*He rises.*] That's a bit rough, isn't it?—A bit extreme!—He may have had his faults—I admit he was a fickle old ... Who did this, and why?

> [MOON *turns to face her. He stands up and makes swiftly for his seat. Before he gets there he is stopped by the sound of voices.*]
> [SIMON *and* HOUND *are occupying the critics' seats.*]
> [MOON *freezes.*]

SIMON: To say that it is without pace, point, focus, interest, drama, wit or originality is to say simply that it does not happen to be my cup of tea. One has only to compare this ragbag with the masters of the genre to see that here we have a trifle that is not my cup of tea at all.

HOUND: I'm sorry to be blunt but there is no getting away from it. It lacks pace. A complete ragbag.

SIMON: I will go further. Those of you who were fortunate enough to be at the Comedie Française on Wednesday last, will not need to be reminded that hysterics are no substitute for *éclat*.

HOUND: It lacks *élan*.

SIMON: Some of the cast seem to have given up acting altogether, apparently aghast, with every reason, at finding themselves involved in an evening that would, and indeed will, make the angels weep.

HOUND: I am not a prude but I fail to see any reason for the shower of filth and sexual allusion foisted on to an unsuspecting public in the guise of modernity at all costs....

> [*Behind* MOON, FELICITY, MAGNUS *and* MRS. DRUDGE *have made their entrances, so that he turns to face their semicircle.*]

MAGNUS: [*pointing to* BIRDBOOT's *body*] Well, Inspector, is this your man?

MOON: [*warily*] ... Yes.... Yes....

CYNTHIA: It's Simon ...

MOON: Yes ... yes ... poor.... [*Up.*] Is this some kind of joke?

MAGNUS: If it is, Inspector, it's in very poor taste.

> [MOON *pulls himself together and becomes galvanic, a little wild, in grief for* BIRDBOOT.]

MOON: All right! I'm going to find out who did this! I want everyone to go to the positions they occupied when the shot was fired—[*they move; hysterically*]: No one will leave the house! [*They move back.*]

MAGNUS: I think we all had the opportunity to fire the shot, Inspector—

MOON: [*furious*] I am not—

MAGNUS: —but which of us would want to?

MOON: Perhaps you, Major Magnus!

MAGNUS: Why should I want to kill him?

MOON: Because he was on to you—yes, he tumbled you right from the start—and you shot him just when he was about to reveal that you killed—[MOON *points, pauses and then crosses to Higgs's body and falters*]— killed—[*he turns Higgs over*]—this . . . chap.

MAGNUS: But what motive would there be for killing him? [*Pause.*] Who *is* this chap? [*Pause.*] Inspector?

MOON: [*rising*] I don't know. Quite unlike anyone I've ever met. [*Long pause.*] Well . . . now . . .

MRS. DRUDGE: Inspector?

MOON: [*eagerly*] Yes? Yes, what is it, dear lady?

MRS. DRUDGE: Happening to enter this room earlier in the day to close the windows, I chanced to overhear a remark made by the deceased Simon Gascoyne to her ladyship, viz.[2]—"I will kill anyone who comes between us."

MOON: Ah—yes—well, that's it, then. This . . . chap . . . [*pointing*] was obviously killed by [*pointing*] er . . . by [*pause*] Simon.

CYNTHIA: But he didn't come between us!

MAGNUS: And who, then, killed Simon?

MRS. DRUDGE: Subsequent to that reported remark, I also happened to be in earshot of a remark made by Lady Muldoon to the deceased, to the effect, "I will kill you, Simon Gascoyne!" I hope you don't mind my mentioning it.

MOON: Not at all. I'm glad you did. It is from these chance remarks that we in the force build up our complete picture before moving in to make the arrest. It will not be long now, I fancy, and I must warn you, Lady Muldoon that anything you say—

CYNTHIA: Yes!—I hated Simon Gascoyne, for he had me in his power!—But I didn't kill him!

MRS. DRUDGE: Prior to that, Inspector, I also chanced to overhear a remark made by Miss Cunningham, no doubt in the heat of the moment, but it stuck in my mind as these things do, viz., "I will kill you for this, Simon Gascoyne!"

MOON: Ah! The final piece of the jigsaw! I think I am now in a position to reveal the mystery. This man [*the corpse*] was, of course, McCoy, the Canadian who, as we heard, meeting Gascoyne in the street and being solicited for sixpence for a toffee apple, smacked him across the ear, with the cry, "How's that for a grudge to harbour, you sniffling little workshy!"[3] all those many years ago. Gascoyne bided his time, but in due course tracked McCoy down to this house, having, on the way, met, in the neighbourhood, a simple ambitious girl from the provinces. He was charming, persuasive—told her, I have no doubt, that she would go straight to the top—and she, flattered by his sophistication, taken in by his promises to see her all right on the night, gave in to his simple desires. Perhaps she loved him. We shall never know. But in the very

2. Common abbreviation of *videlicet*, a Latin term meaning "namely" or "that is to say."
3. Shirker.

hour of her promised triumph, his eye fell on another—yes, I refer to
Lady Cynthia Muldoon. From the moment he caught sight of her there
was no other woman for him—he was in her spell, willing to sacrifice anything, even you, Felicity Cunningham. It was only today—unexpectedly
finding him here—that you learned the truth. There was a bitter argument which ended with your promise to kill him—a promise that you
carried out in this very room at your first opportunity! And I must warn
you that anything you say—

FELICITY: But it doesn't make sense!

MOON: Not at first glance, *perhaps.*

MAGNUS: Could not Simon have been killed by the same person who killed
McCoy?

FELICITY: But why should any of us want to kill a perfect stranger?

MAGNUS: Perhaps he was not a stranger to *one* of us.

MOON: [*faltering*] But Simon was the madman, wasn't he?

MAGNUS: We only have your word for that, Inspector. We only have your
word for a lot of things. For instance—McCoy. Who is he? Is his name
McCoy? Is there any truth in that fantastic and implausible tale of the
insult inflicted in the Canadian streets? Or is there something else,
something quite unknown to us, behind all this? Suppose for a moment
that the madman, having killed this unknown stranger for private and
inscrutable reasons of his own, was disturbed before he could dispose
of the body, so having cut the telephone wires he decided to return to
the scene of the crime, masquerading as—Police Inspector Hound!

MOON: But . . . I'm not mad . . . I'm almost sure I'm not mad . . .

MAGNUS: . . . only to discover that in the house was a man, Simon Gascoyne, who recognized the corpse as a man against whom you had held
a deep-seated grudge—!

MOON: But I didn't kill—I'm almost sure I—

MAGNUS: I put it to you!—are you the real Inspector Hound?!

MOON: You know damn well I'm not! What's it all about?

MAGNUS: I thought as much.

MOON: I only dreamed . . . sometimes I dreamed—

CYNTHIA: So it was you!

MRS. DRUDGE: The madman!

FELICITY: The killer!

CYNTHIA: Oh, it's horrible, horrible.

MRS. DRUDGE: The stranger in our midst!

MAGNUS: Yes, we had a shrewd suspicion he would turn up here—and he
walked into the trap!

MOON: What *trap?*

MAGNUS: I am not the real Magnus Muldoon!—It was a mere subterfuge!—
and [*standing up and removing his mustaches.*] I now reveal myself as—

CYNTHIA: You mean—?

MAGNUS: Yes!—I am the real Inspector Hound!

MOON: [*pause*] *Puckeridge!*

MAGNUS: [*with pistol*] Stand where you are, or I shoot!

MOON: [*backing*] Puckeridge! You killed Higgs—and Birdboot tried to tell me—

MAGNUS: Stop in the name of the law!

> [MOON *turns to run.* MAGNUS *fires.* MOON *drops to his knees.*]

I have waited a long time for this moment.

CYNTHIA: So you are the real Inspector Hound.

MAGNUS: Not only that!—I have been leading a double life—at *least*!

CYNTHIA: You mean——?

MAGNUS: Yes!—It's been ten long years, but don't you know me?

CYNTHIA: You mean——?

MAGNUS: Yes!—it is me, Albert!—who lost his memory and joined the force, rising by merit to the rank of Inspector, his past blotted out—until fate cast him back into the home he left behind, back to the beautiful woman he had brought here as his girlish bride—in short, my darling, my memory has returned and your long wait is over!

CYNTHIA: Oh, Albert!

> [*They embrace.*]

MOON: [*with a trace of admiration*] Puckeridge . . . you cunning bastard.

> [MOON *dies.*]

THE END

1968

QUESTIONS

1. How does Stoppard differentiate Moon from Birdboot? What can the reader infer about their respective characters—education and class background, attitude toward drama, and so forth—from their speeches in the play?

2. If you were the set designer for a production of *The Real Inspector Hound*, how would you create the illusion that the audience is actually backstage, looking out over the stage and the "audience" that includes the critics Moon and Birdboot? How would you position the actors onstage so that their faces could be seen clearly by the real audience?

3. When does the imaginary barrier between the critics and the actors onstage first become blurred? When does it disappear entirely?

4. What is the dramatic function of Mrs. Drudge in the play? Is she a "static" character or "dynamic"—that is, does her character change over the course of the play?

5. For the comedy of *The Real Inspector Hound* to "work," what conventions of fiction and drama (standard settings, plots, characters) must be familiar to the audience? What must an audience know about the theater world of critics and reviews?

RESPONDING TO DRAMA

When reading a play in order to write about it, you will need to keep a record of your responses and insights as the action unfolds. Recording your thoughts before you've finished a play may help you clarify your expectations, much as Moon and Birdboot in *The Real Inspector Hound* guess out loud who the murderer is and rehearse the reviews they will write. Below you will find examples showing two ways of responding to a play. The first example, in response to *The Real Inspector Hound*, shows how you might jot down your initial impressions in the margins of a play as you read. The second example shows how one reader used the questions on pages 746–47 to take more comprehensive, methodical notes on *Trifles*. Each of these methods of note-taking has certain advantages, and you might find that using a combination of the two works best.

SAMPLE WRITING: ANNOTATING A PLAY

Any passage in *The Real Inspector Hound* would reward close analysis. The passage chosen here comes after the two main characters, Moon and Birdboot, continue their parallel monologues, daydreaming about murder and romance, respectively. They have been ignoring each other and the play, although they both try out some lines for the different reviews they will write for tomorrow's papers. In this passage, just at the beginning of the third act of the mystery at Muldoon Manor, Moon and Birdboot unwillingly become part of the action, which includes comic repetition of dialogue from the first act.

BIRDBOOT: A rattling good evening out. I was held.

> Birdboot's review appeals to popular audience.

[*The phone starts to ring on the empty stage.* MOON *tries to ignore it.*]

MOON: Harder still— Harder still if possible— Harder still if it is possible to be— Neither do I find it easy—Dante and Dorothy L. Sayers. Harder still—

> Moon struggles to impress a sophisticated audience.

BIRDBOOT: Others taking part included—*Moon!*

> Double meaning: At this point, Moon does start to take part.

[*For* MOON *has lost patience and is bearing down on the ringing phone. He is frankly irritated.*]

MOON: [*picking up phone, barks*] Hel-lo! [*Pause, turns to* BIRDBOOT, *quietly.*] It's for you. [*Pause.*]

> Now Birdboot takes part.

[BIRDBOOT *gets up. He approaches cautiously.* MOON *gives him the phone and moves back to his seat.* BIRDBOOT *watches him go. He looks round and smiles weakly, expiating himself.*]

BIRDBOOT: [*into phone*] Hello . . . [*Explosion.*] Oh, for God's sake, Myrtle!—I've told you never to phone me at work! [*He is naturally embarrassed, looking about with surreptitious fury.*] What? Last night? Good God, woman, this is hardly the time to—I assure you, Myrtle, there is absolutely nothing — Hypocrisy. going on between me and—I took her to dinner simply by way of keeping *au fait* with the world of the paint and the motley—— Yes, I promise—— Yes, I do—— Yes, I *said* yes—I *do*—and you are mine too, Myrtle—darling—I can't—[*whispers*] I'm not alone—[*up*]. No, she's not!—[*he looks around furtively, licks his lips and mumbles*]. All *right!* I love your little pink ears — Has to use embarrassing and you are my own fluffy bunny-boo—— Now for God's baby talk to get off the hook. sake—— Good-bye, Myrtle—[*puts down phone*].

[BIRDBOOT *mops his brow with his handkerchief. As he turns, a tennis ball bounces in through the french windows, followed by* FELICITY, *as before, in tennis outfit. The lighting is as it was. Everything is as it was. It is, let us say, the same moment of time.*] — Stage direction seems intended to be read.

FELICITY: [*calling*] Out! [*She catches sight of* BIRDBOOT *and is amazed.*] You!————————————— Haven't we heard this before?

BIRDBOOT: Er, yes—hello again.——————————— Birdboot "becomes" Simon.

FELICITY: What are you doing here?! Blurs line between "reality" and play.

BIRDBOOT: Well, I . . .

FELICITY: Honestly, darling, you really are extraordinary——

BIRDBOOT: Yes, well, here I am. [*He looks round sheepishly.*]

FELICITY: You must have been desperate to see me—I mean, I'm flattered, but couldn't it wait till I got back?

BIRDBOOT: No, no, you've got it all wrong——

> Here he breaks from earlier dialogue. Why?

FELICITY: What is it?

BIRDBOOT: And about last night—perhaps I gave you the wrong impression—got carried away a bit, perhaps—

FELICITY: [*stiffly*] What are you trying to say?

BIRDBOOT: I want to call it off.

> Why doesn't he say he loves another? Simon did.

FELICITY: I see.

BIRDBOOT: I didn't promise anything—and the fact is, I have my reputation—people do talk—

FELICITY: You don't have to say any more—

BIRDBOOT: And my wife, too—I don't know how she got to hear of it, but—

FELICITY: Of all the nerve! To march in here and—

BIRDBOOT: I'm sorry you had to find out like this—the fact is I didn't mean it this way—

FELICITY: You philandering coward!

BIRDBOOT: I'm sorry—but I want you to know that I meant those things I said—oh yes—shows brilliant promise—I shall say so—

FELICITY: I'll kill you for this, Simon Gascoyne!

> Birdboot is talking to the actress, but the character replies to Simon.

[*She leaves in tears, passing* MRS. DRUDGE *who has entered in time to overhear her last remark.*]

SAMPLE WRITING: READING NOTES ON *TRIFLES*

Below are examples of the questions an experienced reader might ask when reading the play *Trifles* for the first time, as well as responses to those questions. (See pp. 746–47.) Any of these notes might inspire ideas for essay topics on *Trifles*. This is just a selection of the many details that could be observed about this lasting play, in which details certainly matter.

Expectations

Do you know anything about the playwright or other works by her or him?
I could check the short biography in this anthology or do a Google search if I
wanted to learn more about Glaspell. I expect a realistic play about everyday
people; I expect neither old-fashioned poetic language nor abstract and ironic
dialogue.

When was it written? According to the date at the end of the play, it was
written and first staged in 1916, during World War I.

Does the title suggest anything? "*Trifles*" sounds like a comedy (a trifle is
something trivial), but it might be ironic. But why does Hale say that "women
are used to worrying over trifles"? I expect to find out that the title is
significant in some way.

Characterization

Who are the characters? What are they like? Three men and two women in the
cast of characters. After I read the stage directions and part of the dialogue, I
check the list again to keep straight who is who. What kind of situation
would bring together a sheriff, a county attorney, a farmer, and two wives?
No actors are needed to play either Mr. Wright or Mrs. Wright. Some men who
help Mr. Hale (Harry) and Mr. Peters (deputy Frank) are mentioned as coming
and going but are never on stage.

The "county attorney" acts like a detective; he seems businesslike and thinks
he's smarter than farmers and women. The stage directions specify that he
speaks "With the gallantry of a young politician," but his flattery toward the
women doesn't work. We find out his name is Mr. Henderson.

According to the stage directions, Mrs. Peters, the sheriff's wife, is "a slight
wiry woman, a thin nervous face"; Mrs. Hale, the farmer's wife, is "larger and
would ordinarily be called more comfortable looking." The casting of the two
women would be important for contrast; a wider range of physical types
would be suitable for the men. Everyone is cold, but only the men take
comfort by the fire in the kitchen; the women are upset.

Is there a protagonist, an antagonist, or other types? There isn't a young hero
or heroine of this play, and I wouldn't call anyone the villain unless it's the
dead man.

Are the characters' names significant? There's nothing especially meaningful or unusual about the names, although "Hale" means healthy (as in "hale and hearty"), and "Wright" sounds just like "right," though obviously something's wrong in this house where the woman has no rights?

Plot

What happens? The big event has already happened; this is the scene of the crime. The men are looking for clues and leave the women in the kitchen, where they discover possible causes or motives for the crime, such as the uneven sewing on the quilt piece, a broken birdcage, and the dead bird in the box. The women decide not to tell the men about their suspicion that John Wright wrung the bird's neck and Minnie Wright strangled him in revenge; instead they hide the bird.

Are there scene changes? The whole scene is a fairly short uninterrupted time in one part of a farmhouse. Characters go offstage to other rooms or outdoors to the barn.

How is exposition handled? The county attorney asks Hale to "tell just what happened"; Hale explains what happened before the play started, describing how Mrs. Wright behaved. It comes as a shock to learn that Mrs. Wright told Hale he couldn't see John Wright " 'Cause [he was] dead." Shouldn't she have run to tell someone about the murder or have told Hale as soon as he arrived? When Hale reports that Mrs. Wright said her husband "died of a rope around his neck," it sounds suspicious. Could she have slept so soundly that she didn't realize someone had strangled Mr. Wright?

What events mark the rising action? When the men go upstairs and Mrs. Hale says "I'd hate to have men coming into my kitchen, and snooping and criticizing," the women have a chance to notice more in the kitchen. Mrs. Hale recalls her relationship to Mrs. Wright, and the women discuss whether the wife really murdered her husband.

The men return to the kitchen on their way out to the barn just after the women discover the quilt pieces with the bad stitching. The next dialogue between the women is more open and brings out Mrs. Hale's regret for not having visited and supported Mrs. Wright in her unhappy marriage. They notice the empty birdcage.

What is the climax? Mrs. Hale finds the dead bird in the pretty box, and the two women understand what it means just before the men return to the kitchen briefly. From then on the women utter small lies to the men. Mrs. Peters for the first time reveals her own memories that suggest she can imagine Mrs. Wright's motives.

What is the resolution? As everyone prepares to leave, Mrs. Peters pretends the bird is insignificant, joining Mrs. Hale in protecting Mrs. Wright and playing along with the men's idea that there's nothing to notice in the kitchen. The women collaborate in hiding the bird.

What kind of play or plot is it? Like some detective stories, the play doesn't ask "whodunnit?" but asks why the murder was committed. Its mode of representation is a familiar type—domestic realism—in which the places, people, things, and even events are more or less ordinary. (Unfortunately, domestic violence is quite common.)

Setting

When does the action occur? The play appears to be contemporary with 1916 (a stove heater, party-line telephones, a horse-drawn wagon). It is a winter morning, and the scene takes perhaps an hour.

Where does the action occur? It is obviously farm country, perhaps in the Midwest, where farms are very far apart. The Dickson County attorney has just returned from Omaha—so it may be Nebraska, though the original event took place in Iowa. There's a Dickson County in Nebraska, a Dickinson County in Iowa.

What is the atmosphere? The freezing weather reflects the feeling of the play and gives the characters a motivation for gathering in the kitchen. John Wright is described as a chilly wind. The frozen house has ruined Mrs. Wright's preserves of summer fruit. The mess in the kitchen, especially the sticky spill of red fruit in the cupboard, seems related to the unhappiness and horror of the marriage and the crime.

Are there scene changes? Instead of several scenes over a longer time, showing the deteriorating marriage, the crisis over the bird, the murder itself, Mrs. Wright's sleepless night, and Mr. Hale's visit, the story unfolds in a single scene, in one room, on the second morning after the murder, between the entrance and exit of Mrs. Hale and Mrs. Peters. It is essential that the play focus on "kitchen things" and what the women visitors notice and think.

Style, Tone, Imagery

What is the style of the dialogue? The dialogue seems similar to everyday speech. There are some differences in speaking style that show the Hales are more rustic than the Peters and the county attorney. Hale has a relaxed way of telling a story: "then I says," etc. Mrs. Hale: "Those towels get dirty awful quick" and "If I was you, I wouldn't tell her the fruit was gone. Tell her it *ain't.*"

How do nonverbal gestures and actions convey meaning? Many specific actions given in the stage directions are crucial to the play: everyone looking at the rocking chair, pointing to the room upstairs, looking at the loaf of bread that should have been put back in the bread box, etc.

Do any of the props seem to have symbolic meaning? Some objects in the play are so important they seem symbolic, though the play tries not to be too heavily poetic. All kinds of "trifles" are clues. For instance, the women get Mrs. Wright's clothes to bring to her in jail. "MRS. HALE: [*Examining the skirt.*] Wright was close," meaning stingy. Mrs. Hale's words convey a quick impression: The skirt looks "shabby" because John Wright didn't give his wife any money for clothes (he was "good" but stingy and cold).

There would be some colorful props on stage—the jar of cherries, the red cloth and other quilt material, the pretty box—all of them signs of what has gone wrong. The room itself is "gloomy" and has some dirty and messy things in plain sight; other things in the cupboards are eventually revealed. These props would add to the uncomfortable feeling of the play.

The closest thing to a symbol is the caged songbird. Even the men notice the broken door and missing bird. Mrs. Hale underlines the comparison to Mrs. Wright twice: "she was kind of like a bird," and later, "No, Wright wouldn't like the bird—a thing that sang. She used to sing. He killed that, too."

Theme

What is the theme of the play? The title calls attention to what the play is about. Glaspell didn't call it *The Caged Songbird* or *Murder in the Midwest* or something heavy-handed. The main action is a search for a motive to confirm what everyone believes, that Minnie Wright must have strangled her husband while he was sleeping in bed. But the underlying theme of the play seems to be about men's and women's different perspectives. How can women's everyday things be important? Why would anyone charged with murder worry about preserves? Even the women hope that Mrs. Wright's worry about having her apron and shawl in jail means she didn't commit the crime. The kitchen things—the trifles in her own house—"turn against her," but the women are able to hide evidence that the men consider insignificant.

WRITING ABOUT DRAMA

Writing an essay about drama, like writing about fiction or poetry, can sharpen your responses and focus your reading; at the same time, it can demonstrate effects in the work that other readers may have missed. When you write about drama, in a very real sense you perform the role that directors and actors take on in a stage performance: You offer your "reading" of the text, interpreting it in order to guide other readers' responses. But you also shape and refine your own response by attempting to express it clearly.

Using the notes you have taken while reading a play, try to locate the specific lines that have contributed to your expectations or your discoveries. Are these lines at the beginning, the middle, or the end of the play? Who gives most of the hints or misleading information? If there is one character who is especially unseeing, especially devious, or especially insightful, you might decide to write an essay describing the function of that character in the play. A good way to undertake such a study of a character in drama (as in fiction) is to imagine the work without that character. Mrs. Hale in *Trifles* is certainly the cleverest "detective," so why do we need Mrs. Peters as well? Similarly, Moon is cleverer than Birdboot, but *The Real Inspector Hound* would be incomplete without Moon's more conservative and complacent counterpart. Why? One answer is that plays need dialogue, and we would find it artificial if Mrs. Hale and Moon talked mainly to themselves. But a more interesting answer is that in each play the audience learns by witnessing characters with different temperaments responding to a situation. Mrs. Peters speaks for our misgivings about protecting a murderer, and Birdboot stands in for our ordinary appetites, whether for chocolates or romance. As these remarks suggest, you can also develop essays that compare characters with similar roles in two plays. To do so, however, you need to take into account the different styles and forms of the respective plays. A brief essay comparing two characters is usually best limited to a single play.

In addition to character studies, essays on drama can focus on the kinds of observations made above: expectations and plot structure; the presence and absence of characters or actions onstage; the different degrees of awareness of characters and audience at various points in the action; titles, stage directions, and other stylistic details, including metaphors or other imagery; and, of course, themes such as the importance of feminine "trifles" or the illusoriness of reality, onstage or off. As you write, you will probably discover that you can imagine directing or acting in a performance of the play, and you'll realize that interpreting a play is a crucial step in bringing it to life.

SUGGESTIONS FOR WRITING

1. How do your sympathies for Mrs. Peters change over the course of *Trifles*? What might Mrs. Peters be said to represent in the clash of attitudes at the heart of the play? Write an essay in which you examine both Mrs. Peters's evolving character as it is revealed in *Trifles* and her dramatic function in relation to the other characters and to the plot.

2. How would you characterize Susan Glaspell's feminism as revealed in *Trifles*—does it seem radical or moderate? How does it compare to feminist political and social ideas of our own time? (Consult three or more educational or library Web sites for biographical background on Glaspell; there are several sites offering teaching materials on *Trifles* as well. If time allows, you might also pursue sources that provide an overview of women's movements in the United States in the twentieth century.) Write an essay in which you explore the political leanings apparent in *Trifles*, both in the context of Glaspell's play (published in 1920) and in the broader historical context of the struggle for women's rights over the past century.

3. Write an essay in which you propose a production of *Trifles*, complete with details of how you would handle the casting, costumes, set design, lighting, and direction of the actors. What would be your overall controlling vision for the production? Would you attempt to reproduce faithfully the look and feel of the play as it might have been in 1916, or would you introduce innovations? How would you justify your choices in terms of dramatic effectiveness?

4. Can a farce like *The Real Inspector Hound* be considered a "serious" play? What is *Inspector Hound* really about—drama? illusion? identity? Write an essay in which you argue that Stoppard's play should be taken seriously, that his aim is more than mere entertainment. What would you say is the play's main theme?

5. In *The Real Inspector Hound*, what does it mean that Moon and Birdboot seem to have formulated their reviews of the play-within-a-play in advance, or that they become more and more involved in the action onstage? Write an essay in which you examine the different critical approaches of Moon and Birdboot, as well as Stoppard's depiction of the relationship between drama and drama criticism.

6. How would you stage *The Real Inspector Hound*? Write a proposal for all aspects of a production—casting, direction, costumes, set design, lighting, sound,

etc. What special challenges and opportunities does *Inspector Hound* present? What would be your overarching vision for a production of the play?

7. Glaspell's play has the manner of domestic realism that was current when the play was first performed in 1916, whereas Stoppard's play, which premiered in 1968, is an absurdist or postmodern farce. Yet each play uses a single set that represents a house in the country in which a murder has taken place. Write an essay in which you compare the setting, style, and tone of the realist and the farcical "whodunnit?" plots of these plays.

SAMPLE WRITING

In the following short essay, Linda Durai writes about the repetition and the stage directions in *The Real Inspector Hound* and argues that these elements make it a play that is better appreciated when read than when seen in a theater. Consider this essay as an example of good student work that needs to be edited in order to correct some common errors and enhance its effect. As you read it, note what works well and what could be improved. Notice, on the positive side, that the thesis is significant—beyond what anyone would simply agree on about the play. The author supports her thesis with specific evidence, quoting accurately from the text. She strengthens her argument by acknowledging other perspectives—as when she notes that some of the humor of the play would work better in a performance than on the page.

What other positive qualities can you observe in Durai's essay? How might you revise it to make it even stronger? For example, could she organize her essay differently? Are there places in the essay that could be clearer and more focused? How might you edit Durai's choices of words or the structure of her sentences to be more precise or economical? Like many student essays, this one has a few common errors that are easy to catch on rereading. Can you find where the antecedent or reference for a pronoun is unclear? Can you locate where a plural pronoun is used for a singular subject (the number should be consistent)? Are there any incomplete sentences?

Linda Durai
Professor Paul Ridgeway
English 282

Reading a "Whodunnit?": Stage Directions and Repetition
in *The Real Inspector Hound*

Most plays have stage directions to guide the director and actors as well as readers. Comedies use repetition to make the audience laugh. Tom Stoppard's *The Real Inspector Hound* (1968) uses both stage directions and

---

repetition in unusual and funny ways. In this play, different kinds of stage directions add to the humor, usually with repetitions that don't seem to make sense. Further, the stage directions go beyond what is necessary for performing the play. Some of the italicized words crack jokes for the reader, and sometimes what would usually be in the printed script is spoken aloud by characters. One of the characters, Mrs. Drudge, is a major source of this ridiculous repetition, as to what she says and the stage directions of what she does. *The Real Inspector Hound* is a really complicated play that needs to be read again and again to be fully understood. A reader can reread and compare the stage directions that connect the murder mystery at Muldoon Manor with the play about the theater critics Moon and Birdboot.

    The Real Inspector Hound is a parody of Agatha Christie's *The Mousetrap*, and it also makes fun of theater critics and plays that have a "play-within-the-play" (Ridgeway, Hodgson, Stoppard, "Conversation"). This is a device that Shakespeare used in *Hamlet* and *A Midsummer Night's Dream* (Ridgeway). A frame and an inner play usually mirror each other, with comic results. The printed play of *The Real Inspector Hound* makes it more obvious that there is a frame or a mirroring of an inside and an outside play. This is something that you wouldn't notice in a theater. It begins with several paragraphs in italics that no one in the theater would read. What a live audience would *see* is something like "their own reflection." Stoppard's note declares: "Impossible" (759; all page references are to *The Norton Introduction to Literature*, Portable Edition); no mirror could really reflect everyone sitting in the actual seats. The reader knows that Stoppard describes the set of the play-within-the-play as a realistic drawing room, and knows that Stoppard instructs directors to cast two different types, "plumpish middle-aged Birdboot and younger taller, less-relaxed Moon" (760). Theatergoers would probably be slower to realize that this play is not going to proceed like other plays do, though they would know the play has started, whereas the reader sees continuing stage directions.

    Alone on stage, Moon follows directions that Stoppard drags out to entertain the reader; it could be summarized "*Moon stares around the stage for several minutes and then reads the program cover to cover.*" Instead the prose is dramatic: "*Silence. The room. The body.* MOON. . . . *He turns over the page and reads. . . . Pause.* MOON *picks up his programme. . . . Pause . . .*" I count seven sentences that tell us how Moon reads the program. When performed, this would make the audience impatient like Moon, and laugh at seeing him act the way they might feel. But it is also a funny imitation of a reader *reading* the play and waiting to find out the plot. We feel like Birdboot objecting when Moon says the play has started with a pause, "You can't start with a *pause!*" (761). That's already a joke about the kind of experimental theater that Stoppard writes.

There are many "straight" stage directions not meant for laughs. These help the reader put themselves in the place of actors, directors, and crew. I can't note all of the fun effects here. But Moon and Birdboot are always talking over and over about the same themes, Moon about his jealousy of the lead reviewer and wanting to murder him, Birdboot about his affairs and his lusting after actresses. There are lots of jokes about the way the two reviewers see the same thing differently, one very intellectual and fancy and the other crude or vulgar. It's interesting that most of the dialogue directions are about Birdboot, who is always shifting his tone to keep up appearances: "conspiratorially," "suspiciously," "instantly outraged," "urbanely." His repeated loud chewing on chocolates would be funnier onstage. But the reader can enjoy the stage-direction descriptions, and only a reader knows that Stoppard thinks Birdboot "grasps reality in the form of his box of chocolates" (761). The audience would just see him as a lover of candy, a kind of big baby, and he even uses baby talk to his wife.

Besides the beginning with a "pause," the play has a bunch of jokes, out loud and in the written play, about stage directions, programs, and exposition—information that you might find in a program or printed stage directions. Many of these jokes are around Mrs. Drudge, who is always repeating things in a crazy overdone way. We read that "the char" comes in to dust the room "on the trot," giving a very English picture of a servant (familiar from lots of comedies and farces). And then Moon reads out loud from the program: "Mrs. Drudge the Help"—a little like labeling her Mrs. Clean the Maid, to be really sure everyone gets it. Her job is obviously to "help" the play, doing the chores of getting information across and making the audience laugh because she doesn't see what the audience sees. It's like a game where she's blind-folded and can't see the corpse *and* the suspicious intruder. She is the one who turns on the radio announcement that sounds like a warning in an old scary movie. And she is the one who answers the phone by saying aloud the information about the scene, what ought to be in the program. It's especially funny to read what is happening while Mrs. Drudge keeps waiting for the sound technician to make the phone ring.

Durai 4

Her answer makes no sense only as a parody of stage directions: "Hello, the drawing-room of Lady Muldoon's country residence one morning in early spring?" Most of Mrs. Drudge's speeches rattle off the background about all the people and the time and place of the play that is happening on the stage. Sometimes they sound like a silly idea of the country life: "now that the cuckoo-beard is in bud" (765).

The play gets incredibly ridiculous as things repeat more and more. Especially with the repeating of Mrs. Drudge's stage business and speeches. She is the center of several scenes that seem to go nowhere, especially in the episode where she serves coffee (beginning of "act two"). Again she seems to *ask* the person on the telephone what would actually be the information about the next scene: "the same, half an hour later?" (776). Then she sets up a silly round of asking characters how they take their coffee. Stoppard winks at the reader by first spelling it all out and then getting impatient: "[*Mrs. Drudge pours.*]" becomes "[*Ditto.*]" and so on through cream, sugar, and starting to offer biscuits. Birdboot writes a note out loud about how dull the beginning of the second act is, and Felicity jumps up and says, "If you ask me, there's something funny going on." This is a double irony that is easier to catch on paper because you can stop and read it again. That is, if Mrs. Drudge *asks her* about a biscuit, it's ridiculous, *and* Felicity thinks there's something suspicious like a crime going on. This meaning comes out when Felicity turns on the radio so the warning is broadcast again. Felicity is another character type, the romantic leading lady, as much as Mrs. Drudge is the type of a wise servant, and she also mostly repeats whatever she says or does, including her threats to kill Simon Gascoyne. A lot of times Mrs. Drudge happens to come onstage "in time to overhear" such remarks.

There are scenes that repeat as if the actors have gotten stuck in the first act, and the stage directions seem to be aware of this. When "[a tennis ball bounces in through the french windows, followed by FELICITY . . .]," for the second time, things are a little different because Birdboot is onstage. The stage directions make a big deal of the idea that the scene is being acted over again: "as before. . . . The lighting is as it was. Everything is as it was. It is, let us say, the same moment in time."] (783). The last two sentences just can't be staged. Stoppard seems to be talking to us as readers. We can turn back the pages to check that the words are almost identical, and that the actress who plays Felicity says her lines the same no matter which man is playing "Simon."

Durai 5

The inner play is obviously a "whodunnit" or murder mystery. It is also a farce, a kind of play with lots of coincidences, running in and out of entrances, disguises, and funny repetitions and discoveries that get people in trouble. The whole play depends on physical situation, the kind of thing viewers see, even though a character like Mrs. Drudge ignores it. But at the same time it involves puns and wordplay, also noticed by the audience while the characters may not be aware. The audience and readers are going to enjoy the way the Moon's long speeches about theater are also comments by the playwright about his own work. Although some actions, for instance the two times that Magnus runs over characters in a wheelchair, are probably funnier live than reading about it, other repetitions are going to be more obvious to a reader than if we were watching in a real theater. I think the stage directions make all the repetitions in *The Real Inspector Hound* funnier than they would be in performance. As a parody of all sorts of theater conventions, it is a play that should be read and reread.

Works Cited

Hodgson, Terry. "The Plays of Tom Stoppard." As quoted in "*The Real Inspector Hound*: Drama Criticism of the Play by Tom Stoppard." *Theatre Database*. Web. http://www.theatredatabase.com/20th_century/real_inspector_hound.htm. Accessed 7 March 2009.

Ridgeway, Paul. Class lecture, English 282 Introduction to Literature, February 10, 2009.

Stoppard, Tom. "Tom Stoppard in Conversation." As quoted in "*The Real Inspector Hound*: Drama Criticism of the Play by Tom Stoppard." *Theatre Database*. Web. http://www.theatredatabase.com/20th_century/real_inspector_hound.htm. Accessed 7 March 2009.

Understanding the Text

14 ELEMENTS OF DRAMA

Most of us read more fiction than drama and are likely to encounter drama by watching filmed versions of it. Nonetheless, the skills you have developed in reading stories and poems come in handy when you read plays. And just as with fiction and poetry, you will understand and appreciate drama more fully by becoming familiar with the various elements of the genre.

CHARACTER

Character is possibly the most familiar and accessible of the elements; both fiction and drama feature one or more imaginary persons who take part in the action. The word "character" refers not only to a person represented in an imagined plot, whether narrated or acted out, but also to the unique qualities that make up a personality. From one point of view, "character" as a part in a plot and "character" as a kind of personality are both predictions: This sort of person is likely to see things from a certain angle and behave in certain ways. Notice that the idea of character includes both the individual differences among people and the classification of similar people into types. Whereas much realistic fiction emphasizes unique individuals rather than general character types, drama often compresses and simplifies personalities—a play has only about two hours in which to show situations, appearances, and behaviors, without description or background other than exposition spoken by the actors. The advantage of portraying character in broader strokes is that it heightens the contrasts between character types, adding to the drama: Differences provoke stronger reactions.

Plays are especially concerned with characters because of the concrete manner in which they portray people on the stage. With a few exceptions (such as experiments in multimedia performance), the only words in the performance of a play are spoken by actors, and usually these actors are *in character*—that is, speaking as though they really were the people they play in the drama. (Some plays have a narrator who observes and comments on the action from the sidelines, and in some plays a character may address the audience directly, but even when the actors apparently step outside of the imaginary frame, they are still part of the play and are still playing characters.) In fiction, the narrator's description and commentary can guide a reader's judgment about characters. Reading a play, you will have no such guide because most drama relies almost exclusively on *indirect characterization*. Apart from some clues about characters in the stage directions, you will need to imagine the appearance, manners, and movement of someone speaking the lines assigned to any one character. You can do this even as you read through a play for the first time, discovering the characters' attitudes and motivations as the scenes unfold. This ability to predict character and then to revise expectations as situations change is based not only on our experiences of people in real life but also on our familiarity with types of characters or roles that occur in many dramatic forms.

Consider the patterns of characters in many stories that are narrated or acted out, whether in novels, comic books, television series, Hollywood films, or even some video games. In many of these forms, there is a leading role, a main character: the **protagonist**. The titles of plays such as *Hamlet* and *Antigone* imply that the play will be about a central character, the chief object of the playwright's and the reader's or audience's concern. Understanding the character of the protagonist—sometimes in contrast with an **antagonist**, the opponent of the main character—becomes the consuming interest of such a play. Especially in more traditional or popular genres, the protagonist may be called a **hero** or **heroine**, and the antagonist may be called the **villain**. Most characterization in professional theater, however, avoids depicting pure good and pure evil in a fight to the death. Most characters possess both negative and redeeming qualities.

As in other genres that represent people in action, in drama there are minor characters or supporting roles. At least since ancient Rome, romantic comedies have been structured around a leading man and woman, along with a comparable pair (often the "buddies" of the leads) whose problems may be less serious, whose characters may be less complex, or who in other ways support rather than lead the action. Sometimes a minor character can be said to be a **foil**, a character designed to bring out qualities in another character by contrast. The main point to remember is that all the characters in a drama are interdependent and help characterize each other. Through dialogue and behavior, each brings out what is characteristic in the others.

Like movies and other "shows," plays must respect certain limitations: the time an audience can be expected to sit and watch, the attention and sympathy an audience is likely to give to various characters, the amount of **exposition** that can be shown rather than spoken aloud. Because of these constraints, playwrights, screenwriters, casting directors, and actors must rely on shortcuts to convey character. Everyone involved, including the audience, consciously or unconsciously relies on stereotypes of various social roles to flesh out the dramatic action that is concentrated into two hours, more or less. Even a play that seeks to undermine stereotypes must still invoke them. In the United States today, casting—or typecasting— usually relies on an actor's social identity, from gender and race to occupation, region, and age. However, plays or other dramatic forms can rely too much on stereotypes, positive or negative, and the familiarity leaves everyone disappointed (or offended); a role that defies stereotypes can be more interesting to perform and to watch. Alternatively, a character can be so exceptional and unfamiliar that audiences will fail to recognize any connection to people they might meet, and their responses will fall flat. All dramatic roles, then, must have some connection to types of personality, and good roles modify such types just enough to make the character deeper and more interesting. Playwrights often overturn or modify expectations of character in order to surprise an audience. So, too, do the actors who play those parts.

Questions about Character

1. Who is the protagonist? Why and how so? Which other characters, if any, are main or major characters? Which are minor characters?

2. What are the protagonist's most distinctive traits, and what is most distinctive about his or her outlook and values? What motivates the character? What is it about the character that creates internal and/or external conflict? Which lines or stage directions reveal most about the character?

3. What are the roles of other characters? Which, if any, functions as an antagonist? Which, if any, serves as a foil? Does any character function as a narrator or chorus, providing background information and commentary? Why and how so?

4. To what extent are any of the characters in the play "types"? How might this affect an audience's experience of the play? In what ways might a director or actor choose to go against the expected types, and how would this complicate the overall effect of the play?

5. Which of the characters, or which aspects of the characters, does the play encourage us to sympathize with or to admire? to view negatively? Why and how so? Are there characters who might be more or less sympathetic, depending on how the role is cast and interpreted?

6. If you were directing a production of this play, whom among your friends and acquaintances would you cast in each role, and why? If you were directing a movie version, what professional actors would you cast?

Every performance of a given character, like every production of a play, is an interpretation. Not just "adaptations"—Greek or Elizabethan plays set in modern times and performed in modern dress, for example—but even productions that seek to adhere faithfully to the written play are interpretations of what is vital or essential in it. John Malkovich, in the 1983–84 production of *Death of a Salesman*, did not project Biff Loman as an outgoing, successful, hail-fellow-well-met jock, though that is what Arthur Miller intended and how he wanted the part played. Malkovich saw Biff as only pretending to be a jock. Big-time athletes, he insisted, don't glad-hand people; they wait for people to come to them. The actor did not change the author's words, but by intonation, body language, and "stage business" (wordless gestures and actions) he suggested his own view of the character's nature. In other words, he broke with the expectations associated with the character's type. As you read and develop your own interpretation of a play, try adding unexpected qualities to one or more of the characters in order to reveal different possible meanings in the drama.

PLOT AND STRUCTURE

An important part of any storyteller's task, whether in narrative or dramatic genres, is the invention, selection, and arrangement of some **action**. Even carefully structured action cannot properly be called a full-scale **plot** without some unifying sense of purpose. That is, what happens should seem to happen for meaningful reasons. This does not mean, of course, that characters or the audience must be satisfied in their hopes or expectations, or that effective plays need to wrap up every loose end. It does mean that a reader or theatergoer should feel that the playwright has completed *this* play—that nothing essential is missing—though the play's outcome or overall effect may be difficult to sum up.

Conflict is the engine that drives plot, and the presentation of conflict shapes the dramatic structure of a play. A conflict whose outcome is never in doubt may have other kinds of interest, but it is not truly dramatic. In a dramatic conflict, each of the opposing forces must at some point seem likely to triumph or worthy of such triumph—whether it is *external* (one character versus another, or one group of characters versus another group, each of whom may represent a different worldview) or *internal* (within a single character torn between competing views, duties, needs, or desires), or even one idea or ideology versus another one. In *Hamlet*, for example, our interest in the struggle between Hamlet and Claudius depends on their being evenly matched, though few viewers would ever wish that the new king would defeat the young hero. Claudius has possession of the throne and the queen, but Hamlet's role as the heir to the late king and his popularity with the people offset his opponent's strength.

The typical plot in drama, as in fiction, involves five stages: exposition, rising action, climax, falling action, and conclusion. **Exposition**, the first phase of plot, provides essential background information about the characters and situation as they exist at the beginning of a play and perhaps also about the events that got the characters to this point—as when, early in *Trifles*, Mr. Hale describes what happened before the play opens. The second phase, **rising action**, begins when an **inciting incident** leads to open conflict either within a single character or among two or more characters—as when, in *Trifles*, the men leave the women alone with what the latter soon discover to be crucial evidence. The moment when the conflict reaches its greatest pitch of intensity and its outcome is decided is the plot's third phase, its **climax** or **turning point**—in *Trifles*, perhaps the discovery of the dead bird and the act of covering up the evidence. The fourth stage, **falling action**, brings a release of emotional tension and moves the characters toward the **resolution** of their conflict and the plot itself toward its fifth and final stage, the **conclusion**. In *Trifles*, the men's return to the kitchen because, they believe, no evidence has been found can be called the falling action. The women's apparent decision to remain mute about what they have discovered can be called the resolution. The play concludes as the characters leave the Wrights' house with a few things for Mrs. Wright in the jailhouse. *Trifles*, then, contains all five stages, while some lengthy plays (Shakespeare's *Hamlet*, for example) feature more than one plot. In such cases, the plot to which less time and attention is devoted is called the **subplot**.

Many older plays in the Western tradition, such as Shakespeare's, have five acts, each act roughly corresponding to—and thus emphasizing—a particular phase of plot. Acts are often further subdivided into scenes, each of which usually takes place in a somewhat different time and place and features a somewhat different combination of characters. Ancient Greek plays such as *Antigone* are structured differently, such that individual scenes or *episodes* are separated by choral songs—that is, odes spoken or sung by the group of characters known as the chorus. Modern plays tend to have fewer acts and scenes than those of earlier eras, and plays such as *Trifles* and *The Real Inspector Hound*—in which the action unfolds continuously and, usually, in a single time and place—have become so common that they have their own name: the *one-act play*.

In the performance of a play longer than one act, it has become customary to have at least one intermission, in part for the practical reason that the audience may need restrooms or refreshments. Breaks may be signaled by turning down stage lights, turning up the house lights, and lowering the curtain (if there is one).

On rare occasions, very long plays (such as Tony Kushner's *Angels in America*) are performed over more than one evening, with the obvious challenge of finding an audience willing and able to pay and find the time for more than one performance; those who read such play "cycles" or **sequences** at their own pace at home have a certain advantage.

The key point is that the form of a play and the breaks between scenes or acts result from the nature of the play. Breaks can create suspense—a curtain comes down after an unexplained gunshot—or they can provide relief from tension or an emotional crisis.

Questions about Plot

1. Read the first scene or the first few pages and then stop. What potential for conflict do you see here? What do you expect to happen in the rest of the play?

2. How is the play divided into acts, scenes, or episodes, if at all? What is the effect of this division? Does the division of the play correspond, more or less, to the five stages of plot development—exposition, rising action, climax, resolution, conclusion?

3. Does the play show a relatively clear progression through the traditional stages of plot development, or does it seem to defy such conventions? If so, how, and what might the playwright achieve through these departures from tradition?

4. What is the inciting incident or destabilizing event? How and why does this event destabilize the initial situation? How would you describe the conflict that develops? To what extent is it external, internal, or both?

5. What is the climax, or turning point? Why and how so? How is the conflict resolved? How and why might this resolution fulfill or defy your expectations?

STAGES, SETS, AND SETTING

Most of us have been to a theater at one time or another, if only for a school play, and we know what a conventional modern stage (the **proscenium stage**) looks like: a room with the wall missing between us and it (the so-called *fourth wall*). So when we read a modern play—that is, one written during the past two or three hundred years—and imagine it taking place before us, we think of it as happening on this kind of stage. But there are also other modern types of stages—the **thrust stage**, where the audience sits around three sides of the major acting area, and the **arena stage**, where the audience sits all the way around the acting area and players make their entrances and their exits through the auditorium—but most plays today are performed on a proscenium stage. Most of the plays in this book can be readily imagined as taking place on such a stage.

Ancient Greek plays and the plays of Shakespeare were originally staged quite differently from most modern plays, and although they may be played today on a proscenium stage, we might be confused as we read if we are unaware of the layout of the theaters for which they were first written. In the Greek theater, the audience sat on a raised semicircle of seats (**amphi-theater**) halfway around a circular area (**orchestra**) used primarily for dancing by the chorus. At the back of the orchestra was the **skene**, or stage house, representing the palace or temple before which the action took place. Shakespeare's stage, in contrast, basically involved a rectangular area built inside one end of a large enclosure like a circular walled-in yard; the audience stood on the ground or sat in stacked balconies around three sides of the principal acting area (rather like a thrust stage). There were additional acting areas on either side of this stage, as well as a recessed area at its back (which could represent Gertrude's chamber in *Hamlet*, for example) and an upper acting area (which could serve as Juliet's balcony). A trap door in the stage floor was used for occasional effects; the ghost of Hamlet's father probably entered and exited this way. Until three centuries ago—and certainly in Shakespeare's time—plays for large paying audiences were performed outdoors in daylight because of the difficulty and expense of lighting. If you are curious about Shakespeare's stage, you can visit a reconstruction of his Globe Theatre in Southwark, London, England, either in person or online at <www.shakespeares-globe.org>. Every summer, plays by Shakespeare are performed there for large international audiences willing to sit on hard benches around the arena or to stand as "groundlings" (a lucky few of whom can lean on the stage near the feet of the actors). The walls in the background of the stage are beautifully carved and painted, but there is no painted scenery, minimal furniture, few costume changes, no lighting, and no curtain around the stage (a cloth hanging usually covers the recessed area at the back of the stage). Three or four musicians may play period instruments on the balcony.

As the design of the Globe suggests, the conventions of dramatic writing and stage production have changed considerably over the centuries. Certainly this is true of the way playwrights convey a sense of place—one of the two key ingredients that make up a play's **setting**. Usually the audience is asked to imagine that the featured section of the auditorium is actually a particular place somewhere else. The audience of course knows it is a stage, more or less bare or elaborately disguised, but they accept it as a kitchen, a public square, a wooded park, an open road, or a room in a castle or a hut. *Antigone* takes place entirely before the palace at Thebes. Following the general convention of ancient Greek drama, the play's setting never changes. When the action demands the presence of Teiresias, for example, the scene does not shift to him; instead, escorts bring him to the front of the palace.

Similarly, important events that take place elsewhere are described by witnesses who arrive on the scene.

In Shakespeare's theater the conventions of place are quite different: The acting arena does not represent a single specific place but assumes a temporary identity according to the characters who inhabit it, their costumes, and their speeches. At the opening of *Hamlet* we know we are at a sentry station because a man dressed as a soldier challenges two others. By line 15, we know that we are in Denmark because the actors profess to be "liegemen to the Dane." At the end of the scene the actors leave the stage and in a sense take the sentry station with them. Shortly thereafter, a group of people dressed in court costumes and a man and a woman wearing crowns appear. As a theater audience, we must surmise from the costumes and dialogue that the acting area has now become a royal court; when we read the play, the stage directions give us a cue that the place has changed.

In a modern play, there are likely to be several changes of scene, each marked by the lowering of the curtain or the darkening of the stage while different sets and props are arranged. **Sets** (the design, decoration, and scenery) and **props** (articles or objects used on stage) vary greatly in modern productions of plays written in any period. Sometimes space is merely suggested—a circle of sand at one end of the stage, a blank wall behind—to emphasize abstraction and universal themes, or to stimulate the audience's imagination. More typically, a set uses realistic aids to the imagination. The set of *Trifles*, for example, must include at least a sink, a cupboard, a stove, a small table, a large kitchen table, and a rocking chair, as well as certain props: a bird cage, quilting pieces, and an ornamental box.

Time is the second key ingredient of setting, and conventions for representing time have also altered across the centuries. Three or four centuries ago, European dramatists and critics admired the conventions of classical Greek drama which, they believed, dictated that the action of a play should represent a very short time—sometimes as short as the actual performance time (two or three hours), and certainly no longer than a single day. This unity of time, one of the so-called **classical unities**, impels a dramatist to select the moment when a stable situation should change and to fill in the necessary prior details by exposition. (These same critics maintained that a play should be unified in place and action as well; the kind of leaping from Denmark to England, or from court to forest, that happens in Shakespeare's plays was off-limits according to such standards.) Thus, in *Trifles*, all the action before the investigators' visit to the farmhouse is summarized by characters during their brief visit, and the kitchen is the only part of the house seen by the audience.

When there are gaps and shifts in time, they are often indicated between scenes with the help of scenery, sound effects, stage directions, or notes in the program. An actor must assist in conveying the idea of time if his or her character appears at different ages. Various conventions of classical or Elizabethan drama have also worked effectively to communicate to the audience the idea of the passage of time, from the choral odes in *Antigone* to the breaks between scenes in Shakespeare plays. There is a short time between Hamlet's departure to see his mother at the end of act 3, scene 2, and the entrance of the king with Rosencrantz and Guildenstern at the beginning of the next scene; in other parts of the play, the elapsed time might be as long as that between scenes 4 and 5 of act 4, during which the news of Polonius's death reaches Paris and Laertes returns to Denmark and there rallies his friends.

Action within a play thus can take place in a wide range of locations and over many years rather than in the one place and the twenty-four-hour period demanded by critics who believed in the classical unities. And we can learn much about how a particular play works and what it means by paying attention to the way it handles setting and sets.

Questions about Setting and Staging

1. Does all the action occur in one time and place, or in more than one? If the latter, what are those times and places? How much time tends to pass between scenes or episodes?

2. How important do the general time and place seem to be, and in what ways are they important? What about the plot and characters would remain the same if a director chose to set the play in a different time and place? What wouldn't?

3. What patterns do you notice regarding where and when things happen? Which characters are associated with each setting? How do different characters relate to the same setting? When, how, and why do scenes change from one setting to another? Are there significant deviations?

4. Do the stage directions describe particular settings and props in detail? If so, what seems significant about the details? How might they establish mood, reveal character, and affect individual characters and the characters' interactions with one another? Is there anything in the stage directions that seems to be intended more for readers than for a director staging a production?

5. Does the date of the play tell you anything about the way it was originally intended to be staged? Does the representation of time and place in the play implicitly call for a certain type of stage? If you were staging the play today, what kind of stage, sets, and props might you use, and why? How might your choices affect how the play works on audiences and what it means to them?

TONE, LANGUAGE, AND SYMBOL

In plays as in other literary genres, the **tone**—that is, the style or manner of expression—is difficult to specify or explain. Perhaps tone is more important in drama than in other genres because it is, in performance, a spoken form, and vocal tone always affects the meaning of spoken words to some extent, in any culture or language. The actor—and any reader who wishes to imagine a play as spoken aloud—must infer from the written language just how to read a line, what tone of voice to use. The choice of tone must be a negotiation between the words of the playwright and the interpretation and skill of the actor or reader. At times stage directions will specify the tone of a line of dialogue, though even that must be only a hint, since there are many ways of speaking "intensely" or "angrily." Find a line in one of the plays printed here that has a stage direction telling the actor how to deliver it, and with one or two other people take turns saying it that way. (*Trifles* and *The Real Inspector Hound* have many such instructions on tone.) If nothing else, such an experiment may help you appreciate the talent of good actors who can put on a certain tone of voice and make it seem natural and convincing. But it will also show you the many options for interpreting tone.

Dramatic **irony**, in which a character's perception is contradicted by what the audience knows, and even *situational irony*, in which a character's (and the audience's) expectations about what will happen are contradicted by what actually does happen, are relatively easy to detect. But *verbal irony*, in which a statement implies a meaning quite different from its obvious, literal meaning, can be fairly subtle and easy to miss. In the absence of clear stage directions, verbal irony—like other aspects of tone—can also be a matter of interpretation. That is, directors and actors, as well as readers and audiences, will often have to decide which lines in a play should be interpreted ironically. All three types of irony are nonetheless crucial to drama. As the very term *dramatic irony* suggests, drama—even more than fiction—depends for its effects on gaps between what the various characters and the audience know. And situational irony—the gap between expectations and outcomes and even between what characters seem to deserve and what they get—is an especially key component and even a characteristic element of **tragedy**.

Never hesitate to apply the skills you have developed in interpreting poetry to drama; after all, most early plays were written in some form of verse. Aspects of poetry often emerge in modern plays; for example, **monologues** or extended speeches by one character, while they rarely rhyme or have regular meter, may allow greater eloquence than is usual in everyday speech and may include revealing imagery and **figures of speech**. Moon in *The Real Inspector Hound*, for instance, often embarks on strange fantasy monologues, as in his description of his dream of the violent uprising of "the stand-ins of the world," or more briefly, his comment on his name and role: "It is merely that it is not enough to wax at another's wane, to be held in reserve . . . to step in or not at all, the substitute . . . for I am Moon, continuous Moon, in my own shoes, Moon in June, April, September and no member of the human race keeps warm my bit of space. . . ." Without line breaks, you may not notice that "moon" and "June," "September" and "member," "race" and "space" rhyme, and you may miss at first the point that Moon, like the moon itself, is in shadow (or wanes) when the first-string critic is in place. Stoppard is not using poetic devices seriously, but in parodic fun. Other playwrights may use poetic devices more straightforwardly, giving characters and places names that have deeper significance.

Simple actions or objects, too, often have metaphorical significance or turn into **symbols**. Effective plays often use props in this way, as *Trifles* does with the bird and its cage. And some plays, like some poems, may even be organized around *controlling metaphors*—such as the piano lessons in August Wilson's *The Piano Lesson* (later in this chapter). As you read, pay close attention to metaphors or images, whether in language or more concrete form.

Allusions, references to other works of literature or art or something else external to the play, can enrich the text in similar ways. The title (and title character) of *The Real Inspector Hound*, for example, seems to be an allusion to Sir Arthur Conan Doyle's novel *The Hound of the Baskervilles*, featuring Sherlock Holmes. Doyle's novel is a classic in the detective fiction genre, which Stoppard's *Inspector Hound* parodies. Awareness of all the stylistic choices in the work can help you reach a clearer interpretation of the whole play.

Questions about Tone, Language, and Symbol

1. Which lines in the play strike you as most ambiguous when it comes to the tone in which they should be spoken? Why and how so? What is the effect of that ambiguity, or how might an actor's or reader's decision about tone here affect the play as a whole?

2. How would you describe the overall tone of the whole play? Do any moments or entire scenes or acts in the play seem interestingly different in terms of their tone?

3. How do the play's characters differ from one another in terms of their tone? Does any character's tone change over the course of the play?

4. Are any details—such as names; actions or statements; references to objects, props, or other details of setting; or allusions, metaphors, or other figures of speech—repeated throughout the play? Do any of these repeated details seem to have special significance? If so, what might that significance be?

5. What types of irony, if any, are at work in the play? What is the effect of the irony?

THEME

Theme—usually defined as a statement a work seems to make about a given issue or subject—is by its very nature the most comprehensive of the elements, embracing the impact of the entire work. Indeed, theme is not part of the work but is abstracted from it by the reader or audience. Since we, as interpreters, infer the theme and put it in our own words, we understandably often disagree about it. To arrive at your own statement of a theme, you need to consider all the elements of a play together: character, structure, setting (including time and place), tone, and other aspects of the style or the potential staging that create the entire effect.

Above all, try to understand a play on its own terms and to separate interpretation from evaluation. You may dislike symbolic or unrealistic drama until you get more used to it; if a play is not supposed to represent what real people would do in everyday life in that place and time, then it should not be criticized for failing to do so. Or you may find realistic plays about ordinary adults in middle America in the mid-twentieth century to be lacking in excitement or appeal. Yet if you read carefully, you may discover vigorous, moving portrayals of people trapped in situations all too familiar to them, if alien to you. Tastes may vary as widely as tones of speech, but if you are familiar with the elements of drama and the ways dramatic **conventions** vary over time and across cultures, you can become a good judge of theatrical literature, and you will notice more and more of the fine effects it can achieve. Nothing replaces the exhilaration and immediacy of a live theater performance, but reading and rereading plays can yield a rich and rewarding appreciation of the dramatic art.

Tips for Identifying Theme

Because theme emerges from a work in its entirety and from all the other elements working together, there's no one-size-fits-all method for discovering theme. Here, however, are some things to look for and consider as you read and reread a play.

1. Pay attention to the title. A title will seldom indicate a play's theme directly, but some titles do suggest a central topic or a key question. Probe the rest of the play to see what insights, if any, about that topic or answers to that question it ultimately seems to offer.

2. Identify any statements that the characters make about a general concept, issue, or topic such as human nature, the natural world, and so on, particularly in monologues or in debates between major characters.

(Continued on next page)

(Continued)

Look, too, for statements that potentially have a general meaning or application beyond the play, even if they refer to a specific situation. Then consider whether and how the play as a whole corroborates, overturns, or complicates any one such view or statement.

3. If a character changes over the course of the play, try to articulate the truth or insight that he or she seems to discover. Then consider whether and how the play as a whole corroborates or complicates that insight.

4. Identify a conflict depicted in the play and state it in general terms or turn it into a general question, leaving out any reference to specific characters, setting, and so on. Then think about the insight or theme that might be implied by the way the conflict is resolved.

HENRIK IBSEN

A Doll House[1]

CHARACTERS

TORVALD HELMER, *a lawyer*	THE HELMERS' THREE SMALL CHILDREN
NORA, *his wife*	ANNE-MARIE, *their nurse*
DR. RANK	HELENE, *a maid*
MRS. LINDE	A DELIVERY BOY
NILS KROGSTAD, *a bank clerk*	

The action takes place in HELMER*'s residence.*

ACT I

A comfortable room, tastefully but not expensively furnished. A door to the right in the back wall leads to the entryway; another to the left leads to HELMER*'s study. Between these doors, a piano. Midway in the left-hand wall a door, and further back a window. Near the window a round table with an armchair and a small sofa. In the right-hand wall, toward the rear, a door, and nearer the foreground a porcelain stove with two armchairs and a rocking chair beside it. Between the stove and the side door, a small table. Engravings on the walls. An etagère with china figures and other small art objects; a small bookcase with richly bound books; the floor carpeted; a fire burning in the stove. It is a winter day.*

A bell rings in the entryway; shortly after we hear the door being unlocked. NORA *comes into the room, humming happily to herself; she is wearing street clothes and*

---

1. Translated by Rolf Fjelde.

*carries an armload of packages, which she puts down on the table to the right. She has
left the hall door open; and through it a* DELIVERY BOY *is seen, holding a Christmas
tree and a basket, which he gives to the* MAID *who let them in.*

NORA: Hide the tree well, Helene. The children mustn't get a glimpse of it
till this evening, after it's trimmed. [*To the* DELIVERY BOY, *taking out her
purse.*] How much?

DELIVERY BOY: Fifty, ma'am.

NORA: There's a crown. No, keep the change. [*The* BOY *thanks her and leaves.*
NORA *shuts the door. She laughs softly to herself while taking off her street things.
Drawing a bag of macaroons from her pocket, she eats a couple, then steals over
and listens at her husband's study door.*] Yes, he's home. [*Hums again as she
moves to the table right.*]

HELMER: [*From the study.*] Is that my little lark twittering out there?

NORA: [*Busy opening some packages.*] Yes, it is.

HELMER: Is that my squirrel rummaging around?

NORA: Yes!

HELMER: When did my squirrel get in?

NORA: Just now. [*Putting the macaroon bag in her pocket and wiping her mouth.*]
Do come in, Torvald, and see what I've bought.

HELMER: Can't be disturbed. [*After a moment he opens the door and peers in, pen
in hand.*] Bought, you say? All that there? Has the little spendthrift been
out throwing money around again?

NORA: Oh, but Torvald, this year we really should let ourselves go a bit. It's
the first Christmas we haven't had to economize.

HELMER: But you know we can't go squandering.

NORA: Oh yes, Torvald, we can squander a little now. Can't we? Just a tiny,
wee bit. Now that you've got a big salary and are going to make piles
and piles of money.

HELMER: Yes—starting New Year's. But then it's a full three months till the
raise comes through.

NORA: Pooh! We can borrow that long.

HELMER: Nora! [*Goes over and playfully takes her by the ear.*] Are your scatter-
brains off again? What if today I borrowed a thousand crowns, and you
squandered them over Christmas week, and then on New Year's Eve a
roof tile fell on my head, and I lay there—

NORA: [*Putting her hand on his mouth.*] Oh! Don't say such things!

HELMER: Yes, but what if it happened—then what?

NORA: If anything so awful happened, then it just wouldn't matter if I had
debts or not.

HELMER: Well, but the people I'd borrowed from?

NORA: Them? Who cares about them! They're strangers.

HELMER: Nora, Nora, how like a woman! No, but seriously, Nora, you know
what I think about that. No debts! Never borrow! Something of free-

dom's lost—and something of beauty, too—from a home that's founded on borrowing and debt. We've made a brave stand up to now, the two of us; and we'll go right on like that the little while we have to.

NORA: [*Going toward the stove.*] Yes, whatever you say, Torvald.

HELMER: [*Following her.*] Now, now, the little lark's wings mustn't droop. Come on, don't be a sulky squirrel. [*Taking out his wallet.*] Nora, guess what I have here.

NORA: [*Turning quickly.*] Money!

HELMER: There, see. [*Hands her some notes.*] Good grief, I know how costs go up in a house at Christmastime.

NORA: Ten—twenty—thirty—forty. Oh, thank you, Torvald; I can manage no end on this.

HELMER: You really will have to.

NORA: Oh yes, I promise I will. But come here so I can show you everything I bought. And so cheap! Look, new clothes for Ivar here—and a sword. Here a horse and a trumpet for Bob. And a doll and a doll's bed here for Emmy; they're nothing much, but she'll tear them to bits in no time anyway. And here I have dress material and handkerchiefs for the maids. Old Anne-Marie really deserves something more.

HELMER: And what's in that package there?

NORA: [*With a cry.*] Torvald, no! You can't see that till tonight!

HELMER: I see. But tell me now, you little prodigal, what have you thought of for yourself?

NORA: For myself? Oh, I don't want anything at all.

HELMER: Of course you do. Tell me just what—within reason—you'd most like to have.

NORA: I honestly don't know. Oh, listen, Torvald—

HELMER: Well?

NORA: [*Fumbling at his coat buttons, without looking at him.*] If you want to give me something, then maybe you could—you could—

HELMER: Come, on, out with it.

NORA: [*Hurriedly.*] You could give me money, Torvald. No more than you think you can spare; then one of these days I'll buy something with it.

HELMER: But Nora—

NORA: Oh, please, Torvald darling, do that! I beg you, please. Then I could hang the bills in pretty gilt paper on the Christmas tree. Wouldn't that be fun?

HELMER: What are those little birds called that always fly through their fortunes?

NORA: Oh yes, spendthrifts; I know all that. But let's do as I say, Torvald; then I'll have time to decide what I really need most. That's very sensible, isn't it?

HELMER: [*Smiling.*] Yes, very—that is, if you actually hung onto the money I give you, and you actually used it to buy yourself something. But it goes for the house and for all sorts of foolish things, and then I only have to lay out some more.

NORA: Oh, but Torvald—

HELMER: Don't deny it, my dear little Nora. [*Putting his arm around her waist.*] Spendthrifts are sweet, but they use up a frightful amount of money. It's incredible what it costs a man to feed such birds.

NORA: Oh, how can you say that! Really, I save everything I can.

HELMER: [*Laughing.*] Yes, that's the truth. Everything you can. But that's nothing at all.

NORA: [*Humming, with a smile of quiet satisfaction.*] Hm, if you only knew what expenses we larks and squirrels have, Torvald.

HELMER: You're an odd little one. Exactly the way your father was. You're never at a loss for scaring up money; but the moment you have it, it runs right out through your fingers; you never know what you've done with it. Well, one takes you as you are. It's deep in your blood. Yes, these things are hereditary, Nora.

NORA: Ah, I could wish I'd inherited many of Papa's qualities.

HELMER: And I couldn't wish you anything but just what you are, my sweet little lark. But wait; it seems to me you have a very—what should I call it?—a very suspicious look today—

NORA: I do?

HELMER: You certainly do. Look me straight in the eye.

NORA: [*Looking at him.*] Well?

HELMER: [*Shaking an admonitory finger.*] Surely my sweet tooth hasn't been running riot in town today, has she?

NORA: No. Why do you imagine that?

HELMER: My sweet tooth really didn't make a little detour through the confectioner's?

NORA: No, I assure you, Torvald—

HELMER: Hasn't nibbled some pastry?

NORA: No, not at all.

HELMER: Not even munched a macaroon or two?

NORA: No, Torvald, I assure you, really—

HELMER: There, there now. Of course I'm only joking.

NORA: [*Going to the table, right.*] You know I could never think of going against you.

HELMER: No, I understand that; and you *have* given me your word. [*Going over to her.*] Well, you keep your little Christmas secrets to yourself, Nora darling. I expect they'll come to light this evening, when the tree is lit.

NORA: Did you remember to ask Dr. Rank?

HELMER: No. But there's no need for that; it's assumed he'll be dining with us. All the same, I'll ask him when he stops by here this morning. I've ordered some fine wine. Nora, you can't imagine how I'm looking forward to this evening.

NORA: So am I. And what fun for the children, Torvald!

HELMER: Ah, it's so gratifying to know that one's gotten a safe, secure job, and with a comfortable salary. It's a great satisfaction, isn't it?

NORA: Oh, it's wonderful!

HELMER: Remember last Christmas? Three whole weeks before, you shut yourself in every evening till long after midnight, making flowers for the Christmas tree, and all the other decorations to surprise us. Ugh, that was the dullest time I've ever lived through.

NORA: It wasn't at all dull for me.

HELMER: [*Smiling.*] But the outcome *was* pretty sorry, Nora.

NORA: Oh, don't tease me with that again. How could I help it that the cat came in and tore everything to shreds.

HELMER: No, poor thing, you certainly couldn't. You wanted so much to please us all, and that's what counts. But it's just as well that the hard times are past.

NORA: Yes, it's really wonderful.

HELMER: Now I don't have to sit here alone, boring myself, and you don't have to tire your precious eyes and your fair little delicate hands—

NORA: [*Clapping her hands.*] No, is it really true, Torvald, I don't have to? Oh, how wonderfully lovely to hear! [*Taking his arm.*] Now I'll tell you just how I've thought we should plan things. Right after Christmas—[*The doorbell rings.*] Oh, the bell. [*Straightening the room up a bit.*] Somebody would have to come. What a bore!

HELMER: I'm not at home to visitors, don't forget.

MAID: [*From the hall doorway.*] Ma'am, a lady to see you—

NORA: All right, let her come in.

MAID: [*To* HELMER.] And the doctor's just come too.

HELMER: Did he go right to my study?

MAID: Yes, he did.

[HELMER *goes into his room. The* MAID *shows in* MRS. LINDE, *dressed in traveling clothes, and shuts the door after her.*]

MRS. LINDE: [*In a dispirited and somewhat hesitant voice.*] Hello, Nora.

NORA: [*Uncertain.*] Hello—

MRS. LINDE: You don't recognize me.

NORA: No, I don't know—but wait, I think—[*Exclaiming.*] What! Kristine! Is it really you?

MRS. LINDE: Yes, it's me.

NORA: Kristine! To think I didn't recognize you. But then, how could I? [*More quietly.*] How you've changed, Kristine!

MRS. LINDE: Yes, no doubt I have. In nine—ten long years.

NORA: Is it so long since we met! Yes, it's all of that. Oh, these last eight years have been a happy time, believe me. And so now you've come in to town, too. Made the long trip in the winter. That took courage.

MRS. LINDE: I just got here by ship this morning.

NORA: To enjoy yourself over Christmas, of course. Oh, how lovely! Yes, enjoy ourselves, we'll do that. But take your coat off. You're not still cold? [*Helping her.*] There now, let's get cozy here by the stove. No, the easy chair there! I'll take the rocker here. [*Seizing her hands.*] Yes, now you have your old look again; it was only in that first moment. You're a bit more pale, Kristine— and maybe a bit thinner.

MRS. LINDE: And much, much older, Nora.

NORA: Yes, perhaps a bit older; a tiny, tiny bit; not much at all. [*Stopping short; suddenly serious.*] Oh, but thoughtless me, to sit here, chattering away. Sweet, good Kristine, can you forgive me?

MRS. LINDE: What do you mean, Nora?

NORA: [*Softly.*] Poor Kristine, you've become a widow.

MRS. LINDE: Yes, three years ago.

NORA: Oh, I knew it, of course; I read it in the papers. Oh, Kristine, you must believe me; I often thought of writing you then, but I kept postponing it, and something always interfered.

MRS. LINDE: Nora dear, I understand completely.

NORA: No, it was awful of me, Kristine. You poor thing, how much you must have gone through. And he left you nothing?

MRS. LINDE: No.

NORA: And no children?

MRS. LINDE: No.

NORA: Nothing at all, then?

MRS. LINDE: Not even a sense of loss to feed on.

NORA: [*Looking incredulously at her.*] But Kristine, how could that be?

MRS. LINDE: [*Smiling wearily and smoothing her hair.*] Oh, sometimes it happens, Nora.

NORA: So completely alone. How terribly hard that must be for you. I have three lovely children. You can't see them now; they're out with the maid. But now you must tell me everything—

MRS. LINDE: No, no, no, tell me about yourself.

NORA: No, you begin. Today I don't want to be selfish. I want to think only of you today. But there *is* something I must tell you. Did you hear of the wonderful luck we had recently?

MRS. LINDE: No, what's that?

NORA: My husband's been made manager in the bank, just think!

MRS. LINDE: Your husband? How marvelous!

NORA: Isn't it? Being a lawyer is such an uncertain living, you know, especially if one won't touch any cases that aren't clean and decent. And of course Torvald would never do that, and I'm with him completely there. Oh, we're simply delighted, believe me! He'll join the bank right after New Year's and start getting a huge salary and lots of commissions. From now on we can live quite differently—just as we want. Oh, Kristine,

I feel so light and happy! Won't it be lovely to have stacks of money and not a care in the world?

MRS. LINDE: Well, anyway, it would be lovely to have enough for necessities.

NORA: No, not just for necessities, but stacks and stacks of money!

MRS. LINDE: [*Smiling.*] Nora, Nora, aren't you sensible yet? Back in school you were such a free spender.

NORA: [*With a quiet laugh.*] Yes, that's what Torvald still says. [*Shaking her finger.*] But "Nora, Nora" isn't as silly as you all think. Really, we've been in no position for me to go squandering. We've had to work, both of us.

MRS. LINDE: You too?

NORA: Yes, at odd jobs—needlework, crocheting, embroidery, and such— [*Casually.*] and other things too. You remember that Torvald left the department when we were married? There was no chance of promotion in his office, and of course he needed to earn more money. But that first year he drove himself terribly. He took on all kinds of extra work that kept him going morning and night. It wore him down, and then he fell deathly ill. The doctors said it was essential for him to travel south.

MRS. LINDE: Yes, didn't you spend a whole year in Italy?

NORA: That's right. It wasn't easy to get away, you know. Ivar had just been born. But of course we had to go. Oh, that was a beautiful trip, and it saved Torvald's life. But it cost a frightful sum, Kristine.

MRS. LINDE: I can well imagine.

NORA: Four thousand, eight hundred crowns it cost. That's really a lot of money.

MRS. LINDE: But it's lucky you had it when you needed it.

NORA: Well, as it was, we got it from Papa.

MRS. LINDE: I see. It was just about the time your father died.

NORA: Yes, just about then. And, you know, I couldn't make that trip out to nurse him. I had to stay here, expecting Ivar any moment, and with my poor sick Torvald to care for. Dearest Papa, I never saw him again, Kristine. Oh, that was the worst time I've known in all my marriage.

MRS. LINDE: I know how you loved him. And then you went off to Italy?

NORA: Yes. We had the means now, and the doctors urged us. So we left a month after.

MRS. LINDE: And your husband came back completely cured?

NORA: Sound as a drum!

MRS. LINDE: But—the doctor?

NORA: Who?

MRS. LINDE: I thought the maid said he was a doctor, the man who came in with me.

NORA: Yes, that was Dr. Rank—but he's not making a sick call. He's our closest friend, and he stops by at least once a day. No, Torvald hasn't had a sick moment since, and the children are fit and strong, and I am, too. [*Jumping up and clapping her hands.*] Oh, dear God, Kristine, what a lovely thing to live and be happy! But how disgusting of me—I'm talking of nothing but my own affairs. [*Sits on a stool close by* KRISTINE, *arms resting across her knees.*] Oh, don't be angry with me! Tell me, is it really true that you weren't in love with your husband? Why did you marry him, then?

MRS. LINDE: My mother was still alive, but bedridden and helpless—and I had my two younger brothers to look after. In all conscience, I didn't think I could turn him down.

NORA: No, you were right there. But was he rich at the time?

MRS. LINDE: He was very well off, I'd say. But the business was shaky, Nora. When he died, it all fell apart, and nothing was left.

NORA: And then—?

MRS. LINDE: Yes, so I had to scrape up a living with a little shop and a little teaching and whatever else I could find. The last three years have been like one endless workday without a rest for me. Now it's over, Nora. My poor mother doesn't need me, for she's passed on. Nor the boys, either; they're working now and can take care of themselves.

NORA: How free you must feel—

MRS. LINDE: No—only unspeakably empty. Nothing to live for now. [*Standing up anxiously.*] That's why I couldn't take it any longer out in that desolate hole. Maybe here it'll be easier to find something to do and keep my mind occupied. If I could only be lucky enough to get a steady job, some office work—

NORA: Oh, but Kristine, that's so dreadfully tiring, and you already look so tired. It would be much better for you if you could go off to a bathing resort.

MRS. LINDE: [*Going toward the window.*] I have no father to give me travel money, Nora.

NORA: [*Rising.*] Oh, don't be angry with me.

MRS. LINDE: [*Going to her.*] Nora dear, don't you be angry with me. The worst of my kind of situation is all the bitterness that's stored away. No one to work for, and yet you're always having to snap up your opportunities. You have to live; and so you grow selfish. When you told me the happy change in your lot, do you know I was delighted less for your sakes than for mine?

NORA: How so? Oh, I see. You think maybe Torvald could do something for you.

MRS. LINDE: Yes, that's what I thought.

NORA: And he will, Kristine! Just leave it to me; I'll bring it up so delicately—find something attractive to humor him with. Oh, I'm so eager to help you.

MRS. LINDE: How very kind of you, Nora, to be so concerned over me—doubly kind, considering you really know so little of life's burdens yourself.

NORA: I—? I know so little—?

MRS. LINDE: [*Smiling.*] Well, my heavens—a little needlework and such—Nora, you're just a child.

NORA: [*Tossing her head and pacing the floor.*] You don't have to act so superior.

MRS. LINDE: Oh?

NORA: You're just like the others. You all think I'm incapable of anything serious—

MRS. LINDE: Come now—

NORA: That I've never had to face the raw world.

MRS. LINDE: Nora dear, you've just been telling me all your troubles.

NORA: Hm! Trivia! [*Quietly.*] I haven't told you the big thing.

MRS. LINDE: Big thing? What do you mean?

NORA: You look down on me so, Kristine, but you shouldn't. You're proud that you worked so long and hard for your mother.

MRS. LINDE: I don't look down on a soul. But it *is* true: I'm proud—and happy, too—to think it was given to me to make my mother's last days almost free of care.

NORA: And you're also proud thinking of what you've done for your brothers.

MRS. LINDE: I feel I've a right to be.

NORA: I agree. But listen to this, Kristine—I've also got something to be proud and happy for.

MRS. LINDE: I don't doubt it. But whatever do you mean?

NORA: Not so loud. What if Torvald heard! He mustn't, not for anything in the world. Nobody must know, Kristine. No one but you.

MRS. LINDE: But what is it, then?

NORA: Come here. [*Drawing her down beside her on the sofa.*] It's true—I've also got something to be proud and happy for. I'm the one who saved Torvald's life.

MRS. LINDE: Saved—? Saved how?

NORA: I told you about the trip to Italy. Torvald never would have lived if he hadn't gone south—

MRS. LINDE: Of course; your father gave you the means—

NORA: [*Smiling.*] That's what Torvald and all the rest think, but—

MRS. LINDE: But—?

NORA: Papa didn't give us a pin. I was the one who raised the money.

MRS. LINDE: You? That whole amount?

NORA: Four thousand, eight hundred crowns. What do you say to that?

MRS. LINDE: But Nora, how was it possible? Did you win the lottery?

NORA: [*Disdainfully.*] The lottery? Pooh! No art to that.

MRS. LINDE: But where did you get it from then?

NORA: [*Humming, with a mysterious smile.*] Hmm, tra-la-la-la.

MRS. LINDE: Because you couldn't have borrowed it.

NORA: No? Why not?

MRS. LINDE: A wife can't borrow without her husband's consent.

NORA: [*Tossing her head.*] Oh, but a wife with a little business sense, a wife who knows how to manage—

MRS. LINDE: Nora, I simply don't understand—

NORA: You don't have to. Whoever said I *borrowed* the money? I could have gotten it other ways. [*Throwing herself back on the sofa.*] I could have gotten it from some admirer or other. After all, a girl with my ravishing appeal—

MRS. LINDE: You lunatic.

NORA: I'll bet you're eaten up with curiosity, Kristine.

MRS. LINDE: Now listen here, Nora—you haven't done something indiscreet?

NORA: [*Sitting up again.*] Is it indiscreet to save your husband's life?

MRS. LINDE: I think it's indiscreet that without his knowledge you—

NORA: But that's the point: he mustn't know! My Lord, can't you understand? He mustn't ever know the close call he had. It was to *me* the doctors came to say his life was in danger—that nothing could save him but a stay in the south. Didn't I try strategy then! I began talking about how lovely it would be for me to travel abroad like other young wives; I begged and I cried; I told him please to remember my condition, to be kind and indulge me; and then I dropped a hint that he could easily take out a loan. But at that, Kristine, he nearly exploded. He said I was frivolous, and it was his duty as man of the house not to indulge me in whims and fancies—as I think he called them. Aha, I thought, now you'll just have to be saved—and that's when I saw my chance.

MRS. LINDE: And your father never told Torvald the money wasn't from him?

NORA: No, never. Papa died right about then. I'd considered bringing him into my secret and begging him never to tell. But he was too sick at the time—and then, sadly, it didn't matter.

MRS. LINDE: And you've never confided in your husband since?

NORA: For heaven's sake, no! Are you serious? He's so strict on that subject. Besides—Torvald, with all his masculine pride—how painfully humiliating for him if he ever found out he was in debt to me. That would just ruin our relationship. Our beautiful, happy home would never be the same.

MRS. LINDE: Won't you ever tell him?

NORA: [*Thoughtfully.*] Yes—maybe sometime years from now, when I'm no longer so attractive. Don't laugh! I only mean when Torvald loves me less than now, when he stops enjoying my dancing and dressing up and reciting for him. Then it might be wise to have something in reserve— [*Breaking off.*] How ridiculous! That'll never happen—Well, Kristine, what do you think of my big secret? I'm capable of something too, hm? You can imagine, of course, how this thing hangs over me. It really hasn't been easy meeting the payments on time. In the business world there's what they call quarterly interest and what they call amortization, and these are always so terribly hard to manage. I've had to skimp a little here and there, wherever I could, you know. I could hardly spare anything from my house allowance, because Torvald has to live well. I couldn't let the children go poorly dressed; whatever I got for them, I felt I had to use up completely—the darlings!

MRS. LINDE: Poor Nora, so it had to come out of your own budget, then?

NORA: Yes, of course. But I was the one most responsible, too. Every time Torvald gave me money for new clothes and such, I never used more than half; always bought the simplest, cheapest outfits. It was a godsend that everything looks so well on me that Torvald never noticed. But it did weigh me down at times, Kristine. It *is* such a joy to wear fine things. You understand.

MRS. LINDE: Oh, of course.

NORA: And then I found other ways of making money. Last winter I was lucky enough to get a lot of copying to do. I locked myself in and sat writing every evening till late in the night. Ah, I was tired so often, dead tired. But still it was wonderful fun, sitting and working like that, earning money. It was almost like being a man.

MRS. LINDE: But how much have you paid off this way so far?

NORA: That's hard to say, exactly. These accounts, you know, aren't easy to figure. I only know that I've paid out all I could scrape together. Time and again I haven't known where to turn. [*Smiling.*] Then I'd sit here dreaming of a rich old gentleman who had fallen in love with me—

MRS. LINDE: What! Who is he?

NORA: Oh, really! And that he'd died, and when his will was opened, there in big letters it said, "All my fortune shall be paid over in cash, immediately, to that enchanting Mrs. Nora Helmer."

MRS. LINDE: But Nora dear—who *was* this gentleman?

NORA: Good grief, can't you understand? The old man never existed; that was only something I'd dream up time and again whenever I was at my wits' end for money. But it makes no difference now; the old fossil can go where he pleases for all I care; I don't need him or his will—because now I'm free. [*Jumping up.*] Oh, how lovely to think of that, Kristine! Carefree! To know you're carefree, utterly carefree; to be able to romp and play with the children, and to keep up a beautiful, charming home—everything just the way Torvald likes it! And think, spring is coming, with big blue skies. Maybe we can travel a little then. Maybe I'll see the ocean again. Oh yes, it *is* so marvelous to live and be happy!

[*The front doorbell rings.*]

MRS. LINDE: [*Rising.*] There's the bell. It's probably best that I go.

NORA: No, stay. No one's expected. It must be for Torvald.

MAID: [*From the hall doorway.*] Excuse me, ma'am—there's a gentleman here to see Mr. Helmer, but I didn't know—since the doctor's with him—

NORA: Who is the gentleman?

KROGSTAD: [*From the doorway.*] It's me, Mrs. Helmer.

[MRS. LINDE *starts and turns away toward the window.*]

NORA: [*Stepping toward him, tense, her voice a whisper.*] You? What is it? Why do you want to speak to my husband?

KROGSTAD: Bank business—after a fashion. I have a small job in the investment bank, and I hear now your husband is going to be our chief—

NORA: In other words, it's—

KROGSTAD: Just dry business, Mrs. Helmer. Nothing but that.

NORA: Yes, then please be good enough to step into the study. [*She nods indifferently as she sees him out by the hall door, then returns and begins stirring up the stove.*]

MRS. LINDE: Nora—who was that man?

NORA: That was a Mr. Krogstad—a lawyer.

MRS. LINDE: Then it really was him.

NORA: Do you know that person?

MRS. LINDE: I did once—many years ago. For a time he was a law clerk in our town.

NORA: Yes, he's been that.

MRS. LINDE: How he's changed.

NORA: I understand he had a very unhappy marriage.

MRS. LINDE: He's a widower now.

NORA: With a number of children. There now, it's burning. [*She closes the stove door and moves the rocker a bit to one side.*]

MRS. LINDE: They say he has a hand in all kinds of business.

NORA: Oh? That may be true; I wouldn't know. But let's not think about business. It's so dull.

[DR. RANK *enters from* HELMER'S *study.*]

RANK: [*Still in the doorway.*] No, no, really—I don't want to intrude, I'd just as soon talk a little while with your wife. [*Shuts the door, then notices* MRS. LINDE.] Oh, beg pardon. I'm intruding here too.

NORA: No, not at all. [*Introducing him.*] Dr. Rank, Mrs. Linde.

RANK: Well now, that's a name much heard in this house. I believe I passed the lady on the stairs as I came.

MRS. LINDE: Yes, I take the stairs very slowly. They're rather hard on me.

RANK: Uh-hm, some touch of internal weakness?

MRS. LINDE: More overexertion, I'd say.

RANK: Nothing else? Then you're probably here in town to rest up in a round of parties?

MRS. LINDE: I'm here to look for work.

RANK: Is that the best cure for overexertion?

MRS. LINDE: One has to live, Doctor.

RANK: Yes, there's a common prejudice to that effect.

NORA: Oh, come on, Dr. Rank—you really do want to live yourself.

RANK: Yes, I really do. Wretched as I am, I'll gladly prolong my torment indefinitely. All my patients feel like that. And it's quite the same, too, with the morally sick. Right at this moment there's one of those moral invalids in there with Helmer—

MRS. LINDE: [*Softly.*] Ah!

NORA: Who do you mean?

RANK: Oh, it's a lawyer, Krogstad, a type you wouldn't know. His character is rotten to the root—but even he began chattering all-importantly about how he had to *live.*

NORA: Oh? What did he want to talk to Torvald about?

RANK: I really don't know. I only heard something about the bank.

NORA: I didn't know that Krog—that this man Krogstad had anything to do with the bank.

RANK: Yes, he's gotten some kind of berth down there. [*To* MRS. LINDE.] I don't know if you also have, in your neck of the woods, a type of person who scuttles about breathlessly, sniffing out hints of moral corruption, and then maneuvers his victim into some sort of key position where he can keep an eye on him. It's the healthy these days that are out in the cold.

MRS. LINDE: All the same, it's the sick who most need to be taken in.

RANK: [*With a shrug.*] Yes, there we have it. That's the concept that's turning society into a sanatorium.

[NORA, *lost in her thoughts, breaks out into quiet laughter and claps her hands.*]

RANK: Why do you laugh at that? Do you have any real idea of what society is?

NORA: What do I care about dreary old society? I was laughing at something quite different—something terribly funny. Tell me, Doctor—is everyone who works in the bank dependent now on Torvald?

RANK: Is that what you find so terribly funny?

NORA: [*Smiling and humming.*] Never mind, never mind [*Pacing the floor.*] Yes, that's really immensely amusing: that we—that Torvald has so much power now over all those people. [*Taking the bag out of her pocket.*] Dr. Rank, a little macaroon on that?

RANK: See here, macaroons! I thought they were contraband here.

NORA: Yes, but these are some that Kristine gave me.

MRS. LINDE: What? I—?

NORA: Now, now, don't be afraid. You couldn't possibly know that Torvald had forbidden them. You see, he's worried they'll ruin my teeth. But hmp! Just this once! Isn't that so, Dr. Rank? Help yourself! [*Puts a macaroon in his mouth.*] And you too, Kristine. And I'll also have one, only a little one—or two, at the most. [*Walking about again.*] Now I'm really tremendously happy. Now there's just one last thing in the world that I have an enormous desire to do.

RANK: Well! And what's that?

NORA: It's something I have such a consuming desire to say so Torvald could hear.

RANK: And why can't you say it?

NORA: I don't dare. It's quite shocking.

MRS. LINDE: Shocking?

RANK: Well, then it isn't advisable. But in front of us you certainly can. What do you have such a desire to say so Torvald could hear?

NORA: I have such a huge desire to say—to hell and be damned!

RANK: Are you crazy?

MRS. LINDE: My goodness, Nora!

RANK: Go on, say it. Here he is.

NORA: [*Hiding the macaroon bag.*] Shh, shh, shh!

[HELMER *comes in from his study, hat in hand, overcoat over his arm.*]

NORA: [*Going toward him.*] Well, Torvald dear, are you through with him?

HELMER: Yes, he just left.

NORA: Let me introduce you—this is Kristine, who's arrived here in town.

HELMER: Kristine—? I'm sorry, but I don't know—

NORA: Mrs. Linde, Torvald dear. Mrs. Kristine Linde.

HELMER: Of course. A childhood friend of my wife's, no doubt?

MRS. LINDE: Yes, we knew each other in those days.

NORA: And just think, she made the long trip down here in order to talk with you.

HELMER: What's this?

MRS. LINDE: Well, not exactly—

NORA: You see, Kristine is remarkably clever in office work, and so she's terribly eager to come under a capable man's supervision and add more to what she already knows—

HELMER: Very wise, Mrs. Linde.

NORA: And then when she heard that you'd become a bank manager—the story was wired out to the papers—then she came in as fast as she could and—Really, Torvald, for my sake you can do a little something for Kristine, can't you?

HELMER: Yes, it's not at all impossible. Mrs. Linde, I suppose you're a widow?

MRS. LINDE: Yes.

HELMER: Any experience in office work?

MRS. LINDE: Yes, a good deal.

HELMER: Well, it's quite likely that I can make an opening for you—

NORA: [*Clapping her hands.*] You see, you see!

HELMER: You've come at a lucky moment, Mrs. Linde.

MRS. LINDE: Oh, how can I thank you?

HELMER: Not necessary. [*Putting his overcoat on.*] But today you'll have to excuse me—

RANK: Wait, I'll go with you. [*He fetches his coat from the hall and warms it at the stove.*]

NORA: Don't stay out long, dear.

HELMER: An hour; no more.

NORA: Are you going too, Kristine?

MRS. LINDE: [*Putting on her winter garments.*] Yes, I have to see about a room now.

HELMER: Then perhaps we can all walk together.

NORA: [*Helping her.*] What a shame we're so cramped here, but it's quite impossible for us to—

MRS. LINDE: Oh, don't even think of it! Good-bye, Nora dear, and thanks for everything.

NORA: Good-bye for now. Of course you'll be back this evening. And you too, Dr. Rank. What? If you're well enough? Oh, you've got to be! Wrap up tight now.

[*In a ripple of small talk the company moves out into the hall; children's voices are heard outside on the steps.*]

NORA: There they are! There they are! [*She runs to open the door. The children come in with their nurse,* ANNE-MARIE.] Come in, come in! [*Bends down and kisses them.*] Oh, you darlings—! Look at them, Kristine. Aren't they lovely!

RANK: No loitering in the draft here.

HELMER: Come, Mrs. Linde—this place is unbearable now for anyone but mothers.

[DR. RANK, HELMER, *and* MRS. LINDE *go down the stairs.* ANNE-MARIE *goes into the living room with the children.* NORA *follows, after closing the hall door.*]

NORA: How fresh and strong you look. Oh, such red cheeks you have! Like apples and roses. [*The children interrupt her throughout the following.*] And it was so much fun? That's wonderful. Really? You pulled both Emmy and Bob on the sled? Imagine, all together! Yes, you're a clever boy, Ivar. Oh, let me hold her a bit, Anne-Marie. My sweet little doll baby! [*Takes the smallest from the nurse and dances with her.*] Yes, yes, Mama will dance with Bob as well. What? Did you throw snowballs? Oh, if I'd only been there! No, don't bother, Anne-Marie—I'll undress them myself. Oh yes, let me. It's such fun. Go in and rest; you look half frozen. There's hot coffee waiting for you on the stove. [*The nurse goes into the room to the left.* NORA *takes the children's winter things off, throwing them about, while the children talk to her all at once.*] Is that so? A big dog chased you? But it didn't

bite? No, dogs never bite little, lovely doll babies. Don't peek in the
packages, Ivar! What is it? Yes, wouldn't you like to know. No, no, it's an
ugly something. Well? Shall we play? What shall we play? Hide-and-
seek? Yes, let's play hide-and-seek. Bob must hide first. I must? Yes, let
me hide first. [*Laughing and shouting, she and the children play in and out of
the living room and the adjoining room to the right. At last* NORA *hides under the
table. The children come storming in, search, but cannot find her, then hear her
muffled laughter, dash over to the table, lift the cloth up and find her. Wild shouting. She creeps forward as if to scare them. More shouts. Meanwhile, a knock at the
hall door; no one has noticed it. Now the door half opens, and* KROGSTAD *appears.
He waits a moment; the game goes on.*]

KROGSTAD: Beg pardon, Mrs. Helmer—

NORA: [*With a strangled cry, turning and scrambling to her knees.*] Oh! What do
you want?

KROGSTAD: Excuse me. The outer door was ajar; it must be someone forgot
to shut it—

NORA: [*Rising.*] My husband isn't home, Mr. Krogstad.

KROGSTAD: I know that.

NORA: Yes—then what do you want here?

KROGSTAD: A word with you.

NORA: With—? [*To the children, quietly.*] Go in to Anne-Marie. What? No, the
strange man won't hurt Mama. When he's gone, we'll play some more.
[*She leads the children into the room to the left and shuts the door after them.
Then, tense and nervous:*] You want to speak to me?

KROGSTAD: Yes, I want to.

NORA: Today? But it's not yet the first of the month—

KROGSTAD: No, it's Christmas Eve. It's going to be up to you how merry a
Christmas you have.

NORA: What is it you want? Today I absolutely can't—

KROGSTAD: We won't talk about that till later. This is something else. You
do have a moment to spare, I suppose?

NORA: Oh yes, of course—I do, except—

KROGSTAD: Good. I was sitting over at Olsen's Restaurant when I saw your
husband go down the street—

NORA: Yes?

KROGSTAD: With a lady.

NORA: Yes. So?

KROGSTAD: If you'll pardon my asking: wasn't that lady a Mrs. Linde?

NORA: Yes.

KROGSTAD: Just now come into town?

NORA: Yes, today.

KROGSTAD: She's a good friend of yours?

NORA: Yes, she is. But I don't see—

KROGSTAD: I also knew her once.

NORA: I'm aware of that.

KROGSTAD: Oh? You know all about it. I thought so. Well, then let me ask you short and sweet: is Mrs. Linde getting a job in the bank?

NORA: What makes you think you can cross-examine me, Mr. Krogstad— you, one of my husband's employees? But since you ask, you might as well know—yes, Mrs. Linde's going to be taken on at the bank. And I'm the one who spoke for her, Mr. Krogstad. Now you know.

KROGSTAD: So I guessed right.

NORA: [*Pacing up and down.*] Oh, one does have a tiny bit of influence, I should hope. Just because I am a woman, don't think it means that— When one has a subordinate position, Mr. Krogstad, one really ought to be careful about pushing somebody who—hm—

KROGSTAD: Who has influence?

NORA: That's right.

KROGSTAD: [*In a different tone.*] Mrs. Helmer, would you be good enough to use your influence on my behalf?

NORA: What? What do you mean?

KROGSTAD: Would you please make sure that I keep my subordinate position in the bank?

NORA: What does that mean? Who's thinking of taking away your position?

KROGSTAD: Oh, don't play the innocent with me. I'm quite aware that your friend would hardly relish the chance of running into me again; and I'm also aware now whom I can thank for being turned out.

NORA: But I promise you—

KROGSTAD: Yes, yes, yes, to the point: there's still time, and I'm advising you to use your influence to prevent it.

NORA: But Mr. Krogstad, I have absolutely no influence.

KROGSTAD: You haven't? I thought you were just saying—

NORA: You shouldn't take me so literally. I! How can you believe that I have any such influence over my husband?

KROGSTAD: Oh, I've known your husband from our student days. I don't think the great bank manager's more steadfast than any other married man.

NORA: You speak insolently about my husband, and I'll show you the door.

KROGSTAD: The lady has spirit.

NORA: I'm not afraid of you any longer. After New Year's, I'll soon be done with the whole business.

KROGSTAD: [*Restraining himself.*] Now listen to me, Mrs. Helmer. If necessary, I'll fight for my little job in the bank as if it were life itself.

NORA: Yes, so it seems.

KROGSTAD: It's not just a matter of income; that's the least of it. It's something else—All right, out with it! Look, this is the thing. You know, just like all the others, of course, that once, a good many years ago, I did something rather rash.

NORA: I've heard rumors to that effect.

KROGSTAD: The case never got into court; but all the same, every door was closed in my face from then on. So I took up those various activities you know about. I had to grab hold somewhere; and I dare say I haven't been among the worst. But now I want to drop all that. My boys are growing up. For their sakes, I'll have to win back as much respect as possible here in town. That job in the bank was like the first rung in my ladder. And now your husband wants to kick me right back down in the mud again.

NORA: But for heaven's sake, Mr. Krogstad, it's simply not in my power to help you.

KROGSTAD: That's because you haven't the will to—but I have the means to make you.

NORA: You certainly won't tell my husband that I owe you money?

KROGSTAD: Hm—what if I told him that?

NORA: That would be shameful of you. [*Nearly in tears.*] This secret—my joy and my pride—that he should learn it in such a crude and disgusting way—learn it from you. You'd expose me to the most horrible unpleasantness—

KROGSTAD: Only unpleasantness?

NORA: [*Vehemently.*] But go on and try. It'll turn out the worse for you, because then my husband will really see what a crook you are, and then you'll *never* be able to hold your job.

KROGSTAD: I asked if it was just domestic unpleasantness you were afraid of?

NORA: If my husband finds out, then of course he'll pay what I owe at once, and then we'd be through with you for good.

KROGSTAD: [*A step closer.*] Listen, Mrs. Helmer—you've either got a very bad memory, or else no head at all for business. I'd better put you a little more in touch with the facts.

NORA: What do you mean?

KROGSTAD: When your husband was sick, you came to me for a loan of four thousand, eight hundred crowns.

NORA: Where else could I go?

KROGSTAD: I promised to get you that sum—

NORA: And you got it.

KROGSTAD: I promised to get you that sum, on certain conditions. You were so involved in your husband's illness, and so eager to finance your trip, that I guess you didn't think out all the details. It might just be a good idea to remind you. I promised you the money on the strength of a note I drew up.

NORA: Yes, and that I signed.

KROGSTAD: Right. But at the bottom I added some lines for your father to guarantee the loan. He was supposed to sign down there.

NORA: Supposed to? He did sign.

KROGSTAD: I left the date blank. In other words, your father would have dated his signature himself. Do you remember that?

NORA: Yes, I think—

KROGSTAD: Then I gave you the note for you to mail to your father. Isn't that so?

NORA: Yes.

KROGSTAD: And naturally you sent it at once—because only some five, six days later you brought me the note, properly signed. And with that, the money was yours.

NORA: Well, then; I've made my payments regularly, haven't I?

KROGSTAD: More or less. But—getting back to the point—those were hard times for you then, Mrs. Helmer.

NORA: Yes, they were.

KROGSTAD: Your father was very ill, I believe.

NORA: He was near the end.

KROGSTAD: He died soon after?

NORA: Yes.

KROGSTAD: Tell me, Mrs. Helmer, do you happen to recall the date of your father's death? The day of the month, I mean.

NORA: Papa died the twenty-ninth of September.

KROGSTAD: That's quite correct; I've already looked into that. And now we come to a curious thing—[*Taking out a paper.*] which I simply cannot comprehend.

NORA: Curious thing? I don't know—

KROGSTAD: This is the curious thing: that your father co-signed the note for your loan three days after his death.

NORA: How—? I don't understand.

KROGSTAD: Your father died the twenty-ninth of September. But look. Here your father dated his signature October second. Isn't that curious, Mrs. Helmer? [NORA *is silent.*] Can you explain it to me? [NORA *remains silent.*] It's also remarkable that the words "October second" and the year aren't written in your father's hand, but rather in one that I think I know. Well, it's easy to understand. Your father forgot perhaps to date his signature, and then someone or other added it, a bit sloppily, before anyone knew of his death. There's nothing wrong in that. It all comes down to the signature. And there's no question about *that*, Mrs. Helmer. It really *was* your father who signed his own name here, wasn't it?

NORA: [*After a short silence, throwing her head back and looking squarely at him.*] No, it wasn't. I signed papa's name.

KROGSTAD: Wait, now—are you fully aware that this is a dangerous confession?

NORA: Why? You'll soon get your money.

KROGSTAD: Let me ask you a question—why didn't you send the paper to your father?

NORA: That was impossible. Papa was so sick. If I'd asked him for his signature, I also would have had to tell him what the money was for. But I couldn't tell him, sick as he was, that my husband's life was in danger. That was just impossible.

KROGSTAD: Then it would have been better if you'd given up the trip abroad.

NORA: I couldn't possibly. The trip was to save my husband's life. I couldn't give that up.

KROGSTAD: But didn't you ever consider that this was a fraud against me?

NORA: I couldn't let myself be bothered by that. You weren't any concern of mine. I couldn't stand you, with all those cold complications you made, even though you knew how badly off my husband was.

KROGSTAD: Mrs. Helmer, obviously you haven't the vaguest idea of what you've involved yourself in. But I can tell you this: it was nothing more and nothing worse that I once did—and it wrecked my whole reputation.

NORA: You? Do you expect me to believe that you ever acted bravely to save your wife's life?

KROGSTAD: Laws don't inquire into motives.

NORA: Then they must be very poor laws.

KROGSTAD: Poor or not—if I introduce this paper in court, you'll be judged according to law.

NORA: This I refuse to believe. A daughter hasn't a right to protect her dying father from anxiety and care? A wife hasn't a right to save her husband's life? I don't know much about laws, but I'm sure that somewhere in the books these things are allowed. And you don't know anything about it—you who practice the law? You must be an awful lawyer, Mr. Krogstad.

KROGSTAD: Could be. But business—the kind of business we two are mixed up in—don't you think I know about that? All right. Do what you want now. But I'm telling you *this*: if I get shoved down a second time, you're going to keep me company. [*He bows and goes out through the hall.*]

NORA: [*Pensive for a moment, then tossing her head.*] Oh, really! Trying to frighten me! I'm not so silly as all that. [*Begins gathering up the children's clothes, but soon stops.*] But—? No, but that's impossible! I did it out of love.

THE CHILDREN: [*In the doorway, left.*] Mama, that strange man's gone out the door.

NORA: Yes, yes, I know it. But don't tell anyone about the strange man. Do you hear? Not even Papa!

THE CHILDREN: No, Mama. But now will you play again?

NORA: No, not now.

THE CHILDREN: Oh, but Mama, you promised.

NORA: Yes, but I can't now. Go inside; I have too much to do. Go in, go in, my sweet darlings. [*She herds them gently back in the room and shuts the door after them. Settling on the sofa, she takes up a piece of embroidery and makes some stitches, but soon stops abruptly.*] No! [*Throws the work aside, rises, goes to the hall door and calls out.*] Helene! Let me have the tree in here. [*Goes to the table, left, opens the table drawer, and stops again.*] No, but that's utterly impossible!

MAID: [*With the Christmas tree.*] Where should I put it, ma'am?

NORA: There. The middle of the floor.

MAID: Should I bring anything else?

NORA: No, thanks. I have what I need.

[*The* MAID, *who has set the tree down, goes out.*]

NORA: [*Absorbed in trimming the tree.*] Candles here—and flowers here. That terrible creature! Talk, talk, talk! There's nothing to it at all. The tree's going to be lovely. I'll do anything to please you, Torvald. I'll sing for you, dance for you—

[HELMER *comes in from the hall, with a sheaf of papers under his arm.*]

NORA: Oh! You're back so soon?

HELMER: Yes. Has anyone been here?

NORA: Here? No.

HELMER: That's odd. I saw Krogstad leaving the front door.

NORA: So? Oh yes, that's true. Krogstad was here a moment.

HELMER: Nora, I can see by your face that he's been here, begging you to put in a good word for him.

NORA: Yes.

HELMER: And it was supposed to seem like your own idea? You were to hide it from me that he'd been here. He asked you that, too, didn't he?

NORA: Yes, Torvald, but—

HELMER: Nora, Nora, and you could fall for that? Talk with that sort of person and promise him anything? And then in the bargain, tell me an untruth.

NORA: An untruth—?

HELMER: Didn't you say that no one had been here? [*Wagging his finger.*] My little songbird must never do that again. A songbird needs a clean beak to warble with. No false notes. [*Putting his arm about her waist.*] That's the way it should be, isn't it? Yes, I'm sure of it. [*Releasing her.*] And so, enough of that. [*Sitting by the stove.*] Ah, how snug and cozy it is here. [*Leafing among his papers.*]

NORA: [*Busy with the tree, after a short pause.*] Torvald!

HELMER: Yes.

NORA: I'm so much looking forward to the Stenborgs' costume party, day after tomorrow.

HELMER: And I can't wait to see what you'll surprise me with.

NORA: Oh, that stupid business!

HELMER: What?

NORA: I can't find anything that's right. Everything seems so ridiculous, so inane.

HELMER: So my little Nora's come to *that* recognition?

NORA: [*Going behind his chair, her arms resting on its back.*] Are you very busy, Torvald?

HELMER: Oh—

NORA: What papers are those?

HELMER: Bank matters.

NORA: Already?

HELMER: I've gotten full authority from the retiring management to make all necessary changes in personnel and procedure. I'll need Christmas week for that. I want to have everything in order by New Year's.

NORA: So that was the reason this poor Krogstad—

HELMER: Hm.

NORA: [*Still leaning on the chair and slowly stroking the nape of his neck.*] If you weren't so very busy, I would have asked you an enormous favor, Torvald.

HELMER: Let's hear. What is it?

NORA: You know, there isn't anyone who has your good taste—and I want so much to look well at the costume party. Torvald, couldn't you take over and decide what I should be and plan my costume?

HELMER: Ah, is my stubborn little creature calling for a lifeguard?

NORA: Yes, Torvald, I can't get anywhere without your help.

HELMER: All right—I'll think it over. We'll hit on something.

NORA: Oh, how sweet of you. [*Goes to the tree again. Pause.*] Aren't the red flowers pretty—? But tell me, was it really such a crime that this Krogstad committed?

HELMER: Forgery. Do you have any idea what that means?

NORA: Couldn't he have done it out of need?

HELMER: Yes, or thoughtlessness, like so many others. I'm not so heartless that I'd condemn a man categorically for just one mistake.

NORA: No, of course not, Torvald!

HELMER: Plenty of men have redeemed themselves by openly confessing their crimes and taking their punishment.

NORA: Punishment—?

HELMER: But now Krogstad didn't go that way. He got himself out by sharp practices, and that's the real cause of his moral breakdown.

NORA: Do you really think that would—?

HELMER: Just imagine how a man with that sort of guilt in him has to lie and cheat and deceive on all sides, has to wear a mask even with the nearest and dearest he has, even with his own wife and children. And with the children, Nora—that's where it's most horrible.

NORA: Why?

HELMER: Because that kind of atmosphere of lies infects the whole life of a home. Every breath the children take in is filled with the germs of something degenerate.

NORA: [*Coming closer behind him.*] Are you sure of that?

HELMER: Oh, I've seen it often enough as a lawyer. Almost everyone who goes bad early in life has a mother who's a chronic liar.

NORA: Why just—the mother?

HELMER: It's usually the mother's influence that's dominant, but the father's works in the same way, of course. Every lawyer is quite familiar with it. And still this Krogstad's been going home year in, year out, poisoning his own children with lies and pretense; that's why I call him morally lost. [*Reaching his hands out toward her.*] So my sweet little Nora must promise me never to plead his cause. Your hand on it. Come, come, what's this? Give me your hand. There, now. All settled. I can tell you it'd be impossible for me to work alongside of him. I literally feel physically revolted when I'm anywhere near such a person.

NORA: [*Withdraws her hand and goes to the other side of the Christmas tree.*] How hot it is here! And I've got so much to do.

HELMER: [*Getting up and gathering his papers.*] Yes, and I have to think about getting some of these read through before dinner. I'll think about your costume, too. And something to hang on the tree in gilt paper, I may even see about that. [*Putting his hand on her head.*] Oh you, my darling little songbird. [*He goes into his study and closes the door after him.*]

NORA: [*Softly, after a silence.*] Oh, really! it isn't so. It's impossible. It must be impossible.

ANNE-MARIE: [*In the doorway, left.*] The children are begging so hard to come in to Mama.

NORA: No, no, no, don't let them in to me! You stay with them, Anne-Marie.

ANNE-MARIE: Of course, ma'am. [*Closes the door.*]

NORA: [*Pale with terror*]. Hurt my children—! Poison my home? [*A moment's pause; then she tosses her head.*] That's not true. Never. Never in all the world.

ACT II

Same room. Beside the piano the Christmas tree now stands stripped of ornament, burned-down candle stubs on its ragged branches. NORA's *street clothes lie on the sofa.* NORA, *alone in the room, moves restlessly about; at last she stops at the sofa and picks up her coat.*

NORA: [*Dropping the coat again.*] Someone's coming! [*Goes toward the door, listens.*] No—there's no one. Of course—nobody's coming today, Christmas Day—or tomorrow, either. But maybe—[*Opens the door and looks out.*] No, nothing in the mailbox. Quite empty. [*Coming forward.*] What nonsense! He won't do anything serious. Nothing terrible could happen. It's impossible. Why, I have three small children.

[ANNE-MARIE, *with a large carton, comes in from the room to the left.*]

ANNE-MARIE: Well, at last I found the box with the masquerade clothes.

NORA: Thanks. Put it on the table.

ANNE-MARIE: [*Does so.*] But they're all pretty much of a mess.

NORA: Ahh! I'd love to rip them in a million pieces!

ANNE-MARIE: Oh, mercy, they can be fixed right up. Just a little patience.

NORA: Yes, I'll go get Mrs. Linde to help me.

ANNE-MARIE: Out again now? In this nasty weather? Miss Nora will catch cold—get sick.

NORA: Oh, worse things could happen—How are the children?

ANNE-MARIE: The poor mites are playing with their Christmas presents, but—

NORA: Do they ask for me much?

ANNE-MARIE: They're so used to having Mama around, you know.

NORA: Yes, but Anne-Marie, I *can't* be together with them as much as I was.

ANNE-MARIE: Well, small children get used to anything.

NORA: You think so? Do you think they'd forget their mother if she was gone for good?

ANNE-MARIE: Oh, mercy—gone for good!

NORA: Wait, tell me, Anne-Marie—I've wondered so often—how could you ever have the heart to give your child over to strangers?

ANNE-MARIE: But I had to, you know, to become little Nora's nurse.

NORA: Yes, but how could you *do* it?

ANNE-MARIE: When I could get such a good place? A girl who's poor and who's gotten in trouble is glad enough for that. Because that slippery fish, he didn't do a thing for me, you know.

NORA: But your daughter's surely forgotten you.

ANNE-MARIE: Oh, she certainly has not. She's written to me, both when she was confirmed and when she was married.

NORA: [*Clasping her about the neck.*] You old Anne-Marie, you were a good mother for me when I was little.

ANNE-MARIE: Poor little Nora, with no other mother but me.

NORA: And if the babies didn't have one, then I know that you'd—What silly talk! [*Opening the carton.*] Go in to them. Now I'll have to—Tomorrow you can see how lovely I'll look.

ANNE-MARIE: Oh, there won't be anyone at the party as lovely as Miss Nora. [*She goes off into the room, left.*]

NORA: [*Begins unpacking the box, but soon throws it aside.*] Oh, if I dared to go out. If only nobody would come. If only nothing would happen here while I'm out. What craziness—nobody's coming. Just don't think. This muff—needs a brushing. Beautiful gloves, beautiful gloves. Let it go. Let it go! One, two, three, four, five, six—[*With a cry.*] Oh, there they are! [*Poises to move toward the door, but remains irresolutely standing.* MRS. LINDE *enters from the hall, where she has removed her street clothes.*]

NORA: Oh, it's you, Kristine. There's no one else out there? How good that you've come.

MRS. LINDE: I hear you were up asking for me.

NORA: Yes, I just stopped by. There's something you really can help me with. Let's get settled on the sofa. Look, there's going to be a costume party tomorrow evening at the Stenborgs' right above us, and now Torvald wants me to go as a Neapolitan peasant girl and dance the tarantella[2] that I learned in Capri.

MRS. LINDE: Really, are you giving a whole performance?

NORA: Torvald says yes, I should. See, here's the dress. Torvald had it made for me down there; but now it's all so tattered that I just don't know—

MRS. LINDE: Oh, we'll fix that up in no time. It's nothing more than the trimmings—they're a bit loose here and there. Needle and thread? Good, now we have what we need.

NORA: Oh, how sweet of you!

MRS. LINDE: [*Sewing.*] So you'll be in disguise tomorrow, Nora. You know what? I'll stop by then for a moment and have a look at you all dressed up. But listen, I've absolutely forgotten to thank you for that pleasant evening yesterday.

NORA: [*Getting up and walking about.*] I don't think it was as pleasant as usual yesterday. You should have come to town a bit sooner, Kristine—Yes, Torvald really knows how to give a home elegance and charm.

MRS. LINDE: And you do, too, if you ask me. You're not your father's daughter for nothing. But tell me, is Dr. Rank always so down in the mouth as yesterday?

NORA: No, that was quite an exception. But he goes around critically ill all the time—tuberculosis of the spine, poor man. You know, his father was a disgusting thing who kept mistresses and so on—and that's why the son's been sickly from birth.

MRS. LINDE: [*Lets her sewing fall to her lap.*] But my dearest Nora, how do you know about such things?

NORA: [*Walking more jauntily.*] Hmp! When you've had three children, then you've had a few visits from—from women who know something of medicine, and they tell you this and that.

MRS. LINDE: [*Resumes sewing; a short pause.*] Does Dr. Rank come here every day?

NORA: Every blessed day. He's Torvald's best friend from childhood, and *my* good friend, too. Dr. Rank almost belongs to this house.

---

2. Lively folk dance of southern Italy, thought to cure the bite of the tarantula.

MRS. LINDE: But tell me—is he quite sincere? I mean, doesn't he rather enjoy flattering people?

NORA: Just the opposite. Why do you think that?

MRS. LINDE: When you introduced us yesterday, he was proclaiming that he'd often heard my name in this house; but later I noticed that your husband hadn't the slightest idea who I really was. So how could Dr. Rank—?

NORA: But it's all true, Kristine. You see, Torvald loves me beyond words, and, as he puts it, he'd like to keep me all to himself. For a long time he'd almost be jealous if I even mentioned any of my old friends back home. So of course I dropped that. But with Dr. Rank I talk a lot about such things, because he likes hearing about them.

MRS. LINDE: Now listen, Nora; in many ways you're still like a child. I'm a good deal older than you, with a little more experience. I'll tell you something: you ought to put an end to all this with Dr. Rank.

NORA: What should I put an end to?

MRS. LINDE: Both parts of it, I think. Yesterday you said something about a rich admirer who'd provide you with money—

NORA: Yes, one who doesn't exist—worse luck. So?

MRS. LINDE: Is Dr. Rank well off?

NORA: Yes, he is.

MRS. LINDE: With no dependents?

NORA: No, no one. But—

MRS. LINDE: And he's over here every day?

NORA: Yes, I told you that.

MRS. LINDE: How can a man of such refinement be so grasping?

NORA: I don't follow you at all.

MRS. LINDE: Now don't try to hide it, Nora. You think I can't guess who loaned you the forty-eight hundred crowns?

NORA: Are you out of your mind? How could you think such a thing! A friend of ours, who comes here every single day. What an intolerable situation that would have been!

MRS. LINDE: Then it really wasn't him.

NORA: No, absolutely not. It never even crossed my mind for a moment— And he had nothing to lend in those days; his inheritance came later.

MRS. LINDE: Well, I think that was a stroke of luck for you, Nora dear.

NORA: No, it never would have occurred to me to ask Dr. Rank—Still, I'm quite sure that if I had asked him—

MRS. LINDE: Which you won't, of course.

NORA: No, of course not. I can't see that I'd ever need to. But I'm quite positive that if I talked to Dr. Rank—

MRS. LINDE: Behind your husband's back?

NORA: I've got to clear up this other thing; *that's* also behind his back. I've *got* to clear it all up.

MRS. LINDE: Yes, I was saying that yesterday, but—

NORA: [*Pacing up and down.*] A man handles these problems so much better than a woman—

MRS. LINDE: One's husband does, yes.

NORA: Nonsense. [*Stopping.*] When you pay everything you owe, then you get your note back, right?

MRS. LINDE: Yes, naturally.

NORA: And can rip it into a million pieces and burn it up—that filthy scrap of paper!

MRS. LINDE: [*Looking hard at her, laying her sewing aside, and rising slowly.*] Nora, you're hiding something from me.

NORA: You can see it in my face?

MRS. LINDE: Something's happened to you since yesterday morning. Nora, what is it?

NORA: [*Hurrying toward her.*] Kristine! [*Listening.*] Shh! Torvald's home. Look, go in with the children a while. Torvald can't bear all this snipping and stitching. Let Anne-Marie help you.

MRS. LINDE: [*Gathering up some of the things.*] All right, but I'm not leaving here until we've talked this out. [*She disappears into the room, left, as* TORVALD *enters from the hall.*]

NORA: Oh, how I've been waiting for you, Torvald dear.

HELMER: Was that the dressmaker?

NORA: No, that was Kristine. She's helping me fix up my costume. You know, it's going to be quite attractive.

HELMER: Yes, wasn't that a bright idea I had?

NORA: Brilliant! But then wasn't I good as well to give in to you?

HELMER: Good—because you give in to your husband's judgment? All right, you little goose, I know you didn't mean it like that. But I won't disturb you. You'll want to have a fitting, I suppose.

NORA: And you'll be working?

HELMER: Yes. [*Indicating a bundle of papers.*] See. I've been down to the bank. [*Starts toward his study.*]

NORA: Torvald.

HELMER: [*Stops.*] Yes.

NORA: If your little squirrel begged you, with all her heart and soul, for something—?

HELMER: What's that?

NORA: Then would you do it?

HELMER: First, naturally, I'd have to know what it was.

NORA: Your squirrel would scamper about and do tricks, if you'd only be sweet and give in.

HELMER: Out with it.

NORA: Your lark would be singing high and low in every room—

HELMER: Come on, she does that anyway.

NORA: I'd be a wood nymph and dance for you in the moonlight.

HELMER: Nora—don't tell me it's that same business from this morning?

NORA: [*Coming closer.*] Yes, Torvald, I beg you, please!

HELMER: And you actually have the nerve to drag that up again?

NORA: Yes, yes, you've got to give in to me; you *have* to let Krogstad keep his job in the bank.

HELMER: My dear Nora, I've slated his job for Mrs. Linde.

NORA: That's awfully kind of you. But you could just fire another clerk instead of Krogstad.

HELMER: This is the most incredible stubbornness! Because you go and give an impulsive promise to speak up for him, I'm expected to—

NORA: That's not the reason, Torvald. It's for your own sake. That man does writing for the worst papers; you said it yourself. He could do you any amount of harm. I'm scared to death of him—

HELMER: Ah, I understand. It's the old memories haunting you.

NORA: What do you mean by that?

HELMER: Of course, you're thinking about your father.

NORA: Yes, all right. Just remember how those nasty gossips wrote in the papers about Papa and slandered him so cruelly. I think they'd have had him dismissed if the department hadn't sent you up to investigate, and if you hadn't been so kind and open-minded toward him.

HELMER: My dear Nora, there's a notable difference between your father and me. Your father's official career was hardly above reproach. But mine is; and I hope it'll stay that way as long as I hold my position.

NORA: Oh, who can ever tell what vicious minds can invent? We could be so snug and happy now in our quiet, carefree home—you and I and the children, Torvald! That's why I'm pleading with you so—

HELMER: And just by pleading for him you make it impossible for me to keep him on. It's already known at the bank that I'm firing Krogstad. What if it's rumored around now that the new bank manager was vetoed by his wife—

NORA: Yes, what then—?

HELMER: Oh yes—as long as our little bundle of stubbornness gets her way—! I should go and make myself ridiculous in front of the whole office—give people the idea I can be swayed by all kinds of outside pressure. Oh, you can bet I'd feel the effects of that soon enough! Besides—there's something that rules Krogstad right out at the bank as long as I'm the manager.

NORA: What's that?

HELMER: His moral failings I could maybe overlook if I had to—

NORA: Yes, Torvald, why not?

HELMER: And I hear he's quite efficient on the job. But he was a crony of mine back in my teens—one of those rash friendships that crop up again and again to embarrass you later in life. Well, I might as well say it straight out: we're on a first-name basis. And that tactless fool makes no effort at all to hide it in front of others. Quite the contrary—he thinks that entitles him to take a familiar air around me, and so every other second he comes booming out with his "Yes, Torvald!" and "Sure thing, Torvald!" I tell you, it's been excruciating for me. He's out to make my place in the bank unbearable.

NORA: Torvald, you can't be serious about all this.

HELMER: Oh no? Why not?

NORA: Because these are such petty considerations.

HELMER: What are you saying? Petty? You think I'm petty!

NORA: No, just the opposite, Torvald dear. That's exactly why—

HELMER: Never mind. You call my motives petty; then I might as well be just that. Petty! All right! We'll put a stop to this for good. [*Goes to the hall door and calls.*] Helene!

NORA: What do you want?

HELMER: [*Searching among his papers.*] A decision. [*The* MAID *comes in.*] Look here; take this letter; go out with it at once. Get hold of a messenger and have him deliver it. Quick now. It's already addressed. Wait, here's some money.

MAID: Yes, sir. [*She leaves with the letter.*]

HELMER: [*Straightening his papers.*] There, now, little Miss Willful.

NORA: [*Breathlessly.*] Torvald, what was that letter?

HELMER: Krogstad's notice.

NORA: Call it back, Torvald! There's still time. Oh, Torvald, call it back! Do it for my sake—for your sake, for the children's sake! Do you hear, Torvald; do it! You don't know how this can harm us.

HELMER: Too late.

NORA: Yes, too late.

HELMER: Nora dear, I can forgive you this panic, even though basically you're insulting me. Yes, you are! Or isn't it an insult to think that *I* should be afraid of a courtroom hack's revenge? But I forgive you anyway, because this shows so beautifully how much you love me. [*Takes her in his arms.*] This is the way it should be, my darling Nora. Whatever comes, you'll see: when it really counts, I have strength and courage enough as a man to take on the whole weight myself.

NORA: [*Terrified.*] What do you mean by that?

HELMER: The whole weight, I said.

NORA: [*Resolutely.*] No, never in all the world.

HELMER: Good. So we'll share it, Nora, as man and wife. That's as it should be. [*Fondling her.*] Are you happy now? There, there, there—not these frightened dove's eyes. It's nothing at all but empty fantasies—Now you should run through your tarantella and practice your tambourine. I'll go to the inner office and shut both doors, so I won't hear a thing; you can make all the noise you like. [*Turning in the doorway.*] And when Rank comes, just tell him where he can find me. [*He nods to her and goes with his papers into the study, closing the door.*]

NORA: [*Standing as though rooted, dazed with fright, in a whisper.*] He really could do it. He will do it. He'll do it in spite of everything. No, not that, never, never! Anything but that! Escape! A way out—[*The doorbell rings.*] Dr. Rank! Anything but that! *Anything*, whatever it is! [*Her hands pass over her face, smoothing it; she pulls herself together, goes over and opens the hall door.* DR. RANK *stands outside, hanging his fur coat up. During the following scene, it begins getting dark.*]

NORA: Hello, Dr. Rank. I recognized your ring. But you mustn't go in to Torvald yet; I believe he's working.

RANK: And you?

NORA: For you, I always have an hour to spare—you know that. [*He has entered, and she shuts the door after him.*]

RANK: Many thanks. I'll make use of these hours while I can.

NORA: What do you mean by that? While you can?

RANK: Does that disturb you?

NORA: Well, it's such an odd phrase. Is anything going to happen?

RANK: What's going to happen is what I've been expecting so long—but I honestly didn't think it would come so soon.

NORA: [*Gripping his arm.*] What is it you've found out? Dr. Rank, you have to tell me!

RANK: [*Sitting by the stove.*] It's all over with me. There's nothing to be done about it.

NORA: [*Breathing easier.*] Is it you—then—?

RANK: Who else? There's no point in lying to one's self. I'm the most miserable of all my patients, Mrs. Helmer. These past few days I've been auditing my internal accounts. Bankrupt! Within a month I'll probably be laid out and rotting in the churchyard.

NORA: Oh, what a horrible thing to say.

RANK: The thing itself is horrible. But the worst of it is all the other horror before it's over. There's only one final examination left; when I'm finished with that, I'll know about when my disintegration will begin. There's something I want to say. Helmer with his sensitivity has such a sharp distaste for anything ugly. I don't want him near my sickroom.

NORA: Oh, but Dr. Rank—

RANK: I won't have him in there. Under no condition. I'll lock my door to him—As soon as I'm completely sure of the worst, I'll send you my calling card marked with a black cross, and you'll know then the wreck has started to come apart.

NORA: No, today you're completely unreasonable. And I wanted you so much to be in a really good humor.

RANK: With death up my sleeve? And then to suffer this way for somebody else's sins. Is there any justice in that? And in every single family, in some way or another, this inevitable retribution of nature goes on—

NORA: [*Her hands pressed over her ears.*] Oh, stuff! Cheer up! Please—be gay!

RANK: Yes, I'd just as soon laugh at it all. My poor, innocent spine, serving time for my father's gay army days.

NORA: [*By the table, left.*] He was so infatuated with asparagus tips and *pâté de foie gras*, wasn't that it?

RANK: Yes—and with truffles.

NORA: Truffles, yes. And then with oysters, I suppose?

RANK: Yes, tons of oysters, naturally.

NORA: And then the port and champagne to go with it. It's so sad that all these delectable things have to strike at our bones.

RANK: Especially when they strike at the unhappy bones that never shared in the fun.

NORA: Ah, that's the saddest of all.

RANK: [*Looks searchingly at her.*] Hm.

NORA: [*After a moment.*] Why did you smile?

RANK: No, it was you who laughed.

NORA: No, it was you who smiled, Dr. Rank!

RANK: [*Getting up.*] You're even a bigger tease than I'd thought.

NORA: I'm full of wild ideas today.

RANK: That's obvious.

NORA: [*Putting both hands on his shoulders.*] Dear, dear Dr. Rank, you'll never die for Torvald and me.

RANK: Oh, that loss you'll easily get over. Those who go away are soon forgotten.

NORA: [*Looks fearfully at him.*] You believe that?

RANK: One makes new connections, and then—

NORA: Who makes new connections?

RANK: Both you and Torvald will when I'm gone. I'd say you're well under way already. What was that Mrs. Linde doing here last evening?

NORA: Oh, come—you can't be jealous of poor Kristine?

RANK: Oh yes, I am. She'll be my successor here in the house. When I'm down under, that woman will probably—

NORA: Shh! Not so loud. She's right in there.

RANK: Today as well. So you see.

NORA: Only to sew on my dress. Good gracious, how unreasonable you are. [*Sitting on the sofa.*] Be nice now, Dr. Rank. Tomorrow you'll see how beautifully I'll dance; and you can imagine then that I'm dancing only for you— yes, and of course for Torvald, too—that's understood. [*Takes various items out of the carton.*] Dr. Rank, sit over here and I'll show you something.

RANK: [*Sitting.*] What's that?

NORA: Look here. Look.

RANK: Silk stockings.

NORA: Flesh-colored. Aren't they lovely? Now it's so dark here, but tomorrow— No, no, no, just look at the feet. Oh well, you might as well look at the rest.

RANK: Hm—

NORA: Why do you look so critical? Don't you believe they'll fit?

RANK: I've never had any chance to form an opinion on that.

NORA: [*Glancing at him a moment.*] Shame on you. [*Hits him lightly on the ear with the stockings.*] That's for you. [*Puts them away again.*]

RANK: And what other splendors am I going to see now?

NORA: Not the least bit more, because you've been naughty. [*She hums a little and rummages among her things.*]

RANK: [*After a short silence.*] When I sit here together with you like this, completely easy and open, then I don't know—I simply can't imagine—whatever would have become of me if I'd never come into this house.

NORA: [*Smiling.*] Yes, I really think you feel completely at ease with us.

RANK: [*More quietly, staring straight ahead.*] And then to have to go away from it all—

NORA: Nonsense, you're not going away.

RANK: [*His voice unchanged.*]—and not even be able to leave some poor show of gratitude behind, scarcely a fleeting regret—no more than a vacant place that anyone can fill.

NORA: And if I asked you now for—? No—

RANK: For what?

NORA: For a great proof of your friendship—

RANK: Yes, yes?

NORA: No, I mean—for an exceptionally big favor—

RANK: Would you really, for once, make me so happy?

NORA: Oh, you haven't the vaguest idea what it is.

RANK: All right, then tell me.

NORA: No, but I can't, Dr. Rank—it's all out of reason. It's advice and help, too—and a favor—

RANK: So much the better. I can't fathom what you're hinting at. Just speak out. Don't you trust me?

NORA: Of course. More than anyone else. You're my best and truest friend, I'm sure. That's why I want to talk to you. All right, then, Dr. Rank: there's something you can help me prevent. You know how deeply, how inexpressibly dearly Torvald loves me; he'd never hesitate a second to give up his life for me.

RANK: [*Leaning close to her.*] Nora—do you think he's the only one—

NORA: [*With a slight start.*] Who—?

RANK: Who'd gladly give up his life for you.

NORA: [*Heavily.*] I see.

RANK: I swore to myself you should know this before I'm gone. I'll never find a better chance. Yes, Nora, now you know. And also you know now that you can trust me beyond anyone else.

NORA: [*Rising, natural and calm.*] Let me by.

RANK: [*Making room for her, but still sitting.*] Nora—

NORA: [*In the hall doorway.*] Helene, bring the lamp in. [*Goes over to the stove.*] Ah, dear Dr. Rank, that was really mean of you.

RANK: [*Getting up.*] That I've loved you just as deeply as somebody else? Was *that* mean?

NORA: No, but that you came out and told me. That was quite unnecessary—

RANK: What do you mean? Have you known—?

[*The* MAID *comes in with the lamp, sets it on the table, and goes out again.*]

RANK: Nora—Mrs. Helmer—I'm asking you: have you known about it?

NORA: Oh, how can I tell what I know or don't know? Really, I don't know what to say—Why did you have to be so clumsy, Dr. Rank! Everything was so good.

RANK: Well, in any case, you now have the knowledge that my body and soul are at your command. So won't you speak out?

NORA: [*Looking at him.*] After that?

RANK: Please, just let me know what it is.

NORA: You can't know anything now.

RANK: I have to. You mustn't punish me like this. Give me the chance to do whatever is humanly possible for you.

NORA: Now there's nothing you can do for me. Besides, actually, I don't need any help. You'll see—it's only my fantasies. That's what it is. Of course! [*Sits in the rocker, looks at him, and smiles.*] What a nice one you are, Dr. Rank. Aren't you a little bit ashamed, now that the lamp is here?

RANK: No, not exactly. But perhaps I'd better go—for good?

NORA: No, you certainly can't do that. You must come here just as you always have. You know Torvald can't do without you.

RANK: Yes, but *you*?

NORA: You know how much I enjoy it when you're here.

RANK: That's precisely what threw me off. You're a mystery to me. So many times I've felt you'd almost rather be with me than with Helmer.

NORA: Yes—you see, there are some people that one loves most and other people that one would almost prefer being with.

RANK: Yes, there's something to that.

NORA: When I was back home, of course I loved Papa most. But I always thought it was so much fun when I could sneak down to the maids' quarters, because they never tried to improve me, and it was always so amusing, the way they talked to each other.

RANK: Aha, so it's *their* place that I've filled.

NORA: [*Jumping up and going to him.*] Oh, dear, sweet Dr. Rank, that's not what I meant at all. But you can understand that with Torvald it's just the same as with Papa—

[*The* MAID *enters from the hall.*]

MAID: Ma'am—please! [*She whispers to* NORA *and hands her a calling card.*]

NORA: [*Glancing at the card.*] Ah! [*Slips it into her pocket.*]

RANK: Anything wrong?

NORA: No, no, not at all. It's only some—it's my new dress—

RANK: Really? But—there's your dress.

NORA: Oh, that. But this is another one—I ordered it—Torvald mustn't know—

RANK: Ah, now we have the big secret.

NORA: That's right. Just go in with him—he's back in the inner study. Keep him there as long as—

RANK: Don't worry. He won't get away. [*Goes into the study.*]

NORA: [*To the* MAID.] And he's standing waiting in the kitchen?

MAID: Yes, he came up by the back stairs.

NORA: But didn't you tell him somebody was here?

MAID: Yes, but that didn't do any good.

NORA: He won't leave?

MAID: No, he won't go till he's talked with you, ma'am.

NORA: Let him come in, then—but quietly. Helene, don't breathe a word about this. It's a surprise for my husband.

MAID: Yes, yes, I understand—[*Goes out.*]

NORA: This horror—it's going to happen. No, no, no, it can't happen, it mustn't.

> [*She goes and bolts* HELMER's *door. The* MAID *opens the hall door for* KROG-STAD *and shuts it behind him. He is dressed for travel in a fur coat, boots, and a fur cap.*]

NORA: [*Going toward him.*] Talk softly. My husband's home.

KROGSTAD: Well, good for him.

NORA: What do you want?

KROGSTAD: Some information.

NORA: Hurry up, then. What is it?

KROGSTAD: You know, of course, that I got my notice.

NORA: I couldn't prevent it, Mr. Krogstad. I fought for you to the bitter end, but nothing worked.

KROGSTAD: Does your husband's love for you run so thin? He knows everything I can expose you to, and all the same he dares to—

NORA: How can you imagine he knows anything about this?

KROGSTAD: Ah, no—I can't imagine it either, now. It's not at all like my fine Torvald Helmer to have so much guts—

NORA: Mr. Krogstad, I demand respect for my husband!

KROGSTAD: Why, of course—all due respect. But since the lady's keeping it so carefully hidden, may I presume to ask if you're also a bit better informed than yesterday about what you've actually done?

NORA: More than you ever could teach me.

KROGSTAD: Yes, I *am* such an awful lawyer.

NORA: What is it you want from me?

KROGSTAD: Just a glimpse of how you are, Mrs. Helmer. I've been thinking about you all day long. A cashier, a night-court scribbler, a—well, a type like me also has a little of what they call a heart, you know.

NORA: Then show it. Think of my children.

KROGSTAD: Did you or your husband ever think of mine? But never mind. I simply wanted to tell you that you don't need to take this thing too seriously. For the present, I'm not proceeding with any action.

NORA: Oh no, really! Well—I knew that.

KROGSTAD: Everything can be settled in a friendly spirit. It doesn't have to get around town at all; it can stay just among us three.

NORA: My husband must never know anything of this.

KROGSTAD: How can you manage that? Perhaps you can pay me the balance?

NORA: No, not right now.

KROGSTAD: Or you know some way of raising the money in a day or two?

NORA: No way that I'm willing to use.

KROGSTAD: Well, it wouldn't have done you any good, anyway. If you stood in front of me with a fistful of bills, you still couldn't buy your signature back.

NORA: Then tell me what you're going to do with it.

KROGSTAD: I'll just hold onto it—keep it on file. There's no outsider who'll even get wind of it. So if you've been thinking of taking some desperate step—

NORA: I have.

KROGSTAD: Been thinking of running away from home—

NORA: I have!

KROGSTAD: Or even of something worse—

NORA: How could you guess that?

KROGSTAD: You can drop those thoughts.

NORA: How could you guess I was thinking of *that*?

KROGSTAD: Most of us think about *that* at first. I thought about it too, but I discovered I hadn't the courage—

NORA: [*Lifelessly.*] I don't either.

KROGSTAD: [*Relieved.*] That's true, you haven't the courage? You too?

NORA: I don't have it—I don't have it.

KROGSTAD: It would be terribly stupid, anyway. After that first storm at home blows out, why, then—I have here in my pocket a letter for your husband—

NORA: Telling everything?

KROGSTAD: As charitably as possible.

NORA: [*Quickly.*] He mustn't ever get that letter. Tear it up. I'll find some way to get money.

KROGSTAD: Beg pardon, Mrs. Helmer, but I think I just told you—

NORA: Oh, I don't mean the money I owe you. Let me know how much you want from my husband, and I'll manage it.

KROGSTAD: I don't want any money from your husband.

NORA: What do you want, then?

KROGSTAD: I'll tell you what. I want to recoup, Mrs. Helmer; I want to get on in the world—and there's where your husband can help me. For a year and a half I've kept myself clean of anything disreputable—all that time struggling with the worst conditions; but I was satisfied, working my way up step by step. Now I've been written right off, and I'm just not in the mood to come crawling back. I tell you, I want to move on. I want to get back in the bank—in a better position. Your husband can set up a job for me—

NORA: He'll never do that!

KROGSTAD: He'll do it. I know him. He won't dare breathe a word of protest. And once I'm in there together with him, you just wait and see! Inside of a year, I'll be the manager's right-hand man. It'll be Nils Krogstad, not Torvald Helmer, who runs the bank.

NORA: You'll never see the day!

KROGSTAD: Maybe you think you can—

NORA: I have the courage now—for *that.*

KROGSTAD: Oh, you don't scare me. A smart, spoiled lady like you—

NORA: You'll see; you'll see!

KROGSTAD: Under the ice, maybe? Down in the freezing, coal-black water? There, till you float up in the spring, ugly, unrecognizable, with your hair falling out—

NORA: You don't frighten me.

KROGSTAD: Nor do you frighten me. One doesn't do these things, Mrs. Helmer. Besides, what good would it be? I'd still have him safe in my pocket.

NORA: Afterwards? When I'm no longer—?

KROGSTAD: Are you forgetting that *I'll* be in control then over your final reputation? [NORA *stands speechless, staring at him.*] Good; now I've warned you. Don't do anything stupid. When Helmer's read my letter, I'll be waiting for his reply. And bear in mind that it's your husband himself who's forced me back to my old ways. I'll never forgive him for that. Good-bye, Mrs. Helmer. [*He goes out through the hall.*]

NORA: [*Goes to the hall door, opens it a crack, and listens.*] He's gone. Didn't leave the letter. Oh no, no, that's impossible too! [*Opening the door more and more.*] What's that? He's standing outside—not going downstairs. He's thinking it over? Maybe he'll—? [*A letter falls in the mailbox; then* KROGSTAD's *footsteps are heard, dying away down a flight of stairs.* NORA *gives a muffled cry and runs over toward the sofa table. A short pause.*] In the mailbox. [*Slips warily over to the hall door.*] It's lying there. Torvald, Torvald—now we're lost!

MRS. LINDE: [*Entering with the costume from the room, left.*] There now, I can't see anything else to mend. Perhaps you'd like to try—

NORA: [*In a hoarse whisper.*] Kristine, come here.

MRS. LINDE: [*Tossing the dress on the sofa.*] What's wrong? You look upset.

NORA: Come here. See that letter? *There!* Look—through the glass in the mailbox.

MRS. LINDE: Yes, yes, I see it.

NORA: That letter's from Krogstad—

MRS. LINDE: Nora—it's Krogstad who loaned you the money!

NORA: Yes, and now Torvald will find out everything.

MRS. LINDE: Believe me, Nora, it's best for both of you.

NORA: There's more you don't know. I forged a name.

MRS. LINDE: But for heaven's sake—?

NORA: I only want to tell you that, Kristine, so that you can be my witness.

MRS. LINDE: Witness? Why should I—?

NORA: If I should go out of my mind—it could easily happen—

MRS. LINDE: Nora!

NORA: Or anything else occurred—so I couldn't be present here—

MRS. LINDE: Nora, Nora, you aren't yourself at all!

NORA: And someone should try to take on the whole weight, all of the guilt, you follow me—

MRS. LINDE: Yes, of course, but why do you think—?

NORA: Then you're the witness that it isn't true, Kristine. I'm very much myself; my mind right now is perfectly clear; and I'm telling you: nobody else has known about this; I alone did everything. Remember that.

MRS. LINDE: I will. But I don't understand all this.

NORA: Oh, how could you ever understand it? It's the miracle now that's going to take place.

MRS. LINDE: The miracle?

NORA: Yes, the miracle. But it's so awful, Kristine. It mustn't take place, not for anything in the world.

MRS. LINDE: I'm going right over and talk with Krogstad.

NORA: Don't go near him; he'll do you some terrible harm!

MRS. LINDE: There was a time once when he'd gladly have done anything for me.

NORA: He?

MRS. LINDE: Where does he live?

NORA: Oh, how do I know? Yes. [*Searches in her pocket.*] Here's his card. But the letter, the letter—!

HELMER: [*From the study, knocking on the door.*] Nora!

NORA: [*With a cry of fear.*] Oh! What is it? What do you want?

HELMER: Now, now, don't be so frightened. We're not coming in. You locked the door—are you trying on the dress?

NORA: Yes, I'm trying it. I'll look just beautiful, Torvald.

MRS. LINDE: [*Who has read the card.*] He's living right around the corner.

NORA: Yes, but what's the use? We're lost. The letter's in the box.

MRS. LINDE: And your husband has the key?

NORA: Yes, always.

MRS. LINDE: Krogstad can ask for his letter back unread; he can find some excuse—

NORA: But it's just this time that Torvald usually—

MRS. LINDE: Stall him. Keep him in there. I'll be back as quick as I can. [*She hurries out through the hall entrance.*]

NORA: [*Goes to* HELMER's *door, opens it, and peers in.*] Torvald!

HELMER: [*From the inner study.*] Well—does one dare set foot in one's own living room at last? Come on, Rank, now we'll get a look—[*In the doorway.*] But what's this?

NORA: What, Torvald dear?

HELMER: Rank had me expecting some grand masquerade.

RANK: [*In the doorway.*] That was my impression, but I must have been wrong.

NORA: No one can admire me in my splendor—not till tomorrow.

HELMER: But Nora dear, you look so exhausted. Have you practiced too hard?

NORA: No, I haven't practiced at all yet.

HELMER: You know, it's necessary—

NORA: Oh, it's absolutely necessary, Torvald. But I can't get anywhere without your help. I've forgotten the whole thing completely.

HELMER: Ah, we'll soon take care of that.

NORA: Yes, take care of me, Torvald, please! Promise me that? Oh, I'm so nervous. That big party—You must give up everything this evening for me. No business—don't even touch your pen. Yes? Dear Torvald, promise?

HELMER: It's a promise. Tonight I'm totally at your service—you little helpless thing. Hm—but first there's one thing I want to—[*Goes toward the hall door.*]

NORA: What are you looking for?

HELMER: Just to see if there's any mail.

NORA: No, no, don't do that, Torvald!

HELMER: Now what?

NORA: Torvald, please. There isn't any.

HELMER: Let me look, though. [*Starts out.* NORA, *at the piano, strikes the first notes of the tarantella.* HELMER, *at the door, stops.*] Aha!

NORA: I can't dance tomorrow if I don't practice with you.

HELMER: [*Going over to her.*] Nora dear, are you really so frightened?

NORA: Yes, so terribly frightened. Let me practice right now; there's still time before dinner. Oh, sit down and play for me, Torvald. Direct me. Teach me, the way you always have.

HELMER: Gladly, if it's what you want. [*Sits at the piano.*]

NORA: [*Snatches the tambourine up from the box, then a long, varicolored shawl, which she throws around herself, whereupon she springs forward and cries out:*] Play for me now! Now I'll dance!

[HELMER *plays and* NORA *dances.* RANK *stands behind* HELMER *at the piano and looks on.*]

HELMER: [*As he plays.*] Slower. Slow down.
NORA: Can't change it.
HELMER: Not so violent, Nora!
NORA: Has to be just like this.
HELMER: [*Stopping.*] No, no, that won't do at all.
NORA: [*Laughing and swinging her tambourine.*] Isn't that what I told you?
RANK: Let me play for her.
HELMER: [*Getting up.*] Yes, go on. I can teach her more easily then.

[RANK *sits at the piano and plays;* NORA *dances more and more wildly.* HELMER *has stationed himself by the stove and repeatedly gives her directions; she seems not to hear them; her hair loosens and falls over her shoulders; she does not notice, but goes on dancing.* MRS. LINDE *enters.*]

MRS. LINDE: [*Standing dumbfounded at the door.*] Ah—!
NORA: [*Still dancing.*] See what fun, Kristine!
HELMER: But Nora darling, you dance as if your life were at stake.
NORA: And it is.
HELMER: Rank, stop! This is pure madness. Stop it, I say!

[RANK *breaks off playing, and* NORA *halts abruptly.*]

HELMER: [*Going over to her.*] I never would have believed it. You've forgotten everything I taught you.
NORA: [*Throwing away the tambourine.*] You see for yourself.
HELMER: Well, there's certainly room for instruction here.
NORA: Yes, you see how important it is. You've got to teach me to the very last minute. Promise me that, Torvald?
HELMER: You can bet on it.
NORA: You mustn't, either today or tomorrow, think about anything else but me; you mustn't open any letters—or the mailbox—
HELMER: Ah, it's still the fear of that man—
NORA: Oh yes, yes, that too.
HELMER: Nora, it's written all over you—there's already a letter from him out there.
NORA: I don't know. I guess so. But you mustn't read such things now; there mustn't be anything ugly between us before it's all over.
RANK: [*Quietly to* HELMER.] You shouldn't deny her.
HELMER: [*Putting his arm around her.*] The child can have her way. But tomorrow night, after you've danced—
NORA: Then you'll be free.
MAID: [*In the doorway, right.*] Ma'am, dinner is served.
NORA: We'll be wanting champagne, Helene.
MAID: Very good, ma'am. [*Goes out.*]
HELMER: So—a regular banquet, hm?

NORA: Yes, a banquet—champagne till daybreak! [*Calling out.*] And some macaroons, Helene. Heaps of them—just this once.

HELMER: [*Taking her hands.*] Now, now, now—no hysterics. Be my own little lark again.

NORA: Oh, I will soon enough. But go on in—and you, Dr. Rank. Kristine, help me put up my hair.

RANK: [*Whispering, as they go.*] There's nothing wrong—really wrong, is there?

HELMER: Oh, of course not. It's nothing more than this childish anxiety I was telling you about. [*They go out, right.*]

NORA: Well?

MRS. LINDE: Left town.

NORA: I could see by your face.

MRS. LINDE: He'll be home tomorrow evening. I wrote him a note.

NORA: You shouldn't have. Don't try to stop anything now. After all, it's a wonderful joy, this waiting here for the miracle.

MRS. LINDE: What is it you're waiting for?

NORA: Oh, you can't understand that. Go in to them; I'll be along in a moment.

[MRS. LINDE *goes into the dining room.* NORA *stands a short while as if composing herself; then she looks at her watch.*]

NORA: Five. Seven hours to midnight. Twenty-four hours to the midnight after, and then the tarantella's done. Seven and twenty-four? Thirty-one hours to live.

HELMER: [*In the doorway, right.*] What's become of the little lark?

NORA: [*Going toward him with open arms.*] Here's your lark!

ACT III

Same scene. The table, with chairs around it, has been moved to the center of the room. A lamp on the table is lit. The hall door stands open. Dance music drifts down from the floor above. MRS. LINDE *sits at the table, absently paging through a book, trying to read, but apparently unable to focus her thoughts. Once or twice she pauses, tensely listening for a sound at the outer entrance.*

MRS. LINDE: [*Glancing at her watch.*] Not yet—and there's hardly any time left. If only he's not—[*Listening again.*] Ah, there he is. [*She goes out in the hall and cautiously opens the outer door. Quiet footsteps are heard on the stairs. She whispers:*] Come in. Nobody's here.

KROGSTAD: [*In the doorway.*] I found a note from you at home. What's back of all this?

MRS. LINDE: I just *had* to talk to you.

KROGSTAD: Oh? And it just *had* to be here in this house?

MRS. LINDE: At my place it was impossible; my room hasn't a private entrance. Come in; we're all alone. The maid's asleep, and the Helmers are at the dance upstairs.

KROGSTAD: [*Entering the room.*] Well, well, the Helmers are dancing tonight? Really?

MRS. LINDE: Yes, why not?

KROGSTAD: How true—why not?

MRS. LINDE: All right, Krogstad, let's talk.

KROGSTAD: Do we two have anything more to talk about?

MRS. LINDE: We have a great deal to talk about.

KROGSTAD: I wouldn't have thought so.

MRS. LINDE: No, because you've never understood me, really.

KROGSTAD: Was there anything more to understand—except what's all too common in life? A calculating woman throws over a man the moment a better catch comes by.

MRS. LINDE: You think I'm so thoroughly calculating? You think I broke it off lightly?

KROGSTAD: Didn't you?

MRS. LINDE: Nils—is that what you really thought?

KROGSTAD: If you cared, then why did you write me the way you did?

MRS. LINDE: What else could I do? If I had to break off with you, then it was my job as well to root out everything you felt for me.

KROGSTAD: [*Wringing his hands.*] So that was it. And this—all this, simply for money!

MRS. LINDE: Don't forget I had a helpless mother and two small brothers. We couldn't wait for you, Nils; you had such a long road ahead of you then.

KROGSTAD: That may be; but you still hadn't the right to abandon me for somebody else's sake.

MRS. LINDE: Yes—I don't know. So many, many times I've asked myself if I did have that right.

KROGSTAD: [*More softly.*] When I lost you, it was as if all the solid ground dissolved from under my feet. Look at me; I'm a half-drowned man now, hanging onto a wreck.

MRS. LINDE: Help may be near.

KROGSTAD: It was near—but then you came and blocked it off.

MRS. LINDE: Without my knowing it, Nils. Today for the first time I learned that it's you I'm replacing at the bank.

KROGSTAD: All right—I believe you. But now that you know, will you step aside?

MRS. LINDE: No, because that wouldn't benefit you in the slightest.

KROGSTAD: Not "benefit" me, hm! I'd step aside anyway.

MRS. LINDE: I've learned to be realistic. Life and hard, bitter necessity have taught me that.

KROGSTAD: And life's taught me never to trust fine phrases.

MRS. LINDE: Then life's taught you a very sound thing. But you do have to trust in actions, don't you?

KROGSTAD: What does that mean?

MRS. LINDE: You said you were hanging on like a half-drowned man to a wreck.

KROGSTAD: I've good reason to say that.

MRS. LINDE: I'm also like a half-drowned woman on a wreck. No one to suffer with; no one to care for.

KROGSTAD: You made your choice

MRS. LINDE: There wasn't any choice then.

KROGSTAD: So—what of it?

MRS. LINDE: Nils, if only we two shipwrecked people could reach across to each other.

KROGSTAD: What are you saying?

MRS. LINDE: Two on one wreck are at least better off than each on his own.

KROGSTAD: Kristine!

MRS. LINDE: Why do you think I came into town?

KROGSTAD: Did you really have some thought of me?

MRS. LINDE: I have to work to go on living. All my born days, as long as I can remember, I've worked, and it's been my best and my only joy. But now I'm completely alone in the world; it frightens me to be so empty and lost. To work for yourself—there's no joy in that. Nils, give me something—someone to work for.

KROGSTAD: I don't believe all this. It's just some hysterical feminine urge to go out and make a noble sacrifice.

MRS. LINDE: Have you ever found me to be hysterical?

KROGSTAD: Can you honestly mean this? Tell me—do you know everything about my past?

MRS. LINDE: Yes.

KROGSTAD: And you know what they think I'm worth around here.

MRS. LINDE: From what you were saying before, it would seem that with me you could have been another person.

KROGSTAD: I'm positive of that.

MRS. LINDE: Couldn't it happen still?

KROGSTAD: Kristine—you're saying this in all seriousness? Yes, you are! I can see it in you. And do you really have the courage, then—?

MRS. LINDE: I need to have someone to care for; and your children need a mother. We both need each other. Nils, I have faith that you're good at heart—I'll risk everything together with you.

KROGSTAD: [Gripping her hands.] Kristine, thank you, thank you—Now I know I can win back a place in their eyes. Yes—but I forgot—

MRS. LINDE: [Listening.] Shh! The tarantella. Go now! Go on!

KROGSTAD: Why? What is it?

MRS. LINDE: Hear the dance up there? When that's over, they'll be coming down.

KROGSTAD: Oh, then I'll go. But—it's all pointless. Of course, you don't know the move I made against the Helmers.

MRS. LINDE: Yes, Nils, I know.

KROGSTAD: And all the same, you have the courage to—?

MRS. LINDE: I know how far despair can drive a man like you.

KROGSTAD: Oh, if I only could take it all back.

MRS. LINDE: You easily could—your letter's still lying in the mailbox.

KROGSTAD: Are you sure of that?

MRS. LINDE: Positive. But—

KROGSTAD: [*Looks at her searchingly.*] Is that the meaning of it, then? You'll save your friend at any price. Tell me straight out. Is that it?

MRS. LINDE: Nils—anyone who's sold herself for somebody else once isn't going to do it again.

KROGSTAD: I'll demand my letter back.

MRS. LINDE: No, no.

KROGSTAD: Yes, of course. I'll stay here till Helmer comes down; I'll tell him to give me my letter again—that it only involves my dismissal—that he shouldn't read it—

MRS. LINDE: No, Nils, don't call the letter back.

KROGSTAD: But wasn't that exactly why you wrote me to come here?

MRS. LINDE: Yes, in that first panic. But it's been a whole day and night since then, and in that time I've seen such incredible things in this house. Helmer's got to learn everything; this dreadful secret has to be aired; those two have to come to a full understanding; all these lies and evasions can't go on.

KROGSTAD: Well, then, if you want to chance it. But at least there's one thing I can do, and do right away—

MRS. LINDE: [*Listening.*] Go now, go, quick! The dance is over. We're not safe another second.

KROGSTAD: I'll wait for you downstairs.

MRS. LINDE: Yes, please do; take me home.

KROGSTAD: I can't believe it; I've never been so happy. [*He leaves by way of the outer door; the door between the room and the hall stays open.*]

MRS. LINDE: [*Straightening up a bit and getting together her street clothes.*] How different now! How different! Someone to work for, to live for—a home to build. Well, it is worth the try! Oh, if they'd only come! [*Listening.*] Ah, there they are. Bundle up. [*She picks up her hat and coat.* NORA's *and* HELMER's *voices can be heard outside; a key turns in the lock, and* HELMER *brings* NORA *into the hall almost by force. She is wearing the Italian costume with a large black shawl about her; he has on evening dress, with a black domino*[3] *open over it.*]

---

3. Hood worn by members of some religious orders.

NORA: [*Struggling in the doorway.*] No, no, no, not inside! I'm going up again. I don't want to leave so soon.

HELMER: But Nora dear—

NORA: Oh, I beg you, please, Torvald. From the bottom of my heart, *please—* only an hour more!

HELMER: Not a single minute, Nora darling. You know our agreement. Come on, in we go; you'll catch cold out here. [*In spite of her resistance, he gently draws her into the room.*]

MRS. LINDE: Good evening.

NORA: Kristine!

HELMER: Why, Mrs. Linde—are you here so late?

MRS. LINDE: Yes, I'm sorry, but I did want to see Nora in costume.

NORA: Have you been sitting here, waiting for me?

MRS. LINDE: Yes. I didn't come early enough; you were all upstairs; and then I thought I really couldn't leave without seeing you.

HELMER: [*Removing* NORA's *shawl.*] Yes, take a good look. She's worth looking at, I can tell you that, Mrs. Linde. Isn't she lovely?

MRS. LINDE: Yes, I should say—

HELMER: A dream of loveliness, isn't she? That's what everyone thought at the party, too. But she's horribly stubborn—this sweet little thing. What's to be done with her? Can you imagine, I almost had to use force to pry her away.

NORA: Oh, Torvald, you're going to regret you didn't indulge me, even for just a half hour more.

HELMER: There, you see. She danced her tarantella and got a tumultuous hand—which was well earned, although the performance may have been a bit too naturalistic—I mean it rather overstepped the proprieties of art. But never mind—what's important is, she made a success, an overwhelming success. You think I could let her stay on after that and spoil the effect? Oh no; I took my lovely little Capri girl—my capricious little Capri girl, I should say—took her under my arm; one quick tour of the ballroom, a curtsy to every side, and then—as they say in novels—the beautiful vision disappeared. An exit should always be effective, Mrs. Linde, but that's what I can't get Nora to grasp. Phew, it's hot in here. [*Flings the domino on a chair and opens the door to his room.*] Why's it dark in here? Oh yes, of course. Excuse me. [*He goes in and lights a couple of candles.*]

NORA: [*In a sharp, breathless whisper.*] So?

MRS. LINDE: [*Quietly.*] I talked with him.

NORA: And—?

MRS. LINDE: Nora—you must tell your husband everything.

NORA: [*Dully.*] I knew it.

MRS. LINDE: You've got nothing to fear from Krogstad, but you have to speak out.

NORA: I won't tell.

MRS. LINDE: Then the letter will.

NORA: Thanks, Kristine. I know now what's to be done. Shh!

HELMER: [*Reentering.*] Well, then, Mrs. Linde—have you admired her?

MRS. LINDE: Yes, and now I'll say good night.

HELMER: Oh, come, so soon? Is this yours, this knitting?

MRS. LINDE: Yes, thanks. I nearly forgot it.

HELMER: Do you knit, then?

MRS. LINDE: Oh yes.

HELMER: You know what? You should embroider instead.

MRS. LINDE: Really? Why?

HELMER: Yes, because it's a lot prettier. See here, one holds the embroidery so, in the left hand, and then one guides the needle with the right— so—in an easy, sweeping curve—right?

MRS. LINDE: Yes, I guess that's—

HELMER: But, on the other hand, knitting—it can never be anything but ugly. Look, see here, the arms tucked in, the knitting needles going up and down—there's something Chinese about it. Ah, that was really a glorious champagne they served.

MRS. LINDE: Yes, good night, Nora, and don't be stubborn anymore.

HELMER: Well put, Mrs. Linde!

MRS. LINDE: Good night, Mr. Helmer.

HELMER: [*Accompanying her to the door.*] Good night, good night. I hope you get home all right. I'd be very happy to—but you don't have far to go. Good night, good night. [*She leaves. He shuts the door after her and returns.*] There, now, at last we got her out the door. She's a deadly bore, that creature.

NORA: Aren't you pretty tired, Torvald?

HELMER: No, not a bit.

NORA: You're not sleepy?

HELMER: Not at all. On the contrary, I'm feeling quite exhilarated. But you? Yes, you really look tired and sleepy.

NORA: Yes, I'm very tired. Soon now I'll sleep.

HELMER: See! You see! I was right all along that we shouldn't stay longer.

NORA: Whatever you do is always right.

HELMER: [*Kissing her brow.*] Now my little lark talks sense. Say, did you notice what a time Rank was having tonight?

NORA: Oh, was he? I didn't get to speak with him.

HELMER: I scarcely did either, but it's a long time since I've seen him in such high spirits. [*Gazes at her a moment, then comes nearer her.*] Hm—it's marvelous, though, to be back home again—to be completely alone with you. Oh, you bewitchingly lovely young woman!

NORA: Torvald, don't look at me like that!

HELMER: Can't I look at my richest treasure? At all that beauty that's mine, mine alone—completely and utterly.

NORA: [*Moving around to the other side of the table.*] You mustn't talk to me that way tonight.

HELMER: [*Following her.*] The tarantella is still in your blood, I can see—and it makes you even more enticing. Listen. The guests are beginning to go. [*Dropping his voice.*] Nora—it'll soon be quiet through this whole house.

NORA: Yes, I hope so.

HELMER: You do, don't you, my love? Do you realize—when I'm out at a party like this with you—do you know why I talk to you so little, and keep such a distance away; just send you a stolen look now and then— you know why I do it? It's because I'm imagining then that you're my secret darling, my secret young bride-to-be, and that no one suspects there's anything between us.

NORA: Yes, yes; oh, yes, I know you're always thinking of me.

HELMER: And then when we leave and I place the shawl over those fine young rounded shoulders—over that wonderful curving neck—then I pretend that you're my young bride, that we're just coming from the wedding, that for the first time I'm bringing you into my house—that for the first time I'm alone with you—completely alone with you, your trembling young beauty! All this evening I've longed for nothing but you. When I saw you turn and sway in the tarantella—my blood was pounding till I couldn't stand it—that's why I brought you down here so early—

NORA: Go away, Torvald! Leave me alone. I don't want all this.

HELMER: What do you mean? Nora, you're teasing me. You will, won't you? Aren't I your husband—?

[*A knock at the outside door.*]

NORA: [*Startled.*] What's that?

HELMER: [*Going toward the half.*] Who is it?

RANK: [*Outside.*] It's me. May I come in a moment?

HELMER: [*With quiet irritation.*] Oh, what does he want now? [*Aloud.*] Hold on. [*Goes and opens the door.*] Oh, how nice that you didn't just pass us by!

RANK: I thought I heard your voice, and then I wanted so badly to have a look in. [*Lightly glancing about.*] Ah, me, these old familiar haunts. You have it snug and cozy in here, you two.

HELMER: You seemed to be having it pretty cozy upstairs, too.

RANK: Absolutely. Why shouldn't I? Why not take in everything in life? As much as you can, anyway, and as long as you can. The wine was superb—

HELMER: The champagne especially.

RANK: You noticed that too? It's amazing how much I could guzzle down.

NORA: Torvald also drank a lot of champagne this evening.

RANK: Oh?

NORA: Yes, and that always makes him so entertaining.

RANK: Well, why shouldn't one have a pleasant evening after a well-spent day?

HELMER: Well spent? I'm afraid I can't claim that.

RANK: [*Slapping him on the back.*] But I can, you see!

NORA: Dr. Rank, you must have done some scientific research today.

RANK: Quite so.

HELMER: Come now—little Nora talking about scientific research!

NORA: And can I congratulate you on the results?

RANK: Indeed you may.

NORA: Then they were good?

RANK: The best possible for both doctor and patient—certainty.

NORA: [*Quickly and searchingly.*] Certainty?

RANK: Complete certainty. So don't I owe myself a gay evening afterwards?

NORA: Yes, you're right, Dr. Rank.

HELMER: I'm with you—just so long as you don't have to suffer for it in the morning.

RANK: Well, one never gets something for nothing in life.

NORA: Dr. Rank—are you very fond of masquerade parties?

RANK: Yes, if there's a good array of odd disguises—

NORA: Tell me, what should we two go as at the next masquerade?

HELMER: You little featherhead—already thinking of the next!

RANK: We two? I'll tell you what: you must go as Charmed Life—

HELMER: Yes, but find a costume for *that!*

RANK: Your wife can appear just as she looks every day.

HELMER: That was nicely put. But don't you know what you're going to be?

RANK: Yes, Helmer, I've made up my mind.

HELMER: Well?

RANK: At the next masquerade I'm going to be invisible.

HELMER: That's a funny idea.

RANK: They say there's a hat—black, huge—have you never heard of the hat that makes you invisible? You put it on, and then no one on earth can see you.

HELMER: [*Suppressing a smile.*] Ah, of course.

RANK: But I'm quite forgetting what I came for. Helmer, give me a cigar, one of the dark Havanas.

HELMER: With the greatest pleasure. [*Holds out his case.*]

RANK: Thanks. [*Takes one and cuts off the tip.*]

NORA: [*Striking a match*] Let me give you a light.

RANK: Thank you. [*She holds the match for him; he lights the cigar.*] And now good-bye.

HELMER: Good-bye, good-bye, old friend.

NORA: Sleep well, Doctor.

RANK: Thanks for that wish.

NORA: Wish me the same.

RANK: You? All right, if you like—Sleep well. And thanks for the light. [*He nods to them both and leaves.*]

HELMER: [*His voice subdued.*] He's been drinking heavily.

NORA: [*Absently.*] Could be. [HELMER *takes his keys from his pocket and goes out in the hall.*] Torvald—what are you after?

HELMER: Got to empty the mailbox; it's nearly full. There won't be room for the morning papers.

NORA: Are you working tonight?

HELMER: You know I'm not. Why—what's this? Someone's been at the lock.

NORA: At the lock—?

HELMER: Yes, I'm positive. What do you suppose—? I can't imagine one of the maids—? Here's a broken hairpin. Nora, it's yours—

NORA: [*Quickly.*] Then it must be the children—

HELMER: You'd better break them of that. Hm, hm—well, opened it after all. [*Takes the contents out and calls into the kitchen.*] Helene! Helene, would you put out the lamp in the hall. [*He returns to the room, shutting the hall door, then displays the handful of mail.*] Look how it's piled up. [*Sorting through them.*] Now what's this?

NORA: [*At the window.*] The letter! Oh, Torvald, no!

HELMER: Two calling cards—from Rank.

NORA: From Dr. Rank?

HELMER: [*Examining them.*] "Dr. Rank, Consulting Physician." They were on top. He must have dropped them in as he left.

NORA: Is there anything on them?

HELMER: There's a black cross over the name. See? That's a gruesome notion. He could almost be announcing his own death.

NORA: That's just what he's doing.

HELMER: What! You've heard something? Something he's told you?

NORA: Yes. That when those cards came, he'd be taking his leave of us. He'll shut himself in now and die.

HELMER: Ah, my poor friend! Of course I knew he wouldn't be here much longer. But so soon—And then to hide himself away like a wounded animal.

NORA: If it has to happen, then it's best it happens in silence—don't you think so, Torvald?

HELMER: [*Pacing up and down.*] He'd grown right into our lives. I simply can't imagine him gone. He with his suffering and loneliness—like a dark cloud setting off our sunlit happiness. Well, maybe it's best this way. For him, at least. [*Standing still.*] And maybe for us too, Nora. Now we're thrown back on each other, completely. [*Embracing her.*] Oh you, my darling wife, how can I hold you close enough? You know what, Nora—time and again I've wished you were in some terrible danger, just so I could stake my life and soul and everything, for your sake.

NORA: [*Tearing herself away, her voice firm and decisive.*] Now you must read your mail, Torvald.

HELMER: No, no, not tonight. I want to stay with you, dearest.

NORA: With a dying friend on your mind?

HELMER: You're right. We've both had a shock. There's ugliness between us—these thoughts of death and corruption. We'll have to get free of them first. Until then—we'll stay apart.

NORA: [*Clinging about his neck.*] Torvald—good night! Good night!

HELMER: [*Kissing her on the cheek.*] Good night, little songbird. Sleep well, Nora. I'll be reading my mail now. [*He takes the letters into his room and shuts the door after him.*]

NORA: [*With bewildered glances, groping about, seizing* HELMER's *domino, throwing it around her, and speaking in short, hoarse, broken whispers.*] Never see him again. Never, never. [*Putting her shawl over her head.*] Never see the children either—them, too. Never, never. Oh, the freezing black water! The depths—down—Oh, I wish it were over—He has it now; he's reading it—now. Oh no, no, not yet. Torvald, good-bye, you and the children—[*She starts for the hall; as she does,* HELMER *throws open his door and stands with an open letter in his hand.*]

HELMER: Nora!

NORA: [*Screams.*] Oh—!

HELMER: What is this? You know what's in this letter?

NORA: Yes, I know. Let me go! Let me out!

HELMER: [*Holding her back.*] Where are you going?

NORA: [*Struggling to break loose.*] You can't save me, Torvald!

HELMER: [*Slumping back.*] True! Then it's true what he writes? How horrible! No, no, it's impossible—it can't be true.

NORA: It *is* true. I've loved you more than all this world.

HELMER: Ah, none of your slippery tricks.

NORA: [*Taking one step toward him.*] Torvald—!

HELMER: What *is* this you've blundered into!

NORA: Just let me loose. You're not going to suffer for my sake. You're not going to take on my guilt.

HELMER: No more playacting. [*Locks the hall door.*] You stay right here and give me a reckoning. You understand what you've done? Answer! You understand?

NORA: [*Looking squarely at him, her face hardening.*] Yes. I'm beginning to understand everything now.

HELMER: [*Striding about.*] Oh, what an awful awakening! In all these eight years—she who was my pride and joy—a hypocrite, a liar—worse, worse—a criminal! How infinitely disgusting it all is! The shame! [*NORA says nothing and goes on looking straight at him. He stops in front of her.*] I should have suspected something of the kind. I should have known. All your father's flimsy values—Be still! All your father's flimsy values have come out in you. No religion, no morals, no sense of duty—Oh, how I'm punished for letting him off! I did it for your sake, and you repay me like this.

NORA: Yes, like this.

HELMER: Now you've wrecked all my happiness—ruined my whole future. Oh, it's awful to think of. I'm in a cheap little grafter's hands; he can do anything he wants with me, ask for anything, play with me like a puppet—and I can't breathe a word. I'll be swept down miserably into the depths on account of a featherbrained woman.

NORA: When I'm gone from this world, you'll be free.

HELMER: Oh, quit posing. Your father had a mess of those speeches too. What good would that ever do me if you were gone from this world, as you say? Not the slightest. He can still make the whole thing known; and if he does, I could be falsely suspected as your accomplice. They might even think that I was behind it—that I put you up to it. And all that I can thank you for—you that I've coddled the whole of our marriage. Can you see now what you've done to me?

NORA: [*Icily calm.*] Yes.

HELMER: It's so incredible, I just can't grasp it. But we'll have to patch up whatever we can. Take off the shawl. I said, take it off! I've got to appease him somehow or other. The thing has to be hushed up at any cost. And as for you and me, it's got to seem like everything between us is just as it was—to the outside world, that is. You'll go right on living in this house, of course. But you can't be allowed to bring up the children; I don't dare trust you with them—Oh, to have to say this to someone I've loved so much, and that I still—! Well, that's done with. From now on happiness doesn't matter; all that matters is saving the bits and pieces, the appearance—[*The doorbell rings.* HELMER *starts.*] What's that? And so late. Maybe the worst—? You think he'd—? Hide, Nora! Say you're sick. [NORA *remains standing motionless.* HELMER *goes and opens the door.*]

MAID: [*Half dressed, in the hall.*] A letter for Mrs. Helmer.

HELMER: I'll take it. [*Snatches the letter and shuts the door.*] Yes, it's from him. You don't get it; I'm reading it myself.

NORA: Then read it.

HELMER: [*By the lamp.*] I hardly dare. We may be ruined, you and I. But—I've got to know. [*Rips open the letter, skims through a few lines, glances at an enclosure, then cries out joyfully.*] Nora! [NORA *looks inquiringly at him.*] Nora! Wait—better check it again—Yes, yes, it's true. I'm saved. Nora, I'm saved!

NORA: And I?

HELMER: You too, of course. We're both saved, both of us. Look. He's sent back your note. He says he's sorry and ashamed—that a happy development in his life—oh, who cares what he says! Nora, we're saved! No one can hurt you. Oh, Nora, Nora—but first, this ugliness all has to go. Let me see—[*Takes a look at the note.*] No, I don't want to see it; I want the whole thing to fade like a dream. [*Tears the note and both letters to pieces, throws them into the stove and watches them burn.*] There—now there's nothing left—He wrote that since Christmas Eve you—Oh, they must have been three terrible days for you, Nora.

HELMER: Not—not happy!

NORA: No, only lighthearted. And you've always been so kind to me. But our home's been nothing but a playpen. I've been your doll-wife here, just as at home I was Papa's doll-child. And in turn the children have been my dolls. I thought it was fun when you played with me, just as they thought it fun when I played with them. That's been our marriage, Torvald.

HELMER: There's some truth in what you're saying—under all the raving exaggeration. But it'll all be different after this. Playtime's over; now for the schooling.

NORA: Whose schooling—mine or the children's?

HELMER: Both yours and the children's, dearest.

NORA: Oh, Torvald, you're not the man to teach me to be a good wife to you.

HELMER: And you can say that?

NORA: And I—how am I equipped to bring up children?

HELMER: Nora!

NORA: Didn't you say a moment ago that that was no job to trust me with?

HELMER: In a flare of temper! Why fasten on that?

NORA: Yes, but you were so very right. I'm not up to the job. There's another job I have to do first. I have to try to educate myself. You can't help me with that. I've got to do it alone. And that's why I'm leaving you now.

HELMER: [*Jumping up.*] What's that?

NORA: I have to stand completely alone, if I'm ever going to discover myself and the world out there. So I can't go on living with you.

HELMER: Nora, Nora!

NORA: I want to leave right away. Kristine should put me up for the night—

HELMER: You're insane! You've no right! I forbid you!

NORA: From here on, there's no use forbidding me anything. I'll take with me whatever is mine. I don't want a thing from you, either now or later.

HELMER: What kind of madness is this!

NORA: Tomorrow I'm going home—I mean, home where I came from. It'll be easier up there to find something to do.

HELMER: Oh, you blind, incompetent child!

NORA: I must learn to be competent, Torvald.

HELMER: Abandon your home, your husband, your children! And you're not even thinking what people will say.

NORA: I can't be concerned about that. I only know how essential this is.

HELMER: Oh, it's outrageous. So you'll run out like this on your most sacred vows.

NORA: What do you think are my most sacred vows?

HELMER: And I have to tell you that! Aren't they your duties to your husband and children?

NORA: I have other duties equally sacred.

HELMER: That isn't true. What duties are they?

NORA: Duties to myself.

HELMER: Before all else, you're a wife and a mother.

NORA: I don't believe in that anymore. I believe that, before all else, I'm a human being, no less than you—or anyway, I ought to try to become one. I know the majority thinks you're right, Torvald, and plenty of books agree with you, too. But I can't go on believing what the majority says, or what's written in books. I have to think over these things myself and try to understand them.

HELMER: Why can't you understand your place in your own home? On a point like that, isn't there one everlasting guide you can turn to? Where's your religion?

NORA: Oh, Torvald, I'm really not sure what religion is.

HELMER: What—?

NORA: I only know what the minister said when I was confirmed. He told me religion was this thing and that. When I get clear and away by myself, I'll go into that problem too. I'll see if what the minister said was right, or, in any case, if it's right for me.

HELMER: A young woman your age shouldn't talk like that. If religion can't move you, I can try to rouse your conscience. You do have some moral feeling? Or, tell me—has that gone too?

NORA: It's not easy to answer that, Torvald. I simply don't know. I'm all confused about these things. I just know I see them so differently from you. I find out, for one thing, that the law's not at all what I'd thought—but I can't get it through my head that the law is fair. A woman hasn't a right to protect her dying father or save her husband's life! I can't believe that.

HELMER: You talk like a child. You don't know anything of the world you live in.

NORA: No, I don't. But now I'll begin to learn for myself. I'll try to discover who's right, the world or I.

HELMER: Nora, you're sick; you've got a fever. I almost think you're out of your head.

NORA: I've never felt more clearheaded and sure in my life.

HELMER: And—clearheaded and sure—you're leaving your husband and children?

NORA: Yes.

HELMER: Then there's only one possible reason.

NORA: What?

HELMER: You no longer love me.

NORA: No. That's exactly it.

HELMER: Nora! You can't be serious!

NORA: Oh, this is so hard, Torvald—you've been so kind to me always. But I can't help it. I don't love you anymore.

HELMER: [*Struggling for composure.*] Are you also clearheaded and sure about that?

NORA: Yes, completely. That's why I can't go on staying here.

HELMER: Can you tell me what I did to lose your love?

NORA: Yes, I can tell you. It was this evening when the miraculous thing didn't come—then I knew you weren't the man I'd imagined.

HELMER: Be more explicit; I don't follow you.

NORA: I've waited now so patiently eight long years—for, my Lord, I know miracles don't come every day. Then this crisis broke over me, and such a certainty filled me: *now* the miraculous event would occur. While Krogstad's letter was lying out there, I never for an instant dreamed that you could give in to his terms. I was so utterly sure you'd say to him: go on, tell your tale to the whole wide world. And when he'd done that—

HELMER: Yes, what then? When I'd delivered my own wife into shame and disgrace—!

NORA: When he'd done that, I was so utterly sure that you'd step forward, take the blame on yourself and say: I am the guilty one.

HELMER: Nora—!

NORA: You're thinking I'd never accept such a sacrifice from you? No, of course not. But what good would my protests be against you? That was the miracle I was waiting for, in terror and hope. And to stave that off, I would have taken my life.

HELMER: I'd gladly work for you day and night, Nora—and take on pain and deprivation. But there's no one who gives up honor for love.

NORA: Millions of women have done just that.

HELMER: Oh, you think and talk like a silly child.

NORA: Perhaps. But you neither think nor talk like the man I could join myself to. When your big fright was over—and it wasn't from any threat against me, only for what might damage you—when all the danger was past, for you it was just as if nothing had happened. I was exactly the same, your little lark, your doll, that you'd have to handle with double care now that I'd turned out so brittle and frail. [*Gets up.*] Torvald—in that instant it dawned on me that for eight years I've been living here with a stranger, and that I'd even conceived three children—oh, I can't stand the thought of it! I could tear myself to bits.

HELMER: [*Heavily.*] I see. There's a gulf that's opened between us—that's clear. Oh, but Nora, can't we bridge it somehow?

NORA: The way I am now, I'm no wife for you.

HELMER: I have the strength to make myself over.

NORA: Maybe—if your doll gets taken away.

HELMER: But to part! To part from you! No, Nora, no—I can't imagine it.

NORA: [*Going out, right.*] All the more reason why it has to be. [*She reenters with her coat and a small overnight bag, which she puts on a chair by the table.*]

HELMER: Nora, Nora, not now! Wait till tomorrow.

NORA: I can't spend the night in a strange man's room.

HELMER: But couldn't we live here like brother and sister—

NORA: You know very well how long that would last. [*Throws her shawl about her.*] Good-bye, Torvald. I won't look in on the children. I know they're in better hands than mine. The way I am now, I'm no use to them.

HELMER: But someday, Nora—someday—?

NORA: How can I tell? I haven't the least idea what'll become of me.

HELMER: But you're my wife, now and wherever you go.

NORA: Listen, Torvald—I've heard that when a wife deserts her husband's house just as I'm doing, then the law frees him from all responsibility. In any case, I'm freeing you from being responsible. Don't feel yourself bound, any more than I will. There has to be absolute freedom for us both. Here, take your ring back. Give me mine.

HELMER: That too?

NORA: That too.

HELMER: There it is.

NORA: Good. Well, now it's all over. I'm putting the keys here. The maids know all about keeping up the house—better than I do. Tomorrow, after I've left town, Kristine will stop by to pack up everything that's mine from home. I'd like those things shipped up to me.

HELMER: Over! All over! Nora, won't you ever think about me?

NORA: I'm sure I'll think of you often, and about the children and the house here.

HELMER: May I write you?

NORA: No—never. You're not to do that.

HELMER: Oh, but let me send you—

NORA: Nothing. Nothing.

HELMER: Or help you if you need it.

NORA: No. I accept nothing from strangers.

HELMER: Nora—can I never be more than a stranger to you?

NORA: [*Picking up the overnight bag.*] Ah, Torvald—it would take the greatest miracle of all—

HELMER: Tell me the greatest miracle!

NORA: You and I both would have to transform ourselves to the point that—Oh, Torvald, I've stopped believing in miracles.

HELMER: But I'll believe. Tell me! Transform ourselves to the point that—?

NORA: That our living together could be a true marriage. [*She goes out down the hall.*]

HELMER: [*Sinks down on a chair by the door, face buried in his hands.*] Nora! Nora! [*Looking about and rising.*] Empty. She's gone. [*A sudden hope leaps in him.*] The greatest miracle—?

[*From below, the sound of a door slamming shut.*]

QUESTIONS

1. Though the three acts of *A Doll House* are not formally divided into scenes, each does unfold as a series of relatively discreet, though continuous, episodes. In the first act, for example, the initial encounter between Nora and Helmer is followed by Nora's conversation with Mrs. Linde; a conversation among Mrs. Linde, Dr. Rank, and Nora, and then Torvald as well; a brief interlude in which Nora plays with her children; and, finally, her conversations first with Krogstad and then with her husband. What might the episodic structure itself tell us about Nora's character and situation? How is each of these episodes both similar to and different from the others, especially in terms of justifying or complicating Nora's assertion that everyone sees her the same way? What does each episode contribute to your impression of Nora's character and situation? to your degree of sympathy with her? In these terms, why and how does the order of the episodes matter? For example, what is the effect of Ibsen's choice to delay exposition regarding past events until the second episode (the conversation between Nora and Mrs. Linde)? By the end of this act, what do you see as the play's central conflict or conflicts?

2. How, if at all, has Nora or Torvald, or your impression of their characters and their marriage, changed by the beginning of act II? by its end? How has your interpretation of the conflict changed by this point? In these terms, what is the effect and significance of the way this act is plotted and structured? Why does Nora decide not to confide everything to Dr. Rank and seek his help? What can you surmise at this stage about Nora's plans and expectations for the immediate future? For what "miracle" is she "waiting" (p. 860)?

3. Act III begins with the first and only episode in which Nora does not appear. What is the effect and significance of her absence? of the scene itself? How might this scene compare to the later one between Nora and Torvald? More generally, how does the relationship between Mrs. Linde and Krogstad compare to, and comment on, that between Nora and Torvald?

4. At the end of the play, Nora declares, "It's a great sin what you and Papa did to me. You're to blame that nothing's become of me" (p. 872). How does the play as a whole both endorse and complicate Nora's assessment?

5. To what extent and how might the play as a whole suggest that Nora is right or wrong—or both—to leave her family at the play's end? Why is or isn't this an appropriate or satisfying resolution of the conflict?

6. In what various ways might one interpret the very end of the play? That is, what "sudden hope leaps in" Helmer? What might he mean when he says, "The greatest miracle—"? What is the effect and significance of the fact that we then hear "the sound of a door slamming shut"? Based on evidence from the rest of the play, what interpretation seems most valid to you? How does your interpretation of these words and actions affect your interpretation of the play's theme(s)?

7. In what way does *A Doll House* make use of dramatic or situational irony? By the end of the play, what statements in earlier acts might seem like instances of verbal irony?

8. In act III, Mrs. Linde tells Krogstad that she believes he "could have been another person" had he married her (p. 862), implying that it is, at least in part, forces outside ourselves that shape who we are and how we behave, regardless of our gender. Does the play as a whole seem to endorse that view? If so, what are the most important forces? What role, for example, do different characters—and the play as a whole—assign to heredity or parentage, to parenting, and to economics? In terms of the latter, why might it matter that characters in the play tend to use economic language and metaphors, as when, in act II, Dr. Rank tells Nora, "I've been auditing my internal accounts. Bankrupt!" (p. 850)?

9. What is the effect and significance of Ibsen's choice to have all the action in *A Doll House* take place in one location? to make that location the interior of the Helmer home? to describe this interior as he does in the stage directions that begin each act? What is the effect and significance of the fact that the play opens on Christmas Eve? that each act takes place on a different day? that the play ends 48 hours after it began? What other aspects of setting seem especially effective or important?

10. In terms of the play's conflict, theme(s), and characterization of Nora, Torvald, and their marriage, what role is played by each of the minor characters—Dr. Rank, Anne-Marie, and the Helmer children?

SUGGESTIONS FOR WRITING

1. Do any characters besides Nora change over the course of the play, or is it merely our perception of them that changes? Write an essay that answers this question with regard to Torvald, Mrs. Linde, or Krogstad, making sure to explain precisely when, how, and why either the character or your perception of the character changes and why and how that change affects how the play as a whole works and what it means.

2. Write an essay exploring the symbolic or metaphorical significance of the masquerade and/or tarantella.

3. In a brief essay, explore the validity and significance of Nora's claim that Dr. Rank is her "best and truest friend" (p. 852).

4. Write an essay that draws on evidence from Ibsen's play to make an argument about what most likely happens after the play ends, either to Mrs. Linde and Mr. Krogstad or to Nora and/or Torvald. What reasons, if any, for example, might the play give you for believing that Mrs. Linde and Krogstad will enjoy what Nora calls "a true marriage" (p. 876), or that "Those who go away are soon forgotten" and, perhaps, replaced (p. 851)?

5. *A Doll House* was first performed in 1879, and its portrait of women's roles as daughters, wives, and mothers is in certain ways specific to the late nineteenth century, when—for example—a woman couldn't legally borrow money without her father's or husband's consent and seldom got custody of her children in cases of separation or divorce. Write an essay in which you analyze both how the play characterizes the role nineteenth-century women were expected to

play as daughters, wives, *or* mothers, and why and how that characterization is and/or isn't relevant or accurate today.

6. Religion is explicitly discussed only at the very end of the play, when Torvald asks, "Where's your religion?" and Nora answers him (p. 874). Yet the play takes place during a Christian holiday, and there is frequent talk of "miracles." Write an essay exploring what the play as a whole ultimately seems to suggest about Christianity, its status in the social world depicted in the play, and its role in generating conflict.

AUGUST WILSON

The Piano Lesson

> *Gin my cotton*
> *Sell my seed*
> *Buy my baby*
> *Everything she need*
> —Skip James[1]

CHARACTERS

DOAKER	MARETHA
BOY WILLIE	AVERY
LYMON	WINING BOY
BERNIECE	GRACE

Romare Bearden, *Piano Lesson*, 1983. Collage of various papers with paint, ink, and graphite on paper. Art © Romare Bearden Foundation/Licensed by VAGA, New York NY.

THE SETTING: *The action of the play takes place in the kitchen and parlor of the house where* DOAKER CHARLES *lives with his niece,* BERNIECE, *and her eleven-year-old daughter,* MARETHA. *The house is sparsely furnished, and although there is evidence of a woman's touch, there is a lack of warmth and vigor.* BERNIECE *and* MARETHA *occupy the upstairs rooms.* DOAKER'S *room is prominent and opens onto the kitchen. Dominating the parlor is an old upright piano. On the legs of the piano, carved in the manner of African sculpture, are mask-like figures resembling totems. The carvings are rendered with a grace and power of invention that lifts them out of the realm of craftsmanship and into the realm of art. At left is a staircase leading to the upstairs.*

---

1. Mississippi-born blues musician and minister (1902–69); the quoted lines come from his "Illinois Blues."

ACT I

Scene 1

[*The lights come up on the Charles household. It is five o'clock in the morning. The dawn is beginning to announce itself, but there is something in the air that belongs to the night. A stillness that is a portent, a gathering, a coming together of something akin to a storm. There is a loud knock at the door.*]

BOY WILLIE: [*Off stage, calling.*] Hey, Doaker . . . Doaker! [*He knocks again and calls.*] Hey, Doaker! Hey, Berniece! Berniece!

[DOAKER *enters from his room. He is a tall, thin man of forty-seven, with severe features, who has for all intents and purposes retired from the world though he works full-time as a railroad cook.*]

DOAKER: Who is it?

BOY WILLIE: Open the door, nigger! It's me . . . Boy Willie!

DOAKER: Who?

BOY WILLIE: Boy Willie! Open the door!

[DOAKER *opens the door and* BOY WILLIE *and* LYMON *enter.* BOY WILLIE *is thirty years old. He has an infectious grin and a boyishness that is apt for his name. He is brash and impulsive, talkative and somewhat crude in speech and manner.* LYMON *is twenty-nine.* BOY WILLIE'*s partner, he talks little, and then with a straightforwardness that is often disarming.*]

DOAKER: What you doing up here?

BOY WILLIE: I told you, Lymon. Lymon talking about you might be sleep. This is Lymon. You remember Lymon Jackson from down home? This my Uncle Doaker.

DOAKER: What you doing up here? I couldn't figure out who that was. I thought you was still down in Mississippi.

BOY WILLIE: Me and Lymon selling watermelons. We got a truck out there. Got a whole truckload of watermelons. We brought them up here to sell. Where's Berniece? [*Calls.*] Hey, Berniece!

DOAKER: Berniece up there sleep.

BOY WILLIE: Well, let her get up. [*Calls.*] Hey, Berniece!

DOAKER: She got to go to work in the morning.

BOY WILLIE: Well she can get up and say hi. It's been three years since I seen her. [*Calls.*] Hey, Berniece! It's me . . . Boy Willie.

DOAKER: Berniece don't like all that hollering now. She got to work in the morning.

BOY WILLIE: She can go on back to bed. Me and Lymon been riding two days in that truck . . . the least she can do is get up and say hi.

DOAKER: [*Looking out the window.*] Where you all get that truck from?

BOY WILLIE: It's Lymon's. I told him let's get a load of watermelons and bring them up here.

LYMON: Boy Willie say he going back, but I'm gonna stay. See what it's like up here.

BOY WILLIE: You gonna carry me down there first.

LYMON: I told you I ain't going back down there and take a chance on that truck breaking down again. You can take the train. Hey, tell him Doaker, he can take the train back. After we sell them watermelons he have enough money he can buy him a whole railroad car.

DOAKER: You got all them watermelons stacked up there no wonder the truck broke down. I'm surprised you made it this far with a load like that. Where you break down at?

BOY WILLIE: We broke down three times! It took us two and a half days to get here. It's a good thing we picked them watermelons fresh.

LYMON: We broke down twice in West Virginia. The first time was just as soon as we got out of Sunflower. About forty miles out she broke down. We got it going and got all the way to West Virginia before she broke down again.

BOY WILLIE: We had to walk about five miles for some water.

LYMON: It got a hole in the radiator but it runs pretty good. You have to pump the brakes sometime before they catch. Boy Willie have his door open and be ready to jump when that happens.

BOY WILLIE: Lymon think that's funny. I told the nigger I give him ten dollars to get the brakes fixed. But he thinks that funny.

LYMON: They don't need fixing. All you got to do is pump them till they catch.

[BERNIECE *enters on the stairs. Thirty-five years old, with an eleven-year-old daughter, she is still in mourning for her husband after three years.*]

BERNIECE: What you doing all that hollering for?

BOY WILLIE: Hey, Berniece. Doaker said you was sleep. I said at least you could get up and say hi.

BERNIECE: It's five o'clock in the morning and you come in here with all this noise. You can't come like normal folks. You got to bring all that noise with you.

BOY WILLIE: Hell, I ain't done nothing but come in and say hi. I ain't got in the house good.

BERNIECE: That's what I'm talking about. You start all that hollering and carry on as soon as you hit the door.

BOY WILLIE: Aw hell, woman, I was glad to see Doaker. You ain't had to come down if you didn't want to. I come eighteen hundred miles to see my sister I figure she might want to get up and say hi. Other than that you can go back upstairs. What you got, Doaker? Where your bottle? Me and Lymon want a drink. [*To* BERNIECE.] This is Lymon. You remember Lymon Jackson from down home.

LYMON: How you doing, Berniece. You look just like I thought you looked.

BERNIECE: Why you all got to come in hollering and carrying on? Waking the neighbors with all that noise.

BOY WILLIE: They can come over and join the party. We fixing to have a party. Doaker, where your bottle? Me and Lymon celebrating. The Ghosts of the Yellow Dog got Sutter.

BERNIECE: Say what?

BOY WILLIE: Ask Lymon, they found him the next morning. Say he drowned in his well.

DOAKER: When this happen, Boy Willie?

BOY WILLIE: About three weeks ago. Me and Lymon was over in Stoner County when we heard about it. We laughed. We thought it was funny. A great big old three-hundred-and-forty-pound man gonna fall down his well.

LYMON: It remind me of Humpty Dumpty.

BOY WILLIE: Everybody say the Ghosts of the Yellow Dog pushed him.

BERNIECE: I don't want to hear that nonsense. Somebody down there pushing them people in their wells.

DOAKER: What was you and Lymon doing over in Stoner County?

BOY WILLIE: We was down there working. Lymon got some people down there.

LYMON: My cousin got some land down there. We was helping him.

BOY WILLIE: Got near about a hundred acres. He got it set up real nice. Me and Lymon was down there chopping down trees. We was using Lymon's truck to haul the wood. Me and Lymon used to haul wood all around them parts. [*To* BERNIECE.] Me and Lymon got a truckload of watermelons out there.

[BERNIECE *crosses to the window to the parlor.*]

Doaker, where your bottle? I know you got a bottle stuck up in your room. Come on, me and Lymon want a drink.

[DOAKER *exits into his room.*]

BERNIECE: Where you all get that truck from?

BOY WILLIE: I told you it's Lymon's.

BERNIECE: Where you get the truck from, Lymon?

LYMON: I bought it.

BERNIECE: Where he get that truck from, Boy Willie?

BOY WILLIE: He told you he bought it. Bought it for a hundred and twenty dollars. I can't say where he got that hundred and twenty dollars from . . . but he bought that old piece of truck from Henry Porter. [*To* LYMON.] Where you get that hundred and twenty dollars from, nigger?

LYMON: I got it like you get yours. I know how to take care of money.

[DOAKER *brings a bottle and sets it on the table.*]

BOY WILLIE: Aw hell, Doaker got some of that good whiskey. Don't give Lymon none of that. He ain't used to good whiskey. He liable to get sick.

LYMON: I done had good whiskey before.

BOY WILLIE: Lymon bought that truck so he have him a place to sleep. He down there wasn't doing no work or nothing. Sheriff looking for him. He bought that truck to keep away from the sheriff. Got Stovall looking for him too. He down there sleeping in that truck ducking and dodging both of them. I told him come on let's go up and see my sister.

BERNIECE: What the sheriff looking for you for, Lymon?

BOY WILLIE: The man don't want you to know all his business. He's my company. He ain't asking you no questions.

LYMON: It wasn't nothing. It was just a misunderstanding.

BERNIECE: He in my house. You say the sheriff looking for him, I wanna know what he looking for him for. Otherwise you all can go back out there and be where nobody don't have to ask you nothing.

LYMON: It was just a misunderstanding. Sometimes me and the sheriff we don't think alike. So we just got crossed on each other.

BERNIECE: Might be looking for him about that truck. He might have stole that truck.

BOY WILLIE: We ain't stole no truck, woman. I told you Lymon bought it.

DOAKER: Boy Willie and Lymon got more sense than to ride all the way up here in a stolen truck with a load of watermelons. Now they might have stole them watermelons, but I don't believe they stole that truck.

BOY WILLIE: You don't even know the man good and you calling him a thief. And we ain't stole them watermelons either. Them old man Pitterford's watermelons. He give me and Lymon all we could load for ten dollars.

DOAKER: No wonder you got them stacked up out there. You must have five hundred watermelons stacked up out there.

BERNIECE: Boy Willie, when you and Lymon planning on going back?

BOY WILLIE: Lymon say he staying. As soon as we sell them watermelons I'm going on back.

BERNIECE: [*Starts to exit up the stairs.*] That's what you need to do. And you need to do it quick. Come in here disrupting the house. I don't want all that loud carrying on around here. I'm surprised you ain't woke Maretha up.

BOY WILLIE: I was fixing to get her now. [*Calls.*] Hey, Maretha!

DOAKER: Berniece don't like all that hollering now.

BERNIECE: Don't you wake that child up!

BOY WILLIE: You going up there . . . wake her up and tell her her uncle's here. I ain't seen her in three years. Wake her up and send her down here. She can go back to bed.

BERNIECE: I ain't waking that child up . . . and don't you be making all that noise. You and Lymon need to sell them watermelons and go on back.

[BERNIECE *exits up the stairs.*]

BOY WILLIE: I see Berniece still try to be stuck up.

DOAKER: Berniece alright. She don't want you making all that noise. Maretha up there sleep. Let her sleep until she get up. She can see you then.

BOY WILLIE: I ain't thinking about Berniece. You hear from Wining Boy? You know Cleotha died?

DOAKER: Yeah, I heard that. He come by here about a year ago. Had a whole sack of money. He stayed here about two weeks. Ain't offered nothing. Berniece asked him for three dollars to buy some food and he got mad and left.

LYMON: Who's Wining Boy?

BOY WILLIE: That's my uncle. That's Doaker's brother. You heard me talk about Wining Boy. He play piano. He done made some records and everything. He still doing that, Doaker?

DOAKER: He made one or two records a long time ago. That's the only ones I ever known him to make. If you let him tell it he a big recording star.

BOY WILLIE: He stopped down home about two years ago. That's what I hear. I don't know. Me and Lymon was up on Parchman Farm[2] doing them three years.

DOAKER: He don't never stay in one place. Now, he been here about eight months ago. Back in the winter. Now, you subject not to see him for another two years. It's liable to be that long before he stop by.

BOY WILLIE: If he had a whole sack of money you liable never to see him. You ain't gonna see him until he get broke. Just as soon as that sack of money is gone you look up and he be on your doorstep.

LYMON: [*Noticing the piano.*] Is that the piano?

BOY WILLIE: Yeah . . . look here, Lymon. See how it's carved up real nice and polished and everything? You never find you another piano like that.

LYMON: Yeah, that look real nice.

BOY WILLIE: I told you. See how it's polished? My mama used to polish it every day. See all them pictures carved on it? That's what I was talking about. You can get a nice price for that piano.

LYMON: That's all Boy Willie talked about the whole trip up here. I got tired of hearing him talk about the piano.

BOY WILLIE: All you want to talk about is women. You ought to hear this nigger, Doaker. Talking about all the women he gonna get when he get up here. He ain't had none down there but he gonna get a hundred when he get up here.

2. Former name of the Mississippi State Penitentiary, a work farm operated with the labor of convicts.

DOAKER: How your people doing down there, Lymon?

LYMON: They alright. They still there. I come up here to see what it's like up here. Boy Willie trying to get me to go back and farm with him.

BOY WILLIE: Sutter's brother selling the land. He say he gonna sell it to me. That's why I come up here. I got one part of it. Sell them watermelons and get me another part. Get Berniece to sell that piano and I'll have the third part.

DOAKER: Berniece ain't gonna sell that piano.

BOY WILLIE: I'm gonna talk to her. When she see I got a chance to get Sutter's land she'll come around.

DOAKER: You can put that thought out your mind. Berniece ain't gonna sell that piano.

BOY WILLIE: I'm gonna talk to her. She been playing on it?

DOAKER: You know she won't touch that piano. I ain't never known her to touch it since Mama Ola died. That's over seven years now. She say it got blood on it. She got Maretha playing on it though. Say Maretha can go on and do everything she can't do. Got her in an extra school down at the Irene Kaufman Settlement House. She want Maretha to grow up and be a schoolteacher. Say she good enough she can teach on the piano.

BOY WILLIE: Maretha don't need to be playing on no piano. She can play on the guitar.

DOAKER: How much land Sutter got left?

BOY WILLIE: Got a hundred acres. Good land. He done sold it piece by piece, he kept the good part for himself. Now he got to give that up. His brother come down from Chicago for the funeral . . . he up there in Chicago got some kind of business with soda fountain equipment. He anxious to sell the land, Doaker. He don't want to be bothered with it. He called me to him and said cause of how long our families done known each other and how we been good friends and all, say he wanted to sell the land to me. Say he'd rather see me with it than Jim Stovall. Told me he'd let me have it for two thousand dollars cash money. He don't know I found out the most Stovall would give him for it was fifteen hundred dollars. He trying to get that extra five hundred out of me telling me he doing me a favor. I thanked him just as nice. Told him what a good man Sutter was and how he had my sympathy and all. Told him to give me two weeks. He said he'd wait on me. That's why I come up here. Sell them watermelons. Get Berniece to sell that piano. Put them two parts with the part I done saved. Walk in there. Tip my hat. Lay my money down on the table. Get my deed and walk on out. This time I get to keep all the cotton. Hire me some men to work it for me. Gin my cotton. Get my seed. And I'll see you again next year. Might even plant some tobacco or some oats.

DOAKER: You gonna have a hard time trying to get Berniece to sell that piano. You know Avery Brown from down there don't you? He up here now. He followed Berniece up here trying to get her to marry him after Crawley got killed. He been up here about two years. He call himself a preacher now.

BOY WILLIE: I know Avery. I know him from when he used to work on the Willshaw place. Lymon know him too.

DOAKER: He after Berniece to marry him. She keep telling him no but he won't give up. He keep pressing her on it.

BOY WILLIE: Avery think all white men is bigshots. He don't know there some white men ain't got as much as he got.

DOAKER: He supposed to come past here this morning. Berniece going down to the bank with him to see if he can get a loan to start his church. That's why I know Berniece ain't gonna sell that piano. He tried to get her to sell it to help him start his church. Sent the man around and everything.

BOY WILLIE: What man?

DOAKER: Some white fellow was going around to all the colored people's houses looking to buy up musical instruments. He'd buy anything. Drums. Guitars. Harmonicas. Pianos. Avery sent him past here. He looked at the piano and got excited. Offered her a nice price. She turned him down and got on Avery for sending him past. The man kept on her about two weeks. He seen where she wasn't gonna sell it, he gave her his number and told her if she ever wanted to sell it to call him first. Say he'd go one better than what anybody else would give her for it.

BOY WILLIE: How much he offer her for it?

DOAKER: Now you know me. She didn't say and I didn't ask. I just know it was a nice price.

LYMON: All you got to do is find out who he is and tell him somebody else wanna buy it from you. Tell him you can't make up your mind who to sell it to, and if he like Doaker say, he'll give you anything you want for it.

BOY WILLIE: That's what I'm gonna do. I'm gonna find out who he is from Avery.

DOAKER: It ain't gonna do you no good. Berniece ain't gonna sell that piano.

BOY WILLIE: She ain't got to sell it. I'm gonna sell it. I own just as much of it as she does.

BERNIECE: [Offstage, hollers.] Doaker! Go on get away. Doaker!

DOAKER: [Calling.] Berniece?

[DOAKER and BOY WILLIE rush to the stairs, BOY WILLIE runs up the stairs, passing BERNIECE as she enters, running.]

DOAKER: Berniece, what's the matter? You alright? What's the matter?

[BERNIECE tries to catch her breath. She is unable to speak.]

DOAKER: That's alright. Take your time. You alright. What's the matter? [*He calls.*] Hey, Boy Willie?

BOY WILLIE: [*Offstage.*] Ain't nobody up here.

BERNIECE: Sutter . . . Sutter's standing at the top of the steps.

DOAKER: [*Calls.*] Boy Willie!

[LYMON *crosses to the stairs and looks up.* BOY WILLIE *enters from the stairs.*]

BOY WILLIE: Hey Doaker, what's wrong with her? Berniece, what's wrong? Who was you talking to?

DOAKER: She say she seen Sutter's ghost standing at the top of the stairs.

BOY WILLIE: Seen what? Sutter? She ain't seen no Sutter.

BERNIECE: He was standing right up there.

BOY WILLIE: [*Entering on the stairs.*] That's all in Berniece's head. Ain't nobody up there. Go on up there, Doaker.

DOAKER: I'll take your word for it. Berniece talking about what she seen. She say Sutter's ghost standing at the top of the steps. She ain't just make all that up.

BOY WILLIE: She up there dreaming. She ain't seen no ghost.

LYMON: You want a glass of water, Berniece? Get her a glass of water, Boy Willie.

BOY WILLIE: She don't need no water. She ain't seen nothing. Go on up there and look. Ain't nobody up there but Maretha.

DOAKER: Let Berniece tell it.

BOY WILLIE: I ain't stopping her from telling it.

DOAKER: What happened, Berniece?

BERNIECE: I come out my room to come back down here and Sutter was standing there in the hall.

BOY WILLIE: What he look like?

BERNIECE: He look like Sutter. He look like he always look.

BOY WILLIE: Sutter couldn't find his way from Big Sandy to Little Sandy. How he gonna find his way all the way up here to Pittsburgh? Sutter ain't never even heard of Pittsburgh.

DOAKER: Go on, Berniece.

BERNIECE: Just standing there with the blue suit on.

BOY WILLIE: The man ain't never left Marlin County when he was living . . . and he's gonna come all the way up here now that he's dead?

DOAKER: Let her finish. I want to hear what she got to say.

BOY WILLIE: I'll tell you this. If Berniece had seen him like she think she seen him she'd still be running.

DOAKER: Go on, Berniece. Don't pay Boy Willie no mind.

BERNIECE: He was standing there . . . had his hand on top of his head. Look like he might have thought if he took his hand down his head might have fallen off.

LYMON: Did he have on a hat?

BERNIECE: Just had on that blue suit ... I told him to go away and he just stood there looking at me ... calling Boy Willie's name.

BOY WILLIE: What he calling my name for?

BERNIECE: I believe you pushed him in the well.

BOY WILLIE: Now what kind of sense that make? You telling me I'm gonna go out there and hide in the weeds with all them dogs and things he got around there ... I'm gonna hide and wait till I catch him looking down his well just right ... then I'm gonna run over and push him in. A great big old three-hundred-and-forty-pound man.

BERNIECE: Well, what he calling your name for?

BOY WILLIE: He bending over looking down his well, woman ... how he know who pushed him? It could have been anybody. Where was you when Sutter fell in his well? Where was Doaker? Me and Lymon was over in Stoner County. Tell her, Lymon. The Ghosts of the Yellow Dog got Sutter. That's what happened to him.

BERNIECE: You can talk all that Ghosts of the Yellow Dog stuff if you want. I know better.

LYMON: The Ghosts of the Yellow Dog pushed him. That's what the people say. They found him in his well and all the people say it must be the Ghosts of the Yellow Dog. Just like all them other men.

BOY WILLIE: Come talking about he looking for me. What he come all the way up here for? If he looking for me all he got to do is wait. He could have saved himself a trip if he looking for me. That ain't nothing but in Berniece's head. Ain't no telling what she liable to come up with next.

BERNIECE: Boy Willie, I want you and Lymon to go ahead and leave my house. Just go on somewhere. You don't do nothing but bring trouble with you everywhere you go. If it wasn't for you Crawley would still be alive.

BOY WILLIE: Crawley what? I ain't had nothing to do with Crawley getting killed. Crawley three time seven.[3] He had his own mind.

BERNIECE: Just go on and leave. Let Sutter go somewhere else looking for you.

BOY WILLIE: I'm leaving. Soon as we sell them watermelons. Other than that I ain't going nowhere. Hell, I just got here. Talking about Sutter looking for me. Sutter was looking for that piano. That's what he was looking for. He had to die to find out where that piano was at ... If I was you I'd get rid of it. That's the way to get rid of Sutter's ghost. Get rid of that piano.

BERNIECE: I want you and Lymon to go on and take all this confusion out of my house!

BOY WILLIE: Hey, tell her, Doaker. What kind of sense that make? I told you, Lymon, as soon as Berniece see me she was gonna start something.

---

3. That is, Crawley was 21 years old—an adult.

Didn't I tell you that? Now she done made up that story about Sutter just so she could tell me to leave her house. Well, hell, I ain't going nowhere till I sell them watermelons.

BERNIECE: Well why don't you go out there and sell them! Sell them and go on back!

BOY WILLIE: We waiting till the people get up.

LYMON: Boy Willie say if you get out there too early and wake the people up they get mad at you and won't buy nothing from you.

DOAKER: You won't be waiting long. You done let the sun catch up with you. This the time everybody be getting up around here.

BERNIECE: Come on, Doaker, walk up here with me. Let me get Maretha up and get her started. I got to get ready myself. Boy Willie, just go on out there and sell them watermelons and you and Lymon leave my house.

[BERNIECE *and* DOAKER *exit up the stairs.*]

BOY WILLIE: [*Calling after them.*] If you see Sutter up there . . . tell him I'm down here waiting on him.

LYMON: What if she see him again?

BOY WILLIE: That's all in her head. There ain't no ghost up there. [*Calls.*] Hey, Doaker . . . I told you ain't nothing up there.

LYMON: I'm glad he didn't say he was looking for me.

BOY WILLIE: I wish I would see Sutter's ghost. Give me a chance to put a whupping on him.

LYMON: You ought to stay up here with me. You be down there working his land . . . he might come looking for you all the time.

BOY WILLIE: I ain't thinking about Sutter. And I ain't thinking about staying up here. You stay up here. I'm going back and get Sutter's land. You think you ain't got to work up here. You think this the land of milk and honey. But I ain't scared of work. I'm going back and farm every acre of that land.

[DOAKER *enters from the stairs.*]

I told you there ain't nothing up there, Doaker. Berniece dreaming all that.

DOAKER: I believe Berniece seen something. Berniece levelheaded. She ain't just made all that up. She say Sutter had on a suit. I don't believe she ever seen Sutter in a suit. I believe that's what he was buried in, and that's what Berniece saw.

BOY WILLIE: Well, let her keep on seeing him then. As long as he don't mess with me.

[DOAKER *starts to cook his breakfast.*]

I heard about you, Doaker. They say you got all the women looking out for you down home. They be looking to see you coming. Say you got a different one every two weeks. Say they be fighting one another for you to stay with them. [*To* LYMON.] Look at him, Lymon. He know it's true.

DOAKER: I ain't thinking about no women. They never get me tied up with them. After Coreen I ain't got no use for them. I stay up on Jack Slattery's place when I be down there. All them women want is somebody with a steady payday.

BOY WILLIE: That ain't what I hear. I hear every two weeks the women all put on their dresses and line up at the railroad station.

DOAKER: I don't get down there but once a month. I used to go down there every two weeks but they keep switching me around. They keep switching all the fellows around.

BOY WILLIE: Doaker can't turn that railroad loose. He was working the railroad when I was walking around crying for sugartit. My mama used to brag on him.

DOAKER: I'm cooking now, but I used to line track. I pieced together the Yellow Dog stitch by stitch. Rail by rail. Line track all up around there. I lined track all up around Sunflower and Clarksdale. Wining Boy worked with me. He helped put in some of that track. He'd work it for six months and quit. Go back to playing piano and gambling.

BOY WILLIE: How long you been with the railroad now?

DOAKER: Twenty-seven years. Now, I'll tell you something about the railroad. What I done learned after twenty-seven years. See, you got North. You got West. You look over here you got South. Over there you got East. Now, you can start from anywhere. Don't care where you at. You got to go one of them four ways. And whichever way you decide to go they got a railroad that will take you there. Now, that's something simple. You think anybody would be able to understand that. But you'd be surprised how many people trying to go North get on a train going West. They think the train's supposed to go where they going rather than where it's going.

Now, why people going? Their sister's sick. They leaving before they kill somebody . . . and they sitting across from somebody who's leaving to keep from getting killed. They leaving cause they can't get satisfied. They going to meet someone. I wish I had a dollar for every time that someone wasn't at the station to meet them. I done seen that a lot. In between the time they sent the telegram and the time the person get there . . . they done forgot all about them.

They got so many trains out there they have a hard time keeping them from running into each other. Got trains going every whichaway. Got people on all of them. Somebody going where somebody just left. If everybody stay in one place I believe this would be a better world. Now what I done learned after twenty-seven years of railroading is this . . . if the train stays on the track . . . it's going to get where it's going. It might not be where you going. If it ain't, then all you got to do is sit and wait cause the train's coming back to get you. The train don't never stop. It'll come back every time. Now I'll tell you another thing . . .

BOY WILLIE: What you cooking over there, Doaker? Me and Lymon's hungry.

DOAKER: Go on down there to Wylie and Kirkpatrick to Eddie's restaurant. Coffee cost a nickel and you can get two eggs, sausage, and grits for fifteen cents. He even give you a biscuit with it.

BOY WILLIE: That look good what you got. Give me a little piece of that grilled bread.

DOAKER: Here . . . go on take the whole piece.

BOY WILLIE: Here you go, Lymon . . . you want a piece?

[*He gives* LYMON *a piece of toast.* MARETHA *enters from the stairs.*]

BOY WILLIE: Hey, sugar. Come here and give me a hug. Come on give Uncle Boy Willie a hug. Don't be shy. Look at her, Doaker. She done got bigger. Ain't she got big?

DOAKER: Yeah, she getting up there.

BOY WILLIE: How you doing, sugar?

MARETHA: Fine.

BOY WILLIE: You was just a little old thing last time I seen you. You remember me, don't you? This your Uncle Boy Willie from down South. That there's Lymon. He my friend. We come up here to sell watermelons. You like watermelons?

[MARETHA *nods.*]

We got a whole truckload out front. You can have as many as you want. What you been doing?

MARETHA: Nothing.

BOY WILLIE: Don't be shy now. Look at you getting all big. How old is you?

MARETHA: Eleven. I'm gonna be twelve soon.

BOY WILLIE: You like it up here? You like the North?

MARETHA: It's alright.

BOY WILLIE: That there's Lymon. Did you say hi to Lymon?

MARETHA: Hi.

LYMON: How you doing? You look just like your mama. I remember you when you was wearing diapers.

BOY WILLIE: You gonna come down South and see me? Uncle Boy Willie gonna get him a farm. Gonna get a great big old farm. Come down there and I'll teach you how to ride a mule. Teach you how to kill a chicken, too.

MARETHA: I seen my mama do that.

BOY WILLIE: Ain't nothing to it. You just grab him by his neck and twist it. Get you a real good grip and then you just wring his neck and throw him in the pot. Cook him up. Then you got some good eating. What you like to eat? What kind of food you like?

MARETHA: I like everything . . . except I don't like no black-eyed peas.

BOY WILLIE: Uncle Doaker tell me your mama got you playing that piano. Come on play something for me.

[BOY WILLIE *crosses over to the piano followed by* MARETHA.]

Show me what you can do. Come on now. Here . . . Uncle Boy Willie give you a dime . . . show me what you can do. Don't be bashful now. That dime say you can't be bashful.

[MARETHA *plays. It is something any beginner first learns.*]

Here, let me show you something.

[BOY WILLIE *sits and plays a simple boogie-woogie.*]

See that? See what I'm doing? That's what you call the boogie-woogie. See now . . . you can get up and dance to that. That's how good it sound. It sound like you wanna dance. You can dance to that. It'll hold you up. Whatever kind of dance you wanna do you can dance to that right there. See that? See how it go? Ain't nothing to it. Go on you do it.

MARETHA: I got to read it on the paper.

BOY WILLIE: You don't need no paper. Go on. Do just like that there.

BERNIECE: Maretha! You get up here and get ready to go so you be on time. Ain't no need you trying to take advantage of company.

MARETHA: I got to go.

BOY WILLIE: Uncle Boy Willie gonna get you a guitar. Let Uncle Doaker teach you how to play that. You don't need to read no paper to play the guitar. Your mama told you about that piano? You know how them pictures got on there?

MARETHA: She say it just always been like that since she got it.

BOY WILLIE: You hear that, Doaker? And you sitting up here in the house with Berniece.

DOAKER: I ain't got nothing to do with that. I don't get in the way of Berniece's raising her.

BOY WILLIE: You tell your mama to tell you about that piano. You ask her how them pictures got on there. If she don't tell you I'll tell you.

BERNIECE: Maretha!

MARETHA: I got to get ready to go.

BOY WILLIE: She getting big, Doaker. You remember her, Lymon?

LYMON: She used to be real little.

[*There is a knock on the door.* DOAKER *goes to answer it.* AVERY *enters. Thirty-eight years old, honest and ambitious, he has taken to the city like a fish to water, finding in it opportunities for growth and advancement that did not exist for him in the rural South. He is dressed in a suit and tie with a gold cross around his neck. He carries a small Bible.*]

DOAKER: Hey, Avery, come on in. Berniece upstairs.

BOY WILLIE: Look at him ... look at him ... he don't know what to say. He wasn't expecting to see me.

AVERY: Hey, Boy Willie. What you doing up here?

BOY WILLIE: Look at him, Lymon.

AVERY: Is that Lymon? Lymon Jackson?

BOY WILLIE: Yeah, you know Lymon.

DOAKER: Berniece be ready in a minute, Avery.

BOY WILLIE: Doaker say you a preacher now. What ... we supposed to call you Reverend? You used to be plain old Avery. When you get to be a preacher, nigger?

LYMON: Avery say he gonna be a preacher so he don't have to work.

BOY WILLIE: I remember when you was down there on the Willshaw place planting cotton. You wasn't thinking about no Reverend then.

AVERY: That must be your truck out there. I saw that truck with them watermelons, I was trying to figure out what it was doing in front of the house.

BOY WILLIE: Yeah, me and Lymon selling watermelons. That's Lymon's truck.

DOAKER: Berniece say you all going down to the bank.

AVERY: Yeah, they give me a half day off work. I got an appointment to talk to the bank about getting a loan to start my church.

BOY WILLIE: Lymon say preachers don't have to work. Where you working at, nigger?

DOAKER: Avery got him one of them good jobs. He working at one of them skyscrapers downtown.

AVERY: I'm working down there at the Gulf Building running an elevator. Got a pension and everything. They even give you a turkey on Thanksgiving.

LYMON: How you know the rope ain't gonna break? Ain't you scared the rope's gonna break?

AVERY: That's steel. They got steel cables hold it up. It take a whole lot of breaking to break that steel. Naw, I ain't worried about nothing like that. It ain't nothing but a little old elevator. Now, I wouldn't get in none of them airplanes. You couldn't pay me to do nothing like that.

LYMON: That be fun. I'd rather do that than ride in one of them elevators.

BOY WILLIE: How many of them watermelons you wanna buy?

AVERY: I thought you was gonna give me one seeing as how you got a whole truck full.

BOY WILLIE: You can get one, get two. I'll give you two for a dollar.

AVERY: I can't eat but one. How much are they?

BOY WILLIE: Aw, nigger, you know I'll give you a watermelon. Go on, take as many as you want. Just leave some for me and Lymon to sell.

AVERY: I don't want but one.

BOY WILLIE: How you get to be a preacher, Avery? I might want to be a preacher one day. Have everybody call me Reverend Boy Willie.

AVERY: It come to me in a dream. God called me and told me he wanted me to be a shepherd for his flock. That's what I'm gonna call my church . . . The Good Shepherd Church of God in Christ.

DOAKER: Tell him what you told me. Tell him about the three hobos.

AVERY: Boy Willie don't want to hear all that.

LYMON: I do. Lots a people say your dreams can come true.

AVERY: Naw. You don't want to hear all that.

DOAKER: Go on. I told him you was a preacher. He didn't want to believe me. Tell him about the three hobos.

AVERY: Well, it come to me in a dream. See . . . I was sitting out in this railroad yard watching the trains go by. The train stopped and these three hobos got off. They told me they had come from Nazareth and was on their way to Jerusalem. They had three candles. They gave me one and told me to light it . . . but to be careful that it didn't go out. Next thing I knew I was standing in front of this house. Something told me to go knock on the door. This old woman opened the door and said they had been waiting on me. Then she led me into this room. It was a big room and it was full of all kinds of different people. They looked like anybody else except they all had sheep heads and was making noise like sheep make. I heard somebody call my name. I looked around and there was these same three hobos. They told me to take off my clothes and they give me a blue robe with gold thread. They washed my feet and combed my hair. Then they showed me these three doors and told me to pick one.

I went through one of them doors and that flame leapt off that candle and it seemed like my whole head caught fire. I looked around and there was four or five other men standing there with these same blue robes on. Then we heard a voice tell us to look out across this valley. We looked out and saw the valley was full of wolves. The voice told us that these sheep people that I had seen in the other room had to go over to the other side of this valley and somebody had to take them. Then I heard another voice say, "Who shall I send?" Next thing I knew I said, "Here I am. Send me." That's when I met Jesus. He say, "If you go, I'll go with you." Something told me to say, "Come on. Let's go." That's when I woke up. My head still felt like it was on fire . . . but I had a peace about myself that was hard to explain. I knew right then that I had been filled with the Holy Ghost and called to be a servant of the Lord. It took me a while before I could accept that. But then a lot of little ways God showed me that it was true. So I became a preacher.

LYMON: I see why you gonna call it the Good Shepherd Church. You dreaming about them sheep people. I can see that easy.

BOY WILLIE: Doaker say you sent some white man past the house to look at that piano. Say he was going around to all the colored people's houses looking to buy up musical instruments.

AVERY: Yeah, but Berniece didn't want to sell that piano. After she told me about it . . . I could see why she didn't want to sell it.

BOY WILLIE: What's this man's name?

AVERY: Oh, that's a while back now. I done forgot his name. He give Berniece a card with his name and telephone number on it, but I believe she throwed it away.

[BERNIECE *and* MARETHA *enter from the stairs.*]

BERNIECE: Maretha, run back upstairs and get my pocketbook. And wipe that hair grease off your forehead. Go ahead, hurry up.

[MARETHA *exits up the stairs.*]

How you doing, Avery? You done got all dressed up. You look nice. Boy Willie, I thought you and Lymon was going to sell them watermelons.

BOY WILLIE: Lymon done got sleepy. We liable to get some sleep first.

LYMON: I ain't sleepy.

DOAKER: As many watermelons as you got stacked up on that truck out there, you ought to have been gone.

BOY WILLIE: We gonna go in a minute. We going.

BERNIECE: Doaker. I'm gonna stop down there on Logan Street. You want anything?

DOAKER: You can pick up some ham hocks if you going down there. See if you can get the smoked ones. If they ain't got that get the fresh ones. Don't get the ones that got all that fat under the skin. Look for the long ones. They nice and lean. [*He gives her a dollar.*] Don't get the short ones lessen they smoked. If you got to get the fresh ones make sure that they the long ones. If they ain't got them smoked then go ahead and get the short ones. [*Pause.*] You may as well get some turnip greens while you down there. I got some buttermilk . . . if you pick up some cornmeal I'll make me some cornbread and cook up them turnip greens.

[MARETHA *enters from the stairs.*]

MARETHA: We gonna take the streetcar?

BERNIECE: Me and Avery gonna drop you off at the settlement house. You mind them people down there. Don't be going down there showing your color. Boy Willie, I done told you what to do. I'll see you later, Doaker.

AVERY: I'll be seeing you again, Boy Willie.

BOY WILLIE: Hey, Berniece . . . what's the name of that man Avery sent past say he want to buy the piano?

BERNIECE: I knew it. I knew it when I first seen you. I knew you was up to something.

BOY WILLIE: Sutter's brother say he selling the land to me. He waiting on me now. Told me he'd give me two weeks. I got one part. Sell them watermelons get me another part. Then we can sell that piano and I'll have the third part.

BERNIECE: I ain't selling that piano, Boy Willie. If that's why you come up here you can just forget about it. [*To* DOAKER.] Doaker, I'll see you later. Boy Willie ain't nothing but a whole lot of mouth. I ain't paying him no mind. If he come up here thinking he gonna sell that piano then he done come up here for nothing.

[BERNIECE, AVERY, *and* MARETHA *exit the front door.*]

BOY WILLIE: Hey, Lymon! You ready to go sell these watermelons.

[BOY WILLIE *and* LYMON *start to exit. At the door* BOY WILLIE *turns to* DOAKER.]

Hey, Doaker . . . if Berniece don't want to sell that piano . . . I'm gonna cut it in half and go on and sell my half.

[BOY WILLIE *and* LYMON *exit.*]

[*The lights go down on the scene.*]

Scene 2

[*The lights come up on the kitchen. It is three days later.* WINING BOY *sits at the kitchen table. There is a half-empty pint bottle on the table.* DOAKER *busies himself washing pots.* WINING BOY *is fifty-six years old.* DOAKER'S *older brother, he tries to present the image of a successful musician and gambler, but his music, his clothes, and even his manner of presentation are old. He is a man who looking back over his life continues to live it with an odd mixture of zest and sorrow.*]

WINING BOY: So the Ghosts of the Yellow Dog got Sutter. That just go to show you I believe I always lived right. They say every dog gonna have his day and time it go around it sure come back to you. I done seen that a thousand times. I know the truth of that. But I'll tell you outright . . . if I see Sutter's ghost I'll be on the first thing I find that got wheels on it.

[DOAKER *enters from his room.*]

DOAKER: Wining Boy!

WINING BOY: And I'll tell you another thing . . . Berniece ain't gonna sell that piano.

DOAKER: That's what she told him. He say he gonna cut it in half and go on and sell his half. They been around here three days trying to sell them watermelons. They trying to get out to where the white folks live but the truck keep breaking down. They go a block or two and it break down again. They trying to get out to Squirrel Hill and can't get around the corner. He say soon as he can get that truck empty to where he can set the piano up in there he gonna take it out of here and go sell it.

WINING BOY: What about them boys Sutter got? How come they ain't farming that land?

DOAKER: One of them going to school. He left down there and come North to school. The other one ain't got as much sense as that frying pan over yonder. That is the dumbest white man I ever seen. He'd stand in the river and watch it rise till it drown him.

WINING BOY: Other than seeing Sutter's ghost how's Berniece doing?

DOAKER: She doing alright. She still got Crawley on her mind. He been dead three years but she still holding on to him. She need to go out here and let one of these fellows grab a whole handful of whatever she got. She act like it done got precious.

WINING BOY: They always told me any fish will bite if you got good bait.

DOAKER: She stuck up on it. She think it's better than she is. I believe she messing around with Avery. They got something going. He a preacher now. If you let him tell it the Holy Ghost sat on his head and heaven opened up with thunder and lightning and God was calling his name. Told him to go out and preach and tend to his flock. That's what he gonna call his church. The Good Shepherd Church.

WINING BOY: They had that joker down in Spear walking around talking about he Jesus Christ. He gonna live the life of Christ. Went through the Last Supper and everything. Rented him a mule on Palm Sunday and rode through the town. Did everything . . . talking about he Christ. He did everything until they got up to that crucifixion part. Got up to that part and told everybody to go home and quit pretending. He got up to the crucifixion part and changed his mind. Had a whole bunch of folks come down there to see him get nailed to the cross. I don't know who's the worse fool. Him or them. Had all them folks come down there . . . even carried the cross up this little hill. People standing around waiting to see him get nailed to the cross and he stop everything and preach a little sermon and told everybody to go home. Had enough nerve to tell them to come to church on Easter Sunday to celebrate his resurrection.

DOAKER: I'm surprised Avery ain't thought about that. He trying every little thing to get him a congregation together. They meeting over at his house till he get him a church.

WINING BOY: Ain't nothing wrong with being a preacher. You got the preacher on one hand and the gambler on the other. Sometimes there ain't too much difference in them.

DOAKER: How long you been in Kansas City?

WINING BOY: Since I left here. I got tied up with some old gal down there. [*Pause.*] You know Cleotha died.

DOAKER: Yeah, I heard that last time I was down there. I was sorry to hear that.

WINING BOY: One of her friends wrote and told me. I got the letter right here. [*He takes the letter out of his pocket.*] I was down in Kansas City and she wrote and told me Cleotha had died. Name of Willa Bryant. She say she know cousin Rupert. [*He opens the letter and reads.*] Dear Wining Boy: I am writing this letter to let you know Miss Cleotha Holman passed on Saturday the first of May she departed this world in the loving arms of her sister Miss Alberta Samuels. I know you would want to know this and am writing as a friend of Cleotha. There have been many hardships since last you seen her but she survived them all and to the end was a good woman whom I hope have God's grace and is in His Paradise. Your cousin Rupert Bates is my friend also and he give me your address and I pray this reaches you about Cleotha. Miss Willa Bryant. A friend. [*He folds the letter and returns it to his pocket.*] They was nailing her coffin shut by the time I heard about it. I never knew she was sick. I believe it was that yellow jaundice. That's what killed her mama.

DOAKER: Cleotha wasn't but forty-some.

WINING BOY: She was forty-six. I got ten years on her. I met her when she was sixteen. You remember I used to run around there. Couldn't nothing keep me still. Much as I loved Cleotha I loved to ramble. Couldn't nothing keep me still. We got married and we used to fight about it all the time. Then one day she asked me to leave. Told me she loved me before I left. Told me, Wining Boy, you got a home as long as I got mine. And I believe in my heart I always felt that and that kept me safe.

DOAKER: Cleotha always did have a nice way about her.

WINING BOY: Man that woman was something. I used to thank the Lord. Many a night I sat up and looked out over my life. Said, well, I had Cleotha. When it didn't look like there was nothing else for me, I said, thank God, at least I had that. If ever I go anywhere in this life I done known a good woman. And that used to hold me till the next morning. [*Pause.*] What you got? Give me a little nip. I know you got something stuck up in your room.

DOAKER: I ain't seen you walk in here and put nothing on the table. You done sat there and drank up your whiskey. Now you talking about what you got.

WINING BOY: I got plenty money. Give me a little nip.

[DOAKER *carries a glass into his room and returns with it half-filled. He sets it on the table in front of* WINING BOY.]

WINING BOY: You hear from Coreen?

DOAKER: She up in New York. I let her go from my mind.

WINING BOY: She was something back then. She wasn't too pretty but she had a way of looking at you made you know there was a whole lot of woman there. You got married and snatched her out from under us and we all got mad at you.

DOAKER: She up in New York City. That's what I hear.

[*The door opens and* BOY WILLIE *and* LYMON *enter.*]

BOY WILLIE: Aw hell . . . look here! We was just talking about you. Doaker say you left out of here with a whole sack of money. I told him we wasn't going see you till you got broke.

WINING BOY: What you mean broke? I got a whole pocketful of money.

DOAKER: Did you all get that truck fixed?

BOY WILLIE: We got it running and got halfway out there on Centre and it broke down again. Lymon went out there and messed it up some more. Fellow told us we got to wait till tomorrow to get it fixed. Say he have it running like new. Lymon going back down there and sleep in the truck so the people don't take the watermelons.

LYMON: Lymon nothing. You go down there and sleep in it.

BOY WILLIE: You was sleeping in it down home, nigger! I don't know nothing about sleeping in no truck.

LYMON: I ain't sleeping in no truck.

BOY WILLIE: They can take all the watermelons. I don't care. Wining Boy, where you coming from? Where you been?

WINING BOY: I been down in Kansas City.

BOY WILLIE: You remember Lymon? Lymon Jackson.

WINING BOY: Yeah, I used to know his daddy.

BOY WILLIE: Doaker say you don't never leave no address with nobody. Say he got to depend on your whim. See when it strike you to pay a visit.

WINING BOY: I got four or five addresses.

BOY WILLIE: Doaker say Berniece asked you for three dollars and you got mad and left.

WINING BOY: Berniece try and rule over you too much for me. That's why I left. It wasn't about no three dollars.

BOY WILLIE: Where you getting all these sacks of money from? I need to be with you. Doaker say you had a whole sack of money . . . turn some of it loose.

WINING BOY: I was just fixing to ask you for five dollars.

BOY WILLIE: I ain't got no money. I'm trying to get some. Doaker tell you about Sutter? The Ghosts of the Yellow Dog got him about three weeks ago. Berniece done seen his ghost and everything. He right upstairs. [*Calls.*] Hey Sutter! Wining Boy's here. Come on, get a drink!

WINING BOY: How many that make the Ghosts of the Yellow Dog done got?

BOY WILLIE: Must be about nine or ten, eleven or twelve. I don't know.

DOAKER: You got Ed Saunders. Howard Peterson. Charlie Webb.

WINING BOY: Robert Smith. That fellow that shot Becky's boy . . . say he was stealing peaches . . .

DOAKER: You talking about Bob Mallory.

BOY WILLIE: Berniece say she don't believe all that about the Ghosts of the Yellow Dog.

WINING BOY: She ain't got to believe. You go ask them white folks in Sunflower County if they believe. You go ask Sutter if he believe. I don't care
if Berniece believe or not. I done been to where the Southern cross the
Yellow Dog and called out their names. They talk back to you, too.

LYMON: What they sound like? The wind or something?

BOY WILLIE: You done been there for real, Wining Boy?

WINING BOY: Nineteen thirty. July of nineteen thirty I stood right there on
that spot. It didn't look like nothing was going right in my life. I said
everything can't go wrong all the time . . . let me go down there and
call on the Ghosts of the Yellow Dog, see if they can help me. I went
down there and right there where them two railroads cross each
other . . . I stood right there on that spot and called out their names.
They talk back to you, too.

LYMON: People say you can ask them questions. They talk to you like that?

WINING BOY: A lot of things you got to find out on your own. I can't say how
they talked to nobody else. But to me it just filled me up in a strange
sort of way to be standing there on that spot. I didn't want to leave. It
felt like the longer I stood there the bigger I got. I seen the train coming
and it seem like I was bigger than the train. I started not to move. But
something told me to go ahead and get on out the way. The train passed
and I started to go back up there and stand some more. But something
told me not to do it. I walked away from there feeling like a king. Went
on and had a stroke of luck that run on for three years. So I don't care if
Berniece believe or not. Berniece ain't got to believe. I know cause I been
there. Now Doaker'll tell you about the Ghosts of the Yellow Dog.

DOAKER: I don't try and talk that stuff with Berniece. Avery got her all tied
up in that church. She just think it's a whole lot of nonsense.

BOY WILLIE: Berniece don't believe in nothing. She just think she believe.
She believe in anything if it's convenient for her to believe. But when
that convenience run out then she ain't got nothing to stand on.

WINING BOY: Let's not get on Berniece now. Doaker tell me you talking
about selling that piano.

BOY WILLIE: Yeah . . . hey, Doaker, I got the name of that man Avery was talking about. The man what's fixing the truck gave me his name. Everybody
know him. Say he buy up anything you can make music with. I got his
name and his telephone number. Hey, Wining Boy, Sutter's brother say
he selling the land to me. I got one part. Sell them watermelons get me
the second part. Then . . . soon as I get them watermelons out that truck
I'm gonna take and sell that piano and get the third part.

DOAKER: That land ain't worth nothing no more. The smart white man's
up here in these cities. He cut the land loose and step back and watch
you and the dumb white man argue over it.

WINING BOY: How you know Sutter's brother ain't sold it already? You talking about selling the piano and the man's liable to sold the land two or
three times.

BOY WILLIE: He say he waiting on me. He say he give me two weeks. That's two weeks from Friday. Say if I ain't back by then he might gonna sell it to somebody else. He say he wanna see me with it.

WINING BOY: You know as well as I know the man gonna sell the land to the first one walk up and hand him the money.

BOY WILLIE: That's just who I'm gonna be. Look, you ain't gotta know he waiting on me. I know. Okay. I know what the man told me. Stovall already done tried to buy the land from him and he told him no. The man say he waiting on me . . . he waiting on me. Hey, Doaker . . . give me a drink. I see Wining Boy got his glass.

[DOAKER *exits into his room.*]

Wining Boy, what you doing in Kansas City? What they got down there?

LYMON: I hear they got some nice-looking women in Kansas City. I sure like to go down there and find out.

WINING BOY: Man, the women down there is something else.

[DOAKER *enters with a bottle of whiskey. He sets it on the table with some glasses.*]

DOAKER: You wanna sit up here and drink up my whiskey, leave a dollar on the table when you get up.

BOY WILLIE: You ain't doing nothing but showing your hospitality. I know we ain't got to pay for your hospitality.

WINING BOY: Doaker say they had you and Lymon down on the Parchman Farm. Had you on my old stomping grounds.

BOY WILLIE: Me and Lymon was down there hauling wood for Jim Miller and keeping us a little bit to sell. Some white fellows tried to run us off of it. That's when Crawley got killed. They put me and Lymon in the penitentiary.

LYMON: They ambushed us right there where that road dip down and around that bend in the creek. Crawley tried to fight them. Me and Boy Willie got away but the sheriff got us. Say we was stealing wood. They shot me in my stomach.

BOY WILLIE: They looking for Lymon down there now. They rounded him up and put him in jail for not working.

LYMON: Fined me a hundred dollars. Mr. Stovall come and paid my hundred dollars and the judge say I got to work for him to pay him back his hundred dollars. I told them I'd rather take my thirty days but they wouldn't let me do that.

BOY WILLIE: As soon as Stovall turned his back, Lymon was gone. He down there living in that truck dodging the sheriff and Stovall. He got both of them looking for him. So I brought him up here.

LYMON: I told Boy Willie I'm gonna stay up here. I ain't going back with him.

BOY WILLIE: Ain't nobody twisting your arm to make you go back. You can do what you want to do.

WINING BOY: I'll go back with you. I'm on my way down there. You gonna take the train? I'm gonna take the train.

LYMON: They treat you better up here.

BOY WILLIE: I ain't worried about nobody mistreating me. They treat you like you let them treat you. They mistreat me I mistreat them right back. Ain't no difference in me and the white man.

WINING BOY: Ain't no difference as far as how somebody supposed to treat you. I agree with that. But I'll tell you the difference between the colored man and the white man. Alright. Now you take and eat some berries. They taste real good to you. So you say I'm gonna go out and get me a whole pot of these berries and cook them up to make a pie or whatever. But you ain't looked to see them berries is sitting in the white fellow's yard. Ain't got no fence around them. You figure anybody want something they'd fence it in. Alright. Now the white man come along and say that's my land. Therefore everything that grow on it belong to me. He tell the sheriff, "I want you to put this nigger in jail as a warning to all the other niggers. Otherwise first thing you know these niggers have everything that belong to us."

BOY WILLIE: I'd come back at night and haul off his whole patch while he was sleep.

WINING BOY: Alright. Now Mr. So and So, he sell the land to you. And he come to you and say, "John, you own the land. It's all yours now. But them is my berries. And come time to pick them I'm gonna send my boys over. You got the land . . . but them berries, I'm gonna keep them. They mine." And he go and fix it with the law that them is his berries. Now that's the difference between the colored man and the white man. The colored man can't fix nothing with the law.

BOY WILLIE: I don't go by what the law say. The law's liable to say anything. I go by if it's right or not. It don't matter to me what the law say. I take and look at it for myself.

LYMON: That's why you gonna end up back down there on the Parchman Farm.

BOY WILLIE: I ain't thinking about no Parchman Farm. You liable to go back before me.

LYMON: They work you too hard down there. All that weeding and hoeing and chopping down trees. I didn't like all that.

WINING BOY: You ain't got to like your job on Parchman. Hey, tell him, Doaker, the only one got to like his job is the waterboy.

DOAKER: If he don't like his job he need to set that bucket down.

BOY WILLIE: That's what they told Lymon. They had Lymon on water and everybody got mad at him cause he was lazy.

LYMON: That water was heavy.

BOY WILLIE: They had Lymon down there singing:

[*Sings.*]

O Lord Berta Berta O Lord gal oh-ah
O Lord Berta Berta O Lord gal well

[LYMON *and* WINING BOY *join in.*]

Go 'head marry don't you wait on me oh-ah
Go 'head marry don't you wait on me well
Might not want you when I go free oh-ah
Might not want you when I go free well

BOY WILLIE: Come on, Doaker. Doaker know this one.

[*As* DOAKER *joins in the men stamp and clap to keep time. They sing in harmony with great fervor and style.*]

O Lord Berta Berta O Lord gal oh-ah
O Lord Berta Berta O Lord gal well

Raise them up higher, let them drop on down oh-ah
Raise them up higher, let them drop on down well
Don't know the difference when the sun go down oh-ah
Don't know the difference when the sun go down well

Berta in Meridan and she living at ease oh-ah
Berta in Meridan and she living at ease well
I'm on old Parchman, got to work or leave oh-ah
I'm on old Parchman, got to work or leave well

O Alberta, Berta, O Lord gal oh-ah
O Alberta, Berta, O Lord gal well

When you marry, don't marry no farming man oh-ah
When you marry, don't marry no farming man well
Everyday Monday, hoe handle in your hand oh-ah
Everyday Monday, hoe handle in your hand well

When you marry, marry a railroad man, oh-ah
When you marry, marry a railroad man, well
Everyday Sunday, dollar in your hand oh-ah
Everyday Sunday, dollar in your hand well

O Alberta, Berta, O Lord gal oh-ah
O Alberta, Berta, O Lord gal well

BOY WILLIE: Doaker like that part. He like that railroad part.
LYMON: Doaker sound like Tangleye.[4] He can't sing a lick.

4. Or Tangle Eye, one of the prisoners field-recorded at Parchman Farm by Alan Lomax in the 1930s and 1940s.

BOY WILLIE: Hey, Doaker, they still talk about you down on Parchman. They ask me, "You Doaker Boy's nephew?" I say, "Yeah, me and him is family." They treated me alright soon as I told them that. Say, "Yeah, he my uncle."

DOAKER: I don't never want to see none of them niggers no more.

BOY WILLIE: I don't want to see them either. Hey, Wining Boy, come on play some piano. You a piano player, play some piano. Lymon wanna hear you.

WINING BOY: I give that piano up. That was the best thing that ever happened to me, getting rid of that piano. That piano got so big and I'm carrying it around on my back. I don't wish that on nobody. See, you think it's all fun being a recording star. Got to carrying that piano around and man did I get slow. Got just like molasses. The world just slipping by me and I'm walking around with that piano. Alright. Now, there ain't but so many places you can go. Only so many road wide enough for you and that piano. And that piano get heavier and heavier. Go to a place and they find out you play piano, the first thing they want to do is give you a drink, find you a piano, and sit you right down. And that's where you gonna be for the next eight hours. They ain't gonna let you get up! Now, the first three or four years of that is fun. You can't get enough whiskey and you can't get enough women and you don't never get tired of playing that piano. But that only last so long. You look up one day and you hate the whiskey, and you hate the women, and you hate the piano. But that's all you got. You can't do nothing else. All you know how to do is play that piano. Now, who am I? Am I me? Or am I the piano player? Sometime it seem like the only thing to do is shoot the piano player cause he the cause of all the trouble I'm having.

DOAKER: What you gonna do when your troubles get like mine?

LYMON: If I knew how to play it, I'd play it. That's a nice piano.

BOY WILLIE: Whoever playing better play quick. Sutter's brother say he waiting on me. I sell them watermelons. Get Berniece to sell that piano. Put them two parts with the part I done saved . . .

WINING BOY: Berniece ain't gonna sell that piano. I don't see why you don't know that.

BOY WILLIE: What she gonna do with it? She ain't doing nothing but letting it sit up there and rot. That piano ain't doing nobody no good.

LYMON: That's a nice piano. If I had it I'd sell it. Unless I knew how to play like Wining Boy. You can get a nice price for that piano.

DOAKER: Now I'm gonna tell you something, Lymon don't know this . . . but I'm gonna tell you why me and Wining Boy say Berniece ain't gonna sell that piano.

BOY WILLIE: She ain't got to sell it! I'm gonna sell it! Berniece ain't got no more rights to that piano than I do.

DOAKER: I'm talking to the man . . . let me talk to the man. See, now . . . to understand why we say that . . . to understand about that piano . . . you got to go back to slavery time. See, our family was owned by a fellow named Robert Sutter. That was Sutter's grandfather. Alright. The piano was owned by a fellow named Joel Nolander. He was one of the Nolander brothers from down in Georgia. It was coming up on Sutter's wedding anniversary and he was looking to buy his wife . . . Miss Ophelia was her name . . . he was looking to buy her an anniversary present. Only thing with him . . . he ain't had no money. But he had some niggers. So he asked Mr. Nolander to see if maybe he could trade off some of his niggers for that piano. Told him he would give him one and a half niggers for it. That's the way he told him. Say he could have one full grown and one half grown. Mr. Nolander agreed only he say he had to pick them. He didn't want Sutter to give him just any old nigger. He say he wanted to have the pick of the litter. So Sutter lined up his niggers and Mr. Nolander looked them over and out of the whole bunch he picked my grandmother . . . her name was Berniece . . . same like Berniece . . . and he picked my daddy when he wasn't nothing but a little boy nine years old. They made the trade off and Miss Ophelia was so happy with that piano that it got to be just about all she would do was play on that piano.

WINING BOY: Just get up in the morning, get all dressed up and sit down and play on that piano.

DOAKER: Alright. Time go along. Time go along. Miss Ophelia got to missing my grandmother . . . the way she would cook and clean the house and talk to her and what not. And she missed having my daddy around the house to fetch things for her. So she asked to see if maybe she could trade back that piano and get her niggers back. Mr. Nolander said no. Said a deal was a deal. Him and Sutter had a big falling out about it and Miss Ophelia took sick to the bed. Wouldn't get out of the bed in the morning. She just lay there. The doctor said she was wasting away.

WINING BOY: That's when Sutter called our granddaddy up to the house.

DOAKER: Now, our granddaddy's name was Boy Willie. That's who Boy Willie's named after . . . only they called him Willie Boy. Now, he was a worker of wood. He could make you anything you wanted out of wood. He'd make you a desk. A table. A lamp. Anything you wanted. Them white fellows around there used to come up to Mr. Sutter and get him to make all kinds of things for them. Then they'd pay Mr. Sutter a nice price. See, everything my granddaddy made Mr. Sutter owned cause he owned him. That's why when Mr. Nolander offered to buy him to keep the family together Mr. Sutter wouldn't sell him. Told Mr. Nolander he didn't have enough money to buy him. Now . . . am I telling it right, Wining Boy?

WINING BOY: You telling it.

DOAKER: Sutter called him up to the house and told him to carve my grandmother and my daddy's picture on the piano for Miss Ophelia. And he took and carved this . . .

[DOAKER *crosses over to the piano.*]

See that right there? That's my grandmother, Berniece. She looked just like that. And he put a picture of my daddy when he wasn't nothing but a little boy the way he remembered him. He made them up out of his memory. Only thing . . . he didn't stop there. He carved all this. He got a picture of his mama . . . Mama Esther . . . and his daddy, Boy Charles.

WINING BOY: That was the first Boy Charles.

DOAKER: Then he put on the side here all kinds of things. See that? That's when him and Mama Berniece got married. They called it jumping the broom. That's how you got married in them days. Then he got here when my daddy was born . . . and here he got Mama Esther's funeral . . . and down here he got Mr. Nolander taking Mama Berniece and my daddy away down to his place in Georgia. He got all kinds of things what happened with our family. When Mr. Sutter seen the piano with all them carvings on it he got mad. He didn't ask for all that. But see . . . there wasn't nothing he could do about it. When Miss Ophelia seen it . . . she got excited. Now she had her piano and her niggers too. She took back to playing it and played on it right up till the day she died. Alright . . . now see, our brother Boy Charles . . . that's Berniece and Boy Willie's daddy . . . he was the oldest of us three boys. He's dead now. But he would have been fifty-seven if he had lived. He died in 1911 when he was thirty-one years old. Boy Charles used to talk about that piano all the time. He never could get it off his mind. Two or three months go by and he be talking about it again. He be talking about taking it out of Sutter's house. Say it was the story of our whole family and as long as Sutter had it . . . he had us. Say we was still in slavery. Me and Wining Boy tried to talk him out of it but it wouldn't do any good. Soon as he quiet down about it he'd start up again. We seen where he wasn't gonna get it off his mind . . . so, on the Fourth of July, 1911 . . . when Sutter was at the picnic what the county give every year . . . me and Wining Boy went on down there with him and took that piano out of Sutter's house. We put it on a wagon and me and Wining Boy carried it over into the next county with Mama Ola's people. Boy Charles decided to stay around there and wait until Sutter got home to make it look like business as usual.

Now, I don't know what happened when Sutter came home and found that piano gone. But somebody went up to Boy Charles's house and set it on fire. But he wasn't in there. He must have seen them coming cause he went down and caught the 3:57 Yellow Dog. He didn't know they was gonna come down and stop the train. Stopped the train and found Boy Charles in the boxcar with four of them hobos. Must have got mad when they couldn't find the piano cause they set the boxcar afire and killed everybody. Now, nobody know who done that. Some people say it was Sutter cause it was his piano. Some people say it was Sheriff Carter. Some people say it was Robert Smith and Ed Saunders. But don't nobody know for sure. It was about two months after that that Ed Saunders fell down his well. Just upped and fell down his well for no reason. People say it was the ghost of them men who burned up in the boxcar that pushed him in his well. They started calling them the Ghosts of the Yellow Dog. Now, that's how all that got started and that why we say Berniece ain't gonna sell that piano. Cause her daddy died over it.

BOY WILLIE: All that's in the past. If my daddy had seen where he could have traded that piano in for some land of his own, it wouldn't be sitting up here now. He spent his whole life farming on somebody else's land. I ain't gonna do that. See, he couldn't do no better. When he come along he ain't had nothing he could build on. His daddy ain't had nothing to give him. The only thing my daddy had to give me was that piano. And he died over giving me that. I ain't gonna let it sit up there and rot without trying to do something with it. If Berniece can't see that, then I'm gonna go ahead and sell my half. And you and Wining Boy know I'm right.

DOAKER: Ain't nobody said nothing about who's right and who's wrong. I was just telling the man about the piano. I was telling him why we say Berniece ain't gonna sell it.

LYMON: Yeah, I can see why you say that now. I told Boy Willie he ought to stay up here with me.

BOY WILLIE: You stay! I'm going back! That's what I'm gonna do with my life! Why I got to come up here and learn to do something I don't know how to do when I already know how to farm? You stay up here and make your own way if that's what you want to do. I'm going back and live my life the way I want to live it.

[WINING BOY *gets up and crosses to the piano.*]

WINING BOY: Let's see what we got here. I ain't played on this thing for a while.

DOAKER: You can stop telling that. You was playing on it the last time you was through here. We couldn't get you off of it. Go on and play something.

[WINING BOY *sits down at the piano and plays and sings. The song is one which has put many dimes and quarters in his pocket, long ago, in dimly remembered towns and way stations. He plays badly, without hesitation, and sings in a forceful voice.*]

WINING BOY: [*Singing.*]

> I am a rambling gambling man
> I gambled in many towns
> I rambled this wide world over
> I rambled this world around
> I had my ups and downs in life
> And bitter times I saw
> But I never knew what misery was
> Till I lit on old Arkansas.
>
> I started out one morning
> To meet that early train
> He said, "You better work for me
> I have some land to drain.
> I'll give you fifty cents a day,
> Your washing, board and all
> And you shall be a different man
> In the state of Arkansas."
>
> I worked six months for the rascal
> Joe Herrin was his name
> He fed me old corn dodgers[5]
> They was hard as any rock
> My tooth is all got loosened
> And my knees begin to knock
> That was the kind of hash I got
> In the state of Arkansas.
>
> Traveling man
> I've traveled all around this world
> Traveling man
> I've traveled from land to land
> Traveling man
> I've traveled all around this world
> Well it ain't no use
> Writing no news
> I'm a traveling man.

[*The door opens and* BERNIECE *enters with* MARETHA.]

BERNIECE: Is that . . . Lord, I know that ain't Wining Boy sitting there.

WINING BOY: Hey, Berniece.

BERNIECE: You all had this planned. You and Boy Willie had this planned.

---

5. Cornbread dumplings.

WINING BOY: I didn't know he was gonna be here. I'm on my way down home. I stopped by to see you and Doaker first.

DOAKER: I told the nigger he left out of here with that sack of money, we thought we might never see him again. Boy Willie say he wasn't gonna see him till he got broke. I looked up and seen him sitting on the doorstep asking for two dollars. Look at him laughing. He know it's the truth.

BERNIECE: Boy Willie, I didn't see that truck out there. I thought you was out selling watermelons.

BOY WILLIE: We done sold them all. Sold the truck too.

BERNIECE: I don't want to go through none of your stuff. I done told you to go back where you belong.

BOY WILLIE: I was just teasing you, woman. You can't take no teasing?

BERNIECE: Wining Boy, when you get here?

WINING BOY: A little while ago. I took the train from Kansas City.

BERNIECE: Let me go upstairs and change and then I'll cook you something to eat.

BOY WILLIE: You ain't cooked me nothing when I come.

BERNIECE: Boy Willie, go on and leave me alone. Come on, Maretha, get up here and change your clothes before you get them dirty.

[BERNIECE *exits up the stairs, followed by* MARETHA.]

WINING BOY: Maretha sure getting big, ain't she, Doaker. And just as pretty as she want to be. I didn't know Crawley had it in him.

[BOY WILLIE *crosses to the piano.*]

BOY WILLIE: Hey, Lymon . . . get up on the other side of this piano and let me see something.

WINING BOY: Boy Willie, what is you doing?

BOY WILLIE: I'm seeing how heavy this piano is. Get up over there, Lymon.

WINING BOY: Go on and leave that piano alone. You ain't taking that piano out of here and selling it.

BOY WILLIE: Just as soon as I get them watermelons out that truck.

WINING BOY: Well, I got something to say about that.

BOY WILLIE: This my daddy's piano.

WINING BOY: He ain't took it by himself. Me and Doaker helped him.

BOY WILLIE: He died by himself. Where was you and Doaker at then? Don't come telling me nothing about this piano. This is me and Berniece's piano. Am I right, Doaker?

DOAKER: Yeah, you right.

BOY WILLIE: Let's see if we can lift it up, Lymon. Get a good grip on it and pick it up on your end. Ready? Lift!

[*As they start to move the piano, the sound of* SUTTER'S GHOST *is heard.* DOAKER *is the only one to hear it. With difficulty they move the piano a little bit so it is out of place.*]

BOY WILLIE: What you think?

LYMON: It's heavy . . . but you can move it. Only it ain't gonna be easy.

BOY WILLIE: It wasn't that heavy to me. Okay, let's put it back.

[*The sound of* SUTTER's GHOST *is heard again. They all hear it as* BERNIECE *enters on the stairs.*]

BERNIECE: Boy Willie . . . you gonna play around with me one too many times. And then God's gonna bless you and West is gonna dress you. Now set that piano back over there. I done told you a hundred times I ain't selling that piano.

BOY WILLIE: I'm trying to get me some land, woman. I need that piano to get me some money so I can buy Sutter's land.

BERNIECE: Money can't buy what that piano cost. You can't sell your soul for money. It won't go with the buyer. It'll shrivel and shrink to know that you ain't taken on to it. But it won't go with the buyer.

BOY WILLIE: I ain't talking about all that, woman. I ain't talking about selling my soul. I'm talking about trading that piece of wood for some land. Get something under your feet. Land the only thing God ain't making no more of. You can always get you another piano. I'm talking about some land. What you get something out the ground from. That's what I'm talking about. You can't do nothing with that piano but sit up there and look at it.

BERNIECE: That's just what I'm gonna do. Wining Boy, you want me to fry you some pork chops?

BOY WILLIE: Now, I'm gonna tell you the way I see it. The only thing that make that piano worth something is them carvings Papa Willie Boy put on there. That's what make it worth something. That was my great-grandaddy. Papa Boy Charles brought that piano into the house. Now, I'm supposed to build on what they left me. You can't do nothing with that piano sitting up here in the house. That's just like if I let them watermelons sit out there and rot. I'd be a fool. Alright now, if you say to me, Boy Willie, I'm using that piano. I give out lessons on it and that help me make my rent or whatever. Then that be something else. I'd have to go on and say, well, Berniece using that piano. She building on it. Let her go on and use it. I got to find another way to get Sutter's land. But Doaker say you ain't touched that piano the whole time it's been up here. So why you wanna stand in my way? See, you just looking at the sentimental value. See, that's good. That's alright. I take my hat off whenever somebody say my daddy's name. But I ain't gonna be no fool about no sentimental value. You can sit up here and look at the piano for the next hundred years and it's just gonna be a piano. You can't make more than that. Now I want to get Sutter's land with that piano. I get Sutter's land and I can go down and cash in the crop and get my seed. As long as I got the land and the seed then I'm alright. I can always get me a little something else. Cause that land give back to you. I can make me another crop and cash that in. I still got the land and the seed. But that piano don't put out nothing else. You ain't got nothing working for you. Now, the kind of man my daddy was he would have understood that. I'm sorry you can't see it that way. But that's why I'm gonna take that piano out of here and sell it.

BERNIECE: You ain't taking that piano out of my house. [*She crosses to the piano.*] Look at this piano. Look at it. Mama Ola polished this piano with her tears for seventeen years. For seventeen years she rubbed on it till her hands bled. Then she rubbed the blood in . . . mixed it up with the rest of the blood on it. Every day that God breathed life into her body she rubbed and cleaned and polished and prayed over it. "Play something for me, Berniece. Play something for me, Berniece." Every day. "I cleaned it up for you, play something for me, Berniece." You always talking about your daddy but you ain't never stopped to look at what his foolishness cost your mama. Seventeen years' worth of cold nights and an empty bed. For what? For a piano? For a piece of wood? To get even with somebody? I look at you and you're all the same. You, Papa Boy Charles, Wining Boy, Doaker, Crawley . . . you're all alike. All this thieving and killing and thieving and killing. And what it ever lead to? More killing and more thieving. I ain't never seen it come to nothing. People getting burned up. People getting shot. People falling down their wells. It don't never stop.

DOAKER: Come on now, Berniece, ain't no need in getting upset.

BOY WILLIE: I done a little bit of stealing here and there, but I ain't never killed nobody. I can't be speaking for nobody else. You all got to speak for yourself, but I ain't never killed nobody.

BERNIECE: You killed Crawley just as sure as if you pulled the trigger.

BOY WILLIE: See, that's ignorant. That's downright foolish for you to say something like that. You ain't doing nothing but showing your ignorance. If the nigger was here I'd whup his ass for getting me and Lymon shot at.

BERNIECE: Crawley ain't knew about the wood.

BOY WILLIE: We told the man about the wood. Ask Lymon. He knew all about the wood. He seen we was sneaking it. Why else we gonna be out there at night? Don't come telling me Crawley ain't knew about the wood. Them fellows come up on us and Crawley tried to bully them. Me and Lymon seen the sheriff with them and give in. Wasn't no sense in getting killed over fifty dollars' worth of wood.

BERNIECE: Crawley ain't knew you stole that wood.

BOY WILLIE: We ain't stole no wood. Me and Lymon was hauling wood for Jim Miller and keeping us a little bit on the side. We dumped our little bit down there by the creek till we had enough to make a load. Some fellows seen us and we figured we better get it before they did. We come up there and got Crawley to help us load it. Figured we'd cut him in. Crawley trying to keep the wolf from his door . . . we was trying to help him.

LYMON: Me and Boy Willie told him about the wood. We told him some fellows might be trying to beat us to it. He say let me go back and get my thirty-eight. That's what caused all the trouble.

BOY WILLIE: If Crawley ain't had the gun he'd be alive today.

LYMON: We had it about half loaded when they come up on us. We seen the sheriff with them and we tried to get away. We ducked around near the bend in the creek . . . but they was down there too. Boy Willie say let's give in. But Crawley pulled out his gun and started shooting. That's when they started shooting back.

BERNIECE: All I know is Crawley would be alive if you hadn't come up there and got him.

BOY WILLIE: I ain't had nothing to do with Crawley getting killed. That was his own fault.

BERNIECE: Crawley's dead and in the ground and you still walking around here eating. That's all I know. He went off to load some wood with you and ain't never come back.

BOY WILLIE: I told you, woman . . . I ain't had nothing to do with . . .

BERNIECE: He ain't here, is he? He ain't here!

[BERNIECE *hits* BOY WILLIE.]

I said he ain't here. Is he?

[BERNIECE *continues to hit* BOY WILLIE, *who doesn't move to defend himself, other than back up and turning his head so that most of the blows fall on his chest and arms.*]

DOAKER: [*Grabbing* BERNIECE.] Come on, Berniece . . . let it go, it ain't his fault.

BERNIECE: He ain't here, is he? Is he?

BOY WILLIE: I told you I ain't responsible for Crawley.

BERNIECE: He ain't here.

BOY WILLIE: Come on now, Berniece . . . don't do this now. Doaker get her. I ain't had nothing to do with Crawley . . .

BERNIECE: You come up there and got him!

BOY WILLIE: I done told you now. Doaker, get her. I ain't playing.

DOAKER: Come on. Berniece.

[MARETHA *is heard screaming upstairs. It is a scream of stark terror.*]

MARETHA: Mama! . . . Mama!

[*The lights go down to black. End of Act One.*]

ACT II

Scene 1

[The lights come up on the kitchen. It is the following morning. DOAKER *is ironing the pants to his uniform. He has a pot cooking on the stove at the same time. He is singing a song. The song provides him with the rhythm for his work and he moves about the kitchen with the ease born of many years as a railroad cook.]*

DOAKER:

Gonna leave Jackson Mississippi
And go to Memphis
And double back to Jackson
Come on down to Hattiesburg
Change cars on the Y.D.
Coming through the territory to
Meridian
And Meridian to Greenville
And Greenville to Memphis
I'm on my way and I know where

Change cars on the Katy
Leaving Jackson
And going through Clarksdale
Hello Winona!
Courtland!
Bateville!
Como!
Senitobia!
Lewisberg!
Sunflower!
Glendora!
Sharkey!
And double back to Jackson
Hello Greenwood
I'm on my way Memphis
Clarksdale
Moorhead
Indianola
Can a highball pass through?
Highball on through sir
Grand Carson!
Thirty First Street Depot
Fourth Street Depot
Memphis!

[WINING BOY *enters carrying a suit of clothes.*]

DOAKER: I thought you took that suit to the pawnshop?

WINING BOY: I went down there and the man tell me the suit is too old. Look at this suit. This is one hundred percent silk! How a silk suit gonna get too old? I know what it was he just didn't want to give me five dollars for it. Best he wanna give me is three dollars. I figure a silk suit is worth five dollars all over the world. I wasn't gonna part with it for no three dollars so I brought it back.

DOAKER: They got another pawnshop up on Wylie.

WINING BOY: I carried it up there. He say he don't take no clothes. Only thing he take is guns and radios. Maybe a guitar or two. Where's Berniece?

DOAKER: Berniece still at work. Boy Willie went down there to meet Lymon this morning. I guess they got that truck fixed, they had been out there all day and ain't come back yet. Maretha scared to sleep up there now. Berniece don't know, but I seen Sutter before she did.

WINING BOY: Say what?

DOAKER: About three weeks ago. I had just come back from down there. Sutter couldn't have been dead more than three days. He was sitting over there at the piano. I come out to go to work . . . and he was sitting right there. Had his hand on top of his head just like Berniece said. I believe he broke his neck when he fell in the well. I kept quiet about it. I didn't see no reason to upset Berniece.

WINING BOY: Did he say anything? Did he say he was looking for Boy Willie?

DOAKER: He was just sitting there. He ain't said nothing. I went on out the door and left him sitting there. I figure as long as he was on the other side of the room everything be alright. I don't know what I would have done if he had started walking toward me.

WINING BOY: Berniece say he was calling Boy Willie's name.

DOAKER: I ain't heard him say nothing. He was just sitting there when I seen him. But I don't believe Boy Willie pushed him in the well. Sutter here cause of that piano. I heard him playing on it one time. I thought it was Berniece but then she don't play that kind of music. I come out here and ain't seen nobody, but them piano keys was moving a mile a minute. Berniece need to go on and get rid of it. It ain't done nothing but cause trouble.

WINING BOY: I agree with Berniece. Boy Charles ain't took it to give it back. He took it cause he figure he had more right to it than Sutter did. If Sutter can't understand that . . . then that's just the way that go. Sutter dead and in the ground . . . don't care where his ghost is. He can hover around and play on the piano all he want. I want to see him carry it out the house. That's what I want to see. What time Berniece get home? I don't see how I let her get away from me this morning.

DOAKER: You up there sleep. Berniece leave out of here early in the morning. She out there in Squirrel Hill cleaning house for some bigshot down there at the steel mill. They don't like you to come late. You come late they won't give you your carfare. What kind of business you got with Berniece?

WINING BOY: My business. I ain't asked you what kind of business you got.

DOAKER: Berniece ain't got no money. If that's why you was trying to catch her. She having a hard enough time trying to get by as it is. If she go ahead and marry Avery . . . he working every day . . . she go ahead and marry him they could do alright for themselves. But as it stands she ain't got no money.

WINING BOY: Well, let me have five dollars.

DOAKER: I just give you a dollar before you left out of here. You ain't gonna take my five dollars out there and gamble and drink it up.

WINING BOY: Aw, nigger, give me five dollars. I'll give it back to you.

DOAKER: You wasn't looking to give me five dollars when you had that sack of money. You wasn't looking to throw nothing my way. Now you wanna come in here and borrow five dollars. If you going back with Boy Willie you need to be trying to figure out how you gonna get train fare.

WINING BOY: That's why I need the five dollars. If I had five dollars I could get me some money.

[DOAKER *goes into his pocket.*]

Make it seven.

DOAKER: You take this five dollars . . . and you bring my money back here too.

[BOY WILLIE *and* LYMON *enter. They are happy and excited. They have money in all of their pockets and are anxious to count it.*]

DOAKER: How'd you do out there?

BOY WILLIE: They was lining up for them.

LYMON: Me and Boy Willie couldn't sell them fast enough. Time we got one sold we'd sell another.

BOY WILLIE: I seen what was happening and told Lymon to up the price on them.

LYMON: Boy Willie say charge them a quarter more. They didn't care. A couple of people give me a dollar and told me to keep the change.

BOY WILLIE: One fellow bought five. I say now what he gonna do with five watermelons? He can't eat them all. I sold him the five and asked him did he want to buy five more.

LYMON: I ain't never seen nobody snatch a dollar fast as Boy Willie.

BOY WILLIE: One lady asked me say, "Is they sweet?" I told her say, "Lady, where we grow these watermelons we put sugar in the ground." You know, she believed me. Talking about she had never heard of that before.

Lymon was laughing his head off. I told her, "Oh, yeah, we put the sugar right in the ground with the seed." She say, "Well, give me another one." Them white folks is something else . . . ain't they, Lymon?

LYMON: Soon as you holler watermelons they come right out their door. Then they go and get their neighbors. Look like they having a contest to see who can buy the most.

WINING BOY: I got something for Lymon.

[WINING BOY *goes to get his suit.* BOY WILLIE *and* LYMON *continue to count their money.*]

BOY WILLIE: I know you got more than that. You ain't sold all them watermelons for that little bit of money.

LYMON: I'm still looking. That ain't all you got either. Where's all them quarters?

BOY WILLIE: You let me worry about the quarters. Just put the money on the table.

WINING BOY: [*Entering with his suit.*] Look here, Lymon . . . see this? Look at his eyes getting big. He ain't never seen a suit like this. This is one hundred percent silk. Go ahead . . . put it on. See if it fit you.

[LYMON *tries the suit coat on.*]

Look at that. Feel it. That's one hundred percent genuine silk. I got that in Chicago. You can't get clothes like that nowhere but New York and Chicago. You can't get clothes like that in Pittsburgh. These folks in Pittsburgh ain't never seen clothes like that.

LYMON: This is nice, feel real nice and smooth.

WINING BOY: That's a fifty-five-dollar suit. That's the kind of suit the big-shots wear. You need a pistol and a pocketful of money to wear that suit. I'll let you have it for three dollars. The women will fall out their windows they see you in a suit like that. Give me three dollars and go on and wear it down the street and get you a woman.

BOY WILLIE: That looks nice, Lymon. Put the pants on. Let me see it with the pants.

[LYMON *begins to try on the pants.*]

WINING BOY: Look at that . . . see how it fits you? Give me three dollars and go on and take it. Look at that, Doaker . . . don't he look nice?

DOAKER: Yeah . . . that's a nice suit.

WINING BOY: Got a shirt to go with it. Cost you an extra dollar. Four dollars you got the whole deal.

LYMON: How this look, Boy Willie?

BOY WILLIE: That look nice . . . if you like that kind of thing. I don't like them dress-up kind of clothes. If you like it, look real nice.

WINING BOY: That's the kind of suit you need for up here in the North.

LYMON: Four dollars for everything? The suit and the shirt?

WINING BOY: That's cheap. I should be charging you twenty dollars. I give you a break cause you a homeboy. That's the only way I let you have it for four dollars.

LYMON: [*Going into his pocket.*] Okay . . . here go the four dollars.

WINING BOY: You got some shoes? What size you wear?

LYMON: Size nine.

WINING BOY: That's what size I got! Size nine. I let you have them for three dollars.

LYMON: Where they at? Let me see them.

WINING BOY: They real nice shoes, too. Got a nice tip to them. Got pointy toe just like you want.

[WINING BOY *goes to get his shoes.*]

LYMON: Come on, Boy Willie, let's go out tonight. I wanna see what it looks like up here. Maybe we go to a picture show. Hey, Doaker, they got picture shows up here?

DOAKER: The Rhumba Theater. Right down there on Fullerton Street. Can't miss it. Got the speakers outside on the sidewalk. You can hear it a block away. Boy Willie know where it's at.

[DOAKER *exits into his room.*]

LYMON: Let's go to the picture show, Boy Willie. Let's go find some women.

BOY WILLIE: Hey, Lymon, how many of them watermelons would you say we got left? We got just under a half a load . . . right?

LYMON: About that much. Maybe a little more.

BOY WILLIE: You think that piano will fit up in there?

LYMON: If we stack them watermelons you can sit it up in the front there.

BOY WILLIE: I'm gonna call that man tomorrow.

WINING BOY: [*Returns with his shoes.*] Here you go . . . size nine. Put them on. Cost you three dollars. That's a Florsheim shoe. That's the kind Staggerlee[6] wore.

LYMON: [*Trying on the shoes.*] You sure these size nine?

WINING BOY: You can look at my feet and see we wear the same size. Man, you put on that suit and them shoes and you got something there. You ready for whatever's out there. But is they ready for you? With them shoes on you be the King of the Walk. Have everybody stop to look at your shoes. Wishing they had a pair. I'll give you a break. Go on and take them for two dollars.

[LYMON *pays* WINING BOY *two dollars.*]

---

6. In African American folklore, a flashy figure (also called Stagger Lee, Stagolee, Stagalee, Stackolee, Stack O'Lee, Stack-o-lee, and so on) who murdered the man who stole his Stetson hat. The story is frequently retold (and reinterpreted) in song.

LYMON: Come on, Boy Willie . . . let's go find some women. I'm gonna go upstairs and get ready. I'll be ready to go in a minute. Ain't you gonna get dressed?

BOY WILLIE: I'm gonna wear what I got on. I ain't dressing up for these city niggers.

[LYMON *exits up the stairs.*]

That's all Lymon think about is women.

WINING BOY: His daddy was the same way. I used to run around with him. I know his mama too. Two strokes back and I would have been his daddy! His daddy's dead now . . . but I got the nigger out of jail one time. They was fixing to name him Daniel and walk him through the Lion's Den.[7] He got in a tussle with one of them white fellows and the sheriff lit on him like white on rice. That's how the whole thing come about between me and Lymon's mama. She knew me and his daddy used to run together and he got in jail and she went down there and took the sheriff a hundred dollars. Don't get me to lying about where she got it from. I don't know. The sheriff looked at that hundred dollars and turned his nose up. Told her, say, "That ain't gonna do him no good. You got to put another hundred on top of that." She come up there and got me where I was playing at this saloon . . . said she had all but fifty dollars and asked me if I could help. Now the way I figured it . . . without that fifty dollars the sheriff was gonna turn him over to Parchman. The sheriff turn him over to Parchman it be three years before anybody see him again. Now I'm gonna say it right . . . I will give anybody fifty dollars to keep them out of jail for three years. I give her the fifty dollars and she told me to come over to the house. I ain't asked her. I figure if she was nice enough to invite me I ought to go. I ain't had to say a word. She invited me over just as nice. Say, "Why don't you come over to the house?" She ain't had to say nothing else. Them words rolled off her tongue just as nice. I went on down there and sat about three hours. Started to leave and changed my mind. She grabbed hold to me and say, "Baby, it's all night long." That was one of the shortest nights I have ever spent on this earth! I could have used another eight hours. Lymon's daddy didn't even say nothing to me when he got out. He just looked at me funny. He had a good notion something had happened between me an' her. L. D. Jackson. That was one bad-luck nigger. Got killed at some dance. Fellow walked in and shot him thinking he was somebody else.

[DOAKER *enters from his room.*]

Hey, Doaker, you remember L. D. Jackson?

---

7. See Daniel 6.23: "My God has sent his angel and closed the lions' mouths so that they have not hurt me."

DOAKER: That's Lymon's daddy. That was one bad-luck nigger.

BOY WILLIE: Look like you ready to railroad some.

DOAKER: Yeah, I got to make that run.

[LYMON *enters from the stairs. He is dressed in his new suit and shoes, to which he has added a cheap straw hat.*]

LYMON: How I look?

WINING BOY: You look like a million dollars. Don't he look good, Doaker? Come on, let's play some cards. You wanna play some cards?

BOY WILLIE: We ain't gonna play no cards with you. Me and Lymon gonna find some women. Hey, Lymon, don't play no cards with Wining Boy. He'll take all your money.

WINING BOY: [*To* LYMON.] You got a magic suit there. You can get you a woman easy with that suit . . . but you got to know the magic words. You know the magic words to get you a woman?

LYMON: I just talk to them to see if I like them and they like me.

WINING BOY: You just walk right up to them and say, "If you got the harbor I got the ship." If that don't work ask them if you can put them in your pocket. The first thing they gonna say is, "It's too small." That's when you look them dead in the eye and say, "Baby, ain't nothing small about me." If that don't work then you move on to another one. Am I telling him right, Doaker?

DOAKER: That man don't need you to tell him nothing about no women. These women these days ain't gonna fall for that kind of stuff. You got to buy them a present. That's what they looking for these days.

BOY WILLIE: Come on, I'm ready. You ready, Lymon? Come on, let's go find some women.

WINING BOY: Here, let me walk out with you. I wanna see the women fall out their window when they see Lymon.

[*They all exit and the lights go down on the scene.*]

Scene 2

[*The lights come up on the kitchen. It is late evening of the same day.* BERNIECE *has set a tub for her bath in the kitchen. She is heating up water on the stove. There is a knock at the door.*]

BERNIECE: Who is it?

AVERY: It's me, Avery.

[BERNIECE *opens the door and lets him in.*]

BERNIECE: Avery, come on in. I was just fixing to take my bath.

AVERY: Where Boy Willie? I see that truck out there almost empty. They done sold almost all them watermelons.

BERNIECE: They was gone when I come home. I don't know where they went off to. Boy Willie around here about to drive me crazy.

AVERY: They sell them watermelons . . . he'll be gone soon.

BERNIECE: What Mr. Cohen say about letting you have the place?

AVERY: He say he'll let me have it for thirty dollars a month. I talked him out of thirty-five and he say he'll let me have it for thirty.

BERNIECE: That's a nice spot next to Benny Diamond's store.

AVERY: Berniece . . . I be at home and I get to thinking you up here an' I'm down there. I get to thinking how that look to have a preacher that ain't married. It makes for a better congregation if the preacher was settled down and married.

BERNIECE: Avery . . . not now. I was fixing to take my bath.

AVERY: You know how I feel about you, Berniece. Now . . . I done got the place from Mr. Cohen. I get the money from the bank and I can fix it up real nice. They give me a ten cents a hour raise down there on the job . . . now Berniece, I ain't got much in the way of comforts. I got a hole in my pockets near about as far as money is concerned. I ain't never found no way through life to a woman I care about like I care about you. I need that. I need somebody on my bond side. I need a woman that fits in my hand.

BERNIECE: Avery, I ain't ready to get married now.

AVERY: You too young a woman to close up, Berniece.

BERNIECE: I ain't said nothing about closing up. I got a lot of woman left in me.

AVERY: Where's it at? When's the last time you looked at it?

BERNIECE: [Stunned by his remark.] That's a nasty thing to say. And you call yourself a preacher.

AVERY: Anytime I get anywhere near you . . . you push me away.

BERNIECE: I got enough on my hands with Maretha. I got enough people to love and take care of.

AVERY: Who you got to love you? Can't nobody get close enough to you. Doaker can't half say nothing to you. You jump all over Boy Willie. Who you got to love you, Berniece?

BERNIECE: You trying to tell me a woman can't be nothing without a man. But you alright, huh? You can just walk out of here without me—without a woman—and still be a man. That's alright. Ain't nobody gonna ask you, "Avery, who you got to love you?" That's alright for you. But everybody gonna be worried about Berniece. "How Berniece gonna take care of herself? How she gonna raise that child without a man? Wonder what she do with herself. How she gonna live like that?" Everybody got all kinds of questions for Berniece. Everybody telling me I can't be a woman unless I got a man. Well, you tell me, Avery—you know—how much woman am I?

AVERY: It wasn't me, Berniece. You can't blame me for nobody else. I'll own up to my own shortcomings. But you can't blame me for Crawley or nobody else.

BERNIECE: I ain't blaming nobody for nothing. I'm just stating the facts.

AVERY: How long you gonna carry Crawley with you, Berniece? It's been over three years. At some point you got to let go and go on. Life's got all kinds of twists and turns. That don't mean you stop living. That don't mean you cut yourself off from life. You can't go through life carrying Crawley's ghost with you. Crawley's been dead three years. Three years, Berniece.

BERNIECE: I know how long Crawley's been dead. You ain't got to tell me that. I just ain't ready to get married right now.

AVERY: What is you ready for, Berniece? You just gonna drift along from day to day. Life is more than making it from one day to another. You gonna look up one day and it's all gonna be past you. Life's gonna be gone out of your hands—there won't be enough to make nothing with. I'm standing here now, Berniece—but I don't know how much longer I'm gonna be standing here waiting on you.

BERNIECE: Avery, I told you . . . when you get your church we'll sit down and talk about this. I got too many other things to deal with right now. Boy Willie and the piano . . . and Sutter's ghost. I thought I might have been seeing things, but Maretha done seen Sutter's ghost, too.

AVERY: When this happen, Berniece?

BERNIECE: Right after I came home yesterday. Me and Boy Willie was arguing about the piano and Sutter's ghost was standing at the top of the stairs. Maretha scared to sleep up there now. Maybe if you bless the house he'll go away.

AVERY: I don't know, Berniece. I don't know if I should fool around with something like that.

BERNIECE: I can't have Maretha scared to go to sleep up there. Seem like if you bless the house he would go away.

AVERY: You might have to be a special kind of preacher to do something like that.

BERNIECE: I keep telling myself when Boy Willie leave he'll go on and leave with him. I believe Boy Willie pushed him in the well.

AVERY: That's been going on down there a long time. The Ghosts of the Yellow Dog been pushing people in their wells long before Boy Willie got grown.

BERNIECE: Somebody down there pushing them people in their wells. They ain't just upped and fell. Ain't no wind pushed nobody in their well.

AVERY: Oh, I don't know. God works in mysterious ways.

BERNIECE: He ain't pushed nobody in their wells.

AVERY: He caused it to happen. God is the Great Causer. He can do anything. He parted the Red Sea.[8] He say I will smite my enemies. Reverend Thompson used to preach on the Ghosts of the Yellow Dog as the hand of God.

---

8. See Exodus 14.21: "Then Moses stretched out his hand over the sea, and the Lord swept the sea with a strong east wind throughout the night and so turned it into dry land."

BERNIECE: I don't care who preached what. Somebody down there pushing them people in their wells. Somebody like Boy Willie. I can see him doing something like that. You ain't gonna tell me that Sutter just upped and fell in his well. I believe Boy Willie pushed him so he could get his land.

AVERY: What Doaker say about Boy Willie selling the piano?

BERNIECE: Doaker don't want no part of that piano. He ain't never wanted no part of it. He blames himself for not staying behind with Papa Boy Charles. He washed his hands of that piano a long time ago. He didn't want me to bring it up here—but I wasn't gonna leave it down there.

AVERY: Well, it seems to me somebody ought to be able to talk to Boy Willie.

BERNIECE: You can't talk to Boy Willie. He been that way all his life. Mama Ola had her hands full trying to talk to him. He don't listen to nobody. He just like my daddy. He get his mind fixed on something and can't nobody turn him from it.

AVERY: You ought to start a choir at the church. Maybe if he seen you was doing something with it—if you told him you was gonna put it in my church—maybe he'd see it different. You ought to put it down in the church and start a choir. The Bible say "Make a joyful noise unto the Lord." Maybe if Boy Willie see you was doing something with it he'd see it different.

BERNIECE: I done told you I don't play on that piano. Ain't no need in you to keep talking this choir stuff. When my mama died I shut the top on that piano and I ain't never opened it since. I was only playing it for her. When my daddy died seem like all her life went into that piano. She used to have me playing on it . . . had Miss Eula come in and teach me . . . say when I played it she could hear my daddy talking to her. I used to think them pictures came alive and walked through the house. Sometime late at night I could hear my mama talking to them. I said that wasn't gonna happen to me. I don't play that piano cause I don't want to wake them spirits. They never be walking around in this house.

AVERY: You got to put all that behind you, Berniece.

BERNIECE: I got Maretha playing on it. She don't know nothing about it. Let her go on and be a schoolteacher or something. She don't have to carry all of that with her. She got a chance I didn't have. I ain't gonna burden her with that piano.

AVERY: You got to put all of that behind you. Berniece. That's the same thing like Crawley. Everybody got stones in their passway. You got to step over them or walk around them. You picking them up and carrying them with you. All you got to do is set them down by the side of the road. You ain't got to carry them with you. You can walk over there right now and play that piano. You can walk over there right now and

God will walk over there with you. Right now you can set that sack of stones down by the side of the road and walk away from it. You don't have to carry it with you. You can do it right now.

[AVERY *crosses over to the piano and raises the lid.*]

Come on, Berniece . . . set it down and walk away from it. Come on, play "Old Ship of Zion." Walk over here and claim it as an instrument of the Lord. You can walk over here right now and make it into a celebration.

[BERNIECE *moves toward the piano.*]

BERNIECE: Avery . . . I done told you I don't want to play that piano. Now or no other time.

AVERY: The Bible say, "The Lord is my refuge . . . and my strength!" With the strength of God you can put the past behind you, Berniece. With the strength of God you can do anything! God got a bright tomorrow. God don't ask what you done . . . God ask what you gonna do. The strength of God can move mountains! God's got a bright tomorrow for you . . . all you got to do is walk over here and claim it.

BERNIECE: Avery, just go on and let me finish my bath. I'll see you tomorrow.

AVERY: Okay, Berniece. I'm gonna go home. I'm gonna go home and read up on my Bible. And tomorrow . . . if the good Lord give me strength tomorrow . . . I'm gonna come by and bless the house . . . and show you the power of the Lord.

[AVERY *crosses to the door.*]

It's gonna be alright, Berniece. God say he will soothe the troubled waters. I'll come by tomorrow and bless the house.

[*The lights go down to black.*]

Scene 3

[*Several hours later. The house is dark.* BERNIECE *has retired for the night.* BOY WILLIE *enters the darkened house with* GRACE.]

BOY WILLIE: Come on in. This is my sister's house. My sister live here. Come on, I ain't gonna bite you.

GRACE: Put some light on. I can't see.

BOY WILLIE: You don't need to see nothing, baby. This here is all you need to see. All you need to do is see me. If you can't see me you can feel me in the dark. How's that, sugar? [*He attempts to kiss her.*]

GRACE: Go on now . . . wait!

BOY WILLIE: Just give me one little old kiss.

GRACE: [*Pushing him away.*] Come on, now. Where I'm gonna sleep at?

BOY WILLIE: We got to sleep out here on the couch. Come on, my sister don't mind. Lymon come back he just got to sleep on the floor. He run off with Dolly somewhere he better stay there. Come on, sugar.

GRACE: Wait now . . . you ain't told me nothing about no couch. I thought you had a bed. Both of us can't sleep on that little old couch.

BOY WILLIE: It don't make no difference. We can sleep on the floor. Let Lymon sleep on the couch.

GRACE: You ain't told me nothing about no couch.

BOY WILLIE: What difference it make? You just wanna be with me.

GRACE: I don't want to be with you on no couch. Ain't you got no bed?

BOY WILLIE: You don't need no bed, woman. My granddaddy used to take women on the backs of horses. What you need a bed for? You just want to be with me.

GRACE: You sure is country. I didn't know you was this country.

BOY WILLIE: There's a lot of things you don't know about me. Come on, let me show you what this country boy can do.

GRACE: Let's go to my place. I got a room with a bed if Leroy don't come back there.

BOY WILLIE: Who's Leroy? You ain't said nothing about no Leroy.

GRACE: He used to be my man. He ain't coming back. He gone off with some other gal.

BOY WILLIE: You let him have your key?

GRACE: He ain't coming back.

BOY WILLIE: Did you let him have your key?

GRACE: He got a key but he ain't coming back. He took off with some other gal.

BOY WILLIE: I don't wanna go nowhere he might come. Let's stay here. Come on, sugar. [He pulls her over to the couch.] Let me heist your hood and check your oil. See if your battery needs charged. [He pulls her to him. They kiss and tug at each other's clothing. In their anxiety they knock over a lamp.]

BERNIECE: Who's that . . . Wining Boy?

BOY WILLIE: It's me . . . Boy Willie. Go on back to sleep. Everything's alright. [To GRACE.] That's my sister. Everything's alright, Berniece. Go on back to sleep.

BERNIECE: What you doing down there? What you done knocked over?

BOY WILLIE: It wasn't nothing. Everything's alright. Go on back to sleep. [To GRACE.] That's my sister. We alright. She gone back to sleep.

[They begin to kiss. BERNIECE enters from the stairs dressed in a nightgown. She cuts on the light.]

BERNIECE: Boy Willie, what you doing down here?

BOY WILLIE: It was just that there lamp. It ain't broke. It's okay. Everything's alright. Go on back to bed.

BERNIECE: Boy Willie, I don't allow that in my house. You gonna have to take your company someplace else.

BOY WILLIE: It's alright. We ain't doing nothing. We just sitting here talking. This here is Grace. That's my sister Berniece.

BERNIECE: You know I don't allow that kind of stuff in my house.

BOY WILLIE: Allow what? We just sitting here talking.

BERNIECE: Well, your company gonna have to leave. Come back and talk in the morning.

BOY WILLIE: Go on back upstairs now.

BERNIECE: I got an eleven-year-old girl upstairs. I can't allow that around here.

BOY WILLIE: Ain't nobody said nothing about that. I told you we just talking.

GRACE: Come on . . . let's go to my place. Ain't nobody got to tell me to leave but once.

BOY WILLIE: You ain't got to be like that, Berniece.

BERNIECE: I'm sorry, Miss. But he know I don't allow that in here.

GRACE: You ain't got to tell me but once. I don't stay nowhere I ain't wanted.

BOY WILLIE: I don't know why you want to embarrass me in front of my company.

GRACE: Come on, take me home.

BERNIECE: Go on, Boy Willie. Just go on with your company.

[BOY WILLIE *and* GRACE *exit.* BERNIECE *puts the light on in the kitchen and puts on the teakettle. Presently there is a knock at the door.* BERNIECE *goes to answer it.* BERNIECE *opens the door.* LYMON *enters.*]

LYMON: How you doing, Berniece? I thought you'd be asleep. Boy Willie been back here?

BERNIECE: He just left out of here a minute ago.

LYMON: I went out to see a picture show and never got there. We always end up doing something else. I was with this woman she just wanted to drink up all my money. So I left her there and came back looking for Boy Willie.

BERNIECE: You just missed him. He just left out of here.

LYMON: They got some nice-looking women in this city. I'm gonna like it up here real good. I like seeing them with their dresses on. Got them high heels. I like that. Make them look like they real precious. Boy Willie met a real nice one today. I wish I had met her before he did.

BERNIECE: He come by here with some woman a little while ago. I told him to go on and take all that out of my house.

LYMON: What she look like, the woman he was with? Was she a brown-skinned woman about this high? Nice and healthy? Got nice hips on her?

BERNIECE: She had on a red dress.

LYMON: That's her! That's Grace. She real nice. Laugh a lot. Lot of fun to be with. She don't be trying to put on. Some of these woman act like they the Queen of Sheba. I don't like them kind. Grace ain't like that. She real nice with herself.

BERNIECE: I don't know what she was like. He come in here all drunk knocking over the lamp, and making all kind of noise. I told them to take that somewhere else. I can't really say what she was like.

LYMON: She real nice. I seen her before he did. I was trying not to act like I seen her. I wanted to look at her a while before I said something. She seen me when I come into the saloon. I tried to act like I didn't see her. Time I looked around Boy Willie was talking to her. She was talking to him kept looking at me. That's when her friend Dolly came. I asked her if she wanted to go to the picture show. She told me to buy her a drink while she thought about it. Next thing I knew she done had three drinks talking about she too tired to go. I bought her another drink, then I left. Boy Willie was gone and I thought he might have come back here. Doaker gone, huh? He say he had to make a trip.

BERNIECE: Yeah, he gone on his trip. This is when I can usually get me some peace and quiet, Maretha asleep.

LYMON: She look just like you. Got them big eyes. I remember her when she was in diapers.

BERNIECE: Time just keep on. It go on with or without you. She going on twelve.

LYMON: She sure is pretty. I like kids.

BERNIECE: Boy Willie say you staying . . . what you gonna do up here in this big city? You thought about that?

LYMON: They never get me back down there. The sheriff looking for me. All because they gonna try and make me work for somebody when I don't want to. They gonna try and make me work for Stovall when he don't pay nothing. It ain't like that up here. Up here you more or less do what you want to. I figure I find me a job and try to get set up and then see what the year brings. I tried to do that two or three times down there . . . but it never would work out. I was always in the wrong place.

BERNIECE: This ain't a bad city once you get to know your way around.

LYMON: Up here is different. I'm gonna get me a job unloading boxcars or something. One fellow told me say he know a place. I'm gonna go over there with him next week. Me and Boy Willie finish selling them watermelons I'll have enough money to hold me for a while. But I'm gonna go over there and see what kind of jobs they have.

BERNIECE: You shouldn't have too much trouble finding a job. It's all in how you present yourself. See now, Boy Willie couldn't get no job up here. Somebody hire him they got a pack of trouble on their hands. Soon as they find that out they fire him. He don't want to do nothing unless he do it his way.

LYMON: I know. I told him let's go to the picture show first and see if there was any women down there. They might get tired of sitting at home and walk down to the picture show. He say he wanna look around first. We never did get down there. We tried a couple of places and then we went to this saloon where he met Grace. I tried to meet her before he did but he beat me to her. We left Wining Boy sitting down there running his mouth. He told me if I wear this suit I'd find me a woman. He was almost right.

BERNIECE: You don't need to be out there in them saloons. Ain't no telling what you liable to run into out there. This one liable to cut you as quick as that one shoot you. You don't need to be out there. You start out that fast life you can't keep it up. It makes you old quick. I don't know what them women out there be thinking about.

LYMON: Mostly they be lonely and looking for somebody to spend the night with them. Sometimes it matters who it is and sometimes it don't. I used to be the same way. Now it got to matter. That's why I'm here now. Dolly liable not to even recognize me if she sees me again. I don't like women like that. I like my women to be with me in a nice and easy way. That way we can both enjoy ourselves. The way I see it we the only two people like us in the world. We got to see how we fit together. A woman that don't want to take the time to do that I don't bother with. Used to. Used to bother with all of them. Then I woke up one time with this woman and I didn't know who she was. She was the prettiest woman I had ever seen in my life. I spent the whole night with her and didn't even know it. I had never taken the time to look at her. I guess she kinda knew I ain't never really looked at her. She must have known that cause she ain't wanted to see me no more. If she had wanted to see me I believe we might have got married. How come you ain't married? It seem like to me you would be married. I remember Avery from down home. I used to call him plain old Avery. Now he Reverend Avery. That's kinda funny about him becoming a preacher. I like when he told about how that come to him in a dream about them sheep people and them hobos. Nothing ever come to me in a dream like that. I just dream about women. Can't never seem to find the right one.

BERNIECE: She out there somewhere. You just got to get yourself ready to meet her. That's what I'm trying to do. Avery's alright. I ain't really got nobody in mind.

LYMON: I get me a job and a little place and get set up to where I can make a woman comfortable I might get married. Avery's nice. You ought to go ahead and get married. You be a preacher's wife you won't have to work. I hate living by myself. I didn't want to be no strain on my mama so I left home when I was about sixteen. Everything I tried seem like it just didn't work out. Now I'm trying this.

BERNIECE: You keep trying it'll work out for you.

LYMON: You ever go down there to the picture show?

BERNIECE: I don't go in for all that.

LYMON: Ain't nothing wrong with it. It ain't like gambling and sinning. I went to one down in Jackson once. It was fun.

BERNIECE: I just stay home most of the time. Take care of Maretha.

LYMON: It's getting kind of late. I don't know where Boy Willie went off to. He's liable not to come back. I'm gonna take off these shoes. My feet hurt. Was you in bed? I don't mean to be keeping you up.

BERNIECE: You ain't keeping me up. I couldn't sleep after that Boy Willie woke me up.

LYMON: You got on that nightgown. I likes women when they wear them fancy nightclothes and all. It makes their skin look real pretty.

BERNIECE: I got this at the five-and-ten-cents store. It ain't so fancy.

LYMON: I don't too often get to see a woman dressed like that. [*There is a long pause.* LYMON *takes off his suit coat.*] Well, I'm gonna sleep here on the couch. I'm supposed to sleep on the floor but I don't reckon Boy Willie's coming back tonight. Wining Boy sold me this suit. Told me it was a magic suit. I'm gonna put it on again tomorrow. Maybe it bring me a woman like he say. [*He goes into his coat pocket and takes out a small bottle of perfume.*] I almost forgot I had this. Some man sold me this for a dollar. Say it come from Paris. This is the same kind of perfume the Queen of France wear. That's what he told me. I don't know if it's true or not. I smelled it. It smelled good to me. Here . . . smell it see if you like it. I was gonna give it to Dolly. But I didn't like her too much.

BERNIECE: [*Takes the bottle.*] It smells nice.

LYMON: I was gonna give it to Dolly if she had went to the picture with me. Go on, you take it.

BERNIECE: I can't take it. Here . . . go on you keep it. You'll find somebody to give it to.

LYMON: I wanna give it to you. Make you smell nice. [*He takes the bottle and puts perfume behind* BERNIECE'*s ear.*] They tell me you supposed to put it right here behind your ear. Say if you put it there you smell nice all day.

[BERNIECE *stiffens at his touch.* LYMON *bends down to smell her.*]

There . . . you smell real good now. [*He kisses her neck.*] You smell real good for Lymon.

[*He kisses her again.* BERNIECE *returns the kiss, then breaks the embrace and crosses to the stairs. She turns and they look silently at each other.* LYMON *hands her the bottle of perfume.* BERNIECE *exits up the stairs.* LYMON *picks up his suit coat and strokes it lovingly with the full knowledge that it is indeed a magic suit. The lights go down on the scene.*]

Scene 4

[*It is late the next morning. The lights come up on the parlor.* LYMON *is asleep on the sofa.* BOY WILLIE *enters the front door.*]

BOY WILLIE: Hey, Lymon! Lymon, come on get up.

LYMON: Leave me alone.

BOY WILLIE: Come on, get up, nigger! Wake up, Lymon.

LYMON: What you want?

BOY WILLIE: Come on, let's go. I done called the man about the piano.

LYMON: What piano?

BOY WILLIE: [*Dumps* LYMON *on the floor.*] Come on, get up!

LYMON: Why you leave, I looked around and you was gone.

BOY WILLIE: I come back here with Grace, then I went looking for you. I figured you'd be with Dolly.

LYMON: She just want to drink and spend up your money. I come on back here looking for you to see if you wanted to go to the picture show.

BOY WILLIE: I been up at Grace's house. Some nigger named Leroy come by but I had a chair up against the door. He got mad when he couldn't get in. He went off somewhere and I got out of there before he could come back. Berniece got mad when we came here.

LYMON: She say you was knocking over the lamp busting up the place.

BOY WILLIE: That was Grace doing all that.

LYMON: Wining Boy seen Sutter's ghost last night.

BOY WILLIE: Wining Boy's liable to see anything. I'm surprised he found the right house. Come on, I done called the man about the piano.

LYMON: What he say?

BOY WILLIE: He say to bring it on out. I told him I was calling for my sister, Miss Berniece Charles. I told him some man wanted to buy it for eleven hundred dollars and asked him if he would go any better. He said yeah, he would give me eleven hundred and fifty dollars for it if it was the same piano. I described it to him again and he told me to bring it out.

LYMON: Why didn't you tell him to come and pick it up?

BOY WILLIE: I didn't want to have no problem with Berniece. This way we just take it on out there and it be out the way. He want to charge twenty-five dollars to pick it up.

LYMON: You should have told him the man was gonna give you twelve hundred for it.

BOY WILLIE: I figure I was taking a chance with that eleven hundred. If I had told him twelve hundred he might have run off. Now I wish I had told him twelve-fifty. It's hard to figure out white folks sometimes.

LYMON: You might have been able to tell him anything. White folks got a lot of money.

BOY WILLIE: Come on, let's get it loaded before Berniece come back. Get that end over there. All you got to do is pick it up on that side. Don't worry about this side. You wanna stretch you' back for a minute?

LYMON: I'm ready.

BOY WILLIE: Get a real good grip on it now.

[*The sound of* SUTTER's GHOST *is heard. They do not hear it.*]

LYMON: I got this end. You get that end.

BOY WILLIE: Wait till I say ready now. Alright. You got it good? You got a grip on it?

LYMON: Yeah, I got it. You lift up on that end.

BOY WILLIE: Ready? Lift!

[*The piano will not budge.*]

LYMON: Man, this piano is heavy! It's gonna take more than me and you to move this piano.

BOY WILLIE: We can do it. Come on—we did it before.

LYMON: Nigger—you crazy! That piano weighs five hundred pounds!

BOY WILLIE: I got three hundred pounds of it! I know you can carry two hundred pounds! You be lifting them cotton sacks! Come on lift this piano!

[*They try to move the piano again without success.*]

LYMON: It's stuck. Something holding it.

BOY WILLIE: How the piano gonna be stuck? We just moved it. Slide you' end out.

LYMON: Naw—we gonna need two or three more people. How this big old piano get in the house?

BOY WILLIE: I don't know how it got in the house. I know how it's going out though! You get on this end. I'll carry three hundred and fifty pounds of it. All you got to do is slide your end out. Ready?

[*They switch sides and try again without success.* DOAKER *enters from his room as they try to push and shove it.*]

LYMON: Hey, Doaker . . . how this piano get in the house?

DOAKER: Boy Willie, what you doing?

BOY WILLIE: I'm carrying this piano out the house. What it look like I'm doing? Come on, Lymon, let's try again.

DOAKER: Go on let the piano sit there till Berniece come home.

BOY WILLIE: You ain't got nothing to do with this, Doaker. This my business.

DOAKER: This is my house, nigger! I ain't gonna let you or nobody else carry nothing out of it. You ain't gonna carry nothing out of here without my permission!

BOY WILLIE: This is my piano. I don't need your permission to carry my belongings out of your house. This is mine. This ain't got nothing to do with you.

DOAKER: I say leave it over there till Berniece come home. She got part of it too. Leave it set there till you see what she say.

BOY WILLIE: I don't care what Berniece say. Come on, Lymon. I got this side.

DOAKER: Go on and cut it half in two if you want to. Just leave Berniece's half sitting over there. I can't tell you what to do with your piano. But I can't let you take her half out of here.

BOY WILLIE: Go on, Doaker. You ain't got nothing to do with this. I don't want you starting nothing now. Just go on and leave me alone. Come on, Lymon. I got this end.

[DOAKER *goes into his room.* BOY WILLIE *and* LYMON *prepare to move the piano.*]

LYMON: How we gonna get it in the truck?

BOY WILLIE: Don't worry about how we gonna get it on the truck. You got to get it out the house first.

LYMON: It's gonna take more than me and you to move this piano.

BOY WILLIE: Just lift up on that end, nigger!

[DOAKER *comes to the doorway of his room and stands.*]

DOAKER: [*Quietly with authority.*] Leave that piano set over there till Berniece come back. I don't care what you do with it then. But you gonna leave it sit over there right now.

BOY WILLIE: Alright.... I'm gonna tell you this, Doaker. I'm going out of here ... I'm gonna get me some rope ... find me a plank and some wheels ... and I'm coming back. Then I'm gonna carry that piano out of here ... sell it and give Berniece half the money. See ... now that's what I'm gonna do. And you ... or nobody else is gonna stop me. Come on, Lymon ... let's go get some rope and stuff. I'll be back, Doaker.

[BOY WILLIE *and* LYMON *exit. The lights go down on the scene.*]

Scene 5

[*The lights come up.* BOY WILLIE *sits on the sofa, screwing casters on a wooden plank.* MARETHA *is sitting on the piano stool.* DOAKER *sits at the table playing solitaire.*]

BOY WILLIE: [*To* MARETHA.] Then after that them white folks down around there started falling down their wells. You ever seen a well? A well got a wall around it. It's hard to fall down a well. You got to be leaning way over. Couldn't nobody figure out too much what was making these fellows fall down their well ... so everybody says the Ghosts of the Yellow

Dog must have pushed them. That's what everybody called them four men what got burned up in the boxcar.

MARETHA: Why they call them that?

BOY WILLIE: Cause the Yazoo Delta railroad got yellow boxcars. Sometime the way the whistle blow sound like an old dog howling so the people call it the Yellow Dog.

MARETHA: Anybody ever see the Ghosts?

BOY WILLIE: I told you they like the wind. Can you see the wind?

MARETHA: No.

BOY WILLIE: They like the wind you can't see them. But sometimes you be in trouble they might be around to help you. They say if you go where the Southern cross the Yellow Dog . . . you go to where them two railroads cross each other . . . and call out their names . . . they say they talk back to you. I don't know, I ain't never done that. But Uncle Wining Boy he say he been down there and talked to them. You have to ask him about that part.

[BERNIECE *has entered from the front door.*]

BERNIECE: Maretha, you go on and get ready for me to do your hair.

[MARETHA *crosses to the steps.*]

Boy Willie, I done told you to leave my house. [*To* MARETHA.] Go on, Maretha.

[MARETHA *is hesitant about going up the stairs.*]

BOY WILLIE: Don't be scared. Here, I'll go up there with you. If we see Sutter's ghost I'll put a whupping on him. Come on, Uncle Boy Willie going with you.

[BOY WILLIE *and* MARETHA *exit up the stairs.*]

BERNIECE: Doaker—what is going on here?

DOAKER: I come home and him and Lymon was moving the piano. I told them to leave it over there till you got home. He went out and got that board and them wheels. He say he gonna take that piano out of here and ain't nobody gonna stop him.

BERNIECE: I ain't playing with Boy Willie. I got Crawley's gun upstairs. He don't know but I'm through with it. Where Lymon go?

DOAKER: Boy Willie sent him for some rope just before you come in.

BERNIECE: I ain't studying Boy Willie or Lymon—or the rope. Boy Willie ain't taking that piano out this house. That's all there is to it.

[BOY WILLIE *and* MARETHA *enter on the stairs.* MARETHA *carries a hot comb and a can of hair grease.* BOY WILLIE *crosses over and continues to screw the wheels on the board.*]

MARETHA: Mama, all the hair grease is gone. There ain't but this little bit left.

BERNIECE: [*Gives her a dollar.*] Here . . . run across the street and get another can. You come straight back, too. Don't you be playing around out there. And watch the cars. Be careful when you cross the street.

[MARETHA *exits out the front door.*]

Boy Willie, I done told you to leave my house.

BOY WILLIE: I ain't in you' house. I'm in Doaker's house. If he ask me to leave then I'll go on and leave. But consider me done left your part.

BERNIECE: Doaker, tell him to leave. Tell him to go on.

DOAKER: Boy Willie ain't done nothing for me to put him out of the house. I told you if you can't get along just go on and don't have nothing to do with each other.

BOY WILLIE: I ain't thinking about Berniece. [*He gets up and draws a line across the floor with his foot.*] There! Now I'm out of your part of the house. Consider me done left your part. Soon as Lymon come back with that rope. I'm gonna take that piano out of here and sell it.

BERNIECE: You ain't gonna touch that piano.

BOY WILLIE: Carry it out of here just as big and bold. Do like my daddy would have done come time to get Sutter's land.

BERNIECE: I got something to make you leave it over there.

BOY WILLIE: It's got to come better than this thirty-two-twenty.[9]

DOAKER: Why don't you stop all that! Boy Willie, go on and leave her alone. You know how Berniece get. Why you wanna sit there and pick with her?

BOY WILLIE: I ain't picking with her. I told her the truth. She the one talking about what she got. I just told her what she better have.

BERNIECE: That's alright, Doaker. Leave him alone.

BOY WILLIE: She trying to scare me. Hell, I ain't scared of dying. I look around and see people dying every day. You got to die to make room for somebody else. I had a dog that died. Wasn't nothing but a puppy. I picked it up and put it in a bag and carried it up there to Reverend C. L. Thompson's church. I carried it up there and prayed and asked Jesus to make it live like he did the man in the Bible.[1] I prayed real hard. Knelt down and everything. Say ask in Jesus' name. Well, I must have called Jesus' name two hundred times. I called his name till my mouth got sore. I got up and looked in the bag and the dog still dead. It ain't moved a muscle! I say, "Well, ain't nothing precious." And then I went out and killed me a cat. That's when I discovered the power of death. See, a nigger that ain't afraid to die is the worse kind of nigger for the white man.

9. That is, this thirty-two-twenty-caliber gun I'm (figuratively) holding.
1. Lazarus, who was raised from the dead by Jesus; see John 11.1–44.

He can't hold that power over you. That's what I learned when I killed that cat. I got the power of death too. I can command him. I can call him up. The white man don't like to see that. He don't like for you to stand up and look him square in the eye and say, "I got it too." Then he got to deal with you square up.

BERNIECE: That's why I don't talk to him, Doaker. You try and talk to him and that's the only kind of stuff that comes out his mouth.

DOAKER: You say Avery went home to get his Bible?

BOY WILLIE: What Avery gonna do? Avery can't do nothing with me. I wish Avery would say something to me about this piano.

DOAKER: Berniece ain't said about that. Avery went home to get his Bible. He coming by to bless the house see if he can get rid of Sutter's ghost.

BOY WILLIE: Ain't nothing but a house full of ghosts down there at the church. What Avery look like chasing away somebody's ghost?

[MARETHA *enters the front door.*]

BERNIECE: Light that stove and set that comb over there to get hot. Get something to put around your shoulders.

BOY WILLIE: The Bible say an eye for an eye, a tooth for a tooth, and a life for a life.[2] Tit for tat. But you and Avery don't want to believe that. You gonna pass up that part and pretend it ain't in there. Everything else you gonna agree with. But if you gonna agree with part of it you got to agree with all of it. You can't do nothing halfway. You gonna go at the Bible halfway. You gonna act like that part ain't in there. But you pull out the Bible and open it and see what it say. Ask Avery. He a preacher. He'll tell you it's in there. He the Good Shepherd. Unless he gonna shepherd you to heaven with half the Bible.

BERNIECE: Maretha, bring me that comb. Make sure it's hot.

[MARETHA *brings the comb.* BERNIECE *begins to do her hair.*]

BOY WILLIE: I will say this for Avery. He done figured out a path to go through life. I don't agree with it. But he done fixed it so he can go right through it real smooth. Hell, he liable to end up with a million dollars that he done got from selling bread and wine.

MARETHA: OWWWWWWW!

BERNIECE: Be still, Maretha. If you was a boy I wouldn't be going through this.

BOY WILLIE: Don't you tell that girl that. Why you wanna tell her that?

BERNIECE: You ain't got nothing to do with this child.

BOY WILLIE: Telling her you wished she was a boy. How's that gonna make her feel?

BERNIECE: Boy Willie, go on and leave me alone.

2. See Exodus 21. 23–25.

DOAKER: Why don't you leave her alone? What you got to pick with her for? Why don't you go on out and see what's out there in the streets? Have something to tell the fellows down home.

BOY WILLIE: I'm waiting on Lymon to get back with that truck. Why don't you go on out and see what's out there in the streets? You ain't got to work tomorrow. Talking about me . . . why don't you go out there? It's Friday night.

DOAKER: I got to stay around here and keep you all from killing one another.

BOY WILLIE: You ain't got to worry about me. I'm gonna be here just as long as it takes Lymon to get back here with that truck. You ought to be talking to Berniece. Sitting up there telling Maretha she wished she was a boy. What kind of thing is that to tell a child? If you want to tell her something tell her about that piano. You ain't even told her about that piano. Like that's something to be ashamed of. Like she supposed to go off and hide somewhere about that piano. You ought to mark down on the calendar the day that Papa Boy Charles brought that piano into the house. You ought to mark that day down and draw a circle around it . . . and every year when it come up throw a party. Have a celebration. If you did that she wouldn't have no problem in life. She could walk around here with her head held high. I'm talking about a big party!

Invite everybody! Mark that day down with a special meaning. That way she know where she at in the world. You got her going out here thinking she wrong in the world. Like there ain't no part of it belong to her.

BERNIECE: Let me take care of my child. When you get one of your own then you can teach it what you want to teach it.

[DOAKER *exits into his room.*]

BOY WILLIE: What I want to bring a child into this world for? Why I wanna bring somebody else into all this for? I'll tell you this . . . If I was Rockefeller[3] I'd have forty or fifty. I'd make one every day. Cause they gonna start out in life with all the advantages. I ain't got no advantages to offer nobody. Many is the time I looked at my daddy and seen him staring off at his hands. I got a little older I know what he was thinking. He sitting there saying, "I got these big old hands but what I'm gonna do with them? Best I can do is make a fifty-acre crop for Mr. Stovall. Got these big old hands capable of doing anything. I can take and build something with these hands. But where's the tools? All I got is these hands. Unless I go out here and kill me somebody and take what they got . . . it's a long row to hoe for me to get something of my own. So what I'm gonna do with these big old hands? What would you do?"

---

3. John D. Rockefeller (1839–1937), American oil magnate and philanthropist; the Rockefeller family is known for its wealth.

See now . . . if he had his own land he wouldn't have felt that way. If he had something under his feet that belonged to him he could stand up taller. That's what I'm talking about. Hell, the land is there for everybody. All you got to do is figure out how to get you a piece. Ain't no mystery to life. You just got to go out and meet it square on. If you got a piece of land you'll find everything else fall right into place. You can stand right up next to the white man and talk about the price of cotton . . . the weather, and anything else you want to talk about. If you teach that girl that she living at the bottom of life, she's gonna grow up and hate you.

BERNIECE: I'm gonna teach her the truth. That's just where she living. Only she ain't got to stay there. [*To* MARETHA.] Turn you' head over to the other side.

BOY WILLIE: This might be your bottom but it ain't mine. I'm living at the top of life. I ain't gonna just take my life and throw it away at the bottom. I'm in the world like everybody else. The way I see it everybody else got to come up a little taste to be where I am.

BERNIECE: You right at the bottom with the rest of us.

BOY WILLIE: I'll tell you this . . . and ain't a living soul can put a come back on it. If you believe that's where you at then you gonna act that way. If you act that way then that's where you gonna be. It's as simple as that. Ain't no mystery to life. I don't know how you come to believe that stuff. Crawley didn't think like that. He wasn't living at the bottom of life. Papa Boy Charles and Mama Ola wasn't living at the bottom of life. You ain't never heard them say nothing like that. They would have taken a strap to you if they heard you say something like that.

[DOAKER *enters from his room.*]

Hey, Doaker . . . Berniece say the colored folks is living at the bottom of life. I tried to tell her if she think that . . . that's where she gonna be. You think you living at the bottom of life? Is that how you see yourself?

DOAKER: I'm just living the best way I know how. I ain't thinking about no top or no bottom.

BOY WILLIE: That's what I tried to tell Berniece. I don't know where she got that from. That sound like something Avery would say. Avery think cause the white man give him a turkey for Thanksgiving that makes him better than everybody else. That's gonna raise him out of the bottom of life. I don't need nobody to give me a turkey. I can get my own turkey. All you have to do is get out my way. I'll get me two or three turkeys.

BERNIECE: You can't even get a chicken let alone two or three turkeys. Talking about get out your way. Ain't nobody in your way. [*To* MARETHA.] Straighten your head, Maretha! Don't be bending down like that. Hold your head up! [*To* BOY WILLIE.] All you got going for you is talk. You' whole life that's all you ever had going for you.

BOY WILLIE: See now . . . I'll tell you something about me. I done strung along and strung along. Going this way and that. Whatever way would lead me to a moment of peace. That's all I want. To be as easy with everything. But I wasn't born to that. I was born to a time of fire. The world ain't wanted no part of me. I could see that since I was about seven. The world say it's better off without me. See, Berniece accept that. She trying to come up to where she can prove something to the world. Hell, the world a better place cause of me. I don't see it like Berniece. I got a heart that beats here and it beats just as loud as the next fellow's. Don't care if he black or white. Sometime it beats louder. When it beats louder, then everybody can hear it. Some people get scared of that. Like Berniece. Some people get scared to hear a nigger's heart beating. They think you ought to lay low with that heart. Make it beat quiet and go along with everything the way it is. But my mama ain't birthed me for nothing. So what I got to do? I got to mark my passing on the road. Just like you write on a tree, "Boy Willie was here."

That's all I'm trying to do with that piano. Trying to put my mark on the road. Like my daddy done. My heart say for me to sell that piano and get me some land so I can make a life for myself to live in my own way. Other than that I ain't thinking about nothing Berniece got to say.

[*There is a knock at the door.* BOY WILLIE *crosses to it and yanks it open thinking it is* LYMON. AVERY *enters. He carries a Bible.*]

BOY WILLIE: Where you been, nigger? Aw . . . I thought you was Lymon. Hey, Berniece, look who's here.
BERNIECE: Come on in, Avery. Don't you pay Boy Willie no mind.
BOY WILLIE: Hey . . . Hey, Avery . . . tell me this . . . can you get to heaven with half the Bible?
BERNIECE: Boy Willie . . . I done told you to leave me alone.
BOY WILLIE: I just ask the man a question. He can answer. He don't need you to speak for him. Avery . . . if you only believe on half the Bible and don't want to accept the other half . . . you think God let you in heaven? Or do you got to have the whole Bible? Tell Berniece . . . if you only believe in part of it . . . when you see God he gonna ask you why you ain't believed in the other part . . . then he gonna send you straight to Hell.
AVERY: You got to be born again. Jesus say unless a man be born again he cannot come unto the Father and who so ever heareth my words and believeth them not shall be cast into a fiery pit.[4]
BOY WILLIE: That's what I was trying to tell Berniece. You got to believe in it all. You can't go at nothing halfway. She think she going to heaven with half the Bible. [*To* BERNIECE.] You hear that . . . Jesus say you got to believe in it all.

4. See John 3.3.

BERNIECE: You keep messing with me.

BOY WILLIE: I ain't thinking about you.

DOAKER: Come on in, Avery, and have a seat. Don't pay neither one of them no mind. They been arguing all day.

BERNIECE: Come on in, Avery.

AVERY: How's everybody in here?

BERNIECE: Here, set this comb back over there on that stove. [*To* AVERY.] Don't pay Boy Willie no mind. He been around here bothering me since I come home from work.

BOY WILLIE: Boy Willie ain't bothering you. Boy Willie ain't bothering nobody. I'm just waiting on Lymon to get back. I ain't thinking about you. You heard the man say I was right and you still don't want to believe it. You just wanna go and make up anythin'. Well there's Avery . . . there's the preacher . . . go on and ask him.

AVERY: Berniece believe in the Bible. She been baptized.

BOY WILLIE: What about that part that say an eye for an eye a tooth for a tooth and a life for a life? Ain't that in there?

DOAKER: What they say down there at the bank, Avery?

AVERY: Oh, they talked to me real nice. I told Berniece . . . they say maybe they let me borrow the money. They done talked to my boss down at work and everything.

DOAKER: That's what I told Berniece. You working every day you ought to be able to borrow some money.

AVERY: I'm getting more people in my congregation every day. Berniece says she gonna be the Deaconess. I get me my church I can get married and settled down. That's what I told Berniece.

DOAKER: That be nice. You all ought to go ahead and get married. Berniece don't need to be by herself. I tell her that all the time.

BERNIECE: I ain't said nothing about getting married. I said I was thinking about it.

DOAKER: Avery get him his church you all can make it nice. [*To* AVERY.] Berniece said you was coming by to bless the house.

AVERY: Yeah, I done read up on my Bible. She asked me to come by and see if I can get rid of Sutter's ghost.

BOY WILLIE: Ain't no ghost in this house. That's all in Berniece's head. Go on up there and see if you see him. I'll give you a hundred dollars if you see him. That's all in her imagination.

DOAKER: Well, let her find that out then. If Avery blessing the house is gonna make her feel better . . . what you got to do with it?

AVERY: Berniece say Maretha seen him too. I don't know, but I found a part in the Bible to bless the house. If he is here then that ought to make him go.

BOY WILLIE: You worse than Berniece believing all that stuff. Talking about . . . if he here. Go on up there and find out. I been up there I ain't seen him. If you reading from that Bible gonna make him leave out of Berniece imagination, well, you might be right. But if you talking about . . .

DOAKER: Boy Willie, why don't you just be quiet? Getting all up in the man's business. This ain't got nothing to do with you. Let him go ahead and do what he gonna do.

BOY WILLIE: I ain't stopping him. Avery ain't got no power to do nothing.

AVERY: Oh, I ain't got no power. God got the power! God got power over everything in His creation. God can do anything. God say, "As I commandeth so it shall be." God said, "Let there be light," and there was light.[5] He made the world in six days and rested on the seventh. God's got a wonderful power. He got power over life and death. Jesus raised Lazareth from the dead. They was getting ready to bury him and Jesus told him say, "Rise up and walk." He got up and walked and the people made great rejoicing at the power of God. I ain't worried about him chasing away a little old ghost!

[*There is a knock at the door.* BOY WILLIE *goes to answer it.* LYMON *enters carrying a coil of rope.*]

BOY WILLIE: Where you been? I been waiting on you and you run off somewhere.

LYMON: I ran into Grace. I stopped and bought her drink. She say she gonna go to the picture show with me.

BOY WILLIE: I ain't thinking about no Grace nothing.

LYMON: Hi, Berniece.

BOY WILLIE: Give me that rope and get up on this side of the piano.

DOAKER: Boy Willie, don't start nothing now. Leave the piano alone.

BOY WILLIE: Get that board there, Lymon. Stay out of this, Doaker.

[BERNIECE *exits up the stairs.*]

DOAKER: You just can't take the piano. How you gonna take the piano? Berniece ain't said nothing about selling that piano.

BOY WILLIE: She ain't got to say nothing. Come on, Lymon. We got to lift one end at a time up on the board. You got to watch so that the board don't slide up under there.

LYMON: What we gonna do with the rope?

BOY WILLIE: Let me worry about the rope. You just get up on this side over here with me.

[BERNIECE *enters from the stairs. She has her hand in her pocket where she has Crawley's gun.*]

AVERY: Boy Willie . . . Berniece . . . why don't you all sit down and talk this out now?

BERNIECE: Ain't nothing to talk out.

---

5. See Genesis 1.3. *Lazareth:* Lazarus.

BOY WILLIE: I'm through talking to Berniece. You can talk to Berniece till you get blue in the face, and it don't make no difference. Get up on that side, Lymon. Throw that rope around there and tie it to the leg.

LYMON: Wait a minute . . . wait a minute, Boy Willie. Berniece got to say. Hey, Berniece . . . did you tell Boy Willie he could take this piano?

BERNIECE: Boy Willie ain't taking nothing out of my house but himself. Now you let him go ahead and try.

BOY WILLIE: Come on, Lymon, get up on this side with me.

[LYMON *stands undecided.*]

Come on, nigger! What you standing there for?

LYMON: Maybe Berniece is right, Boy Willie. Maybe you shouldn't sell it.

AVERY: You all ought to sit down and talk it out. See if you can come to an agreement.

DOAKER: That's what I been trying to tell them. Seem like one of them ought to respect the other one's wishes.

BERNIECE: I wish Boy Willie would go on and leave my house. That's what I wish. Now, he can respect that. Cause he's leaving here one way or another.

BOY WILLIE: What you mean one way or another? What's that supposed to mean? I ain't scared of no gun.

DOAKER: Come on, Berniece, leave him alone with that.

BOY WILLIE: I don't care what Berniece say. I'm selling my half. I can't help it if her half got to go along with it. It ain't like I'm trying to cheat her out of her half. Come on, Lymon.

LYMON: Berniece . . . I got to do this . . . Boy Willie say he gonna give you half of the money . . . say he want to get Sutter's land.

BERNIECE: Go on, Lymon. Just go on . . . I done told Boy Willie what to do.

BOY WILLIE: Here, Lymon . . . put that rope up over there.

LYMON: Boy Willie, you sure you want to do this? The way I figure it . . . I might be wrong . . . but I figure she gonna shoot you first.

BOY WILLIE: She just gonna have to shoot me.

BERNIECE: Maretha, get on out the way. Get her out the way, Doaker.

DOAKER: Go on, do what your mama told you.

BERNIECE: Put her in your room.

[MARETHA *exits to Doaker's room.* BOY WILLIE *and* LYMON *try to lift the piano. The door opens and* WINING BOY *enters. He has been drinking.*]

WINING BOY: Man, these niggers around here! I stopped down there at Seefus. . . . These folks standing around talking about Patchneck Red's coming. They jumping back and getting off the sidewalk talking about Patchneck Red this and Patchneck Red that. Come to find out . . . you know who they was talking about? Old John D. from up around Tyler! Used to run around with Otis Smith. He got everybody scared of him.

Calling him Patchneck Red. They don't know I whupped the nigger's head in one time.

BOY WILLIE: Just make sure that board don't slide, Lymon.

LYMON: I got this side. You watch that side.

WINING BOY: Hey, Boy Willie, what you got? I know you got a pint stuck up in your coat.

BOY WILLIE: Wining Boy, get out the way!

WINING BOY: Hey, Doaker. What you got? Gimme a drink. I want a drink.

DOAKER: It look like you had enough of whatever it was. Come talking about "What you got?" You ought to be trying to find somewhere to lay down.

WINING BOY: I ain't worried about no place to lay down. I can always find me a place to lay down in Berniece's house. Ain't that right, Berniece?

BERNIECE: Wining Boy, sit down somewhere. You been out there drinking all day. Come in here smelling like an old polecat. Sit on down there, you don't need nothing to drink.

DOAKER: You know Berniece don't like all that drinking.

WINING BOY: I ain't disrespecting Berniece. Berniece, am I disrespecting you? I'm just trying to be nice. I been with strangers all day and they treated me like family. I come in here to family and you treat me like a stranger. I don't need your whiskey. I can buy my own. I wanted your company, not your whiskey.

DOAKER: Nigger, why don't you go upstairs and lay down? You don't need nothing to drink.

WINING BOY: I ain't thinking about no laying down. Me and Boy Willie fixing to party. Ain't that right, Boy Willie? Tell him. I'm fixing to play me some piano. Watch this.

[WINING BOY *sits down at the piano.*]

BOY WILLIE: Come on, Wining Boy! Me and Lymon fixing to move the piano.

WINING BOY: Wait a minute . . . wait a minute. This a song I wrote for Cleotha. I wrote this song in memory of Cleotha. [*He begins to play and sing.*]

Hey little woman what's the matter with you now
Had a storm last night and blowed the line all down

Tell me how long
Is I got to wait
Can I get it now
Or must I hesitate

It takes a hesitating stocking in her hesitating shoe
It takes a hesitating woman wanna sing the blues

> Tell me how long
> Is I got to wait
> Can I kiss you now
> Or must I hesitate.

BOY WILLIE: Come on, Wining Boy, get up! Get up, Wining Boy! Me and Lymon's fixing to move the piano.

WINING BOY: Naw . . . Naw . . . you ain't gonna move this piano!

BOY WILLIE: Get out the way, Wining Boy.

[WINING BOY, *his back to the piano, spreads his arms out over the piano.*]

WINING BOY: You ain't taking this piano out the house. You got to take me with it!

BOY WILLIE: Get on out the way, Wining Boy! Doaker get him!

[*There is a knock on the door.*]

BERNIECE: I got him, Doaker. Come on, Wining Boy. I done told Boy Willie he ain't taking the piano.

[BERNIECE *tries to take* WINING BOY *away from the piano.*]

WINING BOY: He got to take me with it!

[DOAKER *goes to answer the door.* GRACE *enters.*]

GRACE: Is Lymon here?

DOAKER: Lymon.

WINING BOY: He ain't taking that piano.

BERNIECE: I ain't gonna let him take it.

GRACE: I thought you was coming back. I ain't gonna sit in that truck all day.

LYMON: I told you I was coming back.

GRACE: [Sees BOY WILLIE.] Oh, hi, Boy Willie. Lymon told me you was gone back down South.

LYMON: I said he was going back. I didn't say he had left already.

GRACE: That's what you told me.

BERNIECE: Lymon, you got to take your company someplace else.

LYMON: Berniece, this is Grace. That there is Berniece. That's Boy Willie's sister.

GRACE: Nice to meet you. [To LYMON.] I ain't gonna sit out in that truck all day. You told me you was gonna take me to the movie.

LYMON: I told you I had something to do first. You supposed to wait on me.

BERNIECE: Lymon, just go on and leave. Take Grace or whoever with you. Just go on get out my house.

BOY WILLIE: You gonna help me move this piano first, nigger!

LYMON: [To GRACE.] I got to help Boy Willie move the piano first.

[*Everybody but* GRACE *suddenly senses* SUTTER's *presence.*]

GRACE: I ain't waiting on you. Told me you was coming right back. Now you got to move a piano. You just like all the other men. [GRACE *now senses something.*] Something ain't right here. I knew I shouldn't have come back up in this house. [GRACE *exits.*]

LYMON: Hey, Grace! I'll be right back, Boy Willie.

BOY WILLIE: Where you going, nigger?

LYMON: I'll be back. I got to take Grace home.

BOY WILLIE: Come on, let's move the piano first!

LYMON: I got to take Grace home. I told you I'll be back.

[LYMON *exits.* BOY WILLIE *exits and calls after him.*]

BOY WILLIE: Come on, Lymon! Hey . . . Lymon! Lymon . . . come on!

[*Again, the presence of* SUTTER *is felt.*]

WINING BOY: Hey, Doaker, did you feel that? Hey, Berniece . . . did you get cold? Hey, Doaker . . .

DOAKER: What you calling me for?

WINING BOY: I believe that's Sutter.

DOAKER: Well, let him stay up there. As long as he don't mess with me.

BERNIECE: Avery, go on and bless the house.

DOAKER: You need to bless that piano. That's what you need to bless. It ain't done nothing but cause trouble. If you gonna bless anything go on and bless that.

WINING BOY: Hey, Doaker, if he gonna bless something let him bless everything. The kitchen . . . the upstairs. Go on and bless it all.

BOY WILLIE: Ain't no ghost in this house. He need to bless Berniece's head. That's what he need to bless.

AVERY: Seem like that piano's causing all the trouble. I can bless that. Berniece, put me some water in that bottle.

[AVERY *takes a small bottle from his pocket and hands it to* BERNIECE, *who goes into the kitchen to get water.* AVERY *takes a candle from his pocket and lights it. He gives it to* BERNIECE *as she gives him the water.*]

Hold this candle. Whatever you do make sure it don't go out.

O Holy Father we gather here this evening in the Holy Name to cast out the spirit of one James Sutter. May this vial of water be empowered with thy spirit. May each drop of it be a weapon and a shield against the presence of all evil and may it be a cleansing and blessing of this humble abode.

Just as Our Father taught us how to pray so He say, "I will prepare a table for you in the midst of mine enemies,"[6] and in His hands we place

6. Psalm 23.5.

ourselves to come unto his presence. Where there is Good so shall it cause Evil to scatter to the Four Winds. [*He throws water at the piano at each commandment.*] Get thee behind me, Satan! Get thee behind the face of Righteousness as we Glorify His Holy Name! Get thee behind the Hammer of Truth that breaketh down the Wall of Falsehood! Father. Father. Praise. Praise. We ask in Jesus' name and call forth the power of the Holy Spirit as it is written. . . . [*He opens the Bible and reads from it.*] I will sprinkle clean water upon thee and ye shall be clean.

BOY WILLIE: All this old preaching stuff. Hell, just tell him to leave.

[AVERY *continues reading throughout* BOY WILLIE's *outburst.*]

AVERY: I will sprinkle clean water upon you and you shall be clean: from all your uncleanliness, and from all your idols, will I cleanse you. A new heart also will I give you, and a new spirit will I put within you: and I will take out of your flesh the heart of stone, and I will give you a heart of flesh. And I will put my spirit within you, and cause you to walk in my statutes, and ye shall keep my judgments, and do them.

[BOY WILLIE *grabs a pot of water from the stove and begins to fling it around the room.*]

BOY WILLIE: Hey Sutter! Sutter! Get your ass out this house! Sutter! Come on and get some of this water! You done drowned in the well, come on and get some more of this water!

[BOY WILLIE *is working himself into a frenzy as he runs around the room throwing water and calling* SUTTER's *name.* AVERY *continues reading.*]

BOY WILLIE: Come on, Sutter! [*He starts up the stairs.*] Come on, get some water! Come on, Sutter!

[*The sound of* SUTTER's GHOST *is heard. As* BOY WILLIE *approaches the steps he is suddenly thrown back by the unseen force, which is choking him. As he struggles he frees himself, then dashes up the stairs.*]

BOY WILLIE: Come on, Sutter!

AVERY: [*Continuing.*] A new heart also will I give you and a new spirit will I put within you: and I will take out of your flesh the heart of stone, and I will give you a heart of flesh. And I will put my spirit within you, and cause you to walk in my statutes, and ye shall keep my judgments, and do them.

[*There are loud sounds heard from upstairs as* BOY WILLIE *begins to wrestle with* SUTTER's GHOST. *It is a life-and-death struggle fraught with perils and faultless terror.* BOY WILLIE *is thrown down the stairs.* AVERY *is stunned into silence.* BOY WILLIE *picks himself up and dashes back upstairs.*]

AVERY: Berniece, I can't do it.

[*There are more sounds heard from upstairs.* DOAKER *and* WINING BOY *stare at one another in stunned disbelief. It is in this moment, from somewhere old, that* BERNIECE *realizes what she must do. She crosses to the piano. She begins to play. The song is found piece by piece. It is an old urge to song that is both a commandment and a plea. With each repetition it gains in strength. It is intended as an exorcism and a dressing for battle. A rustle of wind blowing across two continents.*]

BERNIECE: [*Singing.*]

I want you to help me
I want you to help me
I want you to help me
I want you to help me
I want you to help me
I want you to help me
Mama Berniece
I want you to help me
Mama Esther
I want you to help me
Papa Boy Charles
I want you to help me
Mama Ola
I want you to help me

I want you to help me
I want you to help me
I want you to help me
I want you to help me
I want you to help me
I want you to help me
I want you to help me
I want you to help me

[*The sound of a train approaching is heard. The noise upstairs subsides.*]

BOY WILLIE: Come on, Sutter! Come back, Sutter!

[BERNIECE *begins to chant:*]

BERNIECE:

Thank you.
Thank you.
Thank you.

[*A calm comes over the house.* MARETHA *enters from* DOAKER'*s room.* BOY WILLIE *enters on the stairs. He pauses a moment to watch* BERNIECE *at the piano.*]

BERNIECE:

> Thank you.
> Thank you.
> Thank you.

BOY WILLIE: Wining Boy, you ready to go back down home? Hey, Doaker, what time the train leave?

DOAKER: You still got time to make it.

[MARETHA *crosses and embraces* BOY WILLIE.]

BOY WILLIE: Hey Berniece ... if you and Maretha don't keep playing on that piano ... ain't no telling ... me and Sutter both liable to be back. [*He exits.*]

BERNIECE: Thank you.

[*The lights go down to black.*]

1987

QUESTIONS

1. What, specifically, do the carvings on the piano represent? What different past does the piano represent for each of the characters? How important is the past ownership of the piano? What is the significance of the way the family acquired it? In what ways do different characters' attitudes toward the piano reveal their feelings about the past?

2. Why is Boy Willie portrayed in the first scene as so loud and intrusive? What does this behavior achieve for the play dramatically? What aspects of Boy Willie's character does the opening scene illustrate? What aspects of his character are revealed later? What does "land" represent to him?

3. How would you describe Doaker's role in the play? Is he a minor character? How does he contribute to the play thematically? How does he affect the way events unfold, or the dramatic climax? Given the importance of family in this play and his role as the family's acting patriarch, could we call him a hero?

4. What functions does Maretha have in the play? In what ways is her age important? If you were directing the play, how would you have Maretha behave? How would she be costumed?

5. In what ways is geography important to the play? What does Mississippi represent to the different characters? What does Pittsburgh represent to the different characters? What does Doaker's continued employment with the railroad symbolize, and what is the significance of his description of how the railroad works (in the play's opening scene)?

6. What does the truckload of watermelons represent to Boy Willie? to Lymon? In what sense does the offstage presence of the watermelons keep time for the play and mark the progression of the plot? Describe the rising action and climax of the play in relation to the truck's load.

7. Describe the the conflict between Berniece and Boy Willie and the way it develops throughout the play. Where do other characters fit into the opposition? What role might gender, as well as race, play in this conflict?
8. What plot functions does Grace perform? In what ways does her presence complicate the play's portrayal of African American women's experience and options?
9. What does Avery represent to Berniece? What attracts her to him, and what, on the other hand, makes her hesitate in accepting his offer of marriage? If you were directing the play, how would you present the critical scene of Avery preaching? Of the exorcism?
10. What does "Lesson" in the title mean? What lesson does the piano teach each of the characters?

SUGGESTIONS FOR WRITING

1. What is the role of music in *The Piano Lesson*? How does the music function to reveal character and to provide a counterpoint to the action? What is the thematic importance of the music? Write an essay in which you explore the many uses of music in Wilson's play.
2. What is the legacy of slavery in the lives of the African American characters in *The Piano Lesson*? How fully does each character acknowledge slavery's influence on the mid-twentieth-century lives depicted in the play? How does each character try to break free of this influence? Write an essay in which you explore slavery's lingering power to shape the attitudes and behavior of the characters in *The Piano Lesson*.
3. How does *The Piano Lesson* present gender roles and sexual politics? What expectations do the men and women in the play have of each other? Write an essay in which you discuss the play's representation of gender differences.
4. Were you surprised by the play's ending? A longstanding "rule" for playwrights is that if a gun appears onstage, it must be fired by the end of the play. *The Piano Lesson*, though, seems to build steadily toward a violent climax that is averted at the last moment. Write an essay in which you examine the way August Wilson both uses and subverts the audience's conventional expectation that drama is resolved by violence.
5. Write an essay exploring Sutter's role in and significance to the play, especially in terms of conflict and theme. Why might it matter that we aren't informed about Sutter's race until the second act? What is the significance of the timing of his appearances and of the way other characters respond to and interpret them? Why is Berniece able to rid the house of Sutter by playing the piano whereas Avery's approach proves ineffectual?
6. Write a series of "newsy" letters from Boy Willie, Berniece, Maretha, and Lymon, in which each character, in turn, describes the conflict over the piano. How would they describe their own feelings and actions? How would they account for the values and motivations of the other characters? What resolution of the conflict would each character hope for?

Authors on Their Work: AUGUST WILSON (1945–2005)

From "August Wilson: The Art of Theater XIV"
(1999)*

INTERVIEWER

Can you talk about the genesis of a work? *The Piano Lesson?*

WILSON

I started with the idea from one of Romare Bearden's paintings—*The Piano Lesson*, the subtitle of which was *Homage to Mary Lou Williams*, who was a jazz pianist in Pittsburgh. I started with a question: Can you acquire a sense of self worth by denying your past, or is implicit in that denial a repudiation of the worth of the self? Once deciding that, I had to construct a series of events that posed that question and illustrated some possible answers. I started by having four guys carry the piano into the house. I wrote eight pages of dialogue.... Once they got it in the house they began arguing about where to put it. I thought, Wait a minute, where am I going? What am I doing? So I threw those pages out and started over. And then I got the idea of the brother coming into the house like a tornado, bringing in the past that his sister is trying to deny. I usually start with a line of dialogue, which contains elements of the plot, character, and the thematic idea.

From "An Interview with August Wilson" (1999)**

Q. Is *The Piano Lesson* a kind of debate between Berniece and Boy Willie?

A. That play sets up the question of whether you can develop a sense of self-worth by denying the past. Everyone sees the play differently than I do. Because Boy Willie wants to sell the piano, they think he is trying to deny the past. But Berniece cannot even touch the piano—she's the one who is denying everything, she's the one trying to run away from the past. (15–16)

• • •

Q. One playwright has said that drama is made up of sound and silence. Do you see drama that way?

A. No doubt drama is made up of sound and silence, but I see conflict at the center. What you do is set up a character who has certain beliefs

(Continued on next page)

(Continued)

and you establish a situation where those beliefs are challenged and that character is forced to examine those beliefs and perhaps change them. That's the kind of dramatic situation which engages an audience.

Q. Then is the conflict primarily internal rather than external, between characters?

A. Internal, right, where the character has to reexamine his whole body of beliefs. The play has to shake the very foundation of his whole system of beliefs and force him to make a choice. Then I think you as a playwright have accomplished something, because that process also forces the audience to go through the same inner struggle.

*From George Plimpton and August Wilson, "August Wilson: The Art of Theater XIV," *The Paris Review* 41.153 (Winter 1999): 67–94.
**Bonnie Lyons, "An Interview with August Wilson," *Contemporary Literature* 40.1 (Spring 1999): 1–21.

.

Reading More Drama

A Raisin in the Sun

What happens to a dream deferred?

Does it dry up
Like a raisin in the sun?
Or fester like a sore—
And then run?
Does it stink like rotten meat?
Or crust and sugar over—
Like a syrupy sweet?
Maybe it just sags
Like a heavy load.

Or does it explode?

—LANGSTON HUGHES[1]

CAST OF CHARACTERS

RUTH YOUNGER	JOSEPH ASAGAI
TRAVIS YOUNGER	GEORGE MURCHISON
WALTER LEE YOUNGER (BROTHER)	KARL LINDNER
BENEATHA YOUNGER	BOBO
LENA YOUNGER (MAMA)	MOVING MEN

The action of the play is set in Chicago's Southside, sometime between World War II and the present.

ACT I

Scene One

The Younger living room would be a comfortable and well-ordered room if it were not for a number of indestructible contradictions to this state of being. Its furnishings are typical and undistinguished and their primary feature now is that they have clearly had to accommodate the living of too many people for too many years—and

---

1. Hughes's poem, published in 1951, is titled "Harlem (A Dream Deferred)."

Ruby Dee as Ruth, Sidney Poitier as Walter Lee Younger, and Diana
Sands as Beneatha in the original 1959 Broadway production of
A Raisin in the Sun

*they are tired. Still, we can see that at some time, a time probably no longer remem-
bered by the family (except perhaps for* MAMA), *the furnishings of this room were
actually selected with care and love and even hope—and brought to this apartment
and arranged with taste and pride.*

*That was a long time ago. Now the once loved pattern of the couch upholstery has
to fight to show itself from under acres of crocheted doilies and couch covers which
have themselves finally come to be more important than the upholstery. And here a
table or a chair has been moved to disguise the worn places in the carpet; but the carpet has fought back by showing its weariness, with depressing uniformity, elsewhere
on its surface.*

*Weariness has, in fact, won in this room. Everything has been polished, washed,
sat on, used, scrubbed too often. All pretenses but living itself have long since vanished
from the very atmosphere of this room.*

Moreover, a section of this room, for it is not really a room unto itself, though the landlord's lease would make it seem so, slopes backward to provide a small kitchen area, where the family prepares the meals that are eaten in the living room proper, which must also serve as dining room. The single window that has been provided for these "two" rooms is located in this kitchen area. The sole natural light the family may enjoy in the course of a day is only that which fights its way through this little window.

At left, a door leads to a bedroom which is shared by MAMA *and her daughter,* BENEATHA. *At right, opposite, is a second room (which in the beginning of the life of this apartment was probably a breakfast room) which serves as a bedroom for* WAL-TER *and his wife,* RUTH.

Time: Sometime between World War II and the present.

Place: Chicago's Southside.

At Rise: It is morning dark in the living room. TRAVIS *is asleep on the make-down bed at center. An alarm clock sounds from within the bedroom at right, and presently* RUTH *enters from that room and closes the door behind her. She crosses sleepily toward the window. As she passes her sleeping son she reaches down and shakes him a little. At the window she raises the shade and a dusky Southside morning light comes in feebly. She fills a pot with water and puts it on to boil. She calls to the boy, between yawns, in a slightly muffled voice.*

RUTH *is about thirty. We can see that she was a pretty girl, even exceptionally so, but now it is apparent that life has been little that she expected, and disappointment has already begun to hang in her face. In a few years, before thirty-five even, she will be known among her people as a "settled woman."*

She crosses to her son and gives him a good, final, rousing shake.

RUTH: Come on now, boy, it's seven thirty! [*Her son sits up at last, in a stupor of sleepiness.*] I say hurry up, Travis! You ain't the only person in the world got to use a bathroom! [*The child, a sturdy, handsome little boy of ten or eleven, drags himself out of the bed and almost blindly takes his towels and "today's clothes" from drawers and a closet and goes out to the bathroom, which is in an outside hall and which is shared by another family or families on the same floor.* RUTH *crosses to the bedroom door at right and opens it and calls in to her husband.*] Walter Lee! . . . It's after seven thirty! Lemme see you do some waking up in there now! [*She waits.*] You better get up from there, man! It's after seven thirty I tell you. [*She waits again.*] All right, you just go ahead and lay there and next thing you know Travis be finished and Mr. Johnson'll be in there and you'll be fussing and cussing round here like a mad man! And be late too! [*She waits, at the end of patience.*] Walter Lee—it's time for you to get up!

[*She waits another second and then starts to go into the bedroom, but is apparently satisfied that her husband has begun to get up. She stops, pulls the door to, and returns to the kitchen area. She wipes her face with a moist cloth and runs her fingers through her sleep-disheveled hair in a vain effort and ties an apron*] *around her housecoat. The bedroom door at right opens and her husband stands in the doorway in his pajamas, which are rumpled and mismated. He is a lean, intense young man in his middle thirties, inclined to quick nervous movements and erratic speech habits—and always in his voice there is a quality of indictment.*]

WALTER: Is he out yet?

RUTH: What you mean *out*? He ain't hardly got in there good yet.

WALTER: [*Wandering in, still more oriented to sleep than to a new day.*] Well, what was you doing all that yelling for if I can't even get in there yet? [*Stopping and thinking.*] Check coming today?

RUTH: They *said* Saturday and this is just Friday and I hopes to God you ain't going to get up here first thing this morning and start talking to me 'bout no money—'cause I 'bout don't want to hear it.

WALTER: Something the matter with you this morning?

RUTH: No—I'm just sleepy as the devil. What kind of eggs you want?

WALTER: Not scrambled. [RUTH *starts to scramble eggs.*] Paper come? [RUTH *points impatiently to the rolled up* Tribune *on the table, and he gets it and spreads it out and vaguely reads the front page.*] Set off another bomb yesterday.

RUTH: [*Maximum indifference.*] Did they?

WALTER: [*Looking up.*] What's the matter with you?

RUTH: Ain't nothing the matter with me. And don't keep asking me that this morning.

WALTER: Ain't nobody bothering you. [*Reading the news of the day absently again.*] Say Colonel McCormick[2] is sick.

RUTH: [*Affecting tea-party interest.*] Is he now? Poor thing.

WALTER: [*Sighing and looking at his watch.*] Oh, me. [*He waits.*] Now what is that boy doing in that bathroom all this time? He just going to have to start getting up earlier. I can't be late to work on account of him fooling around in there.

RUTH: [*Turning on him.*] Oh, no he ain't going to be getting up no earlier no such thing! It ain't his fault that he can't get to bed no earlier nights 'cause he got a bunch of crazy good-for-nothing clowns sitting up running their mouths in what is supposed to be his bedroom after ten o'clock at night . . .

WALTER: That's what you mad about, ain't it? The things I want to talk about with my friends just couldn't be important in your mind, could they?

[*He rises and finds a cigarette in her handbag on the table and crosses to the little window and looks out, smoking and deeply enjoying this first one.*]

---

2. Robert Rutherford McCormick (1880-1955), owner-publisher of the *Chicago Tribune*.

954 READING MORE DRAMA

RUTH: [*Almost matter of factly, a complaint too automatic to deserve emphasis.*] Why you always got to smoke before you eat in the morning?

WALTER: [*At the window.*] Just look at 'em down there . . . Running and racing to work . . . [*He turns and faces his wife and watches her a moment at the stove, and then, suddenly.*] You look young this morning, baby.

RUTH: [*Indifferently.*] Yeah?

WALTER: Just for a second—stirring them eggs. It's gone now—just for a second it was—you looked real young again. [*Then, drily.*] It's gone now—you look like yourself again.

RUTH: Man, if you don't shut up and leave me alone.

WALTER: [*Looking out to the street again.*] First thing a man ought to learn in life is not to make love to no colored woman first thing in the morning. You all some evil people at eight o'clock in the morning.

[TRAVIS *appears in the hall doorway, almost fully dressed and quite wide awake now, his towels and pajamas across his shoulders. He opens the door and signals for his father to make the bathroom in a hurry.*]

TRAVIS: [*Watching the bathroom.*] Daddy, come on!

[WALTER *gets his bathroom utensils and flies out to the bathroom.*]

RUTH: Sit down and have your breakfast, Travis.

TRAVIS: Mama, this is Friday. [*Gleefully.*] Check coming tomorrow, huh?

RUTH: You get your mind off money and eat your breakfast.

TRAVIS: [*Eating.*] This is the morning we supposed to bring the fifty cents to school.

RUTH: Well, I ain't got no fifty cents this morning.

TRAVIS: Teacher say we have to.

RUTH: I don't care what teacher say. I ain't got it. Eat your breakfast, Travis.

TRAVIS: I *am* eating.

RUTH: Hush up now and just eat!

[*The boy gives her an exasperated look for her lack of understanding, and eats grudgingly.*]

TRAVIS: You think Grandmama would have it?

RUTH: No! And I want you to stop asking your grandmother for money, you hear me?

TRAVIS: [*Outraged.*] Gaaaleee! I don't ask her, she just gimme it sometimes!

RUTH: Travis Willard Younger—I got too much on me this morning to be—

TRAVIS: Maybe Daddy—

RUTH: *Travis!*

[*The boy hushes abruptly. They are both quiet and tense for several seconds.*]

TRAVIS: [*Presently.*] Could I maybe go carry some groceries in front of the supermarket for a little while after school then?

RUTH: Just hush, I said. [TRAVIS *jabs his spoon into his cereal bowl viciously, and rests his head in anger upon his fists.*] If you through eating, you can get over there and make up your bed.

[*The boy obeys stiffly and crosses the room, almost mechanically, to the bed and more or less carefully folds the covering. He carries the bedding into his mother's room and returns with his books and cap.*]

TRAVIS: [*Sulking and standing apart from her unnaturally.*] I'm gone.

RUTH: [*Looking up from the stove to inspect him automatically.*] Come here. [*He crosses to her and she studies his head.*] If you don't take this comb and fix this here head, you better! [TRAVIS *puts down his books with a great sigh of oppression, and crosses to the mirror. His mother mutters under her breath about his "slubbornness."*] 'Bout to march out of here with that head looking just like chickens slept in it! I just don't know where you get your slubborn ways . . . And get your jacket, too. Looks chilly out this morning.

TRAVIS: [*With conspicuously brushed hair and jacket.*] I'm gone.

RUTH: Get carfare and milk money—[*Waving one finger.*]—and not a single penny for no caps, you hear me?

TRAVIS: [*With sullen politeness.*] Yes'm.

[*He turns in outrage to leave. His mother watches after him as in his frustration he approaches the door almost comically. When she speaks to him, her voice has become a very gentle tease.*]

RUTH: [*Mocking; as she thinks he would say it.*] Oh, Mama makes me so mad sometimes, I don't know what to do! [*She waits and continues to his back as he stands stock-still in front of the door.*] I wouldn't kiss that woman good-bye for nothing in this world this morning! [*The boy finally turns around and rolls his eyes at her, knowing the mood has changed and he is vindicated; he does not, however, move toward her yet.*] Not for nothing in this world! [*She finally laughs aloud at him and holds out her arms to him and we see that it is a way between them, very old and practiced. He crosses to her and allows her to embrace him warmly but keeps his face fixed with masculine rigidity. She holds him back from her presently and looks at him and runs her fingers over the features of his face. With utter gentleness—*] Now—whose little old angry man are you?

TRAVIS: [*The masculinity and gruffness start to fade at last.*] Aw gaalee—Mama . . .

RUTH: [*Mimicking.*] Aw—gaaaaalleeeee, Mama! [*She pushes him, with rough playfulness and finality, toward the door.*] Get on out of here or you going to be late.

TRAVIS: [*In the face of love, new aggressiveness.*] Mama, could I *please* go carry groceries?

RUTH: Honey, it's starting to get so cold evenings.

WALTER: [*Coming in from the bathroom and drawing a make-believe gun from a make-believe holster and shooting at his son.*] What is it he wants to do?

RUTH: Go carry groceries after school at the supermarket.

WALTER: Well, let him go . . .

TRAVIS: [*Quickly, to the ally.*] I *have* to—she won't gimme the fifty cents . . .

WALTER: [*To his wife only.*] Why not?

RUTH: [*Simply, and with flavor.*] 'Cause we don't have it.

WALTER: [*To* RUTH *only.*] What you tell the boy things like that for? [*Reaching down into his pants with a rather important gesture.*] Here, son—

[*He hands the boy the coin, but his eyes are directed to his wife's.* TRAVIS *takes the money happily.*]

TRAVIS: Thanks, Daddy.

[*He starts out.* RUTH *watches both of them with murder in her eyes.* WALTER *stands and stares back at her with defiance, and suddenly reaches into his pocket again on an afterthought.*]

WALTER: [*Without even looking at his son, still staring hard at his wife.*] In fact, here's another fifty cents . . . Buy yourself some fruit today—or take a taxicab to school or something!

TRAVIS: Whoopee—

[*He leaps up and clasps his father around the middle with his legs, and they face each other in mutual appreciation; slowly* WALTER LEE *peeks around the boy to catch the violent rays from his wife's eyes and draws his head back as if shot.*]

WALTER: You better get down now—and get to school, man.

TRAVIS: [*At the door.*] O.K. Good-bye.

[*He exits.*]

WALTER: [*After him, pointing with pride.*] That's *my* boy. [*She looks at him in disgust and turns back to her work.*] You know what I was thinking 'bout in the bathroom this morning?

RUTH: No.

WALTER: How come you always try to be so pleasant!

RUTH: What is there to be pleasant 'bout!

WALTER: You want to know what I was thinking 'bout in the bathroom or not!

RUTH: I know what you thinking 'bout.

WALTER: [*Ignoring her.*] 'Bout what me and Willy Harris was talking about last night.

RUTH: [*Immediately—a refrain.*] Willy Harris is a good-for-nothing loud mouth.

WALTER: Anybody who talks to me has got to be a good-for-nothing loud mouth, ain't he? And what you know about who is just a good-for-nothing loud mouth? Charlie Atkins was just a "good-for-nothing loud mouth" too, wasn't he! When he wanted me to go in the dry-cleaning business with him. And now—he's grossing a hundred thousand a year. A hundred thousand dollars a year! You still call *him* a loudmouth!

RUTH: [*Bitterly.*] Oh, Walter Lee . . .

[*She folds her head on her arms over the table.*]

WALTER: [*Rising and coming to her and standing over her.*] You tired, ain't you? Tired of everything. Me, the boy, the way we live—this beat-up hole—everything. Ain't you? [*She doesn't look up, doesn't answer.*] So tired—moaning and groaning all the time, but you wouldn't do nothing to help, would you? You couldn't be on my side that long for nothing, could you?

RUTH: Walter, please leave me alone.

WALTER: A man needs for a woman to back him up . . .

RUTH: Walter—

WALTER: Mama would listen to you. You know she listen to you more than she do me and Bennie. She think more of you. All you have to do is just sit down with her when you drinking your coffee one morning and talking 'bout things like you do and— [*He sits down beside her and demonstrates graphically what he thinks her methods and tone should be.*] —you just sip your coffee, see, and say easy like that you been thinking 'bout that deal Walter Lee is so interested in, 'bout the store and all, and sip some more coffee, like what you saying ain't really that important to you—And the next thing you know, she be listening good and asking you questions and when I come home—I can tell her the details. This ain't no fly-by-night proposition, baby. I mean we figured it out, me and Willy and Bobo.

RUTH: [*With a frown.*] Bobo?

WALTER: Yeah. You see, this little liquor store we got in mind cost seventy-five thousand and we figured the initial investment on the place be 'bout thirty thousand, see. That be ten thousand each. Course, there's a couple of hundred you got to pay so's you don't spend your life just waiting for them clowns to let your license get approved—

RUTH: You mean graft?

WALTER: [*Frowning impatiently.*] Don't call it that. See there, that just goes to show you what women understand about the world. Baby, don't *nothing* happen for you in this world 'less you pay *somebody* off!

RUTH: Walter, leave me alone! [*She raises her head and stares at him vigorously—then says, more quietly.*] Eat your eggs, they gonna be cold.

WALTER: [*Straightening up from her and looking off.*] That's it. There you are.
Man say to his woman: I got me a dream. His woman say: Eat your eggs.
[*Sadly, but gaining in power.*] Man say: I got to take hold of this here
world, baby! And a woman will say: Eat your eggs and go to work. [*Passionately now.*] Man say: I got to change my life, I'm choking to death,
baby! And his woman say— [*In utter anguish as he brings his fists down on his
thighs.*] —Your eggs is getting cold!

RUTH: [*Softly.*] Walter, that ain't none of our money.

WALTER: [*Not listening at all or even looking at her.*] This morning, I was lookin'
in the mirror and thinking about it . . . I'm thirty-five years old; I been
married eleven years and I got a boy who sleeps in the living room—
[*Very, very quietly.*] —and all I got to give him is stories about how rich
white people live . . .

RUTH: Eat your eggs, Walter.

WALTER: *Damn my eggs . . . damn all the eggs that ever was!*

RUTH: Then go to work.

WALTER: [*Looking up at her.*] See—I'm trying to talk to you 'bout myself—
[*Shaking his head with the repetition.*] —and all you can say is eat them eggs
and go to work.

RUTH: [*Wearily.*] Honey, you never say nothing new. I listen to you every day,
every night and every morning, and you never say nothing new. [*Shrugging.*] So you would rather *be* Mr. Arnold than be his chauffeur. So—I
would *rather* be living in Buckingham Palace.[3]

WALTER: That is just what is wrong with the colored woman in this world . . .
Don't understand about building their men up and making 'em feel
like they somebody. Like they can do something.

RUTH: [*Drily, but to hurt.*] There *are* colored men who do things.

WALTER: No thanks to the colored woman.

RUTH: Well, being a colored woman, I guess I can't help myself none.

[*She rises and gets the ironing board and sets it up and attacks a huge pile of
rough-dried clothes, sprinkling them in preparation for the ironing and then
rolling them into tight fat balls.*]

WALTER: [*Mumbling.*] We one group of men tied to a race of women with
small minds.

[*His sister BENEATHA enters. She is about twenty, as slim and intense as her
brother. She is not as pretty as her sister-in-law, but her lean, almost intellectual face has a handsomeness of its own. She wears a bright-red flannel nightie,
and her thick hair stands wildly about her head. Her speech is a mixture of
many things; it is different from the rest of the family's insofar as education has
permeated her sense of English—and perhaps the Midwest rather than the*

3. Where the queen of Great Britain resides in London.

South has finally—at last—won out in her inflection; but not altogether, because over all of it is a soft slurring and transformed use of vowels which is the decided influence of the Southside. She passes through the room without looking at either RUTH *or* WALTER *and goes to the outside door and looks, a little blindly, out to the bathroom. She sees that it has been lost to the Johnsons. She closes the door with a sleepy vengeance and crosses to the table and sits down a little defeated.*]

BENEATHA: I am going to start timing those people.

WALTER: You should get up earlier.

BENEATHA: [*Her face in her hands. She is still fighting the urge to go back to bed.*] Really—would you suggest dawn? Where's the paper?

WALTER: [*Pushing the paper across the table to her as he studies her almost clinically, as though he has never seen her before.*] You a horrible-looking chick at this hour.

BENEATHA: [*Drily.*] Good morning, everybody.

WALTER: [*Senselessly.*] How is school coming?

BENEATHA: [*In the same spirit.*] Lovely. Lovely. And you know, biology is the greatest. [*Looking up at him.*] I dissected something that looked just like you yesterday.

WALTER: I just wondered if you've made up your mind and everything.

BENEATHA: [*Gaining in sharpness and impatience.*] And what did I answer yesterday morning—and the day before that?

RUTH: [*From the ironing board, like someone disinterested and old.*] Don't be so nasty, Bennie.

BENEATHA: [*Still to her brother.*] And the day before that and the day before that!

WALTER: [*Defensively.*] I'm interested in you. Something wrong with that? Ain't many girls who decide—

WALTER AND BENEATHA: [*In unison.*]—"to be a doctor."

[*Silence.*]

WALTER: Have we figured out yet just exactly how much medical school is going to cost?

RUTH: Walter Lee, why don't you leave that girl alone and get out of here to work?

BENEATHA: [*Exits to the bathroom and bangs on the door.*] Come on out of there, please!

[*She comes back into the room.*]

WALTER: [*Looking at his sister intently.*] You know the check is coming tomorrow.

BENEATHA: [*Turning on him with a sharpness all her own.*] That money belongs to Mama, Walter, and it's for her to decide how she wants to use it. I don't care if she wants to buy a house or a rocket ship or just nail it up somewhere and look at it. It's hers. Not ours—*hers.*

WALTER: [*Bitterly.*] Now ain't that fine! You just got your mother's interest at heart, ain't you, girl? You such a nice girl—but if Mama got that money she can always take a few thousand and help you through school too—can't she?

BENEATHA: I have never asked anyone around here to do anything for me.

WALTER: No! And the line between asking and just accepting when the time comes is big and wide—ain't it!

BENEATHA: [*With fury.*] What do you want from me, Brother—that I quit school or just drop dead, which!

WALTER: I don't want nothing but for you to stop acting holy 'round here. Me and Ruth done made some sacrifices for you—why can't you do something for the family?

RUTH: Walter, don't be dragging me in it.

WALTER: You are in it—Don't you get up and go work in somebody's kitchen for the last three years to help put clothes on her back?

RUTH: Oh, Walter—that's not fair . . .

WALTER: It ain't that nobody expects you to get on your knees and say thank you, Brother; thank you, Ruth; thank you, Mama—and thank you, Travis, for wearing the same pair of shoes for two semesters—

BENEATHA: [*Dropping to her knees.*] Well—I *do*—all right?—thank everybody . . . and forgive me for ever wanting to be anything at all . . . forgive me, forgive me!

RUTH: Please stop it! Your mama'll hear you.

WALTER: Who the hell told you you had to be a doctor? If you so crazy 'bout messing 'round with sick people—then go be a nurse like other women—or just get married and be quiet . . .

BENEATHA: Well—you finally got it said . . . it took you three years but you finally got it said. Walter, give up; leave me alone—it's Mama's money.

WALTER: *He was my father, too!*

BENEATHA: So what? He was mine, too—and Travis' grandfather—but the insurance money belongs to Mama. Picking on me is not going to make her give it to you to invest in any liquor stores— [*Underbreath, dropping into a chair.*] —and I for one say, God bless Mama for that!

WALTER: [*To* RUTH.] See—did you hear? Did you hear!

RUTH: Honey, please go to work.

WALTER: Nobody in this house is ever going to understand me.

BENEATHA: Because you're a nut.

WALTER: Who's a nut?

BENEATHA: You—you are a nut. Thee is mad, boy.

WALTER: [*Looking at his wife and his sister from the door, very sadly.*] The world's most backward race of people, and that's a fact.

BENEATHA: [*Turning slowly in her chair.*] And then there are all those prophets who would lead us out of the wilderness—. [WALTER *slams out of the house.*] —into the swamps!

RUTH: Bennie, why you always gotta be pickin' on your brother? Can't you be a little sweeter sometimes? [*Door opens.* WALTER *walks in.*]

WALTER: [*To* RUTH.] I need some money for carfare.

RUTH: [*Looks at him, then warms; teasing, but tenderly.*] Fifty cents? [*She goes to her bag and gets money.*] Here, take a taxi.

[WALTER *exits.* MAMA *enters. She is a woman in her early sixties, full-bodied and strong. She is one of those women of a certain grace and beauty who wear it so unobtrusively that it takes a while to notice. Her dark-brown face is surrounded by the total whiteness of her hair, and, being a woman who has adjusted to many things in life and overcome many more, her face is full of strength. She has, we can see, wit and faith of a kind that keep her eyes lit and full of interest and expectancy. She is, in a word, a beautiful woman. Her bearing is perhaps most like the noble bearing of the women of the Hereros of Southwest Africa—rather as if she imagines that as she walks she still bears a basket or a vessel upon her head. Her speech, on the other hand, is as careless as her carriage is precise—she is inclined to slur everything—but her voice is perhaps not so much quiet as simply soft.*]

MAMA: Who that 'round here slamming doors at this hour?

[*She crosses through the room, goes to the window, opens it, and brings in a feeble little plant growing doggedly in a small pot on the window sill. She feels the dirt and puts it back out.*]

RUTH: That was Walter Lee. He and Bennie was at it again.

MAMA: My children and they tempers. Lord, if this little old plant don't get more sun than it's been getting it ain't never going to see spring again. [*She turns from the window.*] What's the matter with you this morning, Ruth? You looks right peaked. You aiming to iron all them things? Leave some for me. I'll get to 'em this afternoon. Bennie honey, it's too drafty for you to be sitting 'round half dressed. Where's your robe?

BENEATHA: In the cleaners.

MAMA: Well, go get mine and put it on.

BENEATHA: I'm not cold, Mama, honest.

MAMA: I know—but you so thin . . .

BENEATHA: [*Irritably.*] Mama, I'm not cold.

MAMA: [*Seeing the make-down bed as* TRAVIS *has left it.*] Lord have mercy, look at that poor bed. Bless his heart—he tries, don't he?

[*She moves to the bed* TRAVIS *has sloppily made up.*]

RUTH: No—he don't half try at all 'cause he knows you going to come along behind him and fix everything. That's just how come he don't know how to do nothing right now—you done spoiled that boy so.

MAMA: Well—he's a little boy. Ain't supposed to know 'bout housekeeping. My baby, that's what he is. What you fix for his breakfast this morning?

RUTH: [*Angrily.*] I feed my son, Lena!

MAMA: I ain't meddling— [*Underbreath; busy-bodyish.*] I just noticed all last week he had cold cereal, and when it starts getting this chilly in the fall a child ought to have some hot grits or something when he goes out in the cold—

RUTH: [*Furious.*] I gave him hot oats—is that all right!

MAMA: I ain't meddling. [*Pause.*] Put a lot of nice butter on it? [RUTH *shoots her an angry look and does not reply.*] He likes lots of butter.

RUTH: [*Exasperated.*] Lena—

MAMA: [*To* BENEATHA. MAMA *is inclined to wander conversationally sometimes.*] What was you and your brother fussing 'bout this morning?

BENEATHA: It's not important, Mama.

[*She gets up and goes to look out at the bathroom, which is apparently free, and she picks up her towels and rushes out.*]

MAMA: What was they fighting about?

RUTH: Now you know as well as I do.

MAMA: [*Shaking her head.*] Brother still worrying hisself sick about that money?

RUTH: You know he is.

MAMA: You had breakfast?

RUTH: Some coffee.

MAMA: Girl, you better start eating and looking after yourself better. You almost thin as Travis.

RUTH: Lena—

MAMA: Un-hunh?

RUTH: What are you going to do with it?

MAMA: Now don't you start, child. It's too early in the morning to be talking about money. It ain't Christian.

RUTH: It's just that he got his heart set on that store—

MAMA: You mean that liquor store that Willy Harris want him to invest in?

RUTH: Yes—

MAMA: We ain't no business people, Ruth. We just plain working folks.

RUTH: Ain't nobody business people till they go into business. Walter Lee say colored people ain't never going to start getting ahead till they start gambling on some different kinds of things in the world—investments and things.

MAMA: What done got into you, girl? Walter Lee done finally sold you on investing.

RUTH: No. Mama, something is happening between Walter and me. I don't know what it is—but he needs something—something I can't give him anymore. He needs this chance, Lena.

MAMA: [*Frowning deeply.*] But liquor, honey—

RUTH: Well—like Walter say—I spec people going to always be drinking themselves some liquor.

MAMA: Well—whether they drinks it or not ain't none of my business. But whether I go into business selling it to 'em *is*, and I don't want that on my ledger this late in life. [*Stopping suddenly and studying her daughter-in-law.*] Ruth Younger, what's the matter with you today? You look like you could fall over right there.

RUTH: I'm tired.

MAMA: Then you better stay home from work today.

RUTH: I can't stay home. She'd be calling up the agency and screaming at them, "My girl didn't come in today—send me somebody! My girl didn't come in!" Oh, she just have a fit . . .

MAMA: Well, let her have it. I'll just call her up and say you got the flu—

RUTH: [*Laughing.*] Why the flu?

MAMA: 'Cause it sounds respectable to 'em. Something white people get, too. They know 'bout the flu. Otherwise they think you been cut up or something when you tell 'em you sick.

RUTH: I got to go in. We need the money.

MAMA: Somebody would of thought my children done all but starved to death the way they talk about money here late. Child, we got a great big old check coming tomorrow.

RUTH: [*Sincerely, but also self-righteously.*] Now that's your money. It ain't got nothing to do with me. We all feel like that—Walter and Bennie and me—even Travis.

MAMA: [*Thoughtfully, and suddenly very far away.*] Ten thousand dollars—

RUTH: Sure is wonderful.

MAMA: Ten thousand dollars.

RUTH: You know what you should do, Miss Lena? You should take yourself a trip somewhere. To Europe or South America or someplace—

MAMA: [*Throwing up her hands at the thought.*] Oh, child!

RUTH: I'm serious. Just pack up and leave! Go on away and enjoy yourself some. Forget about the family and have yourself a ball for once in your life—

MAMA: [*Drily.*] You sound like I'm just about ready to die. Who'd go with me? What I look like wandering 'round Europe by myself?

RUTH: Shoot—these here rich white women do it all the time. They don't think nothing of packing up they suitcases and piling on one of them big steamships and—swoosh!—they gone, child.

MAMA: Something always told me I wasn't no rich white woman.

RUTH: Well—what are you going to do with it then?

MAMA: I ain't rightly decided. [*Thinking. She speaks now with emphasis.*] Some of it got to be put away for Beneatha and her schoolin'—and ain't nothing going to touch that part of it. Nothing. [*She waits several seconds, trying to make up her mind about something, and looks at* RUTH *a little tentatively before going on.*] Been thinking that we maybe could meet the notes on a little old two-story somewhere, with a yard where Travis could play in the summertime, if we use part of the insurance for a down payment and everybody kind of pitch in. I could maybe take on a little day work again, few days a week—

RUTH: [*Studying her mother-in-law furtively and concentrating on her ironing, anxious to encourage without seeming to.*] Well, Lord knows, we've put enough rent into this here rat trap to pay for four houses by now . . .

MAMA: [*Looking up at the words "rat trap" and then looking around and leaning back and sighing—in a suddenly reflective mood—*] "Rat trap"—yes, that's all it is. [*Smiling.*] I remember just as well the day me and Big Walter moved in here. Hadn't been married but two weeks and wasn't planning on living here no more than a year. [*She shakes her head at the dissolved dream.*] We was going to set away, little by little, don't you know, and buy a little place out in Morgan Park. We had even picked out the house. [*Chuckling a little.*] Looks right dumpy today. But Lord, child, you should know all the dreams I had 'bout buying that house and fixing it up and making me a little garden in the back— [*She waits and stops smiling.*] And didn't none of it happen.

[*Dropping her hands in a futile gesture.*]

RUTH: [*Keeps her head down, ironing.*] Yes, life can be a barrel of disappointments, sometimes.

MAMA: Honey, Big Walter would come in here some nights back then and slump down on that couch there and just look at the rug, and look at me and look at the rug and then back at me—and I'd know he was down then . . . really down. [*After a second very long and thoughtful pause; she is seeing back to times that only she can see.*] And then, Lord, when I lost that baby—little Claude—I almost thought I was going to lose Big Walter too. Oh, that man grieved hisself! He was one man to love his children.

RUTH: Ain't nothin' can tear at you like losin' your baby.

MAMA: I guess that's how come that man finally worked hisself to death like he done. Like he was fighting his own war with this here world that took his baby from him.

RUTH: He sure was a fine man, all right. I always liked Mr. Younger.

MAMA: Crazy 'bout his children! God knows there was plenty wrong with Walter Younger—hard-headed, mean, kind of wild with women—plenty wrong with him. But he sure loved his children. Always wanted them to have something—be something. That's where Brother gets all these notions, I reckon. Big Walter used to say, he'd get right wet in the eyes sometimes, lean his head back with the water standing in his eyes and say, "Seem like God didn't see fit to give the black man nothing but dreams—but He did give us children to make them dreams seem worthwhile." [*She smiles.*] He could talk like that, don't you know.

RUTH: Yes, he sure could. He was a good man, Mr. Younger.

MAMA: Yes, a fine man—just couldn't never catch up with his dreams, that's all.

[BENEATHA *comes in, brushing her hair and looking up to the ceiling, where the sound of a vacuum cleaner has started up.*]

BENEATHA: What could be so dirty on that woman's rugs that she has to vacuum them every single day?

RUTH: I wish certain young women 'round here who I could name would take inspiration about certain rugs in a certain apartment I could also mention.

BENEATHA: [*Shrugging.*] How much cleaning can a house need, for Christ's sakes.

MAMA: [*Not liking the Lord's name used thus.*] Bennie!

RUTH: Just listen to her—just listen!

BENEATHA: Oh, God!

MAMA: If you use the Lord's name just one more time—

BENEATHA: [*A bit of a whine.*] Oh, Mama—

RUTH: Fresh—just fresh as salt, this girl!

BENEATHA: [*Drily.*] Well—if the salt loses its savor—[4]

MAMA: Now that will do. I just ain't going to have you 'round here reciting the scriptures in vain—you hear me?

BENEATHA: How did I manage to get on everybody's wrong side by just walking into a room?

RUTH: If you weren't so fresh—

BENEATHA: Ruth, I'm twenty years old.

MAMA: What time you be home from school today?

BENEATHA: Kind of late. [*With enthusiasm.*] Madeline is going to start my guitar lessons today.

[MAMA *and* RUTH *look up with the same expression.*]

MAMA: Your *what* kind of lessons?

BENEATHA: Guitar.

RUTH: Oh, Father!

MAMA: How come you done taken it in your mind to learn to play the guitar?

4. See Matthew 5.13: "You are the salt of the earth. But if the salt loses its taste, with what can it be seasoned? It is no longer good for anything but to be thrown out and trampled underfoot."

BENEATHA: I just want to, that's all.

MAMA: [*Smiling.*] Lord, child, don't you know what to do with yourself? How long it going to be before you get tired of this now—like you got tired of that little play-acting group you joined last year? [*Looking at* RUTH.] And what was it the year before that?

RUTH: The horseback-riding club for which she bought that fifty-five-dollar riding habit that's been hanging in the closet ever since!

MAMA: [*To* BENEATHA.] Why you got to flit so from one thing to another, baby?

BENEATHA: [*Sharply.*] I just want to learn to play the guitar. Is there anything wrong with that?

MAMA: Ain't nobody trying to stop you. I just wonders sometimes why you has to flit so from one thing to another all the time. You ain't never done nothing with all that camera equipment you brought home—

BENEATHA: I don't flit! I—I experiment with different forms of expression—

RUTH: Like riding a horse?

BENEATHA: —People have to express themselves one way or another.

MAMA: What is it you want to express?

BENEATHA: [*Angrily.*] Me! [MAMA *and* RUTH *look at each other and burst into raucous laughter.*] Don't worry—I don't expect you to understand.

MAMA: [*To change the subject.*] Who you going out with tomorrow night?

BENEATHA: [*With displeasure.*] George Murchison again.

MAMA: [*Pleased.*] Oh—you getting a little sweet on him?

RUTH: You ask me, this child ain't sweet on nobody but herself— [*Under breath.*] Express herself!

[*They laugh.*]

BENEATHA: Oh—I like George all right, Mama. I mean I like him enough to go out with him and stuff, but—

RUTH: [*For devilment.*] What does *and stuff* mean?

BENEATHA: Mind your own business.

MAMA: Stop picking at her now, Ruth. [*A thoughtful pause, and then a suspicious sudden look at her daughter as she turns in her chair for emphasis.*] What *does* it mean?

BENEATHA: [*Wearily.*] Oh, I just mean I couldn't ever really be serious about George. He's—he's so shallow.

RUTH: Shallow—what do you mean he's shallow? He's *rich!*

MAMA: Hush, Ruth.

BENEATHA: I know he's rich. He knows he's rich, too.

RUTH: Well—what other qualities a man got to have to satisfy you, little girl?

BENEATHA: You wouldn't even begin to understand. Anybody who married Walter could not possibly understand.

MAMA: [*Outraged.*] What kind of way is that to talk about your brother?

BENEATHA: Brother is a flip—let's face it.

MAMA: [*To* RUTH, *helplessly.*] What's a flip?

RUTH: [*Glad to add kindling.*] She's saying he's crazy.

BENEATHA: Not crazy. Brother isn't really crazy yet—he—he's an elaborate neurotic.

MAMA: Hush your mouth!

BENEATHA: As for George. Well. George looks good—he's got a beautiful car and he takes me to nice places and, as my sister-in-law says, he is probably the richest boy I will ever get to know and I even like him sometimes—but if the Youngers are sitting around waiting to see if their little Bennie is going to tie up the family with the Murchisons, they are wasting their time.

RUTH: You mean you wouldn't marry George Murchison if he asked you someday? That pretty, rich thing? Honey, I knew you was odd—

BENEATHA: No I would not marry him if all I felt for him was what I feel now. Besides, George's family wouldn't really like it.

MAMA: Why not?

BENEATHA: Oh, Mama—The Murchisons are honest-to-God-real-*live*-rich colored people, and the only people in the world who are more snobbish than rich white people are rich colored people. I thought everybody knew that. I've met Mrs. Murchison. She's a scene!

MAMA: You must not dislike people 'cause they well off, honey.

BENEATHA: Why not? It makes just as much sense as disliking people 'cause they are poor, and lots of people do that.

RUTH: [*A wisdom-of-the-ages manner. To* MAMA.] Well, she'll get over some of this—

BENEATHA: Get over it? What are you talking about, Ruth? Listen, I'm going to be a doctor. I'm not worried about who I'm going to marry yet—if I ever get married.

MAMA AND RUTH: *If!*

MAMA: Now, Bennie—

BENEATHA: Oh, I probably will . . . but first I'm going to be a doctor, and George, for one, still thinks that's pretty funny. I couldn't be bothered with that. I am going to be a doctor and everybody around here better understand that!

MAMA: [*Kindly.*] 'Course you going to be a doctor, honey, God willing.

BENEATHA: [*Drily.*] God hasn't got a thing to do with it.

MAMA: Beneatha—that just wasn't necessary.

BENEATHA: Well—neither is God. I get sick of hearing about God.

MAMA: Beneatha!

BENEATHA: I mean it! I'm just tired of hearing about God all the time. What has He got to do with anything? Does He pay tuition?

MAMA: You 'bout to get your fresh little jaw slapped!

RUTH: That's just what she needs, all right!

BENEATHA: Why? Why can't I say what I want to around here, like everybody else?

MAMA: It don't sound nice for a young girl to say things like that—you wasn't brought up that way. Me and your father went to trouble to get you and Brother to church every Sunday.

BENEATHA: Mama, you don't understand. It's all a matter of ideas, and God is just one idea I don't accept. It's not important. I am not going out and be immoral or commit crimes because I don't believe in God. I don't even think about it. It's just that I get tired of Him getting credit for all the things the human race achieves through its own stubborn effort. There simply is no blasted God—there is only man and it is he who makes miracles!

[MAMA *absorbs this speech, studies her daughter and rises slowly and crosses to* BENEATHA *and slaps her powerfully across the face. After, there is only silence and the daughter drops her eyes from her mother's face, and* MAMA *is very tall before her.*]

MAMA: Now—you say after me, in my mother's house there is still God. [*There is a long pause and* BENEATHA *stares at the floor wordlessly.* MAMA *repeats the phrase with precision and cool emotion.*] In my mother's house there is still God.

BENEATHA: In my mother's house there is still God.

[*A long pause.*]

MAMA: [*Walking away from* BENEATHA, *too disturbed for triumphant posture. Stopping and turning back to her daughter.*] There are some ideas we ain't going to have in this house. Not long as I am at the head of this family.

BENEATHA: Yes, ma'am.

[MAMA *walks out of the room.*]

RUTH: [*Almost gently, with profound understanding.*] You think you a woman, Bennie—but you still a little girl. What you did was childish—so you got treated like a child.

BENEATHA: I see. [*Quietly.*] I also see that everybody thinks it's all right for Mama to be a tyrant. But all the tyranny in the world will never put a God in the heavens!

[*She picks up her books and goes out.*]

RUTH: [*Goes to* MAMA's *door.*] She said she was sorry.

MAMA: [*Coming out, going to her plant.*] They frightens me, Ruth. My children.

RUTH: You got good children, Lena. They just a little off sometimes—but they're good.

MAMA: No—there's something come down between me and them that don't let us understand each other and I don't know what it is. One done almost lost his mind thinking 'bout money all the time and the other done commence to talk about things I can't seem to understand in no form or fashion. What is it that's changing, Ruth?

RUTH: [*Soothingly, older than her years.*] Now . . . you taking it all too seriously. You just got strong-willed children and it takes a strong woman like you to keep 'em in hand.

MAMA: [*Looking at her plant and sprinkling a little water on it.*] They spirited all right, my children. Got to admit they got spirit—Bennie and Walter. Like this little old plant that ain't never had enough sunshine or nothing—and look at it . . .

[*She has her back to* RUTH, *who has had to stop ironing and lean against something and put the back of her hand to her forehead.*]

RUTH: [*Trying to keep* MAMA *from noticing.*] You . . . sure . . . loves that little old thing, don't you? . . .

MAMA: Well, I always wanted me a garden like I used to see sometimes at the back of the houses down home. This plant is close as I ever got to having one. [*She looks out of the window as she replaces the plant.*] Lord, ain't nothing as dreary as the view from this window on a dreary day, is there? Why ain't you singing this morning, Ruth? Sing that "No Ways Tired." That song always lifts me up so— [*She turns at last to see that* RUTH *has slipped quietly into a chair, in a state of semiconsciousness.*] Ruth! Ruth honey—what's the matter with you . . . Ruth!

[CURTAIN.]

Scene Two

It is the following morning; a Saturday morning, and house cleaning is in progress at the Youngers. Furniture has been shoved hither and yon and MAMA *is giving the kitchen-area walls a washing down.* BENEATHA, *in dungarees, with a handkerchief tied around her face, is spraying insecticide into the cracks in the walls. As they work, the radio is on and a Southside disk-jockey program is inappropriately filling the house with a rather exotic saxophone blues.* TRAVIS, *the sole idle one, is leaning on his arms, looking out of the window.*

TRAVIS: Grandmama, that stuff Bennie is using smells awful. Can I go downstairs, please?

MAMA: Did you get all them chores done already? I ain't seen you doing much.

TRAVIS: Yes'm—finished early. Where did Mama go this morning?

MAMA: [*Looking at* BENEATHA.] She had to go on a little errand.

TRAVIS: Where?

MAMA: To tend to her business.

TRAVIS: Can I go outside then?

MAMA: Oh, I guess so. You better stay right in front of the house, though . . . and keep a good lookout for the postman.

TRAVIS: Yes'm. [*He starts out and decides to give his aunt* BENEATHA *a good swat on the legs as he passes her.*] Leave them poor little old cockroaches alone, they ain't bothering you none.

[*He runs as she swings the spray gun at him both viciously and playfully.* WALTER *enters from the bedroom and goes to the phone.*]

MAMA: Look out there, girl, before you be spilling some of that stuff on that child!

TRAVIS: [*Teasing.*] That's right—look out now!

[*He exits.*]

BENEATHA: [*Drily.*] I can't imagine that it would hurt him—it has never hurt the roaches.

MAMA: Well, little boys' hides ain't as tough as Southside roaches.

WALTER: [*Into phone.*] Hello—Let me talk to Willy Harris.

MAMA: You better get over there behind the bureau. I seen one marching out of there like Napoleon yesterday.

WALTER: Hello, Willy? It ain't come yet. It'll be here in a few minutes. Did the lawyer give you the papers?

BENEATHA: There's really only one way to get rid of them, Mama—

MAMA: How?

BENEATHA: Set fire to this building.

WALTER: Good. Good. I'll be right over.

BENEATHA: Where did Ruth go, Walter?

WALTER: I don't know.

[*He exits abruptly.*]

BENEATHA: Mama, where did Ruth go?

MAMA: [*Looking at her with meaning.*] To the doctor, I think.

BENEATHA: The doctor? What's the matter? [*They exchange glances.*] You don't think—

MAMA: [*With her sense of drama.*] Now I ain't saying what I think. But I ain't never been wrong 'bout a woman neither.

[*The phone rings.*]

BENEATHA: [*At the phone.*] Hay-lo . . . [*Pause, and a moment of recognition.*] Well—when did you get back! . . . And how was it? . . . Of course I've missed you—in my way . . . This morning? No . . . house cleaning and all that and Mama hates it if I let people come over when the house is like this . . . You *have?* Well, that's different . . . What is it—Oh, what the hell, come on over . . . Right, see you then.

[*She hangs up.*]

MAMA: [*Who has listened vigorously, as is her habit.*] Who is that you inviting over here with this house looking like this? You ain't got the pride you was born with!

BENEATHA: Asagai doesn't care how houses look, Mama—he's an intellectual.

MAMA: *Who?*

BENEATHA: Asagai—Joseph Asagai. He's an African boy I met on campus. He's been studying in Canada all summer.

MAMA: What's his name?

BENEATHA: Asagai, Joseph. Ah-sah-guy . . . He's from Nigeria.

MAMA: Oh, that's the little country that was founded by slaves way back . . .

BENEATHA: No, Mama—that's Liberia.

MAMA: I don't think I never met no African before.

BENEATHA: Well, do me a favor and don't ask him a whole lot of ignorant questions about Africans. I mean, do they wear clothes and all that—

MAMA: Well, now, I guess if you think we so ignorant 'round here maybe you shouldn't bring your friends here—

BENEATHA: It's just that people ask such crazy things. All anyone seems to know about when it comes to Africa is Tarzan—

MAMA: [*Indignantly.*] Why should I know anything about Africa?

BENEATHA: Why do you give money at church for the missionary work?

MAMA: Well, that's to help save people.

BENEATHA: You mean save them from *heathenism*—

MAMA: [*Innocently.*] Yes.

BENEATHA: I'm afraid they need more salvation from the British and the French.

[RUTH *comes in forlornly and pulls off her coat with dejection. They both turn to look at her.*]

RUTH: [*Dispiritedly.*] Well, I guess from all the happy faces—everybody knows.

BENEATHA: You pregnant?

MAMA: Lord have mercy, I sure hope it's a little old girl. Travis ought to have a sister.

[BENEATHA *and* RUTH *give her a hopeless look for this grandmotherly enthusiasm.*]

BENEATHA: How far along are you?

RUTH: Two months.

BENEATHA: Did you mean to? I mean did you plan it or was it an accident?

MAMA: What do you know about planning or not planning?

BENEATHA: Oh, Mama.

RUTH: [*Wearily.*] She's twenty years old, Lena.

BENEATHA: Did you plan it, Ruth?

RUTH: Mind your own business.

BENEATHA: It is my business—where is he going to live, on the roof? [*There is silence following the remark as the three women react to the sense of it.*] Gee—I didn't mean that, Ruth, honest. Gee, I don't feel like that at all. I—I think it is wonderful.

RUTH: [*Dully.*] Wonderful.

BENEATHA: Yes—really.

MAMA: [*Looking at* RUTH, *worried.*] Doctor say everything going to be all right?

RUTH: [*Far away.*] Yes—she says everything is going to be fine . . .

MAMA: [*Immediately suspicious.*] "She"—What doctor you went to?

[RUTH *folds over, near hysteria.*]

MAMA: [*Worriedly hovering over* RUTH.] Ruth honey—what's the matter with you—you sick?

[RUTH *has her fists clenched on her thighs and is fighting hard to suppress a scream that seems to be rising in her.*]

BENEATHA: What's the matter with her, Mama?

MAMA: [*Working her fingers in* RUTH'*s shoulder to relax her.*] She be all right. Women gets right depressed sometimes when they get her way. [*Speaking softly, expertly, rapidly.*] Now you just relax. That's right . . . just lean back, don't think 'bout nothing at all . . . nothing at all—

RUTH: I'm all right . . .

[*The glassy-eyed look melts and then she collapses into a fit of heavy sobbing. The bell rings.*]

BENEATHA: Oh, my God—that must be Asagai.

MAMA: [*To* RUTH.] Come on now, honey. You need to lie down and rest awhile . . . then have some nice hot food.

[*They exit,* RUTH'*s weight on her mother-in-law.* BENEATHA, *herself profoundly disturbed, opens the door to admit a rather dramatic-looking young man with a large package.*]

ASAGAI: Hello, Alaiyo—

BENEATHA: [*Holding the door open and regarding him with pleasure.*] Hello . . . [*Long pause.*] Well—come in. And please excuse everything. My mother was very upset about my letting anyone come here with the place like this.

ASAGAI: [*Coming into the room.*] You look disturbed too . . . Is something wrong?

BENEATHA: [*Still at the door, absently.*] Yes . . . we've all got acute ghetto-itus. [*She smiles and comes toward him, finding a cigarette and sitting.*] So—sit down! How was Canada?

ASAGAI: [*A sophisticate.*] Canadian.

BENEATHA: [*Looking at him.*] I'm very glad you are back.

ASAGAI: [*Looking back at her in turn.*] Are you really?

BENEATHA: Yes—very.

ASAGAI: Why—you were quite glad when I went away. What happened?

BENEATHA: You went away.

ASAGAI: Ahhhhhhhh.

BENEATHA: Before—you wanted to be so serious before there was time.

ASAGAI: How much time must there be before one knows what one feels?

BENEATHA: [*Stalling this particular conversation. Her hands pressed together, in a deliberately childish gesture.*] What did you bring me?

ASAGAI: [*Handing her the package.*] Open it and see.

BENEATHA: [*Eagerly opening the package and drawing out some records and the colorful robes of a Nigerian woman.*] Oh, Asagai! . . . You got them for me! . . . How beautiful . . . and the records too! [*She lifts out the robes and runs to the mirror with them and holds the drapery up in front of herself.*]

ASAGAI: [*Coming to her at the mirror.*] I shall have to teach you how to drape it properly. [*He flings the material about her for the moment and stands back to look at her.*] Ah—Oh-pay-gay-day, oh-gbah-mu-shay. [*A Yoruba exclamation for admiration.*] You wear it well . . . very well . . . mutilated hair and all.

BENEATHA: [*Turning suddenly.*] My hair—what's wrong with my hair?

ASAGAI: [*Shrugging.*] Were you born with it like that?

BENEATHA: [*Reaching up to touch it.*] No . . . of course not.

[*She looks back to the mirror, disturbed.*]

ASAGAI: [*Smiling.*] How then?

BENEATHA: You know perfectly well how . . . as crinkly as yours . . . that's how.

ASAGAI: And it is ugly to you that way?

BENEATHA: [*Quickly.*] Oh, no—not ugly . . . [*More slowly, apologetically.*] But it's so hard to manage when it's, well—raw.

ASAGAI: And so to accommodate that—you mutilate it every week?

BENEATHA: It's not mutilation!

ASAGAI: [*Laughing aloud at her seriousness.*] Oh . . . please! I am only teasing you because you are so very serious about these things. [*He stands back from her and folds his arms across his chest as he watches her pulling at her hair and frowning in the mirror.*] Do you remember the first time you met me at school? . . . [*He laughs.*] You came up to me and you said—and I thought you were the most serious little thing I had ever seen—you said: [*He imitates her.*] "Mr. Asagai—I want very much to talk with you. About Africa. You see, Mr. Asagai, I am looking for my *identity*!"

[*He laughs.*]

BENEATHA: [*Turning to him, not laughing.*] Yes—

[*Her face is quizzical, profoundly disturbed.*]

ASAGAI: [*Still teasing and reaching out and taking her face in his hands and turning her profile to him.*] Well . . . it is true that this is not so much a profile of a

Hollywood queen as perhaps a queen of the Nile— [*A mock dismissal of the importance of the question.*] But what does it matter? Assimilationism is so popular in your country.

BENEATHA: [*Wheeling, passionately, sharply.*] I am not an assimilationist!

ASAGAI: [*The protest hangs in the room for a moment and* ASAGAI *studies her, his laughter fading.*] Such a serious one. [*There is a pause.*] So—you like the robes? You must take excellent care of them—they are from my sister's personal wardrobe.

BENEATHA: [*With incredulity.*] You—you sent all the way home—for me?

ASAGAI: [*With charm.*] For you—I would do much more . . . Well, that is what I came for. I must go.

BENEATHA: Will you call me Monday?

ASAGAI: Yes . . . We have a great deal to talk about. I mean about identity and time and all that.

BENEATHA: Time?

ASAGAI: Yes. About how much time one needs to know what one feels.

BENEATHA: You never understood that there is more than one kind of feeling which can exist between a man and a woman—or, at least, there should be.

ASAGAI: [*Shaking his head negatively but gently.*] No. Between a man and a woman there need be only one kind of feeling. I have that for you . . . Now even . . . right this moment . . .

BENEATHA: I know—and by itself—it won't do. I can find that anywhere.

ASAGAI: For a woman it should be enough.

BENEATHA: I know—because that's what it says in all the novels that men write. But it isn't. Go ahead and laugh—but I'm not interested in being someone's little episode in America or— [*With feminine vengeance.*] —one of them! [ASAGAI *has burst into laughter again.*] That's funny as hell, huh!

ASAGAI: It's just that every American girl I have known has said that to me. White—black—in this you are all the same. And the same speech, too!

BENEATHA: [*Angrily.*] Yuk, yuk, yuk!

ASAGAI: It's how you can be sure that the world's most liberated women are not liberated at all. You all talk about it too much!

[MAMA *enters and is immediately all social charm because of the presence of a guest.*]

BENEATHA: Oh—Mama—this is Mr. Asagai.

MAMA: How do you do?

ASAGAI: [*Total politeness to an elder.*] How do you do, Mrs. Younger. Please forgive me for coming at such an outrageous hour on a Saturday.

MAMA: Well, you are quite welcome. I just hope you understand that our house don't always look like this. [*Chatterish.*] You must come again. I would love to hear all about— [*Not sure of the name.*] —your country. I think it's so sad the way our American Negroes don't know nothing about Africa 'cept Tarzan and all that. And all that money they pour into these churches when they ought to be helping you people over there drive out them French and Englishmen done taken away your land.

[*The mother flashes a slightly superior look at her daughter upon completion of the recitation.*]

ASAGAI: [*Taken aback by this sudden and acutely unrelated expression of sympathy.*] Yes . . . yes . . .

MAMA: [*Smiling at him suddenly and relaxing and looking him over.*] How many miles is it from here to where you come from?

ASAGAI: Many thousands.

MAMA: [*Looking at him as she would* WALTER.] I bet you don't half look after yourself, being away from your mama either. I spec you better come 'round here from time to time and get yourself some decent home-cooked meals . . .

ASAGAI: [*Moved.*] Thank you. Thank you very much. [*They are all quiet, then—*] Well . . . I must go. I will call you Monday, Alaiyo.

MAMA: What's that he call you?

ASAGAI: Oh—"Alaiyo." I hope you don't mind. It is what you would call a nickname, I think. It is a Yoruba word. I am a Yoruba.

MAMA: [*Looking at* BENEATHA.] I—I thought he was from—

ASAGAI: [*Understanding.*] Nigeria is my country. Yoruba is my tribal origin—

BENEATHA: You didn't tell us what Alaiyo means . . . for all I know—you might be calling me Little Idiot or something . . .

ASAGAI: Well . . . let me see . . . I do not know how just to explain it . . . The sense of a thing can be so different when it changes languages.

BENEATHA: You're evading.

ASAGAI: No—really it is difficult . . . [*Thinking.*] It means . . . it means One for Whom Bread—Food—Is Not Enough. [*He looks at her.*] Is that all right?

BENEATHA: [*Understanding, softly.*] Thank you.

MAMA: [*Looking from one to the other and not understanding any of it.*] Well . . . that's nice . . . You must come see us again—Mr.—

ASAGAI: Ah-sah-guy . . .

MAMA: Yes . . . Do come again.

ASAGAI: Good-bye.

[*He exits.*]

MAMA: [*After him.*] Lord, that's a pretty thing just went out here! [*Insinuatingly, to her daughter.*] Yes, I guess I see why we done commence to get so interested in Africa 'round here. Missionaries my aunt Jenny!

[*She exits.*]

BENEATHA: Oh, Mama! . . .

[*She picks up the Nigerian dress and holds it up to her in front of the mirror again. She sets the headdress on haphazardly and then notices her hair again and clutches at it and then replaces the headdress and frowns at herself. Then she starts to wriggle in front of the mirror as she thinks a Nigerian woman might.* TRAVIS *enters and regards her.*]

TRAVIS: You cracking up?

BENEATHA: Shut up.

[*She pulls the headdress off and looks at herself in the mirror and clutches at her hair again and squinches her eyes as if trying to imagine something. Then, suddenly, she gets her raincoat and kerchief and hurriedly prepares for going out.*]

MAMA: [*Coming back into the room.*] She's resting now. Travis, baby, run next door and ask Miss Johnson to please let me have a little kitchen cleanser. This here can is empty as Jacob's kettle.

TRAVIS: I just came in.

MAMA: Do as you told. [*He exits and she looks at her daughter.*] Where you going?

BENEATHA: [*Halting at the door.*] To become a queen of the Nile!

[*She exits in a breathless blaze of glory.* RUTH *appears in the bedroom doorway.*]

MAMA: Who told you to get up?

RUTH: Ain't nothing wrong with me to be lying in no bed for. Where did Bennie go?

MAMA: [*Drumming her fingers.*] Far as I could make out—to Egypt. [RUTH *just looks at her.*] What time is it getting to?

RUTH: Ten twenty. And the mailman going to ring that bell this morning just like he done every morning for the last umpteen years.

[TRAVIS *comes in with the cleanser can.*]

TRAVIS: She say to tell you that she don't have much.

MAMA: [*Angrily.*] Lord, some people I could name sure is tight-fisted! [*Directing her grandson.*] Mark two cans of cleanser down on the list there. If she that hard up for kitchen cleanser, I sure don't want to forget to get her none!

RUTH: Lena—maybe the woman is just short on cleanser—

MAMA: [*Not listening.*] —Much baking powder as she done borrowed from me all these years, she could of done gone into the baking business!

[*The bell sounds suddenly and sharply and all three are stunned—serious and silent—mid-speech. In spite of all the other conversations and distractions of the morning, this is what they have been waiting for, even* TRAVIS, *who looks helplessly from his mother to his grandmother.* RUTH *is the first to come to life again.*]

RUTH: [*To* TRAVIS.] *Get down them steps, boy!*

[TRAVIS *snaps to life and flies out to get the mail.*]

MAMA: [*Her eyes wide, her hand to her breast.*] You mean it done really come?

RUTH: [*Excited.*] Oh, Miss Lena!

MAMA: [*Collecting herself.*] Well ... I don't know what we all so excited about 'round here for. We known it was coming for months.

RUTH: That's a whole lot different from having it come and being able to hold it in your hands ... a piece of paper worth ten thousand dollars ... [TRAVIS *bursts back into the room. He holds the envelope high above his head, like a little dancer, his face is radiant and he is breathless. He moves to his grandmother with sudden slow ceremony and puts the envelope into her hands. She accepts it, and then merely holds it and looks at it.*] Come on! Open it ... Lord have mercy, I wish Walter Lee was here!

TRAVIS: Open it, Grandmama!

MAMA: [*Staring at it.*] Now you all be quiet. It's just a check.

RUTH: Open it ...

MAMA: [*Still staring at it.*] Now don't act silly ... We ain't never been no people to act silly 'bout no money—

RUTH: [*Swiftly.*] We ain't never had none before—*open it!*

[MAMA *finally makes a good strong tear and pulls out the thin blue slice of paper and inspects it closely. The boy and his mother study it raptly over* MAMA's *shoulders.*]

MAMA: *Travis!* [*She is counting off with doubt.*] Is that the right number of zeros.

TRAVIS: Yes'm ... ten thousand dollars. Gaalee, Grandmama, you rich.

MAMA: [*She holds the check away from her, still looking at it. Slowly her face sobers into a mask of unhappiness.*] Ten thousand dollars. [*She hands it to* RUTH.] Put it away somewhere, Ruth. [*She does not look at* RUTH; *her eyes seem to be seeing something somewhere very far off.*] Ten thousand dollars they give you. Ten thousand dollars.

TRAVIS: [*To his mother, sincerely.*] What's the matter with Grandmama—don't she want to be rich?

RUTH: [*Distractedly.*] You go on out and play now, baby. [TRAVIS *exits.* MAMA *starts wiping dishes absently, humming intently to herself.* RUTH *turns to her, with kind exasperation.*] You've gone and got yourself upset.

MAMA: [*Not looking at her.*] I spec if it wasn't for you all ... I would just put that money away or give it to the church or something.

RUTH: Now what kind of talk is that. Mr. Younger would just be plain mad if he could hear you talking foolish like that.

MAMA: [*Stopping and staring off.*] Yes . . . he sure would. [*Sighing.*] We got enough to do with that money, all right. [*She halts then, and turns and looks at her daughter-in-law hard;* RUTH *avoids her eyes and* MAMA *wipes her hands with finality and starts to speak firmly to* RUTH.] Where did you go today, girl?

RUTH: To the doctor.

MAMA: [*Impatiently.*] Now, Ruth . . . you know better than that. Old Doctor Jones is strange enough in his way but there ain't nothing 'bout him make somebody slip and call him "she"—like you done this morning.

RUTH: Well, that's what happened—my tongue slipped.

MAMA: You went to see that woman, didn't you?

RUTH: [*Defensively, giving herself away.*] What woman you talking about?

MAMA: [*Angrily.*] That woman who—

[WALTER *enters in great excitement.*]

WALTER: Did it come?

MAMA: [*Quietly.*] Can't you give people a Christian greeting before you start asking about money?

WALTER: [*To* RUTH.] Did it come? [RUTH *unfolds the check and lays it quietly before him, watching him intently with thoughts of her own.* WALTER *sits down and grasps it close and counts off the zeros.*] Ten thousand dollars— [*He turns suddenly, frantically to his mother and draws some papers out of his breast pocket.*] Mama—look. Old Willy Harris put everything on paper—

MAMA: Son—I think you ought to talk to your wife . . . I'll go on out and leave you alone if you want—

WALTER: I can talk to her later—Mama, look—

MAMA: Son—

WALTER: WILL SOMEBODY PLEASE LISTEN TO ME TODAY!

MAMA: [*Quietly.*] I don't 'low no yellin' in this house, Walter Lee, and you know it— [WALTER *stares at them in frustration and starts to speak several times.*] And there ain't going to be no investing in no liquor stores. I don't aim to have to speak on that again.

[*A long pause.*]

WALTER: Oh—so you don't aim to have to speak on that again? So you have decided . . . [*Crumpling his papers.*] Well, *you* tell that to my boy tonight when you put him to sleep on the living-room couch . . . [*Turning to* MAMA *and speaking directly to her.*] Yeah—and tell it to my wife, Mama, tomorrow when she has to go out of here to look after somebody else's kids. And tell it to *me*, Mama, every time we need a new pair of curtains and I have to watch *you* go out and work in somebody's kitchen. Yeah, you tell me then!

[WALTER *starts out.*]

RUTH: Where you going?

WALTER: I'm going out!

RUTH: Where?

WALTER: Just out of this house somewhere—

RUTH: [*Getting her coat.*] I'll come too.

WALTER: I don't want you to come!

RUTH: I got something to talk to you about, Walter.

WALTER: That's too bad.

MAMA: [*Still quietly.*] Walter Lee— [*She waits and he finally turns and looks at her.*] Sit down.

WALTER: I'm a grown man, Mama.

MAMA: Ain't nobody said you wasn't grown. But you still in my house and my presence. And as long as you are—you'll talk to your wife civil. Now sit down.

RUTH: [*Suddenly.*] Oh, let him go on out and drink himself to death! He makes me sick to my stomach! [*She flings her coat against him.*]

WALTER: [*Violently.*] And you turn mine too, baby! [RUTH *goes into their bedroom and slams the door behind her.*] That was my greatest mistake—

MAMA: [*Still quietly.*] Walter, what is the matter with you?

WALTER: Matter with me? Ain't nothing the matter with *me*!

MAMA: Yes there is. Something eating you up like a crazy man. Something more than me not giving you this money. The past few years I been watching it happen to you. You get all nervous acting and kind of wild in the eyes—[WALTER *jumps up impatiently at her words.*] I said sit there now, I'm talking to you!

WALTER: Mama—I don't need no nagging at me today.

MAMA: Seem like you getting to a place where you always tied up in some kind of knot about something. But if anybody ask you 'bout it you just yell at 'em and bust out the house and go out and drink somewheres. Walter Lee, people can't live with that. Ruth's a good, patient girl in her way—but you getting to be too much. Boy, don't make the mistake of driving that girl away from you.

WALTER: Why—what she do for me?

MAMA: She loves you.

WALTER: Mama—I'm going out. I want to go off somewhere and be by myself for a while.

MAMA: I'm sorry 'bout your liquor store, son. It just wasn't the thing for us to do. That's what I want to tell you about—

WALTER: I got to go out, Mama—

[*He rises.*]

MAMA: It's dangerous, son.

WALTER: What's dangerous?

MAMA: When a man goes outside his home to look for peace.

WALTER: [*Beseechingly.*] Then why can't there never be no peace in this house then?

MAMA: You done found it in some other house?

WALTER: No—there ain't no woman! Why do women always think there's a woman somewhere when a man gets restless. [*Coming to her.*] Mama—Mama—I want so many things . . .

MAMA: Yes, son—

WALTER: I want so many things that they are driving me kind of crazy . . . Mama—look at me.

MAMA: I'm looking at you. You a good-looking boy. You got a job, a nice wife, a fine boy and—

WALTER: A job. [*Looks at her.*] Mama, a job? I open and close car doors all day long. I drive a man around in his limousine and I say, "Yes, sir; no, sir; very good, sir; shall I take the Drive, sir?" Mama, that ain't no kind of job . . . that ain't nothing at all. [*Very quietly.*] Mama, I don't know if I can make you understand.

MAMA: Understand what, baby?

WALTER: [*Quietly.*] Sometimes it's like I can see the future stretched out in front of me—just plain as day. The future, Mama. Hanging over there at the edge of my days. Just waiting for me—a big, looming blank space—full of *nothing.* Just waiting for *me.* [*Pause.*] Mama—sometimes when I'm downtown and I pass them cool, quiet-looking restaurants where them white boys are sitting back and talking 'bout things . . . sitting there turning deals worth millions of dollars . . . sometimes I see guys don't look much older than me—

MAMA: Son—how come you talk so much 'bout money?

WALTER: [*With immense passion.*] Because it is life, Mama!

MAMA: [*Quietly.*] Oh— [*Very quietly.*] So now it's life. Money is life. Once upon a time freedom used to be life—now it's money. I guess the world really do change . . .

WALTER: No—it was always money, Mama. We just didn't know about it.

MAMA: No . . . something has changed. [*She looks at him.*] You something new, boy. In my time we was worried about not being lynched and getting to the North if we could and how to stay alive and still have a pinch of dignity too . . . Now here come you and Beneatha—talking 'bout things we ain't never even thought about hardly, me and your daddy. You ain't satisfied or proud of nothing we done. I mean that you had a home; that we kept you out of trouble till you was grown; that you don't have to ride to work on the back of nobody's streetcar—You my children—but how different we done become.

WALTER: You just don't understand, Mama, you just don't understand.

MAMA: Son—do you know your wife is expecting another baby? [WALTER *stands, stunned, and absorbs what his mother has said.*] That's what she wanted to talk to you about. [WALTER *sinks down into a chair.*] This ain't for me to be telling—but you ought to know. [*She waits.*] I think Ruth is thinking 'bout getting rid of that child.[5]

WALTER: [*Slowly understanding.*] No—no—Ruth wouldn't do that.

MAMA: When the world gets ugly enough—a woman will do anything for her family. *The part that's already living.*

WALTER: You don't know Ruth, Mama, if you think she would do that.

[RUTH *opens the bedroom door and stands there a little limp.*]

RUTH: [*Beaten.*] Yes I would too, Walter. [*Pause.*] I gave her a five-dollar down payment.

[*There is total silence as the man stares at his wife and the mother stares at her son.*]

MAMA: [*Presently.*] Well— [*Tightly.*] Well—son, I'm waiting to hear you say something . . . I'm waiting to hear how you be your father's son. Be the man he was . . . [*Pause.*] Your wife say she going to destroy your child. And I'm waiting to hear you talk like him and say we a people who give children life, not who destroys them— [*She rises.*] I'm waiting to see you stand up and look like your daddy and say we done give up one baby to poverty and that we ain't going to give up nary another one . . . I'm waiting.

WALTER: Ruth—

MAMA: If you a son of mine, tell her! [WALTER *turns, looks at her and can say nothing. She continues, bitterly.*] You . . . you are a disgrace to your father's memory. Somebody get me my hat.

[CURTAIN.]

ACT II

Scene One

Time: Later the same day.

At rise: RUTH *is ironing again. She has the radio going. Presently* BENEATHA's *bedroom door opens and* RUTH's *mouth falls and she puts down the iron in fascination.*

RUTH: What have we got on tonight!

BENEATHA: [*Emerging grandly from the doorway so that we can see her thoroughly robed in the costume* ASAGAI *brought.*] You are looking at what a well-dressed Nigerian woman wears— [*She parades for* RUTH, *her hair completely hidden by the headdress; she is coquettishly fanning herself with an ornate oriental fan,*

---

5. Abortions were illegal and dangerous in the United States at that time.

mistakenly more like Butterfly⁶ than any Nigerian that ever was.] Isn't it beautiful? [*She promenades to the radio and, with an arrogant flourish, turns off the good loud blues that is playing.*] Enough of this assimilationist junk! [RUTH *follows her with her eyes as she goes to the phonograph and puts on a record and turns and waits ceremoniously for the music to come up. Then, with a shout—*] OCOMOGOSIAY!

[RUTH *jumps. The music comes up, a lovely Nigerian melody.* BENEATHA *listens, enraptured, her eyes far away—"back to the past." She begins to dance.* RUTH *is dumbfounded.*]

RUTH: What kind of dance is that?
BENEATHA: A folk dance.
RUTH: [*Pearl Bailey.*]⁷ What kind of folks do that, honey?
BENEATHA: It's from Nigeria. It's a dance of welcome.
RUTH: Who you welcoming?
BENEATHA: The men back to the village.
RUTH: Where they been?
BENEATHA: How should I know—out hunting or something. Anyway, they are coming back now . . .
RUTH: Well, that's good.
BENEATHA: [*With the record.*]

*Alundi, alundi
Alundi alunya
Jop pu a jeepua
Ang gu sooooooooooo*

*Ai yai yae . . .
Ayehaye—alundi . . .*

[WALTER *comes in during this performance; he has obviously been drinking. He leans against the door heavily and watches his sister, at first with distaste. Then his eyes look off—"back to the past"—as he lifts both his fists to the roof, screaming.*]

WALTER: YEAH . . . AND ETHIOPIA STRETCH FORTH HER HANDS AGAIN! . . .⁸
RUTH: [*Drily, looking at him.*] Yes—and Africa sure is claiming her own tonight. [*She gives them both up and starts ironing again.*]

---

6. Madame Butterfly, a Japanese woman married to and then abandoned by an American man in the opera *Madama Butterfly* (1904), by the Italian composer Giacomo Puccini (1858–1924).
7. That is, in the manner of the popular African American singer and entertainer (1918–90).
8. See Psalms 68.31: "Princes shall come out of Egypt; Ethiopia shall soon stretch out her hands unto God."

WALTER: [*All in a drunken, dramatic shout.*] Shut up! ... I'm digging them drums ... them drums move me! ... [*He makes his weaving way to his wife's face and leans in close to her.*] In my heart of hearts— [*He thumps his chest.*] —I am much warrior!

RUTH: [*Without even looking up.*] In your heart of hearts you are much drunkard.

WALTER: [*Coming away from her and starting to wander around the room, shouting.*] Me and Jomo ... [*Intently, in his sister's face. She has stopped dancing to watch him in this unknown mood.*] That's my man, Kenyatta.[9] [*Shouting and thumping his chest.*] FLAMING SPEAR! HOT DAMN! [*He is suddenly in possession of an imaginary spear and actively spearing enemies all over the room.*] OCOMOGOSIAY ... THE LION IS WAKING ... OWIMOWEH! [*He pulls his shirt open and leaps up on a table and gestures with his spear. The bell rings.* RUTH *goes to answer.*]

BENEATHA: [*To encourage* WALTER, *thoroughly caught up with this side of him.*] OCOMOGOSIAY, FLAMING SPEAR!

WALTER: [*On the table, very far gone, his eyes pure glass sheets. He sees what we cannot, that he is a leader of his people, a great chief, a descendant of Chaka,*[1] *and that the hour to march has come.*] Listen, my black brothers—

BENEATHA: OCOMOGOSIAY!

WALTER: —Doyouhearthewatersrushingagainsttheshoresofthecoastlands—

BENEATHA: OCOMOGOSIAY!

WALTER: —Do you hear the screeching of the cocks in yonder hills beyond where the chiefs meet in council for the coming of the mighty war—

BENEATHA: OCOMOGOSIAY!

WALTER: —Do you hear the beating of the wings of the birds flying low over the mountains and the low places of our land—

[RUTH *opens the door.* GEORGE MURCHISON *enters.*]

BENEATHA: OCOMOGOSIAY!

WALTER: —Do you hear the singing of the women, singing the war songs of our fathers to the babies in the great houses ... singing the sweet war songs? OH, DO YOU HEAR, MY BLACK BROTHERS!

BENEATHA: [*Completely gone.*] We hear you, Flaming Spear—

WALTER: Telling us to prepare for the greatness of the time— [*To* GEORGE.] Black Brother!

[*He extends his hand for the fraternal clasp.*]

GEORGE: Black Brother, hell!

---

9. Jomo Kenyatta (1893–1978), African political leader and first president of Kenya (1964–78).
1. Zulu chief (1786–1828), also known as "Shaka" and called "The Black Napoleon" for his strategic and organizational genius.

RUTH: [*Having had enough, and embarrassed for the family.*] Beneatha, you got company—what's the matter with you? Walter Lee Younger, get down off that table and stop acting like a fool ...

[WALTER *comes down off the table suddenly and makes a quick exit to the bathroom.*]

RUTH: He's had a little to drink ... I don't know what her excuse is.

GEORGE: [*To* BENEATHA.] Look honey, we're going *to* the theatre—we're not going to be *in* it ... so go change, huh?

RUTH: You expect this boy to go out with you looking like that?

BENEATHA:[*Looking at*GEORGE.]That's up to George.If he's ashamed of his heritage—

GEORGE: Oh, don't be so proud of yourself, Bennie—just because you look eccentric.

BENEATHA: How can something that's natural be eccentric?

GEORGE: That's what being eccentric means—being natural. Get dressed.

BENEATHA: I don't like that, George.

RUTH: Why must you and your brother make an argument out of everything people say?

BENEATHA: Because I hate assimilationist Negroes!

RUTH: Will somebody please tell me what assimila-who-ever means!

GEORGE: Oh, it's just a college girl's way of calling people Uncle Toms—but that isn't what it means at all.

RUTH: Well, what does it mean?

BENEATHA: [*Cutting* GEORGE *off and staring at him as she replies to* RUTH.] It means someone who is willing to give up his own culture and submerge himself completely in the dominant, and in this case, *oppressive* culture!

GEORGE: Oh, dear, dear, dear! Here we go! A lecture on the African past! On our Great West African Heritage! In one second we will hear all about the great Ashanti empires; the great Songhay civilizations; and the great sculpture of Bénin—and then some poetry in the Bantu—and the whole monologue will end with the word *heritage!* [*Nastily.*] Let's face it, baby, your heritage is nothing but a bunch of raggedy-assed spirituals and some grass huts!

BENEATHA: *Grass huts!* [RUTH *crosses to her and forcibly pushes her toward the bedroom.*] See there ... you are standing there in your splendid ignorance talking about people who were the first to smelt iron on the face of the earth! [RUTH *is pushing her through the door.*] The Ashanti were performing surgical operations when the English— [RUTH *pulls the door to, with* BENEATHA *on the other side, and smiles graciously at* GEORGE. BENEATHA *opens the door and shouts the end of the sentence defiantly at* GEORGE.] —were still tattooing themselves with blue dragons ... [*She goes back inside.*]

RUTH: Have a seat, George. [*They both sit.* RUTH *folds her hands rather primly on her lap, determined to demonstrate the civilization of the family.*] Warm, ain't it? I mean for September. [*Pause.*] Just like they always say about Chicago weather: If it's too hot or cold for you, just wait a minute and it'll change. [*She smiles happily at this cliché of clichés.*] Everybody say it's got to do with them bombs and things they keep setting off.[2] [*Pause.*] Would you like a nice cold beer?

GEORGE: No, thank you. I don't care for beer. [*He looks at his watch.*] I hope she hurries up.

RUTH: What time is the show?

GEORGE: It's an eight-thirty curtain. That's just Chicago, though. In New York standard curtain time is eight forty.

[*He is rather proud of this knowledge.*]

RUTH: [*Properly appreciating it.*] You get to New York a lot?

GEORGE: [*Offhand.*] Few times a year.

RUTH: Oh—that's nice. I've never been to New York.

[WALTER *enters. We feel he has relieved himself, but the edge of unreality is still with him.*]

WALTER: New York ain't got nothing Chicago ain't. Just a bunch of hustling people all squeezed up together—being "Eastern."

[*He turns his face into a screw of displeasure.*]

GEORGE: Oh—you've been?

WALTER: *Plenty* of times.

RUTH: [*Shocked at the lie.*] Walter Lee Younger!

WALTER: [*Staring her down.*] Plenty! [*Pause.*] What we got to drink in this house? Why don't you offer this man some refreshment. [*To* GEORGE.] They don't know how to entertain people in this house, man.

GEORGE: Thank you—I don't really care for anything.

WALTER: [*Feeling his head; sobriety coming.*] Where's Mama?

RUTH: She ain't come back yet.

WALTER: [*Looking* MURCHISON *over from head to toe, scrutinizing his carefully casual tweed sports jacket over cashmere V-neck sweater over soft eyelet shirt and tie, and soft slacks, finished off with white buckskin shoes.*] Why all you college boys wear them fairyish-looking white shoes?

RUTH: Walter Lee!

[GEORGE MURCHISON *ignores the remark.*]

WALTER: [*To* RUTH.] Well, they look crazy as hell—white shoes, cold as it is.

RUTH: [*Crushed.*] You have to excuse him—

WALTER: No he don't! Excuse me for what? What you always excusing me for! I'll excuse myself when I needs to be excused! [*A pause.*] They look as

2. In the 1950s, people commonly blamed weather fluctuations on atomic testing.

funny as them black knee socks Beneatha wears out of here all the
time.

RUTH: It's the college *style*, Walter.

WALTER: Style, hell, She looks like she got burnt legs or something!

RUTH: Oh, Walter—

WALTER: [*An irritable mimic.*] Oh, Walter! Oh, Walter! [*To* MURCHISON.] How's
your old man making out? I understand you all going to buy that big
hotel on the Drive?[3] [*He finds a beer in the refrigerator, wanders over to*
MURCHISON, *sipping and wiping his lips with the back of his hand, and straddling
a chair backwards to talk to the other man.*] Shrewd move. Your old man is all
right, man. [*Tapping his head and half winking for emphasis.*] I mean he
knows how to operate. I mean he thinks *big*, you know what I mean, I
mean for a *home*, you know? But I think he's kind of running out of ideas
now. I'd like to talk to him. Listen, man, I got some plans that could turn
this city upside down. I mean I think like he does. *Big.* Invest big, gamble
big, hell, lose *big* if you have to, you know what I mean. It's hard to find a
man on this whole Southside who understands my kind of thinking—
you dig? [*He scrutinizes* MURCHISON *again, drinks his beer, squints his eyes and
leans in close, confidential, man to man.*] Me and you ought to sit down and
talk sometimes, man. Man, I got me some ideas . . .

GEORGE: [*With boredom.*] Yeah—sometimes we'll have to do that, Walter.

WALTER: [*Understanding the indifference, and offended.*] Yeah—well, when you
get the time, man. I know you a busy little boy.

RUTH: Walter, please—

WALTER: [*Bitterly, hurt.*] I know ain't nothing in this world as busy as you
colored college boys with your fraternity pins and white shoes . . .

RUTH: [*Covering her face with humiliation.*] Oh, Walter Lee—

WALTER: I see you all the time—with the books tucked under your arms—
going to your [*British A—a mimic.*] "clahsses." And for what! What the
hell you learning over there? Filling up your heads— [*Counting off on his
fingers.*] —with the sociology and the psychology—but they teaching you
how to be a man? How to take over and run the world? They teaching
you how to run a rubber plantation or a steel mill? Naw—just to talk
proper and read books and wear white shoes . . .

GEORGE: [*Looking at him with distaste, a little above it all.*] You're all wacked up
with bitterness, man.

WALTER: [*Intently, almost quietly, between the teeth, glaring at the boy.*] And you—
ain't you bitter, man? Ain't you just about had it yet? Don't you see no
stars gleaming that you can't reach out and grab? You happy?—You contented son-of-a-bitch—you happy? You got it made? Bitter? Man, I'm a
volcano. Bitter? Here I am a giant—surrounded by ants! Ants who can't
even understand what it is the giant is talking about.

---

3. Lake Shore Drive, a scenic thoroughfare along Lake Michigan.

RUTH: [*Passionately and suddenly.*] Oh, Walter—ain't you with nobody!

WALTER: [*Violently.*] No! 'Cause ain't nobody with me! Not even my own mother!

RUTH: Walter, that's a terrible thing to say!

[BENEATHA *enters, dressed for the evening in a cocktail dress and earrings.*]

GEORGE: Well—hey, you look great.

BENEATHA: Let's go, George. See you all later.

RUTH: Have a nice time.

GEORGE: Thanks. Good night. [*To* WALTER, *sarcastically.*] Good night, *Prometheus.*[4]

[BENEATHA *and* GEORGE *exit.*]

WALTER: [*To* RUTH.] Who is Prometheus?

RUTH: I don't know. Don't worry about it.

WALTER: [*In fury, pointing after* GEORGE.] See there—they get to a point where they can't insult you man to man—they got to go talk about something ain't nobody never heard of!

RUTH: How do you know it was an insult? [*To humor him.*] Maybe Prometheus is a nice fellow.

WALTER: Prometheus! I bet there ain't even no such thing! I bet that simple-minded clown—

RUTH: Walter—

[*She stops what she is doing and looks at him.*]

WALTER: [*Yelling.*] Don't start!

RUTH: Start what?

WALTER: Your nagging! Where was I? Who was I with? How much money did I spend?

RUTH: [*Plaintively.*] Walter Lee—why don't we just try to talk about it . . .

WALTER: [*Not listening.*] I been out talking with people who understand me. People who care about the things I got on my mind.

RUTH: [*Wearily.*] I guess that means people like Willy Harris.

WALTER: Yes, people like Willy Harris.

RUTH: [*With a sudden flash of impatience.*] Why don't you all just hurry up and go into the banking business and stop talking about it!

WALTER: Why? You want to know why? 'Cause we all tied up in a race of people that don't know how to do nothing but moan, pray and have babies!

[*The line is too bitter even for him and he looks at her and sits down.*]

---

4. In Greek mythology, Prometheus represented the bold creative spirit; he stole fire from Olympus (the locale of the gods) and gave it to humankind.

RUTH: Oh, Walter . . . [*Softly.*] Honey, why can't you stop fighting me?

WALTER: [*Without thinking.*] Who's fighting you? Who even cares about you?

[*This line begins the retardation of his mood.*]

RUTH: Well— [*She waits a long time, and then with resignation starts to put away her things.*] I guess I might as well go on to bed . . . [*More or less to herself.*] I don't know where we lost it . . . but we have . . . [*Then, to him.*] I—I'm sorry about this new baby, Walter. I guess maybe I better go on and do what I started . . . I guess I just didn't realize how bad things was with us . . . I guess I just didn't really realize— [*She starts out to the bedroom and stops.*] You want some hot milk?

WALTER: Hot milk?

RUTH: Yes—hot milk.

WALTER: Why hot milk?

RUTH: 'Cause after all that liquor you come home with you ought to have something hot in your stomach.

WALTER: I don't want no milk.

RUTH: You want some coffee then?

WALTER: No, I don't want no coffee. I don't want nothing hot to drink. [*Almost plaintively.*] Why you always trying to give me something to eat?

RUTH: [*Standing and looking at him helplessly.*] What else can I give you, Walter Lee Younger?

[*She stands and looks at him and presently turns to go out again. He lifts his head and watches her going away from him in a new mood which began to emerge when he asked her "Who cares about you?"*]

WALTER: It's been rough, ain't it, baby? [*She hears and stops but does not turn around and he continues to her back.*] I guess between two people there ain't never as much understood as folks generally thinks there is. I mean like between me and you— [*She turns to face him.*] How we gets to the place where we scared to talk softness to each other. [*He waits, thinking hard himself.*] Why you think it got to be like that? [*He is thoughtful, almost as a child would be.*] Ruth, what is it gets into people ought to be close?

RUTH: I don't know, honey. I think about it a lot.

WALTER: On account of you and me, you mean? The way things are with us. The way something done come down between us.

RUTH: There ain't so much between us, Walter . . . Not when you come to me and try to talk to me. Try to be with me . . . a little even.

WALTER: [*Total honesty.*] Sometimes . . . sometimes . . . I don't even know how to try.

RUTH: Walter—

WALTER: Yes?

RUTH: [*Coming to him, gently and with misgiving, but coming to him.*] Honey . . . life don't have to be like this. I mean sometimes people can do things so that things are better . . . You remember how we used to talk when Travis was born . . . about the way we were going to live . . . the kind of house . . . [*She is stroking his head.*] Well, it's all starting to slip away from us . . .

[MAMA *enters, and* WALTER *jumps up and shouts at her.*]

WALTER: Mama, where have you been?

MAMA: My—them steps is longer than they used to be. Whew! [*She sits down and ignores him.*] How you feeling this evening, Ruth?

[RUTH *shrugs, disturbed some at having been prematurely interrupted and watching her husband knowingly.*]

WALTER: Mama, where have you been all day?

MAMA: [*Still ignoring him and leaning on the table and changing to more comfortable shoes.*] Where's Travis?

RUTH: I let him go out earlier and he ain't come back yet. Boy, is he going to get it!

WALTER: Mama!

MAMA: [*As if she has heard him for the first time.*] Yes, son?

WALTER: Where did you go this afternoon?

MAMA: I went downtown to tend to some business that I had to tend to.

WALTER: What kind of business?

MAMA: You know better than to question me like a child, Brother.

WALTER: [*Rising and bending over the table.*] Where were you, Mama? [*Bringing his fists down and shouting.*] Mama, you didn't go do something with that insurance money, something crazy?

[*The front door opens slowly, interrupting him, and* TRAVIS *peeks his head in, less than hopefully.*]

TRAVIS: [*To his mother.*] Mama, I—

RUTH: "Mama I" nothing! You're going to get it, boy! Get on in that bedroom and get yourself ready!

TRAVIS: But I—

MAMA: Why don't you all never let the child explain hisself.

RUTH: Keep out of it now, Lena.

[MAMA *clamps her lips together, and* RUTH *advances toward her son menacingly.*]

RUTH: A thousand times I have told you not to go off like that—

MAMA: [*Holding out her arms to her grandson.*] Well—at least let me tell him something. I want him to be the first one to hear . . . Come here, Travis. [*The boy obeys, gladly.*] Travis— [*She takes him by the shoulder and looks into his face.*] —you know that money we got in the mail this morning?

TRAVIS: Yes'm—

MAMA: Well—what you think your grandmama gone and done with that money?

TRAVIS: I don't know, Grandmama.

MAMA: [*Putting her finger on his nose for emphasis.*] She went out and she bought you a house! [*The explosion comes from* WALTER *at the end of the revelation and he jumps up and turns away from all of them in a fury.* MAMA *continues, to* TRAVIS.] You glad about the house? It's going to be yours when you get to be a man.

TRAVIS: Yeah—I always wanted to live in a house.

MAMA: All right, gimme some sugar then— [TRAVIS *puts his arms around her neck as she watches her son over the boy's shoulder. Then, to* TRAVIS, *after the embrace.*] Now when you say your prayers tonight, you thank God and your grandfather—'cause it was him who give you the house—in his way.

RUTH: [*Taking the boy from* MAMA *and pushing him toward the bedroom.*] Now you get out of here and get ready for your beating.

TRAVIS: Aw, Mama—

RUTH: Get on in there— [*Closing the door behind him and turning radiantly to her mother-in-law.*] So you went and did it!

MAMA: [*Quietly, looking at her son with pain.*] Yes, I did.

RUTH: [*Raising both arms classically.*] Praise God! [*Looks at* WALTER *a moment, who says nothing. She crosses rapidly to her husband.*] Please, honey—let me be glad . . . you be glad too. [*She has laid her hands on his shoulders, but he shakes himself free of her roughly, without turning to face her.*] Oh, Walter . . . a home . . . a home. [*She comes back to* MAMA.] Well—where is it? How big is it? How much it going to cost?

MAMA: Well—

RUTH: When we moving?

MAMA: [*Smiling at her.*] First of the month.

RUTH: [*Throwing back her head with jubilance.*] Praise God!

MAMA: [*Tentatively, still looking at her son's back turned against her and* RUTH.] It's—it's a nice house too . . . [*She cannot help speaking directly to him. An imploring quality in her voice, her manner, makes her almost like a girl now.*] Three bedrooms—nice big one for you and Ruth . . . Me and Beneatha still have to share our room, but Travis have one of his own—and [*With difficulty.*] I figure if the—new baby—is a boy, we could get one of them double-decker outfits . . . And there's a yard with a little patch of dirt where I could maybe get to grow me a few flowers . . . And a nice big basement . . .

RUTH: Walter honey, be glad—

MAMA: [*Still to his back, fingering things on the table.*] 'Course I don't want to make it sound fancier than it is . . . It's just a plain little old house—but it's made good and solid—and it will be *ours*. Walter Lee—it makes a difference in a man when he can walk on floors that belong to *him* . . .

RUTH: Where is it?

MAMA: [*Frightened at this telling.*] Well—well—it's out there in Clybourne Park—[5]

[RUTH's *radiance fades abruptly, and* WALTER *finally turns slowly to face his mother with incredulity and hostility.*]

RUTH: Where?

MAMA: [*Matter-of-factly.*] Four o six Clybourne Street, Clybourne Park.

RUTH: Clybourne Park? Mama, there ain't no colored people living in Clybourne Park.

MAMA: [*Almost idiotically.*] Well, I guess there's going to be some now.

WALTER: [*Bitterly.*] So that's the peace and comfort you went out and bought for us today!

MAMA: [*Raising her eyes to meet his finally.*] Son—I just tried to find the nicest place for the least amount of money for my family.

RUTH: [*Trying to recover from the shock.*] Well—well—'course I ain't one never been 'fraid of no crackers[6] mind you—but—well, wasn't there no other houses nowhere?

MAMA: Them houses they put up for colored in them areas way out all seem to cost twice as much as other houses. I did the best I could.

RUTH: [*Struck senseless with the news, in its various degrees of goodness and trouble, she sits a moment, her fists propping her chin in thought, and then she starts to rise, bringing her fists down with vigor, the radiance spreading from cheek to cheek again.*] Well—well!—All I can say is—if this is my time in life—*my time*—to say good-bye— [*And she builds with momentum as she starts to circle the room with an exuberant, almost tearfully happy release.*] —to these God-damned cracking walls!— [*She pounds the walls.*] —and these marching roaches!— [*She wipes at an imaginary army of marching roaches.*] —and this cramped little closet which ain't now or never was no kitchen! . . . then I say it loud and good, *Hallelujah! and good-bye misery . . . I don't never want to see your ugly face again!* [*She laughs joyously, having practically destroyed the apartment, and flings her arms up and lets them come down happily, slowly, reflectively, over her abdomen, aware for the first time perhaps that the life therein pulses with happiness and not despair.*] Lena?

MAMA: [*Moved, watching her happiness.*] Yes, honey?

RUTH: [*Looking off.*] Is there—is there a whole lot of sunlight?

MAMA: [*Understanding.*] Yes, child, there's a whole lot of sunlight.

[*Long pause.*]

RUTH: [*Collecting herself and going to the door of the room* TRAVIS *is in.*] Well—I guess I better see 'bout Travis. [*To* MAMA.] Lord, I sure don't feel like whipping nobody today!

---

5. On Chicago's Near North Side. 6. Derogatory term for poor whites.

[*She exits.*]

MAMA: [*The mother and son are left alone now and the mother waits a long time, considering deeply, before she speaks.*] Son—you—you understand what I done, don't you? [WALTER *is silent and sullen.*] I—I just seen my family falling apart today . . . just falling to pieces in front of my eyes . . . We couldn't of gone on like we was today. We was going backwards 'stead of forwards—talking 'bout killing babies and wishing each other was dead . . . When it gets like that in life—you just got to do something different, push on out and do something bigger . . . [*She waits.*] I wish you say something, son . . . I wish you'd say how deep inside you you think I done the right thing—

WALTER: [*Crossing slowly to his bedroom door and finally turning there and speaking measuredly.*] What you need me to say you done right for? *You* the head of this family. You run our lives like you want to. It was your money and you did what you wanted with it. So what you need for me to say it was all right for? [*Bitterly, to hurt her as deeply as he knows is possible.*] So you butchered up a dream of mine—you—who always talking 'bout your children's dreams . . .

MAMA: Walter Lee—

[*He just closes the door behind him.* MAMA *sits alone, thinking heavily.*]

[CURTAIN.]

Scene Two

Time: Friday night. A few weeks later.
At rise: Packing crates mark the intention of the family to move. BENEATHA *and* GEORGE *come in, presumably from an evening out again.*

GEORGE: O.K. . . . O.K., whatever you say . . . [*They both sit on the couch. He tries to kiss her. She moves away.*] Look, we've had a nice evening; let's not spoil it, huh? . . .

[*He again turns her head and tries to nuzzle in and she turns away from him, not with distaste but with momentary lack of interest; in a mood to pursue what they were talking about.*]

BENEATHA: I'm *trying* to talk to you.
GEORGE: We always talk.
BENEATHA: Yes—and I love to talk.
GEORGE: [*Exasperated; rising.*] I know it and I don't mind it sometimes . . . I want you to cut it out, see—The moody stuff, I mean. I don't like it. You're a nice-looking girl . . . all over. That's all you need, honey, forget the atmosphere. Guys aren't going to go for the atmosphere—they're

going to go for what they see. Be glad for that. Drop the Garbo[7] routine.
It doesn't go with you. As for myself, I want a nice— [*Groping.*] —simple
[*Thoughtfully.*] —sophisticated girl . . . not a poet— O.K.?

[*She rebuffs him again and he starts to leave.*]

BENEATHA: Why are you angry?

GEORGE: Because this is stupid! I don't go out with you to discuss the
nature of "quiet desperation"[8] or to hear all about your thoughts—
because the world will go on thinking what it thinks regardless—

BENEATHA: Then why read books? Why go to school?

GEORGE: [*With artificial patience, counting on his fingers.*] It's simple. You read
books—to learn facts—to get grades—to pass the course—to get a degree.
That's all—it has nothing to do with thoughts.

[*A long pause.*]

BENEATHA: I see. [*A longer pause as she looks at him.*] Good night, George.

[GEORGE *looks at her a little oddly, and starts to exit. He meets* MAMA *coming in.*]

GEORGE: Oh—hello, Mrs. Younger.

MAMA: Hello, George, how you feeling?

GEORGE: Fine—fine, how are you?

MAMA: Oh, a little tired. You know them steps can get you after a day's
work. You all have a nice time tonight?

GEORGE: Yes—a fine time. Well, good night.

MAMA: Good night. [*He exits.* MAMA *closes the door behind her.*] Hello, honey.
What you sitting like that for?

BENEATHA: I'm just sitting.

MAMA: Didn't you have a nice time?

BENEATHA: No.

MAMA: No? What's the matter?

BENEATHA: Mama, George is a fool—honest. [*She rises.*]

MAMA: [*Hustling around unloading the packages she has entered with. She stops.*] Is
he, baby?

BENEATHA: Yes.

[BENEATHA *makes up* TRAVIS' *bed as she talks.*]

MAMA: You sure?

BENEATHA: Yes.

MAMA: Well—I guess you better not waste your time with no fools.

7. Greta Garbo (1905–90), Swedish-born American film star whose sultry, remote, and European
femininity was widely imitated.
8. In *Walden* (1854), Henry Thoreau asserted that "the mass of men lead lives of quiet desperation."

[BENEATHA *looks up at her mother, watching her put groceries in the refrigerator. Finally she gathers up her things and starts into the bedroom. At the door she stops and looks back at her mother.*]

BENEATHA: Mama—
MAMA: Yes, baby—
BENEATHA: Thank you.
MAMA: For what?
BENEATHA: For understanding me this time.

[*She exits quickly and the mother stands, smiling a little, looking at the place where* BENEATHA *just stood.* RUTH *enters.*]

RUTH: Now don't you fool with any of this stuff, Lena—
MAMA: Oh, I just thought I'd sort a few things out.

[*The phone rings.* RUTH *answers.*]

RUTH: [*At the phone.*] Hello—Just a minute. [*Goes to door.*] Walter, it's Mrs. Arnold. [*Waits. Goes back to the phone. Tense.*] Hello. Yes, this is his wife speaking . . . He's lying down now. Yes . . . well, he'll be in tomorrow. He's been very sick. Yes—I know we should have called, but we were so sure he'd be able to come in today. Yes—yes, I'm very sorry. Yes . . . Thank you very much. [*She hangs up.* WALTER *is standing in the doorway of the bedroom behind her.*] That was Mrs. Arnold.
WALTER: [*Indifferently.*] Was it?
RUTH: She said if you don't come in tomorrow that they are getting a new man . . .
WALTER: Ain't that sad—ain't that crying sad.
RUTH: She said Mr. Arnold has had to take a cab for three days . . . Walter, you ain't been to work for three days! [*This is a revelation to her.*] Where you been, Walter Lee Younger? [WALTER *looks at her and starts to laugh.*] You're going to lose your job.
WALTER: That's right . . .
RUTH: Oh, Walter, and with your mother working like a dog every day—
WALTER: That's sad too—Everything is sad.
MAMA: What you been doing for these three days, son?
WALTER: Mama—you don't know all the things a man what got leisure can find to do in this city . . . What's this—Friday night? Well—Wednesday I borrowed Willy Harris' car and I went for a drive . . . just me and myself and I drove and drove . . . Way out . . . way past South Chicago, and I parked the car and I sat and looked at the steel mills all day long. I just sat in the car and looked at them big black chimneys for hours. Then I drove back and I went to the Green Hat. [*Pause.*] And Thursday—Thursday I borrowed the car again and I got in it and I pointed it the other way and I drove the other way—for hours—way, way up to Wiscon-

sin, and I looked at the farms. I just drove and looked at the farms. Then I drove back and I went to the Green Hat. [*Pause.*] And today—today I didn't get the car. Today I just walked. All over the Southside. And I looked at the Negroes and they looked at me and finally I just sat down on the curb at Thirty-ninth and South Parkway and I just sat there and watched the Negroes go by. And then I went to the Green Hat. You all sad? You all depressed? And you know where I am going right now—

[RUTH *goes out quietly.*]

MAMA: Oh, Big Walter, is this the harvest of our days?

WALTER: You know what I like about the Green Hat? [*He turns the radio on and a steamy, deep blues pours into the room.*] I like this little cat they got there who blows a sax . . . He blows. He talks to me. He ain't but 'bout five feet tall and he's got a conked head[9] and his eyes is always closed and he's all music—

MAMA: [*Rising and getting some papers out of her handbag.*] Walter—

WALTER: And there's this other guy who plays the piano . . . and they got a sound. I mean they can work on some music . . . They got the best little combo in the world in the Green Hat . . . You can just sit there and drink and listen to them three men play and you realize that don't nothing matter worth a damn, but just being there—

MAMA: I've helped do it to you, haven't I, son? Walter, I been wrong.

WALTER: Naw—you ain't never been wrong about nothing, Mama.

MAMA: Listen to me, now. I say I been wrong, son. That I been doing to you what the rest of the world been doing to you. [*She stops and he looks up slowly at her and she meets his eyes pleadingly.*] Walter—what you ain't never understood is that I ain't got nothing, don't own nothing, ain't never really wanted nothing that wasn't for you. There ain't nothing as precious to me . . . There ain't nothing worth holding on to, money, dreams, nothing else—if it means—if it means it's going to destroy my boy. [*She puts her papers in front of him and he watches her without speaking or moving.*] I paid the man thirty-five hundred dollars down on the house. That leaves sixty-five hundred dollars. Monday morning I want you to take this money and take three thousand dollars and put it in a savings account for Beneatha's medical schooling. The rest you put in a checking account—with your name on it. And from now on any penny that come out of it or that go in it is for you to look after. For you to decide. [*She drops her hands a little helplessly.*] It ain't much, but it's all I got in the world and I'm putting it in your hands. I'm telling you to be the head of this family from now on like you supposed to be.

WALTER: [*Stares at the money.*] You trust me like that, Mama?

MAMA: I ain't never stop trusting you. Like I ain't never stop loving you.

9. Straightened hair.

[*She goes out, and* WALTER *sits looking at the money on the table as the music continues in its idiom, pulsing in the room. Finally, in a decisive gesture, he gets up, and, in mingled joy and desperation, picks up the money. At the same moment,* TRAVIS *enters for bed.*]

TRAVIS: What's the matter, Daddy? You drunk?

WALTER: [*Sweetly, more sweetly than we have ever known him.*] No, Daddy ain't drunk. Daddy ain't going to never be drunk again. . . .

TRAVIS: Well, good night, Daddy.

[*The father has come from behind the couch and leans over, embracing his son.*]

WALTER: Son, I feel like talking to you tonight.

TRAVIS: About what?

WALTER: Oh, about a lot of things. About you and what kind of man you going to be when you grow up . . . Son—son, what do you want to be when you grow up?

TRAVIS: A bus driver.

WALTER: [*Laughing a little.*] A what? Man, that ain't nothing to want to be!

TRAVIS: Why not?

WALTER: 'Cause, man—it ain't big enough—you know what I mean.

TRAVIS: I don't know then. I can't make up my mind. Sometimes Mama asks me that too. And sometimes when I tell her I just want to be like you—she says she don't want me to be like that and sometimes she says she does . . .

WALTER: [*Gathering him up in his arms.*] You know what, Travis? In seven years you going to be seventeen years old. And things is going to be very different with us in seven years, Travis . . . One day when you are seventeen I'll come home—home from my office downtown somewhere—

TRAVIS: You don't work in no office, Daddy.

WALTER: No—but after tonight. After what your daddy gonna do tonight, there's going to be offices—a whole lot of offices . . .

TRAVIS: What you gonna do tonight, Daddy?

WALTER: You wouldn't understand yet, son, but your daddy's gonna make a transaction . . . a business transaction that's going to change our lives . . . That's how come one day when you 'bout seventeen years old I'll come home and I'll be pretty tired, you know what I mean, after a day of conferences and secretaries getting things wrong the way they do . . . 'cause an executive's life is hell, man— [*The more he talks the farther away he gets.*] And I'll pull the car up on the driveway . . . just a plain black Chrysler, I think, with white walls—no—black tires. More elegant. Rich people don't have to be flashy . . . though I'll have to get something a little sportier for Ruth—maybe a Cadillac convertible to do her shopping in . . . And I'll come up the steps to the house and the gardener will be clipping away at the hedges and he'll say, "Good evening, Mr. Younger." And I'll say, "Hello, Jefferson, how are you this evening?" And I'll go inside and Ruth will come downstairs and meet me at the door and we'll kiss each other and she'll take my arm and we'll go up to your room to see you sitting on the floor with the catalogues of all the great schools in America around you . . . All the great schools in the world. And—and I'll say, all right son—it's your seventeenth birthday, what is it you've decided? . . . Just tell me where you want to go to school and you'll go. Just tell me, what it is you want to be—and you'll *be* it . . . Whatever you want to be—Yessir! [*He holds his arms open for* TRAVIS.] You just name it, son . . . [TRAVIS *leaps into them.*] and I hand you the world!

> [WALTER's *voice has risen in pitch and hysterical promise and on the last line he lifts* TRAVIS *high.*]

> [BLACKOUT.]

Scene Three

Time: Saturday, moving day, one week later.

Before the curtain rises, RUTH's *voice, a strident, dramatic church alto, cuts through the silence.*

It is, in the darkness, a triumphant surge, a penetrating statement of expectation: "Oh, Lord, I don't feel no ways tired! Children, oh, glory hallelujah!"

As the curtain rises we see that RUTH *is alone in the living room, finishing up the family's packing. It is moving day. She is nailing crates and tying cartons.* BENEATHA *enters, carrying a guitar case, and watches her exuberant sister-in-law.*

RUTH: Hey!

BENEATHA: [*Putting away the case.*] Hi.

RUTH: [*Pointing at a package.*] Honey—look in that package there and see what I found on sale this morning at the South Center. [RUTH *gets up and moves to the package and draws out some curtains.*] Lookahere—hand-turned hems!

BENEATHA: How do you know the window size out there?

RUTH: [*Who hadn't thought of that.*] Oh—Well, they bound to fit something in the whole house. Anyhow, they was too good a bargain to pass up. [RUTH *slaps her head, suddenly remembering something.*] Oh, Bennie—I meant to put a special note on that carton over there. That's your mama's good china and she wants 'em to be very careful with it.

BENEATHA: I'll do it.

> [BENEATHA *finds a piece of paper and starts to draw large letters on it.*]

RUTH: You know what I'm going to do soon as I get in that new house?

BENEATHA: What?

RUTH: Honey—I'm going to run me a tub of water up to here ... [*With her fingers practically up to her nostrils.*] And I'm going to get in it—and I am going to sit ... and sit ... and sit in that hot water and the first person who knocks to tell *me* to hurry up and come out—

BENEATHA: Gets shot at sunrise.

RUTH: [*Laughing happily.*] You said it, sister! [*Noticing how large* BENEATHA *is absent-mindedly making the note.*] Honey, they ain't going to read that from no airplane.

BENEATHA: [*Laughing herself.*] I guess I always think things have more emphasis if they are big, somehow.

RUTH: [*Looking up at her and smiling.*] You and your brother seem to have that as a philosophy of life. Lord, that man—done changed so 'round here. You know—you know what we did last night? Me and Walter Lee?

BENEATHA: What?

RUTH: [*Smiling to herself.*] We went to the movies. [*Looking at* BENEATHA *to see if she understands.*] We went to the movies. You know the last time me and Walter went to the movies together?

BENEATHA: No.

RUTH: Me neither. That's how long it been. [*Smiling again.*] But we went last night.
The picture wasn't much good, but that didn't seem to matter. We went—and we held hands.

BENEATHA: Oh, Lord!

RUTH: We held hands—and you know what?

BENEATHA: What?

RUTH: When we come out of the show it was late and dark and all the stores and things was closed up ... and it was kind of chilly and there wasn't many people on the streets ... and we was still holding hands, me and Walter.

BENEATHA: You're killing me.

[WALTER *enters with a large package. His happiness is deep in him; he cannot keep still with his new-found exuberance. He is singing and wiggling and snapping his fingers. He puts his package in a corner and puts a phonograph record, which he has brought in with him, on the record player. As the music comes up he dances over to* RUTH *and tries to get her to dance with him. She gives in at last to his raunchiness and in a fit of giggling allows herself to be drawn into his mood and together they deliberately burlesque an old social dance of their youth.*]

BENEATHA: [*Regarding them a long time as they dance, then drawing in her breath for a deeply exaggerated comment which she does not particularly mean.*] Talk about—olddddddddddd-fashionedddddddd—Negroes!

WALTER: [*Stopping momentarily.*] What kind of Negroes?

[*He says this in fun. He is not angry with her today, nor with anyone. He starts to dance with his wife again.*]

BENEATHA: Old-fashioned.

WALTER: [*As he dances with* RUTH.] You know, when these *New Negroes* have their convention— [*Pointing at his sister.*] —that is going to be the chairman of the Committee on Unending Agitation. [*He goes on dancing, then stops.*] Race, race, race! . . . Girl, I do believe you are the first person in the history of the entire human race to successfully brainwash yourself. [BENEATHA *breaks up and he goes on dancing. He stops again, enjoying his tease.*] Damn, even the N double A C P¹ takes a holiday sometimes! [BENEATHA *and* RUTH *laugh. He dances with* RUTH *some more and starts to laugh and stops and pantomimes someone over an operating table.*] I can just see that chick someday looking down at some poor cat on an operating table before she starts to slice him, saying . . . [*Pulling his sleeves back maliciously.*] "By the way, what are your views on civil rights down there? . . ."

[*He laughs at her again and starts to dance happily. The bell sounds.*]

BENEATHA: Sticks and stones may break my bones but . . . words will never hurt me!

[BENEATHA *goes to the door and opens it as* WALTER *and* RUTH *go on with the clowning.* BENEATHA *is somewhat surprised to see a quiet-looking middle-aged white man in a business suit holding his hat and a briefcase in his hand and consulting a small piece of paper.*]

MAN: Uh—how do you do, miss. I am looking for a Mrs.— [*He looks at the slip of paper.*] Mrs. Lena Younger?

BENEATHA: [*Smoothing her hair with slight embarrassment.*] Oh—yes, that's my mother. Excuse me [*She closes the door and turns to quiet the other two.*] Ruth! Brother! Somebody's here. [*Then she opens the door. The* MAN *casts a curious quick glance at all of them.*] Uh—come in please.

MAN: [*Coming in.*] Thank you.

BENEATHA: My mother isn't here just now. Is it business?

MAN: Yes . . . well, of a sort.

WALTER: [*Freely, the Man of the House.*] Have a seat. I'm Mrs. Younger's son. I look after most of her business matters.

[RUTH *and* BENEATHA *exchange amused glances.*]

MAN: [*Regarding* WALTER, *and sitting.*] Well—My name is Karl Lindner . . .

WALTER: [*Stretching out his hand.*] Walter Younger. This is my wife— [RUTH *nods politely.*] —and my sister.

LINDNER: How do you do.

WALTER: [*Amiably, as he sits himself easily on a chair, leaning with interest forward on his knees and looking expectantly into the newcomer's face.*] What can we do for you, Mr. Lindner!

1. National Association for the Advancement of Colored People, civil rights organization founded in 1909.

LINDNER: [*Some minor shuffling of the hat and briefcase on his knees.*] Well—I am a
representative of the Clybourne Park Improvement Association—

WALTER: [*Pointing.*] Why don't you sit your things on the floor?

LINDNER: Oh—yes. Thank you. [*He slides the briefcase and hat under the chair.*] And
as I was saying—I am from the Clybourne Park Improvement Association
and we have had it brought to our attention at the last meeting that you
people—or at least your mother—has bought a piece of residential property at— [*He digs for the slip of paper again.*] —four o six Clybourne Street . . .

WALTER: That's right. Care for something to drink? Ruth, get Mr. Lindner a
beer.

LINDNER: [*Upset for some reason.*] Oh—no, really. I mean thank you very much,
but no thank you.

RUTH: [*Innocently.*] Some coffee?

LINDNER: Thank you, nothing at all.

   [BENEATHA *is watching the man carefully.*]

LINDNER: Well, I don't know how much you folks know about our organization. [*He is a gentle man; thoughtful and somewhat labored in his manner.*] It
is one of these community organizations set up to look after—oh, you
know, things like block upkeep and special projects and we also have
what we call our New Neighbors Orientation Committee . . .

BENEATHA: [*Drily.*] Yes—and what do they do?

LINDNER: [*Turning a little to her and then returning the main force to* WALTER.]
Well—it's what you might call a sort of welcoming committee, I guess. I
mean they, we, I'm the chairman of the committee—go around and see
the new people who move into the neighborhood and sort of give them
the lowdown on the way we do things out in Clybourne Park.

BENEATHA: [*With appreciation of the two meanings, which escape* RUTH *and* WAL-
TER.] Un-huh.

LINDNER: And we also have the category of what the association calls— [*He
looks elsewhere.*] —uh—special community problems . . .

BENEATHA: Yes—and what are some of those?

WALTER: Girl, let the man talk.

LINDNER: [*With understated relief.*] Thank you. I would sort of like to explain
this thing in my own way. I mean I want to explain to you in a certain
way.

WALTER: Go ahead.

LINDNER: Yes. Well. I'm going to try to get right to the point. I'm sure we'll
all appreciate that in the long run.

BENEATHA: Yes.

WALTER: Be still now!

LINDNER: Well—

RUTH: [*Still innocently.*] Would you like another chair—you don't look
comfortable.

LINDNER: [*More frustrated than annoyed.*] No, thank you very much. Please. Well—to get right to the point I— [*A great breath, and he is off at last.*] I am sure you people must be aware of some of the incidents which have happened in various parts of the city when colored people have moved into certain areas— [BENEATHA *exhales heavily and starts tossing a piece of fruit up and down in the air.*] Well—because we have what I think is going to be a unique type of organization in American community life—not only do we deplore that kind of thing—but we are trying to do something about it. [BENEATHA *stops tossing and turns with a new and quizzical interest to the man.*] We feel— [*Gaining confidence in his mission because of the interest in the faces of the people he is talking to.*] —we feel that most of the trouble in this world, when you come right down to it— [*He hits his knee for emphasis.*] —most of the trouble exists because people just don't sit down and talk to each other.

RUTH: [*Nodding as she might in church, pleased with the remark.*] You can say that again, mister.

LINDNER: [*More encouraged by such affirmation.*] That we don't try hard enough in this world to understand the other fellow's problem. The other guy's point of view.

RUTH: Now that's right.

[BENEATHA *and* WALTER *merely watch and listen with genuine interest.*]

LINDNER: Yes—that's the way we feel out in Clybourne Park. And that's why I was elected to come here this afternoon and talk to you people. Friendly like, you know, the way people should talk to each other and see if we couldn't find some way to work this thing out. As I say, the whole business is a matter of *caring* about the other fellow. Anybody can see that you are a nice family of folks, hard working and honest I'm sure. [BENEATHA *frowns slightly, quizzically, her head tilted regarding him.*] Today everybody knows what it means to be on the outside of something. And of course, there is always somebody who is out to take the advantage of people who don't always understand.

WALTER: What do you mean?

LINDNER: Well—you see our community is made up of people who've worked hard as the dickens for years to build up that little community. They're not rich and fancy people; just hard-working, honest people who don't really have much but those little homes and a dream of the kind of community they want to raise their children in. Now, I don't say we are perfect and there is a lot wrong in some of the things they want. But you've got to admit that a man, right or wrong, has the right to want to have the neighborhood he lives in a certain kind of way. And at the moment the overwhelming majority of our people out there feel that people get along better, take more of a common interest in the life of the community, when they share a common background. I want you to believe me when I tell you that race prejudice simply doesn't enter into it. It is a matter of the people of Clybourne Park believing, rightly or wrongly, as I say, that for the happiness of all concerned that our Negro families are happier when they live in their *own* communities.

BENEATHA: [*With a grand and bitter gesture.*] This, friends, is the Welcoming Committee!

WALTER: [*Dumfounded, looking at* LINDNER.] Is this what you came marching all the way over here to tell us?

LINDNER: Well, now we've been having a fine conversation. I hope you'll hear me all the way through.

WALTER: [*Tightly.*] Go ahead, man.

LINDNER: You see—in the face of all things I have said, we are prepared to make your family a very generous offer . . .

BENEATHA: Thirty pieces and not a coin less![2]

WALTER: Yeah?

LINDNER: [*Putting on his glasses and drawing a form out of the briefcase.*] Our association is prepared, through the collective effort of our people, to buy the house from you at a financial gain to your family.

RUTH: Lord have mercy, ain't this the living gall!

WALTER: All right, you through?

LINDNER: Well, I want to give you the exact terms of the financial arrangement—

WALTER: We don't want to hear no exact terms of no arrangements. I want to know if you got any more to tell us 'bout getting together?

LINDNER: [*Taking off his glasses.*] Well—I don't suppose that you feel . . .

WALTER: Never mind how I feel—you got any more to say 'bout how people ought to sit down and talk to each other? . . . Get out of my house, man.

[*He turns his back and walks to the door.*]

LINDNER: [*Looking around at the hostile faces and reaching and assembling his hat and briefcase.*] Well—I don't understand why you people are reacting this way. What do you think you are going to gain by moving into a neighborhood where you just aren't wanted and where some elements—well—people can get awful worked up when they feel that their whole way of life and everything they've ever worked for is threatened.

WALTER: Get out.

LINDNER: [*At the door, holding a small card.*] Well—I'm sorry it went like this.

WALTER: Get out.

LINDNER: [*Almost sadly regarding* WALTER.] You just can't force people to change their hearts, son.

---

2. See Matthew 26.15, in which Judas Iscariot is paid 30 pieces of silver to betray Jesus.

[*He turns and puts his card on a table and exits.* WALTER *pushes the door to with stinging hatred, and stands looking at it.* RUTH *just sits and* BENEATHA *just stands. They say nothing.* MAMA *and* TRAVIS *enter.*]

MAMA: Well—this all the packing got done since I left out of here this morning. I testify before God that my children got all the energy of the dead. What time the moving men due?

BENEATHA: Four o'clock. You had a caller, Mama.

[*She is smiling, teasingly.*]

MAMA: Sure enough—who?

BENEATHA: [*Her arms folded saucily.*] The Welcoming Committee.

[WALTER *and* RUTH *giggle.*]

MAMA: [*Innocently.*] Who?

BENEATHA: The Welcoming Committee. They said they're sure going to be glad to see you when you get there.

WALTER: [*Devilishly.*] Yeah, they said they can't hardly wait to see your face.

[*Laughter.*]

MAMA: [*Sensing their facetiousness.*] What's the matter with you all?

WALTER: Ain't nothing the matter with us. We just telling you 'bout the gentleman who came to see you this afternoon. From the Clybourne Park Improvement Association.

MAMA: What he want?

RUTH: [*In the same mood as* BENEATHA *and* WALTER.] To welcome you, honey.

WALTER: He said they can't hardly wait. He said the one thing they don't have, that they just *dying* to have out there is a fine family of colored people! [*To* RUTH *and* BENEATHA.] Ain't that right!

RUTH AND BENEATHA: [*Mockingly.*] Yeah! He left his card in case—

[*They indicate the card, and* MAMA *picks it up and throws it on the floor— understanding and looking off as she draws her chair up to the table on which she has put her plant and some sticks and some cord.*]

MAMA: Father, give us strength. [*Knowingly—and without fun.*] Did he threaten us?

BENEATHA: Oh—Mama—they don't do it like that anymore. He talked Brotherhood. He said everybody ought to learn how to sit down and hate each other with good Christian fellowship.

[*She and* WALTER *shake hands to ridicule the remark.*]

MAMA: [*Sadly.*] Lord, protect us . . .

RUTH: You should hear the money those folks raised to buy the house from us. All we paid and then some.

BENEATHA: What they think we going to do—eat 'em?

RUTH: No, honey, marry 'em.

MAMA: [Shaking her head.] Lord, Lord, Lord . . .

RUTH: Well—that's the way the crackers crumble. Joke.

BENEATHA: [Laughingly noticing what her mother is doing.] Mama, what are you doing?

MAMA: Fixing my plant so it won't get hurt none on the way . . .

BENEATHA: Mama, you going to take *that* to the new house?

MAMA: Un-huh—

BENEATHA: That raggedy-looking old thing?

MAMA: [Stopping and looking at her.] It expresses me.

RUTH: [With delight, to BENEATHA.] So there, Miss Thing!

[WALTER *comes to* MAMA *suddenly and bends down behind her and squeezes her in his arms with all his strength. She is overwhelmed by the suddenness of it and, though delighted, her manner is like that of* RUTH *with* TRAVIS.]

MAMA: Look out now, boy! You make me mess up my thing here!

WALTER: [His face lit, he slips down on his knees beside her, his arms still about her.] Mama . . . you know what it means to climb up in the chariot?

MAMA: [Gruffly, very happy.] Get on away from me now . . .

RUTH: [Near the gift-wrapped package, trying to catch WALTER's eye.] Psst—

WALTER: What the old song say, Mama . . .

RUTH: Walter—Now?

[She is pointing at the package.]

WALTER: [Speaking the lines, sweetly, playfully, in his mother's face.]

I got wings . . . you got wings . . .
All God's Children got wings[3] . . .

MAMA: Boy—get out of my face and do some work . . .

WALTER:

When I get to heaven gonna put on my wings,
Gonna fly all over God's heaven . . .

BENEATHA: [Teasingly, from across the room.] Everybody talking 'bout heaven ain't going there!

WALTER: [To RUTH, who is carrying the box across to them.] I don't know, you think we ought to give her that . . . Seems to me she ain't been very appreciative around here.

MAMA: [Eying the box, which is obviously a gift.] What is that?

---

3. Lines from an African American spiritual. Walter's and Beneatha's next lines are also from the song.

WALTER: [*Taking it from* RUTH *and putting it on the table in front of* MAMA.] Well— what you all think? Should we give it to her?

RUTH: Oh—she was pretty good today.

MAMA: I'll good you—

[*She turns her eyes to the box again.*]

BENEATHA: Open it, Mama.

[*She stands up, looks at it, turns and looks at all of them, and then presses her hands together and does not open the package.*]

WALTER: [*Sweetly.*] Open it, Mama. It's for you. [MAMA *looks in his eyes. It is the first present in her life without its being Christmas. Slowly she opens her package and lifts out, one by one, a brand-new sparkling set of gardening tools.* WALTER *continues, prodding.*] Ruth made up the note—read it . . .

MAMA: [*Picking up the card and adjusting her glasses.*] "To our own Mrs. Miniver[4]— Love from Brother, Ruth and Beneatha." Ain't that lovely . . .

TRAVIS: [*Tugging at his father's sleeve.*] Daddy, can I give her mine now?

WALTER: All right, son. [TRAVIS *flies to get his gift.*] Travis didn't want to go in with the rest of us, Mama. He got his own. [*Somewhat amused.*] We don't know what it is . . .

TRAVIS: [*Racing back in the room with a large hatbox and putting it in front of his grandmother.*] Here!

MAMA: Lord have mercy, baby. You done gone and bought your grand-mother a hat?

TRAVIS: [*Very proud.*] Open it!

[*She does and lifts out an elaborate, but very elaborate, wide gardening hat, and all the adults break up at the sight of it.*]

RUTH: Travis, honey, what is that?

TRAVIS: [*Who thinks it is beautiful and appropriate.*] It's a gardening hat! Like the ladies always have on in the magazines when they work in their gardens.

BENEATHA: [*Giggling fiercely.*] Travis—we were trying to make Mama Mrs. Miniver—not Scarlett O'Hara![5]

MAMA: [*Indignantly.*] What's the matter with you all! This here is a beautiful hat! [*Absurdly.*] I always wanted me one just like it!

[*She pops it on her head to prove it to her grandson, and the hat is ludicrous and considerably oversized.*]

RUTH: Hot dog! Go, Mama!

---

4. Courageous, charismatic title character of a 1942 film starring Greer Garson.
5. Glamorous, headstrong heroine of Margaret Mitchell's 1936 novel *Gone with the Wind*.

WALTER: [*Doubled over with laughter.*] I'm sorry, Mama—but you look like you ready to go out and chop you some cotton sure enough!

[*They all laugh except* MAMA, *out of deference to* TRAVIS' *feelings.*]

MAMA: [*Gathering the boy up to her.*] Bless your heart—this is the prettiest hat I ever owned— [WALTER, RUTH *and* BENEATHA *chime in—noisily, festively and insincerely congratulating* TRAVIS *on his gift.*] What are we all standing around here for? We ain't finished packin' yet. Bennie, you ain't packed one book.

[*The bell rings.*]

BENEATHA: That couldn't be the movers . . . it's not hardly two good yet—

[BENEATHA *goes into her room.* MAMA *starts for door.*]

WALTER: [*Turning, stiffening.*] Wait—wait—I'll get it.

[*He stands and looks at the door.*]

MAMA: You expecting company, son?

WALTER: [*Just looking at the door.*] Yeah—yeah . . .

[MAMA *looks at* RUTH, *and they exchange innocent and unfrightened glances.*]

MAMA: [*Not understanding.*] Well, let them in, son.

BENEATHA: [*From her room.*] We need some more string.

MAMA: Travis—you run to the hardware and get me some string cord.

[MAMA *goes out and* WALTER *turns and looks at* RUTH. TRAVIS *goes to a dish for money.*]

RUTH: Why don't you answer the door, man?

WALTER: [*Suddenly bounding across the floor to her.*] 'Cause sometimes it hard to let the future begin! [*Stooping down in her face.*]

I got wings! You got wings!
All God's children got wings!

[*He crosses to the door and throws it open. Standing there is a very slight little man in a not too prosperous business suit and with haunted frightened eyes and a hat pulled down tightly, brim up, around his forehead.* TRAVIS *passes between the men and exits.* WALTER *leans deep in the man's face, still in his jubilance.*]

When I get to heaven gonna put on my wings,
Gonna fly all over God's heaven . . .

[*The little man just stares at him.*]

Heaven—

[*Suddenly he stops and looks past the little man into the empty hallway.*] Where's Willy, man?

BOBO: He ain't with me.

WALTER: [*Not disturbed.*] Oh—come on in. You know my wife.

BOBO: [*Dumbly, taking off his hat.*] Yes—h'you, Miss Ruth.

RUTH: [*Quietly, a mood apart from her husband already, seeing* BOBO.] Hello, Bobo.

WALTER: You right on time today . . . Right on time. That's the way! [*He slaps* BOBO *on his back.*] Sit down . . . lemme hear.

[RUTH *stands stiffly and quietly in back of them, as though somehow she senses death, her eyes fixed on her husband.*]

BOBO: [*His frightened eyes on the floor, his hat in his hands.*] Could I please get a drink of water, before I tell you about it, Walter Lee?

[WALTER *does not take his eyes off the man.* RUTH *goes blindly to the tap and gets a glass of water and brings it to* BOBO.]

WALTER: There ain't nothing wrong, is there?

BOBO: Lemme tell you—

WALTER: Man—didn't nothing go wrong?

BOBO: Lemme tell you—Walter Lee. [*Looking at* RUTH *and talking to her more than to* WALTER.] You know how it was. I got to tell you how it was. I mean first I got to tell you how it was all the way . . . I mean about the money I put in, Walter Lee . . .

WALTER: [*With taut agitation now.*] What about the money you put in?

BOBO: Well—it wasn't much as we told you—me and Willy— [*He stops.*] I'm sorry, Walter. I got a bad feeling about it. I got a real bad feeling about it . . .

WALTER: Man, what you telling me about all this for? . . . Tell me what happened in Springfield . . .

BOBO: Springfield.

RUTH: [*Like a dead woman.*] What was supposed to happen in Springfield?

BOBO: [*To her.*] This deal that me and Walter went into with Willy—Me and Willy was going to go down to Springfield and spread some money 'round so's we wouldn't have to wait so long for the liquor license . . . That's what we were going to do. Everybody said that was the way you had to do, you understand, Miss Ruth?

WALTER: Man—what happened down there?

BOBO: [*A pitiful man, near tears.*] I'm trying to tell you, Walter.

WALTER: [*Screaming at him suddenly.*] THEN TELL ME, GODDAMMIT . . . WHAT'S THE MATTER WITH YOU?

BOBO: Man . . . I didn't go to no Springfield, yesterday.

WALTER: [*Halted, life hanging in the moment.*] Why not?

BOBO: [*The long way, the hard way to tell.*] 'Cause I didn't have no reasons to . . .

WALTER: Man, what are you talking about!

BOBO: I'm talking about the fact that when I got to the train station yesterday morning—eight o'clock like we planned . . . Man—*Willy didn't never show up.*

WALTER: Why . . . where was he . . . where is he?

BOBO: That's what I'm trying to tell you . . . I don't know . . . I waited six hours . . . I called his house . . . and I waited . . . six hours . . . I waited in that train station six hours . . . [*Breaking into tears.*] That was all the extra money I had in the world . . . [*Looking up at* WALTER *with the tears running down his face.*] Man, *Willy is gone.*

WALTER: Gone, what you mean Willy is gone? Gone where? You mean he went by himself. You mean he went off to Springfield by himself—to take care of getting the license— [*Turns and looks anxiously at* RUTH.] You mean maybe he didn't want too many people in on the business down there? [*Looks to* RUTH *again, as before.*] You know Willy got his own ways. [*Looks back to* BOBO.] Maybe you was late yesterday and he just went on down there without you. Maybe—maybe—he's been callin' you at home tryin' to tell you what happened or something. Maybe—maybe—he just got sick. He's somewhere—he's got to be somewhere. We just got to find him—me and you got to find him. [*Grabs* BOBO *senselessly by the collar and starts to shake him.*] We got to!

BOBO: [*In sudden angry, frightened agony.*] What's the matter with you, Walter! *When a cat take off with your money he don't leave you no maps!*

WALTER: [*Turning madly, as though he is looking for* WILLY *in the very room.*] Willy! . . . Willy . . . don't do it . . . Please don't do it . . . Man, not with that money . . . Man, please, not with that money . . . Oh, God . . . Don't let it be true . . . [*He is wandering around, crying out for* WILLY *and looking for him or perhaps for help from God.*] Man . . . I trusted you . . . Man, I put my life in your hands . . . [*He starts to crumple down on the floor as* RUTH *just covers her face in horror.* MAMA *opens the door and comes into the room, with* BENEATHA *behind her.*] Man . . . [*He starts to pound the floor with his fists, sobbing wildly.*] That money is made out of my father's flesh . . .

BOBO: [*Standing over him helplessly.*] I'm sorry, Walter . . . [*Only* WALTER's *sobs reply.* BOBO *puts on his hat.*] I had my life staked on this deal, too . . .

[*He exits.*]

MAMA: [*To* WALTER.] Son— [*She goes to him, bends down to him, talks to his bent head.*] Son . . . Is it gone? Son, I gave you sixty-five hundred dollars. Is it gone? All of it? Beneatha's money too?

WALTER: [*Lifting his head slowly.*] Mama . . . I never . . . went to the bank at all . . .

MAMA: [*Not wanting to believe him.*] You mean . . . your sister's school money . . . you used that too . . . Walter? . . .

WALTER: Yessss! . . . All of it . . . It's all gone . . . [*There is total silence.* RUTH *stands with her face covered with her hands;* BENEATHA *leans forlornly against a wall, fingering a piece of red ribbon from the mother's gift.* MAMA *stops and looks at her son without recognition and then, quite without thinking about it, starts to beat him senselessly in the face.* BENEATHA *goes to them and stops it.*]

BENEATHA: Mama!

[MAMA *stops and looks at both of her children and rises slowly and wanders vaguely, aimlessly away from them.*]

MAMA: I seen . . . him . . . night after night . . . come in . . . and look at that rug . . . and then look at me . . . the red showing in his eyes . . . the veins moving in his head . . . I seen him grow thin and old before he was forty . . . working and working and working like somebody's old horse . . . killing himself . . . and you—you give it all away in a day . . .

BENEATHA: Mama—

MAMA: Oh, God . . . [*She looks up to Him.*] Look down here—and show me the strength.

BENEATHA: Mama—

MAMA: [*Folding over.*] Strength . . .

BENEATHA: [*Plaintively.*] Mama . . .

MAMA: Strength!

[CURTAIN.]

ACT III

An hour later.

At curtain, there is a sullen light of gloom in the living room, gray light not unlike that which began the first scene of Act I. At left we can see WALTER *within his room, alone with himself. He is stretched out on the bed, his shirt out and open, his arms under his head. He does not smoke, he does not cry out, he merely lies there, looking up at the ceiling, much as if he were alone in the world.*

In the living room BENEATHA *sits at the table, still surrounded by the now almost ominous packing crates. She sits looking off. We feel that this is a mood struck perhaps an hour before, and it lingers now, full of the empty sound of profound disappointment. We see on a line from her brother's bedroom the sameness of their attitudes. Presently the bell rings and* BENEATHA *rises without ambition or interest in answering. It is* ASAGAI, *smiling broadly, striding into the room with energy and happy expectation and conversation.*

ASAGAI: I came over . . . I had some free time. I thought I might help with the packing. Ah, I like the look of packing crates! A household in preparation for a journey! It depresses some people . . . but for me . . . it is another feeling. Something full of the flow of life, do you understand? Movement, progress . . . It makes me think of Africa.

BENEATHA: Africa!

ASAGAI: What kind of a mood is this? Have I told you how deeply you move me?

BENEATHA: He gave away the money, Asagai . . .

ASAGAI: Who gave away what money?

BENEATHA: The insurance money. My brother gave it away.

ASAGAI: Gave it away?

BENEATHA: He made an investment! With a man even Travis wouldn't have trusted.

ASAGAI: And it's gone?

BENEATHA: Gone!

ASAGAI: I'm very sorry . . . And you, now?

BENEATHA: Me? . . . Me? . . . Me, I'm nothing . . . Me. When I was very small . . . we used to take our sleds out in the wintertime and the only hills we had were the ice-covered stone steps of some houses down the street. And we used to fill them in with snow and make them smooth and slide down them all day . . . and it was very dangerous you know . . . far too steep . . . and sure enough one day a kid named Rufus came down too fast and hit the sidewalk . . . and we saw his face just split open right there in front of us . . . And I remember standing there looking at his bloody open face thinking that was the end of Rufus. But the ambulance came and they took him to the hospital and they fixed the broken bones and they sewed it all up . . . and the next time I saw Rufus he just had a little line down the middle of his face . . . I never got over that . . .

[WALTER *sits up, listening on the bed. Throughout this scene it is important that we feel his reaction at all times, that he visibly respond to the words of his sister and* ASAGAI.]

ASAGAI: What?

BENEATHA: That that was what one person could do for another, fix him up—sew up the problem, make him all right again. That was the most marvelous thing in the world . . . I wanted to do that. I always thought it was the one concrete thing in the world that a human being could do. Fix up the sick, you know—and make them whole again. This was truly being God . . .

ASAGAI: You wanted to be God?

BENEATHA: No—I wanted to cure. It used to be so important to me. I wanted to cure. It used to matter. I used to care. I mean about people and how their bodies hurt . . .

ASAGAI: And you've stopped caring?

BENEATHA: Yes—I think so.

ASAGAI: Why?

[WALTER *rises, goes to the door of his room and is about to open it, then stops and stands listening, leaning on the door jamb.*]

BENEATHA: Because it doesn't seem deep enough, close enough to what ails mankind—I mean this thing of sewing up bodies or administering drugs. Don't you understand? It was a child's reaction to the world. I thought that doctors had the secret to all the hurts . . . That's the way a child sees things—or an idealist.

ASAGAI: Children see things very well sometimes—and idealists even better.

BENEATHA: I know that's what you think. Because you are still where I left off—you still care. This is what you see for the world, for Africa. You with the dreams of the future will patch up all Africa—you are going to cure the Great Sore of colonialism with Independence—

ASAGAI: Yes!

BENEATHA: Yes—and you think that one word is the penicillin of the human spirit: "Independence!" But then what?

ASAGAI: That will be the problem for another time. First we must get there.

BENEATHA: And where does it end?

ASAGAI: End? Who even spoke of an end? To life? To living?

BENEATHA: An end to misery!

ASAGAI: [*Smiling.*] You sound like a French intellectual.

BENEATHA: No! I sound like a human being who just had her future taken right out of her hands! While I was sleeping in my bed in there, things were happening in this world that directly concerned me—and nobody asked me, consulted me—they just went out and did things—and changed my life. Don't you see there isn't any real progress, Asagai, there is only one large circle that we march in, around and around, each of us with our own little picture—in front of us—our own little mirage that we think is the future.

ASAGAI: That is the mistake.

BENEATHA: What?

ASAGAI: What you just said—about the circle. It isn't a circle—it is simply a long line—as in geometry, you know, one that reaches into infinity. And because we cannot see the end—we also cannot see how it changes. And it is very odd but those who see the changes are called "idealists"—and those who cannot, or refuse to think, they are the "realists." It is very strange, and amusing too, I think.

BENEATHA: You—you are almost religious.

ASAGAI: Yes . . . I think I have the religion of doing what is necessary in the world—and of worshipping man—because he is so marvelous, you see.

BENEATHA: Man is foul! And the human race deserves its misery!

ASAGAI: You see: *you* have become the religious one in the old sense. Already, and after such a small defeat, you are worshipping despair.

BENEATHA: From now on, I worship the truth—and the truth is that people are puny, small and selfish . . .

ASAGAI: Truth? Why is it that you despairing ones always think that only you have the truth? I never thought to see *you* like that. You! Your brother made a stupid, childish mistake—and you are grateful to him. So that now you can give up the ailing human race on account of it. You talk about what good is struggle; what good is anything? Where are we all going? And why are we bothering?

BENEATHA: *And you cannot answer it!* All your talk and dreams about Africa and Independence. Independence and then what? What about all the crooks and petty thieves and just plain idiots who will come into power to steal and plunder the same as before—only now they will be black and do it in the name of the new Independence—You cannot answer that.

ASAGAI: [*Shouting over her.*] *I live the answer!* [*Pause.*] In my village at home it is the exceptional man who can even read a newspaper . . . or who ever *sees* a book at all. I will go home and much of what I will have to say will seem strange to the people of my village . . . But I will teach and work and things will happen, slowly and swiftly. At times it will seem that nothing changes at all . . . and then again . . . the sudden dramatic events which make history leap into the future. And then quiet again. Retrogression even. Guns, murder, revolution. And I even will have moments when I wonder if the quiet was not better than all that death and hatred. But I will look about my village at the illiteracy and disease and ignorance and I will not wonder long. And perhaps . . . perhaps I will be a great man . . . I mean perhaps I will hold on to the substance of truth and find my way always with the right course . . . and perhaps for it I will be butchered in my bed some night by the servants of empire . . .

BENEATHA: *The martyr!*

ASAGAI: . . . or perhaps I shall live to be a very old man, respected and esteemed in my new nation . . . And perhaps I shall hold office and this is what I'm trying to tell you, Alaiyo; perhaps the things I believe now for my country will be wrong and outmoded, and I will not understand and do terrible things to have things my way or merely to keep my power. Don't you see that there will be young men and women, not British soldiers then, but my own black countrymen . . . to step out of the shadows some evening and slit my then useless throat? Don't you see they have always been there . . . that they always will be. And that such a thing as my own death will be an advance? They who might kill me even . . . actually replenish me!

BENEATHA: Oh, Asagai, I know all that.

ASAGAI: Good! Then stop moaning and groaning and tell me what you plan to do.

BENEATHA: Do?

ASAGAI: I have a bit of a suggestion.

BENEATHA: What?

ASAGAI: [*Rather quietly for him.*] That when it is all over—that you come home with me—

BENEATHA: [*Slapping herself on the forehead with exasperation born of misunderstanding.*] Oh—Asagai—at this moment you decide to be romantic!

ASAGAI: [*Quickly understanding the misunderstanding.*] My dear, young creature of the New World—I do not mean across the city—I mean across the ocean; home—to Africa.

BENEATHA: [*Slowly understanding and turning to him with murmured amazement.*] To—to Nigeria?

ASAGAI: Yes! . . . [*Smiling and lifting his arms playfully.*] Three hundred years later the African Prince rose up out of the seas and swept the maiden back across the middle passage[6] over which her ancestors had come—

BENEATHA: [*Unable to play.*] Nigeria?

ASAGAI: Nigeria. Home. [*Coming to her with genuine romantic flippancy.*] I will show you our mountains and our stars; and give you cool drinks from gourds and teach you the old songs and the ways of our people—and, in time, we will pretend that— [*Very softly.*] —you have only been away for a day—

[*She turns her back to him, thinking. He swings her around and takes her full in his arms in a long embrace which proceeds to passion.*]

BENEATHA: [*Pulling away.*] You're getting me all mixed up—

ASAGAI: Why?

BENEATHA: Too many things—too many things have happened today. I must sit down and think. I don't know what I feel about anything right this minute.

[*She promptly sits down and props her chin on her fist.*]

ASAGAI: [*Charmed.*] All right, I shall leave you. No—don't get up. [*Touching her, gently, sweetly.*] Just sit awhile and think . . . Never be afraid to sit awhile and think. [*He goes to door and looks at her.*] How often I have looked at you and said, "Ah—so this is what the New World hath finally wrought . . ."[7]

[*He exits.* BENEATHA *sits on alone. Presently* WALTER *enters from his room and starts to rummage through things, feverishly looking for something. She looks up and turns in her seat.*]

6. Term denoting the route traveled by slaves transported from Africa to the Americas.
7. Allusion to the biblical exclamation "What hath God wrought!" (Numbers 23.23).

BENEATHA: [*Hissingly.*] Yes—just look at what the New World hath wrought! . . . Just look! [*She gestures with bitter disgust.*] There he is! *Monsieur le petit bourgeois noir*[8]—himself! There he is—Symbol of a Rising Class! Entrepreneur! Titan of the system! [WALTER *ignores her completely and continues frantically and destructively looking for something and hurling things to the floor and tearing things out of their place in his search.* BENEATHA *ignores the eccentricity of his actions and goes on with the monologue of insult.*] Did you dream of yachts on Lake Michigan, Brother? Did you see yourself on that Great Day sitting down at the Conference Table, surrounded by all the mighty bald-headed men in America? All halted, waiting, breathless, waiting for your pronouncements on industry? Waiting for you—Chairman of the Board? [WALTER *finds what he is looking for—a small piece of white paper—and pushes it in his pocket and puts on his coat and rushes out without ever having looked at her. She shouts after him.*] I look at you and I see the final triumph of stupidity in the world!

[*The door slams and she returns to just sitting again.* RUTH *comes quickly out of* MAMA's *room.*]

RUTH: Who was that?

BENEATHA: Your husband.

RUTH: Where did he go?

BENEATHA: Who knows—maybe he has an appointment at U.S. Steel.

RUTH: [*Anxiously, with frightened eyes.*] You didn't say nothing bad to him, did you?

BENEATHA: Bad? Say anything bad to him? No—I told him he was a sweet boy and full of dreams and everything is strictly peachy keen, as the ofay[9] kids say!

[MAMA *enters from her bedroom. She is lost, vague, trying to catch hold, to make some sense of her former command of the world, but it still eludes her. A sense of waste overwhelms her gait; a measure of apology rides on her shoulders. She goes to her plant, which has remained on the table, looks at it, picks it up and takes it to the window sill and sits it outside, and she stands and looks at it a long moment. Then she closes the window, straightens her body with effort and turns around to her children.*]

MAMA: Well—ain't it a mess in here, though? [*A false cheerfulness, a beginning of something.*] I guess we all better stop moping around and get some work done. All this unpacking and everything we got to do. [RUTH *raises her head slowly in response to the sense of the line; and* BENEATHA *in similar manner turns very slowly to look at her mother.*] One of you all better call the moving people and tell 'em not to come.

RUTH: Tell 'em not to come?

8. Mister Black Middle-Class (French).   9. White.

MAMA: Of course, baby. Ain't no need in 'em coming all the way here and having to go back. They charges for that too. [*She sits down, fingers to her brow, thinking.*] Lord, ever since I was a little girl, I always remembers people saying, "Lena—Lena Eggleston, you aims too high all the time. You needs to slow down and see life a little more like it is. Just slow down some." That's what they always used to say down home—"Lord, that Lena Eggleston is a high-minded thing. She'll get her due one day!"

RUTH: No, Lena . . .

MAMA: Me and Big Walter just didn't never learn right.

RUTH: Lena, no! We gotta go. Bennie—tell her . . . [*She rises and crosses to* BENEATHA *with her arms outstretched.* BENEATHA *doesn't respond.*] Tell her we can still move . . . the notes ain't but a hundred and twenty-five a month. We got four grown people in this house—we can work . . .

MAMA: [*To herself.*] Just aimed too high all the time—

RUTH: [*Turning and going to* MAMA *fast—the words pouring out with urgency and desperation.*] Lena—I'll work . . . I'll work twenty hours a day in all the kitchens in Chicago . . . I'll strap my baby on my back if I have to and scrub all the floors in America and wash all the sheets in America if I have to—but we got to move . . . We got to get out of here . . .

[MAMA *reaches out absently and pats* RUTH's *hand.*]

MAMA: No—I sees things differently now. Been thinking 'bout some of the things we could do to fix this place up some. I seen a second-hand bureau over on Maxwell Street[1] just the other day that could fit right there. [*She points to where the new furniture might go.* RUTH *wanders away from her.*] Would need some new handles on it and then a little varnish and then it look like something brand-new. And—we can put up them new curtains in the kitchen . . . Why this place be looking fine. Cheer us all up so that we forget trouble ever came . . . [*To* RUTH.] And you could get some nice screens to put up in your room round the baby's bassinet . . . [*She looks at both of them, pleadingly.*] Sometimes you just got to know when to give up some things . . . and hold on to what you got.

[WALTER *enters from the outside, looking spent and leaning against the door, his coat hanging from him.*]

MAMA: Where you been, son?

WALTER: [*Breathing hard.*] Made a call.

MAMA: To who, son?

WALTER: To The Man.

MAMA: What man, baby?

WALTER: The Man, Mama. Don't you know who The Man is?

1. Street market southwest of the Loop.

RUTH: Walter Lee?

WALTER: *The Man*. Like the guys in the streets say—The Man. Captain Boss—Mistuh Charley . . . Old Captain Please Mr. Bossman . . .

BENEATHA: [*Suddenly.*] Lindner!

WALTER: That's right! That's good. I told him to come right over.

BENEATHA: [*Fiercely, understanding.*] For what? What do you want to see him for!

WALTER: [*Looking at his sister.*] We going to do business with him.

MAMA: What you talking 'bout, son?

WALTER: Talking 'bout life, Mama. You all always telling me to see life like it is. Well—I laid in there on my back today . . . and I figured it out. Life just like it is. Who gets and who don't get. [*He sits down with his coat on and laughs.*] Mama, you know it's all divided up. Life is. Sure enough. Between the takers and the "tooken." [*He laughs.*] I've figured it out finally. [*He looks around at them.*] Yeah. Some of us always getting "tooken." [*He laughs.*] People like Willy Harris, they don't never get "tooken." And you know why the rest of us do? 'Cause we all mixed up. Mixed up bad. We get to looking 'round for the right and the wrong, and we worry about it and cry about it and stay up nights trying to figure out 'bout the wrong and the right of things all the time . . . And all the time, man, them takers is out there operating, just taking and taking. Willy Harris? Shoot—Willy Harris don't even count. He don't even count in the big scheme of things. But I'll say one thing for old Willy Harris . . . he's taught me something. He's taught me to keep my eye on what counts in this world. Yeah— [*Shouting out a little.*] Thanks, Willy!

RUTH: What did you call that man for, Walter Lee?

WALTER: Called him to tell him to come on over to the show. Gonna put on a show for the man. Just what he wants to see. You see, Mama, the man came here today and he told us that them people out there where you want us to move—well they so upset they willing to pay us not to move out there. [*He laughs again.*] And—and oh, Mama—you would of been proud of the way me and Ruth and Bennie acted. We told him to get out . . . Lord have mercy! We told the man to get out. Oh, we was some proud folks this afternoon, yeah. [*He lights a cigarette.*] We were still full of that old-time stuff . . .

RUTH: [*Coming toward him slowly.*] You talking 'bout taking them people's money to keep us from moving in that house?

WALTER: I ain't just talking 'bout it, baby—I'm telling you that's what's going to happen.

BENEATHA: Oh, God! Where is the bottom! Where is the real honest-to-God bottom so he can't go any farther!

WALTER: See—that's the old stuff. You and that boy that was here today. You all want everybody to carry a flag and a spear and sing some marching songs, huh? You wanna spend your life looking into things and trying to find the right and the wrong part, huh? Yeah. You know what's going to happen to that boy someday—he'll find himself sitting in a dungeon, locked in forever—and the takers will have the key! Forget it, baby! There ain't no causes—there ain't nothing but taking in this world, and he who takes most is smartest—and it don't make a damn bit of difference *how.*

MAMA: You making something inside me cry, son. Some awful pain inside me.

WALTER: Don't cry, Mama. Understand. That white man is going to walk in that door able to write checks for more money than we ever had. It's important to him and I'm going to help him . . . I'm going to put on the show, Mama.

MAMA: Son—I come from five generations of people who was slaves and sharecroppers—but ain't nobody in my family never let nobody pay 'em no money that was a way of telling us we wasn't fit to walk the earth. We ain't never been that poor. [*Raising her eyes and looking at him.*] We ain't never been that dead inside.

BENEATHA: Well—we are dead now. All the talk about dreams and sunlight that goes on in this house. All dead.

WALTER: What's the matter with you all! I didn't make this world! It was give to me this way! Hell, yes, I want me some yachts someday! Yes, I want to hang some real pearls 'round my wife's neck. Ain't she supposed to wear no pearls? Somebody tell me—tell me, who decides which women is suppose to wear pearls in this world. I tell you I am a *man*—and I think my wife should wear some pearls in this world!

[*This last line hangs a good while and* WALTER *begins to move about the room. The word "Man" has penetrated his consciousness; he mumbles it to himself repeatedly between strange agitated pauses as he moves about.*]

MAMA: Baby, how you going to feel on the inside?

WALTER: Fine! . . . Going to feel fine . . . a man . . .

MAMA: You won't have nothing left then, Walter Lee.

WALTER: [*Coming to her.*] I'm going to feel fine, Mama. I'm going to look that son-of-a-bitch in the eyes and say— [*He falters.*] —and say, "All right, Mr. Lindner— [*He falters even more.*] —that's your neighborhood out there. You got the right to keep it like you want. You got the right to have it like you want. Just write the check and—the house is yours." And, and I am going to say— [*His voice almost breaks.*] And you—you people just put the money in my hand and you won't have to live next to this bunch of stinking niggers! . . . [*He straightens up and moves away from his mother, walking around the room.*] Maybe—maybe I'll just get down on my black knees . . . [*He does so;* RUTH *and* BENNIE *and* MAMA *watch him in frozen horror.*] Captain, Mistuh, Bossman. [*He starts crying.*] A-hee-hee-hee! [*Wringing his hands in profoundly anguished imitation.*] Yassss-suh! Great White

Father, just gi' ussen de money, fo' God's sake, and we's ain't gwine come out deh and dirty up yo' white folks neighborhood . . .

[*He breaks down completely, then gets up and goes into the bedroom.*]

BENEATHA: That is not a man. That is nothing but a toothless rat.

MAMA: Yes—death done come in this here house. [*She is nodding, slowly, reflectively.*] Done come walking in my house. On the lips of my children. You what supposed to be my beginning again. You—what supposed to be my harvest. [*To* BENEATHA.] You—you mourning your brother?

BENEATHA: He's no brother of mine.

MAMA: What you say?

BENEATHA: I said that that individual in that room is no brother of mine.

MAMA: That's what I thought you said. You feeling like you better than he is today? [BENEATHA *does not answer.*] Yes? What you tell him a minute ago? That he wasn't a man? Yes? You give him up for me? You done wrote his epitaph too—like the rest of the world? Well, who give you the privilege?

BENEATHA: Be on my side for once! You saw what he just did, Mama! You saw him—down on his knees. Wasn't it you who taught me—to despise any man who would do that. Do what he's going to do.

MAMA: Yes—I taught you that. Me and your daddy. But I thought I taught you something else too . . . I thought I taught you to love him.

BENEATHA: Love him? There is nothing left to love.

MAMA: There is always something left to love. And if you ain't learned that, you ain't learned nothing. [*Looking at her.*] Have you cried for that boy today? I don't mean for yourself and for the family 'cause we lost the money. I mean for him; what he been through and what it done to him. Child, when do you think is the time to love somebody the most; when they done good and made things easy for everybody? Well then, you ain't through learning—because that ain't the time at all. It's when he's at his lowest and can't believe in hisself 'cause the world done whipped him so. When you starts measuring somebody, measure him right, child, measure him right. Make sure you done taken into account what hills and valleys he come through before he got to wherever he is.

[TRAVIS *bursts into the room at the end of the speech, leaving the door open.*]

TRAVIS: Grandmama—the moving men are downstairs! The truck just pulled up.

MAMA: [*Turning and looking at him.*] Are they, baby? They downstairs?

[*She sighs and sits.* LINDNER *appears in the doorway. He peers in and knocks lightly, to gain attention, and comes in. All turn to look at him.*]

LINDNER: [*Hat and briefcase in hand.*] Uh—hello . . . [RUTH *crosses mechanically to the bedroom door and opens it and lets it swing open freely and slowly as the lights come up on* WALTER *within, still in his coat, sitting at the far corner of the room. He looks up and out through the room to* LINDNER.]

RUTH: He's here.

[*A long minute passes and* WALTER *slowly gets up.*]

LINDNER: [*Coming to the table with efficiency, putting his briefcase on the table and starting to unfold papers and unscrew fountain pens.*] Well, I certainly was glad to hear from you people. [WALTER *has begun the trek out of the room, slowly and awkwardly, rather like a small boy, passing the back of his sleeve across his mouth from time to time.*] Life can really be so much simpler than people let it be most of the time. Well—with whom do I negotiate? You, Mrs. Younger, or your son here? [MAMA *sits with her hands folded on her lap and her eyes closed as* WALTER *advances.* TRAVIS *goes close to* LINDNER *and looks at the papers curiously.*] Just some official papers, sonny.

RUTH: Travis, you go downstairs.

MAMA: [*Opening her eyes and looking into* WALTER'S.] No. Travis, you stay right here. And you make him understand what you doing, Walter Lee. You teach him good. Like Willy Harris taught you. You show where our five generations done come to. Go ahead, son—

WALTER: [*Looks down into his boy's eyes.* TRAVIS *grins at him merrily and* WALTER *draws him beside him with his arm lightly around his shoulders.*] Well, Mr. Lindner. [BENEATHA *turns away.*] We called you— [*There is a profound, simple groping quality in his speech.*] —because, well, me and my family [*He looks around and shifts from one foot to the other.*] Well—we are very plain people . . .

LINDNER: Yes—

WALTER: I mean—I have worked as a chauffeur most of my life—and my wife here, she does domestic work in people's kitchens. So does my mother. I mean—we are plain people . . .

LINDNER: Yes, Mr. Younger—

WALTER: [*Really like a small boy, looking down at his shoes and then up at the man.*] And—uh—well, my father, well, he was a laborer most of his life.

LINDNER: [*Absolutely confused.*] Uh, yes—

WALTER: [*Looking down at his toes once again.*] My father almost beat a man to death once because this man called him a bad name or something, you know what I mean?

LINDNER: No, I'm afraid I don't.

WALTER: [*Finally straightening up.*] Well, what I mean is that we come from people who had a lot of pride. I mean—we are very proud people. And that's my sister over there and she's going to be a doctor—and we are very proud—

LINDNER: Well—I am sure that is very nice, but—

WALTER: [*Starting to cry and facing the man eye to eye.*] What I am telling you is that we called you over here to tell you that we are very proud and that this is—this is my son, who makes the sixth generation of our family in this country, and that we have all thought about your offer and we have decided to move into our house because my father—my father—he earned it. [MAMA *has her eyes closed and is rocking back and forth as though she were in church, with her head nodding the amen yes.*] We don't want to make no trouble for nobody or fight no causes—but we will try to be good neighbors. That's all we got to say. [*He looks the man absolutely in the eyes.*] We don't want your money.

[*He turns and walks away from the man.*]

LINDNER: [*Looking around at all of them.*] I take it then that you have decided to occupy.

BENEATHA: That's what the man said.

LINDNER: [*To* MAMA *in her reverie.*] Then I would like to appeal to you, Mrs. Younger. You are older and wiser and understand things better I am sure . . .

MAMA: [*Rising.*] I am afraid you don't understand. My son said we was going to move and there ain't nothing left for me to say. [*Shaking her head with double meaning.*] You know how these young folks is nowadays, mister. Can't do a thing with 'em. Good-bye.

LINDNER: [*Folding up his materials.*] Well—if you are that final about it . . . There is nothing left for me to say. [*He finishes. He is almost ignored by the family, who are concentrating on* WALTER LEE. *At the door* LINDNER *halts and looks around.*] I sure hope you people know what you're doing.

[*He shakes his head and exits.*]

RUTH: [*Looking around and coming to life.*] Well, for God's sake—if the moving men are here—LET'S GET THE HELL OUT OF HERE!

MAMA: [*Into action.*] Ain't it the truth! Look at all this here mess. Ruth, put Travis' good jacket on him . . . Walter Lee, fix your tie and tuck your shirt in, you look just like somebody's hoodlum. Lord have mercy, where is my plant? [*She flies to get it amid the general bustling of the family, who are deliberately trying to ignore the nobility of the past moment.*] You all start on down . . . Travis child, don't go empty-handed . . . Ruth, where did I put that box with my skillets in it? I want to be in charge of it myself . . . I'm going to make us the biggest dinner we ever ate tonight . . . Beneatha, what's the matter with them stockings? Pull them things up, girl . . .

[*The family starts to file out as two moving men appear and begin to carry out the heavier pieces of furniture, bumping into the family as they move about.*]

BENEATHA: Mama, Asagai—asked me to marry him today and go to Africa—

MAMA: [*In the middle of her getting-ready activity.*] He did? You ain't old enough to marry nobody— [*Seeing the moving men lifting one of her chairs precari-*

ously.] Darling, that ain't no bale of cotton, please handle it so we can sit in it again. I had that chair twenty-five years . . .

[*The movers sigh with exasperation and go on with their work.*]

BENEATHA: [*Girlishly and unreasonably trying to pursue the conversation.*] To go to Africa, Mama—be a doctor in Africa . . .

MAMA: [*Distracted.*] Yes, baby—

WALTER: Africa! What he want you to go to Africa for?

BENEATHA: To practice there . . .

WALTER: Girl, if you don't get all them silly ideas out your head! You better marry yourself a man with some loot . . .

BENEATHA: [*Angrily, precisely as in the first scene of the play.*] What have you got to do with who I marry!

WALTER: Plenty. Now I think George Murchison—

[*He and* BENEATHA *go out yelling at each other vigorously;* BENEATHA *is heard saying that she would not marry* GEORGE MURCHISON *if he were Adam and she were Eve, etc. The anger is loud and real till their voices diminish.* RUTH *stands at the door and turns to* MAMA *and smiles knowingly.*]

MAMA: [*Fixing her hat at last.*] Yeah—they something all right, my children . . .

RUTH: Yeah—they're something. Let's go, Lena.

MAMA: [*Stalling, starting to look around at the house.*] Yes—I'm coming. Ruth—

RUTH: Yes?

MAMA: [*Quietly, woman to woman.*] He finally come into his manhood today, didn't he? Kind of like a rainbow after the rain . . .

RUTH: [*Biting her lip lest her own pride explode in front of* MAMA.] Yes, Lena.

[WALTER's *voice calls for them raucously.*]

MAMA: [*Waving* RUTH *out vaguely.*] All right, honey—go on down. I be down directly.

[RUTH *hesitates, then exits.* MAMA *stands, at last alone in the living room, her plant on the table before her as the lights start to come down. She looks around at all the walls and ceilings and suddenly, despite herself, while the children call below, a great heaving thing rises in her and she puts her fist to her mouth, takes a final desperate look, pulls her coat about her, pats her hat and goes out. The lights dim down. The door opens and she comes back in, grabs her plant, and goes out for the last time.*]

[CURTAIN.]

1959

Authors on Their Work: LORRAINE HANSBERRY

From *Village Voice* (1959)*

... Walter Younger is an American more than he is any-thing else. His ordeal ... is not extraordinary but intensely familiar like Willy [Loman]'s [in Arthur Miller's *Death of a Salesman*]. The two of them have virtually no values which have not come out of their culture, and to a significant point, no view of the possible solutions to their problems which do not also come out of the selfsame culture. Walter can find no peace with that part of society which seems to permit him no entry into that which has willfully excluded him. He shares with Willy Loman the acute awareness that *something* is obstructing some abstract progress that he feels he *should* be making; that *something* is in the way of his ascendancy. It does not occur to either of them to question the nature of this desired "ascendancy." Walter accepts, he believes in the "world" as it has been presented to him. When we first meet him, he does not wish to alter *it*; merely to change *his* position in it. His mentors and his associates all take the view that the institutions which frustrate him are somehow impeccable, or, at best, "unfortunate." "Things being as they are," he must look to *himself* as the only source of any rewards he may expect. Within himself, he is encouraged to believe, are the only seeds of defeat or victory within the universe. And Walter believes this and when opportunity, haphazard and rooted in death, prevails, he acts.

Huge Obstacles

But the obstacles ... are gigantic; the weight of the loss of the money is in fact, the weight of death. In Walter Lee Younger's life, somebody *has* to die for ten thousand bucks to pile up—if then. Elsewhere in the world, in the face of catastrophe, he might be tempted to don the saffron robes of acceptance and sit on a mountain top all day contemplating the divine justice of his misery. Or, history being what it is turning out to be, he might wander down to his first Communist Party meeting. But here in the dynamic and confusing postwar years on the Southside of Chicago, his choices of action are equal to those gestures only in symbolic terms. The American ghetto hero may give up and contemplate his misery in rose-colored bars to the melodies of hypnotic saxophones, but revolution seems alien to him in his circumstances (America), and it is easier to

(Continued on next page)

(Continued)

dream of personal wealth than of a communal state wherein universal dignity is supposed to be a corollary. Yet his position in time and space does allow for one other alternative; he may take his place on any one of a number of frontiers of challenge. Challenges (such as helping to break down restricted neighborhoods) which are admittedly limited because they most certainly do not threaten the basic social order.

Not So Small

But why is even this final choice possible . . . ? Well, that is where Walter departs from Willy Loman; there is a second pulse in his still-dual culture. His people have had "somewhere" they have been trying to get for so long that more sophisticated confusions do not yet bind them. . . . Walter is, despite his lack of consciousness of it, inextricably as much wedded to his special mass as Willy was to his, and the moods of each are able to decisively determine the dramatic typicality. Furthermore, the very nature of the situation of American Negroes can force their representative hero to recognize that for his *true* ascendancy he must ultimately be at cross-purposes with at least certain of his culture's values. . . .

In other words, the symbolism of moving into the new house is quite as small as it seems and quite as significant. For if there are no waving flags and marching songs at the barricades as Walter marches out with his little battalion, it is not because the battle lacks nobility. On the contrary, he has picked up in his way, still imperfect and wobbly in his small view of human destiny, what I believe Arthur Miller once called "the golden thread of history." He becomes, in spite of those who are too intrigued with despair and hatred of man to see it, King Oedipus refusing to tear out his eyes, but attacking the Oracle instead. He is that last Jewish patriot manning his rifle in the burning ghetto at Warsaw; . . . he is the nine small heroes of Little Rock; he is Michelangelo creating David and Beethoven bursting forth with the Ninth Symphony. He is all those things because he has finally reached out in his tiny moment and caught that sweet essence which is human dignity, and it shines like the gold star-touched dream that it is in his eyes. We see, in the moment, I think, what becomes, and not for Negroes alone, but for Willy and all of us, entirely an American responsibility.

Out in the darkness where we watch, most of us are not afraid to cry.

*Lorraine Hansberry, "Willie Loman, Walter Younger, and He Who Must Live," *Village Voice* 12 (Aug. 1959): 7–8.

Hamlet

CHARACTERS

CLAUDIUS, *King of Denmark*
HAMLET, *son of the former king and*
   nephew to the present king
POLONIUS, *Lord Chamberlain*
HORATIO, *friend of Hamlet*
LAERTES, *son of Polonius*
VOLTEMAND ⎤
CORNELIUS   ⎥
ROSENCRANTZ ⎥ *courtiers*
GUILDENSTERN ⎥
OSRIC   ⎥
A GENTLEMAN ⎦
A PRIEST

MARCELLUS ⎤ *officers*
BERNARDO ⎦
FRANCISCO, *a soldier*
REYNALDO, *servant to Polonius*
PLAYERS
TWO CLOWNS, *gravediggers*
FORTINBRAS, *Prince of Norway*
A NORWEGIAN CAPTAIN
ENGLISH AMBASSADORS
GERTRUDE, *Queen of Denmark, and*
   mother of Hamlet
OPHELIA, *daughter of Polonius*
GHOST OF HAMLET'S FATHER

LORDS, LADIES, OFFICERS, SOLDIERS, SAILORS, MESSENGERS, AND ATTENDANTS

SCENE: *The action takes place in or near the royal castle of Denmark at Elsinore.*

ACT I

Scene 1

A guard station atop the castle. Enter BERNARDO *and* FRANCISCO, *two sentinels.*

BERNARDO: Who's there?
FRANCISCO: Nay, answer me. Stand and unfold yourself.
BERNARDO: Long live the king!
FRANCISCO: Bernardo?
5 BERNARDO: He.
FRANCISCO: You come most carefully upon your hour.
BERNARDO: 'Tis now struck twelve. Get thee to bed, Francisco.
FRANCISCO: For this relief much thanks. 'Tis bitter cold,
   And I am sick at heart.
BERNARDO: Have you had quiet guard?
10 FRANCISCO: Not a mouse stirring.
BERNARDO: Well, good night.
   If you do meet Horatio and Marcellus,
   The rivals[1] of my watch, bid them make haste.

     [*Enter* HORATIO *and* MARCELLUS.]

---

1. Companions.

FRANCISCO: I think I hear them. Stand, ho! Who is there?
HORATIO: Friends to this ground.
MARCELLUS: And liegemen to the Dane.[2]   15
FRANCISCO: Give you good night.
MARCELLUS: O, farewell, honest soldier!
    Who hath relieved you?
FRANCISCO: Bernardo hath my place.
    Give you good night.   [*Exit* FRANCISCO.]
MARCELLUS: Holla, Bernardo!
BERNARDO: Say—
    What, is Horatio there?
HORATIO: A piece of him.
BERNARDO: Welcome, Horatio. Welcome, good Marcellus.   20
HORATIO: What, has this thing appeared again tonight?
BERNARDO: I have seen nothing.
MARCELLUS: Horatio says 'tis but our fantasy,
    And will not let belief take hold of him
    Touching this dreaded sight twice seen of us.   25
    Therefore I have entreated him along
    With us to watch the minutes of this night,
    That if again this apparition come,
    He may approve[3] our eyes and speak to it.
HORATIO: Tush, tush, 'twill not appear.
BERNARDO: Sit down awhile,   30
    And let us once again assail your ears,
    That are so fortified against our story,
    What we have two nights seen.
HORATIO: Well, sit we down.
    And let us hear Bernardo speak of this.
BERNARDO: Last night of all,   35
    When yond same star that's westward from the pole[4]
    Had made his course t' illume that part of heaven
    Where now it burns, Marcellus and myself,
    The bell then beating one—

        [*Enter* GHOST.]

MARCELLUS: Peace, break thee off. Look where it comes again.   40
BERNARDO: In the same figure like the king that's dead.
MARCELLUS: Thou art a scholar; speak to it, Horatio.
BERNARDO: Looks 'a[5] not like the king? Mark it, Horatio.

---

2. The "Dane" is the king of Denmark, who is also called "Denmark," as in line 48 of this scene.
In line 61 a similar reference is used for the king of Norway.
3. Confirm the testimony of.   4. Polestar.   5. He.

HORATIO: Most like. It harrows me with fear and wonder.

BERNARDO: It would be spoke to.

45 MARCELLUS: Speak to it, Horatio.

HORATIO: What art thou that usurp'st this time of night
    Together with that fair and warlike form
    In which the majesty of buried Denmark
    Did sometimes march? By heaven I charge thee, speak.

MARCELLUS: It is offended.

50 BERNARDO: See, it stalks away.

HORATIO: Stay. Speak, speak. I charge thee, speak.   [*Exit* GHOST.]

MARCELLUS: 'Tis gone and will not answer.

BERNARDO: How now, Horatio! You tremble and look pale.
    Is not this something more than fantasy?
55   What think you on't?

HORATIO: Before my God, I might not this believe
    Without the sensible[6] and true avouch
    Of mine own eyes.

MARCELLUS: It is not like the king?

HORATIO: As thou art to thyself.
60   Such was the very armor he had on
    When he the ambitious Norway combated.
    So frowned he once when, in an angry parle,[7]
    He smote the sledded Polacks on the ice.
    'Tis strange.

65 MARCELLUS: Thus twice before, and jump[8] at this dead hour,
    With martial stalk hath he gone by our watch.

HORATIO: In what particular thought to work I know not,
    But in the gross and scope of mine opinion,
    This bodes some strange eruption to our state.

70 MARCELLUS: Good now, sit down, and tell me he that knows,
    Why this same strict and most observant watch
    So nightly toils the subject[9] of the land,
    And why such daily cast of brazen cannon
    And foreign mart for implements of war;
75   Why such impress of shipwrights, whose sore task
    Does not divide the Sunday from the week.
    What might be toward that this sweaty haste
    Doth make the night joint-laborer with the day?
    Who is't that can inform me?

HORATIO: That can I.
80   At least, the whisper goes so. Our last king,
    Whose image even but now appeared to us,

6. Perceptible.   7. Parley.   8. Precisely.   9. People.

Was as you know by Fortinbras of Norway,
Thereto pricked on by a most emulate pride,
Dared to the combat; in which our valiant Hamlet
(For so this side of our known world esteemed him) 85
Did slay this Fortinbras; who by a sealed compact
Well ratifièd by law and heraldry,
Did forfeit, with his life, all those his lands
Which he stood seized of,[1] to the conqueror;
Against the which a moiety competent[2] 90
Was gagèd[3] by our king; which had returned
To the inheritance of Fortinbras,
Had he been vanquisher; as, by the same covenant
And carriage of the article designed,
His fell to Hamlet. Now, sir, young Fortinbras, 95
Of unimprovèd mettle hot and full,
Hath in the skirts of Norway here and there
Sharked up a list of lawless resolutes
For food and diet to some enterprise
That hath a stomach in't; which is no other, 100
As it doth well appear unto our state,
But to recover of us by strong hand
And terms compulsatory, those foresaid lands
So by his father lost; and this, I take it,
Is the main motive of our preparations, 105
The source of this our watch, and the chief head
Of this post-haste and romage[4] in the land.
BERNARDO: I think it be no other but e'en so.
　Well may it sort[5] that this portentous figure
　Comes armèd through our watch so like the king 110
　That was and is the question of these wars.
HORATIO: A mote[6] it is to trouble the mind's eye.
　In the most high and palmy state of Rome,
　A little ere the mightiest Julius fell,
　The graves stood tenantless, and the sheeted dead 115
　Did squeak and gibber in the Roman streets;
　As stars with trains of fire, and dews of blood,
　Disasters in the sun; and the moist star,
　Upon whose influence Neptune's empire stands,[7]
　Was sick almost to doomsday with eclipse. 120
　And even the like precurse[8] of feared events,

---

1. Possessed.　2. Portion of similar value.　3. Pledged.　4. Stir.　5. Chance.
6. Speck of dust.　7. Neptune was the Roman sea god; the "moist star" is the moon.
8. Precursor.

As harbingers preceding still the fates
And prologue to the omen coming on,
Have heaven and earth together demonstrated
125 Unto our climatures[9] and countrymen.

[*Enter* GHOST.]

But soft, behold, lo where it comes again!
I'll cross it[1] though it blast me.—Stay, illusion.

[*It spreads (its) arms.*]

If thou hast any sound or use of voice,
Speak to me.
130 If there be any good thing to be done,
That may to thee do ease, and grace to me,
Speak to me.
If thou art privy to thy country's fate,
Which happily foreknowing may avoid,
135 O, speak!
Or if thou hast uphoarded in thy life[1]
Extorted treasure in the womb of earth,
For which, they say, you spirits oft walk in death,

[*The cock crows.*]

Speak of it. Stay, and speak. Stop it, Marcellus.
140 MARCELLUS: Shall I strike at it with my partisan?[2]
HORATIO: Do, if it will not stand.
BERNARDO: 'Tis here.
HORATIO: 'Tis here.
MARCELLUS: 'Tis gone.   [*Exit* GHOST.]
We do it wrong, being so majestical,
To offer it the show of violence;
145 For it is as the air, invulnerable,
And our vain blows malicious mockery.
BERNARDO: It was about to speak when the cock crew.
HORATIO: And then it started like a guilty thing
Upon a fearful summons. I have heard
150 The cock, that is the trumpet to the morn,
Doth with his lofty and shrill-sounding throat

[handwritten: not a lot of stage directions]

9. Regions.
1. Horatio means either that he will move across the ghost's path in order to stop him or that he will make the sign of the cross to gain power over him. The stage direction that follows is somewhat ambiguous. "It" seems to refer to the ghost, but the movement would be appropriate to Horatio.
2. Halberd.

Awake the god of day, and at his warning,
Whether in sea or fire, in earth or air,
Th' extravagant and erring³ spirit hies
To his confine; and of the truth herein   155
This present object made probation.⁴
MARCELLUS: It faded on the crowing of the cock.
Some say that ever 'gainst that season comes
Wherein our Savior's birth is celebrated,
This bird of dawning singeth all night long,   160
And then, they say, no spirit dare stir abroad,
The nights are wholesome, then no planets strike,
No fairy takes,⁵ nor witch hath power to charm,
So hallowed and so gracious is that time.
HORATIO: So have I heard and do in part believe it.   165
But look, the morn in russet mantle clad
Walks o'er the dew of yon high eastward hill.
Break we our watch up, and by my advice
Let us impart what we have seen tonight
Unto young Hamlet, for upon my life   170
This spirit, dumb to us, will speak to him.
Do you consent we shall acquaint him with it,
As needful in our loves, fitting our duty?
MARCELLUS: Let's do't, I pray, and I this morning know
Where we shall find him most conveniently.   [*Exeunt.*] 175

Scene 2

A chamber of state. Enter KING CLAUDIUS, QUEEN GERTRUDE, HAMLET, POLO-
NIUS, LAERTES, VOLTEMAND, CORNELIUS *and other members of the court.*

KING: Though yet of Hamlet our dear brother's death
The memory be green, and that it us befitted
To bear our hearts in grief, and our whole kingdom
To be contracted in one brow of woe,
Yet so far hath discretion fought with nature   5
That we with wisest sorrow think on him,
Together with remembrance of ourselves.
Therefore our sometime sister, now our queen,
Th' imperial jointress⁶ to this warlike state,
Have we, as 'twere with a defeated joy,   10
With an auspicious and a dropping eye,

---

3. Errant, wandering out of bounds.   4. Proof.   5. Enchants.
6. A "jointress" is a widow who holds a *jointure* or life interest in the estate of her deceased husband.

With mirth in funeral, and with dirge in marriage,
In equal scale weighing delight and dole,
Taken to wife; nor have we herein barred

15   Your better wisdoms, which have freely gone
With this affair along. For all, our thanks.
Now follows that you know young Fortinbras,
Holding a weak supposal of our worth,
Or thinking by our late dear brother's death

20   Our state to be disjoint and out of frame,
Colleaguèd with this dream of his advantage,
He hath not failed to pester us with message
Importing the surrender of those lands
Lost by his father, with all bonds of law,

25   To our most valiant brother. So much for him.
Now for ourself, and for this time of meeting,
Thus much the business is: we have here writ
To Norway, uncle of young Fortinbras—
Who, impotent and bedrid, scarcely hears

30   Of this his nephew's purpose—to suppress
His further gait⁷ herein, in that the levies,
The lists, and full proportions are all made
Out of his subject; and we here dispatch
You, good Cornelius, and you, Voltemand,

35   For bearers of this greeting to old Norway,
Giving to you no further personal power
To business with the king, more than the scope
Of these dilated⁸ articles allow.
Farewell, and let your haste commend your duty.

40   CORNELIUS: ⎤
       VOLTEMAND: ⎦ In that, and all things will we show our duty.

KING: We doubt it nothing, heartily farewell.

                          [*Exeunt* VOLTEMAND *and* CORNELIUS.]

And now, Laertes, what's the news with you?
You told us of some suit. What is't, Laertes?
You cannot speak of reason to the Dane

45   And lose your voice. What wouldst thou beg, Laertes,
That shall not be my offer, not thy asking?
The head is not more native to the heart,
The hand more instrumental⁹ to the mouth,
Than is the throne of Denmark to thy father.
What wouldst thou have, Laertes?

50 LAERTES: My dread lord,

---

7. Progress.   8. Fully expressed.   9. Serviceable.

Your leave and favor to return to France,
From whence, though willingly, I came to Denmark
To show my duty in your coronation,
Yet now I must confess, that duty done,
My thoughts and wishes bend again toward France,   55
And bow them to your gracious leave and pardon.
KING: Have you your father's leave? What says Polonius?
POLONIUS: He hath, my lord, wrung from me my slow leave
  By laborsome petition, and at last
  Upon his will I sealed my hard consent.   60
  I do beseech you give him leave to go.
KING: Take thy fair hour, Laertes. Time be thine,
  And thy best graces spend it at thy will.
  But now, my cousin¹ Hamlet, and my son—
HAMLET: [*Aside.*] A little more than kin, and less than kind.   65
KING: How is it that the clouds still hang on you?
HAMLET: Not so, my lord. I am too much in the sun.
QUEEN: Good Hamlet, cast thy nighted color off,
  And let thine eye look like a friend on Denmark.
  Do not for ever with thy vailèd lids²   70
  Seek for thy noble father in the dust.
  Thou know'st 'tis common—all that lives must die,
  Passing through nature to eternity.
HAMLET: Ay, madam, it is common.
QUEEN: If it be,
  Why seems it so particular with thee?   75
HAMLET: Seems, madam? Nay, it is. I know not "seems."
  'Tis not alone my inky cloak, good mother,
  Nor customary suits of solemn black,
  Nor windy suspiration of forced breath,
  No, nor the fruitful river in the eye,   80
  Nor the dejected havior³ of the visage,
  Together with all forms, moods, shapes of grief,
  That can denote me truly. These indeed seem,
  For they are actions that a man might play,
  But I have that within which passes show—   85
  These but the trappings and the suits of woe.
KING: 'Tis sweet and commendable in your nature, Hamlet,
  To give these mourning duties to your father,
  But you must know your father lost a father,
  That father lost, lost his, and the survivor bound   90
  In filial obligation for some term

---

1. "Cousin" is used here as a general term of kinship.   2. Lowered eyes.   3. Appearance.

To do obsequious[4] sorrow. But to persever
In obstinate condolement is a course
Of impious stubbornness. 'Tis unmanly grief.
95   It shows a will most incorrect to[5] heaven,
A heart unfortified, a mind impatient,
An understanding simple and unschooled.
For what we know must be, and is as common
As any the most vulgar thing to sense,
100   Why should we in our peevish opposition
Take it to heart? Fie, 'tis a fault to heaven,
A fault against the dead, a fault to nature,
To reason most absurd, whose common theme
Is death of fathers, and who still hath cried,
105   From the first corse[6] till he that died today,
"This must be so." We pray you throw to earth
This unprevailing woe, and think of us
As of a father, for let the world take note
You are the most immediate[7] to our throne,
110   And with no less nobility of love
Than that which dearest father bears his son
Do I impart toward you. For your intent
In going back to school in Wittenberg,
It is most retrograde[8] to our desire,
115   And we beseech you, bend you to remain
Here in the cheer and comfort of our eye,
Our chiefest courtier, cousin, and our son.
QUEEN: Let not thy mother lose her prayers, Hamlet.
I pray thee stay with us, go not to Wittenberg.
120 HAMLET: I shall in all my best obey you, madam.
KING: Why, 'tis a loving and a fair reply.
Be as ourself in Denmark. Madam, come.
This gentle and unforced accord of Hamlet
Sits smiling to my heart, in grace whereof,
125   No jocund health that Denmark drinks today
But the great cannon to the clouds shall tell,
And the king's rouse the heaven shall bruit[9] again,
Respeaking earthly thunder. Come away.

[Flourish. Exeunt all but HAMLET.]

HAMLET: O, that this too too solid flesh would melt,
130   Thaw, and resolve itself into a dew,
Or that the Everlasting had not fixed
His canon[1] 'gainst self-slaughter. O God, God,

---

4. Suited for funeral obsequies.   5. Unsubmissive toward.   6. Corpse.   7. Next in line.
8. Contrary.   9. Echo. *Rouse:* carousal.   1. Law.

How weary, stale, flat, and unprofitable
Seem to me all the uses of this world!
Fie on't, ah, fie, 'tis an unweeded garden   135
That grows to seed. Things rank and gross in nature
Possess it merely.[2] That it should come to this,
But two months dead, nay, not so much, not two.
So excellent a king, that was to this
Hyperion to a satyr,[3] so loving to my mother,   140
That he might not beteem[4] the winds of heaven
Visit her face too roughly. Heaven and earth,
Must I remember? Why, she would hang on him
As if increase of appetite had grown
By what it fed on, and yet, within a month—   145
Let me not think on't. Frailty, thy name is woman—
A little month, or ere those shoes were old
With which she followed my poor father's body
Like Niobe,[5] all tears, why she, even she—
O God, a beast that wants discourse of reason   150
Would have mourned longer—married with my uncle,
My father's brother, but no more like my father
Than I to Hercules.[6] Within a month,
Ere yet the salt of most unrighteous tears
Had left the flushing in her gallèd eyes,   155
She married. O, most wicked speed, to post
With such dexterity to incestuous sheets!
It is not, nor it cannot come to good.
But break my heart, for I must hold my tongue.

[*Enter* HORATIO, MARCELLUS, *and* BERNARDO.]

HORATIO: Hail to your lordship!
HAMLET: I am glad to see you well.   160
    Horatio—or I do forget myself.
HORATIO: The same, my lord, and your poor servant ever.
HAMLET: Sir, my good friend, I'll change that name with you.
    And what make you from[7] Wittenberg, Horatio?
    Marcellus?   165
MARCELLUS: My good lord!

2. Entirely.
3. Hyperion, a Greek god, stands here for beauty in contrast to the monstrous satyr, a lecherous creature, half man and half goat.   4. Permit.
5. In Greek mythology, Niobe was turned to stone after a tremendous fit of weeping over the death of her fourteen children, a misfortune brought about by her boasting over her fertility.
6. The demigod Hercules was noted for his strength and the series of spectacular labors that he accomplished.   7. What are you doing away from? *Change*: exchange.

HAMLET: I am very glad to see you. [*To* BERNARDO.] Good even, sir.—
But what, in faith, make you from Wittenberg?
HORATIO: A truant disposition, good my lord.
170 HAMLET: I would not hear your enemy say so,
Nor shall you do my ear that violence
To make it truster of your own report
Against yourself. I know you are no truant.
But what is your affair in Elsinore?
175 We'll teach you to drink deep ere you depart.
HORATIO: My lord, I came to see your father's funeral.
HAMLET: I prithee do not mock me, fellow-student,
I think it was to see my mother's wedding.
HORATIO: Indeed, my lord, it followed hard upon.
180 HAMLET: Thrift, thrift, Horatio. The funeral-baked meats
Did coldly furnish forth the marriage tables.
Would I had met my dearest[8] foe in heaven
Or ever I had seen that day, Horatio!
My father—methinks I see my father.
HORATIO: Where, my lord?
185 HAMLET: In my mind's eye, Horatio.
HORATIO: I saw him once, 'a was a goodly king.
HAMLET: 'A was a man, take him for all in all,
I shall not look upon his like again.
HORATIO: My lord, I think I saw him yesternight.
190 HAMLET: Saw who?
HORATIO: My lord, the king your father.
HAMLET: The king my father?
HORATIO: Season your admiration[9] for a while
With an attent ear till I may deliver[1]
Upon the witness of these gentlemen
This marvel to you.
195 HAMLET: For God's love, let me hear!
HORATIO: Two nights together had these gentlemen,
Marcellus and Bernardo, on their watch
In the dead waste and middle of the night
Been thus encountered. A figure like your father,
200 Armèd at point exactly, cap-a-pe,[2]
Appears before them, and with solemn march
Goes slow and stately by them. Thrice he walked
By their oppressed and fear-surprisèd eyes
Within his truncheon's[3] length, whilst they, distilled

8. Bitterest.   9. Moderate your wonder.   1. Relate. *Attent*: attentive.
2. From head to toe. *Exactly*: completely.   3. Baton of office.

Almost to jelly with the act of fear, 205
Stand dumb and speak not to him. This to me
In dreadful secrecy impart they did,
And I with them the third night kept the watch,
Where, as they had delivered, both in time,
Form of the thing, each word made true and good, 210
The apparition comes. I knew your father.
These hands are not more like.

HAMLET: But where was this?

MARCELLUS: My lord, upon the platform where we watch.

HAMLET: Did you not speak to it?

HORATIO: My lord, I did,
But answer made it none. Yet once methought 215
It lifted up it head and did address
Itself to motion, like as it would speak;
But even then the morning cock crew loud,
And at the sound it shrunk in haste away
And vanished from our sight.

HAMLET: 'Tis very strange. 220

HORATIO: As I do live, my honored lord, 'tis true,
And we did think it writ down in our duty
To let you know of it.

HAMLET: Indeed, sirs, but
This troubles me. Hold you the watch tonight?

ALL: We do, my lord.

HAMLET: Armed, say you?

ALL: Armed, my lord. 225

HAMLET: From top to toe?

ALL: My lord, from head to foot.

HAMLET: Then saw you not his face.

HORATIO: O yes, my lord, he wore his beaver[4] up.

HAMLET: What, looked he frowningly?

HORATIO: A countenance more in sorrow than in anger. 230

HAMLET: Pale or red?

HORATIO: Nay, very pale.

HAMLET: And fixed his eyes upon you?

HORATIO: Most constantly.

HAMLET: I would I had been there.

HORATIO: It would have much amazed you.

HAMLET: Very like.
Stayed it long? 235

HORATIO: While one with moderate haste might tell[5] a hundred.

---

4. Hinged face protector.   5. Count.

BOTH: Longer, longer.

HORATIO: Not when I saw't.

HAMLET: His beard was grizzled, no?

HORATIO: It was as I have seen it in his life,
     A sable silvered.

240 HAMLET: I will watch tonight.
     Perchance 'twill walk again.

HORATIO: I warr'nt it will.

HAMLET: If it assume my noble father's person,
     I'll speak to it though hell itself should gape
     And bid me hold my peace. I pray you all,

245   If you have hitherto concealed this sight,
     Let it be tenable[6] in your silence still,
     And whatsomever else shall hap tonight,
     Give it an understanding but no tongue.
     I will requite your loves. So fare you well.

250   Upon the platform 'twixt eleven and twelve
     I'll visit you.

ALL: Our duty to your honor.

HAMLET: Your loves, as mine to you. Farewell.   [*Exeunt all but* HAMLET.]
     My father's spirit in arms? All is not well.
     I doubt[7] some foul play. Would the night were come!

255   Till then sit still, my soul. Foul deeds will rise,
     Though all the earth o'erwhelm them, to men's eyes.   [*Exit.*]

Scene 3

The dwelling of POLONIUS. *Enter* LAERTES *and* OPHELIA.

LAERTES: My necessaries are embarked. Farewell.
     And, sister, as the winds give benefit
     And convoy is assistant,[8] do not sleep,
     But let me hear from you.

OPHELIA: Do you doubt that?

5 LAERTES: For Hamlet, and the trifling of his favor,
     Hold it a fashion and a toy in blood,
     A violet in the youth of primy[9] nature,
     Forward, not permanent, sweet, not lasting,
     The perfume and suppliance of a minute,
     No more.

OPHELIA: No more but so?

10 LAERTES: Think it no more.
     For nature crescent[1] does not grow alone

---

6. Held.   7. Suspect.   8. Means of transport is available.   9. Of the spring.   1. Growing.

In thews and bulk, but as this temple[2] waxes
The inward service of the mind and soul
Grows wide withal. Perhaps he loves you now,
And now no soil nor cautel[3] doth besmirch   15
The virtue of his will, but you must fear,
His greatness weighted,[4] his will is not his own,
For he himself is subject to his birth.
He may not, as unvalued persons do,
Carve for himself, for on his choice depends   20
The safety and health of this whole state,
And therefore must his choice be circumscribed
Unto the voice[5] and yielding of that body
Whereof he is the head. Then if he says he loves you,
It fits your wisdom so far to believe it   25
As he in his particular act and place
May give his saying deed, which is no further
Than the main voice of Denmark goes withal.
Then weigh what loss your honor may sustain
If with too credent ear you list[6] his songs,   30
Or lose your heart, or your chaste treasure open
To his unmastered importunity.
Fear it, Ophelia, fear it, my dear sister,
And keep you in the rear of your affection,
Out of the shot and danger of desire.   35
The chariest[7] maid is prodigal enough
If she unmask her beauty to the moon.
Virtue itself scapes not calumnious strokes.
The canker[8] galls the infants of the spring
Too oft before their buttons[9] be disclosed,   40
And in the morn and liquid dew of youth
Contagious blastments[1] are most imminent.
Be wary then; best safety lies in fear.
Youth to itself rebels, though none else near.

OPHELIA: I shall the effect of this good lesson keep   45
  As watchman to my heart. But, good my brother,
  Do not as some ungracious pastors do,
  Show me the steep and thorny way to heaven,
  Whiles like a puffed and reckless libertine
  Himself the primrose path of dalliance treads   50
  And recks not his own rede.[2]
LAERTES: O, fear me not.

2. Body. *Thews*: muscles.   3. Deceit.   4. Rank considered.   5. Assent.
6. Too credulous an ear you listen to.   7. Most circumspect.   8. Cankerworm.   9. Buds.
1. Blights.   2. Heeds not his own advice.

[*Enter* POLONIUS.]

I stay too long. But here my father comes.
A double blessing is a double grace;
Occasion smiles upon a second leave.

55 POLONIUS: Yet here, Laertes? Aboard, aboard, for shame!
The wind sits in the shoulder of your sail,
And you are stayed for. There—my blessing with thee,
And these few precepts in thy memory
Look thou character.³ Give thy thoughts no tongue,
60   Nor any unproportioned thought his act.
Be thou familiar, but by no means vulgar.
Those friends thou hast, and their adoption tried,
Grapple them unto thy soul with hoops of steel;
But do not dull⁴ thy palm with entertainment
65   Of each new-hatched, unfledged comrade. Beware
Of entrance to a quarrel, but being in,
Bear't that th' opposèd⁵ may beware of thee.
Give every man thy ear, but few thy voice;⁶
Take each man's censure, but reserve thy judgment.
70   Costly thy habit as thy purse can buy,
But not expressed in fancy; rich not gaudy,
For the apparel oft proclaims the man,
And they in France of the best rank and station
Are of a most select and generous chief⁷ in that.
75   Neither a borrower nor a lender be,
For loan oft loses both itself and friend,
And borrowing dulls th' edge of husbandry.
This above all, to thine own self be true,
And it must follow as the night the day
80   Thou canst not then be false to any man.
Farewell. My blessing season this in thee!

LAERTES: Most humbly do I take my leave, my lord.

POLONIUS: The time invests you. Go, your servants tend.⁸

LAERTES: Farewell, Ophelia, and remember well
What I have said to you.

85 OPHELIA: 'Tis in my memory locked,
And you yourself shall keep the key of it.

LAERTES: Farewell.   [*Exit.*]

POLONIUS: What is't, Ophelia, he hath said to you?

OPHELIA: So please you, something touching the Lord Hamlet.

---

3. Write.   4. Make callous.   5. Conduct it so that the opponent.   6. Approval.
7. Eminence.   8. Await.

POLONIUS: Marry, well bethought.   90
'Tis told me he hath very oft of late
Given private time to you, and you yourself
Have of your audience been most free and bounteous.
If it be so—as so 'tis put on me,
And that in way of caution—I must tell you,   95
You do not understand yourself so clearly
As it behooves my daughter and your honor.
What is between you? Give me up the truth.
OPHELIA: He hath, my lord, of late made many tenders
Of his affection to me.   100
POLONIUS: Affection? Pooh! You speak like a green girl,
Unsifted in such perilous circumstance.
Do you believe his tenders, as you call them?
OPHELIA: I do not know, my lord, what I should think.
POLONIUS: Marry, I will teach you. Think yourself a baby   105
That you have ta'en these tenders for true pay
Which are not sterling. Tender yourself more dearly,
Or (not to crack the wind of the poor phrase,
Running it thus) you'll tender me a fool.
OPHELIA: My lord, he hath importuned me with love   110
In honorable fashion.
POLONIUS: Ay, fashion you may call it. Go to, go to.
OPHELIA: And hath given countenance⁹ to his speech, my lord,
With almost all the holy vows of heaven.
POLONIUS: Ay, springes¹ to catch woodcocks. I do know,   115
When the blood burns, how prodigal the soul
Lends the tongue vows. These blazes, daughter,
Giving more light than heat, extinct in both
Even in their promise, as it is a-making,
You must not take for fire. From this time   120
Be something scanter of your maiden presence.
Set your entreatments² at a higher rate
Than a command to parle. For Lord Hamlet,
Believe so much in him that he is young,
And with a larger tether may he walk   125
Than may be given you. In few, Ophelia,
Do not believe his vows, for they are brokers,³
Not of that dye which their investments⁴ show,
But mere implorators⁵ of unholy suits,
Breathing like sanctified and pious bawds,   130

9. Confirmation.   1. Snares.   2. Negotiations before a surrender.   3. Panderers.
4. Garments.   5. Solicitors.

The better to beguile. This is for all:
I would not, in plain terms, from this time forth
Have you so slander any moment leisure
As to give words or talk with the Lord Hamlet.
135   Look to't, I charge you. Come your ways.
OPHELIA: I shall obey, my lord.   [*Exeunt.*]

Scene 4

The guard station. Enter HAMLET, HORATIO *and* MARCELLUS.

HAMLET: The air bites shrewdly;[6] it is very cold.
HORATIO: It is a nipping and an eager[7] air.
HAMLET: What hour now?
HORATIO: I think it lacks of twelve.
MARCELLUS: No, it is struck.
HORATIO: Indeed? I heard it not.
5   It then draws near the season
Wherein the spirit held his wont to walk.

[*A flourish of trumpets, and two pieces go off.*]

What does this mean, my lord?
HAMLET: The king doth wake tonight and takes his rouse,
Keeps wassail, and the swagg'ring up-spring reels,
10   And as he drains his draughts of Rhenish[8] down,
The kettledrum and trumpet thus bray out
The triumph of his pledge.
HORATIO: Is it a custom?
HAMLET: Ay, marry, is't,
But to my mind, though I am native here
15   And to the manner born, it is a custom
More honored in the breach than the observance.
This heavy-headed revel east and west
Makes us traduced and taxed of other nations.
They clepe[9] us drunkards, and with swinish phrase
20   Soil our addition,[1] and indeed it takes
From our achievements, though performed at height,
The pith and marrow of our attribute.[2]
So oft it chances in particular men,
That for some vicious mole of nature in them,
25   As in their birth, wherein they are not guilty

6. Sharply.   7. Keen.   8. Rhine wine. *Up-spring*: a German dance.   9. Call.   1. Reputation.
2. Honor.

(Since nature cannot choose his origin),
By their o'ergrowth of some complexion,
Oft breaking down the pales[3] and forts of reason,
Or by some habit that too much o'er-leavens
The form of plausive[4] manners—that these men,   30
Carrying, I say, the stamp of one defect,
Being nature's livery or fortune's star,
His virtues else, be they as pure as grace,
As infinite as man may undergo,
Shall in the general censure take corruption   35
From that particular fault. The dram of evil
Doth all the noble substance often doubt[5]
To his own scandal.

      [*Enter* GHOST.]

HORATIO: Look, my lord, it comes.
HAMLET: Angels and ministers of grace defend us!
  Be thou a spirit of health or goblin damned,   40
  Bring with thee airs from heaven or blasts from hell,
  Be thy intents wicked or charitable,
  Thou com'st in such a questionable[6] shape
  That I will speak to thee. I'll call thee Hamlet,
  King, father, royal Dane. O, answer me!   45
  Let me not burst in ignorance, but tell
  Why thy canonized[7] bones, hearsèd in death,
  Have burst their cerements;[8] why the sepulchre
  Wherein we saw thee quietly inurned
  Hath oped his ponderous and marble jaws   50
  To cast thee up again. What may this mean
  That thou, dead corse, again in complete steel[9]
  Revisits thus the glimpses of the moon,
  Making night hideous, and we fools of nature
  So horridly to shake our disposition   55
  With thoughts beyond the reaches of our souls?
  Say, why is this? Wherefore? What should we do?

      [GHOST *beckons*.]

HORATIO: It beckons you to go away with it,
  As if it some impartment[1] did desire
  To you alone.

---

3. Barriers.   4. Pleasing.   5. Extinguish.   6. Prompting question.
7. Buried in accordance with church canons.   8. Gravecloths.   9. Armor.   1. Communication.

60 MARCELLUS: Look with what courteous action
       It waves you to a more removèd[2] ground.
       But do not go with it.
   HORATIO: No, by no means.
   HAMLET: It will not speak; then I will follow it.
   HORATIO: Do not, my lord.
   HAMLET: Why, what should be the fear?
65   I do not set my life at a pin's fee,[3]
       And for my soul, what can it do to that,
       Being a thing immortal as itself?
       It waves me forth again. I'll follow it.
   HORATIO: What if it tempt you toward the flood, my lord,
70   Or to the dreadful summit of the cliff
       That beetles[4] o'er his base into the sea,
       And there assume some other horrible form,
       Which might deprive your sovereignty of reason[5]
       And draw you into madness? Think of it.
75   The very place puts toys of desperation,[6]
       Without more motive, into every brain
       That looks so many fathoms to the sea
       And hears it roar beneath.
   HAMLET: It wafts me still.
       Go on. I'll follow thee.
   MARCELLUS: You shall not go, my lord.
80 HAMLET: Hold off your hands.
   HORATIO: Be ruled. You shall not go.
   HAMLET: My fate cries out
       And makes each petty artere in this body
       As hardy as the Nemean lion's nerve.[7]
       Still am I called. Unhand me, gentlemen.
85   By heaven, I'll make a ghost of him that lets[8] me.
       I say, away! Go on. I'll follow thee.   [*Exeunt* GHOST *and* HAMLET.]
   HORATIO: He waxes desperate with imagination.
   MARCELLUS: Let's follow. 'Tis not fit thus to obey him.
   HORATIO: Have after. To what issue will this come?
90 MARCELLUS: Something is rotten in the state of Denmark.
   HORATIO: Heaven will direct it.
   MARCELLUS: Nay, let's follow him.   [*Exeunt.*]

---

2. Beckons you to a more distant.   3. Price.   4. Juts out.
5. Rational power. *Deprive*: take away.   6. Desperate fancies. *Artere*: artery.
7. The Nemean lion was a mythological monster slain by Hercules as one of his twelve labors.
8. Hinders.

Scene 5

Near the guard station. Enter GHOST *and* HAMLET.

HAMLET: Whither wilt thou lead me? Speak. I'll go no further.
GHOST: Mark me.
HAMLET: I will.
GHOST: My hour is almost come,
  When I to sulph'rous and tormenting flames
  Must render up myself.
HAMLET: Alas, poor ghost!
GHOST: Pity me not, but lend thy serious hearing   5
  To what I shall unfold.
HAMLET: Speak. I am bound to hear.
GHOST: So art thou to revenge, when thou shalt hear.
HAMLET: What?
GHOST: I am thy father's spirit,
  Doomed for a certain term to walk the night,   10
  And for the day confined to fast in fires,
  Till the foul crimes done in my days of nature[9]
  Are burnt and purged away. But that I am forbid
  To tell the secrets of my prison house,
  I could a tale unfold whose lightest word   15
  Would harrow up thy soul, freeze thy young blood,
  Make thy two eyes like stars start from their spheres,
  Thy knotted and combinèd[1] locks to part,
  And each particular hair to stand an end,
  Like quills upon the fretful porpentine.[2]   20
  But this eternal blazon[3] must not be
  To ears of flesh and blood. List, list, O, list!
  If thou didst ever thy dear father love—
HAMLET: O God!
GHOST: Revenge his foul and most unnatural murder.   25
HAMLET: Murder!
GHOST: Murder most foul, as in the best it is,
  But this most foul, strange, and unnatural.
HAMLET: Haste me to know't, that I, with wings as swift
  As meditation or the thoughts of love,   30
  May sweep to my revenge.
GHOST: I find thee apt.
  And duller shouldst thou be than the fat weed

---

9. That is, while I was alive.   1. Tangled.   2. Porcupine.   3. Description of eternity.

That rots itself in ease on Lethe[4] wharf,—
Wouldst thou not stir in this. Now, Hamlet, hear.
35 'Tis given out that, sleeping in my orchard,
A serpent stung me. So the whole ear of Denmark
Is by a forgèd process[5] of my death
Rankly abused. But know, thou noble youth,
The serpent that did sting thy father's life
Now wears his crown.
40 HAMLET: O my prophetic soul!
My uncle!
GHOST: Ay, that incestuous, that adulterate beast,
With witchcraft of his wits, with traitorous gifts—
O wicked wit and gifts that have the power
45 So to seduce!—won to his shameful lust
The will of my most seeming virtuous queen.
O Hamlet, what a falling off was there,
From me, whose love was of that dignity
That it went hand in hand even with the vow
50 I made to her in marriage, and to decline[6]
Upon a wretch whose natural gifts were poor
To those of mine!
But virtue, as it never will be moved,
Though lewdness court it in a shape of heaven,
55 So lust, though to a radiant angel linked,
Will sate itself in a celestial bed
And prey on garbage.
But soft, methinks I scent the morning air.
Brief let me be. Sleeping within my orchard,
60 My custom always of the afternoon,
Upon my secure hour thy uncle stole,
With juice of cursed hebona[7] in a vial,
And in the porches of my ears did pour
The leperous distilment, whose effect
65 Holds such an enmity with blood of man
That swift as quicksilver it courses through
The natural gates and alleys of the body,
And with a sudden vigor it doth posset[8]
And curd, like eager[9] droppings into milk,
70 The thin and wholesome blood. So did it mine,
And a most instant tetter barked about[1]

---

4. The waters of the Lethe, one of the rivers of the classical underworld, when drunk, induced forgetfulness. The "fat weed" is the asphodel that grew there; some texts have "roots" for "rots."
5. False report. 6. Sink. 7. A poison. 8. Coagulate. 9. Acid. *Curd*: curdle.
1. Covered like bark. *Tetter*: a skin disease.

Most lazar-like[2] with vile and loathsome crust
All my smooth body.
Thus was I sleeping by a brother's hand
Of life, of crown, of queen at once dispatched,   75
Cut off even in the blossoms of my sin,
Unhouseled, disappointed, unaneled,[3]
No reck'ning made, but sent to my account
With all my imperfections on my head.
O, horrible! O, horrible, most horrible!   80
If thou hast nature in thee, bear it not.
Let not the royal bed of Denmark be
A couch of luxury[4] and damnèd incest.
But howsomever thou pursues this act,
Taint not thy mind, nor let thy soul contrive   85
Against thy mother aught. Leave her to heaven,
And to those thorns that in her bosom lodge
To prick and sting her. Fare thee well at once.
The glowworm shows the matin[5] to be near,
And gins to pale his uneffectual fire.   90
Adieu, adieu, adieu. Remember me.   [*Exit.*]
HAMLET: O all you host of heaven! O earth! What else?
And shall I couple hell? O, fie! Hold, hold, my heart,
And you, my sinews, grow not instant old,
But bear me stiffly up. Remember thee?   95
Ay, thou poor ghost, whiles memory holds a seat
In this distracted globe.[6] Remember thee?
Yea, from the table[7] of my memory
I'll wipe away all trivial fond[8] records,
All saws of books, all forms, all pressures past   100
That youth and observation copied there,
And thy commandment all alone shall live
Within the book and volume of my brain,
Unmixed with baser matter. Yes, by heaven!
O most pernicious woman!   105
O villain, villain, smiling, damnèd villain!
My tables—meet it is I set it down
That one may smile, and smile, and be a villain.
At least I am sure it may be so in Denmark.
So, uncle, there you are. Now to my word:[9]   110

---

2. Leperlike.
3. The ghost means that he died without the customary rites of the church, that is, without
receiving the Sacrament, without confession, and without Extreme Unction.   4. Lust.
5. Morning.   6. Skull.   7. Writing tablet.   8. Foolish.   9. For my motto.

It is "Adieu, adieu. Remember me."
I have sworn't.

[*Enter* HORATIO *and* MARCELLUS.]

HORATIO: My lord, my lord!
MARCELLUS: Lord Hamlet!
HORATIO: Heavens secure him!
HAMLET: So be it!
115 MARCELLUS: Illo, ho, ho,[1] my lord!
HAMLET: Hillo, ho, ho, boy! Come, bird, come.
MARCELLUS: How is't, my noble lord?
HORATIO: What news, my lord?
HAMLET: O, wonderful!
HORATIO: Good my lord, tell it.
HAMLET: No, you will reveal it.
HORATIO: Not I, my lord, by heaven.
120 MARCELLUS: Nor I, my lord.
HAMLET: How say you then, would heart of man once think it?
    But you'll be secret?
BOTH: Ay, by heaven, my lord.
HAMLET: There's never a villain dwelling in all Denmark
    But he's an arrant knave.
125 HORATIO: There needs no ghost, my lord, come from the grave
    To tell us this.
HAMLET: Why, right, you are in the right,
    And so without more circumstance at all
    I hold it fit that we shake hands and part,
    You, as your business and desire shall point you,
130   For every man hath business and desire
    Such as it is, and for my own poor part,
    Look you, I'll go pray.
HORATIO: These are but wild and whirling words, my lord.
HAMLET: I am sorry they offend you, heartily;
    Yes, faith, heartily.
135 HORATIO: There's no offence, my lord.
HAMLET: Yes, by Saint Patrick, but there is, Horatio,
    And much offence too. Touching this vision here,
    It is an honest ghost, that let me tell you.
    For your desire to know what is between us,
140   O'ermaster't as you may. And now, good friends,
    As you are friends, scholars, and soldiers,
    Give me one poor request.

1. A falconer's cry.

HORATIO: What is't, my lord? We will.
HAMLET: Never make known what you have seen tonight.
BOTH: My lord, we will not.
HAMLET: Nay, but swear't.
HORATIO: In faith, 145
    My lord, not I.
MARCELLUS: Nor I, my lord, in faith.
HAMLET: Upon my sword.
MARCELLUS: We have sworn, my lord, already.
HAMLET: Indeed, upon my sword, indeed.

   [GHOST *cries under the stage.*]

GHOST: Swear.
HAMLET: Ha, ha, boy, say'st thou so? Art thou there, truepenny?[2]
    Come on. You hear this fellow in the cellarage.[3] 150
    Consent to swear.
HORATIO: Propose the oath, my lord.
HAMLET: Never to speak of this that you have seen,
    Swear by my sword.
GHOST: [*Beneath.*] Swear.
HAMLET: Hic et ubique?[4] Then we'll shift our ground. 155
    Come hither, gentlemen,
    And lay your hands again upon my sword.
    Swear by my sword
    Never to speak of this that you have heard.
GHOST: [*Beneath.*] Swear by his sword. 160
HAMLET: Well said, old mole! Canst work i' th' earth so fast?
    A worthy pioneer![5] Once more remove, good friends.
HORATIO: O day and night, but this is wondrous strange!
HAMLET: And therefore as a stranger give it welcome.
    There are more things in heaven and earth, Horatio, 165
    Than are dreamt of in your philosophy.
    But come.
    Here as before, never, so help you mercy,
    How strange or odd some'er I bear myself
    (As I perchance hereafter shall think meet 170
    To put an antic[6] disposition on),
    That you, at such times, seeing me, never shall,
    With arms encumbered[7] thus, or this head-shake,
    Or by pronouncing of some doubtful phrase,
    As "Well, we know," or "We could, and if we would" 175

2. Trusty old fellow. 3. Below. 4. Here and everywhere? (Latin).
5. Soldier who digs trenches. 6. Mad. 7. Folded.

Or "If we list to speak," or "There be, and if they might"
Or such ambiguous giving out, to note
That you know aught of me—this do swear,
So grace and mercy at your most need help you.
180 GHOST: [*Beneath.*] Swear.   [*They swear.*]
HAMLET: Rest, rest, perturbèd spirit! So, gentlemen,
With all my love I do commend me to you,
And what so poor a man as Hamlet is
May do t'express his love and friending[8] to you,
185 God willing, shall not lack. Let us go in together,
And still your fingers on your lips, I pray.
The time is out of joint. O cursèd spite
That ever I was born to set it right!
Nay, come, let's go together.   [*Exeunt.*]

ACT II

Scene 1

The dwelling of POLONIUS. *Enter* POLONIUS *and* REYNALDO.

POLONIUS: Give him this money and these notes, Reynaldo.
REYNALDO: I will, my lord.
POLONIUS: You shall do marvellous wisely, good Reynaldo,
Before you visit him, to make inquire[9]
Of his behavior.
5 REYNALDO: My lord, I did intend it.
POLONIUS: Marry, well said, very well said. Look you, sir.
Enquire me first what Danskers[1] are in Paris,
And how, and who, what means, and where they keep,[2]
What company, at what expense; and finding
10 By this encompassment[3] and drift of question
That they do know my son, come you more nearer
Than your particular demands[4] will touch it.
Take you as 'twere some distant knowledge of him,
As thus, "I know his father and his friends,
15 And in part him." Do you mark this, Reynaldo?
REYNALDO: Ay, very well, my lord.
POLONIUS: "And in part him, but," you may say, "not well,
But if't be he I mean, he's very wild,
Addicted so and so." And there put on him
20 What forgeries you please; marry, none so rank[5]

8. Friendship.   9. Inquiry.   1. Danes.   2. Live.   3. Indirect means.   4. Direct questions.
5. Foul. *Forgeries*: lies.

As may dishonor him. Take heed of that.
But, sir, such wanton, wild, and usual slips
As are companions noted and most known
To youth and liberty.
REYNALDO: As gaming, my lord.
POLONIUS: Ay, or drinking, fencing, swearing,
   Quarrelling, drabbing[6]—you may go so far.   25
REYNALDO: My lord, that would dishonor him.
POLONIUS: Faith, no, as you may season it in the charge.[7]
   You must not put another scandal on him,
   That he is open to incontinency.[8]   30
   That's not my meaning. But breathe his faults so quaintly[9]
   That they may seem the taints of liberty,[1]
   The flash and outbreak of a fiery mind,
   A savageness in unreclaimèd[2] blood,
   Of general assault.[3]
REYNALDO: But, my good lord—   35
POLONIUS: Wherefore should you do this?
REYNALDO: Ay, my lord,
   I would know that.
POLONIUS: Marry, sir, here's my drift,
   And I believe it is a fetch of warrant.[4]
   You laying these slight sullies on my son,
   As 'twere a thing a little soiled wi' th' working,   40
   Mark you,
   Your party in converse,[5] him you would sound,
   Having ever seen in the prenominate[6] crimes
   The youth you breathe[7] of guilty, be assured
   He closes with you in this consequence,   45
   "Good sir," or so, or "friend," or "gentleman,"
   According to the phrase or the addition
   Of man and country.
REYNALDO: Very good, my lord.
POLONIUS: And then, sir, does 'a this—'a does—What was I about to say?
   By the mass, I was about to say something.   50
   Where did I leave?
REYNALDO: At "closes in the consequence."
POLONIUS: At "closes in the consequence"—ay, marry,
   He closes thus: "I know the gentleman.
   I saw him yesterday, or th' other day,   55
   Or then, or then, with such, or such, and as you say,

---

6. Whoring.   7. Soften the accusation.   8. Sexual excess.   9. With delicacy.
1. Faults of freedom.   2. Untamed.   3. Touching everyone.   4. Permissible trick.
5. Conversation.   6. Already named.   7. Speak.

There was 'a gaming, there o'ertook in's rouse,
There falling out at tennis," or perchance
"I saw him enter such a house of sale,"
60 Videlicet,[8] a brothel, or so forth.
See you, now—
Your bait of falsehood takes this carp of truth,
And thus do we of wisdom and of reach,[9]
With windlasses and with assays of bias,[1]
65 By indirections find directions out;
So by my former lecture and advice
Shall you my son. You have me, have you not?
REYNALDO: My lord, I have.
POLONIUS: God b'wi' ye; fare ye well.
REYNALDO: Good my lord.
70 POLONIUS: Observe his inclination in yourself.
REYNALDO: I shall, my lord.
POLONIUS: And let him ply[2] his music.
REYNALDO: Well, my lord.
POLONIUS: Farewell.   [*Exit* REYNALDO.]

    [*Enter* OPHELIA.]
                         How now, Ophelia, what's the matter?
OPHELIA: O my lord, my lord, I have been so affrighted!
75 POLONIUS: With what, i' th' name of God?
OPHELIA: My lord, as I was sewing in my closet,[3]
    Lord Hamlet with his doublet all unbraced,[4]
    No hat upon his head, his stockings fouled,
    Ungartered and down-gyvèd[5] to his ankle,
80 Pale as his shirt, his knees knocking each other,
    And with a look so piteous in purport
    As if he had been loosèd out of hell
    To speak of horrors—he comes before me.
POLONIUS: Mad for thy love?
OPHELIA: My lord, I do not know,
    But truly I do fear it.
85 POLONIUS: What said he?
OPHELIA: He took me by the wrist, and held me hard,
    Then goes he to the length of all his arm,
    And with his other hand thus o'er his brow,
    He falls to such perusal of my face
90 As 'a would draw it. Long stayed he so.

8. Namely.   9. Ability.   1. Indirect tests.   2. Practice.   3. Chamber.
4. Unlaced. *Doublet*: jacket.   5. Fallen down like fetters.

At last, a little shaking of mine arm,
And thrice his head thus waving up and down,
He raised a sigh so piteous and profound
As it did seem to shatter all his bulk,[6]
And end his being. That done, he lets me go,
And with his head over his shoulder turned
He seemed to find his way without his eyes,
For out adoors he went without their helps,
And to the last bended[7] their light on me.

POLONIUS: Come, go with me. I will go seek the king.   100
This is the very ecstasy of love,
Whose violent property fordoes[8] itself,
And leads the will to desperate undertakings
As oft as any passion under heaven
That does afflict our natures. I am sorry.   105
What, have you given him any hard words of late?

OPHELIA: No, my good lord, but as you did command
I did repel[9] his letters, and denied
His access to me.

POLONIUS: That hath made him mad.
I am sorry that with better heed and judgment   110
I had not quoted[1] him. I feared he did but trifle,
And meant to wrack[2] thee; but beshrew my jealousy.
By heaven, it is as proper to our age
To cast beyond ourselves in our opinions
As it is common for the younger sort   115
To lack discretion. Come, go we to the king.
This must be known, which being kept close, might move
More grief to hide than hate to utter love.
Come.   [*Exeunt.*]

Scene 2

A public room. Enter KING, QUEEN, ROSENCRANTZ *and* GUILDENSTERN.

KING: Welcome, dear Rosencrantz and Guildenstern.
Moreover that[3] we much did long to see you,
The need we have to use you did provoke
Our hasty sending. Something have you heard
Of Hamlet's transformation—so call it,   5
Sith[4] nor th' exterior nor the inward man
Resembles that it was. What it should be,

6. Body.   7. Directed.   8. Destroys. *Property:* character.   9. Refuse.   1. Observed.   2. Harm.
3. In addition to the fact that.   4. Since.

her's death, that thus hath put him
ch' understanding of himself,
Mor..n of. I entreat you both
Sc..g of so young days[5] brought up with him,
so neighbored[6] to his youth and havior,
10   ou vouchsafe your rest here in our court
.e little time, so by your companies
draw him on to pleasures, and to gather
So much as from occasion you may glean,
Whether aught to us unknown afflicts him thus,
That opened lies within our remedy.
QUEEN: Good gentlemen, he hath much talked of you,
20   And sure I am two men there are not living
To whom he more adheres. If it will please you
To show us so much gentry[7] and good will
As to expend your time with us awhile
For the supply and profit of our hope,
25   Your visitation shall receive such thanks
As fits a king's remembrance.
ROSENCRANTZ: Both your majesties
Might, by the sovereign power you have of us,
Put your dread pleasures more into command
Than to entreaty.
GUILDENSTERN: But we both obey,
30   And here give up ourselves in the full bent[8]
To lay our service freely at your feet,
To be commanded.
KING: Thanks, Rosencrantz and gentle Guildenstern.
QUEEN: Thanks, Guildenstern and gentle Rosencrantz.
35   And I beseech you instantly to visit
My too much changed son. Go, some of you,
And bring these gentlemen where Hamlet is.
GUILDENSTERN: Heavens make our presence and our practices
Pleasant and helpful to him!
QUEEN: Ay, amen!
                        [*Exeunt* ROSENCRANTZ *and* GUILDENSTERN.]

[*Enter* POLONIUS.]

40   POLONIUS: Th' ambassadors from Norway, my good lord,
Are joyfully returned.

5. From childhood.   6. Closely allied.   7. Courtesy.   8. Completely.

KING: Thou still⁹ hast been the father of good news.

POLONIUS: Have I, my lord? I assure you, my good liege,
  I hold my duty as I hold my soul,
  Both to my God and to my gracious king;   45
  And I do think—or else this brain of mine
  Hunts not the trail of policy¹ so sure
  As it hath used to do—that I have found
  The very cause of Hamlet's lunacy.

KING: O, speak of that, that do I long to hear.   50

POLONIUS: Give first admittance to th' ambassadors.
  My news shall be the fruit² to that great feast.

KING: Thyself do grace to them, and bring them in.   [*Exit* POLONIUS.]
  He tells me, my dear Gertrude, he hath found
  The head and source of all your son's distemper.   55

QUEEN: I doubt it is no other but the main,
  His father's death and our o'erhasty marriage.

KING: Well, we shall sift³ him.

[*Enter Ambassadors (*VOLTEMAND *and* CORNELIUS*) with* POLONIUS.]

                        Welcome, my good friends,
  Say, Voltemand, what from our brother Norway?

VOLTEMAND: Most fair return of greetings and desires.   60
  Upon our first,⁴ he sent out to suppress
  His nephew's levies, which to him appeared
  To be a preparation 'gainst the Polack,
  But better looked into, he truly found
  It was against your highness, whereat grieved,   65
  That so his sickness, age, and impotence
  Was falsely borne in hand, sends out arrests⁵
  On Fortinbras, which he in brief obeys,
  Receives rebuke from Norway, and in fine,
  Makes vow before his uncle never more   70
  To give th' assay⁶ of arms against your majesty.
  Whereon old Norway, overcome with joy,
  Gives him three thousand crowns in annual fee,
  And his commission to employ those soldiers,
  So levied as before, against the Polack,   75
  With an entreaty, herein further shown,   [*Gives* CLAUDIUS *a paper.*]
  That it might please you to give quiet pass⁷
  Through your dominions for this enterprise,

9. Ever.   1. Statecraft.   2. Dessert.   3. Examine.   4. That is, first appearance.
5. Orders to stop. *Falsely borne in hand:* deceived.   6. Trial.   7. Safe conduct.

On such regards of safety and allowance
As therein are set down.

80 KING: It likes[8] us well,
And at our more considered time[9] we'll read,
Answer, and think upon this business.
Meantime we thank you for your well-took[1] labor.
Go to your rest; at night we'll feast together.
Most welcome home!   [*Exeunt* AMBASSADORS.]

85 POLONIUS: This business is well ended.
My liege and madam, to expostulate[2]
What majesty should be, what duty is,
Why day is day, night night, and time is time,
Were nothing but to waste night, day, and time.
90 Therefore, since brevity is the soul of wit,
And tediousness the limbs and outward flourishes,[3]
I will be brief. Your noble son is mad.
Mad call I it, for to define true madness,
What is't but to be nothing else but mad?
But let that go.

95 QUEEN: More matter with less art.
POLONIUS: Madam, I swear I use no art at all.
That he is mad, 'tis true: 'tis true 'tis pity,
And pity 'tis 'tis true. A foolish figure,
But farewell it, for I will use no art.
100 Mad let us grant him, then, and now remains
That we find out the cause of this effect,
Or rather say the cause of this defect,
For this effect defective comes by cause.
Thus it remains, and the remainder thus.
105 Perpend.[4]
I have a daughter—have while she is mine—
Who in her duty and obedience, mark,
Hath given me this. Now gather, and surmise.
[*Reads*] *the letter.*
    "To the celestial, and my soul's idol, the most beautified Ophelia."—
110 That's an ill phrase, a vile phrase, "beautified" is a vile phrase. But you
shall hear. Thus:
    "In her excellent white bosom, these, etc."
QUEEN: Came this from Hamlet to her?
POLONIUS: Good madam, stay awhile. I will be faithful.

---

8. Pleases.   9. Time for more consideration.   1. Successful.   2. Discuss.   3. Adornments.
4. Consider.

"Doubt thou the stars are fire,   115
   Doubt that the sun doth move;
   Doubt truth to be a liar;
   But never doubt I love.

O dear Ophelia, I am ill at these numbers.[5] I have not art to reckon
my groans, but that I love thee best, O most best, believe it. Adieu.   120
   Thine evermore, most dear lady,
      whilst this machine[6] is to him, Hamlet."
This in obedience hath my daughter shown me,
And more above, hath his solicitings,
As they fell out by time, by means, and place,   125
All given to mine ear.
KING: But how hath she
Received his love?
POLONIUS: What do you think of me?
KING: As of a man faithful and honorable.
POLONIUS: I would fain prove so. But what might you think,
   When I had seen this hot love on the wing.   130
   (As I perceived it, I must tell you that,
   Before my daughter told me), what might you,
   Or my dear majesty your queen here, think,
   If I had played the desk or table-book,
   Or given my heart a winking, mute and dumb,   135
   Or looked upon this love with idle sight,[7]
   What might you think? No, I went round[8] to work,
   And my young mistress thus I did bespeak:
   "Lord Hamlet is a prince out of thy star.[9]
   This must not be." And then I prescripts[1] gave her,   140
   That she should lock herself from his resort,
   Admit no messengers, receive no tokens.
   Which done, she took[2] the fruits of my advice;
   And he repelled, a short tale to make,
   Fell into a sadness, then into a fast,   145
   Thence to a watch, thence into a weakness,
   Thence to a lightness, and by this declension,
   Into the madness wherein now he raves,
   And all we mourn for.
KING: Do you think 'tis this?

5. Verses.   6. Body.
7. Polonius means that he would have been at fault if, having seen Hamlet's attention to Ophelia,
he had winked at it or not paid attention, an "idle sight," and if he had remained silent and kept
the information to himself, as if it were written in a "desk" or "table-book."   8. Directly.
9. Beyond your sphere.   1. Orders.   2. Followed.

150 QUEEN: It may be, very like.

POLONIUS: Hath there been such a time—I would fain know that—
    That I have positively said "'Tis so,"
    When it proved otherwise?

KING: Not that I know.

POLONIUS: [*Pointing to his head and shoulder.*] Take this from this, if this be
    otherwise.

155   If circumstances lead me, I will find
    Where truth is hid, though it were hid indeed
    Within the centre.[3]

KING: How may we try it further?

POLONIUS: You know sometimes he walks four hours together
    Here in the lobby.

QUEEN: So he does, indeed.

160 POLONIUS: At such a time I'll loose[4] my daughter to him.
    Be you and I behind an arras[5] then.
    Mark the encounter. If he love her not,
    And be not from his reason fall'n thereon,
    Let me be no assistant for a state,
    But keep a farm and carters.

165 KING: We will try it.

[*Enter* HAMLET *reading a book.*]

QUEEN: But look where sadly the poor wretch comes reading.

POLONIUS: Away, I do beseech you both away,
    I'll board[6] him presently.   [*Exeunt* KING *and* QUEEN.]
           O, give me leave.
    How does my good Lord Hamlet?

170 HAMLET: Well, God-a-mercy.

POLONIUS: Do you know me, my lord?

HAMLET: Excellent well, you are a fishmonger.

POLONIUS: Not I, my lord.

HAMLET: Then I would you were so honest a man.

175 POLONIUS: Honest, my lord?

HAMLET: Ay, sir, to be honest as this world goes, is to be one man picked out
    of ten thousand.

POLONIUS: That's very true, my lord.

HAMLET: For if the sun breed maggots in a dead dog, being a god kissing
180   carrion[7]—Have you a daughter?

POLONIUS: I have, my lord.

---

3. Of the earth.   4. Let loose.   5. Tapestry.   6. Accost.

7. A reference to the belief of the period that maggots were produced spontaneously by the action
of sunshine on carrion.

HAMLET: Let her not walk i' th' sun. Conception is a blessing, but as your daughter may conceive—friend, look to't.

POLONIUS: How say you by that? [*Aside.*] Still harping on my daughter. Yet he knew me not at first. 'A said I was a fishmonger. 'A is far gone. And 185 truly in my youth I suffered much extremity for love. Very near this. I'll speak to him again.—What do you read, my lord?

HAMLET: Words, words, words.

POLONIUS: What is the matter, my lord?

HAMLET: Between who? 190

POLONIUS: I mean the matter that you read, my lord.

HAMLET: Slanders, sir; for the satirical rogue says here that old men have grey beards, that their faces are wrinkled, their eyes purging thick amber and plumtree gum, and that they have a plentiful lack of wit, together with most weak hams[8]—all which, sir, though I most powerfully and potently 195 believe, yet I hold it not honesty to have it thus set down, for yourself, sir, shall grow old as I am, if like a crab you could go backward.

POLONIUS: [*Aside.*] Though this be madness, yet there is method in't.—Will you walk out of the air, my lord?

HAMLET: Into my grave? 200

POLONIUS: [*Aside.*] Indeed, that's out of the air. How pregnant sometime his replies are! a happiness that often madness hits on, which reason and sanity could not so prosperously be delivered of. I will leave him, and suddenly contrive the means of meeting between him and my daughter.— My honorable lord. I will most humbly take my leave of you. 205

HAMLET: You cannot take from me anything that I will more willingly part withal—except my life, except my life, except my life.

[*Enter* GUILDENSTERN *and* ROSENCRANTZ.]

POLONIUS: Fare you well, my lord.

HAMLET: These tedious old fools!

POLONIUS: You go to seek the Lord Hamlet. There he is. 210

ROSENCRANTZ: [*To* POLONIUS.] God save you, sir!   [*Exit* POLONIUS.]

GUILDENSTERN: My honored lord!

ROSENCRANTZ: My most dear lord!

HAMLET: My excellent good friends! How dost thou, Guildenstern? 215
    Ah, Rosencrantz! Good lads, how do you both?

ROSENCRANTZ: As the indifferent[9] children of the earth.

GUILDENSTERN: Happy in that we are not over-happy;
    On Fortune's cap we are not the very button.[1]

HAMLET: Nor the soles of her shoe?

ROSENCRANTZ: Neither, my lord. 220

HAMLET: Then you live about her waist, or in the middle of her favors?

8. Limbs.   9. Ordinary.   1. That is, on top.

GUILDENSTERN: Faith, her privates we.

HAMLET: In the secret parts of Fortune? O, most true, she is a strumpet.[2]
What news?

225 ROSENCRANTZ: None, my lord, but that the world's grown honest.

HAMLET: Then is doomsday near. But your news is not true. Let me question more in particular. What have you, my good friends, deserved at the hands of Fortune, that she sends you to prison hither?

GUILDENSTERN: Prison, my lord?

230 HAMLET: Denmark's a prison.

ROSENCRANTZ: Then is the world one.

HAMLET: A goodly one, in which there are many confines, wards[3] and dungeons. Denmark being one o' th' worst.

ROSENCRANTZ: We think not so, my lord.

235 HAMLET: Why then 'tis none to you; for there is nothing either good or bad, but thinking makes it so. To me it is a prison.

ROSENCRANTZ: Why then your ambition makes it one. 'Tis too narrow for your mind.

HAMLET: O God, I could be bounded in a nutshell and count myself a king
240 of infinite space, were it not that I have bad dreams.

GUILDENSTERN: Which dreams indeed are ambition; for the very substance of the ambitious is merely the shadow of a dream.

HAMLET: A dream itself is but a shadow.

ROSENCRANTZ: Truly, and I hold ambition of so airy and light a quality that
245 it is but a shadow's shadow.

HAMLET: Then are our beggars bodies, and our monarchs and outstretched heroes the beggars' shadows. Shall we to th' court? for, by my fay,[4] I cannot reason.

BOTH: We'll wait upon you.

250 HAMLET: No such matter. I will not sort[5] you with the rest of my servants; for to speak to you like an honest man, I am most dreadfully attended. But in the beaten way of friendship, what make you at Elsinore?

ROSENCRANTZ: To visit you, my lord; no other occasion.

HAMLET: Beggar that I am, I am even poor in thanks, but I thank you; and sure, dear friends, my thanks are too dear a halfpenny.[6] Were you not
255 sent for? Is it your own inclining? Is it a free visitation? Come, come, deal justly with me. Come, come, nay speak.

GUILDENSTERN: What should we say, my lord?

HAMLET: Anything but to th' purpose. You were sent for, and there is a kind of confession in your looks, which your modesties have not craft enough
260 to color. I know the good king and queen have sent for you.

---

2. Prostitute. Hamlet is indulging in characteristic ribaldry. Guildenstern means that they are "privates" = ordinary citizens, but Hamlet takes him to mean "privates" = sexual organs and "middle of her favors" = waist = sexual organs.   3. Cells.   4. Faith.   5. Include.
6. Not worth a halfpenny.

ROSENCRANTZ: To what end, my lord?

HAMLET: That you must teach me. But let me conjure you by the rights of our fellowship, by the consonancy of our youth, by the obligation of our ever preserved love, and by what more dear a better proposer can charge you withal, be even and direct[7] with me whether you were sent 265 for or no.

ROSENCRANTZ: [*Aside to* GUILDENSTERN.] What say you?

HAMLET: [*Aside.*] Nay, then, I have an eye of you.—If you love me, hold not off.

GUILDENSTERN: My lord, we were sent for.

HAMLET: I will tell you why; so shall my anticipation prevent your discovery,[8] 270 and your secrecy to the king and queen moult no feather. I have of late—but wherefore I know not—lost all my mirth, forgone all custom of exercises; and indeed it goes so heavily with my disposition, that this goodly frame the earth seems to me a sterile promontory, this most excellent canopy the air, look you, this brave o'er-hanging firmament, this majes- 275 tical roof fretted[9] with golden fire, why it appeareth nothing to me but a foul and pestilent congregation of vapors. What a piece of work is a man, how noble in reason, how infinite in faculties, in form and moving, how express[1] and admirable in action, how like an angel in apprehension, how like a god: the beauty of the world, the paragon of animals. 280 And yet to me, what is this quintessence of dust? Man delights not me, nor woman neither, though by your smiling you seem to say so.

ROSENCRANTZ: My lord, there was no such stuff in my thoughts.

HAMLET: Why did ye laugh, then, when I said "Man delights not me"?

ROSENCRANTZ: To think, my lord, if you delight not in man, what lenten 285 entertainment the players shall receive from you. We coted[2] them on the way, and hither are they coming to offer you service.

HAMLET: He that plays the king shall be welcome—his majesty shall have tribute of me; the adventurous knight shall use his foil and target; the lover shall not sigh gratis; the humorous[3] man shall end his part in 290 peace; the clown shall make those laugh whose lungs are tickle o' th' sere;[4] and the lady shall say her mind freely, or the blank verse shall halt for't. What players are they?

ROSENCRANTZ: Even those you were wont to take such delight in, the tragedians of the city.

295

HAMLET: How chances it they travel? Their residence, both in reputation and profit, was better both ways.

ROSENCRANTZ: I think their inhibition comes by the means of the late innovation.

HAMLET: Do they hold the same estimation they did when I was in the city? 300 Are they so followed?

ROSENCRANTZ: No, indeed, are they not.

---

7. Straightforward. 8. Disclosure. 9. Ornamented with fretwork. 1. Well built.
2. Passed. *Lenten:* scanty. 3. Eccentric. *Foil and target:* sword and shield. 4. Easily set off.

HAMLET: How comes it? Do they grow rusty?

ROSENCRANTZ: Nay, their endeavor keeps in the wonted pace; but there is,
305   sir, an eyrie of children, little eyases,⁵ that cry out on the top of question,⁶
and are most tyrannically clapped for't. These are now the fashion, and
so berattle the common stages (so they call them) that many wearing
rapiers are afraid of goose quills⁷ and dare scarce come thither.⁸

HAMLET: What, are they children? Who maintains 'em? How are they
310   escoted?⁹ Will they pursue the quality no longer than they can sing? Will
they not say afterwards, if they should grow themselves to common players (as it is most like, if their means are no better), their writers do them
wrong to make them exclaim against their own succession?¹

ROSENCRANTZ: Faith, there has been much todo on both sides; and the
nation holds it no sin to tarre² them to controversy. There was for a while
315   no money bid for argument,³ unless the poet and the player went to
cuffs⁴ in the question.

HAMLET: Is't possible?

GUILDENSTERN: O, there has been much throwing about of brains.

320 HAMLET: Do the boys carry it away?

ROSENCRANTZ: Ay, that they do, my lord. Hercules and his load too.⁵

HAMLET: It is not very strange, for my uncle is King of Denmark, and those
that would make mouths⁶ at him while my father lived give twenty,
forty, fifty, a hundred ducats apiece for his picture in little.⁷ 'Sblood,
there is something in this more than natural, if philosophy could find it
325   out.

    [A flourish.]

GUILDENSTERN: There are the players.

HAMLET: Gentlemen, you are welcome to Elsinore. Your hands. Come then,
th' appurtenance of welcome is fashion and ceremony. Let me comply
with you in this garb, lest my extent⁸ to the players, which I tell you
330   must show fairly outwards should more appear like entertainment⁹
than yours. You are welcome. But my uncle-father and aunt-mother are
deceived.

GUILDENSTERN: In what, my dear lord?

---

5. Little hawks.   6. With a loud, high delivery.   7. Pens of satirical writers.
8. The passage refers to the emergence at the time of the play of theatrical companies made up of
children from London choir schools. Their performances became fashionable and hurt the business of the established companies. Hamlet says that if they continue to act, "pursue the quality,"
when they are grown, they will find that they have been damaging their own future careers.
9. Supported.   1. Future careers.   2. Urge.   3. Paid for a play plot.   4. Blows.
5. During one of his labors Hercules assumed for a time the burden of the Titan Atlas, who supported the heavens on his shoulders. Also a reference to the effect on business at Shakespeare's theater, the Globe.   6. Sneer.   7. Miniature.   8. Fashion. *Comply with:* welcome.   9. Cordiality.

HAMLET: I am but mad north-north-west; when the wind is southerly I know a hawk from a handsaw.[1]

[*Enter* POLONIUS.]

POLONIUS: Well be with you, gentlemen. 335
HAMLET: Hark you, Guildenstern—and you too—at each ear a hearer. That great baby you see there is not yet out of his swaddling clouts.[2]
ROSENCRANTZ: Happily he is the second time come to them, for they say an old man is twice a child.
HAMLET: I will prophesy he comes to tell me of the players. Mark it.—You 340 say right, sir, a Monday morning, 'twas then indeed.
POLONIUS: My lord, I have news to tell you.
HAMLET: My lord, I have news to tell you. When Roscius was an actor in Rome—[3]
POLONIUS: The actors are come hither, my lord.
HAMLET: Buzz, buzz.
POLONIUS: Upon my honor— 345
HAMLET: Then came each actor on his ass—
POLONIUS: The best actors in the world, either for tragedy, comedy, history, pastoral, pastoral-comical, historical-pastoral, tragical-historical, tragical-comical historical-pastoral, scene individable, or poem unlimited. Seneca cannot be too heavy nor Plautus too light. For the law of 350 writ and the liberty, these are the only men.[4]
HAMLET: O Jephtha, judge of Israel, what a treasure hadst thou![5]
POLONIUS: What a treasure had he, my lord?
HAMLET: Why— 355

"One fair daughter, and no more,
The which he loved passing well."

POLONIUS: [*Aside.*] Still on my daughter.
HAMLET: Am I not i' th' right, old Jephtha?
POLONIUS: If you call me Jephtha, my lord, I have a daughter that I love 360 passing well.
HAMLET: Nay, that follows not.
POLONIUS: What follows then, my lord?

1. A "hawk" is a plasterer's tool; Hamlet may also be using "handsaw" = hernshaw = heron.
2. Wrappings for an infant. 3. Roscius was the most famous actor of classical Rome.
4. Seneca and Plautus were Roman writers of tragedy and comedy, respectively. The "law of writ" refers to plays written according to such rules as the three unities; the "liberty" to those written otherwise.
5. To ensure victory, Jephtha promised to sacrifice the first creature to meet him on his return. Unfortunately, his only daughter outstripped his dog and was the victim of his vow. The biblical story is told in Judges 11.

HAMLET: Why—

365   "As by lot, God wot"

and then, you know,

"It came to pass, as most like it was."

The first row of the pious chanson[6] will show you more, for look where
my abridgement[7] comes.

[*Enter the* PLAYERS.]

370   You are welcome, masters; welcome, all.—I am glad to see thee well.—
Welcome, good friends.—O, old friend! Why, thy face is valanced[8] since
I saw thee last. Com'st thou to beard me in Denmark?—What, my young
lady and mistress? By'r lady, your ladyship is nearer to heaven than
when I saw you last by the altitude of a chopine.[9] Pray God your voice,
375   like a piece of uncurrent gold, be not cracked within the ring.—Masters,
you are all welcome. We'll e'en to't like French falconers, fly at anything
we see. We'll have a speech straight. Come give us a taste of your quality,[1]
come a passionate speech.

FIRST PLAYER: What speech, my good lord?

HAMLET: I heard thee speak me a speech once, but it was never acted, or if it
380   was, not above once, for the play, I remember, pleased not the million;
'twas caviary to the general.[2] But it was—as I received it, and others
whose judgments in such matters cried in the top of[3] mine—an excellent play, well digested[4] in the scenes, set down with as much modesty
as cunning. I remember one said there were no sallets[5] in the lines to
385   make the matter savory, nor no matter in the phrase that might indict
the author of affectation, but called it an honest method, as wholesome
as sweet, and by very much more handsome than fine. One speech in't I
chiefly loved. 'Twas Æneas' tale to Dido, and thereabout of it especially
where he speaks of Priam's slaughter.[6] If it live in your memory, begin at
this line—let me see, let me see:

390   "The rugged Pyrrhus, like th' Hyrcanian beast"[7]—

'tis not so; it begins with Pyrrhus—

---

6. Song. *Row*: stanza.   7. That which cuts short by interrupting.   8. Fringed (with a beard).
9. A reference to the contemporary theatrical practice of using boys to play women's parts. The
company's "lady" has grown in height by the size of a woman's thick-soled shoe, "chopine," since
Hamlet saw him last. The next sentence refers to the possibility, suggested by his growth, that the
young actor's voice may soon begin to change.   1. Trade.
2. Caviar to the masses (i.e., pearls before swine).   3. Were weightier than.   4. Arranged.
5. Spicy passages.
6. Aeneas, fleeing with his band from fallen Troy (Ilium), arrives in Carthage, where he tells Dido,
the queen of Carthage, of the fall of Troy. Here he is describing the death of Priam, the aged king
of Troy, at the hands of Pyrrhus, the son of the slain Achilles.   7. Tiger.

"The rugged Pyrrhus, he whose sable arms,
Black as his purpose, did the night resemble
When he lay couchéd in th' ominous horse,[8]
Hath now this dread and black complexion smeared   395
With heraldry more dismal; head to foot
Now is he total gules, horridly tricked[9]
With blood of fathers, mothers, daughters, sons,
Baked and impasted with the parching[1] streets,
That lend a tyrannous and a damnèd light   400
To their lord's murder. Roasted in wrath and fire,
And thus o'er-sizèd with coagulate[2] gore,
With eyes like carbuncles, the hellish Pyrrhus
Old grandsire Priam seeks."

    So proceed you.   405
POLONIUS: Fore God, my lord, well spoken, with good accent and good
    discretion.
FIRST PLAYER: "Anon he finds him[3]
Striking too short at Greeks. His antique[4] sword,
Rebellious[5] to his arm, lies where it falls,   410
Repugnant to command. Unequal matched,
Pyrrhus at Priam drives, in rage strikes wide.
But with the whiff and wind of his fell sword
Th' unnervèd father falls. Then senseless[6] Ilium,
Seeming to feel this blow, with flaming top   415
Stoops[7] to his base, and with a hideous crash
Takes prisoner Pyrrhus' ear. For, lo! his sword,
Which was declining[8] on the milky head
Of reverend Priam, seemed i' th' air to stick.
So as a painted tyrant Pyrrhus stood,   420
And like a neutral to his will and matter,[9]
Did nothing.
But as we often see, against some storm,
A silence in the heavens, the rack[1] stand still,
The bold winds speechless, and the orb below   425
As hush as death, anon the dreadful thunder
Doth rend the region; so, after Pyrrhus' pause,
A rousèd vengeance sets him new awork,[2]
And never did the Cyclops' hammers fall

---

8. That is, the Trojan horse.   9. Adorned. *Total gules*: completely red.
1. Burning. *Impasted*: crusted.   2. Clotted. *O'er-sizèd*: glued over.
3. That is, Pyrrhus finds Priam.   4. Which he used when young.   5. Refractory.
6. Without feeling.   7. Falls.   8. About to fall.   9. Between his will and the fulfillment of it.
1. Clouds.   2. To work.

430 On Mars's armor, forged for proof eterne,[3]
With less remorse than Pyrrhus' bleeding sword
Now falls on Priam.
Out, out, thou strumpet, Fortune! All you gods,
In general synod take away her power,
435 Break all the spokes and fellies[4] from her wheel,
And bowl the round nave[5] down the hill of heaven
As low as to the fiends."

POLONIUS: This is too long.

HAMLET: It shall to the barber's with your beard.—Prithee say on. He's for a
440 jig,[6] or a tale of bawdry, or he sleeps. Say on; come to Hecuba.[7]

FIRST PLAYER: "But who, ah woe! had seen the mobled[8] queen—"

HAMLET: "The mobled queen"?

POLONIUS: That's good. "Mobled queen" is good.

FIRST PLAYER: "Run barefoot up and down, threat'ning the flames
445 With bisson rheum, a clout[9] upon that head
Where late the diadem stood, and for a robe,
About her lank and all o'er-teemed loins,
A blanket, in the alarm of fear caught up—
Who this had seen, with tongue in venom steeped,
450 'Gainst Fortune's state[1] would treason have pronounced.
But if the gods themselves did see her then,
When she saw Pyrrhus make malicious sport
In mincing[2] with his sword her husband's limbs,
The instant burst of clamor that she made,
455 Unless things mortal move them not at all,
Would have made milch[3] the burning eyes of heaven,
And passion in the gods."

POLONIUS: Look whe'r[4] he has not turned his color, and has tears in's eyes.
Prithee no more.

460 HAMLET: 'Tis well. I'll have thee speak out the rest of this soon.—Good my
lord, will you see the players well bestowed?[5] Do you hear, let them be
well used, for they are the abstract[6] and brief chronicles of the time;
after your death you were better have a bad epitaph than their ill report
while you live.

POLONIUS: My lord, I will use them according to their desert.

---

3. Mars, as befits a Roman war god, had armor made for him by the blacksmith god Vulcan and
his assistants, the Cyclopes. It was suitably impenetrable, of "proof eterne."
4. Parts of the rim.   5. Hub. *Bowl*: roll.   6. A comic act.
7. Hecuba was the wife of Priam and queen of Troy. Her "loins" are described below as "o'erteemed"
because of her unusual fertility. The number of her children varies in different accounts, but
twenty is a safe minimum.   8. Muffled (in a hood).   9. Cloth. *Bisson rheum*: blinding tears.
1. Government.   2. Cutting up.   3. Tearful (literally, milk-giving).   4. Whether.
5. Provided for.   6. Summary.

HAMLET: God's bodkin, man, much better. Use every man after his desert, 465
and who shall 'scape whipping? Use them after your own honor and
dignity. The less they deserve, the more merit is in your bounty. Take
them in.
POLONIUS: Come, sirs.
HAMLET: Follow him, friends. We'll hear a play tomorrow.
[*Aside to* FIRST PLAYER.]
Dost thou hear me, old friend, can you play "The Murder of Gonzago"? 470
FIRST PLAYER: Ay, my lord.
HAMLET: We'll ha't tomorrow night. You could for a need study a speech of
some dozen or sixteen lines which I would set down and insert in't,
could you not?
FIRST PLAYER: Ay, my lord.
HAMLET: Very well. Follow that lord, and look you mock him not. 475
[*Exeunt* POLONIUS *and* PLAYERS.]
My good friends, I'll leave you till night. You are welcome to Elsinore.
ROSENCRANTZ: Good my lord. [*Exeunt* ROSENCRANTZ *and* GUILDENSTERN.]
HAMLET: Ay, so God b'wi'ye. Now I am alone.
O, what a rogue and peasant slave am I!
Is it not monstrous that this player here, 480
But in a fiction, in a dream of passion,
Could force his soul so to his own conceit[7]
That from her working all his visage wanned;[8]
Tears in his eyes, distraction in his aspect[9]
A broken voice, and his whole function suiting 485
With forms to his conceit? And all for nothing,
For Hecuba!
What's Hecuba to him or he to Hecuba,
That he should weep for her? What would he do
Had he the motive and the cue for passion 490
That I have? He would drown the stage with tears,
And cleave the general ear with horrid speech,
Make mad the guilty, and appal the free,
Confound the ignorant, and amaze indeed
The very faculties of eyes and ears. 495
Yet I,
A dull and muddy-mettled rascal, peak[1]
Like John-a-dreams, unpregnant[2] of my cause,
And can say nothing; no, not for a king
Upon whose property and most dear life 500

7. Imagination. 8. Grew pale. 9. Face. 1. Mope. *Muddy-mettled*: dull-spirited.
2. Not quickened by. *John-a-dreams*: a man dreaming.

A damned defeat was made. Am I a coward?
Who calls me villain, breaks my pate across,
Plucks off my beard and blows it in my face,
Tweaks me by the nose, gives me the lie i' th' throat
505 As deep as to the lungs? Who does me this?
Ha, 'swounds, I should take it; for it cannot be
But I am pigeon-livered and lack gall[3]
To make oppression bitter, or ere this
I should 'a fatted all the region kites[4]
510 With this slave's offal. Bloody, bawdy villain!
Remorseless, treacherous, lecherous, kindless[5] villain!
O, vengeance!
Why, what an ass am I! This is most brave,
That I, the son of a dear father murdered,
515 Prompted to my revenge by heaven and hell,
Must like a whore unpack[6] my heart with words,
And fall a-cursing like a very drab,
A scullion![7] Fie upon't! foh!
About, my brains. Hum—I have heard
520 That guilty creatures sitting at a play,
Have by the very cunning of the scene
Been struck so to the soul that presently
They have proclaimed[8] their malefactions;
For murder, though it have no tongue, will speak
525 With most miraculous organ. I'll have these players
Play something like the murder of my father
Before mine uncle. I'll observe his looks.
I'll tent him to the quick. If 'a do blench,[9]
I know my course. The spirit that I have seen
530 May be a devil, and the devil hath power
T' assume a pleasing shape, yea, and perhaps
Out of my weakness and my melancholy,
As he is very potent with such spirits,
Abuses me to damn me. I'll have grounds
535 More relative[1] than this. The play's the thing
Wherein I'll catch the conscience of the king.   [*Exit.*]

---

3. Bitterness.   4. Birds of prey of the area.   5. Unnatural.   6. Relieve.
7. In some versions of the play, the word "stallion," a slang term for a prostitute, appears in place
of "scullion."   8. Admitted.   9. Turn pale. *Tent*: try.   1. Conclusive.

ACT III

Scene 1

A room in the castle. Enter KING, QUEEN, POLONIUS, OPHELIA, ROSENCRANTZ *and* GUILDENSTERN.

KING: And can you by no drift of conference²
    Get from him why he puts on this confusion,
    Grating so harshly all his days of quiet
    With turbulent³ and dangerous lunacy?
ROSENCRANTZ: He does confess he feels himself distracted,   5
    But from what cause 'a will by no means speak.
GUILDENSTERN: Nor do we find him forward to be sounded,⁴
    But with a crafty madness keeps aloof
    When we would bring him on to some confession
    Of his true state.
QUEEN: Did he receive you well?   10
ROSENCRANTZ: Most like a gentleman.
GUILDENSTERN: But with much forcing of his disposition.⁵
ROSENCRANTZ: Niggard of question, but of our demands⁶
    Most free in his reply.
QUEEN: Did you assay⁷ him
    To any pastime?   15
ROSENCRANTZ: Madam, it so fell out that certain players
    We o'er-raught⁸ on the way. Of these we told him,
    And there did seem in him a kind of joy
    To hear of it. They are here about the court,
    And as I think, they have already order   20
    This night to play before him.
POLONIUS: 'Tis most true,
    And he beseeched me to entreat your majesties
    To hear and see the matter.⁹
KING: With all my heart, and it doth much content me
    To hear him so inclined.   25
    Good gentlemen, give him a further edge,
    And drive his purpose¹ into these delights.
ROSENCRANTZ: We shall, my lord.
                    [*Exeunt* ROSENCRANTZ *and* GUILDENSTERN.]
KING: Sweet Gertrude, leave us too,
    For we have closely sent for Hamlet hither,

---

2. Line of conversation.   3. Disturbing.   4. Questioned. *Forward*: eager.   5. Mood.
6. To our questions.   7. Tempt.   8. Passed.   9. Performance.   1. Sharpen his intention.

30   That he, as 'twere by accident, may here
       Affront² Ophelia.
       Her father and myself (lawful espials³)
       Will so bestow ourselves that, seeing unseen,
       We may of their encounter frankly judge,
35   And gather by him, as he is behaved,
       If't be th' affliction of his love or no
       That thus he suffers for.
       QUEEN: I shall obey you.—
       And for your part, Ophelia, I do wish
       That your good beauties be the happy cause
40   Of Hamlet's wildness. So shall I hope your virtues
       Will bring him to his wonted⁴ way again,
       To both your honors.
       OPHELIA: Madam, I wish it may.   [*Exit* QUEEN.]
       POLONIUS: Ophelia, walk you here.—Gracious,⁵ so please you,
       We will bestow ourselves.—[*To* OPHELIA.] Read on this book,
45   That show of such an exercise may color⁶
       Your loneliness.—We are oft to blame in this,
       'Tis too much proved, that with devotion's visage
       And pious action we do sugar o'er
       The devil himself.
50 KING: [*Aside.*]   O, 'tis too true.
       How smart a lash that speech doth give my conscience!
       The harlot's cheek, beautied with plast'ring⁷ art,
       Is not more ugly to the thing that helps it
       Than is my deed to my most painted word.
       O heavy burden!
55 POLONIUS: I hear him coming. Let's withdraw, my lord.
                                 [*Exeunt* KING *and* POLONIUS.]

       [*Enter* HAMLET.]

       HAMLET: To be, or not to be, that is the question:
       Whether 'tis nobler in the mind to suffer
       The slings and arrows of outrageous fortune,
       Or to take arms against a sea of troubles,
60   And by opposing end them. To die, to sleep—
       No more; and by a sleep to say we end
       The heartache, and the thousand natural shocks
       That flesh is heir to. 'Tis a consummation
       Devoutly to be wished—to die, to sleep—

2. Confront.   3. Justified spies.   4. Usual.   5. Majesty.   6. Explain. *Exercise*: act of devotion.
7. Thickly painted.

To sleep, perchance to dream, ay there's the rub;   65
For in that sleep of death what dreams may come
When we have shuffled off this mortal coil⁸
Must give us pause—there's the respect⁹
That makes calamity of so long life.
For who would bear the whips and scorns of time,   70
Th' oppressor's wrong, the proud man's contumely,¹
The pangs of despised love, the law's delay,
The insolence of office, and the spurns²
That patient merit of th' unworthy takes,
When he himself might his quietus³ make   75
With a bare bodkin? Who would fardels⁴ bear,
To grunt and sweat under a weary life,
But that the dread of something after death,
The undiscovered country, from whose bourn⁵
No traveller returns, puzzles the will,   80
And makes us rather bear those ills we have
Than fly to others that we know not of?
Thus conscience does make cowards of us all;
And thus the native⁶ hue of resolution
Is sicklied o'er with the pale cast of thought,   85
And enterprises of great pitch and moment⁷
With this regard their currents turn awry
And lose the name of action.—Soft you now,
The fair Ophelia.—Nymph, in thy orisons⁸
Be all my sins remembered.
OPHELIA: Good my lord,   90
How does your honor for this many a day?
HAMLET: I humbly thank you, well, well, well.
OPHELIA: My lord, I have remembrances of yours
That I have longèd long to re-deliver.
I pray you now receive them.
HAMLET: No, not I,   95
I never gave you aught.
OPHELIA: My honored lord, you know right well you did,
And with them words of so sweet breath composed
As made the things more rich. Their perfume lost,
Take these again, for to the noble mind   100
Rich gifts wax⁹ poor when givers prove unkind.
There, my lord.
HAMLET: Ha, ha! are you honest?¹

---

8. Turmoil.   9. Consideration.   1. Insulting behavior.   2. Rejections.   3. Settlement.
4. Burdens. *Bodkin*: dagger.   5. Boundary.   6. Natural.   7. Importance. *Pitch*: height.
8. Prayers.   9. Become.   1. Chaste.

OPHELIA: My lord?

105 HAMLET: Are you fair?

OPHELIA: What means your lordship?

HAMLET: That if you be honest and fair, your honesty should admit no discourse to your beauty.

OPHELIA: Could beauty, my lord, have better commerce[2] than with honesty?

110 HAMLET: Ay, truly, for the power of beauty will sooner transform honesty
from what it is to a bawd than the force of honesty can translate beauty
into his likeness. This was sometimes a paradox, but now the time gives
it proof. I did love you once.

OPHELIA: Indeed, my lord, you made me believe so.

115 HAMLET: You should not have believed me, for virtue cannot so inoculate[3]
our old stock but we shall relish of it. I loved you not.

OPHELIA: I was the more deceived.

HAMLET: Get thee to a nunnery.[4] Why wouldst thou be a breeder of sinners?
I am myself indifferent[5] honest, but yet I could accuse me of such things
that it were better my mother had not borne me: I am very proud,
120 revengeful, ambitious, with more offences at my beck[6] than I have
thoughts to put them in, imagination to give them shape, or time to act
them in. What should such fellows as I do crawling between earth and
heaven? We are arrant[7] knaves all; believe none of us. Go thy ways to a
nunnery. Where's your father?

125 OPHELIA: At home, my lord.

HAMLET: Let the doors be shut upon him, that he may play the fool nowhere
but in's own house. Farewell.

OPHELIA: O, help him, you sweet heavens!

HAMLET: If thou dost marry, I'll give thee this plague for thy dowry: be
thou as chaste as ice, as pure as snow, thou shalt not escape calumny.
130 Get thee to a nunnery, farewell. Or if thou wilt needs marry, marry a
fool, for wise men know well enough what monsters[8] you make of them.
To a nunnery, go, and quickly too. Farewell.

OPHELIA: Heavenly powers, restore him!

135 HAMLET: I have heard of your paintings, too, well enough. God hath given
you one face, and you make yourselves another. You jig, you amble, and
you lisp;[9] you nickname God's creatures, and make your wantonness
your ignorance.[1] Go to, I'll no more on't, it hath made me mad. I say we
will have no more marriage. Those that are married already, all but one,
140 shall live. The rest shall keep as they are. To a nunnery, go.   [Exit.]

2. Intercourse. 3. Change by grafting.
4. With typical ribaldry Hamlet uses "nunnery" in two senses, the second as a slang term for
brothel. 5. Moderately. 6. Command. 7. Thorough. 8. Horned because cuckolded.
9. Walk and talk affectedly.
1. Hamlet means that women call things by pet names and then blame the affectation on
ignorance.

OPHELIA: O, what a noble mind is here o'erthrown!
The courtier's, soldier's, scholar's, eye, tongue, sword,
Th' expectancy and rose[2] of the fair state,
The glass of fashion and the mould[3] of form,
Th' observed of all observers, quite quite down!   145
And I of ladies most deject and wretched,
That sucked the honey of his music[4] vows,
Now see that noble and most sovereign reason
Like sweet bells jangled, out of time and harsh;
That unmatched form and feature of blown[5] youth   150
Blasted with ecstasy. O, woe is me
T' have seen what I have seen, see what I see!

    [*Enter* KING *and* POLONIUS.]

KING: Love! His affections do not that way tend,
Nor what he spake, though it lacked form a little,
Was not like madness. There's something in his soul   155
O'er which his melancholy sits on brood,[6]
And I do doubt the hatch and the disclose[7]
Will be some danger; which to prevent,
I have in quick determination
Thus set it down: he shall with speed to England   160
For the demand of our neglected tribute.
Haply the seas and countries different,
With variable objects, shall expel
This something-settled matter in his heart
Whereon his brains still beating puts him thus   165
From fashion of himself. What think you on't?
POLONIUS: It shall do well. But yet do I believe
The origin and commencement of his grief
Sprung from neglected love.—How now, Ophelia?
You need not tell us what Lord Hamlet said,   170
We heard it all.—My lord, do as you please,
But if you hold it fit, after the play
Let his queen-mother all alone entreat him
To show his grief. Let her be round[8] with him,
And I'll be placed, so please you, in the ear[9]   175
Of all their conference. If she find him not,[1]
To England send him; or confine him where
Your wisdom best shall think.

---

2. Ornament. *Expectancy:* hope.   3. Model. *Glass:* mirror.   4. Musical.   5. Full-blown.
6. That is, like a hen.   7. Result. *Doubt:* fear.   8. Direct.   9. Hearing.
1. Does not discover his problem.

KING: It shall be so.
Madness in great ones must not unwatched go.   [*Exeunt.*]

Scene 2

A public room in the castle. Enter HAMLET *and three of the* PLAYERS.

HAMLET: Speak the speech, I pray you, as I pronounced it to you, trippingly
on the tongue; but if you mouth it as many of our players do, I had as
lief the town-crier spoke my lines. Nor do not saw the air too much with
your hand thus, but use all gently, for in the very torrent, tempest, and
as I may say, whirlwind of your passion, you must acquire and beget a
5   temperance that may give it smoothness. O, it offends me to the soul to
hear a robustious periwig-pated[2] fellow tear a passion to tatters, to very
rags, to split the ears of the groundlings, who for the most part are capable of [3] nothing but inexplicable dumb shows and noise. I would have
such a fellow whipped for o'erdoing Termagant. It out-herods Herod.[4]
10   Pray you avoid it.
FIRST PLAYER: I warrant your honor.
HAMLET: Be not too tame neither, but let your own discretion be your tutor.
Suit the action to the word, the word to the action, with this special
observance, that you o'erstep not the modesty of nature; for anything
so o'erdone is from[5] the purpose of playing, whose end both at the first,
15   and now, was and is, to hold as 'twere the mirror up to nature, to show
virtue her own feature, scorn her own image, and the very age and body
of the time his form and pressure.[6] Now this overdone, or come tardy
off, though it makes the unskilful[7] laugh, cannot but make the judi-
cious grieve, the censure[8] of the which one must in your allowance
20   o'erweigh a whole theatre of others. O, there be players that I have seen
play—and heard others praise, and that highly—not to speak it pro-
fanely, that neither having th' accent of Christians, nor the gait of Christian, pagan, nor man, have so strutted and bellowed that I have thought
some of nature's journeymen[9] had made men, and not made them well,
25   they imitated humanity so abominably.
FIRST PLAYER: I hope we have reformed that indifferently[1] with us, sir.
HAMLET: O, reform it altogether. And let those that play your clowns speak
no more than is set down for them, for there be of them that will themselves laugh, to set on some quantity of barren[2] spectators to laugh too,

---

2. Bewigged. *Robustious:* noisy.
3. That is, capable of understanding. *Groundlings:* the spectators who paid least.
4. Termagant, a "Saracen" deity, and the biblical Herod were stock characters in popular drama
noted for the excesses of sound and fury used by their interpreters.   5. Contrary to.
6. Shape.   7. Ignorant.   8. Judgment.   9. Inferior craftsmen.   1. Somewhat.
2. Dull-witted.

though in the meantime some necessary question of the play be then to
be considered. That's villainous, and shows a most pitiful ambition in 30
the fool that uses it. Go, make you ready.   [*Exeunt* PLAYERS.]

[*Enter* POLONIUS, GUILDENSTERN, *and* ROSENCRANTZ.]

How now, my lord? Will the king hear this piece of work?
POLONIUS: And the queen too, and that presently.
HAMLET: Bid the players make haste.   [*Exit* POLONIUS.] 35
Will you two help to hasten them?
ROSENCRANTZ: Ay, my lord.   [*Exeunt they two.*]
HAMLET: What, ho, Horatio!

[*Enter* HORATIO.]

HORATIO: Here, sweet lord, at your service.
HAMLET: Horatio, thou art e'en as just a man   40
As e'er my conversation coped[3] withal.
HORATIO: O my dear lord!
HAMLET: Nay, do not think I flatter,
For what advancement may I hope from thee,
That no revenue hast but thy good spirits
To feed and clothe thee? Why should the poor be flattered?   45
No, let the candied tongue lick absurd pomp,
And crook the pregnant[4] hinges of the knee
Where thrift[5] may follow fawning. Dost thou hear?
Since my dear soul was mistress of her choice
And could of men distinguish her election,   50
S'hath sealed thee for herself, for thou hast been
As one in suff'ring all that suffers nothing,
A man that Fortune's buffets and rewards
Hast ta'en with equal thanks; and blest are those
Whose blood and judgment are so well commingled   55
That they are not a pipe[6] for Fortune's finger
To sound what stop[7] she please. Give me that man
That is not passion's slave, and I will wear him
In my heart's core, ay, in my heart of heart,
As I do thee. Something too much of this.   60
There is a play tonight before the king.
One scene of it comes near the circumstance
Which I have told thee of my father's death.
I prithee, when thou seest that act afoot,
Even with the very comment[8] of thy soul   65

---

3. Encountered.   4. Quick to bend.   5. Profit.   6. Musical instrument.   7. Note. *Sound:* play.
8. Keenest observation.

Observe my uncle. If his occulted[9] guilt
Do not itself unkennel[1] in one speech,
It is a damnèd ghost that we have seen,
And my imaginations are as foul
70 As Vulcan's stithy. Give him heedful note,[2]
For I mine eyes will rivet to his face,
And after we will both our judgments join
In censure of his seeming.[3]
HORATIO: Well, my lord.
If 'a steal aught the whilst this play in playing,
75 And 'scape detecting, I will pay[4] the theft.

[*Enter Trumpets and Kettledrums,* KING, QUEEN, POLONIUS, OPHELIA, ROSENCRANTZ, GUILDENSTERN, *and other* LORDS *attendant.*]

HAMLET: They are coming to the play. I must be idle.
     Get you a place.
KING: How fares our cousin Hamlet?
HAMLET: Excellent, i' faith, of the chameleon's dish. I eat the air, promise-crammed. You cannot feed capons[5] so.
80 KING: I have nothing with this answer, Hamlet. These words are not mine.
HAMLET: No, nor mine now. [*To* POLONIUS.] My lord, you played once i' th' university, you say?
POLONIUS: That did I, my lord, and was accounted a good actor.
HAMLET: What did you enact?
85 POLONIUS: I did enact Julius Cæsar. I was killed i' th' Capitol; Brutus killed me.[6]
HAMLET: It was a brute part of him to kill so capital a calf there. Be the players ready?
ROSENCRANTZ: Ay, my lord, they stay upon your patience.[7]
QUEEN: Come hither, my dear Hamlet, sit by me.
90 HAMLET: No, good mother, here's metal more attractive.
POLONIUS: [*To the* KING.] O, ho! do you mark that?
HAMLET: Lady, shall I lie in your lap?

     [*Lying down at* OPHELIA's *feet.*]

OPHELIA: No, my lord.
HAMLET: I mean, my head upon your lap?
95 OPHELIA: Ay, my lord.

9. Hidden.   1. Break loose.   2. Careful attention. *Stithy*: smithy.   3. Manner.   4. Repay.
5. Castrated male chickens fattened for slaughter; also a term for fool. *Chameleon's dish*: a reference to a popular belief that the chameleon subsisted on a diet of air. Hamlet has deliberately misunderstood the king's question.
6. The assassination of Julius Caesar by Brutus and others is the subject of another play by Shakespeare.   7. Leisure. *Stay*: wait.

HAMLET: Do you think I meant country matters?[8]
OPHELIA: I think nothing, my lord.
HAMLET: That's a fair thought to lie between maids' legs.
OPHELIA: What is, my lord?
HAMLET: Nothing.   100
OPHELIA: You are merry, my lord.
HAMLET: Who, I?
OPHELIA: Ay, my lord.
HAMLET: O God, your only jig-maker![9] What should a man do but be merry?
For look you how cheerfully my mother looks, and my father died with-
in's two hours.   105
OPHELIA: Nay, 'tis twice two months, my lord.
HAMLET: So long? Nay then, let the devil wear black, for I'll have a suit of
sables. O heavens! die two months ago, and not forgotten yet? Then
there's hope a great man's memory may outlive his life half a year, but
by'r lady 'a must build churches then, or else shall 'a suffer not thinking   110
on, with the hobby-horse, whose epitaph is "For O, for O, the hobby-
horse is forgot!"[1]

> *The trumpets sound. Dumb Show follows. Enter a* KING *and a* QUEEN *very*
> *lovingly; the* QUEEN *embracing him and he her. She kneels, and makes show of*
> *protestation unto him. He takes her up, and declines[2] his head upon her neck. He*
> *lies him down upon a bank of flowers; she, seeing him asleep, leaves him. Anon*
> *come in another man, takes off his crown, kisses it, pours poison in the sleeper's*
> *ears, and leaves him. The* QUEEN *returns, finds the* KING *dead, makes passionate*
> *action. The* POISONER *with some three or four come in again, seem to condole*
> *with her. The dead body is carried away. The* POISONER *woos the* QUEEN *with*
> *gifts; she seems harsh awhile, but in the end accepts love.*   [*Exeunt.*]

OPHELIA: What means this, my lord?
HAMLET: Marry, this is miching mallecho;[3] it means mischief.
OPHELIA: Belike this show imports the argument[4] of the play.   115

[*Enter* PROLOGUE.]

HAMLET: We shall know by this fellow. The players cannot keep counsel;
they'll tell all.
OPHELIA: Will 'a tell us what this show meant?
HAMLET: Ay, or any show that you will show him. Be not you ashamed to
show, he'll not shame to tell you what it means.   120

---

8. Presumably, rustic misbehavior, but here and elsewhere in this exchange Hamlet treats Ophelia to some ribald double meanings.   9. Writer of comic scenes.
1. In traditional games and dances one of the characters was a man represented as riding a horse.
The horse was made of something like cardboard and was worn about the "rider's" waist.
2. Lays.   3. Sneaking crime (from the Spanish *malhecho*, "evil deed").   4. Plot. *Imports*: explains.

OPHELIA: You are naught, you are naught. I'll mark[5] the play.

PROLOGUE: *For us, and for our tragedy,*
  Here stooping to your clemency,
  We beg your hearing patiently. [*Exit.*]

125 HAMLET: Is this a prologue, or the posy[6] of a ring?

OPHELIA: 'Tis brief, my lord.

HAMLET: As woman's love.

[*Enter the* PLAYER KING *and* QUEEN.]

PLAYER KING: *Full thirty times hath Phœbus' cart gone round*
  Neptune's salt wash and Tellus' orbèd ground,
130 *And thirty dozen moons with borrowed sheen[7]*
  About the world have times twelve thirties been,
  Since love our hearts and Hymen did our hands
  Unite comutual in most sacred bands.[8]

PLAYER QUEEN: *So many journeys may the sun and moon*
135 *Make us again count o'er ere love be done!*
  But woe is me, you are so sick of late,
  So far from cheer and from your former state,
  That I distrust[9] you. Yet though I distrust,
  Discomfort you, my lord, it nothing must.
140 *For women's fear and love hold quantity,[1]*
  In neither aught, or in extremity.[2]
  Now what my love is proof hath made you know,
  And as my love is sized,[3] my fear is so.
  Where love is great, the littlest doubts are fear;
145 *Where little fears grow great, great love grows there.*

PLAYER KING: *Faith, I must leave thee, love, and shortly too;*
  My operant powers their functions leave[4] to do.
  And thou shalt live in this fair world behind,
  Honored, beloved, and haply one as kind
  For husband shalt thou—

150 PLAYER QUEEN: *O, confound the rest!*
  Such love must needs be treason in my breast.
  In second husband let me be accurst!
  None wed the second but who killed the first.[5]

---

5. Attend to. *Naught*: obscene.   6. Motto engraved inside.   7. Light.
8. The speech contains several references to Greek mythology. Phoebus was the sun god, and his chariot or "cart" is the sun. The "salt wash" of Neptune is the ocean; Tellus was an earth goddess, and her "orbed ground" is the Earth, or globe. Hymen was the god of marriage. *Comutual*: mutually.
9. Fear for.   1. Agree in weight.   2. Without regard to too much or too little.   3. In size.
4. Cease. *Operant powers*: active forces.   5. Though there is some ambiguity, she seems to mean that the only kind of woman who would remarry is one who has killed or would kill her first husband.

HAMLET: That's wormwood.[6]

PLAYER QUEEN: *The instances[7] that second marriage move*   155
Are base respects[8] of thrift, but none of love.
A second time I kill my husband dead,
When second husband kisses me in bed.

PLAYER KING: *I do believe you think what now you speak,*
But what we do determine oft we break.   160
Purpose is but the slave to memory,
Of violent birth, but poor validity;
Which now, like fruit unripe, sticks on the tree,
But fall unshaken when they mellow be.
Most necessary 'tis that we forget   165
To pay ourselves what to ourselves is debt.
What to ourselves in passion we propose,
The passion ending, doth the purpose lose.
The violence of either grief or joy
Their own enactures[9] with themselves destroy.   170
Where joy most revels, grief doth most lament;
Grief joys, joy grieves, on slender accident.
This world is not for aye,[1] nor 'tis not strange
That even our loves should with our fortunes change;
For 'tis a question left us yet to prove,   175
Whether love lead fortune, or else fortune love.
The great man down, you mark his favorite flies;
The poor advanced makes friends of enemies;
And hitherto doth love on fortune tend,
For who not needs shall never lack a friend,   180
And who in want a hollow[2] friend doth try,
Directly seasons him[3] his enemy.
But orderly to end where I begun,
Our wills and fates do so contrary run
That our devices[4] still are overthrown;   185
Our thoughts are ours, their ends none of our own.
So think thou wilt no second husband wed,
But die thy thoughts when thy first lord is dead.

PLAYER QUEEN: *Nor earth to me give food, nor heaven light,*
Sport and repose lock from me day and night,   190
To desperation turn my trust and hope,
An anchor's cheer[5] in prison be my scope,
Each opposite that blanks[6] the face of joy
Meet what I would have well, and it destroy,

---

6. *Wormwood:* bitter medicine. 7. Causes. 8. Concerns. 9. Actions. 1. Eternal. 2. False.
3. Ripens him into. 4. Plans. 5. Anchorite's (hermit's) food. 6. Blanches.

195   *Both here and hence[7] pursue me lasting strife,*
      If once a widow, ever I be wife!
      HAMLET: If she should break it now!
      PLAYER KING: 'Tis deeply sworn. *Sweet, leave me here awhile.*
      My spirits grow dull, and fain I would beguile
      The tedious day with sleep.   [*Sleeps.*]
200   PLAYER QUEEN: *Sleep rock thy brain,*
      And never come mischance between us twain!   [*Exit.*]
      HAMLET: Madam, how like you this play?
      QUEEN: The lady doth protest too much, methinks.
      HAMLET: O, but she'll keep her word.
205   KING: Have you heard the argument? Is there no offence in't?
      HAMLET: No, no, they do but jest, poison in jest; no offence i' th' world.
      KING: What do you call the play?
      HAMLET: "The Mouse-trap." Marry, how? Tropically.[8] This play is the image
      of a murder done in Vienna. Gonzago is the duke's name; his wife, Bap-
210   tista. You shall see anon. 'Tis a knavish piece of work, but what of that?
      Your majesty, and we that have free souls, it touches us not. Let the
      galled jade wince, our withers are unwrung.[9]

      [*Enter* LUCIANUS.]

      This is one Lucianus, nephew to the king.
      OPHELIA: You are as good as a chorus, my lord.
215   HAMLET: I could interpret between you and your love, if I could see the pup-
      pets dallying.
      OPHELIA: You are keen, my lord, you are keen.
      HAMLET: It would cost you a groaning to take off mine edge.
      OPHELIA: Still better, and worse.
220   HAMLET: So you mistake your husbands.—Begin, murderer. Leave thy dam-
      nable faces and begin. Come, the croaking raven doth bellow for revenge.
      LUCIANUS: *Thoughts black, hands apt, drugs fit, and time agreeing,*
      Confederate season,[1] else no creature seeing,
      Thou mixture rank, of midnight weeds collected,
225   *With Hecate's ban thrice blasted, thrice infected,[2]*
      Thy natural magic[3] and dire property
      On wholesome life usurp immediately.   [*Pours the poison in his ears.*]
      HAMLET: 'A poisons him i' th' garden for his estate. His name's Gonzago.
      The story is extant, and written in very choice Italian. You shall see
230   anon how the murderer gets the love of Gonzago's wife.

---

7. In the next world.   8. Figuratively.
9. A "galled jade" is a horse, particularly one of poor quality, with a sore back. The "withers" are
the ridge between a horse's shoulders; "unwrung withers" are not chafed by the harness.
1. A helpful time for the crime.   2. Hecate was a classical goddess of witchcraft.
3. Native power.

OPHELIA: The king rises.
HAMLET: What, frighted with false fire?
QUEEN: How fares my lord?
POLONIUS: Give o'er the play.
KING: Give me some light. Away!   235
POLONIUS: Lights, lights, lights!   [*Exeunt all but* HAMLET *and* HORATIO.]
HAMLET:

> Why, let the strucken deer go weep,
>   The hart ungallèd[4] play.
> For some must watch while some must sleep;
>   Thus runs the world away.   240

Would not this, sir, and a forest of feathers[5]—if the rest of my fortunes
turn Turk with me—with two Provincial roses on my razed shoes, get
me a fellowship in a cry of players?[6]
HORATIO: Half a share.
HAMLET: A whole one, I.   245

> For thou dost know, O Damon dear,[7]
>   This realm dismantled was
> Of Jove himself, and now reigns here
>   A very, very—peacock.

HORATIO: You might have rhymed.   250
HAMLET: O good Horatio, I'll take the ghost's word for a thousand pound.
    Didst perceive?
HORATIO: Very well, my lord.
HAMLET: Upon the talk of the poisoning.
HORATIO: I did very well note[8] him.   255
HAMLET: Ah, ha! Come, some music. Come, the recorders.[9]

> For if the king like not the comedy.
> Why then, belike he likes it not, perdy.[1]

Come, some music.

[*Enter* ROSENCRANTZ *and* GUILDENSTERN.]

---

4. Uninjured.   5. Plumes.
6. Hamlet asks Horatio if "this" recitation, accompanied with a player's costume, including
plumes and rosettes on shoes that have been slashed for decorative effect, might not entitle him to
become a shareholder in a theatrical company in the event that Fortune goes against him, "turn
Turk." *Cry:* company.
7. Damon was a common name for a young man or a shepherd in lyric, especially pastoral poetry.
Jove was the chief god of the Romans. Readers may supply for themselves the rhyme referred to by
Horatio.   8. Observe.   9. Wooden, end-blown flutes.
1. *Perdy*, that is, *par Dieu* (French for "by God").

260 GUILDENSTERN: Good my lord, vouchsafe me a word with you.

HAMLET: Sir, a whole history.

GUILDENSTERN: The king, sir—

HAMLET: Ay, sir, what of him?

GUILDENSTERN: Is in his retirement marvellous distempered.[2]

265 HAMLET: With drink, sir?

GUILDENSTERN: No, my lord, with choler.[3]

HAMLET: Your wisdom should show itself more richer to signify this to the doctor, for for me to put him to his purgation[4] would perhaps plunge him into more choler.

270 GUILDENSTERN: Good my lord, put your discourse into some frame,[5] and start not so wildly from my affair.

HAMLET: I am tame, sir. Pronounce.

GUILDENSTERN: The queen your mother, in most great affliction of spirit, hath sent me to you.

275 HAMLET: You are welcome.

GUILDENSTERN: Nay, good my lord, this courtesy is not of the right breed. If it shall please you to make me a wholesome[6] answer, I will do your mother's commandment. If not, your pardon and my return[7] shall be the end of my business.

280 HAMLET: Sir, I cannot.

ROSENCRANTZ: What, my lord?

HAMLET: Make you a wholesome answer; my wit's diseased. But, sir, such answer as I can make, you shall command, or rather, as you say, my mother. Therefore no more, but to the matter. My mother, you say—

285 ROSENCRANTZ: Then thus she says: your behavior hath struck her into amazement and admiration.[8]

HAMLET: O wonderful son, that can so stonish a mother! But is there no sequel at the heels of his mother's admiration? Impart.[9]

ROSENCRANTZ: She desires to speak with you in her closet[1] ere you go to bed.

290 HAMLET: We shall obey, were she ten times our mother. Have you any further trade[2] with us?

ROSENCRANTZ: My lord, you once did love me.

HAMLET: And do still, by these pickers and stealers.[3]

ROSENCRANTZ: Good my lord, what is your cause of distemper? You do

295 surely bar the door upon your own liberty, if you deny your griefs to your friend.

HAMLET: Sir, I lack advancement.

ROSENCRANTZ: How can that be, when you have the voice of the king himself for your succession in Denmark?

---

2. Vexed. *Retirement*: place to which he has retired.   3. Bile (anger).
4. Treatment with a laxative.   5. Order. *Discourse*: speech.   6. Reasonable.
7. That is, to the queen.   8. Wonder.   9. Tell me.   1. Bedroom.   2. Business.   3. Hands.

HAMLET: Ay, sir, but "while the grass grows"—the proverb[4] is something musty.

[*Enter the* PLAYERS *with recorders.*]

O, the recorders! Let me see one. To withdraw with you[5]—why do you 300 go about to recover the wind of me, as if you would drive me into a toil?[6]

GUILDENSTERN: O my lord, if my duty be too bold, my love is too unmannerly.

HAMLET: I do not well understand that. Will you play upon this pipe?[7]

GUILDENSTERN: My lord, I cannot. 305

HAMLET: I pray you.

GUILDENSTERN: Believe me, I cannot.

HAMLET: I do beseech you.

GUILDENSTERN: I know no touch of it,[8] my lord.

HAMLET: It is as easy as lying. Govern these ventages[9] with your fingers and 310 thumb, give it breath with your mouth, and it will discourse most eloquent music. Look you, these are the stops.[1]

GUILDENSTERN: But these cannot I command to any utt'rance of harmony. I have not the skill.

HAMLET: Why, look you now, how unworthy a thing you make of me! You 315 would play upon me, you would seem to know my stops, you would pluck out the heart of my mystery, you would sound[2] me from my lowest note to the top of my compass;[3] and there is much music, excellent voice, in this little organ, yet cannot you make it speak. 'Sblood, do you think I am easier to be played on than a pipe? Call me what instrument you will, though you can fret[4] me, you cannot play upon me. 320

[*Enter* POLONIUS.]

God bless you, sir!

POLONIUS: My lord, the queen would speak with you, and presently.[5]

HAMLET: Do you see yonder cloud that's almost in shape of a camel?

POLONIUS: By th' mass, and 'tis like a camel indeed. 325

HAMLET: Methinks it is like a weasel.

POLONIUS: It is backed like a weasel.

HAMLET: Or like a whale.

POLONIUS: Very like a whale.

HAMLET: Then I will come to my mother by and by. [*Aside.*] They fool me to 330 the top of my bent.[6]—I will come by and by.

---

4. The proverb ends "the horse starves."   5. Let me step aside.
6. The figure is from hunting. Hamlet asks why Guildenstern is attempting to get windward of him, as if he would drive him into a net.   7. Recorder.   8. Have no ability.
9. Holes. *Govern:* cover and uncover.   1. Wind-holes.   2. Play.   3. Range.
4. "Fret" is used in a double sense, to annoy and to play a guitar or similar instrument using the "frets" or small bars on the neck.   5. At once.   6. Treat me as an utter fool.

POLONIUS: I will say so.   [*Exit.*]
HAMLET: "By and by" is easily said. Leave me, friends.
                                                              [*Exeunt all but* HAMLET.]
'Tis now the very witching time of night,
335   When churchyards yawn, and hell itself breathes out
Contagion to this world. Now could I drink hot blood,
And do such bitter business as the day
Would quake to look on. Soft, now to my mother.
O heart, lose not thy nature; let not ever
340   The soul of Nero[7] enter this firm bosom.
Let me be cruel, not unnatural;
I will speak daggers to her, but use none.
My tongue and soul in this be hypocrites—
How in my words somever she be shent,[8]
345   To give them seals[9] never, my soul, consent!   [*Exit.*]

Scene 3

A room in the castle. Enter KING, ROSENCRANTZ *and* GUILDENSTERN.

KING: I like him not,[1] nor stands it safe with us
To let his madness range.[2] Therefore prepare you.
I your commission will forthwith dispatch,
And he to England shall along with you.
5   The terms of our estate[3] may not endure
Hazard so near's as doth hourly grow
Out of his brows.
GUILDENSTERN: We will ourselves provide,[4]
Most holy and religious fear it is
To keep those many many bodies safe
10   That live and feed upon your majesty.
ROSENCRANTZ: The single and peculiar[5] life is bound
With all the strength and armor of the mind
To keep itself from noyance,[6] but much more
That spirit upon whose weal[7] depends and rests
15   The lives of many. The cess[8] of majesty
Dies not alone, but like a gulf[9] doth draw
What's near it with it. It is a massy[1] wheel
Fixed on the summit of the highest mount,
To whose huge spokes ten thousand lesser things

---

7. The Roman emperor Nero, known for his excesses, was believed to have been responsible for the death of his mother.   8. Shamed.   9. Fulfillment in action.   1. Distrust him.
2. Roam freely.   3. Condition of the state.   4. Equip (for the journey).   5. Individual.
6. Harm.   7. Welfare.   8. Cessation.   9. Whirlpool.   1. Massive.

Are mortised and adjoined,[2] which when it falls,   20
Each small annexment, petty consequence,
Attends[3] the boist'rous ruin. Never alone
Did the king sigh, but with a general groan.
KING: Arm you, I pray you, to this speedy voyage,
For we will fetters put about this fear,   25
Which now goes too free-footed.
ROSENCRANTZ: We will haste us.
                    [*Exeunt* ROSENCRANTZ *and* GUILDENSTERN.]
    [*Enter* POLONIUS.]

POLONIUS: My lord, he's going to his mother's closet.
Behind the arras I'll convey[4] myself
To hear the process. I'll warrant she'll tax him home,[5]
And as you said, and wisely was it said,   30
'Tis meet that some more audience than a mother,
Since nature makes them partial, should o'erhear
The speech, of vantage.[6] Fare you well, my liege.
I'll call upon you ere you go to bed,
And tell you what I know.
KING: Thanks, dear my lord.   [*Exit* POLONIUS.] 35
O, my offence is rank, it smells to heaven;
It hath the primal eldest curse[7] upon't,
A brother's murder. Pray can I not,
Though inclination be as sharp as will.
My stronger guilt defeats my strong intent,   40
And like a man to double business[8] bound,
I stand in pause where I shall first begin,
And both neglect. What if this cursèd hand
Were thicker than itself with brother's blood,
Is there not rain enough in the sweet heavens   45
To wash it white as snow? Whereto serves mercy
But to confront the visage of offence?
And what's in prayer but this twofold force,
To be forestallèd[9] ere we come to fall,
Or pardoned being down?[1] Then I'll look up.   50
My fault is past, But, O, what form of prayer
Can serve my turn? "Forgive me my foul murder"?
That cannot be, since I am still possessed
Of those effects[2] for which I did the murder—

---

2. Attached.   3. Joins in.   4. Station.   5. Sharply. *Process*: proceedings.
6. From a position of vantage.   7. That is, of Cain.   8. Two mutually opposed interests.
9. Prevented (from sin).   1. Having sinned.   2. Gains.

55 My crown, mine own ambition, and my queen.
    May one be pardoned and retain th' offence?[3]
    In the corrupted currents of this world
    Offence's gilded[4] hand may shove by justice,
    And oft 'tis seen the wicked prize itself
60 Buys out the law. But 'tis not so above.
    There is no shuffling; there the action[5] lies
    In his true nature, and we ourselves compelled,
    Even to the teeth and forehead of[6] our faults,
    To give in evidence. What then? What rests?[7]
65 Try what repentance can. What can it not?
    Yet what can it when one cannot repent?
    O wretched state! O bosom black as death!
    O limèd[8] soul, that struggling to be free
    Art more engaged! Help, angels! Make assay.
70 Bow, stubborn knees, and heart with strings of steel,
    Be soft as sinews of the new-born babe.
    All may be well.   [*He kneels.*]

        [*Enter* HAMLET.]

HAMLET: Now might I do it pat,[9] now 'a is a-praying,
    And now I'll do't—and so 'a goes to heaven,
75 And so am I revenged. That would be scanned.[1]
    A villain kills my father, and for that,
    I, his sole son, do this same villain send
    To heaven.
    Why, this is hire and salary, not revenge.
80 'A took my father grossly, full of bread,[2]
    With all his crimes broad blown, as flush[3] as May;
    And how his audit stands who knows save heaven?
    But in our circumstance and course of thought
    'Tis heavy with him; and am I then revenged
85 To take him in the purging of his soul,
    When he is fit and seasoned[4] for his passage?
    No.
    Up, sword, and know thou a more horrid hent.[5]
    When he is drunk, asleep, or in his rage,
90 Or in th' incestuous pleasure of his bed,
    At game a-swearing, or about some act

---

3. That is, benefits of the offense.   4. Bearing gold as a bribe.   5. Case at law.
6. Face-to-face with.   7. Remains.   8. Caught as with birdlime.   9. Easily.
1. Deserves consideration.   2. In a state of sin and without fasting.
3. Vigorous. *Broad blown*: full-blown.   4. Ready.   5. Opportunity.

That has no relish⁶ of salvation in't—
Then trip him, that his heels may kick at heaven,
And that his soul may be as damned and black
As hell, whereto it goes. My mother stays.   95
This physic⁷ but prolongs thy sickly days.   [*Exit.*]
KING: [*Rising.*] My words fly up, my thoughts remain below.
Words without thoughts never to heaven go.   [*Exit.*]

Scene 4

The Queen's chamber. Enter QUEEN *and* POLONIUS.

POLONIUS: 'A will come straight. Look you lay home to⁸ him.
Tell him his pranks have been too broad⁹ to bear with,
And that your grace hath screen'd¹ and stood between
Much heat and him. I'll silence me even here.
Pray you be round with him.   5
HAMLET: [*Within.*] Mother, mother, mother!
QUEEN: I'll warrant you. Fear² me not.
Withdraw, I hear him coming.

        [POLONIUS *goes behind the arras. Enter* HAMLET.]

HAMLET: Now, mother, what's the matter?
QUEEN: Hamlet, thou hast thy father much offended.   10
HAMLET: Mother, you have my father much offended.
QUEEN: Come, come, you answer with an idle tongue.
HAMLET: Go, go, you question with a wicked tongue.
QUEEN: Why, how now, Hamlet?
HAMLET: What's the matter now?
QUEEN: Have you forgot me?
HAMLET: No, by the rood,³ not so.   15
You are the queen, your husband's brother's wife,
And would it were not so, you are my mother.
QUEEN: Nay, then I'll set those to you that can speak.
HAMLET: Come, come, and sit you down. You shall not budge.
You go not till I set you up a glass⁴   20
Where you may see the inmost part of you.
QUEEN: What wilt thou do? Thou wilt not murder me?
Help, ho!
POLONIUS: [*Behind.*] What, ho! help!
HAMLET: [*Draws.*] How now, a rat?   25
Dead for a ducat, dead!

6. Flavor.   7. Medicine.   8. Be sharp with.   9. Outrageous.   1. Acted as a fire screen.
2. Doubt.   3. Cross.   4. Mirror.

[*Kills* POLONIUS *with a pass through the arras.*]

POLONIUS: [*Behind.*] O, I am slain!
QUEEN: O me, what hast thou done?
HAMLET: Nay, I know not.
    Is it the king?
30 QUEEN: O, what a rash and bloody deed is this!
HAMLET: A bloody deed!—almost as bad, good mother,
    As kill a king and marry with his brother.
QUEEN: As kill a king?
HAMLET: Ay, lady, it was my word.   [*Parting the arras.*]
    Thou wretched, rash, intruding fool, farewell!
35 I took thee for thy better. Take thy fortune.
    Thou find'st to be too busy⁵ is some danger.—
    Leave wringing of your hands. Peace, sit you down
    And let me wring your heart, for so I shall
    If it be made of penetrable stuff,
40 If damnèd custom have not brazed it⁶ so
    That it be proof and bulwark against sense.⁷
QUEEN: What have I done that thou dar'st wag thy tongue
    In noise so rude against me?
HAMLET: Such an act
    That blurs the grace and blush of modesty,
45 Calls virtue hypocrite, takes off the rose
    From the fair forehead of an innocent love.
    And sets a blister⁸ there, makes marriage-vows
    As false as dicers' oaths. O, such a deed
    As from the body of contraction⁹ plucks
50 The very soul, and sweet religion makes
    A rhapsody of words. Heaven's face does glow
    O'er this solidity and compound mass¹
    With heated visage, as against the doom²—
    Is thought-sick at the act.
QUEEN: Ay me, what act
55 That roars so loud and thunders in the index?³
HAMLET: Look here upon this picture⁴ and on this,
    The counterfeit presentment of two brothers.
    See what a grace was seated on this brow:
    Hyperion's curls, the front⁵ of Jove himself,
60 An eye like Mars, to threaten and command,

---

5. Officious.   6. Plated it with brass.   7. Feeling. *Proof*: armor.   8. Brand.
9. The marriage contract.   1. Meaningless mass (Earth).   2. Judgment Day.
3. Table of contents.   4. Portrait.   5. Forehead.

A station like the herald Mercury[6]
New lighted[7] on a heaven-kissing hill—
A combination and a form indeed
Where every god did seem to set his seal,[8]
To give the world assurance of a man.   65
This was your husband. Look you now what follows.
Here is your husband, like a mildewed ear
Blasting his wholesome brother. Have you eyes?
Could you on this fair mountain leave to feed,
And batten[9] on this moor? Ha! have you eyes?   70
You cannot call it love, for at your age
The heyday in the blood is tame, it's humble,
And waits upon the judgment, and what judgment
Would step from this to this? Sense sure you have
Else could you not have motion, but sure that sense   75
Is apoplexed[1] for madness would not err,
Nor sense to ecstasy was ne'er so thralled
But it reserved some quantity[2] of choice
To serve in such a difference. What devil was't
That thus hath cozened you at hoodman-blind?[3]   80
Eyes without feeling, feeling without sight,
Ears without hands or eyes, smelling sans[4] all,
Or but a sickly part of one true sense
Could not so mope.[5] O shame! where is thy blush?
Rebellious hell,   85
If thou canst mutine[6] in a matron's bones,
To flaming youth let virtue be as wax
And melt in her own fire. Proclaim no shame
When the compulsive ardor gives the charge,[7]
Since frost itself as actively doth burn,   90
And reason panders[8] will.
QUEEN: O Hamlet, speak no more!
Thou turn'st my eyes into my very soul;
And there I see such black and grainèd[9] spots
As will not leave their tinct.[1]
HAMLET: Nay, but to live
In the rank sweat of an enseamèd[2] bed,   95
Stewed in curruption, honeying and making love
Over the nasty sty—

6. In Roman mythology, Mercury served as the messenger of the gods. *Station*: bearing.
7. Newly alighted.   8. Mark of approval.   9. Feed greedily.   1. Paralyzed.   2. Power.
3. Blindman's buff. *Cozened*: cheated.   4. Without.   5. Be stupid.   6. Commit mutiny.
7. Attacks.   8. Pimps for.   9. Ingrained.   1. Lose their color.   2. Greasy.

QUEEN: O, speak to me no more!
These words like daggers enter in my ears;
No more, sweet Hamlet.

HAMLET: A murderer and a villain,

100   A slave that is not twentieth part the tithe[3]
Of your precedent lord, a vice of kings,[4]
A cutpurse[5] of the empire and the rule,
That from a shelf the precious diadem stole
And put it in his pocket—

105 QUEEN: No more.

       [*Enter* GHOST.]

HAMLET: A king of shreds and patches—
Save me and hover o'er me with your wings,
You heavenly guards! What would your gracious figure?

QUEEN: Alas, he's mad.

110 HAMLET: Do you not come your tardy[6] son to chide,
That lapsed in time and passion lets go by
Th' important acting of your dread command?
O, say!

GHOST: Do not forget. This visitation

115   Is but to whet thy almost blunted purpose.
But look, amazement on thy mother sits.
O, step between her and her fighting soul!
Conceit[7] in weakest bodies strongest works.
Speak to her, Hamlet.

HAMLET: How is it with you, lady?

120 QUEEN: Alas, how is't with you,
That you do bend[8] your eye on vacancy,
And with th' incorporal air do hold discourse?
Forth at your eyes your spirits wildly peep,
And as the sleeping soldiers in th' alarm,

125   Your bedded hairs like life in excrements[9]
Start up and stand an end. O gentle son,
Upon the heat and flame of thy distemper
Sprinkle cool patience. Whereon do you look?

HAMLET: On him, on him! Look you how pale he glares.

130   His form and cause conjoined,[1] preaching to stones,
Would make them capable.[2]—Do not look upon me,

---

3. One-tenth.
4. The "Vice," a common figure in the popular drama, was a clown or buffoon. *Precedent lord*: first husband.   5. Pickpocket.   6. Slow to act.   7. Imagination.   8. Turn.   9. Nails and hair.
1. Working together.   2. Of responding.

Lest with this piteous action you convert
My stern effects.[3] Then what I have to do
Will want true color—tears perchance for blood.
QUEEN: To whom do you speak this?   135
HAMLET: Do you see nothing there?
QUEEN: Nothing at all, yet all that is I see.
HAMLET: Nor did you nothing hear?
QUEEN: No, nothing but ourselves.
HAMLET: Why, look you there. Look how it steals away.   140
My father, in his habit[4] as he lived!
Look where he goes even now out at the portal.   [*Exit* GHOST.]
QUEEN: This is the very coinage[5] of your brain.
This bodiless creation ecstasy[6]
Is very cunning[7] in.
HAMLET: Ecstasy?   145
My pulse as yours doth temperately keep time,
And makes as healthful music. It is not madness
That I have uttered. Bring me to the test,
And I the matter will re-word, which madness
Would gambol[8] from. Mother, for love of grace,   150
Lay not that flattering unction[9] to your soul,
That not your trespass but my madness speaks.
It will but skin and film the ulcerous place
Whiles rank corruption, mining[1] all within,
Infects unseen. Confess yourself to heaven,   155
Repent what's past, avoid what is to come.
And do not spread the compost on the weeds,
To make them ranker. Forgive me this my virtue,
For in the fatness of these pursy[2] times
Virtue itself of vice must pardon beg,   160
Yea, curb[3] and woo for leave to do him good.
QUEEN: O Hamlet, thou hast cleft my heart in twain.
HAMLET: O, throw away the worser part of it,
And live the purer with the other half.
Good night—but go not to my uncle's bed.   165
Assume a virtue, if you have it not.
That monster custom[4] who all sense doth eat
Of habits devil, is angel yet in this,
That to the use of actions fair and good
He likewise gives a frock or livery   170
That aptly[5] is put on. Refrain tonight,

---

3. Deeds.   4. Clothing.   5. Invention.   6. Madness.   7. Skilled.   8. Shy away.
9. Ointment.   1. Undermining.   2. Bloated.   3. Bow.   4. Habit.   5. Easily.

And that shall lend a kind of easiness
To the next abstinence; the next more easy;
For use almost can change the stamp of nature,
175   And either curb the devil, or throw him out
With wondrous potency. Once more, good night,
And when you are desirous to be blest,
I'll blessing beg of you. For this same lord
I do repent; but heaven hath pleased it so,
180   To punish me with this, and this with me,
That I must be their scourge and minister.
I will bestow[6] him and will answer well
The death I gave him. So, again, good night.
I must be cruel only to be kind.
185   Thus bad begins and worse remains behind.
One word more, good lady.

QUEEN: What shall I do?

HAMLET: Not this, by no means, that I bid you do:
Let the bloat[7] king tempt you again to bed,
Pinch wanton[8] on your cheek, call you his mouse,
190   And let him, for a pair of reechy[9] kisses,
Or paddling in your neck with his damned fingers,
Make you to ravel[1] all this matter out,
That I essentially am not in madness,
But mad in craft. 'Twere good you let him know,
195   For who that's but a queen, fair, sober, wise,
Would from a paddock, from a bat, a gib,[2]
Such dear concernings hide? Who would so do?
No, in despite of sense and secrecy,
Unpeg the basket on the house's top,
200   Let the birds fly, and like the famous ape,
To try conclusions, in the basket creep
And break your own neck down.[3]

QUEEN: Be thou assured, if words be made of breath
And breath of life, I have no life to breathe
205   What thou hast said to me.

HAMLET: I must to England; you know that?

QUEEN: Alack,
I had forgot. 'Tis so concluded on.

HAMLET: There's letters sealed, and my two school-fellows,
Whom I will trust as I will adders fanged,

---

6. Dispose of.   7. Bloated.   8. Lewdly.   9. Foul.   1. Reveal.   2. Tomcat. *Paddock*: toad.
3. Apparently a reference to a now-lost fable in which an ape, finding a basket containing a cage of
birds on a housetop, opens the cage. The birds fly away. The ape, thinking that if he were in the
basket he too could fly, enters, jumps out, and breaks his neck.

They bear the mandate; they must sweep[4] my way   210
And marshal me to knavery. Let it work,
For 'tis the sport to have the enginer
Hoist with his own petard;[5] and't shall go hard
But I will delve[6] one yard below their mines
And blow them at the moon. O, 'tis most sweet   215
When in one line two crafts directly meet.
This man shall set me packing.
I'll lug the guts into the neighbor room.
Mother, good night. Indeed, this counsellor
Is now most still, most secret, and most grave,   220
Who was in life a foolish prating knave.
Come sir, to draw toward an end with you.
Good night, mother.
                    [*Exit the* QUEEN. *Then exit* HAMLET *tugging* POLONIUS.]

ACT IV

Scene 1

A room in the castle. Enter KING, QUEEN, ROSENCRANTZ *and* GUILDENSTERN.

KING: There's matter in these sighs, these profound heaves,
     You must translate;[7] 'tis fit we understand them.
     Where is your son?
QUEEN: Bestow this place on us a little while.
                    [*Exeunt* ROSENCRANTZ *and* GUILDENSTERN.]
     Ah, mine own lord, what have I seen tonight!   5
KING: What, Gertrude? How does Hamlet?
QUEEN: Mad as the sea and wind when both contend
     Which is the mightier. In his lawless fit,
     Behind the arras hearing something stir,
     Whips out his rapier, cries "A rat, a rat!"   10
     And in this brainish apprehension[8] kills
     The unseen good old man.
KING: O heavy deed!
     It had been so with us had we been there.
     His liberty is full of threats to all—
     To you yourself, to us, to every one.   15

---

4. Prepare. *Mandate*: command.
5. The "enginer," or engineer, is a military man who is here described as being blown up by a bomb of his own construction, "hoist with his own petard." The military figure continues in the succeeding lines where Hamlet describes himself as digging a countermine or tunnel beneath the one Claudius is digging to defeat Hamlet. In line 216 the two tunnels unexpectedly meet.
6. Dig.   7. Explain.   8. Insane notion.

Alas, how shall this bloody deed be answered?
It will be laid to us, whose providence[9]
Should have kept short, restrained, and out of haunt,[1]
This mad young man. But so much was our love,
20   We would not understand what was most fit;
But, like the owner of a foul disease,
To keep it from divulging, let it feed
Even on the pith of life. Where is he gone?
QUEEN: To draw apart the body he hath killed,
25   O'er whom his very madness, like some ore
Among a mineral of metals base,
Shows itself pure: 'a weeps for what is done.
KING: O Gertrude, come away!
The sun no sooner shall the mountains touch
30   But we will ship him hence, and this vile deed
We must with all our majesty and skill
Both countenance and excuse. Ho, Guildenstern!

[*Enter* ROSENCRANTZ *and* GUILDENSTERN.]

Friends both, go join you with some further aid.
Hamlet in madness hath Polonius slain,
35   And from his mother's closet hath he dragged him.
Go seek him out; speak fair, and bring the body
Into the chapel. I pray you haste in this.
                              [*Exeunt* ROSENCRANTZ *and* GUILDENSTERN.]
Come, Gertrude, we'll call up our wisest friends
And let them know both what we mean to do
40   And what's untimely done;
Whose whisper o'er the world's diameter,
As level as the cannon to his blank,[2]
Transports his poisoned shot—may miss our name,
And hit the woundless air. O, come away!
45   My soul is full of discord and dismay.   [*Exeunt.*]

Scene 2

A passageway. Enter HAMLET.

HAMLET: Safely stowed.
ROSENCRANTZ *and* GUILDENSTERN: [*Within.*] Hamlet! Lord Hamlet!
HAMLET: But soft, what noise? Who calls on Hamlet?
      O, here they come.

---

9. Prudence.   1. Away from public gatherings   2. Mark. *Level:* direct.

[*Enter* ROSENCRANTZ, GUILDENSTERN, *and* OTHERS.]

ROSENCRANTZ: What have you done, my lord, with the dead body?   5
HAMLET: Compounded it with dust, whereto 'tis kin.
ROSENCRANTZ: Tell us where 'tis, that we may take it thence
   And bear it to the chapel.
HAMLET: Do not believe it.
ROSENCRANTZ: Believe what?   10
HAMLET: That I can keep your counsel and not mine own. Besides, to be
   demanded of a sponge—what replication[3] should be made by the son of
   a king?
ROSENCRANTZ: Take you me for a sponge, my lord?
HAMLET: Ay, sir, that soaks up the king's countenance,[4] his rewards, his   15
   authorities. But such officers do the king best service in the end. He
   keeps them like an apple in the corner of his jaw, first mouthed to be
   last swallowed. When he needs what you have gleaned, it is but squeez-
   ing you and, sponge, you shall be dry again.
ROSENCRANTZ: I understand you not, my lord.   20
HAMLET: I am glad of it. A knavish speech sleeps in a foolish ear.
ROSENCRANTZ: My lord, you must tell us where the body is, and go with us
   to the king.
HAMLET: The body is with the king, but the king is not with the body.
   The king is a thing—   25
GUILDENSTERN: A thing, my lord!
HAMLET: Of nothing. Bring me to him. Hide fox, and all after.[5]   [*Exeunt.*]

Scene 3

A room in the castle. Enter KING.

KING: I have sent to seek him, and to find the body.
   How dangerous is it that this man goes loose!
   Yet must not we put the strong law on him.
   He's loved of the distracted[6] multitude,
   Who like not in their judgment but their eyes,   5
   And where 'tis so, th' offender's scourge[7] is weighed,
   But never the offence. To bear all smooth and even,
   This sudden sending him away must seem
   Deliberate pause.[8] Diseases desperate grown
   By desperate appliance are relieved,   10
   Or not at all.

---

3. Answer. *Demanded of:* questioned by.   4. Favor.
5. Apparently a reference to a children's game like hide-and-seek.   6. Confused.
7. Punishment.   8. That is, not an impulse.

[*Enter* ROSENCRANTZ, GUILDENSTERN, *and all the rest.*]

            How now! what hath befall'n?

ROSENCRANTZ: Where the dead body is bestowed, my lord,
    We cannot get from him.

KING: But where is he?

ROSENCRANTZ: Without, my lord; guarded, to know[9] your pleasure.

KING: Bring him before us.

15 ROSENCRANTZ: Ho! bring in the lord.

[*They enter with* HAMLET.]

KING: Now, Hamlet, where's Polonius?

HAMLET: At supper.

KING: At supper? Where?

HAMLET: Not where he eats, but where 'a is eaten. A certain convocation of
20   politic[1] worms are e'en at him. Your worm is your only emperor for diet.
    We fat all creatures else to fat us, and we fat ourselves for maggots. Your
    fat king and your lean beggar is but variable service—two dishes, but to
    one table. That's the end.

KING: Alas, alas!

25 HAMLET: A man may fish with the worm that hath eat of a king, and eat of
    the fish that hath fed of that worm.

KING: What dost thou mean by this?

HAMLET: Nothing but to show you how a king may go a progress through
    the guts of a beggar.

30 KING: Where is Polonius?

HAMLET: In heaven. Send thither to see. If your messenger find him not
    there, seek him i' th' other place yourself. But if, indeed, you find him
    not within this month, you shall nose[2] him as you go up the stairs into
    the lobby.

KING: [*To* ATTENDANTS.] Go seek him there.

35 HAMLET: 'A will stay till you come.   [*Exeunt* ATTENDANTS.]

KING: Hamlet, this deed, for thine especial safety—
    Which we do tender, as we dearly[3] grieve
    For that which thou hast done—must send thee hence
    With fiery quickness. Therefore prepare thyself.
40   The bark is ready, and the wind at help,
    Th' associates tend, and everything is bent
    For England.

HAMLET: For England?

KING: Ay, Hamlet.

HAMLET: Good.

---

9. Await.   1. Scheming. *Convocation*: gathering.   2. Smell.   3. Deeply. *Tender*: consider.

KING: So it is, if thou knew'st our purposes.
HAMLET: I see a cherub that sees them. But come, for England!
  Farewell, dear mother.   45
KING: Thy loving father, Hamlet.
HAMLET: My mother. Father and mother is man and wife, man and wife is
  one flesh. So, my mother. Come, for England.   [*Exit.*]
KING: Follow him at foot;⁴ tempt him with speed aboard.
  Delay it not; I'll have him hence tonight.   50
  Away! for everything is sealed and done
  That else leans on th' affair. Pray you make haste.
                                          [*Exeunt all but the* KING.]
  And, England, if my love thou hold'st at aught—
  As my great power thereof may give thee sense,⁵
  Since yet thy cicatrice⁶ looks raw and red   55
  After the Danish sword, and thy free awe
  Pays homage to us—thou mayst not coldly set⁷
  Our sovereign process,⁸ which imports at full
  By letters congruing⁹ to that effect
  The present death of Hamlet. Do it, England,   60
  For like the hectic¹ in my blood he rages,
  And thou must cure me. Till I know 'tis done,
  Howe'er my haps, my joys were ne'er begun.   [*Exit.*]

Scene 4

Near Elsinore. Enter FORTINBRAS *with his army.*

FORTINBRAS: Go, captain, from me greet the Danish king.
  Tell him that by his license Fortinbras
  Craves the conveyance² of a promised march
Over his kingdom. You know the rendezvous.
  If that his majesty would aught with us,   5
  We shall express our duty in his eye,³
  And let him know so.
CAPTAIN: I will do't, my lord.
FORTINBRAS: Go softly on.   [*Exeunt all but the* CAPTAIN.]

  [*Enter* HAMLET, ROSENCRANTZ, GUILDENSTERN, *and* OTHERS.]

HAMLET: Good sir, whose powers are these?
CAPTAIN: They are of Norway, sir.   10
HAMLET: How purposed, sir, I pray you?
CAPTAIN: Against some part of Poland.

4. Closely.   5. Of its value.   6. Wound scar.   7. Set aside.   8. Mandate.   9. Agreeing.
1. Chronic fever.   2. Escort.   3. Presence.

HAMLET: Who commands them, sir?

CAPTAIN: The nephew to old Norway, Fortinbras.

15 HAMLET: Goes it against the main[4] of Poland, sir,
    Or for some frontier?

CAPTAIN: Truly to speak, and with no addition,[5]
    We go to gain a little patch of ground
    That hath in it no profit but the name.

20   To pay five ducats,[6] five, I would not farm it;
    Nor will it yield to Norway or the Pole
    A ranker rate should it be sold in fee.[7]

HAMLET: Why, then the Polack never will defend it.

CAPTAIN: Yes, it is already garrisoned.

25 HAMLET: Two thousand souls and twenty thousand ducats
    Will not debate the question of this straw.
    This is th' imposthume[8] of much wealth and peace,
    That inward breaks, and shows no cause without
    Why the man dies. I humbly thank you, sir.

CAPTAIN: God b'wi'ye, sir.   [Exit.]

30 ROSENCRANTZ: Will't please you go, my lord?

HAMLET: I'll be with you straight. Go a little before.
                                    [Exeunt all but HAMLET.]

    How all occasions do inform against me,
    And spur my dull revenge! What is a man,
    If his chief good and market[9] of his time
35   Be but to sleep and feed? A beast, no more.
    Sure he that made us with such large discourse,[1]
    Looking before and after, gave us not
    That capability and godlike reason
    To fust[2] in us unused. Now, whether it be
40   Bestial oblivion, or some craven scruple
    Of thinking too precisely on th' event[3]—
    A thought which, quartered, hath but one part wisdom
    And ever three parts coward—I do not know
    Why yet I live to say "This thing's to do,"
45   Sith[4] I have cause, and will, and strength, and means,
    To do't. Examples gross as earth exhort me.
    Witness this army of such mass and charge,[5]
    Led by a delicate and tender prince,
    Whose spirit, with divine ambition puffed,
50   Makes mouths at[6] the invisible event,
    Exposing what is mortal and unsure

---

4. Central part.   5. Exaggeration.   6. That is, in rent.   7. Outright. *Ranker*: higher.
8. Abscess.   9. Occupation.   1. Ample reasoning power.   2. Grow musty.
3. Outcome.   4. Since.   5. Expense.   6. Scorns.

To all that fortune, death, and danger dare,
Even for an eggshell. Rightly to be great
Is not to stir without great argument,
But greatly to find quarrel in a straw   55
When honor's at the stake. How stand I then,
That have a father killed, a mother stained,
Excitements of my reason and my blood,
And let all sleep, while to my shame I see
The imminent death of twenty thousand men   60
That for a fantasy and trick of fame
Go to their graves like beds, fight for a plot
Whereon the numbers cannot try the cause,
Which is not tomb enough and continent
To hide the slain?⁷ O, from this time forth,   65
My thoughts be bloody, or be nothing worth!   [*Exit.*]

Scene 5

A room in the castle. Enter QUEEN, HORATIO *and a* GENTLEMAN.

QUEEN: I will not speak with her.
GENTLEMAN: She is importunate, indeed distract.
  Her mood will needs to be pitied.
QUEEN: What would she have?
GENTLEMAN: She speaks much of her father, says she hears
  There's tricks i' th' world, and hems, and beats her heart,   5
  Spurns enviously at straws,⁸ speaks things in doubt
  That carry but half sense. Her speech is nothing,
  Yet the unshapèd use of it doth move
  The hearers to collection;⁹ they yawn at it,
  And botch the words up fit to their own thoughts,   10
  Which, as her winks and nods and gestures yield them,
  Indeed would make one think there might be thought,
  Though nothing sure, yet much unhappily.
HORATIO: 'Twere good she were spoken with, for she may strew
  Dangerous conjectures in ill-breeding minds.   15
QUEEN: Let her come in.   [*Exit* GENTLEMAN.]
  [*Aside.*] To my sick soul, as sin's true nature is,
  Each toy seems prologue to some great amiss.¹
  So full of artless jealousy is guilt,
  It spills itself in fearing to be spilt.   20

---

7. The plot of ground involved is so small that it cannot contain the number of men involved in
fighting or furnish burial space for the number of those who will die.
8. Takes offense at trifles.   9. An attempt to order.   1. Catastrophe. *Toy*: trifle.

[*Enter* OPHELIA *distracted.*]

OPHELIA: Where is the beauteous majesty of Denmark?

QUEEN: How now, Ophelia!

OPHELIA:

> [*Sings.*]
>
> How should I your true love know
>   From another one?
> 25   By his cockle hat and staff,[2]
>   And his sandal shoon.[3]

QUEEN: Alas, sweet lady, what imports this song?

OPHELIA: Say you? Nay, pray you mark.

> [*Sings.*]
>
> He is dead and gone, lady,
> 30   He is dead and gone;
>   At his head a grass-green turf,
>   At his heels a stone.

> O, ho!

QUEEN: Nay, but Ophelia—

OPHELIA: Pray you mark.

> [*Sings.*]
>
> White his shroud as the mountain snow—

[*Enter* KING.]

35 QUEEN: Alas, look here, my lord.

OPHELIA:

> [*Sings.*]
>
> Larded all with sweet flowers;
> Which bewept to the grave did not go
>   With true-love showers.

KING: How do you, pretty lady?

40 OPHELIA: Well, God dild you! They say the owl was a baker's daughter.[4]
Lord, we know what we are, but know not what we may be. God be at
your table!

---

2. A cockle hat, one decorated with a shell, indicated that the wearer had made a pilgrimage to the shrine of St. James at Compostela in Spain. The staff also marked the carrier as a pilgrim.

3. Shoes.

4. Reference to a folktale about a young woman who was transformed into an owl when she failed to offer generosity to Jesus, who had asked for bread in her father's shop. *Dild*: yield, repay.

KING: Conceit[5] upon her father.

OPHELIA: Pray let's have no words of this, but when they ask you what it
means, say you this:

    [*Sings.*]

    Tomorrow is Saint Valentine's day, 45
      All in the morning betime,
    And I a maid at your window,
      To be your Valentine.

    Then up he rose, and donn'd his clo'es,
      And dupped[6] the chamber-door, 50
    Let in the maid, that out a maid
      Never departed more.

KING: Pretty Ophelia!

OPHELIA: Indeed, without an oath, I'll make an end on't.

    [*Sings.*]

    By Gis[7] and by Saint Charity, 55
      Alack, and fie for shame!
    Young men will do't, if they come to't;
      By Cock,[8] they are to blame.
    Quoth she "before you tumbled me,
      You promised me to wed." 60

    He answers:

    "So would I'a done, by yonder sun,
      An thou hadst not come to my bed."

KING: How long hath she been thus?

OPHELIA: I hope all will be well. We must be patient, but I cannot choose but 65
weep to think they would lay him i' th' cold ground. My brother shall
know of it, and so I thank you for your good counsel. Come, my coach!
Good night, ladies, good night. Sweet ladies, good night, good night.
                      [*Exit.*]

KING: Follow her close; give her good watch, I pray you.
            [*Exeunt* HORATIO *and* GENTLEMAN.]
O, this is the poison of deep grief; it springs 70
All from her father's death, and now behold!
O Gertrude, Gertrude!
When sorrows come, they come not single spies,
But in battalions: first, her father slain;
Next, your son gone, and he most violent author 75

5. Thought.   6. Opened.   7. Jesus.   8. Corruption of "God," with a sexual pun.

Of his own just remove; the people muddied,[9]
Thick and unwholesome in their thoughts and whispers
For good Polonius' death; and we have done but greenly[1]
In hugger-mugger[2] to inter him; poor Ophelia
80   Divided from herself and her fair judgment,
Without the which we are pictures, or mere beasts;
Last, and as much containing as all these,
Her brother is in secret come from France,
Feeds on his wonder, keeps himself in clouds,
85   And wants not buzzers to infect his ear
With pestilent speeches of his father's death,
Wherein necessity, of matter beggared,[3]
Will nothing stick our person to arraign[4]
In ear and ear.[5] O my dear Gertrude, this,
90   Like to a murd'ring piece,[6] in many places
Gives me superfluous death.   [A noise within.]
QUEEN: Alack, what noise is this?
KING: Attend!
Where are my Switzers?[7] Let them guard the door.
What is the matter?
95   MESSENGER: Save yourself, my lord.
The ocean, overpeering of his list,[8]
Eats not the flats with more impiteous[9] haste
Than young Laertes, in a riotous head,[1]
O'erbears your officers. The rabble call him lord,
100   And as the world were now but to begin,
Antiquity forgot, custom not known,
The ratifiers and props of every word,
They cry "Choose we, Laertes shall be king."
Caps, hands, and tongues, applaud it to the clouds,
105   "Laertes shall be king, Laertes king."
QUEEN: How cheerfully on the false trail they cry![2]

[A noise within.]

O, this is counter,[3] you false Danish dogs!
KING: The doors are broke.

[Enter LAERTES, with OTHERS.]

LAERTES: Where is this king?—Sirs, stand you all without.

---

9. Disturbed.   1. Without judgment.   2. Haste.   3. Short on facts.
4. Accuse. *Stick*: hesitate.   5. From both sides.   6. A weapon designed to scatter its shot.
7. Swiss guards.   8. Towering above its limits.   9. Pitiless.   1. With an armed band.
2. As if following the scent.   3. Backward.

ALL: No, let's come in.
LAERTES: I pray you give me leave.   110
ALL: We will, we will.
LAERTES: I thank you. Keep⁴ the door.   [*Exeunt his followers.*]
                    O thou vile king,
  Give me my father!
QUEEN: Calmly, good Laertes.
LAERTES: That drop of blood that's calm proclaims me bastard,
  Cries cuckold to my father, brands the harlot   115
  Even here between the chaste unsmirchèd brow
  Of my true mother.
KING: What is the cause, Laertes,
  That thy rebellion looks so giant-like?
  Let him go, Gertrude. Do not fear⁵ our person.
  There's such divinity doth hedge a king   120
  That treason can but peep to⁶ what it would,
  Acts little of his will. Tell me, Laertes.
  Why thou art thus incensed. Let him go, Gertrude.
  Speak, man.
LAERTES: Where is my father?
KING: Dead.
QUEEN: But not by him.
KING: Let him demand⁷ his fill.   125
LAERTES: How came he dead? I'll not be juggled with.
  To hell allegiance, vows to the blackest devil,
  Conscience and grace to the profoundest pit!
  I dare damnation. To this point I stand,
  That both the worlds I give to negligence,⁸   130
  Let come what comes, only I'll be revenged
  Most throughly for my father.
KING: Who shall stay you?
LAERTES: My will, not all the world's.
  And for my means, I'll husband⁹ them so well
  They shall go far with little.
KING: Good Laertes,   135
  If you desire to know the certainty
  Of your dear father, is't writ in your revenge
  That, swoopstake,¹ you will draw both friend and foe,
  Winner and loser?
LAERTES: None but his enemies.
KING: Will you know them, then?   140

4. Guard.   5. Fear for.   6. Look at over or through a barrier.   7. Question.
8. Disregard. *Both the worlds*: that is, this and the next.   9. Manage.   1. Sweeping the board.

LAERTES: To his good friends thus wide I'll ope my arms,
 And like the kind life-rend'ring pelican,[2]
 Repast them with my blood.
KING: Why, now you speak
 Like a good child and a true gentleman.
145 That I am guiltless of your father's death,
 And am most sensibly in grief for it,
 It shall as level[3] to your judgment 'pear
 As day does to your eye.

[*A noise within:* "Let her come in."]

LAERTES: How now? What noise is that?

[*Enter* OPHELIA.]

150 O, heat dry up my brains! tears seven times salt
 Burn out the sense and virtue[4] of mine eye!
 By heaven, thy madness shall be paid with weight
 Till our scale turn the beam. O rose of May,
 Dear maid, kind sister, sweet Ophelia!
155 O heavens, is't possible a young maid's wits
 Should be as mortal as an old man's life?
 Nature is fin[5] in love, and where 'tis fine
 It sends some precious instances of itself
 After the thing it loves.[6]
OPHELIA:

[*Sings.*]

160 They bore him barefac'd on the bier;
  Hey non nonny, nonny, hey nonny;
  And in his grave rain'd many a tear—

 Fare you well, my dove!
LAERTES: Hadst thou thy wits, and didst persuade revenge,
165 It could not move thus.
OPHELIA: You must sing "A-down, a-down, and you call him a-down-a." O,
 how the wheel becomes it! It is the false steward, that stole his master's
 daughter.[7]

---

2. The pelican was believed to feed her young with her own blood.   3. Plain.
4. Function. *Sense:* feeling.   5. Refined.
6. Laertes means that Ophelia, because of her love for her father, gave up her sanity as a token of grief at his death.
7. The "wheel" refers to the "burden" or refrain of a song, in this case "A-down, a-down, and you call him a-down-a." The ballad to which she refers was about a false steward. Others have suggested that the "wheel" is the Wheel of Fortune, a spinning wheel to whose rhythm such a song might have been sung or a kind of dance movement performed by Ophelia as she sings.

LAERTES: This nothing's more than matter.

OPHELIA: There's a rosemary, that's for remembrance. Pray you, love, remember.
And there is pansies, that's for thoughts.   170

LAERTES: A document[8] in madness, thoughts and remembrance fitted.

OPHELIA: There's fennel for you, and columbines. There's rue for you, and here's some for me. We may call it herb of grace a Sundays. O, you must wear your rue with a difference. There's a daisy. I would give you some violets, but they withered all when my father died. They say 'a made a good end.   175

[*Sings.*]

For bonny sweet Robin is all my joy.

LAERTES: Thought and affliction, passion, hell itself,
She turns to favor[9] and to prettiness.

OPHELIA:

[*Sings.*]

And will 'a not come again?
And will 'a not come again?   180
  No, no, he is dead,
  Go to thy death-bed,
He never will come again.

His beard was as white as snow,   185
All flaxen was his poll;[1]
  He is gone, he is gone,
  And we cast away moan:
God-a-mercy on his soul!

And of all Christian souls, I pray God. God b'wi'you.   [*Exit.*]

LAERTES: Do you see this, O God?   190

KING: Laertes, I must commune with your grief,
Or you deny me right. Go but apart,
Make choice of whom your wisest friends you will,
And they shall hear and judge 'twixt you and me.
If by direct or by collateral[2] hand   195
They find us touched,[3] we will our kingdom give,
Our crown, our life, and all that we call ours,
To you in satisfaction; but if not,
Be you content to lend your patience to us,
And we shall jointly labor with your soul   200
To give it due content.

---

8. Lesson.   9. Beauty.   1. Head.   2. Indirect.   3. By guilt.

LAERTES: Let this be so.
His means of death, his obscure funeral—
No trophy, sword, nor hatchment,[4] o'er his bones,
No noble rite nor formal ostentation[5]—
205   Cry to be heard, as 'twere from heaven to earth,
That I must call't in question.
KING: So you shall;
And where th' offence is, let the great axe fall.
I pray you go with me.   [*Exeunt.*]

Scene 6

Another room in the castle. Enter HORATIO *and a* GENTLEMAN.

HORATIO: What are they that would speak with me?
GENTLEMAN: Sea-faring men, sir. They say they have letters for you.
HORATIO: Let them come in.   [*Exit* GENTLEMAN.]
   I do not know from what part of the world
5   I should be greeted, if not from Lord Hamlet.

      [*Enter* SAILORS.]

SAILOR: God bless you, sir.
HORATIO: Let him bless thee too.
SAILOR: 'A shall, sir, an't please him. There's a letter for you, sir—it came
   from th' ambassador that was bound for England—if your name be
10   Horatio, as I am let to know[6] it is.
HORATIO: [*Reads.*] "Horatio, when thou shalt have overlooked[7] this, give
   these fellows some means[8] to the king. They have letters for him. Ere we
   were two days old at sea, a pirate of very warlike appointment[9] gave us
   chase. Finding ourselves too slow of sail, we put on a compelled valor,
   and in the grapple I boarded them. On the instant they got clear of our
15   ship, so I alone became their prisoner. They have dealt with me like
   thieves of mercy, but they knew what they did; I am to do a good turn
   for them. Let the king have the letters I have sent, and repair thou to me
   with as much speed as thou wouldest fly death. I have words to speak in
   thine ear will make thee dumb; yet are they much too light for the bore
20   of the matter.[1] These good fellows will bring thee where I am. Rosencrantz and Guildenstern hold their course for England. Of them I have
   much to tell thee. Farewell.
                    He that thou knowest thine, Hamlet."
   Come, I will give you way[2] for these your letters,

4. Coat of arms.   5. Pomp.   6. Informed.   7. Read through.   8. Access.   9. Equipment.
1. A figure from gunnery, referring to shot that is too small for the size of the weapons to be
fired.   2. Means of delivery.

And do't the speedier that you may direct me   25
To him from whom you brought them.   [*Exeunt.*]

Scene 7

Another room in the castle. Enter KING *and* LAERTES.

KING: Now must your conscience my acquittance seal,[3]
   And you must put me in your heart for friend,
   Sith you have heard, and with a knowing ear,
   That he which hath your noble father slain
   Pursued my life.
LAERTES: It well appears. But tell me   5
   Why you proceeded not against these feats,
   So criminal and so capital in nature,
   As by your safety, greatness, wisdom, all things else,
   You mainly were stirred up.
KING: O, for two special reasons,
   Which may to you, perhaps, seem much unsinewed,[4]   10
   But yet to me th' are strong. The queen his mother
   Lives almost by his looks, and for myself—
   My virtue or my plague, be it either which—
   She is so conjunctive[5] to my life and soul
   That, as the star moves not but in his sphere,[6]   15
   I could not but by her. The other motive,
   Why to a public count[7] I might not go,
   Is the great love the general gender[8] bear him,
   Who, dipping all his faults in their affection,
   Work like the spring that turneth wood to stone,[9]   20
   Convert his gyves[1] to graces; so that my arrows,
   Too slightly timbered[2] for so loud a wind,
   Would have reverted to my bow again,
   But not where I had aimed them.
LAERTES: And so have I a noble father lost,   25
   A sister driven into desp'rate terms,
   Whose worth, if praises may go back again,
   Stood challenger on mount of all the age
   For her perfections. But my revenge will come.
KING: Break not your sleeps for that. You must not think   30

---

3. Grant me innocent.   4. Weak.   5. Closely joined.
6. A reference to the Ptolemaic cosmology, in which planets and stars were believed to revolve in
crystalline spheres concentrically about the Earth.   7. Reckoning.   8. Common people.
9. Certain English springs contain so much lime that a limestone covering will be deposited on a
log placed in one of them for a length of time.   1. Fetters.   2. Shafted.

That we are made of stuff so flat and dull
That we can let our beard be shook with danger,
And think it pastime. You shortly shall hear more.
I loved your father, and we love our self,
35   And that, I hope, will teach you to imagine—

[*Enter a* MESSENGER *with letters.*]

How now? What news?
MESSENGER: Letters, my lord, from Hamlet.
These to your majesty; this to the queen.
KING: From Hamlet! Who brought them?
MESSENGER: Sailors, my lord, they say. I saw them not.
40   They were given me by Claudio; he received them
Of him that brought them.
KING: Laertes, you shall hear them.—
Leave us.   [*Exit* MESSENGER.]
[*Reads.*] "High and mighty, you shall know I am set naked on your
kingdom. Tomorrow shall I beg leave to see your kingly eyes; when I
shall, first asking your pardon thereunto, recount the occasion of my
45   sudden and more strange return.
                              Hamlet."
What should this mean? Are all the rest come back?
Or is it some abuse,[3] and no such thing?
LAERTES: Know you the hand?
50   KING: 'Tis Hamlet's character.[4] "Naked"!
And in a postscript here, he says "alone."
Can you devise[5] me?
LAERTES: I am lost in it, my lord. But let him come.
It warms the very sickness in my heart
55   That I shall live and tell him to his teeth
"Thus didest thou."
KING: If it be so, Laertes—
As how should it be so, how otherwise?—
Will you be ruled by me?
LAERTES: Ay, my lord,
So you will not o'errule me to a peace.
60   KING: To thine own peace. If he be now returned,
As checking at[6] his voyage, and that he means
No more to undertake it, I will work him
To an exploit now ripe in my device,
Under the which he shall not choose but fall;
65   And for his death no wind of blame shall breathe

3. Trick.   4. Handwriting.   5. Explain it to.   6. Turning aside from.

But even his mother shall uncharge[7] the practice
And call it accident.

LAERTES: My lord, I will be ruled;
The rather if you could devise it so
That I might be the organ.[8]

KING: It falls right.
You have been talked of since your travel much,   70
And that in Hamlet's hearing, for a quality
Wherein they say you shine. Your sum of parts
Did not together pluck such envy from him
As did that one, and that, in my regard,
Of the unworthiest siege.[9]

LAERTES: What part is that, my lord?   75

KING: A very riband in the cap of youth,
Yet needful too, for youth no less becomes
The light and careless livery that it wears
Than settled age his sables and his weeds,[1]
Importing health and graveness. Two months since   80
Here was a gentleman of Normandy.
I have seen myself, and served against, the French,
And they can[2] well on horseback, but this gallant
Had witchcraft in't. He grew unto his seat,
And to such wondrous doing brought his horse,   85
As had he been incorpsed and demi-natured
With the brave beast. So far he topped my thought
That I, in forgery[3] of shapes and tricks,
Come short of what he did.[4]

LAERTES: A Norman was't?

KING: A Norman.   90

LAERTES: Upon my life, Lamord.

KING: The very same.

LAERTES: I know him well. He is the brooch indeed
And gem of all the nation.

KING: He made confession[5] of you,
And gave you such a masterly report   95
For art and exercise in your defence,[6]
And for your rapier most especial,

7. Not accuse.   8. Instrument.   9. Lowest rank.   1. Dignified clothing.   2. Perform.
3. Imagination.
4. The gentleman referred to was so skilled in horsemanship that he seemed to share one body with the horse, "incorpsed." The king further extends the compliment by saying that he appeared like the mythical centaur, a creature who was man from the waist up and horse from the waist down, therefore "demi-natured."
5. Gave a report.   6. Skill in fencing.

That he cried out 'twould be a sight indeed
If one could match you. The scrimers[7] of their nation
100   He swore had neither motion, guard, nor eye,
If you opposed them. Sir, this report of his
Did Hamlet so envenom with his envy
That he could nothing do but wish and beg
Your sudden coming o'er, to play with you.
Now out of this—
105 LAERTES: What out of this, my lord?
      KING: Laertes, was your father dear to you?
Or are you like the painting of a sorrow,
A face without a heart?
      LAERTES: Why ask you this?
      KING: Not that I think you did not love your father,
110   But that I know love is begun by time,
And that I see in passages of proof,[8]
Time qualifies the spark and fire of it.
There lives within the very flame of love
A kind of wick or snuff that will abate it,
115   And nothing is at a like goodness still,
For goodness, growing to a plurisy,[9]
Dies in his own too much.[1] That we would do,
We should do when we would; for this "would" changes,
And hath abatements and delays as many
120   As there are tongues, are hands, are accidents,
And then this "should" is like a spendthrift's sigh
That hurts by easing. But to the quick of th' ulcer—[2]
Hamlet comes back; what would you undertake
To show yourself in deed your father's son
More than in words?
125 LAERTES: To cut his throat i' th' church.
      KING: No place indeed should murder sanctuarize;[3]
Revenge should have no bounds. But, good Laertes,
Will you do this? Keep close within your chamber.
Hamlet returned shall know you are come home.
130   We'll put on those shall praise your excellence,
And set a double varnish on the fame
The Frenchman gave you, bring you in fine[4] together,
And wager on your heads. He, being remiss,[5]

---

7. Fencers.   8. Tests of experience.   9. Fullness.   1. Excess.
2. Heart of the matter. *Spendthrift's sigh*: a sigh was believed to draw a drop of blood from the heart
and thus to "hurt" by "easing" sadness.   3. Provide sanctuary for murder.   4. In short.
5. Careless.

Most generous, and free from all contriving,
Will not peruse[6] the foils, so that with ease,   135
Or with a little shuffling, you may choose
A sword unbated,[7] and in a pass of practice
Requite him for your father.
LAERTES: I will do't,
And for that purpose I'll anoint my sword.
I bought an unction of a mountebank   140
So mortal that but dip a knife in it,
Where it draws blood no cataplasm[8] so rare,
Collected from all simples[9] that have virtue
Under the moon, can save the thing from death
That is but scratched withal. I'll touch my point   145
With this contagion, that if I gall[1] him slightly,
It may be death.
KING: Let's further think of this,
Weigh what convenience both of time and means
May fit us to our shape. If this should fail,
And that our drift look[2] through our bad performance,   150
'Twere better not assayed. Therefore this project
Should have a back or second that might hold
If this did blast in proof.[3] Soft, let me see.
We'll make a solemn wager on your cunnings—
I ha't.   155
When in your motion you are hot and dry—
As make your bouts more violent to that end—
And that he calls for drink, I'll have prepared him
A chalice for the nonce, whereon but sipping,
If he by chance escape your venomed stuck,[4]   160
Our purpose may hold there.—But stay, what noise?

[*Enter* QUEEN.]

QUEEN: One woe doth tread upon another's heel,
So fast they follow. Your sister's drowned, Laertes.
LAERTES: Drowned? O, where?
QUEEN: There is a willow grows aslant the brook   165
That shows his hoar leaves in the glassy stream.
Therewith fantastic garlands did she make
Of crowflowers, nettles, daisies, and long purples
That liberal shepherds give a grosser[5] name,

6. Examine. 7. Not blunted. 8. Poultice. 9. Herbs. 1. Scratch.
2. Intent become obvious. 3. Fail when tried. 4. Thrust.
5. Coarser. The "long purples" are purple orchises, a type of orchid known as "dog's cullions" (testicles) or "goat's cullions." *Liberal*: vulgar.

170 But our cold[6] maids do dead men's fingers call them.
There on the pendent boughs her coronet weeds
Clamb'ring to hang, an envious[7] sliver broke,
When down her weedy trophies and herself
Fell in the weeping brook. Her clothes spread wide,
175 And mermaid-like awhile they bore her up,
Which time she chanted snatches of old tunes,
As one incapable[8] of her own distress,
Or like a creature native and indued[9]
Unto that element. But long it could not be
180 Till that her garments, heavy with their drink,
Pulled the poor wretch from her melodious lay
To muddy death.
LAERTES: Alas, then she is drowned?
QUEEN: Drowned, drowned.
LAERTES: Too much of water hast thou, poor Ophelia,
185 And therefore I forbid my tears; but yet
It is our trick; nature her custom holds,
Let shame say what it will. When these are gone,
The woman will be out. Adieu, my lord.
I have a speech o' fire that fain would blaze
But that this folly drowns it.   [*Exit.*]
190 KING: Let's follow, Gertrude.
How much I had to do to calm his rage!
Now fear I this will give it start again;
Therefore let's follow.   [*Exeunt.*]

ACT V

Scene 1

A churchyard. Enter two CLOWNS.[1]

CLOWN: Is she to be buried in Christian burial when she wilfully seeks her
own salvation?
OTHER: I tell thee she is. Therefore make her grave straight. The crowner
hath sat on her,[2] and finds it Christian burial.
5 CLOWN: How can that be, unless she drowned herself in her own defence?
OTHER: Why, 'tis found so.
CLOWN: It must be "se offendendo";[3] it cannot be else. For here lies the
point: if I drown myself wittingly, it argues an act, and an act hath three

---

6. Chaste.   7. Malicious.   8. Unaware.   9. Habituated.   1. Rustics.
2. Held an inquest. *Crowner:* coroner.   3. An error for *se defendendo*, in self-defense.

branches—it is to act, to do, to perform; argal,[4] she drowned herself wittingly.

OTHER: Nay, but hear you, Goodman Delver.   10

CLOWN: Give me leave. Here lies the water; good. Here stands the man; good. If the man go to this water and drown himself, it is, will he, nill he, he goes—mark you that. But if the water come to him and drown him, he drowns not himself. Argal, he that is not guilty of his own death shortens not his own life.   15

OTHER: But is this law?

CLOWN: Ay, marry, is't; crowner's quest[5] law.

OTHER: Will you ha' the truth on't? If this had not been a gentlewoman, she should have been buried out o' Christian burial.

CLOWN: Why, there thou say'st. And the more pity that great folk should 20 have count'nance[6] in this world to drown or hang themselves more than their even-Christen.[7] Come, my spade. There is no ancient gentlemen but gard'ners, ditchers, and grave-makers. They hold up Adam's profession.

OTHER: Was he a gentleman?

CLOWN: 'A was the first that ever bore arms.   25

OTHER: Why, he had none.

CLOWN: What, art a heathen? How dost thou understand the Scripture? The Scripture says Adam digged. Could he dig without arms? I'll put another question to thee. If thou answerest me not to the purpose, confess thyself—

OTHER: Go to.   30

CLOWN: What is he that builds stronger than either the mason, the shipwright, or the carpenter?

OTHER: The gallows-maker, for that frame outlives a thousand tenants.

CLOWN: I like thy wit well, in good faith. The gallows does well. But how does it well? It does well to those that do ill. Now thou dost ill to say the gallows is built stronger than the church. Argal, the gallows may do 35 well to thee. To't again,[8] come.

OTHER: Who builds stronger than a mason, a shipwright, or a carpenter?

CLOWN: Ay tell me that, and unyoke.[9]

OTHER: Marry, now I can tell.   40

CLOWN: To't.

OTHER: Mass, I cannot tell.

CLOWN: Cudgel thy brains no more about it, for your dull ass will not mend his pace with beating. And when you are asked this question next, say "a grave maker." The houses he makes lasts till doomsday. Go, get thee in, 45 and fetch me a stoup[1] of liquor.   [*Exit* OTHER CLOWN.]

---

4. "Ergo," therefore.   5. Inquest.   6. Approval.   7. Fellow Christians.   8. Guess again.
9. Finish the matter.   1. Mug.

[*Enter* HAMLET *and* HORATIO *as* CLOWN *digs and sings.*]

In youth, when I did love, did love,
  Methought it was very sweet,
To contract the time for-a my behove,[2]
50   O, methought there-a was nothing-a meet.[3]

HAMLET: Has this fellow no feeling of his business, that 'a sings in grave-
  making?
HORATIO: Custom hath made it in him a property of easiness.
HAMLET: 'Tis e'en so. The hand of little employment hath the daintier
  sense.
CLOWN:

  [*Sings.*]

But age, with his stealing steps,
55   Hath clawed me in his clutch,
And hath shipped me into the land,
  As if I had never been such.

  [*Throws up a skull.*]

HAMLET: That skull had a tongue in it, and could sing once. How the knave
  jowls[4] it to the ground, as if 'twere Cain's jawbone, that did the first
60 murder! This might be the pate of a politician, which this ass now
  o'erreaches;[5] one that would circumvent God, might it not?
HORATIO: It might, my lord.
HAMLET: Or of a courtier, which could say, "Good morrow, sweet lord! How
  does thou, sweet lord?" This might be my Lord Such-a-one, that praised
65 my Lord Such-a-one's horse, when 'a meant to beg it, might it not?
HORATIO: Ay, my lord.
HAMLET: Why, e'en so, and now my Lady Worm's, chapless,[6] and knock'd
  about the mazzard with a sexton's spade. Here's fine revolution,[7] an we
  had the trick to see't. Did these bones cost no more the breeding but to
70 play at loggets with them?[8] Mine ache to think on't.
CLOWN:

  [*Sings.*]

A pick-axe and a spade, a spade,
  For and a shrouding sheet:

---

2. Advantage. *Contract*: shorten.
3. The gravedigger's song is a free version of "The aged lover renounceth love" by Thomas, Lord
Vaux, published in *Tottel's Miscellany*, 1557.   4. Hurls.   5. Gets the better of.
6. Lacking a lower jaw.   7. Skill. *Mazzard*: head.
8. "Loggets" were small pieces of wood thrown as part of a game.

O, a pit of clay for to be made
For such a guest is meet.

[*Throws up another skull.*]

HAMLET: There's another. Why may not that be the skull of a lawyer? Where 75
be his quiddities now, his quillets, his cases, his tenures, and his tricks?
Why does he suffer this mad knave now to knock him about the sconce[9]
with a dirty shovel, and will not tell him of his action of battery? Hum!
This fellow might be in's time a great buyer of land, with his statutes,
his recognizances, his fines, his double vouchers, his recoveries. Is this
the fine[1] of his fines, and the recovery of his recoveries, to have his fine 80
pate full of fine dirt? Will his vouchers vouch him no more of his pur-
chases, and double ones too, than the length and breadth of a pair of
indentures?[2] The very conveyances of his lands will scarcely lie in this
box, and must th' inheritor himself have no more, ha?[3]
HORATIO: Not a jot more, my lord. 85
HAMLET: Is not parchment made of sheepskins?
HORATIO: Ay, my lord, and of calves' skins too.
HAMLET: They are sheep and calves which seek out assurance in that. I will
speak to this fellow. Whose grave's this, sirrah?
CLOWN: Mine, sir. 90

[*Sings.*]

O, a pit of clay for to be made
For such a guest is meet.

HAMLET: I think it be thine indeed, for thou liest in't.
CLOWN: You lie out on't, sir, and therefore 'tis not yours. For my part, I do
not lie in't, yet it is mine. 95
HAMLET: Thou dost lie in't, to be in't and say it is thine. 'Tis for the dead,
not for the quick;[4] therefore thou liest.
CLOWN: 'Tis a quick lie, sir; 'twill away again from me to you.
HAMLET: What man dost thou dig it for?
CLOWN: For no man, sir. 100
HAMLET: What woman, then?
CLOWN: For none neither.
HAMLET: Who is to be buried in't?
CLOWN: One that was a woman, sir; but, rest her soul, she's dead.
HAMLET: How absolute the knave is! We must speak by the card,[5] or equivo- 105
cation will undo us. By the Lord, Horatio, this three years I have took
note of it, the age is grown so picked[6] that the toe of the peasant comes

9. Head. 1. End. 2. Contracts.
3. In this speech Hamlet reels off a list of legal terms relating to property transactions.
4. Living. 5. Exactly. *Absolute*: precise. 6. Refined.

so near the heel of the courtier, he galls his kibe.[7] How long hast thou
been a grave-maker?

CLOWN: Of all the days i' th' year, I came to't that day that our last King
110   Hamlet overcame Fortinbras.

HAMLET: How long is that since?

CLOWN: Cannot you tell that? Every fool can tell that. It was that very day
that young Hamlet was born—he that is mad, and sent into England.

HAMLET: Ay, marry, why was he sent into England?

115 CLOWN: Why, because 'a was mad. 'A shall recover his wits there; or, if 'a do
not, 'tis no great matter there.

HAMLET: Why?

CLOWN: 'Twill not be seen in him there. There the men are as mad as he.

HAMLET: How came he mad?

120 CLOWN: Very strangely, they say.

HAMLET: How strangely?

CLOWN: Faith, e'en with losing his wits.

HAMLET: Upon what ground?

CLOWN: Why, here in Denmark. I have been sexton here, man and boy,
125   thirty years.

HAMLET: How long will a man lie i' th' earth ere he rot?

CLOWN: Faith, if 'a be not rotten before 'a die—as we have many pocky[8]
corses now-a-days that will scarce hold the laying in—'a will last you
some eight year or nine year. A tanner will last you nine year.

130 HAMLET: Why he more than another?

CLOWN: Why, sir, his hide is so tanned with his trade that 'a will keep out
water a great while; and your water is a sore decayer of your whoreson
dead body. Here's a skull now hath lien[9] you i' th' earth three and
twenty years.

HAMLET: Whose was it?

135 CLOWN: A whoreson mad fellow's it was. Whose do you think it was?

HAMLET: Nay, I know not.

CLOWN: A pestilence on him for a mad rogue! 'A poured a flagon of Rhenish on my head once. This same skull, sir, was, sir, Yorick's skull, the
king's jester.

HAMLET: [*Takes the skull.*] This?

140 CLOWN: E'en that.

HAMLET: Alas, poor Yorick! I knew him, Horatio—a fellow of infinite jest, of
most excellent fancy. He hath bore me on his back a thousand times,
and now how abhorred in my imagination it is! My gorg[1] rises at it. Here
hung those lips that I have kissed I know not how oft. Where be your
145 gibes now, your gambols, your songs, your flashes of merriment that

7. Rubs a blister on his heel. 8. Corrupted by syphilis.
9. Lain. *Whoreson:* bastard (not literally). 1. Throat.

were wont to set the table on a roar? Not one now to mock your own
grinning? Quite chap-fall'n?² Now get you to my lady's chamber, and
tell her, let her paint an inch thick, to this favor³ she must come. Make
her laugh at that. Prithee, Horatio, tell me one thing.
HORATIO: What's that, my lord?   150
HAMLET: Dost thou think Alexander looked o' this fashion i' th' earth?
HORATIO: E'en so.
HAMLET: And smelt so? Pah!   [*Throws down the skull.*]
HORATIO: E'en so, my lord.
HAMLET: To what base uses we may return, Horatio! Why may not imagina-   155
tion trace the noble dust of Alexander till 'a find it stopping a bung-
hole?⁴
HORATIO: 'Twere to consider too curiously⁵ to consider so.
HAMLET: No, faith, not a jot, but to follow him thither with modesty⁶
enough, and likelihood to lead it. Alexander died, Alexander was buried, Alexander returneth to dust; the dust is earth; of earth we make
loam; and why of that loam whereto he was converted might they not   160
stop a beerbarrel?

Imperious Cæsar, dead and turned to clay,
Might stop a hole to keep the wind away.
O, that that earth which kept the world in awe
Should patch a wall t'expel the winter's flaw!⁷   165

But soft, but soft awhile! Here comes the king,
The queen, the courtiers.

[*Enter* KING, QUEEN, LAERTES, *and the Corse with a* PRIEST *and* LORDS
attendant.]

          Who is this they follow?
And with such maimèd⁸ rites? This doth betoken
The corse they follow did with desperate hand
Fordo its own life. 'Twas of some estate.⁹   170
Couch¹ we awhile and mark.   [*Retires with* HORATIO.]
LAERTES: What ceremony else?²
HAMLET: That is Laertes, a very noble youth. Mark.
LAERTES: What ceremony else?
PRIEST: Here obsequies have been as far enlarged³   175
As we have warranty. Her death was doubtful,
And but that great command o'ersways the order,⁴
She should in ground unsanctified been lodged

2. Lacking a lower jaw. 3. Appearance. 4. Used as a cork in a cask. 5. Precisely.
6. Moderation. 7. Gusty wind. 8. Shortened. 9. Rank. *Fordo*: destroy.
1. Conceal ourselves. 2. More. 3. Extended. 4. Usual rules.

Till the last trumpet. For charitable prayers,
180 Shards, flints, and pebbles, should be thrown on her.
Yet here she is allowed her virgin crants,[5]
Her maiden strewments,[6] and the bringing home
Of bell and burial.

LAERTES: Must there no more be done?

PRIEST: No more be done.
185 We should profane the service of the dead
To sing a requiem and such rest to her
As to peace-parted souls.

LAERTES: Lay her i' th' earth,
And from her fair and unpolluted flesh
May violets spring! I tell thee, churlish priest,
190 A minist'ring angel shall my sister be
When thou liest howling.[7]

HAMLET: What, the fair Ophelia!

QUEEN: Sweets to the sweet. Farewell!   [Scatters flowers.]
I hoped thou shouldst have been my Hamlet's wife.
I thought thy bride-bed to have decked, sweet maid,
And not t' have strewed thy grave.

195 LAERTES: O, treble woe
Fall ten times treble on that cursèd head
Whose wicked deed thy most ingenious sense[8]
Deprived thee of! Hold off the earth awhile,
Till I have caught her once more in mine arms.   [Leaps into the grave.]
200 Now pile your dust upon the quick and dead,
Till of this flat a mountain you have made
T' o'er-top old Pelion or the skyish head
Of blue Olympus.[9]

HAMLET: [Coming forward.] What is he whose grief
Bears such an emphasis, whose phrase of sorrow
205 Conjures[1] the wand'ring stars, and makes them stand
Like wonder-wounded hearers? This is I,
Hamlet the Dane.

         [HAMLET leaps into the grave and they grapple.]

LAERTES: The devil take thy soul!

HAMLET: Thou pray'st not well.

---

5. Wreaths.   6. Flowers strewn on the grave.   7. In Hell.   8. Lively mind.
9. The rivalry between Laertes and Hamlet in this scene extends even to their rhetoric. Pelion and Olympus, mentioned here by Laertes, and Ossa, mentioned below by Hamlet, are Greek mountains noted in mythology for their height. Olympus was the reputed home of the gods, and the other two were piled one on top of the other by the Giants in an attempt to reach the top of Olympus and overthrow the gods.   1. Casts a spell on.

I prithee take thy fingers from my throat,
For though I am not splenitive[2] and rash,   210
Yet have I in me something dangerous,
Which let thy wisdom fear. Hold off thy hand.
KING: Pluck them asunder.
QUEEN: Hamlet! Hamlet!
ALL: Gentlemen!   215
HORATIO: Good my lord, be quiet.

[*The* ATTENDANTS *part them, and they come out of the grave.*]

HAMLET: Why, I will fight with him upon this theme
    Until my eyelids will no longer wag.[3]
QUEEN: O my son, what theme?
HAMLET: I loved Ophelia. Forty thousand brothers   220
    Could not with all their quantity of love
    Make up my sum. What wilt thou do for her?
KING: O, he is mad, Laertes.
QUEEN: For love of God, forbear[4] him.
HAMLET: 'Swounds, show me what th'owt do.   225
    Woo't[5] weep, woo't fight, woo't fast, woo't tear thyself,
    Woo't drink up eisel,[6] eat a crocodile?
    I'll do't. Dost come here to whine?
    To outface[7] me with leaping in her grave?
    Be buried quick with her, and so will I.   230
    And if thou prate of mountains, let them throw
    Millions of acres on us, till our ground,
    Singeing his pate against the burning zone,[8]
    Make Ossa like a wart! Nay, an thou'lt mouth,
    I'll rant as well as thou.
QUEEN: This is mere madness   235
    And thus awhile the fit will work on him.
    Anon, as patient as the female dove
    When that her golden couplets[9] are disclosed,
    His silence will sit drooping.
HAMLET: Hear you, sir.
    What is the reason that you use me thus?   240
    I loved you ever. But it is no matter.
    Let Hercules himself do what he may,
    The cat will mew, and dog will have his day.   [*Exit.*]
KING: I pray thee, good Horatio, wait upon[1] him.

    [*Exit* HORATIO.]

2. Hot-tempered.   3. Move.   4. Bear with.   5. Will you.   6. Vinegar.
7. Get the best of.   8. Sky in the torrid zone.   9. Pair of eggs.   1. Attend.

245 [*To* LAERTES.] Strengthen your patience in our last night's speech.
We'll put the matter to the present push.[2]—
Good Gertrude, set some watch over your son.—
This grave shall have a living monument.
An hour of quiet shortly shall we see;
250 Till then in patience our proceeding be.   [*Exeunt.*]

Scene 2

A hall or public room. Enter HAMLET *and* HORATIO.

HAMLET: So much for this, sir; now shall you see the other.
You do remember all the circumstance?
HORATIO: Remember it, my lord!
HAMLET: Sir, in my heart there was a kind of fighting
5   That would not let me sleep. Methought I lay
Worse than the mutines in the bilboes.[3] Rashly,
And praised be rashness for it—let us know,
Our indiscretion sometime serves us well,
When our deep plots do pall; and that should learn[4] us
10   There's a divinity that shapes our ends,
Rough-hew them how we will—
HORATIO: That is most certain.
HAMLET: Up from my cabin,
My sea-gown scarfed[5] about me, in the dark
Groped I to find out them, had my desire,
15   Fingered their packet, and in fine[6] withdrew
To mine own room again, making so bold,
My fears forgetting manners, to unseal
Their grand commission; where I found, Horatio—
Ah, royal knavery!—an exact[7] command,
20   Larded[8] with many several sorts of reasons,
Importing Denmark's health, and England's too,
With, ho! such bugs and goblins in my life,[9]
That on the supervise,[1] no leisure bated,
No, not to stay the grinding of the axe,
My head should be struck off.
25 HORATIO: Is't possible?
HAMLET: Here's the commission; read it at more leisure.
But wilt thou hear now how I did proceed?
HORATIO: I beseech you.

2. Immediate trial.   3. Stocks. *Mutines*: mutineers.   4. Teach.   5. Wrapped.
6. Quickly. *Fingered*: stole.   7. Precisely stated.   8. Garnished.
9. Such dangers if I remained alive.   1. As soon as the commission was read.

HAMLET: Being thus benetted[2] round with villainies,
Ere I could make a prologue to my brains,   30
They had begun the play. I sat me down,
Devised a new commission, wrote it fair.[3]
I once did hold it, as our statists[4] do,
A baseness to write fair, and labored much
How to forget that learning; but sir, now   35
It did me yeoman's service.[5] Wilt thou know
Th' effect[6] of what I wrote?
HORATIO: Ay, good my lord.
HAMLET: An earnest conjuration from the king,
As England was his faithful tributary,[7]
As love between them like the palm might flourish,   40
As peace should still her wheaten garland wear
And stand a comma 'tween their amities[8]
And many such like as's of great charge,[9]
That on the view and knowing of these contents,
Without debatement[1] further more or less,   45
He should those bearers put to sudden death,
Not shriving-time allowed.[2]
HORATIO: How was this sealed?
HAMLET: Why, even in that was heaven ordinant,[3]
I had my father's signet in my purse,
Which was the model of that Danish seal,   50
Folded the writ up in the form of th' other,
Subscribed it, gave't th' impression,[4] placed it safely,
The changeling[5] never known. Now, the next day
Was our sea-fight, and what to this was sequent[6]
Thou knowest already.   55
HORATIO: So Guildenstern and Rosencrantz go to't.
HAMLET: Why, man, they did make love to this employment.
They are not near my conscience; their defeat[7]
Does by their own insinuation grow.
'Tis dangerous when the baser nature comes   60
Between the pass and fell[8] incensèd points
Of mighty opposites.
HORATIO: Why, what a king is this!
HAMLET: Does it not, think thee, stand me now upon—
He that hath killed my king and whored my mother,

---

2. Caught in a net.   3. Legibly. *Devised*: made.   4. Politicians.   5. Served me well.
6. Contents.   7. Vassal.   8. Link friendships.   9. Import.   1. Consideration.
2. Without time for confession.   3. Operative.   4. With the seal.   5. Replacement.
6. Followed.   7. Death. *Are not near*: do not touch.   8. Cruel. *Pass*: thrust.

65 Popped in between th' election and my hopes,
    Thrown out his angle[9] for my proper life,
    And with such coz'nage[1]—is't not perfect conscience
    To quit[2] him with this arm? And is't not to be damned
    To let this canker of our nature come
70 In further evil?
    HORATIO: It must be shortly known to him from England
    What is the issue[3] of the business there.
    HAMLET: It will be short;[4] the interim is mine.
    And a man's life's no more than to say "one."
75 But I am very sorry, good Horatio,
    That to Laertes I forgot myself;
    For by the image of my cause I see
    The portraiture of his. I'll court his favors.
    But sure the bravery[5] of his grief did put me
    Into a tow'ring passion.
80 HORATIO: Peace; who comes here?

        [*Enter* OSRIC.]

    OSRIC: Your lordship is right welcome back to Denmark.
    HAMLET: I humbly thank you, sir. [*Aside to* HORATIO.] Dost know this water-
    fly?
    HORATIO: [*Aside to* HAMLET.] No, my good lord.
    HAMLET: [*Aside to* HORATIO.] Thy state is the more gracious, for 'tis a vice to
85 know him. He hath much land, and fertile. Let a beast be lord of beasts,
    and his crib shall stand at the king's mess. 'Tis a chough,[6] but as I say,
    spacious in the possession of dirt.
    OSRIC: Sweet lord, if your lordship were at leisure, I should impart a thing
    to you from his majesty.
90 HAMLET: I will receive it, sir, with all diligence of spirit. Put your bonnet to
    his right use. 'Tis for the head.[7]
    OSRIC: I thank your lordship, it is very hot.
    HAMLET: No, believe me, 'tis very cold; the wind is northerly.
    OSRIC: It is indifferent[8] cold, my lord, indeed.
95 HAMLET: But yet methinks it is very sultry and hot for my complexion.[9]
    OSRIC: Exceedingly, my lord; it is very sultry, as 'twere—I cannot tell how.
    My lord, his majesty bade me signify to you that 'a has laid a great wager
    on your head. Sir, this is the matter—
    HAMLET: I beseech you, remember.   [*Moves him to put on his hat.*]

---

9. Fishhook.   1. Trickery.   2. Repay.   3. Outcome.   4. Soon.   5. Exaggerated display.
6. Jackdaw.   7. Osric has evidently removed his hat in deference to the prince.
8. Moderately.   9. Temperament.

OSRIC: Nay, good my lord; for my ease, in good faith. Sir, here is newly come 100
to court Laertes; believe me, an absolute[1] gentleman, full of most excellent differences of very soft society and great showing.[2] Indeed, to speak
feelingly of him, he is the card or calendar of gentry, for you shall find
in him the continent[3] of what part a gentleman would see.

HAMLET: Sir, his definement[4] suffers no perdition in you, though I know to 105
divide him inventorially would dozy[5] th' arithmetic of memory, and yet
but yaw neither in respect of his quick sail. But in the verity of extol-
ment, I take him to be a soul of great article,[6] and his infusion of such
dearth and rareness as, to make true diction of him, his semblage is his
mirror,[7] and who else would trace him, his umbrage,[8] nothing more. 110

OSRIC: Your lordship speaks most infallibly of him.

HAMLET: The concernancy,[9] sir? Why do we wrap the gentleman in our
more rawer breath?[1]

OSRIC: Sir?

HORATIO: Is't not possible to understand in another tongue? You will to't, 115
sir, really.

HAMLET: What imports the nomination[2] of this gentleman?

OSRIC: Of Laertes?

HORATIO: [*Aside.*] His purse is empty already. All's golden words are spent.

HAMLET: Of him, sir. 120

OSRIC: I know you are not ignorant—

HAMLET: I would you did, sir; yet, in faith, if you did, it would not much
approve me. Well, sir.

OSRIC: You are not ignorant of what excellence Laertes is—

HAMLET: I dare not confess that, lest I should compare[3] with him in excel- 125
lence; but to know a man well were to know himself.

OSRIC: I mean, sir, for his weapon; but in the imputation[4] laid on him by
them, in his meed he's unfellowed.[5]

HAMLET: What's his weapon?

OSRIC: Rapier and dagger. 130

HAMLET: That's two of his weapons—but well.

OSRIC: The king, sir, hath wagered with him six Barbary horses, against the
which he has impawned,[6] as I take it, six French rapiers and poniards,
with their assigns, as girdle, hangers,[7] and so. Three of the carriages, in

---

1. Perfect.   2. Good manners. *Excellent differences*: qualities.
3. Sum total. *Calendar*: measure.   4. Description.
5. Steer wildly. *Dozy*: daze. *Divide him inventorially*: examine bit by bit.
6. Nature. *Article*: scope.
7. That is, his likeness ("semblage") is (only) his own mirror image; he is unrivaled. *Diction*: telling.   8. Shadow. *Trace*: keep pace with.
9. Meaning. (Hamlet is mocking Osric's affected speech.)   1. Cruder words.   2. Naming.
3. That is, compare myself.   4. Reputation.   5. Unequaled in his excellence.   6. Staked.
7. Sword belts. *Assigns*: appurtenances.

135   faith, are very dear to fancy,[8] very responsive to the hilts, most delicate
       carriages, and of very liberal conceit.[9]
       HAMLET: What call you the carriages?
       HORATIO: [*Aside to* HAMLET.] I knew you must be edified by the margent[1] ere
       you had done.
140   OSRIC: The carriages, sir, are the hangers.
       HAMLET: The phrase would be more germane to the matter if we could
       carry a cannon by our sides. I would it might be hangers till then. But
       on! Six Barbary horses against six French swords, their assigns, and
       three liberal conceited carriages; that's the French bet against the Dan-
145   ish. Why is this all impawned, as you call it?
       OSRIC: The king, sir, hath laid, sir, that in a dozen passes between yourself
       and him he shall not exceed you three hits; he hath laid on twelve for
       nine, and it would come to immediate trial if your lordship would
       vouchsafe the answer.
       HAMLET: How if I answer no?
150   OSRIC: I mean, my lord, the opposition of your person in trial.
       HAMLET: Sir, I will walk here in the hall. If it please his majesty, it is the
       breathing time[2] of day with me. Let the foils be brought, the gentleman
       willing, and the king hold his purpose; I will win for him an I can. If
       not, I will gain nothing but my shame and the odd hits.
155   OSRIC: Shall I deliver you so?
       HAMLET: To this effect, sir, after what flourish your nature will.
       OSRIC: I commend my duty to your lordship.
       HAMLET: Yours, yours. [*Exit* OSRIC.] He does well to commend it himself;
       there are no tongues else for's turn.
160   HORATIO: This lapwing runs away with the shell on his head.[3]
       HAMLET: 'A did comply, sir, with his dug[4] before 'a sucked it. Thus has he,
       and many more of the same bevy that I know the drossy age dotes on,
       only got the tune of the time; and out of an habit of encounter, a king of
       yesty[5] collection which carries them through and through the most
       fanned and winnowed opinions; and do but blow them to their trial,
165   the bubbles are out.

       [*Enter a* LORD.]

       LORD: My lord, his majesty commended him to you by young Osric, who
       brings back to him that you attend[6] him in the hall. He sends to know

8. Finely designed.   9. Elegant design. *Delicate*: well adjusted.   1. Marginal gloss.
2. Time for exercise.
3. The lapwing was thought to be so precocious that it could run immediately after being
hatched, even, as here, with bits of the shell still on its head.
4. Mother's breast. *Comply*: deal formally.   5. Yeasty.   6. Await.

if your pleasure hold to play with Laertes, or that you will take longer time.

HAMLET: I am constant to my purposes; they follow the king's pleasure. If his fitness speaks, mine is ready; now or whensoever, provided I be so 170 able as now.

LORD: The king and queen and all are coming down.

HAMLET: In happy time.

LORD: The queen desires you to use some gentle entertainment[7] to Laertes before you fall to play.

HAMLET: She well instructs me.   [*Exit* LORD.] 175

HORATIO: You will lose this wager, my lord.

HAMLET: I do not think so. Since he went into France I have been in continual practice. I shall win at the odds. But thou wouldst not think how ill[8] all's here about my heart. But it's no matter.

HORATIO: Nay, good my lord—   180

HAMLET: It is but foolery, but it is such a kind of gaingiving[9] as would perhaps trouble a woman.

HORATIO: If your mind dislike anything, obey it. I will forestall their repair[1] hither, and say you are not fit.

HAMLET: Not a whit, we defy augury. There is special providence in the fall 185 of a sparrow. If it be now, 'tis not to come; if it be not to come, it will be now; if it be not now, yet it will come. The readiness is all. Since no man of aught he leaves knows, what is't to leave betimes? Let be.

[*A table prepared. Enter* TRUMPETS, DRUMS, *and* OFFICERS *with cushions;* KING, QUEEN, OSRIC *and* ATTENDANTS *with foils, daggers, and* LAERTES.]

KING: Come, Hamlet, come and take this hand from me.

[*The* KING *puts* LAERTES' *hand into* HAMLET'*s.*]

HAMLET: Give me your pardon, sir. I have done you wrong,   190
But pardon 't as you are a gentleman.
This presence[2] knows, and you must needs have heard,
How I am punished with a sore distraction.
What I have done
That might your nature, honor, and exception,[3]   195
Roughly awake, I here proclaim was madness.
Was 't Hamlet wronged Laertes? Never Hamlet.
If Hamlet from himself be ta'en away,
And when he's not himself does wrong Laertes,
Then Hamlet does it not, Hamlet denies it.   200
Who does it then? His madness. If't be so,
Hamlet is of the faction that is wronged;

7. Cordiality. 8. Uneasy. 9. Misgiving. 1. Coming. 2. Company. 3. Resentment.

His madness is poor Hamlet's enemy.
Sir, in this audience,
205   Let my disclaiming from[4] a purposed evil
Free[5] me so far in your most generous thoughts
That I have shot my arrow o'er the house
And hurt my brother.

LAERTES: I am satisfied in nature,
Whose motive in this case should stir me most
210   To my revenge. But in my terms of honor
I stand aloof, and will no reconcilement
Till by some elder masters of known honor
I have a voice[6] and precedent of peace
To keep my name ungored.[7] But till that time
215   I do receive your offered love like love,
And will not wrong it.

HAMLET: I embrace it freely,
And will this brother's wager frankly[8] play.
Give us the foils. Come on.

LAERTES: Come, one for me.

HAMLET: I'll be your foil, Laertes. In mine ignorance
220   Your skill shall, like a star i' th' darkest night,
Stick fiery off[9] indeed.

LAERTES: You mock me, sir.

HAMLET: No, by this hand.

KING: Give them the foils, young Osric. Cousin Hamlet,
You know the wager?

HAMLET: Very well, my lord;
225   Your Grace has laid the odds o' th' weaker side.

KING: I do not fear it, I have seen you both;
But since he is bettered[1] we have therefore odds.

LAERTES: This is too heavy; let me see another.

HAMLET: This likes me well. These foils have all a[2] length?

[*They prepare to play.*]

230 OSRIC: Ay, my good lord.

KING: Set me the stoups of wine upon that table.
If Hamlet give the first or second hit,
Or quit in answer of[3] the third exchange,
Let all the battlements their ordnance fire.
235   The king shall drink to Hamlet's better breath,
And in the cup an union[4] shall he throw,

4. Denying of.   5. Absolve.   6. Authority.   7. Unshamed.   8. Freely.
9. Shine brightly.   1. Reported better.   2. The same. *Likes:* suits.   3. Repay.   4. Pearl.

Richer than that which four successive kings
In Denmark's crown have worn. Give me the cups,
And let the kettle[5] to the trumpet speak,
The trumpet to the cannoneer without,
The cannons to the heavens, the heaven to earth,   240
"Now the king drinks to Hamlet." Come, begin—

    [*Trumpets the while.*]

And you, the judges, bear a wary eye.
HAMLET: Come on, sir.
LAERTES: Come, my lord.

    [*They play.*]

HAMLET: One.
LAERTES: No.
HAMLET: Judgment?
OSRIC: A hit, a very palpable hit.   245

    [*Drums, trumpets, and shot. Flourish; a piece goes off.*]

LAERTES: Well, again.
KING: Stay, give me drink. Hamlet, this pearl is thine.
  Here's to thy health. Give him the cup.
HAMLET: I'll play this bout first; set it by awhile.
  Come.   250

    [*They play.*]

Another hit; what say you?
LAERTES: A touch, a touch, I do confess't.
KING: Our son shall win.
QUEEN: He's fat,[6] and scant of breath.
  Here, Hamlet, take my napkin, rub thy brows.
  The queen carouses to thy fortune, Hamlet.   255
HAMLET: Good madam!
KING: Gertrude, do not drink.
QUEEN: I will, my lord; I pray you pardon me.
KING: [*Aside.*] It is the poisoned cup; it is too late.
HAMLET: I dare not drink yet, madam; by and by.   260
QUEEN: Come, let me wipe thy face.
LAERTES: My lord, I'll hit him now.
KING: I do not think't.
LAERTES: [*Aside.*] And yet it is almost against my conscience.
HAMLET: Come, for the third, Laertes. You do but dally.

5. Kettledrum.   6. Out of shape.

265   I pray you pass[7] with your best violence;
        I am afeard you make a wanton of me.[8]
        LAERTES: Say you so? Come on.

        [*They play.*]

        OSRIC: Nothing, neither way.
        LAERTES: Have at you now!

        [LAERTES *wounds* HAMLET: *then, in scuffling, they change rapiers, and*
        HAMLET *wounds* LAERTES.]

270   KING: Part them. They are incensed.
        HAMLET: Nay, come again.

        [*The* QUEEN *falls.*]

        OSRIC: Look to the queen there, ho!
        HORATIO: They bleed on both sides. How is it, my lord?
        OSRIC: How is't, Laertes?
275   LAERTES: Why, as a woodcock to mine own springe,[9] Osric.
        I am justly killed with mine own treachery.
        HAMLET: How does the queen?
        KING: She swoons to see them bleed.
        QUEEN: No, no, the drink, the drink! O my dear Hamlet!
        The drink, the drink! I am poisoned.   [*Dies.*]
280   HAMLET: O, villainy! Ho! let the door be locked.
        Treachery! seek it out.
        LAERTES: It is here, Hamlet. Hamlet, thou art slain;
        No med'cine in the world can do thee good.
        In thee there is not half an hour's life.
285   The treacherous instrument is in thy hand,
        Unbated[1] and envenomed. The foul practice
        Hath turned itself on me. Lo, here I lie,
        Never to rise again. Thy mother's poisoned.
        I can no more. The king, the king's to blame.
290   HAMLET: The point envenomed too?
        Then, venom, to thy work.   [*Hurts the* KING.]
        ALL: Treason! treason!
        KING: O, yet defend me, friends. I am but hurt.[2]
        HAMLET: Here, thou incestuous, murd'rous, damnèd Dane,
295   Drink off this potion. Is thy union here?
        Follow my mother.

        [*The* KING *dies.*]

7. Attack.   8. Trifle with me.   9. Snare.   1. Unblunted.   2. Wounded.

LAERTES: He is justly served.
It is a poison tempered³ by himself.
Exchange forgiveness with me, noble Hamlet.
Mine and my father's death come not upon thee,
Nor thine on me!   [*Dies.*] 300
HAMLET: Heaven make thee free of⁴ it! I follow thee.
I am dead, Horatio. Wretched queen, adieu!
You that look pale and tremble at this chance,⁵
That are but mutes or audience to this act,
Had I but time, as this fell sergeant Death   305
Is strict in his arrest,⁶ O, I could tell you—
But let it be. Horatio, I am dead:
Thou livest; report me and my cause aright
To the unsatisfied.⁷
HORATIO: Never believe it.
I am more an antique Roman than a Dane.   310
Here's yet some liquor left.
HAMLET: As th'art a man,
Give me the cup. Let go. By heaven, I'll ha't.
O God, Horatio, what a wounded name,
Things standing thus unknown, shall live behind me!
If thou didst ever hold me in thy heart,   315
Absent thee from felicity awhile,
And in this harsh world draw thy breath in pain,
To tell my story.
        [*A march afar off.*]
                What warlike noise is this?
OSRIC: Young Fortinbras, with conquest come from Poland,
To th' ambassadors of England gives   320
This warlike volley.⁸
HAMLET: O, I die, Horatio!
The potent poison quite o'er-crows⁹ my spirit.
I cannot live to hear the news from England,
But I do prophesy th' election¹ lights
On Fortinbras. He has my dying voice.²   325
So tell him, with th' occurrents,³ more and less,

---

3. Mixed.   4. Forgive.   5. Circumstance.   6. Summons to court.   7. Uninformed.
8. The staging presents some difficulties here. Unless Osric is clairvoyant, he must have left the
stage at some point and returned. One possibility is that he might have left to carry out Hamlet's
order to lock the door (line 280) and returned when the sound of the distant march is
heard.   9. Overcomes.   1. (Of a new king for Denmark.)   2. Support.   3. Circumstances.

Which have solicited[4]—the rest is silence.   [*Dies.*]

HORATIO: Now cracks a noble heart. Good night, sweet prince,
And flights of angels sing thee to thy rest!

[*March within.*]

330   Why does the drum come hither?

[*Enter* FORTINBRAS, *with the* AMBASSADORS *and with drum, colors, and*
ATTENDANTS.]

FORTINBRAS: Where is this sight?

HORATIO: What is it you would see?
If aught of woe or wonder, cease your search.

FORTINBRAS: This quarry cries on havoc.[5] O proud death,
What feast is toward[6] in thine eternal cell

335   That thou so many princes at a shot
So bloodily hast struck?

AMBASSADORS: The sight is dismal;
And our affairs from England come too late.
The ears are senseless[7] that should give us hearing
To tell him his commandment is fulfilled,

340   That Rosencrantz and Guildenstern are dead.
Where should we have our thanks?

HORATIO: Not from his mouth,
Had it th' ability of life to thank you.
He never gave commandment for their death.
But since, so jump[8] upon this bloody question,

345   You from the Polack wars, and you from England,
Are here arrived, give orders that these bodies
High on a stage be placèd to the view,
And let me speak to th' yet unknowing world
How these things came about. So shall you hear

350   Of carnal, bloody, and unnatural acts;
Of accidental judgments, casual[9] slaughters;
Of deaths put on by cunning and forced cause;
And, in this upshot,[1] purposes mistook
Fall'n on th' inventors' heads. All this can I
Truly deliver.

355 FORTINBRAS: Let us haste to hear it,
And call the noblest to the audience.[2]
For me, with sorrow I embrace my fortune.

---

4. Brought about this scene.   5. The game killed in the hunt proclaims a slaughter.
6. In preparation.   7. Without sense of hearing.   8. Exactly.
9. Brought about by apparent accident.   1. Result.   2. Hearing.

I have some rights of memory[3] in this kingdom,
Which now to claim my vantage[4] doth invite me.
HORATIO: Of that I shall have also cause to speak,   360
And from his mouth whose voice will draw on more.
But let this same be presently performed,
Even while men's minds are wild, lest more mischance
On plots and errors happen.
FORTINBRAS: Let four captains
Bear Hamlet like a soldier to the stage,   365
For he was likely, had he been put on,[5]
To have proved most royal; and for his passage
The soldier's music and the rite of war
Speak loudly for him.
Take up the bodies. Such a sight as this   370
Becomes the field,[6] but here shows much amiss.
Go, bid the soldiers shoot.   [*Exeunt marching. A peal of ordnance shot off.*]

                                                              ca. 1600

SOPHOCLES

Antigone[1]

CHARACTERS

ANTIGONE	HAEMON
ISMENE	TEIRESIAS
CHORUS OF THEBAN ELDERS	A MESSENGER
CREON	EURYDICE
A SENTRY	SECOND MESSENGER

The two sisters ANTIGONE *and* ISMENE *meet in front of the palace gates in Thebes.*

ANTIGONE: Ismene, my dear sister,
     whose father was my father, can you think of any
     of all the evils that stem from Oedipus[2]
     that Zeus does not bring to pass for us, while we yet live?

3. Succession.   4. Position.   5. Elected king.   6. Battlefield.   1. Translated by David Grene.
2. In Greek legend, Oedipus became king of Thebes by inadvertently fulfilling the prophecy that he was destined to kill his father and marry his mother (as depicted in Sophocles' *Oedipus the King*); for these offenses against nature and the gods, Creon sent Oedipus, along with his daughters Antigone and Ismene, into exile at Colonus. Soon Oedipus's sons, Eteocles and Polyneices, battled to the death for the throne of Thebes.

A production of *Antigone*
(New York Shakespeare Festival, 1982)

5   No pain, no ruin, no shame, and no dishonor
        but I have seen it in our mischiefs,
        yours and mine.
        And now what is the proclamation that they tell of
        made lately by the commander, publicly,
10   to all the people? Do you know it? Have you heard it?
        Don't you notice when the evils due to enemies
        are headed towards those we love?
   ISMENE: Not a word, Antigone, of those we love,
        either sweet or bitter, has come to me since the moment
15   when we lost our two brothers,
        on one day, by their hands dealing mutual death.
        Since the Argive[3] army fled in this past night,
        I know of nothing further, nothing
        of better fortune or of more destruction.
20 ANTIGONE: *I* knew it well; that is why I sent for you
        to come outside the palace gates
        to listen to me, privately.
   ISMENE: What is it? Certainly your words
        come of dark thoughts.
25 ANTIGONE: Yes, indeed; for those two brothers of ours, in burial
        has not Creon honored the one, dishonored the other?
        Eteocles, they say he has used justly

3. From Argos, a rival Greek city-state.

with lawful rites and hid him in the earth
to have his honor among the dead men there.
But the unhappy corpse of Polyneices   30
he has proclaimed to all the citizens,
they say, no man may hide
in a grave nor mourn in funeral,
but leave unwept, unburied, a dainty treasure
for the birds that see him, for their feast's delight.   35
That is what, they say, the worthy Creon
has proclaimed for you and me—for me, I tell you—
and he comes here to clarify to the unknowing
his proclamation; he takes it seriously;
for whoever breaks the edict death is prescribed,   40
and death by stoning publicly.
There you have it; soon you will show yourself
as noble both in your nature and your birth,
or yourself as base, although of noble parents.
ISMENE: If things are as you say, poor sister, how   45
can I better them? how loose or tie the knot?
ANTIGONE: Decide if you will share the work, the deed.
ISMENE: What kind of danger is there? How far have your thoughts gone?
ANTIGONE: Here is this hand. Will you help it to lift the dead man?
ISMENE: Would you bury him, when it is forbidden the city?   50
ANTIGONE: At least he is my brother—and yours, too,
though you deny him. *I* will not prove false to him.
ISMENE: You are so headstrong. Creon has forbidden it.
ANTIGONE: It is not for him to keep me from my own.
ISMENE: O God!   55
Consider, sister, how our father died,
hated and infamous; how he brought to light
his own offenses; how he himself struck out
the sight of his two eyes;
his own hand was their executioner.   60
Then, mother and wife, two names in one, did shame
violently on her life, with twisted cords.
Third, our two brothers, on a single day,
poor wretches, themselves worked out their mutual doom.
Each killed the other, hand against brother's hand.   65
Now there are only the two of us, left behind,
and see how miserable our end shall be
if in the teeth of law we shall transgress
against the sovereign's decree and power.
You ought to realize we are only women,   70
not meant in nature to fight against men,

and that we are ruled, by those who are stronger,
to obedience in this and even more painful matters.
I do indeed beg those beneath the earth
75 to give me their forgiveness,
since force constrains me,
that I shall yield in this to the authorities.
Extravagant action is not sensible.
ANTIGONE: I would not urge you now; nor if you wanted
80 to act would I be glad to have you with me.
Be as you choose to be; but for myself
I myself will bury him. It will be good
to die, so doing. I shall lie by his side,
loving him as he loved me; I shall be
85 a criminal—but a religious one.
The time in which I must please those that are dead
is longer than I must please those of this world.
For there I shall lie forever. You, if you like,
can cast dishonor on what the gods have honored.
90 ISMENE: I will not put dishonor on them, but
to act in defiance of the citizenry,
my nature does not give me means for that.
ANTIGONE: Let that be your excuse. But I will go
to heap the earth on the grave of my loved brother.
95 ISMENE: How I fear for you, my poor sister!
ANTIGONE: Do not fear for me. Make straight your own path to destiny.
ISMENE: At least do not speak of this act to anyone else;
bury him in secret; I will be silent, too.
ANTIGONE: Oh, oh, no! shout it out. I will hate you still worse
100 for silence—should you not proclaim it,
to everyone.
ISMENE: You have a warm heart for such chilly deeds.
ANTIGONE: I know I am pleasing those I should please most.
ISMENE: *If* you can do it. But you are in love
105 with the impossible.
ANTIGONE: No. When I can no more, then I will stop.
ISMENE: It is better not to hunt the impossible
at all.
ANTIGONE: If you will talk like this I will loathe you,
110 and you will be adjudged an enemy—
justly—by the dead's decision. Let me alone
and my folly with me, to endure this terror.
No suffering of mine will be enough
to make me die ignobly.
115 ISMENE: Well, if you will, go on.

Know this; that though you are wrong to go, your friends
are right to love you.
CHORUS: Sun's beam, fairest of all
    that ever till now shone
    on seven-gated Thebes;   120
    O golden eye of day, you shone
    coming over Dirce's stream;[4]
    You drove in headlong rout
    the whiteshielded man from Argos,
    complete in arms;   125
    his bits rang sharper
    under your urging.

    Polyneices brought him here
    against our land, Polyneices,
    roused by contentious quarrel;   130
    like an eagle he flew into our country,
    with many men-at-arms,
    with many a helmet crowned with horsehair.

    He stood above the halls, gaping with murderous lances,
    encompassing the city's   135
    seven-gated mouth[5]
    But before his jaws would be sated
    with our blood, before the fire,
    pine fed, should capture our crown of towers,
    he went hence—   140
    such clamor of war stretched behind his back,
    from his dragon foe, a thing he could not overcome.

    For Zeus, who hates the most
    the boasts of a great tongue,
    saw them coming in a great tide,   145
    insolent in the clang of golden armor.
    The god struck him down with hurled fire,
    as he strove to raise the victory cry,
    now at the very winning post.

    The earth rose to strike him as he fell swinging.   150
    In his frantic onslaught, possessed, he breathed upon us
    with blasting winds of hate.
    Sometimes the great god of war was on one side,

---

4. River near Thebes.
5. Thebes was known throughout the ancient world for having seven gateways through the walls
protecting the city.

155   and sometimes he struck a staggering blow on the other;
       the god was a very wheel horse[6] on the right trace.

       At seven gates stood seven captains,
       ranged equals against equals, and there left
       their brazen suits of armor
       to Zeus, the god of trophies.
160   Only those two wretches born of one father and mother
       set their spears to win a victory on both sides;
       they worked out their share in a common death.

       Now Victory, whose name is great, has come
       to Thebes of many chariots
165   with joy to answer her joy,
       to bring forgetfulness of these wars;
       let us go to all the shrines of the gods
       and dance all night long.
       Let Bacchus lead the dance,
170   shaking Thebes to trembling.

       But here is the king of our land,
       Creon,[7] son of Menoeceus;
       in our new contingencies with the gods,
       he is our new ruler.
175   He comes to set in motion some design—
       what design is it? Because he has proposed
       the convocation of the elders.
       He sent a public summons for our discussion.
CREON: Gentlemen: as for our city's fortune,
180 the gods have shaken her, when the great waves broke,
     but the gods have brought her through again to safety.
     For yourselves, I chose you out of all and summoned you
     to come to me, partly because I knew you
     as always loyal to the throne—at first,
185 when Laïus[8] was king, and then again
     when Oedipus saved our city and then again
     when he died and you remained with steadfast truth
     to their descendants,
     until they met their double fate upon one day,
190 striking and stricken, defiled each by a brother's murder.
     Now here I am, holding all authority

---

6. Strongest and ablest horse in a team pulling a vehicle, harnessed nearest the front wheels "on the right trace."
7. Brother of Jocasta, mother and wife of Oedipus; he became king of Thebes after the deaths of Oedipus's sons.   8. Father of Oedipus.

and the throne, in virtue of kinship with the dead.
It is impossible to know any man—
I mean his soul, intelligence, and judgment—
until he shows his skill in rule and law.   195
I think that a man supreme ruler of a whole city,
if he does not reach for the best counsel for her,
but through some fear, keeps his tongue under lock and key,
him I judge the worst of any;
I have always judged so; and anyone thinking   200
another man more a friend than his own country,
I rate him nowhere. For my part, God is my witness,
who sees all, always, I would not be silent
if I saw ruin, not safety, on the way
towards my fellow citizens. I would not count   205
any enemy of my country as a friend—
because of what I know, that she it is
which gives us our security. If she sails upright
and we sail on her, friends will be ours for the making.
In the light of rules like these, I will make her greater still.   210

In consonance with this, I here proclaim
to the citizens about Oedipus' sons.
For Eteocles, who died this city's champion,
showing his valor's supremacy everywhere,
he shall be buried in his grave with every rite   215
of sanctity given to heroes under earth.
However, his brother, Polyneices, a returned exile,
who sought to burn with fire from top to bottom
his native city, and the gods of his own people;
who sought to taste the blood he shared with us,   220
and lead the rest of us to slavery—
I here proclaim to the city that this man
shall no one honor with a grave and none shall mourn.
You shall leave him without burial; you shall watch him
chewed up by birds and dogs and violated.   225
Such is my mind in the matter; never by me
shall the wicked man have precedence in honor
over the just. But he that is loyal to the state
in death, in life alike, shall have my honor.
CHORUS: Son of Menoeceus, so it is your pleasure   230
to deal with foe and friend of this our city.
To use any legal means lies in your power,
both about the dead and those of us who live.
CREON: I understand, then, you will do my bidding.

235 CHORUS: Please lay this burden on some younger man.
CREON: Oh, watchers of the corpse I have already.
CHORUS: What else, then, do your commands entail?
CREON: That you should not side with those who disagree.
CHORUS: There is none so foolish as to love his own death.
240 CREON: Yes, indeed those are the wages, but often greed
has with its hopes brought men to ruin.

> [*The* SENTRY *whose speeches follow represents a remarkable experiment in
> Greek tragedy in the direction of naturalism of speech. He speaks with marked
> clumsiness, partly because he is excited and talks almost colloquially. But also
> the royal presence makes him think apparently that he should be rather grand
> in his show of respect. He uses odd bits of archaism or somewhat stale poetical
> passages, particularly in catch phrases. He sounds something like lower-level
> Shakespearean characters, e.g. Constable Elbow, with his uncertainty about
> benefactor and malefactor.*]

SENTRY: My lord, I will never claim my shortness of breath
is due to hurrying; nor were there wings in my feet.
I stopped at many a lay-by in my thinking;
245 I circled myself till I met myself coming back.
My soul accosted me with different speeches.
"Poor fool, yourself, why are you going somewhere
when once you get there you will pay the piper?"
"Well, aren't you the daring fellow! stopping again?
250 and suppose Creon hears the news from someone else—
don't you realize that you will smart for that?"
I turned the whole matter over. I suppose I may say
"I made haste slowly" and the short road became long.
However, at last I came to a resolve:
255 I must go to you; even if what I say
is nothing, really, still I shall say it.
I come here, a man with a firm clutch on the hope
that nothing can betide him save what is fated.
CREON: What is it then that makes you so afraid?
260 SENTRY: No, I want first of all to tell you my side of it.
I didn't do the thing; I never saw who did it.
It would not be fair for me to get into trouble.
CREON: You hedge, and barricade the thing itself.
Clearly you have some ugly news for me.
265 SENTRY: Well, you know how disasters make a man
hesitate to be their messenger.
CREON: For God's sake, tell me and get out of here!
SENTRY: Yes, I *will* tell you. Someone just now
buried the corpse and vanished. He scattered on the skin

some thirsty dust; he did the ritual,   270
  duly, to purge the body of desecration.
CREON: What! Now who on earth could have done that?
SENTRY: I do not know. For there was there no mark
  of axe's stroke nor casting up of earth
  of any mattock; the ground was hard and dry,   275
  unbroken; there were no signs of wagon wheels.
  The doer of the deed had left no trace.
  But when the first sentry of the day pointed it out,
  there was for all of us a disagreeable
  wonder. For the body had disappeared;   280
  not in a grave, of course; but there lay upon him
  a little dust as of a hand avoiding
  the curse of violating the dead body's sanctity.
  There were no signs of any beast nor dog
  that came there; he had clearly not been torn.   285
  There was a tide of bad words at one another,
  guard taunting guard, and it might well have ended
  in blows, for there was no one there to stop it.
  Each one of us was the criminal but no one
  manifestly so; all denied knowledge of it.   290
  We were ready to take hot bars in our hands
  or walk through fire,[9] and call on the gods with oaths
  that we had neither done it nor were privy
  to a plot with anyone, neither in planning
  nor yet in execution.   295
  At last when nothing came of all our searching,
  there was one man who spoke, made every head
  bow to the ground in fear. For we could not
  either contradict him nor yet could we see how
  if we did what he said we would come out all right.   300
  His word was that we must lay information
  about the matter to yourself; we could not cover it.
  This view prevailed and the lot of the draw chose me,
  unlucky me, to win that prize. So here
  I am. I did not want to come,   305
  and you don't want to have me. I know that.
  For no one likes the messenger of bad news.
CHORUS: My lord: I wonder, could this be God's doing?
  This is the thought that keeps on haunting me.

---

9. Ancient legal customs in which an accused person was required to undergo a "trial by ordeal,"
such as walking through fire; if the resulting injuries were not serious, the person was thought to
be innocent and therefore divinely protected.

310   CREON: Stop, before your words fill even me with rage,
       that you should be exposed as a fool, and you so old.
       For what you say is surely insupportable
       when you say the gods took forethought for this corpse.
       Is it out of excess of honor for the man,
315   for the favors that he did them, they should cover him?
       This man who came to burn their pillared temples,
       their dedicated offerings—and this land
       and laws he would have scattered to the winds?
       Or do you see the gods as honoring
320   criminals? This is not so. But what I am doing
       now, and other things before this, some men disliked,
       within this very city, and muttered against me,
       secretly shaking their heads; they would not bow
       justly beneath the yoke to submit to me.
325   I am very sure that these men hired others
       to do this thing. I tell you the worse currency
       that ever grew among mankind is money. This
       sacks cities, this drives people from their homes,
       this teaches and corrupts the minds of the loyal
330   to acts of shame. This displays
       all kinds of evil for the use of men,
       instructs in the knowledge of every impious act.
       Those that have done this deed have been paid to do it,
       but in the end they will pay for what they have done.

335   It is as sure as I still reverence Zeus—
       know this right well—and I speak under oath—
       if you and your fellows do not find this man
       who with his own hand did the burial
       and bring him here before me face to face,
340   your death alone will not be enough for me.
       You will hang alive till you open up this outrage.
       That will teach you in the days to come from what
       you may draw profit—safely—from your plundering.
       It's not from anything and everything
345   you can grow rich. You will find out
       that ill-gotten gains ruin more than they save.
       SENTRY: Have I your leave to say something—or should
       I just turn and go?
       CREON: Don't you know your talk is painful enough already?
350   SENTRY: Is the ache in your ears or in your mind?
       CREON: Why do you dissect the whereabouts of my pain?
       SENTRY: Because it is he who did the deed who hurts your

mind. I only hurt your ears that listen.
CREON: I am sure you have been a chatterbox since you were born.
SENTRY: All the same, I did not do this thing.   355
CREON: You might have done this, too, if you sold your soul.
SENTRY: It's a bad thing if one judges and judges wrongly.
CREON: You may talk as wittily as you like of judgment.
Only, if you don't bring to light those men
who have done this, you will yet come to say   360
that your wretched gains have brought bad consequences.
SENTRY: [*Aside.*] It were best that he were found, but whether
the criminal is taken or he isn't—
for that chance will decide—one thing is certain,
you'll never see me coming here again.   365
I never hoped to escape, never thought I could.
But now I have come off safe, I thank God heartily.
CHORUS: Many are the wonders, none
        is more wonderful than what is man.
        This it is that crosses the sea   370
        with the south winds storming and the waves swelling,
        breaking around him in roaring surf.
        He it is again who wears away
        the Earth, oldest of gods, immortal, unwearied,
        as the ploughs wind across her from year to year   375
        when he works her with the breed that comes from horses.

        The tribe of the lighthearted birds he snares
        and takes prisoner the races of savage beasts
        and the brood of the fish of the sea,
        with the close-spun web of nets.   380
        A cunning fellow is man. His contrivances
        make him master of beasts of the field
        and those that move in the mountains.
        So he brings the horse with the shaggy neck
        to bend underneath the yoke;   385
        and also the untamed mountain bull;
        and speech and windswift thought
        and the tempers that go with city living
        he has taught himself, and how to avoid
        the sharp frost, when lodging is cold   390
        under the open sky
        and pelting strokes of the rain.
        He has a way against everything,
        and he faces nothing that is to come
        without contrivance.   395

Only against death
can he call on no means of escape;
but escape from hopeless diseases
he has found in the depths of his mind.
400   With some sort of cunning, inventive
beyond all expectation
he reaches sometimes evil,
and sometimes good.

If he honors the laws of earth,
405   and the justice of the gods he has confirmed by oath,
high is his city; no city
has he with whom dwells dishonor
prompted by recklessness.
He who is so, may he never
410   share my hearth!
may he never think my thoughts!

Is this a portent sent by God?
I cannot tell.
I know her. How can I say
415   that this is not Antigone?
Unhappy girl, child of unhappy Oedipus,
what is this?
Surely it is not you they bring here
as disobedient to the royal edict,
420   surely not you, taken in such folly.
SENTRY: She is the one who did the deed;
    we took her burying him. But where is Creon?
CHORUS: He is just coming from the house, when you most need him.
CREON: What is this? What has happened that I come
425   so opportunely?
SENTRY: My lord, there is nothing
    that a man should swear he would never do.
    Second thoughts make liars of the first resolution.
    I would have vowed it would be long enough
430   before I came again, lashed hence by your threats.
    But since the joy that comes past hope, and against all hope,
    is like no other pleasure in extent,
    I have come here, though I break my oath in coming.
    I bring this girl here who has been captured
435   giving the grace of burial to the dead man.
    This time no lot chose me; this was my jackpot,
    and no one else's. Now, my lord, take her
    and as you please judge her and test her; I

am justly free and clear of all this trouble.

CREON: This girl—how did you take her and from where? 440

SENTRY: She was burying the man. Now you know all.

CREON: Do you know what you are saying? Do you mean it?

SENTRY: She is the one; I saw her burying
the dead man you forbade the burial of.
Now, do I speak plainly and clearly enough? 445

CREON: How was she seen? How was she caught in the act?

SENTRY: This is how it was. When we came there,
with those dreadful threats of yours upon us,
we brushed off all the dust that lay upon
the dead man's body, heedfully 450
leaving it moist and naked.
We sat on the brow of the hill, to windward,
that we might shun the smell of the corpse upon us.
Each of us wakefully urged his fellow
with torrents of abuse, not to be careless 455
in this work of ours. So it went on,
until in the midst of the sky the sun's bright circle
stood still; the heat was burning. Suddenly
a squall lifted out of the earth a storm of dust,
a trouble in the sky. It filled the plain, 460
ruining all the foliage of the wood
that was around it. The great empty air
was filled with it. We closed our eyes, enduring
this plague sent by the gods. When at long last
we were quit of it, why, then we saw the girl. 465

She was crying out with the shrill cry
of an embittered bird
that sees its nest robbed of its nestlings
and the bed empty. So, too, when she saw
the body stripped of its cover, she burst out in groans, 470
calling terrible curses on those that had done that deed;
and with her hands immediately
brought thirsty dust to the body; from a shapely brazen
urn, held high over it, poured a triple stream
of funeral offerings; and crowned the corpse. 475
When we saw that, we rushed upon her and
caught our quarry then and there, not a bit disturbed.
We charged her with what she had done, then and the first time.
She did not deny a word of it—to my joy,
but to my pain as well. It is most pleasant 480
to have escaped oneself out of such troubles

but painful to bring into it those whom we love.
However, it is but natural for me
to count all this less than my own escape.
485 CREON: You there, that turn your eyes upon the ground,
do you confess or deny what you have done?
ANTIGONE: Yes, I confess; I will not deny my deed.
CREON: [*To the* SENTRY.] You take yourself off where you like.
You are free of a heavy charge.
490 Now, Antigone, tell me shortly and to the point,
did you know the proclamation against your action?
ANTIGONE: I knew it; of course I did. For it was public.
CREON: And did you dare to disobey that law?
ANTIGONE: Yes, it was not Zeus that made the proclamation;
495 nor did Justice, which lives with those below, enact
such laws as that, for mankind. I did not believe
your proclamation had such power to enable
one who will someday die to override
God's ordinances, unwritten and secure.
500 *They* are not of today and yesterday;
they live forever; none knows when first they were.
These are the laws whose penalties I would not
incur from the gods, through fear of any man's temper.

I know that I will die—of course I do—
505 even if you had not doomed me by proclamation.
If I shall die before my time, I count that
a profit. How can such as I, that live
among such troubles, not find a profit in death?
So for such as me, to face such a fate as this
510 is pain that does not count. But if I dared to leave
the dead man, my mother's son, dead and unburied,
that would have been real pain. The other is not.
Now, if you think me a fool to act like this,
perhaps it is a fool that judges so.
515 CHORUS: The savage spirit of a savage father
shows itself in this girl. She does not know
how to yield to trouble.
CREON: I would have you know the most fanatic spirits
fall most of all. It is the toughest iron,
520 baked in the fire to hardness, you may see
most shattered, twisted, shivered to fragments.
I know hot horses are restrained
by a small curb. For he that is his neighbor's slave cannot
be high in spirit. This girl had learned her insolence

before this, when she broke the established laws.   525
But here is still another insolence
in that she boasts of it, laughs at what she did.
I swear I am no man and she the man
if she can win this and not pay for it.
No; though she were my sister's child or closer   530
in blood than all that my hearth god acknowledges
as mine, neither she nor her sister should escape
the utmost sentence—death. For indeed I accuse her,
the sister, equally of plotting the burial.
Summon her. I saw her inside, just now,   535
crazy, distraught. When people plot
mischief in the dark, it is the mind which first
is convicted of deceit. But surely I hate indeed
the one that is caught in evil and then makes
that evil look like good.   540
ANTIGONE: Do you want anything
beyond my taking and my execution?
CREON: Oh, nothing! Once I have that I have everything.
ANTIGONE: Why do you wait, then? Nothing that you say
pleases me; God forbid it ever should.   545
So my words, too, naturally offend you.
Yet how could I win a greater share of glory
than putting my own brother in his grave?
All that are here would surely say that's true,
if fear did not lock their tongues up. A prince's power   550
is blessed in many things, not least in this,
that he can say and do whatever he likes.
CREON: You are alone among the people of Thebes
to see things in that way.
ANTIGONE: No, these do, too,   555
but keep their mouths shut for the fear of you.
CREON: Are you not ashamed to think so differently
from them?
ANTIGONE: There is nothing shameful in honoring my brother.
CREON: Was not he that died on the other side your brother?   560
ANTIGONE: Yes, indeed, of my own blood from father and mother.
CREON: Why then do you show a grace that must be impious
in *his* sight?
ANTIGONE: *That* other dead man
would never bear you witness in what you say.   565
CREON: Yes he would, if you put him only on equality
with one that was a desecrator.
ANTIGONE: It was his brother, not his slave, that died.

CREON: He died destroying the country the other defended.

570 ANTIGONE: The god of death demands these rites for both.

CREON: But the good man does not seek an *equal* share only,
with the bad.

ANTIGONE: Who knows
if in that other world this is true piety?

CREON: My enemy is still my enemy, even in death.

575 ANTIGONE: My nature is to join in love, not hate.

CREON: Go then to the world below, yourself, if you
must love. Love *them*. When I am alive no woman shall rule.

CHORUS: Here before the gates comes Ismene
shedding tears for the love of a brother.

580   A cloud over her brow casts shame
on her flushed face, as the tears wet
her fair cheeks.

CREON: You there, who lurked in my house, viper-like—
secretly drawing its lifeblood; I never thought

585   that I was raising two sources of destruction,
two rebels against my throne. Come tell me now,
will you, too, say you bore a hand in the burial
or will you swear that you know nothing of it?

ISMENE: I did it, yes—if she will say I did it

590   I bear my share in it, bear the guilt, too.

ANTIGONE: Justice will not allow you what you refused
and I will have none of your partnership.

ISMENE: But in your troubles I am not ashamed
to sail with you the sea of suffering.

595 ANTIGONE: Where the act was death, the dead are witnesses.
I do not love a friend who loves in words.

ISMENE: Sister, do not dishonor me, denying me
a common death with you, a common honoring
of the dead man.

600 ANTIGONE: Don't die with me, nor make your own
what you have never touched. I that die am enough.

ISMENE: What life is there for me, once I have lost you?

ANTIGONE: Ask Creon; all your care was on his behalf.

ISMENE: Why do you hurt me, when you gain nothing by it?

605 ANTIGONE: I am hurt by my own mockery—if I mock you.

ISMENE: Even now—what can I do to help you still?

ANTIGONE: Save yourself; I do not grudge you your escape.

ISMENE: I cannot bear it! Not even to share your death!

ANTIGONE: Life was your choice, and death was mine.

610 ISMENE: You cannot say I accepted that choice in silence.

ANTIGONE: You were right in the eyes of one party, I in the other.

ISMENE: Well then, the fault is equally between us.
ANTIGONE: Take heart; you are alive, but my life died
   long ago, to serve the dead.
CREON: Here are two girls; I think that one of them   615
   has suddenly lost her wits—the other was always so.
ISMENE: Yes, for, my lord, the wits that they are born with
   do not stay firm for the unfortunate.
   They go astray.
CREON: Certainly yours do,
   when you share troubles with the troublemaker.   620
ISMENE: What life can be mine alone without her?
CREON: Do not
   speak of *her*. *She* isn't, anymore.
ISMENE: Will you kill your son's wife to be?[1]
CREON: Yes, there are other fields for him to plough.
ISMENE: Not with the mutual love of him and her.   625
CREON: I hate a bad wife for a son of mine.
ANTIGONE: Dear Haemon, how your father dishonors you.
CREON: There is too much of you—and of your marriage!
CHORUS: Will you rob your son of this girl?
CREON: Death—it is death that will stop the marriage for me.   630
CHORUS: Your decision it seems is taken: she shall die.
CREON: Both you and I have decided it. No more delay.

   [*He turns to the* SERVANTS.]

   Bring her inside, you. From this time forth,
   these must be women, and not free to roam.
   For even the stout of heart shrink when they see   635
   the approach of death close to their lives.
CHORUS: Lucky are those whose lives
      know no taste of sorrow.
     But for those whose house has been shaken by God
     there is never cessation of ruin;   640
     it steals on generation after generation
     within a breed. Even as the swell
     is driven over the dark deep
     by the fierce Thracian winds
     I see the ancient evils of Labdacus' house[2]   645
     are heaped on the evils of the dead.
     No generation frees another, some god
     strikes them down; there is no deliverance.

1. Antigone, betrothed to Creon's son Haemon.
2. Theban royal lineage that included Labdacus; his son, Laïus; and his grandson, Oedipus.

650 Here was the light of hope stretched
over the last roots of Oedipus' house,
and the bloody dust due to the gods below
has mowed it down—that and the folly of speech
and ruin's enchantment of the mind.

655 Your power, O Zeus, what sin of man can limit?
All-aging sleep does not overtake it,
nor the unwearied months of the gods; and you,
for whom time brings no age,
you hold the glowing brightness of Olympus.

660 For the future near and far,
and the past, this law holds good:
nothing very great
comes to the life of mortal man
without ruin to accompany it.

665 For Hope, widely wandering, comes to many of mankind
as a blessing,
but to many as the deceiver,
using light-minded lusts;
she comes to him that knows nothing
till he burns his foot in the glowing fire.

670 With wisdom has someone declared
a word of distinction:
that evil seems good to one whose mind
the god leads to ruin,
and but for the briefest moment of time

675 is his life outside of calamity.
Here is Haemon, youngest of your sons.
Does he come grieving
for the fate of his bride to be,
in agony at being cheated of his marriage?

680 CREON: Soon we will know that better than the prophets.
My son, can it be that you have not heard
of my final decision on your betrothed?
Can you have come here in your fury against your father?
Or have I your love still, no matter what I do?

685 HAEMON: Father, I am yours; with your excellent judgment
you lay the right before me, and I shall follow it.
No marriage will ever be so valued by me
as to override the goodness of your leadership.

CREON: Yes, my son, this should always be
690 in your very heart, that everything else
shall be second to your father's decision.

It is for this that fathers pray to have
obedient sons begotten in their halls,
that they may requite with ill their father's enemy
and honor his friend no less than he would himself.   695
If a man have sons that are no use to him,
what can one say of him but that he has bred
so many sorrows to himself, laughter to his enemies?
Do not, my son, banish your good sense
through pleasure in a woman, since you know   700
that the embrace grows cold
when an evil woman shares your bed and home.
What greater wound can there be than a false friend?
No. Spit on her, throw her out like an enemy,
this girl, to marry someone in Death's house.   705
I caught her openly in disobedience
alone out of all this city and I shall not make
myself a liar in the city's sight. No, I will kill her.
So let her cry if she will on the Zeus of kinship;
for if I rear those of my race and breeding   710
to be rebels, surely I will do so with those outside it.
For he who is in his household a good man
will be found a just man, too, in the city.
But he that breaches the law or does it violence
or thinks to dictate to those who govern him   715
shall never have my good word.
The man the city sets up in authority
must be obeyed in small things and in just
but also in their opposites.
I am confident such a man of whom I speak   720
will be a good ruler, and willing to be well ruled.
He will stand on his country's side, faithful and just,
in the storm of battle. There is nothing worse
than disobedience to authority.
It destroys cities, it demolishes homes;   725
it breaks and routs one's allies. Of successful lives
the most of them are saved by discipline.
So we must stand on the side of what is orderly;
we cannot give victory to a woman.
If we must accept defeat, let it be from a man;   730
we must not let people say that a woman beat us.
CHORUS: We think, if we are not victims of Time the Thief,
    that you speak intelligently of what you speak.
HAEMON: Father, the natural sense that the gods breed
    in men is surely the best of their possessions.   735

I certainly could not declare you wrong—
may I never know how to do so!—Still there might
be something useful that some other than you might think.
It is natural for me to be watchful on your behalf
740   concerning what all men say or do or find to blame.
Your face is terrible to a simple citizen;
it frightens him from words you dislike to hear.
But what *I* can hear, in the dark, are things like these:
the city mourns for this girl; they think she is dying
745   most wrongly and most undeservedly
of all womenkind, for the most glorious acts.
Here is one who would not leave her brother unburied,
a brother who had fallen in bloody conflict,
to meet his end by greedy dogs or by
750   the bird that chanced that way. Surely what she merits
is golden honor, isn't it? That's the dark rumor
that spreads in secret. Nothing I own
I value more highly, father, than your success.
What greater distinction can a son have than the glory
755   of a successful father, and for a father
the distinction of successful children?
Do not bear this single habit of mind, to think
that what you say and nothing else is true.
A man who thinks that he alone is right,
760   or what he says, or what he *is* himself,
unique, such men, when opened up, are seen
to be quite empty. For a man, though he be wise,
it is no shame to learn—learn many things,
and not maintain his views too rigidly.
765   You notice how by streams in wintertime
the trees that yield preserve their branches safely,
but those that fight the tempest perish utterly.
The man who keeps the sheet[3] of his sail tight
and never slackens capsizes his boat
770   and makes the rest of his trip keel uppermost.
Yield something of your anger, give way a little.
If a much younger man, like me, may have
a judgment, I would say it were far better
to be one altogether wise by nature, but,
775   as things incline not to be so, then it is good
also to learn from those who advise well.
CHORUS: My lord, if he says anything to the point,

_____

3. Rope attached to the corner of a sail to hold it at the proper angle to the wind.

you should learn from him, and you, too, Haemon,
learn from your father. Both of you
have spoken well.   780
CREON: Should we that are my age learn wisdom
from young men such as he is?
HAEMON: Not learn injustice, certainly. If I am young,
do not look at my years but what I do.
CREON: Is what you do to have respect for rebels?
HAEMON: I   785
would not urge you to be scrupulous
towards the wicked.
CREON: Is *she* not tainted by the disease of wickedness?
HAEMON: The entire people of Thebes says no to that.
CREON: Should the city tell me how I am to rule them?   790
HAEMON: Do you see what a young man's words these are of yours?
CREON: Must I rule the land by someone else's judgment
rather than my own?
HAEMON: There is no city
possessed by one man only.
CREON: Is not the city thought to be the ruler's?   795
HAEMON: You would be a fine dictator of a desert.
CREON: It seems this boy is on the woman's side.
HAEMON: If you are a woman—my care is all for you.
CREON: You villain, to bandy words with your own father!
HAEMON: I see your acts as mistaken and unjust.   800
CREON: Am I mistaken, reverencing my own office?
HAEMON: There is no reverence in trampling on God's honor.
CREON: Your nature is vile, in yielding to a woman.
HAEMON: You will not find me yield to what is shameful.
CREON: At least, your argument is all for her.   805
HAEMON: Yes, and for you and me—and for the gods below.
CREON: You will never marry her while her life lasts.
HAEMON: Then she must die—and dying destroy another.
CREON: Has your daring gone so far, to threaten me?
HAEMON: What threat is it to speak against empty judgments?   810
CREON: Empty of sense yourself, you will regret
your schooling of me in sense.
HAEMON: If you were not
my father, I would say you are insane.
CREON: You woman's slave, do not try to wheedle me.
HAEMON: You want to talk but never to hear and listen.   815
CREON: Is that so? By the heavens above you will not—
be sure of that—get off scot-free, insulting,
abusing me.

[He speaks to the SERVANTS.*]*

You people bring out this creature,
this hated creature, that she may die before
820   his very eyes, right now, next her would-be husband.
HAEMON: Not at my side! Never think that! She will not
die by my side. But you will never again
set eyes upon my face. Go then and rage
with such of your friends as are willing to endure it.
825 CHORUS: The man is gone, my lord, quick in his anger.
A young man's mind is fierce when he is hurt.
CREON: Let him go, and do and think things superhuman.
But these two girls he shall not save from death.
CHORUS: Both of them? Do you mean to kill them both?
830 CREON: No, not the one that didn't do anything.
You are quite right there.
CHORUS: And by what form of death do you mean to kill her?
CREON: I will bring her where the path is loneliest,
and hide her alive in a rocky cavern there.
835   I'll give just enough of food as shall suffice
for a bare expiation, that the city may avoid pollution.
In that place she shall call on Hades, god of death,
in her prayers. That god only she reveres.
Perhaps she will win from him escape from death
840   or at least in that last moment will recognize
her honoring of the dead is labor lost.
CHORUS: Love undefeated in the fight,
    Love that makes havoc of possessions,
    Love who lives at night in a young girl's soft cheeks,
845   Who travels over sea, or in huts in the countryside—
    there is no god able to escape you
    nor anyone of men, whose life is a day only,
    and whom you possess is mad.

    You wrench the minds of just men to injustice,
850   to their disgrace; this conflict among kinsmen
    it is you who stirred to turmoil.
    The winner is desire. She gleaming kindles
    from the eyes of the girl good to bed.
    Love shares the throne with the great powers that rule.
855   For the golden Aphrodite[4] holds her play there
    and then no one can overcome her.

---

4. Goddess of love and beauty.

Here I too am borne out of the course of lawfulness
when I see these things, and I cannot control
the springs of my tears
when I see Antigone making her way   860
to her bed—but the bed
that is rest for everyone.

ANTIGONE: You see me, you people of my country,
as I set out on my last road of all,
looking for the last time on this light of this sun—   865
never again. I am alive but Hades who gives sleep to everyone
is leading me to the shores of Acheron,⁵
though I have known nothing of marriage songs
nor the chant that brings the bride to bed.
My husband is to be the Lord of Death.   870

CHORUS: Yes, you go to the place where the dead are hidden,
but you go with distinction and praise.
You have not been stricken by wasting sickness;
you have not earned the wages of the sword;
it was your own choice and alone among mankind   875
you will descend, alive,
to that world of death.

ANTIGONE: But indeed I have heard of the saddest of deaths—
of the Phrygian stranger,⁶ daughter of Tantalus,
whom the rocky growth subdued, like clinging ivy.   880
The rains never leave her, the snow never fails,
as she wastes away. That is how men tell the story.
From streaming eyes her tears wet the crags;
most like to her the god brings me to rest.

CHORUS: Yes, but she was a god, and god born,   885
and you are mortal and mortal born.
Surely it is great renown
for a woman that dies, that in life and death
her lot is a lot shared with demigods.

ANTIGONE: You mock me. In the name of our fathers' gods   890
why do you not wait till I am gone to insult me?
Must you do it face to face?
My city! Rich citizens of my city!
You springs of Dirce, you holy groves of Thebes,
famed for its chariots! I would still have you as my witnesses,   895
with what dry-eyed friends, under what laws

---

5. River in Hades.
6. Niobe, whose children were slain because of her boastfulness and who was herself turned into a stone on Mount Siphylus. Her tears became the mountain's streams.

I make my way to my prison sealed like a tomb.
Pity me. Neither among the living nor the dead
do I have a home in common—
900   neither with the living nor the dead.
CHORUS: You went to the extreme of daring
and against the high throne of Justice
you fell, my daughter, grievously.
But perhaps it was for some ordeal of your father
905   that you are paying requital.
ANTIGONE: You have touched the most painful of my cares—
the pity for my father, ever reawakened,
and the fate of all of our race, the famous Labdacids;
the doomed self-destruction of my mother's bed
910   when she slept with her own son,
my father.
What parents I was born of, God help me!
To them I am going to share their home,
the curse on me, too, and unmarried.
915   Brother, it was a luckless marriage you made,
and dying killed my life.
CHORUS: There *is* a certain reverence for piety.
But for him in authority,
he cannot see that authority defied;
920   it is your own self-willed temper
that has destroyed you.
ANTIGONE: No tears for me, no friends, no marriage. Brokenhearted
I am led along the road ready before me.
I shall never again be suffered
925   to look on the holy eye of the day.
But my fate claims no tears—
no friend cries for me.
CREON: [*To the* SERVANTS.] Don't you know that weeping and wailing before
       death
would never stop if one is allowed to weep and wail?
930   Lead her away at once. Enfold her
in that rocky tomb of hers—as I told you to.
There leave her alone, solitary,
to die if she so wishes
or live a buried life in such a home;
935   we are guiltless in respect of her, this girl.
But living above, among the rest of us, this life
she shall certainly lose.
ANTIGONE: Tomb, bridal chamber, prison forever
dug in rock, it is to you I am going

to join my people, that great number that have died, 940
whom in their death Persephone⁷ received.
I am the last of them and I go down
in the worst death of all—for I have not lived
the due term of my life. But when I come
to that other world my hope is strong 945
that my coming will be welcome to my father,
and dear to you, my mother, and dear to you,
my brother deeply loved. For when you died,
with my own hands I washed and dressed you all,
and poured the lustral offerings on your graves. 950
And now, Polyneices, it was for such care of your body
that I have earned these wages.
Yet those who think rightly will think I did right
in honoring you. Had I been a mother
of children, and my husband been dead and rotten, 955
I would not have taken this weary task upon me
against the will of the city. What law backs me
when I say this? I will tell you:
If my husband were dead, I might have had another,
and child from another man, if I lost the first. 960
But when father and mother both were hidden in death
no brother's life would bloom for me again.
That is the law under which I gave you precedence,
my dearest brother, and that is why Creon thinks me
wrong, even a criminal, and now takes me 965
by the hand and leads me away,
unbedded, without bridal, without share
in marriage and in nurturing of children;
as lonely as you see me; without friends;
with fate against me I go to the vault of death 970
while still alive. What law of God have I broken?
Why should I still look to the gods in my misery?
Whom should I summon as ally? For indeed
because of piety I was called impious.
If this proceeding is good in the gods' eyes 975
I shall know my sin, once I have suffered.
But if Creon and his people are the wrongdoers
let their suffering be no worse than the injustice
they are meting out to me.

---

7. Abducted by Pluto (known to the Greeks as Hades), god of the underworld, who made her his queen.

980 CHORUS: It is the same blasts, the tempests of the soul,
    possess her.
  CREON: Then for this her guards,
    who are so slow, will find themselves in trouble.
  ANTIGONE: [*Cries out.*] Oh, that word has come
    very close to death.
985 CREON: I will not comfort you
    with hope that the sentence will not be accomplished.
  ANTIGONE: O my father's city, in Theban land,
    O gods that sired my race,
    I am led away, I have no more stay.
990   Look on me, princes of Thebes,
    the last remnant of the old royal line;
    see what I suffer and who makes me suffer
    because I gave reverence to what claims reverence.
  CHORUS: Danae suffered, too, when, her beauty lost, she gave
995   the light of heaven in exchange for brassbound walls,
    and in the tomb-like cell was she hidden and held;
    yet she was honored in her breeding, child,
    and she kept, as guardian, the seed of Zeus
    that came to her in a golden shower.[8]
1000   But there is some terrible power in destiny
    and neither wealth nor war
    nor tower nor black ships, beaten by the sea,
    can give escape from it.

    The hot-tempered son of Dryas,[9] the Edonian king,
1005   in fury mocked Dionysus,
    who then held him in restraint
    in a rocky dungeon.
    So the terrible force and flower of his madness
    drained away. He came to know the god
1010   whom in frenzy he had touched with his mocking tongue,
    when he would have checked the inspired women
    and the fire of Dionysus,
    when he provoked the Muses[1] that love the lyre.
    By the black rocks, dividing the sea in two,
1015   are the shores of the Bosporus, Thracian Salmydessus.[2]

---

8. Danae was locked away because it was prophesized that her son would kill her father. Zeus entered her cell as a shower of gold, impregnated her, and thus fathered Perseus, the child who fulfilled the prophecy. 9. Stricken with madness by Dionysus.
1. Nine sister goddesses of poetry, music, and the arts.
2. City in the land of Thrace, in ancient times erroneously believed to lie on the Bosporus, the strait separating Europe and Asia at the outlet of the Black Sea.

There the god of war who lives near the city
saw the terrible blinding wound
dealt by his savage wife
on Phineus' two sons.[3]
She blinded and tore with the points of her shuttle,   1020
and her bloodied hands, those eyes
that else would have looked on her vengefully.
As they wasted away, they lamented
their unhappy fate that they were doomed
to be born of a mother cursed in her marriage.   1025
She traced her descent from the seed
of the ancient Erechtheidae.
In far-distant caves she was raised
among her father's storms, that child of Boreas[4]
quick as a horse, over the steep hills,   1030
a daughter of the gods.
But, my child, the long-lived Fates[5]
bore hard upon her, too.

[*Enter* TEIRESIAS, *the blind prophet, led by a* BOY.]

TEIRESIAS: My lords of Thebes, we have come here together,
one pair of eyes serving us both. For the blind   1035
such must be the way of going, by a guide's leading.
CREON: What is the news, my old Teiresias?
TEIRESIAS: I will tell you; and you, listen to the prophet.
CREON: Never in the past have I turned from your advice.
TEIRESIAS: And so you have steered well the ship of state.   1040
CREON: I have benefited and can testify to that.
TEIRESIAS: Then realize you are on the razor edge
of danger.
CREON: What can that be? I shudder to hear those words.
TEIRESIAS: When you learn the signs recognized by my art   1045
you will understand.
I sat at my ancient place of divination
for watching the birds, where every bird finds shelter;
and I heard an unwonted voice among them;
they were horribly distressed, and screamed unmeaningly.   1050
I knew they were tearing each other murderously;
the beating of their wings was a clear sign.

---

3. King Phineus's second wife blinded the children of his first wife, whom Phineus had imprisoned in a cave.   4. God of the cold north wind, who sometimes took the form of a stallion.
5. Supernatural forces, usually represented as three old women, who determine the quality and length of life.

I was full of fear; at once on all the altars,
as they were fully kindled, I tasted the offerings,
1055 but the god of fire refused to burn from the sacrifice,
and from the thighbones a dark stream of moisture
oozed from the embers, smoked and sputtered.
The gall bladder burst and scattered to the air
and the streaming thighbones lay exposed
1060 from the fat wrapped round them—
so much I learned from this boy here,
the fading prophecies of a rite that failed.
This boy here is my guide, as I am others'.
This is the city's sickness—and your plans are the cause of it.
1065 For our altars and our sacrificial hearths
are filled with the carrion meat of birds and dogs,
torn from the flesh of Oedipus' poor son.
So the gods will not take our prayers or sacrifice
nor yet the flame from the thighbones, and no bird
1070 cries shrill and clear, so glutted
are they with fat of the blood of the killed man.
Reflect on these things, son. All men
can make mistakes; but, once mistaken,
a man is no longer stupid nor accursed
1075 who, having fallen on ill, tries to cure that ill,
not taking a fine undeviating stand.
It is obstinacy that convicts of folly.
Yield to the dead man; do not stab him—
now he is gone—what bravery is this,
1080 to inflict another death upon the dead?
I mean you well and speak well for your good.
It is never sweeter to learn from a good counselor
than when he counsels to your benefit.
CREON: Old man, you are all archers, and I am your mark.
1085 I must be tried by your prophecies as well.
By the breed of you I have been bought and sold
and made a merchandise, for ages now.
But I tell you: make your profit from silver-gold
from Sardis[6] and the gold from India
1090 if you will. But this dead man you shall not hide
in a grave, not though the eagles of Zeus should bear
the carrion, snatching it to the throne of Zeus itself.
Even so, I shall not so tremble at the pollution

---

6. Capital of the ancient kingdom of Lydia, part of modern-day Turkey; it was an important trading center, famed for its wealth.

to let you bury him.
        No, I am certain
no human has the power to pollute the gods.   1095
They fall, you old Teiresias, those men,
—so very clever—in a bad fall whenever
they eloquently speak vile words for profit.
TEIRESIAS: I wonder if there's a man who dares consider—
CREON: What do you mean? What sort of generalization   1100
is this talk of yours?
TEIRESIAS: How much the best of possessions is the ability
to listen to wise advice?
CREON: As I should imagine that the worst
injury must be native stupidity.   1105
TEIRESIAS: Now that is exactly where your mind is sick.
CREON: I do not like to answer a seer with insults.
TEIRESIAS: But you do, when you say my prophecies are lies.
CREON: Well,
the whole breed of prophets certainly loves money.   1110
TEIRESIAS: And the breed that comes from princes loves to take
advantage—base advantage.
CREON: Do you realize
you are speaking in such terms of your own prince?
TEIRESIAS: I know. But it is through me you have saved the city.
CREON: You are a wise prophet, but what you love is wrong.   1115
TEIRESIAS: You will force me to declare what should be hidden
in my own heart.
CREON: Out with it—
but only if your words are not for gain.
TEIRESIAS: They won't be for *your* gain—that I am sure of.
CREON: But realize you will not make a merchandise   1120
of my decisions.
TEIRESIAS: And you must realize
that you will not outlive many cycles more
of this swift sun before you give in exchange
one of your own loins bred, a corpse for a corpse,
for you have thrust one that belongs above   1125
below the earth, and bitterly dishonored
a living soul by lodging her in the grave;
while one that belonged indeed to the underworld
gods you have kept on this earth without due share
of rites of burial, of due funeral offerings,   1130
a corpse unhallowed. With all of this you, Creon,
have nothing to do, nor have the gods above.
These acts of yours are violence, on your part.

And in requital the avenging Spirits
1135   of Death itself and the gods' Furies shall
after *your* deeds, lie in ambush for you, and
in their hands you shall be taken cruelly.
Now, look at this and tell me I was bribed
to say it! The delay will not be long
1140   before the cries of mourning in your house,
of men and women. All the cities will stir in hatred
against you, because their sons in mangled shreds
received their burial rites from dogs, from wild beasts
or when some bird of the air brought a vile stink
1145   to each city that contained the hearths of the dead.
These are the arrows that archer-like I launched—
you vexed me so to anger—at your heart.
You shall not escape their sting. You, boy,
lead me away to my house, so he may discharge
1150   his anger on younger men; so may he come to know
to bear a quieter tongue in his head and a better
mind than that now he carries in him.
CHORUS: That was a terrible prophecy, my lord.
The man has gone. Since these hairs of mine grew white
1155   from the black they once were, he has never spoken
a word of a lie to our city.
CREON: I know, I know.
My mind is all bewildered. To yield is terrible.
But by opposition to destroy my very being
1160   with a self-destructive curse must also be reckoned
in what is terrible.
CHORUS: You need good counsel, son of Menoeceus,
and need to take it.
CREON: What must I do, then? Tell me; I shall agree.
1165 CHORUS: The girl—go now and bring her up from her cave,
and for the exposed dead man, give him his burial.
CREON: That is really your advice? You would have me yield.
CHORUS: And quickly as you may, my lord. Swift harms
sent by the gods cut off the paths of the foolish.
1170 CREON: Oh, it is hard; I must give up what my heart
would have me do. But it is ill to fight
against what must be.
CHORUS: Go now, and do this;
do not give the task to others.
1175 CREON: I will go,
just as I am. Come, servants, all of you;
take axes in your hands; away with you
to the place you see, there.

For my part, since my intention is so changed,
as I bound her myself, myself will free her.   1180
I am afraid it may be best, in the end
of life, to have kept the old accepted laws.
CHORUS: You of many names,[7] glory of the Cadmeian
bride, breed of loud thundering Zeus;
you who watch over famous Italy;   1185
you who rule where all are welcome in Eleusis;
in the sheltered plains of Deo—
O Bacchus that dwells in Thebes,
the mother city of Bacchanals,
by the flowing stream of Ismenus,   1190
in the ground sown by the fierce dragon's teeth.

You are he on whom the murky gleam of torches glares,
above the twin peaks of the crag
where come the Corycean nymphs
to worship you, the Bacchanals;   1195
and the stream of Castalia has seen you, too;
and you are he that the ivy-clad
slopes of Nisaean hills,
and the green shore ivy-clustered,
sent to watch over the roads of Thebes,   1200
where the immortal Evoe chant[8] rings out.

It is Thebes which you honor most of all cities,
you and your mother both,
she who died by the blast of Zeus' thunderbolt.
And now when the city, with all its folk,   1205
is gripped by a violent plague,
come with healing foot, over the slopes of Parnassus,[9]
over the moaning strait.
You lead the dance of the fire-breathing stars,
you are master of the voices of the night.   1210
True-born child of Zeus, appear,
my lord, with your Thyiad attendants,
who in frenzy all night long
dance in your house, Iacchus,
dispenser of gifts.   1215

---

7. Refers to Dionysus, known also as Bacchus (especially to the later Romans); his father was Zeus
and his mortal mother, Semele, was a princess of Thebes. As god of wine, Dionysus presided over
frenzied rites known as Bacchanals.   8. Come forth, come forth!
9. Mountain in central Greece sacred to Apollo, Dionysus, and the Muses; Apollo's shrine, Delphi, lies at the foot of Parnassus.

MESSENGER: You who live by the house of Cadmus and Amphion,[1]
hear me. There is no condition of man's life
that stands secure. As such I would not
praise it or blame. It is chance that sets upright;
1220   it is chance that brings down the lucky and the unlucky,
each in his turn. For men, that belong to death,
there is no prophet of established things.
Once Creon was a man worthy of envy—
of my envy, at least. For he saved this city
1225   of Thebes from her enemies, and attained
the throne of the land, with all a king's power.
He guided it right. His race bloomed
with good children. But when a man forfeits joy
I do not count his life as life, but only
1230   a life trapped in a corpse.
Be rich within your house, yes greatly rich,
if so you will, and live in a prince's style.
If the gladness of these things is gone, I would not
give the shadow of smoke for the rest,
1235   as against joy.
CHORUS: What is the sorrow of our princes
of which you are the messenger?
MESSENGER: Death; and the living are guilty of their deaths.
CHORUS: But who is the murderer? Who the murdered? Tell us.
1240 MESSENGER: Haemon is dead; the hand that shed his blood
was his very own.
CHORUS: Truly his own hand? Or his father's?
MESSENGER: His own hand, in his anger
against his father for a murder.
1245 CHORUS: Prophet, how truly you have made good your word!
MESSENGER: These things are so; you may debate the rest.
Here I see Creon's wife Eurydice
approaching. Unhappy woman!
Does she come from the house as hearing about her son
1250   or has she come by chance?
EURYDICE: I heard your words, all you men of Thebes, as I
was going out to greet Pallas[2] with my prayers.
I was just drawing back the bolts of the gate
to open it when a cry struck through my ears
1255   telling of my household's ruin. I fell backward
in terror into the arms of my servants; I fainted.
But tell me again, what is the story? I

---

1. A name for Thebes.   2. Athena, goddess of wisdom.

will hear it as one who is no stranger to sorrow.
MESSENGER: Dear mistress, I will tell you, for I was there,
and I will leave out no word of the truth.   1260
Why should I comfort you and then tomorrow
be proved a liar? The truth is always best.
I followed your husband, at his heels, to the end of the plain
where Polyneices' body still lay unpitied,
and torn by dogs. We prayed to Hecate, goddess   1265
of the crossroads, and also to Pluto³
that they might restrain their anger and turn kind.
And him we washed with sacred lustral water
and with fresh-cut boughs we burned what was left of him
and raised a high mound of his native earth;   1270
then we set out again for the hollowed rock,
death's stone bridal chamber for the girl.
Someone then heard a voice of bitter weeping
while we were still far off, coming from that unblest room.
The man came to tell our master Creon of it.   1275
As the king drew nearer, there swarmed about him
a cry of misery but no clear words.
He groaned and in an anguished mourning voice
cried "Oh, am I a true prophet? Is this the road
that I must travel, saddest of all my wayfaring?   1280
It is my son's voice that haunts my ear. Servants,
get closer, quickly. Stand around the tomb
and look. There is a gap there where the stones
have been wrenched away; enter there, by the very mouth,
and see whether I recognize the voice of Haemon   1285
or if the gods deceive me." On the command
of our despairing master we went to look.
In the furthest part of the tomb we saw her, hanging
by her neck. She had tied a noose of muslin on it.
Haemon's hands were about her waist embracing her,   1290
while he cried for the loss of his bride gone to the dead,
and for all his father had done, and his own sad love.
When Creon saw him he gave a bitter cry,
went in and called to him with a groan: "Poor son!
what have you done? What can you have meant?   1295
What happened to destroy you? Come out, I pray you!"
The boy glared at him with savage eyes, and then
spat in his face, without a word of answer.
He drew his double-hilted sword. As his father

---

3. King of the underworld, known to the Greeks as Hades. *Hecate:* goddess of witchcraft.

1300 ran to escape him, Haemon failed to strike him,
and the poor wretch in anger at himself
leaned on his sword and drove it halfway in,
into his ribs. Then he folded the girl to him,
in his arms, while he was conscious still,
1305 and gasping poured a sharp stream of bloody drops
on her white cheeks. There they lie,
the dead upon the dead. So he has won
the pitiful fulfillment of his marriage
within death's house. In this human world he has shown
1310 how the wrong choice in plans is for a man
his greatest evil.
CHORUS: What do you make of this? My lady is gone,
without a word of good or bad.
MESSENGER: I, too,
am lost in wonder. I am inclined to hope
1315 that hearing of her son's death she could not
open her sorrow to the city, but chose rather
within her house to lay upon her maids
the mourning for the household grief. Her judgment
is good; she will not make any false step.
1320 CHORUS: I do not know. To me this over-heavy silence
seems just as dangerous as much empty wailing.
MESSENGER: I will go in and learn if in her passionate
heart she keeps hidden some secret purpose.
You are right; there is sometimes danger in too much silence.
1325 CHORUS: Here comes our king himself. He bears in his hands
a memorial all too clear;
it is a ruin of none other's making,
purely his own if one dare to say that.
CREON: The mistakes of a blinded man
1330 are themselves rigid and laden with death.
You look at us the killer and the killed
of the one blood. Oh, the awful blindness
of those plans of mine. My son, you were so young,
so young to die. You were freed from the bonds of life
1335 through no folly of your own—only through mine.
CHORUS: I think you have learned justice—but too late.
CREON: Yes, I have learned it to my bitterness. At this moment
God has sprung on my head with a vast weight
and struck me down. He shook me in my savage ways;
1340 he has overturned my joy, has trampled it,
underfoot. The pains men suffer
are pains indeed.

SECOND MESSENGER: My lord, you have troubles and a store besides;
  some are there in your hands, but there are others
  you will surely see when you come to your house.   1345
CREON: What trouble can there be beside these troubles?
SECOND MESSENGER: The queen is dead. She was indeed true mother
  of the dead son. She died, poor lady,
  by recent violence upon herself.
CREON: Haven of death, you can never have enough.   1350
  Why, why do you destroy me?
  You messenger, who have brought me bitter news,
  what is this tale you tell?
  It is a dead man that you kill again—
  what new message of yours is this, boy?   1355
  Is this new slaughter of a woman
  a doom to lie on the pile of the dead?
CHORUS: You can see. It is no longer
  hidden in a corner.

[*By some stage device, perhaps the so-called eccyclema,*[4] *the inside of the palace
  is shown, with the body of the dead* QUEEN.]

CREON: Here is yet another horror   1360
  for my unhappy eyes to see.
  What doom still waits for me?
  I have but now taken in my arms my son,
  and again I look upon another dead face.
  Poor mother and poor son!   1365
SECOND MESSENGER: She stood at the altar, and with keen whetted knife
  she suffered her darkening eyes to close.
  First she cried in agony recalling the noble fate of Megareus,[5]
  who died before all this,
  and then for the fate of this son; and in the end   1370
  she cursed you for the evil you had done
  in killing her sons.
CREON: I am distracted with fear. Why does not someone
  strike a two-edged sword right through me?
  I am dissolved in an agony of misery.   1375
SECOND MESSENGER: You were indeed accused
  by her that is dead
  of Haemon's and of Megareus' death.
CREON: By what kind of violence did she find her end?
SECOND MESSENGER: Her own hand struck her to the entrails   1380

---

4. Wheeled platform rolled forward onto the stage to depict interior scenes; often used in tragedies to reveal dead bodies.   5. Another son of Creon who died defending Thebes.

when she heard of her son's lamentable death.

CREON: These acts can never be made to fit another
to free me from the guilt. It was I that killed her.
Poor wretch that I am, I say it is true!

1385 Servants, lead me away, quickly, quickly.
I am no more a live man than one dead.

CHORUS: What you say is for the best—if there be a best
in evil such as this. For the shortest way
is best with troubles that lie at our feet.

1390 CREON: O, let it come, let it come,
that best of fates that waits on my last day.
Surely best fate of all. Let it come, let it come!
That I may never see one more day's light!

CHORUS: These things are for the future. We must deal

1395 with what impends. What in the future is to care for
rests with those whose duty it is
to care for them.

CREON: At least, all that *I* want
is in that prayer of mine.

1400 CHORUS: Pray for no more at all. For what is destined
for us, men mortal, there is no escape.

CREON: Lead me away, a vain silly man
who killed you, son, and you, too, lady.
I did not mean to, but I did.

1405 I do not know where to turn my eyes
to look to, for support.
Everything in my hands is crossed. A most unwelcome fate
has leaped upon me.

CHORUS: Wisdom is far the chief element in happiness

1410 and, secondly, no irreverence towards the gods.
But great words of haughty men exact
in retribution blows as great
and in old age teach wisdom.

THE END

ca. 441 B.C.E.

TENNESSEE WILLIAMS

A Streetcar Named Desire

And so it was I entered the broken
world
To trace the visionary company of
love, its voice
An instant in the wind (I know not
whither hurled)
But not for long to hold each desperate choice.

—"THE BROKEN TOWER" BY HART
CRANE[1]

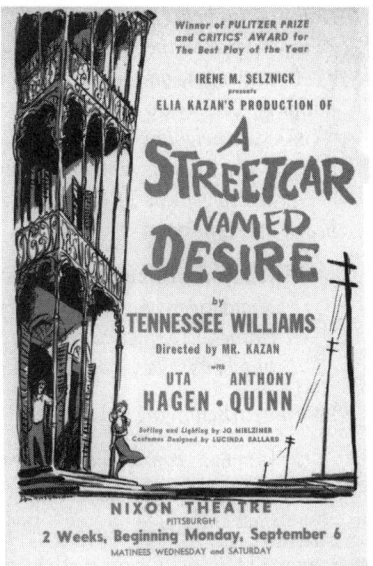

CHARACTERS

BLANCHE	EUNICE	A DOCTOR
STELLA	STEVE	A NURSE (MATRON)
STANLEY	PABLO	A YOUNG COLLECTOR
MITCH	A NEGRO WOMAN	A MEXICAN WOMAN

Scene 1

The exterior of a two-story corner building on a street in New Orleans which is
named Elysian Fields and runs between the L & N tracks and the river.[2] The section
is poor but, unlike corresponding sections in other American cities, it has a raffish
charm. The houses are mostly white frame, weathered grey, with rickety outside
stairs and galleries and quaintly ornamented gables. This building contains two flats,
upstairs and down. Faded white stairs ascend to the entrances of both.

It is first dark of an evening early in May. The sky that shows around the dim white
building is a peculiarly tender blue, almost a turquoise, which invests the scene with a
kind of lyricism and gracefully attenuates the atmosphere of decay. You can almost
feel the warm breath of the brown river beyond the river warehouses with their faint
redolences of bananas and coffee. A corresponding air is evoked by the music of
Negro entertainers at a barroom around the corner. In this part of New Orleans you
are practically always just around the corner, or a few doors down the street, from a

---

1. American poet (1899–1932).
2. Elysian Fields is in fact a New Orleans street at the northern tip of the French Quarter, between
the Louisville & Nashville railroad tracks and the Mississippi River. In Greek mythology, the Elysian Fields are the abode of the blessed in the afterlife; in Paris, the Champs-Élysées ("Elysian
Fields") is a grand boulevard.

tinny piano being played with the infatuated fluency of brown fingers. This "Blue Piano" expresses the spirit of the life which goes on here.

Two women, one white and one colored, are taking the air on the steps of the building. The white woman is EUNICE, *who occupies the upstairs flat; the* NEGRO WOMAN, *a neighbor, for New Orleans is a cosmopolitan city where there is a relatively warm and easy intermingling of races in the old part of town.*

Above the music of the "Blue Piano" the voices of people on the street can be heard overlapping.

[*Two men come around the corner,* STANLEY KOWALSKI *and* MITCH. *They are about twenty-eight, or thirty years old, roughly dressed in blue denim work clothes.* STANLEY *carries his bowling jacket and a red-stained package from a butcher's. They stop at the foot of the steps.*]

STANLEY: [*Bellowing.*] Hey there! Stella, baby!

[STELLA *comes out on the first floor landing, a gentle young woman, about twenty-five, and of a background obviously quite different from her husband's.*]

STELLA: [*Mildly.*] Don't holler at me like that. Hi, Mitch.

STANLEY: Catch!

STELLA: What?

STANLEY: Meat!

[*He heaves the package at her. She cries out in protest but manages to catch it: then she laughs breathlessly. Her husband and his companion have already started back around the corner.*]

STELLA: [*Calling after him.*] Stanley! Where are you going?

STANLEY: Bowling!

STELLA: Can I come watch?

STANLEY: Come on. [*He goes out.*]

STELLA: Be over soon. [*To the* WHITE WOMAN.] Hello, Eunice. How are you?

EUNICE: I'm all right. Tell Steve to get him a poor boy's sandwich[3] 'cause nothing's left here.

[*They all laugh; the* NEGRO WOMAN *does not stop.* STELLA *goes out.*]

NEGRO WOMAN: What was that package he th'ew at 'er? [*She rises from steps, laughing louder.*]

EUNICE: You hush, now!

NEGRO WOMAN: Catch *what*!

[*She continues to laugh.* BLANCHE *comes around the corner, carrying a valise. She looks at a slip of paper, then at the building, then again at the slip and again*]

---

3. Usually called just "poor boy" or "po' boy"; similar to a hero or submarine sandwich.

at the building. Her expression is one of shocked disbelief. Her appearance is incongruous to this setting. She is daintily dressed in a white suit with a fluffy bodice, necklace and earrings of pearl, white gloves and hat, looking as if she were arriving at a summer tea or cocktail party in the garden district.[4] *She is about five years older than* STELLA. *Her delicate beauty must avoid a strong light. There is something about her uncertain manner, as well as her white clothes, that suggests a moth.*]

EUNICE: [*Finally.*] What's the matter, honey? Are you lost?

BLANCHE: [*With faintly hysterical humor.*] They told me to take a street-car named Desire, and then transfer to one called Cemeteries[5] and ride six blocks and get off at—Elysian Fields!

EUNICE: That's where you are now.

BLANCHE: At Elysian Fields?

EUNICE: This here is Elysian Fields.

BLANCHE: They mustn't have—understood—what number I wanted. . . .

EUNICE: What number you lookin' for?

[BLANCHE *wearily refers to the slip of paper.*]

BLANCHE: Six thirty-two.

EUNICE: You don't have to look no further.

BLANCHE: [*Uncomprehendingly.*] I'm looking for my sister, Stella DuBois, I mean—Mrs. Stanley Kowalski.

EUNICE: That's the party.—You just did miss her, though.

BLANCHE: This—can this be—her home?

EUNICE: She's got the downstairs here and I got the up.

BLANCHE: Oh. She's—out?

EUNICE: You noticed that bowling alley around the corner?

BLANCHE: I'm—not sure I did.

EUNICE: Well, that's where she's at, watchin' her husband bowl. [*There is a pause.*] You want to leave your suitcase here an' go find her?

BLANCHE: No.

NEGRO WOMAN: I'll go tell her you come.

BLANCHE: Thanks.

NEGRO WOMAN: You welcome. [*She goes out.*]

EUNICE: She wasn't expecting you?

BLANCHE: No. No, not tonight.

EUNICE: Well, why don't you just go in and make yourself at home till they get back.

BLANCHE: How could I—do that?

EUNICE: We own this place so I can let you in.

---

4. Wealthy, fashionable section of New Orleans.

5. Desire is a street in New Orleans; Cemeteries is the end of a streetcar line that stopped at a cemetery.

[*She gets up and opens the downstairs door. A light goes on behind the blind, turning it light blue.* BLANCHE *slowly follows her into the downstairs flat. The surrounding areas dim out as the interior is lighted. Two rooms can be seen, not too clearly defined. The one first entered is primarily a kitchen but contains a folding bed to be used by* BLANCHE. *The room beyond this is a bedroom. Off this room is a narrow door to a bathroom.*]

EUNICE: [*Defensively, noticing* BLANCHE'*s look.*] It's sort of messed up right now but when it's clean it's real sweet.

BLANCHE: Is it?

EUNICE: Uh-huh, I think so. So you're Stella's sister?

BLANCHE: Yes. [*Wanting to get rid of her.*] Thanks for letting me in.

EUNICE: *Por nada,* as the Mexicans say, *por nada!*[6] Stella spoke of you.

BLANCHE: Yes?

EUNICE: I think she said you taught school.

BLANCHE: Yes.

EUNICE: And you're from Mississippi, huh?

BLANCHE: Yes.

EUNICE: She showed me a picture of your home-place, the plantation.

BLANCHE: Belle Reve?[7]

EUNICE: A great big place with white columns.

BLANCHE: Yes . . .

EUNICE: A place like that must be awful hard to keep up.

BLANCHE: If you will excuse me, I'm just about to drop.

EUNICE: Sure, honey. Why don't you set down?

BLANCHE: What I meant was I'd like to be left alone.

EUNICE: [*Offended.*] Aw. I'll make myself scarce, in that case.

BLANCHE: I didn't mean to be rude, but—

EUNICE: I'll drop by the bowling alley an' hustle her up. [*She goes out the door.*]

[BLANCHE *sits in a chair very stiffly with her shoulders slightly hunched and her legs pressed close together and her hands tightly clutching her purse as if she were quite cold. After a while the blind look goes out of her eyes and she begins to look slowly around. A cat screeches. She catches her breath with a startled gesture. Suddenly she notices something in a half opened closet. She springs up and crosses to it, and removes a whiskey bottle. She pours a half tumbler of whiskey and tosses it down. She carefully replaces the bottle and washes out the tumbler at the sink. Then she resumes her seat in front of the table.*]

BLANCHE: [*Faintly to herself.*] I've got to keep hold of myself!

[STELLA *comes quickly around the corner of the building and runs to the door of the downstairs flat.*]

6. It's nothing. 7. Beautiful Dream.

STELLA: [*Calling out joyfully.*] *Blanche!*

[*For a moment they stare at each other. Then* BLANCHE *springs up and runs to her with a wild cry.*]

BLANCHE: Stella, oh, Stella, Stella! Stella for Star!⁸ [*She begins to speak with feverish vivacity as if she feared for either of them to stop and think. They catch each other in a spasmodic embrace.*] Now, then, let me look at you. But don't you look at me, Stella, no, no, no, not till later, not till I've bathed and rested! And turn that over-light off! Turn that off! I won't be looked at in this merciless glare! [STELLA *laughs and complies.*] Come back here now! Oh, my baby! Stella! Stella for Star! [*She embraces her again.*] I thought you would never come back to this horrible place! What am I saying? I didn't mean to say that. I meant to be nice about it and say—Oh, what a convenient location and such—Ha-a-ha! Precious lamb! You haven't said a *word* to me.

STELLA: You haven't given me a chance to, honey! [*She laughs, but her glance at* BLANCHE *is a little anxious.*]

BLANCHE: Well, now you talk. Open your pretty mouth and talk while I look around for some liquor! I know you must have some liquor on the place! Where could it be, I wonder? Oh, I spy, I spy! [*She rushes to the closet and removes the bottle; she is shaking all over and panting for breath as she tries to laugh. The bottle nearly slips from her grasp.*]

STELLA: [*Noticing.*] Blanche, you sit down and let me pour the drinks. I don't know what we've got to mix with. Maybe a Coke in the icebox. Look'n see, honey, while I'm—

BLANCHE: No Coke, honey, not with my nerves tonight! Where—where—where is—?

STELLA: Stanley? Bowling! He loves it. They're having a—found some soda!—tournament. . . .

BLANCHE: Just water, baby, to chase it! Now don't get worried, your sister hasn't turned into a drunkard, she's just all shaken up and hot and tired and dirty! You sit down, now, and explain this place to me! What are you doing in a place like this?

STELLA: Now, Blanche—

BLANCHE: Oh, I'm not going to be hypocritical, I'm going to be honestly critical about it! Never, never, never in my worst dreams could I picture—Only Poe! Only Mr. Edgar Allan Poe!—could do it justice! Out there I suppose is the ghoul-haunted woodland of Weir!⁹ [*She laughs.*]

STELLA: No, honey, those are the L & N tracks.

BLANCHE: No, now seriously, putting joking aside. Why didn't you tell me, why didn't you write me, honey, why didn't you let me know?

STELLA: [*Carefully, pouring herself a drink.*] Tell you what, Blanche?

8. *Stella* is "star" in Latin.   9. From the refrain of Poe's gothic ballad "Ulalume" (1847).

BLANCHE: Why, that you had to live in these conditions!

STELLA: Aren't you being a little intense about it? It's not that bad at all! New Orleans isn't like other cities.

BLANCHE: This has got nothing to do with New Orleans. You might as well say—forgive me, blessed baby! [*She suddenly stops short.*] The subject is closed!

STELLA: [*A little drily.*] Thanks.

> [*During the pause,* BLANCHE *stares at her. She smiles at* BLANCHE.]

BLANCHE: [*Looking down at her glass, which shakes in her hand.*] You're all I've got in the world, and you're not glad to see me!

STELLA: [*Sincerely.*] Why, Blanche, you know that's not true.

BLANCHE: No?—I'd forgotten how quiet you were.

STELLA: You never did give me a chance to say much, Blanche. So I just got in the habit of being quiet around you.

BLANCHE: [*Vaguely.*] A good habit to get into . . . [*Then, abruptly.*] You haven't asked me how I happened to get away from the school before the spring term ended.

STELLA: Well, I thought you'd volunteer that information—if you wanted to tell me.

BLANCHE: You thought I'd been fired?

STELLA: No, I—thought you might have—resigned. . . .

BLANCHE: I was so exhausted by all I'd been through my—nerves broke. [*Nervously tamping cigarette.*] I was on the verge of—lunacy, almost! So Mr. Graves—Mr. Graves is the high school superintendent—he suggested I take a leave of absence. I couldn't put all of those details into the wire.[1] . . . [*She drinks quickly.*] Oh, this buzzes right through me and feels so *good*!

STELLA: Won't you have another?

BLANCHE: No, one's my limit.

STELLA: Sure?

BLANCHE: You haven't said a word about my appearance.

STELLA: You look just fine.

BLANCHE: God love you for a liar! Daylight never exposed so total a ruin! But you—you've put on some weight, yes, you're just as plump as a little partridge! And it's so becoming to you!

STELLA: Now, Blanche—

BLANCHE: Yes, it is, it is or I wouldn't say it! You just have to watch around the hips a little. Stand up.

STELLA: Not now.

BLANCHE: You hear me? I said stand up! [STELLA *complies reluctantly.*] You messy child, you, you've spilt something on that pretty white lace col-

---

1. Telegram.

lar! About your hair—you ought to have it cut in a feather bob with your dainty features. Stella, you have a maid, don't you?

STELLA: No. With only two rooms it's—

BLANCHE: What? *Two* rooms, did you say?

STELLA: This one and— [*She is embarrassed.*]

BLANCHE: The other one? [*She laughs sharply. There is an embarrassed silence.*] I am going to take just one little tiny nip more, sort of to put the stopper on, so to speak. . . . Then put the bottle away so I won't be tempted. [*She rises.*] I want you to look at *my* figure! [*She turns around.*] You know I haven't put on one ounce in ten years, Stella? I weigh what I weighed the summer you left Belle Reve. The summer Dad died and you left us. . . .

STELLA: [*A little wearily.*] It's just incredible, Blanche, how well you're looking.

BLANCHE: [*They both laugh uncomfortably.*] But, Stella, there's only two rooms, I don't see where you're going to put me!

STELLA: We're going to put you in here.

BLANCHE: What kind of bed's this—one of those collapsible things? [*She sits on it.*]

STELLA: Does it feel all right?

BLANCHE: [*Dubiously.*] Wonderful, honey. I don't like a bed that gives much. But there's no door between the two rooms, and Stanley—will it be decent?

STELLA: Stanley is Polish, you know.

BLANCHE: Oh, yes. They're something like Irish, aren't they?

STELLA: Well—

BLANCHE: Only not so—highbrow? [*They both laugh again in the same way.*] I brought some nice clothes to meet all your lovely friends in.

STELLA: I'm afraid you won't think they are lovely.

BLANCHE: What are they like?

STELLA: They're Stanley's friends.

BLANCHE: Polacks?

STELLA: They're a mixed lot, Blanche.

BLANCHE: Heterogeneous—types?

STELLA: Oh, yes. Yes, types is right!

BLANCHE: Well—anyhow—I brought nice clothes and I'll wear them. I guess you're hoping I'll say I'll put up at a hotel, but I'm not going to put up at a hotel. I want to be *near* you, got to be *with* somebody, I *can't* be *alone*! Because—as you must have noticed—I'm—*not* very *well*. . . . [*Her voice drops and her look is frightened.*]

STELLA: You seem a little bit nervous or overwrought or something.

BLANCHE: Will Stanley like me, or will I be just a visiting in-law, Stella? I couldn't stand that.

STELLA: You'll get along fine together, if you'll just try not to—well—compare him with men that we went out with at home.

BLANCHE: Is he so—different?

STELLA: Yes. A different species.

BLANCHE: In what way; what's he like?

STELLA: Oh, you can't describe someone you're in love with! Here's a picture of him! [*She hands a photograph to* BLANCHE.]

BLANCHE: An officer?

STELLA: A Master Sergeant in the Engineers' Corps. Those are decorations!

BLANCHE: He had those on when you met him?

STELLA: I assure you I wasn't just blinded by all the brass.

BLANCHE: That's not what I—

STELLA: But of course there were things to adjust myself to later on.

BLANCHE: Such as his civilian background! [STELLA *laughs uncertainly.*] How did he take it when you said I was coming?

STELLA: Oh, Stanley doesn't know yet.

BLANCHE: [*Frightened.*] You—haven't told him?

STELLA: He's on the road a good deal.

BLANCHE: Oh. Travels?

STELLA: Yes.

BLANCHE: Good. I mean—isn't it?

STELLA: [*Half to herself.*] I can hardly stand it when he is away for a night . . .

BLANCHE: Why, Stella!

STELLA: When he's away for a week I nearly go wild!

BLANCHE: Gracious!

STELLA: And when he comes back I cry on his lap like a baby. . . . [*She smiles to herself.*]

BLANCHE: I guess that is what is meant by being in love. . . . [STELLA *looks up with a radiant smile.*] Stella—

STELLA: What?

BLANCHE: [*In an uneasy rush.*] I haven't asked you the things you probably thought I was going to ask. And so I'll expect you to be understanding about what *I* have to tell *you.*

STELLA: What, Blanche? [*Her face turns anxious.*]

BLANCHE: Well, Stella—you're going to reproach me, I know that you're bound to reproach me—but before you do—take into consideration—you left! I stayed and struggled! You came to New Orleans and looked out for yourself! *I* stayed at Belle Reve and tried to hold it together! I'm not meaning this in any reproachful way, but *all* the burden descended on *my* shoulders.

STELLA: The best I could do was make my own living, Blanche.

[BLANCHE *begins to shake again with intensity.*]

BLANCHE: I know, I know. But you are the one that abandoned Belle Reve, not I! I stayed and fought for it, bled for it, almost died for it!

STELLA: Stop this hysterical outburst and tell me what's happened? What do you mean fought and bled? What kind of—
BLANCHE: I knew you would, Stella. I knew you would take this attitude about it!
STELLA: About—what?—please!
BLANCHE: [*Slowly.*] The loss—the loss . . .
STELLA: Belle Reve? Lost, is it? No!
BLANCHE: Yes, Stella.

[*They stare at each other across the yellow-checked linoleum of the table.* BLANCHE *slowly nods her head and* STELLA *looks slowly down at her hands folded on the table. The music of the "Blue Piano" grows louder.* BLANCHE *touches her handkerchief to her forehead.*]

STELLA: But how did it go? What happened?
BLANCHE: [*Springing up.*] You're a fine one to ask me how it went!
STELLA: Blanche!
BLANCHE: You're a fine one to sit there *accusing me* of it!
STELLA: *Blanche!*
BLANCHE: I, I, *I* took the blows in my face and my body! All of those deaths! The long parade to the graveyard! Father, Mother! Margaret, that dreadful way! So big with it, it couldn't be put in a coffin! But had to be burned like rubbish! You just came home in time for the funerals, Stella. And funerals are pretty compared to deaths. Funerals are quiet, but deaths—not always. Sometimes their breathing is hoarse, and sometimes it rattles, and sometimes they even cry out to you, "Don't let me go!" Even the old, sometimes, say, "Don't let me go." As if you were able to stop them! But funerals are quiet, with pretty flowers. And, oh, what gorgeous boxes they pack them away in! Unless you were there at the bed when they cried out, "Hold me!" you'd never suspect there was the struggle for breath and bleeding. You didn't dream, but I saw! *Saw! Saw!* And now you sit there telling me with your eyes that I let the place go! How in hell do you think all that sickness and dying was paid for? Death is expensive, Miss Stella! And old Cousin Jessie's right after Margaret's, hers! Why, the Grim Reaper[2] had put up his tent on our doorstep! . . . Stella. Belle Reve was his headquarters! Honey—that's how it slipped through my fingers! Which of them left us a fortune? Which of them left a cent of insurance even? Only poor Jessie—one hundred to pay for her coffin. That was all, Stella! And I with my pitiful salary at the school. Yes, accuse me! Sit there and stare at me, thinking I let the place go! *I* let the place go? Where were *you!* In bed with your—Polack!
STELLA: [*Springing.*] Blanche! You be still! That's enough! [*She starts out.*]
BLANCHE: Where are you going?

2. Death.

STELLA: I'm going into the bathroom to wash my face.
BLANCHE: Oh, Stella, Stella, you're crying!
STELLA: Does that surprise you?
BLANCHE: Forgive me—I didn't mean to—

[*The sound of men's voices is heard.* STELLA *goes into the bathroom, closing the door behind her. When the men appear, and* BLANCHE *realizes it must be* STANLEY *returning, she moves uncertainly from the bathroom door to the dressing table, looking apprehensively toward the front door.* STANLEY *enters, followed by* STEVE *and* MITCH. STANLEY *pauses near his door,* STEVE *by the foot of the spiral stair, and* MITCH *is slightly above and to the right of them, about to go out. As the men enter, we hear some of the following dialogue.*]

STANLEY: Is that how he got it?
STEVE: Sure that's how he got it. He hit the old weather-bird for 300 bucks on a six-number-ticket.³
MITCH: Don't tell him those things; he'll believe it. [MITCH *starts out.*]
STANLEY: [*Restraining* MITCH.] Hey, Mitch—come back here.

[BLANCHE, *at the sound of voices, retires in the bedroom. She picks up* STANLEY's *photo from dressing table, looks at it, puts it down. When* STANLEY *enters the apartment, she darts and hides behind the screen at the head of bed.*]

STEVE: [*To* STANLEY *and* MITCH.] Hey, are we playin' poker tomorrow?
STANLEY: Sure—at Mitch's.
MITCH: [*Hearing this, returns quickly to the stair rail.*] No—not at my place. My mother's still sick!
STANLEY: Okay, at my place . . . [MITCH *starts out again.*] But you bring the beer!

[MITCH *pretends not to hear—calls out "Good night, all," and goes out, singing.* EUNICE's *voice is heard, above.*]

EUNICE: Break it up down there! I made the spaghetti dish and ate it myself.
STEVE: [*Going upstairs.*] I told you and phoned you we was playing. [*To the men.*] Jax⁴ beer!
EUNICE: You never phoned me once.
STEVE: I told you at breakfast—and phoned you at lunch. . . .
EUNICE: Well, never mind about that. You just get yourself home here once in a while.
STEVE: You want it in the papers?

---

3. That is, he won $300 in a lottery. To "hit the weather-bird" in target shooting, means to shoot at a barn and hit the ornamental rooster on the weathervane—an extraordinarily lucky shot.
4. A local brand.

[*More laughter and shouts of parting come from the men.* STANLEY *throws the screen door of the kitchen open and comes in. He is of medium height, about five feet eight or nine, and strongly, compactly built. Animal joy in his being is implicit in all his movements and attitudes. Since earliest manhood the center of his life has been pleasure with women, the giving and taking of it, not with weak indulgence, dependently, but with the power and pride of a richly feathered male bird among hens. Branching out from this complete and satisfying center are all the auxiliary channels of his life, such as his heartiness with men, his appreciation of rough humor, his love of good drink and food and games, his car, his radio, everything that is his, that bears his emblem of the gaudy seed-bearer. He sizes women up at a glance, with sexual classifications, crude images flashing into his mind and determining the way he smiles at them.*]

BLANCHE: [*Drawing involuntarily back from his stare.*] You must be Stanley. I'm Blanche.

STANLEY: Stella's sister?

BLANCHE: Yes.

STANLEY: H'lo. Where's the little woman?

BLANCHE: In the bathroom.

STANLEY: Oh. Didn't know you were coming in town.

BLANCHE: I—uh—

STANLEY: Where you from, Blanche?

BLANCHE: Why, I—live in Laurel.

[*He has crossed to the closet and removed the whiskey bottle.*]

STANLEY: In Laurel, huh? Oh, yeah. Yeah, in Laurel, that's right. Not in my territory. Liquor goes fast in hot weather. [*He holds the bottle to the light to observe its depletion.*] Have a shot?

BLANCHE: No, I—rarely touch it.

STANLEY: Some people rarely touch it, but it touches them often.

BLANCHE: [*Faintly.*] Ha-ha.

STANLEY: My clothes're stickin' to me. Do you mind if I make myself comfortable?

[*He starts to remove his shirt.*]

BLANCHE: Please, please do.

STANLEY: Be comfortable is my motto.

BLANCHE: It's mine, too. It's hard to stay looking fresh. I haven't washed or even powdered my face and—here you are!

STANLEY: You know you can catch cold sitting around in damp things, especially when you been exercising hard like bowling is. You're a teacher, aren't you?

BLANCHE: Yes.

STANLEY: What do you teach, Blanche?

BLANCHE: English.

STANLEY: I never was a very good English student. How long you here for, Blanche?

BLANCHE: I—don't know yet.

STANLEY: You going to shack up here?

BLANCHE: I thought I would if it's not inconvenient for you all.

STANLEY: Good.

BLANCHE: Traveling wears me out.

STANLEY: Well, take it easy.

[*A cat screeches near the window.* BLANCHE *springs up.*]

BLANCHE: What's that?

STANLEY: Cats, . . . Hey, Stella!

STELLA: [*Faintly, from the bathroom.*] Yes, Stanley.

STANLEY: Haven't fallen in, have you? [*He grins at* BLANCHE. *She tries unsuccessfully to smile back. There is a silence.*] I'm afraid I'll strike you as being the unrefined type. Stella's spoke of you a good deal. You were married once, weren't you?

[*The music of the polka rises up, faint in the distance.*]

BLANCHE: Yes. When I was quite young.

STANLEY: What happened?

BLANCHE: The boy—the boy died. [*She sinks back down.*] I'm afraid I'm—going to be sick! [*Her head falls on her arms.*]

Scene 2

It is six o'clock the following evening. BLANCHE *is bathing.* STELLA *is completing her toilette.* BLANCHE*'s dress, a flowered print, is laid out on* STELLA*'s bed.*

STANLEY *enters the kitchen from outside, leaving the door open on the perpetual "Blue Piano" around the corner.*

STANLEY: What's all this monkey doings?

STELLA: Oh, Stan! [*She jumps up and kisses him, which he accepts with lordly composure.*] I'm taking Blanche to Galatoire's[5] for supper and then to a show, because it's your poker night.

STANLEY: How about my supper, huh? I'm not going to no Galatoire's for supper!

STELLA: I put you a cold plate on ice.

STANLEY: Well, isn't that just dandy!

STELLA: I'm going to try to keep Blanche out till the party breaks up because I don't know how she would take it. So we'll go to one of the little places in the Quarter afterward and you'd better give me some money.

5. A famous old restaurant on Bourbon Street, the principal street in the French Quarter.

STANLEY: Where is she?

STELLA: She's soaking in a hot tub to quiet her nerves. She's terribly upset.

STANLEY: Over what?

STELLA: She's been through such an ordeal.

STANLEY: Yeah?

STELLA: Stan, we've—lost Belle Reve!

STANLEY: The place in the country?

STELLA: Yes.

STANLEY: How?

STELLA: [*Vaguely.*] Oh, it had to be—sacrificed or something. [*There is a pause while* STANLEY *considers.* STELLA *is changing into her dress.*] When she comes in be sure to say something nice about her appearance. And, oh! Don't mention the baby. I haven't said anything yet, I'm waiting until she gets in a quieter condition.

STANLEY: [*Ominously.*] So?

STELLA: And try to understand her and be nice to her, Stan.

BLANCHE: [*Singing in the bathroom.*] "From the land of the sky blue water, They brought a captive maid!"[6]

STELLA: She wasn't expecting to find us in such a small place. You see I'd tried to gloss things over a little in my letters.

STANLEY: So?

STELLA: And admire her dress and tell her she's looking wonderful. That's important with Blanche. Her little weakness!

STANLEY: Yeah. I get the idea. Now let's skip back a little to where you said the country place was disposed of.

STELLA: Oh!—yes . . .

STANLEY: How about that? Let's have a few more details on that subjeck.

STELLA: It's best not to talk much about it until she's calmed down.

STANLEY: So that's the deal, huh? Sister Blanche cannot be annoyed with business details right now!

STELLA: You saw how she was last night.

STANLEY: Uh-hum, I saw how she was. Now let's have a gander at the bill of sale.

STELLA: I haven't seen any.

STANLEY: She didn't show you no papers, no deed of sale or nothing like that, huh?

STELLA: It seems like it wasn't sold.

STANLEY: Well, what in hell was it then, give away? To charity?

STELLA: Shhh! She'll hear you.

STANLEY: I don't care if she hears me. Let's see the papers!

---

6. From the song "From the Land of Sky-Blue Water" (1908), by Nelle Richmond Eberhart (1871–1944) and Charles Wakefield Cadman (1881–1946), popularized by the Andrews Sisters in the late 1930s.

STELLA: There weren't any papers, she didn't show any papers, I don't care about papers.

STANLEY: Have you ever heard of the Napoleonic code?[7]

STELLA: No, Stanley, I haven't heard of the Napoleonic code and if I have, I don't see what it—

STANLEY: Let me enlighten you on a point or two, baby.

STELLA: Yes?

STANLEY: In the state of Louisiana we have the Napoleonic code according to which what belongs to the wife belongs to the husband and vice versa. For instance if I had a piece of property, or you had a piece of property—

STELLA: My head is swimming!

STANLEY: All right. I'll wait till she gets through soaking in a hot tub and then I'll inquire if *she* is acquainted with the Napoleonic code. It looks to me like you have been swindled, baby, and when you're swindled under the Napoleonic code I'm swindled *too*. And I don't like to be *swindled.*

STELLA: There's plenty of time to ask her questions later but if you do now she'll go to pieces again. I don't understand what happened to Belle Reve but you don't know how ridiculous you are being when you suggest that my sister or I or anyone of our family could have perpetrated a swindle on anyone else.

STANLEY: Then where's the money if the place was sold?

STELLA: Not sold—*lost, lost!* [*He stalks into bedroom, and she follows him.*] Stanley!

[*He pulls open the wardrobe trunk standing in middle of room and jerks out an armful of dresses.*]

STANLEY: Open your eyes to this stuff! You think she got them out of a teacher's pay?

STELLA: Hush!

STANLEY: Look at these feathers and furs that she come here to preen herself in! What's this here? A solid-gold dress, I believe! And this one! What is these here? Fox-pieces! [*He blows on them.*] Genuine fox fur-pieces, a half a mile long! Where are your fox-pieces, Stella? Bushy snow-white ones, no less! Where are your white fox-pieces?

STELLA: Those are inexpensive summer furs that Blanche has had a long time.

STANLEY: I got an acquaintance who deals in this sort of merchandise. I'll have him in here to appraise it. I'm willing to bet you there's thousands of dollars invested in this stuff here!

STELLA: Don't be such an idiot, Stanley!

---

7. This codification of French law (1802), made by Napoleon as emperor, is the basis for Louisiana's civil law.

[*He hurls the furs to the day bed. Then he jerks open a small drawer in the trunk and pulls up a fistful of costume jewelry.*]

STANLEY: And what have we here? The treasure chest of a pirate!

STELLA: Oh, Stanley!

STANLEY: Pearls! Ropes of them! What is this sister of yours, a deep-sea diver? Bracelets of solid gold, too! Where are your pearls and gold bracelets?

STELLA: Shhh! Be still, Stanley!

STANLEY: And diamonds! A crown for an empress!

STELLA: A rhinestone tiara she wore to a costume ball.

STANLEY: What's rhinestone?

STELLA: Next door to glass.

STANLEY: Are you kidding? I have an acquaintance that works in a jewelry store. I'll have him in here to make an appraisal of this. Here's your plantation, or what was left of it, here!

STELLA: You have no idea how stupid and horrid you're being! Now close that trunk before she comes out of the bathroom!

[*He kicks the trunk partly closed and sits on the kitchen table.*]

STANLEY: The Kowalskis and the DuBoises have different notions.

STELLA: [*Angrily.*] Indeed they have, thank heavens!—*I'm* going outside. [*She snatches up her white hat and gloves and crosses to the outside door.*] You come out with me while Blanche is getting dressed.

STANLEY: Since when do you give me orders?

STELLA: Are you going to stay here and insult her?

STANLEY: You're damn tootin' I'm going to stay here.

[STELLA *goes out to the porch.* BLANCHE *comes out of the bathroom in a red satin robe.*]

BLANCHE: [*Airily.*] Hello, Stanley! Here I am, all freshly bathed and scented, and feeling like a brand new human being!

[*He lights a cigarette.*]

STANLEY: That's good.

BLANCHE: [*Drawing the curtains at the windows.*] Excuse me while I slip on my pretty new dress!

STANLEY: Go right ahead, Blanche.

[*She closes the drapes between the rooms.*]

BLANCHE: I understand there's to be a little card party to which we ladies are cordially *not* invited!

STANLEY: [*Ominously.*] Yeah?

[BLANCHE *throws off her robe and slips into a flowered print dress.*]

BLANCHE: Where's Stella?

STANLEY: Out on the porch.

BLANCHE: I'm going to ask a favor of you in a moment.

STANLEY: What could that be, I wonder?

BLANCHE: Some buttons in back! You may enter! [*He crosses through drapes with a smoldering look.*] How do I look?

STANLEY: You look all right.

BLANCHE: Many thanks! Now the buttons!

STANLEY: I can't do nothing with them.

BLANCHE: You men with your big clumsy fingers. May I have a drag on your cig?

STANLEY: Have one for yourself.

BLANCHE: Why, thanks! . . . It looks like my trunk has exploded.

STANLEY: Me an' Stella were helping you unpack.

BLANCHE: Well, you certainly did a fast and thorough job of it!

STANLEY: It looks like you raided some stylish shops in Paris.

BLANCHE: Ha-ha! Yes—clothes are my passion!

STANLEY: What does it cost for a string of fur-pieces like that?

BLANCHE: Why, those were a tribute from an admirer of mine!

STANLEY: He must have had a lot of—admiration!

BLANCHE: Oh, in my youth I excited some admiration. But look at me now! [*She smiles at him radiantly.*] Would you think it possible that I was once considered to be—attractive?

STANLEY: Your looks are okay.

BLANCHE: I was fishing for a compliment, Stanley.

STANLEY: I don't go in for that stuff.

BLANCHE: What—stuff?

STANLEY: Compliments to women about their looks. I never met a woman that didn't know if she was good-looking or not without being told, and some of them give themselves credit for more than they've got. I once went out with a doll who said to me, "I am the glamorous type, I am the glamorous type!" I said, "So what?"

BLANCHE: And what did she say then?

STANLEY: She didn't say nothing. That shut her up like a clam.

BLANCHE: Did it end the romance?

STANLEY: It ended the conversation—that was all. Some men are took in by this Hollywood glamor stuff and some men are not.

BLANCHE: I'm sure you belong in the second category.

STANLEY: That's right.

BLANCHE: I cannot imagine any witch of a woman casting a spell over you.

STANLEY: That's—right.

BLANCHE: You're simple, straightforward and honest, a little bit on the primitive side I should think. To interest you a woman would have to— [*She pauses with an indefinite gesture.*]

STANLEY: [*Slowly.*] Lay . . . her cards on the table.

BLANCHE: [*Smiling.*] Well, I never cared for wishy-washy people. That was why, when you walked in here last night, I said to myself—"My sister has married a man!"—Of course that was all that I could tell about you.

STANLEY: [*Booming.*] Now let's cut the re-bop![8]

BLANCHE: [*Pressing hands to her ears.*] Ouuuuu!

STELLA: [*Calling from the steps.*] Stanley! You come out here and let Blanche finish dressing!

BLANCHE: I'm through dressing, honey.

STELLA: Well, you come out, then.

STANLEY: Your sister and I are having a little talk.

BLANCHE: [*Lightly.*] Honey, do me a favor. Run to the drugstore and get me a lemon Coke with plenty of chipped ice in it!—Will you do that for me, sweetie?

STELLA: [*Uncertainly.*] Yes. [*She goes around the corner of the building.*]

BLANCHE: The poor little thing was out there listening to us, and I have an idea she doesn't understand you as well as I do. . . . All right; now, Mr. Kowalski, let us proceed without any more double-talk. I'm ready to answer all questions. I've nothing to hide. What is it?

STANLEY: There is such a thing in this state of Louisiana as the Napoleonic code, according to which whatever belongs to my wife is also mine—and vice versa.

BLANCHE: My, but you have an impressive judicial air!

[*She sprays herself with her atomizer; then playfully sprays him with it. He seizes the atomizer and slams it down on the dresser. She throws back her head and laughs.*]

STANLEY: If I didn't know that you was my wife's sister I'd get ideas about you!

BLANCHE: Such as what!

STANLEY: Don't play so dumb. You know what!

BLANCHE: [*She puts the atomizer on the table.*] All right. Cards on the table. That suits me. [*She turns to* STANLEY.] I know I fib a good deal. After all, a woman's charm is fifty per cent illusion, but when a thing is important I tell the truth, and this is the truth: I haven't cheated my sister or you or anyone else as long as I have lived.

STANLEY: Where's the papers? In the trunk?

BLANCHE: Everything that I own is in that trunk. [STANLEY *crosses to the trunk, shoves it roughly open and begins to open compartments.*] What in the name of heaven are you thinking of! What's in the back of that little boy's mind of yours? That I am absconding with something, attempting

---

8. Nonsense (from "bop," a form of jazz).

some kind of treachery on my sister?—Let me do that! It will be faster and simpler. . . . [*She crosses to the trunk and takes out a box.*] I keep my papers mostly in this tin box. [*She opens it.*]

STANLEY: What's them underneath? [*He indicates another sheaf of paper.*]

BLANCHE: These are love-letters, yellowing with antiquity, all from one boy. [*He snatches them up. She speaks fiercely.*] Give those back to me!

STANLEY: I'll have a look at them first!

BLANCHE: The touch of your hands insults them!

STANLEY: Don't pull that stuff!

[*He rips off the ribbon and starts to examine them.* BLANCHE *snatches them from him, and they cascade to the floor.*]

BLANCHE: Now that you've touched them I'll burn them!

STANLEY: [*Staring, baffled.*] What in hell are they?

BLANCHE: [*On the floor gathering them up.*] Poems a dead boy wrote. I hurt him the way that you would like to hurt me, but you can't! I'm not young and vulnerable any more. But my young husband was and I—never mind about that! Just give them back to me!

STANLEY: What do you mean by saying you'll have to burn them?

BLANCHE: I'm sorry, I must have lost my head for a moment. Everyone has something he won't let others touch because of their—intimate nature. . . . [*She now seems faint with exhaustion and she sits down with the strong box and puts on a pair of glasses and goes methodically through a large stack of papers.*] Ambler & Ambler. Hmmmmm. . . . Crabtree. . . . More Ambler & Ambler.

STANLEY: What is Ambler & Ambler?

BLANCHE: A firm that made loans on the place.

STANLEY: Then it *was* lost on a mortgage?

BLANCHE: [*Touching her forehead.*] That must've been what happened.

STANLEY: I don't want no ifs, ands or buts! What's all the rest of them papers?

[*She hands him the entire box. He carries it to the table and starts to examine the papers.*]

BLANCHE: [*Picking up a large envelope containing more papers.*] There are thousands of papers, stretching back over hundreds of years, affecting Belle Reve as, piece by piece, our improvident grandfathers and father and uncles and brothers exchanged the land for their epic fornications—to put it plainly! [*She removes her glasses with an exhausted laugh.*] The four-letter word deprived us of our plantation, till finally all that was left—and Stella can verify that!—was the house itself and about twenty acres of ground, including a graveyard, to which now all but Stella and I have retreated. [*She pours the contents of the envelope on the table.*] Here all of them are, all papers! I hereby endow you with them! Take them, peruse them—commit them to memory, even! I think it's wonderfully fitting that Belle

Reve should finally be this bunch of old papers in your big, capable hands!... I wonder if Stella's come back with my lemon Coke.... [*She leans back and closes her eyes.*]

STANLEY: I have a lawyer acquaintance who will study these out.

BLANCHE: Present them to him with a box of aspirin tablets.

STANLEY: [*Becoming somewhat sheepish.*] You see, under the Napoleonic code—a man has to take an interest in his wife's affairs—especially now that she's going to have a baby.

[BLANCHE *opens her eyes. The "Blue Piano" sounds louder.*]

BLANCHE: Stella? Stella going to have a baby? [*Dreamily.*] I didn't know she was going to have a baby! [*She gets up and crosses to the outside door.* STELLA *appears around the corner with a carton from the drugstore.* STANLEY *goes into the bedroom with the envelope and the box. The inner rooms fade to darkness and the outside wall of the house is visible.* BLANCHE *meets* STELLA *at the foot of the steps to the sidewalk.*] Stella, Stella for star! How lovely to have a baby! It's all right. Everything's all right.

STELLA: I'm sorry he did that to you.

BLANCHE: Oh, I guess he's just not the type that goes for jasmine perfume, but maybe he's what we need to mix with our blood now that we've lost Belle Reve. We thrashed it out. I feel a bit shaky, but I think I handled it nicely, I laughed and treated it all as a joke. [STEVE *and* PABLO *appear, carrying a case of beer.*] I called him a little boy and laughed and flirted. Yes, I was flirting with your husband! [*As the men approach.*] The guests are gathering for the poker party. [*The two men pass between them, and enter the house.*] Which way do we go now, Stella—this way?

STELLA: No, this way. [*She leads* BLANCHE *away.*]

BLANCHE: [*Laughing.*] The blind are leading the blind![9]

[*A tamale* VENDOR *is heard calling.*]

VENDOR'S VOICE: Red-hot!

Scene 3. The Poker Night

*There is a picture of Van Gogh's of a billiard-parlor at night.[1] The kitchen now suggests that sort of lurid nocturnal brilliance, the raw colors of childhood's spectrum. Over the yellow linoleum of the kitchen table hangs an electric bulb with a vivid green glass shade. The poker players—*STANLEY, STEVE, MITCH *and* PABLO—*wear colored shirts, solid blues, a purple, a red-and-white check, a light green, and they are men at the peak of their physical manhood, as coarse and direct and powerful*

9. See Matthew 15.14—"If a blind person leads a blind person, both will fall into a pit." *Red-hot!*: Hot dog!
1. *The Night Café,* by Vincent van Gogh (1853–90), Dutch Postimpressionist painter. *The Poker Night* was Williams's first working title for *A Streetcar Named Desire.*

as the primary colors. There are vivid slices of watermelon on the table, whiskey bottles and glasses. The bedroom is relatively dim with only the light that spills between the portieres and through the wide window on the street.

For a moment, there is absorbed silence as a hand is dealt.

STEVE: Anything wild this deal?

PABLO: One-eyed jacks are wild.

STEVE: Give me two cards.

PABLO: You, Mitch?

MITCH: I'm out.

PABLO: One.

MITCH: Anyone want a shot?

STANLEY: Yeah. Me.

PABLO: Why don't somebody go to the Chinaman's and bring back a load of chop suey?

STANLEY: When I'm losing you want to eat! Ante up! Openers? Openers! Get y'r ass off the table, Mitch. Nothing belongs on a poker table but cards, chips and whiskey. [*He lurches up and tosses some watermelon rinds to the floor.*]

MITCH: Kind of on your high horse, ain't you?

STANLEY: How many?

STEVE: Give me three.

STANLEY: One.

MITCH: I'm out again. I oughta go home pretty soon.

STANLEY: Shut up.

MITCH: I gotta sick mother. She don't go to sleep until I come in at night.

STANLEY: Then why don't you stay home with her?

MITCH: She says to go out, so I go, but I don't enjoy it. All the while I keep wondering how she is.

STANLEY: Aw, for the sake of Jesus, go home, then!

PABLO: What've you got?

STEVE: Spade flush.

MITCH: You all are married. But I'll be alone when she goes.—I'm going to the bathroom.

STANLEY: Hurry back and we'll fix you a sugar-tit.[2]

MITCH: Aw, go rut. [*He crosses through the bedroom into the bathroom.*]

STEVE: [*Dealing a hand.*] Seven card stud. [*Telling his joke as he deals.*] This ole farmer is out in back of his house sittin' down th'owing corn to the chickens when all at once he hears a loud cackle and this young hen comes lickety split around the side of the house with the rooster right behind her and gaining on her fast.

STANLEY: [*Impatient with the story.*] Deal!

2. Baby's pacifier dipped in sugar.

STEVE: But when the rooster catches sight of the farmer th'owing the corn he puts on the brakes and lets the hen get away and starts pecking corn. And the old farmer says, "Lord God, I hopes I never gits *that* hongry!"

[STEVE *and* PABLO *laugh. The sisters appear around the corner of the building.*]

STELLA: The game is still going on.

BLANCHE: How do I look?

STELLA: Lovely, Blanche.

BLANCHE: I feel so hot and frazzled. Wait till I powder before you open the door. Do I look done in?

STELLA: Why no. You are as fresh as a daisy.

BLANCHE: One that's been picked a few days.

[STELLA *opens the door and they enter.*]

STELLA: Well, well, well. I see you boys are still at it?

STANLEY: Where you been?

STELLA: Blanche and I took in a show. Blanche, this is Mr. Gonzales and Mr. Hubbell.

BLANCHE: Please don't get up.

STANLEY: Nobody's going to get up, so don't be worried.

STELLA: How much longer is this game going to continue?

STANLEY: Till we get ready to quit.

BLANCHE: Poker is so fascinating. Could I kibitz?[3]

STANLEY: You could not. Why don't you women go up and sit with Eunice?

STELLA: Because it is nearly two-thirty. [BLANCHE *crosses into the bedroom and partially closes the portieres.*] Couldn't you call it quits after one more hand?

[*A chair scrapes.* STANLEY *gives a loud whack of his hand on her thigh.*]

STELLA: [*Sharply.*] That's not fun, Stanley. [*The men laugh.* STELLA *goes into the bedroom.*] It makes me so mad when he does that in front of people.

BLANCHE: I think I will bathe.

STELLA: Again?

BLANCHE: My nerves are in knots. Is the bathroom occupied?

STELLA: I don't know.

[BLANCHE *knocks.* MITCH *opens the door and comes out, still wiping his hands on a towel.*]

BLANCHE: Oh!—good evening.

MITCH: Hello. [*He stares at her.*]

STELLA: Blanche, this is Harold Mitchell. My sister, Blanche DuBois.

MITCH: [*With awkward courtesy.*] How do you do, Miss DuBois.

---

3. That is, watch a card player from behind and offer advice.

STELLA: How is your mother now, Mitch?
MITCH: About the same, thanks. She appreciated your sending over that custard.—Excuse me, please.

[*He crosses slowly back into the kitchen, glancing back at* BLANCHE *and coughing a little shyly. He realizes he still has the towel in his hands and with an embarrassed laugh hands it to* STELLA. BLANCHE *looks after him with a certain interest.*]

BLANCHE: That one seems—superior to the others.
STELLA: Yes, he is.
BLANCHE: I thought he had a sort of sensitive look.
STELLA: His mother is sick.
BLANCHE: Is he married?
STELLA: No.
BLANCHE: Is he a wolf?
STELLA: Why, Blanche! [BLANCHE *laughs.*] I don't think he would be.
BLANCHE: What does—what does he do? [*She is unbuttoning her blouse.*]
STELLA: He's on the precision bench in the spare parts department. At the plant Stanley travels for.
BLANCHE: Is that something much?
STELLA: No. Stanley's the only one of his crowd that's likely to get anywhere.
BLANCHE: What makes you think Stanley will?
STELLA: Look at him.
BLANCHE: I've looked at him.
STELLA: Then you should know.
BLANCHE: I'm sorry, but I haven't noticed the stamp of genius even on Stanley's forehead.

[*She takes off the blouse and stands in her pink silk brassiere and white skirt in the light through the portieres. The game has continued in undertones.*]

STELLA: It isn't on his forehead and it isn't genius.
BLANCHE: Oh. Well, what is it, and where? I would like to know.
STELLA: It's a drive that he has. You're standing in the light, Blanche!
BLANCHE: Oh, am I!

[*She moves out of the yellow streak of light.* STELLA *has removed her dress and put on a light blue satin kimona.*[4]]

STELLA: [*With girlish laughter.*] You ought to see their wives.
BLANCHE: [*Laughingly.*] I can imagine. Big, beefy things, I suppose.
STELLA: You know that one upstairs? [*More laughter.*] One time [*Laughing.*] the plaster— [*Laughing.*] cracked—
STANLEY: You hens cut out that conversation in there!

4. Kimono.

STELLA: You can't hear us.

STANLEY: Well, you can hear me and I said to hush up!

STELLA: This is my house and I'll talk as much as I want to!

BLANCHE: Stella, don't start a row.

STELLA: He's half drunk!—I'll be out in a minute.

[*She goes into the bathroom.* BLANCHE *rises and crosses leisurely to a small white radio and turns it on.*]

STANLEY: Awright, Mitch, you in?

MITCH: What? Oh!—No, I'm out!

[BLANCHE *moves back into the streak of light. She raises her arms and stretches, as she moves indolently back to the chair. Rhumba music comes over the radio.* MITCH *rises at the table.*]

STANLEY: Who turned that on in there?

BLANCHE: I did. Do you mind?

STANLEY: Turn it off!

STEVE: Aw, let the girls have their music.

PABLO: Sure, that's good, leave it on!

STEVE: Sounds like Xavier Cugat!⁵ [STANLEY *jumps up and, crossing to the radio, turns it off. He stops short at the sight of* BLANCHE *in the chair. She returns his look without flinching. Then he sits again at the poker table. Two of the men have started arguing hotly.*] I didn't hear you name it.

PABLO: Didn't I name it, Mitch?

MITCH: I wasn't listenin'.

PABLO: What were you doing, then?

STANLEY: He was looking through them drapes. [*He jumps up and jerks roughly at curtains to close them.*] Now deal the hand over again and let's play cards or quit. Some people get ants when they win.

[MITCH *rises as* STANLEY *returns to his seat.*]

STANLEY: [*Yelling.*] Sit down!

MITCH: I'm going to the "head." Deal me out.

PABLO: Sure he's got ants now. Seven five-dollar bills in his pants pocket folded up tight as spitballs.

STEVE: Tomorrow you'll see him at the cashier's window getting them changed into quarters.

STANLEY: And when he goes home he'll deposit them one by one in a piggy bank his mother give him for Christmas. [*Dealing.*] This game is Spit in the Ocean.

[MITCH *laughs uncomfortably and continues through the portieres. He stops just inside.*]

5. Spanish-born Cuban bandleader (1900–90), well known for composing and playing rhumbas.

BLANCHE: [*Softly.*] Hello! The Little Boys' Room is busy right now.

MITCH: We've—been drinking beer.

BLANCHE: I hate beer.

MITCH: It's—a hot weather drink.

BLANCHE: Oh, I don't think so; it always makes me warmer. Have you got any cigs?

[*She has slipped on the dark red satin wrapper.*]

MITCH: Sure.

BLANCHE: What kind are they?

MITCH: Luckies.

BLANCHE: Oh, good. What a pretty case. Silver?

MITCH: Yes. Yes; read the inscription.

BLANCHE: Oh, is there an inscription? I can't make it out. [*He strikes a match and moves closer.*] Oh! [*Reading with feigned difficulty.*] "And if God choose,/I shall but love thee better—after—death!" Why, that's from my favorite sonnet by Mrs. Browning![6]

MITCH: You know it?

BLANCHE: Certainly I do!

MITCH: There's a story connected with that inscription.

BLANCHE: It sounds like a romance.

MITCH: A pretty sad one.

BLANCHE: Oh?

MITCH: The girl's dead now.

BLANCHE: [*In a tone of deep sympathy.*] Oh!

MITCH: She knew she was dying when she give me this. A very strange girl, very sweet—very!

BLANCHE: She must have been fond of you. Sick people have such deep, sincere attachments.

MITCH: That's right, they certainly do.

BLANCHE: Sorrow makes for sincerity, I think.

MITCH: It sure brings it out in people.

BLANCHE: The little there is belongs to people who have experienced some sorrow.

MITCH: I believe you are right about that.

BLANCHE: I'm positive that I am. Show me a person who hasn't known any sorrow and I'll show you a shuperficial—Listen to me! My tongue is a little—thick! You boys are responsible for it. The show let out at eleven and we couldn't come home on account of the poker game so we had to go somewhere and drink. I'm not accustomed to having more than one drink. Two is the limit—and *three*! [*She laughs.*] Tonight I had three.

---

6. Elizabeth Barrett Browning (1806-61), British poet, famous for her sequence of love poems, *Sonnets from the Portuguese,* which includes the poem quoted here, "How Do I Love Thee?"

STANLEY: Mitch!

MITCH: Deal me out. I'm talking to Miss—

BLANCHE: DuBois.

MITCH: Miss DuBois?

BLANCHE: It's a French name. It means woods and Blanche means white, so the two together mean white woods! Like an orchard in spring! You can remember it by that.

MITCH: You're French?

BLANCHE: We are French by extraction. Our first American ancestors were French Huguenots.[7]

MITCH: You are Stella's sister, are you not?

BLANCHE: Yes, Stella is my precious little sister. I call her little in spite of the fact she's somewhat older than I. Just slightly. Less than a year. Will you do something for me?

MITCH: Sure. What?

BLANCHE: I bought this adorable little colored paper lantern at a Chinese shop on Bourbon. Put it over the light bulb! Will you, please?

MITCH: Be glad to.

BLANCHE: I can't stand a naked light bulb, any more than I can a rude remark or a vulgar action.

MITCH: [*Adjusting the lantern.*] I guess we strike you as being a pretty rough bunch.

BLANCHE: I'm very adaptable—to circumstances.

MITCH: Well, that's a good thing to be. You are visiting Stanley and Stella?

BLANCHE: Stella hasn't been so well lately, and I came down to help her for a while. She's very run down.

MITCH: You're not—?

BLANCHE: Married? No, no. I'm an old maid schoolteacher!

MITCH: You may teach school but you're certainly not an old maid.

BLANCHE: Thank you, sir! I appreciate your gallantry!

MITCH: So you are in the teaching profession?

BLANCHE: Yes. Ah, yes . . .

MITCH: Grade school or high school or—

STANLEY: [*Bellowing.*] Mitch!

MITCH: Coming!

BLANCHE: Gracious, what lung-power! . . . I teach high school. In Laurel.

MITCH: What do you teach? What subject?

BLANCHE: Guess!

MITCH: I bet you teach art or music? [BLANCHE *laughs delicately.*] Of course I could be wrong. You might teach arithmetic.

7. Protestants who fled persecution in Catholic France after the Edict of Nantes (1685); many settled in the American South.

BLANCHE: Never arithmetic, sir; never arithmetic! [*With a laugh.*] I don't even know my multiplication tables! No, I have the misfortune of being an English instructor. I attempt to instill a bunch of bobby-soxers and drug-store Romeos with reverence for Hawthorne and Whitman and Poe!

MITCH: I guess that some of them are more interested in other things.

BLANCHE: How very right you are! Their literary heritage is not what most of them treasure above all else! But they're sweet things! And in the spring, it's touching to notice them making their first discovery of love! As if nobody had ever known it before! [*The bathroom door opens and* STELLA *comes out.* BLANCHE *continues talking to* MITCH.] Oh! Have you finished? Wait—I'll turn on the radio.

[*She turns the knobs on the radio and it begins to play "Wien, Wien, nur du allein."*[8] BLANCHE *waltzes to the music with romantic gestures.* MITCH *is delighted and moves in awkward imitation like a dancing bear.* STANLEY *stalks fiercely through the portieres into the bedroom. He crosses to the small white radio and snatches it off the table. With a shouted oath, he tosses the instrument out the window.*]

STELLA: Drunk—drunk—animal thing, you! [*She rushes through to the poker table.*] All of you—please go home! If any of you have one spark of decency in you—

BLANCHE: [*Wildly.*] Stella, watch out, he's—

[STANLEY *charges after* STELLA.]

MEN: [*Feebly.*] Take it easy, Stanley. Easy, fellow.—Let's all—

STELLA: You lay your hands on me and I'll—

[*She backs out of sight. He advances and disappears. There is the sound of a blow.* STELLA *cries out.* BLANCHE *screams and runs into the kitchen. The men rush forward and there is grappling and cursing. Something is overturned with a crash.*]

BLANCHE: [*Shrilly.*] My sister is going to have a baby!

MITCH: This is terrible.

BLANCHE: Lunacy, absolute lunacy!

MITCH: Get him in here, men.

[STANLEY *is forced, pinioned by the two men, into the bedroom. He nearly throws them off. Then all at once he subsides and is limp in their grasp. They speak quietly and lovingly to him and he leans his face on one of their shoulders.*]

STELLA: [*In a high, unnatural voice, out of sight.*] I want to go away, I want to go away!

MITCH: Poker shouldn't be played in a house with women.

8. "Vienna, Vienna, you are my only," a waltz from an operetta by Franz Lehár (1870–1948).

[BLANCHE *rushes into the bedroom.*]

BLANCHE: I want my sister's clothes! We'll go to that woman's upstairs!

MITCH: Where is the clothes?

BLANCHE: [*Opening the closet.*] I've got them! [*She rushes through to* STELLA.] Stella, Stella, precious! Dear, dear little sister, don't be afraid!

[*With her arm around* STELLA, BLANCHE *guides her to the outside door and upstairs.*]

STANLEY: [*Dully.*] What's the matter; what's happened?

MITCH: You just blew your top, Stan.

PABLO: He's okay, now.

STEVE: Sure, my boy's okay!

MITCH: Put him on the bed and get a wet towel.

PABLO: I think coffee would do him a world of good, now.

STANLEY: [*Thickly.*] I want water.

MITCH: Put him under the shower!

[*The men talk quietly as they lead him to the bathroom.*]

STANLEY: Let the rut go of me, you sons of bitches!

[*Sounds of blows are heard. The water goes on full tilt.*]

STEVE: Let's get quick out of here!

[*They rush to the poker table and sweep up their winnings on their way out.*]

MITCH: [*Sadly but firmly.*] Poker should not be played in a house with women.

[*The door closes on them and the place is still. The Negro entertainers in the bar around the corner play "Paper Doll"*[9] *slow and blue. After a moment* STANLEY *comes out of the bathroom dripping water and still in his clinging wet polka dot drawers.*]

STANLEY: Stella! [*There is a pause.*] My baby doll's left me! [*He breaks into sobs. Then he goes to the phone and dials, still shuddering with sobs.*] Eunice? I want my baby! [*He waits a moment; then he hangs up and dials again.*] Eunice! I'll keep on ringin' until I talk with my baby! [*An indistinguishable shrill voice is heard. He hurls phone to floor. Dissonant brass and piano sounds as the rooms dim out to darkness and the outer walls appear in the night light. The "Blue Piano" plays for a brief interval. Finally,* STANLEY *stumbles half-dressed out to the porch and down the wooden steps to the pavement before the building. There he throws back his head like a baying hound and bellows his wife's name:* "STELLA! STELLA, *sweetheart!* STELLA!"] Stell-lahhhh!

---

9. Song by Johnny S. Black (1915), popularized by the Mills Brothers in the early 1940s.

EUNICE: [*Calling down from the door of her upper apartment.*] Quit that howling out there an' go back to bed!

STANLEY: I want my baby down here. Stella, Stella!

EUNICE: She ain't comin' down so you quit! Or you'll git th' law on you!

STANLEY: Stella!

EUNICE: You can't beat on a woman an' then call 'er back! She won't come! And her goin' t' have a baby! . . . You stinker! You whelp of a Polack, you! I hope they do haul you in and turn the fire hose on you, same as the last time!

STANLEY: [*Humbly.*] Eunice, I want my girl to come down with me!

EUNICE: Hah! [*She slams her door.*]

STANLEY: [*With heaven-splitting violence.*] STELL-LAHHHHH!

[*The low-tone clarinet moans. The door upstairs opens again.* STELLA *slips down the rickety stairs in her robe. Her eyes are glistening with tears and her hair loose about her throat and shoulders. They stare at each other. Then they come together with low, animal moans. He falls to his knees on the steps and presses his face to her belly, curving a little with maternity. Her eyes go blind with tenderness as she catches his head and raises him level with her. He snatches the screen door open and lifts her off her feet and bears her into the dark flat.* BLANCHE *comes out the upper landing in her robe and slips fearfully down the steps.*]

BLANCHE: Where is my little sister? Stella? Stella?

[*She stops before the dark entrance of her sister's flat. Then catches her breath as if struck. She rushes down to the walk before the house. She looks right and left as if for a sanctuary. The music fades away.* MITCH *appears from around the corner.*]

MITCH: Miss DuBois?

BLANCHE: Oh!

MITCH: All quiet on the Potomac now?[1]

BLANCHE: She ran downstairs and went back in there with him.

MITCH: Sure she did.

BLANCHE: I'm terrified!

MITCH: Ho-ho! There's nothing to be scared of. They're crazy about each other.

BLANCHE: I'm not used to such—

MITCH: Naw, it's a shame this had to happen when you just got here. But don't take it serious.

BLANCHE: Violence! Is so—

MITCH: Set down on the steps and have a cigarette with me.

1. "All Quiet on the Potomac" was a Civil War catchphrase, attributed to Union general George McClellan, who pushed the Confederate army back over the Potomac River in 1862.

BLANCHE: I'm not properly dressed.

MITCH: That don't make no difference in the Quarter.

BLANCHE: Such a pretty silver case.

MITCH: I showed you the inscription, didn't I?

BLANCHE: Yes. [*During the pause, she looks up at the sky.*] There's so much—so much confusion in the world. . . . [*He coughs diffidently.*] Thank you for being so kind! I need kindness now.

Scene 4

It is early the following morning. There is a confusion of street cries like a choral chant.

STELLA *is lying down in the bedroom. Her face is serene in the early morning sunlight. One hand rests on her belly, rounding slightly with new maternity. From the other dangles a book of colored comics. Her eyes and lips have that almost narcotized tranquility that is in the faces of Eastern idols.*

The table is sloppy with remains of breakfast and the debris of the preceding night, and STANLEY'S *gaudy pyjamas lie across the threshold of the bathroom. The outside door is slightly ajar on a sky of summer brilliance.*

BLANCHE *appears at this door. She has spent a sleepless night and her appearance entirely contrasts with* STELLA'S. *She presses her knuckles nervously to her lips as she looks through the door, before entering.*

BLANCHE: Stella?

STELLA: [*Stirring lazily.*] Hmmh?

[BLANCHE *utters a moaning cry and runs into the bedroom, throwing herself down beside* STELLA *in a rush of hysterical tenderness.*]

BLANCHE: Baby, my baby sister!

STELLA: [*Drawing away from her.*] Blanche, what is the matter with you?

[BLANCHE *straightens up slowly and stands beside the bed looking down at her sister with knuckles pressed to her lips.*]

BLANCHE: He's left?

STELLA: Stan? Yes.

BLANCHE: Will he be back?

STELLA: He's gone to get the car greased. Why?

BLANCHE: Why! I've been half crazy, Stella! When I found out you'd been insane enough to come back in here after what happened—I started to rush in after you!

STELLA: I'm glad you didn't.

BLANCHE: What were you thinking of? [STELLA *makes an indefinite gesture.*] Answer me! What? What?

STELLA: Please, Blanche! Sit down and stop yelling.

BLANCHE: All right, Stella. I will repeat the question quietly now. How could you come back in this place last night? Why, you must have slept with him!

[STELLA *gets up in a calm and leisurely way.*]

STELLA: Blanche, I'd forgotten how excitable you are. You're making much too much fuss about this.

BLANCHE: Am I?

STELLA: Yes, you are, Blanche. I know how it must have seemed to you and I'm awful sorry it had to happen, but it wasn't anything as serious as you seem to take it. In the first place, when men are drinking and playing poker anything can happen. It's always a powder-keg. He didn't know what he was doing. . . . He was as good as a lamb when I came back and he's really very, very ashamed of himself.

BLANCHE: And that—that makes it all right?

STELLA: No, it isn't all right for anybody to make such a terrible row, but— people do sometimes. Stanley's always smashed things. Why, on our wedding night—soon as we came in here—he snatched off one of my slippers and rushed about the place smashing light bulbs with it.

BLANCHE: He did—*what*?

STELLA: He smashed all the lightbulbs with the heel of my slipper! [*She laughs.*]

BLANCHE: And you—you *let* him? Didn't *run*, didn't *scream*?

STELLA: I was—sort of—thrilled by it. [*She waits for a moment.*] Eunice and you had breakfast?

BLANCHE: Do you suppose I wanted any breakfast?

STELLA: There's some coffee left on the stove.

BLANCHE: You're so—matter-of-fact about it, Stella.

STELLA: What other can I be? He's taken the radio to get it fixed. It didn't land on the pavement so only one tube was smashed.

BLANCHE: And you are standing there smiling!

STELLA: What do you want me to do?

BLANCHE: Pull yourself together and face the facts.

STELLA: What are they, in your opinion?

BLANCHE: In my opinion? You're married to a madman!

STELLA: No!

BLANCHE: Yes, you are, your fix is worse than mine is! Only you're not being sensible about it. I'm going to *do* something. Get hold of myself and make myself a new life!

STELLA: Yes?

BLANCHE: But you've given in. And that isn't right, you're not old! You can get out.

STELLA: [*Slowly and emphatically.*] I'm not in anything I want to get out of.

BLANCHE: [*Incredulously.*] What—Stella?

STELLA: I said I am not in anything that I have a desire to get out of. Look at the mess in this room! And those empty bottles! They went through two cases last night! He promised this morning that he was going to quit having these poker parties, but you know how long such a promise is going to keep. Oh, well, it's his pleasure, like mine is movies and bridge. People have got to tolerate each other's habits, I guess.

BLANCHE: I don't understand you. [STELLA *turns toward her.*] I don't understand your indifference. Is this a Chinese philosophy you've—cultivated?

STELLA: Is what—what?

BLANCHE: This—shuffling about and mumbling—"One tube smashed—beer bottles—mess in the kitchen!"—as if nothing out of the ordinary has happened! [STELLA *laughs uncertainly and picking up the broom, twirls it in her hands.*] Are you deliberately shaking that thing in my face?

STELLA: No.

BLANCHE: Stop it. Let go of that broom. I won't have you cleaning up for him!

STELLA: Then who's going to do it? Are you?

BLANCHE: I? I!

STELLA: No, I didn't think so.

BLANCHE: Oh, let me think, if only my mind would function! We've got to get hold of some money, that's the way out!

STELLA: I guess that money is always nice to get hold of.

BLANCHE: Listen to me. I have an idea of some kind. [*Shakily she twists a cigarette into her holder.*] Do you remember Shep Huntleigh? [STELLA *shakes her head.*] Of course you remember Shep Huntleigh. I went out with him at college and wore his pin for a while. Well—

STELLA: Well?

BLANCHE: I ran into him last winter. You know I went to Miami during the Christmas holidays?

STELLA: No.

BLANCHE: Well, I did. I took the trip as an investment, thinking I'd meet someone with a million dollars.

STELLA: Did you?

BLANCHE: Yes. I ran into Shep Huntleigh—I ran into him on Biscayne Boulevard, on Christmas Eve, about dusk . . . getting into his car—Cadillac convertible; must have been a block long!

STELLA: I should think it would have been—inconvenient in traffic!

BLANCHE: You've heard of oil wells?

STELLA: Yes—remotely.

BLANCHE: He has them, all over Texas. Texas is literally spouting gold in his pockets.

STELLA: My, my.

BLANCHE: Y'know how indifferent I am to money. I think of money in terms of what it does for you. But he could do it, he could certainly do it!

STELLA: Do what, Blanche?

BLANCHE: Why—set us up in a—shop!

STELLA: What kind of shop?

BLANCHE: Oh, a—shop of some kind! He could do it with half what his wife throws away at the races.

STELLA: He's married?

BLANCHE: Honey, would I be here if the man weren't married? [STELLA *laughs a little.* BLANCHE *suddenly springs up and crosses to phone. She speaks shrilly.*] How do I get Western Union?[2]—Operator! Western Union!

STELLA: That's a dial phone, honey.

BLANCHE: I can't dial, I'm too—

STELLA: Just dial O.

BLANCHE: O?

STELLA: Yes, "O" for Operator!

[BLANCHE *considers a moment; then she puts the phone down.*]

BLANCHE: Give me a pencil. Where is a slip of paper? I've got to write it down first—the message, I mean. . . . [*She goes to the dressing table, and grabs up a sheet of Kleenex and an eyebrow pencil for writing equipment.*] Let me see now. . . . [*She bites the pencil.*] "Darling Shep. Sister and I in desperate situation."

STELLA: I beg your pardon!

BLANCHE: "Sister and I in desperate situation. Will explain details later. Would you be interested in—?" [*She bites the pencil again.*] "Would you be—interested—in . . ." [*She smashes the pencil on the table and springs up.*] You never get anywhere with direct appeals!

STELLA: [*With a laugh.*] Don't be so ridiculous, darling!

BLANCHE: But I'll think of something, I've *got* to think of—*some*thing! Don't laugh at me, Stella! Please, please don't—I—I want you to look at the contents of my purse! Here's what's in it! [*She snatches her purse open.*] Sixty-five measly cents in coin of the realm!

STELLA: [*Crossing to bureau.*] Stanley doesn't give me a regular allowance, he likes to pay bills himself, but—this morning he gave me ten dollars to smooth things over. You take five of it, Blanche, and I'll keep the rest.

BLANCHE: Oh, no. No, Stella.

STELLA: [*Insisting.*] I know how it helps your morale just having a little pocket-money on you.

BLANCHE: No, thank you—I'll take to the streets!

STELLA: Talk sense! How did you happen to get so low on funds?

BLANCHE: Money just goes—it goes places. [*She rubs her forehead.*] Sometime today I've got to get hold of a Bromo![3]

---

2. The largest American telegraph company throughout most of the twentieth century.

3. Short for "Bromo Seltzer," a headache remedy.

STELLA: I'll fix you one now.

BLANCHE: Not yet—I've got to keep thinking!

STELLA: I wish you'd just let things go, at least for a—while.

BLANCHE: Stella, I can't live with him! You can, he's your husband. But how could I stay here with him, after last night, with just those curtains between us?

STELLA: Blanche, you saw him at his worst last night.

BLANCHE: On the contrary, I saw him at his best! What such a man has to offer is animal force and he gave a wonderful exhibition of that! But the only way to live with such a man is to—go to bed with him! And that's your job—not mine!

STELLA: After you've rested a little, you'll see it's going to work out. You don't have to worry about anything while you're here. I mean—expenses . . .

BLANCHE: I have to plan for us both, to get us both—out!

STELLA: You take it for granted that I am in something that I want to get out of.

BLANCHE: I take it for granted that you still have sufficient memory of Belle Reve to find this place and these poker players impossible to live with.

STELLA: Well, you're taking entirely too much for granted.

BLANCHE: I can't believe you're in earnest.

STELLA: No?

BLANCHE: I understand how it happened—a little. You saw him in uniform, an officer, not here but—

STELLA: I'm not sure it would have made any difference where I saw him.

BLANCHE: Now don't say it was one of those mysterious electric things between people! If you do I'll laugh in your face.

STELLA: I am not going to say anything more at all about it!

BLANCHE: All right, then, don't!

STELLA: But there are things that happen between a man and a woman in the dark—that sort of make everything else seem—unimportant. [*Pause.*]

BLANCHE: What you are talking about is brutal desire—just—Desire!—the name of that rattle-trap streetcar that bangs through the Quarter, up one old narrow street and down another. . . .

STELLA: Haven't you ever ridden on that streetcar?

BLANCHE: It brought me here.—Where I'm not wanted and where I'm ashamed to be. . . .

STELLA: Then don't you think your superior attitude is a bit out of place?

BLANCHE: I am not being or feeling at all superior, Stella. Believe me I'm not! It's just this. This is how I look at it. A man like that is someone to go out with—once—twice—three times when the devil is in you. But live with? Have a child by?

STELLA: I have told you I love him.

BLANCHE: Then I *tremble* for you! I just—*tremble* for you. . . .
STELLA: I can't help your trembling if you insist on trembling!

[*There is a pause.*]

BLANCHE: May I—speak—*plainly?*
STELLA: Yes, do. Go ahead. As plainly as you want to.

[*Outside, a train approaches. They are silent till the noise subsides. They are both in the bedroom. Under cover of the train's noise* STANLEY *enters from outside. He stands unseen by the women, holding some packages in his arms, and overhears their following conversation. He wears an undershirt and grease-stained seersucker pants.*]

BLANCHE: Well—if you'll forgive me—he's *common!*
STELLA: Why, yes, I suppose he is.
BLANCHE: Suppose! You can't have forgotten that much of our bringing up, Stella, that you just *suppose* that any part of a gentleman's in his nature! *Not one particle, no!* Oh, if he was just—*ordinary!* Just *plain*—but good and wholesome, but—*no.* There's something downright—*bestial*—about him! You're hating me saying this, aren't you?
STELLA: [*Coldly.*] Go on and say it all, Blanche.
BLANCHE: He acts like an animal, has an animal's habits! Eats like one, moves like one, talks like one! There's even something—sub-human—something not quite to the stage of humanity yet! Yes, something—ape-like about him, like one of those pictures I've seen in—anthropological studies! Thousands and thousands of years have passed him right by, and there he is—Stanley Kowalski—survivor of the Stone Age! Bearing the raw meat home from the kill in the jungle! And you—*you* here—*waiting* for him! Maybe he'll strike you or maybe grunt and kiss you! That is, if kisses have been discovered yet! Night falls and the other apes gather! There in the front of the cave, all grunting like him, and swilling and gnawing and hulking! His poker night! you call it—this party of apes! Somebody growls—some creature snatches at something—the fight is on! *God!* Maybe we are a long way from being made in God's image, but Stella—my sister—there has been *some* progress since then! Such things as art—as poetry and music—such kinds of new light have come into the world since then! In some kinds of people some tenderer feelings have had some little beginning! That we have got to make *grow!* And *cling* to, and hold as our flag! In this dark march toward whatever it is we're approaching. . . . *Don't—don't hang back with the brutes!*

[*Another train passes outside.* STANLEY *hesitates, licking his lips. Then suddenly he turns stealthily about and withdraws through front door. The women are still unaware of his presence. When the train has passed he calls through the closed front door.*]

STANLEY: Hey! Hey, Stella!
STELLA: [*Who has listened gravely to* BLANCHE.] Stanley!
BLANCHE: Stell, I—

[*But* STELLA *has gone to the front door.* STANLEY *enters casually with his packages.*]

STANLEY: Hiyuh, Stella. Blanche back?
STELLA: Yes, she's back.
STANLEY: Hiyuh, Blanche. [*He grins at her.*]
STELLA: You must've got under the car.
STANLEY: Them darn mechanics at Fritz's don't know their ass fr'm—Hey!

[STELLA *has embraced him with both arms, fiercely, and full in the view of* BLANCHE. *He laughs and clasps her head to him. Over her head he grins through the curtains at* BLANCHE. *As the lights fade away, with a lingering brightness on their embrace, the music of the "Blue Piano" and trumpet and drums is heard.*]

Scene 5

BLANCHE *is seated in the bedroom fanning herself with a palm leaf as she reads over a just-completed letter. Suddenly she bursts into a peal of laughter.* STELLA *is dressing in the bedroom.*

STELLA: What are you laughing at, honey?
BLANCHE: Myself, myself, for being such a liar! I'm writing a letter to Shep. [*She picks up the letter.*] "Darling Shep. I am spending the summer on the wing, making flying visits here and there. And who knows, perhaps I shall take a sudden notion to *swoop* down on *Dallas*! How would you feel about that? Ha-ha! [*She laughs nervously and brightly, touching her throat as if actually talking to Shep.*] Forewarned is forearmed, as they say!"—How does that sound?
STELLA: Uh-huh . . .
BLANCHE: [*Going on nervously.*] "Most of my sister's friends go north in the summer but some have homes on the Gulf and there has been a continued round of entertainments, teas, cocktails, and luncheons—"

[*A disturbance is heard upstairs at the Hubbells' apartment.*]

STELLA: Eunice seems to be having some trouble with Steve. [EUNICE's *voice shouts in terrible wrath.*]
EUNICE: I heard about you and that blonde!
STEVE: That's a damn lie!
EUNICE: You ain't pulling the wool over my eyes! I wouldn't mind if you'd stay down at the Four Deuces, but you always going up.
STEVE: Who ever seen me up?

EUNICE: I seen you chasing her 'round the balcony—I'm gonna call the vice squad!

STEVE: Don't you throw that at me!

EUNICE: [*Shrieking.*] You hit me! I'm gonna call the police!

[*A clatter of aluminum striking a wall is heard, followed by a man's angry roar, shouts, and overturned furniture. There is a crash; then a relative hush.*]

BLANCHE: [*Brightly.*] Did he *kill* her?

[EUNICE *appears on the steps in daemonic disorder.*]

STELLA: No! She's coming downstairs.

EUNICE: Call the police, I'm going to call the police! [*She rushes around the corner.*]

[*They laugh lightly.* STANLEY *comes around the corner in his green and scarlet silk bowling shirt. He trots up the steps and bangs into the kitchen.* BLANCHE *registers his entrance with nervous gestures.*]

STANLEY: What's a matter with Eun-uss?

STELLA: She and Steve had a row. Has she got the police?

STANLEY: Naw. She's gettin' a drink.

STELLA: That's much more practical!

[STEVE *comes down nursing a bruise on his forehead and looks in the door.*]

STEVE: She here?

STANLEY: Naw, naw. At the Four Deuces.

STEVE: That rutting hunk! [*He looks around the corner a bit timidly, then turns with affected boldness and runs after her.*]

BLANCHE: I must jot that down in my notebook. Ha-ha! I'm compiling a notebook of quaint little words and phrases I've picked up here.

STANLEY: You won't pick up nothing here you ain't heard before.

BLANCHE: Can I count on that?

STANLEY: You can count on it up to five hundred.

BLANCHE: That's a mighty high number. [*He jerks open the bureau drawer, slams it shut and throws shoes in a corner. At each noise* BLANCHE *winces slightly. Finally she speaks.*] What sign were you born under?

STANLEY: [*While he is dressing.*] Sign?

BLANCHE: Astrological sign. I bet you were born under Aries. Aries people are forceful and dynamic. They dote on noise! They love to bang things around! You must have had lots of banging around in the army and now that you're out, you make up for it by treating inanimate objects with such a fury!

[STELLA *has been going in and out of closet during this scene. Now she pops her head out of the closet.*]

STELLA: Stanley was born just five minutes after Christmas.

BLANCHE: Capricorn—the Goat!

STANLEY: What sign were *you* born under?

BLANCHE: Oh, my birthday's next month, the fifteenth of September; that's under Virgo.

STANLEY: What's Virgo?

BLANCHE: Virgo is the Virgin.

STANLEY: [*Contemptuously.*] Hah! [*He advances a little as he knots his tie.*] Say, do you happen to know somebody named Shaw?

[*Her face expresses a faint shock. She reaches for the cologne bottle and dampens her handkerchief as she answers carefully.*]

BLANCHE: Why, everybody knows somebody named Shaw!

STANLEY: Well, this somebody named Shaw is under the impression he met you in Laurel, but I figure he must have got you mixed up with some other party because this other party is someone he met at a hotel called the Flamingo.

[BLANCHE *laughs breathlessly as she touches the cologne-dampened handkerchief to her temples.*]

BLANCHE: I'm afraid he does have me mixed up with this "other party." The Hotel Flamingo is not the sort of establishment I would dare to be seen in!

STANLEY: You know of it?

BLANCHE: Yes, I've seen it and smelled it.

STANLEY: You must've got pretty close if you could smell it.

BLANCHE: The odor of cheap perfume is penetrating.

STANLEY: That stuff you use is expensive?

BLANCHE: Twenty-five dollars an ounce! I'm nearly out. That's just a hint if you want to remember my birthday! [*She speaks lightly but her voice has a note of fear.*]

STANLEY: Shaw must've got you mixed up. He goes in and out of Laurel all the time so he can check on it and clear up any mistake.

[*He turns away and crosses to the portieres.* BLANCHE *closes her eyes as if faint. Her hand trembles as she lifts the handkerchief again to her forehead.* STEVE *and* EUNICE *come around corner.* STEVE'*s arm is around* EUNICE'*s shoulder and she is sobbing luxuriously and he is cooing love-words. There is a murmur of thunder as they go slowly upstairs in a tight embrace.*]

STANLEY: [*To* STELLA.] I'll wait for you at the Four Deuces!

STELLA: Hey! Don't I rate one kiss?

STANLEY: Not in front of your sister.

[*He goes out.* BLANCHE *rises from her chair. She seems faint; looks about her with an expression of almost panic.*]

BLANCHE: Stella! What have you heard about me?

STELLA: Huh?

BLANCHE: What have people been telling you about me?

STELLA: Telling?

BLANCHE: You haven't heard any—unkind—gossip about me?

STELLA: Why, no, Blanche, of course not!

BLANCHE: Honey, there was—a good deal of talk in Laurel.

STELLA: About *you*, Blanche?

BLANCHE: I wasn't so good the last two years or so, after Belle Reve had started to slip through my fingers.

STELLA: All of us do things we—

BLANCHE: I never was hard or self-sufficient enough. When people are soft—soft people have got to shimmer and glow—they've got to put on soft colors, the colors of butterfly wings, and put a—paper lantern over the light. . . . It isn't enough to be soft *and attractive*. And I—I'm fading now! I don't know how much longer I can turn the trick. [*The afternoon has faded to dusk.* STELLA *goes into the bedroom and turns on the light under the paper lantern. She holds a bottled soft drink in her hand.*] Have you been listening to me?

STELLA: I don't listen to you when you are being morbid! [*She advances with the bottled Coke.*]

BLANCHE: [*With abrupt change to gaiety.*] Is that Coke for me?

STELLA: Not for anyone else!

BLANCHE: Why, you precious thing, you! Is it just Coke?

STELLA: [*Turning.*] You mean you want a shot in it!

BLANCHE: Well, honey, a shot never does a Coke any harm! Let me! You mustn't wait on me!

STELLA: I like to wait on you, Blanche. It makes it seem more like home. [*She goes into the kitchen, finds a glass and pours a shot of whiskey into it.*]

BLANCHE: I have to admit I love to be waited on . . . [*She rushes into the bedroom.* STELLA *goes to her with the glass.* BLANCHE *suddenly clutches* STELLA's *free hand with a moaning sound and presses the hand to her lips.* STELLA *is embarrassed by her show of emotion.* BLANCHE *speaks in a choked voice.*] You're—you're—so *good* to me! And I—

STELLA: Blanche.

BLANCHE: I know, I won't! You hate me to talk sentimental! But honey, *believe* I feel things more than I *tell* you! I *won't* stay long! I won't, I *promise* I—

STELLA: Blanche!

BLANCHE: [*Hysterically.*] I won't, I promise, *I'll* go! Go *soon*! I will *really*! I *won't* hang around until he—throws me out. . . .

STELLA: Now will you stop talking foolish?

BLANCHE: Yes, honey. Watch how you pour—that fizzy stuff foams over!

[BLANCHE *laughs shrilly and grabs the glass, but her hand shakes so it almost slips from her grasp.* STELLA *pours the Coke into the glass. It foams over and spills.* BLANCHE *gives a piercing cry.*]

STELLA: [*Shocked by the cry.*] Heavens!

BLANCHE: Right on my pretty white skirt!

STELLA: Oh . . . Use my hanky. Blot gently.

BLANCHE: [*Slowly recovering.*] I know—gently—gently . . .

STELLA: Did it stain?

BLANCHE: Not a bit. Ha-ha! Isn't that lucky? [*She sits down shakily, taking a grateful drink. She holds the glass in both hands and continues to laugh a little.*]

STELLA: Why did you scream like that?

BLANCHE: I don't know why I screamed! [*Continuing nervously.*] Mitch—Mitch is coming at seven. I guess I am just feeling nervous about our relations. [*She begins to talk rapidly and breathlessly.*] He hasn't gotten a thing but a good-night kiss, that's all I have given him, Stella. I want his respect. And men don't want anything they get too easy. But on the other hand men lose interest quickly. Especially when the girl is over—thirty. They think a girl over thirty ought to—the vulgar term is—"put out." . . . And I—I'm not "putting out." Of course he—he doesn't know—I mean I haven't informed him—of my real age!

STELLA: Why are you sensitive about your age?

BLANCHE: Because of hard knocks my vanity's been given. What I mean is—he thinks I'm sort of—prim and proper, you know! [*She laughs out sharply.*] I want to *deceive* him enough to make him—want me . . .

STELLA: Blanche, do you want *him*?

BLANCHE: I want to *rest*! I want to breathe quietly again! Yes—I *want* Mitch . . . *very badly*! Just think! If it happens! I can leave here and not be anyone's problem. . . .

[STANLEY *comes around the corner with a drink under his belt.*]

STANLEY: [*Bawling.*] Hey, Steve! Hey, Eunice! Hey, Stella!

[*There are joyous calls from above. Trumpet and drums are heard from around the corner.*]

STELLA: [*Kissing* BLANCHE *impulsively.*] It *will* happen!

BLANCHE: [*Doubtfully.*] It will?

STELLA: It *will*! [*She goes across into the kitchen, looking back at* BLANCHE.] It will, honey, it *will*. . . . But don't take another drink! [*Her voice catches as she goes out the door to meet her husband.*]

[BLANCHE *sinks faintly back in her chair with her drink.* EUNICE *shrieks with laughter and runs down the steps.* STEVE *bounds after her with goat-like screeches and chases her around corner.* STANLEY *and* STELLA *twine arms as they follow, laughing. Dusk settles deeper. The music from the Four Deuces is slow and blue.*]

BLANCHE: Ah, me, ah, me, ah, me . . . [*Her eyes fall shut and the palm leaf fan drops from her fingers. She slaps her hand on the chair arm a couple of times. There is a little glimmer of lightning about the building. A* YOUNG MAN *comes along the street and rings the bell.*] Come in. [*The* YOUNG MAN *appears through the portieres. She regards him with interest.*] Well, well! What can I do for *you?*

YOUNG MAN: I'm collecting for *The Evening Star.*

BLANCHE: I didn't know that stars took up collections.

YOUNG MAN: It's the paper.

BLANCHE: I know, I was joking—feebly! Will you—have a drink?

YOUNG MAN: No, ma'am. No, thank you. I can't drink on the job.

BLANCHE: Oh, well, now, let's see. . . . No, I don't have a dime! I'm not the lady of the house. I'm her sister from Mississippi. I'm one of those poor relations you've heard about.

YOUNG MAN: That's all right. I'll drop by later. [*He starts to go out. She approaches a little.*]

BLANCHE: Hey! [*He turns back shyly. She puts a cigarette in a long holder.*] Could you give me a light? [*She crosses toward him. They meet at the door between the two rooms.*]

YOUNG MAN: Sure. [*He takes out a lighter.*] This doesn't always work.

BLANCHE: It's temperamental? [*It flares.*] Ah!—thank you. [*He starts away again.*] Hey! [*He turns again, still more uncertainly. She goes close to him.*] Uh—what time is it?

YOUNG MAN: Fifteen of seven, ma'am.

BLANCHE: So late? Don't you just love these long rainy afternoons in New Orleans when an hour isn't just an hour—but a little piece of eternity dropped into your hands—and who knows what to do with it? [*She touches his shoulders.*] You—uh—didn't get wet in the rain?

YOUNG MAN: No, ma'am. I stepped inside.

BLANCHE: In a drugstore? And had a soda?

YOUNG MAN: Uh-huh.

BLANCHE: Chocolate?

YOUNG MAN: No, ma'am. Cherry.

BLANCHE: [*Laughing.*] Cherry!

YOUNG MAN: A cherry soda.

BLANCHE: You make my mouth water. [*She touches his cheek lightly, and smiles. Then she goes to the trunk.*]

YOUNG MAN: Well, I'd better be going—

BLANCHE: [*Stopping him.*] Young man! [*He turns. She takes a large, gossamer scarf from the trunk and drapes it about her shoulders. In the ensuing pause, the "Blue Piano" is heard. It continues through the rest of this scene and the opening of the next. The* YOUNG MAN *clears his throat and looks yearningly at the door.*] Young man! Young, young, young man! Has anyone ever told you that you look like a young Prince out of the Arabian Nights?[4] [*The* YOUNG MAN *laughs uncomfortably and stands like a bashful kid.* BLANCHE *speaks softly to him.*] Well, you do, honey lamb! Come here. I want to kiss you, just once, softly and sweetly on your mouth! [*Without waiting for him to accept, she crosses quickly to him and presses her lips to his.*] Now run along, now, quickly! It would be nice to keep you, but I've got to be good—and keep my hands off children.

[*He stares at her a moment. She opens the door for him and blows a kiss at him as he goes down the steps with a dazed look. She stands there a little dreamily after he has disappeared. Then* MITCH *appears around the corner with a bunch of roses.*]

BLANCHE: [*Gaily.*] Look who's coming! My Rosenkavalier! Bow to me first . . . now present them! Ahhhh—Merciiii![5] [*She looks at him over them, coquettishly pressing them to her lips. He beams at her self-consciously.*]

Scene 6

It is about two a.m. on the same evening. The outer wall of the building is visible. BLANCHE *and* MITCH *come in. The utter exhaustion which only a neurasthenic personality[6] can know is evident in* BLANCHE*'s voice and manner.* MITCH *is stolid but depressed. They have probably been out to the amusement park on Lake Pontchartrain,[7] for* MITCH *is bearing, upside down, a plaster statuette of Mae West, the sort of prize won at shooting galleries and carnival games of chance.*

BLANCHE: [*Stopping lifelessly at the steps.*] Well—[MITCH *laughs uneasily.*] Well . . .
MITCH: I guess it must be pretty late—and you're tired.
BLANCHE: Even the hot tamale man has deserted the street, and he hangs on till the end. [MITCH *laughs uneasily again.*] How will you get home?
MITCH: I'll walk over to Bourbon and catch an owl-car.[8]
BLANCHE: [*Laughing grimly.*] Is that street-car named Desire still grinding along the tracks at this hour?
MITCH: [*Heavily.*] I'm afraid you haven't gotten much fun out of this evening, Blanche.
BLANCHE: I spoiled it for *you.*

---

4. *The Arabian Nights* is a collection of Persian, Indian, and Arabic folktales.
5. *Merci*: thank you (French). *Rosenkavalier*: Knight of the Rose (German), title of a romantic opera (1911) by Richard Strauss (1864–1949).
6. Nineteenth-century diagnostic term for a psychological disorder characterized by nervous exhaustion and other physical symptoms.
7. Large coastal inlet in southern Louisiana; New Orleans is located on its south shore. *Mae West*: American star of stage and film (1892–1980).   8. All-night streetcar.

MITCH: No, you didn't, but I felt all the time that I wasn't giving you much—entertainment.

BLANCHE: I simply couldn't rise to the occasion. That was all. I don't think I've ever tried so hard to be gay and made such a dismal mess of it. I get ten points for trying!—I *did* try.

MITCH: Why did you try if you didn't feel like it, Blanche?

BLANCHE: I was just obeying the law of nature.

MITCH: Which law is that?

BLANCHE: The one that says the lady must entertain the gentleman—or no dice! See if you can locate my door key in this purse. When I'm so tired my fingers are all thumbs!

MITCH: [*Rooting in her purse.*] This it?

BLANCHE: No, honey, that's the key to my trunk which I must soon be packing.

MITCH: You mean you are leaving here soon?

BLANCHE: I've outstayed my welcome.

MITCH: This it?

[*The music fades away.*]

BLANCHE: Eureka! Honey, you open the door while I take a last look at the sky. [*She leans on the porch rail. He opens the door and stands awkwardly behind her.*] I'm looking for the Pleiades,[9] the Seven Sisters, but these girls are not out tonight. Oh, yes they are, there they are! God bless them! All in a bunch going home from their little bridge party. . . . Y' get the door open? Good boy! I guess you—want to go now. . . .

[*He shuffles and coughs a little.*]

MITCH: Can I—uh—kiss you—good night?

BLANCHE: Why do you always ask me if you may?

MITCH: I don't know whether you want me to or not.

BLANCHE: Why should you be so doubtful?

MITCH: That night when we parked by the lake and I kissed you, you—

BLANCHE: Honey, it wasn't the kiss I objected to. I liked the kiss very much. It was the other little—familiarity—that I—felt obliged to—discourage. . . . I didn't resent it! Not a bit in the world! In fact, I was somewhat flattered that you—desired me! But, honey, you know as well as I do that a single girl, a girl alone in the world, has got to keep a firm hold on her emotions or she'll be lost!

MITCH: [*Solemnly.*] Lost?

BLANCHE: I guess you are used to girls that like to be lost. The kind that get lost immediately, on the first date!

---

9. Constellation named for the seven daughters of Atlas who were changed into stars.

MITCH: I like you to be exactly the way that you are, because in all my—experience—I have never known anyone like you. [BLANCHE *looks at him gravely; then she bursts into laughter and then claps a hand to her mouth.*] Are you laughing at me?

BLANCHE: No, honey. The lord and lady of the house have not yet returned, so come in. We'll have a nightcap. Let's leave the lights off. Shall we?

MITCH: You just—do what you want to.

[BLANCHE *precedes him into the kitchen. The outer wall of the building disappears and the interiors of the two rooms can be dimly seen.*]

BLANCHE: [*Remaining in the first room.*] The other room's more comfortable—go on in. This crashing around in the dark is my search for some liquor.

MITCH: You want a drink?

BLANCHE: I want *you* to have a drink! You have been so anxious and solemn all evening, and so have I; we have both been anxious and solemn and now for these few last remaining moments of our lives together—I want to create—*joie de vivre!*[1] I'm lighting a candle.

MITCH: That's good.

BLANCHE: We are going to be very Bohemian. We are going to pretend that we are sitting in a little artists' cafe on the Left Bank in Paris! [*She lights a candle stub and puts it in a bottle.*] Je suis la Dame aux Camellias! Vous êtes—Armand![2] Understand French?

MITCH: [*Heavily.*] Naw. Naw, I—

BLANCHE: Voulez-vous couchez avec moi ce soir? Vous ne comprenez pas? Ah, quelle dommage![3]—I mean it's a damned good thing. . . . I've found some liquor! Just enough for two shots without any dividends, honey. . . .

MITCH: [*Heavily.*] That's—good.

[*She enters the bedroom with the drinks and the candle.*]

BLANCHE: Sit down! Why don't you take off your coat and loosen your collar?

MITCH: I better leave it on.

BLANCHE: No. I want you to be comfortable.

MITCH: I am ashamed of the way I perspire. My shirt is sticking to me.

BLANCHE: Perspiration is healthy. If people didn't perspire they would die in five minutes. [*She takes his coat from him.*] This is a nice coat. What kind of material is it?

1. Joy of life (French).
2. I am the Lady of the Camellias! You are—Armand! (French) Both are characters in the popular romantic play *La Dame aux Camélias* (1852) by the French author Alexandre Dumas (1824–95); she is a courtesan who gives up her true love, Armand. *Left Bank*: section of Paris on the westward ("left") bank of the river Seine, long associated with students and artists.
3. Would you like to sleep with me this evening? You don't understand? Ah, what a pity! (French).

MITCH: They call that stuff alpaca.

BLANCHE: Oh. Alpaca.

MITCH: It's very light-weight alpaca.

BLANCHE: Oh. Light-weight alpaca.

MITCH: I don't like to wear a wash-coat[4] even in summer because I sweat through it.

BLANCHE: Oh.

MITCH: And it don't look neat on me. A man with a heavy build has got to be careful of what he puts on him so he don't look too clumsy.

BLANCHE: You are not too heavy.

MITCH: You don't think I am?

BLANCHE: You are not the delicate type. You have a massive bone-structure and a very imposing physique.

MITCH: Thank you. Last Christmas I was given a membership to the New Orleans Athletic Club.

BLANCHE: Oh, good.

MITCH: It was the finest present I ever was given. I work out there with the weights and I swim and I keep myself fit. When I started there, I was getting soft in the belly but now my belly is hard. It is so hard now that a man can punch me in the belly and it don't hurt me. Punch me! Go on! See? [She pokes lightly at him.]

BLANCHE: Gracious. [Her hand touches her chest.]

MITCH: Guess how much I weigh, Blanche?

BLANCHE: Oh, I'd say in the vicinity of—one hundred and eighty?

MITCH: Guess again.

BLANCHE: Not that much?

MITCH: No. More.

BLANCHE: Well, you're a tall man and you can carry a good deal of weight without looking awkward.

MITCH: I weigh two hundred and seven pounds and I'm six feet one and one half inches tall in my bare feet—without shoes on. And that is what I weigh stripped.

BLANCHE: Oh, my goodness, me! It's awe-inspiring.

MITCH: [Embarrassed.] My weight is not a very interesting subject to talk about. [He hesitates for a moment.] What's yours?

BLANCHE: My weight?

MITCH: Yes.

BLANCHE: Guess!

MITCH: Let me lift you.

BLANCHE: Samson![5] Go on, lift me. [He comes behind her and puts his hands on her waist and raises her lightly off the ground.] Well?

MITCH: You are light as a feather.

---

4. Light washable jacket.   5. Legendary strong man, an Israelite in the Old Testament.

BLANCHE: Ha-ha! [*He lowers her but keeps his hands on her waist.* BLANCHE *speaks with an affectation of demureness.*] You may release me now.

MITCH: Huh?

BLANCHE: [*Gaily.*] I said unhand me, sir. [*He fumblingly embraces her. Her voice sounds gently reproving.*] Now, Mitch. Just because Stanley and Stella aren't at home is no reason why you shouldn't behave like a gentleman.

MITCH: Just give me a slap whenever I step out of bounds.

BLANCHE: That won't be necessary. You're a natural gentleman, one of the very few that are left in the world. I don't want you to think that I am severe and old maid school-teacherish or anything like that. It's just—well—

MITCH: Huh?

BLANCHE: I guess it is just that I have—old-fashioned ideals! [*She rolls her eyes, knowing he cannot see her face.* MITCH *goes to the front door. There is a considerable silence between them.* BLANCHE *sighs and* MITCH *coughs self-consciously.*]

MITCH: [*Finally.*] Where's Stanley and Stella tonight?

BLANCHE: They have gone out. With Mr. and Mrs. Hubbell upstairs.

MITCH: Where did they go?

BLANCHE: I think they were planning to go to a midnight prevue at Loew's State.

MITCH: We should all go out together some night.

BLANCHE: No. That wouldn't be a good plan.

MITCH: Why not?

BLANCHE: You are an old friend of Stanley's?

MITCH: We was together in the Two-forty-first.[6]

BLANCHE: I guess he talks to you frankly?

MITCH: Sure.

BLANCHE: Has he talked to you about me?

MITCH: Oh—not very much.

BLANCHE: The way you say that, I suspect that he has.

MITCH: No, he hasn't said much.

BLANCHE: But what he *has* said. What would you say his attitude toward me was?

MITCH: Why do you want to ask that?

BLANCHE: Well—

MITCH: Don't you get along with him?

BLANCHE: What do you think?

MITCH: I don't think he understands you.

BLANCHE: That is putting it mildly. If it weren't for Stella about to have a baby, I wouldn't be able to endure things here.

MITCH: He isn't—nice to you?

BLANCHE: He is insufferably rude. Goes out of his way to offend me.

MITCH: In what way, Blanche?

6. Battalion of engineers, in World War II.

BLANCHE: Why, in every conceivable way.

MITCH: I'm surprised to hear that.

BLANCHE: Are you?

MITCH: Well, I—don't see how anybody could be rude to you.

BLANCHE: It's really a pretty frightful situation. You see, there's no privacy here. There's just these portieres between the two rooms at night. He stalks through the rooms in his underwear at night. And I have to ask him to close the bathroom door. That sort of commonness isn't necessary. You probably wonder why I don't move out. Well, I'll tell you frankly. A teacher's salary is barely sufficient for her living expenses. I didn't save a penny last year and so I had to come here for the summer. That's why I have to put up with my sister's husband. And he has to put up with me, apparently so much against his wishes. . . . Surely he must have told you how much he hates he!

MITCH: I don't think he hates you.

BLANCHE: He hates me. Or why would he insult me? The first time I laid eyes on him I thought to myself, that man is my executioner! That man will destroy me, unless—

MITCH: Blanche—

BLANCHE: Yes, honey?

MITCH: Can I ask you a question?

BLANCHE: Yes. What?

MITCH: How old are you?

[*She makes a nervous gesture.*]

BLANCHE: Why do you want to know?

MITCH: I talked to my mother about you and she said, "How old is Blanche?" And I wasn't able to tell her. [*There is another pause.*]

BLANCHE: You talked to your mother about me?

MITCH: Yes.

BLANCHE: Why?

MITCH: I told my mother how nice you were, and I liked you.

BLANCHE: Were you sincere about that?

MITCH: You know I was.

BLANCHE: Why did your mother want to know my age?

MITCH: Mother is sick.

BLANCHE: I'm sorry to hear it. Badly?

MITCH: She won't live long. Maybe just a few months.

BLANCHE: Oh.

MITCH: She worries because I'm not settled.

BLANCHE: Oh.

MITCH: She wants me to be settled down before she— [*His voice is hoarse and he clears his throat twice, shuffling nervously around with his hands in and out of his pockets.*]

BLANCHE: You love her very much, don't you?
MITCH: Yes.
BLANCHE: I think you have a great capacity for devotion. You will be lonely when she passes on, won't you? [MITCH *clears his throat and nods.*] I understand what that is.
MITCH: To be lonely?
BLANCHE: I loved someone, too, and the person I loved I lost.
MITCH: Dead? [*She crosses to the window and sits on the sill, looking out. She pours herself another drink.*] A man?
BLANCHE: He was a boy, just a boy, when I was a very young girl. When I was sixteen, I made the discovery—love. All at once and much, much too completely. It was like you suddenly turned a blinding light on something that had always been half in shadow, that's how it struck the world for me. But I was unlucky. Deluded. There was something different about the boy, a nervousness, a softness and tenderness which wasn't like a man's, although he wasn't the least bit effeminate looking—still— that thing was there.... He came to me for help. I didn't know that. I didn't find out anything till after our marriage when we'd run away and come back and all I knew was I'd failed him in some mysterious way and wasn't able to give the help he needed but couldn't speak of! He was in the quicksands and clutching at me—but I wasn't holding him out, I was slipping in with him! I didn't know that. I didn't know anything except I loved him unendurably but without being able to help him or help myself. Then I found out. In the worst of all possible ways. By coming suddenly into a room that I thought was empty—which wasn't empty, but had two people in it ... the boy I had married and an older man who had been his friend for years.... [*A locomotive is heard approaching outside. She claps her hands to her ears and crouches over. The headlight of the locomotive glares into the room as it thunders past. As the noise recedes she straightens slowly and continues speaking.*] Afterward we pretended that nothing had been discovered. Yes, the three of us drove out to Moon Lake Casino,[7] very drunk and laughing all the way. [*Polka music sounds, in a minor key faint with distance.*] We danced the "Varsouviana!"[8] Suddenly in the middle of the dance the boy I had married broke away from me and ran out of the casino. A few moments later—a shot! [*The polka stops abruptly.* BLANCHE *rises stiffly. Then, the polka resumes in a major key.*] I ran out—all did!—all ran and gathered about the terrible thing at the edge of the lake! I couldn't get near for the crowding. Then somebody caught my arm. "Don't go any closer! Come back! You don't want to see!" See? See what! Then I heard voices say—Allan! Allan! The Grey boy! He'd stuck the revolver into his mouth, and fired—so that the back of his head had been—blown away!

7. Casino and night club in Dundee, Mississippi, popular during the 1940s.
8. Fast Polish dance, similar to the polka.

[*She sways and covers her face.*] It was because—on the dance floor—unable to stop myself—I'd suddenly said—"I saw! I know! You disgust me. . . ." And then the searchlight which had been turned on the world was turned off again and never for one moment since has there been any light that's stronger than this—kitchen—candle. . . .

[MITCH *gets up awkwardly and moves toward her a little. The polka music increases.* MITCH *stands beside her.*]

MITCH: [*Drawing her slowly into his arms.*] You need somebody. And I need somebody, too. Could it be—you and me, Blanche?

[*She stares at him vacantly for a moment. Then with a soft cry huddles in his embrace. She makes a sobbing effort to speak but the words won't come. He kisses her forehead and her eyes and finally her lips. The polka tune fades out. Her breath is drawn and released in long, grateful sobs.*]

BLANCHE: Sometimes—there's God—so quickly!

Scene 7

It is late afternoon in mid-September.
The portieres are open and a table is set for a birthday supper, with cake and flowers.
STELLA *is completing the decorations as* STANLEY *comes in.*

STANLEY: What's all this stuff for?
STELLA: Honey, it's Blanche's birthday.
STANLEY: She here?
STELLA: In the bathroom.
STANLEY: [*Mimicking.*] "Washing out some things"?
STELLA: I reckon so.
STANLEY: How long she been in there?
STELLA: All afternoon.
STANLEY: [*Mimicking.*] "Soaking in a hot tub"?
STELLA: Yes.
STANLEY: Temperature 100 on the nose, and she soaks herself in a hot tub.
STELLA: She says it cools her off for the evening.
STANLEY: And you run out an' get her cokes, I suppose? And serve 'em to Her Majesty in the tub? [STELLA *shrugs.*] Set down here a minute.
STELLA: Stanley, I've got things to do.
STANLEY: Set down! I've got th' dope on your big sister, Stella.
STELLA: Stanley, stop picking on Blanche.
STANLEY: That girl calls *me* common!
STELLA: Lately you been doing all you can think of to rub her the wrong way, Stanley, and Blanche is sensitive and you've got to realize that

Blanche and I grew up under very different circumstances than you did.

STANLEY: So I been told. And told and told and told! You know she's been feeding us a pack of lies here?

STELLA: No, I don't and—

STANLEY: Well, she has, however. But now the cat's out of the bag! I found out some things!

STELLA: What—things?

STANLEY: Things I already suspected. But now I got proof from the most reliable sources—which I have checked on!

[BLANCHE *is singing in the bathroom a saccharine*[9] *popular ballad which is used contrapuntally with* STANLEY'S *speech.*]

STELLA: [*To* STANLEY.] Lower your voice!

STANLEY: Some canary bird, huh!

STELLA: Now please tell me quietly what you think you've found out about my sister.

STANLEY: Lie Number One: All this squeamishness she puts on! You should just know the line she's been feeding to Mitch. He thought she had never been more than kissed by a fellow! But Sister Blanche is no lily! Ha-ha! Some lily she is!

STELLA: What have you heard and who from?

STANLEY: Our supply-man down at the plant has been going through Laurel for years and he knows all about her and everybody else in the town of Laurel knows all about her. She is as famous in Laurel as if she was the President of the United States, only she is not respected by any party! This supply-man stops at a hotel called the Flamingo.

BLANCHE: [*Singing blithely.*] "Say, it's only a paper moon, Sailing over a cardboard sea /—But it wouldn't be make-believe If you believed in me!"[1]

STELLA: What about the—Flamingo?

STANLEY: She stayed there, too.

STELLA: My sister lived at Belle Reve.

STANLEY: This is after the home-place had slipped through her lily-white fingers! She moved to the Flamingo! A second-class hotel which has the advantage of not interfering in the private social life of the personalities there! The Flamingo is used to all kinds of goings-on. But even the management of the Flamingo was impressed by Dame Blanche! In fact they was so impressed by Dame Blanche that they requested her to turn in her room key—for permanently! This happened a couple of weeks before she showed here.

9. Cloyingly sweet; overly sentimental. *Contrapuntally*: musical term meaning "in an alternating or contrasting manner."

1. From "It's Only a Paper Moon" (1933), a popular song by Harold Arlen (1905–86).

BLANCHE: [*Singing.*] "It's a Barnum and Bailey[2] world, Just as phony as it can be—/ But it wouldn't be make-believe If you believed in me!"

STELLA: What—contemptible—lies!

STANLEY: Sure, I can see how you would be upset by this. She pulled the wool over your eyes as much as Mitch's!

STELLA: It's pure invention! There's not a word of truth in it and if I were a man and this creature had dared to invent such things in my presence—

BLANCHE: [*Singing.*] "Without your love, / it's a honky-tonk parade! / Without your love, / It's a melody played / In a penny arcade . . ."

STANLEY: Honey, I told you I thoroughly checked on these stories! Now wait till I finish. The trouble with Dame Blanche was that she couldn't put on her act anymore in Laurel! They got wised up after two or three dates with her and then they quit, and she goes on to another, the same old line, same old act, same old hooey! But the town was too small for this to go on forever! And as time went by she became a town character. Regarded as not just different but downright loco—nuts. [STELLA *draws back.*] And for the last year or two she has been washed up like poison. That's why she's here this summer, visiting royalty, putting on all this act—because she's practically told by the mayor to get out of town! Yes, did you know there was an army camp near Laurel and your sister's was one of the places called "Out-of-Bounds"?

BLANCHE: "It's only a paper moon, / Just as phony as it can be— / But it wouldn't be make-believe / If you believed in me!"

STANLEY: Well, so much for her being such a refined and particular type of girl. Which brings us to Lie Number Two.

STELLA: I don't want to hear any more!

STANLEY: She's not going back to teach school! In fact I am willing to bet you that she never had no idea of returning to Laurel! She didn't resign temporarily from the high school because of her nerves! No, siree, Bob! She didn't. They kicked her out of that high school before the spring term ended—and I hate to tell you the reason that step was taken! A seventeen-year-old boy—she'd gotten mixed up with!

BLANCHE: "It's a Barnum and Bailey world, / Just as phony as it can be—"

[*In the bathroom the water goes on loud; little breathless cries and peals of laughter are heard as if a child were frolicking in the tub.*]

STELLA: This is making me—sick!

STANLEY: The boy's dad learned about it and got in touch with the high school superintendent. Boy, oh, boy, I'd like to have been in that office when Dame Blanche was called on the carpet! I'd like to have seen her trying to squirm out of that one! But they had her on the hook good

---

2. P. T. Barnum (1810–91) and James Bailey (1847–1906), circus promoters of "The Greatest Show on Earth."

and proper that time and she knew that the jig was all up! They told her she better move on to some fresh territory. Yep, it was practickly a town ordinance passed against her!

[*The bathroom door is opened and* BLANCHE *thrusts her head out, holding a towel about her hair.*]

BLANCHE: Stella!

STELLA: [*Faintly.*] Yes, Blanche?

BLANCHE: Give me another bath-towel to dry my hair with. I've just washed it.

STELLA: Yes, Blanche. [*She crosses in a dazed way from the kitchen to the bathroom door with a towel.*]

BLANCHE: What's the matter, honey?

STELLA: Matter? Why?

BLANCHE: You have such a strange expression on your face!

STELLA: Oh—[*She tries to laugh.*] I guess I'm a little tired!

BLANCHE: Why don't you bathe, too, soon as I get out?

STANLEY: [*Calling from the kitchen.*] How soon is that going to be?

BLANCHE: Not so terribly long! Possess your soul in patience!³

STANLEY: It's not my soul, it's my kidneys I'm worried about! [BLANCHE *slams the door.* STANLEY *laughs harshly.* STELLA *comes slowly back into the kitchen.*] Well, what do you think of it?

STELLA: I don't believe all of those stories and I think your supply-man was mean and rotten to tell them. It's possible that some of the things he said are partly true. There are things about my sister I don't approve of—things that caused sorrow at home. She was always—flighty!

STANLEY: Flighty!

STELLA: But when she was young, very young, she married a boy who wrote poetry.... He was extremely good-looking. I think Blanche didn't just love him but worshipped the ground he walked on! Adored him and thought him almost too fine to be human! But then she found out—

STANLEY: What?

STELLA: This beautiful and talented young man was a degenerate. Didn't your supply-man give you that information?

STANLEY: All we discussed was recent history. That must have been a pretty long time ago.

STELLA: Yes, it was—a pretty long time ago....

[STANLEY *comes up and takes her by the shoulders rather gently. She gently withdraws from him. Automatically she starts sticking little pink candles in the birthday cake.*]

STANLEY: How many candles you putting in that cake?

3. "In your patience you will possess your souls" (Luke 21.19).

STELLA: I'll stop at twenty-five.

STANLEY: Is company expected?

STELLA: We asked Mitch to come over for cake and ice-cream.

[STANLEY *looks a little uncomfortable. He lights a cigarette from the one he has just finished.*]

STANLEY: I wouldn't be expecting Mitch over tonight.

[STELLA *pauses in her occupation with candles and looks slowly around at* STANLEY.]

STELLA: *Why?*

STANLEY: Mitch is a buddy of mine. We were in the same outfit together—Two-forty-first Engineers. We work in the same plant and now on the same bowling team. You think I could face him if—

STELLA: Stanley Kowalski, did you—did you repeat what that—?

STANLEY: You're goddam right I told him! I'd have that on my conscience the rest of my life if I knew all that stuff and let my best friend get caught!

STELLA: Is Mitch through with her?

STANLEY: Wouldn't you be if—?

STELLA: I said, *Is Mitch through with her?*

[BLANCHE'*s voice is lifted again, serenely as a bell. She sings "But it wouldn't be make-believe / If you believed in me."*]

STANLEY: No, I don't think he's necessarily through with her—just wised up!

STELLA: Stanley, she thought Mitch was—going to—going to marry her. I was hoping so, too.

STANLEY: Well, he's not going to marry her. Maybe he *was*, but he's not going to jump in a tank with a school of sharks—now! [*He rises.*] Blanche! Oh, Blanche! Can I please get in my bathroom? [*There is a pause.*]

BLANCHE: Yes, indeed, sir! Can you wait one second while I dry?

STANLEY: Having waited one hour I guess one second ought to pass in a hurry.

STELLA: And she hasn't got her job? Well, what will she do!

STANLEY: She's not stayin' here after Tuesday. You know that, don't you? Just to make sure I bought her ticket myself. A bus ticket.

STELLA: In the first place, Blanche wouldn't go on a bus.

STANLEY: She'll go on a bus and like it.

STELLA: No, she won't, no, she won't, Stanley!

STANLEY: *She'll go!* Period. P.S. She'll go *Tuesday*!

STELLA: [*Slowly.*] What'll—she—do? What on earth will she—do!

STANLEY: Her future is mapped out for her.

STELLA: What do you mean?

[BLANCHE *sings.*]

STANLEY: Hey, canary bird! Toots! Get *OUT* of the *BATHROOM!*

[*The bathroom door flies open and* BLANCHE *emerges with a gay peal of laughter, but as* STANLEY *crosses past her, a frightened look appears in her face, almost a look of panic. He doesn't look at her but slams the bathroom door shut as he goes in.*]

BLANCHE: [*Snatching up a hairbrush.*] Oh, I feel so good after my long, hot bath, I feel so good and cool and—rested!

STELLA: [*Sadly and doubtfully from the kitchen.*] Do you, Blanche?

BLANCHE: [*Snatching up a hairbrush.*] Yes, I do, so refreshed! [*She tinkles her highball glass.*] A hot bath and a long, cold drink always give me a brand new outlook on life! [*She looks through the portieres at* STELLA, *standing between them, and slowly stops brushing.*] Something has happened!—What is it?

STELLA: [*Turning away quickly.*] Why, nothing has happened, Blanche.

BLANCHE: You're lying! Something has! [*She stares fearfully at* STELLA, *who pretends to be busy at the table. The distant piano goes into a hectic breakdown.*]

Scene 8

Three quarters of an hour later.

The view through the big windows is fading gradually into a still-golden dusk. A torch of sunlight blazes on the side of a big water-tank or oil-drum across the empty lot toward the business district which is now pierced by pinpoints of lighted windows or windows reflecting the sunset.

The three people are completing a dismal birthday supper. STANLEY *looks sullen.* STELLA *is embarrassed and sad.*

BLANCHE *has a tight, artificial smile on her drawn face. There is a fourth place at the table which is left vacant.*

BLANCHE: [*Suddenly.*] Stanley, tell us a joke, tell us a funny story to make us all laugh. I don't know what's the matter, we're all so solemn. Is it because I've been stood up by my beau? [STELLA *laughs feebly.*] It's the first time in my entire experience with men, and I've had a good deal of all sorts, that I've actually been stood up by anybody! Ha-ha! I don't know how to take it. . . . Tell us a funny little story, Stanley! Something to help us out.

STANLEY: I didn't think you liked my stories, Blanche.

BLANCHE: I like them when they're amusing but not indecent.

STANLEY: I don't know any refined enough for your taste.

BLANCHE: Then let me tell one.

STELLA: Yes, you tell one, Blanche. You used to know lots of good stories.

[*The music fades.*]

BLANCHE: Let me see, now. . . . I must run through my repertoire! Oh, yes—I love parrot stories! Do you all like parrot stories? Well, this one's about the old maid and the parrot. This old maid, she had a parrot that cursed a blue streak and knew more vulgar expressions than Mr. Kowalski!

STANLEY: Huh.

BLANCHE: And the only way to hush the parrot up was to put the cover back on its cage so it would think it was night and go back to sleep. Well, one morning the old maid had just uncovered the parrot for the day—when who should she see coming up the front walk but the preacher! Well, she rushed back to the parrot and slipped the cover back on the cage and then she let in the preacher. And the parrot was perfectly still, just as quiet as a mouse, but just as she was asking the preacher how much sugar he wanted in his coffee—the parrot broke the silence with a loud— [*She whistles.*] —and said—"God *damn*, but that was a short day!" [*She throws back her head and laughs.* STELLA *also makes an ineffectual effort to seem amused.* STANLEY *pays no attention to the story but reaches way over the table to spear his fork into the remaining chop which he eats with his fingers.*] Apparently Mr. Kowalski was not amused.

STELLA: Mr. Kowalski is too busy making a pig of himself to think of anything else!

STANLEY: That's right, baby.

STELLA: Your face and your fingers are disgustingly greasy. Go and wash up and then help me clear the table.

[*He hurls a plate to the floor.*]

STANLEY: That's how I'll clear the table! [*He seizes her arm.*] Don't ever talk that way to me! "Pig—Polack—disgusting—vulgar—greasy!"—them kind of words have been on your tongue and your sister's too much around here! What do you two think you are? A pair of queens? Remember what Huey Long[4] said—"Every Man is a King!" And I am the king around here, so don't forget it! [*He hurls a cup and saucer to the floor.*] My place is cleared! You want me to clear your places?

[STELLA *begins to cry weakly.* STANLEY *stalks out on the porch and lights a cigarette. The Negro entertainers around the corner are heard.*]

BLANCHE: What happened while I was bathing? What did he tell you, Stella?

STELLA: Nothing, nothing, nothing!

BLANCHE: I think he told you something about Mitch and me! You know why Mitch didn't come but you won't tell me! [STELLA *shakes her head helplessly.*] I'm going to call him!

STELLA: I wouldn't call him, Blanche.

BLANCHE: I am, I'm going to call him on the phone.

---

4. Louisiana political leader, governor, and senator (1893-1935); a fiery and flamboyant populist.

STELLA: [*Miserably.*] I wish you wouldn't.

BLANCHE: I intend to be given some explanation from someone!

[*She rushes to the phone in the bedroom.* STELLA *goes out on the porch and stares reproachfully at her husband. He grunts and turns away from her.*]

STELLA: I hope you're pleased with your doings. I never had so much trouble swallowing food in my life, looking at that girl's face and the empty chair! [*She cries quietly.*]

BLANCHE: [*At the phone.*] Hello. Mr. Mitchell, please.... Oh.... I would like to leave a number if I may. Magnolia 9047. And say it's important to call.... Yes, very important.... Thank you. [*She remains by the phone with a lost, frightened look.*]

[STANLEY *turns slowly back toward his wife and takes her clumsily in his arms.*]

STANLEY: Stell, it's gonna be all right after she goes and after you've had the baby. It's gonna be all right again between you and me the way that it was. You remember the way that it was? Them nights we had together? God, honey, it's gonna be sweet when we can make noise in the night the way that we used to and get the colored lights going with nobody's sister behind the curtains to hear us! [*Their upstairs neighbors are heard in bellowing laughter at something.* STANLEY *chuckles.*] Steve an' Eunice...

STELLA: Come on back in. [*She returns to the kitchen and starts lighting the candles on the white cake.*] Blanche?

BLANCHE: Yes. [*She returns from the bedroom to the table in the kitchen.*] Oh, those pretty, pretty little candles! Oh, don't burn them, Stella.

STELLA: I certainly will.

[STANLEY *comes back in.*]

BLANCHE: You ought to save them for baby's birthdays. Oh, I hope candles are going to glow in his life and I hope that his eyes are going to be like candles, like two blue candles lighted in a white cake!

STANLEY: [*Sitting down.*] What poetry!

BLANCHE: [*She pauses reflectively for a moment.*] I shouldn't have called him.

STELLA: There's lots of things could have happened.

BLANCHE: There's no excuse for it, Stella. I don't have to put up with insults. I won't be taken for granted.

STANLEY: Goddamn, it's hot in here with the steam from the bathroom.

BLANCHE: I've said I was sorry three times. [*The piano fades out.*] I take hot baths for my nerves. Hydrotherapy, they call it. You healthy Polack, without a nerve in your body, of course you don't know what anxiety feels like!

STANLEY: I am not a Polack. People from Poland are Poles, not Polacks. But what I am is a one-hundred-per-cent American, born and raised in the greatest country on earth and proud as hell of it, so don't ever call me a Polack.

[*The phone rings.* BLANCHE *rises expectantly.*]

BLANCHE: Oh, that's for me, I'm sure.

STANLEY: *I'm* not sure. Keep your seat. [*He crosses leisurely to phone.*] H'lo. Aw, yeh, hello, Mac.

[*He leans against wall, staring insultingly in at* BLANCHE. *She sinks back in her chair with a frightened look.* STELLA *leans over and touches her shoulder.*]

BLANCHE: Oh, keep your hands off me, Stella. What is the matter with you? Why do you look at me with that pitying look?

STANLEY: [*Bawling.*] QUIET IN THERE!—We've got a noisy woman on the place.—Go on, Mac. At Riley's? No, I don't wanta bowl at Riley's. I had a little trouble with Riley last week. I'm the team captain, ain't I? All right, then, we're not gonna bowl at Riley's, we're gonna bowl at the West Side or the Gala! All right, Mac. See you! [*He hangs up and returns to the table.* BLANCHE *fiercely controls herself, drinking quickly from her tumbler of water. He doesn't look at her but reaches in a pocket. Then he speaks slowly and with false amiability.*] Sister Blanche, I've got a little birthday remembrance for you.

BLANCHE: Oh, have you, Stanley? I wasn't expecting any, I—I don't know why Stella wants to observe my birthday! I'd much rather forget it—when you—reach twenty-seven! Well—age is a subject that you'd prefer to—ignore!

STANLEY: Twenty-seven?

BLANCHE: [*Quickly.*] What is it? Is it for *me*?

[*He is holding a little envelope toward her.*]

STANLEY: Yes, I hope you like it!

BLANCHE: Why, why—Why, it's a—

STANLEY: Ticket! Back to Laurel! On the Greyhound![5] Tuesday! [*The "Varsouviana" music steals in softly and continues playing.* STELLA *rises abruptly and turns her back.* BLANCHE *tries to smile. Then she tries to laugh. Then she gives both up and springs from the table and runs into the next room. She clutches her throat and then runs into the bathroom. Coughing, gagging sounds are heard.*] Well!

STELLA: You didn't need to do that.

STANLEY: Don't forget all that I took off her.

STELLA: You needn't have been so cruel to someone alone as she is.

STANLEY: Delicate piece she is.

STELLA: She is. She was. You didn't know Blanche as a girl. Nobody, nobody, was tender and trusting as she was. But people like you abused her, and forced her to change. [*He crosses into the bedroom, ripping off his shirt, and*

---

5. Long-distance bus company.

changes into a brilliant silk bowling shirt. She follows him.] Do you think you're going bowling now?

STANLEY: Sure.

STELLA: You're not going bowling. [*She catches hold of his shirt.*] Why did you do this to her?

STANLEY: I done nothing to no one. Let go of my shirt. You've torn it.

STELLA: I want to know why. Tell me why.

STANLEY: When we first met, me and you, you thought I was common. How right you was, baby. I was common as dirt. You showed me the snapshot of the place with the columns. I pulled you down off them columns and how you loved it, having them colored lights going! And wasn't we happy together, wasn't it all okay till she showed here? [STELLA *makes a slight movement. Her look goes suddenly inward as if some interior voice had called her name. She begins a slow, shuffling progress from the bedroom to the kitchen, leaning and resting on the back of the chair and then on the edge of a table with a blind look and listening expression.* STANLEY, *finishing with his shirt, is unaware of her reaction.*] And wasn't we happy together? Wasn't it all okay? Till she showed here. Hoity-Toity, describing me as an ape. [*He suddenly notices the change in* STELLA.] Hey, what is it, Stell? [*He crosses to her.*]

STELLA: [*Quietly.*] Take me to the hospital.

[*He is with her now, supporting her with his arm, murmuring indistinguishably as they go outside.*]

Scene 9

A while later that evening. BLANCHE *is seated in a tense hunched position in a bedroom chair that she has recovered with diagonal green and white stripes. She has on her scarlet satin robe. On the table beside chair is a bottle of liquor and a glass. The rapid, feverish polka tune, the "Varsouviana," is heard. The music is in her mind; she is drinking to escape it and the sense of disaster closing in on her, and she seems to whisper the words of the song. An electric fan is turning back and forth across her.*

MITCH *comes around the corner in work clothes: blue denim shirt and pants. He is unshaven. He climbs the steps to the door and rings.* BLANCHE *is startled.*

BLANCHE: Who is it, please?

MITCH: [*Hoarsely.*] Me. Mitch.

[*The polka tune stops.*]

BLANCHE: Mitch!—Just a minute. [*She rushes about frantically, hiding the bottle in a closet, crouching at the mirror and dabbing her face with cologne and powder. She is so excited that her breath is audible as she dashes about. At last she rushes to the door in the kitchen and lets him in.*] Mitch!—Y'know, I really shouldn't let you in after the treatment I have received from you this evening! So utterly uncavalier! But hello, beautiful! [*She offers him her lips. He ignores it and pushes past her into the flat. She looks fearfully after him as he stalks into the bedroom.*] My, my, what a cold shoulder! And such uncouth apparel! Why, you haven't even shaved! The unforgivable insult to a lady! But I forgive you. I forgive you because it's such a relief to see you. You've stopped that polka tune that I had caught in my head. Have you ever had anything caught in your head? No, of course you haven't, you dumb angel-puss, you'd never get anything awful caught in your head!

[*He stares at her while she follows him while she talks. It is obvious that he has had a few drinks on the way over.*]

MITCH: Do we have to have that fan on?

BLANCHE: No!

MITCH: I don't like fans.

BLANCHE: Then let's turn it off, honey. I'm not partial to them! [*She presses the switch and the fan nods slowly off. She clears her throat uneasily as* MITCH *plumps himself down on the bed in the bedroom and lights a cigarette.*] I don't know what there is to drink. I—haven't investigated.

MITCH: I don't want Stan's liquor.

BLANCHE: It isn't Stan's. Everything here isn't Stan's. Some things on the premises are actually mine! How is your mother? Isn't your mother well?

MITCH: Why?

BLANCHE: Something's the matter tonight, but never mind. I won't cross-examine the witness. I'll just— [*She touches her forehead vaguely. The polka tune starts up again.*]—pretend I don't notice anything different about you! That—music again . . .

MITCH: What music?

BLANCHE: The "Varsouviana"! The polka tune they were playing when Allan—Wait! [*A distant revolver shot is heard.* BLANCHE *seems relieved.*] There now, the shot! It always stops after that. [*The polka music dies out again.*] Yes, now it's stopped.

MITCH: Are you boxed out of your mind?

BLANCHE: I'll go and see what I can find in the way of—[*She crosses into the closet, pretending to search for the bottle.*] Oh, by the way, excuse me for not being dressed. But I'd practically given you up! Had you forgotten your invitation to supper?

MITCH: I wasn't going to see you anymore.

BLANCHE: Wait a minute. I can't hear what you're saying and you talk so little that when you do say something, I don't want to miss a single syllable of it. . . . What am I looking around here for? Oh, yes—liquor! We've had so much excitement around here this evening that I *am* boxed out of my mind! [*She pretends suddenly to find the bottle. He draws his foot up on the bed and stares at her contemptuously.*] Here's something. Southern Comfort![6] What is that, I wonder?

---

6. Peach-flavored bourbon liqueur.

MITCH: If you don't know, it must belong to Stan.

BLANCHE: Take your foot off the bed. It has a light cover on it. Of course you boys don't notice things like that. I've done so much with this place since I've been here.

MITCH: I bet you have.

BLANCHE: You saw it before I came. Well, look at it now! This room is almost—dainty! I want to keep it that way. I wonder if this stuff ought to be mixed with something? Ummm, it's sweet! It's terribly, terribly sweet! Why, it's a *liqueur*, I believe! Yes, that's what it *is*, a liqueur! [MITCH *grunts*.] I'm afraid you won't like it, but try it, and maybe you will.

MITCH: I told you already I don't want none of his liquor and I mean it. You ought to lay off his liquor. He says you been lapping it up all summer like a wild cat!

BLANCHE: What a fantastic statement! Fantastic of him to say it, fantastic of you to repeat it! I won't descend to the level of such cheap accusations to answer them, even!

MITCH: Huh.

BLANCHE: What's in your mind? I see something in your eyes!

MITCH: [*Getting up.*] It's dark in here.

BLANCHE: I like it dark. The dark is comforting to me.

MITCH: I don't think I ever seen you in the light. [BLANCHE *laughs breathlessly.*] That's a fact!

BLANCHE: Is it?

MITCH: I've never seen you in the afternoon.

BLANCHE: Whose fault is that?

MITCH: You never want to go out in the afternoon.

BLANCHE: Why, Mitch, you're at the plant in the afternoon!

MITCH: Not Sunday afternoon. I've asked you to go out with me sometimes on Sundays but you always make an excuse. You never want to go out till after six and then it's always some place that's not lighted much.

BLANCHE: There is some obscure meaning in this but I fail to catch it.

MITCH: What it means is I've never had a real good look at you, Blanche. Let's turn the light on here.

BLANCHE: [*Fearfully.*] Light? Which light? What for?

MITCH: This one with the paper thing on it.

[*He tears the paper lantern off the light bulb. She utters a frightened gasp.*]

BLANCHE: What did you do that for?

MITCH: So I can take a look at you good and plain!

BLANCHE: Of course you don't really mean to be insulting!

MITCH: No, just realistic.

BLANCHE: I don't want realism. I want magic! [MITCH *laughs.*] Yes, yes, magic! I try to give that to people. I misrepresent things to them. I don't tell truth, I tell what *ought* to be truth. And if that is sinful, then let me be damned for it!—Don't turn the light on!

[MITCH *crosses to the switch. He turns the light on and stares at her. She cries out and covers her face. He turns the lights off again.*]

MITCH: [*Slowly and bitterly.*] I don't mind you being older than what I thought. But all the rest of it—Christ! That pitch about your ideals being so old-fashioned and all the malarkey that you've dished out all summer. Oh, I knew you weren't sixteen anymore. But I was a fool enough to believe you was straight.

BLANCHE: Who told you I wasn't—"straight"? My loving brother-in-law. And you believed him.

MITCH: I called him a liar at first. And then I checked on the story. First I asked our supply-man who travels through Laurel. And then I talked directly over long-distance to this merchant.

BLANCHE: Who is this merchant?

MITCH: Kiefaber.

BLANCHE: The merchant Kiefaber of Laurel! I know the man. He whistled at me. I put him in his place. So now for revenge he makes up stories about me.

MITCH: Three people, Kiefaber, Stanley, and Shaw, swore to them!

BLANCHE: Rub-a-dub-dub, three men in a tub! And such a filthy tub!

MITCH: Didn't you stay at a hotel called The Flamingo?

BLANCHE: Flamingo? No! Tarantula was the name of it! I stayed at a hotel called The Tarantula Arms!

MITCH: [*Stupidly.*] Tarantula?

BLANCHE: Yes, a big spider! That's where I brought my victims. [*She pours herself another drink.*] Yes, I had many intimacies with strangers. After the death of Allan—intimacies with strangers was all I seemed able to fill my empty heart with. . . . I think it was panic, just panic, that drove me from one to another, hunting for some protection—here and there, in the most—unlikely places—even, at last, in a seventeen-year-old boy but—somebody wrote the superintendent about it—"This woman is morally unfit for her position!" [*She throws back her head with convulsive, sobbing laughter. Then she repeats the statement, gasps, and drinks.*] True? Yes, I suppose—unfit somehow—anyway. . . . So I came here. There was nowhere else I could go. I was played out. You know what played out is? My youth was suddenly gone up the water-spout, and—I met you. You said you needed somebody. Well, I needed somebody, too. I thanked God for you, because you seemed to be gentle—a cleft in the rock of the world that I could hide in! But I guess I was asking, hoping—too much! Kiefaber, Stanley, and Shaw have tied an old tin can to the tail of the kite.

[*There is a pause.* MITCH *stares at her dumbly.*]

MITCH: You lied to me, Blanche.
BLANCHE: Don't say I lied to you.
MITCH: Lies, lies, inside and out, all lies.
BLANCHE: Never inside, I didn't lie in my heart. . . .

> [*A vendor comes around the corner. She is a blind* MEXICAN WOMAN *in a dark shawl, carrying bunches of those gaudy tin flowers that lower-class Mexicans display at funerals and other festive occasions. She is calling barely audibly. Her figure is only faintly visible outside the building.*]

MEXICAN WOMAN: *Flores. Flores, Flores para los muertos.*[7] *Flores. Flores.*
BLANCHE: What? Oh! Somebody outside . . . [*She goes to the door, opens it and stares at the* MEXICAN WOMAN.]
MEXICAN WOMAN: [*She is at the door and offers* BLANCHE *some of her flowers.*] *Flores? Flores para los muertos?*
BLANCHE: [*Frightened.*] No, no! Not now! Not now! [*She darts back into the apartment, slamming the door.*]
MEXICAN WOMAN: [*She turns away and starts to move down the street.*] *Flores para los muertos.*

> [*The polka tune fades in.*]

BLANCHE: [*As if to herself.*] Crumble and fade and—regrets—recriminations . . . "If you'd done this, it wouldn't've cost me that!"
MEXICAN WOMAN: *Corones*[8] *para los muertos. Corones . . .*
BLANCHE: Legacies! Huh. . . . And other things such as bloodstained pillowslips—"Her linen needs changing"—"Yes, Mother. But couldn't we get a colored girl to do it?" No, we couldn't of course. Everything gone but the—
MEXICAN WOMAN: *Flores.*
BLANCHE: Death—I used to sit here and she used to sit over there and death was as close as you are. . . . We didn't dare even admit we had ever heard of it!
MEXICAN WOMAN: *Flores para los muertos, flores—flores . . .*
BLANCHE: The opposite is desire. So do you wonder? How could you possibly wonder! Not far from Belle Reve, before we had lost Belle Reve, was a camp where they trained young soldiers. On Sunday nights they would go in town to get drunk—
MEXICAN WOMAN: [*Softly.*] *Corones . . .*
BLANCHE: —and on the way back they would stagger onto my lawn and call—"Blanche! Blanche!"—the deaf old lady remaining suspected nothing. But sometimes I slipped outside to answer their calls. . . . Later the paddy-wagon[9] would gather them up like daisies . . . the long way home. . . . [*The* MEXICAN WOMAN *turns slowly and drifts back off with her soft mournful cries.* BLANCHE *goes to the dresser and leans forward on it. After a*

7. Flowers for the dead (Spanish). 8. Wreaths (Spanish). 9. Police van.

moment, MITCH *rises and follows her purposefully. The polka music fades away. He places his hands on her waist and tries to turn her about.*] What do you want?

MITCH: [*Fumbling to embrace her.*] What I been missing all summer.

BLANCHE: Then marry me, Mitch!

MITCH: I don't think I want to marry you anymore.

BLANCHE: No?

MITCH: [*Dropping his hands from her waist.*] You're not clean enough to bring in the house with my mother.

BLANCHE: Go away, then. [*He stares at her.*] Get out of here quick before I start screaming fire! [*Her throat is tightening with hysteria.*] Get out of here quick before I start screaming fire. [*He still remains staring. She suddenly rushes to the big window with its pale blue square of the soft summer light and cries wildly.*] Fire! Fire! Fire!

[*With a startled gasp,* MITCH *turns and goes out the outer door, clatters awkwardly down the steps and around the corner of the building.* BLANCHE *staggers back from the window and falls to her knees. The distant piano is slow and blue.*]

Scene 10

It is a few hours later that night.

BLANCHE *has been drinking fairly steadily since* MITCH *left. She has dragged her wardrobe trunk into the center of the bedroom. It hangs open with flowery dresses thrown across it. As the drinking and packing went on, a mood of hysterical exhilaration came into her and she has decked herself out in a somewhat soiled and crumpled white satin evening gown and a pair of scuffed silver slippers with brilliants[1] set in their heels.*

Now she is placing the rhinestone tiara on her head before the mirror of the dressing-table and murmuring excitedly as if to a group of spectral admirers.

BLANCHE: How about taking a swim, a moonlight swim at the old rock-quarry? If anyone's sober enough to drive a car! Ha-ha! Best way in the world to stop your head buzzing! Only you've got to be careful to dive where the deep pool is—if you hit a rock you don't come up till tomorrow . . . [*Tremblingly she lifts the hand mirror for a closer inspection. She catches her breath and slams the mirror face down with such violence that the glass cracks. She moans a little and attempts to rise.* STANLEY *appears around the corner of the building. He still has on the vivid green silk bowling shirt. As he rounds the corner the honky-tonk music is heard. It continues softly throughout the scene. He enters the kitchen, slamming the door. As he peers in at* BLANCHE, *he gives a low whistle.*

1. Sparkling gems.

He has had a few drinks on the way and has brought some quart beer bottles home with him.] How is my sister?

STANLEY: She is doing okay.

BLANCHE: And how is the baby?

STANLEY: [*Grinning amiably.*] The baby won't come before morning so they told me to go home and get a little shut-eye.

BLANCHE: Does that mean we are to be alone in here?

STANLEY: Yep. Just me and you, Blanche. Unless you got somebody hid under the bed. What've you got on those fine feathers for?

BLANCHE: Oh, that's right. You left before my wire came.

STANLEY: You got a wire?

BLANCHE: I received a telegram from an old admirer of mine.

STANLEY: Anything good?

BLANCHE: I think so. An invitation.

STANLEY: What to? A fireman's ball?

BLANCHE: [*Throwing back her head.*] A cruise of the Caribbean on a yacht!

STANLEY: Well, well. What do you know?

BLANCHE: I have never been so surprised in my life.

STANLEY: I guess not.

BLANCHE: It came like a bolt from the blue!

STANLEY: Who did you say it was from?

BLANCHE: An old beau of mine.

STANLEY: The one that give you the white fox-pieces?

BLANCHE: Mr. Shep Huntleigh. I wore his ATO[2] pin my last year at college. I hadn't seen him again until last Christmas. I ran in to him on Biscayne Boulevard. Then—just now—this wire—inviting me on a cruise of the Caribbean! The problem is clothes. I tore into my trunk to see what I have that's suitable for the tropics!

STANLEY: And come up with that—gorgeous—diamond—tiara?

BLANCHE: This old relic? Ha-ha! It's only rhinestones.

STANLEY: Gosh. I thought it was Tiffany diamonds. [*He unbuttons his shirt.*]

BLANCHE: Well, anyhow, I shall be entertained in style.

STANLEY: Uh-huh. It goes to show, you never know what is coming.

BLANCHE: Just when I thought my luck had begun to fail me—

STANLEY: Into the picture pops this Miami millionaire.

BLANCHE: This man is not from Miami. This man is from Dallas.

STANLEY: This man is from Dallas?

BLANCHE: Yes, this man is from Dallas where gold spouts out of the ground!

STANLEY: Well, just so he's from somewhere! [*He starts removing his shirt.*]

BLANCHE: Close the curtains before you undress any further.

STANLEY: [*Amiably.*] This is all I'm going to undress right now. [*He rips the sack off a quart beer bottle.*] Seen a bottle-opener? [*She moves slowly toward*

---

2. Probably Alpha Tau Omega, a college fraternity.

the dresser, where she stands with her hands knotted together.] I used to have a cousin who could open a beer bottle with his teeth. [*Pounding the bottle cap on the corner of table.*] That was his only accomplishment, all he could do—he was just a human bottle-opener. And then one time, at a wedding party, he broke his front teeth off! After that he was so ashamed of himself he used t' sneak out of the house when company came . . . [*The bottle cap pops off and a geyser of foam shoots up.* STANLEY *laughs happily, holding up the bottle over his head.*] Ha-ha! Rain from heaven! [*He extends the bottle toward her.*] Shall we bury the hatchet and make it a loving-cup? Huh?

BLANCHE: No, thank you.

STANLEY: Well, it's a red-letter night for us both. You having an oil millionaire and me having a baby. [*He goes to the bureau in the bedroom and crouches to remove something from the bottom drawer.*]

BLANCHE: [*Drawing back.*] What are you doing in here?

STANLEY: Here's something I always break out on special occasions like this. The silk pyjamas I wore on my wedding night!

BLANCHE: Oh.

STANLEY: When the telephone rings and they say, "You've got a son!" I'll tear this off and wave it like a flag! [*He shakes out a brilliant pyjama coat.*] I guess we are both entitled to put on the dog. [*He goes back to the kitchen with the coat over his arm.*]

BLANCHE: When I think of how divine it is going to be to have such a thing as privacy once more—I could weep with joy!

STANLEY: This millionaire from Dallas is not going to interfere with your privacy any?

BLANCHE: It won't be the sort of thing you have in mind. This man is a gentleman and he respects me. [*Improvising feverishly.*] What he wants is my companionship. Having great wealth sometimes makes people lonely! A cultivated woman, a woman of intelligence and breeding, can enrich a man's life—immeasurably! I have those things to offer, and this doesn't take them away. Physical beauty is passing. A transitory possession. But beauty of the mind and richness of the spirit and tenderness of the heart—and I have all of those things—aren't taken away, but grow! Increase with the years! How strange that I should be called a destitute woman! When I have all of these treasures locked in my heart. [*A choked sob comes from her.*] I think of myself as a very, very rich woman! But I have been foolish—casting my pearls before swine![3]

STANLEY: Swine, huh?

BLANCHE: Yes, swine! Swine! And I'm thinking not only of you but of your friend, Mr. Mitchell. He came to see me tonight. He dared to come here

_____

3. See Matthew 7.6: "Do not give what is holy to dogs, or throw your pearls before swine, lest they trample them underfoot, and turn and tear you to pieces."

in his work clothes! And to repeat slander to me, vicious stories that he had gotten from you! I gave him his walking papers . . .

STANLEY: You did, huh?

BLANCHE: But then he came back. He returned with a box of roses to beg my forgiveness! He implored my forgiveness. But some things are not forgivable. Deliberate cruelty is not forgivable. It is the one unforgivable thing in my opinion and it is the one thing of which I have never, ever been guilty. And so I told him, I said to him, "Thank you," but it was foolish of me to think that we could ever adapt ourselves to each other. Our ways of life are too different. Our attitudes and our backgrounds are incompatible. We have to be realistic about such things. So farewell, my friend! And let there be no hard feelings. . . .

STANLEY: Was this before or after the telegram came from the Texas oil millionaire?

BLANCHE: What telegram? No! No, after! As a matter of fact, the wire came just as—

STANLEY: As a matter of fact there wasn't no wire at all!

BLANCHE: Oh, oh!

STANLEY: There isn't no millionaire! And Mitch didn't come back with roses 'cause I know where he is—

BLANCHE: Oh!

STANLEY: There isn't a goddam thing but imagination!

BLANCHE: Oh!

STANLEY: And lies and conceit and tricks!

BLANCHE: Oh!

STANLEY: And look at yourself! Take a look at yourself in that worn-out Mardi Gras[4] outfit, rented for fifty cents from some ragpicker! And with the crazy crown on! What queen do you think you are?

BLANCHE: Oh—God . . .

STANLEY: I've been on to you from the start! Not once did you pull any wool over this boy's eyes! You come in here and sprinkle the place with powder and spray perfume and cover the light-bulb with a paper lantern, and lo and behold the place has turned into Egypt and you are the Queen of the Nile![5] Sitting on your throne and swilling down my liquor! I say— Ha!—Ha! Do you hear me? Ha—ha—ha! [*He walks into the bedroom.*]

BLANCHE: Don't come in here! [*Lurid reflections appear on the walls around* BLANCHE. *The shadows are of a grotesque and menacing form. She catches her breath, crosses to the phone and jiggles the hook.* STANLEY *goes into the bathroom and closes the door.*] Operator, operator! Give me long-distance, please. . . . I want to get in touch with Mr. Shep Huntleigh of Dallas. He's so well known he doesn't require any address. Just ask anybody who—Wait!!—

---

4. Literally, "Fat Tuesday" (French), the carnival before Lent, the Christian period of self-denial, which begins on Ash Wednesday. 5. Cleopatra, Queen of Egypt.

No, I couldn't find it right now. . . . Please understand, I—No! No, wait! . . . One moment! Someone is—Nothing! Hold on, please! [*She sets the phone down and crosses warily into the kitchen. The night is filled with inhuman voices like cries in a jungle. The shadows and lurid reflections move sinuously as flames along the wall spaces. Through the back wall of the rooms, which have become transparent, can be seen the sidewalk. A prostitute has rolled[6] a drunkard. He pursues her along the walk, overtakes her and there is a struggle. A policeman's whistle breaks it up. The figures disappear. Some moments later the* NEGRO WOMAN *appears around the corner with a sequined bag which the prostitute had dropped on the walk. She is rooting excitedly through it.* BLANCHE *presses her knuckles to her lips and returns slowly to the phone. She speaks in a hoarse whisper.*] Operator! Operator! Never mind long-distance. Get Western Union. There isn't time to be—Western—Western Union! [*She waits anxiously.*] Western Union? Yes! I—want to—Take down this message! "In desperate, desperate circumstances! Help me! Caught in a trap. Caught in—" *Oh!*

[*The bathroom door is thrown open and* STANLEY *comes out in the brilliant silk pyjamas. He grins at her as he knots the tassled sash about his waist. She gasps and backs away from the phone. He stares at her for a count of ten. Then a clicking becomes audible from the telephone, steady and rasping.*]

STANLEY: You left th' phone off th' hook.

[*He crosses to it deliberately and sets it back on the hook. After he has replaced it, he stares at her again, his mouth slowly curving into a grin, as he weaves between* BLANCHE *and the outer door. The barely audible "Blue Piano" begins to drum up louder. The sound of it turns into the roar of an approaching locomotive.* BLANCHE *crouches, pressing her fists to her ears until it has gone by.*]

BLANCHE: [*Finally straightening.*] Let me—let me get by you!
STANLEY: Get by me? Sure. Go ahead. [*He moves back a pace in the doorway.*]
BLANCHE: You—you stand over there! [*She indicates a further position.*]
STANLEY: You got plenty of room to walk by me now.
BLANCHE: Not with you there! But I've got to get out somehow!
STANLEY: You think I'll interfere with you? Ha-ha! [*The "Blue Piano" goes softly. She turns confusedly and makes a faint gesture. The inhuman jungle voices rise up. He takes a step toward her, biting his tongue, which protrudes between his lips. Softly.*] Come to think of it—maybe you wouldn't be bad to—interfere with. . . .

[BLANCHE *moves backward through the door into the bedroom.*]

BLANCHE: Stay back! Don't you come toward me another step or I'll—
STANLEY: What?

6. Robbed.

BLANCHE: Some awful thing will happen! It will!

STANLEY: What are you putting on now?

[*They are now both inside the bedroom.*]

BLANCHE: I warn you, don't, I'm in danger!

[*He takes another step. She smashes a bottle on the table and faces him, clutching the broken top.*]

STANLEY: What did you do that for?

BLANCHE: So I could twist the broken end in your face!

STANLEY: I bet you would do that!

BLANCHE: I would! I will if you—

STANLEY: Oh! So you want some roughhouse! All right, let's have some roughhouse! [*He springs toward her, overturning the table. She cries out and strikes at him with the bottle top but he catches her wrist.*] Tiger—tiger! Drop the bottle-top! Drop it! We've had this date with each other from the beginning!

[*She moans. The bottle-top falls. She sinks to her knees: He picks up her inert figure and carries her to the bed. The hot trumpet and drums from the Four Deuces sound loudly.*]

Scene 11

It is some weeks later. STELLA *is packing* BLANCHE's *things. Sounds of water can be heard running in the bathroom.*

*The portieres are partly open on the poker players—*STANLEY, STEVE, MITCH *and* PABLO—*who sit around the table in the kitchen. The atmosphere of the kitchen is now the same raw, lurid one of the disastrous poker night.*

The building is framed by the sky of turquoise. STELLA *has been crying as she arranges the flowery dresses in the open trunk.*

EUNICE *comes down the steps from her flat above and enters the kitchen. There is an outburst from the poker table.*

STANLEY: Drew to an inside straight and made it, by God.

PABLO: *Maldita sea tu suerto!*

STANLEY: Put it in English, greaseball.

PABLO: I am cursing your rutting luck.

STANLEY: [*Prodigiously elated.*] You know what luck is? Luck is believing you're lucky. Take at Salerno.[7] I believed I was lucky. I figured that 4 out of 5 would not come through but I would . . . and I did. I put that down as a

---

7. Important beachhead in the Allied invasion of Italy in World War II.

rule. To hold front position in this rat-race you've got to believe you are lucky.

MITCH: You . . . you . . . you . . . Brag . . . brag . . . bull . . . bull.

[STELLA *goes into the bedroom and starts folding a dress.*]

STANLEY: What's the matter with him?

EUNICE: [*Walking past the table.*] I always did say that men are callous things with no feelings but this does beat anything. Making pigs of yourselves. [*She comes through the portieres into the bedroom.*]

STANLEY: What's the matter with her?

STELLA: How is my baby?

EUNICE: Sleeping like a little angel. Brought you some grapes. [*She puts them on a stool and lowers her voice.*] Blanche?

STELLA: Bathing.

EUNICE: How is she?

STELLA: She wouldn't eat anything but asked for a drink.

EUNICE: What did you tell her?

STELLA: I—just told her that—we'd made arrangements for her to rest in the country. She's got it mixed in her mind with Shep Huntleigh.

[BLANCHE *opens the bathroom door slightly.*]

BLANCHE: Stella.

STELLA: Yes.

BLANCHE: That cool yellow silk—the bouclé.[8] See if it's crushed. If it's not too crushed I'll wear it and on the lapel that silver and turquoise pin in the shape of a seahorse. You will find them in the heart-shaped box I keep my accessories in. And Stella . . . Try and locate a bunch of artificial violets in that box, too, to pin with the seahorse on the lapel of the jacket.

[*She closes the door.* STELLA *turns to* EUNICE.]

STELLA: I don't know if I did the right thing.

EUNICE: What else could you do?

STELLA: I couldn't believe her story and go on living with Stanley.

EUNICE: Don't ever believe it. Life has got to go on. No matter what happens, you've got to keep on going.

[*The bathroom door opens a little.*]

BLANCHE: [*Looking out.*] Is the coast clear?

STELLA: Yes, Blanche. [*To* EUNICE.] Tell her how well she's looking.

BLANCHE: Please close the curtains before I come out.

STELLA: They're closed.

---

8. Textile woven with uneven yarn to produce a rough, uneven surface.

STANLEY: —How many for you?
PABLO: Two.
STEVE: Three.

[BLANCHE *appears in the amber light of the door. She has a tragic radiance in her red satin robe following the sculptural lines of her body. The "Varsouviana" rises audibly as* BLANCHE *enters the bedroom.*]

BLANCHE: [*With faintly hysterical vivacity.*] I have just washed my hair.
STELLA: Did you?
BLANCHE: I'm not sure I got the soap out.
EUNICE: Such fine hair!
BLANCHE: [*Accepting the compliment.*] It's a problem. Didn't I get a call?
STELLA: Who from, Blanche?
BLANCHE: Shep Huntleigh . . .
STELLA: Why, not yet, honey!
BLANCHE: How strange! I—

[*At the sound of* BLANCHE'*s voice* MITCH'*s arm supporting his cards has sagged and his gaze is dissolved into space.* STANLEY *slaps him on the shoulder.*]

STANLEY: Hey, Mitch, come to!

[*The sound of this new voice shocks* BLANCHE. *She makes a shocked gesture, forming his name with her lips.* STELLA *nods and looks quickly away.* BLANCHE *stands quite still for some moments—the silver-backed mirror in her hand and a look of sorrowful perplexity as though all human experience shows on her face.* BLANCHE *finally speaks but with sudden hysteria.*]

BLANCHE: What's going on here? [*She turns from* STELLA *to* EUNICE *and back to* STELLA. *Her rising voice penetrates the concentration of the game.* MITCH *ducks his head lower but* STANLEY *shoves back his chair as if about to rise.* STEVE *places a restraining hand on his arm. Continuing.*] What's happened here? I want an explanation of what's happened here.
STELLA: [*Agonizingly.*] Hush! Hush!
EUNICE: Hush! Hush! Honey.
STELLA: Please, Blanche.
BLANCHE: Why are you looking at me like that? Is something wrong with me?
EUNICE: You look wonderful, Blanche. Don't she look wonderful?
STELLA: Yes.
EUNICE: I understand you are going on a trip.
STELLA: Yes, Blanche *is.* She's going on a vacation.
EUNICE: I'm green with envy.
BLANCHE: Help me, help me get dressed!
STELLA: [*Handing her dress.*] Is this what you—
BLANCHE: Yes, it will do! I'm anxious to get out of here—this place is a trap!

EUNICE: What a pretty blue jacket.

STELLA: It's lilac colored.

BLANCHE: You're both mistaken. It's Della Robbia blue.[9] The blue of the robe in the old Madonna pictures. Are these grapes washed? [*She fingers the bunch of grapes which* EUNICE *had brought in.*]

EUNICE: Huh?

BLANCHE: Washed, I said. Are they washed?

EUNICE: They're from the French Market.

BLANCHE: That doesn't mean they've been washed. [*The cathedral bells chime.*] Those cathedral bells—they're the only clean thing in the Quarter. Well, I'm going now. I'm ready to go.

EUNICE: [*Whispering.*] She's going to walk out before they get here.

STELLA: Wait, Blanche.

BLANCHE: I don't want to pass in front of those men.

EUNICE: Then wait'll the game breaks up.

STELLA: Sit down and . . .

[BLANCHE *turns weakly, hesitantly about. She lets them push her into a chair.*]

BLANCHE: I can smell the sea air. The rest of my time I'm going to spend on the sea. And when I die, I'm going to die on the sea. You know what I shall die of? [*She plucks a grape.*] I shall die of eating an unwashed grape one day out on the ocean. I will die—with my hand in the hand of some nice-looking ship's doctor, a very young one with a small blond mustache and a big silver watch. "Poor lady," they'll say, "the quinine[1] did her no good. That unwashed grape has transported her soul to heaven." [*The cathedral chimes are heard.*] And I'll be buried at sea sewn up in a clean white sack and dropped overboard—at noon—in the blaze of summer— and into an ocean as blue as [*Chimes again.*] my first lover's eyes!

[*A* DOCTOR *and a* MATRON[2] *have appeared around the corner of the building and climbed the steps to the porch. The gravity of their profession is exaggerated—the unmistakable aura of the state institution with its cynical detachment. The* DOCTOR *rings the doorbell. The murmur of the game is interrupted.*]

EUNICE: [*Whispering to* STELLA.] That must be them.

[STELLA *presses her fists to her lips.*]

BLANCHE: [*Rising slowly.*] What is it?

EUNICE: [*Affectedly casual.*] Excuse me while I see who's at the door.

STELLA: Yes.

---

9. A shade of light blue seen in terra cottas made by the Della Robbia family during the Italian Renaissance.   1. Medicinal salt used to treat malaria.

2. Female supervisor at a hospital or other institution.

[EUNICE *goes into the kitchen.*]

BLANCHE: [*Tensely.*] I wonder if it's for me.

[*A whispered colloquy takes place at the door.*]

EUNICE: [*Returning, brightly.*] Someone is calling for Blanche.

BLANCHE: It *is* for me, then! [*She looks fearfully from one to the other and then to the portieres. The "Varsouviana" faintly plays.*] Is it the gentleman I was expecting from Dallas?

EUNICE: I think it is, Blanche.

BLANCHE: I'm not quite ready.

STELLA: Ask him to wait outside.

BLANCHE: I . . .

[EUNICE *goes back to the portieres. Drums sound very softly.*]

STELLA: Everything packed?

BLANCHE: My silver toilet articles are still out.

STELLA: Ah!

EUNICE: [*Returning.*] They're waiting in front of the house.

BLANCHE: They! Who's "they"?

EUNICE: There's a lady with him.

BLANCHE: I cannot imagine who this "lady" could be! How is she dressed?

EUNICE: Just—just a sort of a—plain-tailored outfit.

BLANCHE: Possibly she's—[*Her voice dies out nervously.*]

STELLA: Shall we go, Blanche?

BLANCHE: Must we go through that room?

STELLA: I will go with you.

BLANCHE: How do I look?

STELLA: Lovely.

EUNICE: [*Echoing.*] Lovely.

[BLANCHE *moves fearfully to the portieres.* EUNICE *draws them open for her.* BLANCHE *goes into the kitchen.*]

BLANCHE: [*To the men.*] Please don't get up. I'm only passing through.

[*She crosses quickly to outside door.* STELLA *and* EUNICE *follow. The poker players stand awkwardly at the table—all except* MITCH, *who remains seated, looking down at the table.* BLANCHE *steps out on a small porch at the side of the door. She stops short and catches her breath.*]

DOCTOR: How do you do?

BLANCHE: You are not the gentleman I was expecting. [*She suddenly gasps and starts back up the steps. She stops by* STELLA, *who stands just outside the door, and speaks in a frightening whisper.*] That man isn't Shep Huntleigh.

[*The "Varsouviana" is playing distantly.* STELLA *stares back at* BLANCHE. EUNICE *is holding* STELLA's *arm. There is a moment of silence—no sound but that of* STANLEY *steadily shuffling the cards.* BLANCHE *catches her breath again and slips back into the flat. She enters the flat with a peculiar smile, her eyes wide and brilliant. As soon as her sister goes past her,* STELLA *closes her eyes and clenches her hands.* EUNICE *throws her arms comfortingly about her. Then she starts up to her flat.* BLANCHE *stops just inside the door.* MITCH *keeps staring down at his hands on the table, but the other men look at her curiously. At last she starts around the table toward the bedroom. As she does,* STANLEY *suddenly pushes back his chair and rises as if to block her way. The* MATRON *follows her into the flat.*]

STANLEY: Did you forget something?
BLANCHE: [*Shrilly.*] Yes! Yes, I forgot something!

[*She rushes past him into the bedroom. Lurid reflections appear on the walls in odd, sinuous shapes. The "Varsouviana" is filtered into a weird distortion, accompanied by the cries and noises of the jungle.* BLANCHE *seizes the back of a chair as if to defend herself.*]

STANLEY: [*Sotto voce.*[3]] Doc, you better go in.
DOCTOR: [*Sotto voce, motioning to the* MATRON.] Nurse, bring her out.

[*The* MATRON *advances on one side,* STANLEY *on the other. Divested of all the softer properties of womanhood, the* MATRON *is a peculiarly sinister figure in her severe dress. Her voice is bold and toneless as a firebell.*]

MATRON: Hello, Blanche.

[*The greeting is echoed and re-echoed by other mysterious voices behind the walls, as if reverberated through a canyon of rock.*]

STANLEY: She says that she forgot something.

[*The echo sounds in threatening whispers.*]

MATRON: That's all right.
STANLEY: What did you forget, Blanche?
BLANCHE: I—I—
MATRON: It don't matter. We can pick it up later.
STANLEY: Sure. We can send it along with the trunk.
BLANCHE: [*Retreating in panic.*] I don't know you—I don't know you. I want to be—left alone—please!
MATRON: Now, Blanche!
ECHOES: [*Rising and falling.*] Now, Blanche—now, Blanche—now, Blanche!
STANLEY: You left nothing here but spilt talcum and old empty perfume bottles—unless it's the paper lantern you want to take with you. You want the lantern?

3. In an undertone (Italian).

[*He crosses to dressing table and seizes the paper lantern, tearing it off the light bulb, and extends it toward her. She cries out as if the lantern was herself. The* MATRON *steps boldly toward her. She screams and tries to break past the* MATRON. *All the men spring to their feet.* STELLA *runs out to the porch, with* EUNICE *following to comfort her, simultaneously with the confused voices of the men in the kitchen.* STELLA *rushes into* EUNICE'*s embrace on the porch.*]

STELLA: Oh, my God, Eunice help me! Don't let them do that to her, don't let them hurt her! Oh, God, oh, please God, don't hurt her! What are they doing to her? What are they doing? [*She tries to break from* EUNICE'*s arms.*]

EUNICE: No, honey, no, no, honey. Stay here. Don't go back in there. Stay with me and don't look.

STELLA: What have I done to my sister? Oh, God, what have I done to my sister?

EUNICE: You done the right thing, the only thing you could do. She couldn't stay here; there wasn't no other place for her to go.

[*While* STELLA *and* EUNICE *are speaking on the porch the voices of the men in the kitchen overlap them.* MITCH *has started toward the bedroom.* STANLEY *crosses to block him.* STANLEY *pushes him aside.* MITCH *lunges and strikes at* STANLEY. STANLEY *pushes* MITCH *back.* MITCH *collapses at the table, sobbing. During the preceding scenes, the* MATRON *catches hold of* BLANCHE'*s arm and prevents her flight.* BLANCHE *turns wildly and scratches at the* MATRON. *The heavy woman pinions her arms.* BLANCHE *cries out hoarsely and slips to her knees.*]

MATRON: These fingernails have to be trimmed. [*The* DOCTOR *comes into the room and she looks at him.*] Jacket,[4] Doctor?

DOCTOR: Not unless necessary. [*He takes off his hat and now he becomes personalized. The unhuman quality goes. His voice is gentle and reassuring as he crosses to* BLANCHE *and crouches in front of her. As he speaks her name, her terror subsides a little. The lurid reflections fade from the walls, the inhuman cries and noises die out and her own hoarse crying is calmed.*] Miss DuBois. [*She turns her face to him and stares at him with desperate pleading. He smiles; then he speaks to the* MATRON.] It won't be necessary.

BLANCHE: [*Faintly.*] Ask her to let go of me.

DOCTOR: [*To the* MATRON.] Let go.

[*The* MATRON *releases her.* BLANCHE *extends her hands toward the* DOCTOR. *He draws her up gently and supports her with his arm and leads her through the portieres.*]

---

4. That is, straitjacket, used to restrain the mentally ill from violence.

BLANCHE: [*Holding tight to his arm.*] Whoever you are—I have always depended on the kindness of strangers.

[*The poker players stand back as* BLANCHE *and the* DOCTOR *cross the kitchen to the front door. She allows him to lead her as if she were blind. As they go out on the porch,* STELLA *cries out her sister's name from where she is crouched a few steps up on the stairs.*]

STELLA: Blanche! Blanche, Blanche!

[BLANCHE *walks on without turning, followed by the* DOCTOR *and the* MATRON. *They go around the corner of the building.* EUNICE *descends to* STELLA *and places the child in her arms. It is wrapped in a pale blue blanket.* STELLA *accepts the child, sobbingly.* EUNICE *continues downstairs and enters the kitchen where the men, except for* STANLEY, *are returning silently to their places about the table.* STANLEY *has gone out on the porch and stands at the foot of the steps looking at* STELLA.]

STANLEY: [*A bit uncertainly.*] Stella? [*She sobs with inhuman abandon. There is something luxurious in her complete surrender to crying now that her sister is gone. Voluptuously, soothingly.*] Now, honey. Now, love. Now, now, love. [*He kneels beside her and his fingers find the opening of her blouse.*] Now, now, love. Now, love. . . .

[*The luxurious sobbing, the sensual murmur fade away under the swelling music of the "Blue Piano" and the muted trumpet.*]

STEVE: This game is seven-card stud.

CURTAIN

1947

Biographical Sketches: Playwrights

SUSAN GLASPELL
(1876–1948)

Born and raised in Davenport, Iowa, Susan Glaspell graduated from Drake University and worked on the staff of the Des Moines *Daily News* until her stories began appearing in magazines such as *Harper's* and *Ladies' Home Journal*. In 1911, Glaspell moved to New York City, where, two years later, she married the theater director George Cram Cook. In 1915 they founded the Provincetown Playhouse (later the Playwright's Theater), an extraordinary Cape Cod gathering of actors, directors, and playwrights, including Eugene O'Neill, Edna St. Vincent Millay, and John Reed. The Provincetown Players produced several of Glaspell's early plays, including *Trifles* (1916); her later plays include *The Inheritors* (1921), *The Verge* (1921), *Bernice* (1924), and *Alison's House* (1930), for which she won the Pulitzer Prize. Glaspell spent the last part of her life writing fiction in Provincetown; among her many books are *Visioning* (1911), *Lifted Masks: Stories* (1912), *Fidelity* (1915), *The Road to the Temple* (1926), and *The Morning Is Near Us* (1940).

LORRAINE HANSBERRY
(1930–1965)

The first African American woman to have a play produced on Broadway, Lorraine Hansberry was born in Chicago to a prominent family and even at a young age showed an interest in writing. She attended the University of Wisconsin, the Art Institute of Chicago, and Roosevelt University, then moved to New York City in order to concentrate on writing for the stage. After extensive fund-raising, Hansberry's play *A Raisin in the Sun* (loosely based on events involving her own family) opened in 1959 at the Ethel Barrymore Theatre on Broadway, received critical acclaim, and won the New York Drama Critics' Circle Award for Best Play. Hansberry's second production, *The Sign in Sidney Brustein's Window*, had a short run on Broadway in 1964. Shortly after, Hansberry died of cancer. *To Be Young, Gifted, and Black*, adapted from her writing, was produced off-Broadway in 1969 and published the next year, when her drama *Les Blancs* was also produced.

HENRIK IBSEN
(1828–1906)

Born in Skien, Norway, Henrik Ibsen was apprenticed to an apothecary until 1850, when he left for Oslo and published his first play, *Catilina*, a verse tragedy. By 1857 Ibsen was director of Oslo's Norwegian Theater, but his early plays, such as *Love's Comedy* (1862), were poorly received. Disgusted with what he saw as Norway's backwardness, Ibsen left in 1864 for Rome, where he wrote two more verse plays, *Brand* (1866) and *Peer Gynt* (1867), before turning to the realistic style and harsh criticism of traditional social mores for which he is best known. *The League of Youth* (1869), *Pillars of Society* (1877), *A Doll House* (1879), *Ghosts* (1881), *An Enemy of the People* (1882), *The Wild Duck* (1884), and *Hedda Gabler* (1890)

won him a reputation throughout Europe as a controversial and outspoken advocate of moral and social reform. Near the end of his life, Ibsen explored the human condition in the explicitly symbolic terms of *The Master Builder* (1892) and *When We Dead Awaken* (1899). Ibsen's works had enormous influence over the drama of the twentieth century.

WILLIAM SHAKESPEARE
(1554–1616)

Considering the great and well-deserved fame of his work, surprisingly little is known of William Shakespeare's life. Between 1585 and 1592, he left his birthplace of Stratford-upon-Avon for London to begin a career as playwright and actor. No dates of his professional career are recorded, however, nor can the order in which he composed his plays and poetry be determined with certainty. By 1594, he had established himself as a poet with two long works—*Venus and Adonis* and *The Rape of Lucrece*; his more than 150 sonnets are supreme expressions of the form. His matchless reputation, though, rests on his works for the theater. Shakespeare produced perhaps thirty-five plays in twenty-five years, proving himself a master of every dramatic genre: tragedy (in works such as *Macbeth, Hamlet, King Lear,* and *Othello*); historical drama (for example, *Richard III* and *Henry IV*); comedy (*A Midsummer Night's Dream, Twelfth Night, As You Like It,* and many more); and romance or "tragi-comedy" (in plays such as *The Tempest* and *Cymbeline*). Without question, Shakespeare is the most quoted, discussed, and beloved writer in English literature.

SOPHOCLES
(496?–406 BCE)

Sophocles lived at a time when Athens and Greek civilization were at the peak of their power and influence. He not only

served as a general under Pericles and played a prominent role in the city's affairs but also was arguably the greatest of the Greek tragic playwrights, winning the annual dramatic competition about twenty times, a feat unmatched by even his great contemporaries, Aeschylus and Euripides. An innovator, Sophocles fundamentally changed the nature of dramatic performance by adding a third actor, enlarging the chorus, and introducing the use of painted scenery. Aristotle held that Sophocles' *Oedipus the King* (c. 429 BCE) was the perfect tragedy and used it as his model when he discussed the nature of tragedy in his *Poetics.* Today only seven of Sophocles' tragedies survive—the Oedipus trilogy (*Oedipus the King, Oedipus at Colonus,* and *Antigone*), *Philoctetes, Ajax, Trachiniae,* and *Electra*—though he is believed to have written as many as 123 plays.

TOM STOPPARD
(b. 1937)

Tom Stoppard was born in Zlin, Czechoslovakia. In 1939 his family moved to Singapore to escape the Nazis. His mother then fled with Tom and his brother to Darjeeling, India, in advance of the Japanese invasion of Singapore; his father, who remained behind, was killed. In 1946 the family moved to England, where Tom's mother married Kenneth Stoppard, a major in the British army. Stoppard dropped out of high school before his junior year, worked as a journalist and freelance drama critic, and began to write plays for radio and television. His first television play, *A Walk on the Water* (1963), was later adapted for the stage as *Enter a Free Man* (1968). Stoppard's first major success was *Rosencrantz and Guildenstern Are Dead* (1966), which won a Tony Award for Best Play in 1968. Subsequent popular dramas include *The Real Inspector Hound* (1968), *Jumpers* (1972), and *Travesties* (1974). *Every Good Boy Deserves Favour* (1977), *Dogg's Hamlet* (1979), and *Squaring the Circle* (1984) attack the oppressive regimes of

Eastern Europe. Among Stoppard's more recent plays are *Arcadia* (1993) and *The Invention of Love* (1997). Stoppard has written a number of screenplays, including *Shakespeare in Love* (1998), which he coauthored with Marc Norman and which won the 1999 Academy Award for Best Screenplay.

TENNESSEE WILLIAMS
(1911–1983)

Born in Columbus, Mississippi, Thomas Lanier Williams moved to St. Louis with his family at the age of seven. Williams's father was a violent alcoholic, his mother was ill, and his sister, Rose, suffered from a variety of mental illnesses; each of them became a model for the domineering men and sensitive women of his plays. He attended the University of Missouri and Washington University in St. Louis, but earned his B.A. from the University of Iowa. While there, Williams won prizes for his fiction and began to write plays. His extensive body of work, with its explosive dramatic tension and dazzling dialogue, confronts issues of adultery, homosexuality, incest, and mental illness. In 1944, *The Glass Menagerie* won the New York Drama Critics' Circle Award. In 1948, he earned his first Pulitzer Prize, for *A Streetcar Named Desire;* in 1955, he won a second Pulitzer Prize, for *Cat on a Hot Tin Roof.* His other dramas include *Camino Real* (1953), *Suddenly Last Summer* (1958), *The Night of the Iguana* (1961), *The Two-Character Play* (1969; later revised as *Out Cry*), and *Clothes for a Summer Hotel* (1980). Williams also published short fiction, poetry, and a film script.

AUGUST WILSON
(1945–2005)

Frederick August Kittel was born in a lower-class black neighborhood of Pittsburgh, Pennsylvania. At fifteen, disgusted by treatment he considered racist, he left school and sought to educate himself at the local library. A black nationalist and participant in the Black Arts Movement during the 1960s and '70s, Wilson disavowed his white father and adopted his black mother's surname. In 1968 he cofounded the Black Horizons Theater Company, in St. Paul, Minnesota; he later founded the Playwrights Center in Minneapolis. The 1984 Broadway production of *Ma Rainey's Black Bottom* established his theatrical reputation; much of the rest of his career was devoted to completing the ten-play "Pittsburgh Cycle" dealing with the black experience in America, each play set during a different decade of the twentieth century. Among his plays are *Jitney* (1982); *Fences* (1985), winner of the 1987 Pulitzer Prize; *Joe Turner's Come and Gone* (1986); *The Piano Lesson* (1987), which won a Tony Award, the Drama Critics Circle Award, the American Theater Critics Outstanding Play Award, and the 1990 Pulitzer Prize; *Two Trains Running* (1992); *Seven Guitars* (1995); *King Hedley II* (2001); and *Gem of the Ocean* (2003).

Writing about Literature

When it comes to the study of literature, reading and writing are closely interrelated—even mutually dependent—activities. On the one hand, the quality of whatever we write about a literary text depends entirely on the quality of our work as readers. On the other hand, our reading isn't truly complete until we've tried to capture our sense of a text in writing. Indeed, we often read a literary work much more actively and attentively when we integrate informal writing into the reading process—pausing periodically to mark especially important or confusing passages, to jot down significant facts, to describe the impressions and responses the text provokes—or when we imagine our reading (and our informal writing) as preparation for writing about the work in a more sustained and formal way.

Writing about literature can take any number of forms, ranging from the very informal and personal to the very formal and public. In fact, your instructor may well ask you to try your hand at more than one form. However, the essay is by far the most common and complex form that writing about literature takes. As a result, the following chapters will focus on the essay.* A first, short chapter covers three basic ways of writing about literature. The second chapter, "The Elements of the Essay," seeks to answer a very basic set of questions: *When an instructor says, "Write an essay," what precisely does that mean? What is the purpose of an essay, and what form does it need to take in order to achieve that purpose?* The third chapter, "The Writing Process," addresses questions about how an essay is produced, while the fourth chapter explores the special steps and strategies involved in writing a research essay—a type of essay about literature that draws on secondary sources. "Quotation, Citation, and Documentation" explains the rules and strategies involved in quoting and citing both literary texts and secondary sources using the documentation system recommended by the Modern Language Association (MLA). And, finally, we present a sample research essay, annotated to point out some of its most important features.

*In chapters 15–20, unless otherwise specified, page numbers in the examples refer to this volume, *The Norton Introduction to Literature*, 10th Portable Edition.

15 PARAPHRASE, SUMMARY, DESCRIPTION

Before turning to the essay, let's briefly consider three other basic ways of writing about literature: *paraphrase, summary,* and *description.* Each of these can be useful both as an exercise to prepare for writing an essay and as part of a completed essay. That is, an essay about a literary text must do more than paraphrase, summarize, or describe the text, yet a good essay about a literary text almost always incorporates some paraphrase, summary, and description of the literature and, in the case of a research essay, of secondary sources as well.

15.1 PARAPHRASE

To paraphrase a statement is to restate it in your own words. Since the goal of paraphrase is to represent a statement fully and faithfully, paraphrases tend to be at least as long as the original, and you usually wouldn't try to paraphrase an entire work of any length. The following examples offer paraphrases of sentences from a work of fiction (Jane Austen's *Pride and Prejudice*), a poem (W. B. Yeats's "All Things Can Tempt Me"), and an essay (George L. Dillon's "Styles of Reading").

ORIGINAL SENTENCE	PARAPHRASE
It is a truth universally acknowledged that a single man in possession of a good fortune must be in want of a wife.	Everyone agrees that a propertied bachelor needs (or wants) to find a woman to marry.
All things can tempt me from this craft of verse: One time it was a woman's face, or worse— The seeming needs of my fool-driven land; Now nothing but comes readier to the hand Than this accustomed toil. . . .	Anything can distract me from writing poetry: One time I was distracted by a woman's face, but I was even more distracted by (or I found an even less worthy distraction in) the attempt to fulfill what I imagined to be the needs of a country governed by idiots. At this point in my life I find any task easier than the work I'm used to doing (writing poetry).
. . . making order out of Emily's life is a complicated matter, since the narrator recalls the details through a nonlinear filter.	It's difficult to figure out the order in which events in Emily's life occurred because the narrator doesn't relate them chronologically.

Paraphrase resembles translation. Indeed, the paraphrase of Yeats is essentially a "translation" of poetry into prose, and the paraphrases of Austen and of Dillon are "translations" of one kind of prose (formal nineteenth-century British prose, the equally formal but quite different prose of a twentieth-century literary critic) into another kind (colloquial twentieth-century American prose).

But what good is that? First, paraphrasing tests that you truly understand what you've read; it can be especially helpful when an author's diction and syntax seem difficult, complex, or "foreign" to you. Second, paraphrasing can direct your attention to nuances of tone or potentially significant details. For example, paraphrasing Austen's sentence might highlight its irony and call attention to the multiple meanings of phrases such as *a good fortune* and *in want of*. Similarly, paraphrasing Yeats might help you to think about all that he gains by making himself the object rather than the subject of his sentence. Third, paraphrase can help you begin generating the kind of interpretive questions that can drive an essay. For example, the Austen paraphrase might suggest the following questions: *What competing definitions of "a good fortune" are set out in* Pride and Prejudice*? Which definition, if any, does the novel as a whole seem to endorse?*

15.2 SUMMARY

A summary is a fairly succinct restatement or overview of the content of an entire text or source (or a significant portion thereof). Like paraphrases, summaries should always be stated in your own words.

A summary of a literary text is generally called a *plot summary* because it focuses on the **action** or **plot**. Here, for example, is a summary of Edgar Allan Poe's "The Raven":

> The speaker of Poe's "The Raven" is sitting in his room late at night reading in order to forget the death of his beloved Lenore. There's a tap at the door; after some hesitation he opens it and calls Lenore's name, but there is only an echo. When he goes back into his room he hears the rapping again, this time at his window, and when he opens it a raven enters. He asks the raven its name, and it answers very clearly, "Nevermore." As the speaker's thoughts run back to Lenore, he realizes the aptness of the raven's word: She shall sit there nevermore. But, he says, sooner or later he will forget her, and the grief will lessen. "Nevermore," the raven says again, too aptly. Now the speaker wants the bird to leave, but "Nevermore," the raven says once again. At the end, the speaker knows he'll never escape the raven or its dark message.

Though a summary should be significantly shorter than the original, it can be any length you need it to be. Above, the 108 lines of Poe's poem have been reduced to about 160 words. But one could summarize this or any other work in as little as one sentence. Here, for example, are three viable one-sentence summaries of *Hamlet*:

> A young man seeking to avenge his uncle's murder of his father kills his uncle, while also bringing about his own and many others' deaths.

> A young Danish prince avenges the murder of his father, the king, by his uncle, who has usurped the throne, but the prince himself is killed, as are others, and a well-led foreign army has no trouble successfully invading the decayed and troubled state.

> When a young prince learns, from the ghost of his murdered father, that his uncle, who has married the prince's mother, is the father's murderer, the prince plots revenge, feigning madness, acting erratically—even insulting the woman he loves—and, though gaining his revenge, causes the suicide of his beloved and the deaths of others and, finally, of himself.

As these *Hamlet* examples suggest, different readers—or even the same reader on different occasions—will almost certainly summarize the same text in dramatically different ways. Summarizing entails selection and emphasis. As a result, any summary reflects a particular point of view and may even imply a particular interpretation or argument. When writing a summary, you should try to be as objective as possible; nevertheless, your summary will reflect your own understanding and attitudes. For this reason, summarizing a literary text may help you begin to figure out just what your particular understanding of a text is, especially if you then compare your summary to those of other readers.

15.3 DESCRIPTION

Whereas both summary and paraphrase focus on content, a description of a literary text focuses on its overall form or structure or some particular aspect thereof. Here, for example, is a description (rather than a summary) of the rhyme scheme of "The Raven":

> Poe's "The Raven" is a poem of 108 lines divided into eighteen six-line stanzas. If you were to look just at the ends of the lines, you would notice only one or two unusual features: Not only is there only one rhyme sound per stanza—lines 2, 4, 5, and 6 rhyming—but one rhyme sound is the same in all eighteen stanzas, so that seventy-two lines end with the sound "ore." In addition, the fourth and fifth lines of each stanza end with an identical word; in six of the stanzas that word is "door" and in four others "Lenore." There is even more repetition: The last line of six of the first seven stanzas ends with the words

"nothing more," and the last eleven stanzas end with the word "Nevermore." In each stanza, lines 1, 2, and 3 are sixteen syllables long; lines 4 and 5 fifteen, and line 6 only seven. The longer lines give the effect of shorter ones, however, and add still further to the frequency of repeated sounds, for the first half of each opening line rhymes with the second half of the line, and so do the halves of line 3. There is still more: The first half of line 4 rhymes with the halves of line 3 (in the first stanza the rhymes are "dreary" / "weary" and "napping" / "tapping" / "rapping"). So at least nine words in each six-line stanza are involved in the regular rhyme scheme, and many stanzas have added instances of rhyme or repetition. As if this were not enough, all the half-line rhymes are rich feminine rhymes, where both the accented and the following unaccented syllables rhyme—"dreary" / "wary."

You could similarly describe many other formal elements of the poem—images and **symbols**, for example. You can describe a play in comparable terms—acts, scenes, settings, time lapses, perhaps—and you might describe a novel in terms of chapters, books, summary narration, dramatized scenes. In addition to describing the narrative structure or focus and voice of a short story, you might describe the **diction** (word choice), the sentence structure, the amount and kind of description of characters or landscape, and so on.

16 THE ELEMENTS OF THE ESSAY

As you move from reading literary works to writing essays about them, remember that the essay—like the short story, poem, or play—is a distinctive subgenre with unique elements and conventions. Just as you come to a poem or play with a certain set of expectations, so will readers approach your essay. They will be looking for particular elements, anticipating that the work will unfold in a specific way. This chapter explains and explores those elements so that you can develop a clear sense of what makes a piece of writing an essay and why some essays are more effective than others.

An essay has particular elements and a particular form because it serves a specific purpose. Keeping this in mind, consider what an essay is and what it does. An essay is a relatively short written composition that articulates, supports, and develops an idea or claim. Like any work of expository prose, it aims to explain something complex. Explaining in this case entails both *analysis* (breaking the complex "thing" down into its constituent parts and showing how they work together to form a meaningful whole) and *argument* (working to convince someone that the analysis is valid). In an essay about literature, the literary work is the complex thing that you are helping a reader understand better. The essay needs to show the reader a particular way to understand the work, to interpret or read it. That interpretation or reading starts with the essayist's own personal response. But an essay also needs to persuade the reader that this interpretation is reasonable and enlightening—that though it is distinctive and new, it is more than merely idiosyncratic or subjective.

To achieve these ends, an essay must incorporate four elements: an appropriate *tone*, a clear *thesis*, a coherent *structure*, and ample, appropriate *evidence*.

16.1 TONE (AND AUDIENCE)

Although your reader or audience isn't an element *in* your essay, tone is. And tone and audience are closely interrelated. In everyday life, the tone we adopt has everything to do with whom we are talking to and what situation we're in. For example, we talk very differently to our parents than to our best friends. And in different situations we talk to the same person in different ways. What tone do you adopt with your best friends when you want to borrow money? when you need advice? when you're giving advice? when you're deciding whether to eat pizza or sushi? In each case you act on your knowledge of who your friends are, what information they already have, and what their response is likely to be. But you also try to adopt a tone that will encourage them to respond in a certain way.

In writing, as in everyday life, your audience, situation, and purpose should shape your tone. Conversely, your tone will shape your audience's response. You need to figure out both who your readers are and what response you want to elicit. Who is your audience? When you write an essay for class, the obvious answer is your instructor. But in an important sense, that is the wrong answer. Although your instructor could literally be the only person besides you who will ever read your essay, you write about literature to learn how to write for an audience of peers—people a lot like you who are sensible and educated and who will appreciate having a literary work explained so that they can understand it more fully. Picture your reader as someone about your own age with roughly the same educational background. Assume the person has some experience in reading literature, but that he or she has read this particular work only once and has not yet closely analyzed it. You should neither be insulting and explain the obvious nor assume that your reader has noticed, considered, and remembered every detail.

Should you, then, altogether ignore the obvious fact that an instructor—who probably has a master's degree or doctorate in literature—is your actual reader? Not altogether: You don't want to get so carried away with speaking to people of your own age and interests that you slip into slang, or feel the need to explain what a stanza is, or leave unexplained an allusion to your favorite movie. Even though you do want to learn from the advice and guidelines your instructor has given, try not to be preoccupied with the idea that you are writing for someone "in authority" or someone utterly different from yourself.

Above all, don't think of yourself as writing for a captive audience, for readers who have to read what you write or who already see the text as you do. (If that were the case, there wouldn't be much point in writing at all.) It is not always easy to know how interested your readers will be or how their views might differ from yours, so you must make the most of every word. Remember that the purpose of your essay is to persuade readers to see the text your way. That process begins with persuading them that you deserve their attention and respect. The tone of your paper should be serious and straightforward, respectful toward your readers and the literary work. But its approach and vocabulary, while formal enough for academic writing, should be lively enough to interest someone like you. Try to imagine, as your ideal reader, the person in class whom you most respect but who often seems to see things differently from you. Write to capture and hold that person's attention and respect. Encourage your reader to adopt a desirable stance *toward* your essay by adopting that same stance *in* your essay. Engage and convince your reader by demonstrating your engagement and conviction. Encourage your reader to keep an open mind by showing that you have done the same.

16.2 THESIS

A thesis is to an essay what a **theme** is to a short story, play, or poem: the governing idea, proposition, claim, or point. Good theses come in many shapes and sizes. A thesis cannot always be conveyed in one sentence, nor will it always appear in the same place in every essay. But you will risk both appearing confused and confusing the reader if you can't state the thesis in one to three sentences or if the thesis doesn't appear somewhere in your introduction, usually near its end.

Regardless of its length or location, a thesis must be debatable—a claim that all readers won't automatically accept. It's a proposition that *can* be proved with evidence from the text. Yet it's one that *has* to be proved, that isn't obviously true or factual, that must be supported with evidence in order to be fully understood or accepted by the reader. The following examples juxtapose a series of inarguable topics or fact statements—ones that are merely factual or descriptive—with thesis statements, each of which makes a debatable claim about the topic or fact.

TOPIC OR FACT STATEMENTS	THESIS STATEMENTS
"The Story of an Hour" explores the topic of marriage.	In "The Story of an Hour," Chopin poses a troubling question: Does marriage inevitably encourage people to "impose [their] private will upon a fellow-creature" (307)?
"Cathedral" features a character with a physical handicap.	"Cathedral" features a protagonist who learns about his own emotional and spiritual shortcomings through an encounter with a physically handicapped person. In this way, the story invites us to question traditional definitions of "disability."
"London" consists of three discrete stanzas that each end with a period; two-thirds of the lines are end-stopped.	In "London," William Blake uses a variety of formal techniques to suggest the unnatural rigidity and constraints of urban life.
Creon and Antigone are both similar and different.	Creon and Antigone are alike in several ways, especially the inconsistency of their values and the way they are driven by passion below the surface of rational argument. Both are also one-sided in their commitments. . . . This does not mean, however, that they are equally limited in the values to which they adhere. —Mary Whitlock Blundell, *Helping Friends and Harming Enemies*

All of the thesis statements above are arguable, but they share other traits as well. All are clear and emphatic. Each implicitly answers a compelling interpretive question—for instance, *What do Antigone and Creon stand for? Which character and worldview, if any, does the play as a whole ultimately champion?* Yet each statement entices us to read further by generating more questions in our minds—*How and why do Creon and Antigone demonstrate "inconsistency" and "one-sidedness"? If these two characters are not equally limited, which of them is more limited?* An effective thesis enables the reader to enter the essay with a clear sense of what its writer will try to prove, and it inspires the reader with the desire to see the writer do it. We want to understand how the writer arrived at this view, to test whether it's valid, and to see how the writer will answer the other questions the thesis has generated in our minds. A good thesis captures the reader's interest and shapes his or her expectations. It also makes promises that the rest of the essay should fulfill.

At the same time, an arguable claim is not one-sided or narrow-minded. A thesis needs to stake out a position, but a position can and should admit complexity. Literary texts tend to focus more on exploring problems, conflicts, and questions than on offering solutions, resolutions, and answers. Their goal is to complicate, not simplify, our way of looking at the world. The best essays about literature and the theses that drive them often share a similar quality.

16.2.1 Interpretive versus Evaluative Claims

All the theses in the previous examples involve *interpretive* claims—claims about how a literary text works, what it says, how one should understand it. And interpretive claims generally work best as theses.

Yet it's useful to remember that in reading and writing about literature we often make (and debate) a different type of claim—the *evaluative*. Evaluation entails judging or assessing. Evaluative claims about literature tend to be of two kinds. The first involves aesthetic judgment—whether a text (or a part or element thereof) succeeds in artistic terms. (This kind of claim features prominently in book reviews, for example.) The second involves philosophical, ethical, or even socially or politically based judgment—whether an idea or action is wise or good, valid or admirable. All interpretive and evaluative claims involve informed opinion (which is why they are debatable). But whereas interpretive claims aim to elucidate the opinions expressed *in* and *by* the text, the second kind of evaluative claim assesses the value or validity of those opinions, often by comparing them with the writer's own.

The following examples juxtapose a series of interpretive claims with evaluative claims of both types.

INTERPRETIVE CLAIMS	EVALUATIVE CLAIMS
"A Conversation with My Father" explores the relative values of realistic and fantastic fiction. Rather than advocating one type of fiction, however, the story ends up affirming just how much we need stories of any and every kind.	"A Conversation with My Father" fails because it ends up being more a stilted Platonic dialogue about works of fiction than a true work of fiction in its own right.
	The father in "A Conversation with My Father" is absolutely right: Realistic stories are more effective and satisfying than fantastic ones.
The speaker of John Donne's "Song" is an angry and disillusioned man obsessed with the infidelity of women.	In "Song," John Donne does a very effective job of characterizing the speaker, an angry and disillusioned man obsessed with the infidelity of women.
	John Donne's "Song" is a horribly misogynistic poem because it ends up endorsing the idea that women are incapable of fidelity.
"How I Learned to Drive" demonstrates that, in Paula Vogel's words, "it takes a whole village to molest a child."	"How I Learned to Drive" is at once too preachy and too self-consciously theatrical to be dramatically effective.
	By insisting that sexual abuse is a crime perpetrated by a "whole village" rather than by an individual, Paula Vogel lets individual abusers off the hook, encouraging us to see them as victims rather than as the villains they really are.

In practice, the line between these different types of claims can become very thin. For instance, an essay claiming that a play conveys a socially dangerous or morally bad message may also claim that it is, as a result, an aesthetically flawed play. Further, an essay defending an interpretive claim about a text implies that it is at least aesthetically or philosophically worthy enough to merit interpretation. Conversely, defending and developing an evaluative claim about a text always requires a certain amount of interpretation. (You have to figure out what the text says in order to figure out whether the text says it well or says something worthwhile.)

To some extent, then, the distinctions are ones of emphasis. But they are important nonetheless. And unless instructed otherwise, you should generally make your thesis an interpretive claim, reserving evaluative claims for conclusions. (On conclusions, see 16.3.3.)

16.3 STRUCTURE

Like any literary text, an essay needs to have a beginning (or introduction), a middle (or body), and an ending (or conclusion). Each of these parts has a distinct function.

16.3.1 Beginning: The Introduction

Your essay's beginning, or introduction, should draw readers in and prepare them for what's to come by

- articulating the thesis;
- providing whatever basic information—about the text, the author, and/or the topic—readers will need to follow the argument; and
- creating interest in the thesis by demonstrating that there is a problem or question that it resolves or answers.

This final task involves showing readers why your thesis isn't dull or obvious, establishing a specific *motive* for the essay and its readers. There are numerous possible motives, but writing expert Gordon Harvey has identified three especially common ones:

1. The truth isn't what one would expect or what it might appear to be on a first reading.
2. There's an interesting wrinkle in the text—a paradox, a contradiction, a tension.
3. A seemingly tangential or insignificant matter is actually important or interesting.

(On motives specific to research essays, see 16.1.1.)

16.3.2 Middle: The Body

The middle, or body, of your essay is its beating heart, the place where you do the essential work of supporting and developing the thesis by presenting and analyzing evidence. Each of the body paragraphs needs to articulate, support, and develop one specific claim—a debatable idea directly related to, but smaller and more specific than, the thesis. This claim should be stated fairly early in the paragraph in a *topic sentence*. And every sentence in the paragraph should help prove, or elaborate on, that claim. Indeed, each paragraph ideally should build from an initial, general statement of the claim to the more complex form of it that you develop by presenting and analyzing evidence. In this way, each paragraph functions like a miniature essay with its own thesis, body, and conclusion.

Your essay as a whole should develop logically just as each paragraph does. To ensure that happens, you need to do the following:

- Order your paragraphs so that each builds on the last, with one idea following another in a logical sequence. The goal is to lay out a clear path for the reader. Like any path, it should go somewhere. Don't just prove your point; develop it.

- Present each idea/paragraph so that the logic behind the sequential order is clear. Try to start each paragraph with a sentence that functions as a bridge, carrying the reader from one point to the next. The reader shouldn't have to leap.

16.3.3 Ending: The Conclusion

In terms of their purpose (not their content), conclusions are introductions in reverse. Whereas introductions draw readers away from their world and into your essay, conclusions send them back. Introductions work to convince readers that they should read the essay. Conclusions work to show them why and how the experience was worthwhile. You should approach conclusions, then, by thinking about what sort of lasting impression you want to create. What precisely do you want readers to take with them as they journey back into the "real world"?

Effective conclusions often consider three things:

1. *Implications*—What picture of your author's work or worldview does your argument imply? Alternatively, what might your argument imply about some real-world issue or situation? Implications don't have to be earth-shattering. For example, it's unlikely that your reading of a work will rock your readers' world. Moreover, trying to convince readers that it can may well have opposite effect. Yet your argument should in some small but significant way change the way readers see the work.

2. *Evaluation*—What might your argument about the text reveal about the literary quality or effectiveness of the text as a whole or of some specific element? Alternatively, to what extent and how do you agree and/or disagree with the author's conclusions about a particular issue?

3. *Areas of ambiguity or unresolved questions*—Are there any remaining puzzles or questions that your argument or the text itself doesn't resolve or answer? Alternatively, might your argument suggest a new question or puzzle worth investigating?

Above all, don't repeat what you've already said. If the essay has done its job to this point, and especially if the essay is relatively short, your readers may feel bored and insulted if they get a mere summary. You should clarify anything that needs clarifying, but go a little beyond that. The best essays are rounded wholes in which conclusions do, in a sense, circle back to the place where they started. However, the best essays remind readers of where they began only in order to give them a more palpable sense of how far they've come.

16.4 EVIDENCE

In terms of convincing readers that your claims are valid, both the amount and the quality of your evidence count. And the quality of your evidence will depend, in great part, on how you prepare and present it. Each of the ideas that makes up the body of your essay must be supported and developed with ample, appropriate evidence. Colloquially speaking, the term *evidence* simply refers to facts. But it's helpful to remember that a fact by itself isn't really evidence for anything, or rather that—as lawyers well know—any one fact can be evidence for many things. Like lawyers, essayists turn a fact into evidence by interpreting it, drawing an inference from it, giving the reader a vivid sense of why and how the fact supports a specific claim. You need, then, both to present specific facts and to actively interpret them. *Show* readers why and how each fact matters.

Quotations are an especially important form of evidence in essays about literature; indeed, an essay about literature that contains no quotations is likely to be relatively weak. The reader of such an essay may doubt whether its argument emerges out of a thorough knowledge of the work. However, quotations are by no means the only facts on which you should draw. Indeed, a quotation will lead your reader to expect commentary on, and interpretation of, its language. As a general rule, you should quote directly from the text only when its wording is significant. Otherwise, simply paraphrase, describe, or summarize. The following example demonstrates the use of both summary and quotation. (On effective quotation, see 19.1; on paraphrase, summary, and description, see chapter 15.)

> At many points in the novel, religion is represented as having degenerated into a system of social control by farmers over workers. Only respectable young men can come courting at Upper Weatherbury farm, and no swearing is allowed (ch. 8). Similarly, the atmosphere in Boldwood's farm kitchen is "like a Puritan Sunday lasting all the week." Bathsheba tries to restrict her workers to drinking mild liquor, and church attendance is taken as the mark of respectability.
>
> —Fred Reid, "Art and Ideology in *Far from the Madding Crowd*,"
> *Thomas Hardy Annual* 4 (1986): 91ff. Print.

> NOTE: Pay special attention to the way this writer uses paraphrase, summary, and quotation. At the beginning of the paragraph, he simply paraphrases certain rules; at its end, he summarizes or describes one character's action. Here, he can use his own words because the rules and actions illustrate his point, not the words that the novelist uses to describe them. However, Reid does quote the text when its (religious) language is the crucial, evidentiary element.

16.5 CONVENTIONS THAT CAN CAUSE PROBLEMS

A mastery of basic mechanics and writing conventions is essential to convincing your readers that you are a knowledgeable and careful writer whose ideas they should respect. This section explores three conventions that are especially crucial to essays about literature.

16.5.1 Tenses

Essays about literature tend to function almost wholly in the present tense, a practice that can take some getting used to. The rationale is that the action within any literary work never stops: A text simply, always *is*. Thus yesterday, today, and tomorrow, Ophelia *goes* mad, "The Lost World" *asks* what it means to grow up, Wordsworth *sees* nature as an avenue to God, and so on. When in doubt, stick to the present tense when writing about literature.

An important exception to this general rule is demonstrated in the following example. As you read the excerpt, pay attention to the way the writer shifts between tenses, using various past tenses to refer to completed actions that took place in the actual past, and using the present tense to refer to actions that occur within, or are performed by, the text.

> In 1959 Plath **did not** consciously **attempt** to write in the domestic poem genre, perhaps because she **was not** yet ready to assume her majority. Her journal entries of that period **bristle** with an impatience at herself that **may derive** from this reluctance. . . . But by fall 1962, when she **had** already **lost** so much, she **was** ready. . . . In "Daddy" she **achieved** her victory in two ways. First, . . . she symbolically **assaults** a father figure who **is identified** with male control of language.
> —Steven Gould Axelrod, "Jealous Gods," from *Sylvia Plath: The Wound and the Cure of Words* (Baltimore: Johns Hopkins UP, 1990), 51–70.

16.5.2 Titles

Underline or italicize the titles of all books and works published independently, including

- long poems (*Endymion*; *Paradise Lost*)
- plays (*A Midsummer Night's Dream*; *Death and the King's Horseman*)
- periodicals: newspapers, magazines, scholarly journals, and the like (*New York Times*; *College English*)

Use quotation marks for the titles of works that have been published as part of longer works, including

- short stories ("A Rose for Emily"; "Happy Endings")
- essays and periodical articles ("A Rose for 'A Rose for Emily'"; "Art and Ideology in *Far from the Madding Crowd*")
- poems ("Daddy"; "Ode to a Nightingale")

Generally speaking, you should capitalize the first word of every title, as well as all the other words that aren't either articles (e.g., *the, a*); prepositions (e.g., *among, in, through*); or conjunctions (e.g., *and, but*). One exception to this rule is the poem in which the first line substitutes for a missing title (a category that includes everything by Emily Dickinson, as well as the sonnets of Shakespeare and Edna St. Vincent Millay). In such cases, only the first word is capitalized. Often, the entire phrase is placed in brackets—as in "[Let me not to the marriage of true minds]"—but you will just as often see such titles without brackets.

16.5.3 Names

When first referring to an author, use his or her full name; thereafter, use the last name. (For example, although you may feel a real kinship with Robert Frost, you will appear disrespectful if you refer to him as Robert.)

With characters' names, use the literary work as a guide. Because "Bartleby, the Scrivener" always refers to its characters as Bartleby, Turkey, and Nippers, so should you. But because "The Management of Grief" refers to Judith Templeton either by her full name or by her first name, it would be odd and confusing to call her Templeton.

17 THE WRITING PROCESS

It's fairly easy to describe the purpose and formal elements of an essay. Actually writing one is more difficult. So, too, is prescribing a precise formula for how to do so. In practice, the writing process will vary from writer to writer and from assignment to assignment. No one can give you a recipe. However, this chapter presents a menu of possible approaches and exercises, which you should test out and refine for yourself.

As you do so, keep in mind that writing needn't be a solitary enterprise. Most writers—working in every genre, at every level—get inspiration, guidance, help, and feedback from other people throughout the writing process, and so can you. Your instructor may well create opportunities for collaboration, having you and your colleagues work together to plan essays, critique drafts, and so on. Even if that isn't the case, you can always reach out to others on your own. Since every essay will ultimately have to engage readers, why not bring some actual readers and fellow writers into the writing process? Use class discussions to generate and test out essay topics and theses. Ask your instructor to clarify assignments or to talk with you about your plans. Have classmates, friends, or roommates read your drafts.

Of course, your essay ultimately needs to be your own work. You, the individual writer, must be the ultimate arbiter, critically scrutinizing the advice you receive, differentiating valid reader responses from groundless ones. But in writing about literature, as in reading it, we all can get a much better sense of what we think by considering others' views.

17.1 GETTING STARTED

17.1.1 Scrutinizing the Assignment

For student essayists, as for most professional ones, the writing process usually begins with an assignment. Though assignments vary greatly, all impose certain restrictions. These are designed not to hinder your creativity but to direct it into productive channels, ensuring that you hone certain skills, try out various approaches, and avoid common pitfalls. Your first task as a writer is thus to scrutinize the assignment. Make sure that you fully understand what you are being asked to do (and not do), and ask questions about anything unclear or puzzling.

Almost all assignments restrict the length of the essay by giving word or page limits. Keep those limits in mind as you generate and evaluate potential essay topics, making sure that you choose a topic you can handle in the space allowed. Many assignments impose further restrictions, often indicating the texts and/or topics to be explored. As a result, any given assignment will significantly shape the rest of the writing process—determining, for example, whether and how you should tackle a step such as "Choosing a Text" or "Identifying Topics."

Here are three representative essay assignments, each of which imposes a different set of restrictions:

1. Choose any story in this anthology and write an essay analyzing the way in which its protagonist changes.

2. Write an essay analyzing one of the following sonnets: "Nuns Fret Not," "Range-Finding," or "London, 1802." Be sure to consider how the poem's form contributes to its meaning.

3. Write an essay exploring the significance of references to eyes and vision in *A Midsummer Night's Dream*. What, through them, does the play suggest about both the power and the limitations of human vision?

The first assignment dictates the topic and main question. It also provides the kernel of a thesis: *In [story title], [protagonist's name] goes from being a* _____ *to a* _____ OR *By the end of [story title], [protagonist's name] has learned that* _____. The assignment leaves you free to choose which story you will write about, although it limits you to those in which the protagonist clearly changes or learns a lesson of some kind. The second assignment limits your choice of texts to three. Though it also requires that your essay address the effects of the poet's choice to use the sonnet form, it doesn't require that this be the main topic of the essay. Rather, it leaves you free to pursue any topic that focuses on the poem's meaning. The third assignment is the most restrictive. It indicates both the text and the general topic to be explored, while requiring you to narrow the topic and formulate a specific thesis.

17.1.2 Choosing a Text

If the assignment allows you to choose which text to write about, try letting your initial impressions or "gut reactions" guide you. If you do so, your first impulse may be to choose a text that you like or "get" right away. Perhaps its language resembles your own; it depicts speakers, characters, or situations that you easily relate to; or it explores issues that you care deeply about. Following that first impulse can be a great idea. Writing an engaging essay requires being engaged with whatever we're writing about, and we all find it easier to engage with texts, authors, and/or characters that we like immediately.

You may discover, however, that you have little interesting or new to say about such a text. Perhaps you're too emotionally invested to analyze it closely, or maybe its meaning seems so obvious that there's no puzzle or problem to drive an argument. You might, then, find it more productive to choose a work that provokes the opposite reaction—one that initially puzzles or angers you, one whose characters or situations seem alien, one that investigates an issue you haven't previously thought much about or that articulates a theme you don't agree with. Sometimes such negative responses can have surprisingly positive results when it comes to writing. One student writer, for example, summed up her basic response to William Blake's *The Marriage of Heaven and Hell* with the words "He's crazy." Initially, the book made no sense to her. And that's precisely why she decided to write about it: She needed to do so, to make sense of it for other readers, in order to make sense of it for herself. In the end, she wrote a powerful essay exploring how the book defined, and why it celebrated, seeming insanity.

When writing about a text that you've discussed in class, you might make similar use of your "gut responses" to that conversation. Did you strongly agree or disagree with one of your classmate's interpretations of a particular text? If so, why not write about it?

17.1.3 Identifying Topics

When an assignment allows you to create your own topic, you are much more likely to build a lively and engaging essay from a particular insight or question that captures your attention and makes you want to say something, solve a problem, or stake out a position. The best papers originate in an individual response to a text and focus on a genuine question about it. Even when an instructor assigns a topic, the effectiveness of your essay will largely depend on whether or not you have made the topic your own, turning it into a question to which you discover your own answer.

Often we refer to "finding" a topic, as if there are a bevy of topics "out there" just waiting to be plucked like ripe fruit off the topic-tree. In at least two ways, that's true. For one thing, as we read a literary work, certain topics often do jump out and say, "Hey, look at me! I'm a topic!" A title alone may have that effect: What makes the "hills like white elephants" important to Hemingway's story? Why is Keats so keen on that darn nightingale; what does it symbolize for him? Why does Ibsen call Nora's home "a doll house"?

For another thing, certain general topics can be adapted to fit almost any literary work. In fact, that's just another way of saying that there are certain common types (or subgenres) of literary essays, just as there are of short stories, plays, and poems. For example, one very common kind of literary essay explores the significance of a seemingly insignificant aspect or element of a work—a word or group of related words, an image or image-cluster, a minor character, an incident or action, and so on. Equally common are character-focused essays of three types. The first explores the outlook or worldview of a character and its consequences. The second considers the way a major character develops from the beginning of a literary work to its end. The third analyzes the nature and significance of a conflict between two characters (or two groups of characters) and the way this conflict is ultimately resolved. Especially when you're utterly befuddled about where to begin, it can be very useful to keep in mind these generic topics and essay types and to use them as starting points. But remember that they are just starting points. One always has to adapt and narrow a generic topic such as "imagery" or "character change" in order to produce an effective essay. In practice, then, no writer simply "finds" a topic; he or she *makes* one.

Similarly, though the topic that leaps out at you immediately might end up being the one you find most interesting, you can only discover that by giving yourself some options. It's always a good idea to initially come up with as many topics as you can. Test out various topics to see which one will work best. Making yourself identify multiple topics will lead you to think harder, look more closely, and reach deeper into yourself and the work.

Here are some additional techniques to identify potential topics. In each case, write your thoughts down. Don't worry at this point about what form your writing takes or how good it is.

- *Analyze your initial response.*
  If you've chosen a text that you feel strongly about, start with those responses. Try to describe your feelings and trace them to their source. Be as specific as possible. What moments, aspects, or elements of the text most affected you? Exactly how and why did they affect you? What was most puzzling? amusing? annoying? intriguing? Try to articulate the question behind your feelings. Often, strong responses result when a work either challenges or affirms an expectation, assumption, or conviction that you, the reader, bring to the work. Think about whether and how that's true here. Define the specific expectation, assumption, or conviction. How, where, and why does the text challenge it? fulfill and affirm it? Which of your responses and expectations are objectively valid, likely to be shared by other readers?

- *Think through the elements.*
  Start with a list of elements and work your way through them, thinking about what's unique or interesting or puzzling about the text in terms of each. What stands out about the **tone**? What about the **speaker**? the situation? other elements? Come up with a statement about each. Look for patterns among your statements. Also, think about the questions implied or overlooked by your statements.

- *Pose motive questions.*

In articulating a motive in your essay's introduction, your concern is primarily with the readers, your goal being to give them a solid reason to keep reading. But you can often work your way toward a topic (or topics) by considering motive. As suggested earlier (16.3.1), there are three common motives. Turn each one into a question in order to identify potential topics:

1. What element(s) of this work might a casual reader misinterpret?
2. What interesting paradox(es), contradiction(s), or tension(s) do you see in this text?
3. What seemingly minor, insignificant, easily ignored element(s) or aspect(s) of this text might in fact have major significance?

17.1.4 Formulating a Question and a Thesis

Almost any element, aspect, or point of interest in a text can become a topic for a short essay. Before you can begin writing an essay on that topic, however, you need to come up with a thesis or hypothesis—an arguable statement about the topic. Quite often, one comes up with topic and thesis simultaneously: You might well decide to write about a topic precisely because you've got a specific claim to make about it. At other times, that's not the case: The topic comes much more easily than the thesis. In those cases, it helps to formulate a specific question about the topic and to develop a specific answer. That answer will be your thesis.

Again, remember that your question and thesis should focus on something specific, yet they need to be generally valid, involving more than your personal feelings. Who, after all, can really argue with you about how you feel? The following example demonstrates the way you might freewrite your way from an initial, subjective response to an arguable thesis:

> I really admire Bartleby.
>
> But why? What in the story encourages me to respond that way to him? Well, he sticks to his guns and insists on doing only what he "prefers" to do. He doesn't just follow orders. That makes him really different from all the other characters in the story (especially the narrator). And also from a lot of people I know, even me. He's a nonconformist.
>
> Do I think other readers should feel the same way? Maybe, but maybe not. After all, his refusal to conform does cause problems for everyone around him. And actually it doesn't do him a lot of good either. Plus, he would be annoying in real life. And, even if you admire him, you can't really care about him because he doesn't seem to care about anybody else.
>
> Maybe that's the point. Through Bartleby, Melville explores both how rare and important, and how dangerous, nonconformity can be.

Regardless of how you arrive at your thesis or how strongly you believe in it, it's still helpful at this early stage to think of it as a working hypothesis—a claim that's provisional, still open to rethinking and revision.

17.2 PLANNING

Once you've formulated a tentative thesis, you need to (1) identify the relevant evidence and (2) figure out how to structure your argument, articulating and ordering your claims or sub-ideas. Generally speaking, it works best to tackle structure first—that is, to first figure out your claims and create an outline—because doing so will help you get a sense of what kind of evidence you need. However, you may sometimes get stuck and need to reverse this process, gathering evidence first in order to then formulate and order your claims.

17.2.1 Moving from Claims to Evidence

If you want to focus first on structure, start by looking closely at your thesis. As in many other aspects of writing, it helps to temporarily fill your readers' shoes, trying to see your thesis and the promises it makes from the readers' point of view. What will they need to be shown, and in what order?

If a good thesis shapes readers' expectations, it can also guide you, as a writer. A good thesis often implies what the essay's claims should be and how they should be ordered. For instance, a thesis that focuses on the development of a character implies both that the first body paragraphs will explain what the character is initially like and that later paragraphs will explore how and why that character changes over the course of the story, poem, or play. Similarly, the Bartleby thesis developed in the previous example—*Through Bartleby, Melville explores both how rare and important, and how dangerous, nonconformity can be.*—implies that the writer's essay will address four major issues and will thus have four major parts. The first part must show that Bartleby is a nonconformist. The second part should establish that this nonconformity is rare, a quality that isn't shared by the other characters in the story. Finally, the third and fourth parts should explore, respectively, the positive and negative aspects or consequences of Bartleby's nonconformist behavior. Some or all of these parts may need to include multiple paragraphs, each devoted to a more specific claim.

At this stage, it's very helpful to create an outline. Write down or type out your thesis, and then list each claim (to create a *sentence outline*) or each of the topics to be covered (to create a *topic outline*). Now you can return to the text, rereading it in order to gather evidence for each claim. In the process, you might discover facts that seem relevant to the thesis but that don't relate directly to any of the claims you've articulated. In that case, you may need to insert a new claim into the outline. Additionally, you may find (and should actively look for) facts that challenge your argument. Test and reassess your claims against those facts.

17.2.2 Moving from Evidence to Claims

If you are focusing first on evidence, start by rereading the literary work in a more strategic way, searching for everything relevant to your topic—words, phrases, structural devices, changes of tone, and so forth. As you read (slowly and single-mindedly, with your thesis in mind), keep your pen constantly poised to mark or note down useful facts. Be ready to say something about the facts as you come upon them; immediately write down any ideas that occur to you. Some of these will appear in your essay; some won't. Just like most of the footage shot in making a film, many of your notes will end up on the cutting-room floor. As in filmmaking, however, having too much raw material is preferable to not having enough.

No one can tell you exactly how to take notes. But here is one process that you might try. Be forewarned: This process involves using notecards or uniform sheets of paper. Having your notes on individual cards makes it easier to separate and sort them, a concrete, physical process that can aid the mental process of organizing thoughts and facts. If you are working on a computer, create notecards by putting page breaks between each note or by leaving enough space so that you can cut each page down to a uniform size.

1. Keep your thesis constantly in mind as you reread and take notes. Mark all the passages in the text that bear on your thesis. For each, create a notecard that contains both (a) a single sentence describing how the passage relates to your thesis and (b) the specific information about the passage's location that you will need to create a parenthetical citation. (The information you need will depend on the kind of text you're working with; for specifics, see 19.2.1.) Also, make cards for other relevant, evidentiary facts—like aspects of a poem's rhyme scheme.

2. Keep reading and taking notes until any of the following occur:
   - You get too tired and lose your concentration. (Stop, take a break, come back later.)
   - You stop finding relevant evidence or perceive a noticeable drying up of your ideas. (Again, it's time to pause. Later, when your mind is fresh, read the text one more time to ensure that you didn't miss anything.)
   - You find yourself annotating every sentence or line, so that the evidence all runs together into a single blob. (If this happens, your thesis is probably too broad. Simplify and narrow it. Then continue notetaking.)

- You become impatient with your notetaking and can't wait to get started writing. (Start drafting immediately. But be prepared to go back to systematic notetaking if your ideas stop coming or your energy fades.)
- You find that the evidence is insufficient for your thesis, that it points in another direction, or that it contradicts your thesis. (Revise your thesis to accommodate the evidence, and begin rereading once more.)

3. When you think you have finished notetaking, read all your notecards over slowly, one by one, and jot down any further ideas as they occur to you, each one on a separate notecard.

Use your notecards to work toward an outline. Again, there are many ways to go about doing this. Here's one process.

1. Sort your cards into logical groups or clusters. Come up with a keyword for that group, and write that word at the top of each card in the group.

2. Set your notecards aside. On a fresh sheet of paper or in a separate document on your computer, write all the major points you want to make. Write them randomly, as they occur to you. Then read quickly through your notecards, and add to your list any important points you have left out.

3. Now it's time to order your points. Putting your points in order is something of a guess at this point, and you may well want to reorder later. For now, make your best guess. Taking your random list, put a "1" in front of the point you will probably begin with, a "2" before the probable second point, and so on.

4. Copy the list in numerical order, revising (if necessary) as you go.

5. Match up your notes (and examples) with the points on your outline. Prepare a title card for each point in the outline, writing on it the point and its probable place in the essay. Then line them up in order before you begin writing. If you're working on a computer, use the search function to find each instance of a keyword, phrase, or name. Then cut and paste in order to arrange your electronic "cards" under the headings you've identified.

6. At this point, you may discover cards that resist classification, cards that belong in two or more places, and/or cards that don't belong anywhere at all. If a card relates to more than one point, put it in the pile with the lowest number, but write on it the number or numbers of other possible locations. Try to find a place for the cards that don't seem to fit, and then put any that remain unsorted into a special file marked "?" or "use in revision."

Before you begin drafting, you may want to develop a more elaborate outline, incorporating examples and including topic sentences for each paragraph. Or you may wish to work directly from your sketchy outline and cards.

17.3 DRAFTING

If you've taken enough time with the planning process, you may already be quite close to a first draft. If you've instead jumped straight into writing, you may have to move back and forth between composing and taking some of the steps described in the last section. Either way, remember that first drafts are often called *rough drafts* for a reason. Think of yourself as a painter "roughing out" a sketch in preparation for the more detailed painting to come. The most important thing is to start writing and keep at it.

Try to start with your thesis and work your way step by step through the entire body of the essay at one sitting. (However, you don't actually have to sit the whole time; if you get stuck, jump up and down, walk around the room, water your plants. Then get back to work.) You will almost certainly feel frustrated at times—as you search for the right word, struggle to decide how the next sentence should begin, or discover that you need to tackle ideas in a different order than you had originally planned.

Stick to it. If you become truly stuck, try to explain your point to another person, or get out a piece of paper or open a new computer file and try working out your ideas or freewriting for a few minutes before returning to your draft. Or, if you get to a section you simply can't write at the moment, make a note about what needs to go in that spot. Then move on and come back to that point later.

Whatever it takes, stay with your draft until you've at least got a middle, or body, that you're relatively satisfied with. Then take a break. Later or even tomorrow come back and take another shot, attaching an introduction and conclusion to the body, filling in any gaps, doing your utmost to create a relatively satisfying whole. Now pat yourself on the back and take another break.

17.4 REVISING

Revision is one of the most important and difficult tasks for any writer. It's a crucial stage in the writing process, yet one that is all too easy to ignore or mismanage. The difference between a so-so essay and a good one, between a good essay and a great one, often depends entirely on effective revision. Give yourself time to revise and develop revision strategies that work for you; the investment in time and effort will pay rich dividends.

Ideally, the process of revision should involve three distinct tasks: assessing the elements, improving the argument, and editing and proofreading.

Each of these may require a separate draft. Before considering those three tasks, however, you should be aware of the following three general tips.

First, effective revision requires you to temporarily play the role of reader, as well as writer, of your essay. Take a step back from your draft, doing your utmost to look at it from a more objective point of view. Revision demands re-vision—looking again, seeing anew. As a result, this is an especially good time to involve other people. Have a classmate or friend read and critique your draft.

Second, at this stage it helps to think less in absolute terms (right and wrong, good and bad) than in terms of strengths and weaknesses (elements and aspects of the draft that work well and those that can be improved through revision). If you can understand what's making your essay work, as well as what's detracting from it, then you're better able to improve it. Don't get distracted from this important work by grammatical errors, spelling mistakes, or other minutiae; there will be time to correct them later.

Third, learn to take full advantage of all the capabilities of the computer, but also recognize its limitations. Cutting and pasting make experimenting with different organizational strategies a breeze; word-processing programs identify problems with grammar, spelling, and syntax; the search function can locate repetitive or problematic wording; and so on. You should familiarize yourself with, and use, all the tools your computer provides and be thankful that you barely know the meaning of the word *white-out*. But you should also remember that the computer is just a tool with limits and that you must be its master. Like any tool, it can create new problems in the process of solving old ones. When it comes to grammar, syntax, and spelling, for instance, you should always pay attention to your program's queries and suggestions. But if you let it make all the decisions, you may end up with an essay full of malapropisms at once hilarious and tragic (one student essay consistently referred to human beings as *human beans*!) or of sentences that are all exactly the same size and shape—all perfectly correct, and all perfectly boring. Also, because the computer makes cutting and pasting so easy and only shows an essay one screen at a time, it's much easier to reorganize but much harder to recognize the effects of doing so. During revision, then, you should at times move away from the computer screen. Print out a hard copy periodically so that you can assess your essay as a whole, identifying problems that you can return to the computer to fix.

17.4.1 Assessing the Elements

The first step in revision is to make sure that all the elements or working parts of the essay are indeed working. To help with that process, run through the following checklist in order to identify the strengths and weaknesses of your draft. Try to answer each question honestly.

Thesis

- ☐ Is there *one* claim that effectively controls the essay?
- ☐ Is the claim debatable?
- ☐ Does the claim demonstrate real thought? Does it truly illuminate the text and the topic?

Structure

BEGINNING

- ☐ Does the introduction establish a clear motive for readers, effectively convincing them that there's something worth thinking, reading, and writing about here?
- ☐ Does it give readers all (and only) the basic information they need about the text, author, and topic?
- ☐ Does the introduction clearly state the central claim or thesis? Is it obvious which claim is the thesis?

MIDDLE

- ☐ Does each paragraph state one debatable claim? Is the main claim always obvious? Does everything in the paragraph relate to, and help support and develop, that claim?
- ☐ Is each of those claims clearly related to (but different from) the thesis?
- ☐ Are the claims/paragraphs logically ordered?
- ☐ Is that logic clear? Is each claim clearly linked to those that come before and after? Are there any logical "leaps" that readers might have trouble taking?
- ☐ Does each claim/paragraph clearly build on the last one? Does the argument move forward, or does it seem more like a list or a tour through a museum of interesting observations?
- ☐ Do any key claims or steps in the argument seem to be missing?

TIP: You may be better able to discover structural weaknesses if you
  1. re-outline your draft as it is. Copy your thesis statement and each of your topic sentences into a separate document. Then pose the above questions. OR
  2. read through the essay with highlighters of various colors in hand. As you read, color-code parts that could be restatements of the same or closely related ideas. Then reorganize to match up the colors.

ENDING

- ☐ Does the conclusion give readers the sense that they've gotten somewhere and that the journey has been worthwhile?
- ☐ Does it indicate the implications of the argument, consider relevant evaluative questions, or discuss questions that remain unanswered?

Evidence

☐ Is there ample, appropriate evidence for each claim?

☐ Are the appropriateness and significance of each fact—its relevance to the claim—perfectly clear?

☐ Are there any weak examples or inferences that aren't reasonable? Are there moments when readers might ask, "But couldn't that fact instead mean this?"

☐ Is all the evidence considered? What about facts that might complicate or contradict the argument? Are there moments when readers might think, "But what about this other fact?"

☐ Is each piece of evidence clearly presented? Do readers have all the contextual information they need to understand a quotation?

☐ Is each piece of evidence gracefully presented? Are quotations varied by length and presentation? Are they ever too long? Are there any unnecessary block quotations, or block quotations that require additional analysis? (For more specific explanations and advice on effective quotation, see 19.1.)

Though you want to pay attention to all of the elements, first drafts often have similar weaknesses. There are three especially common ones:

• *Mismatch between thesis and argument or between introduction and body*
  Sometimes a first or second draft ends up being a tool for discovering what your thesis really is. As a result, you may find that the thesis of your draft (or your entire introduction) doesn't fit the argument you've ended up making. You thus need to start your revision by reworking the thesis and introduction. Then work your way back through the essay, making sure that each claim or topic sentence fits the new thesis.

• *The list, or "museum tour," structure*
  In a draft, writers sometimes present each claim as if it were just an item on a list (*First, second,* and so on) or as a stop on a tour of ideas (*And this is also important . . .*). But presenting your ideas in this way keeps you and your readers from making logical connections between ideas. It may also prevent your argument from developing. Sometimes it can even be a sign that you've ceased arguing entirely, falling into mere plot summary or description. Check to see if number-like words or phrases appear prominently at the beginning of your paragraphs or if your paragraphs could be put into a different order without fundamentally changing what you're saying. At times, solving this problem will require wholesale rethinking and reorganizing. But at other times, you will just need to add or rework topic sentences. Make sure that there's a clearly stated, debatable claim at the beginning of each paragraph and that each claim relates to, but differs from, the thesis.

- *Missing sub-ideas*

  You may find that you've skipped a logical step in your argument—that the claim you make in, say, body paragraph 3 actually depends on, or makes sense only in light of, a more basic claim that you took for granted in your draft. In that case, you'll need to create and insert a new paragraph that articulates, supports, and develops this key claim.

17.4.2 Enriching the Argument

Step 1 of the revision process aims to ensure that your essay does the best possible job of making your argument. But revision is also an opportunity to go beyond that—to think about ways in which your overall argument might be made more thorough and complex. In drafting an essay our attention is often and rightly focused on emphatically staking out a particular position and proving its validity. This is the fundamental task of any essay, and you certainly don't want to do anything at this stage to compromise that. At the same time, you do want to make sure that you haven't purchased clarity at the cost of oversimplification by, for example, ignoring evidence that might undermine or complicate your claims, alternative interpretations of the evidence you do present, or alternative claims or points of view. Remember, you have a better chance of persuading readers to accept your point of view if you show them that it's based on a thorough, open-minded exploration of the text and topic. Don't invent unreasonable or irrelevant complications or counterarguments. Do try to assess your argument objectively and honestly, perhaps testing it against the text one more time. Think like a reader rather than a writer: Are there points where a reasonable reader might object to, or disagree with, the argument? Have you ignored or glossed over any questions or issues that a reasonable reader might expect an essay on this topic to address?

17.4.3 Editing and Proofreading

Once you've gotten the overall argument in good shape, it's time to focus on the small but important stuff—words and sentences. Your prose should not only convey your ideas to your readers but also demonstrate how much you care about your essay. Flawless prose can't disguise a vapid or illogical argument, but faulty, flabby prose can destroy a potentially persuasive and thoughtful one. Don't sabotage all your hard work by failing to correct misspelled words, grammatical problems, misquotations, incorrect citations, or typographical errors. Little oversights make all the difference when it comes to clarity and credibility.

Though you will want to check all of the following aspects of your essay, it will probably be easier to spot mistakes and weaknesses if you read through the essay several times, concentrating each time on one specific aspect.

Every writer has individual weaknesses and strengths, and every writer tends to be overly fond of certain phrases and sentence structures. With practice, you will learn to watch out for the kinds of mistakes to which you are most prone. Eventually, you can and should develop your own *personalized* editing checklist.

Sentences
☐ Does each one read clearly and crisply?
☐ Are they varied in length, structure, and word order?
☐ Is the phrasing direct rather than roundabout?

TIPS:
1. Try circling, or using your computer to search for, every preposition and *to be* verb. Since these can lead to confusion or roundabout phrasing, weed out as many as you can.
2. Try reading your paper aloud or having your roommate read it to you. Note places where you stumble, and listen for sentences that are hard to get through or understand.

Words
☐ Have I used any words whose meaning I'm not sure of?
☐ Are the idioms used correctly? Is my terminology correct?
☐ Do my key words always mean *exactly* the same thing?
☐ Do I ever use a fancy word or phrase where a simpler one might do?
☐ Are there any unnecessary words or phrases?
☐ Do my **metaphors** and **figures of speech** make literal sense?
☐ Are my verbs active and precise?
☐ Are my pronoun references clear and correct?
☐ Do my subjects and verbs always agree?

Mechanics
☐ Is every quotation correctly worded and punctuated?
☐ Is the source of each quotation clearly indicated through parenthetical citation?
☐ Have I checked the spelling of words I'm not sure of? (Remember that spell-checks won't indicate how to spell every word and that they sometimes create mistakes by substituting the wrong word for the misspelled one.)
☐ Are my pages numbered?
☐ Does the first page of my essay clearly indicate my name (and any other required identifying information), as well as my essay's title?

17.5 CRAFTING A TITLE

Complete your essay by giving it a title. As any researcher trying to locate and assess sources by browsing titles will tell you, titles are extremely important. They're the first thing readers encounter and a writer's first opportunity to create a good impression and to shape readers' expectations. Every good essay deserves a good title. And a good title is one that both *informs* and *interests*. Inform readers by telling them both the work(s) your essay will analyze and something about your topic. Interest them with an especially vivid and telling word or a short phrase from the literary work ("'We all said, "she will kill herself"': The Narrator/Detective in William Faulkner's 'A Rose for Emily'"), with a bit of wordplay ("'Tintern Abbey' and the Art of Artlessness"), or with a little of both ("A Rose for 'A Rose for Emily'").

18 THE RESEARCH ESSAY

Writing a research essay may seem like a daunting task that requires specialized skills and considerable time and effort. Research does add a few more steps to the writing process, so that process will take more time. And those steps require you to draw on, and develop, skills somewhat different from those involved in creating other kinds of essays. But a research essay is, after all, an essay. Its core elements are those of any essay, its basic purpose exactly the same—to articulate and develop a debatable claim about a literary text. As a result, this kind of essay draws on many of the same skills and strategies you've already begun to develop. Similarly, though you will need to add a few new steps, the writing process still involves getting started, planning, drafting, and revising—exactly the same dance whose rhythms you've already begun to master.

Indeed, the only distinctive thing about a research essay is that it requires the use of secondary sources. Though that adds to your burden in some ways, it can lighten it in others. Think of secondary sources not as another ball you have to juggle but as another tool you get to add to your toolbelt: You're still being asked to build a cabinet, but now you get to use a hammer *and* a screwdriver. This chapter will help you make the best use of this powerful tool.

18.1 TYPES AND FUNCTIONS OF SECONDARY SOURCES

Whenever we write an essay about literature, we engage in a conversation with other readers about the meaning and significance of a particular work (or works). Effective argumentation always depends on imagining how other readers are likely to respond to, and interpret, the literary text. Almost all texts and authors are the subject of actual public conversations, however, often extending over many years and involving numerous scholarly readers. A research essay can be an opportunity to investigate this conversation and to contribute to it. In this case, your secondary sources will be works in which literary scholars analyze a specific text or an author's body of work.

In addition, every literary work is significantly shaped by, and speaks to, its author's unique experience and outlook, as well as the events and debates of the era in which the author lived. So a research assignment can be an opportunity to learn more about a particular author, about that author's body of work, or about the place and time in which the author lived and wrote. The goal of the essay will be to show how context informs text or vice versa. Secondary sources for this sort of research essay will be biographies of the author, essays or letters by the author, and/or historical works of some kind.

Generally speaking, three types of secondary sources are used in essays about literature: *literary criticism, biography,* and *history.* The goal of a particular essay and the kinds of questions it raises will determine which kind of sources you use.

In practice, however, many secondary sources cross these boundaries. Biographies of a particular author often offer literary critical interpretations of that author's work; works of **literary criticism** sometimes make use of historical or biographical information; and so on. And you, too, may want or need to draw on more than one kind of source in a single essay. Your instructor will probably give you guidance about what kinds of sources and research topics or questions are appropriate. So make sure that you have a clear sense of the assignment before you get started.

Unless your instructor indicates otherwise, *your* argument should be the focus of your essay, and secondary sources should be just that—secondary. They should merely serve as tools that you use to deepen and enrich your argument about the literary text. They shouldn't substitute for it. Your essay should never simply repeat or report on what other people have already said.

Thus even though secondary sources are important to the development of your research essay, they should not be the source of your ideas. Instead, as one popular guide to writing suggests,* they are sources of

- *opinion* (or *debatable claims*)—other readers' views and interpretations of the text, author, or topic, which "you support, criticize, or develop";
- *information*—facts (which "you interpret") about the author's life; the text's composition, publication, or reception; the era during, or about which, the author wrote; or the literary movement of which the author was a part;
- *concept*—general terms or theoretical frameworks that you borrow and apply to your author or text.

Again, any one source will likely offer more than one of these things. For example, a literary critic may provide an *opinion* on (or interpretation of) a work, *information* about the context in which the work was written, and *concepts* drawn from other fields, such as psychology or philosophy.

Nonetheless, the distinction between opinion (debatable claim) and information (factual statement) is crucial. As you read a source, you must discriminate between the two. And when drawing on sources in your essay,

*Gordon Harvey, *Writing with Sources.* Indianapolis: Hackett, 1998.

remember that an opinion about a text, no matter how well informed, isn't the same as evidence. Only facts can serve that function. Suppose, for example, that you are writing an essay on Sylvia Plath's poem "Daddy." You claim that the speaker adopts two voices, that of her child self and that of her adult self—an opinion also set forth in Steven Gould Axelrod's article "Jealous Gods." You cannot prove this claim to be true by merely saying that Axelrod makes the same claim. Like any debatable claim, this one must be backed up with evidence from the primary text.

In this situation, however, you must indicate that a source has made the same claim that you do in order to

- give the source credit for having this idea or stating this opinion before you did (see 18.4.1);
- encourage readers to see you as a knowledgeable and trustworthy writer, one who has taken the time to explore, digest, and fairly represent others' opinions;
- demonstrate that your opinion isn't merely idiosyncratic because another informed, even "expert," reader agrees with you.

Were you to disagree with the source's opinion, you would need to acknowledge that disagreement in order to demonstrate the originality of your own interpretation, while also (again) encouraging readers to see you as a knowledgeable, careful, trustworthy writer.

You will need to cite sources throughout your essay whenever you make (1) a claim that complements or contradicts the opinion-claim of a source, or (2) a claim that requires secondary-source information or concepts. In essays that draw on literary critical sources, those sources may prove especially helpful when articulating motive (see 18.1.1).

18.1.1 Source-Related Motives

Not all research essays use sources to establish motive. However, doing so is one way to ensure that your own ideas are the focus of your essay and to demonstrate that (and how) your essay contributes to a literary critical conversation rather than just reporting on it or repeating what others have already said.

In addition to the general motives described above (16.3.1), writing expert Gordon Harvey has identified three common source-related motives:

1. Sources offer different opinions about a particular issue, thus suggesting that there is still a problem or a puzzle worth investigating.

> Almost all interpreters of [*Antigone*] have agreed that the play shows Creon to be morally defective, though they might not agree about the particular nature of his defect. [examples] . . . I want to suggest [instead] that. . . .
> —Martha Nussbaum, *The Fragility of Goodness: Luck and Ethics in Greek Tragedy and Philosophy* (Cambridge and New York: Cambridge UP, 1986)

2. A source (or sources) makes a faulty claim that needs to be challenged or clarified.

> Modern critics who do not share Sophocles' conviction about the paramount duty of burying the dead and who attach more importance than he did to the claims of political authority have tended to underestimate the way in which he justifies Antigone against Creon. [examples]
> —Maurice Bowra, *Sophoclean Tragedy* (Oxford: Clarenden, 1944)

3. Sources neglect a significant aspect or element of the text, or they make a claim that needs to be further developed or applied in a new way.

> At first sight, there appears little need for further study of the lovers in *Far from the Madding Crowd*, and even less of their environment. To cite but a few critics, David Cecil has considered the courtship of Bathsheba, Virginia Hyman her moral development through her varied experience in love, George Wing her suitors, Douglas Brown her relation to the natural environment, Merryn Williams that of Gabriel Oak in contrast to Sergeant Troy's alienation from nature, and, most recently, Peter Casagrande Bathsheba's reformation through her communion with both Gabriel and the environment. To my knowledge, none has considered the modes or styles in which those and other characters express love and how far these may result from or determine their attitude to the land and its dependents, nor the tragic import in the Wessex novels of incompatibility in this sense between human beings, as distinct from that between the human psyche and the cosmos.
> —Lionel Adey, "Styles of Love in *Far from the Madding Crowd.*"
> *Thomas Hardy Annual 5* (1987): 47–62.

18.2 RESEARCH AND THE WRITING PROCESS

Keeping in mind the overall goal of making secondary sources secondary, you have two options about when and how to integrate research into the writing process: (1) You may consult sources in the exploratory phase, using them to generate potential topics and theses for your essay, or (2) you may consult sources during (or even after) the planning or drafting phases, using them to refine and test a tentative thesis. Each approach has advantages and disadvantages.

18.2.1 Using Research to Generate Topic and Thesis

You may consult secondary sources very early in the writing process, using them to help generate your essay topic and thesis (or several potential ones from which you will need to choose). This approach has three advantages. First, you approach the research with a thoroughly open mind and formulate your own opinion about the text(s) only after having considered the range of opinions and information that the sources offer. Second, as you investigate others' opinions, you may find yourself disagreeing, thereby discovering that your mind isn't nearly as open as you'd thought—that you do, indeed, have an opinion of which you weren't fully aware. (Since you've discovered this by disagreeing with a published opinion, you're well on your way to having a motive as well as a thesis.) Third, because you begin by informing yourself about what others have already said, you may be in less danger of simply repeating or reporting.

The potential disadvantage is that you may become overwhelmed by the sheer number of sources or by the amount and diversity of information and opinion they offer. You may agree with everyone, being unable to discriminate among others' opinions or to formulate your own. Or you may find that the conversation seems so exhaustive that you despair of finding anything new to add. If you take this approach, you should maximize the advantages and minimize the disadvantages by keeping in mind a set of clear motive-related questions.

If your sources are works of literary criticism, your goal is to answer two general questions: *What's the conversation about? How can I contribute to it?* To answer those questions, it helps to recall the various motives described in section 18.1.1. Turn them into questions that you can pose about each source:

☐ Do the critics tend to disagree about a particular issue? Might I take one side or another in this debate? Might I offer an alternative?

☐ Do any critics make a claim that I think deserves to be challenged or clarified?

☐ Do the critics ignore a particular element or aspect of the text that I think needs to be investigated? Do any of the critics make a claim that they don't really develop? Or do they make a claim about one text that I might apply to another?

If your sources are historical or biographical, you will instead need to ask questions such as:

☐ Is there information here that might help readers understand some aspect of the literary work in a new way?

☐ Does any of this information challenge or complicate my previous interpretation of the text, or an interpretation that I think other readers might adopt if they weren't aware of these facts?

18.2.2 Using Research to Refine and Test a Thesis

Because of the potential problems of consulting secondary sources in the exploratory phase of the writing process (18.2.1), your instructor may urge you to delay research until later—after you've formulated a tentative thesis, gathered evidence, or written a complete rough draft. This approach may be especially appealing when you begin an assignment with a firm sense of what you want to write. The chief advantage of this approach is that you can look at secondary sources more selectively and critically, seeking information and opinions that will deepen, confirm, or challenge your argument. And since you've already formulated your opinion, you may be in less danger of becoming overwhelmed by others'.

There are, however, several things to watch out for if you take this approach. First, you must be especially careful not to ignore, distort, or misrepresent any source's argument in the interest of maintaining your own. Second, you must strive to keep your mind open, remembering that the goal of your research is to *test* and *refine* your opinion, not just to *confirm* it. A compelling argument or new piece of information may well require you to modify or broaden your original argument. Third, you still need to pose the general questions outlined above (18.2.1).

18.3 THE RESEARCH PROCESS

Regardless of when you begin your research, the process will involve four tasks:

- creating and maintaining a working bibliography;
- identifying and locating potentially useful secondary sources;
- evaluating the credibility of sources;
- taking notes.

18.3.1 Creating a Working Bibliography

A working bibliography lists all the sources that you *might* use in your research essay. It is a "working" document in two ways. For one thing, it will change throughout the research process—expanding each time you add a potentially useful source and contracting when you omit sources that turn out to be less relevant than you anticipated. Also, once you have written your essay, your working bibliography will evolve one last time, becoming your list of works cited. For another thing, you can use your bibliography to organize and keep track of your research "work." To this end, some researchers divide the bibliography into three parts: (1) sources that they need to locate, (2) sources that they have located and think they will use, and (3) sources that they have located but think they probably won't use. (Keeping track of "rejects" ensures, first, that you won't have to start from scratch if you later change your mind; second, that you won't forget that you've already located and rejected a source if you come across another reference to it.)

Because you will need to update your bibliography regularly and because it will ultimately become the kernel of your list of works cited, you should consider using a computer. In that case, you'll need to print a copy or take your laptop along each time you head to the library. However, some researchers find it helpful to also or instead use notecards, creating a separate card for each source. You can then physically separate cards dedicated to sources to be located, sources already located, and "rejected" sources. Just in case your cards get mixed up, however, you should also always note the status of the source on the card (by writing at the top "find," "located," or "rejected").

Regardless of the format you use, your record for each source should include all the information you will need in order both to locate the source and to cite it in your essay. Helpful location information might include the library in which it's found (if you're using multiple libraries), the section of the library in which it's held (e.g., "Reference," "Stacks"), and its call number. As for citation or publication information, it's tempting to ignore this until the very end of the writing process, and some writers do. But if you give in to that temptation, you will, at best, create much more work for yourself down the road. At worst, you'll find yourself unable to use a great source in your essay because you can't relocate the necessary information about it. To avoid these problems, note down all facts you will need for a works cited entry (see 19.2.2). Finally, consider noting where you first discovered each source, just in case you later need to double-check citation information or to remind yourself why you considered a source potentially useful or authoritative. (Though you can use abbreviations, make sure they're ones you'll recognize later.)

Here are two sample entries from the working bibliography of a student researching Adrienne Rich's poetry. Each entry includes all the required citation information, as well as notes on where the student discovered the source and where it is located.

Sample Working Bibliography Entries

Boyers, Robert. "On Adrienne Rich: Intelligence and Will." *Salmagundi* 22–23 (Spring–Summer 1973): 132–48. Source: *DLB* 5. Loc.: UNLV LASR AS30.S33

Martin, Wendy. *American Triptych: Anne Bradstreet, Emily Dickinson, Adrienne Rich.* U of North Carolina P, 1984. Source: *LRC/CLC.* UNLV Stacks PS310.F45 M3 1984

Once you locate a source, double-check the accuracy and thoroughness of your citation information and update your working bibliography. (Notice, for example, that this student will need to check *American Triptych* to find out the city where it was published and then add this information to her bibliography.)

18.3.2 Identifying and Locating Sources

Regardless of your author, text, or topic, you will almost certainly find a wealth of sources to consult. Your first impulse may be to head straight for the library catalog. But the conversation about literature occurs in periodicals as well as books, and not all contributions to that conversation are equally credible or relevant. For all these reasons, consider starting with one of the reference works or bibliographies described in this section. Then you can head to the catalog armed with a clear sense of what you're looking for.

Once you find one good secondary source, you can use its bibliography to refine your own. Checking the footnotes and bibliographies of several (especially recent) sources will give you a good sense of what other sources are available and which ones experts consider the most significant.

REFERENCE WORKS

Your library will contain many reference works that can be helpful starting points, and some may be accessible via the library's Web page. Here are six especially useful ones.

Literature Resource Center (LRC)

One online source to which your library may subscribe is Gale's *Literature Resource Center*. Designed with undergraduate researchers in mind, it's an excellent place to start. Here you can access and search

- all the material in two of the reference works described below (*Dictionary of Literary Biography* and *Contemporary Authors*) and in both Merriam-Webster's *Encyclopedia of Literature* and Gale's For Students series (*Novels for Students, Literature of Developing Nations for Students,* etc.);
- much (though not all) of the material contained in Gale's Literary Criticism series (another of the reference works described below);
- selected full-text critical essays (or articles) from more than 250 literary journals.

Depending on your library's subscription arrangement, *LRC* may also give you access to the *MLA Bibliography* (from 1963) and/or to the Twayne's Authors series (both described below).

You can search the database in numerous ways, but you should probably start with an author search. Results will appear as a list of sources divided into four files: Biographies; Literary Criticism, Articles, and Work Overviews; Bibliographies (of works by and about the author); Additional Resources (such as author-focused Web sites). You can access each file or list by simply clicking on the appropriate tab. (There will be a good deal of overlap among the files.) You can then click any item on the list in order to open and read it. Once an item is open, you can also print or e-mail it by clicking on the appropriate icons and following the directions.

If your library doesn't subscribe to *LRC*, consider starting with the printed reference works listed below. Because each is a multivolume work, you will need to consult its cumulative index to find out which volumes contain entries on your author. None of these series can keep up to the minute with the literary critical conversation about a particular author or work, and all offer only selective bibliographies. Such selectivity is both the greatest strength and the greatest limitation of these reference works.

Dictionary of Literary Biography (DLB)

One of the most important and authoritative reference works for students of literature, the *Dictionary of Literary Biography* covers primarily British and American authors, both living and dead. Each volume focuses on writers working in a particular genre and period. (Volume 152, 4th series, for example, covers *American Novelists since World War II.*) Written by a scholar in the field, each entry includes a photo or sketch of the author, a list of his or her publications, a bibliography of selected secondary sources, and an overview of the author's life and work. The overviews are often very thorough, incorporating brief quotations from letters, interviews, reviews, and so on. You will find multiple entries on any major author, each focusing on a particular portion of his or her canon. The volume titles will give you a good sense of which entry will be most relevant to you. Entries on W. B. Yeats, for example, appear in volume 10, *Modern British Dramatists, 1900–1945*; volume 19, *British Poets, 1880–1914*; volume 98, *Modern British Essayists*, First Series; and volume 156, *British Short-Fiction Writers, 1880–1914: The Romantic Tradition.*

Contemporary Authors: A Biobibliographical Guide to Current Authors and Their Works (CA)

Gale's *Contemporary Authors* focuses on twentieth- and twenty-first-century writers from around the world and in a range of fields (including the social and natural sciences). In terms of content, its entries closely resemble those in the *DLB* (see above). But *CA* entries tend to be much shorter.

Literary Criticism (LC)

Also published by Gale, the Literary Criticism series is, in effect, a series of series, each of which covers a particular historical period. (See below for individual series titles, as well as information about the periods covered by each one.) Each entry includes a very brief overview of the author's life and work. (There is often overlap between these overviews and those in *CA*.) But there are two key differences between the *LC* series and both the *DLB* and *CA*. First, the *LC* series includes entries devoted entirely to some individual works, as well as entries on an author's entire canon. (For example, Nineteenth-Century Literature Criticism contains both a general entry on Charlotte Brontë and one devoted exclusively to *Jane Eyre*.) Second, the bulk of each entry is devoted to excerpts (often lengthy) from some of the most important reviews and literary criticism on an author and/or work, and coverage extends from the author's day up to the time when the *LC* entry was written. Each entry concludes with a bibliography of additional secondary sources. The *LC* series thus gives plenty of guidance in identifying authoritative sources, as well as access to excerpts from sources that your library doesn't own.

Here are the titles of the five series, along with information about the period each one covers. To identify the appropriate series, you will need to know the year in which your author died.

- Contemporary Literary Criticism (living authors and those who died from 1960 on)
- Twentieth-Century Literary Criticism (authors who died 1900–1959)
- Nineteenth-Century Literature Criticism (authors who died 1800–1899)
- Literature Criticism from 1400 to 1800 (authors [except Shakespeare] who died 1400–1799)
- Shakespearean Criticism

The Critical Heritage

For some major authors, you can find information and excerpts like those offered by *LC* within the individual volumes of the Critical Heritage series. Unlike the reference works described above, this series is a collection of discrete publications such as *The Brontës: The Critical Heritage*. Each will be held not in the reference department but in the section of the stacks devoted to scholarship on a specific author. You will thus need to search your library's catalog to find it. These volumes are not regularly updated, so each will give a good sense of your author's reception only up to the time it was published.

Twayne's Authors

The Twayne's Authors series incorporates three distinct series: Twayne's United States Authors, Twayne's English Authors, and Twayne's World Authors. Each volume in each series is a distinct book focusing on one author and typically offering both biographical information and interpretation of major works. All aim to be generally accessible and introductory. (As the publishers themselves put it, "The intent of each volume in these series is to present a critical-analytical study of the works of the writer; to include biographical and historical material that may be necessary for understanding, appreciation, and critical appraisal of the writer; and to present all material in clear, concise English.") Yet because each volume is the work of an individual specialist, it represents that scholar's particular point of view (or opinion), and volumes differ widely in their organization, approach, and level of difficulty.

Each volume will be held not in the reference department but in the section of the stacks devoted to scholarship on a specific author. To find it, you will need to search the catalog.

MLA INTERNATIONAL BIBLIOGRAPHY

For much more thorough, up-to-date lists of secondary sources—especially periodical articles—you should consult scholarly bibliographies. In terms of literary criticism, the most comprehensive and useful general bibliography is *The MLA International Bibliography of Books and Articles on the Modern Languages and Literatures.* Since 1969, the *MLA Bibliography* has aimed to provide a comprehensive list of all scholarship published anywhere in the world on literature and modern languages, including books, dissertations, book chapters, and articles in over two thousand periodicals. Though it doesn't quite live up to that aim, it comes closer than any other reference work. (The *Bibliography* in fact began in 1922 but initially included only American scholarship; international coverage began in 1956, but the range of publications remained limited until 1969.) Updated annually, the bibliography is available in print, CD-ROM, and online versions, so what the bibliography encompasses, how many years it covers, and how you use it will depend on the version you consult.

In the print version, each volume lists articles and books published in a specific year, so you should start with the most recent volume and then work your way backward through earlier volumes. Each volume is arranged by nationality or language, then by period, then by author and title.

The CD-ROM and online versions allow you to do topic or keyword searches to find all relevant publications, regardless of the year of publication. Ask a librarian for help with accessing and searching the database.

ONLINE AND CARD CATALOGS

Your library's catalog will guide you to books about the author's work. However, the title of a potentially useful book may be too general to indicate whether it covers the text and topic in which you're interested. If your library's catalog is online, use keyword searches to limit the number and range of books that the computer finds. For example, if you're writing about William Faulkner's "A Rose for Emily," first limit the search to items that include both "Faulkner" and "A Rose for Emily." If you find few matches or none, broaden the search to include all books about William Faulkner.

The books that you find through a catalog search will lead you to a section of the library where other books on your subject are held (because each will have a similar Library of Congress call number). Even if you locate the books you were looking for right away, take a moment to browse. Books shelved nearby probably cover similar topics, and they may prove even more useful than the ones you originally sought. You can also do this kind of browsing online because most online catalogs offer the option of moving from the record of one book to the records of those that appear just before and after it in the catalog.

THE INTERNET

With its innumerable links and pathways, the Internet seems the perfect resource for research of any kind. And in fact some excellent online resources are available to students of literature. *Bartleby.com* is a good, general information site. Here you can access and search several reference works, as well as full-text versions of numerous poems and works of fiction and nonfiction.

There are also many scholarly sites dedicated to specific authors, works, and literary periods. Most sites provide links to others. One site especially useful as a gateway to thousands of more specific sites is *The Voice of the Shuttle* <http://vos.ucsb.edu/>.

If you don't find an appropriate link on *The Voice of the Shuttle*, you will probably want to conduct a search using one of the commonly available search engines. Searches using keywords such as "Chekhov" or "poetry" will lead you to thousands of possible matches, however, so you should limit your search by creating search strings longer than one word. Read onscreen directions carefully to make sure that the search engine treats the search string as a unit and doesn't find every mention of each individual word.

Despite the obvious benefits of the Internet, you should be cautious in your use of online sources for two reasons. First, although many sites provide solid information and informed opinion, many more offer misinformation or unsubstantiated opinion. Unlike journal articles and books, which are rigorously reviewed by experts before they are accepted for publication, many Internet sources are posted without any sort of review process, and authorship is often difficult to pin down. As a result, you need to be especially careful to identify and evaluate the ultimate source of the information and opinions you find in cyberspace. (For more on evaluating sources, see 18.3.3.)

Second, because the Internet enables you to jump easily from one site to another and to copy whole pages of text merely by cutting and pasting, you may lose your place and be unable to provide readers with precise citations. You may lose track of where your own words end and those of your source begin, thereby putting yourself at risk of plagiarizing (see 18.4.1). In addition, the Internet is itself constantly mutating; what's there today may not be there tomorrow. All this makes it difficult to achieve the goal of all citation: to enable readers to retrace your steps and check your sources. When you find sites that seem potentially useful, bookmark them if you can. If not, make sure that you accurately write down (or, better, copy directly into a document) the URL of each, as well as the other information you will need for your list of works cited: the author's name, if available; the site or page title; the date the site was last revised or originally published; and the date you accessed it. If the material on the site has been taken from a printed source, note all of the particulars about this source as well.

As a general rule, Internet sources should supplement print sources, not substitute for them.

18.3.3 Evaluating Sources

Not all sources are equally reliable or credible. The credibility and persuasiveness of your essay will depend, in part, on the credibility of the sources you draw on. This is a good reason to start with reference works that will guide you to credible sources.

Nonetheless, it is very important to learn how to gauge for yourself the credibility of sources. As you do so, keep in mind that finding a source to be credible isn't the same as agreeing with everything it says. At this stage, concentrate on whether the opinions expressed in a source are worthy of serious consideration, not on whether you agree with them. Here are some especially important questions to consider:

1. *How credible is the publisher (in the case of books), the periodical (in the case of essays, articles, and reviews), or the sponsoring organization (in the case of Internet sources)?*

   Generally speaking, academics give most credence to books published by academic and university presses and to articles published in scholarly or professional journals because all such publications undergo a rigorous peer-review process. As a result, you can trust that these publications have been judged credible by more than one recognized expert. For periodicals aimed at a more general audience, you should prefer prominent, highly respected publications such as the *Los Angeles Times* or the *New Yorker* to, say, the *National Enquirer* or *People* magazine.

   Internet sources are not subjected to rigorous review processes, but many sites are created and sponsored by organizations. Be sure to identify the sponsoring organization and carefully consider its nature, status, and purpose. The last part of the domain name will indicate the kind of organization it is: The suffix *.com* indicates that the ultimate source is a *company* or commercial, for-profit enterprise; *.org*, a nonprofit or charitable *organization*; *.gov*, a *government* agency; and *.edu*, an *educational* institution. Though you will often find more reliable information on *.gov* or *.edu* sites, this won't always be the case. *Bartleby.com* is, for example, only one of many extremely useful commercial sites, whereas many *.edu* sites feature the work of students who may have much less expertise than you do.

2. *How credible is the author? Is he or she a recognized expert in the relevant field or on the relevant subject?*

   Again, publication by a reputable press or in a reputable periodical generally indicates that its author is considered an expert. But you can also investigate further by checking the thumbnail biographies that usually appear within the book or journal (typically near the beginning or end). Has this person been trained or held positions at respected institutions? What else has he or she published?

3. *How credible is the actual argument?*

Assess the source's argument by applying all that you've learned about what makes an argument effective. Does it draw on ample, appropriate, convincing evidence? Does it consider all the relevant evidence? Are its inferences reasonable? Are its claims sound? Does the whole seem fair, balanced, and thorough? Has the author considered possible counterarguments or alternative points of view?

Finally, researchers in many fields would encourage you to consider the source's publication date and the currency of the information it contains. In the sciences, for example, preference is almost always given to the most recently published work on a given topic because new scholarly works tend to render older ones obsolete. In the humanities, too, new scholarly works build on old ones. You should consult recently published sources in order to get a sense of what today's scholars consider the most significant, debatable questions and what answers they offer. Though originality is as important in the humanities as in other scholarly fields, new work in the humanities doesn't necessarily render older work utterly obsolete. For example, a 1922 article on Shakespeare's *Hamlet* may still be as valid and influential as one published in 2009. As a result, you should consider the date of publication in evaluating a source, but don't let age alone determine its credibility or value.

18.3.4 Taking Notes

Once you've acquired the books and articles you determine to be most credible and potentially useful, it's a good idea to skim each one. (In the case of a book, concentrate on the introduction and on the chapter that seems most relevant.) Focus at this point on assessing the relevance of each source to your topic. Or, if you're working your way toward a topic, look for things that spark your interest. Either way, try to get a rough sense of the overall conversation—of the issues and topics that come up again and again across the various sources.

After identifying the sources most pertinent to your argument, begin reading more carefully and taking notes. Again, some researchers find it easier to organize (and reorganize) notes by using notecards, creating one card for each key point. (If you use this method, make sure that each card clearly indicates the source author and short title because cards have a tendency to get jumbled.) Today, however, most researchers take notes on the computer, creating a separate document or file for each source.

Regardless of their form, your notes should be as thorough and accurate as possible. Be thorough because memory is a treacherous thing; it's best not to rely too heavily on it. Accuracy helps you avoid a range of serious problems, including plagiarism (see 18.4.1).

Your notes for each source should include four things: summary, paraphrase, and quotation, as well as your own comments and thoughts. It's crucial to visually discriminate among these by, for instance, always recording your own comments and thoughts in a separate computer document or file or on a separate set of clearly labeled or differently colored notecards.

Whenever you write down, type out, or paste in more than two consecutive words from a source, you should

- place these words in quotation marks so that you will later recognize them as quotations;
- make sure to quote with absolute accuracy every word and punctuation mark;
- record the page where the quotation is found (in the case of print sources).

Keep such quotations to a minimum, recording only the most vivid or telling.

In lieu of extensive quotations, try to summarize and paraphrase as much as possible. You can't decide how to use the source or whether you agree with its argument unless you've first understood it, and you can best understand and test your understanding through summary and paraphrase. Start with a two- or three-sentence summary of the author's overall argument. Then summarize each of the relevant major subsections of the argument. Paraphrase especially important points, making sure to note the page on which each appears.

You may want to try putting your notes in the form of an outline. Again, start with a brief general summary. Then paraphrase each of the major relevant subclaims, incorporating summaries and quotations where appropriate.

Especially if you're dealing with literary criticism, it can be useful to complete the notetaking process by writing a summary that covers all of your sources. Your goal is to show how all the arguments fit together to form one coherent conversation. Doing so will require that you both define the main questions at issue in the conversation and indicate what stance each source takes on each question—where and how their opinions coincide and differ. One might say, for example, that two of the main questions about *Antigone* that preoccupy scholars are (1) *What is the exact nature of the conflict between Creon and Antigone, or what two conflicting worldviews do they represent?* and (2) *How is that conflict resolved? Which, if any, character and worldview does the play as a whole endorse?* A synthetic summary of these sources would explain how each critic answers each question. This kind of summary can be especially helpful when you haven't yet identified a specific essay topic or crafted a thesis because it may help you to see gaps in the conversation, places where you can enter and contribute.

18.4 INTEGRATING SOURCE MATERIAL INTO THE ESSAY

In research essays, you can refer to sources in a number of ways. You can

briefly allude to them:

> Many critics, including Maurice Bowra and Bernard Knox, see Creon as morally inferior to Antigone.

summarize or paraphrase their contents:

> According to Maurice Bowra, Creon's arrogance is his downfall. However prideful Antigone may occasionally seem, Bowra insists that Creon is genuinely, deeply, and consistently so (1526).

quote them directly:

> For Bowra, Creon is the prototypical "proud man" (1526); where Antigone's arrogance is only "apparent," Creon's is all too "real" (1526).

With secondary sources, be very careful about how often you quote and when and how you do so. Keep the number and length of quotations to a minimum. After all, this is *your* essay, and you should use your own words whenever possible, even to describe someone else's ideas. Save quotations for when you really need them: when the source's author has expressed an idea with such precision, clarity, or vividness that you simply can't say it any better, or when a key passage from your source is so rich or difficult that you need to analyze its ideas and language closely. As with primary texts, lengthy quotation will lead the reader to expect sustained analysis. And only rarely will you want to devote a large amount of your limited time and space to thoroughly analyzing the language of a source (as opposed to a primary text). (For more on responsible and effective quotation, see 19.1.)

One advantage of direct quotation is that it's an easy way to indicate that ideas derive from a source rather than from you. But whether you are quoting, summarizing, or paraphrasing a source, use other techniques as well to ensure that there's no doubt about where your ideas and words leave off and those of a source begin (see 18.4.1). A parenthetical citation within a sentence indicates that something in it comes from a specific source, but unless you indicate otherwise, it will also imply that the entire sentence is a paraphrase of the source. For clarity's sake, then, you should also mention the source or its author in your text, using signal phrases (*According to X*; *As X argues*; *X notes that*; etc.) to announce that you are about to introduce someone else's ideas. If your summary of a source goes on for more than a sentence or two, keep using signal phrases to remind readers that you're still summarizing someone else's ideas rather than stating your own, as Lawrence Rodgers does in the example below.

> The ways of interpreting Emily's decision to murder Homer are numerous.... For simple clarification, they can be summarized along two lines. One group finds the murder growing out of Emily's demented attempt to forestall the inevitable passage of time—toward her abandonment by Homer, toward her own death, and toward the steady encroachment of the North and the New South on something loosely defined as the "tradition" of the Old South. Another view sees the murder in more psychological terms. It grows out of Emily's complex relationship to her father, who, by elevating her above all of the eligible men of Jefferson, insured that to yield what one commentator called the "normal emotions" associated with desire, his daughter had to "retreat into a marginal world, into fantasy" (O'Connor 416).
>
> These lines of interpretation complement more than critique each other.... Together, they de-emphasize the element of detection, viewing the murder and its solution not as the central action but as manifestations of the principal element, the decline of the Grierson lineage and all it represents. Recognizing the way in which the story makes use of the detective genre, however, adds another interpretive layer to the story by making the narrator ... a central player in the pattern of action.
>
> —Lawrence R. Rodgers, " 'We All Said, 'she will kill herself' "

> Note: In the first paragraph, Rodgers summarizes other critics' arguments in his own words, briefly but clearly. To ensure that we know he's about to summarize, he announces this intention (*"For simple clarification, they can be summarized..."*). As he begins summarizing each view, he reminds us that it is a "view," that he's still not describing his own thoughts. Finally, he uses this unusually long summary to make a very clear and important point: *Everyone except me has ignored this element!*

18.4.1 Using Sources Responsibly

Both the clarity and the credibility of any research essay depend on the responsible use of sources. And using sources responsibly entails accurately representing them and clearly discriminating between your own words and ideas and those that come from sources. Since ideas, words, information, and concepts not directly and clearly attributed to a source will be taken as your own, any lack of clarity on this score amounts to *plagiarism*. Representing anyone else's ideas or data as your own, even if you state them in your own words, is plagiarism—whether you do so intentionally or unintentionally; whether ideas are taken from a published book or article, another student's paper, the Internet, or any other source. Plagiarism is the most serious of offenses within academe because it amounts to stealing ideas, the resource most precious to this community and its members. As a result, the punishments for plagiarism are severe—including failure, suspension, and expulsion.

To avoid both the offense and its consequences, you must always

- put quotation marks around any quotation from a source (a quotation being any two or more consecutive words or any one especially distinctive word, label, or concept);
- credit a source whenever you take from it any of the following:
  —a quotation (as described above);
  —a nonfactual or debatable claim (an idea, opinion, interpretation, evaluation, or conclusion) stated in your own words;
  —a fact or piece of data that isn't common knowledge; or
  —a distinctive way of organizing factual information.

To clarify, a fact counts as common knowledge—and therefore doesn't need to be credited to a source—whenever you can find it in multiple, readily available sources, none of which seriously question its validity. For example, it is common knowledge that Sherman Alexie is Native American, that he was born in 1966, and that he published a collection of short stories entitled *Ten Little Indians*. No source can "own" or get credit for these facts. However, a source can still "own" a particular way of arranging or presenting such facts. If, for example, you begin your essay by stating—in your own words—a series of facts about Alexie's life in exactly the same order they appear in, say, the *Dictionary of Literary Biography*, then you would need to acknowledge that by citing the *Dictionary*. When in doubt, cite. (For guidance about *how* to do so, see 19.2.)

19 QUOTATION, CITATION, AND DOCUMENTATION

The bulk of any essay you write should consist of your own ideas expressed in your own words. Yet you can develop your ideas and persuade readers to accept them only if you present and analyze evidence. In essays about literature, quotations are an especially privileged kind of evidence. If your essay also makes use of secondary sources, you will need to quote (selectively) from some of these as well. In either case, your clarity and credibility will depend on how responsibly, effectively, and gracefully you move between others' words and your own. Clarity and credibility will also depend on letting your readers know—through precise citation and documentation—exactly where they can find each quotation and each fact or idea that you paraphrase. This chapter addresses the issue of *how* to quote, cite, and document texts and sources. (For a discussion of *when* to do so, see 16.4 and 18.4.)

19.1 EFFECTIVE QUOTATION

When it comes to quoting, there are certain rules that you must follow and certain strategies that, though not required, will help make your argument more clear and effective.

19.1.1 Rules You Must Follow

1. Generally speaking, you should reproduce a quotation exactly as it appears in the original: Include every word and preserve original spelling, capitalization, italics, and so on. However, there are a few exceptions:

   - When absolutely necessary, you may make minor changes to the quotation as long as (a) they do not distort the sense of the quotation, and (b) you clearly acknowledge them. For instance:

     —Additions and substitutions (e.g., of verb endings or pronouns) may be necessary in order to reconcile the quotation's grammar and syntax with your own or to ensure that the quotation makes sense out of its original context. Enclose these additions and changes in brackets.

—Omit material from quotations to ensure you stay focused only on what's truly essential. Indicate omissions with ellipsis points unless the quotation is obviously a sentence fragment.

Notice how these rules are followed in the two examples below:

Sethe, like Jacobs, experiences the wish to give up the fight for survival and die, but while Jacobs says she was "willing to bear on" "for the children's sakes" (127), the reason that Sethe gives for enduring is the physical presence of the baby in her womb: "[I]t didn't seem such a bad idea [to die], . . . but the thought of herself stretched out dead while the little antelope lived on . . . in her lifeless body grieved her so" that she persevered (31).

When Denver tries to leave the haunted house to get food for her mother and Beloved, she finds herself imprisoned within her mother's time—a time that, clinging to places, is always happening again: "Out there . . . were places in which things so bad had happened that when you went near them it would happen again. . . ."
        —Jean Wyatt, "Giving Body to the Word: The Maternal Symbolic in
           Toni Morrison's *Beloved.*" *PMLA* 108 (May 1993): 474–88.

NOTE: In the first example, Wyatt uses brackets to indicate two changes, the capitalization of "it" and the addition of the words "to die." Ellipses indicate that she's omitted a word or words within the sentence that follows the colon. However, she doesn't need to begin or end the phrases *"willing to bear on"* and *"for the children's sake"* with ellipses because both are obviously sentence fragments. In the second example, notice that Wyatt does need to end the quotation with ellipsis points. Even though it reads like a complete sentence, this isn't the case; the sentence continues in the original text.

—Occasionally, you may want to draw your readers' attention to a particular word or phrase within the quotation by using italics. Indicate this change by putting the words "emphasis added" into your parenthetical citation.

Like his constant references to "Tragedy," the wording of the father's question demonstrates that he is almost as hesitant as his daughter to confront death head-on: "When will you look *it* in the face?" he asks her (69; emphasis added).

- Although you should also accurately reproduce original punctuation, there is one exception to this rule: When incorporating a quotation into a sentence, you may *end* it with whatever punctuation mark your sentence requires. You do not need to indicate this particular change with brackets.

Whether portrayed as "queen," "saint," or "angel," the same "nameless girl" "looks out from all his canvases" (lines 5–7, 1).

NOTE: In the poem quoted ("In an Artist's Studio"), the words *queen* and *angel* are not followed by commas. Yet the syntax of this sentence requires that commas be added, and commas are always enclosed by concluding quotation marks. Similarly, the word *canvases* is followed by a comma in the poem, but the sentence requires that this comma be changed to a period.

2. When incorporating short quotations into a sentence, put them in quotation marks and make sure that they fit into the sentence grammatically and syntactically. If necessary, you may make changes to the quotation (e.g., altering verb endings or pronouns) in order to reconcile its grammar and syntax with your own. But you should—again—always indicate changes with brackets.

   It isn't until Mr. Kapasi sees the "topless women" carved on the temple that it "occur[s] to him . . . that he had never seen his own wife fully naked" (415).

3. When quoting fewer than three lines of poetry, indicate any line break with a slash mark, any stanza break with a double slash mark.

   Before Milton's speaker can question his "Maker" for allowing him to go blind, "Patience" intervenes "to prevent / That murmur" (lines 8–9), urging him to see that "God doth not need / Either man's work or his own gifts . . ." (lines 9–10).

   "The cane appears // in our dreams," the speaker explains (lines 15–16).

4. Long quotations—four or more lines of prose, three of poetry—should be indented and presented without quotation marks to create a *block quotation*. In the case of poetry, reproduce original line and stanza breaks.

   Whereas the second stanza individualizes the dead martyrs, the third considers the characteristics they shared with each other and with all those who dedicate themselves utterly to any one cause:

   > Hearts with one purpose alone
   > Through summer and winter seem
   > Enchanted to a stone
   > To trouble the living stream. (lines 41–44)

   Whereas all other "living" people and things are caught up in the "stream" of change represented by the shift of seasons, those who fill their "Hearts with one purpose alone" become as hard, unchanging, and immoveable as stones.

5. Unless they are indented, quotations belong in double quotation marks; quotations within quotations get single quotation marks. However, if everything in your quotation appears in quotation

marks in the original, you do not need to reproduce the single quotation marks.

The words of The Misfit come ringing back to the reader: " 'I don't want no hep,' he said. 'I'm doing all right by myself' " (308).

As The Misfit says to the grandmother, "I'm doing all right by myself" (308).

6. Follow a word or phrase introducing a quotation with whatever punctuation is appropriate to your sentence. For instance:

—If you introduce a quotation with a full independent clause (other than something like *She says*), separate the two with a colon.

Ironically, Mr. Lindner's description of the neighborhood's white residents makes them sound exactly like the Youngers, the very family he's trying to exclude: "They're not rich and fancy people; just hard-working, honest people who don't really have much but . . . a dream of the kind of community they want to raise their children in" (1627).

—If you introduce or interrupt a quotation with an expression such as *she says* or *he writes*, use a comma (or commas) or add a *that*. Likewise, use a comma if you end a quotation with an expression such as *he says*, unless the quotation ends with a question mark or exclamation point.

Alvarez claims, "The whole poem works on one single, returning note and rhyme . . ." (992).

Alvarez suggests that "The whole poem works on one single, returning note and rhyme . . ." (992).

"The whole poem," Alvarez argues, "works on one single, returning note and rhyme . . ." (992).

"Here comes one," says Puck. "Where art thou, proud Demetrius?" asks Lysander (Shakespeare 3.2.400–401).

—If quoted words are blended into your sentence, use the same punctuation (or lack thereof) that you would if the words *were not* quoted.

Miriam Allott suggests that the odes, like "all Keats's major poetry," trace the same one "movement of thought and feeling," which "at first carries the poet . . . into an ideal world of beauty and permanence, and finally returns him to what is actual and inescapable."

Keats's poetry just as powerfully evokes the beauty of ordinary, natural things—of "the sun, the moon, / Trees," and "simple sheep"; of "daffodils" and "musk-rose blooms" (*Endymion*, lines 13–14, 15, 19); of nightingales, grasshoppers, and crickets; of "the stubble-plains" and "barred clouds" of a "soft-dying" autumn day ("To Autumn," lines 25–26).

When the narrator's eighty-six-year-old father asks her to tell him a "simple story" with "recognizable people" and a plot that explains "what happened to them next" (65), he gets "an unadorned and miserable tale" whose protagonist ends up "Hopeless and alone" (65).

7. Commas and periods belong inside quotation marks, semicolons outside. Question marks and exclamation points go inside quotation marks if they are part of the quotation, outside if they aren't. (Since parenthetical citations may alter your punctuation, they are omitted in the following examples. On the placement and punctuation of parenthetical citations, see 19.2.1.)

"You have a nice sense of humor," the narrator's father notes, but "you can't tell a plain story."

Wordsworth calls nature a "homely Nurse"; she has "something of a Mother's Mind."

What does Johnson mean when he says, "I don't care if he's good or not. He ain't *right*!"?

Bobby Lee speaks volumes about the grandmother when he says, "She was a talker, wasn't she?"

19.1.2 Useful Strategies

1. Make the connection between quotations and inferences as seamless as possible. Try to put them next to each other (in one sentence, if possible).

INEFFECTIVE QUOTING	EFFECTIVE QUOTING
Wordsworth calls nature a "homely Nurse" and says she has "something of a Mother's mind" (lines 81, 79). This diction supports the idea that he sees nature as a beneficent, maternal force. He is saying that nature is an educator and a healer.	Wordsworth describes nature as a beneficent, maternal force. A "homely Nurse" with "something of a Mother's Mind," nature both heals and educates (lines 81, 79).
Tennyson advocates decisive action, even as he highlights the forces that often prohibited his contemporaries from taking it. This is suggested by the lines "Made weak by time and fate, but strong in will, / To strive, to seek, to find, and not to yield" (lines 69–70).	Tennyson advocates forceful action, encouraging his contemporaries "To strive, to seek, to find, and not to yield" (line 70). Yet he recognizes that his generation is more tempted to "yield" than earlier ones because they have been "Made weak by time and fate" (line 69).

Avoid drawing attention to your evidence as evidence. Don't waste time with phrases such as *This statement is proof that . . .* ; *This phrase is significant because . . .* ; *This idea is illustrated by . . .* ; *There is good evidence for this . . .* ; and the like. Show why facts are meaningful or interesting rather than simply saying that they are.

2. Introduce or follow a quotation from a source (as well as a paraphrase or summary) with a *signal phrase* that includes the source author's name; you might also include the author's title and/or a bit of information about his or her status, if that information helps establish credibility.

In his study of the Frankenstein myth, Chris Baldick claims that "[m]ost myths, in literate societies at least, prolong their lives not by being retold at great length, but by being alluded to" (3)—a claim that definitely applies to the Hamlet myth.

Oyin Ogunba, himself a scholar of Yoruban descent, suggests that many of Soyinka's plays attempt to capture the mood and rhythm of traditional Yoruban festivals (8).

As historian R. K. Webb observes, "Britain is a country in miniature" (1).

To avoid boring your readers, vary the content and placement of these phrases while always choosing the most accurate verb. (*Says*, for example, implies that words are spoken, not written.) You may find it useful to consult the following list of verbs that describe what sources do.

Verbs to Use in Signal Phrases

affirms	considers	explains	insists	shows
argues	contends	explores	investigates	sees
asks	demonstrates	finds	maintains	speculates
asserts	describes	focuses on	notes	states
believes	discusses	identifies	observes	stresses
claims	draws atten-	illustrates	points out	suggests
comments	tion to	implies	remarks	surmises
concludes	emphasizes	indicates	reports	writes

3. Lead your readers into fairly long quotations by giving them
   • a clear sense of what to look for in the quotation;
   • any information they need to understand the quotation and to appreciate its significance. Quite often, contextual information—for instance, about who's speaking to whom and in what situation—is crucial to a quotation's meaning; this is especially true when quoting dialogue. Also pay attention to pronouns: If the

quotation contains a pronoun without an obvious referent, either indicate the specific referent in advance or add the appropriate noun into the quotation. (Again, place added words in brackets.)

INEFFECTIVE QUOTING	EFFECTIVE QUOTING
A Raisin in the Sun seems to endorse traditional gender roles: "I'm telling you to be the head of this family . . . like you supposed to be" (995); "the colored woman" should be "building their men up and making 'em feel like they somebody" (958).	*A Raisin in the Sun* seems to endorse traditional gender roles. When Mama tells Walter "to be the head of this family from now on like you supposed to be" (995), she affirms that Walter, rather than she or Ruth or Beneatha, is the rightful leader of the family. Implicitly she's also doing what Walter elsewhere says "the colored woman" should do—"building their men up and making 'em feel like they somebody" (958).
Julian expresses disgust for the class distinctions so precious to his mother: "Rolling his eyes upward, he put his tie back on. 'Restored to my class,' he muttered" (326).	Julian professes disgust for the class distinctions so precious to his mother. At her request, he puts back on his tie, but he can't do so without "[r]olling his eyes" and making fun of the idea that he is thereby "[r]estored to [his] class" (326).

NOTE: Here, the more effective examples offer crucial information about who is speaking (*"When Lena tells Walter"*) or what is happening (*"At her request, he puts back on his tie"*). They also include statements about the implications of the quoted words (*"she affirms that Walter . . . is the rightful leader of the family"*). At the same time, background facts are subordinated to the truly important, evidentiary ones.

4. Follow each block quotation with a sentence or more of analysis. It often helps to incorporate into that analysis certain key words and phrases from the quotation.

The second stanza of the poem refers back to the title poem of *The Colossus*, where the speaker's father, representative of the gigantic male other, so dominated her world that her horizon was bounded by his scattered pieces. In "Daddy," she describes him as

> Marble-heavy, a bag full of God,
> Ghastly statue with one grey toe
> Big as a Frisco seal
>
> And a head in the freakish Atlantic
> Where it pours bean green over blue
> In the waters off beautiful Nanset.

... Here the image of her father, grown larger than the earlier Colossus of Rhodes, stretches across and subsumes the whole of the United States, from the Pacific to the Atlantic ocean.

—Pamela J. Annas, *A Disturbance of Mirrors: The Poetry of Sylvia Plath.*
Contributions in Women's Studies 89 (New York,
Westport, and London: Greenwood, 1988)

5. Be aware that even though long (especially block) quotations can be effective, they should be used sparingly. Long quotations can create information overload or confusion for readers, making it hard for them to see what is most significant. When you quote only individual words or short phrases, weaving them into your sentences, readers stay focused on what's significant, and it's easier to show them why it's significant, to get inferences and facts right next to each other.

6. Vary the length of quotations and the way you present them, using a variety of strategies. Choose the strategy that best suits your purpose at a specific moment in your essay, while fairly and fully representing the text. It can be very tempting to fall into a pattern—always, for example, choosing quotations that are at least a sentence long and introducing each with an independent clause and a colon. But overusing any one technique can easily render your essay monotonous. It might even prompt readers to focus more on the (inelegant) way you present evidence than on its appropriateness and significance.

19.2 CITATION AND DOCUMENTATION

In addition to indicating which facts, ideas, or words derive from someone else, always let your readers know where each can be found. You want to enable readers not only to "check up" on you but also to follow in your footsteps and build on your work. After all, you hope that your analysis of a text will entice readers to reread certain passages from a different point of view.

At the same time, you don't want information about how to find others' work to interfere with readers' engagement with *your* work. Who, after all, could really make sense of an essay full of sentences such as these: (1) *"I know not 'seems,'" Hamlet claims in line 76 of act 1, scene 2*, and (2) *On the fourth page of her 1993* PMLA *article (which was in that journal's 108th volume), Jean Wyatt insists that Morrison's "plot . . . cannot move forward because Sethe's space is crammed with the past."*

To ensure that doesn't happen, it is important to have a system for conveying this information in a concise, unobtrusive way. There are, in fact, many such systems currently in use. Different disciplines, publications, and even instructors prefer or require different systems. In literary studies (and the humanities generally), the preferred system is that developed by the Modern Language Association (MLA).

In this system, parenthetical citations embedded in an essay are keyed to an alphabetized list of works cited that appears at its end. Parenthetical citations allow the writer to briefly indicate where an idea, fact, or quotation appears, while the list of works cited gives readers all the information they need to find that source. Here is a typical sentence with parenthetical citation, as well as the works-cited entry to which it refers.

Sample Parenthetical Citation

> In one critic's view, "Ode on a Grecian Urn" explores "what great art means" not to the ordinary person, but only "to those who create it" (Bowra 148).

> NOTE: Here, the parenthetical citation indicates that readers can find this quotation on page 148 of some work by an author named Bowra. To find out more, readers must turn to the list of works cited and scan it for an entry, like the following, that begins with the name "Bowra."

Sample Works Cited Entry

> Bowra, C. M. *The Romantic Imagination*. Oxford: Oxford UP, 1950. Print.

This example gives a basic sense of how parenthetical citations and the list of works cited work together in the MLA system. Note that each parenthetical citation must "match up" with one (and only one) works-cited entry.

The exact content of each parenthetical citation and works-cited entry will depend on a host of factors. The next two sections focus on these factors.

19.2.1 Parenthetical Citation

THE GENERIC PARENTHETICAL CITATION: AUTHOR(S) AND PAGE NUMBER(S)

The generic MLA parenthetical citation includes an author's name and a page number (or numbers). If the source has two or three authors, include all last names, as in (Gilbert and Gubar 57). If it has four or more, use the first author's name followed by "et al." (Latin for "and others"), as in the second example below. In all cases, nothing but a space separates author's name(s) from page number(s).

> Most domestic poems of the 1950s foreground the parent-child relationship (Axelrod 1002).

> Given their rigid structure, it is perhaps "[n]ot surprisin[g]" that many sonnets explore the topic of "confinement" (Booth et al. 832).

Notice the placement of the parenthetical citations in these examples. In each one the citation comes at the end of the sentence, yet it appears *inside* the period (because it is part of the sentence) and *outside* the quotation marks (because it isn't part of the quotation). Such placement of parenthetical citations should be your practice in all but two situations (both described in the next section).

VARIATIONS IN PLACEMENT

In terms of placement, the first exception is the block quotation. In this case, the parenthetical citation should immediately *follow* (not precede) the punctuation mark that ends the quotation.

> As historian Michael Crowder insists, Western-style education was the single "most radical influence on Nigeria introduced by the British" because it came to be seen as a means not only of economic better ment but of social elevation. It opened doors to an entirely new world, the world of the white man. Since missionaries had a virtual monopoly on schools, they were able to use them as a means of further proselytization, and continued to warn their pupils of the evils of their former way of life. (195)

The second exception is the sentence that either incorporates material from multiple sources or texts (as in the first example below) or refers both to something from a source or text and to your own idea (as in the second example below). In either situation, you will need to put the appropriate parenthetical citation in mid-sentence right next to the material to which it refers, even at the risk of interrupting the flow of the sentence.

> Critics describe Caliban as a creature with an essentially "unalterable natur[e]" (Garner 458), "incapable of comprehending the good or of learn-ing from the past" (Peterson 442), "impervious to genuine moral improve-ment" (Wright 451).

> If Caliban is "incapable of . . . learning from the past" (Peterson 442), then how do we explain the changed attitude he seems to demonstrate at the end of the play?

VARIATIONS IN CONTENT

The generic MLA citation may contain the author's name(s) and the rel-evant page number(s), but variations are the rule when it comes to content. The six most common variations occur when you do the following:

1. *Name the author in a signal phrase*
   Parenthetical citations should include only information that isn't crucial to the sense and credibility of your argument. Yet in nine cases out of ten, information about *whose* ideas, data, or words you are referring to is crucial in precisely this way. As a result, it is usually a

good idea to indicate this in your text. When you do so, the parenthetical citation need only include the relevant page number(s).

Jefferson's "new generation" are, in Judith Fetterley's words, just "as much bound by the code of gentlemanly behavior as their fathers were" (409).

According to Steven Gould Axelrod, most domestic poems of the 1950s foreground the parent-child relationship (1002).

2. *Cite a poem or play*
In the case of most poetry, refer to line (not page) numbers.

Ulysses encourages his men "To strive, to seek, to find, and not to yield" (line 70).

In the case of classic plays, indicate act, scene, and line numbers, and separate them with periods.

"I know not 'seems,'" Hamlet claims (1.2.76).

3. *Cite multiple works by the same author or a work whose author is unknown*
When citing multiple works by the same author or an anonymous work, you will need to indicate the title of the specific work to which you refer. Either indicate the title in your text, putting only the page number(s) in a parenthetical citation (as in the first example below), or create a parenthetical citation in which the first word or two of the title is followed by the page number(s) (as in the third example below). In the latter case, you should format the title words exactly as you would the full title, using quotation marks for essays, short stories, and short poems, and using italics or underlining for books.

As Judith Fetterley argues in "A Rose for 'A Rose for Emily,'" Jefferson's younger generation is just "as much bound by the code of gentlemanly behavior as their fathers were" (409).

Jefferson's "new generation" is, in Judith Fetterley's words, just "as much bound by the code of gentlemanly behavior as their fathers were" ("A Rose" 409).

Arguably, Jefferson's "new generation" is just "as much bound by the code of gentlemanly behavior as their fathers were" (Fetterley, "A Rose" 409).

4. *Cite a source quoted in another source*
When quoting the words of one person as they appear in another author's work, mention the person's name in a signal phrase. Then create a parenthetical citation in which the abbreviation "qtd. in" is followed by the author's name and the relevant page number(s).

Hegel describes Creon as "a moral power," "not a tyrant" (qtd. in Knox 2072).

5. *Cite multiple authors with the same last name*
In this case, you should either use the author's full name in a signal phrase (as above) or add the author's first initial to the parenthetical citation (as below).

Beloved depicts a "a specifically female quest powered by the desire to get one's milk to one's baby" (J. Wyatt 475).

6. *Cite multiple sources for the same idea or fact*
In this case, put both citations within a single set of parentheses and separate them with a semicolon.

Though many scholars attribute Caliban's bestiality to a seemingly innate inability to learn or change (Garner 458; Peterson 442; Wright 451), others highlight how inefficient or problematic Prospero's teaching methods are (Willis 443) and how invested Prospero might be in keeping Caliban ignorant (Taylor 384).

7. *Cite a work without numbered pages*
Omit page numbers from parenthetical citations if you cite

- an electronic work that isn't paginated;
- a print work whose pages aren't numbered;
- a print work that is only one page long;
- a print work, such as an encyclopedia, that is organized alphabetically.

If at all possible, mention the author's name and/or the work's title in your text (so that you don't need any parenthetical citation). Otherwise, create a parenthetical citation that contains, as appropriate, the author's name and/or the first word(s) of the title.

8. *Italicize words that aren't italicized in the original*
If you draw your readers' attention to a particular word or phrase within a quotation by using italics or underlining, your parenthetical citation must include the words "emphasis added."

Like his constant references to "Tragedy," the wording of the father's question demonstrates that he is almost as hesitant as his daughter to confront death head-on: "When will you look *it* in the face?" he asks her (69; emphasis added).

19.2.2 The List of Works Cited

The alphabetized list of works cited should appear at the end of your completed essay. It must include all, and only, the texts and sources that you cite in your essay; it also must provide full publication information about each one. If you're writing a research essay and have created and maintained a working bibliography (see 18.3.1), that bibliography will become the core of your works-cited list. To turn the former into the latter, you will need to

- delete sources that you did not ultimately cite in your essay;
- add an entry for each primary text you did cite;
- delete notes about where you found sources (library call numbers, etc.).

FORMATTING THE LIST OF WORKS CITED

The list of works cited should appear on a separate page (or pages) at the end of your essay. (If you conclude your essay on page 5, for example, you would start the list of works cited on page 6.) Center the heading "Works Cited" (without quotation marks) at the top of the first page, and double-space throughout.

The first line of each entry should begin at the left margin; the second and subsequent lines should be indented 5 spaces or 1/2 inch.

Alphabetize your list by the last names of the authors or editors. In the case of anonymous works, alphabetize by the first word of the title other than *A*, *An*, or *The*.

If your list includes multiple works by the same author, begin the first entry with the author's name and each subsequent entry with three hyphens followed by a period. Alphabetize these listings by the first word of the title, again ignoring the words *A*, *An*, or *The*.

FORMATTING WORKS-CITED ENTRIES

The exact content and style of each entry in your list of works cited will depend on the type of source it is. Following are examples of some of the most frequently used types of entries in lists of works cited. For all other types, consult the seventh edition of the *MLA Handbook*.

Book by a single author or editor

Webb, R. K. *Modern England: From the Eighteenth Century to the Present.* New York: Columbia UP, 1969. Print.

Wu, Duncan, ed. *A Companion to Romanticism.* Oxford: Blackwell, 1998. Print.

Book with an author and an editor

Keats, John. *Complete Poems*. Ed. Jack Stillinger. Cambridge: Belknap-Harvard UP, 1982. Print.

Book by two or three authors or editors

Gallagher, Catherine, and Thomas Laqueur, eds. *The Making of the Modern Body: Sexuality and Society in the Nineteenth Century*. Berkeley: U of California P, 1987. Print.

Book by more than three authors or editors

Zipes, Jack, et al. *The Norton Anthology of Children's Literature*. New York: Norton, 2005. Print.

Introduction, preface, or foreword

O'Prey, Paul. Introduction. *Heart of Darkness*. By Joseph Conrad. New York: Viking, 1983. 7–24. Print.

Essay, poem, or any other work in an edited collection or anthology

Shaw, Philip. "Britain at War: The Historical Context." *A Companion to Romanticism*. Ed. Duncan Wu. Oxford: Blackwell, 1998. 48–60. Print.

Yeats, W. B. "The Lake Isle of Innisfree." *The Norton Introduction to Literature*. 10th ed. Ed. Alison Booth and Kelly J. Mays. New York: Norton, 2010. 1173. Print.

portable — add

Multiple short works from one collection or anthology

Booth, Alison and Kelly J. Mays, eds. *The Norton Introduction to Literature*. 10th ed. New York: Norton, 2010. Print.

Frost, Robert. "The Road Not Taken." Booth and Mays. 1019. Print.

Keats, John. "Ode to a Nightingale." Booth and Mays. 1031–33. Print.

Article in a reference work

"Magna Carta." *Encyclopaedia Britannica*. 14th ed. 630–35. Print.

Article in a scholarly journal

Wyatt, Jean. "Giving Body to the Word: The Maternal Symbolic in Toni Morrison's *Beloved*." *PMLA* 108 (May 1993): 474–88. Print.

Article in a newspaper or magazine

McNulty, Charles. "All the World's a Stage Door." *Village Voice* 13 Feb. 2001: 69. Print.

Review or editorial

Leys, Simon. "Balzac's Genius and Other Paradoxes." Rev. of *Balzac: A Life*, by Graham Robb. *New Republic* 20 Dec. 1994: 26–27. Print.

| NOTE: The first name here is that of the reviewer, the second that of the
author whose book is being reviewed.

Web site

U.S. Department of Education (ED) Home Page. U.S. Dept. of Education, 12
Aug. 2009. Web. 26 Aug. 2009.

Yeats Society Sligo Home Page. Yeats Society Sligo, 12 Nov. 2009. Web. 21
Nov. 2009.

Article on a Web site

Padgett, John B. "William Faulkner." The Mississippi Writers Page. 29 Mar.
1999. Web. 9 Sept. 2008.

| NOTE: The first date indicates when material was published or last
updated. The second date indicates when you accessed the site.

20   SAMPLE RESEARCH PAPER

The student essay below was written in response to the following assignment:

> Write an essay of 10–15 pages that analyzes at least two poems by any one author in your text and draws on three or more secondary sources. At least one of these sources must be a work of literary criticism (a book or article in which a scholar interprets your author's work).

Richard Gibson's response to this assignment is an essay that explores the treatment of religion in four poems by Emily Dickinson; Gibson asks how conventional that treatment was in its original historical and social context. Notice that Gibson uses a variety of sources: literary critical studies of Dickinson's poetry, Dickinson biographies, historical studies of nineteenth-century American religious beliefs and practices, letters written by and to Dickinson, and a dictionary. At the same time, notice that Gibson's thesis is an original, debatable interpretive claim about Dickinson's poetry and that he supports and develops that claim by carefully analyzing four poems.

Gibson establishes a motive for his essay by first stating a claim about Dickinson's poetry that a casual reader might be tempted to adopt and then pointing out the problems with that claim in order to set up the more subtle and complex claim that is his thesis.

Richard Gibson

Professor William Barksdale

English 301

4 March 2004

Keeping the Sabbath Separately:

Emily Dickinson's Rebellious Faith

When cataloguing Christian poets, it might be tempting to place Emily Dickinson between Dante and John Donne. She built many poems around biblical quotations, locations, and characters. She meditated often on the afterlife, prayer, and trust in God. Yet Dickinson was also intensely doubtful of the strand of Christianity that she inherited; in fact, she never became a Christian by the standards of her community in nineteenth-century Amherst, Massachusetts. Rather, like many of her contemporaries in Boston, Dickinson recognized the tension between traditional religious teaching and modern ideas. And these tensions, between hope and doubt, between tradition and modernity, animate her poetry. In "Some keep the Sabbath going to church—," "The Brain—is wider than the Sky—," "Because I could not stop for Death—," and "The Bible is an antique Volume," the poet uses traditional religious terms and biblical allusions. But she does so in order both to criticize traditional doctrines and practices and to articulate her own unorthodox beliefs.

In some ways, Emily Dickinson seemed destined by birth and upbringing to be a creature of tradition. After all, her ancestry stretched back to the origin of the Massachusetts Bay Colony; her ancestor Nathaniel Dickinson "was among the four hundred or so settlers who accompanied John Winthrop in the migration that began in 1630" (Lundin 8). Winthrop and his followers were Puritans, a group of zealous Christians who believed in the literal truth and authority of the Bible; the innate corruption of humanity; the doctrine of salvation by faith, not works; and the idea that only certain people were "predestined" for heaven (Noll 21). A few decades after his immigration, Nathaniel Dickinson moved to western Massachusetts, where he and his descendants would become farmers and stalwarts in local churches (Lundin 9). Although Emily Dickinson's grandfather, Samuel Fowler Dickinson, and her father, Edward Dickinson, would give up farming to become lawyers, they, too, subscribed to the articles of their inherited religion (9). In short, for more than three hundred years prior to her birth, Emily Dickinson's family faithfully adhered to the Puritan tradition.

From early life to her year at college, Dickinson received an education that was "overwhelmingly religious" and traditional (Jones 295). The daily routine of the Dickinson household included prayer and readings from the Bible (296). She also received religious teaching regularly at the First Congregational Church and its "Sabbath [Sunday] school" (296). In her weekday schooling, Dickinson read textbooks such as *The New England Primer* and Amherst resident Noah Webster's spelling book that included

Gibson does a great job of establishing key terms— "traditional religious teaching," "modern ideas," and "unorthodox beliefs." Notice how he repeats these terms and variations on them throughout the essay in order to link his various subideas.

Gibson simply paraphrases because his focus is the information in the source, not its words. Nonetheless, Gibson uses parenthetical citations to indicate where in the source one can find this information.

Gibson omits the author's name in this parenthetical citation because he is referring to the source indicated in the preceding parenthetical citation.

Gibson 3

"catechisms," or methodical teachings in religious doctrine and morality (296).

In the early nineteenth century, though, traditional churchgoers in western Massachusetts began to look warily to the east, especially to Boston, where nontraditional religious thinking had developed among both the "liberal Congregationalists" and the "free-thinking rationalists," or "deists" (Noll 138–42, 143–45). Because these theologies were distinctly European and philosophical, they won few converts outside Boston (143, 145). The greater threat was Unitarianism, which had sprung up in Congregational churches. The Unitarians rejected many of the foundational beliefs of the Puritans and instead "promoted a benevolent God, a balanced universe, and a sublime human potential" (284). Former Unitarian minister and transcendentalist philosopher Ralph Waldo Emerson, an author whom Dickinson admired, gained national attention through his writings and speeches on self-reliance and the individual's "direct access" to the "divine spirit" that is behind all "religious systems" (Doriani 18; Norberg xiii–xv). Binding these Bostonian theologies together is an agreement that reason should be applied to religious beliefs. Each then concluded that some—or, in a few minds, most—of the traditional Christian doctrines (to which Amherst adhered) should be abandoned or revised.

Many Bostonian thinkers were influenced by recent developments in science and philosophy that contested the traditional Christian conception of the universe and of the Bible's literal truth. Earlier generations of scientists and philosophers had postulated that the universe obeys fixed laws, which led to ongoing debates about whether the miracles described in the Bible were plausible, even possible (Noll 108). The new astronomy discredited biblical passages describing irregular movements of the sun and the stars. The foremost contemporary dispute, though, concerned the age of the universe. The traditional Christian interpretation of the Bible stated that the universe had existed for about six thousand years (Lundin 32). Early-nineteenth-century geologists, though, had discovered fossils and rock formations that suggested that the Earth was significantly older. Some Christians dug in their heels, while others, like Amherst College professor

Gibson refers readers to all the pages in the source that discuss the debate to which he refers—not just to those pages where the quoted phrases appear.

Gibson 4

Edward Hitchcock, attempted to "reconcile orthodoxy and the new geology"—an effort in which the young Dickinson "took comfort" (32). The intellectual scene of Massachusetts at the time of Dickinson's youth thus offered many competing answers to questions about divinity, the historicity of the Bible, and the cosmos. The reign of the old Puritan beliefs over the minds of New England was beginning to wane.

Dickinson herself began to confess doubts about her ability to join the First Congregational Church while still a teenager. In nineteenth-century Amherst, "to 'become a Christian' and join the church" required "only" that one "subscribe to the articles of faith and offer the briefest of assurance [sic] of belief in Christ" (Lundin 51). At age fifteen, though, Dickinson felt unable to do even this much, writing to her friend Abiah Root that she "had not yet made [her] peace with God." Unable to "feel that [she] could give up all for Christ, were [she] called to die," she asked her friend to pray for her, "that [she] may yet enter into the kingdom [of God], that there may be room left for [her] in the shining courts above" (8 Sept. 1846).

During her stay at Mount Holyoke Women's Seminary, from September 1847 to May 1848, Dickinson was frequently invited, even pressured, to become a Christian. Mary Lyon, headmistress of the college, "laid stress on the salvation of souls" and asked her "students to classify themselves according to their religious condition at the beginning of the year" (Jones 314). Asked to identify herself as a "No-Hoper," "Hoper," or "Christian," Dickinson chose the first of these options (Lundin 40–41). A few months into the school year, she informed Root that "there is a great deal of [religious] interest here and many are flocking to the ark of safety." Dickinson confessed, though, that she "[had] not yet given up to the claims of Christ," but was "not entirely thoughtless on so important & serious a subject" (17 Jan. 1848). In her final letter to Root from Mount Holyoke, Dickinson describes herself as "filled with self-recrimination about the opportunities [for salvation] [she had] missed," fearful that she might never "cast her burden on Christ" (16 May 1848). She thus left Mount Holyoke just as she came to it—a "No-Hoper."

Gibson uses double quotation marks to enclose words he's taken from a source, single quotation marks to enclose words quoted in that source.

The term *sic* indicates that a spelling or grammar problem within the quotation is present in the original. Gibson encloses the term in brackets to indicate that it is his addition.

In order to make quoted material fit grammatically and syntactically into his sentences, Gibson changes pronouns and adds explanatory words, enclosing all changed or added words in brackets.

Gibson 5

Many critics, including recent biographer Roger Lundin, see the year at Mount Holyoke as a turning point in Emily Dickinson's life, the time when it became clear that she would never "become a Christian" according to Amherst's standards (47–48). Dickinson would never join the First Congregationalist Church and, by the age of thirty, stopped going to services altogether (99). She would likewise never join the Unitarians. Many of her spiritual ideas would resemble those of the transcendentalist Emerson, yet important distinctions remained (171). Throughout her life, she wrote to Christian friends, including ministers, on spiritual topics, despite their doctrinal differences (Lease 50–51). Dickinson thus eschewed New England's religious congregations and asserted her independence in spiritual matters. Yet she always remained interested in the traditional perspective, and, as a poet, she relied on the traditional terminology in order to relate her new thinking.

Dickinson's well-known poem "Some keep the Sabbath going to church—," which she wrote around 1860, demonstrates this tendency. The opening line places the poem's events on the "Sabbath," the day of worship in Judeo-Christian traditions (*Oxford*). Thus, while the speaker does not follow her traditional peers "to Church," she nonetheless observes the traditional day (line 1). The speaker finds a "Bobolink," a native bird, to be the service's "Chorister" (line 3), the official term for the leader of a church choir (*Oxford*). A few lines later, the speaker calls this bird "Our little Sexton," the title of the manager of the church grounds. Normally, the sexton "[tolls] the Bell, for Church" (line 7), yet this sexton "sings" (line 8). The "Orchard" where she sits resembles an important part of church architecture, "a Dome." In this intimate setting, "God preaches, a noted Clergyman— / and the sermon is never long" (lines 9–10). The sermon satisfies two desires that most people have at church: first, to encounter God, and, second, not to be bored. In this natural scene "instead of getting to Heaven, at last— / [She's] going, all along" (lines 11–12).

The poem is so pleasant that it is easy to overlook the fact that its central message, that staying at home can be a spiritual experience, is subversive, for church attendance was important in traditional Congregationalist towns like Amherst (Rabinowitz 64–77). In fact, the word "some" might be an understatement, as, in

The author's name is omitted from this parenthetical citation because it is included in the sentence.

This citation refers to a line in the poem, not to a page number. The page number is indicated in the list of works cited.

A slash mark indicates a line break in a poem.

1860, most citizens in Amherst probably attended a church on Sunday. The speaker's situation instead resembles Emerson's 1842 description of the transcendentalists, those "lonely" and "sincere and religious" people who "repel influences" and "shun general society" (104–05). Furthermore, the speaker claims access to God without the aid of a religious community, a pastor, or a sacred text, all of which, as seen above, were essential to Puritan religious experience. In this poem, then, the speaker frames her spiritual experience in traditional terms and even keeps a few of the traditional practices, yet she simultaneously describes the benefits of departing from traditional practice.

While "Some keep the Sabbath going to church—" reveals Dickinson's changes in practice, "The Brain—is wider than the Sky—," composed perhaps two years later, shows her shift in theology. The speaker asserts a confidence in the power of the human intellect that resembles that of Boston's nontraditional thinkers. In each stanza, she invites the reader to measure the brain by comparing it to some other enormous entity. First, she finds that the brain "is wider than the Sky" and urges the reader to "put them side by side" and see that "the one the other will contain / with ease" and the reader "beside" (lines 1–4). Second, she observes that the brain "is deeper than the sea" and, again, urges the reader to "hold them" and see that "the one the other will absorb / as Sponges—Buckets—do" (lines 5–8). The speaker has a complicated imaginative method: Her materials thus far are all physical—brain, sky, sea—but the qualities that she compares are mixed—physical length and depth versus metaphysical length and depth.

In the third stanza, when the speaker observes that the brain "is just the weight of God" (line 9), she introduces theological material into her experiment. She asks the reader to "Heft," or weigh (*Oxford*), the two "Pound for Pound" and forecasts that "they will differ—if they do— / as Syllable from Sound" (lines 10–12). The poet switches from physical science to linguistics in this closing simile, the meaning of which divides scholars. William Sherwood argues that "each syllable is . . . finite" and "includes only a fraction of the total range of sound," yet "at the same time the syllable is the instrument by which sound is articulated" (127–28). Robert Weisbuch tries to take into account the context of the simile, arguing,

Gibson carefully leads the reader from one section of his essay to another with a transitional sentence that first summarizes the claim developed in the last section and then articulates the claim that he will develop in the next section.

Gibson's reference to "scholars" tells the reader that he's about to describe and consider other interpretations.

Gibson 7

Because this quotation is over four lines, it is indented to create a block quotation. Gibson doesn't need to enclose the whole quotation in quotation marks, but he does use quotation marks to set off words quoted within the quotation.

We must take the qualifying "if they do" ironically. The difference of weight between "Syllable" and "Sound" is at once minute and absolute, the difference of a hair. It is the difference between the thing itself and its imperfect, itemized explanation. It is the difference, say, between paraphrase and poetry, poetry and thought. The brain is not quite and not at all the weightless weight of God. (84)

Weisbuch is right to note that the phrase "if they do" is ironic, as "Syllable" and "Sound" undeniably differ. Sherwood helpfully argues that these are differences in quantity and clarity. Thus, though the brain "As Syllable" is, ultimately, less than "the weight of God," it is more intelligible, perhaps more intelligent, than "the total range of sound."

Rather than letting other scholarly interpreters have the last word, Gibson concludes the paragraph by stating his own interpretive claim.

The speaker of this poem is of a scientific bent; her measurements of length, depth, and weight recall the instruction in science that Dickinson received throughout her schooling (Jones 309; Lundin 30). Yet the speaker also believes that there are things beyond or outside the physical world of science and is just as eager to apply her scientific method to them. She perceives both that the human intellect is enormously expansive and that there is a God behind the cosmos. The divinity that she describes, though, is not the one her ancestors worshiped in Amherst: The speaker's God is more like a force than a person, more like the spirit of the universe than its sovereign. In "Some keep the Sabbath going to church—" Dickinson's orchard still seemed planted in Amherst. In "The Brain—is wider than the Sky," it becomes conspicuously a satellite of Boston.

Notice how Gibson touches back on key terms: "Amherst," "Boston," "traditional theology," etc.

This departure from traditional theology caused Dickinson to revise her vision of the afterlife, as suggested by her 1863 "Because I could not stop for Death—." The poem begins by personifying Death as a carriage-driver (lines 1–3). This personification of death echoes several biblical passages; Dickinson's Death "may," for example, "represent one of the Four Horsemen of the Apocalypse" (Bennett 208). The poet's "kindly" personification is, of course, both more benevolent than the destructive biblical figure and, with his

Gibson 8

carriage, more modern (line 2). The carriage ride takes the speaker past a school, "Fields of Gazing Grain," the "Setting Sun," and then "pause[s]" at a "House," before proceeding "toward Eternity" (lines 9, 11, 12, 17, 24). The "House" "seem[s] / a Swelling of the Ground," and is, in fact, a grave (lines 10–11). Thus, the carriage drives the speaker through the stages of life—from youth to maturity, decline, death, and, ultimately, the afterlife.

Although Dickinson may draw her image of Death from the Christian tradition, her Death drives the speaker into a distinctly nontraditional afterlife. The speaker tells the reader early on that Death's carriage holds "Immortality" and then, in the closing stanza, that she has "surmised" that the carriage's direction is "toward Eternity" (lines 3, 4, 23, 24). In the Puritan theological tradition, death leads to Heaven or Hell, paradise or perdition. Yet Dickinson's carriage does not drive toward either destination; rather, the afterlife is just a continuous movement, a continuation of consciousness. "Some keep the Sabbath going to church—" prepared us, quite subtly, for this conception of the afterlife; there, too, Heaven is not a place one "[gets] to," "at last," but a state to which one can be "going all along" (lines 11–12). In "Because I could not stop for Death—," the speaker sounds neither blissful nor pessimistic about this state. Her consciousness has adapted to her new existence: "centuries" pass now, "and yet / [it] feels shorter than the Day" when she "first surmised" the carriage's direction (lines 21–23). The word "surmised," though, signals that she is not entirely certain about what, if anything, is to come.

Uncertainty about the afterlife would remain with Dickinson throughout her life and, in 1882, would result in her asking the Reverend Washington Gladden, a somewhat unorthodox Congregationalist, "Is immortality true?" (Lease 50; Gladden). At this time, one of Dickinson's friends, a pastor, had recently died and another friend had become seriously ill (Gladden). Gladden's attempt to reassure her of the truth of immortality draws mostly from his argument that the authoritative figure "Jesus Christ taught" immortality. At the same time, he admits that "absolute demonstration there can be none of this truth."

In perhaps the same year, Dickinson wrote "The Bible is an antique Volume," which shows a mix of skepticism and optimism

No page number is needed in the parenthetical citations for Gladden because the source is only one page long (see Works Cited).

Notice how Gibson leads the reader from one idea/ paragraph to the next with a transition sentence that states the coming paragraph's main idea (that this poem "shows a mix of skepticism and optimism about the" Bible) by referring back to the concerns of the last paragraph ("Gladden's arguments").

Gibson 9

about the source of Gladden's arguments. The first three lines undermine the Bible's authority; it is an "antique Volume," authored by "faded Men / at the suggestion of Holy Spectres." The poet then provides a list of biblical "Subjects" that "reads like the playbill of a cheap traveling show" (Lundin 203): Eden is "the ancient Homestead"; Satan "the brigadier"; Judas "the Great Defaulter"; David "the Troubadour"; and sin "a distinguished Precipice / others must resist" (lines 4–10). The speaker then uses quotation marks to show her dissatisfaction with religious categories, saying, "Boys that 'believe' are very lonesome / other boys are 'lost' " (lines 11–12). Thus far, the speaker has given us every reason to abandon the Bible—she has discredited its authors, shown the silliness of its subjects, and revealed the tragic culture that surrounds it.

Yet the speaker believes that "had but the Tale [the Bible] a warbling Teller— / all the Boys would come" (lines 13–14). A "warbling Teller" is one whose voice is "thrilling," "ardent," or "friendly" (Bennett 430). For an example, she borrows the poet Orpheus from Greek mythology. His "Sermon," unlike the one the "believing" and "lost" boys now hear, "captivated— / it did not condemn" (lines 15–16). In addition to drawing distinct lines between the saved and the damned, like headmistress Mary Lyon, Puritans often used condemnation, in the now-infamous "fire and brimstone" style, to rouse the immoral to seek salvation (Lundin 11–12; Rabinowitz 5). Instead Dickinson here favors a passionate or intellectual response to a captivating speech over a moral response to a condemning one. She remains a believer in "the emotional force of the Scriptures and [their] expositors," even if she doubts the Bible's historical accuracy and rejects the claims of traditionalist preachers (Doriani 198). The implication of these closing lines, then, is that the Bible is—when read in the right spirit—still a valuable "Volume" for building a community. The Bible has reduced religious authority, but, when performed properly, retains inspirational power. The subtle magic of the poem is that Dickinson herself, in her parodies of biblical "Subjects," enlivens the Bible, "captivates" readers with the old "Tale" through her "warbling" poem.

Though Emily Dickinson might not be a "Christian poet" in the traditional sense of the term, she does beautify and hand down a

Gibson begins his conclusion by returning to the issue he raised in his introduction (Dickinson's status as a "Christian poet"). He then summarizes his argument by briefly reiterating his key points and using a few key words from Dickinson to do so, thus reminding us of how grounded his argument is in textual evidence. Finally, he moves from summarizing his argument to considering its implications for our overall view of Dickinson's poetry.

few beloved pieces of her inheritance, New England Puritanism. She "[keeps] the Sabbath," but at home. She imagines eternity, but without a Heaven or a Hell. She calls the Bible's authors "faded men," but frequently enlivens their "antique" passages in her poems. Over the years, her ideas about God, the universe, and the afterlife changed, but her yearnings to encounter the divine and to experience immortality remained. Emily Dickinson may have physically withdrawn from Amherst society, yet her mind did not withdraw from the intellectual struggles between traditional Amherst and modern Boston. Her spiritual questions and insights are distinctively personal and deeply honest; she is neither a purely skeptical nor a purely religious poet. Her intellect kept her, to her death in 1886, a "No-Hoper" by Mary Lyon's standards, yet, for modern readers, who understand her doubts and share her longings, she is a refreshingly hopeful poet.

WORKS CITED

Bennett, Fordyce R. *A Reference Guide to the Bible in Emily Dickinson's Poetry.* Lanham: Scarecrow, 1997. Print.

Dickinson, Emily. "Because I could not stop for Death." Dickinson, *Complete Poems* 350. Print.

———. "The Bible is an antique Volume." Dickinson, *Complete Poems* 644.

———. "The Brain—is wider than the Sky—." Dickinson, *Complete Poems* 312.

———. *The Complete Poems of Emily Dickinson.* Ed. Thomas H. Johnson. Boston: Little, 1960. Print.

———. *Letters.* Ed. Thomas H. Johnson. Vol. 1. Cambridge: Belknap, 1958. Print.

———. "Some keep the Sabbath going to church." Dickinson, *Complete Poems* 153–54.

———. "To Abiah Root." 8 Sept. 1846. Dickinson, *Letters* 36.

———. "To Abiah Root." 17 Jan. 1848. Dickinson, *Letters* 60.

———. "To Abiah Root." 16 May 1848. Dickinson, *Letters* 67–68.

Doriani, Beth M. *Emily Dickinson: Daughter of Prophecy.* Amherst: U of Massachusetts P, 1996. Print.

Gladden, Washington. "To Emily Dickinson." 27 May 1882. Letter 752a of *Emily Dickinson: Selected Letters.* Ed. Thomas H. Johnson. Cambridge: Belknap, 1971. 282. Print.

Gibson 11

Jones, Rowena Revis. "The Preparation of a Poet: Puritan Directions in Emily Dickinson's Education." *Studies in the American Renaissance, 1982.* Boston: Twayne, 1982. Print.

Lease, Benjamin. "'This World is not Conclusion': Dickinson, Amherst, and 'the local conditions of the soul.'" *Emily Dickinson Journal* 3.2 (1994): 38–55. Print.

Lundin, Roger. *Emily Dickinson and the Art of Belief.* 2nd ed. Grand Rapids: Eerdmans, 2004. Print.

Noll, Mark A. *America's God: From Jonathan Edwards to Abraham Lincoln.* New York: Oxford UP, 2002. Print.

Norberg, Peter. Introduction. *Essays and Poems by Ralph Waldo Emerson.* New York: Barnes and Noble Classics, 2004. xiii–xxxiii. Print.

The Oxford English Dictionary. 2nd ed. 1989. Print.

Rabinowitz, Richard. *The Spiritual Self in Everyday Life: The Transformation of Personal Religious Experience in Nineteenth-Century New England.* Boston: Northeastern UP, 1989. Print.

Sherwood, William R. *Circumference and Circumstance: Stages in the Mind and Art of Emily Dickinson.* New York: Columbia UP, 1968. Print.

Weisbuch, Robert. "The Necessary Veil: A Quest Fiction." *Emily Dickinson.* Ed. Harold Bloom. New York: Chelsea, 1985. Print.

Critical Approaches

F_{ew} human abilities are more remarkable than the ability to read and interpret literature. A computer program or a database can't perform the complex process of reading and interpreting—not to mention writing about—a literary text, although computers can easily exceed human powers of processing codes and information. Readers follow the sequence of printed words and as if by magic re-create a scene between characters in a novel or play, or they respond to the almost inexpressible emotional effect of a poem's figurative language. Experienced readers can pick up on a multitude of literary signals all at once. With rereading and some research, readers can draw on information such as the author's life or the time period when this work and others like it were first published. Varied and complex as the approaches to literary criticism may be, they are not difficult to learn. For the most part schools of criticism and theory have developed to address questions that any reader can begin to answer.

There are essentially three participants in what could be called the literary exchange or interaction: the *text*, the *source* (the *author* and other factors that produce the text), and the *receiver* (the *reader* and other aspects of *reception*). All the varieties of literary analysis concern themselves with these aspects of the literary exchange in varying degrees and with varying emphases. Although each of these elements has a role in any form of literary analysis, systematic studies of literature and its history have defined approaches or methods that focus on the different elements and circumstances of the literary interaction. The first three sections below—"Emphasis on the Text," "Emphasis on the Source," and "Emphasis on the Receiver"—describe briefly those schools or modes of literary analysis that have concentrated on one of the three elements while de-emphasizing the others. These different emphases, plainly speaking, are habits of asking different kinds of questions. Answers or interpretations will vary according to the questions we ask of a literary work. In practice the range of questions can be—to some extent *should* be—combined whenever we develop a literary interpretation. Such questions can always generate the thesis or argument of a critical essay.

Although some approaches to literary analysis treat the literary exchange (text, source, receiver) in isolation from the world surrounding that exchange (the world of economics, politics, religion, cultural tradition, and sexuality—in other words, the world in which we live), most contemporary modes of analysis acknowledge the importance of that world to the literary exchange. These days, even if a literary scholar wants to focus on the text or its source or receiver, she or he will often incorporate some of the observations and methods developed by theorists and critics who have turned their attention toward the changing world surrounding the formal conventions of literature, the writing process and writer's career, and the reception or response to literature. We describe the work of such theorists and critics in the fourth section below, "Historical and Ideological Criticism."

Before expanding on the kinds of critical approaches within these four categories, let's consider one example in which questions concerning the text, source, and receiver, as well as a consideration of historical and ideological questions, would contribute to a richer interpretation of a text. To begin as usual with preliminary questions about the *text*: *What* is "First Fight. Then Fiddle." (see p. 647)? Printed correctly on a separate piece of paper, the text would tell us at once that it is a poem because of its form: rhythm, repeating word sounds, lines that leave very wide margins on the page. Because you are reading this poem in this book, you know even more about its form (in this way, the publication *source* gives clues about the *text*). By putting it in a section with other poetry, we have told you it is a poem worth reading, rereading, and thinking about. (What other ways do you encounter poems, and what does the medium of presenting a poem tell you about it?)

You should pursue other questions focused on the text. What *kind* of poem is it? Here we have helped you, especially if you are not already familiar with the sonnet form, by grouping this poem with other sonnets. Classifying "First Fight. Then Fiddle." as a sonnet might then prompt you to interpret the ways that this poem is or is not like other sonnets. Well and good: You can check off its fourteen lines of (basically) iambic pentameter and note its somewhat unusual rhyme scheme and meter in relation to the rules of Italian and English sonnets. But *why* does this experiment with the sonnet form matter?

To answer questions about the purpose of form, you need to answer some basic questions about *source*, such as *When* was this sonnet written and published? *Who* wrote it? *What* do you know about Gwendolyn Brooks, about 1949, about African American women and/or poets in the United States at that time? A short historical and biographical essay answering such questions might help put the "sonnetness" of "First Fight. Then Fiddle." in context. But assembling all the available information about the source and original context of the poem, even some sort of documented testimony from Brooks about her intentions or interpretation of it, would still leave room for other questions leading to new interpretations.

What about the *receiver* of "First Fight. Then Fiddle."? Even within the poem a kind of audience exists. This sonnet seems to be a set of instructions addressed to "you." (Although many sonnets are addressed by a speaker, "I," to an auditor, "you," such address rarely sounds like a series of military commands, as it does here.) This internal audience is not of course to be confused with real people responding to the poem. How did readers respond to it when it was first published? Can you find any published reviews, or any criticism of this sonnet published in studies of Gwendolyn Brooks?

Questions about the receiver, like those about the author and other sources, readily connect with historical questions. Would a reader or someone listening to this poem read aloud respond differently in the years after World War II than in an age of global terrorism? Does it make a difference if the audience addressed by the speaker inside the poem is imagined as a group of African American men and women or as a group of European American male commanders? (The latter question could be regarded as an inquiry involving the text and the source as well as about the receiver.) Does a reader need to identify with any of the particular groups the poem fictitiously addresses, or would any reader, from any background, respond to it the same way? Even the formal qualities of the text could be examined through historical lenses: The sonnet form has been associated with prestigious European literature, and with themes of love and mortality, since the Renaissance. It is significant that a twentieth-century African American poet chose *this* traditional form to twist "threadwise" into a poem about conflict.

The above are only some of the worthwhile questions that might help illuminate this short, intricate poem. (We will develop a few more thoughts about it in illustrating different approaches to the text and to the source.) Similarly, the complexity of critical approaches far exceeds our four categories. While a great deal of worthwhile scholarship and criticism borrows from a range of theories and methods, below we give necessarily simplified descriptions of various critical approaches that have continuing influence. We cannot trace a history of the issues involved, or the complexity and controversies within these movements. Instead think of what follows as a road map to the terrain of literary analysis. Many available resources describe the entire landscape of literary analysis in more precise detail. If you are interested in learning more about these or any other analytical approaches, consult the works listed in the bibliography at the end of this chapter.

EMPHASIS ON THE TEXT

This broad category encompasses approaches that minimize the elements associated with the author/source or the reader/reception in order to focus on the work. In a sense any writing about literature presupposes recognition of form, in that it deems the object of study to *be* a literary work, and to belong to a genre or subgenre of literature, as Brooks's poem belongs with sonnets. Moreover, almost all literary criticism notes some details of style or structure, some *intrinsic* features such as the relation between dialogue or narrated summary, or the pattern of rhyme and meter. But *formalist* approaches go further by foregrounding the design of the text as inherent to the meaning of the whole work.

Some formalists, reasonably denying the division of content from form (since the form is an aspect of the content or meaning), have more controversially excluded any discussion of *extrinsic* matters such as the author's biography or questions of psychology, sociology, or history. This has led to accusations that formalism, in avoiding relevance to actual authors and readers or to the world of economic power or social change, also avoids political issues or commitments. Some historical or ideological critics have therefore argued that formalism supports the powers that be, since it precludes protest. Conversely, some formalists charge that any extrinsic—that is, historical, political, ideological, as well as biographical or psychological—interpretations of literature reduce the text to a set of more or less cleverly encoded messages or propaganda. A formalist might maintain that the inventive wonders of art exceed any practical function it serves. In practice, influential formalists have generated modes of *close reading* that balance attention to form, significance, and social context, with some acknowledgment of the political implications of literature. In the early twenty-first century the formalist methods of close reading remain influential, especially in classrooms. Indeed, *The Norton Introduction to Literature* adheres to these methods in its presentation of elements and interpretation of form.

New Criticism

One strain of formalism, loosely identified as the New Criticism, dominated literary studies from approximately the 1920s to the 1970s. New Critics rejected both of the approaches that prevailed then in the relatively new field of English studies: the dry analysis of the development of the English language, and the misty appreciation and evaluation of "Great Works." Generally, New Criticism minimizes consideration of both the source and the receiver, favoring the intrinsic qualities of a unified literary work. Psychological or historical information about the author, the intentions or feelings of authors or readers, and any philosophical or socially relevant "messages" derived from the work all are out of bounds in a New Critical reading. The text in a fundamental way refers to itself: Its medium is its message. Although interested in ambiguity and irony as well as figurative language, a New Critical reader establishes the organic unity of the unique work. Like an organism, the work develops in a synergetic relation of parts to whole.

A New Critic might, for example, publish an article titled "A Reading of 'First Fight. Then Fiddle.'" (The method works best with lyric or other short forms because it requires painstaking attention to details such as metaphors or alliteration.) Little if anything would be said of Gwendolyn Brooks or the poem's relation to modernist poetry. The critic's task is to give credit to the poem, not the poet or the period, and if it is a good poem, implicitly, it can't be merely "about" World War II or civil rights. New Criticism presumes that a good literary work symbolically embodies universal human themes and may be interpreted objectively on many levels. These levels may be related more by tension and contradiction than harmony, yet that relation demonstrates the coherence of the whole poem.

Thus the New Critic's essay might include some of the following observations. The title—which reappears as half of the first line—consists of a pair of two-word imperative sentences, and most statements in the poem paraphrase these two sentences, especially the first of them, "First fight." Thus an alliterative two-word command, "Win war" (line 12), follows a longer version of such a command: "But first to arms, to armor" (line 9). Echoes of this sort of exhortation appear throughout. We, as audience, begin to feel "bewitch[ed], bewilder[ed]" (line 4) by a buildup of undesirable urgings, whether at the beginning of a line ("Be deaf," line 11) or the end of a line ("Be remote," line 7; "Carry hate," line 9) or in the middle of a line ("Rise bloody," line 12). It's hardly what we would want to do. Yet the speaker makes a strong case for the practical view that a society needs to take care of defense before it can "devote" itself to "silks and honey" (lines 6-7), that is, the soft and sweet pleasures of art. But what kind of culture would place "hate / In front of . . . harmony" and try to ignore "music" and "beauty" (lines 9-11)? What kind of people are only "remote / A while from malice and from murdering" (lines 6-7)? A society of warlike heroes would rally to this speech. Yet on rereading, many of the words jar with the tone of heroic battle cry.

The New Critic examines not only the speaker's style and words but the order of ideas and lines in the poem. Ironically, the poem defies the speaker's command; it fiddles first, and then fights, as the octave (first eight lines) concern art, and the sestet (last six) concern war. The New Critic might be delighted by the irony that the two segments of the poem in fact unite, in that their topics—octave on how to fiddle, sestet on how to fight—mirror each other. The beginning of the poem plays with metaphors for music and art as means of inflicting "hurting love" (line 3) or emotional conquest, that is, ways to "fight." War and art are both, as far as we know, universal in all human societies. The poem, then, is an organic whole that restates ancient themes.

Later critics have pointed out that New Criticism, despite its avoidance of extrinsic questions, had a political context of its own. The affirmation of unity for the artwork and humanities in general should be regarded as a strategy adapted during the Cold War as a counterbalance to the politicization of art in fascist and communist regimes. New Criticism also provided a program for literary reading that is accessible to beginners regardless of their social background, in keeping with the opening of college-level English studies to more women, minorities, and members of the working class. By the 1970s these same groups had helped generate two sources of opposition to New Criticism's ostensible neutrality and transparency: critical studies that emphasized the politics of social differences (e.g., feminist criticism), and theoretical approaches, based on linguistics, philosophy, and political theory, that effectively distanced nonspecialists once more.

Structuralism

Whereas New Criticism was largely a British and American phenomenon, structuralism and its successor, poststructuralism, derive primarily from French theorists. Strains of structuralism also emerged in the Soviet Union and in Prague, influenced by the demand for a science of criticism that would avoid direct political confrontation. Each of these movements was drawn to scientific objectivity—difficult to attain in literature, arts, and other "humanities"—and at the same time wary of political commitment. Politics, after all, had been the rallying cry for censorship of science, art, and inquiry throughout centuries and in recent memory.

Structuralist philosophy, however, was something rather new. Influenced by the French linguist Ferdinand de Saussure (1857–1913), structuralists sought an objective system for studying the principles of language. Saussure distinguished between individual uses of language, such as the sentences you or I might have just spoken or written (*parole*), and the sets of rules of English or any language (*langue*). Just as a structuralist linguist would study the interrelations of signs in the *langue* rather than the variations in specific utterances in *parole*, a structuralist critic of literature or culture would study shared systems of meaning, such as genres or myths that pass from one country or period to another, rather than a certain poem in isolation (the favored subject of New Criticism).

Another structuralist principle derived from Saussure is the emphasis on the arbitrary association between a word and what it is said to signify— that is, between the *signifier* and the *signified*. The word "horse," for example, has no divine, natural, or necessary connection to that four-legged, domesticated mammal, which is named by other combinations of sounds and letters in other languages. Any language is a network of relations among such arbitrary signifiers, just as each word in the dictionary must be defined using other words in that dictionary. Structuralists largely attribute the meanings of words to rules of differentiation from other words. Such differences may be phonetic (as among the words "cat" and "bat" and "hat") or they may belong to conceptual associations (as among the words "dinky," "puny," "tiny," "small," "miniature," "petite," "compact"). Structuralist thought has particularly called attention to the way that opposites or dualisms such as "night" and "day" or "feminine" and "masculine" define each other through their differences rather than in direct reference to objective reality. For example, the earth's motion around the sun produces changing exposure to sunlight daily and seasonally, but by linguistic convention we call it "night" between, let's say, 8 p.m. and 5 a.m., no matter how light it is. (We may differ in opinions about "evening" or "dawn." But our "day" at work may begin or end in the dark.) The point is that arbitrary labels divide what in fact is continuous.

Structuralism's linguistic insights have greatly influenced literary studies. Like New Criticism, structuralism shows little interest in the creative process or in authors, their intentions, or their circumstances. Similarly, structuralism discounts the idiosyncrasies of particular readings; it takes texts to represent interactions of words and ideas that stand apart from individual human identities or sociopolitical commitments. Structuralist approaches have applied less to lyric poetry than to myths, narratives, and cultural practices, such as sports or fashion. Although structuralism tends to affirm a universal humanity as the New Critics might do, its work in comparative mythology and anthropology challenged the absolute value that New Criticism tended to grant to time-honored canons of great literature.

The structuralist would regard a text not as a self-sufficient icon but as part of a network of conventions. A structuralist essay on "First Fight. Then Fiddle." might ask why the string is plied with the "feathery sorcery" (line 2) of the "bow" (line 7). These words suggest the art of a Native American trickster or primitive sorcerer, while at the same time the instrument is a disguised weapon: a stringed bow with feathered arrows (the term "muzzle" is a similar pun, suggesting an animal's snout and the discharging end of a gun). Or is the fiddle—a violin played in musical forms such as bluegrass—a metaphor for popular art or folk resistance to official culture? In many folk tales a hero is taught to play the fiddle by the devil or tricks the devil with a fiddle or similar instrument. Further, a structuralist reading might attach great significance to the sonnet form as a paradigm that has shaped poetic expression for centuries. The classic "turn" or reversal of thought in a sonnet may imitate the form of many narratives of departure and return, separation and reconciliation. Brooks's poem repeats in the numerous short reversing imperatives, as well as in the structure of octave versus sestet, the eternal oscillation between love and death, creation and destruction.

Poststructuralism

By emphasizing the paradoxes of dualisms and the ways that language constructs our awareness, structuralism planted the seeds of its own destruction or, rather, deconstruction. Dualisms (e.g., masculine/feminine, mind/body, culture/nature) cannot be separate-but-equal; rather, they take effect as differences of power in which one dominates the other. Yet as the German philosopher of history Georg Wilhelm Friedrich Hegel (1770-1831) insisted, the relations of the dominant and subordinate, of master and slave readily invert themselves. The master is dominated by his need for the slave's subordination; the possession of subordinates defines his mastery. As Brooks's poem implies, each society reflects its own identity through an opposing "they," in a dualism of civilized/barbaric. The instability of the speaker's position in this poem (is he or she among the conquerors or the conquered?) is a model of the instability of roles throughout the human world. There is no transcendent ground—except on another planet, perhaps—from which to measure the relative positions of the polar opposites on Earth. Roland Barthes (1915-80) and others, influenced by the radical movements of the 1960s and the increasing complexity of culture in an era of mass consumerism and global media, extended structuralism into more profoundly relativist perspectives.

Poststructuralism is the broad term used to designate the philosophical position that attacks the objective, universalizing claims of most fields of knowledge since the eighteenth century. Poststructuralists, distrusting the optimism of a positivist philosophy that suggests the world is knowable and explainable, ultimately doubt the possibility of certainties of any kind, since language signifies only through a chain of other words rather than through any fundamental link to reality. This argument derives from structuralism, yet it also criticizes structuralist universalism and avoidance of political issues. *Ideology* is a key conceptual ingredient in the poststructuralist argument against structuralism. Ideology is a slippery term that can broadly be defined as a socially shared set of ideas that shape behavior; often it refers to the values that legitimate the ruling interests in a society, and in many accounts it is the hidden code that is officially denied. (We discuss kinds of "ideological" criticism later.) Poststructuralist theory has played a part in a number of critical schools introduced below, not all of them focused on the text. But in literary criticism, poststructuralism has marshaled most forces under the banner of deconstruction.

Deconstruction

Deconstruction insists on the logical impossibility of knowledge that is not influenced or biased by the words used to express it. Deconstruction also claims that language is incapable of representing any sort of reality directly. As practiced by its most famous proponent, the French philosopher Jacques Derrida (1930-2004), deconstruction endeavors to trace the way texts imply the contradiction of their explicit meanings. The deconstructionist delights in the sense of dizziness as the grounds of conviction crumble away; *aporia*, or irresolvable doubt, is the desired, if fleeting, end of an encounter with a text. Deconstruction threatens *humanism*, or the worldview that is centered on human values and the self-sufficient individual, because it denies that there is an ultimate, solid reality on which to base truth or the identity of the self. All values and identities are constructed by the competing systems of meaning, or *discourses*. This is a remarkably influential set of ideas that you will meet again as we discuss other approaches.

The traditional concept of the author as creative origin of the text comes under fire in deconstructionist criticism, which emphasizes instead the creative power of language or the text, and the ingenious work of the critic in detecting gaps and contradictions in writing. Thus, like New Criticism, deconstruction disregards the author and concentrates on textual close reading, but unlike New Criticism, it features the role of the reader as well. Moreover, the text need not be respected as a pure and coherent icon. Deconstructionists might "read" many kinds of writing and representation in other media in much the same way that they might read Milton's *Paradise Lost*, that is, irreverently. Indeed, when deconstruction erupted in university departments of literature, traditional critics and scholars feared the breakdown of the distinctions between literature and criticism and between literature and many other kinds of texts. Many attacks on literary theory have particularly lambasted deconstructionists for apparently rejecting all the reasons to care about literature in the first place and for writing in a style so flamboyantly obscure that no one but specialists can understand. Yet in practice Derrida and others have carried harmony before them, to paraphrase Brooks; their readings can delight in the play of figurative language, thereby enhancing rather than debunking the value of literature.

A deconstructionist might read "First Fight. Then Fiddle." in a manner somewhat similar to the New Critic's, but with even more focus on puns and paradoxes and with resistance to organic unity. For instance, the two alliterative commands, "fight" and "fiddle," might be opposites, twins, or inseparable consequences of each other. The word "fiddle" is tricky. Does it suggest that art is trivial? Does it allude to a dictator who "fiddles while Rome burns," as the saying goes? Someone who "fiddles" is not performing a grand, honest, or even competent act: One fiddles with a hobby, with the books, with car keys in the dark. The artist in this poem defies the orthodoxy of the sonnet form, instead making a kind of harlequin patchwork out of different traditions, breaking the rhythm, intermixing endearments and assaults.

To the deconstructionist the recurring broken antitheses of war and art, art and war cancel each other out. The very metaphors undermine the speaker's summons to war. The command "Be deaf to music and to beauty blind," which takes the form of a *chiasmus*, or X-shaped sequence (adjective, noun; noun, adjective), is a kind of miniature version of this chiasmic poem. (We are supposed to follow a sequence, fight then fiddle, but instead reverse that by imagining ways to do violence with art or to create beauty through destruction.) The poem, a lyric written but imagined as spoken or sung, puts the senses and the arts under erasure; we are somehow not to hear music (by definition audible), not to see beauty (here a visual attribute). "Maybe not too late" comes rather too late: At the end of the poem it will be too late to start over, although "having first to civilize a space / Wherein to play your violin with grace" (lines 12–14) comes across as a kind of beginning. These comforting lines form the only heroic couplet in the poem, the only two lines that run smoothly from end to end. (All the other lines have **caesuras**, **enjambments**, or balanced pairs of concepts, as in "from malice and from murdering" [line 8].) But the violence behind "civilize," the switch to the high-art term "violin," and the use of the Christian term "grace" suggest that the pagan erotic art promised at the outset, the "sorcery" of "hurting love" that can "bewitch," will be suppressed.

Like other formalisms, deconstruction can appear apolitical or conservative because of its skepticism about the referential connection between literature and the world of economics, politics, and other social forms. Yet poststructuralist linguistics provides a theory of *difference* that clearly pertains to the rankings of status and power in society, as in earlier examples of masculine/feminine, master/slave. The *Other*, the negative of the norm, is always less than an equal counterpart. Deconstruction has been a tool for various poststructuralist thinkers—including the historian Michel Foucault (1926–84), the feminist theorist and psychoanalyst Julia Kristeva (b. 1941), and the psychoanalytic theorist Jacques Lacan (1901–81).

Narrative Theory

Before concluding the discussion of text-centered approaches, we should mention the schools of narratology and narrative theory that have shaped study of the novel and other kinds of narrative. Criticism of fiction has been in a boom period since the 1950s, but the varieties of narrative theory per se have had more limited effect than the approaches we have discussed above. Since the 1960s different analysts of the forms and techniques of narrative, most notably the Chicago formalists and the structuralist narratologists, have developed terminology for the various interactions of author, implied author, narrator, and characters; of plot and the treatment of time in the selection and sequence of scenes; of voice, point of view, or focus and other aspects of fiction. As formalisms, narrative theories tend to exclude the author's biography, individual reader response, and the historical context of the work or its actual reception.

Narratology began by presenting itself as a structuralist science; its branches have grown from psychoanalytic theory or extended to reader-response criticism. In recent decades studies of narrative technique and form have responded to Marxist, feminist, and other ideological criticism that insists on the political contexts of literature. One important influence on this shift has been the revival of the work of Mikhail Bakhtin (1895–

1975), which features the novel as a *dialogic* form that pulls together the many discourses and voices of a culture and its history. Part of the appeal of Bakhtin's work has been the fusion of textual close reading with comprehension of material factors such as economics and class, and a sense of the open-endedness and contradictoriness of writing (in the spirit of deconstruction more than of New Criticism). Like other Marxist-trained European formalists, Bakhtin sought to place the complex literary modes of communication in the light of politics and history.

EMPHASIS ON THE SOURCE

As the above examples suggest, a great deal can be drawn from a text without any reference to its source or its author. For millennia many anonymous works were shared in oral or manuscript form, and even after printing spread in Europe few thought it necessary to know the author's name or anything about him or her. Yet criticism from its beginnings in ancient Greece has been interested in the designing intention "behind" the text. Even when no evidence remained about the author, a legendary personality has sometimes been invented to satisfy readers' curiosity. From the legend of blind Homer to the latest debates about biographical evidence and portraits of William Shakespeare, literary criticism has been accompanied by interest in the author's life.

Biographical Criticism

This approach reached its height in an era when humanism prevailed in literary studies (roughly the 1750s to the 1960s). At this time there was widely shared confidence in the ideas that art and literature were the direct expressions of the artist's or writer's genius and that criticism of great works supported veneration of the great persons who created them. The lives of some famous writers became the models that aspiring writers emulated. Criticism at times was skewed by social judgments of personalities, as when Keats was put down as a "Cockney" poet, that is, London-bred and lower-class. Many writers have struggled to get their work taken seriously because of mistaken biographical criticism. Women or minorities have at times used pseudonyms or published anonymously to avoid having their work put down or having it read only through the expectations, negative or positive, of what a woman or person of color might write. Biographical criticism can be diminishing in this respect. Others have objected to reading literature as a reflection of the author's personality. Such critics have supported the idea that the highest literary art is pure form, untouched by gossip or personal emotion. In this spirit some early twentieth-century critics as well as modernist writers such as T. S. Eliot, James Joyce, and Virginia Woolf tried to dissociate the text from the personality or political commitments of the author. (The theories of these writers and their actual practices did not always coincide.)

In the early twentieth century, psychoanalytic interpretations placed the text in light of the author's emotional conflicts, and other interpretations relied heavily on the author's stated intentions. (Although psychoanalytic criticism entails more than analysis of the author, we will introduce it as an approach that primarily concerns the human source[s] of literature; it usually has less to say about the form and receiver of the text.) Author-based readings can be reductive. All the accessible information about a writer's life cannot definitively explain the writings. As a young man D. H. Lawrence might have hated his father and loved his mother, but all men who hate their fathers and love their mothers do not write fiction as powerful as Lawrence's. Indeed, Lawrence himself cautioned that we should "trust the tale, not the teller."

Any kind of criticism benefits, however, from being informed by the writer's life and career to some extent. Certain critical approaches, devoted to recognition of separate literary traditions, make sense only in light of supporting biographical evidence. Studies that concern traditions such as Irish literature, Asian American literature, or literature by Southern women require reliable information about the writers' birth and upbringing and even some judgment of the writers' intentions to write *as* members of such traditions. (We discuss feminist, African American, and other studies of distinct literatures in the "Historical and Ideological Criticism" section, although such studies recognize the biographical "source" as a starting point.)

A reading of "First Fight. Then Fiddle." can become rather different when we know more about Gwendolyn Brooks. An African American, she was raised in Chicago in the 1920s. These facts begin to provide a context for her work. Some of the biographical information has more to do with her time and place than with her race and sex. Brooks began in the 1940s to associate with Harriet Monroe's magazine, *Poetry*, which had been influential in promoting modernist poetry. Brooks early received acclaim for books of poetry that depict the everyday lives of poor, urban African Americans; in 1950 she was the first African American to win a Pulitzer Prize. In 1967 she became an outspoken advocate for the Black Arts movement, which promoted a separate tradition rather than integration into the aesthetic mainstream. But even before this political commitment, her work never sought to "pass" or to distance itself from racial difference, nor did it become any less concerned with poetic tradition and form when she published it through small, independent black presses in her "political" phase.

It is reasonable, then, to read "First Fight. Then Fiddle.," published in 1949, in relation to the role of a racial outsider mastering and adapting the forms of a dominant tradition. Perhaps Brooks's speaker addresses an African American audience in the voice of a revolutionary, calling for violence to gain the right to express African American culture. Perhaps the lines "the music that they wrote / Bewitch, bewilder. Qualify to sing / Threadwise" (lines 3–5) suggest the way that the colonized may transform the empire's music rather than the other way around. Ten years before the poem was published, a famous African American singer, Marian Anderson, had more than "qualif[ied] to sing" opera and classical concert music, but had still encountered the color barrier in the United States. Honored throughout Europe as the greatest living contralto, Anderson was barred in 1939 from performing at Constitution Hall in Washington, DC, because of her race. Instead she performed at the Lincoln Memorial on Easter Sunday to an audience of seventy-five thousand people. It was not easy to find a "space" in which to practice her art. Such a contextual reference, whether or not intended, relates biographically to Brooks's role as an African American woman wisely reweaving classical traditions "threadwise" rather than straining them into "hempen" (line 5) ropes. Beneath the manifest reference to the recent world war, this poem refers to the segregation of the arts in America. (Questions of source and historical context often interrelate.)

Besides readings that derive from biographical and historical information, there are still other ways to read aspects of the *source* rather than the *text* or the *receiver*. The source of the work extends beyond the life of the person who wrote it to include not only the writer's other works but also the circumstances of contemporary publishing; contemporary literary movements; the history of the composition, editing, and publication of this particular text, with all the variations; and other contributing factors. While entire schools of literary scholarship have been devoted to each of these matters, any analyst of a particular work should bear in mind what is known about the circumstances of writers at that time, the material conditions of the work's first publication, and the means of dissemination ever since. It makes a difference in our interpretation to know that a certain sonnet circulated in manuscript in a small courtly audience or that a particular novel was serialized in a weekly journal.

Psychoanalytic Criticism

With the development of psychology and psychoanalysis toward the end of the nineteenth century, many critics were tempted to apply psychological theories to literary analysis. Symbolism, dreamlike imagery, emotional rather than rational logic, and a pleasure in language all suggested that literature profoundly evoked a mental and emotional landscape, often one of disorder or abnormality. From mad poets to patients speaking in verse, imaginative literature might be regarded as a representation of shared irrational structures within all *psyches* (i.e., souls) or selves. While psychoanalytic approaches have developed along with structuralism and poststructuralist linguistics and philosophy, they rarely focus on textual form. Rather, they attribute latent or hidden meaning to unacknowledged desires in some person, usually the author or source behind the character in a narrative or drama. A psychoanalytic critic can also focus on the response of readers and, in recent decades, usually accepts the influence of changing social history on the structures of sexual desire represented in the work. Nevertheless, psychoanalysis has typically aspired to a universal, unchanging theory of the mind and personality, and criticism that applies it has tended to emphasize the authorial source.

FREUDIAN CRITICISM

For most of the twentieth century, the dominant school of psychoanalytic critics was the Freudian, based on the work of Sigmund Freud (1856–1939). Many of its practitioners assert that the meaning of a literary work exists not on its surface but in the psyche (some would even claim, in the neuroses) of the author. Classic psychoanalytic criticism read works as though they were the recorded dreams of patients; interpreted the life histories of authors as keys to the works; or analyzed characters as though like real people they have a set of repressed childhood memories. (In fact, many novels and most plays leave out information about characters' development from infancy through adolescence, the period that psychoanalysis especially strives to reconstruct.)

A well-known Freudian reading of *Hamlet*, for example, insists that Hamlet suffers from an Oedipus complex, a Freudian term for a group of repressed desires and memories that corresponds with the Greek myth that is the basis of Sophocles' play *Oedipus the King*. In this view Hamlet envies his uncle because the son unconsciously wants to sleep with his mother, who was the first object of his desire as a baby. The ghost of Hamlet Sr. may then be a manifestation of Hamlet's unconscious desire or a figure for his guilt for wanting to kill his father, the person who has a right to the desired mother's body. Hamlet's madness is not just acting but the result of this frustrated desire; his cruel mistreatment of Ophelia is a deflection of his disgust at his mother's being "unfaithful" in her love for him. Some Freudian critics stress the author's psyche and so might read *Hamlet* as the expression of Shakespeare's own Oedipus complex. In another mode psychoanalytic critics, reading imaginative literature as symbolic fulfillment of unconscious wishes much as an analyst would interpret a dream, decipher objects, spaces, or actions that appear to relate to sexual anatomy or activity. Much as if tracing out the extended metaphors of an erotic poem by Donne or a blues or Motown lyric, the Freudian reads containers, empty spaces, or bodies of water as female; tools, weapons, towers or trees, trains or planes as male.

Psychoanalytic criticism, learning from Freud's ventures in literary criticism, has favored narrative fiction with uncanny, supernatural, or detective elements. Plots with excessive, inexplicable fatalities seem to express wishes unconsciously shared by readers as well as the writer. The method has often been applied to writers of such stories whose biographies are particularly well documented. The life and works of Edgar Allan Poe (1809–49) therefore have attracted psychoanalytic readings. An orphan who quarreled with the surrogate father who raised him, Poe seems to have been tormented by an unresolved desire for a mother figure. A series of beloved mother figures died prematurely, including his mother and Mrs. Allan, the woman who raised him. He became attached to his aunt and fell in love with her daughter, Virginia Clemm, whom he married in 1836 when she was thirteen, and who died of tuberculosis in 1847. He famously asserted that the most apt subject of poetry is the death of a beautiful woman. In Poe's "The Raven" a macabre talking bird intrudes in the speaker's room and provokes the speaker's obsession with the dead beloved, a woman named Lenore. In a Freudian reading, Poe's "The Cask of Amontillado" appears to transpose a fantasy of return to the womb—an enclosed space holding liquids—into a fulfilled desire to kill a male rival.

JUNGIAN AND MYTH CRITICISM

Just as a Freudian assumes that all human psyches have similar histories and structures, the Jungian critic assumes that we all share a universal or collective unconscious (just as each has a racial and an individual unconscious). According to Carl Gustav Jung (1875–1961) and his followers, the unconscious harbors universal patterns and forms of human experiences, or archetypes. We can never know these archetypes directly, but they surface in art in an imperfect, shadowy way, taking the form of archetypal images—the snake with its tail in its mouth, rebirth, mother, the double, the descent into hell. In the classic quest narrative, the hero struggles to free himself (the gender of the pronoun is significant) from the Great Mother to become a separate, self-sufficient being (combating a demonic antagonist), surviving trials to gain the reward of union with his ideal other, the feminine anima. In a related school of *archetypal criticism*, influenced by Northrop Frye (1912–91), the prevailing myth follows a seasonal cycle of death and rebirth. Frye proposed a system for literary criticism that classified all literary forms in all ages according to a cycle of genres associated with the phases of human experience from birth to death and the natural cycle of seasons (e.g., Spring/Romance).

These approaches have been useful in the study of folklore and early literatures as well as in comparative studies of various national literatures. While most myth critics focus on the hero's quest, there have been forays into feminist archetypal criticism. These emphasize variations on the myths of Isis and Demeter, goddesses of fertility or seasonal renewal, who take different forms to restore either the sacrificed woman (Persephone's season in the underworld) or the sacrificed man (Isis's search for Osiris and her rescue of their son, Horus). Many twentieth-century poets were drawn to the heritage of archetypes and myths. Adrienne Rich's "Diving into the Wreck," for example, self-consciously rewrites a number of gendered archetypes, with a female protagonist on a quest into a submerged world. Most critics today, influenced by poststructuralism, have become wary of universal patterns. Like structuralists, Jungians and archetypal critics strive to compare and unite the ages and peoples of the world and to reveal fundamental truths. Rich, as a feminist poet, suggests that the "book of myths" is an eclectic anthology that needs to be revised. Claims of universality tend to obscure the detailed differences between cultures and often appeal to some idea of *biological determinism*. Such determinism diminishes the power of individuals to design alternative life patterns and even implies that no literature can really surprise us.

LACANIAN CRITICISM

As it has absorbed the indeterminacies of poststructuralism under the influence of thinkers such as Jacques Lacan and Julia Kristeva, psychological criticism has become increasingly complex. Few critics today are direct Freudian analysts of authors or texts, and few maintain that universal archetypes explain the meaning of a tree or water in a text. Yet psychoanalytic theory continues to inform many varieties of criticism, and most new work in this field is affiliated with Lacanian psychoanalysis. Lacan's theory unites poststructuralist linguistics with Freudian theory. The Lacanian critic, like a deconstructionist, focuses on the text that defies conscious authorial control, foregrounding the powerful interpretation of the critic rather than the author or any other reader. Accepting the Oedipal paradigm and the unconscious as the realm of repressed desire, Lacanian theory aligns the development and structure of the individual human *subject* with the development and structure of language. To simplify a purposefully dense theory: The very young infant inhabits the Imaginary, in a preverbal, undifferentiated phase dominated by a sense of union with Mother. Recognition of identity begins with the Mirror Stage, ironically with a disruption of a sense of oneness. For when one first looks into a mirror, one begins to recognize a split or difference between one's body and the image in the mirror. This splitting prefigures a sense that the *object* of desire is Other and distinct from the subject. With difference or the splitting of subject and object comes language and entry into the Symbolic Order, since we use words to summon the absent object of desire (as a child would cry "Mama" to bring her back). But what language signifies most is the lack of that object. The imaginary, perfectly nurturing Mother would never need to be called.

As in the biblical Genesis, the Lacanian "genesis" of the subject tells of a loss of paradise through knowledge of the difference between subject and object or Man and Woman (eating of the Tree of the Knowledge of Good and Evil leads to the sense of shame that teaches Adam and Eve to hide their nakedness). In Lacanian theory the Father governs language or the

Symbolic Order; the Word spells the end of a child's sense of oneness with the Mother. Further, the Father's power claims omnipotence, the possession of male prerogative symbolized by the Phallus, which is not the anatomical difference between men and women but the idea or construction of that difference. Thus it is language or culture rather than nature that generates the difference and inequality between the sexes. Some feminist theorists have adopted aspects of Lacanian psychoanalytic theory, particularly the concept of *the gaze*. This concept notes that the masculine subject is the one who looks, whereas the feminine object is to be looked at.

Another influential concept is *abjection*. Julia Kristeva's theory of abjection most simply reimagines the infant's blissful sense of union with the mother and the darker side of such possible union. To return to the mother's body would be death, as metaphorically we are buried in Mother Earth. Yet according to the theory, people both desire and dread such loss of boundaries. A sense of self or *subjectivity* and hence of independence and power depends on resisting abjection. The association of the maternal body with abjection or with the powerlessness symbolized by the female's Lack of the Phallus can help explain negative cultural images of women. Many narrative genres seem to split the images of women between an angelic and a witchlike type. Lacanian or Kristevan theory has been well adapted to film criticism and to fantasy and other popular forms favored by structuralism or archetypal criticism.

Psychoanalytic literary criticism today—as distinct from specialized discussion of Lacanian theory, for example—treads more lightly than in the past. In James Joyce's "Araby," a young Dublin boy, orphaned and raised by an aunt and uncle, likes to haunt a back room in the house; there the "former tenant, . . . a priest, had died" (paragraph 2). (Disused rooms at the margins of houses resemble the unconscious, and a dead celibate "father" suggests a kind of failure of the Law, conscience, or in Freudian terms, superego.) The priest had left behind a "rusty bicycle-pump" in the "wild garden" with "a central apple tree" (these echoes of the garden of Eden suggesting the impotence of Catholic religious symbolism). The boy seems to gain consciousness of a separate self—or his subjectivity is constructed—through his gaze upon an idealized female object, Mangan's sister, whose "name was like a summons to all my foolish blood" (paragraph 4). Though he secretly watches and follows her, she is not so much a sexual fantasy as a beautiful art object (paragraph 9). He retreats to the back room to think of her in a kind of ecstasy that resembles masturbation. Yet it is not masturbation: It is preadolescent, dispersed through all orifices—the rain feels like "incessant needles . . . playing in the sodden beds"; and it is sublimated, that is, repressed and redirected into artistic or religious forms rather than directly expressed by bodily pleasure: "All my senses seemed to desire to veil themselves" (paragraph 6).

It is not in the back room but on the street that the girl finally speaks to the hero, charging him to go on a quest to Araby. After several trials the hero carrying the talisman arrives in a darkened hall "girdled at half its height by a gallery," an underworld or maternal space that is also a deserted temple (paragraph 25). The story ends without his grasping the prize to carry back, the "chalice" or holy grail (symbolic of female sexuality) that he had once thought to bear "safely through a throng of foes" (paragraph 5).

Such a reading seems likely to raise objections that it is overreading: *You're seeing too much in it; the author didn't mean that.* This has been a popular reaction to psychoanalysis for over a hundred years, but it is only a heightened version of a response to many kinds of criticism. This sample reading pays close attention to the text, but does not really follow a formal approach because its goal is to explain the psychological motivations or sources of the story's details. We have mentioned nothing about the author, though we could have placed the above reading within a psychoanalytic reading of Joyce's biography.

EMPHASIS ON THE RECEIVER

In some sense critical schools develop in reaction to the excesses of other critical schools. By the 1970s, in a time of political upheaval that placed a value on individual expression, a number of critics felt that the various routes toward objective criticism had proved to be dead ends. New Critics, structuralists, and psychoanalytic or myth critics had sought objective, scientific systems that disregarded changing times, political issues, or the reader's personal response. New Critics and other formalists tended to value a literary canon made up of works that were regarded as complete, unchanging objects to be comprehended, as if spatially in a photograph, according to timeless standards.

Reader-Response Criticism

Among critics who challenge New Critical assumptions, the reader-response critics regard the work not as what is printed on the page but as what is experienced temporally through each act of reading. In effect the reader performs the poem into existence from a text the way a musician performs music from a score. Reader-response critics ask not what a work means but what a work does or, rather, what it makes a reader do. Literary texts especially leave gaps that experienced readers fill according to expectations or conventions. Individual readers differ, of course, and gaps in a text provide space for different readings or interpretations. Some of these lacunae are temporary—such as the withholding of the murderer's name until the end of a mystery novel—and are closed by the text sooner or later, though each reader will in the meantime fill them differently. But other lacunae are permanent and can never be filled with certainty; they result in a degree of uncertainty or indeterminacy in the text.

The reader-response critic observes the expectations aroused by a text, how they are satisfied or modified, and how the reader projects a comprehension of the work when all of it has been read, and when it is reread in whole or in part. Such criticism attends to the reading habits associated with different genres and to the shared assumptions of a cultural context that seem to furnish what is left unsaid in the text. Margaret Atwood's "Happy Endings" could almost be an essay on reader response in the guise of do-it-yourself instructions to a simpleminded reader: "John and Mary meet. What happens next? If you want a happy ending, try A" (paragraphs 1–3). This beginning seems to steer the reader to follow alphabetized instructions to assist in designing the narrative. It also satirizes romance plot conventions. Every romance fan knows that if a male and a female character meet, they will fall in love, and that some conflict will delay their marriage until it is resolved—unless the conflict proves insurmountable. As Atwood humorously shows, various love triangles or death will change the outcome. In spite of the scanty details given in the text, each reader will fill in the gaps and imagine "How and Why" (paragraph 23), the realistic details and rounded characterization that he or she has learned to imagine from reading other fiction.

Beyond theoretical formulations about reading, there are other approaches to literary study that concern the receiver rather than the text or source. A critic might examine specific documents of a work's reception, from contemporary reviews to critical essays written across the generations since the work was first published. Sometimes we have available diaries or autobiographical evidence about readers' encounters with particular works. Just as there are histories of publishing and of the book, there are histories of literacy and reading practices. Poetry, fiction, and drama often directly represent the theme of reading as well as writing. Many published works over the centuries have debated the benefits and perils of reading works such as sermons or novels. Different genres and particular works construct different classes or kinds of readers in the way they address them or supply what they are supposed to want. Some scholars have found quantitative measures for reading, from sales and library lending rates to questionnaires.

Finally, the role of the reader or receiver in literary exchange has been portrayed from a political perspective. Literature helps shape social identity, and social status shapes access to different kinds of literature. Feminist critics adapted reader-response criticism, for example, to note that girls often do not identify with many American literary classics as boys do, and thus girls do not simply accept the stereotype of women as angels, temptresses, or scolds who should be abandoned for the sake of all-male adventures. Studies of African American literature and other ethnic literatures have often featured discussion of literacy and of the obstacles for readers who cannot find their counterparts within the texts or who encounter negative stereotypes of their group. Thus, as we will discuss below, most forms of historical and ideological criticism include some consideration of the reader.

HISTORICAL AND IDEOLOGICAL CRITICISM

Approaches to the text, the author, and the reader, outlined above, each may take some note of historical contexts, including changes in formal conventions, the writer's milieu, or audience expectations. In the nineteenth century, historical criticism took the obvious facts that a work is created in a specific historical and cultural context and that the author is a part of that context as reasons to treat literature as a reflection of society. Twentieth-century formalists rejected the *reflectivist* model of art in the old historical criticism, that is, the assumption that literature and other arts straightforwardly express the collective spirit of the society at that time. But as we have remarked, formalist rules for isolating the work of art from social and historical context met resistance in the last decades of the twentieth century. In a revival of historical approaches, critics have replaced the reflectivist model with a *constructivist* model, whereby literature and other cultural discourses help construct social relations and roles rather than merely reflecting them. In other words, art is not just the frosting on the cake but an integral part of the recipe's ingredients and instructions. A society's ideology, its inherent system of representations (ideas, myths, images), is inscribed in and by literature and other cultural forms, which in turn help shape identities and social practices.

Since the 1980s historical approaches have regained great influence in literary studies. Some critical schools have been insistently *materialist*, that is, seeking causes more in concrete conditions such as technology, production, and distribution of wealth, or the exploitation of markets and labor in and beyond Western countries. Such criticism usually owes an acknowledged debt to Marxism. Other historical approaches have been influenced to a degree by Marxist critics and cultural theorists, but work within the realm of ideology, textual production, and interpretation, using some of the methods and concerns of traditional literary history. Still others emerge from the civil rights movement and the struggles for recognition of women and racial, ethnic, and sexual constituencies.

Feminist studies, African American studies, gay and lesbian studies, and studies of the cultures of different immigrant and ethnic populations within the United States have each developed along similar theoretical lines. These schools, like Marxist criticism, adopt a constructivist position: Literature is not simply a reflection of prejudices and norms; it also helps define as well as reshape social identities, such as what it means to be an African American woman. Each of these schools has moved through stages of first claiming *equality* with the literature dominated by white Anglo American men, then affirming the *difference* of their own separate culture, and then theoretically *questioning the terms and standards* of such comparisons. At a certain point in the thought process, each group rejects *essentialism*, the notion of innate or biological bases for the differences between the sexes, races, or other groups. This rejection of essentialism is usually called the constructivist position, in a somewhat different but related sense to our definition above. Constructivism maintains that identity is socially formed rather than biologically determined. Differences of anatomical sex, skin color, first language, parental ethnicity, and eventual sexual preferences have great impact on how one is classified, brought up, and treated socially, and on one's subjectivity or conception of identity. Constructivists maintain that these differences, however, are more constructed by ideology and the resulting behaviors than by any natural programming.

Marxist Criticism

The most insistent and vigorous historical approach through the twentieth century to the present has been Marxism, based on the work of Karl Marx (1818–83). With roots in nineteenth-century historicism, Marxist criticism was initially reflectivist. Economics, the underlying cause of history, was thus the *base*, and culture, including literature and the other arts, was the *superstructure*, an outcome or reflection of the base. Viewed from the Marxist perspective, the literary works of a period were economically determined; they would *reflect* the state of the struggle between classes in any place and time. History enacted recurrent three-step cycles, a pattern that Hegel had defined as *dialectic* (Hegel was cited above on the interdependence of master and slave). Each socioeconomic phase, or *thesis*, is counteracted by its *antithesis*, and the resulting conflict yields a *synthesis*, which becomes the ensuing *thesis*, and so on. As with early Freudian criticism, early Marxist criticism was often preoccupied with labeling and exposing illusions or deceptions. A novel might be read as a thinly disguised defense of the power of bourgeois industrial capital; its appeal on behalf of the suffering poor might be dismissed as an effort to fend off a class rebellion.

As a rationale for state control of the arts, Marxism was abused in the Soviet Union and in other totalitarian states. In the hands of sophisticated critics, however, Marxism has been richly rewarding. Various schools that unite formal close reading and political analysis developed in the early twentieth century under Soviet communism and under fascism in Europe, often in covert resistance. These schools in turn have influenced critical movements in North American universities through translations or through members who came to the United States; New Criticism, structuralist linguistics, deconstruction, and narrative theory have each borrowed from European Marxist critics.

Most recently, a new mode of Marxist theory has developed, largely guided by the thinking of Walter Benjamin (1892–1940) and Theodor

Adorno (1903–69) of the Frankfurt School in Germany, Louis Althusser (1918–90) in France, and Raymond Williams (1921–98) in Britain. This work has generally tended to modify the base/superstructure distinction and to interrelate public and private life, economics and culture. Newer Marxist interpretation assumes that the relation of a literary work to its historical context is *overdetermined*—the relation has multiple determining factors rather than a sole cause or aim. This thinking similarly acknowledges that neither the source nor the receiver of the literary interaction is a mere tool or victim of the ruling powers or state. Representation of all kinds, including literature, always has a political dimension, according to this approach; conversely, political and material conditions such as work, money, or institutions depend on representation.

Showing some influence of psychoanalytic and poststructuralist theories, recent Marxist literary studies examine the effects of ideology by focusing on the works' gaps and silences: Ideology may be conveyed in what is repressed or contradicted. In many ways Marxist criticism has adapted to the conditions of consumer rather than industrial capitalism and to global rather than national economies. The worldwide revolution that was to come when the proletariat or working classes overthrew the capitalists has never taken place; in many countries industrial labor has been swallowed up by the service sector, and workers reject the political Left that would seem their most likely ally. Increasingly, Marxist criticism has acknowledged that the audience of literature may be active rather than passive, just as the text and source may be more than straightforward instructions for toeing a given political line. Marxist criticism has been especially successful with the novel, since that genre more than drama or short fiction is capable of representing numerous people from different classes as they develop over a significant amount of time.

Feminist Criticism

Like Marxist criticism and the schools discussed below, feminist criticism derives from a critique of a history of oppression, in this case the history of women's inequality. Feminist criticism has no single founder like Freud or Marx; it has been practiced to some extent since the 1790s, when praise of women's cultural achievements went hand in hand with arguments that women were rational beings deserving equal rights and education. Contemporary feminist criticism emerged from a "second wave" of feminist activism, in the 1960s and 1970s, associated with the civil rights and antiwar movements. One of the first disciplines in which women's activism took root was literary criticism, but feminist theory and women's studies quickly became recognized methods across the disciplines.

Feminist literary studies began by denouncing the misrepresentation of women in literature and affirming women's writings, before quickly adopting the insights of poststructuralist theory; yet the early strategies continue to have their use. At first, feminist criticism in the 1970s, like early Marxist criticism, regarded literature as a reflection of patriarchal society's sexist base; the demeaning images of women in literature were symptoms of a system that had to be overthrown. Feminist literary studies soon began, however, to claim the *equal* worth if distinctive themes of writings by women and men. Critics such as Elaine Showalter (b. 1941), Sandra M. Gilbert (b. 1936), and Susan Gubar (b. 1944) featured the canonical works by women, relying on close reading with some aid from historical and psychoanalytic methods. Yet by the 1980s it was widely recognized that a New Critical method would leave most of the male-dominated canon intact and most women writers still in obscurity, because many women had written in different genres and styles, on different themes, and for different audiences than had male writers.

To affirm the *difference* of female literary traditions, some feminist studies claimed women's innate or universal affinity for fluidity and cycle rather than solidity and linear progress. Others concentrated on the role of the mother in human psychological development. According to this argument, girls, not having to adopt a gender role different from that of their first object of desire, the mother, grow up with less rigid boundaries of self and a relational rather than judgmental ethic. The dangers of these intriguing generalizations soon became apparent. If the reasons for women's differences from men were biologically based or were due to universal archetypes, there was no solution to women's oppression, which many cultures worldwide had justified in terms of biological reproduction or archetypes of nature.

At this point in the debate, feminist literary studies intersected with poststructuralist linguistic theory in *questioning the terms and standards* of comparison. French feminist theory, articulated most prominently by Hélène Cixous (b. 1935) and Luce Irigaray (b. 1932), deconstructed the supposed archetypes of gender written into the founding discourses of Western culture. We have seen that deconstruction helps expose the power imbalance in every dualism. Thus man is to woman as culture is to nature or mind is to body, and in each case the second term is held to be inferior or Other. The language and hence the worldview and social formations of our culture, not nature or eternal archetypes, constructed woman as Other. This insight was helpful in avoiding essentialism or biological determinism.

Having reached a theoretical criticism of the terms on which women might claim equality or difference from men in the field of literature, feminist studies also confronted other issues in the 1980s. Deconstructionist readings of gender difference in texts by men as well as women could lose sight of the real world, in which women are paid less and are more likely to be victims of sexual violence. Some feminist critics with this in mind pursued links with Marxist or African American studies; gender roles, like those of class and race, were interdependent systems for registering the material consequences of people's differences. It no longer seemed so easy to say what the term "women" referred to, when the interests of different kinds of women had been opposed to each other. African American women asked if feminism was really their cause, when white women had so long enjoyed power over both men and women of their race. In a classic Marxist view, women allied with men of their class rather than with women of other classes. It became more difficult to make universal claims about women's literature, as the horizon of the college-educated North American feminists expanded to recognize the range of conditions of women and of literature worldwide. Feminist literary studies have continued to consider famous and obscure women writers; the way women and gender are portrayed in writings by men as well as women; feminist issues concerning the text, source, or receiver in any national literature; theoretical and historical questions about the representation of differences such as gender, race, class, and nationality, and the way these differences shape each other.

Gender Studies and Queer Theory

From the 1970s, feminists sought recognition for lesbian writers and lesbian culture, which they felt had been even less visible than male homosexual writers and gay culture. Concurrently, feminist studies abandoned the simple dualism of male/female, part of the very binary logic of patriarchy that seemed to cause the oppression of women. Thus feminists recognized a zone of inquiry, the study of gender, as distinct from historical studies of women, and increasingly they included masculinity as a subject of investigation. As gender studies turned to interpretation of the text in ideological context regardless of the sex or intention of the author, it incorporated the ideas of Michel Foucault's *History of Sexuality* (1976). Foucault helped show that there was nothing natural, universal, or timeless in the constructions of sexual difference or sexual practices. Foucault also introduced a history of the concept of homosexuality, which had once been regarded in terms of taboo acts and in the later nineteenth century became defined as a disease associated with a personality type. Literary scholars began to study the history of sexuality as a key to the shifts in modern culture that had also shaped literature.

By the 1980s gender had come to be widely regarded as a discourse that imposed binary social norms on human beings' diversity. Theorists such as Donna Haraway (b. 1944) and Judith Butler (b. 1956) insisted further that sex and sexuality have no natural basis; even the anatomical differences are representations from the moment the newborn is put in a pink or blue blanket. Moreover, these theorists claimed that gender and sexuality are *performative* and malleable positions, enacted in many more than two varieties. From cross-dressing to surgical sex changes, the alternatives chosen by real people have influenced critical theory and generated both writings and literary criticism about those writings. Perhaps biographical and feminist studies face new challenges when identity seems subject to radical change and it is less easy to determine the sex of an author.

Gay and lesbian literary studies have included practices that parallel feminist criticism. At times critics identify oppressive or positive representations of homosexuality in works by men or women, gay, lesbian, or straight. At other times critics seek to establish the equivalent stature of a work by a gay or lesbian writer or, because these identities tended to be hidden in the past, to reveal that a writer *was* gay or lesbian. Again stages of *equality* and *difference* have yielded to a *questioning of the terms of difference*, in this case what has been called queer theory (the stages have not superseded each other). The field of queer theory hopes to leave everyone guessing rather than to identify gay or lesbian writers, characters, or themes. One of its founding texts, *Between Men* (1985), by Eve Kosofsky Sedgwick (b. 1950), drew on structuralist insight into desire as well as anthropological models of kinship to show that, in canonical works of English literature, male characters bond together through their rivalry for and exchange of a woman. Queer theory, because it rejects the idea of a fixed identity or innate or essential gender, likes to discover resistance to heterosexuality in unexpected places. Queer theorists value gay writers such as Oscar Wilde, but they also find queer implications regardless of the author's acknowledged identity. This approach emphasizes not the surface signals of the text but the subtler meanings an audience or receiver might detect. It encompasses elaborate close reading of varieties of work; characteristically, a leading queer theorist, D. A. Miller (b. 1948), has written in loving detail about Jane Austen and about Broadway musicals.

African American and Ethnic Literary Studies

Critics sought to define an African American literary tradition as early as the turn of the twentieth century. A period of literary success in the 1920s, known as the Harlem Renaissance, produced some of the first classic essays on writings by African Americans. Criticism and histories of African American literature tended to ignore and dismiss women writers, while feminist literary histories, guided by Virginia Woolf's classic *A Room of One's Own* (1929), neglected women writers of color. Only after feminist critics began to succeed in the academy and African American studies programs were established did the whiteness of feminist studies and masculinity of African American studies became glaring; both fields have for some time corrected this narrowness of vision. The study of African American literature followed the general pattern that we have noted, first striving to claim equality, on established aesthetic grounds, of works such as Ralph Ellison's magnificent *Invisible Man* (1952). Then in the 1960s the Black Arts or Black

Aesthetic emerged. Once launched in the academy, however, African American studies has been devoted less to celebrating an essential racial difference than to tracing the historical construction of a racial Other and a subordinated literature. The field sought to recover genres in which African Americans have written, such as slave narratives, and traced common elements in fiction or poetry to the conditions of slavery and segregation. By the 1980s feminist and poststructuralist theory had an impact in the work of some African American critics such as Henry Louis Gates Jr. (b. 1950), Houston A. Baker Jr. (b. 1943), Hazel V. Carby (b. 1948), and Deborah E. McDowell (b. 1951), while others objected that the doubts raised by "theory" stood in the way of political commitment. African Americans' cultural contributions to America have gained much more recognition than before. New histories of American culture have been written with the view that racism is not an aberration but inherent to the guiding narratives of national progress. Many critics now regard race as a discourse with only slight basis in genetics but with weighty investments in ideology. This poststructuralist position coexists with scholarship that takes into account the race of the author or reader or that focuses on African American characters or themes.

In recent years a series of fields has arisen in recognition of the literatures of other American ethnic groups, large and small: Asian Americans, Native Americans, and Chicanos. Increasingly, such studies avoid romanticizing an original, pure culture or assuming that these literatures by their very nature undermine the values and power of the dominant culture. Instead, critics emphasize the *hybridity* of all cultures in a global economy. The contact and intermixture of cultures across geographical borders and languages (translations, "creole" speech made up of native and acquired languages, dialects) may be read as enriching themes for literature and art, although they are caused by economic exploitation. In method and in aim these fields have much in common with African American studies, though each cultural and historical context is very different. Each field deserves the separate study that we cannot offer here.

Not so very long ago, critics might have been charged with a fundamental misunderstanding of the nature of literature if they pursued matters considered the business of sociologists, matters—such as class, race, and gender—that seemed extrinsic to the text. The rise of the above-noted fields has made it standard practice that a critic will address questions about class, race, and gender to place a text, its source, and its reception in historical and ideological context. One brief example might illustrate the way Marxist, feminist, queer, and African American criticism can contribute to a literary reading.

Tennessee Williams's *A Streetcar Named Desire* was first produced in 1947 and won the Pulitzer Prize in 1948. Part of its acclaim was likely due to its fashionable blend of naturalism and symbolism: The action takes place in a shabby tenement on an otherworldly street, Elysian Fields—in an "atmosphere of decay" laced with "lyricism," as Williams's stage directions put it. After the Depression and World War II, American audiences welcomed a turn away from world politics into the psychological core of human sexuality. This turn to ostensibly individual conflict was a kind of alibi for at least two sets of issues that Williams and the middle-class theatergoers in New York and elsewhere sought to avoid. First, the racial questions that relate to questions of gender and class: What is the play's attitude to race, and what is Williams's attitude? Biography seems relevant, though not the last word on what the play means. Williams's family had included slave-holding cotton growers, and he chose to spend much of his adult life in the South, which he saw as representing a beautiful but dying way of life. He was deeply attached to women in his family who might be models for the brilliant, fragile, cultivated Southern white woman, Blanche DuBois. Blanche ("white" in French), representative of a genteel, feminine past that has gambled, prostituted, dissipated itself, speaks some of the most eloquent lines in the play when she mourns the faded Delta plantation society. Neither the playwright nor his audience wished to deal with segregation in the South, a region that since the Civil War had stagnated as a kind of agricultural working class in relation to the dominant North—which had its racism, too.

The play scarcely notices race. The main characters are white. The cast includes a "Negro Woman" as servant, and a blind Mexican woman who offers artificial flowers to remember the dead, but these figures seem either stage business or symbolism. Instead, racial difference is transposed as ethnic and class difference, in the story of a working-class Pole intruding into a family clinging to French gentility. Stella warns Blanche that she lives among "heterogeneous types" and that Stanley is "a different species." The play thus transfigures contemporary anxieties about miscegenation, as the virile (black) man dominates the ideal white woman and rapes the spirit of the plantation South. A former army man who works in a factory, Stanley represents as well the defeat of the old, agricultural economy by industrialization.

The second set of issues that neither the playwright nor his audience confronts directly is the disturbance of sexual and gender roles that would in later decades lead to movements for women's and gay rights. It was well known in New Orleans at least that Williams was gay. In the 1940s he lived with his lover, Pancho Rodriguez y Gonzales, in the French Quarter. Like many homosexual writers in different eras, Williams recasts homosexual desire in heterosexual costume. Blanche, performing femininity with a kind of camp excess, might be a fading queen pursuing and failing to capture younger men. Stanley, hypermasculine, might caricature the object of desire of both men and women as well as the anti-intellectual, brute force in postwar America. His conquest of women (he had "the power and pride of a richly feathered male bird among hens") appears to be biologically determined. By the same token it seems natural that Stanley and his buddies go out to work and their wives become homemakers in the way now seen as typical of the 1950s. In this world, artists, homosexuals, or unmarried working women like Blanche would be both vulnerable and threatening. Blanche after all has secret pleasures—drinking and sex—that Stanley indulges in openly. Blanche is the one who is taken into custody by the medical establishment, which in this period diagnosed homosexuality as a form of insanity.

New Historicism

Three interrelated schools of historical and ideological criticism have been important innovations in the past two decades. These are part of the swing of the pendulum away from formal analysis of the text and toward historical analysis of context. New historicism has less obvious political commitments than Marxism, feminism, or queer theory, but it shares their interest in the power of discourse to shape ideology. Old historicism, in the 1850s–1950s, confidently told a story of civilization's progress from the point of view of a Western nation; a historicist critic would offer a close reading of the plays of Shakespeare and then locate them within the prevailing Elizabethan "worldview." "New Historicism," labeled in 1982 by Stephen Greenblatt (b. 1943), rejected the technique of plugging samples of a culture into a history of ideas. Influenced by poststructuralist anthropology, New Historicism tried to take a multilayered impression or "thick description" of a culture at one moment in time, including popular as well as elite forms of representation. As a method, New Historicism belongs with those that deny the unity of the text, defy the authority of the source, and license the receiver—much like deconstructionism. Accordingly, New Historicism doubts the accessibility of the past; all we have is discourse. One model for New Historicism was the historiography of Michel Foucault, who as we have said insisted on the power of discourses, that is, not only writing but all structuring myths or ideologies that underlie social relations. The New Historicist, like Foucault, is interested in the transition from the external powers of the state and church in the feudal order to modern forms of power. The rule of the modern state and middle-class ideology is enforced insidiously by systems of surveillance and by each individual's internalization of discipline (not unlike Freud's idea of the superego).

No longer so "new," the New Historicists have had a lasting influence on a more narrative and concrete style of criticism even among those who espouse poststructuralist and Marxist theories. A New Historicist article begins with an anecdote, often a description of a public spectacle, and teases out the many contributing causes that brought disparate social elements together in that way. It usually applies techniques of close reading to forms that would not traditionally have received such attention. Although it often concentrates on events several hundred years ago, in some ways it defies historicity, flouting the idea that a complete objective impression of the entire context could ever be achieved.

Cultural Studies

Popular culture often gets major attention in the work of New Historicists. Yet today most studies of popular culture would acknowledge their debt instead to cultural studies, as filtered through the now-defunct Center for Contemporary Cultural Studies, founded in 1964 by Stuart Hall (b. 1932) and others at the University of Birmingham in England. Method, style, and subject matter may be similar in New Historicism and cultural studies: Both attend to historical context, theoretical method, political commitment, and textual analysis. But whereas the American movement shares Foucault's paranoid view of state domination through discourse, the British school, influenced by Raymond Williams and his concept of "structures of feeling," emphasizes the possibility that ordinary people, the receivers of cultural forms, may resist dominant ideology. The documents examined in a cultural-studies essay may be recent, such as artifacts of tourism at Shakespeare's birthplace rather than sixteenth-century maps. Cultural studies today influences history, sociology, communications and media, and literature departments; its studies may focus on television, film, romance novels, and advertising, or on museums and the art market, sports and stadiums, New Age religious groups, or other forms and practices.

The questions raised by cultural studies would encourage a critic to place a poem like Marge Piercy's "Barbie Doll" in the context of the history of that toy, a doll whose slender, impossibly long legs, tiptoe feet (not unlike the bound feet of Chinese women of an earlier era), small nose, and torpedo breasts epitomized a 1950s ideal for the female body. A critic influenced by cultural studies might align the poem with other works published around 1973 that express feminist protest concerning cosmetics, body image, consumption, and the objectification of women, while she or he would draw on research into the founding and marketing of Mattel toys. The poem reverses the Sleeping Beauty story: This heroine puts herself into the coffin rather than waking up. The poem omits any hero—Ken?—who would rescue her. "Barbie Doll" protests the pressure a girl feels to fit into a heterosexual plot of romance and marriage; no one will buy her if she is not the right toy or accessory.

Indeed, accessories such as "GE stoves and irons" (line 3) taught girls to plan their lives as domestic consumers, and Barbie's lifestyle is decidedly middle-class and suburban (everyone has a house, car, pool, and lots of handbags). The whiteness of the typical "girlchild" (line 1) goes without saying. Although Mattel produced Barbie's African American friend,

Christie, in 1968, Piercy's title makes the reader imagine Barbie, not Christie. In 1997 Mattel issued Share a Smile Becky, a friend in a wheelchair, as though in answer to the humiliation of the girl in Piercy's poem, who feels so deformed, in spite of her "strong arms and back, / abundant sexual drive and manual dexterity" (lines 8–9), that she finally cripples herself. The icon, in short, responds to changing ideology. Perhaps responding to generations of objections like Piercy's, Barbies over the years have been given feminist career goals, yet women's lives are still plotted according to physical image.

In this manner a popular product might be "read" alongside a literary work. The approach would be influenced by Marxist, feminist, gender, and racial studies, but it would not be driven by a desire to destroy Barbie as sinister, misogynist propaganda. Piercy's kind of protest against indoctrination has gone out of style. Girls have found ways to respond to such messages and divert them into stories of empowerment. Such at least is the outlook of cultural studies, which usually affirms popular culture. A researcher could gather data on Barbie sales and could interview girls or videotape their play, to establish the actual effects of the dolls. Whereas traditional anthropology examined non-European or preindustrial cultures, cultural studies may direct its "field work," or ethnographic research, inward, at home. Nevertheless, many contributions to cultural studies rely on methods of textual close reading or Marxist and Freudian literary criticism developed in the mid-twentieth century.

Postcolonial Criticism and Studies of World Literature

In the middle of the twentieth century, the remaining colonies of the European nations struggled toward independence. French-speaking Frantz Fanon (1925–61) of Martinique was one of the most compelling voices for the point of view of the colonized or exploited countries, which like the feminine Other had been objectified and denied the right to look and talk back. Edward Said (1935–2003), in *Orientalism* (1978), brought a poststructuralist analysis to bear on the history of colonization, illustrating the ways that Western culture feminized and objectified the East. Postcolonial literary studies developed into a distinct field in the 1990s in light of globalization and the replacement of direct colonial power with international corporations. In general this field cannot share the optimism of some cultural studies, given the histories of slavery and economic exploitation of colonies and the violence committed in the name of civilization's progress. Studies by Gayatri Chakravorty Spivak (b. 1942) and Homi K. Bhabha (b. 1949) have further mingled Marxist, feminist, and poststructuralist theory to reread both canonical Western works and the writings of people from beyond centers of dominant culture. Colonial or postcolonial literatures may include works set or published in countries during colonial rule or after independence, or they may feature texts produced in the context of international cultural exchange, such as a novel in English by a woman of Chinese descent writing in Malaysia.

Like feminist studies and studies of African American or other literatures, the field is inspired by recovery of neglected works, redress of a systematic denial of rights and recognition, and increasing realization that the dualisms of opposing groups reveal interdependence. In this field the stage of difference came early, with the celebrations of African heritage known as *Négritude*, but the danger of that essentialist claim was soon apparent: The Dark Continent or wild island might be romanticized and idealized as a source of innate qualities of vitality long repressed in Enlightened Europe. Currently, most critics accept that the context for literature in all countries is hybrid, with immigration and educational intermixing. Close readings of texts are always linked to the author's biography and literary influences and placed within the context of contemporary international politics as well as colonial history. Many fiction writers, from Salman Rushdie to Jhumpa Lahiri, make the theme of cultural mixture or hybridity part of their work, whether in a pastiche of Charles Dickens or a story of an Indian family growing up in New Jersey and returning as tourists to the supposed "native" land. Poststructuralist theories of trauma, and theories of the interrelation of narrative and memory, provide explanatory frames for interpreting writings from Afghanistan to Zambia.

Studies of postcolonial culture retain a clear political mission that feminist and Marxist criticism have found difficult to sustain. Perhaps this is because the scale of the power relations is so vast, between nations rather than the sexes or classes within those nations. Imperialism can be called an absolute evil, and the destruction of local cultures a crime against humanity. Today some of the most exciting literature in English emerges from countries once under the British Empire, and all the techniques of criticism will be brought to bear on it. If history is any guide, in later decades some critical school will attempt to read the diverse literatures of the early twenty-first century in pure isolation from authorship and national origin, as self-enclosed form. The themes of hybridity, indeterminacy, trauma, and memory will be praised as universal. It is even possible that readers' continuing desire to revere authors as creative geniuses in control of their meanings will regain respectability among specialists. The elements of the literary exchange—text, source, and receiver—are always there to provoke questions that generate criticism, which in turn produces articulations of the methods of that criticism. It is an ongoing discussion well worth participating in.

BIBLIOGRAPHY

For more in-depth introductions to these critical approaches, see the following books, from which we have drawn in our discussions and definitions. Some of these books provide bibliographies of the works of critics and schools discussed here.

Alter, Robert. *The Pleasure of Reading in an Ideological Age.* New York: Norton, 1996. Rpt. of *The Pleasures of Reading: Thinking about Literature in an Ideological Age.* 1989. Print.

Barnet, Sylvan, and William E. Cain. *A Short Guide to Writing about Literature.* 10th ed. New York: Longman, 2005. Print.

Barry, Peter. *Beginning Theory: An Introduction to Literary and Cultural Theory.* 2nd ed. Manchester: Manchester UP, 2002. Print.

Bressler, Charles E. *Literary Criticism: An Introduction to Theory and Practice.* 3rd ed. Upper Saddle River: Prentice, 2003. Print.

Culler, Jonathan. *Literary Theory: A Very Short Introduction.* Oxford: Oxford UP, 1997. Print.

Davis, Robert Con, and Ronald Schleifer. *Contemporary Literary Criticism: Literary and Cultural Studies.* 4th ed. New York: Addison, 1999. Print.

During, Simon. *Cultural Studies: A Critical Introduction.* New York: Routledge, 2005. Print.

——. *The Cultural Studies Reader.* New York: Routledge, 1999. Print.

Eagleton, Mary, ed. *Feminist Literary Theory: A Reader.* 2nd ed. Malden: Blackwell, 1996. Print.

Eagleton, Terry. *Literary Theory: An Introduction.* 2nd rev. ed. Minneapolis: U of Minnesota P, 1996. Print.

Groden, Michael, and Martin Kreiswirth. *The Johns Hopkins Guide to Literary Theory and Criticism.* Baltimore: Johns Hopkins UP, 1994. Print.

Hawthorn, Jeremy. *A Glossary of Contemporary Literary Theory.* 3rd ed. London: Arnold, 1998. Print.

Leitch, Vincent B. *American Literary Criticism from the Thirties to the Eighties.* New York: Columbia UP, 1989. Print.

——, et al. *The Norton Anthology of Theory and Criticism.* New York: Norton, 2001. Print.

Lentricchia, Frank. *After the New Criticism.* Chicago: U of Chicago P, 1981. Print.

Macksey, Richard, and Eugenio Donato, eds. *The Structuralist Controversy: The Languages of Criticism and the Sciences of Man.* 1972. Ann Arbor: Books on Demand, n.d. Print.

Moi, Toril. *Sexual-Textual Politics.* New York: Routledge, 1985. Print.

Murfin, Ross, and Supryia M. Ray. *The Bedford Glossary of Critical and Literary Terms.* Boston: Bedford, 1997. Print.

Piaget, Jean. *Structuralism.* Trans. and ed. Chaninah Maschler. New York: Basic, 1970. Print.

Selden, Raman, and Peter Widdowson. *A Reader's Guide to Contemporary Literary Theory.* 3rd ed. Lexington: U of Kentucky P, 1993. Print.

Todorov, Tzvetan. *Mikhail Bakhtin: The Dialogic Principle.* Trans. Wlad Godzich. Minneapolis: U of Minnesota P, 1984. Print.

Turco, Lewis. *The Book of Literary Terms.* Hanover: UP of New England, 1999. Print.

Veeser, Harold, ed. *The New Historicism.* New York: Routledge, 1989. Print.

———. *The New Historicism Reader.* New York: Routledge, 1994. Print.

Warhol, Robyn R., and Diane Price Herndl. *Feminisms.* 2nd ed. New Brunswick: Rutgers UP, 1997. Print.

Wolfreys, Julian. *Literary Theories: A Reader and Guide.* Edinburgh: Edinburgh UP, 1999. Print.

Glossary

Boldface words within definitions are themselves defined in the glossary.

action any event or series of events depicted in a literary work; an event may be verbal as well as physical, so that saying something or telling a story within the story may be an event. *See also* climax, complication, falling action, inciting incident, *and* rising action.

alexandrine a line of verse in iambic hexameter, often with a caesura after the third iambic foot.

allegory a literary work, whether in verse or prose, in which characters, action, and even aspects of setting signify (or serve as symbols for) a second, correlated order of concepts, persons, and actions. One of the most famous English-language allegories is John Bunyan's *Pilgrim's Progress*, in which a character named Christian has to make his way through obstacles such as the Slough of Despond to get to the Celestial City.

alliteration the repetition of usually initial consonant sounds through a sequence of words—for example, "While I nodded, nearly napping" in Edgar Allan Poe's "The Raven."

allusion a brief, often implicit and indirect reference within a literary text to something outside the text, whether another text (e.g., the Bible, a myth, another literary work, a painting, or a piece of music) or any imaginary or historical person, place, or thing. Many of the footnotes in this book explain allusions found in literary selections.

amphitheater a theater consisting of a stage area surrounded by a semicircle of tiered seats.

anapestic referring to a metrical form in which each foot consists of two unstressed syllables followed by a stressed one—for example, "There are mán- | y who sáy | that a dóg | has his dáy" (Dylan Thomas, "The Song of the Mischievous Dog"). A single foot of this type is called an *anapest*.

antagonist a character or a nonhuman force that opposes or is in conflict with the protagonist.

antihero a protagonist who is in one way or another the very opposite of a traditional hero. Instead of being courageous and determined, for instance, an antihero might be timid, hypersensitive, and indecisive to the point of paralysis. Antiheroes are especially common in modern literary works; examples might include the speaker of T. S. Eliot's "The Love Song of J. Alfred Prufrock" or the protagonist of Franz Kafka's *The Metamorphosis*.

archetype a character, ritual, symbol, or plot pattern that recurs in the myth and literature of many cultures; examples include the scapegoat or trickster (character type), the rite of passage (ritual), and the quest or descent into the underworld (plot pattern). The term and our contemporary understanding of it derive from the work of psychologist Carl Jung (1875-1961), who argued that archetypes emerge from—and give us a clue to the workings of—the "collective unconscious," a reservoir of memories and impulses that all humans share but aren't consciously aware of.

arena stage a stage design in which the audience is seated all the way around the acting area; actors make their entrances and exits through the auditorium.

assonance the repetition of vowel sounds in a sequence of words with different endings—for example, "The death of the poet was kept from his poems" in W. H. Auden's "In Memory of W. B. Yeats."

aubade a poem in which the coming of dawn is either celebrated, as in Billy Collins's "Morning," or denounced as a nuisance, as in John Donne's "The Sun Rising."

auditor an imaginary listener within a literary work, as opposed to the reader or audience outside the work.

author the *actual* or *real author* of a work is the historical person who actually wrote it and the focus of biographical criticism, which interprets a work by drawing on facts about the author's life and career. The *implied author*, or authorial **persona**, is the vision of the author's personality and outlook implied by the work as a whole. Thus when we make a claim about the author that relies solely on evidence from the work rather than from other sources, our subject is the implied author; for example, "In *Dubliners*, James Joyce heavily criticizes the Catholic church."

author time *see* **time.**

autobiography *see* **biography.**

ballad a verse **narrative** that is, or originally was, meant to be sung. Characterized by repetition and often by a refrain (a recurrent phrase or series of phrases), ballads were originally a folk creation, transmitted orally from person to person and age to age. An example is "Sir Patrick Spens."

ballad stanza a common **stanza** form, consisting of a quatrain that alternates four-**foot** and three-foot lines; lines 1 and 3 are unrhymed **iambic tetrameter** (four feet), and lines 2 and 4 are rhymed **iambic trimeter** (three feet), as in "Sir Patrick Spens."

bildungsroman literally, "education novel" (German), a **novel** that depicts the intellectual, emotional, and moral development of its **protagonist** from childhood into adulthood; also sometimes called an *apprenticeship novel*. This type of novel tends to envision character as the product of environment, experience, nurture, and education (in the widest sense) rather than of nature, fate, and so on. Charlotte Brontë's *Jane Eyre* is a famous example.

biography a work of **nonfiction** that recounts the life of a real person. If the person depicted in a biography is also its author, then we instead use the term *autobiography*. An autobiography that focuses only on a specific aspect of, or episode in, its author's life is a *memoir*.

blank verse the metrical verse form most like everyday human speech; blank verse consists of unrhymed lines in **iambic pentameter.** Many of Shakespeare's plays are in blank verse, as is William Wordsworth's "Lines Composed a Few Miles above Tintern Abbey."

caesura a short pause within a line of poetry; often but not always signaled by punctuation. Note the two caesuras in this line from Poe's "The Raven": "Once upon a midnight dreary, while I pondered, weak and weary."

canon the range of works that a consensus of scholars, teachers, and readers of a particular time and culture consider "great" or "major."

carpe diem literally, "seize the day" in Latin, a common **theme** of literary works that emphasize the brevity of life and the need to make the most of the present. Andrew Marvell's poem "To His Coy Mistress" is a well-known example.

central consciousness a character whose inner thoughts, perceptions, and feelings are revealed by a *third-person limited* **narrator** who does not reveal the thoughts, perceptions, or feelings of other characters.

character an imaginary personage who acts, appears, or is referred to in a literary work. *Major* or *main characters* are those that receive most attention, *minor characters* least. *Flat characters* are relatively simple, have a few dominant traits, and tend to be predictable. Conversely, *round characters* are complex and multifaceted and act in a way that readers might not expect but accept as possible. *Static characters* do not change; *dynamic characters* do. *Stock characters* represent familiar types that recur frequently in literary works, especially of a particular **genre** (e.g., the "mad scientist" of horror fiction and film or the fool in Renaissance, especially Shakespearean, drama).

characterization the presentation of a fictional personage. A term like "a good character" can, then, be ambiguous—it may mean that the personage is virtuous or that he or she is well presented regardless of his or her characteristics or moral qualities. In fiction, *direct characterization* occurs when a narrator explicitly tells us what a character is like. *Indirect characterization* occurs when a character's traits are revealed implicitly, through his or her speech, behavior, thoughts, appearance, and so on.

chorus a group of actors in a drama who comment on and describe the **action**. In classical Greek theater, members of the chorus often wore masks and relied on song, dance, and recitation to make their commentary.

classical unities as derived from Aristotle's *Poetics*, the three principles of structure that require a play to have one **plot** (*unity of action*) that occurs in one place (*unity of place*) and within one day (*unity of time*); also called the *dramatic unities*. Susan Glaspell's *Trifles* and Sophocles' *Antigone* observe the classical unities.

climax the third part of **plot**, the point at which the **action** stops rising and begins falling or reversing; also called *turning point* or (following Aristotle) *peripeteia*. See also **crisis**.

closet drama *see* drama.

colloquial diction *see* diction.

comedy a broad category of literary, especially dramatic, works intended primarily to entertain and amuse an audience. Comedies take many different forms, but they share three basic characteristics: (1) the values that are expressed and that typically cause **conflict** are determined by the general opinion of society (as opposed to being universal and beyond the control of humankind, as in **tragedy**); (2) **characters** in comedies are often defined primarily in terms of their social identities and roles and tend to be *flat* or *stock characters* rather than highly individualized or *round* ones; (3) comedies conventionally end happily with an act of social reintegration and celebration such as marriage. William Shake-speare's *A Midsummer Night's Dream* is a famous example.

The term *high* or *verbal comedy* may refer either to a particular type of comedy or to a sort of humor found within any literary work that employs subtlety and wit and usually represents high society. Conversely, *low* or *physical comedy* is a type of either comedy or humor that involves burlesque, horseplay, and the representation of unrefined life. See also **farce**.

coming-of-age story *see* initation story.

complication in plot, an **action** or event that introduces a new **conflict** or intensifies the existing one, especially during the **rising action** phase of plot.

conclusion also called *resolution*, the fifth and last phase or part of **plot**, the point at which the situation that was destabilized at the beginning becomes stable once more and the **conflict** is resolved.

concrete poetry poetry in which the words on the page are arranged to look like an object; also called *shaped verse*. George Herbert's "Easter Wings," for example, is arranged to look like two pairs of wings.

conflict a struggle between opposing forces. A conflict is *external* when it pits a **character** against something or someone outside himself or herself—another character or characters or something in nature or society. A conflict is *internal* when the opposing forces are two drives, impulses, or parts of a single character.

connotation what is suggested by a word, apart from what it literally means or how it is defined in the dictionary. *See also* **denotation**.

controlling metaphor *see* metaphor.

convention in literature, a standard or traditional way of presenting or expressing something, or a traditional or characteristic feature of a particular literary **genre** or subgenre. Division into lines and **stanzas** is a convention of poetry. Conventions of the type of poem known as the **epic** include a **plot** that begins *in medias res* and frequent use of **epithets** and extended **similes**.

cosmic irony *see* irony.

couplet two consecutive lines of verse linked by **rhyme** and **meter**; the meter of a *heroic couplet* is **iambic pentameter**.

crisis in **plot**, the moment when the conflict comes to a head, often requiring the character to make a decision; sometimes the crisis is equated with the **climax** or *turning point* and sometimes it is treated as a distinct moment that precedes and prepares for the climax.

criticism *see* **literary criticism**.

cycle *see* **sequence**.

dactylic referring to the metrical pattern in which each **foot** consists of a stressed syllable followed by two unstressed ones—for example, "Fláshed all their/ sábres bare" (Tennyson, "Charge of the Light Brigade"). A single foot of this type is called a *dactyl*.

denotation a word's direct and literal meaning, as opposed to its **connotation**.

dénouement literally, "untying" (as of a knot) in French; a **plot**-related term used in three ways: (1) as a synonym for **falling action**, (2) as a synonym for **conclusion** or resolution, and (3) as the label for a phase following the conclusion in which any loose ends are tied up.

descriptive poem/structure a poem organized as a description of someone or something.

destabilizing event *see* **inciting incident**.

deus ex machina literally, "god out of the machine" (Latin); any improbable, unprepared-for plot contrivance introduced late in a literary work to resolve the **conflict**. The term derives from the ancient Greek theatrical practice of using a mechanical device to lower a god or gods onto the stage to resolve the conflicts of the human characters.

dialogue (1) usually, words spoken by **characters** in a literary work, especially as opposed to words that come directly from the **narrator** in a work of fiction; (2) more rarely, a literary work that consists mainly or entirely of the speech of two or more characters; examples include Thomas Hardy's poem "The Ruined Maid" and Plato's treatise *Republic*.

diction choice of words. Diction is often described as either *informal* or *colloquial*

if it resembles everyday speech, or as *formal* if it is instead lofty, impersonal, and dignified. **Tone** is determined largely through diction.

discriminated occasion a specific, discrete moment portrayed in a fictional work, often signaled by phrases such as "At 5:05 in the morning...," "It was about dusk, one evening during the supreme madness of the carnival season...," or "the day before Maggie fell down...."

discursive poem/structure a poem structured like a treatise, argument, or essay.

drama a literary **genre** consisting of works in which **action** is performed and all words are spoken before an audience by an actor or actors impersonating the **characters**. (Drama typically lacks the **narrators** and **narration** found in fiction.) *Closet drama*, however, is a subgenre of drama that has most of these features yet is intended to be read, either silently by a single reader or out loud in a group setting. As its name suggests, *verse drama* is drama written in verse rather than prose.

dramatic irony *see* **irony**.

dramatic monologue a type or subgenre of poetry in which a **speaker** addresses a silent **auditor** or auditors in a specific situation and setting that is revealed entirely through the speaker's words; this kind of poem's primary aim is the revelation of the speaker's personality, views, and values. For example, T. S. Eliot's "The Love Song of J. Alfred Prufrock" consists of a middle-aged man's words to the unidentified person who is about to accompany him to an evening social event; most of Robert Browning's best-known poems, such as "My Last Duchess," are dramatic monologues.

dramatic poem/structure a poem structured so as to present a **scene** or series of scenes, as in a work of drama, though the term *dramatic poem* is usually not applied to *verse drama*. *See also* **dramatic monologue**.

dramatic unities *see* **classical unities**.

dramatis personae literally, "persons of the drama" (Latin); the list of **characters** that appears either in a play's program or at the top of the first page of the written play.

dynamic character *see* character.

elegy (1) since the Renaissance, usually a formal lament on the death of a particular person, but focusing mainly on the speaker's efforts to come to terms with his or her grief; (2) more broadly, any lyric in sorrowful mood that takes death as its primary subject. An example is W. H. Auden's "In Memory of W. B. Yeats."

end-stopped line a line of verse that contains or concludes a complete clause and usually ends with a punctuation mark. *See also* enjambment.

English sonnet *see* sonnet.

enjambment in poetry, the technique of running over from one line to the next without stop, as in the following lines by William Wordsworth: "My heart leaps up when I behold / A rainbow in the sky." The lines themselves would be described as *enjambed*.

epic a long poem that celebrates, in a continuous narrative, the achievements of mighty heroes and heroines, usually in founding a nation or developing a culture, and uses elevated language and a grand, high style. Other epic conventions include a beginning in medias res, an invocation of the muse, a journey to the underworld, battle scenes, and a scene in which the hero arms himself for battle. Examples include *Beowulf* and Homer's *Iliad*. A *mock epic* is a form of satire in which epic language and conventions are used to depict characters, actions, and settings utterly unlike those in conventional epics, usually (though not always) with the purpose of ridiculing the social milieu or types of people portrayed in the poem. A famous example is Alexander Pope's *The Rape of the Lock*.

epigram a very short, usually witty verse with a quick turn at the end.

epigraph a quotation appearing at the beginning of a literary work or of one section of such a work; not to be confused with epigram.

epilogue (1) in fiction, a short section or chapter that comes after the conclusion, tying up loose ends and often describing what happens to the characters after the resolution of the conflict; (2) in drama, a short speech, often addressed directly to the audience, delivered by a character at the end of a play.

epiphany a sudden revelation of truth, often inspired by a seemingly simple or commonplace event. The term, originally from Christian theology, was first popularized by the Irish fiction writer James Joyce, though Joyce also used the term to describe the individual short stories collected in his book *Dubliners*.

episode a distinct action or series of actions within a plot.

epistolary novel *see* novel.

epithet a characterizing word or phrase that precedes, follows, or substitutes for the name of a person or thing, such as *slain civil rights leader* Martin Luther King Jr., or Zeus, *the god of trophies* (Sophocles, *Antigone*); not to be confused with epitaph.

epitaph an inscription on a tombstone or grave marker; not to be confused with epigram, epigraph, or epithet.

eponymous having a name used in the title of a literary work. For example, Lemuel Gulliver is the eponymous protagonist of Jonathan Swift's *Gulliver's Travels*.

exposition the first phase or part of plot, which sets the scene, introduces and identifies characters, and establishes the situation at the beginning of a story or play. Additional exposition is often scattered throughout the work.

extended metaphor *see* metaphor.

external conflict *see* conflict.

external narration or narrator *see* narrator.

fable an ancient type of short fiction, in verse or prose, illustrating a moral or satirizing human beings. The characters in a fable are often animals that talk and act like human beings. The fable is sometimes treated as a specific type of folktale and sometimes as a fictional subgenre in its own right. An example is Aesop's "The Two Crabs."

fairy tale *see* tale.

falling action the fourth of the five phases or parts of plot, in which the

conflict or conflicts move toward resolution.

fantasy a genre of literary work featuring strange settings and characters and often involving magic or the supernatural; though closely related to horror and science fiction, fantasy is typically less concerned with the macabre or with science and technology. J. R. R. Tolkien's *The Hobbit* is a well-known example.

farce a literary work, especially drama, characterized by broad humor, wild antics, and often slapstick, pratfalls, or other physical humor. *See also* comedy.

fiction any narrative, especially in prose, about invented or imagined characters and action. Today, we tend to divide fiction into three major subgenres based on length—the short story, novella, and novel. Older, originally oral forms of short fiction include the fable, legend, parable, and tale. Fictional works may also be categorized not by their length but by their handling of particular elements such as plot and character. Detective and science fiction, for example, are subgenres that include both novels and novellas such as Frank Herbert's *Dune* and short stories such as Edgar Allan Poe's "The Murders at the Rue Morgue" or Isaac Asimov's "I, Robot." *See also* gothic fiction, historical fiction, nonfiction, and romance.

figurative language language that uses figures of speech.

figure of speech any word or phrase that creates a "figure" in the mind of the reader by effecting an obvious change in the usual meaning or order of words, by comparing or identifying one thing with another; also called *tropes*. Metaphor, simile, metonymy, overstatement, oxymoron, and understatement are common figures of speech.

first-person narrator *see* narrator.

flashback a plot-structuring device whereby a scene from the fictional past is inserted into the fictional present or is dramatized out of order.

flashforward a plot-structuring device whereby a scene from the fictional future is inserted into the fictional present or is dramatized out of order.

flat character *see* character.

focus the visual component of point of view, the point from which people, events, and other details in a story are viewed; also called *focalization*. *See also* voice.

foil a character that serves as a contrast to another.

folktale *see* tale.

foot the basic unit of poetic meter, consisting of any of various fixed patterns of one to three stressed and unstressed syllables. A foot may contain more than one word or just one syllable of a multisyllabic word. In scansion, breaks between feet are usually indicated with a vertical line or slash mark, as in the following example (which contains five feet): "One com- | mon note | on ei- | ther lyre | did strike" (Dryden, "To the Memory of Mr. Oldham"). *For specific examples of metrical feet, see* anapestic, dactylic, iambic, spondee, *and* trochaic.

foreshadowing a hint or clue about what will happen at a later moment in the plot.

formal diction *see* diction.

frame narrative *see* narrative.

free verse poetry characterized by varying line lengths, lack of traditional meter, and nonrhyming lines.

Freytag's pyramid a diagram of plot structure first created by the German novelist and critic Gustav Freytag (1816–95).

general setting *see* setting.

genre a type or category of works sharing particular formal or textual features and conventions; especially used to refer to the largest categories for classifying literature—fiction, poetry, drama, and nonfiction. A smaller division within a genre is usually known as a *subgenre*, such as gothic fiction or epic poetry.

gothic fiction a subgenre of fiction conventionally featuring plots that involve secrets, mystery, and the supernatural (or the seemingly supernatural) and large, gloomy, and usually antiquated (especially medieval) houses as settings. Examples include Horace Walpole's *The Castle of Otranto* and Edgar Allan Poe's "The Fall of the House of Usher."

haiku a poetic form, Japanese in origin, that consists of seventeen syllables arranged in three unrhymed lines of five, seven, and five syllables, respectively.

hero/heroine a character in a literary work, especially the leading male/female character, who is especially virtuous, usually larger than life, sometimes almost godlike. *See also* antihero, protagonist, and villain.

heroic couplet *see* couplet.

hexameter a line of poetry with six feet: "She comes, | she comes | again, | like ring | dove frayed | and fled" (Keats, *The Eve of St. Agnes*). *See* alexandrine.

high (verbal) comedy *see* comedy.

historical fiction a subgenre of fiction, of whatever length, in which the temporal setting, or plot time, is significantly earlier than the time in which the work was written (typically, a period before the birth of the author). Conventionally, such works describe the atmosphere and mores of the setting in vivid detail and explore the influence of historical factors on the characters and action; though focusing mainly on invented or imaginary characters and events, historical fiction sometimes includes some characters and action based on actual historical personages and events. The *historical novel* is a type of historical fiction of which nineteenth-century Scottish writer Walter Scott pioneered in works such as *Rob Roy* and *Ivanhoe*.

hyperbole *see* overstatement. (*See also* understatement.)

iambic referring to a metrical form in which each foot consists of an unstressed syllable followed by a stressed one; this type of foot is an *iamb*. The most common poetic meter in English is *iambic pentameter*—a metrical form in which most lines consist of five iambs: "One cóm- | mon nóte | on éi- | ther lýre | did stríke" (Dryden, "To the Memory of Mr. Oldham").

image/imagery broadly defined, imagery is any sensory detail or evocation in a work; more narrowly, the use of figurative language to evoke a feeling, to call to mind an idea, or to describe an object. Imagery may be described as *auditory*, *tactile*, *visual*, or *olfactory* depending on which sense it primarily appeals to—hearing, touch, vision, or smell. An *image* is a particular instance of imagery.

imitative poem/structure a poem structured so as to mirror as exactly as possible the structure of something that already exists as an object and can be seen.

implied author *see* author.

inciting incident an action that sets a plot in motion by creating conflict; also called *destabilizing event*.

informal diction *see* diction.

initiation story a kind of short story in which a character—often a child or young person—first learns a significant, usually life-changing truth about the universe, society, people, or himself or herself; also called a *coming-of-age story*. James Joyce's "Araby" is a notable example.

in medias res "in the midst of things" (Latin); refers to opening a plot in the middle of the action, and then filling in past details by means of exposition or flashback.

interior monologue *see* monologue.

internal conflict *see* conflict.

internal narration or narrator *see* narrator.

intrusive narration or narrator *see* narrator.

irony a situation or statement characterized by a significant difference between what is expected or understood and what actually happens or is meant. *Verbal irony* occurs when a word or expression in context means something different from, and usually the opposite of, what it appears to mean; when the intended meaning is harshly critical or satiric, verbal irony becomes *sarcasm*. *Situational irony* occurs when a character holds a position or has an expectation that is reversed or fulfilled in an unexpected way. When there is instead a gap between what an audience knows and what a character believes or expects, we have *dramatic irony*; when this occurs in a tragedy, dramatic irony is sometimes called *tragic irony*. Finally, the terms *cosmic irony* and *irony of fate* are sometimes used to refer to situations in which situational irony is the result of fate, chance, the gods, or some other superhuman force or entity.

Italian sonnet *see* sonnet.

legend a type of tale conventionally set in the real world and in either the present or historical past, based on actual historical people and events, and offering an exaggerated or distorted version of the truth about those people and events. American examples might include stories featuring Davy Crockett or Johnny Appleseed or the story about George Washington chopping down the cherry tree. British examples are the legends of King Arthur or Robin Hood.

limerick a light or humorous verse form consisting of mainly anapestic lines of which the first, second, and fifth are of three feet; the third and fourth lines are of two feet; and the rhyme scheme is *aabba*.

limited narrator *see* narrator.

limited point of view *see* point of view.

literary criticism the mainly interpretive (versus evaluative) work written by readers of literary texts, especially professional ones (who are thus known as *literary critics*). It is "criticism" not because it is negative or corrective but rather because those who write criticism ask probing, analytical, "critical" questions about the works they read.

litotes a form of understatement in which one negates the contrary of what one means. Examples from common speech include "Not bad" (meaning "good") and "a novelist of no small repute" (meaning "a novelist with a big reputation"), and so on.

low (physical) comedy *see* comedy.

lyric originally, a poem meant to be sung to the accompaniment of a lyre; now, any relatively short poem in which the **speaker** expresses his or her thoughts and feelings in the first person rather than recounting a **narrative** or portraying a dramatic situation.

magic realism a type of **fiction** that involves the creation of a fictional world in which the kind of familiar, plausible **action** and **characters** one might find

in more straightforwardly realist fiction coexist with utterly fantastic ones straight out of **myths** or dreams. This style of **realism** is associated especially with modern Latin American writers such as Gabriel García Márquez and Jorge Luis Borges. But the label is also sometimes applied to works by other contemporary writers from around the world, including Italo Calvino and Salman Rushdie.

major (main) character *see* character.

memoir *see* biography.

metafiction a subgenre of works that playfully draw attention to their status as **fiction** in order to explore the nature of fiction and the role of authors and readers. Margaret Atwood's "Happy Endings" is an example.

metaphor sometimes, a general term for almost any figure of speech involving comparison; more commonly, a particular **figure of speech** in which two unlike things are compared implicitly—that is, without the use of a signal such as the word *like* or *as*—as in "Love is a rose, but you better not pick it." *See also* simile.

An *extended metaphor* is a detailed and complex metaphor that stretches across a long section of a work. If such a metaphor is so extensive that it dominates or organizes an entire literary work, especially a poem, it is called a *controlling metaphor*. In Linda Pastan's "Marks," for example, the controlling metaphor involves the use of "marks" or grades to talk about the speaker's performance of her familial roles. A *mixed metaphor* occurs when two or more usually incompatible metaphors are entangled together so as to become unclear and often unintentionally humorous, as in "Her blazing words dripped all over him."

meter the more or less regular pattern of stressed and unstressed syllables in a line of poetry. This is determined by the kind of **foot** (iambic or dactylic, for example) and by the number of feet per line (e.g., five feet = pentameter, six feet = hexameter).

metonymy a figure of speech in which the name of one thing is used to refer to another thing associated with it. When we say, "The White House has promised to veto the bill," for example, we use the White House as a metonym for the president and his administration. **Synecdoche** is a specific type of metonymy.

minor character *see* **character.**

mock epic *see* **epic.**

monologue (1) a speech of more than a few sentences, usually in a play but also in other **genres**, spoken by one person and uninterrupted by the speech of anyone else, or (2) an entire work consisting of this sort of speech. In fiction, an *interior monologue* takes place entirely within the mind of a character rather than being spoken aloud. A **soliloquy** is a particular type of monologue occurring in drama, while a **dramatic monologue** is a type of poem.

moral a rule of conduct or a maxim for living (that is, a statement about how one should live or behave) communicated in a literary work. Though **fables** often have morals such as "Don't count your chickens before they hatch," more modern literary works instead tend to have **themes.**

motif a recurrent device, formula, or situation within a literary work. For example, the sound of the breaking harp string is a motif of Anton Chekhov's play *The Cherry Orchard.*

myth (1) originally and narrowly, a **narrative** explaining how the world and humanity developed into their present form and, unlike a folktale, generally considered to be true by the people who develop it. Many, though not all, myths feature supernatural beings and have a religious significance or function within their culture of origin. Two especially common types of myth are the *creation myth*, which explains how the world, human beings, a god or gods, or good and evil came to be (e.g., the myth of Adam and Eve), and the *explanatory myth*, which explains features of the natural landscape or natural processes or events (e.g., "How the Leopard Got His Spots"); (2) more broadly and especially in its adjectival form (*mythic*), any narrative that obviously seeks to work like a myth in the first and more narrow

sense, especially by portraying experiences or conveying truths that it implies are universally valid regardless of culture or time.

narration (1) broadly, the act of telling a story or recounting a **narrative**; (2) more narrowly, the portions of a narrative attributable to the **narrator** rather than words spoken by **characters** (that is, **dialogue**).

narrative a story, whether fictional or true and in prose or verse, related by a **narrator** or narrators (rather than acted out onstage, as in drama). A *frame narrative* is a narrative that recounts the telling of another narrative or story that thus "frames" the inner or framed narrative. An example is Samuel Taylor Coleridge's "The Rime of the Ancient Mariner," in which an anonymous third-person narrator recounts how an old sailor comes to tell a young wedding guest the story of his adventures at sea.

narrative poem/structure a poem that tells a story.

narrator someone who recounts a **narrative** or tells a story. Though we usually instead use the term **speaker** when referring to poetry as opposed to prose fiction, *narrative poems* include at least one speaker who functions as a narrator. *See also* **narrative.**

A narrator or narration is said to be *internal* when the narrator is a **character** within the work, telling the story to an equally fictional **auditor** or listener; internal narrators are usually first- or second-person narrators (*see below*). A narrator or narration is instead said to be *external* when the narrator is not a character.

A *first-person narrator* is an internal narrator who consistently refers to himself or herself using the first-person pronoun *I* (or, infrequently, *we*). A *second-person narrator* consistently uses the second-person pronoun *you* (a very uncommon technique). A *third-person narrator* uses third-person pronouns such as *she, he, they, it,* and so on; third-person narrators are almost always external narrators. Third-person narrators are said to be *omniscient* (literally, "all-knowing") when they describe the inner thoughts and feelings of multiple characters; they are said to be *limited* when they relate the thoughts, feelings, and perceptions of only one character (the central consciousness). If a work encourages us to view a narrator's account of events with suspicion, the narrator (usually first-person) is called *unreliable*. An *intrusive narrator* is a third-person narrator who occasionally disrupts his or her narrative to speak directly to the reader or audience in what is sometimes called *direct address*.

narrator time *see* time.

nonfiction a work or genre of prose works that describe actual, as opposed to imaginary or fictional, characters and events. Subgenres of nonfiction include biography, memoir, and the essay. *See also* fiction.

novel a long work of fiction (approximately 40,000+ words), typically published (or at least publishable) as a stand-alone book; though most novels are written in prose, those written as poetry are called *verse novels*. A novel (as opposed to a short story) conventionally has a complex plot and, often, at least one subplot, as well as a fully realized setting and a relatively large number of characters. One important novelistic subgenre is the *epistolary novel*—a novel composed entirely of letters written by its characters. Another is the bildungsroman.

novella a work of prose fiction that falls somewhere in between a short story and a novel in terms of length, scope, and complexity. Novellas can be, and have been, published either as books in their own right or as parts of books that include other works. Franz Kafka's *The Metamorphosis* is an example.

octameter a line of poetry with eight feet: "Once u- | pon a | midnight | dreary | while I | pondered | weak and | weary."

octave eight lines of verse linked by a pattern of end rhymes, especially the first eight lines of an Italian, or Petrarchan, sonnet. *See also* sestet.

ode a lyric poem characterized by a serious topic and formal tone but without a prescribed formal pattern. Examples

include Keats's odes and Shelley's "Ode to the West Wind."

oeuvre all of the works verifiably written by one author.

omniscient narrator *see* narrator.

omniscient point of view *see* point of view.

onomatopoeia a word capturing or approximating the sound of what it describes; *buzz* is a good example.

orchestra in classical Greek theater, a semicircular area used mostly for dancing by the chorus.

ottava rima literally, "octave (eighth) rhyme" (Italian); a verse form consisting of eight-line stanzas with an *ababbcc* rhyme scheme and iambic meter (usually pentameter). W. B. Yeats's "Sailing to Byzantium" is written in ottava rima.

overplot especially in Shakespearean drama, a subplot that resembles the main plot but stresses the political implications of the depicted action and situation.

overstatement exaggerated language; also called *hyperbole*.

oxymoron a figure of speech that combines two apparently contradictory elements, as in *wise fool*.

parable a short work of fiction that illustrates an explicit moral but that, unlike a fable, lacks fantastic or anthropomorphic characters. Especially familiar examples are the stories attributed to Jesus in the Bible—about the prodigal son, the good Samaritan, and so on.

parody any work that imitates or spoofs another work or genre for comic effect by exaggerating the style and changing the content of the original; parody is a subgenre of satire. Examples include *Scary Movie*, which parodies horror films; *The Colbert Report*, which spoofs conservative talk shows; and Tom Stoppard's *Real Inspector Hound*, a parody of both detective fiction and drama.

particular setting *see* setting.

pastoral literature a work or category of works—whether fiction, poetry, drama, or nonfiction—describing and idealizing the simple life of country folk, usually shepherds who live a painless life in a world full of beauty, music, and love. An example is Christopher Marlowe's "The Passionate Shepherd to His Love."

pentameter a line of poetry with five feet: "Nuns fret | not at | their con- | vent's nar- | row room."

persona the voice or figure of the author who tells and structures the story and who may or may not share the values of the actual author; also called *implied author.*

personification a figure of speech that involves treating something nonhuman, such as an abstraction, as if it were a person by endowing it with human-like qualities, as in "Death entered the room."

Petrarchan sonnet *see* sonnet.

plot the arrangement of the action. The five main parts or phases of plot are exposition, rising action, climax or turning point, falling action, and conclusion or resolution. *See also* subplot, overplot.

plot summary a brief recounting of the principal action of a work of fiction, drama, or narrative poetry, usually in the same order in which the action is recounted in the original work rather than in chronological order.

plot time *see* time.

poetry one of the three major genres of imaginative literature, which has its origins in music and oral performance and is characterized by controlled patterns of rhythm and syntax (often using meter and rhyme); compression and compactness and an allowance for ambiguity; a particularly concentrated emphasis on the sensual, especially visual and aural, qualities and effects of words and word order; and especially vivid, often figurative language.

point of view the perspective from which people, events, and other details in a work of fiction are viewed; also called focus, though the term *point of view* is sometimes used to include both focus and voice. The point of view is said to be *limited* when we see things only from one character's perspective; it is said to be *omniscient* or *unlimited* when we get the perspective of multiple characters.

prop in drama, an object used on the stage.

proscenium arch an arch over the front of a stage; the proscenium serves as a "frame" for the action onstage.

prose the regular form of spoken and written language, measured in sentences rather than lines, as in poetry.

protagonist the most neutral and broadly applicable term for the main character in a work, whether male or female, heroic or not heroic. *See also* antagonist, antihero, and hero/heroine.

psychological realism *see* realism.

quatrain a four-line unit of verse, whether an entire poem, a stanza, or a group of four lines linked by a pattern of rhyme (as in an English or Shakespearean sonnet).

reader time *see* time.

realism (1) generally, the practice in literature, especially fiction and drama, of attempting to describe nature and life as they are without idealization and with attention to detail, especially the everyday life of ordinary people. *See also* verisimilitude.

Just as notions of how life and nature differ widely across cultures and time periods, however, so do notions of what is "realistic." Thus, there are many different kinds of realism. *Psychological realism* refers, broadly, to any literary attempt to accurately represent the workings of the human mind and, more specifically, to the practice of a particular group of late-nineteenth- and early-twentieth-century writers including Joseph Conrad, Henry James, James Joyce, and Virginia Woolf, who developed the stream of consciousness technique of depicting the flow of thought. *See also* magic realism.

(2) more narrowly and especially when capitalized, a mid- to late- nineteenth-century literary and artistic movement, mainly in the U.S. and Europe, that championed realism in the first, more general sense, rejected what its proponents saw as the elitism and idealism of earlier literature and art, and emphasized settings, situations, action, and (especially middle- and working-class) characters ignored or belittled in earlier

literature and art. Writers associated with the movement include Gustave Flaubert and Emile Zola (in France), George Eliot and Thomas Hardy (in Britain), and Theodore Dreiser (in the United States).

reflective (meditative) poem/structure a poem organized primarily around reflection on a subject or event and letting the mind play with it, skipping from one thought or object to another as the mind receives them.

resolution *see* conclusion.

rhetoric the art and scholarly study of effective communication, whether in writing or speech. Many literary terms, especially those for figures of speech, derive from classical and Renaissance rhetoric.

rhyme repetition or correspondence of the terminal sounds of words ("How now, brown cow?"). The most common type, *end rhyme*, occurs when the last words in two or more lines of a poem rhyme with each other. *Internal rhyme* occurs when a word *within* a line of poetry rhymes with another word in the same or adjacent lines, as in "The Dew drew quivering and chill" (Dickinson). An *eye rhyme* or *sight rhyme* involves words that don't actually rhyme but look like they do because of their similar spelling ("cough" and "bough"). *Off, half, near,* or *slant rhyme* is rhyme that is slightly "off" or only approximate, usually because words' final consonant sounds correspond, but not the vowels that proceed them ("phases" and "houses"). When two syllables rhyme and the last is unstressed or unaccented, they create a *feminine rhyme* ("ocean" and "motion"); *masculine rhyme* involves only a single stressed or accented syllable ("cat" and "hat"). *See also* rhyme scheme.

rhyme scheme the pattern of end rhymes in a poem, often noted by small letters, such as *abab* or *abba*.

rhythm the modulation of weak and strong (or stressed and unstressed) elements in the flow of speech. In most poetry written before the twentieth century, rhythm was often expressed in meter; in prose and in free verse, rhythm is present but in a much less predictable and regular manner.

rising action the second of the five phases or parts of plot, in which events complicate the situation that existed at the beginning of a work, intensifying the initial conflict or introducing a new one.

romance (1) originally, a long medieval narrative in verse or prose written in one of the Romance languages (French, Spanish, Italian, etc.) and depicting the quests of knights and other chivalric heroes and the vicissitudes of courtly love; also known as *chivalric romance*; (2) later and more broadly, any literary work, especially a long work of prose fiction, characterized by a nonrealistic and idealizing use of the imagination; (3) commonly today, works of prose fiction aimed at a mass, primarily female, audience and focusing on love affairs (as in *Harlequin Romance*).

round character *see* character.

sarcasm *see* irony.

satire a literary work—whether fiction, poetry, or drama—that holds up human failings to ridicule and censure. Examples include Jonathan Swift's novel *Gulliver's Travels* and Stanley Kubrick's film *Dr. Strangelove*.

scansion the process of analyzing (and sometimes also marking) verse to determine its meter, line by line.

scene a section or subdivision of a play or narrative that presents continuous action in one specific setting.

second-person narrator *see* narrator.

sequence (1) the ordering of action in a fictional plot; (2) a closely linked series or cycle of individual literary works, especially short stories or poems, designed to be read or performed together, as in the sonnet sequences of William Shakespeare and Edna St. Vincent Millay.

sestet six lines of verse linked by a pattern of rhyme, as in the last six lines of the Italian, or Petrarchan, sonnet. *See also* octave.

sestina an elaborate verse structure written in blank verse that consists of six stanzas of six lines each followed by a three-line stanza. The final words of each line in the first stanza appear in variable order in the next five stanzas and are repeated in the middle and at the end of the three lines in the final stanza. Elizabeth Bishop's "Sestina" is an example.

set the design, decoration, and scenery of the stage during a play; not to be confused with **setting**.

setting the time and place of the **action** in a work of fiction, poetry, or drama. The *spatial setting* is the place or places in which action unfolds, the *temporal setting* is the time. (Temporal setting is thus the same as *plot* **time**.) It is sometimes also helpful to distinguish between *general setting*—the general time and place in which all the action unfolds—and *particular settings*—the times and places in which individual **episodes** or **scenes** take place. The film version of *Gone with the Wind*, for example, is generally set in Civil War–era Georgia, while its opening scene takes place on the porch of Tara, Scarlett O'Hara's family home, before the war begins.

Shakespearean sonnet *see* sonnet.

shaped verse *see* concrete poetry.

short story a relatively short work of prose fiction (approximately 500 to 10,000 words) that, according to Edgar Allan Poe, can be read in a single sitting of two hours or less and works to create "a single effect." Two types of short story are the **initiation story** and the *short short story*. (Also sometimes called *microfiction*, a short short story is, as its name suggests, a short story that is especially brief; examples include Linda Brewer's "20/20" and Jamaica Kincaid's "Girl.")

simile a **figure of speech** involving a direct, explicit comparison of one thing to another, usually using the words *like* or *as* to draw the connection, as in "My love is like a red, red rose." An *analogy* is an extended simile. *See also* **metaphor**.

situation the basic circumstances depicted in a literary work, especially when the story, play, or poem begins or at a specific later moment in the **action**. In John Keats's "Ode to a Nightingale," for example, the situation involves a man (the **speaker**) sitting under a tree as he listens to a nightingale's song.

situational irony *see* irony.

skene a low building in the back of the stage area in classical Greek theaters. It represented the palace or temple in front of which the **action** took place.

soliloquy a **monologue** in which the **character** in a play is alone onstage and thinking out loud, as in the famous Hamlet speech that begins "To be or not to be."

sonnet a fixed verse form consisting of fourteen lines usually in **iambic pentameter**. An *Italian sonnet* consists of eight rhyme-linked lines (an **octave**) plus six rhyme-linked lines (a **sestet**), often with either an *abbaabba cdecde* or *abbacddc defdef* **rhyme scheme**. This type of sonnet is also called the *Petrarchan sonnet* in honor of the Italian poet Petrarch (1304–74). An *English* or *Shakespearean sonnet* instead consists of three **quatrains** (four-line units) and a **couplet** and often rhymes *abab cdcd efef gg*.

spatial setting *see* setting.

speaker (1) the person, not necessarily the author, who is the voice of a poem; (2) anyone who speaks **dialogue** in a work of fiction, poetry, or drama.

Spenserian stanza a stanza consisting of eight lines of **iambic pentameter** (five feet) followed by a ninth line of iambic **hexameter** (six feet). The rhyme scheme is *ababbcbcc*. The stanza form takes its name from Edmund Spenser (ca. 1552–99), who used it in *The Faerie Queene*.

spondee a metrical **foot** consisting of a pair of stressed syllables ("Déad sét").

stage directions the words in the printed text of a play that inform the director, crew, actors, and readers how to stage, perform, or imagine the play. Stage directions are not spoken aloud and may appear at the beginning of a play, before any scene, or attached to a line of dialogue; they are often set in italics. The place and time of the action, the design of the set itself, and at times the characters' actions or tone of voice are given through stage directions and interpreted by the group of people who put on a performance.

stanza a section of a poem, marked by extra line spacing before and after, that often has a single pattern of **meter** and/or **rhyme**. Conventional stanza types include **ballad stanza**, **Spenserian stanza**, **ottava rima**, and **terza rima**. *See also* **verse paragraph**.

static character *see* **character**.

stock character *see* **character**.

stream of consciousness a type of third-person **narration** that replicates the thought processes of a **character** without much or any intervention by a **narrator**. The term was originally coined by the nineteenth-century American psychologist William James (brother of novelist Henry James) to describe the workings of the human mind and only later adopted to describe the type of narration that seeks to replicate this process. The technique is closely associated with twentieth-century fiction writers of *psychological realism* such as Virginia Woolf, James Joyce, and William Faulkner, who were all heavily influenced by early psychologists such as William James and Sigmund Freud.

style a distinctive manner of expression; each author's style is expressed through his or her **diction**, **rhythm**, **imagery**, and so on.

subgenre *see* **genre**.

subplot a secondary **plot** in a work of fiction or drama. *See also* **overplot** and **underplot**.

symbol a person, place, thing, or event that figuratively represents or stands for something else. Often the thing or idea represented is more abstract and general, and the symbol is more concrete and particular. A *traditional symbol* is one that recurs frequently in (and beyond) literature and is thus immediately recognizable to those who belong to a given culture. In Western literature and culture, for example, the rose and snake traditionally symbolize love and evil, respectively. Other symbols such as the scarlet letter in Nathaniel Hawthorne's *The Scarlet Letter* instead accrue their complex meanings only within a particular literary work; these are sometimes called *invented symbols*.

symbolic poem a poem in which the use of symbols is so pervasive and internally

consistent that the reference to the outside world being symbolized becomes secondary. William Blake's "The Sick Rose" is an example.

synecdoche a type of **metonymy** in which the part is used to name or stand in for the whole, as when we refer to manual laborers as *hands* or say *wheels* to mean a car.

syntax word order; the way words are put together to form phrases, clauses, and sentences.

tale a brief **narrative** with a simple **plot** and **characters**, an ancient and originally oral form of storytelling. Unlike **fables**, tales typically don't convey or state a simple or single **moral**. An especially common type of tale is the *folktale*, the **conventions** of which include a formulaic beginning and ending ("Once upon a time . . . ," ". . . And so they lived happily ever after."); a **setting** that is not highly particularized in terms of time or place; *flat* and often *stock characters*, animal or human; and fairly simple **plots**. Though the term *fairy tale* is often and broadly used as a synonym for *folktale*, it more narrowly and properly designates a specific type of folktale featuring fairies or other fantastic creatures such as pixies or ogres.

temporal setting *see* **setting**.

terza rima literally, "third rhyme" (Italian); a verse form consisting of three-line **stanzas** in which the second line of each stanza rhymes with the first and third of the next. Percy Bysshe Shelley's "Ode to the West Wind" is written in terza rima.

tetrameter a line of poetry with four **feet**: "The Grass | divides | as with | a comb" (Dickinson).

theme (1) broadly and commonly, a topic explored in a literary work (e.g., "the value of all life"); (2) more narrowly, the insight about a topic communicated in a work (e.g., "All living things are equally precious"). Most literary works have multiple themes, though some people reserve the term *theme* for the central or main insight and refer to others as *subthemes*. Usually, a theme is implicitly communicated by the work as a whole rather than explicitly stated in it, though **fables** are an exception. *See also* **moral**.

thesis the central debatable claim articulated, supported, and developed in an essay or other work of expository prose.

third-person narrator *see* **narrator**.

thrust stage a stage design that allows the audience to sit around three sides of the major acting area.

time in literature, at least four potentially quite different time frames are at issue: (1) *author time*, when the author originally created or published a literary text; (2) *narrator time*, when the **narrator** in a work of fiction supposedly narrated the story; (3) *plot time*, when the **action** depicted in the work supposedly took place (in other words, the work's temporal **setting**); and (4) *reader* (or *audience*) *time*, when an actual reader reads the work or an actual audience sees it performed.

In some cases, author, narrator, plot, and reader time will be roughly the same—as when, for example, in 2008 we read Sherman Alexie's "Flight Patterns," a story published in 2003; set some time after September 11, 2001; and presumably narrated not long after the action ends. But in some cases, some or all of these time frames might differ. Walter Scott's novel *Rob Roy*, for example, was written and published in the early nineteenth century (1817); this is its author time. But the novel (a work of **historical fiction**) is set one hundred years earlier (1715); this is its plot time. The novel's narrator is a **character** supposedly writing down the story of his youthful adventures in his old age and long after the deaths of many of the principal characters; this is the narrator time. Were you to read the novel today, reader time would be almost two hundred years later than author time and almost three hundred years later than plot time.

tone the attitude a literary work takes toward its subject, especially the way this attitude is revealed through **diction**.

traditional symbol *see* **symbol**.

tragedy a work, especially of drama, in which a **character** (traditionally a good and noble person of high rank) is brought to a disastrous end in his or her confron-

tation with a superior force (fortune, the gods, human nature, universal values), but also comes to understand the meaning of his or her deeds and to accept an appropriate punishment. Often the **protagonist**'s downfall is a direct result of a fatal flaw in his or her character. Examples include Sophocles' *Antigone*, William Shakespeare's *Hamlet*.

trimeter a line of poetry with three **feet**: "Little | lamb, who | made thee?" (Blake).

trochaic referring to a metrical form in which the basic **foot** is a *trochee*—a metrical foot consisting of a stressed syllable followed by an unstressed one ("Hómer").

trope *see* **figure of speech**.

turning point *see* **climax**.

underplot a particular type of **subplot**, especially in Shakespeare's plays, that is a parodic or highly romantic version of the main plot. A good example would be the subplot in *A Midsummer Night's Dream* that centers on the character Bottom. *See also* **overplot**.

understatement language that makes it point by self-consciously downplaying its real emphasis, as in "Final exams aren't exactly a walk in the park"; **litotes** is one form of understatement. *See also* **overstatement**.

unity of action *see* **classical unities**.

unity of place *see* **classical unities**.

unity of time *see* **classical unities**.

unlimited point of view *see* **point of view**.

unreliable narrator *see* **narrator**.

verbal irony *see* **irony**.

verisimilitude from the Latin phrase *veri similes* ("like the truth"); the internal truthfulness, lifelikeness, and consistency of the world created within any literary work when we judge that world on its own terms rather than in terms of its correspondence to the real world. Thus, even a work that contains utterly fantastic or supernatural **characters** or **actions** (and doesn't aim at **realism**) may very well achieve a high degree of verisimilitude.

verse drama *see* **drama**.

verse novel *see* **novel**.

verse paragraph though sometimes used as a synonym for **stanza**, this term technically designates passages of verse, often beginning with an indented line, that are unified by topic (as in a prose paragraph) rather than by **rhyme** or **meter.**

villain a **character** who not only opposes the **hero** or **heroine** (and is thus an **antagonist**) but also is characterized as an especially evil person or "bad guy."

villanelle a verse form consisting of nineteen lines divided into six **stanzas**—five tercets (three-line stanzas) and one quatrain (four-line stanza). The first and third lines of the first tercet rhyme with each other, and this rhyme is repeated through each of the next four tercets and in the last two lines of the concluding **quatrain.** The villanelle is also known for its repetition of select lines. An example is Dylan Thomas's "Do Not Go Gentle into That Good Night."

voice the verbal aspect of **point of view,** the acknowledged or unacknowledged source of a story's words; the **speaker;** the "person" telling the story and that person's particular qualities of insight, attitude, and verbal style. *See also* **focus.**

Permissions Acknowledgments

Texts

FICTION

JAMES BALDWIN: "Sonny's Blues" copyright © 1957 by James Baldwin was originally published in *Partisan Review*. Copyright renewed. Collected in *Going to Meet the Man*, published by Vintage Books. Reprinted by arrangement with the James Baldwin Estate.

TONI CADE BAMBARA: "Gorilla, My Love," from *Gorilla, My Love* by Toni Cade Bambara, copyright © 1960, 1963, 1964, 1965, 1968, 1970, 1971, 1972 by Toni Cade Bambara. Used by permission of Random House, Inc.

LINDA BREWER: "20/20" from *Micro Fiction: An Anthology of Really Short Stories*, ed. by Jerome Stern. Reprinted by permission of the author.

RAYMOND CARVER: "Cathedral" from *Cathedral* by Raymond Carver, copyright © 1981, 1982, 1983 by Raymond Carver. Used by permission of Alfred A. Knopf, a division of Random House, Inc.

EDWIDGE DANTICAT: "A Wall of Fire Rising" from *Krik? Krak!* by Edwidge Danticat, copyright © 1955 used by permission of Soho Press, Inc. All rights reserved.

LOUISE ERDRICH: "Love Medicine" from *Love Medicine* (new and expanded version) by Louise Erdrich. Copyright © 1984, 1993 by Louise Erdrich. Reprinted by arrangement with Henry Holt and Company, LLC.

WILLIAM FAULKNER: "A Rose for Emily" from *Collected Stories of William Faulkner* (New York: Random House, 1950). Reprinted by permission.

GABRIEL GARCIA MARQUEZ: "A Very Old Man With Enormous Wings" from *Leaf Storm and Other Stories* by Gabriel Garcia Marquez, trans. by Gregory Rabassa. Copyright © 1971 by Gabriel Garcia Marquez. Reprinted by permission of HarperCollins Publishers.

ERNEST HEMINGWAY: "Hills Like White Elephants" is reprinted with the permission of Scribner, a division of Simon & Schuster, Inc., from *Men Without Women* by Ernest Hemingway. Copyright © 1927 by Charles Scribner's Sons. Copyright © renewed 1955 by Ernest Hemingway.

HA JIN: "In Broad Daylight" was originally published in *The Kenyon Review*. Reprinted by permission of the author.

JAMES JOYCE: "Araby" from *Dubliners* by James Joyce, copyright © 1916 by B.W. Heubsch. Definitive text copyright © 1967 by the Estate of James Joyce. Used by permission of Viking Penguin, a division of Penguin Group (USA) Inc.

FRANZ KAFKA: "A Hunger Artist" from *Franz Kafka: The Complete Stories* by Franz Kafka, edited by Nahum N. Glatzer, copyright 1946, 1947, 1948, 1949, 1954, 1958, 1971 by Schocken Books. Used by permission of Schocken Books, a division of Random House, Inc.

YASUNARI KAWABATA: "The Grasshopper and the Bell Cricket" from *Palm-of-the-Hand Stories* by Yasunari Kawabata. Translated by Lane Dunlop and J. Martin Holman. Translation copyright © 1988 by Lane Dunlop and J. Martin Holman. Reprinted by permission of North Point Press, a division of Farrar, Straus & Giroux, LLC.

JAMAICA KINCAID: "Girl" from *At the Bottom of the River* by Jamaica Kincaid. Copyright © 1983 by Jamaica Kincaid. Reprinted by permission of Farrar, Straus & Giroux, LLC.

D.H. LAWRENCE: "The Rocking-Horse Winner," copyright 1933 by the Estate of D.H. Lawrence, renewed © 1961 by Angelo Ravagli and C.M. Weekley, Executors of the Estate of Frieda Lawrence, from *Complete Short Stories of D.H. Lawrence* by D.H. Lawrence. Used by permission of Viking Penguin, a division of Penguin Group (USA) Inc.

POETRY

DRAMA

Illustrations

FICTION: **p. 3**, "Speed Bump" used with the permission of Dave Coverly and the Cartoonist Group. All rights reserved; **p. 56**, no credit; **p. 62**, Doonesbury ©1985 G. B. Trudeau. Reprinted with permission of Universal Uclick. All rights reserved; **p. 121**, Getty Images/The Bridgeman Art Library; **p. 145**, Christopher Felver/Corbis; **p. 162**, Bettmann/Corbis; **p. 212**, iStockphoto; Michael Brown/Dreamstime; Dreamstime; www.chinesenames.org; **p. 300**, no credit; **p. 425**, Hulton Archive/Getty Images; Sophie Bassouls/Corbis; Courtesy of Vintage/RandomHouse © Joyce Middler; **p. 426**, Bettmann/Corbis; Courtesy of Linda Brewer; Sophie Bassouls/Corbis; Corbis; **p. 427**, Granger Collection; Bettmann/Corbis; AP Photos; **p. 428**, AP Photos; Bettmann/Corbis; Colita/Corbis; **p. 429**, Corbis; Reuters/Corbis; Imagno/Getty Images; **p. 430**, Corbis; John Springer Collection/Corbis; Hulton-Deutsch Collection/Corbis; Bettmann/Corbis; **p. 431**, Bettmann/Corbis; Jeremy Bembaron/Corbis; University of Nottingham library, D.H. Lawrence Collection. Reprinted by permission of the University of Nottingham; **p. 432**, Courtesy of Viking/Penguin; (2) Bettmann/Corbis; Christopher Felver/Corbis; **p. 433**, Photograph by Ralph Morrissey. Reprinted by the courtesy of the Morrissey Collection and the Photographic Archives, Vanderbilt University, Nashville, Tennessee; (2) Bettmann/Corbis; **p. 434**, Christopher Felver/Corbis; Sean Gallup/Getty Images; Nancy Kaszerman/ZUMA/Corbis; **p. 435**, Bettmann/Corbis; Francine Fleischer/Corbis.

POETRY: **p. 468**, Tooga/The Image Bank/Getty Images; **p. 489**, Ariel Skelley/Corbis; Horace Bristol/Corbis; Corbis; **p. 510**, AP Photos; **p. 538**, Rosemary Woods/Illustration Works/Corbis; **p. 542**, Christopher Felver/Corbis; **p. 555**, Pach Brothers/Corbis; **p. 607**, John Cohen/Getty Images; Frank Driggs Collection/Getty Images; Redferns/Getty Images; **p. 729**, Corbis; Bettmann/Corbis; AP Photos; **p. 730**, (4): Bettmann/Corbis; **p. 731**, AP Photos; Oscar White/Corbis; (2): Bettmann/Corbis; **p. 732**, Fred Viebahn; Corbis; E.O. Hoppe/Corbis; **p. 733**, Christopher Felver/Corbis; Granger Collection; Corbis; Pach Brothers/Corbis; **p. 734**, Bettmann/Corbis; Portrait by Joseph Severn. Reprinted by courtesy of the National Portrait Gallery, London; Christopher Felver/Corbis; **p. 735**; **p. 736**, Mary Evans Pictures; Corbis; Underwood & Underwood/Corbis; Stefano Bianchetti/Corbis; **p. 736**, Cheron Bayna; Bettmann/Corbis; Christopher Felver/Corbis; AP Photos; **p. 737**, Margaretta K. Mitchell; Courtesy of the Sylvia Plath Collection, Mortimer Rare Book Room, Smith College; E.O. Hoppe/Corbis; Copyright by Jason Langer, photographer. Reprinted by permission; **p. 738**, Bettmann/Corbis; Chris Hellier/Corbis; Bettmann/Corbis; **p. 739**, Bettmann/Corbis; Hulton-Deutsch Collection/Corbis; Christopher Felver/Corbis; Warder Collection; **p. 740**, Oscar White/Corbis; Pach Brothers/Corbis; Hulton-Deutsch Collection/Corbis; **p. 741**, Bettmann/Corbis.

DRAMA: **p. 879**, Romare Bearden, *Piano Lesson, 1983* Collage of various papers with paint, ink, and graphite on paper. Art © Romare Bearden Foundation/Licensed by VAGA, New York, NY; **p. 948**, AP Photos; **p. 951**, Bettmann/Corbis; **p. 1022**, Bettmann/Corbis; **p. 1165**, Image courtesy of The Advertising Archives; **p. 1239**, AP Photos; (2): Bettmann/Corbis; **p. 1240**, Chris Hellier/Corbis; Christopher Felver/Corbis; Bettmann/Corbis; **p. 1241**, Bettmann/Corbis; AP Photos.

Index of Authors

Aesop
  The Two Crabs, 246
Ali, Agha Shahid
  Postcard from Kashmir,
  543
Angelou, Maya
  Africa, 540
Anonymous
  *The Elephant in the Village
  of the Blind*, 16
Anonymous
  Sir Patrick Spens, 624
Anonymous
  [*There was a young girl
  from St. Paul*], 598
Anonymous
  The Twenty-third Psalm,
  570
Arnold, Matthew
  Dover Beach, 517
Atwood, Margaret
  *Death of a Young Son by
  Drowning*, 500
Auden, W. H.
  In Memory of W. B. Yeats,
  656
  Musée des Beaux Arts, 655
  [*Stop all the clocks, cut off
  the telephone*], 470

Baca, Jimmy Santiago
  Green Chile, 492
Baldwin, James
  Sonny's Blues, 75
Bambara, Toni Cade
  Gorilla, My Love, 294
Behn, Aphra
  *On Her Loving Two
  Equally*, 452
Bernstein, Charles
  Of Time and the Line, 547

Betjeman, John
  In Westminster Abbey,
  518
Bierce, Ambrose
  *An Occurrence at Owl
  Creek Bridge*, 299
Bishop, Elizabeth
  Sestina, 638
Blake, William
  The Chimney Sweeper
  (from *Songs of Experi-
  ence*), 660
  The Chimney Sweeper
  (from *Songs of Inno-
  cence*), 659
  The Lamb, 658
  London, 483
  The Sick Rose, 581
  The Tyger, 658
Borson, Roo
  After a Death, 586
Bradstreet, Anne
  *To My Dear and Loving
  Husband*, 471
Brewer, Linda
  20/20, 19
Brontë, Charlotte
  from *Jane Eyre*, 126
Brontë, Emily
  The Night-Wind, 529
Brooks, Gwendolyn
  First Fight. Then Fiddle.,
  647
  We Real Cool, 509
Browning, Elizabeth
  Barrett
  How Do I Love Thee?, 439
  [*When our two souls stand
  up*], 650
Browning, Robert
  My Last Duchess, 660

  *Soliloquy of the Spanish
  Cloister*, 501
Burns, Robert
  A Red, Red Rose, 568
  To a Louse, 507

Calvino, Italo
  from *Invisible Cities*, 160
Campion, Thomas
  *When to Her Lute Corinna
  Sings*, 608
Carver, Raymond
  Cathedral, 32
Chasin, Helen
  The Word Plum, 587
Chekhov, Anton
  The Lady with the Dog,
  165
Cherry, Kelly
  Alzheimer's, 493
Chopin, Kate
  The Story of an Hour, 306
Cleghorn, Sara
  [*The golf links lie so near
  the mill*], 545
Clover, Joshua
  The Nevada Glassworks,
  531
Coleridge, Samuel Taylor
  Kubla Khan, 662
  Metrical Feet, 596
Collins, Billy
  Morning, 536
  Sonnet, 653
Constable, Henry
  [*My lady's presence makes
  the roses red*], 643
Crane, Stephen
  The Open Boat, 250
Cullen, Countee
  Yet Do I Marvel, 663

Danticat, Edwidge
  A Wall of Fire Rising, 232
De La Mare, Walter
  Slim Cunning Hands, 548
Dickey, James
  Cherrylog Road, 521
  The Leap, 575
Dickinson, Emily
  [*After great pain, a formal
    feeling comes—*], 668
  [*Because I could not stop
    for Death—*], 664
  [*I dwell in Possibility—*],
    554
  [*I stepped from Plank to
    Plank*], 665
  [*My Life had stood—a
    Loaded Gun—*], 667
  [*She dealt her pretty words
    like Blades—*], 666
  [*The Brain—is wider than
    the Sky—*], 666
  [*The Wind begun to knead
    the Grass—*], 627
  [*We do not play on Graves*],
    665
  [*Wild Nights—Wild
    Nights!*], 667
Donne, John
  [*Batter my heart, three-
    personed God*], 571
  The Canonization, 571
  [*Death, be not proud*],
    669
  The Flea, 526
  The Good-Morrow, 535
  Song, 669
  The Sun Rising, 472
  *A Valediction: Forbidding
    Mourning*, 670
Dove, Rita
  Daystar, 514
  *Fifth Grade Autobiogra-
    phy*, 447
Dryden, John
  *To the Memory of Mr. Old-
    ham*, 599
Dunbar, Paul Laurence
  Sympathy, 671
  We Wear the Mask, 672

Dylan, Bob
  Mr. Tambourine Man, 611
Eliot, T. S.
  *The Love Song of J. Alfred
    Prufrock*, 672
Erdrich, Louise
  Love Medicine, 275

Faulkner, William
  A Rose for Emily, 308
Fearing, Kenneth
  Dirge, 588
Ferry, David
  At the Hospital, 573
Finch, Anne, Countess of
    Winchelsea
  There's No To-morrow,
    546
Frost, Robert
  Design, 648
  Fireflies in the Garden, 583
  Home Burial, 678
  Range-Finding, 648
  The Road Not Taken, 677
  *Stopping by Woods on a
    Snowy Evening*, 677

Gilman, Charlotte Perkins
  The Yellow Wallpaper, 315
Glaspell, Susan
  Trifles, 748
Gray, Thomas
  *Elegy Written in a Country
    Churchyard*, 681
Grimké, Angelina
  Tenebris, 685
Grimm, Jacob and
    Wilhelm
  The Little Shroud, 63
Gunn, Thom
  In Time of Plague, 478

Hansberry, Lorraine
  A Raisin in the Sun, 950
Hardy, Thomas
  The Ruined Maid, 496
Harper, Michael
  Dear John, Dear Coltrane,
    610

Harwood, Gwen
  In the Park, 652
Hawthorne, Nathaniel
  The Birth-Mark, 218
Hayden, Robert
  Frederick Douglass, 686
  *Homage to the Empress of
    the Blues*, 610
  Those Winter Sundays,
    491
  The Whipping, 685
Heaney, Seamus
  Digging, 687
  Mid-Term Break, 450
  Punishment, 688
Hemingway, Ernest
  Hills Like White Elephants,
    113
Hopkins, Gerard Manley
  God's Grandeur, 689
  Pied Beauty, 557
  Spring and Fall, 604
  The Windhover, 690
Hudgins, Andrew
  Begotten, 494
Hughes, Langston
  Harlem, 690
  *The Negro Speaks of
    Rivers*, 691

Ibsen, Henrik
  A Doll House, 821

Jarrell, Randall
  *The Death of the Ball
    Turret Gunner*, 573
Jin, Ha
  In Broad Daylight, 146
Jonson, Ben
  [*Come, my Celia, let us
    prove*], 691
  On My First Son, 445
Joyce, James
  Araby, 328

Kafka, Franz
  A Hunger Artist, 333
Kawabata, Yasunara
  *The Grasshopper and the
    Bell Cricket*, 341

Keats, John
  Ode on a Grecian Urn, 694
  Ode to a Nightingale, 692
  On First Looking into
    Chapman's Homer, 4
  On Seeing the Elgin Mar-
    bles, 647
  On the Grasshopper and the
    Cricket, 646
  On the Sonnet, 645
Kennedy, X. J.
  In a Prominent Bar in
    Secaucus One Day, 498
Kincaid, Jamaica
  Girl, 118
Kinnell, Galway
  After Making Love We
    Hear Footsteps, 490
  Blackberry Eating, 696
Knight, Etheridge
  Hard Rock Returns to
    Prison from the Hospital
    for the Criminal Insane,
    479
Kumin, Maxine
  Woodchucks, 484

Lawrence, D. H.
  I Am Like a Rose, 580
  The Rocking Horse Winner,
    343
Lee, Li-Young
  Persimmons, 557
Lowell, Robert
  Skunk Hour, 697

MacLeish, Archibald
  Ars Poetica, 639
Marlowe, Christopher
  The Passionate Shepherd to
    His Love, 698
Márquez, Gabriel García
  A Very Old Man with
    Enormous Wings, 269
Marvell, Andrew
  The Garden, 699
  On a Drop of Dew, 563
  To His Coy Mistress, 527
Mason, Bobbie Ann
  Shiloh, 355

Maupassant, Guy de
  The Jewelry, 69
McKay, Claude
  The Harlem Dancer, 701
  The White House, 702
Melville, Herman
  Bartleby, the Scrivener,
    367
Millay, Edna St. Vincent
  [What lips my lips have
    kissed], 651
  [When I consider how my
    light is spent], 650
  [Women have loved before
    as I love now], 473
Milton, John
  On the Late Massacre in
    Piedmont, 516
Mitchell, Margaret
  from Gone with the Wind,
    161
Moore, Marianne
  Poetry, 637
Mora, Pat
  Elena, 702
  Gentle Communion, 703
  Sonrisas, 620
Morrison, Toni
  Recitatif, 130

Nemerov, Howard
  The Goose Fish, 618
  The Vacuum, 445

O'Connor, Flannery
  A Good Man Is Hard to
    Find, 396
Olds, Sharon
  Sex without Love, 552
  The Victims, 622
Owen, Wilfred
  Dulce et Decorum Est,
    574

Parker, Dorothy
  A Certain Lady, 504
  One Perfect Rose, 580
Pastan, Linda
  love poem, 441
  Marks, 567

To a Daughter Leaving
  Home, 515
Piercy, Marge
  Barbie Doll, 476
Plath, Sylvia
  Daddy, 704
  Lady Lazarus, 706
  Morning Song, 536
  Point Shirley, 530
Poe, Edgar Allan
  The Cask of Amontillado,
    107
  The Raven, 600
Pope, Alexander
  Sound and Sense, 589
Porter, Katherine Anne
  Flowering Judas, 179
Pound, Ezra
  In a Station of the Metro,
    709
  The River-Merchant's Wife:
    A Letter, 469
  A Virginal, 709

Raleigh, Sir Walter
  [The Nymph's Reply to the
    Shepherd], 709
Ramsay, Jarold
  The Tally Stick, 440
Randall, Alice
  from The Wind Done
    Gone, 163
Randall, Dudley
  Ballad of Birmingham,
    640
Ransom, John Crowe
  Bells for John Whiteside's
    Daughter, 710
Rich, Adrienne
  Aunt Jennifer's Tigers, 485
  Diving into the Wreck, 583
  History, 712
  Storm Warnings, 711
Robinson, Edwin
  Arlington
    Mr. Flood's Party, 615
Roethke, Theodore
  My Papa's Waltz, 550
Rosenberg, Liz
  Married Love, 443

Rossetti, Christina
In an Artist's Studio, 651
Rossetti, Dante Gabriel
*A Sonnet Is a Moment's
Monument*, 645

Satrapi, Marjane
from *Persepolis*, 24
Sexton, Anne
The Fury of Overshoes,
448
Shakespeare, William
[*Full many a glorious
morning have I seen*],
533
Hamlet, 1024
[*Let me not to the marriage
of true minds*], 472
[*Like as the waves make
towards the pebbled
shore*], 604
[*My mistress' eyes are noth-
ing like the sun*], 653
[*Not marble, nor the gilded
monuments*], 713
[*Shall I compare thee to a
summer's day?*], 569
Spring, 609
[*That time of year thou
mayest in me behold*],
565
[*Th' expense of spirit in a
waste of shame*], 627
Shelley, Percy Bysshe
Ode to the West Wind, 628
Snodgrass, W. D.
Leaving the Motel, 477
Sophocles
Antigone, 1129

Stevens, Wallace
Anecdote of the Jar, 714
The Emperor of Ice-Cream,
713
Stoppard, Tom
The Real Inspector Hound,
759
Suckling, Sir John
Song, 599

Tan, Amy
A Pair of Tickets, 189
Tennyson, Alfred Lord
from *The Charge of the
Light Brigade*, 598
Tears, Idle Tears, 714
Ulysses, 715
Thomas, Dylan
*Do Not Go Gentle into
That Good Night*, 636
Fern Hill, 717

Updike, John
A & P, 409

Walcott, Derek
A Far Cry from Africa,
541
Midsummer, 533
Waller, Edmund
Song, 579
Welty, Eudora
Why I Live at the P.O., 414
Wheatley, Phillis
*On Being Brought from
Africa to America*, 539
Whitman, Walt
*Facing West from Califor-
nia's Shores*, 719

[*I celebrate myself, and sing
myself*], 510
I Hear America Singing,
719
A Noiseless Patient Spider,
720
Wilbur, Richard
The Beautiful Changes,
562
*Love Calls Us to the Things
of This World*, 720
Wilde, Oscar
Symphony in Yellow, 561
Williams, Tennessee
A Streetcar Named Desire,
1165
Williams, William Carlos
The Dance, 626
The Red Wheelbarrow,
554
This Is Just to Say, 555
Wilson, August
The Piano Lesson, 879
Wordsworth, William
*Lines Written a Few Miles
above Tintern Abbey*,
721
London, 1802, 649
Nuns Fret Not, 643
*She Dwelt among the
Untrodden Ways*, 506
Yeats, W. B.
The Lake Isle of Innisfree,
725
Leda and the Swan, 726
Sailing to Byzantium,
727
The Second Coming, 726

Index of Titles and First Lines

1-2-3 was the number he played but today the number came 3-2-1, 588

20/20 (Brewer), 19

A & P (Updike), 409

About suffering they were never wrong, 655

Africa (Angelou), 540

After a Death (Borson), 586

[After great pain, a formal feeling comes—] (Dickinson), 668

After Making Love We Hear Footsteps (Kinnell), 490

A little black thing among the snow, 660

All we need is fourteen lines, well, thirteen now, 653

Alzheimer's (Cherry), 493

[A narrow Fellow in the Grass] (Dickinson), 605

Anecdote of the Jar (Stevens), 714

A Noiseless Patient Spider, 720

An omnibus across the bridge, 561

Antigone (Sophocles), 1129

A poem should be palpable and mute, 639

Araby (Joyce), 328

Ars Poetica (MacLeish), 639

A single flow'r he sent me, since we met, 580

A Sonnet Is a Moment's Monument (Rossetti), 645

A sudden blow: the great wings beating still, 726

As virtuous men pass mildly away, 670

At the Hospital (Ferry), 573

Aunt Jennifer's Tigers (Rich), 485

Aunt Jennifer's tigers prance across a screen, 485

Avenge, O Lord, thy slaughtered saints, whose bones, 516

A wind is ruffling the tawny pelt, 541

Ballad of Birmingham (Randall), 640

Barbie Doll (Piercy), 476

Bartleby, the Scrivener (Melville), 367

[Batter my heart, three-personed God] (Donne), 571

The Beautiful Changes (Wilbur), 562

[Because I could not stop for Death—] (Dickinson), 664

Because there was a man somewhere in a candystripe silk shirt, 610

Begotten (Hudgins), 494

Bells for John Whiteside's Daughter (Ransom), 710

Bent double, like old beggars under sacks, 574

Between my finger and my thumb, 687

Birth-Mark, The (Hawthorne), 218

Blackberry Eating (Kinnell), 696

Busy old fool, unruly son, 472

But most by numbers judge a poet's song, 589

Call the roller of big cigars, 713

Canonization, The (Donne), 571

Cask of Amontillado, The (Poe), 107

Cathedral (Carver), 32

Certain Lady, A (Parker), 504

Certain things here are quietly American, 533

Charge of the Light Brigade, The (Tennyson), 598

Cherrylog Road (Dickey), 521

Chimney Sweeper, The (from Songs of Experience) (Blake), 660

Chimney Sweeper, The (from Songs of Innocence) (Blake), 659

Come live with me and be my love, 698

[Come, my Celia, let us prove] (Jonson), 691

Daddy (Plath), 704

Dance, The (Williams), 626

Daystar (Dove), 514
Dear John, Dear Coltrane (Harper), 610
[*Death, be not proud*] (Donne), 669
Death of a Young Son by Drowning (Atwood), 500
Death of the Ball Turret Gunner, The (Jarrell), 573
Design (Frost), 648
Digging (Heaney), 687
Dirge (Fearing), 588
Diving into the Wreck (Rich), 583
Doll House, A (Ibsen), 821
Do Not Go Gentle into That Good Night (Thomas), 636
Dover Beach (Arnold), 517
Dulce et Decorum Est (Owen), 574

Elegy Written in a Country Churchyard (Gray), 681
Elena (Mora), 702
Elephant in the Village of the Blind, The (Anonymous), 16
Emperor of Ice-Cream, The (Stevens), 713
Even the long-dead are willing to move, 703

Facing West from California's Shores (Whitman), 719
Far Cry from Africa, A (Walcott), 541
Farewell, thou child of my right hand, and joy, 445
Farewell, too little, and too lately known, 599
Fern Hill (Thomas), 717
Fifth Grade Autobiography (Dove), 447
Fireflies in the Garden (Frost), 583
First Fight. Then Fiddle. (Keats), 647
First fight. Then fiddle. Ply the slipping string, 647
First having read the book of myths, 583
Five years have passed; five summers, with the length, 721
Flea, The (Donne), 526
Flowering Judas (Porter), 179
For God's sake hold your tongue and let me love, 571
For I can snore like a bullhorn, 490
Frederick Douglass (Hayden), 686
From my mother's sleep I fell into the State, 573

[*Full many a glorious morning have I seen*] (Shakespeare), 533
Fury of Overshoes, The (Sexton), 448

Garden, The (Marvell), 699
Gassing the woodchucks didn't turn out right, 484
Gentle Communion (Mora), 703
George Burns likes to insist that he always, 547
Girl (Kincaid), 118
Glory be to God for dappled things, 557
Go, and catch a falling star, 669
God's Grandeur (Hopkins), 689
Go! lovely rose, 579
Gone with the Wind (Mitchell), 161
Good Man Is Hard to Find, A (O'Connor), 396
Good-Morrow, The (Donne), 535
Goose Fish, The (Nemerov), 618
Gorilla, My Love (Bambara), 294
Grasshopper and the Bell Cricket, The (Kawabata), 341
Green Chile (Baca), 492
Gr-r-r—there go, my heart's abhorrence, 501

Had we but world enough, and time, 527
Half a league, half a league, 598
Hamlet (Shakespeare), 1024
Hard Rock Returns to Prison from the Hospital for the Criminal Insane (Knight), 479
Hard Rock was "known not to take no shit, 478
Harlem (Hughes), 690
Ha! whare ya gaun, ye crowlan ferlie, 507
Harlem Dancer, The (McKay), 701
He disappeared in the dead of winter, 656
Here come real stars to fill the upper skies, 583
Here from the start, from our first of days, look, 440
He saw her from the bottom of the stairs, 678
He stands at the door, a crazy old man, 493
He, who navigated with success, 500
Hey! Mr Tambourine Man, play a song for me, 611

Hills Like White Elephants (Hemingway), 113

History (Rich), 712

Homage to the Empress of the Blues (Hayden), 610

Home Burial (Frost), 678

How Do I Love Thee? (Browning), 439

How do I love thee? Let me count the ways, 439

How do they do it, the ones who make love, 552

How strongly does my passion flow, 452

How vainly men themselves amaze, 699

Hunger Artist, A (Kafka), 333

I Am Like a Rose (Lawrence), 580

I am myself at last; now I achieve 580,

I can feel the tug, 688

I caught this morning morning's minion, king, 690

[*I celebrate myself, and sing myself*] (Whitman), 510

I doubt not God is good, well-meaning, kind, 663

[*I dwell in Possibility—*] (Dickinson), 554

If by dull rhymes our English must be chained, 645

If ever two were one, then surely we, 471

I found a dimpled spider, fat and white, 648

I have done it again, 706

I have eaten, 555

I Hear America Singing (Whitman), 719

I hear American singing, the varied carols I hear, 719

I know what the caged bird feels, alas, 671

I live in a doorway, 620

I love to go out in late September, 696

In an Artist's Studio (Rossetti), 651

In a Prominent Bar in Secaucus One Day (Kennedy), 498

In a Station of the Metro (Pound), 709

In Broad Daylight (Jin), 146

In Brueghel's great picture, The Kermess, 626

In Memory of W. B. Yeats (Auden), 656

In sixth grade Mrs. Walker, 557

In summer's mellow midnight, 529

In the Park (Harwood), 652

In Time of Plague (Gunn), 478

Invisible Cities (Calvino), 160

In Westminster Abbey (Betjeman), 518

In Xanadu did Kubla Khan, 662

I placed a jar in Tennessee, 714

I prefer red chile over my eggs, 492

I sat all morning in the college sick bay, 450

[*I stepped from Plank to Plank*] (Dickinson), 665

I've known rivers, 691

I've never, as some children do, 494

I was four in this photograph fishing, 447

I will arise and go now, and go to Innisfree, 725

I wonder, by my troth, what thou and I, 535

Jane Eyre (Brontë), 126

Jewelry, The (de Maupassant), 69

Ka-Boom! They're making glass in Nevada, 531

Kashmir shrinks into my mailbox, 543

Kubla Khan (Coleridge), 662

Lady Lazarus (Plath), 706

Lady with the Dog, The (Chekhov), 165

Lake Isle of Innisfree, The (Yeats), 725

Lamb, The (Blake), 658

Leap, The (Dickey), 575

Leaving the Motel (Snodgrass), 477

Leda and the Swan (Yeats), 726

[*Let me not to the marriage of true minds*] (Shakespeare), 472

Let me take this other glove off, 518

Let us go then, you and I, 672

[*Like as the waves make towards the pebbled shore*] (Shakespeare), 604

Lines Written a Few Miles above Tintern Abbey (Wordsworth), 721

Little Lamb, who made thee, 658

Little Shroud, The (Grimm), 63

London (Blake), 483

London (Wordsworth), 1802, 649

Love Calls Us to the Things of This World (Wilbur), 720

Love Medicine (Erdrich), 275

love poem (Pastan), 441

Love set you going like a fat gold watch, 536

Love Song of J. Alfred Prufrock, The (Eliot), 672

Márgárét, áre you grieving, 604

Mark but this flea, and mark in this, 526

Marks (Pastan), 567

Married Love (Rosenberg), 443

Metrical Feet (Coleridge), 596

Midsummer (Walcott), 533

Mid-Term Break (Heaney), 450

Milton! Thou should'st be living at this hour, 649

Morning (Collins), 536

Morning Song (Plath), 536

"Mother dear, may I go downtown, 640

Mr. Flood's Party (Robinson), 615

Mr. Tambourine Man (Dylan), 611

Much have I traveled in the realms of gold, 4

Musée des Beaux Arts (Auden), 655

My heart aches, and a drowsy numbness pains, 692

My husband gives me an A, 567

[*My lady's presence makes the roses red*] (Constable), 643

My Last Duchess (Browning), 660

[*My Life had stood—a Loaded Gun—*] (Dickinson), 667

[*My mistress' eyes are nothing like the sun*] (Shakespeare), 653

[*My Papa's Waltz*] (Roethke), 550

My Spanish isn't enough, 702

My spirit is too weak—mortality, 647

My thoughts are crowded with death, 478

Nautilus Island's hermit, 697

Negro Speaks of Rivers, The (Hughes), 691

Nevada Glassworks, The (Clover), 531

Night-Wind, The (Brontë), 529

Noiseless Patient Spider, A (Whitman), 720

No, no! Go from me, I have left her lately, 709

[*Not marble, nor the gilded monuments*] (Shakespeare), 713

Now as I was young and easy under the apple boughs, 717

Nuns Fret Not (Wordsworth), 643

Nuns fret not at their convent's narrow room, 643

Nymph's Reply to the Shepherd, The (Raleigh), 709

Occurrence at Owl Creek Bridge, An (Bierce), 299

Ode on a Grecian Urn (Keats), 694

Ode to a Nightingale (Keats), 692

Ode to the West Wind (Shelley), 628

Off Highway 106, 521

Of Time and the Line (Bernstein), 547

Oh, I can smile for you, and tilt my head, 504

Old Eben Flood, climbing alone one night, 615

"O 'Melia, my dear, this does everything crown, 496

O, my luve's like a red, red rose, 568

On a Drop of Dew (Marvell), 563

On Being Brought from Africa to America (Wheatley), 539

Once upon a midnight dreary, while I pondered, weak and weary, 600

One face looks out from all his canvases, 651

One Perfect Rose (Parker), 580

One wading a Fall meadow finds on all sides, 561

On First Looking into Chapman's Homer (Keats), 4

On Her Loving Two Equally (Behn), 452

On My First Son (Jonson), 445

On Seeing the Elgin Marbles (Keats), 647

On the Grasshopper and the Cricket (Keats), 646

On the Late Massacre in Piedmont (Milton), 516

On the long shore, lit by the moon, 618

On the Sonnet (Keats), 645

Open Boat, The (Crane), 250

O rose, thou art sick, 581

Outside, the last kids holler, 477

O wild West Wind, thou breath of Autumn's being, 628

Pair of Tickets, A (Tan), 189

Passionate Shepherd to His Love, The (Marlowe), 698

Persepolis (Satrapi), 24

Persimmons (Lee), 557
Piano Lesson, The (Wilson), 879
Pied Beauty (Hopkins), 557
Poetry (Moore), 637
Point Shirley (Plath), 530
Postcard from Kashmir (Ali), 543
Punishment (Heaney), 688

Raisin in the Sun, A (Hansberry), 950
Range-Finding (Frost), 648
Raven, The (Poe), 600
Real Inspector Hound, The (Stoppard), 759
Recitatif (Morrison), 130
Red, Red Rose, A (Burns), 568
Red Wheelbarrow, The (Williams), 554
River-Merchant's Wife: A Letter, The
  (Pound), 469
Road Not Taken, The (Frost), 677
Rocking Horse Winner, The (Lawrence), 343
Rose for Emily, A (Faulkner), 308
Ruined Maid, The (Hardy),496

Sailing to Byzantium (Yeats), 727
Second Coming, The (Yeats), 726
See how the orient dew, 563
Seeing that there's no other way, 586
September rain falls on the house, 638
Sestina (Bishop), 638
Sex fingers toes, 610
Sex without Love (Olds), 552
[Shall I compare thee to a summer's day?]
  (Shakespeare), 569
[She dealt her pretty words like Blades—]
  (Dickinson), 666
She Dwelt among the Untrodden Ways
  (Wordsworth), 506
She sits in the park. Her clothes are out
  of date, 652
She wanted a little room for thinking,
  514
She was the sentence the cancer spoke
  last, 573
Shiloh (Mason), 355
Should I simplify my life for you, 712
Sick Rose, The (Blake), 581
Sir Patrick Spens (Anonymous), 624
Skunk Hour (Lowell), 697
Slim Cunning Hands (De La Mare), 548
Slim cunning hands at rest, and cozen-
  ing eyes, 548

Soliloquy of the Spanish Cloister (Browning),
  501
so much depends, 554
Song (Donne), 669
Song (Suckling), 599
Song (Waller), 579
Sonnet (Collins), 653
Sonnet Is a Moment's Monument, A (Ros-
  setti), 645
Sonny's Blues (Baldwin), 75
Sonrisas (Mora), 620
Sound and Sense (Pope), 589
Spring (Shakespeare), 609
Spring and Fall (Hopkins), 604
[Stop all the clocks, cut off the telephone]
  (Auden), 470
Stopping by Woods on a Snowy Evening
  (Frost), 677
Storm Warnings (Rich), 711
Story of an Hour, The (Chopin), 306
Streetcar Named Desire, A (Williams), 1165
Sundays too my father got up early, 491
Sun Rising, The (Donne), 472
Sympathy (Dunbar), 671
Symphony in Yellow (Wilde), 561

Tally Stick, The (Ramsay), 440
Tears, Idle Tears (Tennyson), 714
Tears, idle tears, I know not what they
  mean, 714
Tenebris (Grimké), 685
That is no country for old men. The
  young, 727
That's my last Duchess painted on the
  wall, 660
[That time of year thou mayest in me behold]
  (Shakespeare), 565
The apparition of these faces in the
  crowd, 709
The battle rent a cobweb diamond-
  strung, 648
[The Brain—is wider than the Sky—] (Dickin-
  son), 666
The curfew tolls the knell of parting day,
  681
The eyes open to a cry of pulleys, 720
The glass has been falling all the after-
  noon, 711
[The golf links lie so near the mill] (Cleg-
  horn), 545

The house is so quiet now, 445
The king sits in Dumferling toune, 624
The Lord is my shepherd; I shall not want, 570
The old woman across the way, 685
The only thing I have of Jane McNaughton, 575
The poetry of earth is never dead, 646
There is a tree, by day, 685
There's No To-morrow (Finch), 546
[There was a young girl from St. Paul] (Anonymous), 598
There was such speed in her little body, 710
The sea is calm tonight, 517
The trees are uncurling their first, 443
The whiskey on your breath, 550
[The Wind begun to knead the Grass—] (Dickinson), 627
The word plum is delicious, 587,
The world is charged with the grandeur of God, 689
[Th' expense of spirit in a waste of shame] (Shakespeare), 627
They sit in a row, 448
This girlchild was born as usual, 476
This Is Just to Say (Williams), 555
Those Winter Sundays (Hayden), 491
Thou still unravished bride of quietness, 694
Thus she had lain, 540
To a Daughter Leaving Home (Pastan), 515
To a Louse (Burns), 507
To His Coy Mistress (Marvell), 527
To My Dear and Loving Husband (Bradstreet), 471
To the Memory of Mr. Oldham (Dryden), 599
Trifles (Glaspell), 748
Trochee trips from long to short, 596
Turning and turning in the widening gyre, 726
'Twas mercy brought me from my Pagan land, 539
Twenty-third Psalm, The (Anonymous), 570
Two Crabs, The (Aesop), 246
Two long had Lov'd, and now the Nymph desir'd, 546
Two roads diverged in a yellow wood, 677

Tyger, The (Blake), 658
Tyger! tyger! burning bright, 658

Ulysses (Tennyson), 715

Vacuum, The (Nemerov), 445
Valediction: Forbidding Mourning, A (Donne), 670
Very Old Man with Enormous Wings, A (Márquez), 269
Victims, The (Olds), 622
Virginal, A (Pound), 709

Wall of Fire Rising, A (Danticat), 232
[We do not play on Graves] (Dickinson), 665
We Real Cool (Brooks), 509
We real cool. We, 509
We Wear the Mask (Dunbar), 672
We wear the mask that grins and lies, 672
What happens to a dream deferred, 690
[What lips my lips have kissed] (Millay), 651
When daisies pied and violets blue, 609
[When I consider how my light is spent] (Milton), 650
When I taught you, 515
When it is finally ours, this freedom, this liberty, this beautiful, 686
When Mother divorced you, we were glad. She took it and,
When my mother died I was very young, 659
[When our two souls stand up] (Browning), 650
When to Her Lute Corinna Sings (Campion), 608
While my hair was still cut straight across my forehead, 469
Whipping, The (Hayden), 685
White House, The (McKay), 702
Whose woods these are I think I know, 677
Why do we bother with the rest of the day, 536
Why I Live at the P.O. (Welty), 414
Why so pale and wan, fond Lover, 599
[Wild Nights—Wild Nights!] (Dickinson), 667
Wind Done Gone, The (Randall), 163

Windhover, The (Hopkins), 690

[*Women have loved before as I love now*] (Millay), 473

Woodchucks (Kumin), 484

Word Plum, *The* (Chasin), 587

Yellow Wallpaper, The (Gilman), 315

Yet Do I Marvel (Cullen), 663

You do not do, you do not do, 704

Your door is shut against my tightened face, 702

Index of Literary Terms

action 59–60, 66, 456, 616, 812–814, 1245
alexandrine 590
allegory 214–215
alliteration 457, 592, 632
allusion 215, 513, 819
amphitheater 815
anapestic 458, 593, 595
antagonist 18, 122–123, 746, 810
antihero 123
archetype 124, 214, 1331–1332
arena stage 814
assonance 457, 592
aubade 534
auditor 104, 455
author 106–107, 505–506, 1317, 1327
author time 158
autobiography 7, 57

ballad 458
ballad stanza 635
bildungsroman 7
biography 7, 57
blank verse 633, 636

caesura 457, 594, 1326
canon 2
carpe diem 525–526
central consciousness 104
character 7, 121–125, 455, 746, 809–811
characterization 125, 128, 746
chorus 813
classical unities 816–817
climax 63–65, 813
comedy 6, 68, 746
coming-of-age story 106
complication 64, 617
conclusion 63–66, 813, 1254
conflict 61, 63–65, 812–813
connotation 545, 548
controlling metaphor 819
convention 7, 68, 128, 820

couplet 458, 592, 636
crisis 65
criticism 6–7, 1274, 1277
cycle 814

dactylic 593, 595
denotation 545, 548
dénouement 66
descriptive poem/structure 621
destabilizing event 64
deus ex machina 65
dialogue 801
diction 457, 545, 1247
discriminated occasion 61
discursive poem/structure 621
drama 7, 68, 744
dramatic irony 546, 818
dramatic monologue 501
dramatic poem/structure 617–618
dynamic character 124

end-stopped line 457
English sonnet 642
enjambment 457, 594, 1326
epic 7
epilogue 66
epiphany 65
episode 60, 813
epistolary novel 7
epitaph 548
epithet 456
exposition 63–64, 745, 810, 813
extended metaphor 567
external conflict 61, 812
external narration 103–104

fable 246–247
fairy tale 55–56, 246
falling action 63–66, 813
fantasy 158
fiction 14, 56–57

figurative language 212–217, 621
figure of speech 214–215
first-person narrator 104
flashback 60
flashforward 60
flat character 124
focus 102–103
foil 123, 810
folktale 2, 55, 246
foot 592–596
foreshadowing 60
free verse 597, 633, 636
Freytag's pyramid 63–64

general setting 158
genre 2–3, 6–8, 18, 57
gothic fiction 7

hero/heroine 18, 122–123, 746, 810
heroic couplet 636
hexameter 594–595, 635
historical fiction 7, 58, 158

iambic 593–596, 635
image/imagery 18, 163, 214, 747
imitative poem/structure 622
implied author 106–107
inciting incident 63, 813
in medias res 60
internal conflict 61, 812
internal narration/narrator 104
irony 103, 215, 247, 546, 818
Italian sonnet 642

legend 480
limerick 636
limited narrator 104
limited point of view 104
literary criticism 6–7, 1274
lyric 496, 608

magic realism 158
major (main) character 123, 810
memoir 7, 57
metafiction 68
metaphor 5, 215, 457, 564, 1271
meter 457, 592–596, 635–636
metonymy 215–216
minor character 123–124, 810
monologue 443, 818

moral 248
myth 214, 1331

narration 102–107
narrative 14, 55–58, 1326
narrative poem/structure 496, 614,
    617–618
narrator 19, 102–107, 496, 745
nonfiction 7, 56–57
novel 7–8, 57
novella 7, 57

octameter 594–595
octave 642, 1321
ode 458
omniscient narrator 103
omniscient point of view 103
onomatopoeia 587
orchestra 815
oxymoron 216

parable 57
parody 7
particular setting 158
pentameter 594–595, 635
personification 216, 564, 566
Petrarchan sonnet 642
plot 18, 59–61, 63–65, 812–814
plot summary 66, 1245
plot time 158
poetry 7, 438–439, 459
point of view 102–107
prop 816
prose 7, 18–19, 56–58
protagonist 18, 122–123, 746, 810

reflective (meditative) poem/structure
    622
resolution 63–66, 813
rhetoric 214
rhyme 457, 632–635
rhyme scheme 634–635
rhythm 592–593
rising action 63–64, 813
romance 7, 68
round character 124

sarcasm 215
satire 7
scansion 597

scene 813–814
second-person narrator 105
sequence 59–61
sestet 642
sestina 636, 639
set 814–817
setting 7, 158–160, 482, 512–514, 746, 814–817
Shakespearean sonnet 642
short story 7, 57
simile 5, 216, 457, 568–569
situation 64–65, 512–513, 745–746
situational irony 818
skene 815
sonnet 458, 641–643
spatial setting 512
speaker 455, 496–498, 505–506
Spenserian stanza 635
spondee 593
stage directions 745–746, 816
stanza 497, 633–634
static character 124
stock character 124
style 18, 102, 746
subgenre 7
subplot 59–60, 813
symbol 212–217, 457, 560, 575, 819, 1247
symbolic poem 581–582
synecdoche 216
syntax 453, 457, 551–552

tale 55–56
temporal setting 158, 512
terza rima 635
tetrameter 594–595, 635–636
theme 246–249, 457, 475–476, 624, 747, 820, 1250
thesis 1248, 1250–1251
third-person narrator 103–104
thrust stage 814
time 158–160, 162, 512, 746, 816–817
tone 18, 102, 475–476, 622, 747, 818–819, 1248–1250, 1261
traditional symbol 213, 578
tragedy 68, 746, 818,
trimeter 594, 635
trochaic 593–595
trope 214
turning point 64–65, 813

unity of action 816
unity of place 816
unity of time 816
unlimited point of view 103
unreliable narrator 104

verbal irony 215, 818
verse drama 617–618
villain 18, 122, 746, 810
villanelle 636
voice 102–103, 496–497